Association for the Study of Higher Education

Philanthropy, Volunteerism & Fundraising in Higher Education

Lenoar Foster, Series Editor

Association for the Study of Higher Education

Edited by

Andrea Walton

Marybeth Gasman

With a Foreword by

Ellen Condliffe Lagemann

Associate Editors:

Frances Huehls

Amy E. Wells

Noah D. Drezner

PEARSON

Custom Publishing

Cover Art: Philanthropy Stamp Design © 1998 United States Postal Service. All rights reserved. Used with permission.
Photograph of President John F. Kennedy courtesy of Joseph Scherschel/Getty Images.
"Class Bench," courtesy of John Bradley Blankenship.
"Class of 1944 gate," courtesy of John Bradley Blankenship.
Photographs of the Little 500 at Indiana University courtesy of Indiana University.

Printed in the United States of America

10 9 8 7 6 5 4 3 2 1

ISBN 0-536-08332-0

2006220168

SB/SB

Please visit our web site at *www.pearsoncustom.com*

PEARSON CUSTOM PUBLISHING
501 Boylston Street, Suite 900, Boston, MA 02116
A Pearson Education Company

COPYRIGHT ACKNOWLEDGMENTS

"Why College Trustees?" by Ellis Huntingdon Dana, reprinted by permission from the *Journal of Higher Education* 18, no.5 (May 1947).

"The Role of Community College Trustees in Supporting the Foundation," by Norm Nielsen, Wayne Newton and Cheryle W. Mitvalsky, reprinted from *New Directions for Community Colleges*, no.24 (2003), John Wiley & Sons.

"The Roots of Academic Fund Raising," by Frank H. Oliver, reprinted from the *CASE International Journal of Educational Advancement* 3, no.2 (2002), Palgrave Publishers.

"Private Voluntary Support to Public Universities in the United States: Late Nineteenth Century Developments," by Samuel G. Cash, reprinted from the *CASE International Journal of Educational Advancement* 5, no.4 (2005), Palgrave Publishers.

"Fund Raising and the College Presidency in an Era of Uncertainty: From 1975–Present," by W. Bruce Cook, reprinted by permission from the *Journal of Higher Education* 68, no.1 (1997).

"Does Institutional Type Affect Alumnae Donating Patterns in the United States?" by Peter Briechle, reprinted from the *CASE International Journal of Educational Advancement* 4, no.1 (2003), Palgrave Publishers.

"Who Are the Alumni Donors? Giving by Two Generations of Alumni from Selective Colleges," by Charles T. Clotfelter, reprinted from *Nonprofit Management & Leadership* 12, no.2 (winter 2001), Jossey-Bass Publishers, Inc.

"College Relations and Fund-raising Expenditures: Influencing the Probability of Alumni Giving in Higher Education," by William B. Harrison, reprinted from *Economics of Education Review* 14, no.1 (1995), Pergamon Press.

"Winning and Giving: Football Results and Alumni Giving at Selective Private Colleges and Universities," by Sarah E. Turner, Lauren E. Meserve and William G. Bowen, reprinted from *Social Science Quarterly* 82, no.4 (December 2001), Blackwell Publishing, Ltd.

"Institutional Advancement and Community Colleges: A Review of Literature," by S. Renea Akin, reprinted from the *CASE International Journal of Educational Advancement* 6, no.1 (2005), Palgrave Publishers.

"Toward a Theory of Charitable Fund–raising," by James Andreoni, reprinted from *Journal of Political Economy* 106, no.6 (1998), University of Chicago Press.

"Toward Professionalism: Fund Raising Norms and Their Implications for Practice," by Timothy C. Caboni, reprinted from the *CASE International Journal of Educational Advancement* 4, no.1 (2003), Palgrave Publishers.

"Surveying the Major Gifts Literature: Observations and Reflections," by W. Bruce Cook, reprinted from *Nonprofit Management & Leadership* 7, no.3 (spring 1997), Jossey-Bass Publishers, Inc.

"Major Donors, Major Motives: The People and Purposes Behind Major Gifts," by Paul G. Schervish, reprinted from *New Directions for Philanthropic Fundraising*, no.47 (spring 2005), John Wiley & Sons, Inc.

"Charles S. Johnson and Johnetta Cole: Successful Role Models for Fund–raising at Historically Black Colleges and Universities," by Marybeth Gasman, reprinted from the *CASE International Journal of Educational Advancement* 1, no.3 (2001), Palgrave Publishers.

"Black Philanthropy's Past, Present, and Future," by Emmett D. Carson, reprinted from *New Directions for Philanthropic Fundraising*, no.48 (summer 2005), John Wiley & Sons, Inc.

"An Untapped Resource: Bringing African Americans into the College and University Giving Process," by Marybeth Gasman, reprinted from the *CASE International Journal of Educational Advancement* 2, no.3 (2002), Palgrave Publishers.

CONTENTS

FOREWORD

It was once stylish to remark upon the ways the United States was exceptional among OTHER nations around the globe. Even though "exceptionalism," as such thinking was once called, is no longer in favor among scholars of American history and culture, there is no denying that, in its arrangement for postsecondary education and its reliance on volunteerism and fundraising to support those arrangements, the U.S. is unusual, if not entirely unique.

Since the founding of Harvard College in 1636 to ensure orthodoxy and learning in the Massachusetts Bay Colony, higher education has been at the heart of American conceptions of culture and progress. Boasting hundreds of colleges, while older European nations supported only a handful, the U.S. early became the world's leader in offering collegiate education to significant numbers of people. Soon after the Civil War, the possibility of going to college opened to previously excluded categories of people, notably women and African-Americans. By the late 1960s, the numbers and types of postsecondary institutions had grown even further and federal provisions for student financial aid made college-going a common experience for many Americans. In the number, institutional range, and purposes pursued by its institutions of higher learning, the U.S. has a proud and interesting history.

The history of higher education in the U.S. is notable for many reasons, perhaps most especially for the unusual ways in which higher education has been supported. As the oldest of America's colleges, Harvard exemplified much that would become standard elsewhere. From the first, Harvard was supported by public funds, private donations, and student tuitions. The name Harvard derived from the first patron of the College's library, John Harvard's library having early helped actualize the founders' dream that there should be a center of civilization and learning in the small settlement that became Cambridge, MA. Over the years, Harvard slowly accumulated the massive endowments that today make it the most generously endowed university in the U.S., if not in the world. Over the years, too, Harvard has continued to garner significant public funds, now primarily from federal research grants, as well as significant streams of student tuitions. In the mix of its resources, if not in their massive extent, Harvard is representative of American colleges and universities.

Like Harvard, most colleges and universities in the U.S. have funding streams that have been profoundly shaped by the philanthropy of individuals and organizations. Whether the institution is public or private, four-year or two-year, a university with a large array of professional schools or a small, single-purpose college, American colleges are dotted with classroom buildings, laboratories, dormitories, and even athletic facilities that bear the names of loyal, generous alumni/ae, whose post-collegiate lives have enabled them to accumulate sufficient resources to return some of those resources to the institution to which they often attribute their personal success. Personal generosity and a long historical tradition of donating private wealth to realize public purposes have made possible the extraordinary enterprise that is American higher education.

Volunteerism, which represents even more personal gifts of time and service, has also been essential in the history of American higher education. Many people have labored without remuneration to help advance the interests of some particular college or university with which they have been affiliated. Even more notable perhaps, colleges and universities have nurtured recurrent waves of student volunteers, who have left the comfort of their college campuses to serve people in need around the country and the world. In the nineteenth century, the New England colleges sent volunteer ministers to the Western states and later to the Far East; in the twentieth century, those same colleges and many others sent volunteers to Mississippi to work for civil rights and to India and Africa to build schools and hospitals. Volunteerism is not unique to the United States. It is an activity that can be found in many different forms, in most societies around the globe. But volunteerism has been an important force in supporting institutions of higher education in the U.S. and has also been an important manifestation of the ideals and aspirations those colleges and universities have helped nurture in their students, alumni/ae, and also in the men and women who have served on their faculties.

Given the importance of higher education in the history of the U.S., and given the importance of philanthropy and volunteerism in that history, it is vital that all of us understand the ways in which the three have been interconnected over almost 400 hundred years of American history. As no prior volume has done, this ASHE Reader will make that possible. Bringing together cutting edge scholarship pertaining to higher education, philanthropy, and volunteerism, this volume should be helpful in establishing the fact that the history of higher education cannot be understood apart from study of philanthropy and volunteerism. Beyond that, it should be helpful in advancing the importance of studying philanthropy and volunteerism as entities important in their own rights.

As a branch of American intellectual, cultural, and social history, the history of American higher education is well established as an important field of study. Students of history as well as students of leadership and administration in higher education routinely turn to the history of higher education for insight into the ideas, people, and practices that have guided American colleges and university for almost four centuries. Unfortunately, however, the importance of philanthropy and volunteerism within that history has been too rarely recognized. With the exception of the works of the late Merle Curti and a handful of more recent volumes, there are few extant studies that have plumbed this all-important relationship. By editing this comprehensive volume of writings, and introducing it with an essay that carefully notes the intricacies of the relationships among higher education, philanthropy, and volunteerism, Andrea Walton of Indiana University and Marybeth Gasman of the University of Pennsylvania have taken a first step toward filling this void.

Even though PHILANTHROPY, VOLUNTEERISM & FUNDRAISING IN HIGHER EDUCATION would mark a landmark contribution to American history at any moment in time, this volume is especially timely at the beginning of this new millennium. Long secure in its leadership of higher education, the U.S. can no longer rest secure in that status. Other nations now send more young people to college and, in some instance, offer them more productive opportunities for learning. What is more, the establishment of increasing numbers of profit-making colleges and postsecondary institute now challenges long-established traditions of non-profit management in higher education. This makes it even more urgent that all higher education leaders, all citizens who care about the quality of American colleges and universities, and all involved in philanthropy and volunteerism understand the history of these old relationships. Such understanding will ensure that future policies governing this crucially important domain of American education evolve in ways that are historically intelligent. Historical intelligence will not preclude change in the future. Rather, it should help guarantee that future policies are set in ways that are mindful of what can be learned from the past.

PHILANTHROPY, VOLUNTEERISM & FUNDRAISING IN HIGHER EDUCATION is a volume that can be used as a reference, a text, or simply a convenient compendium of useful historical insights. However it is read, Walton and Gasman's volume will long stand as a guide to an aspect of American life that is central to the well being of education in the United States and around the world.

—Ellen Condliffe Lagemann

PREFACE

The idea for a Reader on Philanthropy, Volunteerism, and Fundraising emerged from our teaching. For many years we have offered courses and seminars at our respective institutions on these topics, each of us pulling together classic historical articles, clippings from the *Chronicle of Philanthropy* and the *Chronicle of Higher Education*, and continually looking for fresh scholarship to keep our students abreast of new developments in the field. We wanted to have the chance to share ideas from our research with our students and to encourage them to think in new directions. We talked often about how researchers in many different fields and disciplines studied philanthropy but that the scholarship on the subject was scattered across a range of specialized journals and books, making it difficult to locate and cumbersome to use in teaching. Out of this conversation came the idea for a Reader. We aimed to create a comprehensive document that would be useful to those teaching and studying contemporary philanthropy and fundraising as well as those interested in the history of these topics. We hope that faculty, students, practitioners, and others will find that this Reader illuminates salient issues, furnishes a theoretical foundation for their work, and provides guidance for their practice.

The Reader is divided into three interrelated parts: Philanthropy, Volunteerism, and Fundraising. Each of these three facets is crucial to underscoring the prominent role of private funding and voluntary initiatives in higher education, historically and today. Because philanthropy is so often thought of as merely a financial gift, we wanted to use the cover to introduce the reader to the broader understanding of philanthropy that informs this text. So, we culled through a wide range of photographs before locating the images that appear on the Reader's cover. We hope these images capture the essence of the phenomenon of educational philanthropy in the American setting. Included is a United States postage stamp entitled *Giving & Sharing: An American Tradition*, which shows an image of a bee pollinating a flower and represents the "sharing present in a philanthropic act." The photo of the Class of 1944 campus gate, a donation from grateful alums to their alma mater, represents the tradition of private financial support for the bricks and mortar of campus building. An image of college-aged students helping in a soup kitchen and another image of students helping to build a house in the community depict philanthropy as the giving of time and energy to help others, while the photo of the student bicyclists participating in the Little 500 race, a fundraising event sponsored each spring by Indiana University's Student Foundation, serves as a reminder of the interconnections of the traditions of philanthropy, volunteerism, and fundraising. And, finally, the photo of United Negro College Fund presidents meeting with President John F. Kennedy represents both the importance of fundraising and the interplay between private voluntary initiatives and government activity to advance access to higher education.

Many individuals helped us select materials for this Reader. We are grateful to the advisory board for their candor and expertise and extend our thanks to our three Associate editors—Frances Huehls, Amy E. Wells, and Noah D. Drezner—for their hard work and valuable contributions. We were also assisted by several students on this project, including Christopher Tudico, Katherine V. Sedgwick, Ebony Russ, Deborah Worley, John Bradley Blankenship, Lowell Davis, and Melanie Rago. Their efforts are greatly appreciated. We would like to thank Lenoar Foster, the ASHE Readers Series editor, and the Associate for the Study of Higher Education for their support in making this Reader possible. It was a joy to work with our editor Karen Whitehouse, at Pearson, whose lively personality and support throughout the process of compiling an anthology of this sort were valued and comforting.

On a more personal note, Andrea would like to thank friends and family for their encouragement and support during the project and to thank her students at IU who always contributed thoughtful questions and lively debate to the philanthropy seminar discussions. Marybeth would like to thank her students at the University of Pennsylvania for the interest they expressed in the Reader project and to thank Edward for his constant support and encouragement of her scholarship.

Andrea Walton, Indiana University Bloomington
Marybeth Gasman, University of Pennsylvania

ADVISORY BOARD LIST

Associate Editors

Frances Huehls, Indiana University-Purdue University (Part One)

Amy E. Wells, University of Mississippi (Part Two)

Noah D. Drezner, University of Pennsylvania (Part Three).

Advisory Board

Kathyrn Agard, Dorothy A. Johnnson Center for Philanthropy and Nonprofit Leadership, Grand Valley State University

Robert G. Bringle, Chancellor's Professor, Indiana University-Purdue University, Indianapolis.

Dwight Burlingame, Executive Associate Director, Indiana University Center on Philanthropy, Indianapolis

Mariam Chamberlain, National Council for Research on Women

John Donohue, Executive Vice President, United Negro College Fund

Matt Hartley, Assistant Professor, University of Pennsylvania

Frances Huehls, Librarian, Payton Philanthropic Studies Library, Indiana University-Purdue University

Roger Geiger, Distinguished Professor of Education, The Pennsylvania State University

Julie A. Hatcher, Indiana University-Purdue University

Ellen Condliffe Lagemann, Harvard Graduate School of Education, Harvard University

Linda Perkins, Associate Professor, Claremont Graduate School

Richard Magat, Visiting Fellow, Yale University

Alfred Moss, Associate Professor, University of Maryland, College Park

Kenneth W. Rose, Assistant Director, Rockefeller Archive Center and Adjunct Professor, The Rockefeller University

Auden Thomas, Pennsylvania State University

John Thelin, Professor, University of Kentucky

Wayne J. Urban, Professor and Associate Director of the Education Policy Center, University of Alabama

Harold S. Wechsler, Professor, University of Rochester

Amy E. Wells, Associate Professor, University of Mississippi

Student Advisory Board

ASHE READER SERIES

PHILANTHROPY, VOLUNTEERISM, & FUNDRAISING IN HIGHER EDUCATION

ANDREA WALTON, INDIANA UNIVERSITY
MARYBETH GASMAN, UNIVERSITY OF PENNSYLVANIA

Philanthropy, derived from the Greek word *philanthropia*, means love of humankind. For the purposes of this Reader on philanthropy, volunteerism, and fundraising, we define philanthropy as the voluntary giving of time or money for public purposes. Such a definition, anchored in history and the current literature on philanthropy, includes the financial gifts of individuals, groups, and foundations, as well as the service of trustees and volunteerism of students and faculty.[1] Presenting original introductory essays, research articles covering major approaches and topics, and primary documents for teaching, this Reader introduces students to several important points: among these are the centrality of private giving in shaping the development and diversity of U.S. higher education; the importance of voluntary action in shaping educational policy, even in an era when government intervention has been strong; the role of donors as an external force shaping research as well as campus intellectual life and culture; and the role of philanthropy in access. The reader will give students of philanthropy a firm grasp of the significance of the cultural phenomenon of philanthropy as a salient force shaping higher education, both historically and today.

Because the study of philanthropy is complex, value-laden, and burdened by the issues of the unequal distribution of power in society, scholars have been reticent about the topic. This partly explains the absence of a reader in higher education and philanthropy up to this time. Prior to the mid-1950s, organized philanthropy resisted scholarly inquiry into its inner workings and did little to make archival materials available to scholars. Faculty members themselves avoided the topic, "because it tended to lead them toward the kinds of essentially political concerns with wealth and power that were unlikely to enhance their career prospects."[2] Even up and until the 1980s, when the study of philanthropy and nonprofits was gaining more acceptance, some critics remained skeptical. As the *Chronicle of Higher Education* noted in 1985, "Scholars aren't being named to distinguished professorships in the history of charitable giving, and academic departments don't appear to be designing positions for specialists in the subject."[3]

Since 1985, however, efforts to institutionalize the university study of philanthropy have achieved remarkable success. In fact, the field of philanthropic studies is flourishing. By 1987, twelve research centers had been established, followed by endowed chairs, refereed journals, and most recently, the first Ph.D. program. Equally important, scholarship and teaching about philanthropy can be found across the disciplines and professional fields. This trend is, at least in part, an outgrowth of the 1973 Filer Commission's work* and the subsequent founding of Independent Sector in 1980, which brought growing interest in the study of the voluntary and nonprofit sector, in concerns about civic engagement and the vitality of civil society, and in the realities of devolution. Indeed, not only have applied fields such as business, public administration, teacher preparation, and higher education studies incorporated philanthropy and fundraising courses into the requirements and electives of their degree programs, but so too have liberal arts majors and concentrations, such as history, political science, sociology, psychology, ethics and religious studies. In all of these areas, there is an emphasis on philanthropy as a phenomenon that has been instrumental in shaping our intellectual, civic, and cultural institutions in the U.S.—including higher education. This interest makes it especially timely to produce a reader on the subject of philanthropy, fundraising, and higher education.

Jesse Sears in his 1922 text, *Philanthropy in the History of American Higher Education,* was the first to study systematically the role of philanthropy in the development of higher education.[4] Since then, scholars have researched the politics of patronage, and foundation support in higher education, especially in relation to the university's role in the organization and dissemination of knowledge, the standardizing the professions, and the promotion of equal opportunity. Though higher education today is primarily a fee-based enterprise, the power of private funding is significant and raises a number of crucial questions about higher education policy. Today, the impact of philanthropy on higher education is discussed within standard courses in higher education programs—finance and higher education, economics of higher education, higher education administration, higher education governance, and introduction to higher education, to name a few.

Courses and discussions of philanthropy within the higher education setting are becoming more critical because of the changing philanthropic situation at the national level, as well as the imminent transfer of substantial wealth from an older generation to its children.[5] The problems of weakened endowments and enormous cuts in state appropriations to higher education on the one hand, coupled with the possibility of engaging a broader range of donors (improving outreach to women, communities of color, LGBT populations) on the other, make understanding the motivations of philanthropy and the dynamics and ethics of fundraising even more important. Given the challenges of the changing economic and political climate that higher education faces—resulting, for instance, in the dire situation of some small black colleges and less prestigious women's colleges—providing future faculty and practitioners with adequate knowledge about philanthropy, volunteerism, and fundraising is crucial.

Indeed, the study of philanthropy in higher education is essential to understanding both the rise and the development of higher education as well as the contemporary context. Philanthropy plays a role in the political and financial challenges that all academic institutions—public or private, secular or religious—must face. According to philanthropic studies scholar, Peter Dobkin Hall, "No single force is more responsible for the emergence of the modern university in America than [the] giving by individuals and foundations."[6] A change in the priorities by some national foundations (such as the Atlantic Philanthropies's sudden and unforeseen decision to pull their monies out of higher education) can have disastrous consequences. Equally important, a foundation's decision to fund certain initiatives in higher education—such as Carnegie's efforts to reexamine doctoral education and teacher preparation—can shape the national policy agenda. These complex dynamics make it all the more pressing for future faculty and administrators to understand the historic and contemporary relationship between higher education and philanthropy.[7] Likewise, the increased desire for control on the part of donors raises issues about university governance and academic freedom. As shown by the recent examples of corporate malfeasance and governance fiascos (notably, the case of the Adelphi University board of trustees), greater attentiveness to teaching about concepts such as stewardship and trusteeship would be beneficial. And, lastly, no less than in the days of John D. Rockefeller, colleges and universities must consider the ethical question of whether they have received or can accept "tainted" philanthropic dollars.

Up until now, a researcher or instructor seeking information on philanthropy and higher education would consult "classic" studies like Sears's 1922 book (i.e. texts which are still useful but outdated as secondary sources) and the major survey texts in the philanthropic literature—notably, Charles T. Clotfelter and Thomas Ehrlich's *Philanthropy and the Nonprofit Sector in a Changing America,*[8] David Hammack's *Making the Nonprofit Sector in the United States,*[9] Peter Dobkin Hall's *Inventing the Nonprofit Sector,*[10] Ray Bacchetti and Thomas Ehrlich's *Reconnecting Education and Foundations,*[11] and Michael O'Neill's *The Third America: The Emergence of the Nonprofit Sector in the United States.*[12] These recent books, while providing the important background information that informs our reader, were written for a general audience. They focus on defining the role(s) of the nonprofit sector and philanthropy and generally use examples related to nonprofit activity and philanthropy in the arts (e.g. museums) and health care, directing only limited attention to higher education.[13] Lastly, Michael Worth's book *New Strategies for Educational Fund Raising* (2002), although a necessity for practitioners in the area of fundraising, offers little theoretical perspective.[14]

This Reader—both through its organization and its original introductory essays—provides students with a firm grasp of the context in which philanthropic action in higher education occurs. Moreover, this Reader documents how some of the current interest and research on philanthropy has translated into curricular debates and innovations—such as service learning and efforts to foster civic engagement experiences among today's college students. In all, this reader addresses a significant gap in the available teaching and reference materials on philanthropy, volunteerism, and fundraising.

In order to capture the many facets of philanthropy as a cultural phenomenon that figures prominently in higher education, this reader is divided into three parts. Part I focuses on historical perspectives and classic works on philanthropy. Part II offers material relevant to volunteerism and service learning; in particular, it emphasizes the ways that contemporary pedagogical and curricular issues relate to the intersection of philanthropy and higher education. Part III focuses on issues related to fundraising activities, which support higher education's mission to advance knowledge and provide equal educational opportunity. Although the terms philanthropy and fundraising are frequently lumped together by those outside of the field, these concepts are quite different. Fundraising refers to the act of soliciting funds, specifically money, from potential donors. Thus, fundraising and philanthropy are related activities and both are integral to understanding the private support that has been the hallmark of American higher education.

As noted, each section of the reader begins with an original introductory essay. We include selections that introduce students to the most prevalent individual and institutional forms of educational philanthropy. These selections also expose students to the broader changes and trends within the history of philanthropy that have had a significant impact on philanthropic support of colleges and universities. Because philanthropy is a value-laden enterprise, we paid particular attention to achieving a balanced presentation of the contrasting views that observers of higher education (both historical actors and contemporary figures) have offered. Especially important is the influence that philanthropy has had within the academic life and in the shaping the academy's responsibility to society. Though the literature on philanthropy and higher education is uneven, attention is paid to the dynamics of gender, race, religion, and other forms of difference. The majority of selections in the reader are drawn from social science case studies and histories that offer an in-depth perspective on the intersection of philanthropy and higher education. Selections presenting empirical research are complemented by others offering theoretical frameworks from philanthropic studies and other disciplines that can be usefully applied to higher education.

Notes

1. Robert Payton, *Philanthropy: Voluntary Action for the Public Good* (New York: American Council on Education/Macmillan Pub. Co., 1988); Andrea Walton. "Women and Philanthropy in Education: A Problem of Conceptions." In Andrea Walton (Ed.), *Women and Philanthropy in Education*. (Bloomington, IN: Indiana University Press, 2005), pp. 1–36.

2. Peter Dobkin Hall, "Teaching and Research on Philanthropy, Voluntarism, and Nonprofit Organizations: A Case Study of Academic Innovation." *Teachers College Record*, Vol. 93, No. 3, (Spring, 1992), pp. 403–436, 403.

3. P. Desruisseaux, "Non-Profit Sector is Now a Hot Topic for Researchers in Several Fields." *Chronicle of Higher Education*, (April 10, 1985), p. 836.

4. Jesse B. Sears, *Philanthropy in the History of American Higher Education*. New Brunswick, (New Jersey: Transaction Publishers, 1990).

5. Paul G. Schervish & John J. Havens, "Money and Magnanimity: New Findings on the Distribution of Income, Wealth, and Philanthropy." *Nonprofit Management and Leadership*, Vol. 8, No. 4, (Summer 1998), pp. 421–434.

6. Peter Dobkin Hall, "Teaching and Research on Philanthropy, Voluntarism, and Nonprofit Organizations: A Case Study of Academic Innovation." *Teachers College Record*, Vol. 93, No. 3, (Spring, 1992), pp. 403–436, 403.

7. M. Sinclair, "Changes in Atlantic Philanthropies Funding." *The Nonprofit Times*, (2002), available at http://www.nptimes.com/Oct02/npt1.html (accessed February 9, 2003).

8. Charles T. Clotfelter & Thomas Ehrlich, *Philanthropy and the Nonprofit Sector in a Changing America*. (Bloomington, Indiana: Indiana University Press, 1999).

9. David Hammack, *Making the Nonprofit Sector in the United States*. (Bloomington: Indiana University Press, 1998).

10. Peter Dobkin Hall, *Inventing the Nonprofit Sector and Other Essays on Philanthropy, Volunteerism and Nonprofit Organizations* (Baltimore: Johns Hopkins University Press, 1992).

11. Ray Bacchetti and Thomas Ehrlich (Eds.), *Reconnecting Education and Fundations: Turning Good Intentions into Educational Capital* (San Francisco: Wiley & Sons, 2006).

12. Michael O'Neill, The Third America: *The Emergence of the Nonprofit Sector in the United States*. (San Francisco: Jossey-Bass, 1989).

13. Bacchetti and Ehrlich's recent volume, which appeared while this Reader was in production, stands apart from these texts in that it takes educational philanthropy as its main subject, but its discussion is broad, encompassing both higher education and schooling.

14. Michael Worth, *New Strategies for Educational Fundraising* (Westport, CT; Praeger, 2002).

 * The Filer Commission refers to the Commission on Private Philanthropy and Public Needs. Business leader John H. Filer led the Commission, which lasted for two years, from 1973 to 1975, and produced the most far-reaching and detailed report of American philanthropy ever undertaken.

PART I

HISTORICAL AND THEORETICAL PERSPECTIVES

PHILANTHROPY IN HIGHER EDUCATION: PAST AND PRESENT

ANDREA WALTON

The custom of giving in support of higher learning is deeply embedded in the history of the United States. It has played an instrumental role in the development of colleges and universities in this country, going back to the 1638 gift of John Harvard to aid a fledgling colonial college on the banks of the Charles River in Massachusetts. Although scholars can discern European antecedents for both our institutional forms of higher education (the college and, later, the university) and our tradition of private support to higher education, these models and traditions were, once transplanted, inevitably transformed within the U.S. context.[1]

Here, localism has profoundly influenced the educational enterprise and educational policymaking at all levels, and philanthropy—the gifts of money and time for the public good—helped solidify ties between colleges and universities and their local setting. Gifts of candles and blankets to a colonial college, the American Education Society's support of a poor farmer's son, a statewide subscription drive to fund a denominational college, the recent promise made by Kalamazoo, Michigan's philanthropists (anonymously) to offer free or subsidized college tuition to area residents are all examples of how the tradition of philanthropy has helped to make higher education more responsive to the needs, interests, and priorities of the surrounding community.

The many examples of its local inspiration and sway notwithstanding, philanthropy's influence in shaping our intellectual and cultural institutions and educational traditions and practices has been farther reaching. Especially, but not exclusively, with the advent of large foundations in the late 19th century and early years of the 20th century, philanthropy—thanks in good measure to rising endowments and large-scale grant-making programs—extended its purview and influence beyond a specific locality or region.[2] Indeed, foundations in their efforts to unearth the root causes of social problems and to identify effective remedies or strategies for improvement in a particular area (such as education) have played a formidable role in weaving the fabric of a "national society" or, some might say, a "global society."[3] The gifts of White Northern philanthropists to educate the freedmen in the South after the Civil War, or foundation programs offering technical assistance to developing countries, the establishment of a nationwide pension system to strengthen the professoriate, or a foundation-commissioned report to set standards in professional education (e.g. the Flexner report) are all examples of this phenomenon.

The contours of philanthropy's scope and influence in higher education have been as varied as they have been complex. The motivations underlying giving have been wide-ranging and the differences between philanthropy's expressed aims and its outcomes have at times been striking, making philanthropy in higher education the proper target of scholarly study. Multi-million dollar gifts and a steady stream of small donations have sparked and sustained the innovation and diversity that have characterized American higher education, on one hand, while the actions of large foundations and their grant-making priorities have often exerted a standardizing influence on the "vertical" and "horizontal" landscape of higher education, on the other hand. Knowledge of these dynamics and other related ones is important to the educator and the grant-maker alike.[4]

As the selections in Part I illuminate, whereas philanthropy has been a central and highly visible contributor to the bricks-and-mortar development of campuses, it has also helped to define higher education's relationship to society and policy issues. Private giving has shaped patterns of educational access, advanced disciplinary research and interdisciplinary innovations, fostered specialization and professionalization, and even molded the idea of the university as a distinctive institution committed to research, teaching, and service. Often viewed through the lens of its impact on an individual campus, or through the vision of an individual donor or the agenda of a particular foundation, private giving to higher education can perhaps be understood best as a constant thread in the history of higher education, one that connects higher education across eras, across the increasingly blurred boundaries of "public" and "private," and across types of institutions. Notably, even as the federal government has expanded its funding and policymaking interest in higher education dramatically in the post-World War II era, the tradition of educational philanthropy in higher education (both at private and public institutions) in this country remains salient and vibrant. In 2006, colleges and universities in the U.S. saw a 9.4 percent increase in giving and received a record high of $28 billion dollars in charitable contributions.[5]

Part I of this ASHE Reader focuses on the traditional notion of philanthropy as the giving of financial support for public purposes. The selections address both philanthropy's place in the ideology of capitalism and in U.S. society generally, and the power and politics of private monetary contributions to higher education in particular. In Chapter 1, readers are introduced to three historical figures: Andrew Carnegie, Washington Gladden, and Booker T. Washington, whose commentary on philanthropy during their own day drew attention to the social significance of philanthropic practices and traditions and to private giving's capacity to meet the demands of certain social conditions and historic challenges. These figures were chosen because their ideas struck a chord with contemporaries and typify perspectives on giving that continue to shape discussions about private giving to meet public needs. The chapter also includes the insights of contemporary foundation personnel on the efficacy of large scale-organized philanthropy and the ties between education and philanthropy. Together the documents in this chapter help shed light on the scope, motivations, and influence of private giving to higher education.

Many readers will be familiar with the opening selection, an excerpt from steel magnate Andrew Carnegie's essay, "Wealth," (1889), which was later republished in England's *Pall Mall*, at Gladstone's suggestion, as "The Gospel of Wealth." A benefactor of libraries, research institutes, and several foundations, Carnegie's name became synonymous with the new brand of industrialist-cum-philanthropist in the United States who, reaping the benefits of the late 19th century's economic development, used their great fortunes to usher in an expansive, paradigm-setting era both in philanthropy and educational institution-building. Rejecting the common practice of bequeathing one's wealth, Carnegie instead advocated "administer[ing] it as a public trust during life." From his perspective, old-style charity and almsgiving were counterproductive; individuals, and therefore, society were best helped by being provided the means of self-help and improvement, "ladders to climb." To Carnegie's mind, the larger social significance and impact of dispensing one's wealth could be increased manifold by funding public libraries, research institutes, and colleges and universities.

It is well worth noting, though, that even as Carnegie's "The Gospel of Wealth" captured and helped to fuel the philanthropic imagination of his era (and indeed, generations to follow), words of caution were also voiced, pointing to what critics viewed as the morally ambiguous or darker side of philanthropy. The social gospel minister Washington Gladden's essay "Tainted Money" is a prime example of this tradition of critique—one that can be traced to the present day. Gladden questioned the value of the large-scale philanthropy and educational institutions funded by what he disparaged as the ill-gotten gains of the robber barons. Was this altruism or an effort to assuage a guilt-ridden conscience? Although Gladden makes no direct reference to philanthropist John D. Rockefeller, it would be hard to forget that the University of Chicago—a competitive research university at its founding in 1892 and, thus, one of the era's prominent testaments to the power of the purse—was funded mainly by Rockefeller, whose wealth derived substantially from profits of Standard Oil, a company with questionable labor practices.

Booker T. Washington's "How to Help Men Most With Money" describes the educational situation of children in the rural South circa 1910. Washington called for financial support to public schools in the region not as charity or to bring momentary relief to the poor but rather to create a long-range solution. Emphasizing community-building and self-help through education rather than posing a direct challenge to racial and economic injustice, Washington's focus on saving a generation of children by improving the school situation was akin to Carnegie's emphasis of the importance of "ladders to climb." There were, of course, contemporaries of Washington's who offered alternate views of the educational situation of African Americans and who questioned the wisdom of any reliance on the philanthropy of Whites to advance Black education. Readers will find it helpful to consider Washington's essay in tandem with Marybeth Gasman's article on Charles S. Johnson and W.E.B. Du Bois, appearing in Chapter 4.

The next two selections in this chapter were penned by foundation personnel—"insiders" in the world of large grant-making organizations. Susan Wisely, former Director of Evaluation for the Lilly Endowment, elaborates on the unusual status of the foundation in American society as an entity that is at once "private in its operations yet public in its regard" (p. 1). Wisely's close examination of General Eli Lilly's personal interest in character education and the subsequent history of the Lilly Endowment (chartered in 1937), with its emphasis on religion, education, and community development, underscores the lesson that the values and vision of founding donors inevitably shape the work of foundations and yet the priorities of foundations also change over time, as there are larger shifts in society and as thinking about the aims of philanthropy changes—whether it be an emphasis on relief, improvement, or social reform. As Wisely explains, philanthropic work, as conceptualized by the Lilly Endowment, is inherently about education and the "reweaving bonds" of community—a goal that she points to in Andrew Carnegie's influential philanthropic efforts, for example (p. 1). Guided by its historical moorings, the Lilly Endowment has directed substantial support to liberal arts education, theological education, and Historically Black Colleges and Universities.

James Allen Smith, formerly a staff member at the Twentieth Century Fund (now the Century Foundation) and Senior Advisor to the J. Paul Getty Trust, is currently professor at Georgetown University. He reflects upon his own career as a scholar of European history and a "philanthropoid," asking: "What do the insights of the historian bring to the practice of philanthropy and "What does experience in the philanthropic world bring to the study of history?"[6] Smith contends that his historian's sensibilities have made him more conscious of the context in which foundations operate and of the importance of recordkeeping. At the same time his professional knowledge of the daily workings of a foundation made him more aware of the strategies to be learned from studying earlier generations of grant-makers and firmly grasping the nature of foundations as a legal entity, among other lessons. He shares Wisely's concern about the importance of reflection for foundation personnel and others engaged in philanthropic work.

The final selection in Chapter 1 is a classic in the field of philanthropic studies, Merle Curti's "The History of American Philanthropy as a Field of Research." Appearing in 1957, against the background of Cold War concerns about foundation operations and funding priorities, the article summarized an ambitious agenda for scholarship on philanthropy that was formulated by a group of scholars and foundation personnel at a conference held in Princeton a year earlier, with funding by the Russell Sage and Ford Foundations. Although the scholarly study of philanthropy did not germinate in the 1950s, as Curti and his funders had hoped, this article remains an important outline of work various disciplines might undertake to further our understanding of the scope and significance of philanthropy within the United States.

✳✳✳

Chapter 2 focuses on how scholars in a number of disciplines and within the growing field of philanthropic studies have framed their research on philanthropy. The range of scholarly approaches and the growing knowledge base in areas related to philanthropy and education are far too extensive to cover here—including, for instance, studies of altruism, trust, pro-social behavior, civil society, social capital, civic engagement, and the ramifications of the estate tax on donations, to name only a few. Given space constraints, selections were chosen to capture a number of major developments in the academic study of philanthropy that have been most fruitful in understanding the influences of philanthropy on colleges and universities and the context in which they operate. Additional suggested readings are listed in the "Selected Bibliography" at the end of the chapter.

The first selection in this chapter describes a philosophical approach to studying philanthropy in the American context. The former head of the Exxon Foundation, Robert Payton, has been an instrumental figure in the development of philanthropic studies. Recalling one of Thomas Jefferson's letters to a friend, Payton invokes the metaphor of a "dialogue" between the "head" and the "heart" to consider the act of giving and explains the value of the study of philanthropy to liberal education. Importantly, this approach to the study of philanthropy has important applications at all levels of higher education: undergraduate, graduate, and professional education.

One of the most developed areas of research on philanthropy and centers of lively scholarly debate has been in the discipline of history. The first history selection included is Merle Curti's now classic "Philanthropy and the National Character." Although Curti's work is dated by the "exceptionalism" that Ellen Lagemann comments upon in her Foreword to this Reader, his work points usefully to the heavy reliance in the U.S. setting on philanthropy, rather than the state, to fund education and social welfare. Readers will be interested to consult Curti's *American Philanthropy Abroad: A History* (1963) and his *Philanthropy in the Shaping of American Higher Education* (co-authored with Roderick Nash in 1965), which has recently been reprinted by Harvard's Hauser Center.[7]

In addition to situating the study of philanthropy in the broader context of U.S. history, historians have produced more specialized studies of foundations and personalities whose activities have had a strong impact on colleges, universities, adult education and continuing education programs, and education research and policy. Ellen Lagemann's framework of the "politics of knowledge" helps illuminate Carnegie's widespread influence in helping determine the role of knowledge-producing elites, how experts would communicate to non-experts, and how expert knowledge would guide policy. Although Lagemann's work focuses on the specific history of the Carnegie philanthropies, her discussion of the "politics of knowledge" has been influential in the history of educational philanthropy more generally.

There has also been a critique of philanthropy as a hegemonic form associated with Western capitalism, a theme elaborated upon by Robert F. Arnove and colleagues in their classic *Philanthropy and Cultural Imperialism: The Foundations at Home and Abroad* (1980). Perhaps one of the most sustained debates within studies of philanthropy (and one that is especially relevant to education) has been about the larger question of whether philanthropy is a democratizing force or whether (reflecting a Gramscian analysis) philanthropy, especially foundation activity, is a power that has served the interests of a ruling elite. Not surprisingly much research on the values and class-biases embedded in foundation philanthropy has centered on the rise of social sciences. Salma Ahmad's brief overview traces an exchange in *Sociology* and other platforms between Martin Bulmer and Donald Fisher, two major scholars holding divergent views on philanthropy's influence on knowledge and intellectual life. Adopting a middle ground, Ahmad's reading of the evidence suggests that Bulmer "underestimated" and Fisher "exaggerated" the impact of foundations, particularly the Rockefeller Foundation, on research.

In the past 20 years, philanthropy and the non-profit world, in part because of changes in government policies and changes in public sentiment about the need for greater accountability and transparency on the part of all institutions, has been more self-conscious of its place in U.S. society. The founding of academic centers and organizations, conferences, and journals devoted to philanthropic studies has been part of an attempt to understand better the nature of philanthropy and the nonprofit sector and to make philanthropy more effective. Susan Ostrander and Paul Schervish in their widely cited essay challenge the old linear notion that the donor unilaterally shapes the agenda. Instead, these scholars describe philanthropy as a "giving" and "getting," a dynamic relationship between the two parties. This framework has been exceedingly useful to historians and practitioners to foster "philanthropy that is more responsive to social need" (108).

One of the most relevant tools to illuminate the power of philanthropy, and especially the influence of foundations, a major funding and ideological force in education—has been drawn from sociology—"new institutionalism." As Paul DiMaggio and Walter Powell elaborate, even as organizations within a field change or try to innovate, they may in fact become more homogeneous. An understanding of this phenomenon—"isomorphism"—has been useful to scholars in conceptualizing how foundations operate and how funding patterns influence institutions. For example, Roger Geiger's article later in this chapter uses the concept of isomorphism to discuss how funding shaped the development of universities.

Working within what can be regarded as a still relatively young field, scholars in philanthropic studies have sought ways to bring greater clarity and coherence to their efforts. Roger Lohmann offers the classical paradigm of the "the commons" as a suitable tool for unifying the multi-disciplinary study of nonprofit organizations, voluntarism, and philanthropy. His article provides a view of the rise of academic study in these fields since the 1970s and underscores the conceptual difficulties of using the concept of a "sector" to guide research on the wide range of philanthropic and voluntary activities outside the realm of the state and marketplace. Lohmann believes these difficulties can be overcome by using the idea of "commons" and "common goods."

Jon Van Til, like Lohmann, provides a guide for research and teaching about the "third sector," in his chapter from *Mapping the Nonprofit Sector* (2000). As Van Til describes, the vast areas of activity outside the boundaries of the state and business have been described and studied variously, as reflected in the vast literature on the nonprofit sector, the independent sector, and the third sector. As Van Til discusses, all of these terms are useful guides but have limitations and have generated debate. For example, some theorists add a fourth section to their conceptual map in order to recognize the private role of the family.

The final selection in Chapter 2 crystallizes yet another important connection between the history of higher education and philanthropic traditions in the U.S. Philosopher and foundation staff member William Sullivan argues that "in the popular mind the mission of the academy has remained distinctly public and philanthropic." His conceptual framework of the "university as a citizen" evokes the ideal of service, examined in greater depth in Part II of this Reader—and places universities at the center of a contemporary discussion about the vitality of civic life and democracy in the U.S.

***

In Chapter 3, the focus shifts to a closer examination of individual donors, their gifts, and their approaches to philanthropy. A closer look at the impact of individual donors is exceedingly important to a discussion of educational philanthropy in higher education. Each year nearly three-fourths of the gifts to all causes are given by individuals. Notably, in 2005, individual giving totaled $199.7 billion dollars or 76.5 percent of all philanthropic giving. And, over time, education has been one of the favored targets of both individual and organized philanthropy in the United States, receiving a total of $28 billion dollars from all sources (alumni/ae, foundations, corporate giving, and non-alumni/ae friends) in 2006, according to the Council for Aid to Education (second to religion).[8] This generosity stems in large part from a longstanding belief in education as a tool or a social good as well as from government incentives (through the tax structure) for individuals to give.

"American Millionaires and Their Public Gifts," a commentary based on a list of wealthy donors that appeared in the *New York Tribune*, portrays the social world of the late 19th century, where many of the well-to-do directed their gifts to local educational institutions. The newspaper account describes the phenomenon of individuals who amassed vast fortunes through business ventures related to building the infrastructure of a national society (for example, telegraphs or railroads) and tapping natural resources (the development of the oil, steel, and coal industries). The editors describe these gains not in individual terms but rather as a kind of "social wealth," which carries with it an "obligation" to society—especially in the absence of any government tax or policy to redistribute wealth. The article also provides an example of the media's attention to the great university builders and the donors who aided their work. Today we see increased media attention to large-scale gifts and bequests and their ramifications, perhaps most notably the recent high-profile gift by Warren Buffett to the Bill and Melinda Gates Foundation.

The next three selections focus on the relationship between the donor and the recipient institution. The focus here is not on the simple act of writing a check, but rather on the purposeful donation. History shows that some donors have intended their benefaction to foster or to compel institutional change. One recalls Thomas Hollis's gift in 1719 to endow a divinity chair at Harvard. Others, especially "outsiders" like women and individuals of color, have used gifts by donors to achieve agency within the social structure. The selections that follow illuminate the goals and values that donors brought to the process of giving and the significance of their gifts to the recipients.

Andrea Walton uses the lens of philanthropy to study the history of Columbia University and the contributions of two patrons, Grace Dodge, a founder of Teachers College, and Elsie Clews Parsons, a benefactor of Columbia's anthropology department. Walton discusses how philanthropy became an avenue by which these women were able to overcome the barriers of gender and to participate in discipline- and institution-building at an elite university.

Paul Ritterband and Harold Wechsler consider the role of patronage on curricular innovation as they examine the politics surrounding the naming of Salo Baron, "the most suitable and available man," to an endowed chair in Jewish learning at Columbia University in 1928. In this particular case, the donor, Linda Miller, the widow of a local businessman, aimed to memorialize her husband through the gift of an endowed chair. The search was protracted: The donor held a particular vision of the type of study to be introduced at Columbia and directed the search committee's attention to a particular scholar. However, the university had its own interests and definition of "suitability" and sought both to direct the benefaction to the institution's own ends and to protect the faculty hiring process from any intrusiveness of the donor.

The final selection in this chapter is a brief popular media account of Larry Ellison's decision to withdraw his gift pledge of $115 million dollars from Harvard University. As "The Rich Giveth, and They Taketh Away" underscores, donor-recipient ties can change unpredictably and always need nurturing. Indeed, the pages of the *Chronicle of Higher Education* and the *Chronicle of Philanthropy* in recent years have described a growing number of high-profile tensions between donor interests and institutional interests and the orientation of a new breed of hands-on donors who are concerned with accountability and results. This piece might be read along with Luisa Boverini's essay "When Venture Philanthropy Rocks the Ivory Tower" in Part III.

✳✳✳

Chapter 4 explores the scope and nature of foundation activities and for this reason, reflecting the more extensive literature and complexity of the topic, is the lengthiest chapter in Part I. Although giving by individuals constitutes the lion's share of philanthropic support, the institutionalized form of private giving has become synonymous with giving in the public imagination. Foundations, largely because of their historic concern with addressing root causes of social problems through research and demonstration programs, have had widespread influence on policy and public perceptions through their grant-making. As Barry D. Karl and Stanley N. Katz explore in their now classic article, "The American Private Philanthropic Foundation and the Public Sphere, 1890–1930" the rise of foundations must be considered within the context of perceptions about the federal government's role in reform in light of sweeping economic and organizational developments during these decades, and a recognition that existing traditions of charity and association could not meet the new demands arising. Karl and Katz's article provides an excellent discussion of the history of foundations and the history of critique.

The history of social work, as Linda Shoemaker recounts in "Early Conflicts in Social Work Education," provides insight into the sweeping changes that the U.S. experienced at the end of the 19th century and the beginning of the 20th century. Once dominated by the Charity Organization Society, as social work sought to codify its knowledge base and develop models of preparation and practice it looked to a higher education setting—marked by the opening of the New York School of Philanthropy, the Boston School for Social Workers, and the Chicago School of Social Service Administration.

One of the central areas where foundations have shaped higher education and the broader network of auxiliary institutions that support the creation and dissemination of knowledge is science.

Robert Kohler's essay "Science, Foundations, and American Universities in the 1920s" explores how foundations shifted their priorities and patterns of funding from individual scientists to academic communities of scientists, with the "common cause" of foundations and university scholars. His discussion of the National Research Council (NRC) and the Social Science Research Council (SSRC) speaks to the activity of "trade associations and other voluntary agencies [that] did what in Europe [that which] was done by government agencies" (p. 141).

In "After the Emergence: Voluntary Support and the Building of American Research Universities," Roger Geiger looks at how private funds made possible the bricks-and-mortar building on campuses but also created the conditions necessary for research and its dissemination, truly defining characteristics and culture of the American university. He notes that universities existed "within a new and complex structure of philanthropy and coordinate agencies that transcended the organizational boundaries of individual universities (p. 371). If universities became more alike in the years leading up to 1910, they became more highly differentiated later as foundations began to favor private institutions and endowments, together with alumni support, enabled institutions to cap enrollments.

If the influence of foundation has often been seen as the fulcrum of progress—expansion and "making the peaks higher"—it is worth being reminded that not all observers in the 20th century of philanthropy viewed the burgeoning activities of foundations in the higher education arena in unequivocal or sanguine terms. The critics have included academics like British political scientist Harold Laski, whose essay "Foundations, Universities, and Research," appearing in *Harper's Magazine* in 1928, warned that foundation purse strings had negatively influenced teaching, producing an "executive" type of professor, and promoting collaborative research for the sake of collaboration over perhaps more fruitful independent inquiry—all threatening the autonomy and integrity of the university.

As many scholars have documented, the politicized nature of philanthropy and its impact on education became a major concern for educators seeking to broaden opportunities for African Americans. Differing opinions about the impact of philanthropy and whether it was a democratizing and liberating force that could serve the interests of African Americans or a force that served the interests of an elite ruling class divided educators.

As Marybeth Gasman elaborates in her essay on W.E.B. Du Bois and Charles S. Johnson, these two educators shared a common case of advancing black education but held fundamentally opposed views on the capacity of philanthropy to achieve that goal. Johnson developed personal strategies to work with White philanthropists to achieve his goals, such as the Institute of Race Relations or Basic College at Fisk. In contrast, Du Bois offered a radical critique of the paternalism of White philanthropy and looked instead to the state to advance social and economic equality.

Although foundations themselves have received considerable attention, it is important to look at how their funds have been channeled through private voluntary associations, which are themselves a manifestation of the associational impulse that Tocqueville observed during his trip to this country in the 1830s. Hugh Hawkins's analysis in "The Philanthropic Aegis" (Chapter 5 of his 1992 study *Banding Together: The Rise of National Associations in American Higher Education, 1887–1950*") considers a host of voluntary agencies and associations—notably the National Educational Association (NEA), the College Entrance Examination Board (CEEB), and the American Council on Education (ACE). These organizations carry out voluntarily the types of policymaking functions that in another national setting might be overseen by a ministry of education. These organizations provide the network of professionals through which foundations could exert influence, helping to influence policy and to shape the character of an educational "system."

In addition to their work at the institutional level, foundations have figured in the study and reform of higher education. Rooted in the Cold War of the 1950s, the academic study of higher education blossomed in the 1960s and 1970s. John Aubrey Douglass's "Higher Education as a National Resource: A Retrospective on the Carnegie Commission and Policy Council on Higher Education" discusses these two bodies whose funded work from 1967 to 1973 and 1973 to 1979 advanced the careers of a generation of scholars and respectively represented a landmark systematic study of higher education—resulting, for example, in the Carnegie Classification of 1973 and financial aid programs such as the Basic Educational Opportunity Grant and the Pell Grant.

Finally, whereas foundations were a dominant presence in the late 19th and early 20th centuries and have continued to be formidable actors in the post-World War II era, the Federal government's presence in recent decades has towered over private initiatives. Government funding efforts have provided student aid and crucial research opportunities that have left their mark on disciplines and scholarly careers, and established government philanthropies, such as the National Endowment for the Humanities and the National Science Foundation. Philanthropy must be viewed not in isolation but, rather, within the broader trends of professionalization, bureaucratization, democratization, and globalization, among others, and within the context of a larger web of relationships that include government and think tanks.

Grant-making and patronage have always played a role in introducing and cultivating curricular innovation and reform. Some of the innovations that we take for granted in higher education, especially in the areas of research and the disciplines, were sponsored by foundations. Mariam Chamberlain and Alison Bernstein describe the major achievements of foundation funding to efforts to challenge the male-biases of the academy and academic knowledge in "Philanthropy and the Emergence of Women's Studies." The authors discuss the efflorescence of dissertations for women, research centers (such as the Carnegie-funded Center for Research on Women founded at Wellesley College in 1974), professional organization such as National Women's Studies Association (NWSA), periodicals, and curricular mainstreaming.

Another foundation-funded and -inspired innovation still in its early stages is the effort to reconsider scholarship that was launched by Ernest Boyer during his tenure at the helm of the Carnegie Foundation for the Advancement of Teaching. Partly the outcome of a previous era's philanthropic grant-making and institution-building, the current tensions between teaching and research are a major source of discontent within the academy and the target of criticism. Boyer sought to reconceptualize scholarship as discovery, integration, application, and teaching. In "The Scholarship of Teaching: New Elaborations, New Developments" Pat Hutchings and Lee Shulman provide a progress report on Carnegie-sponsored reforms designed to improve student learning and promote (in line with Boyer's reform ideas) faculty consideration of the classroom as a laboratory for research on teaching and learning.

Many topics related to philanthropic support of colleges and universities could not be represented here. This is the case in part because of space limitations but also because the research literature is still catching up with the rapid changes in the field. For example, we need more studies about the influence of the collective power of giving circles, the rise of community foundations, outreach programs for women donors and graduates of color, the trends pointed to by new data collected on giving (such as Indiana University Center on Philanthropy's panel study of giving behaviors), and the impact of venture philanthropy.

Notes

1. Frederick Rudolph, *American College and University* (New York: Alfred Knopf, 1962). See Merle Curti and Roderick Nash, *Philanthropy in the Shaping of American Higher Education* (Piscataway: Rutgers University Press, 1965) reprinted with a new introduction by Andrea Walton at http://www.ksghauser.harvard.edu/philanthropyclassics/

2. John R. Thelin, *A History of American Higher Education* (Baltimore: Johns Hopkins University Press, 2004), pp. 145–46.

3. Barry D. Karl and Stanley N. Katz , "The American Private Philanthropic Foundation and the Public Sphere, 1890–1930," *Minerva*, Vol. 19 (1981), pp. 236–70.

4. Thelin, *A History*, pp. 145–46.

5. Survey by the Council for Aid to Education, 2006, press release February 21, 2007 accessed at www.cae.org on February 23, 2007. See also Erin Strout, "Private Donations to Colleges Increase for Third Consecutive Year," *Chronicle of Higher Education*, 22 February 2007; and "Private Giving to College Soars," *Inside Higher Education*, 22 February 2007.

6. The name given to professional advisors in philanthropic organizations.
7. See note 1.
8. See *Giving USA, 2005*, a publication of the Giving USA Foundation, accessed at http://www.givingin-stitute. org/about_aafrc/index.cfm?pg=chart1.cfm&ID=xgusa1 See also 2006 data on the "Voluntary Support of Higher Education by Source, 2006" accessed from the Council for Aid to Education, 2007 at www.cae.org and "Private Giving to College Soars."

CHAPTER 1

HISTORICAL OVERVIEW

WEALTH

ANDREW CARNEGIE
JUNE, 1889

The problem of our age is the proper administration of wealth, so that the ties of brotherhood may still bind together the rich and poor in harmonious relationship. The conditions of human life have not only been changed, but revolutionized, within the past few hundred years. In former days there was little difference between the dwelling, dress, food, and environment of the chief and those of his retainers. The Indians are to-day where civilized man then was. When visiting the Sioux, I was led to the wigwam of the chief. It was just like the others in external appearance, and even within the difference was trifling between it and those of the poorest of his braves. The contrast between the palace of the millionaire and the cottage of the laborer with us to-day measures the change which has come with civilization.

This change, however, is not to be deplored, but welcomed as highly beneficial. It is well, nay, essential for the progress of the race, that the houses of some should be homes for all that is highest and best in literature and the arts, and for all the refinements of civilization, rather than that none should be so. Much better this great irregularity than universal squalor. Without wealth there can be no Mæcenas. The "good old times" were not good old times. Neither master nor servant was as well situated then as to-day. A relapse to old conditions would be disastrous to both—not the least so to him who serves—and would sweep away civilization with it. But whether the change be for good or ill, it is upon us, beyond our power to alter, and therefore to be accepted and made the best of. It is a waste of time to criticise the inevitable.

It is easy to see how the change has come. One illustration will serve for almost every phase of the cause. In the manufacture of products we have the whole story. It applies to all combinations of human industry, as stimulated and enlarged by the inventions of this scientific age. Formerly articles were manufactured at the domestic hearth or in small shops which formed part of the household. The master and his apprentices worked side by side, the latter living with the master, and therefore subject to the same conditions. When these apprentices rose to be masters, there was little or no change in their mode of life, and they, in turn, educated in the same routine succeeding apprentices. There was, substantially, social equality, and even political equality, for those engaged in industrial pursuits had then little or no political voice in the State.

But the inevitable result of such a mode of manufacture was crude articles at high prices. To-day the world obtains commodities of excellent quality at prices which even the generation preceding this would have deemed incredible. In the commercial world similar causes have produced similar results, and the race is benefited thereby. The poor enjoy what the rich could not before afford. What were the luxuries have become the necessaries of life. The laborer has now more comforts than the farmer had a few generations ago. The farmer has more luxuries than the landlord had, and is more richly clad and better housed. The landlord has books and pictures rarer, and appointments more artistic, than the King could then obtain.

The price we pay for this salutary change is, no doubt, great. We assemble thousands of operatives in the factory, in the mine, and in the counting-house, of whom the employer can know little or nothing, and to whom the employer is little better than a myth. All intercourse between them is at an end.

14

Rigid Castes are formed, and, as usual, mutual ignorance breeds mutual distrust. Each Caste is without sympathy for the other, and ready to credit anything disparaging in regard to it. Under the law of competition, the employer of thousands is forced into the strictest economies, among which the rates paid to labor figure prominently, and often there is friction between the employer and the employed, between capital and labor, between rich and poor. Human society loses homogeneity.

The price which society pays for the law of competition, like the price it pays for cheap comforts and luxuries, is also great; but the advantages of this law are also greater still, for it is to this law that we owe our wonderful material development, which brings improved conditions in its train. But, whether the law be benign or not, we must say of it, as we say of the change in the conditions of men to which we have referred: It is here; we cannot evade it; no substitutes for it have been found; and while the law may be sometimes hard for the individual, it is best for the race, because it insures the survival of the fittest in every department. We accept and welcome, therefore, as conditions to which we must accommodate ourselves, great inequality of environment, the concentration of business, industrial and commercial, in the hands of a few, and the law of competition between these, as being not only beneficial, but essential for the future progress of the race. Having accepted these, it follows that there must be great scope for the exercise of special ability in the merchant and in the manufacturer who has to conduct affairs upon a great scale. That this talent for organization and management is rare among men is proved by the fact that it invariably secures for its possessor enormous rewards, no matter where or under what laws or conditions. The experienced in affairs always rate the MAN whose services can be obtained as a partner as not only the first consideration, but such as to render the question of his capital scarcely worth considering, for such men soon create capital; while, without the special talent required, capital soon takes wings. Such men become interested in firms or corporations using millions; and estimating only simple interest to be made upon the capital invested, it is inevitable that their income must exceed their expenditures, and that they must accumulate wealth. Nor is there any middle ground which such men can occupy, because the great manufacturing or commercial concern which does not earn at least interest upon its capital soon becomes bankrupt. It must either go forward or fall behind: to stand still is impossible. It is a condition essential for its successful operation that it should be thus far profitable, and even that, in addition to interest on capital, it should make profit. It is a law, as certain as any of the others named, that men possessed of this peculiar talent for affairs, under the free play of economic forces, must, of necessity, soon be in receipt of more revenue than can be judiciously expended upon themselves; and this law is as beneficial for the race as others.

Objections to the foundations upon which society is based are not in order, because the condition of the race is better with these than it has been with any others which have been tried. Of the effect of any new substitutes proposed we cannot be sure. The Socialist or Anarchist who seeks to overturn present conditions is to be regarded as attacking the foundation upon which civilization itself rests, for civilization took its start from the day that the capable, industrious workman said to his incompetent and lazy fellow, "If thou dost not sow, thou shalt not reap," and thus ended primitive Communism by separating the drones from the bees. One who studies this subject will soon be brought face to face with the conclusion that upon the sacredness of property civilization itself depends—the right of the laborer to his hundred dollars in the savings bank, and equally the legal right of the millionaire to his millions. To those who propose to substitute Communism for this intense Individualism the answer, therefore, is: The race has tried that. All progress from that barbarous day to the present time has resulted from its displacement. Not evil, but good, has come to the race from the accumulation of wealth by those who have the ability and energy that produce it. But even if we admit for a moment that it might be better for the race to discard its present foundation, Individualism,—that it is a nobler ideal that man should labor, not for himself alone, but in and for a brotherhood of his fellows, and share with them all in common, realizing Swedenborg's idea of Heaven, where, as he says, the angels derive their happiness, not from laboring for self, but for each other,—even admit all this, and a sufficient answer is, This is not evolution, but revolution. It necessitates the changing of human nature itself—a work of æons, even if it were good to change it, which we cannot know. It is not practicable in our day or in our age. Even if desirable theoretically, it belongs to another and long-succeeding sociological stratum. Our duty is with what is practicable now; with the next step possible in our day and generation. It is criminal to waste our energies in endeavoring to uproot, when all we can profitably or possibly accomplish is to bend the universal tree of humanity a little in the direction most favorable to the production of good fruit under existing circumstances. We might as well urge the destruction of the highest existing type of man because he failed to reach our ideal as to favor the destruction of Individualism, Private Property, the Law of Accumulation of Wealth, and the Law of Competition; for these are the highest results of human experience, the soil in which society so far has produced the best fruit. Unequally or unjustly, perhaps, as these laws sometimes operate, and imperfect as they appear to the Idealist, they are, nevertheless, like the highest type of man, the best and most valuable of all that humanity has yet accomplished.

We start, then, with a condition of affairs under which the best interests of the race are promoted, but which inevitably gives wealth to the few. Thus far, accepting conditions as they exist, the situation can be surveyed and pronounced good. The question then arises,—and, if the foregoing be correct, it is the only question with which we have to deal,—What is the proper mode of administering wealth after the laws upon which civilization is founded have thrown it into the hands of the few? And it is of this great question that I believe I offer the true solution. It will be understood that *fortunes* are here spoken of, not moderate sums saved by many years of effort, the returns from which are required for the comfortable maintenance and education of families. This is not *wealth*, but only *competence*, which it should be the aim of all to acquire.

There are but three modes in which surplus wealth can be disposed of. It can be left to the families of the decedents; or it can be bequeathed for public purposes; or, finally, it can be administered during their lives by its possessors. Under the first and second modes most of the wealth of the world that has reached the few has hitherto been applied. Let us in turn consider each of these modes. The first is the most injudicious. In monarchical countries, the estates and the greatest portion of the wealth are left to the first son, that the vanity of the parent may be gratified by the thought that his name and title are to descend to succeeding generations unimpaired. The condition of this class in Europe to-day teaches the futility of such hopes or ambitions. The successors have become impoverished through their follies or from the fall in the value of land. Even in Great Britain the strict law of entail has been found inadequate to maintain the status of an hereditary class. Its soil is rapidly passing into the hands of the stranger. Under republican institutions the division of property among the children is much fairer, but the question which forces itself upon thoughtful men in all lands is: Why should men leave great fortunes to their children? If this is done from affection, is it not misguided affection? Observation teaches that, generally speaking, it is not well for the children that they should be so burdened. Neither is it well for the state. Beyond providing for the wife and daughters moderate sources of income, and very moderate allowances indeed, if any, for the sons, men may well hesitate, for it is no longer questionable that great sums bequeathed oftener work more for the injury than for the good of the recipients. Wise men will soon conclude that, for the best interests of the members of their families and of the state, such bequests are an improper use of their means.

It is not suggested that men who have failed to educate their sons to earn a livelihood shall cast them adrift in poverty. If any man has seen fit to rear his sons with a view to their living idle lives, or, what is highly commendable, has instilled in them the sentiment that they are in a position to labor for public ends without reference to pecuniary considerations, then, of course, the duty of the parent is to see that such are provided for *in moderation*. There are instances of millionaires' sons unspoiled by wealth, who, being rich, still perform great services in the community. Such are the very salt of the earth, as valuable as, unfortunately, they are rare; still it is not the exception, but the rule, that men must regard, and, looking at the usual result of enormous sums conferred upon legatees, the thoughtful man must shortly say, "I would as soon leave to my son a curse as the almighty dollar," and admit to himself that it is not the welfare of the children, but family pride, which inspires these enormous legacies.

As to the second mode, that of leaving wealth at death for public uses, it may be said that this is only a means for the disposal of wealth, provided a man is content to wait until he is dead before it becomes of much good in the world. Knowledge of the results of legacies bequeathed is not calculated to inspire the brightest hopes of much posthumous good being accomplished. The cases are not few in which the real object sought by the testator is not attained, nor are they few in which his real wishes are thwarted. In many cases the bequests are so used as to become only monuments of his folly. It is well to remember that it requires the exercise of not less ability than that which acquired the wealth to use it so as to be really beneficial to the community. Besides this, it may fairly be said that no man is to be extolled for doing what he cannot help doing, nor is he to be thanked by the community to which he only leaves wealth at death. Men who leave vast sums in this way may fairly be thought men who would not have left it at all, had they been able to take it with them. The memories of such cannot be held in grateful remembrance, for there is no grace in their gifts. It is not to be wondered at that such bequests seem so generally to lack the blessing.

The growing disposition to tax more and more heavily large estates left at death is a cheering indication of the growth of a salutary change in public opinion. The State of Pennsylvania now takes—subject to some exceptions—one-tenth of the property left by its citizens. The budget presented in the British Parliament the other day proposes to increase the death-duties; and, most significant of all, the new tax is to be a graduated one. Of all forms of taxation, this seems the wisest. Men who continue hoarding great sums all their lives, the proper use of which for public ends would work good to the community, should be made to feel that the community, in the form of the state, cannot thus be deprived of its proper share. By taxing estates heavily at death the state marks its condemnation of the selfish millionaire's unworthy life.

It is desirable that nations should go much further in this direction. Indeed, it is difficult to set bounds to the share of a rich man's estate which should go at his death to the public through the agency of the state, and by all means such taxes should be graduated, beginning at nothing upon moderate sums to dependents, and increasing rapidly as the amounts swell, until of the millionaire's hoard, as of Shylock's, at least

> "——The other half
> Comes to the privy coffer of the state."

This policy would work powerfully to induce the rich man to attend to the administration of wealth during his life, which is the end that society should always have in view, as being that by far most fruitful for the people. Nor need it be feared that this policy would sap the root of enterprise and render men less anxious to accumulate, for to the class whose ambition it is to leave great fortunes and be talked about after their death, it will attract even more attention, and, indeed, be a somewhat nobler ambition to have enormous sums paid over to the state from their fortunes.

There remains, then, only one mode of using great fortunes; but in this we have the true antidote for the temporary unequal distribution of wealth, the reconciliation of the rich and the poor—a reign of harmony—another ideal, differing, indeed, from that of the Communist in requiring only the further evolution of existing conditions, not the total overthrow of our civilization. It is founded upon the present most intense individualism, and the race is prepared to put it in practice by degrees whenever it pleases. Under its sway we shall have an ideal state, in which the surplus wealth of the few will become, in the best sense, the property of the many, because administered for the common good, and this wealth, passing through the hands of the few, can be made a much more potent force for the elevation of our race than if it had been distributed in small sums to the people themselves. Even the poorest can be made to see this, and to agree that great sums gathered by some of their fellow-citizens and spent for public purposes, from which the masses reap the principal benefit, are more valuable to them than if scattered among them through the course of many years in trifling amounts.

If we consider what results flow from the Cooper Institute, for instance, to the best portion of the race in New York not possessed of means, and compare these with those which would have arisen for the good of the masses from an equal sum distributed by Mr. Cooper in his lifetime in the form of wages, which is the highest form of distribution, being for work done and not for charity, we can form some estimate of the possibilities for the improvement of the race which lie embedded in the present law of the accumulation of wealth. Much of this sum, if distributed in small quantities among the people, would have been wasted in the indulgence of appetite, some of it in excess, and it may be doubted whether even the part put to the best use, that of adding to the comforts of the home, would have yielded results for the race, as a race, at all comparable to those which are flowing and are to flow from the Cooper Institute from generation to generation. Let the advocate of violent or radical change ponder well this thought.

We might even go so far as to take another instance, that of Mr. Tilden's bequest of five millions of dollars for a free library in the city of New York, but in referring to this one cannot help saying involuntarily, How much better if Mr. Tilden had devoted the last years of his own life to the proper administration of this immense sum; in which case neither legal contest nor any other cause of delay could have interfered with his aims. But let us assume that Mr. Tilden's millions finally become the means of giving to this city a noble public library, where the treasures of the world contained in books will be open to all forever, without money and without price. Considering the good of that part of the race which congregates in and around Manhattan Island, would its permanent benefit have been better promoted had these millions been allowed to circulate in small sums through the hands of the masses? Even the most strenuous advocate of Communism must entertain a doubt upon this subject. Most of those who think will probably entertain no doubt whatever.

Poor and restricted are our opportunities in this life; narrow our horizon; our best work most imperfect; but rich men should be thankful for one inestimable boon. They have it in their power during their lives to busy themselves in organizing benefactions from which the masses of their fellows will derive lasting advantage, and thus dignify their own lives. The highest life is probably to be reached, not by such imitation of the life of Christ as Count Tolstoï gives us, but, while animated by Christ's spirit, by recognizing the changed conditions of this age, and adopting modes of expressing this spirit suitable to the changed conditions under which we live; still laboring for the good of our fellows, which was the essence of his life and teaching, but laboring in a different manner.

This, then, is held to be the duty of the man of Wealth: First, to set an example of modest, unostentatious living, shunning display or extravagance; to provide moderately for the legitimate wants of those dependent upon him; and after doing so to consider all surplus revenues which come to him simply as trust funds, which he is called upon to administer, and strictly bound as a matter of duty to administer in the manner which, in his judgment, is best calculated to produce the most beneficial results for the community—the man of wealth thus becoming the mere agent and trustee for his poorer brethren, bringing to their service his superior wisdom, experience, and ability to administer, doing for them better than they would or could do for themselves.

We are met here with the difficulty of determining what are moderate sums to leave to members of the family; what is modest, unostentatious living; what is the test of extravagance. There must be different standards for different conditions. The answer is that it is as impossible to name exact amounts or actions as it is to define good manners, good taste, or the rules of propriety; but, nevertheless, these are verities, well known although undefinable. Public sentiment is quick to know and to feel what offends these. So in the case of wealth. The rule in regard to good taste in the dress of men or women applies here. Whatever makes one conspicuous offends the canon. If any family be chiefly known for display, for extravagance in home, table, equipage, for enormous sums ostentatiously spent in any form upon itself,—if these be its chief distinctions, we have no difficulty in estimating its nature or culture. So likewise in regard to the use or abuse of its surplus wealth, or to generous, freehanded coöperation in good public uses, or to unabated efforts to accumulate and hoard to the last, whether they administer or bequeath. The verdict rests with the best and most enlightened public sentiment. The community will surely judge, and its judgments will not often be wrong.

The best uses to which surplus wealth can be put have already been indicated. Those who would administer wisely must, indeed, be wise, for one of the serious obstacles to the improvement of our race is indiscriminate charity. It were better for mankind that the millions of the rich were thrown into the sea than so spent as to encourage the slothful, the drunken, the unworthy. Of every thousand dollars spent in so called charity to-day, it is probable that $950 is unwisely spent; so spent, indeed, as to produce the very evils which it proposes to mitigate or cure. A well-known writer of philosophic books admitted the other day that he had given a quarter of a dollar to a man who approached him as he was coming to visit the house of his friend. He knew nothing of the habits of this beggar; knew not the use that would be made of this money, although he had every reason to suspect that it would be spent improperly. This man professed to be a disciple of Herbert Spencer; yet the quarter-dollar given that night will probably work more injury than all the money which its thoughtless donor will ever be able to give in true charity will do good. He only gratified his own feelings, saved himself from annoyance,—and this was probably one of the most selfish and very worst actions of his life, for in all respects he is most worthy.

In bestowing charity, the main consideration should be to help those who will help themselves; to provide part of the means by which those who desire to improve may do so; to give those who desire to rise the aids by which they may rise; to assist, but rarely or never to do all. Neither the individual nor the race is improved by alms-giving. Those worthy of assistance, except in rare cases, seldom require assistance. The really valuable men of the race never do, except in cases of accident or sudden change. Every one has, of course, cases of individuals brought to his own knowledge where temporary assistance can do genuine good, and these he will not overlook. But the amount which can be wisely given by the individual for individuals is necessarily limited by his lack of knowledge of the circumstances connected with each. He is the only true reformer who is as careful and as anxious not to aid the unworthy as he is to aid the worthy, and, perhaps, even more so, for in alms-giving more injury is probably done by rewarding vice than by relieving virtue.

The rich man is thus almost restricted to following the examples of Peter Cooper, Enoch Pratt of Baltimore, Mr. Pratt of Brooklyn, Senator Stanford, and others, who know that the best means of benefiting the community is to place within its reach the ladders upon which the aspiring can rise—parks, and means of recreation, by which men are helped in body and mind; works of art, certain to give pleasure and improve the public taste, and public institutions of various kinds, which will improve the general condition of the people;—in this manner returning their surplus wealth to the mass of their fellows in the forms best calculated to do them lasting good.

Thus is the problem of Rich and Poor to be solved. The laws of accumulation will be left free; the laws of distribution free. Individualism will continue, but the millionaire will be but a trustee for the poor; intrusted for a season with a great part of the increased wealth of the community, but administering it for the community far better than it could or would have done for itself. The best minds will thus have reached a stage in the development of the race in which it is clearly seen that there is no mode of disposing of surplus wealth creditable to thoughtful and earnest men into whose hands it flows save by using it year by year for the general good. This day already dawns. But a little while, and although, without incurring the pity of their fellows, men may die sharers in great business enterprises from which their capital cannot be or has not been withdrawn, and is left chiefly at death for public uses, yet the man who dies leaving behind him millions of available wealth, which was his to administer during life, will pass away "unwept, unhonored, and unsung," no matter to what uses he leaves the dross which he cannot take with him. Of such as these the public verdict will then be : "The man who dies thus rich dies disgraced."

Such, in my opinion, is the true Gospel concerning Wealth, obedience to which is destined some day to solve the problem of the Rich and the Poor, and to bring "Peace on earth, among men Good-Will."

TAINTED MONEY

WASHINGTON GLADDEN

The novelists have been dealing rather freely of late with the question respecting the kind of human beings which the present plutocratic régime is producing. What breed of men is coming out of our gigantic commercial operations? What manner of society does it all produce? What are the habits, sentiments, standards of judgment, forms of social enjoyment, which prevail in these circles? Mrs. Burton Harrison has been trying to answer these questions for us; so has Mr. Marion Crawford, and Mr. Charles Dudley Warner, and so have others. One striking contribution to this discussion is Sir Walter Besant's story, "Beyond the Dreams of Avarice." It is the tale of an ill-gotten fortune and of its influence upon the lives of all who sought to gain possession of it. The old miser, the last proprietor, under whose sordid and infamous manipulations the estate had been twice or thrice doubled, and who had driven his own children from their home by his avarice, dies, apparently intestate, in one of the first chapters, and leaves a property of enormous proportions—enormous for England, only moderate for America—some twelve million pounds. The property, unless an heir appears, escheats to the State: but there is an heir—a grandson, a young physician and rising man of science—who knows himself to be the heir, though the knowledge is shared by no one except his young wife and his lawyer. His father, who had cut himself loose from a family whose traditions were all accursed, and had changed his name and made for himself an honorable reputation, had charged him on his death-bed not to touch that tainted wealth; and when he learns that there is no will, and that the property is legally his, his first inclination is to heed his father's counsel and never reveal his identity. For a considerable time he maintains this resolution, supported therein by his wife, whose intuitions never waver. The whole history of the family becomes known to them; the steps by which the fortune has been amassed are shown them; and the record is one of appalling cruelty and perfidy. Evidently a curse has fallen on all who have had anything to do with the money, from the founder of the house to the last representative. And yet the knowledge that he can, by saying the word, step in and take all this fabulous wealth and make himself rich beyond the dreams of avarice, soon casts its spell over the life of this young physician. Everybody knows the infamy of all the previous possessors of this plunder—his grandfather included; for after the miser's death the newspapers unearthed the family secrets and spread the whole sickening story before the gaze of the world. To take the fortune is to be the inheritor of that infamy. "But, after all," he began to argue, "how am I to blame for the acts of my ancestors? And is it not true that this generation has ceased to be squeamish about the sources of wealth? Should I, after all, lose much social caste on account of the crimes of my forbears? Would not a man with so much money be likely to become an important personage in society, no matter how the money may have been gotten? And then, the good that could be done with it! The great college of science that it would build! The immense enterprises that could be endowed for the enlightenment of mankind!" So the dream wrought upon him, and the effect was melancholy. All his interest in his profession was lost; his nature grew hard and cynical; his moral sense was blunted; all his ideals were dethroned.

Other claimants soon appeared—grandnephews and grandnieces, who, not knowing of the existence of the direct heir, began to gather like moths to a candle. To every one of them the attempt to secure this property brought harm and shame; the nearer they came to it the more sordid grew their natures and the more disturbed their thoughts; lives that had been peaceful and prosperous felt the blight of this Mountain of Mammon as soon as they came within its shadow. And the story makes it easy to see why this must have been: it was no result of superstition; it was a clear case of cause and effect.

It is not necessary to tell the story, but the psychological study is full of suggestion. One is able to see that money secured by extortion or by crime must carry a curse with it to all who, seeing the blood-stains upon it, covet it for themselves. The question of tainted money is a question that this generation must face. There are vast heaps of it on every side of us—accumulations that have been made by methods as heartless, as cynically iniquitous as any that were employed by Roman plunderers or robber barons of the Dark Ages. In the cool brutality with which properties are wrecked, securities destroyed, and people by the hundreds robbed of their little all to build up the fortunes of the multi-millionaires, we have an appalling revelation of the kind of monster that a human being may become. Much of this wealth has been gained by the most daring violation of the laws of the land; by tampering with courts of justice; by the bribery of city councils or legislatures, and even of Congress itself; by practices which have introduced into the body politic a virulent and deadly poison that threatens the very life of the Nation. That many of the largest fortunes in this country have some such origin all intelligent men know. Is this clean money? Can any man, can any institution, knowing its origin, touch it without being defiled?

We often hear it said that the money of Dives is just as good as any other man's money; that if he will only make over some portion of his wealth to us we will find good uses for it and ask no questions about where he got it. Is this a safe principle? Suppose we know that the money was stolen, and from whom it was stolen; should we be justified in accepting it? Should we not be partakers of the crime? If we are morally certain that it was obtained by some kind of robbery, legalized or otherwise, yet do not know from whom it was wrested, is our complicity any less real?

In truth, the gold and the silver that have been obtained by wrong are corroded with a rust which eats the flesh like fire. Every man who covets such gains passes under their curse. Money is not a mere material entity. Its character is symbolic and representative. It always stands for something. It is either the reward of productive labor, of honest commerce, or it is the sign of injustice and fraud. To separate the money from the history of the processes by which it was won is not practicable. To wish for ill-gotten gains is to condone the wrongs by which they were obtained.

Even if this reasoning be thought fanciful, no man can eliminate the personal factor which always enters into the problem. To accept the reward of iniquity is to place upon our lips the seal of silence respecting its perpetrators. Those who recognize no responsibility for the maintenance of public virtue may wear such a muzzle without discomfort; but it would seem that public teachers, of all sorts, should be unwilling to put it on.

Money that has been gained by nefarious methods is often brought to the door of the church, and those who bring it seldom fail of a warm welcome. The liberal contribution can hardly be refused; will not such charity cover a multitude of sins? If this malefactor has done evil in the past, ought we not to be glad that he now seems to be of a better mind? And this money will go just as far in "supporting the Gospel" as any other man's money. Why should we hesitate about taking it? Think of the good that may be done by turning this wealth—which men say has been gotten by iniquity—into channels of mercy! If the liberal donor happen to conceive a special fondness for the parson, and there are handsome gifts now and then, and suggestions of European tours, all this reasoning gains in cogency.

Of course, under such circumstances, the pulpit of this church is not likely to discuss the kind of iniquity by which this money was gained, nor anything near akin to it. It would be extremely ungrateful—it would, indeed, be dishonorable—for this pulpit to touch upon such matters. Having sought and welcomed these liberal donations, it is simply the dictate of ordinary decency to refrain from criticising the financial methods of the donor. People might charge that this plutocrat had stipulated that nothing should be said in the church about his practices, but that is a crude conception; of course he has said nothing about it; nothing has been said by anybody; nothing needs to be said. This minister has never promised that he will be silent on themes of this character; it is not necessary for him to make any promise; the situation speaks for itself; if he has the instincts of a gentleman, he will not assail the man who has put him under such obligations.

This pulpit, then, will have no message respecting wrongs of this particular kind. And, inasmuch as it would seem rather inconsistent to attack other closely related social wrongs and avoid these, this pulpit will probably abstain from all reference to public evils. It will confine itself to what is known as "the simple Gospel"—to a purely abstract religionism which has little or nothing to do with life in this world, but which confines itself to the preparation of men for the world to come. The kind of preaching which Isaiah and Jeremiah and Amos and Paul and James practiced will not be heard from this pulpit. Its moral power will be paralyzed. Its influence upon the social life of the community will be practically nil. Or, if it stands for anything at all, its silent testimony will support the iniquities by which the foundations of the social order are undermined.

Such is the effect of tainted money upon the life of a church. When it is coveted and sought, when those who bring it to the altars of the church are courted and made welcome, consequences like these are simply inevitable.

Similar results must needs appear in the life of a college built on such foundations or largely dependent on resources of this character. Not a little of this tainted money has been turned into the channels of the higher education. It seems to have been assumed by many of those who have this work in charge that all money is pure and holy, and that just as much good can be done with the money of a robber as with the money of an honest merchant or manufacturer. It seems even to have been regarded as a meritorious achievement to pave the highways of learning with the price of blood.

It is passing strange that the implications and consequences of such an alliance should be ignored or disregarded. Is it not plain that an institution which accepts subsidies from notoriously iniquitous sources, by this act virtually resigns the privilege of bearing testimony against such iniquities? When we enter into partnership with corruptionists and extortionists in the business of education, we must, in common decency, refrain from turning round and abusing our partners. Whatever public teaching may be needed respecting the evil conditions out of which this fortune has sprung, this college, at least, can offer none. It is foolish to say that the donor has imposed no restrictions upon the teaching; certainly not; there is not the least need of it. Some things can be taken for granted, among gentlemen. It would be utterly dishonorable for an institution thus founded, or largely befriended, to enter into a thorough investigation of the methods by which its endowments were accumulated. The teaching might deal, in an abstract way, with social subjects; but it could not examine historically and scientifically certain burning questions of its own neighborhood and generation. Its instructors will be constrained to say to themselves—perhaps to one another—"All this is valuable and necessary work, but this is not the institution where such work can be done." Think of a college—above all, a "Christian" college—putting itself in such an attitude as this before the world!

But this is not all. An institution thus allied must needs pay honor to those whose benefactions it is sharing. There will be a place, and a high place, at its feasts for the men to whom it owes so much. Glowing words of eulogy will not be wanting. The young men of the institution who look and listen will thus be aided in forming their theories of life. The whole world will see who it is that these Christian scholars and leaders of the people delight to honor. So it is that public opinion is formed, and that men who are the pirates of industry and the spoilers of the state are advanced to the front rank in modern society.

Is it true that one man's money is worth as much as another's to a church or a college? Is it not rather true that there is a great deal of money with which the hands that are seeking to do the will of God must never defile themselves? For much of this money, under all sound ethical standards, must be considered as stolen money. And do our churches and colleges need to be told that the partaker is as bad as the thief?

But it may be said that a great deal of the money in circulation comes from questionable sources. Fraud and falsehood and extortion, we are told, play a large part in the building of many fortunes. Much of the money that comes into our hands has been tainted by methods of which we are not aware. This may be true; but so long as we are not aware of the evil sources, we are not contaminated. It is impossible for us to investigate the business of all our neighbors; it is our duty to assume that they are honest until there is good evidence to the contrary. But when their transactions are flagrant and notorious, we may at least decline to enter into partnership with them in the business of religion or of education. There is enough of clean money in the country—money that has been gained in honest trade or productive industry—to furnish the churches and the colleges with all necessary resources.

Really—must it be said?—money is not the first requisite of a great church or a great college. Some things are more important. Is it not well for churches and colleges to ask themselves what these things are? What shall it profit a church or a college if it shall gain the whole world and lose its own life?

How to Help Men Most with Money

Educate Six Million Negro Children

Booker T. Washington

Some time ago, in Alabama, one old colored woman met another in the public road and said, "Sister, where is you gwine?" Her friend replied, "I has done been where I's gwine."

It is not often that an individual or a nation has the privilege of dealing close at hand with a new people, of shaping and molding a new race. Most of the races of the world have been "where they is gwine"; the American Negro has yet to go "where he's gwine," and is now on the way. During the next few years the people of this country will have an opportunity, such as will perhaps never occur again, to shape the destiny of the millions of Negroes in this country.

The Negroes in the Southern States occupy nearly one-eighth of all the farming land in the United States. It is safe to say that for a number of years at least Negroes will occupy this territory as farmers, almost to the exclusion of any other race. Since we have, then, nearly seven millions of Negroes occupying nearly one-eighth of the richest farming land in the United States, it is important that every individual Negro be made just as valuable a producer as is possible.

In the agricultural states of the Middle West, the average farmer produces annually more than $1,000 worth of products. In the Southern States, the average Negro farmer produces only $340 worth of produce. This condition can, I am convinced, be speedily changed if the masses of the Negro people, especially those who reside in the farming districts, are given the opportunity for an education that will really help them to live and make the most of their opportunities.

I know perfectly well that when I speak of educating the Negro there are a number of people who will express doubts. They will perhaps refer to the sums that have been already expended on the education of the Negro without any adequate results. Very few people in the United States realize the fact that education has never been tried on the Negro except in spots, and these spots are generally in the larger towns and cities.

In South Carolina last year, for example, every Negro child had spent upon him for his education from the public fund $1.70. At the same time Iowa spent $18.33 on every child, irrespective of color. There is one county in Alabama where the state contributes from the public fund $15.84 for the education of every white child and $1.78 for the education of every Negro child in that county.

Under such circumstances it is impossible to educate the masses of the Negro race, and a little education serves in many cases to hurt rather than to help. When I speak of the small amount per capita spent on the Negro in the rural districts in the South, I have not by any means told the whole story. This small expenditure means a schoolhouse that is not fit for creatures of any kind to remain in, a poor teacher, a school-term of from two to five months during the year.

If I speak confidently concerning the use to which a large sum of money could be put for Negro education in the rural districts of the South, it is because in Macon County, Ala., where I live, the thing has been tried, and the results have justified the expense. In Macon County the Negro children and the Negro people of the rural districts have good schoolhouses. The schools are in session from eight to nine months during the year. The teachers receive good wages. The children are not only taught from the book, but are taught cooking, table-serving, sewing—and especially gardening, farming of all kinds, poultry-raising, pig-raising, and dairying. The teachers in the rural districts of Macon County take pride in their school farms, which are usually found adjoining the schoolhouse and serve to furnish part of the money for the support of the teacher. Where such conditions as I have described exist, the whole life of the community centres in and around the school, and the work of the school touches and changes every part of the life of the people surrounding it.

If it were possible to get sufficient means for the purpose, it would be possible to multiply these thrifty, little farming communities all over the South, and the whole Southern country would prosper as a result.

The colored people of Macon County have learned, as a result of the efforts that have been made to articulate the work of the school with the life of the farm and the community, that education actually means something; that education does not make a fool of an individual, but makes him a sensible, sober, useful person.

The white people in Macon County see the benefit of this kind of education. They have long since learned that it pays to have a good Negro schoolhouse, to have a good teacher, and a school session lasting from eight to nine months—because the people of the county pay less money in punishing criminals, because the land is more valuable, because farm laborers are contented and permanent, and because more friendly relations exist between the races.

Whatever is done in the way of helping Negro rural education, let me add, should be done in connection with the public school. The public school system is permanent, and whatever is contributed ought to be done with the knowledge and coöperation of public-school authorities.

The money spent in this way is used not merely to improve present conditions but to build up a permanent system. Faster than anyone realizes, the masses of the colored people can be taught to help themselves in these matters. In Macon County in one year, the colored people have raised in extra taxation more than $3,800 to be used in building school-houses and extending the school term.

It is a disgrace to our Christian civilization for the outside world to know that, with all of our wealth and intelligence in this country, we are permitting between six and seven millions of children in the rural districts of the South to grow up in almost total ignorance. Here is a rare opportunity, in my opinion, for a large sum of money to accomplish the greatest good in this generation.

A Foundation's Relationship to its Public: Legacies and Lessons for the Lilly Endowment

D. Susan Wisely

As has often been observed, the private foundation is a curious creature on the landscape of American society. It is an institution posed somewhere between public and private—private in its operations, yet public in its regard. The ambiguity of this position has haunted foundations since their inception, and it presents special problems in the late twentieth century, when "the American public" itself seems ready to dissolve into an array of diverse communities, defined less by commonalities than by differences. In such a moment, when all Americans are pressed to think about the nature of their relationship to a larger public, foundation personnel must be especially reflective. How are we, in our institutional capacities, related to the changing arena of public life? And how can we best participate in the pressing task of reweaving the bonds of community in this country, in a way that is respectful of diversity yet hopeful for a common future?[1]

Answers to these questions are not easily forthcoming, perhaps for good reason. We live in a time between times, no longer confidently progressive in our social programs, but not sure, just yet, of our ambitions for the future. The word "change" may be on the tip of every politician's tongue and at the center of every organizational logo; still, no one seems certain about the true direction of change.

Perhaps, even as we strive to move forward, we might acknowledge our uncertainty a little more openly and let this "time between times" be something of an opportunity—an opportunity to reflect, to converse together, and to learn from the past. Obviously, as always, we should try to learn from the mistakes and delusions of the past, especially insofar as those mistakes and delusions determine our present situation. But can we not learn from the hopes and dreams of the past as well—the visions of previous generations which impelled them to think in new ways, to act in new ways and to create new institutions which would carry their work forward?

In order to think about a foundation's relationship to the changing needs of the American public, I have turned to my own institution's past and especially to the traditions of hope that helped give it shape. Those traditions are several: As a private family foundation, the Lilly Endowment is heir to many legacies, familial and regional as well as professional. What, for example, can the Lilly family legacy tell us about a foundation's best contribution to public life? Furthermore, what can we learn from the larger traditions of American philanthropy that have also informed our work?

What follows are my own tentative researches and reflections on one foundation's history, as that history bears upon the question of a foundation's relationship to its public. In any explanation of the past, of course, we see only a part of what is there—and in any institutional history, we illuminate only a portion of the larger societal landscape. This partial illumination is really an invitation to others engaged in American philanthropy to study their own past, too, and to contribute their own understanding to contemporary discussion. I heartily invite the corrections, additions, and complicating thoughts of others who seek to understand and improve philanthropic practice in a democracy.

The Lilly Legacy: The Ideal of an Educated Public

Throughout its history, the Lilly Endowment has invested in three substantive concerns: religion, education, and community development. In a phrase by now deeply familiar to those who work at Lilly, the Endowment's charter of 1937 dedicated the assets of this foundation to "the promotion and support of religious, educational, or charitable purposes."

The early architects of the Endowment also gave these three purposes structural expression in three grantmaking divisions: Religion, Education, and Community Development.

Yet the term "divisions," with its suggestion of clean edges and no overlap, is slightly misleading. In the thinking of the Lilly family, and of one Endowment founder in particular, Eli Lilly, the three purposes were more like aspects of a single and encompassing mission: that mission was the cultivation of an educated and virtuous American citizenry. Eli Lilly stated this mission in his own manner when, in response to a question about the main purpose of his family's foundation, he said, "I would hope we could help improve the character of the American people."

Through its vision of a virtuous, educated public, the Lilly family participated in a long-standing tradition of American thought about education—what Robert Wood Lynn and others have termed the "republican style of educational thought." This tradition has two key assumptions: first, that the future of the Republic depends upon the character, or virtue, of its citizens; and secondly, that the achievement of virtue comes mainly through education.

Today we often hear that America's future depends on the quality of its education. But what is generally meant by this call to educational arms is that the *economic* future of our country depends upon the inculcation of basic skills and habits of discipline. Eli Lilly's sense of the public importance of education was more than economic. Education, he believed, was not only a means to greater earnings and improved material conditions—it was a means to virtue.

Again, we hear a great deal these days about the need for "moral education," by which people usually mean greater attention to values in America's schools. But Eli Lilly's understanding of character education was quite different from the exercises in "values clarification" of recent years. Character education was not simply a solitary pursuit for the sake of individual fulfillment. As his emphasis upon "the American people" suggests, Lilly was interested in how such an education might help us to find common ground with one another—how it might enable us *to see ourselves related to each other as members of the American public*. He believed that education for character formation encourages people to lead more connected lives, lives linked to others beyond their immediate circle of interest.

The task of character formation was a lifelong passion for Eli Lilly, and he made it a central concern of his family foundation as well. The Endowment's first annual report, published in 1950, listed grants for Pitirim Sorokin's work on altruism and Ernest Ligon's work with young people; both efforts were expected to provide "basic research in developing human character, an entirely new field of inquiry." And, in the following year, the annual report described the entire grantmaking program in "Social Science and Humanities, including Religion" as an inquiry into character education. "The grants in this field reflect the interest of the Endowment's board of directors in projects which contain basic American principles influencing character," said the authors of that report, "and in programs containing a spiritual context."

The reference to a "spiritual context" raises an interesting further point about the founding vision of the Lilly family. As I have already noted, in that vision education and community development were treated not as separate but as interdependent concerns. So too, the success of education and community development were seen to depend upon the vitality of one's "spiritual context," or religion. The founders of the Lilly Endowment believed that an education in virtue must be rooted in an ethical or religious tradition.

But, one might reasonably object, can't a civic education in virtue proceed perfectly well without bringing in religion? Indeed, in a country committed to the clear separation of church and state, shouldn't it?

For the Lilly family, as for so many Americans of their day, the answer was, simply, no. As a nation we have long been committed to the separation of church and state; but, as a society, we have predicated many of our practices and institutions on a religious conception of human existence. In the tradition of the Lilly family, a good education was understood to be religious, awakening us to depths and dimensions of our existence that can most appropriately be called spiritual.

Consider the following statement from the Endowment's annual report of 1957:

> What is the most valuable thing a student can gain from his education? Our answer is a vital faith, a framework of fundamental belief, that gives meaning to his life. This should be a faith that has something to say about the inescapable realities of life—good and evil, joy and suffering, death, history, God—a faith that will stand the test of time. . . . It should be, to use the language of an earlier period, a "saving" faith, one capable of transforming a person. (1957 Annual Report, pp. 9–10)

In this vision, education ought to nourish the spirit as much as the intellect. Furthermore, the spirit's nourishment can best be found in a common tradition, a tradition enlivened by the experience and tempered by the wisdom of other human beings:

> [This faith] should be the student's own in the sense that it is a part of him—he has thought it through—though probably not his own in the sense that he invented it. Surely, no fabricated system of ideas could be as profound as a historic faith that survived centuries of experience and changing conditions. (1957 Annual Report, pp. 9–10)

This statement seems to allow for the possibility of several different historical traditions of faith. In reality, though, the character education efforts supported by the Lilly Endowment earlier in this century were very much rooted in one particular tradition: that of Christianity. According to influential grantees like Sorokin and Ligon, for instance, good character education would cultivate the specific virtues recommended in the Sermon on the Mount. Ligon and Sorokin hoped to help future generations aspire to that lofty set of virtues, as set forth and defined by contemporary Christian culture.

The Lillys, like Ligon and Sorokin, believed that good character education relies upon the wisdom of particular religious traditions. They also believed that such an education requires a community of practice extending far beyond the local schoolhouse. Since the nineteenth century at least, Protestant leaders have argued that citizens acquire an education in virtue not only through formal schooling, but through participation in religious and voluntary organizations as well. Eli Lilly's consistent support for a variety of youth-serving groups and for weekday religious education are manifestations of this conviction that the formation of character occurs in many different educational settings.

Eli Lilly is no longer with us, and the 'values-management' approaches of Ernest Ligon and other "character educators" do not seem to hold the promise they once did. Yet, knowingly or unknowingly, those of us at the Lilly Endowment are heirs to the vision inherent in "character education." That vision, of an *American public educated to virtue through participation in religious and community life*, helped inspire the establishment of the Lilly Endowment. And, at least initially, it lent a natural unity to the three "divisions" of religion, education, and community development within which we labor today. Perhaps we need to ask ourselves, from time to time, if that vision persists in our own more pluralistic age—and, if not, what hopes and dreams we do share in common.

The Challenge of a Pluralistic Society

In the Endowment's annual report of 1957, the same writer who had spoken eloquently of "a vital faith" went on to identify three such faiths which have contended for domination in the twentieth century: "Christianity, national socialism, and communism." The author then unabashedly stated the Endowment's preference for the first of these faiths, writing that "Christianity seems to us to offer the intelligent believer the most insight into God and man."

That writer's easy assurance about the "most insightful" faith belongs to a time when the challenges of a pluralistic society had not been deeply felt or acknowledged. Earlier in this nation's history, Christian faith dominated American society and defined our common culture. Today we cannot so easily identify a faith for all to share. We live in a much more diverse mix of cultures and traditions; we also acknowledge a greater diversity of experience and meaning, not simply along cultural lines, but in terms of gender, race, socioeconomic situation, region, and even personal differences of temperament. Most of us would hesitate to prescribe our own faith for the American public as a whole.

Given this newly acknowledged diversity, many people today feel compelled to question and even reject any vision that refers to a common good, a shared or public faith. One respected scholar of American religion. John Wilson, has argued that the term "public" inevitably pretends that "the interests of some (including ourselves) are coincident with the interests of all. Whenever we see the term," he concludes, "we ought to ask whose public and in the service of whose purposes?"[2]

Thoughtful critics such as Wilson have forced us to ask difficult questions about the contributions that a private foundation can make to public life in America. How can an institution like the Lilly Endowment continue to help people discern meaning, not simply as individuals but as a "public," if we cannot presume that one definitive tradition or faith should be binding on us all? Must the concept of a virtuous public be abandoned in a society of diverse convictions? And, if not, how can a foundation contribute to the character education of that public?

Following Wilson's advice, it might seem wisest simply to pack away Eli Lilly's vision of an educated public as the unenlightened creed of an earlier time. And yet, before abandoning this legacy to the new pluralism, I would like to look once more to our institutional heritage for greater understanding. For in that heritage, I suspect that there may be resources to serve us in this new time—clues, or wise hints, about how a foundation can continue to help educate the American people, in ways respectful of the diversity of its members and yet committed to a common world and even a common good.

Prudence and Creativity

One of the most striking features of the Lilly Endowment's ethos or culture is its emphasis on the contrasting virtues of *prudence* and *creativity*. Robert Greenleaf, the late social critic and advisor to business, philanthropic, and educational institutions, first put these two unlikely terms together in a speech to the Endowment's Board of Directors in 1974. "[The] test of creativity urges foundations to produce new solutions," he said. "The test of prudence suggests that foundations probably should not use their funds to influence the choice of a solution."

In this memorable bit from his series of "advices to servants," Greenleaf was articulating a basic tension that has characterized the Endowment's work from the very beginning—a tension between innovation and tradition. As "a conservatively progressive" enterprise, in J. K. Lilly, Sr.'s, phrase, we have consistently acted from the conviction that innovation is not everything, that tradition might in fact be an important resource for thinking about the future. But at the same time, we have argued that fundamental rethinking is often needed to respond fully to the challenges of new circumstances. Thus the ethos of conservative progressivism, like the companion virtues of prudence and creativity, demands a certain modesty in a foundation's relationship with those it would serve. It warns us against asserting that the solutions we most immediately favor are the correct ones, or that we have the answers for others. It encourages us to seek truth not so much in one person or perspective, but instead in the process of people working and talking together: in *civic engagement* and in *public discourse*.

The ethos of conservative progressivism, and the virtues of prudence and creativity, cannot alone solve the dilemma of public life in a pluralistic society. But they might help a foundation achieve an appropriate modesty in relation to those it would serve. For they urge us to act—but to do so reflectively, without assuming that we necessarily know what the public wants, or should want. Here, certainly, are a few "clues and wise hints" from our past, as we face the challenges of our future.

Three Traditions of American Philanthropy

The Lilly Endowment is a family enterprise, shaped by the convictions of a particular family. It is also a private foundation, heir to a variety of philanthropic traditions. Having looked at the Lilly legacy, let's look now at those philanthropic roots: the various traditions of philanthropy which have informed the Endowment's self-understanding, past and present.

Earlier, we spoke of Eli Lilly's vision of philanthropy as a cultivation of the American public—a means of clarifying and fostering connections among the citizenry. This vision of human connectedness is central to the history of philanthropy in our country. As historian Ellen Condliffe Lagemann has written, American philanthropy represents "a long tradition of . . . efforts to establish the values, shape the beliefs, and define the behaviors that would join people to one another."[3] In his 1992 keynote speech to the Council on Foundations, James Joseph paid homage to this central impulse when he said that "it may be that the most fundamental rationale for organized philanthropy is that it can affirm and advance the connectedness of humanity."

And yet, while American philanthropists have sought to cultivate connection among the members of this society, they have not always understood that task in the same way. There have been three distinctive traditions of American philanthropy in the brief history of this nation: those of Relief, Improvement, and Social Reform.[4] Within each of these traditions, the principles and purposes of philanthropic practice have been defined differently.

Philanthropy as Relief	Philanthropy as Improvement	Philanthropy as Social Reform
*	*	*
operates on principle of compassion	operates on principle of progress	operates on principle of Justice
*	*	*
alleviates human suffering	maximizes human potential	solves social problems

Let's take a moment to explore each of these traditions, both in their broadest outlines and in their particular manifestations in the history of one private foundation, the Lilly Endowment.

Philanthropy As Relief

The tradition of benevolence, or *philanthropy as relief*, represents the most ancient form of philanthropy—what is sometimes called "charity." Animated by the principle of compassion, this kind of philanthropy is mainly concerned with alleviating human suffering.

Of all the traditions contributing to the contemporary practice of philanthropy, the tradition of benevolence is most obviously rooted in a religious world view: Charity, from the Latin term *caritas* means other-regarding love, prompted without regard for status or merit, as in God's love for humanity.[5] The benevolent impulse proceeds from the recognition that we are all connected to one another, as part of God's creation: even our accumulated wealth is God's gift, not our own achievement, and therefore is to be shared freely with God's other creatures. In a now famous sermon delivered to his fellow Puritans while sailing to America in 1630, John Winthrop gave these principles exemplary expression. Because we are "knit . . . together in the bond of brotherly affection," argued Winthrop, "it appears plainly that no man is made more honorable than another or more wealthy, etc., out of any particular and singular respect to himself, but for the glory of his creator and the common good of the creature, man." In works of mercy, continued Winthrop, the law of *caritas* demands that "every man afford his help to another in every want or distress." As "members of the same body," he concluded, "We must delight in each other, make other's conditions as our own, rejoice together, mourn together, labor and suffer together."[6]

The religiously grounded tradition of charity has shaped the Lilly Endowment's self-understanding from the very beginning. The Endowment's first gift, in 1938, went to the Community Chest, an Indianapolis organization that enabled citizens to pool their charitable contributions to meet the needs of their neighbors. The same charitable sentiment is still evident in the 1974 annual report: "Of the many justifications for private philanthropy," says the author of that report, "the oldest is the ancient teaching of all the great religions of the world about the obligation of man to give of his resources and his time to aid the widows, the orphans, the sick, the poor, the oppressed." In recent years, Endowment spokespersons have often expressed our charitable obligation in the following way: "Out of gratitude for the gifts of life, we have an obligation to care for others."

Precisely because it is an act of compassion, a matter of "feeling with" others, charitable philanthropy is responsive to the public. Resources are provided in response to clear and pressing needs. At its best, such benevolence is a simple and genuine expression of empathy for others. At its worst, however, charity can display a deep passivity toward the public, reacting to pressing needs rather than trying to change the conditions that create those needs. Winthrop expressed this attitude of acquiescence to "the order of things" in the opening words of his sermon, when he declared that "God Almighty . . . hath so disposed of the condition of mankind as in all times some must be rich, some poor; some high and eminent in power and dignity, others mean in subjection."[7] For better or worse, charity is a tradition resigned to the inevitability of social inequality. "The poor will always be with you" might well be its motto.

Philanthropy As Improvement

The second great tradition of American philanthropy, *philanthropy as improvement*, developed at least partly as a response to the perceived futility and wastefulness of the tradition of relief. In contrast to the latter's emphasis on alleviating human misery, the tradition of improvement is primarily concerned with *maximizing human potential* by providing opportunities for self-improvement. Those who exemplify this sort of philanthropy—Benjamin Franklin and Andrew Carnegie immediately come to mind—established a great American tradition of stimulating public efforts on behalf of individual and civic self-betterment: e.g., by nurturing individual talent, by sponsoring cultural and arts offerings, and by supporting educational and other "improving" organizations.

Andrew Carnegie provides an especially interesting example of philanthropy as improvement. In establishing one of the first modern foundations, he consciously rejected the old tradition of charity. Not unlike those of the benevolent tradition, Carnegie hoped philanthropy would affirm an organic sense of human connectedness. His essay "Wealth" begins: "The problem of our age is the proper administration of wealth, that the ties of brotherhood may still bind together the rich and poor in harmonious relationship." He nonetheless believed that the revolutionary changes wrought by industrialization and urbanization in the last third of the nineteenth century called for a fundamentally new approach to philanthropy.

For Carnegie, as for a number of Victorian philanthropists, the traditional forms of charity and almsgiving perpetuated the very ills they sought to alleviate. In "Wealth," he gives us a defining statement of the principles animating philanthropy as improvement:

> In bestowing charity, the main consideration should be to help those who will help themselves; to provide part of the means by which those who desire to improve may do so; to give those who desire to rise the aids by which they may rise; to assist, but rarely or never to do all. Neither the individual nor the race is improved by almsgiving.

Carnegie continues:

> . . . the best means of benefiting the community is to place within its reach the ladders upon which the aspiring can rise—parks, and means of recreation, by which men are helped in body and mind; works of art, certain to give pleasure and improve the public taste; and public institutions of various kinds, which will improve the general condition of the people.

As Carnegie makes plain here, individuals are responsible for taking advantage of the "ladders" set before them. What philanthropy can do is improve those ladders, by enhancing and equalizing the opportunities available. This kind of philanthropy is practiced *by* the public as much as *on* the public; while a project may be "seeded" by wealthy donors, it is often carried through to completion by public groups and volunteer organizations. Indeed, in the improvement tradition the figure of the passive beneficiary begins to disappear altogether, replaced by a public acting on its own behalf.[8]

Lilly Endowment's participation in the tradition of philanthropy as improvement also dates from its early years. Like Carnegie, our founders wanted to do more than alleviate human suffering—they felt called upon to improve basic opportunities for achievement and fulfillment. The first annual report shows the influence of this second major tradition of American philanthropy:

> The Endowment believes that funds strictly for relief should make up a small portion of its program; and, in contrast to that kind of charity, the Endowment has taken an approach which can best be described by the term "self-help." This principle can and should be taught by education, demonstration, and leading service organizations. It is accepted by most foundations today. (1950 Annual Report, pp. 4–5)

The persistent influence of this tradition is evident in the Endowment's continuing support for liberal arts colleges, historically black institutions, theological schools, youth-serving organizations, museums and other cultural arts institutions, and in a host of other efforts to increase the capacity of institutions of fundamental importance to American society.

Like the tradition of relief, however, the tradition of improvement has some weaknesses as well as some strengths. In the latter half of this century, American philanthropy has increasingly confronted a society in which its improving efforts seemed chiefly to benefit the well-situated and highly motivated members of the community. The concept of "individual opportunities" is of diminished value if entire groups are effectively blocked for social, legal, and economic reasons from taking advantage of such opportunities.

Just as Carnegie reacted to the flaws in the relief tradition, so too more recent foundation leaders have felt it necessary to respond to the flaws in the improvement tradition. In a retrospective published in 1981, a spokesperson for Carnegie's own foundation noted that, in the early 1960s, the staff and board of the Carnegie Corporation had become "painfully aware of the urgent problems of race, poverty, and inequality that were besetting the nation." Looking back on a tradition of encouraging educational opportunities, they concluded that "it was not reasonable to expect that schooling alone could create equality of opportunity when equality did not exist in the world of jobs, of social relations, or of politics."[9] Like the Rockefeller and Ford Foundations, Carnegie shifted its grantmaking strategies in a new direction: it began to attack perceived underlying circumstances of inequality. Many of America's largest foundations now dedicated themselves, not to charity or improvement, but to social change.

Philanthropy As Social Reform

Thus emerged a third great tradition in American philanthropy, the tradition of *social reform*. While of relatively recent origins, this tradition currently dominates the landscape of American philanthropy; it characterizes the self-understanding of most large foundations and, increasingly, of many smaller and more traditional charitable organizations as well. Philanthropy as social reform is, above all, dedicated to *encouraging social change*. Its practitioners believe that societal circumstances are often more powerful in shaping human destiny than the actions of individuals themselves; hence, they argue, philanthropy must help change the circumstances.

Philanthropy as social reform takes a proactive, even directive role in public life. Rather than responding to the requests of others, it actively attempts to define and solve public problems, often through experimentation and the innovative use of venture capital. According to proponents of this approach, a foundation has the resources, freedom, and expertise necessary to experiment on social problems; therefore, they argue, it should seek innovative solutions that can in time be adopted by others. In the early 1970s, a series of government commissions on the public role of foundations gave this perspective classic expression. "Our society . . . is in obvious need of philanthropic institutions standing outside the frame of government but in support of the public interest," declared the Peterson Commission in 1970. "[J]ust as scouts move in advance of a main body of troops to probe what lies ahead," so too "philanthropic institutions . . . can spot emergent problems, diagnose them, and test alternative ways to deal with them."[10]

This shift toward active social experimentation has brought with it some difficulties. Often, when foundations look to others to adopt the experiments they have fostered, they count on public revenue or hope to influence governmental policy. Modern foundations have naturally been tempted to see themselves as a kind of "shadow government," not just as supporters of experiments that might inspire further thinking but as the very makers of future social policy. Paul Ylvisaker indicated just this tendency in *The Handbook on Private Foundations*, when he wrote that modern philanthropy has been dedicated "to finding systemic solutions to underlying causes of poverty and other social ills, and over time has become a recognized social process, in effect a set of private legislatures defining public problems, setting goals and priorities, and allocating resources toward general solutions."[11]

Perhaps more than some other large foundations, the Lilly Endowment has resisted the temptation to conceive of itself as "a private legislature." Our conservative ethos naturally disinclines us from legislating "on behalf" of the public. Yet our foundation, too, has participated in the social reform tradition in key ways. Clearly, our grant-making has influenced public policy—and nowhere more evidently than in the revitalization of our own downtown. Likewise, a social policy focus is explicit in the way we refer to grants in the area of "Economics and Public Policy." The Endowment's school reform and housing initiatives are two other recent efforts that exemplify our participation in the reform tradition.

A Fourth Philanthropic Response?

As the history of the Lilly Endowment suggests, the three types of philanthropy outlined above are not mutually exclusive: indeed, most modern foundations participate to some degree in all three traditions, attempting now to alleviate human suffering, now to maximize human potential, and now to solve social problems. Yet, on the whole, American philanthropy has in recent decades moved increasingly in the direction of social reform, relying on volunteer organizations for civic improvement projects and largely relegating the traditionally charitable work of "relief" to governmental and religious bodies.

The future direction of American philanthropy is less clear. Events of recent years and months have put new pressure upon foundations to rethink their fundamental strategies for serving the American public. Despite the social reform efforts of government and philanthropy alike, ours is more than ever a society divided into rich and poor, a society still very much challenged to alleviate human suffering and to maximize human potential by providing significant opportunities for all its members. Meanwhile, the on-going debate about the size of the deficit and the federal government's distinctive powers and responsibilities suggests that it is unlikely that governmental funds for relief and improvement will be as plentiful in the future as they have been in the past. In these circumstances, philanthropic organizations of all shapes and sizes will need to rethink their own commitments.[12]

And yet, as I suggested in my introduction, this "time between times" may be an opportunity not simply to draw upon the strengths of past traditions but to learn, as well, from their blind spots. Each of the three philanthropic traditions outlined above has made significant contributions to the well-being of the American public; but each, if taken to an extreme, has revealed real weaknesses as well, in the kind of relationship it fosters between a foundation and those whom it would serve. As noted, the tradition of relief can encourage a philanthropy that is somewhat passive, reacting to pressing needs rather than trying to change the conditions that create those needs. The tradition of improvement, on the other hand, can encourage philanthropy which benefits only selected members of the community. The tradition of social reform, finally, can lead foundation workers into unilateral decision-making "on behalf of" the public, but without much openness to the wisdom or will of that public.

In this time of rethinking a foundation's best contribution, then, we might do well to learn from the strengths and the weaknesses of these three traditions. Taken together, they challenge us to cultivate a form of philanthropy which maintains a more balanced relationship between a foundation and its public—a relationship which is at once active and receptive, guiding and listening. And it is here, I believe, that the Lilly legacy of concern for *prudence* and *creativity* can be especially instructive. For when these virtues are cultivated in tandem, they encourage us to listen and reflect even as we act.

On the one hand, the standard of *prudence* in grantmaking warns us against forcing our own solutions on others. Active advocacy of particular options, as in the social reform tradition, may not always be the most prudent use of foundation funds; indeed, it can degenerate into a coercive use of power. On the other hand, the standard of *creativity* in grantmaking encourages us to do more than patch up existing wounds, as in the benevolent tradition—or underwrite opportunities for individual achievement, as in the improvement tradition. Often the problems of American life demand creative thought and imaginative experimentation over time, the kind of experimentation that can best be pursued by informed individuals or groups, and that requires freedom of thought and action. As institutions with the resources necessary to provide such freedom to others, foundations have the unusual opportunity to stimulate much-needed creativity in the solving of social problems.

In short, we are encouraged both by the history of American philanthropy, and by Lilly's more local legacies, to believe that a foundation should not simply impose its own agenda on the public—but neither should the conventional viewpoint necessarily rule the day. People have untapped wisdom and resources for public service in their own cultural and religious traditions and in their own practical experience, which, for a variety of reasons, they have not been able to discover or recover. To put it simply, they need opportunities to *learn*—from themselves and about themselves, from others and about others. A foundation can help those whom it would serve to tap these deep veins of wisdom, thereby discerning more clearly appropriate directions for public service in their own particular places, their own particular ways. Moreover, an encounter with others of diverse perspectives can enlarge and even transform people, if that encounter is grounded in the recognition of a common purpose.

One timely contribution a private foundation like the Lilly Endowment can make, then, is to promote civic engagement and encourage public moral discourse, by cultivating hospitable spaces for reflection and by bringing diverse people and perspectives into conversation. Rather than trying to force a specific vision of the future (which could turn out to be an unexamined extension of the past), we can create the conditions for conversation, in the hope that new vision and fresh action will eventually emerge. In doing so, we are not forcing our own experimental answers on others or simply repeating the predictable answers a little louder for all to hear. Instead, we will be furthering public deliberation and discovery of new ways of seeing.

It seems to me, in short, that by cultivating those virtues nestled at the heart of Lilly's own heritage—namely, the virtues of creativity and prudence—we can begin to craft or discern a "fourth" philanthropic response for American society, one which counters the weaknesses and builds on the strengths of the three great traditions of benevolence, improvement, and social reform.

In Conclusion

At the beginning of this essay, I posed the following question: What do the several legacies of the Lilly Endowment reveal about a foundation's best contribution to public life? I started by looking at Eli Lilly's dream of improving the character of the American people. The continuity between that receding past and the present lies in this foundation's lasting conviction that its best contribution is to assist in the *education* of the public; furthermore, that such an education requires the context of *community*; and finally, that it draws upon the resources of *religion*, awakening us to spiritual dimensions and depths in our life together.

The conditions for an education in virtue have changed during this past century. But even in these altered circumstances, the Endowment's tradition is still powerful and relevant. Along with other foundations, we can help those who serve the larger society to recover and renew a "vital faith," by providing hospitable spaces for reflection, and by fostering conversation among persons of diverse perspectives.

In doing so, we are trusting that the American people have untapped resources for a healthier public life—that they, like us, have legacies to discover, lessons to learn, and wisdom to share with one another.

By making this kind of learning possible, I believe that we will be true to the lessons of our own legacies.

Notes

1. The following essay was prompted by conversations among those planning for a Lilly Endowment staff meeting in 1992, on the topic of a foundation's relationship to its public. The organizers of this event encouraged us to think about the nature and changing needs of American "public life;" they also invited our reflections on the ways in which an institution like ours can make its best contribution to the quality of that life.
2. "The Public as a Problem," in *Caring for the Commonweal*, eds. Parker Palmer. Barbara Wheeler and James W. Fowler (Macon, Georgia: Mercer University Press, 1990), 22.
3. Ellen Condliffe Lagemann, *Private Power for the Public Good* (Middletown, Connecticut: Wesleyan University Press, 1983), 1.
4. In understanding philanthropic traditions and the functions and roles of foundations, I am especially indebted to Brian O'Connell, *Philanthropy in Action* (New York: The Foundation Center, 1987), 3–9 and Paul N. Ylvisaker, "Small Can Be Effective" (Washington, D.C.: Council on Foundations, 1989), 3–4.
5. Augustine gave caritas its classic Christian definition in *On Christian Doctrine:* the double commandment of charity, he wrote, is to love God and one's neighbor as one loves oneself.
6. "A Model of Christian Charity," in *America's Voluntary Spirit*, ed. Brian O'Connell (New York: The Foundation Center, 1983), 29–30; 30; 32.
7. Ibid., 29.
8. Daniel Boorstin describes this as a shift from "conscience to community" in his helpful essay, "From Charity to Philanthropy," in *Hidden History* (New York: Vintage Books, 1989), see especially 204–205.
9. Alan Pifer, Carnegie Corporation of New York Annual Report 1981, 10.
10. O'Connell, *America's Voluntary Spirit*, 290–291.
11. Paul Ylvisaker, "Small Can Be Effective" in *The Handbook on Private Foundations* (New York: The Foundation Center, 1991), 256.
12. Reconstructions of the respective responsibilities of government and philanthropy are, of course, not new. As scholar Peter Dobkin Hall observes, "historians have agreed that a fundamental restructuring of public life began to take place in the 1870s and 1880s, which emerged as a national force with the progressive movement at the turn of the century, and which, despite changes in regimes and electoral moods, framed public life for the rest of the century. In its essentials, this restructuring involved an accommodation between government and private voluntary associations, which coexisted uneasily—and often turbulently—through the first century of the republic's existence." *Inventing the Nonprofit Sector and Other Essays on Philanthropy, Voluntarism and Nonprofit Organizations* (Baltimore: The John Hopkins University Press, 1992), 3.

THE HISTORIAN AS PHILANTHROPOID, THE PHILANTHROPOID AS HISTORIAN

JAMES ALLEN SMITH

DECEMBER 7, 2001

I accepted her invitation to speak readily, rapidly for one paramount reason. Waldemar Nielsen has had a considerable influence on my career. I doubt that he knows this. But I am grateful to have an opportunity to acknowledge it publicly and to say something about the example he set for a young college student.

I wish there were dramatic film of our first meeting as there was when a certain young high school student from Arkansas, and later a Georgetown graduate, visited Washington in 1963 and stepped from the crowd to shake hands with JFK. His political destiny seems to have been foretold in that encounter.

There is no photographic record of my first meeting with Wally Nielsen, nothing in a destiny foreshadowed. But I remember it clearly. The place—a lovely apartment at 72nd and Riverside Drive in Manhattan. The date—an October weekend in 1969. I was then a college senior. One of my closest college pals, Dwight Moore, was dating Wally's daughter, Signe, and I tagged along one weekend when the Nielsen family and the Moore family gathered for dinner. Why can I recall this event from 32 years ago, the late 1960s, with such clarity?

The prospect of meeting Wally Nielsen and the conversation that evening made an indelible mark. I had taken courses in African history and political development the preceding spring. And that Saturday night I found myself with a chance to talk about those topics with Wally Nielsen, the president of the African American Institute and author of a book called, confidently, *Africa*. I probably prepared for dinner as if it were a final exam.

And I still remember what we talked about: Kenyan tribal politics, Jomo Kenyatta's autobiography *Facing Mount Kenya*, and the assassination the preceding July of Tom Mboya, a Luo leader of the Kenyan African National Union. No doubt there were other topics of conversation. But those are the things I've remembered for years. Topics I had merely studied, he had written about. People I had merely read about, he had met and worked with. That evening he might also have mentioned that he was working on another book.

I learned more about that the following summer, 1970, at another dinner. The place: Washington, the Old Occidental Restaurant on Pennsylvania Avenue. The people: Wally, his daughter, and me. The topic of conversation was his research for a book, particularly his interviews in Washington with people responsible for the recent Tax Reform Act. He explained that the legislation would have an impact on foundations. I doubt that I then understood very much as he explained the implications of the Tax Reform Act of 1969. I don't recall what other topics of conversation we pursued that evening. We probably talked about my plans for graduate school that fall, why I was studying European and not African history.

I can't say what these two dinners foreshadowed about my own career, but his lustrous experiences with the Marshall Plan, the Ford Foundation, the African American Institute and the books on foundations and the nonprofit sector that were soon to come from his typewriter certainly opened my eyes to new possibilities, even if those possibilities did not present themselves for another decade. I went on to graduate school to study medieval history with scarcely a thought that I would ever have anything to do with the world of philanthropic foundations, research and writing that Wally Nielsen inhabited.

My plans were to teach European history, which I did for a few years. For most of the past twenty years I have worked variously as a foundation program officer, a foundation executive director, an advisor to a wealthy donor, and a foundation trustee. In other words, I have become more a practicing philanthropoid than academic historian. I have read far more grant proposals than scholarly articles. I have sat through many more foundation board meetings than faculty meetings. I have written thousands of pages of internal memoranda, minutes of meetings, and rejection letters and published far less. But throughout I have approached my work with the temperament of a trained historian and I have, from time to time, reflected and written about the practice of philanthropy.

This lecture gives me a chance to pose two questions:

What do the insights of the historian bring to the practice of philanthropy?
What does experience in the philanthropic world bring to the study of history?

My answers may seem self-indulgently autobiographical. I have certainly begun in that vein. To the extent, that I tell you what I was reading and when and what I was writing and why, I might be experimenting with a new approach that is autobiohistoriographical. Or perhaps it is an older literary form: the confession.

Humbly my tongue confesses (and here I am echoing that extraordinary student of voluntary action, namely St. Augustine, bishop of Hippo) that I began my career as a medieval historian. I studied and wrote about charity and charitable institutions in northern Europe in the twelfth and thirteenth century. As a graduate student and faculty member, I pored over the account books and legal documents of monasteries, leper hospitals, beguinages, alms houses, and parish poor relief systems. Twenty and even thirty years ago, medieval and early modern charity provided very hot topics for aspiring European historians. And my research examined one of the fundamental transformations of western charity as the predominately agrarian economy of the early Middle Ages gave way to a more commercial, money economy and to an increasingly urban society. The burgeoning cities and towns of the Middle Ages were forced to deal in new ways with problems of poverty and disease. The increasingly wealthy inhabitants of those towns confronted the reality of new levels of wealth, the reproaches of sermonizing Dominicans and Franciscans, and the juxtaposition of their wealth with the poverty of others. New charitable institutions were invented and some old ones were adapted to address the new realities.

After several years in European archives and four years of teaching, never getting past the Renaissance and Reformation, indeed, never getting within three hundred years of our own era, I joined the staff, quite improbably, of the Twentieth Century Fund (now called The Century Foundation). The Fund, a venerable public policy research foundation had been created in the 1910s by Edward Filene, the department store magnate. It is one of that generation of foundations, including the Russell Sage Foundation, the Carnegie Corporation, the Commonwealth Fund, and the Rockefeller Foundation, all founded in the first two decades of the twentieth century, all seeking to use the tools of science, especially the social sciences, to address society's problems.

The Fund had begun in the late 1970s to explore two loosely related policy research areas, the nonprofit sector and freedom of expression, especially threats to free expression that seemed to be posed by UNESCO's avowal of a New World Information Order.

The then director of the Fund was a crusty former journalist. His name was M. J. Rossant and my colleague, Ron Chernow, who occupied the office next to mine had described him as "some tornado tearing through [his] life . . . his gaze fierce, his words a howling wind." Ron viewed the Fund in our years there "as a haven for lost souls, a ship of gifted misfits piloted by that piratical captain, M. J. Rossant, who proudly flew the Jolly Roger." I often described it as a Dickensian asylum, a poorhouse or orphanage. And Ron elaborated on that image: "When our trustees were around, Murray was on his best behavior . . . [they were treated like] Victorian trustees visiting a poorhouse and receiving a show prepared by the smiling parochial beadle for the occasion. The next day, however, we were back washing floors and eating crusts of stale bread."

I was the only historian among four economists and two political scientists. In the office that I inherited in our very proper brick townhouse on East 70th Street between Park and Madison were books that had accumulated during the late 1960s and early 1970s during the time Wally Nielsen was working on the book he had mentioned at dinner nine years earlier. It was this book: his Twentieth Century Fund study, *The Big Foundations*. His book, which I read early on, stared down from my shelf throughout my seven years with the Fund.

One paragraph in it has haunted me from the moment I read it: "Why staff members of grant-making foundations enter the profession at all, or remain in it, is something of a mystery, for there is hardly another comparable field of activity that is subject to so much disparagement by its clientele. The general public may regard philanthropic work as relatively prestigious, but in the academic and scientific community foundation officers are often considered second-rate individuals whose credentials would not qualify them for the faculties and staffs of first-rate universities or research centers. Similarly, many figures in intellectual life and the creative arts tend to think of them as bureaucratic functionaries. Although many government officials view foundation employment at times with some envy, they also think of it as a refuge for people who have retired to the periphery of affairs."

What line of work had I gotten myself into? What self-loathing world had I joined? Nielsen's observations drove me to read more about these institutions. And there were other volumes at hand, some of them reflecting the interests that both the Fund and the Russell Sage Foundation had shared in the late 1920s and early 1930s as they systematically gathered and published some of the first information about American foundations and their fields of activity. These projects foreshadowed the Russell Sage Foundation's role in establishing the Foundation Center. I also found memoirs and foundation histories: F. Emerson Andrews' books were in my office and in the library was the hefty two-volume history of Russell Sage's first forty years. The Fund's various directors had been presented with other books and foundation ephemera over the years.

We had shelf space and a well-trained packrat of a librarian, who had worked at the Fund for more than thirty years. And in the basement we had file cabinets, though somewhat disorganized and with numerous gaps, containing material from the Fund's earliest years and on many of its important New Deal and post-World War II era research projects. Since medieval historians are by nature archival creatures, I spent considerable time in the basement. I looked at the files on projects from the 1930s that concerned some of the very same social welfare programs that were under assault in the 1980s.

But that was not the only place to find the Twentieth Century Fund's history. At board meetings I met trustees who had been a part of the New Deal: David Lilienthal, former chairman of the Tennessee Valley Authority; Benjamin Cohen, author of securities legislation in the 1930s and delegate to the first UN General Assembly and the Dumbarton Oaks conference; James Rowe, one of FDR's and LBJ's chief political fixers; even the brain truster Adolf Berle, who had chaired the Fund, continued to cast a long shadow over the Fund through the presence of his son.

I wanted to know what kind of institution the Twentieth Century Fund was and to learn what I could of its history. Indeed, I arrived at the Fund at a time when its history and traditions seemed up for grabs. The Board was increasingly divided between New Deal liberals and New York neo-conservatives. And the Fund's program of research leading to the publication of books seemed increasingly out-moded and under assault from young, upstart conservative think tanks. In asking what kind of institution the Fund was—and employing historical and archival instincts, turning to informal oral history opportunities, drawing on the historical literature about Progressive Era institutions—I was able in internal memoranda and board briefing books to help the Board understand the Fund's role in the new environment it faced in the 1980s. This was a practical, immediate use of the historian's skills, instincts and temperament.

And it seemed particularly important to think seriously about the role of the nonprofit sector as government was retrenching and responsibilities were devolving to states and localities. It was a time to ask about the future of this sector as Nielsen did in this book, *The Endangered Sector*.

Over the next ten years, I began to remake myself as a historian of American think tanks and public policymaking. And with *The Big Foundations* in mind, I proposed to the Fund's director and the board that I be allowed to undertake a similar exploration of another not-well-studied American institution: the public policy think tank. To my astonishment they allowed me to do it, acknowledging that it could indeed serve as a successor study to the foundation book. And the result was my book—*The Idea Brokers*. My gratitude to Wally Nielsen is sincere and enduring since it is his example that set me on course to ask questions that he had begun to pose in *The Big Foundations* and continued to ask in *The Golden Donors* and *Inside American Philanthropy*. He asked fundamental questions:

How can we generate "some plain honest talk about foundations and their problems"?

How can we understand "the nature and role of foundations in the larger context of the institutional structure of American life"?

How can we hold a mirror up to the leading foundations "to show their trustees and officers the urgent need to initiate procedures for self-reform and self-renewal"?

Since his three books on foundations total 1,235 pages, I will not try to provide a cursory summary of his answers.

Instead I want to focus on my first question: what did I bring as a historian to my work in foundations. The most immediate quality is simply the historian's instinctive trait of viewing an institution in historical perspective. The Twentieth Century Fund had (and has) a past; it was born in one historical moment and had come to be situated in quite a different era by the time I worked there. As a historian I tried to link the two historical moments.

It is always possible to think about an institution's present mission through the analytic lens of the historian. Foundations all too often are afflicted with institutional amnesia, looking forward but not looking rigorously back at what they have done or what other foundations have done. Foundations should be much more self-conscious of where they are situated in the flow of history. Or to put it another way: they should think about time and the duration of their commitments and they should think clearly about the forces that are propelling social, economic and other changes.

Endowed foundations, which are as near to being permanent and secure institutions as the human mind and money can invent, are nonetheless intended to deal with change, to be responsive to new circumstances. Foundation staff and trustees ought continually to ask themselves whether their role is to take the long view of social processes and social transformation or to act immediately to resolve pressing needs and crises. Who has the greater claim: the homeless person who needs shelter tonight or the organization with the plan to renovate a building or the policy research and advocacy group working toward new federal housing policies or the research center testing new, cheaper construction materials? What is the perspective on change? Is it tomorrow, six months from now, two years or ten years into the future? Where do foundations situate themselves in this process and how long are they willing to wait for results?

Foundation executives and trustees must also situate themselves in relationship to other institutions. For lack of a better term, they must think about their jurisdiction and they must think about their scale. What is the best scope for the application of private resources? Is it defined by the scale of the project, by geography, or by an explicit decision about the boundaries between public and private sector activity? What can private resources do about a problem? What is their relation to public resources? The shifting commitments of government, the shifting relationships between public and private sector, growth and change in the wider civil society supply the changing context in which foundations operate.

Foundation boards and staffs should also ask whether they need to play the role of institution-builders offering operating support and endowment capital or as program innovators prodding institutions to change and offering opportunistic capital so that old organizations can move in new directions. Probably the greatest change in the century-long history of foundations has been the change in foundations' willingness to act as institution builders making multi-million dollar commitments for ten or fifteen years. It is almost axiomatic that as staffs in the large foundations have grown more professional, the grants have gotten smaller, the length of commitment shorter, the proposal process and reporting requirements more onerous.

Foundations are also engaged in a subtle debate about the public role they wish to play. How closely do they wish to operate to political processes? Where are the boundaries of their role as public advocate? When does an educational role or the use of the foundation pulpit overstep the boundaries of political processes? When do private pools of capital begin to overstep and perhaps even to undermine democratic processes? When does support of social and economic research shade into advocacy? In a society perennially suspicious of large concentrations of wealth most foundations have chosen to remain out of the political limelight, but that does not diminish the tension between the public and private spheres of foundation activity.

Foundations are also a continuing effort to balance lay leadership and practical experience against professional expertise. Foundations are always engaged in a discussion of which constituencies they want to serve. In a society that has increasingly come to value the professional and the specialized expert, the foundation has been a force for enlarging the domain of the expert in many fields, but it has also sought to temper specialization and narrow perspectives. Foundations must hold this tension in balance in their deliberations.

From my vantage point as a historian, these are some of the more important recurring questions in American foundations: What forces of change are foundations working with or against? How do we think about jurisdiction, the boundaries between public and private sector? What are the relative claims to build new institutions, give them general support, and retain capital for investing in innovative programs? How and by what means do foundations engage a democratic policy process? How do we balance practical experience against professional expertise? They are not asked every day about every proposal, but they do shape the discussions that take place at every level of foundation decision making. There are no right and permanent answers to these questions, only an obligation to keep asking them and to hold them in some kind of balance. And it seems to me that historical insights into them are especially valuable.

The less immediate contribution that a historian in the workaday philanthropic setting can make is to the record, for the record, to see that decisions made and deeds done are accurately recorded and that record keeping and archival practices are sound. This may seem like monkish medievalism but it is an obligation I've felt toward the various institutions in which I've worked as well as to the nonprofit sector more generally and to the scholars who will follow us. It is this commitment to maintaining an accessible record of decisions and deeds that makes genuine accountability possible.

After leaving the Fund I spent time as resident scholar at the Rockefeller Archive Center in the late 1980s and understood, as all historians do, how important that single archive has been to the scholarship we all do. It is a repository of records for the Rockefeller philanthropic entities as well as Russell Sage, Commonwealth and other foundations. In those collections are also documents from countless other nonprofits, ephemeral organizations that have not survived. The body of work produced by scholars working in this archive has broadened and deepened the debate about foundations and, most importantly, grounded it solidly in the historical evidence. This obligation to keep and preserve and make the records accessible is harder than it might at first seem. Board members, colleagues, lawyers often stand in the way. But it is a battle that needs to be fought. And it is best waged from the inside by staff members who feel an institutional obligation to future staff members as well as a public duty to those historians, social scientists, and journalists who should someday be able to scrutinize and understand what foundations have done and why.

There is also much in the archives and in foundation files that can make for better philanthropic practice. When you've read the correspondence and memoranda of Frederick T. Gates, Beardsley Ruml, Henry Pritchett, Frederick Keppel (or read about them), you've been tutored by some of your shrewdest predecessors. You've looked over their shoulders as they've built new institutions, shaped new academic fields, invested in human capital, worked with government. It's the very best nonprofit management program you can find anywhere. You can see the entire continuum of foundation activities B from building basic knowledge, applying that knowledge, engaging in policy advocacy, instigating social movements, to experimenting with and delivering various social services. And you can see it in the changing external environment in which foundations operate. If some of the best philanthropy is Aenlightened opportunism," as Edwin Embree of the Julius Rosenwald Fund once put it, one can best gauge and then seize those opportunities by studying the work of others.

I also used history throughout the seven and a half years that I worked with a donor in New York and headed his foundation. I continue to engage the past as I work with several other donors as they contemplate their philanthropic legacies and try to structure their foundations. History offers a kind of peer-to-peer education. In my first meeting with Howard Gilman, I handed him the memo Robert W. DeForest had written for Margaret Olivia Sage, setting out options for the Russell Sage Foundation in 1906. I gave him letters exchanged among Rockefellers Senior and Junior and Frederick Gates as they struggled for a decade before finally establishing the Rockefeller Foundation. I wanted to show him how donors and advisers had thought about the burdens and opportunities of their vast wealth. In particular, I used history to keep several questions in front of the donor:

How is our world in the late twentieth century different from the world of Sage, Rockefeller and Carnegie?

What have we learned from their experiences of institutionalizing their philanthropy, of creating governance structures, of focusing on particular sorts of problems, on moving from individual charitable impulse to enduring organizations?

Engaging these questions—day in and day out—with a donor and building from scratch a foundation staff and program over seven years and then fighting a very bitter battle after the donor's death with his executors and corporate executives leads me to conclude by posing my second large question:

What have my experiences in the philanthropic sector taught me about history? Have they in any way made me a better or more insightful historian of philanthropy? Or, more plaintively, in the spirit of an apologia and confession what do I wish I had known when I first entered the foundation world?

First, I have learned about the inner contest and conflict within the particular foundations where I've worked. Understanding the contours of those battles has given me insights into other foundations. While the outer facade of foundations often appears monolithic—and much scholarship on foundations has portrayed them that way—the teeming, incessant internal argument is the most compelling and interesting feature of any foundation. Whether it is staff members versus staff members, staff versus board or factions of both slugging it out, foundations can seem like one long internal argument. Often these conflicts replicate wider intellectual disputes in our society. Gaining scholarly insight into these contests is difficult but worth the effort.

Second, I have gained a much deeper appreciation of the foundation as a legal entity and, with that, an appreciation of lawyers. Sometimes a foundation is a legal entity in transit from one form to another: private corporate assets intended for a philanthropic purpose embodied in a will; passage into an estate controlled by executors and a corporate-dominated board; and finally a foundation with an evolving governance structure as it matures. I have come to view foundations far more legalistically than I once did. And I see them in evolutionary terms as well—and sometimes subject to shocks and evolutionary reversals.

Third, I tend to see philanthropic institutions as more malleable and adaptive than I had ever thought them to be. Not only do new legal forms emerge—the large general purpose foundation was once, only a hundred years ago, a novelty. Fidelity and Schwab and others have invented something over the past five years that is also new. Moreover, program focus and philanthropic strategic approaches also change, perhaps too rapidly. The most interesting questions about philanthropy are, to my mind, about these changes. They compel us to look outside philanthropy to the changing role of government, to developments in financial and business organizations, to the ways we think and argue about public purposes.

I've recently returned to my roots as a European historian, having been asked by the Bertelsmann Foundation to write an essay on foundations in Europe from antiquity to the twentieth century. Covering some of the same terrain the callow graduate student walked in the 1970s, I brought a grizzled, battle-scarred veteran's eye to the assignment. What I saw this time around was a story grounded in the development of Greek and Roman law, canon law, common law, continental civil law. It was a story of governance practices and their evolution, a story of municipal and state authorities seeking to reform and regulate philanthropic institutions (indeed, there were intense periods of reformist zeal confronting the same sets of abuses century after century) and above all, a continuing debate about large concepts such as duty, obligation, equity, material and spiritual poverty, vices and virtues.

In sweeping through the centuries I returned to a returned to a world and to a vocabulary, quite familiar to a medievalist, but a lexicon far, far different from the contemporary managerial language of the nonprofit sector, with its half-understood business metaphors suggesting thoroughly novel approaches to strategic and venture philanthropy. My recent backward-looking, bi-millennial historical exercise has reinforced two hopes: As a historian I hope I have gained a perspective on what is faddish and what endures in philanthropy. As a practicing philanthropoid, who has experienced both memorable disappointments and greatly satisfying experiences, I hope I have earned the right (in the spirit of Wally Nielsen) to be skeptical of the philanthropic enterprise, even as I remain deeply committed to its potential.

THE HISTORY OF AMERICAN PHILANTHROPY
AS A FIELD OF RESEARCH

MERLE CURTI

In the literature of American social history, one finds certain large themes or areas receiving special attention. These include the social structure and social relations of the family, of work groups, and of social classes, as well as the characteristics and interactions with the rest of the population of the various ethnic and nationality groups. The historian has also described the social aspects of such institutions as religion, education, technology and the arts, politics and, especially of late, business, which has of course come more and more to affect all other occupations.

The time has come to ask whether there are less obvious but possibly almost as important segments of our culture which have received less attention at the hands of social historians than their importance warrants. To be specific, is philanthropy, in all its ramifications, one of these major culture segments? In other words, how important has relatively disinterested benevolence been in giving expression to, and in promoting at home and abroad, a major American value—human welfare? All one can say at the present time, I think, is that the literature of the subject warrants the hypothetical statement, to be tested by investigation, that philanthropy has been one of the major aspects of and keys to American social and cultural development.

In recognition of the need for advancing our knowledge in this field, Russell Sage Foundation, which from its inception has concerned itself with the nature and impact of giving, sponsored a research planning conference, held at Princeton, February 3–4, 1956.

The conference participants[1] take this way of sharing with others some of the suggestions that were developed in the course of their discussions. It is hoped that the suggestions made here may stimulate historians to direct the attention of their graduate students to this field as a promising and important one. It is also hoped that young historians who have finished their formal training may find inviting topics for investigation in our suggestions. It will be apparent that some of the problems mentioned may be best pursued by individual effort. Some, however, invite a cooperative and interdisciplinary approach. If, for example, one were to study the urges that have been satisfied by giving and try to find how these have been related to forms of giving and to manifest explanations of such giving, helpful clues would be found in the writings of anthropologists, sociologists, and psychologists.

In the interest of promoting perspective on the history of American philanthropy, historians can profitably consider the role of charity and philanthropy in other cultures and at other times. Certainly the history of philanthropy in America cannot be understood without taking into account its relationship to the development of philanthropy in western civilization. But it might also be profitable to broaden the comparative approach by taking into account the role of philanthropy in non-Christian cultures—such as those in which Buddhism or Mohammedanism is the prevailing religion.

Perspective may also be broadened, and necessary relationships discovered, by a careful consideration of the role of charity in ancient Israel, in pre-Christian and in post-Christian Greece and Rome, and in the various branches of Christianity, including the eastern orthodox churches, the medieval western church, the Protestant Reformation churches, and the pietistic and evangelical movements in the post-Reformation era. That much of the work in these areas has been done is apparent to any scholar acquainted with such standard works as Ernst Troeltsch's *Social Teachings of the Christian Churches*. But quite possibly scholars in these fields of history may still be able to give us new insights and information about charity and philanthropy in earlier times and in other places. In any case, we need to know more than we do about the ways in which the heritage represented in many of these forms of Christianity was transmitted to this country.

Religion in its American forms contributed to philanthropic habits and institutions through direct gifts to church organizations and, indirectly, by motivating contributions to secular causes and institutions. We need further explorations of the relationship to philanthropy of such more or less distinctively American religious movements as the "federal theology" of Puritan New England, the later "New England theology" of the followers of Jonathan Edwards, the revivalist doctrines and impulses, the Social Gospel, American Quakerism, Mormonism, and the Pentecostal sects. All these contributed in one way or another to the development of an American philanthropy. But precisely in what ways? The story of Jewish charities and of Catholic charities and missionary activities offers another field for study. Kenneth Scott Latourette, in his monumental work on missionary activities, has documented many aspects of the interrelationships between the older program of emphasis on conversion and the newer supplementary activities in education, health, and welfare. But the latest developments still need to be studied, as well as the efforts to develop self-supporting, independent churches in the countries in which missionary efforts have long been made.

Materials for these and related studies are available in many depositories, including libraries at Yale University, the University of Chicago, and Union Theological Seminary. Scholars will also find materials in the collections of the several departments, divisional units, and commissions of the National Council of Churches. Scholars interested in these and related materials would find a helpful response on the part of those who have given special attention to this area; Kenneth Latourette, R. Pierce Baker, M. S. Bates, Frank W. Price, Charles Forman, Robert Bilkeimer, and Father John J. Considine come to mind.

Closely related to religion as a dynamic factor in the history of American philanthropy is humanitarianism. We have, of course, many competent studies of organizations and movements devoted to humanitarian enterprises—world peace, the abolition of slavery, temperance, prison reform, aid for the handicapped, and the rehabilitation of social deviants. But we still need studies exploring some of the aspects of these movements that bear on the larger story of philanthropy. We need studies of motivation, conscious and, so far as it can be sensed, unconscious, in founders and workers. Historians can study changes in fund-raising activities, the development of pressure-group techniques, the stimulus given to government to assume a greater measure of responsibility in a given area, and the impacts of humanitarian crusades on institutions, legislation, and social habits.

But the values associated with religion and humanitarianism did not exist in a vacuum. No study of any aspect of philanthropy can safely ignore economic institutions and values; nor should it ignore other complex economic considerations, including the changes in business policy toward mobile assets, investment, public relations, and the tax structure. It is also important to keep in mind the fact that there is nothing really static in the economic universe. In agrarian economies, giving took the form of giving land. What were the effects of this? In a commercial-industrial economy giving usually takes the form of giving stocks and bonds. Has there been adequate study of the relationship between mobile capital, business policy, and giving, or between the various forms of wealth and giving practices? To come to our recent history, what needs to be learned about the relationship between giving and business expansion and contraction, or between philanthropy and the passage, modification, and repeal of bankruptcy laws, as in the depression of 1837? What is known and what can be learned about giving habits at different income levels, in different periods? Have there been significant changes or trends? What similarities and differences can be detected in a given period between economically stable and economically unstable communities?

The historian might also investigate the effects on philanthropy of changing concepts of the ceiling of welfare. That is, he might show how the pattern of philanthropy has been affected from one period to another by what are considered necessities and what are considered luxuries. We clearly need to know a great deal more than we do about the ways in which our changing world economic relationships have influenced private philanthropy in less developed areas. To what extent, for example, did the development of philanthropic habits on the part of business leaders and corporations at home influence the welfare policies abroad of Firestone, United Fruit, and other corporations?

Let us be more specific. We could try to find out, from existing histories of business firms and corporations, how decisions about giving were made. We can ask when corporations began to feel it was important, in the interest of good business, to have the good will of the community in which operations centered. Has the last word been said on the motives, nature, and effects of the philanthropic activities of the early New England textile manufacturers? What were the implications of Jay Cooke's shift in the focus of giving from the East to the Northwest after he became involved in promoting the Northern Pacific? We know something about the role of the railroads in promoting the Y.M.C.A., but possibly the whole story has not yet been told. Thanks to the studies of Henrietta Larson, Thomas Cochran, and C. Howard Hopkins, a high standard for further inquiries into this area has been set. Surely something can also yet be learned about the origin, nature, course, and effects of philanthropic activities in company towns. We know from the studies of F. Emerson Andrews and of Williams and Croxton, as well as from the reports of the National Bureau of Economic Research, something about the more recent aspects of corporation giving. What would a re-examination of the archives of business firms whose histories have been written reveal, if the investigator approached the materials holding firmly in mind some of the questions we have asked? It would be interesting to know what lies within corporation archives that has not been made available to historical study. Would these tell us more than we know about the reasons why some corporations decided *not* to give? We can ask what role was played by pressure groups, how much responsiveness there has been to community opinion, how much consideration there has been of stockholders and of the labor force, what have been the functions of public relations counsels.

Nor is corporation giving the only type of philanthropy which a consideration of functional economic groups suggests. It is known that many trade unions have engaged in philanthropic activities. We need to know which ones set the pace and why they did. It would also be important to know more than we do about the directions in which labor philanthropies have pointed. What have been the results?

Legal history has, of course, been necessarily concerned with many matters closely related to philanthropy. Such monumental works as Holdsworth's *History of English Law* and Austin Scott's study of trusts have opened new vistas. The studies of English philanthropy by W. K. Jordan and David Owen promise to illuminate certain dark corners of legal relations; but the American field is still largely open.

A study of the explanation of American resistance to certain legal concepts relating to philanthropy, both in common law and in the Statute of Charitable Uses, could be of great interest. What light on this and other points would more exhaustive, perhaps quantitative, study of wills and bequests reveal? What needs to be considered in studying "manifest reason" and "real" motives? We need explorations pointing out how these can be studied. Again, the outlines of our knowledge of the ways in which religious organizations came to be tax exempt after separation of church and state need to be filled in. What were the antecedents of "dead hand?" Someone ought to study further the story of the early exemption of charitable trusts from strict legal restrictions. We need comparisons of this story with recent tax exemption practices. We also need to know more about perpetuities, obsolescent laws, and cy-pres doctrine. What, legally speaking, constituted philanthropy at different periods?

With some exceptions, legal historians have chiefly concerned themselves with the history of a special legal doctrine. Often they have done this because a current problem suggested an ad hoc study. While some of the best of the legal history studies relate legal doctrines involving philanthropy to the economic, social, and cultural context, this is all too infrequently the case. We need more legal historians who are aware of the interdisciplinary approach. We also need historians of philanthropy, especially in some of its aspects, who are acquainted with the more relevant points of law in its technical sense.

Attention has been called to the need for considering the economic basis of philanthropy in any effort to explain its legal relationships and implications. So, too, is it desirable to take the social context into account in legal studies of philanthropy. In fact, every phase of philanthropy needs to be studied in terms of its social context. The historian should, for example, consider the implications of shifts in the role of the family in looking out for its needy members. Another aspect of the history of philanthropy which needs to be explored is its relation to social status and to the social roles of those who receive and those who give, organize, and dispense benefactions.

Of all the social changes in America which have basically affected the course of philanthropy, none seems to be as important as the movement commonly referred to as urbanization. Since Arthur M. Schlesinger, Sr., first called our attention to this basic theme in American history, we have learned much about it and about how to study it. We know, for example, that one may be misled by assuming the adequacy for all purposes of the census definition of a city; for it is clear that many urban centers in the technical sense retained rural values and rural types of conduct for varying periods of time. With this in mind, one may find in the growth of cities, metropolitan areas, and suburban decentralization, important keys to an understanding of many of the most significant developments in philanthropy.

We now have some very competent urban histories, such, for example, as those of Rochester, Milwaukee, and Chicago. In these, the student of the history of philanthropy will find answers to some of the questions he is curious about. He will, for instance, learn a good deal about the establishment, support, and role of particular philanthropic agencies. But there is still much unbroken ground.

It would be worth while to make a comparative study of philanthropy in cities of different sizes and rates of growth, in different sections of the United States, and of differing ethnic composition. What similarities and what differences would be found between Rochester and Milwaukee, Cleveland and San Francisco, Boston and Baltimore? What changes in giving habits did the example of philanthropy such as that of Eastman have on Rochester? It is perhaps not too soon to begin to ask why philanthropic efforts have succeeded in making striking changes in a short period in Pittsburgh, why similar efforts in other places have succeeded less well, and why they have not even been undertaken in still others.

Other aspects of the relations between urban growth and philanthropy could also be further explored with profit—notably the rise and fortunes of the organized charity associations, which initiated the social settlement houses and the substitution of "scientific philanthropy" for traditional face-to-face giving. In his recent suggestive and competent studies, Robert H. Bremner has shown the indebtedness to British patterns of both the charity organization movement and the establishment of social settlement houses and has broadly outlined some of the factors in the Americanization of these agencies. But much remains to be done. While such books as Robert A. Wood's *The Settlement Horizon* (1922) are informative, we have no studies which set this movement in its historical perspective and adequately evaluate it. The autobiographical accounts of settlement residents, often polemical and almost always interesting, have in general not been supplemented with scholarly biographies. A composite portrait of the persons drawn into this movement, illuminating their backgrounds, motives, values, and philosophies, would be welcome. We need to have histories of particular settlement houses which trace their changing functions and analyze their role as spearheads of urban reform, as interpreters between the less advantaged and the favored urban residents, and as agencies for acquainting Americans with the causes of poverty, social dislocation, cultural differences, and "immigrant gifts."

The literature of social work is extensive, but for the most part it has been written by practitioners in the field. The few studies which give some attention to historical perspective only suggest the amount of work yet to be done. We know something about the bearings of the early charity organization movement on social work and the transition from private charity to public relief. But F. D. Watson's *Charity Organization Movement in the United States* (1922) and J. C. Brown's *Public Relief, 1929–1939* (1940) stand practically alone as pioneer works of a systematic sort. The insights of such a thoughtful interpretation as *Life, Liberty, and the Pursuit of Bread* (1940), by Carlisle and Carol Shafer, open many vistas which invite exploration. We need further study of the antecedents of social work, of its development as a profession, of cooperative financing, and of the impacts of prosperity, depression, and war. Biographies of social workers are wanted—the recently completed study of Mary Richmond by Muriel Pumphrey gives promise that this need is now being recognized. We should also have studies of the influence of sociology, psychology, and psychiatry on the philosophy and techniques of social work. Yet to be thoroughly explored are the contributions of social work to the methods of social investigation and to public welfare policy in rural as well as in urban settings. The role of the federal government in the area of social welfare and its impact on social work particularly require attention.

Urban growth also involved changes in fund-raising practices which need to be explored. How did growing specialization, functional to city living, affect patterns of philanthropy, particularly the increasing concern with problems of health, recreation, and delinquency? The story of community chests and federated giving has been told only in small part. How did American urban conditions affect Old World patterns of philanthropy, such as, for example, the charitable traditions which Jewish communities brought from Europe? One can think of many possibilities for the study of the role of urban philanthropy in creating new emphases on the artistic values. How has the trend toward suburban living affected philanthropy? How has philanthropy, before and after the marked growth of cities, been directed to rural areas and rural problems?

Social mobility in America, especially in city life, must have certain relationships to philanthropy. In colonial America, and in certain nineteenth-century communities, men gave to gain standing in the eyes of God; as the nineteenth century moved forward, many gave to gain standing in the eyes of men. Freeman Hunt's *Lives of American Merchants* (1858) clearly indicates that the desire for social approval and status figured in a good deal of philanthropy. We need to know more about the relationship of social mobility and social status to philanthropy. Light might be thrown on this relationship by an examination of the historical development of the practice, during fundraising campaigns, of carefully selecting solicitors from the elite.

Related to all of the problems and issues thus far mentioned is the extremely important question of the interrelations between voluntary giving, by individuals or groups, and the responsibility of government for welfare. Contrary to a fairly widely-held view, the interrelations cannot be described merely in terms of the steady retreat of the one and the corresponding advance of the other. During most of the colonial period, for example, when mercantilistic philosophy was uppermost, government assumed a principal responsibility for poor relief. Thus in some degree the colonial period foreshadowed the modern welfare state.

Historians might well study the relations between this older pattern and such developments as the separation of church and state, the westward movement, the humanitarian reform movements of the nineteenth century, the depressions and the relief agencies they occasioned, the establishment of income taxes, and social security legislation. To what extent did voluntary philanthropic organizations call attention to new problems, arouse public opinion, serve as pressure groups, and lead the way to a larger assumption of responsibility by government agencies? How was this trend illustrated in the matter of the emancipation of the slave, the guaranteeing of civil rights to the Negro, and the care of the immigrant, the Indian, and the handicapped? What about work for peace, temperance, and the care of the aged; the work to curb delinquency and alcoholic drinking? What was back of the shift to a larger measure of government responsibility in areas earlier dominated by voluntary philanthropy? When did the shift take place in the fields of education, health, and recreation? Finally we may ask how our major wars have affected these changes.

We might consider the implications of the fact that many of the consequences of political democracy were not felt until the twentieth century. Until a half century ago, wealth in general was not particularly sensitive to political movements. When it became so in the Populist and Progressive periods, and in a more marked degree perhaps in the depression of the 1930's, philanthropies of the rich may have slowed down some of the trends toward greater government responsibility in many areas; but the question remains an open one. On the other hand, the growth of wealth was associated with new types of taxation which enabled government to perform functions hitherto chiefly performed by private philanthropy, at least since the colonial period.

Another large problem involves the extremely difficult task of evaluating the influences of philanthropy. Here there are many variables. It is hard indeed to separate philanthropy from the many other factors in our country that have been pushing us toward the conception of a widely-based and constantly-advancing standard of welfare. One hardly need mention some of the more important of these factors: an endowment of natural resources in relation to population and available technology which gave a relatively high degree of reality to the concept of abundance, a widely-held conviction that it is possible for man to transform his environment for the better, a high degree of social mobility, and a marked expectation of achievement. We need to know as much as we can about the ways in which philanthropy has interacted with this larger concept.

A major problem in this field of research, then, is to effect some control over certain variables. For example, taking two otherwise comparable cities, we might compare the level of welfare of one in which there was a good deal of philanthropic activity with that of the city in which there was little or no such activity. We might compare a state having a considerable body of social legislation with one which more largely pursued a policy of depending on voluntary giving and philanthropy. A study could be made of two otherwise comparable educational institutions, of which one received consistently large philanthropic benefactions and the other did not, with an effort to assess their relative levels of scholarship and contributions to the wider community. Other, and better, methods of controlling variables will occur to those giving some thought to the problem.

Another matter to be considered is that of the most useful periodizations in the study of the history of philanthropy. The span to the mid-eighteenth century might provide an initial period, one in which there was a transfer from England of the laws of charity and benefactions and in which government assumed a large measure of responsibility for welfare and improvement. Succeeding periods could be (1) the age of Franklin, that is, the period of the growth of commerce and of towns, with rising secular conceptions of worth and of service; (2) the period from, roughly, 1815 to 1860, in which church and state were separated in Massachusetts and Connecticut, in which a new evangelical fervor inspired many efforts at moral reform, and in which social dislocations associated with the westward movement and the advance of the industrial revolution stimulated new types of voluntary philanthropy; and (3) the continuation of these impulses in the period after 1860, with the further industrial expansion and new westward movements. Then we could consider (4) the period from the late 1880's to the Great Depression, when new sources of mobile capital were available, when titans of wealth used philanthropy for various reasons, and when Carnegie was preaching and practicing the doctrine of the stewardship of great riches.[2] Finally, (5) we could deal with the period since the depression, in which we have a shift of control from owners to managers, with the growing importance of public relations, and significant changes in the tax structure.

Of course, there were no sharp breaks between any of these so-called periods; but we can define certain watersheds or turning points. None of these seems to be related alone to economics, social structure, movements of thought, or emphases within the frame of philanthropy itself. All the watersheds seem rather to be defined by a cluster of factors interpenetrating every segment of American life.

It might be well to begin by taking one of these periods and working out a "model" for its careful analysis in terms of philanthropy. This would involve, as must be apparent from the foregoing discussion, consideration of factors such as the economy and changes in it, the shifting nature of the social structure and of social roles, changes in the nature and configuration of the population, and developments in communication and techniques of fund-raising. All these would be related, no doubt, to general movements in thought and to systems of value. No one model would in itself serve for studies of other periods, but it would nevertheless be highly suggestive.

The importance of periodization is clear, but the precise boundaries of any one period need to be held tentatively until a good deal of empirical data are available and until considerable thought has gone into the meaning of the data. The period approach seems well suited to cooperative or team work.

In addition to period studies, we obviously need careful, objective, well-documented studies of particular organizations which run through two or more periods, studies which relate the history of the organization to preceding and contemporary social, economic, cultural, and political developments. A few examples may illustrate: a college or church school, the Interchurch World Movement, the International Christian University Foundation, the Near East Relief and the Near East Foundation, American Friends Service Committee, CARE, the Layman's Inquiry on Foreign Missions, the United Jewish Charities, the National Catholic Welfare Conference, a philanthropically-supported, low-rent housing project. We also need institutional studies of such organizations as the American

Cancer Foundation, the American Foundation for the Blind, the American Heart Association, the Mental Hygiene Association. The many cultural centers, such as privately-supported museums, the MacDowell Colony, and Yaddo, warrant study. Other institutional studies might include histories of such fund-raising organizations as the John Price Jones Company, Marts and Lundy, associations of colleges and universities for fund-raising and fund-pooling, and joint chest funds—to cite only a few examples. Careful studies of "charity rackets" might prove illuminating. We also need histories of the philanthropic activities of corporations, trade unions, and small foundations, as well as many of the larger foundations that have not thus far been adequately studied.

What would mark a first-rate institutional study? We have some models, and others are about to appear, including Shryock's history of the American Tuberculosis Association. Any scholarly institutional study should, of course, be based on unrestricted access to all available material. It should not, in general, be written by anyone who has been closely concerned with the institution. It must avoid being a mere glory story; it must examine failures as well as successes. It should include such topics as origin, sources of support, patterns of fund-raising, relation to tax structure, nature of decision-making, reputation, and impact on the community, the nation, or an overseas area.

In addition to period histories and institutional studies, there is room for a series of biographies of philanthropists whose stories in relation to philanthropy have been inadequately written or not written at all. It is important to make an immediate and concerted effort to save pertinent papers and to broaden the base of materials when possible, through oral interview with the subject or his associates.

Topical studies, already mentioned, are also obviously needed. At the risk of some repetition, one may call attention to the need for a study of laws regulating philanthropy; of the economic aspects of philanthropy; of religion and philanthropy, education and philanthropy, the arts and philanthropy, science and health and philanthropy; and of philanthropic activities abroad. Topical studies of fund-raising and of the interrelations of philanthropy and government are also needed. Ultimately, it is to be hoped that, when the necessary spade work is done, we may have a systematic history of American philanthropy.

No doubt much of the work here suggested will in time be done even without the aid of special planning and encouragement. But more work, and better work, may be done through the planning and cooperative efforts of scholars. The individual scholar, once started on a project, must be free to work it out as he thinks best; but he will need to know how his study is related to others and where he may find related materials. No single question or topic suggested here can really be understood without reference to every other one. The scholar, as he pursues his investigations, will need time and opportunities for travel. This means that he will need financial aid. In view of the difficulties many competent historians have faced in their efforts to secure publication of non-profit scholarly contributions, some plan assuring the publication of superior studies would doubtless encourage many serious and able scholars to undertake such studies as those outlined in this essay.[3]

Quite apart from any bearing a larger knowledge of the history of philanthropy may have on a clearer understanding of various problems currently associated with it, who can doubt that the character and dimensions of American civilization may be illuminated by sustained inquiries into American experience in giving?

University of Wisconsin

Notes

1. The conference was organized by F. Emerson Andrews of Russell Sage Foundation, who, with Donald Young, represented the Foundation at the meeting. Participants included Thomas C. Cochran, Henry Edward Guerlac, W. Stull Holt, Kenneth Scott Latourette, Richard B. Morris, Richard H. Shryock, David B. Truman, Merle Curti (chairman), and two representatives of the Ford Foundation, Carl B. Spaeth, Stanford University, and Mrs. Jackson Chance. There is available a report of the discussions, including a list of topics needing investigation, a topical outline of American philanthropy, and a selected bibliography of the literature of philanthropy by Margaret W. Otto, Chief Librarian of the New York School of Social Work (*Report of the Princeton Conference on the History of Philanthropy in the United States*, Russell Sage Foundation, New York, N. Y., 1956, pp. 84, $1.00).

2. We might also point out that Carnegie emphasized the idea that help to others should enable them to help themselves—as in the case of the public library. Also, in this period philanthropy was increasingly emphasizing prevention, cure, and rehabilitation, rather than mere alleviation of social evils and individual misfortunes. This was also the period of considerable opposition to the use of "tainted money" for philanthropic purposes.

3. There is evidence of growing interest on the part of many agencies in making possible deeper knowledge of the role of philanthropy in American development. It seems clear that further support for well-designed projects in this field can be anticipated.

Bibliography
Chapter 1 Historical Overview

Adam, Thomas, ed. *Philanthropy, Patronage, and Civil Society: Experiences from Germany, Great Britain, and North America*. Bloomington: Indiana University Press, 2004.

Andrews, F. Emerson. *Philanthropic Giving* New York: Russell Sage Foundation, 1950.

Bremner, Robert. *American Philanthropy* 2nd edition. Chicago: University of Chicago Press, 1988.

Brilliant, Eleanor, *Private Charity and Public Inquiry: A History of the Filer and Peterson Commissions*. Bloomington, IN: Indiana University Press, 2000.

Brooks, Arhur C. *Who Really Cares: The Surprising Truth About Compassionate Conservatism*. New York: Basic Books, 2006.

Brooks, Arthur C., ed. *Gifts of Time and Money in America's Communities*. Rowman & Littlefield, 2005.

Burlingame, Dwight. *The Responsibilities of Wealth*. Bloomington, IN: Indiana University Press, 1992.

Cherry, Conrad. *Hurrying Toward Zion: Universities, Divinity Schools, and American Protestantism*. Bloomington, IN: Indiana University Press, 1995.

Crocker, Margaret. *Mrs. Russell Sage: Women's Philanthropy and Activism in Gilded Age and Progressive Era America*. Bloomington: Indiana University Press, 2006.

Crowder, Nancy L. and Virginia A. Hodgkinson. *Academic Centers and Programs Focusing on Philanthropy, Voluntarism, and Not-for-Profit Activity: A Progress Report*. Washington, D.C.: Independent Sector, 1993.

Curti, Merle. "Philanthropy," in *Dictionary of the History of Ideas*, Vol. 3, pp. 487–493.

Curti, Merle and Roderick Nash. *Philanthropy and the Shaping of American Higher Education* Piscataway: Rutgers University Press, 1965; reprint with new introduction by Andrea Walton, available at http://www.ksghauser.harvard.edu/philanthropyclass

Dowie, Mark. *American Foundations: An Investigative History*. Cambridge, MA: MIT Press, 2001.

Ehrlich, Thomas and Ray Bacchetti. *Reconnecting Education and Foundations: Turning Good Intentions into Educational Capital*. San Francisco: Jossey Bass, 2007.

Fleishman, Joel L. *"The Foundation: A Great American Secret: How Private Wealth Is Changing the World."* Public Affairs, 2007.

Friedman, Lawrence J. and Mark D. McGarvie, eds. *Charity, Philanthropy, and Civility in American History*. Cambridge: Cambridge University Press, 2003.

Frumkin, Peter. *Strategic Giving: The Art and Science of Philanthrophy*. Chicago: University of Chicago Press, 2006.

Gardner, John. *Living, Leading and the American Dream*, edited by Francesa Gardner. Foreward by Bill Moyers. San Francisco: Jossey-Bass, 2003.

Hall, Peter Dobkin. *Inventing the Nonprofit Sector and other Essays on Philanthropy, Voluntarism, and Nonprofit Organizations*. Baltimore and London: Johns Hopkins University Press, 1992.

Hammack, David C. *Making the Nonprofit Sector: A Reader*. Bloomington: Indiana University Press, 1998.

Hewa, Soma. "The Protestant Personality and Higher Education: American Philanthropy Beyond the "Progressive Era," *International Journal of Politics, Culture & Society*, Vol. 12, No. 1 (Fall 1998), pp. 135–164.

Hollis, Ernest. *Philanthropy and Higher Education*. New York: Columbia University Press, 1938.

Jeavons, Thomas. *Learning for the Common Good: Liberal Education, Civic Education and Teaching About Philanthropy*. Washington, DC: Association of American Colleges, 1991.

Kass, Amy A, ed. *The Perfect Gift*. Bloomington, IN: Indiana University Press, 2002.

Kramer, Ralph. "A Third Sector in the Third Millenium." *Voluntas: International Journal of Voluntary and Nonprofit Organizations*, Vol. 11, No. 1 (2000), pp. 1–23.

Lagemann, Ellen Condliffe ed. *Philanthropic Foundations: New Scholarship, New Possibilities.* Bloomington, IN: Indiana University Press, 1999.

Layton, Diaphne Niobe. *Philanthropy and Voluntarism: An Annotated Bibliography.* New York: Foundation Center, 1987.

McCarthy, Kathleen. *American Creed: Philanthropy and the Rise of Civil Society 1700–1865.* Chicago: University of Chicago Press, 2003.

Mirbella, R. and Naomi B Wish. "The 'Best Place' Debate: A Comparison of Graduate Education Programs for Nonprofit Managers." *Public Administration Review, Vol.* 60, No. 3, pp. 219–229.

Oates, Mary, *The Catholic Philanthropic Tradition in America.* Bloomington: Indiana University Press.

Ott, J. Stephen. *The Nature of the Nonprofit Sector.* Boulder, CO: Westview, 2001.

———. "Philanthropy, Education, and the Politics of Knowledge," in *Teachers College Record,* Vol. 93 (Spring 1992), pp. 361–369. (The **entire** volume of *Teachers College Record* is devoted to philanthropy.)

———. *Private Power for the Public Good: A History of the Carnegie Foundation for the Advancement of Teaching.* Middletown, CT: Wesleyan University Press, 1989. Putnam, Robert D. *Bowling Alone: The Collapse and Revival of American Community.* New York: Simon Schuster, 2000.

Rose, Kenneth W., Benjamin R. Shute, Jr., Darwin H. Stapleton, *Minerva: A Review of Science, Learning & Policy,* Vol. 35, No. 3 (Fall 1997), pp. 203–05. (The **entire** issue is devoted to the theme of philanthropy and institution building in the 20th century).

Rosenwald, Julius. "Principles of Public Giving." *The Atlantic Monthly.* May 1929, pp. 599–606.

Sears, Jesse Brundage. Philanthropy in the History of American Higher Education (1922), "Introduction," pp. 1–32.

Shankman, Marcy. "Organizational Creation in Higher Education: The Indiana University Center on Philanthropy." PhD Indiana University, 2001.

Sealander, Judith. *Private Wealth and Public Life: Foundation Philanthropy and the Reshaping of American Social Policy from the Progressive Era to the New Deal.* Baltimore: Johns Hopkins University Press, 1997.

Smith, James Allen, *The Idea Brokers: Think Tanks and the Rise of the New Policy Elite.* New York: Macmillan/Free Press, 1991.

Warren, Mark E. *Democracy and Association.* Princeton and Oxford: Oxford University Press, 2001.

Wuthnow, Robert. *Faith and Philanthropy: Exploring the Role of Religion in America's Voluntary Sector.* San Francisco: Jossey-Bass, 1990.

Primary Materials

Bremner, Robert H. "Private Philanthropy and Public Needs: Historical Perspective," in Volume I of Filer Commission Report: *History, Trends, and Current Magnitudes,* pp. 89–114. (See Commission on Private Philanthropy and Public Needs. Giving in America: Toward a Stronger Voluntary Sector. Washington, D.C.: U.S. Department of Treasury, 1975.)

Burlingame, Dwight F. *Philanthropy in America: A Comprehensive Historical Encyclopedia,* Santa Barbara, CA: ABC-CLIO, 2004 (Includes primary documents).

Weitzman, Virginia and Murry et al. "Dimensions of the Voluntary Sector." *Nonprofit Alamanac.* San Francisco: Jossey-Bass, 1992.

Websites

Council for Aid to Higher Education	www.cae.org
Giving USA	www.aafrc.org
Giving Forum	www.givingforum.org
National Education Association	www..nea.org
PRO: Philanthropy Resources Online	http://indiamond6.ulib.iupui.edu/PRO/

CHAPTER 2

INTERPRETIVE FRAMEWORKS

A DIALOGUE BETWEEN THE HEAD AND THE HEART

ROBERT PAYTON

These reflections on reason and emotion in philanthropy are inspired by Thomas Jefferson's famous letter to Maria Cosway.

My theme is philanthropy and liberal education. My text is a letter-essay that Thomas Jefferson once wrote that goes by the title, "A Dialogue Between My Head and My Heart."[1] It is an essay on friendship, charity, the human condition, and the methods and values of science and morals. The letter was written to a married British woman whom Jefferson had met in Paris (and for whom he developed a strong but platonic affection), on the occasion of her departure for America. Jefferson was so moved by their parting that he returned to his apartment and wrote the long letter that same evening.

The body of the letter is in the literary form of a dialogue between Head and Heart, first as an exchange about the joy of friendship and the pain of separation. Jefferson then speaks of the "divided empire" of the self, the dialectic between reason and emotion, between self-interest and altruism, in each of us.

Friendship is at issue because of Jefferson's distress at the departure of his friend. His head tells him that the principle to follow is to avoid becoming entangled with others, with "their follies and their misfortunes," and to play it safe. Don't rush into new relationships; recognize beforehand the anguish they may cause, and cultivate instead the pleasures of privacy and contemplation. In a miserable world, the best course is to avoid adding misery to it.

Jefferson's heart responds that because the world is full of sorrow, it is only sensible to share our burdens: "For assuredly nobody will care for him who cares for nobody." In fact, the balance will tip the other way: ". . . thanks to a benevolent arrangement of things, the greater part of life is sunshine."

Although Jefferson attributes to the Head the hegemony over the world of nature, he claims for the Heart the human virtues of sympathy, love, justice; of benevolence, gratitude, and friendship. The methods and values of science include calculation, and calculation in the form of self-interest in human affairs is a misapplication of science. Morality is too important, he says, "to be risked on the incertain combinations of the head"; the foundation of morality requires "the mechanism of the heart."

There is, on balance, in Jefferson's view, a long-term wisdom in the reliance on the human affections rather than on human cleverness. Jefferson implies that the concessions that the head makes to the heart are the source of some of our most important moral victories. (Although he doesn't make the point, I suspect that Jefferson would agree that the discipline imposed by the head on the heart often saves us from doing harm in our rush to do good. I will return to that later.)

Beyond friendship, in our less personal relations in society at large, Jefferson counsels against the misleading influence of narrow self-interest. The head leads us astray when it intrudes in the affairs of the heart. He illustrates his theme with two examples, the first that of a weary soldier seeking a lift on the back of Jefferson's carriage. Jefferson's self-interest advises against it: His head argues that there will be other soldiers further on; eventually we'll put too much of a burden on the horses. Jefferson rides on, but his conscience gets the better of him: It may not be possible to help everyone, his heart pleads, but we ought to help those we can. The logic of compassion wins out, but too late, because when Jefferson turns back to find the soldier, the soldier has taken another road.

The second illustration is not one of voluntary service, but of voluntary giving. Jefferson's head tells him that a woman seeking alms is in fact a drunkard who will only waste his charity in the taverns. Jefferson's heart again belatedly overrules his head, but this time he is able to seek out the woman and learn the truth about her. She was not a drunkard, after all, but a woman seeking charity to place her child in school.

Jefferson recognizes that there are consequences to these actions of the heart: "We have no rose without it's [sic] thorn; no pleasure without alloy." There are risks to be run, which implies that pain may well be incurred in the search for happiness. But that is better than lonely isolation, better than the security of the contemplative life that his head advises him to choose: "Let the sublimated philosopher grasp visionary happiness while pursuing phantoms dressed in the garb of truth! Their supreme wisdom is supreme folly . . ."

The dialogue between the head and the heart is a metaphor for the study of the philanthropic tradition. Jefferson's letter serves as a useful point of departure. Jefferson himself was a man of strong and developed reason as well as powerful and courageous commitment, presumably a model of the educated person, sensitive to human values, aware of human failings, pragmatic and visionary.

The philanthropic tradition is a setting in which to study the divided empire. We all have learned how our self-interest works, and we could quickly add to Jefferson's reasons for not picking up the soldier on the road: Not only will others be demanding the same help; the next thing you know they'll all want to sit up front with us.

Jefferson's example of the woman seeking alms makes us aware of the ancient moral problem of *desert:* Jefferson gave the woman help because she proved *not* to be a drunkard. Would he have helped her if his first impression had been accurate, had he detected the tell-tale odor on her breath? Today, we might simply evade the issue by contending that drunkenness is a disease, not a vice, and the woman deserves our help because she is sick. And that might then prompt us to ask ourselves—our hearts asking our heads—is there anyone out there who *doesn't* deserve our help?

The issue of the deserving poor and needy of our contemporary society has been debated at length in recent years. It continues to be a controversial issue of public policy. The complexities of the problem are by now familiar: Inspired by our hearts, we have followed our heads and turned the mentally ill out of institutions and into the streets. The consensus seems to be that such people shouldn't be made to live in the streets. At the same time, we have come to know that public shelters and institutions are often dangerous, heartless places. The morally right thing to do, it would seem, would be to find decent homes that will take these people in. Decent homes, presumably, like yours and mine . . .

In Santa Cruz, California, according to newspaper reports, able-bodied young people are found in considerable numbers claiming food, shelter, and freedom of action as the rights and protections belonging to the modern vagabond. They are neither seeking nor interested in employment.

Should we consider the mentally ill on the streets of New York and the idle dropouts on the streets of Santa Cruz equal in their claims on us?

In choosing one's friends, Jefferson said, one should exercise careful judgment. Friendship should not be based on externals or self-interest: "I receive no one into my esteem until they are worthy of it." Did Jefferson apply a test of worthiness to his acts of charity? He apparently took the soldier's plea at its face value; the soldier was worthy simply by virtue of being a soldier on duty. The woman seeking alms, on the other hand, required a test to determine that she was worthy of his assistance. Had she turned out to be a drunkard after all, she would have failed the test. Whether one should make judgments about the moral worth of those seeking aid is one of the recurrent issues of the philanthropic tradition, livelier today perhaps even than it was in Jefferson's time.

Friendship is not the basis for charity, for voluntary giving and service. Acts of philanthropy reach out to total strangers, often in distant places, usually without the ability to screen out the unworthy or otherwise unqualified. Nothing could be more familiar to Americans today, for example, than the drawn faces and swollen bellies of starving children in Africa, yet presumably few of us are personally acquainted with any of them. Our hearts tell us only that we *must* act to help them—even though are heads cannot tell us why.

That African appeal has touched millions of people, perhaps unprecedented numbers around the world. It has enlisted the efforts of people usually identified not with the relief of suffering, but with the manufacture of pleasure and self-indulgence. The rock musicians and other entertainers who produced the "We Are the World" and "Live Aid" fundraising extravaganzas were not more expert about the Ethiopian crisis than the readers of daily newspapers. They were able to condemn the situation as morally intolerable and to use their extraordinary promotional skills and technologies to raise large amounts of money very quickly—yet without any expertise at all in using that money to effect the changes they felt were necessary.

The dialogue between the Head and Heart over what we should do when faced with a human tragedy such as the famine in Ethiopia warns us of the limits of our emotion. The tens of millions of dollars raised by the rock concerts and records are not quickly and easily converted into food for the hungry. Rock stars prove to know little about the logistics of food aid, and seem to have only just recently discovered that Ethiopia is the center of a terrible civil war. We have learned to our dismay that some Ethiopians are willing to starve other Ethiopians for political ends. To seek to bring food for the innocent through that maze of ancient animosity may call for the cleverness of con men as well as for the patient commitment of saints.

Closer to home, and with no Russians to point a finger at, our failures to deal humanely and effectively with the homeless, even when we are inclined to respond to them, are instructive in teaching us that it is difficult to be enlightened and humane. Such failures seem to lead some people to conclude that the effort should not be made in the first place. As a nation, our head is telling us that we are better advised to ignore the "follies and the misfortunes" of others, and to make ourselves comfortable in our studies (or television rooms).

The purpose of liberal education is to bring some semblance of *detente* if not harmony to the divided empire of the human mind and spirit. To study the habits of the heart is to study the consequences of friendship and charity, of high aspiration and low technique, to reflect on knowing when to mind one's business and when not to, on wanting to do good and knowing how.

To study the tradition and practice of philanthropy is to confront liberal education at its best: in the education of the public citizen and the private person, in the continuing education of the Head *and* the Heart.

Note

1. Merrill D. Peterson, ed., *Thomas Jefferson: Writings*, The Library of America, 1984, pp. 866–877.
* This essay is adapted from a "Conversation at Monticello" sponsored by the White Burkett Miller Center of Public Affairs at the University of Virginia, September 12, 1985.

AMERICAN PHILANTHROPY AND THE NATIONAL CHARACTER

MERLE CURTI

In 1875 Thomas Wentworth Higginson, better known for his championship of the slave and of women's rights than for linguistic scholarship, reported that the term philanthropy had appeared for the first time as an English word in *The Guide to Tongues*, published in 1628. The word was simply "Philanthropie; Humanitie; a loving of man." Dryden, in apologizing for his use of the word philanthropy, declared that it had been introduced into English because there was no indigenous word to connote precisely the meaning of the Greek original. Colonial scholars who read in the original such writers as Isocrates, Xenophon, Epictetus, Plutarch and Polybius, knew the word in its Greek form, but the word philanthropy was not generally in English until the time of Addison.[1]

The term found some favor among disciples of the Enlightenment, but it came into common use only in the middle decades of the nineteenth century. It meant the love of man, charity, benevolence, humanitarianism, social reform. To cite an example from the hundreds at hand, Theodore Parker spoke of John Augustus as a philanthropist. This illegitimate, eccentric Lexington shoemaker had, Parker declared, earned the title by giving help to the helpless and love to the unlovely; more concretely, by bailing thousands out of jail, keeping hundreds from crime and redeeming countless fallen women.[2] In the minds of some of Theodore Parker's contemporaries the term suggested a meddling, hypocritical do-gooder. It was no doubt this image that old Count Gorowski had in mind when he cautioned a young lady against mixing with anyone of that class. "Marry thief!" he said, "marry murderer! But never marry philanthropist!"[3] But the more usual meaning was that given in a pamphlet written by Linus Pierpont Brockett in 1864 bearing the title "The Philanthropic Results of the War in America." The author identified the term with charity, benevolence, the love of one's needy fellow men without thought of personal advantage.[4]

After the Civil War certain leaders in the American Social Science Association agreed that philanthropy implies the impulse to relieve a situation, in contrast with social science, which presumably endeavors to prevent poverty and other social problems by probing behind effect to cause.[5] But this use of the term did not entirely catch on. When, early in our own century, the New York Charity Organization Society established a professional training program for social workers the new institution was called "The School of Philanthropy."[6]

Yet even at this time the word philanthropy had come to mean, to many Americans, large-scale giving by such men of great wealth as Peabody, Carnegie and Rockefeller. This of course is the sense in which the word is most commonly used today, despite the distaste both Carnegie and Rockefeller had for being called philanthropists. It might be argued that the change in the meaning of the term from benevolence and humanitarianism to organized large-scale giving reflects a shift in our society to a greater emphasis on the role of wealth.

What indeed has been the relation of philanthropy to the national character? Many social scientists of course reject the validity and usefulness of the concept of national character. Yet the belief that there is a cluster of more or less distinguishing American traits and values has persisted through our history, varying in expression from time to time, from place to place, from subculture to subculture.

In general however there has been agreement that the American national character has emphasized practicality and efficiency; and that it has equated successful achievement with individual freedom, individual effort, individual responsibility and a wide variety of choices. At the same time voluntary association with others in common causes has been thought to be strikingly characteristic of American life.

Other generalizations about "the American character" have been almost as commonly accepted. Americans have commonly identified public and private interest and needs—an identification made the easier by the national plenty and by social mobility. The national character has included an emphasis on equality both as a right and a fact. It has attached importance to the status and role of women. It has assumed the possibility and desirability of progress toward general well-being through the effort and co-operation of individuals, with the aid of education. It has, despite secular interests, found in religion and morality a rationale and a motivating power. Finally, American values have set much store on process, rather than on the finished product: the assumption has been that America is creative, not merely traditional and imitative.

Not all students of our national character have included philanthropy as a component. If mentioned, benevolence or philanthropy is passed over lightly in the studies of Constance Rourke, David Riesman and Max Lerner. But these writers and also the Kluckhohns and others do give a place in the American value-system to benevolence or closely related traits.

Among historians, Turner was appreciatively aware of the role of philanthropy although he did not dwell on it. The Beards, in *The American Spirit*, devoted some thoughtfully discriminating pages to the theme. One is somewhat surprised to find that David Potter, in the stimulating study of the national character in which he makes plenty the key, stopped short of linking this with philanthropy. On the other hand, Arthur M. Schlesinger, Sr., writing in 1953, declared that "unlike Europe, the United States has fathered few misers. . . . The successful . . . have shared their money with others almost as freely as they made it, returning at least part of their substance to channels of social usefulness through munificent gifts and bequests. This philanthropic streak in the national character, an index of the pervasive spirit of neighborliness, appeared early and has in our own day reached fabulous dimensions. "It is," continued Professor Schlesinger, "another of the distinguishing marks of the American way."[7]

Support for the thesis that American philanthropy reflects the national character also comes from our more thoughtful foreign visitors. Tocqueville was not the first of these to comment on the spirit of mutual helpfulness in America, but no one before him had stated it so cogently. The French social philosopher did not believe there was less selfishness among Americans than among Europeans. He did hold that in America selfishness was more enlightened; when an American asked for the help or cooperation of his fellow-citizens, it was seldom refused. It was apt to be given generously and with great goodwill. Whereas in most civilized nations a poor wretch might be as friendless in the midst of a crowd as the savage in the wilds, in America, in case of accident or calamity, "the purse of a thousand strangers" poured in to relieve the distress of the sufferers. "Equality of condition," Tocqueville said, "while it makes men feel their independence, shows them their own weakness; they are free, but exposed to a thousand accidents; and experience soon teaches them that although they do not habitually require the assistance of others, a time almost always comes when they cannot do without it."[8]

American generosity and mutual helpfulness, traits conceded by many of our most severe critics, were the subject of a striking comment on the part of a later distinguished visitor. "In works of active beneficence, no country has surpassed, perhaps none has equalled the United States," wrote James Bryce in 1888. "Not only are the sums collected for all sorts of philanthropic purposes larger relatively to the wealth of America than in any European country," Bryce went on, "but the amount of personal interest and effort devoted to them seems to a European visitor to excel what he knows at home." This informed admirer thought religious impulses in American life largely explained this trait.[9]

Sixty years later Harold Laski, whose critical analysis of our institutions reflected a socialist bias, conceded the striking generosity of well-to-do Americans in endowing education, research and the arts. In speaking of American giving to Europe and Asia in hundreds of thousands of donations, great and small, Laski insisted that no one was "entitled to speak of the material-mindedness of

Americans unless he can produce an instance of comparable and continuous generosity from European experience."[10]

As yet no careful historical and statistical study has been made to test this assumption which has from time to time been challenged by Americans themselves. No one can now say what proportion of men of wealth at given periods saw fit either during their lifetime or in making their last wills, to give generously to philanthropic causes. The evidence at hand does show that many people of wealth gave little to philanthropy.[11] It also seems clear that in the nineteenth century a reputation for philanthropy sometimes rested on giving less than two per cent of an estate. We know that Americans have reacted in various ways to reports of failure to help the less fortunate. Some merely shrugged their shoulders with indifference. Others offered rather limp apologies. Some were openly disapproving. Such, for example, was the phrenological-minded sculptor who was finishing a head of A. T. Stewart, the fabulously rich New York merchant, when he discovered how very little his subject had left to charity. He lost no time in remolding the cranium, leveling off the bumps of benevolence and idealism and building up those indicative of acquisitiveness and all the selfish and animal propensities![12]

Until fuller and more precise knowledge is available about the kind and extent of American philanthropy as compared with that in other countries one must indeed be cautious in discussing philanthropy and the national character. Yet a tentative thesis may be suggested at this time, namely that while American patterns of giving for religion, welfare, education, health, science and the arts owe much to British and Continental example, they have, apart from the question of magnitude, reflected a distinctively American character. They have also helped shape that character. In other words, philanthropy has been both index and agent.

To make such a claim is not to deny that the Old World heritage is basic in American philanthropy. The very word, one recalls, and the idea for which it stands, came from the Greeks. American philanthropy owes much to the ancient Jewish doctrine which taught rules about the duty of giving and the right of those in need to receive. It is hardly too much to say that Jewish, Catholic and Protestant doctrines and practices have been central in the development of philanthropy in America. From the time of the Puritans and Quakers in early seventeenth-century America to our own day it would be hard to overstate the influence of the religious emphasis on the value of individual life, regardless of status, of the injunction to feed the hungry and clothe the naked, of the teaching that man is his brother's keeper. The Pauline doctrine that one is only a steward for the wealth God has given him has profoundly influenced American giving. Habits of giving among those who had relatively little to give have owed a great deal to the missionary movement. Even today somewhat over half of all individual giving finds its way into the church envelope, collection plate or treasury of church-related institutions.

American philanthropy has also operated within a frame of English common and statutory law.[13] The colonists brought with them the Elizabethan poor laws; and the Victorian modifications of these laws influenced our charitable practices. English law guided us in our use of the will, the bequest, the perpetuity and the foundation. The English philosophy that he who gives should control, crystallized by Locke, exerted far-reaching influence in America.

Americans have a notable record in giving for disaster relief at home and abroad; but we did not invent this practice. In 1676, for example, the good ship *Catharine* left Dublin laden with meal, wheat, malt, butter and cheese, to be distributed to all in the three New England colonies who stood in need by reason of the disasters accompanying King Philip's War.[14]

Colonial support for schools, colleges and hospitals followed in good part the British pattern of voluntary private support.[15] A Britisher named Wilson preceded Franklin in establishing loan funds for worthy mechanics. In founding parochial and general libraries, charity schools, and in promoting religious and moral instruction among Indians and Negroes, the British-supported Society for the Propagation of the Gospel in Foreign Parts adapted British giving to special needs and conditions in the colonies and in so doing established a pattern later followed by the Americans themselves.

Nor did British influence on American philanthropy end here. It provided an example of a new approach to the relief of poverty and distress. Isabella Marshall Graham, coming to New York from Scotland in 1796, proceeded to found the Society for the Relief of Poor Widows and Small Children, an agency similar to one that Bernard and Wilberforce had just established in London for the relief of the poor. Mrs. Graham likewise established and devoted her entire time to the Orphan Asylum Society and the Magdalen Society, the first organization of that sort in the young Republic.[16] Much later the influence of the Manchester *laissez faire* school in general and of Dr. Thomas Chalmers of Glasgow in particular were important in the development in the 1830's and 1840's of American voluntary associations for the urban poor.[17] All these activities were associated with the idea that public charity pauperizes and demoralizes the recipient. Nor should one forget the wealthy and childless English scientist, James Smithson, who set an example to well-to-do Americans to give generously for the advancement and diffusion of knowledge.

Yet such British activities and influences should not obscure the fact that for a few decades before the Civil War Americans won an international reputation for leadership in benevolent enterprises. European leaders came here to study prison reform, institutions for the handicapped and agencies for the diffusion of knowledge. In the Old World itself the writings and achievements of our Franklins, Livingstons, Quincys, Rantouls, Manns, Grays and Sumners found admirers and imitators.

In 1867, however, *The Nation*, in reviewing the recent international congresses on charity and philanthropy, sadly admitted that Americans in this field were no longer read and quoted in Europe as they once had been. The wind blew in the other direction. The growing emphasis in Britain on organization, co-operation, non-duplication of effort, districting, friendly visiting, in short, on scientific method in charity, was reflected in the post-Civil War decades in America in the Charity Organization Movement. The movement in England for model tenements was felt on our side of the Atlantic and the influence of Toynbee Hall on the American social settlement movement is of course well known.[18]

If the idea of national character is valid, one would expect that the philanthropic ingredients transferred to our shores from the Old World would be interrelated in a distinctive pattern. We would also expect to find the key to this in unique or characteristically American experiences.

Our federal system has, surely, given American philanthropy some of its hallmarks. The legislatures and courts of the several states have emphasized the need of a flexibility which they did not see in British precedents. New York's repudiation of certain aspects of the English law of bequests and Samuel J. Tilden's failure to appreciate this in bequeathing a large part of his fortune to a trust for a public library, resulted in lengthy litigation and the defeat of Tilden's full purpose.[19] One finds different laws from state to state on the incorporation and degree of public control of charitable institutions and foundations and on bequests and exemptions from taxation for giving. Unlike Britain, then, the United States long had no unified legal code affecting charitable giving in every part of the country. The federal internal revenue legislation, to be sure, has in its provisions for tax-deductible gifts come in many respects to serve as such a code.[20] If on the one hand the diversity of state legislation and court decisions on bequests and gifts has made for uncertainty and confusion, it has also made possible some flexibility and experimentation.

In opening the door to state rights and functions, the federal system has until yesterday minimized the role of the central government in assuming any great responsibility for welfare, education, research and the arts.[21] Since the states themselves have, until our century, supported only a few hospitals, welfare agencies and colleges and even fewer art galleries and museums, private citizens have shouldered the costs for such local institutions—in the Old World all these have long enjoyed the support of national government.

Separation of church and state as well as the federal system has shaped American philanthropy. In the Reformation the new state churches or governments in continental protestant Europe took over the role of the medieval church in supporting hospitals, schools and universities. The Anglican Church was something of an exception in not taking on such far-reaching functions. In America separation of church and state meant that, in the absence of any one state church, the large number of voluntarily supported churches have maintained colleges, orphanages, hospitals and similar agencies. Although America has followed England in the last decades in moving toward the Continental pattern of state support of welfare agencies, our long experience with voluntary maintenance of charitable and educational institutions has encouraged Americans to feel that there are unique values in such non-government operations. These include the control by laymen rather than by experts of privately supported hospitals, art galleries, colleges and welfare institutions. Still another by-product has been the encouragement of competition between rival institutions for gifts and, more recently, of co-operative and highly organized fund-raising.

American philanthropy in greater degree than that of Europe has emphasized the idea of self-help, whether in giving on condition of the matching of gifts or in loans to students to be paid back. This is related to our creed of individual responsibility and achievement, supplemented by mutual aid. It is to be further explained by the concept of plenty. Americans rejected the Old World notion that the poor must always be with us and taken care of by charity. This stress on self-help in philanthropy was functional to the social fluidity that has characterized the industrial growth of our cities and also the frontier process.

American cities, like those of Europe, bred conditions that inspired relief and philanthropic endeavor. But in America the concept of self-help and mutual aid was strengthened by the existence of immigrant groups and by the limited role of local government through long stretches of our municipal history. Thus immigrants, uprooted and often in need until adjustments were made, organized mutual self-help societies, one of the earliest being the Scots Charitable Society in Boston (1657). National and racial pride, related to our cultural pluralism, also help explain why other groups that formed sub-cultures took care of their own: the Jewish groups, the Chinese, the Mormons, to cite only the more striking examples. All this gave a special tone to American charities.[22]

The frontier and the related concept of plenty have also given an American accent to the philanthropic heritage from the Old World. One of the first major philanthropic efforts in the East was inspired by a fear on the part of the established order of "western irreligion" and political deviancy, together with a Puritan sense of obligation to do something about it. But the influence of the frontier on philanthropy was not merely in giving an incentive to the organization of the so-called "benevolent empire" of home missionaries and college founders in the west.[23]

The problems involved in settling new areas did, as Tocqueville noted, not merely favor neighborly co-operation in time of need and trouble—they made it necessary. An example from the frontier history of Trempealeau County, Wisconsin, will illustrate the point. When young William Lincoln became ill and died during the winter of 1853, the neighbors provided what medical and religious services the boy received. Neighbors dug a grave. One, Stuart Butman, laid out the body. In the absence of a minister, two neighbor girls sang a hymn. No money was needed to pay for these services. In re-enforcing over and again this tendency to help others and in making ever evident the horizons of plenty, the frontier must have encouraged generosity.

Moreover, the social mobility which the frontier fostered along with our industrial development, made it hard for rising men and their wives to be sure of their social status. This uncertainty encouraged some to take part in charitable and philanthropic activities to win social recognition. Biographies of philanthropists suggest that in some cases giving was motivated by status considerations. In a fluid society like ours one not only had to make his place but to keep it by further achievement, such as putting success to socially approved uses. If some men of wealth gave quietly, even anonymously, others enjoyed having their gifts publicized and basked in the limelight of community approval.

The American emphasis on individual achievement and on sustained activity to that end have also given a distinct stamp to large-scale giving. Having spent untold effort in getting rich, having tasted the sweets and boredom of extravagant spending, some, driven by a never-ceasing lust to achieve, turned to philanthropy. Carnegie and Rockefeller, each relatively frugal in what he spent on himself, set their hearts on giving with the imagination, organization and efficiency that had marked their activities in steel and oil.

This desire to realize the efficiency which is allegedly so American explained in part the rise of professional middlemen in the philanthropic process. The prototype was the lean and tireless agent that the nineteenth-century college hired for a pittance to travel over the land begging for contributions to keep the wolf from the classroom door. In due course professional administrators of welfare agencies and fund-raisers appeared. So did the foundation official and the chronic solicitor of funds from the foundation. Frederick Keppel, an early head of the Carnegie Corporation, loved to tell of the college president who on one occasion announced that he had not come to ask for any thing that day. "How much is it," asked Mr. Keppel, "that you don't want to ask for?"

Less familiar among the middlemen of philanthropy who seem to be in the American character have been the counselors to the rich in the matter of giving. One thinks of such preachers as the Reverend William Willcox who guided the Boston merchant Daniel Stone and his wife in giving a two million dollar fortune to church-related colleges scattered over the land. One recalls the Reverend Charles Force Deems and the Reverend Frederick T. Gates, whose role in Vanderbilt and Rockefeller giving was crucial. The list of lawyers and bankers who counseled on matters of giving is likewise a long one.

One pioneer figure, neither a preacher, banker nor lawyer, devoted his later years to publicizing unwise or misguided giving and to counseling, without charge, potential donors. Alvin M. West, who made a fortune in California, was shocked on learning that state laws prevented Los Angeles from accepting Colonel Griffith G. Griffith's donation of land for a public park valued at a million dollars. West's search for frustrated donors and unwise giving continued through the first three decades of our century. His list came to include the Sailor's Snug Harbor, whose trustees were unable to spend the income of an early nineteenth-century bequest for a home for seafaring men. West publicized the whittling away of a great part of a St. Louis fortune left for the relief of travelers headed westward in prairie schooners. The courts finally decided, under the *cy pres* doctrine, that the residue might be used to support the Travellers Aid Bureau in railway stations. Then there was the attorney general of Massachusetts who left money to Harvard, Yale and Columbia for the development of "sound public opinion against the tendency to take woman out of the home and to put her into politics"—each institution turned down the gift! Again, the Christian Science Church in Portland refused a gift to establish the White Shield Home for Wayward Girls because the donor had not appreciated the import of an Oregon law requiring the inmates of all homes to be medically examined. By the mid-1920's West estimated that of the approximate $500,000,000 annually given for philanthropic purposes a good proportion was either wasted in duplicating adequate facilities, in inviting disgruntled kinfolk to challenge wills in court with ensuing costly litigation or in passing by truly useful causes.[24]

The effort to bring philanthropy into tune with the national penchant for efficiency has resulted in its rapport with big business. Partly for reasons of tax consideration, partly to enlist public favor and partly to prove the continuing creativity of American business, great firms have increased corporate giving until it has now become a highly specialized function with its own counselors and techniques.[25]

The effort to make philanthropy efficient and socially useful does not exhaust the ways in which American traits, values and actualities have influenced patterns of giving. It has been assumed that American women have played a more telling role in decision making, in civic enterprises and in spending, than those of most other countries. Certainly this has been true in the American Red Cross. In charity and welfare, women's influence has incontestably been notable. In counseling husbands and sons on giving, and in themselves dispensing their inherited wealth, American women have been active agents in philanthropy. Out of hundreds of names, those of Sophia Smith, Phoebe Hearst, Valeria Stone, Nettie Fowler McCormick, Ellen Scripps, the Phelps-Stokes sisters, Mrs. Stephen Harkness and Elizabeth Milbank Anderson, are representative.

One cannot draw a sharp line between American philanthropy as an index of the national character and as an agent of it. But let us examine the claim that in extending the idea that America stands for the creative process, philanthropy has given content and reality to the national character. The argument is that philanthropy in shifting from the lady bountiful type of amelioration to pioneering in education, research, welfare and social policy at home and abroad, has helped realize national values.

This contention has met with sharp criticism. One criticism has linked a good deal of philanthropy with inefficient and unwise giving, with the dead hand. In addition muckrakers, progressives and socialists contended that large-scale giving placed far too much power over public policy in the hands of a few men whose fortunes after all had been created only because of prevailing social and economic conditions. It was argued that philanthropy was intended to patch up the shortcomings in the existing order and thus to preserve a status quo that did not deserve preservation.[26] Verbal evidence issuing from donors and particularly from middlemen solicitors gives some support to this statement.[27] It is also true that only a very small proportion of total giving challenged the status quo. The few sizable gifts to the abolition, women's rights and temperance crusades were overshadowed by small rank and file contributions. This was also true of the peace movement until the twentieth-century munificence of Ginn, Bok, Ford and Carnegie. In finding angels such as Tom Johnson and Joseph Fels, Henry George's crusade was more fortunate than most reform causes: its shadow was to be prolonged by the Robert Schalkenbach Foundation. The socialist crusade found some support from such well-to-do benefactors as Gaylord Wilshire and J. G. Phelps Stokes. Both socialists and communists received donations from the American Fund for Public Service, established in the early 1920's when Charles Garland refused on conscientious grounds to keep a million dollar fortune he inherited. But this was certainly an exceptional foundation.[28]

Many critics felt that philanthropic support of Negro education put a premium on vocational training and retarded the development of liberal and professional education. Nor was the *New Republic* without cause when, in commenting on the Eastman and Duke benefactions, it asked why large gifts to higher education mainly concentrated on institutions of no particular reputation for pioneering. Among the ranks of philanthropists themselves Richard T. Crane criticized giving to higher education and to the mere beautifying of parts of cities while the disadvantaged poor struggled against great odds in grim slums.[29] Certainly much philanthropy was not aimed at remedying basic factors in poverty.

But there was another side of the coin. Emphasis on voluntary initiative in spotting social evils and taking the first steps to remedy them has helped give America her national character. It was private initiative and support that pioneered in constructive efforts to meet the problem of juvenile delinquency, to establish public parks and recreational centers, to build model tenements as pilot examples and to launch many other civic improvements. The roster of pioneers, both donors and those who gave themselves, is a very long one.[30]

When a group of progressive-minded merchants made possible the introduction of scientific study in our colleges in the mid-nineteenth century, a new era in our educational history was under way. The names of Lawrence, Sheffield, the younger Agassiz, Bussey, Peabody, Lick, Ryerson, Scripps and countless others, made possible some of the most notable scientific work in our universities. Private initiative also got under way much needed vocational training, as the names of Rensselaer, Cooper, Pratt, Drexel and Carnegie, to name only a few, suggest. And philanthropists also made possible the establishment of the first professional schools of mines, business and journalism. All these philanthropic initiatives give support to the thesis that philanthropy has helped shape national character in creatively meeting new problems, in implementing the idea that America is process rather than finished product.

Without belittling the part of the state universities in opening the doors of higher education to women, this innovation owes a great deal to such philanthropists as Cornell, Durant, Vassar, Goucher and Sophia Smith. In the making of an American university tradition, Cornell, Hopkins, Clark, Rockefeller and the educational leaders associated with them, played a leading part. So did the generous donors who made possible the transformation of Harvard, Columbia, Princeton and Yale. The Stanfords, the Vanderbilts, the Candlers and the Dukes helped build a university tradition on the West Coast and in the South. The thesis that philanthropy responded to and helped develop the creative impulse in the national character found further support in the introduction of art and music in American higher education. The Carnegie Foundation pioneered in establishing professors' pensions.[31] The Carnegie Foundation and the Rockefeller foundations revolutionized medical education and research.[32] More recently, the innovating process found further expression in the support of various foundations for the area programs, including American studies. Imaginative too was the backing given by a New Jersey merchant and his sister to the establishment at Princeton of the Institute for Advanced Studies.[33] Finally, no one will doubt that American scholarship would be much the poorer were it not for the libraries associated with the names of generous givers at Harvard, Yale, Columbia and Princeton, and for such great collections as the Newberry, the Crerar, the Morgan, the Huntington and the Folger.

Our public schools have been a truly popular achievement. Yet much that is now taken for granted in our educational programs owes a major debt to philanthropy in implementing the national ideal of equality of opportunity. Antislavery men and women dug deep into their purses to finance the first southern schools for Negroes during and after the Civil War. A Connecticut industrialist, John Slater, following in the footsteps of George Peabody, established a fund which did much for Negro education in the South. Daniel Hand, George Foster Peabody, the General Education Board, the Jeanes Fund and the Rosenwald Fund prepared Southern opinion for a more adequate public support for Negro schools and piloted many telling improvements in the meantime.[34]

But the stimulus given to building educational opportunities for Negroes was by no means the only constructive contribution by which philanthropy helped realize the onward and upward theme in our national character through our public schools. A Massachusetts industrialist established the first teacher training institute through an initial gift conditional on state support.[35] The education of the blind, the crippled and the deaf was incorporated into public education only after private philanthropy pointed the way. This was also true of manual training and of school health programs.[36]

In adult education, too, private philanthropy laid the groundwork in helping people who wanted to know. In providing for the institute in Boston bearing his name, John Lowell was a creative giver. Dozens of self-made men, poignantly regretting their own deficiencies in early education, founded public libraries in their home towns long before Carnegie entered the stage. Yet the 2,811 Carnegie libraries, given on condition of community maintenance, marked a new era in the world of reading. The contributions of the Carnegie Corporation and of other foundations to adult education have both stimulated public action, improved the quality of that which existed, and added new dimensions to the movement.

Except during the New Deal, government has played a negligible part in opening the world of art and music to adult Americans. The example of William Corcoran in providing a building for his art collection and in making it available to the public has been followed by far too many to catalogue their names and evaluate their collections. But it may be appropriate to mention Phillips, Frear and Mellon at the nation's capital, the Fricks, Whitneys and others in New York, and the Tafts, Holdens, Walkers, Nelsons and Johnsons in the several cities which now support or contribute to the support of the notable collections these men and women assembled. So, too, our botanic gardens and museums of natural history sprang in most cases from philanthropic gifts. Finally, the great development of musical taste and talent in America cannot be separated from the pioneer support given to the Boston Symphony by Henry Lee Higginson and the generous gifts of well-to-do men and women in New York, Philadelphia, Baltimore, Chicago, Rochester, Cincinnati and Los Angeles. What Otto Kahn and others did for opera, what Elizabeth Sprague Coolidge did for chamber music, and what Eastman, Curtis, Juilliard, Presser and others did for musical training, has been both pioneering in character and significant in effect.

Philanthropy has also forwarded several values in the American creed by broadening the base of contributions to social welfare, to medicine, health and, of course, to the religious life. The democratizing of giving not only reflects, but has added substance and method to democratic faith and practice. Here the roots are deep for at the time of the great fire in Boston in 1760, many people both in the surrounding towns and in neighboring colonies, contributed to the relief of sufferers.[37] In later disasters, whether fires, droughts, floods, pestilences, cyclones or earthquakes, the participation in giving tended to become broader and broader. In part this mass giving owed much to the zeal of the churches in promoting both home and foreign missions—enterprises that required sustained general support from the faithful. In part it was related to the prevalence of plenty and to the relatively high standard of living.

The democratization of giving has not, however, been a merely automatic process. The zest for organization and for "drives" has become increasingly characteristic of American behavior. Parenthetically, this zest owes much to such newspapers as the New York *Herald* and the New York *Tribune*, and to such religious organs as De Witt Talmage's *Christian Herald*, as anyone who reads the sensational appeals for sending street urchins to fresh air camps and the even more sensational appeals for disaster relief, can appreciate. In our own century the Red Cross and the proliferating number of organizations designed to stem mortality in tuberculosis, infantile paralysis, cancer and heart ailments, have also designed unique campaigns for fund-raising.[38] The experience of John Price Jones in mobilizing opinion in World War I for putting across the liberty loan drives, was transferred to a professional fund raising organization which in the 1920's conducted successfully one campaign after another for universities and colleges in the interest of faculty pay, scholarships, plant and endowment.[39] The Community Chest and United Givers are still more recent examples of both high-pressure salesmanship and of wide participation in giving more or less voluntary.

One of the byproducts of the newer techniques of fund-raising has been misrepresentation. Worse, racketeering cloaked as philanthropy exploited millions of givers. This dishonest exploitation for profits of American generosity has no doubt reflected one aspect of American character; but the effort to curb it no less reflects that ambivalent phenomenon.[40]

Both in terms of objects of giving and the wide-scale participation, the evidence at hand suggests as tenable the hypothesis that philanthropy has both reflected and helped create an American middle way between a type of capitalism characteristic of the old world, in which owners surrender little of what they have unless forced to do so, on the one hand, and socialism on the other. With due respect for minority opinion in each situation, it is interesting to note that the first Congressional investigation of foundations on the eve of the first world war criticized them for alleged effects in consolidating an existing status quo; and that the Reece committee in McCarthy's time, damned them for the support they had presumably given to an un-American collectivism.[41] In relieving class and group tensions and in facilitating the growth of social well-being philanthropy has in a sense been the American equivalent for socialism.

We are today deeply concerned with the American reputation abroad and with the best ways and means by which America can contribute to strengthening the western heritage of freedom. A close study of the history of our past experience in voluntary giving to relieve suffering from famines in Ireland, Russia, China and India, earthquakes in Sicily, and malaria and other plagues in many places, as well as study of projects to initiate and strengthen educational enterprises, and to rehabilitate depressed areas, reveals much of importance in our effort to realize the American mission in the larger world. The story is one of failure, partial failure, partial success and amazing success. It is a story of what missionaries, foundations, private donors, the American Friends Service Committee, CARE and dozens of other agencies have undertaken and carried through—more or less. The story both reflects a significant facet in the American character and provides testimony to the degree of creativity and effectiveness our philanthropy has enjoyed when it has traveled abroad.

Perhaps in the magnitude of giving, and certainly in the patterns of philanthropy that have found expression here, American experience in philanthropy has both expressed American character and at the same time has helped to shape it. It will be worth watching the future to see how a plant so rooted grows.

Notes

1. Thomas Wentworth Higginson, "The Word Philanthropy," *Freedom and Fellowship in Religion* (Boston: Roberts Brothers, 1875), pp. 323–37. The Abbè de St. Pierre, writing in 1725, used the word *bienfaisance* as the equivalent for the Greek "philanthropy," *The Nation*, IV (April 18, 1867), 309.
2. John Weiss, *Life and Correspondence of Theodore Parker* (2 vols.: New York: 1864), II, 329–30.
3. Higginson, *Freedom and Fellowship in Religion*, p. 336.
4. *The Philanthropic Results of the War in America. By an American Citizen* (Linus Pierpont Brockett), (New York: Press of Wynkoop, Hallenbeck, and Thomas, 1863), pp. 3 ff.
5. Henry Villard, "Historical Sketch of Social Science," *Journal of Social Science*, I (1869), 5.
6. Daniel Coit Gilman, "Special Training for Philanthropic Work" (Address at the Annual Meeting of the Charity Organization Society of New York, January 27, 1905), in *The Launching of a University* (New York: Dodd, Mead & Co., 1906), p. 365.
7. Arthur M. Schlesinger, "The True American Way of Life," *St. Louis Post-Dispatch*, Part Two (December 13, 1953), 3.
8. Alexis de Tocqueville, *Democracy in America* (The Henry Reeve Text . . . now further corrected and edited . . . by Phillips Bradley [2 vols.; New York: Alfred A. Knopf, 1945]), II, 175.
9. James Bryce, *The American Commonwealth* (3rd ed.; 2 vols.; New York: The Macmillan Co., 1909), II, 723.
10. Harold J. Laski, *The American Democracy. A Commentary and an Interpretation* (New York: The Viking Press, 1948), p. 725.

11. In an article entitled "American Millionaires and Their Gifts" a writer, presumably the editor of *The Review of Reviews: an International Magazine* (VII, February 1893, 48–60), reported the results of his request to correspondents in various cities to rate those of the 4,047 millionaires living in their city—the basis of the inquiry being the list of millionaires in a special supplement of the *New York Tribune Monthly*, IV (June 1892). For the text and illuminating interpretations see Sidney Ratner (ed.), *New Light on the History of Great American Fortunes* (New York: Augustus M. Kelley, Inc., 1953).

12. Henry Clews, *Fifty Years in Wall Street* (New York: Irving Publishing Co., 1908), pp. 533–34.

13. B. Kirman Gray, *A History of English Philanthropy* (London: P.S. King and Son, 1905); Amos G. Warner, *American Charities* (New York: Thomas Y. Crowell & Co., 1908), pp. 389–98.

14. Charles Deane, "The Irish Donation in 1676," *The New England Historical and Geneological Register*, II (1848), 245–50.

15. Beverly McAnear, "The Raising of Funds by Colonial Colleges," *Mississippi Valley Historical Review*, XXXVIII (March, 1952), 591–612.

16. Mrs. Joanna Bethune, *The Life of Mrs. Isabella Graham* (New York: J. S. Taylor, 1838); *The Power of Faith; Exemplified in the Life and Writings of the Late Mrs. Isabella Graham of New York* (New York: Kirk and Mercien, 1817).

17. *Chalmers on Charity. A Selection of Passages and Scenes to Illustrate the Teaching and Practical Work of Thomas Chalmers, D.D.*, Arranged and edited by N. Masterman, M.A. (Westminster: Archibald Constable & Co., 1900); *The Christian and Civic Economy of Large Towns*, Abridged and with an introduction by Charles R. Henderson (New York: Charles Scribner's Sons, 1900).

18. "Philanthropy in America and Europe," *The Nation*, IV (April 18, 1867), 309. See also Robert Bremner, *From the Depths. The Discovery of Poverty in the United States* (New York: New York University Press, 1956), pp. 207–8.

19. Alexander G. Flick, Samuel J. Tilden (New York: Dodd, Mead & Co., 1939), pp. 513 ff.

20. Daniel S. Remsen, *Postmortem Use of Wealth* (New York: G. P. Putnam's Sons, 1911); Harvey W. Peck, *Taxation and Welfare* (New York: The Macmillan Co., 1925); Carl Zollman, *American Law of Charities* (Milwaukee: Bruce Publishing Co., 1924); and F. Emerson Andrews, *Corporation Giving* (New York: Russell Sage Foundation, 1952).

21. For the story of federal support of scientific research see A. Hunter Dupree, *Science in the Federal Government. A History of Policies and Activities to 1940* (Cambridge: The Belknap Press, 1957).

22. Edwin Wolf and Maxwell Whitman, *The History of the Jews of Philadelphia from Colonial Times to the Age of Jackson* (Philadelphia: The Jewish Publication Society of America, 1957).

23. Merle Curti, *The Social Ideas of American Educators* (New York: Charles Scribner's Sons, 1935), pp. 688–70; Clifford S. Griffin, "Religious Benevolence as Social Control, 1815–1860," *Mississippi Valley Historical Review*, XLIV (December, 1957), 423–44.

24. Alvin West, "Biographical Clippings," Hanover Bank and Trust Company, New York City.

25. F. Emerson Andrews, *Corporate Giving* (New York: Russell Sage Foundation, 1952); Berrien C. Eaton, Jr., "Charitable Foundations, Tax Avoidance and Business Expediency," *Virginia Law Review*, L (November, 1949); 809–61 and (December, 1949), 987–1051.

26. Morrison I. Swift, *Vicarious Philanthropy* (No place, ca. 1904), pp. 23–24; *The Nation*, IX (November 11, 1869), 406–7; Robert J. Ingersoll, "The Three Philanthropists," *North American Review*, GLIII (December, 1891), 661–71; Hubert Howe Bancroft, *Retrospection: Political and Personal* (New York: The Bancroft Co., 1912), pp. 452–53; United States Congress, Senate, *Industrial Relations*: Final Report and Testimony submitted to Congress by the Commission on Industrial Relations created by the Act of August 23, 1912. 64th Congress, 1st Session, Senate Document, No. 415 (11 vols.; Washington: Government Printing Office, 1916).

27. Samuel Gompers, "Shall Education be Rockefellerized?" *American Federationist*, XXIV (March, 1917), 206–8; Wayne Andrews, *Battle for Chicago* (New York: Harcourt, Brace & Co., 1946), pp. 162–63; Ferdinand Lundberg, *America's Sixty Families* (New York: The Citadel Press, 1946), pp. 320–73.

28. New York *Times*, January 14, 1924, March 16, 1925, March 8, 1926, March 25, 1929.

29. Andrews, *Battle for Chicago*; "Goose Step and the Golden Eggs," *New Republic* (December 24, 1924), pp. 106–8.

30. See, again, Bremner, *From the Depths, passim*. See also Daniel C. Gilman (ed.), *The Organization of Charities, being a Report of the Sixth Section of the International Congress of Charities, Corrections, and Philanthropy, Chicago, June 1893* (Baltimore: The Johns Hopkins Press, 1894); George S. Hale, "The Charities of Boston," Justin Winsor (ed.), *Memorial History of Boston* (4 vols.; Boston: James R. Osgood & Co., 1881), IV, 641–74; Frances A. Goodale (ed.), *The Literature of Philanthropy* (New York: Harper & Bros., 1893; Alexander Johnson, *Adventures in Social Welfare being the Reminiscences of Things, Thoughts and*

Folks during Forty Years of Social Work (Fort Wayne, Ind.: Fort Wayne Printing Press, 1923); and William H. Matthews, *Adventures in Giving* (New York: Dodd, Mead & Co., 1939).

31. Robert M. Lester, *Forty Years of Carnegie Giving* (New York: Charles Scribner's Sons, 1941), pp. 45, 82; Howard J. Savage, *Fruit of an Impulse: Forty-five Years of the Carnegie Foundation*, 1905–1950 (New York: Harcourt, Brace & Co., 1953).

32. Raymond B. Fosdick, *The Story of the Rockefeller Foundation* (New York: Harper & Bros., 1952), pp. 81 ff, 93 ff; The Rockefeller Foundation, Annual Reports, 1913; Carnegie Corporation of New York, *Reports of the President and Treasurer*, 1922.

33. Abraham Flexner, *I Remember, An Autobiography* (New York: Simon & Schuster, 1940), pp. 356 ff.

34. George R. Bentley, *A History of the Freedmen's Bureau* (Philadelphia: University of Pennsylvania Press, 1955), pp. 34, 31 ff, 63 ff; *Jessie Pearl Rice, J. L. M. Curry, Southerner, Statesman, and Educator* (New York: King's Crown Press, 1949); Horace Mann Bond, *The Education of the Negro in the American Social Order*, (New York: Prentice-Hall Inc., 1934) p. 133; Ullin W. Leavell, *Philanthropy in Negro Education* (Nashville, Tenn.: George Peabody College for Teachers, Contributions to Education, No. 100, 1930); *Charleston News and Courier*, October 7, 1880 (on Daniel Hand); Benjamin Brawley, *Doctor Dillard and the Jeanes Fund* (Chicago: Fleming H, Revell Co., 1930); George Foster Peabody Papers, Library of Congress; Phelps Stokes Fund, *Negro Status and Race Relations 1911–1946: The Thirty-Five Year Report of the Phelps-Stokes Fund* (New York: Phelps-Stokes Fund, 1948); Edwin R. Embree, *Investment in People: The Story of the Julius Rosenwald Fund* (New York: Harper & Bros., 1949).

35. Curti, *Social Ideas of American Education*, p. 113.

36. Ashton R. Willard, "The Rindge Gifts to Cambridge," *New England Magazine*, n.s. III (February 1891), 733 ff; W. R. Odell, *Gifts to the Public Schools* (New York: William R. Odell, Publisher, 1932); Allie Boyd, *Philanthropy in the Form of Gifts and Endowments for Elementary and Secondary Education* (Master's thesis, University of Chicago, 1928); "The Des Moines House of Dreams," *School Executives Magazine*, LI (January 1932), 207–25; Milbank Memorial Fund *Quarterly*, (1940); *Annual Reports of the Milbank Memorial Fund*, 1922–1925, especially *Report* for 1922, pp. 65–69.

37. Extract from Green and Russell's *Boston Post Boy and Advertiser*, No. 136, March 24, 1760, in *New England Historical and Geneological Register*, XXXIV (July 1880), 288–93; *Boston Gazette and County Journal*, March 24, 1760; Documents and Correspondence relating to the Great Boston Fire, Manuscript Division, Boston Public Library, MS. 806.

38. Foster Rhea Dulles, *American Red Cross. A History* (New York: Harper & Bros., 1950); Richard Harrison Shryock has set a high standard for such studies in his *National Tuberculosis Association*, 1904–1954 (New York: National Tuberculosis Association, 1957).

39. John Price Jones Manuscript Collection, Baker Library, Harvard University. See also John Price Jones, *The American Giver* (New York: Inter-River Press, 1954).

40. "Charitable Rackets," *Social Service Review*, XXVIII (March, 1954), 87–88; Jerome Ellison, "Who Gets Your Charity Dollars?," *Saturday Evening Post*, CCXXVI (June 26, 1954), 27 ff; Bernard Thompkins, "When You Give-are you Being Taken?" *Colliers*, CXXXIII (June 25, 1954) 90–93.

41. United States Congress, Senate, *Industrial Relations*. Final Report and Testimony submitted to Congress by the Commission on Industrial Relations created by the Act of August 23, 1912, 64th Congress, 1st Session. Senate Document No. 415 (11 vols.; Washington: Government Printing Office, 1916); John E. Lankford, *Congressional Investigations of the Philanthropic Foundations*, 1902–54 (Master's thesis, University of Wisconsin, 1957).

THE POLITICS OF KNOWLEDGE: THE CARNEGIE CORPORATION AND THE FORMULATION OF PUBLIC POLICY

ELLEN CONDLIFFE LAGEMANN

Thirty years ago, Merle Curti ventured that "philanthropy has been one of the major aspects of and keys to American social and cultural development."[1] It was an apt, challenging, and important observation that was not immediately heeded and has yet to be sufficiently pursued. With Curti's comment in mind, I should like to sketch the development of a politics that took shape in the United States in the early twentieth century, and then to explore a number of relationships between that politics and some of the early activities of one of the large, grant-making foundations established before the First World War—the Carnegie Corporation of New York. Although the argument I shall present derives from a close study of only one foundation, the history of the Carnegie Corporation crosses and even merges with the history of many other institutions, including other foundations, and is inseparable from ideas, national trends, and both national and international events that have touched American society generally. What is more, the size, the longevity, the broad scope, the effectiveness, and the concern for responsible philanthropy that have always characterized the Carnegie Corporation have made it a leader and even a model for many of its peers. To some degree at least, then, in considering relationships between Carnegie Corporation philanthropy and what I shall call the politics of knowledge, one is also considering the validity of Curti's "hypothetical" claim. One is asking, not only whether, but, more importantly, how philanthropic foundations have achieved the significance Curti attributed to them.

I

Although ideas may always have been involved in efforts to gain the power, authority, and deference necessary to shape the minds and behavior of other people, a distinct politics of knowledge arose in the United States in conjunction with the emergence of a large-scale, national state at the beginning of the twentieth century. This politics crystallized in relation to the new importance knowledge assumed at this time in the formulation, implementation, and evaluation of public policy. As regulation of economic activity increased and the management of conflict became more purposive, as the coordination of institutional and social aims became more deliberate, and as localities, local interests, and local groups were increasingly articulated at the national level, both more specialized (expert) knowledge and more general (popular) "intelligence" were required. The former was needed to provide rationales and techniques for public action, the latter, to relate public opinion, local action, and individual behavior to national priorities. Inevitably, as this occurred, a politics concerning the creation, organization, development, and dissemination of knowledge took shape, and this politics, the politics of knowledge, became critical to the processes through which public policy was set.

Three large questions were (and are) central to the politics of knowledge. The first had to do with which fields of knowledge and approaches within different fields would become more or less authoritative and therefore more or less closely associated with the expertise deemed relevant to policy-making. Leaving aside the large secular trends that resulted in increasing authority for knowledge gained through experimental science and decreasing authority for the revealed insights of religion or the tacit, commonsense perceptions associated with experience, questions of what knowledge would become primary to policy were at root questions of who among those studying similar or related problems would gain priority for their substantive and methodological emphases.

Many contests among and within different realms of knowledge could exemplify this, few better than the one that emerged among students of "sociology" at the turn of the century—on the one hand, settlement workers, and, on the other, university scholars. Both groups thought of themselves as sociologists, and both were basically concerned with problems of "social control." But settlement workers favored a more practical, less formal, and more immediately useful approach to the study of these problems than university scholars, who tended to believe that a more "rigorous" and explicitly theoretical approach would yield more cumulatively and universally valid results. Being different, these approaches need not have been in contest, but the necessity for agreement on what would be the basis for a "science of society" that developed with professionalization meant that one would have to take precedence, practice guiding the development of theory or theory guiding the development of practice.

In this instance, as in many others, a contest between different approaches was largely settled by differences in status between two groups, these being related to differences of gender and institutional affiliation, of balance between local versus cosmopolitan interests, and of conceptions of what was "amateur" as opposed to "professional" and of what was "old fashioned" as opposed to "modern." That university scholars gained priority—today, they are *the* sociologists, and settlement workers are social workers, members of what has been described as merely a "semi-profession"— may have been predictable. Settlement workers tended to be women, without university affiliations or advanced degrees, who were more concerned with individual and local circumstances than with "science," and therefore less "professional" and "modern" in outlook. The point, though, is that this outcome was neither inevitable nor certain in 1900. Like contemporary and subsequent contests between other groups with different approaches to other kinds of important problems, the outcome of this contest was an outcome of the politics of knowledge. It depended upon which group could gain the deference, authority, and financial resources necessary to prevail.

In addition to the question of which groups would become the knowledge-producing elites (those groups most able to exercise unusual influence on decisions concerning the nature of public problems and how these would be addressed), a second set of questions central to the politics of knowledge involved issues concerning with whom, to whom, on what occasions, and through what means "experts" would communicate with non-experts. In the early 1920s, Herbert Hoover, as secretary of commerce, wanted to disseminate the results of expert economic studies of unemployment to "the public," which in his mind comprised the public made up of business leaders. At roughly the same time, the historian James Harvey Robinson called for "the humanizing of knowledge," his purpose being to urge the dissemination of arcane, scholarly knowledge, especially scientific knowledge, to general audiences. Granted that the two men were concerned with fundamentally different matters, Hoover with reversing a business depression and Robinson with overcoming the cultural divide that would be symbolized in the 1925 Scopes trial, their different conceptions of audience or "public" nevertheless suggest the degree to which questions of relationship between knowledge-producing elites and various sets of others were in essence questions of who could and should govern, both generally and within different domains of public concern. Should those governing be only the immediately responsible managers, in other words, members of elites, or, through familiarity with the scientific basis for expert knowledge, should they be everyone who would be affected by public policies, in the instance of the Scopes trial, policies having to do with whether "creationist" or "evolutionary" views of science would be taught in the public schools? Obviously, because matters pertaining to the dissemination of knowledge had to do with enfranchisement and different modes of participation in public affairs, they had vital political consequences. It is always useful to recall that for the Greeks the opposite of a "citizen" was an "idiot," one who did not have a place in the polis. The nature of decisions concerning access to the knowledge increasingly necessary to make informed judgments about public matters, the processes by which these decisions were made and by whom, and the implications of these decisions for the distribution of power and knowledge were critical in the politics of knowledge.

Finally, there was the question of who could and would gain entrance to the knowledge-producing elites that emerged and proliferated as the United States became a more nationally and bureaucratically organized society. To a large extent, these elites were related to professions. The two developed simultaneously and in conjunction with one another. This meant that access to knowledge-producing elites was often granted through access to one or another of the professions, which was, in turn, granted via access to the requisite educational credentials. Usually a necessary condition for membership in a knowledge-producing elite, educational credentials were not, however, a sufficient condition. Patterns of personal acquaintance and professional colleagueship, styles of research, political views, manners, and other varied bases for "merit" that were often related to race, gender, ethnicity, and social class were also involved. Louis Brandeis did become a member of the Supreme Court, an old and highly prestigious knowledge-producing elite among lawyers. But his appointment was challenged by some distinguished members of the bar for reasons that included the fact that he was Jewish. W. I. Thomas was well launched upon a brilliant career in sociology when he was fired from the faculty of the University of Chicago in 1918 owing to charges of immoral behavior (adultery) that may well have been intended to embarrass his pacifist wife. From then on Thomas was only able to work as a free lance. The educational and, importantly, the other related and unrelated bases upon which entrance to knowledge-producing elites was granted, achieved, sustained, and lost determined to whom these elites were open. Obviously relevant to the crucial matter of whether and how the existence of elites can be reconciled with democratic theory, questions of the nature and control of elites have also been essential to, and influenced by, the politics of knowledge.

The politics of knowledge developed for many reasons and has been continuously defined and redefined by a great variety of events, technological developments, political movements, ideas, and groups of people. Emerging as an important politics in the United States at roughly the same time that large philanthropic foundations were coming into being, this politics was one that many foundations shaped, participated in, and reacted to. The Carnegie Corporation of New York, which was organized in 1911 as the last and largest of the various benevolent trusts established by the steel baron Andrew Carnegie, was one such foundation.

II

At the time the Carnegie Corporation was organized, Andrew Carnegie was seventy-six years old, weary of the "beggars" who besieged him, and increasingly afraid that he would die without having fulfilled his public pledge personally to dispose of his "surplus wealth" before his death. His close friend and counselor, the lawyer and statesman Elihu Root, offered him a way out. If Carnegie were to establish and endow a foundation, chartered to carry forward his interest in promoting "the advancement and diffusion of knowledge and understanding" and governed by a board of trustees made up of Carnegie, his personal assistants, and the heads of his other (U.S.) trusts, he could personally participate in the distribution of his wealth so long as he was able, and die assured that his millions were no longer his own. Root's scheme pleased Carnegie. After the necessary papers had been drawn, his characteristic ebullience was restored for a time. "Now it is all settled," he wrote to a friend. "We are off for Florida."[2]

Obviously, however, it was not all settled. In creating the Carnegie Corporation and endowing it with $125,000,000 (to which $10,336,867 was added after Carnegie's death in 1919), Carnegie had established what was described as "the greatest endowment ever given to a group of men for the promotion and diffusion of knowledge and understanding amongst the people of a nation."[3] Inherent in the rights and responsibilities he had vested in the Corporation's board of trustees was a potential to yield unusual power. Added to this, as Carnegie's health failed and his spirit was crushed by the outbreak of war in Europe—"Men slaying each other like wild beasts," he wrote in the autobiography he could not bring himself to finish—the Corporation's board moved to formulate policies that would magnify this potential through the adoption of a more "efficient" approach to the pursuit of its chartered mission.

The leader in developing these internal policies was Henry Smith Pritchett, who, as president of the Carnegie Foundation for the Advancement of Teaching since 1905, had already transformed that trust from the single-purpose professorial pension fund Andrew Carnegie had initially envisaged into a pension agency that would also aspire to be what Pritchett described as "one of the Great Agencies . . . in standardizing American education."[4] His more prudent and diplomatic ally at the Corporation was Elihu Root, who tempered the speed with which changes were implemented, thereby, in the long run, facilitating the reorientation that he, no less than Pritchett, thought wise. While Pritchett drafted policy statements and organized new internal administrative procedures, Root brought new grant possibilities to the board. Although not himself a scientist, as Pritchett was, Root was a great admirer of science as both an investigatory enterprise and a basis for the objectivity and disinterest he associated with expertise. Beyond that, the two shared a disdain for partisan politics that, coupled with their deep concern for national policies, led them to believe that "the best men," or, as Pritchett once put it, the "men of discriminating judgment," should lead.[5] These convictions provided a basis for the new approach to philanthropy that Pritchett and Root introduced into the Carnegie Corporation, certainly by 1920, if not a few years earlier.

Two points were central in this. The first was that the Corporation should engage in decision making of a highly purposeful and rather specific kind. Because he had been convinced that access to knowledge was positively related to the awakening of individual "genius," to the inventiveness that led to greater material prosperity for all, and to the humane insights that would foster community well-being, international goodwill, and, most important, peace, Andrew Carnegie had believed that, as a philanthropist, he should assess possibilities for donations only in terms of whether they might, in his personal judgment, foster the development of new knowledge or make available knowledge more accessible to more people. Hence, small, local colleges should receive more money than large, well-established colleges, and public libraries should be built across the United States and in many other English-speaking countries, while funds for already outstanding libraries, for example, the Bodleian at Oxford and the Johns Hopkins University Library in Baltimore, Maryland, should be (and were) denied.

Not without principles to guide his benevolence, even if he was less than scrupulous in the consistency with which he adhered to them, Carnegie relied upon criteria for giving that were notable for what they did *not* include—standards for discriminating between types of knowledge and for establishing priorities concerning the kinds of knowledge that should be advanced and diffused. Although he admired Matthew Arnold and adopted Arnold's phrase "Sweetness and Light" as one of his mottos, Carnegie did not agree with Arnold that "the best which has been thought and said" was necessarily most worthy of study.[6] Not coincidentally, by building the "bookless" public libraries for which he would be famed, he limited the domain in which he would make decisions, judgments concerning book selection being left to localities. If a community possessed a library building, its residents might be encouraged to purchase and study the books they wished to read, whatever those might be—that was Carnegie's hope, with similar hopes also having prompted his gifts to encourage music, art, and science, among many other things. Carnegie's lack of standards for discriminating between types of knowledge should not suggest an absence of values. He believed in, preached, and otherwise tried to foster respect for hard work, self-improvement, and other virtues of the Protestant ethic. That notwithstanding, the point remains that to this self-educated, multimillionaire of radical Scots background, knowledge was good, individuals differed, and no one, not even he, should attempt to determine what knowledge would best serve and most likely spark the initiative of others.

Henry Pritchett and Elihu Root did not agree. "Our nation faces sharp, pressing, insistent questions concerning which the people stand in urgent need of knowledge and understanding," Pritchett wrote in a 1916 memorandum to his fellow trustees. "It seems clearly the duty of the Trustees to inquire if there are means by which this Trust may come to closer grip with these questions than through the giving of library buildings."[7] Already suggesting that the Corporation should promote, not knowledge in general, but knowledge relevant to urgent, public questions, Pritchett clarified the expanded sphere of decision making he was urging in a discussion of possible alternatives to the financing of library buildings. Since, as he put it, "American isolation—political and commercial—has come to an end," one alternative was "an effort to educate the people of the United States into a realization of a *welt politik* and of their obligations in it." This might be done via the dissemination of "popular but adequate information about other countries" to colleges, international polity clubs, chautauqua circles, magazines, and newspapers. Since Americans were in even greater need of accurate information relevant to "their domestic problems," especially their economic problems, Pritchett also suggested the possibility of establishing an "Institute of Economics" that would provide an "antidote" to socialist and anarchist "propaganda" through the "dissemination among the mass of the people of simple, fundamental economic facts told in understandable form."[8] The eventual translation of "provisional suggestions" such as these into actual grants revealed fascinating differences of assumption between Corporation trustees and grantees, and sometimes also between Corporation trustees and the trustees or officers of other foundations. In authorizing funds to the National Bureau of Economic Research in 1920, for example, the trustees thought they were supporting "an Institute of Economics" not different from the one Pritchett had suggested, even though that conception did not precisely square with the conception of the bureau held by Wesley Mitchell, Edwin Gay, and its other founders. However that might have been, by 1920 the Corporation's trustees had decided that they should no longer seek to promote whatever social good might arise through the possibilities for individual enlightenment made available via the "wholesale" development and dissemination of any and all knowledge, but instead should concern themselves specifically and directly with nationally urgent knowledge, knowledge that, in the opinion of "men of discriminating judgement," "the people" needed to have.

Closely related to this first new principle for Carnegie Corporation giving was a second that, as always, Henry Pritchett articulated most clearly and forcefully. In one of the many memoranda he wrote to urge his views upon his brethren trustees, he argued that the Corporation had to decide whether to continue "the passive sorting out of the innumerable petitions from Colleges, hospitals, Settlements and all other causes engaged in their own judgement at least, in the advancement and diffusion of knowledge," or instead to "take the initiative in seeking out those forces in the social order that promise to be significant and fruitful."[9] To have implied that Andrew Carnegie's philanthropy had exemplified the first option was not entirely accurate. Albeit with waning enthusiasm and energy, Carnegie's career as a philanthropist had been marked by considerable initiative. Friends receiving letters asking for suggestions of how to spend $10,000,000 or of what to call some project—"P.S. Prize for the best!"—could have attested to that.[10] But Pritchett was not troubled by that, since what he was really advocating in this 1918 statement was that the Corporation not only become more initiatory but that in so doing it also direct its attention to fostering innovation. In the simplified spelling he sometimes used, Andrew Carnegie had told the trustees: "Conditions upon the erth inevitably change; hence, no wise man will bind Trustees forever to certain paths, causes or institutions. I disclaim any intention of doing so."[11] In establishing the Corporation, he had therefore left room for the initiation of new grant priorities. But, with Elihu Root and eventually the other trustees concurring, Pritchett was now adding to Carnegie's call for flexibility a responsibility for identifying desirable prospects for change and then supporting and encouraging them.

This introduced a more explicitly projective and implicitly directive sense of purpose into the Carnegie Corporation, one that would begin to be fully evident in actual grants and other activities when Frederick P. Keppel, president of the Corporation from 1922 until 1941, would be asked by the trustees to develop a program in adult education. Even though adult education was an age-old enterprise, the Corporation's trustees, in anticipation of increasing leisure time and a greater demand for postschool education, were concerned with establishing and coordinating more organized, regular programs of adult study that would operate with motives of service rather than profit uppermost in mind and offer educational opportunities outside the existing educational "system." The effort floundered partly because Keppel was interested in innovation as highly diverse experimentation rather than as the more deliberate (and implicitly highly directive) fostering of desirable social trends and partly because the 1930s depression spawned many nonschool educational programs in addition to and different from those encouraged by the Corporation. This suggests the subtle but important ways Corporation policies shifted over the years as both its leadership and external environment changed. What is important here, however, is that the decision to develop adult education programs derived at the outset from the institutionalization of a new, more future-oriented, design-level definition of mission.

In initiating policies for the Carnegie Corporation that were based, first, on a willingness to decide what knowledge was needed and, second, on an acceptance of responsibility for identifying and supporting desirable change, Henry Pritchett and Elihu Root moved this foundation out of alignment with a nineteenth-century conception of policy-making and into alignment with a conception more widely held in the twentieth century. The former had been based on a belief in positive but loosely coupled associations between the collective good or national destiny, the free exercise of individual initiative, and the absence of a strong, central, executive power; the latter was based on belief in expert decision making, combined with the wide and deliberate transmission of this expertise, science thus informing "the best men" and instructing "the people" as to how, without involuntary sacrifice of liberty, individuals could reconcile their actions in pursuit of "the public good." Obviously, in aligning the Corporation with this new conception of policy-making, Pritchett and Root did not intend to engage it in politics. Indeed, as I have suggested, their conception of policy-making arose from the hope that science could yield expertise sufficiently objective and disinterested to transcend the corruption, compromise, and other problems then so often grouped together under the rubric of "inefficiency." If, in retrospect, this hope must be recognized as inseparable from an elitism that was a prominent theme in turn-of-the-century American social thought, so, too, must it be acknowledged as sincerely held, in "the public interest," by those who participated in it. That notwithstanding, in aligning "the greatest endowment ever given to a group of men for the promotion and diffusion of knowledge and understanding amongst the people of a nation" with those individuals, groups, and institutions also concerned with transcending politics—what they saw as partisan politics—Pritchett and Root, in fact, involved it in another politics. This was, of course, the politics of knowledge.

III

The Carnegie Corporation's involvement in this politics can be suggested by three examples drawn from its early history. The first was a 1919 grant of $5,000,000 to provide a headquarters and an endowment for the National Academy of Sciences (NAS) and its World War I adjunct, the National Research Council (NRC), which had recruited and organized scientists for wartime government service, its temporary status having been changed to permanent status in 1918. What was unusual about the two organizations was their relation to the federal government. By virtue of its Civil War charter, the NAS was the government's official advisor for scientific affairs, a status indirectly also enjoyed by the NRC, owing to its organization as a subordinate agency of the NAS. Scientists not represented in the NAS, whose members were drawn primarily from the natural science disciplines, could and would establish their own organizations to plan research, solicit funding, and otherwise represent the interests of their disciplines. An example of this was the Social Science Research Council (SSRC), established in 1923, which would also receive Carnegie Corporation dollars, roughly 24 percent of its income having come from the Corporation between 1925 and 1945.[12] That notwithstanding, the SSRC's lack of affiliation with the NAS (and therefore lack of official governmental advisory status) resulted in an important, at least symbolic, difference of location vis-à-vis those most immediately responsible for national defense, foreign policy, and other vital matters of common, public concern.

The NAS and NRC's superiority of status compared to other scientific academies and councils, including the SSRC, was certainly not caused by Carnegie Corporation funding, even if the Corporation's gift of $5,000,000 was unusually large. But the Corporation's trustees did recognize and favor that preeminence and made the 1919 grant with it very much in mind. Indeed, Elihu Root was one of the "most valued and beloved advisors" of George Ellery Hale, the brilliant astrophysicist, entrepreneur for science, and champion of the NAS, who had organized the NRC partly to protect its advisory prerogatives, when, without consulting the NAS, the government had sought advice from non-NAS endorsed scientists and inventors like Thomas Edison at the beginning of World War I.[13] Like Hale, Root saw a possibility for national prominence in greater reliance upon those sciences he thought most directly instrumental to industrial growth, and he believed these should be represented in a formally organized academy of men notable for their learning and cultivation. He also recognized great potential in the NAS's charter, which left the academy free of government control despite its advisory status, and alerted Hale to this, Hale independently expressing sentiments not dissimilar from Root's when he voiced the worry that popularly elected officials (especially Democrats) were all too inclined to favor "the needs of 'the Little Red School House on the hill,' standing for light and leading to the lowly of the land."[14] Owing to all this, Root had tried before World War I to convince Andrew Carnegie to provide the NAS with the funds that were eventually granted in the year of Carnegie's death. But Carnegie had refused those funds because he thought the academy merely one of those "fancy societies" and did not concur in Hale and Root's belief that it should be "the clearing house of American science, and its official center in both a national and international sense."[15] That the Corporation subsequently granted the NAS and NRC $5,000,000 (a higher figure than had initially been sought for the NAS) was therefore not insignificant. Combined with its trustees' willingness financially to assist (at a lower level) but not to suggest or seek equal prominence for the social scientists represented by the SSRC, the grant indicated active awareness and participation in questions concerning which fields and approaches within different fields of knowledge should gain the wherewithal necessary to be considered more or less authoritative bases for public policy.

Two years before authorizing this grant to the NAS and NRC, the Corporation's trustees had taken an action that provides another early illustration of the Corporation's engagement in the politics of knowledge. This one involved the commissioning of a series of studies rather than simply the donation of funds. The series was intended to transmit expertise to "the people" and eventually resulted in the publication of ten volumes, well known collectively as the "Americanization Studies." Some of the volumes, for example, *Old World Traits Transplanted* by W. I. Thomas (whose name was removed from the title page owing to the scandal in Chicago), Robert E. Park, and Herbert Miller, quickly became classics and have remained so.

As an example of the Corporation's engagement in the politics of knowledge, what was interesting about the so-called "Americanization Studies" was that they were intended to present instructive information about *methods* of Americanization.[16] Granted that Americanization was still tantamount to a national crusade in 1917, when the studies were first planned, there was nevertheless an important decision inherent in the determination that the public needed to know *how* to Americanize rather than to be encouraged to debate *whether* to Americanize, one alternative having been to accept the viability of cultural pluralism, a possibility variously urged at the time by John Dewey, Horace Kallen, and Randolph Bourne, among others, in journals like the *New Republic, Nation,* and *Atlantic Monthly*. Inherent in the Corporation's trustees' initiation of the "Americanization Studies" was a decision to transmit answers, not questions; to tell rather than to teach; to use expert knowledge to broaden public participation in the implementation of a policy but not in its initial formulation or design. As it would turn out, some of the experts commissioned to undertake the studies developed monographs that would raise questions and transmit knowledge necessary to the reconsideration of policy objectives. Clearly, philanthropic intentions are not easily achieved, particularly when scholarly inquiry is involved. But that turn of events simply underscores the complexity of the politics in which the Carnegie Corporation had become enmeshed. The "Americanization Studies" exemplify the way in which the Corporation's activities shaped, or were intended to shape, communication between experts and nonexperts and, with that, relative roles in the setting of public agendas and the definition of "the public good."

The last of the three questions central to the politics of knowledge, the question of access to knowledge-producing elites, was also one in which the Carnegie Corporation would participate, as may be shown by its authorization in 1923 of $1,075,000 to launch the American Law Institute (ALI), the initial organization of which had already been assisted with a grant for $25,000 made in the previous year. The ALI grew out of an alliance between prominent members of the bar, including Elihu Root, and leading legal scholars. Its primary official purpose was to simplify the common law, which was growing rapidly at this time and coming increasingly to reflect the complexity of rulings based upon different and changing social circumstances rather than upon (as in Blackstone) settled categories for and principles of the law. It was to do this through "restatements" that would initially be developed by scholars, expert in contracts, property, trusts, torts, and other fields, and then reviewed, revised, and agreed upon by ALI committees in which legal scholars would be joined by judges and practicing attorneys. This cumbersome (and expensive) process was intended to insure, as Root explained, that a restatement "while . . . not itself made law by any political authority . . . would be accepted as being prima facie a correct statement of the law contained in the decisions examined."[17]

Within the context of both the social history of American law and the politics of knowledge, what was noteworthy about the launching of the ALI was that, along with this primary, official purpose, there were also several less well announced, subsidiary purposes. Among these were setting boundaries for the common law and insuring that members of the bench and bar would determine these. Both were rooted in questions having to do with who possessed the knowledge and credentials appropriate to lawmaking. For example, if the common law were allowed to remain in its existing flexible, evolutionary condition, social scientists and psychologists concerned with the law as an expression of customary practice might claim a role alongside or even instead of the legal scholars whose exclusive province legal interpretation might otherwise be. Equally important, if the authority of the common law were not enhanced—via simplification and the prestige conferring consensus process that was to be associated with the ALI's restatements—legislative bodies, susceptible to public pressure and accessible to what one legal scholar described as the "alien races from Eastern Europe and from Asia [that have] been pouring in on us, accustomed to absolute government, accustomed to hate the law, and hostile above all to wealth and power," might attempt to settle questions otherwise amenable to judicial holdings.[18] Fully to clarify all the issues involved would require an analysis of the interconnections between a variety of institutions and the impact upon those of a variety of contemporary attitudes. The early history of the ALI is best set within the context, not only of the law itself (including the development of "legal realism"), but also of early twentieth-century reforms of legal education and licensure and the anti-immigrant (especially anti-Semitic) sentiment so unfortunately pervasive among lawyers at the time. Even without the clarity possible within that context, however, it should be apparent that in helping to establish this organization and in providing it with its major funding for what is now known as its First Restatement, the Carnegie Corporation was taking part in crucial decisions concerning what American law should be and who should determine this on the basis of which statuses and credentials.

IV

Certainly, one could point to many other instances in which activities of the Carnegie Corporation were significantly related to one, several, or all of the large questions that one may discern within "the politics of knowledge." But my argument can be summarized without those. However much this politics may have changed over the course of the twentieth century, its existence, and indeed vitality, has lent significance to the grants the Carnegie Corporation has made, the studies it has commissioned, and the projects, programs, and institutions it has helped to organize and support far beyond whatever these may have immediately achieved. The establishment of the ALI and the publication of its First Restatement were, for example, only the most direct and obvious outcomes of the grants referred to above, which also had indirect but far-reaching consequences for legal education and legal scholarship, as well as for the continuing development of the law itself. Obviously, therefore, one must consider grants such as this within a very broad context. What is more, since discrete grants, even large ones, are often not as revealing as patterns of grants, one must study the overall record of the Carnegie Corporation's activities within such a context. Not coincidentally, it is through context that a politics of knowledge becomes recoverable. One can only understand the political significance of support for the unusual link the NAS–NRC had with the federal government by contrasting that support with a lack of support for the development of a similar link for the SSRC. One can only appreciate the political strategy implicit in the publication of the "Americanization Studies" when one recognizes that there was a sufficient diversity of view and public interest in Americanization to have made possible a campaign of education intended to illuminate choices rather than to offer instruction in techniques. And one can only grasp the relationship between the establishment of the ALI and questions having to do with who should interpret the law by contrasting the social, political, economic, and professional composition of the ALI with that of other contemporary groups also (in a variety of ways) asserting a right and capacity to interpret the law.

Philanthropic decisions have necessitated choices, and the alternatives not acted upon are historically vital. After all, at the time choices were made and contests explicitly and implicitly joined and settled, it was neither clear nor inevitable that things would turn out as they did. The "mainstream" after all, is defined, not given.

Recognizing that, one may venture that large philanthropic foundations like the Carnegie Corporation have tended to play not merely a "gatekeeper's" role but also an umpire's role within the politics of knowledge.[19] Their efforts have not directly or exclusively determined the nature of public policy-making or indeed the substance of public policy in the United States. But insofar as they have played a central role in shaping the politics of knowledge, their efforts have often been vital in determining which intellectual resources and which social groups would be brought to bear in defining the issues and questions that policymakers would address. One would be hard pressed to find better confirmation for Merle Curti's "hypothetical statement" that the history of such organizations should be assessed as "one of the major aspects of and keys to American social and cultural development."

Notes

1. Merle Curti, "The History of American Philanthropy as a Field of Research," *American Historical Review* 62 (Jan. 1957): 352.
2. Quoted in Joseph Frazier Wall, *Andrew Carnegie* (New York, 1970), 884.
3. Henry S. Pritchett, "Fields of Activity Open to the Carnegie Corporation," Trustee Memorandum, 15 Apr. 1916, p. 2, Carnegie Corporation files, New York, N.Y.
4. Henry S. Pritchett to Andrew Carnegie, 16 Nov. 1905, Carnegie Foundation for the Advancement of Teaching files, New York, N.Y. Pritchett's efforts to transform the Carnegie Foundation, which presaged the subsequent transformation of the Carnegie Corporation, as well as the policies that followed from that are fully discussed in Ellen Condliffe Lagemann, *Private Power for the Public Good: A History of the Carnegie Foundation for the Advancement of Teaching* (Middletown, Conn., 1983).
5. The Pritchett phrase is from [Henry S. Pritchett], "The Administration of the Carnegie Corporation," Trustee Memorandum, [1918], p. 8, Carnegie Corporation files. Many studies pertain to the disdain for politics and preference for governance by "the best men" that Pritchett and Root expressed, including older works such as John G. Sproat, *"The Best Men": Liberal Reformers in the Gilded Age* (New York, 1968), and newer ones, for example, Martin J. Schiesl, *The Politics of Efficiency: Municipal Administration and Reform in America, 1800–1920* (Berkeley, Calif., 1977).
6. Matthew Arnold, *Culture and Anarchy*, ed. J. Dover Wilson (1869; London, 1960), 6.
7. Pritchett, "Fields of Activity Open to the Carnegie Corporation," 2.
8. Ibid., 3–9.
9. Pritchett, "The Administration of the Carnegie Corporation," 2.
10. Carnegie to Pritchett, 14 Dec. 1905, Andrew Carnegie Papers, Library of Congress, Washington, D.C.
11. Robert M. Lester, Forty Years of Carnegie Giving: A Summary of the Benefactions of Andrew Carnegie and of the Work of the Philanthropic Trusts Which He Created (New York, 1941), 166.
12. The estimate of Carnegie Corporation contributions to SSRC income was developed by corporation staff in considering a proposal presented in Donald Young to Devereux Josephs, 13 Apr. 1946, Carnegie Corporation files.
13. Hale's description of Root is quoted in Helen Wright, Explorer of the Universe: A Biography of George Ellery Hale (New York, 1966), 308. Among the many works that deal with the NAS and the NRC, those that are most relevant to the argument here, including Hale and Root's close relationship, are: Daniel J. Kevles, "George Ellery Hale, the First World War, and the Advancement of Science in America," Isis 59 (1968): 427–37; and Ronald C. Tobey, The American Ideology of National Science, 1919–1930 (Pittsburgh, 1971).
14. George Ellery Hale to H. H. Turner, 6 Mar. 1916, as quoted in Kevles, "George Ellery Hale, the First World War, and the Advancement of Science in America," 432.
15. Carnegie's comment is quoted in Wright, Explorer of the Universe, 309. The description of the NAS is in a letter from Hale to Carnegie, 8 May 1914, George Ellery Hale Papers, Mount Wilson and Las Campanas Observatories, Pasadena, Calif.
16. Trustee Minutes, 12 Mar. 1918, Carnegie Corporation files.

17. Elihu Root, "The Origin of the Restatement of the Law," *Oklahoma State Bar Journal* 3 (Feb. 1933): 309. Unfortunately, there is no full secondary history of the ALI, but an account by its first director, William Draper Lewis, "'How We Did It': History of the American Law Institute and the First Restatement of the Law," in *The Restatement in the Courts*, permanent ed. (St. Paul, Minn., 1945), 1–42, gives much of the official story.

18. Joseph H. Beale, "The Necessity for a Study of Legal System," American Association of Law Schools, *Proceedings* 14 (1914): 33–34. The sentiments Beale expressed as well as other concerns important in the founding of the ALI are discussed in Jerold S. Auerbach, *Unequal Justice: Lawyers and Social Change in Modern America* (New York, 1976); and Robert Bocking Stevens, *Law School: Legal Education in America from the 1850s to the 1980s* (Chapel Hill, N.C., 1983).

19. The "gatekeeper" conception was first developed in Lewis A. Coser, "Foundations as Gatekeepers of Contemporary Intellectual Life," *in Men of Ideas: A Sociologist's View* (New York, 1965), ch. 25.

American Foundations and the Development of the Social Sciences Between the Wars: Comment on the Debate Between Martin Bulmer and Donald Fisher

Salma Ahmad

Abstract This paper comments on the debate between Martin Bulmer and Donald Fisher, which appears in an earlier issue of this journal, concerning the influence of Rockefeller philanthropy on the social sciences between the wars. Three central issues of contention are distinguished and rival claims are evaluated. I argue that new empirical evidence drawn from the foundations' archives does not support some of their arguments although each interpretation has its merits.

Martin Bulmer and Donald Fisher reached quite different conclusions in their independent studies of the influence of the Rockefeller foundations on British and American social science between the wars. This debate is outlined in *Sociology* (Bulmer 1984b; Fisher 1984) and presented in detail elsewhere (Bulmer 1985; Bulmer 1984a; Bulmer 1982a; Bulmer 1982b; Bulmer 1981; Bulmer and Bulmer 1981; Bulmer 1980; Fisher 1988; Fisher 1986; Fisher 1983; Fisher 1980). My aim is to comment on three central issues of contention between them.[1] The first is whether the Rockefeller foundations (the Memorial and Rockefeller Foundation) represented ruling class interests. I argue that trustees were recruited from the American upper class, at least in the 1930s, and trustee influence on the foundations' policies was greater than Bulmer contends. Although the foundations' policies reflected wider trends in the social sciences, as Bulmer argues, they represented far more than this. Secondly, I consider and question the extent to which the foundations were 'disinterested' as defined by Bulmer. Thirdly, I consider the impact of the foundations on research and argue that this is exaggerated by Fisher and underestimated by Bulmer.

Although the accounts of Fisher and Bulmer differ, they agree that the Memorial was a major patron of social research in the U.S.A. and in Britain (Bulmer and Bulmer 1981:385–86; Fisher 1980:284–87). They also agree that during the 1920s under the directorship of B. Ruml, the Memorial's programme for promoting 'centres of excellence' and international fellowships assumed that the social sciences would only develop and provide useful knowledge if their methods were as rigorous as the natural sciences; if their theoretical propositions were tested with empirical and quantitative data; if the issues they addressed were contemporary and were tackled collaboratively; and if social scientists did not allow political judgements to influence their research (Fisher 1983:210–14; Fisher 1980:278–81; Bulmer 1984b:573; Bulmer and Bulmer 1981:347; 361–99). Ruml, according to Bulmer, also promoted some applied research in child welfare, leisure, recreation, social work, race relations and community work; but Bulmer overlooks two other areas which were sponsored, criminology and international relations (Bulmer and Bulmer 1981 364)[2]. Fisher notes a change in policy during the 1930s, when Edmund Day, the Harvard economist and director of the newly formed Social

Science Division of the Rockefeller Foundation, promoted fields of research (such as 'economic stabilisation') which Day believed could mitigate the worst aspects of the Depression. At the same time the policy of cultivating 'centres of excellence' was gradually abandoned (Fisher 1983:214–23; Fisher 1980:281–84).

Bulmer's and Fisher's accounts begin to diverge when they consider what the Rockefeller policies represented, the first aspect of the debate which I shall comment on. Fisher's proposition is that the '. . . foundations have represented the interests of the ruling class' (Fisher 1983:224) but this is dismissed by Bulmer as a conspiracy theory without foundation or reference to the social and intellectual context.

It seems to me, however, that there is a sense in which the Rockefeller foundations represented the ruling class. As the early Rockefeller trusts, established at the turn of the century with vast profits accrued from the Standard Oil empire, evolved into large corporate foundations, Rockefeller capitalists devolved power and appointed trustees to manage their philanthropies (Collier and Horowitz 1976:30–134). Internal Rockefeller surveys clearly show that those trustees, at least in the 1930s, were drawn from the upper classes (something which is assumed by Fisher) the majority being influential lawyers, businessmen and bankers from the New York region.[3]

For Bulmer, however, the trustees' social class is irrelevant, mainly because '. . . by the early 1920s the various Rockefeller philanthropies were controlled by their officers, who pursued aims independently of the trustees and the family (Bulmer 1984b:573). Yet this demarcation of policy formulation between trustees and officers (administrators) was not so sharp as Bulmer maintains. The possibility of trustee influence should not be dismissed simply because it cannot be *seen* to be exerted; they had the power to reject policies and this may have lead officers to modify their recommendations. Furthermore, trustees sometimes directly influenced policies. As Fisher has also noted, during the Depression three trustees took control of an important emergency relief programme.[4] Another example was the Memorial's sponsorship of research into international policing related to the trustee A. Wood's work as Assessor to the League of Nation's Advisory Committee on Opium.[5]

Bulmer further argues that Fisher does not cite the crucial evidence of F. Gates (J. D. Rockefeller's advisor) who claimed that the foundations were controlled by officers rather than trustees (Bulmer 1984b:573). Yet Bulmer equally disregards other contradictory evidence. In 1944 R. Fosdick recalled trustee involvement in all aspects of policy making:

> '. . . the old Laura Spelman Rockefeller Memorial adopted the policy of shunting to the Executive Committee all questions of specific appropriations and reserving the meetings of the trustees for considerations of policy. This system lasted for about a year and then was given up because, frankly, the trustee wanted some of the fun of making appropriations to specific objects'.[6]

Additionally, in 1935 another influential trustee, J. D. Greene, wrote in a confidential memorandum that the real authority in the Rockefeller Foundation remained in the hands of very few persons '. . . having dealings with the foundation, with the authority of Mr Rockefeller or of the somewhat mystical centre of influence associated with his office'.[7]

Another argument advanced by Bulmer to undermine Fisher's contention that the foundations represented ruling class interests is the lack of evidence to demonstrate '. . . that commercial ends or the advancement of the interests of a particular social and economic class ever entered Ruml's mind' (Bulmer and Bulmer 1981:402). Officers, he maintains, merely promoted their intellectual interests and it is more plausible to regard the Memorial's policy as reflecting contemporaneous trends in the social sciences. Fisher is accused of ignoring this social and intellectual context somewhat unfairly, since Fisher notes that '. . . Rockefeller philanthropy was influenced by and contributed to a general movement towards a scientific approach to all aspects of knowledge' (Fisher 1983:207). Bulmer, admitedly, is far clearer about what those trends involved in each discipline (Bulmer and Bulmer 1981:369–70).

It is true that the Memorial's officers never intended to promote social research for commercial ends. They decided not to sponsor social scientists in companies such as General Motors because their research neglected wider social and economic issues.[8] The Memorial's policy certainly reflected the views of a new generation of social scientists referred to by Bulmer, such as those who sought to create an objective political science addressing contemporary issues or who favoured a more empirical orientation in sociology, but it would be a mistake to assume that officers always shared the concerns of academics. Officers, for example, sponsored the American Social Science Research Council, in part to help them manage social research more effectively; while the political scientist Charles Merriam, a leading advocate of setting up the SSRC, hoped that it would increase funding for political science and enhance its scientific status.[9] The Memorial's policy also represented far more than the intellectual interests of some academics. As Kohler has argued, it was a strategy for 'community development'; an attempt to apply business methods to create collectives of social scientists who would play a central role in reconstructing national institutions after the first world war (Kohler 1989:137; 148). Ruml's policy was also, as Alchon maintains, a manifesto calling for a technocratic social science and enlightened management in industry, government and welfare based on social scientific knowledge (Alchon 1985:118–20).

I have alluded to Bulmer's characterisation of foundations as disinterested agencies, defined in several ways, each of which I shall consider separately. In Bulmer's view, Ruml followed regulations '. . . to ensure that foundations did not and could not influence the social science research that they supported' (Bulmer 1984b:575). This was achieved partly by giving universities block grants which could be administered and evaluated as they wished (Bulmer, 1982a:190; Bulmer and Bulmer 1981:378–81).

Bulmer's thesis contains some truth. Foundations were committed to the principle of 'academic freedom' during the 1920s and block grants were intended to allow technical judgements of research priorities to be delegated to academics leaving philanthropists with the task of assessing the institutions' organisational needs (Karl and Katz 1987:19–20; Kohler 1987:146–47). In practice, however, Rockefeller personnel did attempt to influence research priorities in the social sciences and their methods. One example was at Oxford in the 1930s when, as a trustee reported, a group of economists had apparently moved away from '. . . abstract theoretical work to careful inductive analysis', a development which had been '. . . so desirable that it seemed wise to encourage this line of attack' (with a grant).[10] Similarly, the London School of Economics (LSE) was maintained as the foundations' British 'centre of excellence' throughout most of the interwar period because, compared with other British universities, it best approximated to the Memorial's ideal centre for the social sciences. Officers were also impressed by the directors of the School, W. Beveridge and A. Carr-Saunders, because of their 'scientific' approach and because Beveridge was a government advisor.[11]

Selection between universities and departments was only one strategy adopted by officers to influence research. In the 1930s some academics, starved of resources, would probably have shifted their research proposals to mesh with the foundation's favoured topics. Direct interference in universities to change research priorities was also not excluded. This occurred at the LSE in the 1930s when Beveridge devoted a considerable proportion of the Rockefeller grants to a new Department of Social Biology, which proved to be unpopular with many members of staff and with the foundation's personnel. The latter decided that social biology had no place in their social science programme and pursued various courses of action: they made their views known to Beveridge on several occasions, they enabled the head of the Department of Social Biology to take up an appointment elsewhere by providing a grant for his salary, they declined to fund a research project from the department and, finally, they threatened not to renew future grants to the School if it persisted with social biology.[12] Although the demise of that department, which survived for only eight years, cannot be solely attributed to the Rockefeller Foundation, it certainly played a part.

The above account suggests that there is something amiss with Bulmer's portrayal of foundations as disinterested patrons of research, yet he insists that 'Ruml never attempted to persuade any academic to do something which he was not already interested in doing' (Bulmer and Bulmer 1981:402). This, he argues, was illustrated at the University of Cambridge in 1925 when the Vice-Chancellor accepted Ruml's offer to finance a Chair in Political Science but declined an endowment for a Chair in Sociology because the university authorities were hostile towards the subject. According to Bulmer, Ruml reluctantly accepted the situation and could only suggest in a letter to the Vice-Chancellor that the Memorial would be 'sympathetic' if they decided to develop sociology at a later date. (Bulmer 1981:156–59). Fisher, however, who generally portrays the Rockefeller officers as forcing their ideas upon academics, often rejecting requests for funds, offers a different story (Fisher 1986:6; Fisher 1980:290). It was Ruml, he claims, who decided not to fund a Chair in Sociology until Cambridge developed clearer plans, an invitation never taken up (Fisher 1984:580; Fisher 1980:291).

My reading of the archives suggests that Bulmer's interpretation is more accurate although Ruml was not quite as willing to accept the situation at Cambridge as Bulmer believes. Shortly after Ruml wrote his letter to the Vice-Chancellor, he sent another to a colleague (which has not been quoted in full in either Bulmer's or Fisher's accounts), revealing a long term strategy for achieving his objectives at Cambridge.

> At Cambridge the situation is fairly promising for getting an edge into one of the most conservative of universities . . . when the statement came from Cambridge, however, the outline of what was proposed in Sociology did not seem sufficiently detailed to justify recommending that Chair at this time, but since some of the people in Cambridge know that we are prepared to recommend to our Board such a Chair, I think holding off at this time may cause them to re-examine their position in Social Science a bit. I am somewhat concerned lest the yeast of a Chair in Political Science prove inadequate to leaven the rather substantial lump, but in view of the desirability of taking the chance, and again of meeting the Cambridge people on their own ground and not trying to inject too many of our own notions into a foreign soil, it seemed wise to go ahead. Neither Woods nor I feel that this particular situation is absolutely ideal, but with things as they are, it seemed a good strategy, looking forward toward the possibility of doing something else a little later on.[13]

This letter suggests, contrary to Bulmer's view, that when the officers' proposals were not enthusiastically received they tried to change the situation (sometimes aggressively, as illustrated at the LSE mentioned above). However, Bulmer is right to point out that they were not always successful. Much to Ruml's dismay, Cambridge appointed a political theorist rather than a 'scientist' to their Memorial endowed chair, and a Chair in Sociology was not established until the 1960s (Bulmer 1985:23; Bulmer 1981:156–59).

Finally, Bulmer maintains that the foundations were disinterested because Ruml avoided sponsoring politically controversial topics (Bulmer 1984b:573). However, Bulmer fails to note that the officers and trustees could avoid adverse publicity by working through other agencies. For example, in 1936 a trustee policy document on social security stated that '[s]ince these questions involve legislation and government policy of a controversial nature, the Foundation is working almost entirely through the Social Security Committee of the SSRC'.[14]

While Bulmer assumes that officers always followed bureaucratic regulations, Fisher is equally misled into believing that the missionary zeal with which personnel attempted to modernise social research achieved successful results. This is the third issue of contention between Bulmer and Fisher, the impact of the foundations' policies on research which, I believe, Fisher clearly exaggerates. According to Fisher, American and British social science under Rockefeller influence began to reflect the foundations' interests and the general trend in Britain and at the LSE was towards more empirical, scientific and realistic research (Fisher 1980:294–95). Both the 'size and pace' of the shift from deductive theory to empirical investigation in Britain '. . . had been largely due to Rockefeller influence' (Fisher 1980:295). Furthermore, Rockefeller funding helped to

> . . . produce knowledge that would help preserve the economic structure of Western society. Economic stability was the objective and consequently the vast majority of British economic research focused on studies that would explain why depressions occurred'. Similarly, with anthropology their aim was 'social security' so consequently the vast amount of anthropological research focused on British African territories and almost certainly helped the system of 'Indirect Rule' and exploitation that much more efficient (Fisher 1980:305).

There are several problems with Fisher's scenario. Firstly, he assumes, but does not demonstrate, that Rockefeller funded projects formed part of a tradition of empirical, scientific and realistic research

(Fisher 1980:294). Secondly, while it is conceivable that Rockefeller personnel hoped social scientists would find solutions for the problems noted by Fisher, it does not follow that their expectations were fulfilled, or that the arising social theories informed public policy: this needs to be demonstrated by Fisher. Thirdly, Fisher has a tendency to play down the role of other influences that contributed to the trends he identifies and consequently, exaggerates the foundations' role.[15] Bulmer rightly takes issue with him and argues that in the United States, the interwar movement towards empiricism as well as a more rigorous scientific approach arose for many other reasons including the rise of statistics as a discipline and the desire of social scientists to increase the status of their subjects by emulating the methods of the natural sciences and biology (Bulmer 1984b:574–75; Bulmer and Bulmer 1981:369–70).

A similar argument may be advanced with regard to the development of social sciences at the LSE. I have argued elsewhere that the founders and many directors of the School wanted to create a centre for National and Imperial Efficiency and consequently, encouraged commercial and vocational courses at the School from the turn of the century.[16] Some directors at the School, especially Beveridge, also encouraged empirical based research and the use of scientific methods. Beveridge hoped, for example, that the Joint School of Geography with King's College, which he helped to establish in 1922, would encourage social scientists to use natural science methods. These were just some of the influences that fostered the trends in research Fisher refers to at the LSE *before* Rockefeller funding was received in 1923. They continued and, in some cases, were strengthened, during the interwar period with the help of Rockefeller funding. Fisher, however, is too eager to attribute such developments primarily to Rockefeller activities (Fisher 1980:294).

Fisher also exaggerates the foundations' role in changing social science by drawing attention to those research traditions, in this instance at the LSE, which were favoured and funded by the foundations. One example, among others, was the empirical social survey tradition in the form of the *New Survey of London Life and Labour* which began in 1927. However, other types of research which the foundations did not favour also received funding, or they persisted without Rockefeller support, and the implications of this are not appreciated by Fisher (Fisher 1980:286–94). Bulmer cites the Rockefeller funded work of R. H. Tawney's *Religion and the rise of Capitalism* (1926) (Bulmer 1984b:574). Other examples, overlooked by Bulmer, included their funding or research in abstract economic theory, notably Lionel Robbin's *Nature and Significance of Economic Science* (1932) in which he gave vent to his hostility towards Beveridge's scientific and empirical approach to economics (Robbins 1971:136, 149). Rockefeller grants were used to publish E. Power's and R. H. Tawney's *Tudor Economic Documents* (1924), hardly an example of research into contemporary affairs. Additionally, in sociology M. Ginsberg published two books with Rockefeller funds although he was noted for carrying on the department's philosophical and theoretical tradition and, like his predecessor L. T. Hobhouse, made little attempt to develop empirical research before the second world war (Macrae 1972:52; Hawthorn 1976:167–68).[17]

These examples, and the fact that research in the Department of Sociology at the LSE during the interwar period largely remained theoretical and philosophical and that, outside commerce, economists moved away from their earlier concerns with historical methods and became noted for their highly theoretical, abstract and mathematical works (Winch 1969:64–65, 159, 206; Hayek 1946:5; Seligman 1963:363), suggests that even with the use of selective funding the Rockefeller foundations were not able to control research to the extent suggested by Fisher.[18] But, as I have argued above in contrast to Bulmer, this cannot be attributed entirely to disinterested foundation management. Rather, British social science did not prove to be so easy for the foundations to mould as Fisher contends. One reason for this is that although Rockefeller funds were made available for large scale collaborative projects, research assistants and machines to tabulate data, not all academics required that type of assistance and many happily continued with their 'armchair theorising'.

In conclusion, I suggest that while Fisher and Bulmer both offer interesting insights into the development of social science during the interwar period under Rockefeller influence, neither author has been able to offer a totally convincing account of the foundations' political, social and intellectual role in society.

Notes

1. Other criticisms of Fisher's work have been advanced by Karl and Katz (1987) who argue that the 'Gramscian' approach, used by Fisher and others, is ill-suited to explaining the origins of foundations and their donors' intentions. However, Fisher in my view is not especially concerned with the histories of foundations. Another issue raised, not discussed here, is whether it is appropriate to apply Gramscian analysis to the American context, when discussing the relationship between foundations, politics and political institutions.

2. The archives of the Laura Spelman Rockefeller Memorial (LSRM) and Rockefeller Foundation (RF) are held at the Rockefeller Archive Center (RAC) Hillcrest, Pocantico Hills, North Tarrytown, New York, 10591. For details of the programmes in criminology and international relations see: LSRM S11, Box 2, File 16 (1925–6), RAC; 'Brief resume on International Relations 1923–32', RG. 3, Series 910, Box 7, Folder 66 (20 June 1933), RAC.

3. R. Fosdick to J. D. Rockefeller 3rd, RG. 3, Series 900, Box 1, Folder 2 (20 October 1936), RAC; RG. 3, Box 1, Folder 9 (21 June 1939), RAC.

4. RG. 1.1, Box 393, Folder 4657 (1933), RAC; RG. 3, Series 904, Box 4, Folder 25 (13 November 1933), RAC.

5. LSRM S11, Box 2, File 16 (1925–26), p. 38, RAC.

6. R. Fosdick to H. Dodds, RG. 3, Series 903, Box 1, Folder 3 (18 December 1944), RAC.

7. J. D. Greene, 'Memorandum on the Relation of the Trustees to the Policy and Control of the Rockefeller Foundation', RG. Series 900, Box 19, File 141 (20 October 1935), p. 13, RAC.

8. L. K. Frank, 'The Status Of Social Science in the United States'. LSRM, SIII-6, B63, File 679 (1923), p. 10 and 25, RAC.

9. R. Fosdick to E. M. Hopkins, 'Principles Governing the Memorial's Programme in Social Sciences', RG. 3, Series 910, Box 1 (19 December 1928), RAC; 'Social Science Research Council', RG. 3, Series 910, Box 3, Folder 26 (August 1934), RAC; Karl B. D. (1975), p. 124.

10. John Van Sickle to T. B. Kitteridge, RG. 1.1, 401, Box 71, File 944 (19.1.37) RAC. For other Rockefeller views of British and European social science see Ahmad (1987:106–36).

11. Fisher has also noted the foundations' view of LSE (1980:286). See also Memo. to B. Ruml, LSRM, SIII, Subseries 6, Box 55, File 592 (12 November 1924), RAC Memo. From the Executive Committee to the Board of Directors, LSRM, Series 11, Box 2, File 16 (1925/6), p. 7, RAC; 'General social science policy in Europe', RG. 3, Series 910, Box 3, Folder 16 (1939), RAC.

12. The full story of the demise of the Department of Social Biology, which I argue it only partly related by Fisher and Bulmer, is presented in Ahmad (1987:241–69).

13. B. Ruml to E. M. Hopkins, LSRM, Series 11, Box 4, File 45 (10th August 1926), RAC.

14. 'Extract from Statement of Programme presented at Special Trustee Committee Conference', RG. 3, Series 910, Box 2, 14 (15 December 1936), p. 2, RAC.

15. E. C. Lagemann (1987:470) has noted that others also exaggerate the influence of foundations on academic work. She cites Gunnar Myrdal's (1944) 'An American Dilemma: The Negro Problem and Modern Democracy' which, she maintains, was shaped more by the writings of sociologists from Chicago than by the expectations of personnel from the Carnegie Corporation.

16. See Ahmad (1987:137–79).

17. LSE Review (1938), 'Review of the activities and the development of the London School of Economics during the period 1923–1937, Appendix 6, University of London, London School of Economics Archives. In 1981 these archives were deposited at Connaught House, London School of Economics, Houghton Street, London WC2A 2AE.

18. See Ahmad (1987:197–202). Another example of Rockefeller funding for academics who did not share their view of social science was G. Myrdal, a Rockefeller fellow (1929–30), who had in 1930 argued against the possibility of developing objective (value free) social research (E. Lagemann 1987:458–59).

References

Ahmad, S.P. 1987. 'Institutions and the Growth of Knowledge: the Rockefeller Foundations' Influence on the Social Sciences Between the Wars', (unpublished doctoral thesis). Manchester University.

Alchon, G. 1985. *The Invisible Hand of Planning: Capitalism, Social Science and the State in the 1920s*. Princeton: Princeton University Press.

Bulmer, M. (ed.) 1985. *Essays on the History of British Sociological Research*. Cambridge: Cambridge University Press.

Bulmer, M. 1984a. *The Chicago School of Sociology: Institutionalisation, Diversity and the Rise of Sociological Research.* Cambridge: Cambridge University Press.

Bulmer M. 1984b. 'Philanthropic Foundations and the Development of the Social Sciences in the Early Twentieth Century: A Reply to Donald Fisher'. *Sociology* 18:572–79.

Bulmer M. 1982a. 'Support for Sociology in the 1920s: the Laura Spelman Rockefeller Memorial and the Beginnings of Modern, Large-scale, Sociological Research in the University'. *The American Sociologist* 17:185–92.

Bulmer M. 1982b. 'Beardsley Ruml and the School Between the Wars: An Unsung Benefactor'. *LSE Magazine* 64:5–7.

Bulmer M. 1981. 'Sociology and Political Science at Cambridge in the 1920s: an Opportunity Missed and an Opportunity Taken'. *The Cambridge Review* CII 2262: 156–59.

Bulmer M. and Bulmer, J. 1981. 'Philanthropy and social science in the 1920s: the Case of Beardsley Ruml and the Laura Spelman Rockefeller Memorial, 1922–1929', *Minerva* 19:347–407.

Bulmer M. 1980. 'The Early Institutional Establishment of Social Science Research: the Local Community Research Committee of the University of Chicago, 1923–30'. *Minerva* 18:51–110.

Collier, P. and Horowitz, D. 1976. *The Rockefellers: An American Dynasty*, New York: Holt, Rinehart and Winston.

Fisher, D. 1988. 'Boundary Work: A Model of the Relation Between Power and Knowledge'. *Knowledge* 10:156–76.

Fisher, D. 1986. 'Rockefeller Philanthropy and the Rise of Social Anthropology'. *Anthropology Today* 2:5–8.

Fisher, D. 1984. 'Philanthropic Foundations and the Social Sciences: A Response to Martin Bulmer'. *Sociology* 18:580–7.

Fisher, D. 1983. 'The Role of the Rockefeller Foundations and the Production of Hegemony: Rockefeller Foundations and the Social Sciences'. *Sociology* 17:206–33.

Fisher, D. 1980. 'American Philanthropy and the Social Sciences in Britain 1919–1939: the Reproduction of a Conservative Ideology'. *The Sociology Review* 28:277–315.

Hawthorn, G. 1976. *Enlightenment and Despair. A History of Sociology.* Cambridge: Cambridge University Press.

Hayek, Von F.A. 1946. 'The London School of Economics: 1895–1945'. *Economica* 18:1–31.

Karl, B.D. 1975. *Charles E. Merriam and the Study of Politics.* Chicago: Chicago University Press.

Karl, B.D. and Katz, S.N. 1987. 'Foundations and Ruling Class Elites'. *Daedalus* 116(1):1–40.

Kohler, R.E. 1987. 'Science, Foundations and American Universities in the 1920s'. *Osiris* 2nd Series, 3:135–64.

Lagemann, E.C. 1987. 'A Philanthropic Foundation at Work: Gunnar Myrdal's American Dilemma and the Carnegie Corporation'. *Minerva* 25:441–70.

Macrae, D.G. 1972. 'The Basis of Social Cohesion', in Robson, W.A. (ed.) *Man and the Social Sciences.* London: Allen and Unwin.

Robbins, L. 1971. *An Autobiography of an Economist.* Basingstoke: Macmillan.

Seligman, E. 1963. *Main Currents in Economics. Economic Thought Since 1870.* New York: Free Press.

Winch, D. 1969. *Economics and Policy.* London: Hodder and Stoughton.

Biographical note: S. P. AHMAD B.A. (Manchester Polytechnic), M.Sc. (Manchester University), Ph.D. (Manchester University).

Address: 36, Fulmer Road, Hunters Bar, Sheffield S11 8UF.

Giving and Getting: Philanthropy as a Social Relation

Susan A. Ostrander & Paul G. Schervish

In the decade since the Filer Commission Report, a growing body of research and theory has sought to clarify the nature of philanthropy, the institutional boundaries of the nonprofit sector, and the giving behavior of individuals and organizations. Most of this research conceptualizes and studies the philanthropic world as a world of donors. This work, including some done by the present authors, has focused on explanations of why and how and under what circumstances people give voluntarily of their money and time.

This research is important and should continue. It is also important to recognize that an exclusive focus on donors runs the risk of obscuring issues that are of concern to recipients and therefore to philanthropy as a whole. The common language of giver and receiver used to characterize philanthropy suggests a one-way relationship in which valued goods and services move only in one direction, a point of view we challenge here. A donor focus also ignores the ways in which recipients actively take part in defining what goes on in the world of philanthropy, ways in which recipients are agents in creating philanthropic institutions and relations. Attention tends to be diverted from the social needs that recipients have and that donors seek to address, and from what gifts actually accomplish from the perspective of those who receive them. Strategies that recipients and their advocates use to obtain support are generally left unexplored and unspecified.

Of greatest concern to us here is that the relatively exclusive focus on donors obscures the most fundamental sociological fact about philanthropy; namely, that philanthropy is a social relation of giving and getting between donors and recipients. The major aim of this chapter is to conceptualize and explore philanthropy in this way. This relational understanding of philanthropy elevates the position and priority of the recipient. It brings the recipient into theory, research, and practice in the field. Conceptualizing philanthropy as a social relation has the potential, we believe, for contributing to the making of a better match between the resources and needs of donors and the resources and needs of recipients. It can therefore help to improve philanthropic practice by developing a philanthropy that is more responsive to social need.

We begin this chapter by explaining what we mean by this understanding of philanthropy as social relation. We differentiate philanthropy from two other kinds of social relations, commercial transactions and electoral politics. Next we lay out an array of strategies that the two major parties in the relation—donors and recipients—use to gain the attention and favorable response of the other. Each of the strategies is defined by the relative power with which donors and recipients approach each other, that is, the extent to which each party takes into account the needs and interests of the other. Strategies as we conceive them are composites of three dimensions: complex goals, strategic rationales, and practices. Finally, we consider briefly some implications of our conceptualization of philanthropy and the strategies for philanthropic practices.

Throughout the chapter, we speak of the social relation that is philanthropy as an interaction between what appears to be only two actors: donors and recipients. We recognize, however, that a whole set of actors exist between and within these two sides of the social relation and that mediate the interaction. On the donor side, the relation to recipients is mediated by organizations such as foundations and funding exchanges and by individual office and field staff members who represent such organizations. On the recipient side, the relation to donors is mediated by grant-seeking organizations (including universities, hospitals, museums, churches, and social service agencies) that provide services to clients and consumers and by advocacy groups that work politically for social change. Other organizations and individuals combine donor-side and recipient-side roles, such as the United Way and the Black United Fund, which both raise and disperse funds. Thus, while we speak here of donors and recipients, we in fact mean to include the chain of donor-side and recipient-side agents that represent and carry out the wishes, concerns, and interests of the two ultimate actors at either end of the chain of interaction.

In the following discussion, we speak of recipients most frequently, although not exclusively, as organizations that provide services for clients and consumers or that advocate for social change. In contrast, we tend to speak of donors as individuals who give money to support such organizations. This approach makes sense since over 80 percent of donors are individuals, where virtually all legally recognized tax-exempt recipients of these contributions are organizations.

The strategies we develop here to conceptualize the orientations and actions of recipients and donors in the social relation that is philanthropy emerged from three sources: our own research on philanthropic donors and recipient organizations, the literature on philanthropy and fund raising, and our conversations with other scholars and activists in the world of philanthropy. Donor strategies presented here were developed from the research of Schervish and Herman on wealth and philanthropy.[1] Recipient strategies were developed from what is known about donors and from the trade literature on fund raising[2] as well as indirectly from Ostrander's field work in voluntary social service agencies.[3] A major task for future research is to specify which strategies and under which conditions these are most likely to result in a match between the resources and needs of donors and the resources and needs of recipients.

Philanthropy as a Distinctive Social Relation

Philanthropy, in our way of thinking, is not distinct because of its location in a clearly defined or bounded institutional sector or realm. Philanthropy as we conceive it here is not limited to a "third" or voluntary or nonprofit sector.[4] Our point is that philanthropy is a particular type of social relation that may occur in government and corporate settings, and it most certainly occurs in families and neighborhoods. The other kinds of social relations we look at here—commercial transactions and electoral politics—also are not defined or limited by a particular institutional realm. Commercial transactions occur not only in the economic marketplace but throughout social life wherever goods and services are exchanged for monetary compensation. Electoral politics is not limited to government organizations or the institution of the state but represents a mode of exercising power and decision making wherever votes are taken to establish positions, determine officeholders, and decide policy directions. In the same way, our notion of philanthropy as social relation is more extensive than the notion of philanthropy as institution or organization.

Like other social relations, that between donor-side and recipient-side actors contains identifiable patterns of interaction. Like other social relations, it is a transaction in which both parties get and give as a condition for establishing and maintaining the relation. At the same time, in this and many other social exchanges, the relation between the two parties is not an equal one. For a number of reasons a power difference between donor and recipient emerges from the current character of philanthropy as a social relation. The general tendency is for donors to occupy positions that give them substantially more active choice than recipients about how to define the philanthropic transaction and how to take part in it. Recipients also can and do make choices that affect what happens to themselves and to donors and shape the way philanthropy is organized.

This relative inequality between donors and recipients and the disparity in the extent of active choice available to each party derive from the larger societal context in which philanthropy occurs. We conceptualize this context by drawing on social theory about human agency and societal structure.[5] Social structure both creates and is created by human action and choice in an iterative process. Once created, social structure defines the terms and boundaries of choice, presenting both obstacles and possibilities for action. Donors and recipients, then, are both constrained and facilitated by the structure of philanthropy in what they do and how they think. At the same time, both donors and recipients participate as agents in reinforcing or changing this structure of philanthropy—the structure that then in turn forms the context for their own thinking and acting in the philanthropic world.

Commercial Transactions, Electoral Politics, and Philanthropy

If it is not an institutional or legal boundary that separates philanthropic relations from commerce and politics, then what is it? What distinguishes philanthropy as a particular kind of social relation? The most important distinction we make between philanthropy and commercial and electoral relations revolves around the *media of communication* through which needs are put forth in each case. Each type of relation differs in how a request or demand is made and in how such demand elicits a response. Commercial appeals or demands are made in terms of dollars, while electoral appeals or demands are made in terms of votes. Philanthropic appeals are made in normative or moral or value terms.

In commercial transactions, consumer demands or needs generate a response from suppliers of resources largely to the extent that demands are expressed through dollars. Needs are communicated to suppliers or producers through what economists call "effective demand," that is, demand backed up by and made efficacious by the power of monetary votes or dollars. It is not just the existence of needs or demands that is important in getting a response, but also the fact that these needs can mobilize or generate a response that produces what is demanded. Similarly in electoral politics, needs or interests get attended to largely to the extent that they can be expressed as votes—what one might call another kind of effective demand.

The important question here is just what makes commercial and electoral demands effective in eliciting responses? It is, we believe, that commercial and electoral demands are regulating and "coercive." That is, they are presented through quantifiable media upon which suppliers depend for their very existence in material terms. Elected officials must have votes. Commercial suppliers must have consumer dollars. The demands of voters and consumer dollars cannot in the long run be ignored. In philanthropy the demands are not compelling in the same way.

In philanthropic relations, the media for communicating recipient needs or demands are neither votes nor dollars but rather words and images that are put together in such a way as to make a normative or moral appeal for support. In philanthropy, demand is made efficacious by inviting the supplier or producer to attend primarily to the needs expressed themselves rather than to the medium through which they are expressed. Philanthropy thus recognizes or responds to what can be called "affective" rather than "effective" demand.[6] By this we mean that philanthropy is mobilized and governed by a moral or normative currency that ultimately appeals to the nonmaterial or "affective" aspects of the giver's consciousness rather than to a particular material interest.

This approach to philanthropy should not be interpreted as meaning that demands or needs expressed by institutions or organizations presently defined as "charitable" or philanthropic do in fact always operate according to the moral or normative currency that we see as the defining characteristic of philanthropy defined in these relational terms. Indeed, it is one of our points that the nonprofit sector is no more exclusively the realm of philanthropic relations than the for-profit sector is exclusively the realm of commercial relations or government is the exclusive realm of electoral relations. For instance, nonprofit hospitals may in fact be characterized largely by commercial relations just as for-profit hospitals may in fact respond philanthropically, as we have defined the term, when they mobilize some services around patient need rather than ability to pay. Put simply, when appeals or demands are not expressed primarily in normative or moral terms, they are not philanthropic in the sense we mean that term here, regardless of the social setting from which they come.

The Tendency of Philanthropy to Be Donor-Led

The major consequence for the way that philanthropy works as a social relation arises from its governance more by moral than by material or electoral claims. Because normative appeals do not carry the same kinds of rewards or sanctions as money or votes, philanthropy (unlike commercial transactions or electoral politics) tends to be driven more by the supply of philanthropic resources than by the demand for them based in recipient needs. Because philanthropic appeals are normative or morally based, they tend therefore to be "weaker" and less compelling than when the currency is votes or money. This means that attention to recipient needs may not always remain prominent or determinant in the minds of those providing donor resources or in the minds of those who seek funding on behalf of ultimate beneficiaries.

Commercial and electoral relations retain at least some semblance of consumer and voter sovereignty. That is, they tend to be demand-led in the sense of being responsive in some degree to consumer needs and voter interests. Suppliers or producers in commercial and electoral relations are constrained at least to some extent by the countervailing power of consumers to buy other products from other producers and by voters to cast their ballots for other candidates.

Philanthropic donors—by which we mean suppliers or producers of monetary resources essential for philanthropy—are not similarly constrained by the countervailing power of recipients and their representatives. This is because philanthropy tends to be supply- or donor-led. That is, recipients enjoy little or no ability to ensure or "discipline" the response of donors. Appeals in the form of words and images arranged in a normative display cannot be accumulated as can dollars or votes. As a result, philanthropic donors who supply the resources essential to meeting recipients' needs are not threatened by the withdrawal of the media for expressing the need. The consequences of philanthropy being supply-led are profound for both donors and recipients. We characterize two such major consequences by the terms *donor ascendancy* and *recipient influence*.

Donor Ascendancy and Recipient Influence

Because normative appeals offer little, if any, immediate extrinsic reward or sanction to a potential donor, any single appeal can be refused without any direct negative material consequence. It is, of course, true that donors are not exempt from pressures to give money to "charitable" causes as a part of their climb to success in the corporate world or as a result of belonging to certain social networks.[7] Still, for the most part, the obligation to give money is essentially based on moral grounds—because it is the right and good and sincere gesture to be made—without direct material censure or reward. Normative claims impose this obligation only to the extent that donors recognize and heed them. So recipient groups find themselves dependent on donors not only for funds. Ironically, they depend as well on donors for the very recognition of the legitimacy of the appeals by which recipients make claims on donors in the first place.

The structural tendency in philanthropic relations is, therefore, to grant more power to the donor than to the recipient. As we noted earlier, donors occupy positions that afford them substantially more choice or agency about how they define the social relation that is philanthropy and about how they act and think in it. The concept of agency thus explains more about how the philanthropic world looks and works from the vantage point of the donor. The concept of social structure explains more about the vantage point of the recipient. One of our aims here is to specify the social relation between donor and recipient in such a way as to provide practical guidelines toward empowering recipient groups and the beneficiaries they represent. We want to increase the influence, bargaining power, and choices of strategies available to recipients in their relation with donors and potential donors. Simply defining philanthropy as a social relation in which there is some kind of reciprocal exchange is itself a first step in this direction. As we said earlier, it brings recipients more prominently into the relation.

Given our discussion of philanthropy as donor-led, it is now clearer why and how recipients exercise less choice, power, and influence than donors. Recipients are dependent on donors for their organizational existence and for the well-being of their clients, consumers, and employees. The imperative of finding a donor leads recipients to search actively and continuously, to "prospect" as it is sometimes put in the fund-raising literature. This is done at considerable effort and expense. Small recipient organizations and those whose activities are controversial are at a distinct disadvantage in mounting the fund-raising or "development" efforts. While it is true that some donors choose to search actively for recipients, donors do not have to carry on this kind of activity as a condition of their existence. They can choose among the requests that come to them from grant-seeking recipients. Indeed, one of the problems of being a well-known donor is that one is constantly receiving requests for contributions and having to decide which of them to grant.

Although donors certainly cannot be said to depend on recipients for their actual and material existence, it could be said that donors depend on recipients for the moral and normative and perhaps social meaning of their existence. Recipients have their own influence and their own set of resources to give to donors. In recipient appeals to potential donors, the moral currency that is used is not without value and command. As will be seen in our discussion of philanthropic strategies, donors respond to a whole array of non-material incentives, ranging from making a sincere effort to meet social needs to fulfilling a moral duty, obtaining psychic satisfaction, achieving social and personal legitimation, gaining status in the community, or achieving a social agenda.

Although philanthropy as currently constituted tends toward donor ascendancy, in actual practice the balance of power does not always remain firmly established on the side of the donor. Whenever recipients or their advocates introduce and enforce normative claims or incentives that affect donors, the balance of power begins to shift toward recipients. It is, then, not always the case that philanthropy is governed by the supply of donor resources though this does not refute the structural tendencies we have noted here. Framing the issue in this way does call for a specification of the conditions under which the structural tendencies get modified so that recipients have more influence. The strategies we next consider differ in the extent to which they contain possible directions for creating and strengthening such conditions. As we will show, it is not simply a matter of the degree to which recipients and their needs are taken into account by donors. It is also a matter of the qualitatively different ways in which this comes about.

Strategies in Philanthropy: Modes of Interaction Between Donors and Recipients

By focusing on philanthropic strategies of donors and recipients, we are able to characterize philanthropy in a different way than by types of donor motivations, the size of gifts, or the cause or purpose for which gifts are dedicated. While these matters are certainly important, none really helps us to understand how donors and recipients actively participate in philanthropy. By conceptualizing strategies of philanthropy as modes of consciousness and modes of engagement, we highlight the different ways that people on the donor and recipient sides of the relation come to think about and carry out philanthropy.

The strategies as we conceive them are a composite of three dimensions: a complex goal, a strategic rationale or consciousness, and a strategic practice or mode of engagement. These dimensions can perhaps be best understood as answers to a series of questions. What is the multiple set of goals or ends that each party seeks to accomplish or bring about through participation in the relation? How does each think about or understand the way in which the relationship between them is or ought to be constituted in order to accomplish these ends? How is this presented or communicated to the other so as to gain access and attention? What kinds of claims and appeals are made, and how exactly are they expressed? What does each party actually do? What specific practices are engaged in and how are they carried out?

The strategies, as we have developed them, differ in regard to the quality of the social relation between donor and recipient. We discuss this difference in terms of (1) the kind of involvement, contact, and communication between the two parties or sides; (2) the kind of specific knowledge each has about the other; and (3) the relative priority given by the two parties to what donors want in comparison to what recipients need. An important focus here, as we have said, is one particular aspect of the social relation of philanthropy, namely, the media of expression or communication between donor and recipient. These strategies are not mutually exclusive or exhaustive. A particular donor or recipient probably participates in more than one at a time and the strategies we list are by no means complete. Given our earlier discussion about the donor-led character of philanthropy and the power of the donor, we present donor-side strategies first because we see them as framing an important context within which recipients must think and act.

Donor-Side Philanthropic Strategies. In previous research, Schervish and Herman[8] identified sixteen qualitatively different strategies or "logics" of philanthropy that are carried out by donors, distinguishing them according to differences in goals, modes of consciousness, and modes of practice. Here we discuss nine of those strategies, locating them within three broad approaches by which donors understand and carry out their relation to recipients. The three general donor-side approaches we will consider here are the personal-engagement, mediated-engagement, and donor-oriented strategies (Table 1).

Personal-Engagement Strategies. In the personal-engagement approach, donors attend immediately and directly to the needs of recipients and, as the name implies, are in personal, physical contact with them. We describe three specific types of personal-engagement philanthropy, each of which shares a common set of goals. Individuals who carry out personal-engagement philanthropy are attempting to do more than fulfill their personal aspirations and support a beneficial outcome for recipients. Those who pursue the various types of personal-engagement philanthropy also seek to know and be known by the ultimate beneficiaries of their support and in some cases to allow beneficiaries to actually enforce attention to their needs. The way such donors think about their relationship to recipients reflects a concern to learn as much as possible about the recipients and their specific needs. Accordingly, the distinctive practice that characterizes personal-engagement forms of philanthropy revolves around efforts to be in personal contact with recipients, to learn their appeals, and to ensure that these appeals become binding on them.

   A number of diverse types of philanthropy fall under this general category of personal-engagement philanthropy. The extreme instance of the direct personal matching of donor resources to recipient needs is *consumption philanthropy.* In this approach donors contribute to causes or organizations from which these donors directly benefit. The match is so complete simply because the donor and beneficiary are the same. Consumption philanthropy, it turns out, is the largest single category of philanthropy because

TABLE 1

Donor-Side Strategies

Personal-Engagement Strategies: direct personal contact and exchange of information between donors and beneficiaries, with priority given to recipient needs

   1. *Consumption*: donor is also beneficiary of gift

   2. *Therapeutic/empowering*: donors seek simultaneously to enhance their own sense of self-empowerment and to give over some active organizational control to beneficiaries

   3. *Adoptive*: donors attend personally to recipient needs in an ongoing and multifaceted relationship

Mediated-Engagement Strategies: contact between donors and recipients mediated by organizations or other individuals though knowledge and concern for recipient needs may be high

   1. *Contributory*: donor gives to a cause with no direct contact with recipient

   2. *Brokering*: donors solicit other key donors in their own network

   3. *Catalytic*: organizers donate time to mobilize large number of other donors in a mass appeal

Donor-Oriented Strategies: donors governed and mobilized by their own circumstances rather than by those of recipients

   1. *Exchange*: giving propelled by mutual obligation within a network of donors

   2. *Derivative*: giving based on obligations associated with job expectations or family responsibilities

   3. *Noblesse oblige*: philanthropy grows out of decision to designate part of family money for social involvement

it includes contributions to churches, schools, cultural institutions, and professional organizations, from which givers and their families directly benefit.

Even though the other two forms of personal-engagement philanthropy are much less prominent, they are important to describe because they indicate possible directions for the future development of philanthropy. One such approach is what we call *therapeutic* or *empowerment* philanthropy as it takes form in various funding organizations such as the Vanguard Foundation and the Funding Exchange. The term *therapeutic* is coupled with the term *empowerment* to emphasize how the practice of philanthropy is viewed and concretely organized by donors to come to grips simultaneously with their own need to become personally empowered in regard to their wealth and their desire to empower others. The feelings of donors who pursue this approach that their own needs have been denied or obscured in their lives of wealth lead them to be particularly sensitive to the experience of powerlessness among those at the opposite end of the economic spectrum. The upshot is the creation of an organizational structure with two unique aspects. First, in regard to donors there is a requirement that they contribute relatively equal amounts so that no one donor is overly able to influence decisions. Also, there is the more or less informal expectation that donors will meet among themselves to discuss how they can grow in their self-understanding as socially responsible wealthy individuals. Second, in regard to recipients, such donors constitute boards of directors composed of nondonors, representatives of recipient groups, and beneficiaries. They also establish organizational bylaws that ensure the articulation and enforcement of recipient claims by limiting or even eliminating giver control over funding decisions.

A third form of personal-engagement philanthropy is called *adoptive* philanthropy. In adoptive philanthropy, donors become personally involved in the lives of the beneficiaries they seek to help. This is typified by Eugene Lang's and others' efforts in the I Have a Dream program. In addition to devoting funds to a cause, the goal is for donors to involve themselves directly in the lives of inner-city students in an effort to motivate and guide them toward a college education. Working in and supporting the Boys Club and Girls Club and in Big Sister and Big Brother programs are obvious examples. Others include efforts by suburban churches to assist inner-city churches, corporations that commit themselves to develop a particular neighborhood or assist particular schools, individuals who assist particular artists or scholars as does the MacArthur family, and a respondent in the Study on Wealth and Philanthropy who supports a writer's retreat for women. Many other examples could be enumerated, but the point *is*, again, that personal attention to particular needs of the beneficiaries is foremost in the donor's mind, in part because the recipient is physically in the donor's social world.

Although substantially different in how they come to recognize and heed the moral claims of recipients, adoptive, therapeutic/empowerment, and consumption donors all have in common the highest regard for the needs of the recipients. In fact, by being so directly in contact with the ultimate beneficiaries and not just with their advocates, such donors often go so far as to give over legal governance at least in part to these beneficiaries, their advocates, or third-party professionals such as social workers and academics.

Mediated-Engagement Strategies. A second level and type of attention to recipient issues is represented by a variety of strategies in which contacts with the recipients are indirect or mediated by organizations or individuals who serve as advocates on behalf of recipients. In general terms, the composite goal is to contribute to important concerns while, at the same time, remaining somewhat insulated from having to expend time in contact with ultimate beneficiaries. If the strategy of personal engagement is like retail relations in the commercial sphere, mediated engagement is like wholesale relations. The strategic consciousness revolves around discerning how much and to what one should contribute while the practice tends to be limited to making such contributions and getting others to do so as well.

The most common form of such mediated engagement is termed *contributory* philanthropy. This approach, second only to consumption philanthropy in the amount of giving, is the form most likely to occur in all income groups and is the most familiar popular image of philanthropy. The contributory strategy revolves quite simply around obtaining and mobilizing financial resources on behalf of a cause. The term *contributory* is used to emphasize the fact that philanthropic involvement is primarily in the form of monetary contributions rather than in time or skills. In addition, there is virtually no direct contact between the donor and the ultimate beneficiary. Rather, the moral appeal to which donors respond is formulated and presented by a grant-seeking or advocacy organization. This, of course, is the most common mode of fund raising by such groups as OXFAM America, CARE, the NAACP, universities, hospitals, symphony orchestras, peace groups, and numerous other traditional and progressive organizations devoted to raising funds for important causes and needy recipients. It is important to note that the contributory strategy often reflects a very high level of commitment and devotion by contributors to fulfilling the needs of the ultimate beneficiaries and, indeed, to the beneficiaries themselves. But the relation to them remains indirect and impersonal, mediated by various intermediary organizations and individuals.

A second form of mediated interaction occurs in *brokering* philanthropy. Here organizational officers, board members, or other interested parties devote their efforts to fund raising by seeking contributions from major donors. Once again, a high degree of affective commitment may motivate brokering donors as they demonstrate by spending time and effort to solicit contributions from others. We usually see this strategy exercised by wealthy individuals who turn to their social and business associates to raise funds for a cause. But such brokering is not limited to efforts by the rich to solicit contributions from their peers. The nonwealthy also pursue the brokering strategy by seeking pledges from friends and associates for each mile traversed in the various "walks" and "runs" on behalf of efforts to relieve hunger and cure AIDS, to name just two.

A less widespread but equally visible form of mediated engagement is *catalytic* philanthropy. If the vast majority of participants in the mass-involvement types of philanthropy like Boston's Walk for Hunger are engaging in brokering philanthropy, many of those organizing and directing such efforts are engaging in catalytic philanthropy. Like brokering philanthropy, the major goal is broadening the base for fund raising on behalf of a cherished cause but, again, without requiring any direct involvement with beneficiaries by those giving time and money. In contrast to brokering philanthropy, however, the catalytic strategy—as its name implies—is directed toward mobilizing not a small number of personally known peers but a large number of unknown contributors. Accordingly, catalytic philanthropy is often led by media stars, sports figures, and other celebrities. They lend their names, notoriety, and personal efforts to raise money by eliciting an affective engagement of a broad popular base. What the sociologist Robert Merton discovered more than forty years ago in his study of Kate Smith's dramatic success in getting Americans to invest in war bonds is directly relevant here. The public's perception of personal sacrifice and dedication by celebrities on behalf of a cause induces more contributions than what would be generated by a verbal appeal alone. Even when the central figures who lead such catalytic projects are not publicly known at the inception of a massparticipation drive, they often become so over time. For instance, those of us who live in Boston have witnessed how the dramatic success of the Walk for Hunger coincided with the rise to prominence of its inspirational founder and organizer, Dan Daley.

In contrast to the strategy of personal engagement, then, the strategy of mediated engagement does not entail a direct knowledge of or contact with the final beneficiaries of the philanthropic efforts—although the strategy does not preclude it. The major advantage of this strategy is its relatively efficient fund-raising process—one that appeals to donors because it leaves them relatively unencumbered in that they can retain whatever degree of social distance from the recipients they desire. The most serious disadvantage is that in the absence of a systematic direct contact between donors and recipients, it is possible for extraphilanthropic personal and organizational goals to become substituted for the moral claims of beneficiaries. Donors continue to respond to direct normative appeals in this strategy. However, there is the possibility of substantial slippage between how such normative appeals are recognized and responded to when mediated by advocacy groups and how they might be recognized and responded to if donors were placed in personal contact with those in need.

Donor-Oriented Strategies. A third general strategy encompasses a number of philanthropic approaches that tend to be governed almost exclusively by donor-side rather than recipient-side considerations. The major characteristic of what we call a donor-oriented giving strategy is that it is primarily attentive not to recipient needs but to donor interests and obligations. It is not the pull of engagement with recipients but the push of obligation that governs this strategy. The complex goal or teleology of donor-based philanthropy, then, revolves around fulfilling a set of obligations derived from family, business, or social relationships. Dedication to specific causes remains a goal of philanthropy, but it is not key to what mobilizes philanthropy in the first place. The strategic consciousness centers around learning and recognizing the expectations of one's position in relation to peers rather than in relation to those outside one's personal circle. The major practice is moving back and forth between responding to the expectations derived from one's social position and getting others in one's social purview to do the same.

Concretely, one prominent form of donor-based giving is *exchange* philanthropy. In this strategy, individuals give to a cause at the request of an associate in anticipation that in the future they will be able to call upon that associate to contribute to their cause. Individuals participate in a network of friends and associates each of whom feels free to call upon the other to support a favored project. Again, it is not that the beneficiaries disappear completely from the picture; it is just that the needs of beneficiaries are not what motivates philanthropy in the sense of setting it in motion. In contrast to the affective dedication surrounding personal-engagement and even mediated-engagement philanthropy, exchange philanthropy is matter of fact and dispassionate in tone. Whatever urgency emerges results not from what individual donors deem important but from the need to fulfill a social obligation that reproduces the bonds in a social network of friends and associates.

In a similar vein is *derivative* philanthropy, in which philanthropy is once again starkly supply-led in the sense that giving of money and time is derived from the everyday expectations of employment or social status. Schervish and Herman[9] found that this gets played out most commonly in two arenas. The first is at the workplace. A number of respondents indicated that they expect their senior staff to be engaged in some form of philanthropic activity or community involvement as a condition for working in their firm. Other, respondents, especially attorneys, indicated that they were on the receiving end of such imposed obligation, again in the form of service within the broader community and not simply in the performance of pro bono legal work. The second arena wherein derivative philanthropy is relatively prominent is in volunteer networks of women of the upper class. Here the traditional family and social roles accorded wealthy women become expressed in the realm of philanthropy as the expectation that they devote substantial amounts of time to various volunteer activities, ranging from the simplest clerical tasks to the most arduous of managerial responsibilities. Although younger generations of women eschew the imposition of such roles and many who carry them out are deeply critical of their status, the point is that this is a form of philanthropy that is clearly supply-led. The engagement of donors occurs in response to the mobilization of normative expectations in their own world rather than the mobilization of moral claims in the world of others.

A final form of donor-initiated mobilization is *noblesse oblige* philanthropy. This term is used in a nonpejorative sense to emphasize that for many the inherited practice of philanthropy is derived from the expectation that community involvement is a traditional family obligation. What connects this strategy to inherited wealth is not an attitude of condescending parentalism but the fact that those pursuing this strategy inherit along with their wealth a set of expectations about how they are to use their wealth. Money is conceived as divided into three categories: an untouchable principal or capital, an amount for daily consumption, and an amount for philanthropic endeavors. Once again it is the nature of socialization and an understanding of money derived from a particular status—here, membership in an established family line—that induce philanthropic activity, rather than the pull of moral obligation. Recipient needs may come into play in determining the specific causes to which such individuals devote their time and money, but the fact of involvement is determined from another quarter, namely, a preexistent duty to allocate a certain part of one's time and money to philanthropic endeavors.

As we will also see in the case of the recipient-side strategies, the donor-side strategies can be understood as differing in regard to the kind of relationship that exists and is carried out between donors and recipients. The three specific approaches summarized under the rubric of donor-oriented giving exemplify that pole of the relationship most expressive of the underlying tendency of philanthropy as it is now organized to be supply- or donor-led. Exchange, derivative, and noblesse oblige philanthropy all center around efforts by donors to fulfill obligations derived from relations with those in their social circle rather than from relations with recipients. In the strategies grouped together as mediated-engagement philanthropy, there is a shift in psychological attention toward the needs of beneficiaries and a shift in practice toward heeding and responding to the world of beneficiaries even though personal contact with recipients does not occur. The most direct communication and contact between donors and recipients takes place, as we have said, in the personal-engagement strategies such as consumption, adoption, and therapeutic/empowerment philanthropy. Compared to donor-oriented approaches, especially, personal-engagement strategies shift the direction of concern to the ultimate beneficiaries of philanthropy. It is not just that donors come to heed the needs of recipients in a more direct and responsive manner that distinguishes approaches to philanthropy that bring donors and recipients into personal contact. It is also that a set of conditions are set in motion that have the potential for transforming the very way donors and recipients think about and interact with each other, both individually and as social groups.

Recipient-Side Philanthropic Strategies

We have developed three strategies that recipient organizations can use to gain the attention and favorable response of donors and potential donors. They are needs-based, opportunity-based, and agenda-based strategies (Table 2).

Needs-Based Strategy. The foremost goal of the needs-based strategy is to put forth as straightforwardly and in as unmediated a fashion as possible the preeminence of beneficiaries' needs. The

TABLE 2

Recipient-Side Strategies

Needs-Based Strategy: needs of beneficiaries are presented forthrightly to donors as the sole basis for mobilizing contributions; these needs may be presented either by the beneficiaries themselves or by recipient organizations or groups on their behalf

- Recipient frames need as inherently worthy of attention

- Recipient poses relationship to donor as a collaboration around a shared responsibility

- Recipient appeals revolve around efforts to communicate information about beneficiaries and their need

Opportunity-Based Strategy: needs of beneficiaries are recast and expressed as donor opportunities representing social or political benefit for the donor beyond simply responding to the needs themselves

- Recipients' appeals are formulated to persuade donors that responding to the needs of beneficiaries simultaneously provides donors with valued rewards

- Recipients may present the proposed project or program as an opportunity for the donors to make an innovative or distinctive contribution to the community, to enhance their own status or influence, to make a good investment, or to enter a prominent donor network

- Recipients may offer donors reduced costs or special access to programs or activities of recipient organizations

Agenda-Based Strategy: needs of beneficiaries are submerged and even compromised as recipients offer donors the chance to fulfill interests arising from events or circumstances in the donors' personal, family, or professional life

- Recipients cultivate personal relationships with current and prospective donors by focusing on what donors want or need as the condition or incentive for making a gift

- Recipients remain alert to new and emerging donor agendas as old agendas are fulfilled or fade in importance

- Recipients often maintain and update detailed prospecting files on individual donors

central concern always remains the depth and scope of the needs and interests of the people—potential clients, consumers, beneficiaries—for whom or with whom the philanthropic project is being proposed and carried out. The two major ways that beneficiaries' needs may be directly and forthrightly communicated to donors are, first, for a grant-seeking organization to serve as a broker between donors and beneficiaries and, second, for beneficiaries to frame and express their needs directly to donors on their own. In some cases, the two approaches are joined, as when beneficiaries become an integral part of the group actively seeking funds. This is the case, for example, with a battered-women's shelter whose staff and board members seeking the grant include women who have been or might be in the future residents of the shelter.

Given such a strong focus on the needs and interests of the beneficiaries, beneficiaries are more likely to be involved directly in this strategy than in the opportunity- or agenda-based strategy. Indeed this involvement is itself often one of the goals of the needs-based strategy. If beneficiaries are not involved directly (as is perhaps most often the case), grant seekers still press clearly, forcefully, and sometimes dramatically the import of their need. This is the case, for example, with the appeals made by Mother Teresa. In addition to convincing donors of the import of the need itself and involving ultimate beneficiaries in the philanthropic process, those pursuing the needs-based strategy often seek to educate the community as a whole in an effort to press the needs in a broader arena.

The strategic consciousness or rationale expressed in a needs-based strategy focuses on a relationship between donor and recipient of a shared sense of responsibility and obligation to the community and its needs. Donors are not held in special esteem in this view. Rather, they are often seen as collaborators in a relationship of mutual respect and cooperation. Recipients take it as a given that donors wish to contribute and be involved in projects that seek to address community needs, and that if given the chance to do so, they will come forward and give what they can. Recipient groups are not hesitant in their zeal for seeking funds, and the relationship is conceived as being less hierarchical than is typically the case. The intrinsic rewards for donor contributions are highly valued both by the recipients and by the donors to whom this kind of appeal is attractive. These rewards include the intrinsic worth of being part of a community with connections to others and the inherent satisfaction of doing with and for others.

Recipient-side practices consistent with a needs-based strategy are targeted toward donors who are likely to be responsive to a direct and immediate appeal. Possible specific fund-raising tactics might include mailings to lists of donors who have given to similar programs. Mailings would likely include substantial amounts of concrete, explicit information about the need or interest being addressed. Testimony from potential or actual beneficiaries might be included. Telephoning from known lists and door-to-door campaigning, especially in areas most affected, are other tactics consistent with this strategy. Public speaking engagements, ads in the public media, and opportunities for donors to meet with potential or current beneficiaries could be arranged.

From the point of view of recipient-side organizations, the needs-based strategy has a number of advantages. It allows these recipient groups and the beneficiaries with whom and for whom they work to define the issues or needs that are important and the projects most appropriate and feasible to address them. Because the needs-based strategy focuses the appeal to donors around these points, it is the most recipient centered.

Opportunity-Based Strategy. In the recipient-side strategy we call the opportunity-based strategy, the mode of gaining access to the donor and a favorable response shifts toward the donor. While the importance of the needs addressed and the value of the project designed to address them are not ignored in this or any other strategy, here recipient needs are mediated through and expressed as donor opportunities. The goal of the transaction is to persuade the donor of the value of this opportunity. It is a strategy that requires that the recipient have more specific knowledge about the donor and what the donor might want and value than is the case with a needs-based strategy.

The strategic consciousness or rationale on the part of the recipient in the opportunity-based strategy conceives of the relationship with the donor as one in which the recipient who is seeking the grant must pose some reward—perhaps social or political or even indirectly material—that will induce the donor to make a gift. Giving is not seen as its own reward here, and so the recipients feel indebted to and beholden to the donor. This is less likely to occur in the needs-based strategy, where recipients do not feel compelled to provide something extrinsic in return for a gift.

The basis for asking donor support here is what recipients have to offer to donors beyond the satisfaction of giving itself. Recipients can offer donors the opportunity to be seen as innovators in the community, to make their mark by funding a project posed as a new and exciting solution or an innovative response to a need or interest. Appeals may be expressed so as to persuade donors to give to a program that is professionally managed, fiscally responsible, and efficiently organized—in other words, a good investment. The recipient group may offer, explicitly or implicitly, the donor the chance to be brought into the organization in a decision-making position as a member of the board. This may be presented in such a way as to imply that the donor's position at his or her place of business may be enhanced by such voluntary activity, thus contributing to the donor's economic and social well-being. Becoming a donor may be presented by recipient groups that are seeking a gift as the opportunity to become part of a community network of other donors of high status, thus also enhancing one's own social position and opportunity to have a voice in community affairs. To facilitate such networks and to provide entertainment as well as raise funds, recipient groups that use the opportunity-based strategy may organize events that provide donors a chance to see friends and be seen, to combine pleasure with social conscience. While some donors may view this kind of appeal as an onerous social obligation, to others it is an indispensable part of their social and business lives. The onus is on the recipient group that is seeking the gift to discover what will appeal to which donors and to carry out that particular form of appeal.

The practices used to express the opportunity-based strategy seem likely to include a strong visual packaging of the program as innovative and exciting, as an entrepreneurial opportunity for the donor. A selling package that emphasizes financial reports and evaluations of the program and its organization might be used. Donors with high name recognition and social status or "star" status may be used to appeal to other potential donors. The recipient organization may offer donors free or reduced-cost services, such as discounted subscriptions to symphonies, museums, and theaters, or implicit promises to university donors that members of their family will have an edge in admission. In these instances, the donor also becomes a user, as in the earlier discussion of consumption philanthropy.

In the opportunity-based strategy, groups that are seeking grants must still argue the importance of the need persuasively, but this and the capacity of the proposed project to meet the need are not seen as sufficient to get the gift. In addition, this strategy requires that the recipient group obtain information about potential donors that anticipates what they might want as the basis for an appeal. It requires that recipients learn relevant fund-raising techniques that focus not just on their needs but on the interests of the donors.

Agenda-Based Strategy. The third and final recipient-side strategy for seeking funds we will describe here is the most donor centered of the three. An agenda-based strategy is organized around and mediated through tactics that pose for donors a chance to carry out some preestablished agenda of their own or to fulfill some interest arising from an event in their family, professional, or business life. Recipients approach fund raising by locating specific donors who have some agenda and by persuading them—often indirectly and with discretion—that the agenda can be met in the course of giving to a certain project or organization. This strategy requires that the recipient have detailed and personal knowledge of the donor. It is a strategy that requires an investment on the part of recipient groups that can be made only by the largest, most affluent, and most professionally staffed grant-seeking organizations.

The claims that recipient groups that use this strategy make on donors include some event in the donor's life, such as a recent inheritance, change in marital status or parental status, graduation from college, geographical move, or illness or death of a family member. Files that catalogue this kind of information are kept on current and potential donors. Critical events in business or professional life include a recent promotion, surge in company profits, new position on a board of directors, a geographical move of corporate headquarters, or the need to counter some adverse publicity as a result of a boycott, union strike, industrial accident, or pollution alert.

The specific practices that accompany an agenda-based strategy for grant seeking are articulated in the fund-raising literature on what is called "prospecting" and in advertisements for costly workshops where recipient groups learn the techniques appropriate to this strategy. Expensive reference manuals with names, addresses, and other personal information about wealthy donors are printed and frequently updated. The fund-raising literature that emphasizes this approach advises recipient groups to do "investigative work" on potential donors and to keep elaborate and detailed "prospecting files" on individuals who may be persuaded to give.[10] Information from personal conversations between donors and the staff or volunteers of the grant-seeking organizations and from a wide range of other sources such as newspaper clippings are to be included in these files. Annual reports of the donor's business are collected along with any other information that can be found about the donor's company. Medical records, credit records, family counseling files, and academic records are referred to in one source as "hot potatoes" that should be used with discretion and a sensitivity to the need for confidentiality. Grant seekers are cautioned by one fund-raising manual that though "It may take a long time to establish a real working relationship with the keepers of these records," the rewards will be worth the effort and the grant seeker should stay with it.[11]

The agenda-based strategy seems problematic from the point of view of many recipient groups and, in at least some instances, the donor as well. The outlay of resources on the part of the recipient is very high, and some ethical questions seem troublesome. The use of donors' medical and counseling records does not seem to us justifiable no matter how effective they might be in getting a gift. The need of clients and consumers seems to almost disappear in the agenda-based strategy, and the usefulness of the project in meeting that need is at best seen as secondary. The strategy seems most suited to a donor base of a small number of large donors, given the investment that must be made in order to get the gift. The donor may be personally very involved in the recipient organization if convinced that a personal agenda can be played out and a donor need met. The basis for the donor's involvement, however, may or may not be consistent with what recipients and beneficiaries want or need. Once the donor has fulfilled his or her need, interest in making further gifts to the recipient organization may end. Donors with their own agenda may also expect—or be seen by recipients as expecting—formal and public recognition of their efforts, such as naming opportunities and ceremonies of appreciation that are highly publicized.

The three recipient-side strategies we have outlined here differ according to the kind of involvement between donor and recipient, knowledge about the other, and the relative priority given to donor or recipient interests. Involvement of the various parties and contact among them over time seem highest in the needs-based strategy, where donors, beneficiaries, and recipient groups are all very invested in addressing the need or concern in a collaborative manner. Since the needs-based strategy is centered around beneficiary needs, recipient groups and donors are required to know only of each other's mutual interest and concern as a condition for the gift and for the relationship between them.

In the opportunity-based strategy, the degree of involvement or contact of the various parties with one another is less than in the needs-based strategy. They are required to have enough contact with one another for the recipient to receive the gift and for the donor to fulfill the desired opportunity obtainable through the gift. Recipients would seem to require somewhat more detailed information about donors than is the case in the needs-based strategy. Since the opportunity-based strategy is more donor centered than the needs-based strategy, the recipient organization has to know what opportunities will appeal to which potential donors, and donors have to know what opportunities are being offered beyond the chance to respond to and participate in some community project or program.

The agenda-based strategy requires recipients to accrue perhaps the most intensive knowledge of a personal nature about donors. The appeal for a gift is mediated through a personal, private agenda of the donor's that the recipient discovers through detailed investigation. Since this strategy is almost exclusively donor centered, recipients must have detailed information about the donors in order to ascertain their agenda.

Implications for the Practice of Philanthropy

As we have discussed, philanthropy typically is mobilized and governed more by availability of donor resources than by the existence of recipient needs. The implications of what we have had to say here about reconceptualizing philanthropy as a social relation between donor and recipient and about developing and applying philanthropic strategies that represent the interests and concerns of donors and recipients flow from this tension that is generated by a supply-led or donor-led process. As a counterbalance to the structural tendency of philanthropy to be supply-led—and therefore for donors to have more power in the relation than recipients—conditions need to be specified under which recipients can and do have influence in the philanthropic relation. As we have said, it is our belief that this counterbalance—that bringing recipients in—will improve the quality and performance of philanthropy for donors and recipients.

One principle in particular seems to derive from the arguments we have made here: donors have needs to be fulfilled as well as resources to grant, and recipients have resources to give as well as needs to be met. In other words, *donors and recipients both give and get in the social relation that is philanthropy*. In consumption philanthropy, where donors and recipients are one and the same, we see that recipient needs are the most heeded. We think it is not accidental that such consumption philanthropy turns out to be the largest form of philanthropy in terms of size of contributions. What can be learned from this is not that consumptive philanthropy itself should be extended but rather that contributions are mobilized most strongly when donors see their interests and concerns to be the same as those of recipients or closely identified with them. This is counter to the more traditional view of philanthropic relation in which givers and receivers are socially distant and hierarchically arranged.

In each of the strategies we have laid out here, donors and recipients can be seen both as wanting something from each other and as having something to give that the other values. If recipients could be clearer about this, it would counter their tendency to go "hat in hand" to potential donors. It seems to us that recipients could use the needs-based strategy more often than our review of the fund-raising literature would suggest they do, or at least are advised by that literature to do. A fundamental assumption made over and over in this literature is that donors will not give to a project simply because it is presented as an effective way to address an important community need or interest. The desire on the part of a donor to be a part of a community effort, the satisfaction of being an active participant in creating one's own community and being connected to others in a collaborative project, the enlightened self-interest on the part of donors who recognize that they might benefit directly or indirectly from some philanthropic project—these are not seen as sufficient to motivate donors to give. In *Proven Tips and Secrets for Winning Grant $$*, for example, grant seekers are advised that while they "must present a clear picture of why [their] program is necessary" and they must "solicit community involvement in the grantsmanship process," the most important factor is the ability to "tailor each proposal to the individual requirements of funders."[12] Grant seekers are urged to keep the donors' wants constantly in mind and to "appeal to them often" in the proposal.[13] Even more bluntly, *Grantsmanship: Money and How to Get It* advises, "Tailor the letter [of inquiry] to the [funding] organization's opportunity, not the applicant's need."[14]

This kind of advice, repeated frequently and, as the above quotations illustrate, in very similar language, seems to advocate the use of what we have conceptualized here as the opportunity-based and agenda-based recipient-side strategies of grant seeking. Although these strategies may be effective in one sense, they are the most donor centered, and they require the largest investment and effort on the part of recipients. The agenda-based strategy in particular requires that recipient groups have a substantial amount of information about donors in order to find out what donors want and how they as recipients might satisfy those wants as a condition of "winning" the gift. The fund-raising techniques that are applied, again, especially in the agenda-based approach, often require the counsel of "experts" who constitute a whole new industry that can be called the fund-raising business. Clients and consumers, along with the needs and interests they carry, are the least visible in these strategies and the appeals and practices that derive from them.

The needs-based strategy that we have conceptualized here places the concerns and interests of the grant-seeking organization and the clients and consumers it serves at the center. It is less costly to carry out. It empowers recipients because they are the ones who define the need and the program, ideally in collaboration and in dialogue with clients and consumers and with donors. The depth and scope of the need and the interest in all parties in addressing that need with an effective program are seen as sufficient to win the gift. Donors are envisioned as members of the community who have resources that they are willing to contribute in return for the satisfaction of community involvement and participation. While individual donors may indeed use their philanthropic activities to create opportunities for themselves or to carry out their own personal or professional agendas, these are not the focus of the grant-seeking organization's appeals. They are seen as individual matters not at the center of the social relation that is philanthropy.

Our call for a recipient movement toward the needs-based strategy corresponds to a parallel call for a donor movement away from donor-oriented strategies and toward mediated-engagement, especially personal-engagement, philanthropy. From the point of view of donor strategies, the implication is to encourage increased donor engagement—both personal and psychological—in the needs and interests of recipients. Such engagement may well lead to increased monetary contributions by donors, but this is not the only or even the most important consequence. Engagement between donors and recipients has the potential for transforming the practice of philanthropy in a more profound way. The projects funded may become more in line with what people need and less with what they can get funded. As the hierarchical and nonreciprocal distinction between donor and recipient becomes replaced with more collaborative approaches, philanthropy has the potential of becoming more innovative and creative, not only in regard to types of social projects that it initiates but in regard to the interactive quality of social relations that it exemplifies.[15] A philanthropic practice that emphasizes a personal-engagement strategy for donors and a needs-based strategy for recipients would be organized around the values of reciprocity, cooperation, mutual respect, accountability, and commitment.

By conceptualizing philanthropy as a social relation rather than as an institution, sector, or organization, we have attempted to locate in a positive way the distinctive attribute of philanthropy. What constitutes philanthropy is not the legal tax status of an organization or the deductibility of a contribution. Rather, it is an interaction between donors and recipients that revolves around an effort to match what donors have to give to recipients with what recipients have to give to donors. Much of this matching tends to be talked about as donors giving concrete resources to recipients and recipients giving nonmaterial or intrinsic rewards to donors. This is true enough for much of the current practice of philanthropy. However, our definition of philanthropy as a social relation and how it gets carried out in the more mutual donor and recipient strategies indicates that there is more to it than this. When philanthropy is practiced at its best, donors are given material opportunities—and not just psychic rewards—through their relation to recipients. In turn, recipients are given various kinds of nonmaterial resources—in addition to material support—such as respect, empowerment, and esteem when philanthropy is recognized and carried out as a reciprocal social relation.

In this chapter we have taken the first step toward conceptualizing philanthropy as a reciprocal relation and toward laying out a range of strategies that donors and recipients use in that relation to orient and guide their behavior. It is the task of future research to specify the conditions and circumstances that increase the use of the strategies that are most open to bringing recipients into philanthropy as mutual partners.

Notes

1. Andrew Herman and Paul G. Schervish, "Varieties of Philanthropic Practice Among the Wealthy." Paper presented at Annual Spring Research Forum of INDEPENDENT SECTOR, New York, Mar. 19–20, 1987; Paul G. Schervish and Andrew Herman, *Final Report: The Study on Wealth and Philanthropy*. Submitted to the T. B. Murphy Foundation Charitable Trust, Boston College, 1988.
2. See, for example, *Fundraising Review*, Feb. 1982 through Dec. 1987; Jerald Panas, *Mega-Gifts: Who Gives Them, Who Gets Them*. Chicago: Pluribus Press, 1984; Michael Seltzer, *Securing Your Organization's Future*. New York: Foundation Center, 1987.

3. Susan A. Ostrander, "Voluntary Social Service Agencies in the United States." *Social Services Review*, Sept. 1985, *59*, 435–454; "Elite Domination in Private Social Service Agencies: How It Happens and How It Is Challenged." In Thomas R. Dye and G. William Domhoff (eds.), *Power Elites and Organizations*. Newbury Park, Calif.: Sage, 1987; "Private Social Services: Obstacles to the Welfare State?" *Nonprofit and Voluntary Sector Quarterly* (formerly *Journal of Voluntary Action Research*), 1989, *1*.

4. Peter Dobkin Hall, "Abandoning the Rhetoric of Independence: Reflections on the Nonprofit Sector in the Post-Liberal Era"; Susan A. Ostrander, "Introduction" and "Toward Implications for Research, Theory, and Policy on Nonprofits and Voluntarism"; and Jon Van Til, "The Three Sectors: Voluntarism in a Changing Political Economy." In Susan A. Ostrander, Stuart Langton, and Jon Van Til (eds.), *Shifting the Debate: Public/Private Sector Relations in the Modern Welfare State*. New Brunswick, N.J.: Transaction Books, 1987. See also Paul G. Schervish, "Bringing Recipients Back In: Philanthropy as a Social Relation." Paper presented at INDEPENDENT SECTOR Academic Retreat, Indianapolis, June 7–8, 1988; and Jon Van Til, *Mapping the Third Sector*. New York: Foundation Center, 1988.

5. Anthony Giddens, *The Constitution of Society*. Cambridge, Mass.: Polity Press, 1985; Paul G. Schervish, Andrew Herman, and Lynn Rhenisch, "Towards a General Theory of the Philanthropic Activities of the Wealthy." Paper presented at Annual Spring Research Forum of INDEPENDENT SECTOR, New York, Mar. 13–14, 1986.

6. Schervish and Herman.

7. Joseph Galaskiewicz, *Gifts, Givers, and Getters: Business Philanthropy in an Urban Setting*. New York: Academic Press, 1986; Susan A. Ostrander, *Women of the Upper Class*. Philadelphia: Temple University Press, 1984; Michael Useem, *The Inner Circle*. New York: Oxford University Press, 1984.

8. Schervish and Herman.

9. Schervish and Herman.

10. James K. Hickey and Elizabeth Kochoo, *Prospecting: Searching Out the Philanthropic Dollar*. (2nd ed.) Washington, D.C.: Taft Corporation, 1984; Jeanne B. Jenkins and Marilyn Lucas, *How to Find Philanthropic Prospects*. Ambler, Pa.: Fundraising Institute, 1986.

11. Jenkins and Lucas, p. 16.

12. Education Funding Research Council, *Proven Tips and Secrets for Winning Grant $$*. Arlington, Va.: Government Information Services, 1987, p. 36.

13. Education Funding Research Council, p. 46.

14. Marquis Academic Media, *Grantsmanship: Money and How to Get It*. (2nd ed.) Chicago: Marquis Academic Media, 1987.

15. Susan A. Ostrander, "Why Philanthropy Neglects Poverty: Some Thoughts from History and Theory." In Virginia A. Hodgkinson, Richard Lyman, and Associates, *The Future of the Nonprofit Sector: Challenges, Changes, and Policy Considerations*. San Francisco: Jossey-Bass, 1989.

* The authors are listed in alphabetical order. Paul Schervish would like to gratefully acknowledge Andrew Herman, who helped develop a number of the ideas concerning the theoretical nature of philanthropy and the strategies of philanthropy carried out by donors.

THE IRON CAGE REVISITED: INSTITUTIONAL ISOMORPHISM AND COLLECTIVE RATIONALITY IN ORGANIZATIONAL FIELDS

PAUL J. DIMAGGIO & WALTER W. POWELL

In *The Protestant Ethic and the Spirit of Capitalism*, Max Weber warned that the rationalist spirit ushered in by asceticism had achieved a momentum of its own and that, under capitalism, the rationalist order had become an iron cage in which humanity was, save for the possibility of prophetic revival, imprisoned "perhaps until the last ton of fossilized coal is burnt" (Weber 1952:181–82). In his essay on bureaucracy, Weber returned to this theme, contending that bureaucracy, the rational spirit's organizational manifestation, was so efficient and powerful a means of controlling men and women that, once established, the momentum of bureaucratization was irreversible (Weber [1922] 1978).

The imagery of the iron cage has haunted students of society as the tempo of bureaucratization has quickened. But while bureaucracy has spread continuously in the eighty years since Weber wrote, we suggest that the engine of organizational rationalization has shifted. For Weber, bureaucratization resulted from three related causes: competition among capitalist firms in the marketplace; competition among states, increasing rulers' need to control their staff and citizenry; and bourgeois demands for equal protection under the law. Of these three, the most important was the competitive marketplace. "Today," Weber [1922] 1978:974) wrote, "it is primarily the capitalist market economy which demands that the official business of administration be discharged precisely, unambiguously, continuously, and with as much speed as possible. Normally, the very large, modern capitalist enterprises are themselves unequalled models of strict bureaucratic organization."

We argue that the causes of bureaucratization and rationalization have changed. The bureaucratization of the corporation and the state have been achieved. Organizations are still becoming more homogeneous, and bureaucracy remains the common organizational form. Today, however, structural change in organizations seems less and less driven by competition or by the need for efficiency. Instead, we contend, bureaucratization and other forms of organizational change occur as the result of processes that make organizations more similar without necessarily making them more efficient. Bureaucratization and other forms of homogenization emerge, we argue, out of the structuration (Giddens 1979) of organizational fields. This process, in turn, is effected largely by the state and the professions, which have become the great rationalizers of the second half of the twentieth century. For reasons that we will explain, highly structured organizational fields provide a context in which individual efforts to deal rationally with uncertainty and constraint often lead, in the aggregate, to homogeneity in structure, culture, and output.

Organizational Theory and Organizational Diversity

Much of modern organizational theory posits a diverse and differentiated world of organizations and seeks to explain variation among organizations in structure and behavior (e.g., Woodward 1965; Child and Kieser 1981). Hannan and Freeman begin a major theoretical paper (1977) with the question, "Why are there so many kinds of organizations?" Even our investigatory technologies (for example, those based on least-squares techniques) are geared toward explaining variation rather than its absence.

We ask, instead, why there is such startling homogeneity of organizational forms and practices, and we seek to explain homogeneity, not variation. In the initial stages of their life cycle, organizational fields display considerable diversity in approach and form. Once a field becomes well established, however, there is an inexorable push toward homogenization.

Coser, Kadushin, and Powell (1982) describe the evolution of American college textbook publishing from a period of initial diversity to the current hegemony of only two models, the large bureaucratic generalist and the small specialist. Rothman (1980) describes the winnowing of several competing models of legal education into two dominant approaches. Starr (1980) provides evidence of mimicry in the development of the hospital field; Tyack (1974) and Katz (1975) show a similar process in public schools; Barnouw (1966–68) describes the development of dominant forms in the radio industry; and DiMaggio (1982a, 1982b) depicts the emergence of dominant organizational models for the provision of high culture in the late nineteenth century. What we see in each of these cases is the emergence and structuration of an organizational field as a result of the activities of a diverse set of organizations and, second, the homogenization of these organizations, and of new entrants as well, once the field is established.

By *organizational field* we mean those organizations that, in the aggregate, constitute a recognized area of institutional life: key suppliers, resource and product consumers, regulatory agencies, and other organizations that produce similar services or products. The virtue of this unit of analysis is that it directs our attention not simply to competing firms, as does the population approach of Hannan and Freeman (1977), or to networks of organizations that actually interact, as does the interorganizational network approach of Laumann, Galaskiewicz, and Marsden (1978), but to the totality of relevant actors. In doing this, the field idea comprehends the importance of both *connectedness* (see Laumann, Galaskiewicz, and Marsden 1978) and *structural equivalence* (White, Boorman, and Breiger 1976).[1]

The structure of an organizational field cannot be determined a priori but must be defined on the basis of empirical investigation. Fields only exist to the extent that they are institutionally defined. The process of institutional definition, or "structuration," consists of four parts: an increase in the extent of interaction among organizations in the field; the emergence of sharply defined interorganizational structures of domination and patterns of coalition; an increase in the information load with which organizations in a field must contend; and the development of a mutual awareness among participants in a set of organizations that they are involved in a common enterprise (DiMaggio 1983).

Once disparate organizations in the same line of business are structured into an actual field (as we argue, by competition, the state, or the professions), powerful forces emerge that lead them to become more similar to one another. Organizations may change their goals or develop new practices, and new organizations enter the field. But in the long run, organizational actors making rational decisions construct around themselves an environment that constrains their ability to change further in later years. Early adopters of organizational innovations are commonly driven by a desire to improve performance. But new practices can become, in Selznick's words (1957:17), "infused with value beyond the technical requirements of the task at hand." As an innovation spreads, a threshold is reached beyond which adoption provides legitimacy rather than improves performance (Meyer and Rowan 1977). Strategies that are rational for individual organizations may not be rational if adopted by large numbers. Yet the very fact that they are normatively sanctioned increases the likelihood of their adoption. Thus organizations may try to change constantly; but after a certain point in the structuration of an organizational field, the aggregate effect of individual change is to lessen the extent of diversity within the field.[2] Organizations in a structured field, to paraphrase Schelling (1978:14), respond to an environment that consists of other organizations responding to their environment, which consists of organizations responding to an environment of organizations' responses.

Tolbert and Zucker's (1983) work on the adoption of civil service reform in the United States nicely illustrates this process. Early adoption of civil service reforms was related to internal governmental needs and strongly predicted by such city characteristics as the size of immigrant population, political reform movements, socioeconomic composition, and city size. Later, however, adoption is not predicted by city characteristics, but is related to institutional definitions of the legitimate structural form for municipal administration.[3] Marshall Meyer's (Meyer, Stevenson, and Webster 1985) study of the bureaucratization of urban fiscal agencies has yielded similar findings: strong relationships between city characteristics and organizational attributes at the turn of the century, null relationships in recent years. Carroll and Delacroix's (1982) findings on the birth and death rates of newspapers support the view that selection acts with great force only in the early years of an industry's existence.[4] Freeman (1982:14) suggests that older, larger organizations reach a point where they can dominate their environments rather than adjust to them.

The concept that best captures the process of homogenization is *isomorphism*. In Hawley's (1968) description, isomorphism is a constraining process that forces one unit in a population to resemble other units that face the same set of environmental conditions. At the population level, such an approach suggests that organizational characteristics are modified in the direction of increasing compatibility with environmental characteristics; the number of organizations in a population is a function of environmental carrying capacity; and the diversity of organizational forms is isomorphic to environmental diversity. Hannan and Freeman (1977) have significantly extended Hawley's ideas. They argue that isomorphism can result because nonoptimal forms are selected out of a population of organizations *or* because organizational decision makers learn appropriate responses and adjust their behavior accordingly. Hannan and Freeman's focus is almost solely on the first process—selection.[5]

Following Meyer (1983b) and Fennell (1980), we maintain that there are two types of isomorphism: competitive and institutional. Hannan and Freeman's classic paper (1977), and much of their recent work, deals with competitive isomorphism, assuming a system rationality that emphasizes market competition, niche change, and fitness measures. Such a view, we suggest, is most relevant for those fields in which free and open competition exists. It explains parts of the process of bureaucratization that Weber observed, and may apply to early adoption of innovation, but it does not present a fully adequate picture of the modern world of organizations. For this purpose it must be supplemented by an institutional view of isomorphism of the sort introduced by Kanter (1972:152–54) in her discussion of the forces pressing communities toward accommodation with the outside world. As Aldrich (1979:265) has argued, "the major factors that organizations must take into account are other organizations." Organizations compete not just for resources and customers, but for political power and institutional legitimacy, for social as well as economic fitness.[6] The concept of institutional isomorphism is a useful tool for understanding the politics and ceremony that pervade much modern organizational life.

Three Mechanisms of Institutional Isomorphic Change

We identify three mechanisms through which institutional isomorphic change occurs, each with its own antecedents: (1) *coercive* isomorphism that stems from political influence and the problem of legitimacy; (2) *mimetic* isomorphism resulting from standard responses to uncertainty; and (3) *normative* isomorphism, associated with professionalization. This typology is an analytic one: the types are not always empirically distinct. For example, external actors may induce an organization to conform to its peers by requiring it to perform a particular task and specifying the profession responsible for its performance. Or mimetic change may reflect environmentally constructed uncertainties.[7] Yet, while the three types intermingle in empirical settings, they tend to derive from different conditions and may lead to different outcomes.

Coercive Isomorphism

Coercive isomorphism results from both formal and informal pressures exerted on organizations by other organizations upon which they are dependent and by cultural expectations in the society within which organizations function. Such pressures may be felt as force, as persuasion, or as invitations to join in collusion. In some circumstances, organizational change is a direct response to government mandate: manufacturers adopt new pollution control technologies to conform to environmental regulations; nonprofits maintain accounts and hire accountants in order to meet tax law requirements; and organizations employ affirmative action officers to fend off allegations of discrimination. Schools mainstream special students and hire special education teachers, cultivate PTAs and administrators who get along with them, and promulgate curricula that conform with state standards (Meyer, Scott, and Deal 1981). The fact that these changes may be largely ceremonial does not mean they are inconsequential. As Ritti and Goldner (1979) have argued, staff become involved in advocacy for their functions that can alter power relations within organizations over the long run.

The existence of a common legal environment affects many aspects of an organization's behavior and structure. Weber pointed out the profound impact of a complex, rationalized system of contract law that requires the necessary organizational controls to honor legal commitments. Other legal and technical requirements of the state—the vicissitudes of the budget cycle, the ubiquity of certain fiscal years, annual reports, and financial reporting requirements that ensure eligibility for the receipt of federal contracts or funds—also shape organizations in similar ways. Pfeffer and Salancik (1978:188–224) have discussed how organizations faced with unmanageable interdependence seek to use the greater power of the larger social system and its government to eliminate difficulties or provide for needs. They observe that politically constructed environments have two characteristic features: political decision makers often do not experience directly the consequences of their actions; and political decisions are applied across the board to entire classes of organizations, thus making such decisions less adaptive and less flexible.

Meyer and Rowan (1977) have argued persuasively that as rationalized states and other large rational organizations expand their dominance over more arenas of social life, organizational structures increasingly come to reflect rules institutionalized and legitimated by and within the state (also see Meyer and Hannan 1979). As a result, organizations are increasingly homogeneous within given domains and increasingly organized around rituals of conformity to wider institutions. At the same time, organizations are decreasingly structurally determined by the constraints posed by technical activities and decreasingly held together by output controls. Under such circumstances, organizations employ ritualized controls of credentials and group solidarity.

Direct imposition of standard operating procedures and legitimated rules and structures also occurs outside the governmental arena. Michael Sedlak (1981) has documented the ways that United Charities in the 1930s altered and homogenized the structures, methods, and philosophies of the social service agencies that depended upon it for support. As conglomerate corporations increase in size and scope, standard performance criteria are not necessarily imposed on subsidiaries, but it is common for subsidiaries to be subject to standardized reporting mechanisms (Coser, Kadushin, and Powell 1982). Subsidiaries are compelled to adopt accounting practices, performance evaluations, and budgetary plans that are compatible with the policies of the parent corporation. A variety of service infrastructures, often provided by monopolistic firms—for example, telecommunications and transportation—exerts common pressures over the organizations that use them. Thus, the expansion of the central state, the centralization of capital, and the coordination of philanthropy all support the homogenization of organizational models through direct authority relationships.

We have so far referred only to the direct and explicit imposition of organizational models on dependent organizations. Coercive isomorphism, however, may be more subtle and less explicit than these examples suggest. Milofsky (1981) has described the ways in which neighborhood organizations in urban communities, many of which are committed to participatory democracy, are driven to developing organizational hierarchies in order to gain support from more hierarchically organized donor organizations. Similarly, Swidler (1979) describes the tensions created in the free schools she studied by the need to have a "principal" to negotiate with the district superintendent and to represent the school to outside agencies. In general, the need to lodge responsibility and managerial authority at least ceremonially in a formally defined role in order to interact with hierarchical organizations is a constant obstacle to the maintenance of egalitarian or collectivist organizational forms (Kanter 1972; Rothschild-Whitt 1979).

Mimetic Processes

Not all institutional isomorphism, however, derives from coercive authority. Uncertainty is also a powerful force that encourages imitation. When organizational technologies are poorly understood (March and Olsen 1976), when goals are ambiguous, or when the environment creates symbolic uncertainty, organizations may model themselves on other organizations. The advantages of mimetic behavior in the economy of human action are considerable; when an organization faces a problem with ambiguous causes or unclear solutions, problemistic search may yield a viable solution with little expense (Cyert and March 1963).

Modeling, as we use the term, is a response to uncertainty. The modeled organization may be unaware of the modeling or may have no desire to be copied; it merely serves as a convenient source of practices that the borrowing organization may use. Models may be diffused unintentionally, indirectly through employee transfer or turnover, or explicitly by organizations such as consulting firms or industry trade associations. Even innovation can be accounted for by organizational modeling. As Alchian (1950) has observed:

> While there certainly are those who consciously innovate, there are those who, in their imperfect attempts to imitate others, unconsciously innovate by unwittingly acquiring some unexpected or unsought unique attributes which under the prevailing circumstances prove partly responsible for the success. Others, in turn, will attempt to copy the uniqueness, and the innovation-imitation process continues. (Pp. 218–19)

One of the most dramatic instances of modeling was the effort of Japan's modernizers in the late nineteenth century to model new governmental initiatives on apparently successful Western prototypes. Thus, the imperial government sent its officers to study the courts, army, and police in France, the navy and postal system in Great Britain, and banking and art education in the United States (see Westney 1987). American corporations are now returning the compliment by implementing (their perceptions of) Japanese models to cope with thorny productivity and personnel problems in their own firms. The rapid proliferation of quality circles and quality-of-work-life issues in American firms is, at least in part, an attempt to model Japanese and European successes. These developments also have a ritual aspect; companies adopt these "innovations" to enhance their legitimacy, to demonstrate they are at least trying to improve working conditions. More generally, the wider the population of personnel employed by, or customers served by, an organization, the stronger the pressure felt by the organization to provide the programs and services offered by other organizations. Thus, either a skilled labor force or a broad customer base may encourage mimetic isomorphism.

Much homogeneity in organizational structures stems from the fact that despite considerable search for diversity there is relatively little variation to be selected from. New organizations are modeled upon old ones throughout the economy, and managers actively seek models upon which to build (Kimberly 1980). Thus in the arts one can find textbooks on how to organize a community arts council or how to start a symphony women's guild. Large organizations choose from a relatively small set of major consulting firms, which, like Johnny Appleseeds, spread a few organizational models throughout the land. Such models are powerful because structural changes are observable, whereas changes in policy and strategy are less easily noticed. With the advice of a major consulting firm, a large metropolitan public television station switched from a functional design to a multidivisional structure. The stations' executives were skeptical that the new structure was more efficient; in fact, some services were now duplicated across divisions. But they were convinced that the new design would carry a powerful message to the for-profit firms with whom the station regularly dealt. These firms, whether in the role of corporate underwriters or as potential partners in joint ventures, would view the reorganization as a sign that "the sleepy nonprofit station was becoming more business-minded" (Powell 1988). The history of management reform in U.S. government agencies, which are noted for their goal ambiguity, is almost a textbook case of isomorphic modeling, from the PPPB of the McNamara era to the zero-based budgeting of the Carter administration.

Organizations tend to model themselves after similar organizations in their field that they perceive to be more legitimate or successful. The ubiquity of certain kinds of structural arrangements can more likely be credited to the universality of mimetic processes than to any concrete evidence that the adopted models enhance efficiency. John Meyer (1981) contends that it is easy to predict the organization of a newly emerging nation's administration without knowing anything about the nation itself, since "peripheral nations are far more isomorphic—in administrative form and economic pattern—than any theory of the world system of economic division of labor would lead one to expect."

Normative Pressures

A third source of isomorphic organizational change is normative and stems primarily from professionalization. Following Larson (1977) and Collins (1979), we interpret professionalization as the collective struggle of members of an occupation to define the conditions and methods of their work, to control "the production of producers" (Larson 1977:49–52), and to establish a cognitive base and legitimation for their occupational autonomy. As Larson points out, the professional project is rarely achieved with complete success. Professionals must compromise with nonprofessional clients, bosses, or regulators. The major recent growth in the professions has been among organizational professionals, particularly managers and specialized staff of large organizations. The increased professionalization of workers whose futures are inextricably bound up with the fortunes of the organizations that employ them has rendered obsolescent (if not obsolete) the dichotomy between organizational commitment and professional allegiance that characterized traditional professionals in earlier organizations (Hall 1968). Professions are subject to the same coercive and mimetic pressures as are organizations. Moreover, while various kinds of professionals within an organization may differ from one another, they exhibit much similarity to their professional counterparts in other organizations. In addition, in many cases, professional power is as much assigned by the state as it is created by the activities of the professions.

Two aspects of professionalization are important sources of isomorphism. One is the resting of formal education and of legitimation in a cognitive base produced by university specialists; the second is the growth and elaboration of professional networks that span organizations and across which new models diffuse rapidly. Universities and professional training institutions are important centers for the development of organizational norms among professional managers and their staff. Professional and trade associations are another vehicle for the definition and promulgation of normative rules about organizational and professional behavior. Such mechanisms create a pool of almost interchangeable individuals who occupy similar positions across a range of organizations and possess a similarity of orientation and disposition that may override variations in tradition and control that might otherwise shape organizational behavior (Perrow 1974).

One important mechanism for encouraging normative isomorphism is the filtering of personnel. Within many organizational fields, filtering occurs through the hiring of individuals from firms within the same industry; through the recruitment of fast-track staff from a narrow range of training institutions; through common promotion practices, such as always hiring top executives from financial or legal departments; and from skill-level requirements for particular jobs. Many professional career tracks are so closely guarded, both at the entry level and throughout the career progression, that individuals who make it to the top are virtually indistinguishable. March and March (1977) found that individuals who attained the position of school superintendent in Wisconsin were so alike in background and orientation as to make further career advancement random and unpredictable. Hirsch and Whisler (1982) find a similar absence of variation among Fortune 500 board members. In addition, individuals in an organizational field undergo anticipatory socialization to common expectations about their personal behavior, appropriate style of dress, organizational vocabularies (Cicourel 1970; Williamson 1975), and standard methods of speaking, joking, or addressing others (Ouchi 1980). Particularly in industries with a service or financial orientation (Collins 1979 argues that the importance of credentials is strongest in these areas), the filtering of personnel approaches what Kanter (1977) refers to as the "homosexual reproduction of management." To the extent managers and key staff are drawn from the same universities and filtered on a common set of attributes, they will tend to view problems in a similar fashion, see the same policies, procedures, and structures as normatively sanctioned and legitimated, and approach decisions in much the same way.

Entrants to professional career tracks who somehow escape the filtering process—for example, Jewish naval officers, women stockbrokers, or black insurance executives—are likely to be subjected to pervasive on-the-job socialization. To the extent that organizations in a field differ and primary social-ization occurs on the job, socialization could reinforce, not erode, differences among organizations. But when organizations in a field are similar and occupational socialization is carried out in trade asso-ciation workshops, in-service educational programs, consultant arrangements, employer–professional school networks, and in the pages of trade magazines, socialization acts as an isomorphic force.

The professionalization of management tends to proceed in tandem with the structuration of organizational fields. The exchange of information among professionals helps contribute to a commonly recognized hierarchy of status, of center and periphery, that becomes a matrix for infor-mation flows and personnel movement across organizations. This status ordering occurs through both formal and informal means. The designation of a few large firms in an industry as key bargaining agents in union-management negotiations may make these central firms pivotal in other respects as well. Government recognition of key firms or organizations through the grant or contract process may give these organizations legitimacy and visibility and lead competing firms to copy aspects of their structure or operating procedures in hope of obtaining similar rewards. Professional and trade associations provide other arenas in which center organizations are recognized and their personnel given positions of substantive or ceremonial influence. Managers in highly visible organizations may in turn have their stature reinforced by representation on the boards of other organizations, partic-ipation in industrywide or interindustry councils, and consultation by agencies of government (Useem 1979). In the nonprofit sector, where legal barriers to collusion do not exist, structuration may proceed even more rapidly. Thus executive producers or artistic directors of leading theaters head trade or professional association committees, sit on government and foundation grant-award panels, con-sult as government- or foundation-financed management advisers to smaller theaters, or sit on smaller organizations' boards, even as their stature is reinforced and enlarged by the grants their theaters receive from government, corporate, and foundation funding sources (DiMaggio 1983).

Such central organizations serve as both active and passive models; their policies and structures will be copied throughout their fields. Their centrality is reinforced as upwardly mobile managers and staff seek to secure positions in these central organizations in order to further their own careers. Aspiring managers may undergo anticipatory socialization into the norms and mores of the orga-nizations they hope to join. Career paths may also involve movement from entry positions in the center organizations to middle-management positions in peripheral organizations. Personnel flows within an organizational field are further encouraged by structural homogenization, for example, the existence of common career titles and paths (such as assistant, associate, and full professor) with meanings that are commonly understood.

Each of the institutional isomorphic processes can be expected to proceed in the absence of evidence that it increases internal organizational efficiency. To the extent that organizational effectiveness is enhanced, the reason is often that organizations are rewarded for their similarity to other organizations in their fields. This similarity can make it easier for organizations to transact with other organizations, to attract career-minded staff, to be acknowledged as legitimate and reputable, and to fit into administrative categories that define eligibility for public and private grants and contracts. None of this, however, ensures that con-formist organizations do what they do more efficiently than do their more deviant peers.

Pressures for competitive efficiency are also mitigated in many fields because the number of orga-nizations is limited and there are strong fiscal and legal barriers to entry and exit. Lee (1971:51) maintains this is why hospital administrators are less concerned with the efficient use of resources and more concerned with status competition and parity in prestige. Fennell (1980) notes that hos-pitals are a poor market system because patients lack the needed knowledge of potential exchange partners and prices. She argues that physicians and hospital administrators are the actual consumers. Competition among hospitals is based on "attracting physicians, who, in turn, bring their patients to the hospital." Fennell concludes that

> Hospitals operate according to a norm of social legitimation that frequently conflicts with market considerations of efficiency and system rationality. Apparently, hospitals can increase their range of services not because there is an actual need for a particular service or facility within the patient pop-ulation, but because they will be defined as fit only if they can offer everything other hospitals in the area offer. (P. 505)

These results suggest a more general pattern. Organizational fields that include a large professionally trained labor force will be driven primarily by status competition. Organizational prestige and resources are key elements in attracting professionals. This process encourages homogenization as organizations seek to ensure that they can provide the same benefits and services as their competitors.

Predictors of Isomorphic Change

It follows from our discussion of the mechanisms by which isomorphic change occurs that we should be able to predict empirically which organizational fields will be most homogeneous in structure, process, and behavior. While an empirical test of such predictions is beyond the scope of this chapter, the ultimate value of our perspective lies in its predictive utility. The hypotheses discussed below are not meant to exhaust the universe of predictors, but merely to suggest several hypotheses that may be pursued using data on the characteristics of organizations in a field, either cross-sectionally or, preferably, over time. The hypotheses are implicitly governed by ceteris paribus assumptions, particularly with regard to size, technology, and centralization of external resources.

A. Organizational-Level Predictors

There is variability in the extent to and rate at which organizations in a field change to become more like their peers. Some organizations respond to external pressures quickly; others change only after a long period of resistance. The first two hypotheses derive from our discussion of coercive isomorphism and constraint.

Hypothesis A-1. *The greater the dependence of an organization on another organization, the more similar it will become to that organization in structure, climate, and behavioral focus.* Following Thompson (1967) and Pfeffer and Salancik (1978), this proposition recognizes the greater ability of organizations to resist the demands of organizations on which they are not dependent. A position of dependence leads to isomorphic change. Coercive pressures are built into exchange relationships. As Williamson (1979) has shown, exchanges are characterized by transaction-specific investments in both knowledge and equipment. Once an organization chooses a specific supplier or distributor for particular parts or services, the supplier or distributor develops expertise in the performance of the task as well as idiosyncratic knowledge about the exchange relationship. The organization comes to rely on the supplier or distributor, and such transaction-specific investments give the supplier or distributor considerable advantages in any subsequent competition with other suppliers or distributors.

Hypothesis A-2. *The greater the centralization of organization A's resource supply, the greater the extent to which organization A will change isomorphically to resemble the organizations on which it depends for resources.* As Thompson (1967) notes, organizations that depend on the same sources for funding, personnel, and legitimacy will be more subject to the whims of resource suppliers than will organizations that can play one source of support off against another. In cases where alternative sources are either not readily available or require effort to locate, the stronger party to the transaction can coerce the weaker party to adopt its practices in order to accommodate the stronger party's needs (see Powell 1983).

The third and fourth hypotheses derive from our discussion of mimetic isomorphism, modeling, and uncertainty.

Hypothesis A-3. *The more uncertain the relationship between means and ends, the greater the extent to which an organization will model itself after organizations it perceives as successful.* The mimetic thought process involved in the search for models is characteristic of change in organizations in which key technologies are only poorly understood (March and Cohen 1974). Here our prediction diverges somewhat from Meyer and Rowan (1977), who argue, as we do, that organizations which lack well-defined technologies will import institutionalized rules and practices. Meyer and Rowan posit a loose coupling between legitimated external practices and internal organizational behavior. From an ecologist's point of view, loosely coupled organizations are more likely to vary internally. In contrast, we expect substantive internal changes in tandem with more ceremonial practices, thus greater homogeneity and less variation. Internal consistency of this sort is an important means of interorganizational coordination. It also increases organizational stability.

Hypothesis A-4. *The more ambiguous the goals of an organization, the greater the extent to which the organization will model itself after organizations that it perceives as successful.* There are two reasons for this modeling. First, organizations with ambiguous or disputed goals are likely to be highly dependent upon appearances for legitimacy. Such organizations may find it to their advantage to meet the expectations of important constituencies about how they should be designed and run. In contrast to our view, ecologists would argue that organizations that copy other organizations usually have no competitive advantage. We contend that, in most situations, reliance on established, legitimated procedures enhances organizational legitimacy and survival characteristics. A second reason for modeling behavior is found in situations where conflict over organizational goals is repressed in the interest of harmony; thus participants find it easier to mimic other organizations than to make decisions on the basis of systematic analyses of goals since such analyses would prove painful or disruptive.

The fifth and sixth hypotheses are based on our discussion of normative processes found in professional organizations.

Hypothesis A-5. *The greater the reliance on academic credentials in choosing managerial and staff personnel, the greater the extent to which an organization will become like other organizations in its field.* Applicants with academic credentials have already undergone a socialization process in university programs and are thus more likely than others to have internalized reigning norms and dominant organizational models.

Hypothesis A-6. *The greater the participation of organizational managers in trade and professional associations, the more likely the organization will be, or will become, like other organizations in its field.* This hypothesis is parallel to the institutional view that the more elaborate the relational networks among organizations and their members, the greater the collective organization of the environment (Meyer and Rowan 1977).

B. Field-Level Predictors

The following six hypotheses describe the expected effects of several characteristics of organizational fields on the extent of isomorphism in a particular field. Since the effect of institutional isomorphism is homogenization, the best indicator of isomorphic change is a decrease in variation and diversity, which could be measured by lower standard deviations of the values of selected indicators in a set of organizations. The key indicators would vary with the nature of the field and the interest of the investigator. In all cases, however, field-level measures are expected to affect organizations in a field regardless of each organization's scores on related organizational-level measures.

Hypothesis B-1. *The greater the extent to which an organizational field is dependent upon a single (or several similar) source(s) of support for vital resources, the higher the level of isomorphism.* The centralization of resources within a field both directly causes homogenization by placing organizations under similar pressures from resource suppliers, and interacts with uncertainty and goal ambiguity to increase their impact. This hypothesis is congruent with the ecologist's argument that the number of organizational forms is determined by the distribution of resources in the environment and the terms on which resources are available.

Hypothesis B-2. *The greater the extent to which the organizations in a field transact with agencies of the state, the greater the extent of isomorphism in the field as a whole.* This hypothesis follows not just from the previous one, but from two elements of state/private-sector transactions: their rule-boundedness and formal rationality, and the emphasis of government actors on institutional rules. Moreover, the federal government routinely designates industry standards for an entire field which require adoption by all competing firms. John Meyer (1980) argues convincingly that the aspects of an organization which are affected by state transactions differ to the extent that state participation is unitary or fragmented among several public agencies.

The third and fourth hypotheses follow from our discussion of isomorphic change resulting from uncertainty and modeling.

Hypothesis B-3. *The fewer the number of visible alternative organizational models in a field, the faster the rate of isomorphism in that field.* The predictions of this hypothesis are less specific than those of others and require further refinement; but our argument is that for any relevant dimension of organizational strategies or structures in an organizational field there will be a threshold level, or a tipping point, beyond which adoption of the dominant form will proceed with increasing speed (Granovetter 1978; Boorman and Leavitt 1979).

Hypothesis B-4. *The greater the extent to which technologies are uncertain or goals are ambiguous within a field, the greater the rate of isomorphic change.* Somewhat counterintuitively, abrupt increases in uncertainty and ambiguity should, after brief periods of ideologically motivated experimentation, lead to rapid isomorphic change. As in the case of A-4, ambiguity and uncertainty may be a function of environmental definition and, in any case, interact both with the centralization of resources (A-1, A-2, B-1, B-2) and with professionalization and structuration (A-5, A-6, B-5, B-6). Moreover, in fields characterized by a high degree of uncertainty, new entrants, which could serve as sources of innovation and variation, will seek to overcome the liability of newness by imitating established practices within the field.

The two final hypotheses in this section follow from our discussion of professional filtering, socialization, and structuration.

Hypothesis B-5. *The greater the extent of professionalization in a field, the greater the amount of institutional isomorphic change.* Professionalization may be measured by the universality of credential requirements, the robustness of graduate training programs, or the vitality of professional and trade associations.

Hypothesis B-6. *The greater the extent of structuration of a field, the greater the degree of isomorphism.* Fields that have stable and broadly acknowledged centers, peripheries, and status orders will be more homogeneous both because the diffusion structure for new models and norms is more routine and because the level of interaction among organizations in the field is higher. While structuration may not lend itself to easy measurement, it might be tapped crudely with the use of such familiar measures as concentration ratios, reputational interview studies, or data on network characteristics.

This rather schematic exposition of a dozen hypotheses relating the extent of isomorphism to selected attributes of organizations and of organizational fields does not constitute a complete agenda for empirical assessment of our perspective. We have not discussed the expected nonlinearities and ceiling effects in the relationships we have posited. Nor have we addressed the issue of the indicators that one must use to measure homogeneity. Organizations in a field may be highly diverse on some dimensions, yet extremely homogeneous on others. While we suspect, in general, that the rate at which the standard deviations of structural or behavioral indicators approach zero will vary with the nature of an organizational field's technology and environment, we do not develop these ideas here. This section suggests that the theoretical discussion is susceptible to empirical test and lays out a few testable propositions that may guide future analyses.

Implications for Social Theory

A comparison of macrosocial theories of functionalist or Marxist orientation with theoretical and empirical work in the study of organizations yields a paradoxical conclusion. Societies (or elites), so it seems, are smart, while organizations are dumb. Societies comprise institutions that mesh together comfortably in the interest of efficiency (Clark 1962), the dominant value system (Parsons 1951), or, in the Marxist version, capitalists (Domhoff 1967; Althusser 1969). Organizations, by contrast, are either anarchies (Cohen, March, and Olsen 1972), federations of loosely coupled parts (Weick 1976), or autonomy-seeking agents (Gouldner 1954) laboring under such formidable constraints as bounded rationality (March and Simon 1958), uncertain or contested goals (Sills 1957), and unclear technologies (March and Cohen 1974).

Despite the findings of organizational research, the image of society as consisting of tightly and rationally coupled institutions persists throughout much of modern social theory. Rational administration pushes out nonbureaucratic forms, schools assume the structure of the workplace, hospital and university administrations come to resemble the management of for-profit firms, and the modernization of the world economy proceeds unabated. Weberians point to the continuing homogenization of organizational structures as the formal rationality of bureaucracy extends to the limits of contemporary organizational life. Functionalists describe the rational adaptation of the structure of firms, schools, and states to the values and needs of modern society (Chandler 1977; Parsons 1977). Marxists attribute changes in such organizations as welfare agencies (Pivan and Cloward 1971) and schools (Bowles and Gintis 1976) to the logic of the accumulation process.

We find it difficult to square the extant literature on organizations with these macrosocial views. How can it be that the confused and contentious bumblers who populate the pages of organizational case studies and theories combine to construct the elaborate and well-proportioned social edifice that macrotheorists describe?

The conventional answer to this paradox has been that some version of natural selection occurs in which selection mechanisms operate to weed out those organizational forms that are less fit. Such arguments, as we have contended, are difficult to mesh with organizational realities. Less efficient organizational forms do persist. In some contexts efficiency or productivity cannot even be measured. In government agencies or in faltering corporations selection may occur on political rather than economic grounds. In other contexts, for example, the Metropolitan Opera or the Bohemian Grove, supporters are far more concerned with noneconomic values like aesthetic quality or social status than with efficiency per se. Even in the for-profit sector, where competitive arguments would promise to bear the greatest fruit, Nelson and Winter's work (Winter 1964, 1975; Nelson and Winter 1982) demonstrates that the invisible hand operates with, at best, a light touch.

A second approach to the paradox we have identified comes from Marxists and theorists who assert that key elites guide and control the social system through their command of crucial positions in major organizations (e.g., the financial institutions that dominate monopoly capitalism). In this view, while organizational actors ordinarily proceed undisturbed through mazes of standard operating procedures, at key turning points capitalist elites get their way by intervening in decisions that set the course of an institution for years to come (Katz 1975).

While evidence suggests that this is, in fact, sometimes the case—Barnouw's account (1966–70) of the early days of broadcasting or Weinstein's (1968) work on the Progressives are good examples—other historians have been less successful in their search for class-conscious elites. In such cases as the development of the New Deal programs (Hawley 1966) or the expansion of the Vietnamese conflict (Halperin 1974), the capitalist class appears to have been muddled and disunited.

Moreover, without constant monitoring, individuals pursuing parochial organizational or subunit interests can quickly undo the work that even the most prescient elites have accomplished. Perrow (1976:21) has noted that despite superior resources and sanctioning power, organizational elites are often unable to maximize their preferences because "the complexity of modern organizations makes control difficult." Moreover, organizations have increasingly become the vehicle for numerous "gratifications, necessities, and preferences so that many groups within and without the organization seek to use it for ends that restrict the return to masters."

We reject neither the natural-selection nor the elite-control arguments out of hand. Elites do exercise considerable influence over modern life, and aberrant or inefficient organizations sometimes do expire. But we contend that neither of these processes is sufficient to explain the extent to which organizations have become structurally more similar. We argue that a theory of institutional isomorphism may help explain the observations that organizations are becoming more homogeneous and that elites often get their way, while at the same time enabling us to understand the irrationality, the frustration of power, and the lack of innovation that are so commonplace in organizational life. What is more, our approach is more consonant with the ethnographic and theoretical literature on how organizations work than are either functionalist or elite theories of organizational change.

A focus on institutional isomorphism can also add a much needed perspective on the political struggle for organizational power and survival that is missing from much of population ecology. The institutionalization approach associated with John Meyer and his students posits the importance of myths and ceremony but does not ask how these models arise and whose interest they initially serve. Explicit attention to the genesis of legitimated models and to the definition and elaboration of organizational fields should answer this question. Examination of the diffusion of similar organizational strategies and structures should be productive means for assessing the influence of elite interest. A consideration of isomorphic processes also leads us to a bifocal view of power and its application in modern politics. To the extent that organizational change is unplanned and goes on largely behind the backs of groups that wish to influence it, our attention should be directed to two forms of power. The first, as March and Simon (1958) and Simon (1957) pointed out years ago, is the power to set premises, to define the norms and standards which shape and channel behavior. The second is the point of critical intervention (Domhoff 1979) at which elites can define appropriate models of organizational structure and policy which then go unquestioned for years to come (see Katz 1975). Such a view is consonant with some of the best recent work on power (see Lukes 1974); research on the structuration of organizational fields and on isomorphic processes may help give it more empirical flesh.

Finally, a more developed theory of organizational isomorphism may have important implications for social policy in those fields in which the state works through private organizations. To the extent that pluralism is a guiding value in public policy deliberations, we need to discover new forms of intersectoral coordination that will encourage diversification rather than hastening homogenization. An understanding of the manner in which fields become more homogeneous would prevent policymakers and analysts from confusing the disappearance of an organizational form with its substantive failure. Current efforts to encourage diversity tend to be conducted in an organizational vacuum. Policymakers concerned with pluralism should consider the impact of their programs on the structure of organizational fields as a whole and not simply on the programs of individual organizations.

We believe there is much to be gained by attending to similarity as well as to variation among organizations and, in particular, to change in the degree of homogeneity or variation over time. Our approach seeks to study incremental change as well as selection. We take seriously the observations of organizational theorists about the role of change, ambiguity, and constraint and point to the implications of these organizational characteristics for the social structure as a whole. The foci and motive forces of bureaucratization (and, more broadly, homogenization in general) have, as we argued, changed since Weber's time. But the importance of understanding the trends to which he called attention has never been more immediate.

Acknowledgments

This chapter was originally published in 1983 in the *American Sociological Review* 48(April): 147–60. The chapter incorporates several changes that are not in the 1983 version. The first iteration of the chapter was presented by Powell at the American Sociological Association meetings in Toronto, August 1981. The authors have benefited considerably from careful readings of earlier drafts by Dan Chambliss, Randall Collins, Lewis Coser, Rebecca Friedkin, Connie Gersick, Albert Hunter, Rosabeth Moss Kanter, Charles E. Lindblom, John Meyer, David Morgan, Susan Olzak, Charles Perrow, Richard A. Peterson, Arthur Stinchcombe, and Blair Wheaton. The authors' names are listed in alphabetical order for convenience. This was a fully collaborative effort.

Notes

1. By *connectedness* we mean the existence of transactions tying organizations to one another: such transactions might include formal contractual relationships, participation of personnel in common enterprises such as professional associations, labor unions, or boards of directors, or informal organizational-level ties like personnel flows. A set of organizations strongly connected to one another and only weakly connected to other organizations constitutes a *clique*. By *structural equivalence* we refer to similarity of position in a network structure. For example, two organizations are structurally equivalent if they have ties of the same kind to the same set of other organizations, even if they themselves are not connected; here the key structure is the *role* or *block*.

2. By *organizational change* we refer to change in formal structure, organizational culture, and goals, program, or mission. Organizational change varies in its responsiveness to technical conditions. In this chapter

we are most interested in processes that affect organizations in a given field: in most cases these organizations employ similar technical bases; thus we do not attempt to partial out the relative importance of technically functional versus other forms of organizational change. While we cite many examples of organizational change as we go along, our purpose here is to identify a widespread class of organizational processes relevant to a broad range of substantive problems, rather than to identify deterministically the causes of specific organizational arrangements.

3. Knoke 1982, in a careful event-history analysis of the spread of municipal reform, refutes the conventional explanations of culture clash or hierarchal diffusion and finds but modest support for modernization theory. His major finding is that regional differences in municipal reform adoption arise not from social compositional differences, "but from some type of imitation or contagion effects as represented by the level of neighboring regional cities previously adopting reform government" (p. 1337).

4. A wide range of factors—interorganizational commitments, elite sponsorship, and government support in the form of open-ended contracts, subsidy, tariff barriers and import quotas, or favorable tax laws—reduces selection pressures even in competitive organizational fields. An expanding or a stable, protected market can also mitigate the forces of selection.

5. In contrast to Hannan and Freeman, we emphasize adaptation, but we are not suggesting that managers' actions are necessarily strategic in a long-range sense. Indeed, two of the three forms of isomorphism described below—mimetic and normative—involve managerial behaviors at the level of taken-for-granted assumptions rather than consciously strategic choices. In general, we question the utility of arguments about the motivations of actors that suggest a polarity between the rational and the nonrational. Goal-oriented behavior may be reflexive or prerational in the sense that it reflects deeply embedded predispositions, scripts, schema, or classifications; behavior oriented to a goal may be reinforced without contributing to the accomplishment of that goal. While isomorphic change may often be mediated by the desires of managers to increase the effectiveness of their organizations, we are more concerned with the menu of possible options that managers consider than with their motives for choosing particular alternatives. In other words, we freely concede that actors' understandings of their own behaviors are interpretable in rational terms. The theory of isomorphism addresses not the psychological states of actors but the structural determinants of the range of choices that actors perceive as rational or prudent.

6. Carroll and Delacroix 1982 clearly recognizes this and includes political and institutional legitimacy as a major resource. Aldrich 1979 has argued that the population perspective must attend to historical trends and changes in legal and political institutions.

7. This point was suggested by John Meyer. We are grateful for his extensive comments.

References

Abbott, Andrew. 1988. *The System of Professions: An Essay on the Division of Expert Labor*. Chicago: University of Chicago Press.

Abelson, Robert P. 1976. Script Processing in Attitude Formation and Decision Making. In *Cognition and Social Behavior*, ed. J. S. Carroll and J. W. Payne, 33–45. Hillsdale, N.J.: Erlbaum.

Abernathy, William. 1978. *The Productivity Dilemma*. Baltimore: Johns Hopkins University Press.

Abolafia, Mitchell. 1984. Structured Anarchy: Formal Organization in the Commodity Futures Market. In *The Social Dynamics of Financial Markets*, ed. Patricia Adler and Peter Adler, 129–50. Greenwich, Conn.: JAI Press.

Abrams, M. A. 1985. Art-as-Such: The Sociology of Modern Aesthetics. *Bulletin of the American Academy of Arts and Sciences* 38:8–33.

Adam, T. R. 1939. *The Museum and Popular Culture*. New York: American Association for Adult Education.

Aiken, Michael, and Jerald Hage. 1968. Organizational Interdependence and Intraorganizational Structure. *American Sociological Review* 33:912–30.

Akerlof, George. 1976. The Economics of Caste and of the Rat Race and Other Woeful Tales. *Quarterly Journal of Economics* 90:599–617.

Alchian, Armen, 1950. Uncertainty, Evolution, and Economic Theory. *Journal of Political* Economy 58:214–21.

Alchian, Armen A., and Harold Demsetz. 1972. Production, Information Cost, and Economic Organization. *American Economic Review* 62:777–95.

Aldrich, Howard E. 1972. An Organization-Environment Perspective on Cooperation and Conflict in the Manpower Training System. In *Conflict and Power in Complex Organizations*, ed. A. R. Negandhi, 11–37. Kent, Ohio: Center for Business and Economic Research.

_____. 1978. Centralization versus Decentralization in the Design of Human Service Delivery Systems: A Response to Gouldner's Lament. In *The Management of Human Services*, ed. R. C. Sarri and Y. Hasenfeld, 51–79. New York: Columbia University Press.

_____. 1979. *Organizations and Environments.* Englewood Cliffs, N.J.: PrenticeHall.

Aldrich, Howard E., and Jeffrey Pfeffer. 1976. Environments of Organizations. *Annual Review of Sociology* 2:79–105.

Aldrich, Howard E., and Udo Staber. 1988. Organizing Business Interests: Patterns of Trade Association Foundings, Transformations and Death. In *Ecological Models of Organizations*, ed. Glenn R. Carroll, 111–26. Cambridge, Mass.: Ballinger.

Aldrich, Howard E., and David A. Whetten. 1981. Organization-sets, Action-sets, and Networks: Making the Most of Simplicity. In *Handbook of Organization Design,* ed. P. C. Nystrom and W. H. Starbuck, 1:385–408. New York: Oxford University Press.

Alexander, C. N., Jr., L. G. Zucker, and C. Brody. 1970. Experimental Expectations and Autokinetic Experiences: Consistency Theories and Judgmental Convergence. *Sociometry* 33:108–22.

Alexander, Edward P. 1983. *Museum Masters: Their Museums and Their Influence.* Nashville: American Association for State and Local History.

Alexander, Jeffrey C. 1983. *The Modern Reconstruction of Classical Thought: Talcott Parsons.* Vol. 4 of *Theoretical Logic in Sociology.* Berkeley: University of California Press.

_____. 1987. *Twenty Lectures: Sociological Theory since World War II.* New York: Columbia University Press.

Alexander, Jeffrey C., and W. Richard Scott. 1984. The Impact of Regulation on the Administrative Structure of Hospitals: Toward an Analytic Framework. *Hospital and Health Services Administration* 29:71–85.

Alexander, Victoria D. 1988. Aging as a Societal Sector: Causes and Consequences of the Structuration of the Aging Industry. Paper presented at the annual meetings of the Pale Sociological Association, Las Vegas, April 5–8.

Alford Robert R. 1975. *Health Care Politics: Ideological and Interest Group Barriers to Reform.* Chicago: University of Chicago Press.

Alford, Robert R., and Roger Friedland. 1985. *Powers of Theory: Capitalism, the State and Democracy.* Cambridge: Cambridge University Press.

Alinsky, Saul. 1969. *Rules for Radicals.* Chicago: University of Chicago Press.

Allison, Graham T. 1971. *Essence of Decision: Explaining the Cuban Missile Crisis.* Boston: Little, Brown.

Althusser, Louis. 1969. *For Marx.* London: Allan Lane.

Amburgey, Terry L., and Paul G. Lippert. 1989. Institutional Determinants of Strategy: The Legitimation and Diffusion of Management Buyouts. Manuscript. University of Wisconsin.

American Management Association. 1926. Marketing Policies and Sales Methods that Stabilize Business. Sales Executive Series No. 36. New York: American Management Association.

Anderson , Florence. 1941. *Memorandum on the Use of Art and Music Study Materials.* New York: Carnegie Corporation of New York.

Anderson, Perry. 1974. *Passages from Antiquity to Feudalism.* London: New Left Books.

Angell, Robert C. 1936. Discussion of the Ecological Aspect of Institutions. *American Sociological Review* 1:189–92.

Aoki, Masahiko. 1984. Aspects of the Japanese Firm. In *The Economic Analysis of the Japanese Firm*, ed. M. Aoki, 3–43, Amsterdam: Elsevier.

Aristotle. 1929. *Politics.* Trans. P. H. Wicksted and F. M. Cornford. London: W. Heinemann.

Arthur, W. Brian. 1987. Urban Systems and Historical Path-Dependence. In *Urban Systems and Infrastructure,* ed. R. Herman and J. Ausubel. Washington, D.C.: NAS/NAE.

_____. 1988a. Competing Technologies: An Overview. In *Technical Change and Economic Theory*, ed. G. Dosi et al., 590–607. London: Pinter.

_____. 1988b. Self–Reinforcing Mechanisms in Economics. In *The Economy as an Evolving Complex System*, ed. P. W. Anderson and K. J. Arrow, 9–32. Menlo Park, Calif.: Addison–Wesley.

_____. 1989. Competing Technologies and Lock–in by Historical Events: The Dynamics of Allocation under Increasing Returns. *Economic Journal* 99(394):116–31.

_____. 1990. Positive Feedbacks in the Economy. *Scientific American* 262(2):92–99.

Ashworth, William. 1975. *A Short History of the International Economy since 1850.* London: Longman.

Astley, W. Graham. 1985. The Two Ecologies: Population and Community Perspectives on Organizational Evolution. *Administrative Science Quarterly* 30:224–41.

Astley, W. Graham, and Andrew Van de Ven. 1983. Central Perspectives and Debates in Organization Theory. *Administrative Science Quarterly* 28:245–73.

Bach, Richard F. 1924. *The Place of the Arts in American Life.* Office Memorandum, ser. I, no. 9. Carnegie Corporation, New York.

Badie, Bertrand, and Pierre Birnbaum. 1983. *The Sociology of the State.* Chicago: University of Chicago Press.

Bailes, Kendall. 1978. *Technology and Society under Lenin and Stalin.* Princeton: Princeton University Press.

Baker, Frank, and Gregory O'Brien. 1971. Intersystems Relations and Coordination of Human Service Organizations. *American Journal of Public Health* 61:130–37.

Baker, Wayne. 1984. The Social Structure of a National Securities Market. *American Journal of Sociology* 89:775–811.

Bales, Robert F. 1953. The Equilibrium Problem in Small Groups. In *Working Papers in the Theory of Action*, ed. T. Parsons, R. F. Bales, and E. A. Shils, 111–50. Glencoe, Ill.: Free Press.

Ballarin, E. 1986. *Commercial Banks amid the Financial Revolution.* Cambridge, Mass.: Ballinger Press.

Bankston, Mary. 1982. Organizational Reporting in a School District: State and Federal Programs. Project Report No. 82-A10. Stanford, Calif.: Institute for Research on Educational Finance and Governance, Stanford University.

Barbagli, Mario. 1982. *Educating for Unemployment.* Trans. from the Italian by Robert H. Ross. New York: Columbia University Press.

Barbu, Zevedei. 1960. *Problems of Historical Psychology.* London: Routledge and Kegan Paul.

Bardach, Eugene. 1977. *The Implementation Game: What Happens after a Bill Becomes a Law.* Cambridge: MIT Press.

Barnard, Chester. 1938. *The Function of the Executive.* Cambridge: Harvard University Press.

Barnouw, Erik. 1966–70. *A History of Broadcasting in the United States.* 3 vols. New York: Oxford University Press.

Baron, James P., Frank Dobbin, and P. Devereaux Jennings. 1986. War and Peace: The Evolution of Modern Personnel Administration in U.S. Industry. *American Journal of Sociology* 92:250–83.

Barzelay, Michael, and Rogers Smith. 1987. The One Best System? A Political Analysis of Neoclassical Institutionalist Perspectives on the Modern Corporation. In *Corporations and Society,* ed. W. Samuels and A. S. Miller, 81–110. New York: Greenwood Press.

Beker, Gary. 1981. *A Treatise on the Family.* Cambridge: Harvard University Press.

Bell, Daniel. 1973. *The Coming of Post-Industrial Society.* New York: Basic Books.

_____. 1976. *The Cultural Contradictions of Capitalism.* New York: Basic Books.

Bem, Daryl J. 1970. *Beliefs, Attitudes, and Human Affairs.* Belmont, Calif.: Brooks Cole.

Bendix, Reinhard. 1956. *Work and Authority in Industry.* Berkeley: University of California Press.

_____. 1964. *Nation-Building and Citizenship.* New York: Wiley.

_____. 1968. Bureaucracy. In *International Encyclopedia of the Social Sciences,* ed. David L. Sills, 206–19. New York: Macmillan.

Benson, J. Kenneth. 1975. The Interorganizational Network as a Political Economy. *Administrative Science Quarterly* 20:229–49.

_____. 1981. Networks and Policy Sectors: A Framework for Policy Analysis. In *Interorganizational Coordination,* ed. D. L. Rogers and D. A. Whetten, 137–76. Ames: Iowa State University Press.

Berger, Joseph, B. P. Cohen, and Morris Zelditch. 1966. Status Characteristics and Expectation States. In *Sociological Theories in Progress,* ed. J. Berger et al., 29–46. Boston: Houghton Mifflin.

_____. 1972. Status Characteristics and Social Interaction. *American Sociological Review* 37:241–44.

Berger, Peter L. 1968. *The Sacred Canopy: Elements of a Sociological Theory of Religion.* New York: Doubleday.

Berger, Peter L., Brigitte Berger, and Hansfried Kellner. 1973. *The Homeless Mind: Modernization and Consciousness.* New York: Random House.

Berger, Peter L., and Thomas Luckmann. 1967. *The Social Construction of Reality.* New York: Doubleday.

Berger, Suzanne D., ed. 1981. *Organizing Interests in Western Europe: Pluralism, Corporatism, and the Transformation of Politics*. Cambridge: Cambridge University Press.

Berk, Sarah Fenstermaker. 1985. *The Gender Factory*. New York: Plenum.

Berman, Paul, and Milbrey McLaughlin. 1975–78. *Federal Programs supporting Educational Change*. Vols. 1–8. Santa Monica, Calif.: Rand Corporation.

Berner, Roberta. 1983. Giving in Minnesota—1982: For Corporations, Foundations, Total Giving Tops 180 Million Dollars. *Giving Forum* 6(4):6.

Bernstein, Basil. 1971. *Class, Codes, and Control*. Vol. I. Boston: Routledge and Kegan Paul.

Bertsch, Kenneth. 1982. *Corporate Philanthropy*. Washington, D.C.: Investor Responsibility Research Center, Inc.

Best, Robert S. 1974. Youth Policy. In *Issues in Canadian Public Policy*, ed. G. B. Doern and V. S. Wilson, 137–65. San Francisco: Macmillan.

Bierstedt, Robert. 1970. *The Social Order*. 3rd ed. New York: McGraw-Hill.

Bierstedt, Robert, E. J. Meehan, and P. A. Samuelson. 1964. *Modern Social Science*. New York: McGraw-Hill.

Bingham, Mary, comp. 1933. *Who's Who in the Membership of the American Association of Museums*. Washington, D.C.: American Association of Museums.

Blake, J., and K. Davis. 1964. Norms, Values and Sanctions. In *Handbook of Modern Sociology*, ed. R. E. L. Faris, 247–79. Chicago: Rand McNally.

Blau, Peter M. 1956. *Bureaucracy in Modern Society*. New York: Random House.

_____. 1970. A Formal Theory of Differentiation in Organizations. *American Sociological Review* 35:201–18.

_____. 1977. *Inequality and Heterogeneity*. New York: Free Press.

Blau, Peter M., and Richard A. Schoenherr. 1971. *The Structure of Organizations*. New York: Basic Books.

Blau, Peter M., and W. Richard Scott. 1962. *Formal Organizations*. San Francisco: Chandler.

Block, Fred. 1977. The Ruling Class Does Not Rule. *Socialist Revolution* 7:6–28.

Blum, Alan F., and Peter McHugh. 1971. The Social Ascription of Motives. *American Sociological Review* 36:98–109.

Boltanski, Luc. *The Making of a Class: Cadres in French Society*. Trans. Arthur Goldhammer. New York: Cambridge University Press.

Boomer, D. S. 1959. Subjective Certainty and Resistance to Change. *Journal of Abnormal and Social Psychology* 58:323–28.

Boorman, Scott A., and Paul R. Levitt. 1979. The Cascade Principle for General Disequilibrium Dynamics. Harvard-Yale Reprints in Mathematical Sociology, no. 15.

Borcherding, T. E., and R. T. Deacon. 1972. The Demand for the Services of Non-Federal Government. *American Economic Review* 62:891–901.

Bourdieu, Pierre. [1972] 1977. *Outline of a Theory of Practice*. Cambridge: Cambridge University Press.

_____. 1981. Men and Machines. In *Advances in Social Theory and Methodology*, ed. K. Knorr-Cetina and A. Cicourel, 304–18. Boston: Routledge and Kegan Paul.

_____. 1984. *Distinction: A Social Critique of the Judgement of Taste*. Trans. Richard Nice. Cambridge: Harvard University Press.

_____. 1990. *The Logic of Practice*. Stanford: Stanford University Press.

Bourdieu, Pierre, and Luc Boltanski. 1975. Le titre et le poste: Rapports entre le système de reproduction. *Actes de la Recherche en Sciences Sociales* 2:95–107.

Bourdieu, Pierre, and Jean-Claude Passeron. 1977. *Reproduction in Education, Society, and Culture*. Trans. Richard Nice. Beverly Hills, Calif.: Sage.

Bourricaud, François. 1981. *The Sociology of Talcott Parsons*. Chicago: University of Chicago Press.

Bower, Gordon H., J. Black, and T. Turner. 1979. Scripts in Text Comprehension and Memory. *Cognitive Psychology* 11:177–220.

Bowles, Samuel, and Herbert Gintis. 1976. *Schooling in Capitalist America*. New York: Basic Books.

Braito, Rita, Steve Paulson, and Gerald Klonglon. 1972. Domain Consensus: A Key Variable in Interorganizational Analysis. In *Complex Organizations and Their Environments*, ed. M. B. Brinkerhoff and P. R. Kunz, 176–92. Dubuque, Iowa: Wm. C Brown.

Braudel, Fernand. 1982. *The Wheels of Commerce*. New York: Harper and Row.

Brint, Steven. 1984. "New Class" and Cumulative Trend Explanations of the Liberal Political Attitudes of Professionals. *American Journal of Sociology* 91:30–70.

Brint, Steven, and Jerome Karabel. 1989. *The Diverted Dream: Community Colleges and the Promise of Educational Opportunity in America, 1900–1985.* New York: Oxford University Press.

Brown, John L., and Rodney Schneck. 1979. A Structuralist Comparison between Canadian and American Industrial Organizations. *Administrative Science Quarterly* 24:24–47.

Brown, Lawrence D. 1983. *New Policies, New Politics: Government's Response to Government's Growth.* Washington, D.C.: Brookings Institute.

Brown, Richard H. 1978. Bureaucracy as Praxis: Toward a Phenomenology of Formal Organizations. *Administrative Science Quarterly* 23 (September): 365–82.

Buckley, Walter. 1967. *Sociology and Modern Systems Theory.* Englewood Cliffs, N.J.: Prentice-Hall.

Bull, Hedley, and Alan Watson. 1984. *The Expansion of International Society.* Oxford: Oxford University Press.

Burawoy, Michael. 1983. Between the Labor Process and the State: The Changing Face of Factory Regimes under Advanced Capitalism. *American Sociological Review* 48:587–605.

Burgelman, Robert A., and Jitendra V. Singh. 1988. Strategy and Organization: An Evolutionary Approach. Wharton School, University of Pennsylvania. Manuscript.

Burns, Lawton R., and Douglas R. Wholey. 1990. The Diffusion of Matrix Management: Effects of Task Diversity and Interorganizational Networks. Manuscript. University of Arizona.

Burns, Tom, and Helen Flam. 1987. *The Shaping of Social Organization.* Newbury Park, Calif.: Sage.

Burns, Tom, and G. M. Stalker. 1961. *The Management of Innovation.* London: Tavistock.

Burt, Ronald S. 1983. *Corporate Profits and Cooptation.* New York: Academic Press.

Cahill, Holger. 1944. John Cotton Dana and the Newark Museum. Foreword to *The Newark Museum: A Museum in Action.* Newark, N.J.: Newark Museum.

Callahan, Raymond E. 1962. *Education and the Cult of Efficiency.* Chicago: University of Chicago Press.

Camic, Charles. 1986. The Matter of Habit. *American Journal of Sociology* 91(5):1039–87.

_____. 1989. Structure after 50 Years: The Anatomy of a Charter. *American Journal of Sociology* 95(1):38–107.

Campbell, R. F., and T. L. Mazzoni, Jr. 1976. *State Policy Making for the Public Schools.* Berkeley, Calif.: McCutchan.

Cantor, Nancy, and Walter Mischel. 1977. Traits as Prototypes: Effects on Recognition Memory. *Journal of Personality and Social Psychology* 35:38–49.

Carlson, Richard O. 1962. *Executive Succession and Organizational Change.* Chicago: Midwest Administration Center, University of Chicago.

Carroll, Glenn. 1983. A Stochastic Model of Organizational Mortality: Review and Reanalysis. *Social Science Research* 12:303–29.

_____. 1984. Organizational Ecology. *Annual Review of Sociology* 10:71–93.

_____. 1987. *Publish and Perish: The Organizational Ecology of Newspaper Foundings.* Greenwich, Conn.: JAI Press.

_____. ed. 1988. *Ecological Models of Organization.* Cambridge, Mass.: Ballinger.

Carroll, Glenn R., and Jacques Delacroix. 1982. Organizational Mortality in the Newspaper Industries of Argentina and Ireland: An Ecological Approach. *Administrative Science Quarterly* 27:169–98.

Carroll, Glenn R., J. Delacroix, and J. Goodstein. 1988. The Political Environment of Organizations: An Ecological View. In *Research in Organizational Behavior*, vol. 10. Greenwich, Conn.: JAI Press.

Carroll, Glenn R., Jerry Goodstein. and Antal Gyenes. 1988. Organizations and the State: Effects of the Institutional Environment on Agricultural Cooperatives in Hungary. *Administrative Science Quarterly* 33(2):233–56.

Carroll, Glenn R., and Yang-chung Paul Huo. 1986. Organizational Task and Institutional Environments in Ecological Perspective: Findings from the Local Newspaper Industry, *American Journal of Sociology* 91:838–73.

Caves, Richard E., and Masu Uekusa. 1976. *Industrial Organization in Japan.* Washington, D.C.: Brookings Institute.

Chandler, Alfred D. 1961. *Strategy and Structure.* Cambridge: MIT Press.

_____. 1977. *The Visible Hand: The Managerial Revolution in American Business.* Cambridge: Harvard University Press.

Chang, Chan-sup. 1987. Management of Chaebol: The Conglomerate in South Korea. In *Proceedings of the Pan-Pacific Conference IV*, 42–47. Taipei, Taiwan.

Child, John. 1972. Organization Structure, Environment and Performance: The Role of Strategic Choice. *Sociology* 6:1–22.

Child, John, and Alfred Kieser. 1981. Development of Organizations over Time. In *Handbook of Organizational Design,* ed. P. C. Nystrom and W. H. Starbuck, 28–64. New York: Oxford University Press.

Cicourel, Aaron. 1964. *Method and Measurement in Sociology.* New York: Free Press.

_____. 1970. The Acquisition of Social Structure: Toward a Developmental Sociology of Language. In *Understanding Everyday Life,* ed. J. D. Douglas, 136–68. Chicago: Aldine.

_____. 1974. *Cognitive Sociology.* New York: Free Press.

Ciniglio, Ada V. 1976. Pioneers in American Museums: Paul J. Sachs. *Museum News* 54:48–51, 68–71.

Clark, Burton R. 1956. *Adult Education in Transition.* Berkeley: University of California Press.

_____. 1960a. The "Cooling-Out Function" in Higher Education. *American Journal of Sociology* 65:569–76.

_____. 1960b. *The Open-Door Colleges: A Case Study.* New York: McGraw-Hill.

_____. 1962. *Educating the Expert Society.* San Francisco: Chandler.

_____. 1986. *The Higher Education System: Academic Organization in Cross-National Perspective.* Berkeley; University of California Press.

Coase, Ronald H. 1937. The Nature of the Firm. *Economica* 16:386–405.

_____. 1960. The Problem of Social Cost. *Journal of Law and Economics* 3:1–44.

Cohen, Bernard P. 1980. *Developing Sociological Knowledge: Theory and Method.* Englewood Cliffs, N.J.: Prentice-Hall.

Cohen, Michael D., and James G. March. 1974. *Leadership and Ambiguity: The American College President.* New York: McGraw-Hill.

Cohen, Michael D., James G. March, and Johan P. Olsen. 1972. A Garbage Can Model of Organizational Choice. *Administrative Science Quarterly* 17:1–25.

Cohen, Myron L. 1976. *House United, House Divided: The Chinese Family in Taiwan.* New York: Columbia University Press.

Cole, Robert. 1985. The Macropolitics of Organizational Change: A Comparative Analysis of the Spread of Small-Group Activities. *Administrative Science Quarterly* 30:560–85.

Coleman, J. F., R. R. Blake, and J. S. Mouton. 1958. Task Difficulty and Conformity Pressures. *Journal of Abnormal and Social Psychology* 57:120–22.

Coleman, James S. 1964. *Introduction to Mathematical Sociology.* New York: Free Press.

_____. 1974. *Power and the Structure of Society.* New York: Norton.

_____. 1982. *The Asymmetric Society.* Syracuse, N.Y.: Syracuse University Press.

_____. 1985. Micro Foundations and Macrosocial Theory. In *Approaches to Social Theory*, ed. S. Lindenberg et al., 345–63. New York: Russell Sage.

_____. 1986. Social Theory, Social Research, and a Theory of Action. *American Journal of Sociology* 91:1309–35.

Coleman, James S., and Thomas Hoffer. 1987. *Public and Private High Schools: The Impact of Communities.* New York: Basic Books.

Coleman, Laurence Vail. 1932. Recent Progress and Condition of Museums. In U.S. Commissioner of Education, *Biennial Survey of Education in the United States, 1928–30.* Washington, D.C.: U.S. Government Printing Office.

_____. 1939. *The Museum in America: A Critical Study.* Washington, D. C.: American Association of Museums.

Collins, N., and L. Preston. 1961. The Size Structure of the Largest Industrial Firms, 1900–1958. *American Economic Review* 51:986–1011.

Collins, Randall. 1975. *Conflict Sociology.* New York: Academic Press.

_____. 1979. *The Credential Society.* New York: Academic Press.

_____. 1981. On the Micro-Foundations of Macro-Sociology. *American Journal of Sociology* 86:984–1014.

_____. 1986a. Is Sociology in the Doldrums? *American Journal of Sociology* 91:1336–55.

_____. 1986b. The Weberian Revolution of the High Middle Ages. In *Weberian Sociology Theory*, 45–76. New York: Cambridge University Press.

_____. 1988a. The Durkheimian Tradition in Conflict Sociology. In *Durkeimian Sociology: Cultural Studies*, ed. J. C. Alexander, 107–28. New York: Columbia University Press.

_____. 1988b. The Micro Contribution to Macro Sociology. *Sociological Theory* 6:242–53.

Committee on Youth. 1971. *A Report to the Secretary of State: It's Your Turn.* Ottawa: Information Canada.

Cooke, Edmund. 1934. A Survey of the Educational Activities of Forty-seven Museums. *Museum News* 12:6.

Cooper, S. K., and D. R. Fraser. 1984. *Banking Deregulation and the New Competition in the Financial Services Industry.* Cambridge, Mass.: Ballinger Press.

Copeland, M. 1927. Marketing. In *Recent Economic Changes in the United States,* 321–424. New York: McGraw-Hill.

Cornwell, H. C. 1966. Personality Variables in Autokinetic Figure Writing. *Perceptual and Motor Skills* 22:731–35.

Coser, Lewis, Charles Kadushin, and Walter W. Powell. 1982. *Books: The Culture and Commerce of Publishing.* New York: Basic Books.

Covaleski, Mark A., and Mark W. Dirsmith. 1988. An Institutional Perspective on the Rise, Social Transformation, and Fall of a University Budget Category. *Administrative Science Quarterly* 33(4):562–87.

Cross, K. Patricia. 1971. *Beyond the Open Door.* San Francisco: Jossey-Bass.

Cummings, Bruce. 1984. The Origins and Development of the Northeast Asian Political Economy: Industrial Sectors Product Cycles, and Political Consequences. *International Organization* 381:1–40.

Cyert, Richard M., and James G. March. 1963. *A Behavioral Theory of the Firm.* Englewood Cliffs, N.J.: Prentice-Hall.

Daft, Richard L. 1983. *Organization Theory and Design.* St. Paul, Minn.: West Publishing.

Dahrendorf, Ralf. 1964. *Class and Class Conflict in Industrial Society.* Stanford: Stanford University Press.

Daily Economic News. 1986. *Directory of Korean Firms for 1985.*

Dalton, Melville, 1959. *Men Who Manage.* New York: Wiley.

Dana, John Cotton. 1917. *The Gloom of the Museum.* Woodstock, Vt.: Elm Tree Press.

David, Paul. 1986. Understanding the Economics of QWERTY: The Necessity of History. In *Economic History and the Modern Historian,* ed. W. Parker, 30–49. London: Blackwell.

Davis, Keith. 1973. The Case for and against Business Assumption of Social Responsibilities. *Academy of Management Journal* 16:312–22.

Davis, Kingsley. 1949. *Human Society.* New York: Macmillan.

Davis, Stanley M., and Paul R. Lawrence. 1977. *Matrix.* Reading, Mass.: Addison Wesley.

Deacon, R. T. 1978. A Demand Model for the Local Public Sector. *Review of Economics and Statistics* 50:184–92.

Deci, Edward L. 1971. Effects of Externally Mediated Rewards on Intrinsic Motivation. *Journal of Personality and Social Psychology* 18:105–15.

Delacroix, Jacques, and Glenn R. Carroll. 1983. Organizational Foundings: An Ecological Study of the Newspaper Industry of Argentina and Ireland. *Administrative Science Quarterly* 28:274–91.

Deleuze, Giles. 1988. *Foucault.* Minneapolis: University of Minnesota Press.

Derthick, Martha. 1972. *New Towns In-Town.* Washington, D.C.: Urban Institute.

Dill, William R. 1958. Environment as an Influence on Managerial Autonomy. *Administrative Science Quarterly* 2:409–43.

DiMaggio, Paul J. 1977. Market Structures, the Creative Process, and Popular Culture. *Journal of Popular Culture* 11:436–52.

_____. 1982a. Cultural Entrepreneurship in Nineteenth-Century Boston, Part I: The Creation of an Organizational Base for High Culture in America. *Media, Culture and Society* 4:33–50.

_____. 1982b. Cultural Entrepreneurship in Nineteenth-Century Boston, Part II: The Classification and Framing of American Art. *Media, Culture and Society* 4:303–22.

_____. 1983. State Expansion and Organizational Fields. In *Organizational Theory and Public Policy,* ed. R. H. Hall and R. E. Quinn, 147–61. Beverly Hills, Calif.: Sage.

_____. 1986a. Structural Analysis of Organizational Fields: A Blockmodel Approach. In *Research in Organizational Behavior,* ed. Barry M. Staw and L. L. Cummings, 8:335–70. Greenwich, Conn.: JAI Press.

_____. 1986b. Support for the Arts from Private Foundations. In *Nonprofit Enterprise in the Arts,* ed. Paul DiMaggio, 113–39. New York Oxford University Press.

_____. 1988a. Interest and Agency in Institutional Theory. In *Institutional Patterns and Organizations,* ed. L. G. Zucker, 3–22. Cambridge, Mass.: Ballinger.

_____. 1988b. Progressivism in the Arts. *Society* 25:70–75.

DiMaggio, Paul J. and Walter W. Powell. 1983. The Iron Cage Revisited: Institutional Isomorphism and Collective Rationality in Organizational Fields. *American Sociological Review* 48:147–60.

_____. 1984. Institutional Isomorphism and Structural Conformity. Paper presented at 1984 American Sociological Association Annual meetings. San Antonio, Tex.

Dobbin, Frank R. 1986. The Institutionalization of the State: Industrial Policy in Britain, France, and the United States. Ph.D. diss. Stanford University.

Dobbin, Frank R., Lauren Edelman, John W. Meyer, W. Richard Scott, and Ann Swidler. 1988 The Expansion of Due Process in Organizations. In *Institutional Patterns and Organizations*, ed. L. G. Zucker, 71–98. Cambridge, Mass.: Ballinger.

Dodwell Marketing Consultants, comp. 1984. *Industrial Groupings in Japan*. Rev. ed. Tokyo: Dodwell.

Domhoff, J. William. 1967. *Who Rules America?* Englewood Cliffs, NJ.: Prentice-Hall.

_____.1970. *The Higher Circles*. New York: Random House.

_____. 1979. *The Powers That Be: Processes of Ruling Class Domination in America*. New York: Random House.

_____. 1983. Who Rules America Now? Englewood Cliffs, N.J.: Prentice-Hall.

Donabedian, Avedis. 1966. Evaluating the Quality of Medical Care. *Milbank Memorial Fund Quarterly* 44 (part 2):166ˆ–203.

Dore, Ronald P. 1976. *The Diploma Disease: Education, Qualifications and Development*. Berkeley: University of California Press.

_____. 1983. Goodwill and the Spirit of Market Capitalism. *British Journal of Sociology* 34(4):459–82.

_____. 1986. *Structural Adjustment in Japan, 1970-82*. Geneva: International Labour Office.

Dornbusch, Sanford M., and W. Richard Scott. 1975. *Evaluation and the Exercise of Authority*. San Francisco: Jossey-Ross.

Douglas, Mary. 1986. *How Institutions Think*. Syracuse, N.Y.: Syracuse University Press.

Dowling, John, and Jeffrey Pfeffer. 1975. Organizational Legitimacy: Social Values and Organizational Behavior. *Pacific Sociological Review* 18:122–36.

Downs, Anthony. 1967. *Inside Bureaucracy*. Boston: Little, Brown.

Dumont, Louis. 1982. A Modified View of Our Origins: The Christian Beginnings of Modern Individualism. *Religion* 12:1–27.

Durkheim, Emile. [1901] 1950. *The Rules of Sociological Method*. Glencoe, Ill.: Free Press.

_____. 1933. *The Division of Labor in Society*. New York: Macmillan.

Dye, Thomas R. 1981. *Understanding Public Policy*. 4th ed. Englewood Cliffs, N.J.: Prentice- Hall

_____. 1986. *Who's Running America? The Conservative Years*. 4th ed. Englewood Cliffs, N.J.: Prentice-Hall.

Dyson, Kenneth H. F. 1980. *The State Tradition in Western Europe*. Oxford: Oxford University Press.

Eccles, Robert G., and Harrison C. White. 1988. Price and Authority in Inter-Profit Center Transactions. *American Journal of Sociology* 94:517–52.

Economic Council of Canada. 1976. *People and Jobs: A Study of the Canadian Labour Market*. Ottawa: Information Canada.

_____. 1977. *Into the 80s*. Ottawa: Information Canada.

Edelman, Lauren B. 1985. Organizational Governance and Due Process; The Expansion of Rights in the American Workplace. Ph.D. diss, Stanford University.

_____. 1990. Legal Environments and Organizational Governance: The Expansion of Due Process in the American Workplace. *American Journal of Sociology* 95:1401–40.

Edelman, Murray. 1967. *The Symbolic Uses of Politics*. Urbana: University of Illinois Press.

Eis, C. 1978. *The 1919–1930 Merger Movement in American Industry*. New York: Arno Press.

Eisenstadt, Schmuel N. 1968. Social Institutions: The Concept. In *International Encyclopedia of the Social Sciences*, ed. D. L. Sills, 14:409–21. New York: Macmillan.

_____. 1983. Transcendental Visions—Other Worldliness—And Its Transformations. *Religion* 13:1–17.

_____. 1985. Civilizational Formations and Political Dynamics: The Stein Rokkan Lecture, 1985. *Scandinavian Political Studies* 8:231–51.

Elazar, Daniel J. 1972. *American Federalism: A View from the States*. 2d ed. New York: Harper and Row.

Elias, Norbert. *1978. The Civilizing Process*. New York: Urizen Books.

Ellul, Jacques. 1964. *The Technological Society*. New York: Knopf.

Elster, Jon. 1982. Marxism, Functionalism, and Game Theory. *Theory and Society* 11:453–82.

_____. 1985. *Making Sense of Marx*. Cambridge: Cambridge University Press.

_____. 1986. Introduction. In *Rational Choice*, ed. John Elster, 1–33. New York: New York University Press.

Emery, Fred L., and Eric L. Trist. 1965. The Causal Texture of Organizational Environments. *Human Relations* 18:21–32.

Encarnation. Dennis J. 1983. Public Finance and Regulation of Non-Public Education: Retrospect and Prospect. In *Public Dollars for Private Schools*, ed. T. James and H. M. Levin, 175–95. Philadelphia: Temple University Press.

Estes, Carroll L. 1979. *The Aging Enterprise*. San Francisco: Jossey-Bass.

Evan, William M. 1966. The Organization Set: Toward a Theory of Interorganizational Relations. In *Approaches to Organizational Design*, ed. James D. Thompson, 173–88. Pittsburgh: University of Pittsburgh Press.

Everard, L. C., ed. 1932. Handbook of American Museums. Washington, D.C.: American Association of Museums.

Fararo, Thomas J., and John Skvoretz. 1986. Action and Institution, Network and Function;:The Cybernetic Concept of Social Structure. *Sociological Forum* 1:219–50.

Farr, Robert M., and Serge Moscovici, eds. 1984. *Social Representations*. Cambridge: Cambridge University Press.

Farrow, B. J., J. F. Santos, J. R. Haines, and C. M. Solley. 1965. Influence of Repeated Experience on the Latency and Extent of Autokinetic Movement. *Perceptual and Motor Skills* 20:1113–20.

Faucheux, Claude, Gilles Amado, and Andre Laurent. 1982. Organizational Development and Change. *Annual Review of Psychology* 33:343–70.

Federal Trade Commission. 1957. *Report on Industrial Concentration and Product Diversification in the 1000 Largest Manufacturing Companies*. Washington, D. C.: U. S. Government Printing Office.

Feinberg, Walter. 1980. *Revisionists Respond to Ravitch*. Washington, D. C.: National Academy of Education.

Fennell, Mary L. 1980. The Effects of Environmental Characteristics on the Structure of Hospital Clusters. *Administrative Science Quarterly* 25:484–510.

Field, Alexander J. 1979. On the Explanation of Rules Using Rational Choice Models. *Journal of Economic Issues* 13:49–72.

Firestone, William A. 1985. The Study of Loose Coupling: Problems, Progress, and Prospects. In *Research in Sociology of Education and Socialization*, ed. Ronald G. Corwin, 5:3–30. Greenwich, Conn.: JAI Press.

Fiske, Susan T. 1982. Schema-Triggered Affect: Applications to Social Perception. In *Affect and Cognition: The 17th Annual Carnegie Symposium on Cognition*, ed. M. S. Clarke and S. T. Fiske, 55–78. Hillsdale, N.J.: Erlbaum.

Fiske, Susan T., and Mark A. Pavelchak. 1986. Category-Based versus Piece-meal-Based Affective Responses: Developments in Schema-Triggered Affect. In *Handbook of Motivation and Cognition: Foundations of Social Behavior*, ed. R. M. Sorrentino and E. T. Higgins, 167–203. New York: Guilford.

Fitzpatrick, Sheila. 1979. *Education and Social Mobility in the Soviet Union, 1921–1934*. New York: Columbia University Press.

Flacks, Richard. 1988. *Making History vs. Making Life: Left and Mainstream in American Consciousness*. New York: Columbia University Press.

Fligstein, Neil. 1985. The Spread of the Multidivisional Form among Large Firms, 1919–1979. *American Sociological Review* 50:377–91.

_____. 1987. The Intraorganizational Power Struggle: The Rise of Finance Presidents in Large Firms, 1919–79. *American Sociological Review* 52:44–58.

_____. 1990a. Organizational, Economic, and Demographic Determinants of the Growth Patterns of Large Firms, 1919–79. In *Comparative Social Research*, ed. Craig Calhoun, 12:45–76. Greenwich, Conn.: JAI Press.

_____. 1990b. *The Transformation of Corporate Control*. Cambridge: Harvard University Press.

Flora, Peter, and J. A. Heidenheimer. 1981. *The Development of Welfare States in Europe and America*. New Brunswick, N.J.: Transaction.

Foucault, Michel. 1978. *The History of Sexuality*. Vol. 1. New York: Vintage.

_____. 1979. Governmentality. *Ideology and Consciousness* 6:5–21.

_____. 1980. *Power/Knowledge*. Ed. Colin Gordon. New York: Pantheon.

_____. 1983. The Subject and Power. In *Michel Foucault: Beyond Structuralism and Hermeneutics*, 2d ed., ed. H. Dreyfus and P. Rabinow, 208–23. Chicago: University of Chicago Press.

Fox, Daniel M. 1963. *Engines of Culture. Philanthropy and Art Museums*. Madison: Wisconsin State Historical Society.

Freedman, J. L., J. M. Carlsmith, and D. O. Sears. 1974. *Social Psychology.* 2d ed. Englewood Cliffs, N.J.: Prentice-Hall.

Freeman, John H. 1973. Environment, Technology and Administrative Intensity of Manufacturing Organizations. *American Sociological Review* 38:750–63.

_____. 1979. Going to the Well: School District Administrative Intensity and Environmental Constraint. *Administrative Science Quarterly* 24:119–33.

_____. 1982. Organizational Life Cycles and Natural Selection Processes. In *Research in Organizational Behavior,* ed. B. Staw and L. L. Cummings, 4:1–32. Greenwich, Conn.: JAI Press.

Freeman, John H., Glenn R. Carroll, and Michael T. Hannan. 1983. The Liability of Newness: Age Dependence in Organizational Death Rates. *American Sociological Review* 48:692–710.

Freeman, John H., and Michael T. Hannan. 1983. Niche Width and the Dynamics of Organizational Populations. *American Journal of Sociology* 88:1116–45.

Freidson, Eliot. 1986. *Professional Powers: A Study of the Institutionalization of Formal Knowledge.* Chicago: University of Chicago Press.

Friedland, Roger, and Richard D. Hocht. 1989. Rocks, Roads and Ramot Control: The Other War for Jerusalem. *Soundings* 72(2–3):227–73.

_____. 1990. Jerusalem: Deconstructing the Politics of a Sacred City. Paper presented at the American Academy of Religion, New Orleans.

Friedland, Roger, and A. F. Robertson. 1990. Beyond the Marketplace. In *Beyond the Marketplace: Rethinking Economy and Society.* ed. Roger Friedland and A. F. Robertson, 2–52. New York: Aldine de Gruyter.

Friedman, Debra, and Michael Hechter. 1988. The Contribution of Rational Choice Theory to Macrosociological Research. Paper presented at the annual meetings of the American Sociological Association, Atlanta, Ga.

Friedman, Lawrence M. 1973. *A History of American Law.* New York: Simon and Schuster.

Fukuda, John K. 1983. Transfer of Management: Japanese Practices for the Orientals? *Management Decision* 21:17–26.

Futatsugi, Yusaku. 1982. *Nihon no kabushiki shoyu kozo* (The structure of shareholding in Japan). Tokyo: Dobunkan.

_____. 1986. *Japanese Enterprise Groups.* Monograph No. 4. School of Business Administration, Kobe University.

Galaskiewicz, Joseph. 1984. Interorganizational Relations. *Annual Review of Sociology* 11:281–304.

_____. 1985a. Professional Networks and the Institutionalization of a Single Mind Set. *American Sociological Review* 50:639–58.

_____. 1985b. *Social Organization of an Urban Grants Economy: A Study of Business Philanthropy and Nonprofit Organizations.* Orlando, Fla.: Academic Press.

_____. 1987. The Study of a Business Elite and Corporate Philanthropy in a U.S. Metropolitan Area. In *Research Methods for Elite Studies,* ed. G. Moyser and M. Wagstaffe, 147–65. London: Allen and Unwin.

Galaskiewicz, Joseph, and Ronald S. Burt. 1991. Interorganizational Contagion in Corporate Philanthropy. *Administrative Science Quarterly* 36(1):88–105.

Galaskiewicz, Joseph, and Stanley Wasserman. 1989. Mimetic and Normative Processes within an Interorganizational Field: An Empirical Test. *Administrative Science Quarterly* 34(3):454–79.

Galbraith, Jay. 1973. *Designing Complex Organizations.* Reading, Mass.: Addison-Wesley.

Gamson, William A. 1975. *The Strategy of Social Protest.* Homewood, Ill.: Dorsey Press.

Gans, Sheldon, and Gerald Horton. 1975. *Integration of Human Services: The State and Municipal Levels.* New York: Praeger.

Gardner, Elmer A., and James N. Snipe. 1970. Toward the Coordination and Integration of Personal Health Services. *American Journal of Public Health* 60:2068–78.

Garfinkel, Harold. 1967. *Studies In Ethnomethodology.* Englewood Cliffs, N.J.: Prentice-Hall.

GAUSS. 1985. Program and Documentation.

Geertz, Clifford. 1973. *The Interpretation of Cultures.* New York: Basic Books.

_____. 1975. On the Nature of Anthropological Understanding. *American Scientist* 63:47–53.

_____. 1983. Local Knowledge. New York: Basic Books.

Gerth, Hans, and C. Wright Mills. 1953. *Character and Social Structure.* New York: Harcourt Brace.

Giddens, Anthony. 1976. *The New Rules of the Sociological Method.* New York: Basic Books.

_____. 1979. *Central Problems in Social Theory: Action, Structure, and Contradiction in Social Analysis.* Berkeley: University of California Press.

_____. 1982. *Sociology.* New York: Harcourt Brace Jovanovich.

_____. 1984. *The Constitution of Society.* Berkeley: University of California Press.

_____. 1986. *The Nation-State and Violence.* Berkeley: University of California *Press.*

Gilman, Benjamin Ives. 1918. *Museum Ideals.* Cambridge: Harvard University Press for the Museum of Fine Arts.

Glasberg Davita S., and Michael Schwartz. 1983. Ownership and Control of Corporations. *Annual Review of Sociology* 9:311–32.

Goffman. Erving. 1961. *Asylums: Essays on the Social Situation of Mental Patients and Other Inmates.* New York: Doubleday.

_____. 1967. *Interaction Ritual.* Garden City, N. Y.: Anchor.

_____. 1974. *Frame Analysis.* Cambridge: Harvard University Press.

Gold, Thomas B. 1986. *State and Society in the Taiwan Miracle.* New York: M. E. Sharpe.

Goldner, Fred, and Richard R. Ritti. 1967. Professionalism as Career Immobility. *American Journal of Sociology* 72:489–502.

Goode, George Brown. 1897. Memorial to George Brown Goode, Together with a Selection of His Papers on Museums and on the History of Science in America. In *Annual Report for 1897.* Smithsonian Institution, Washington, D.C.

Goodwin, Gregory. 1971. The Historical Development of the Community-Junior College Ideology. Ph.D. diss., Department of Education, University of Illinois.

Gort, M. 1961. *Diversification and Integration in American Industry.* Princeton: Princeton University Press.

Gouldner, Alvin W. 1954. *Patterns of Industrial Bureaucracy.* Glencoe, Ill.: Free Press.

_____. 1962. Anti-Minotaur The Myth of a Value-Free Sociology. *Social Problems* 9:199–213.

_____. 1970. *The Coming Crisis of Western Sociology.* New York: Basic Books.

_____. 1978. The New Class Project, I. *Theory and Society* 7:153–202

_____. 1979. *The Future of Intellectuals and the Rise of the New Class.* New York: Seabury.

Gramsci, Antonio. 1971. *Selections from the Prison Notebooks.* New York: International Publishers.

Grana, Cesar. 1963. *Fact and Symbol: Essays in the Sociology of Art and Literature.* New York: Oxford University Press.

Granovetter, Mark. 1973. The Strength of Weak Ties. *American Journal of Sociology* 78:1360–80.

_____. 1978. Threshold Models of Collective Behavior. *American Journal of Sociology* 83:1420–43.

_____. 1985. Economic Action and Social Structure: The Problem of Embeddedness. *American Journal of Sociology* 91:481–510.

Greenwood, Royston, and C. R. Hinings. 1988. Organizational Design Types, Tracks and the Dynamics of Strategic Change. *Organization Studies* 9:293–316.

Gregory, R. L., and O. L. Zangweil. 1963. The Origin of the Autokinetic Effect. *Quarterly Journal of Experimental Psychology* 15:252–61.

Grodzins, Morton. 1961. Centralization and Decentralization in the Federal System. In *A Nation of States: Essays on the American Federal System,* ed. Robert A. Goldwin, 1–23. Chicago: Rand McNally.

_____. 1966. *The American System.* Chicago: Rand McNally.

Grossman, Sanford J., and Oliver Hart. 1987. The Costs and Benefits of Ownership: A Theory of Vertical and Lateral Integration. *Journal of Political Economy* 94:691–719.

Gusfield, Joseph. 1955. Social Structure and Moral Reform: A Study of the Womens' Christian Temperance Union. *American Journal of Sociology* 61:221–32.

Gwyn, Sandra. 1972. The Great Ottawa Grant Boom (and How It Grew). *Saturday Night* 87(10):7–20.

Habermas, Jurgen. 1970. *Toward a Rational Society.* Boston: Beacon Press.

_____. 1975. *Legitimation Crisis.* Boston: Beacon Press.

_____. 1984. *The Theory of Communicative Action.* Boston: Beacon Press.

Hadley, Eleanor M. 1970. *Antitrust in Japan.* Princeton: Princeton University Press.

Hahn, Chan K., Yong H. Kim, and Jay S. Kim. 1987. An Analysis of Korean Chaebols: Formation and Growth Pattern. In *Proceedings* of *the Pan-Pacific Conference IV.* 128–33. Taipei, Taiwan.

Hall, John A. 1986. *Powers and Liberties: The Causes and Consequences of the Rise of the West.* New York: Penguin.

Hall, Peter. 1987. A Historical Overview of the Private Nonprofit Sector. In *The Nonprofit Sector: A Research Handbook,* ed. W. W. Powell, 3–26. New Haven: Yale University Press.

Hall, Richard. 1968. Professionalization and Bureaucratization. *American Sociological Review* 33:92–104.

Halperin, Marton H. 1974. *Bureaucratic Politics and Foreign Policy.* Washington, D.C.: Brookings Institution.

Hamilton, Gary G., and Nicole Woolsey Biggart. 1988. Market, Culture, and Authority: A Comparative Analysis of Management and Organization in the Far East. *American Journal of Sociology* 94:S52–S94.

Hankook Ilbo. 1985. *Pal ship o nyndo hankook ui 50 dae jae bul* (The 50 top *chaebol* in Korea). Seoul, Korea.

Hannan, Michael T. 1986a. A Model of Competitive and Institutional Processes in Organizational Ecology. Technical Report No. 86–13. Department of Sociology, Cornell University.

_____. 1986b. Uncertainty, Diversity, and Organizational Change. In *Behavioral and Social Sciences: Fifty Years of Discovery,* ed. N. Smelser and D. Gerstein, 73–94. Washington, D.C.: National Academy Press.

Hannan, Michael T., and John H. Freeman. 1977. The Population Ecology of Organizations. *American Journal of Sociology* 82:929–64.

_____. 1981. Niche Width and the Dynamics of Organizational Populations. Technical Report No. 2. Institute for Mathematical Studies in the Social Sciences, Stanford University.

_____. 1984. Structural Inertia and Organizational Change. *American Sociological Review* 49:149–64.

_____. 1987. The Ecology of Organizational Founding: American Labor Unions, 1836–1985. *American Journal of Sociology* 92:910–43.

_____. 1988. The Ecology of Organizational Mortality: American Labor Unions, 1836–1985. *American Journal of Sociology* 94:25–52.

_____. 1989. *Organizational Ecology.* Cambridge: Harvard University Press.

Harris, Neil. 1962. The Gilded Age Revisited: Boston and the Museum Movement. *American Quarterly* 14:545–66.

Hastings, A., and C. R. Hinings. 1970. Role Relations and Value Adaptation: A Study of the Professional Accountant in Industry. *Sociology* 4:353–66.

Hatch, Elvin. 1989. Theories of Social Honor. *American Anthropologist* 91:341–53.

Hawley, Amos. 1968. Human Ecology. *In International Encyclopedia of the Social Sciences,* ed. David L. Sills, 328–37. New York: Macmillan.

Hawley, Ellis W. 1966. *The New Deal and the Problem of Monopoly: A Study in Economic Ambivalence.* Princeton: Princeton University Press.

Hay, Robert, and Ed Gray. 1974. Social Responsibilities of Business Managers. *Academy of Management Journal* 17:135–43.

Hayek, Friedrich August von. 1973. *Law, Legislation, and Liberty.* Vol. 1. London: Routledge and Kegan Paul.

Hayes, Michael T. 1981. *Lobbyists and Legislators: A Theory of Political Markets.* New Brunswick, N.J.: Rutgers University Press.

Hays, Samuel P. 1957. *The Response to Industrialism, 1985–1914.* Chicago: University of Chicago Press.

_____. 1964. The Politics of Reform in Municipal Government in the Progressive Era. *Pacific Northwest Quarterly* 55:157–69.

_____. 1972. The New Organizational Society. In *Building the Organizational Society,* ed. Jerry Israel, 1–9. New York: Free Press.

Hechter, Michael: 1975. *Internal Colonialism: The Celtic Fringe in British National Development, 1536–1966.* Berkeley: University of California Press.

_____. ed. 1983. *The Micro Foundations of Macrosociology.* Philadelphia: Temple University Press.

Heintz, Kathleen. 1976. State Organizations for Human Services. *Evaluation* 3:106–10.

Heritage, John C. 1984. *Garfinkel and Ethnomethodology.* Cambridge, England: Polity Press.

_____. 1987. Ethnomethodology. In *Social Theory Today,* ed. A. Giddens and J. Turner, 224–72. Stanford: Stanford University Press.

Hernes, Gudmund. 1976. Structural Change in Social Process. *American Journal of Sociology* 82:513–47.

Herriot, Robert E., and William A. Firestone. 1984. Two Images of Schools as Organizations: A Refinement and Elaboration. *Educational Administration Quarterly* 20:48–57.

Hicks, John. 1969. *A Theory of Economic History.* Oxford: Oxford University Press.

Hirsch, Paul M. 1972. Processing Fads and Fashions: An Organization-Set Analysis of Cultural Industry Systems. *American Journal of Sociology* 77:639–59.

_____. 1975. Organizational Effectiveness and the Institutional Environment. *Administrative Science Quarterly* 20:327–44.

_____. 1985. The Study of Industries. In *Research in the Sociology of Organizations,* ed. S. B. Bacharach and S. M. Mitchell, 4:271–309. Greenwich, Conn.: JAI Press.

_____. 1986. From Ambushes to Golden Parachutes: Corporate Takeovers as an Instance of Cultural Framing and Institutional Integration. *American Journal of Sociology* 91:800–837.

Hirsch, Paul M., and Thomas Whisler. 1982. The View from the Boardroom. Paper presented at Academy of Management Meetings, New York, N.Y.

Hirschman, Albert O. 1972. *Exit, Voice, and Loyalty.* Cambridge: Harvard University Press.

_____. 1986. The Concept of Interest: From Euphemis to Tautology. In *Rival Views of Market Society,* 35–55. New York: Viking.

Hiss, Priscilla, and Roberta Fansler. 1934. *Research in Fine Arts in the Colleges and Universities of the United States.* New York: Carnegie Corporation.

Hobbs, C. 1924. Why a Sales Training Makes a Good Manufacturer. *System,* August 1924,147–49.

Hofstadter, Richard. 1955. *The Age of Reform.* New York: Knopf.

Hofstede, Geert. 1980. *Culture's Consequences: International Differences in Work-Related Values.* Beverly Hills, Calif.: Sage.

Hogan, Daniel J. 1985. *Class and Reform: School and Society in Chicago, 1880–1930.* Philadelphia: University of Pennsylvania Press.

Hollis, Martin. 1985. Of Masks and Men. In *The Category of the Person,* ed. Michael Carrithers et al., 217–33. New York: Cambridge University Press.

Holusha, John. 1987. Accounting in Factories Is Criticized as Outdated. *New York Times,* March 23.

Homans, George C. 1950. *The Human Group.* New York: Harcourt, Brace.

_____. 1961. *Social Behavior: Its Elementary Forms.* New York: Harcourt Brace Jovanovich.

Hopwood, Anthony. 1983. On Trying to Study Accounting in the Contexts in Which It Operates. *Accounting, Organizations, and Society* 8:287–305.

Horwitz, Morton J. 1977. *The Transformation of American Law, 1780–1860.* Cambridge: Harvard University Press.

Houston, Lorne F. 1972. The Flowers of Power: A Critique of OFY and LIP Programmes. *Our Generation* 7:52–71.

Hughes, Everett C. 1936. The Ecological Aspect of Institutions. *American Sociological Review* 1:180–89.

_____. 1937. Institutional Office and the Person. *American Journal of Sociology* 63:79–87.

Hunt, Lynn. 1984. *Politics, Culture, and Class in the French Revolution.* Berkeley: University of California Press.

Huntington, Samuel P. 1968. *Political Order in Changing Societies.* New Haven: Yale University Press.

Hurst, James Willard. 1982. *Law and Markets in United States History.* Madison: University of Wisconsin Press.

Inkeles, Alex, and David H. Smith. 1974. *Becoming Modern: Individual Change in Six Developing Countries.* Cambridge: Harvard University Press.

Ishida, Hideto. 1983. Anticompetitive Practices in the Distribution of Goods and Services in Japan: The Problem of Distribution *Keiretsu. Journal of Japanese Studies* 9:319–34.

Jacobs, David, M. Useem, and M. Zald. 1991. Firms, Industries, and Politics. In *Research in Political Sociology* 5:141–65. Greenwich, Conn.: JAI Press.

Jacobs, Norman. 1985. *The Korean Road to Modernization and Development.* Urbana: University of Illinois Press.

Jacobs, R. C., and D. T. Campbell. 1961. The Perpetuation of an Arbitrary Tradition through Successive Generations of a Laboratory Microculture. *Journal of Abnormal and Social Psychology* 62:649–58.

Jacoby, Sanford, 1985. *Employing Bureaucracy.* New York: Columbia University Press.

Janowitz, Morris. 1969. *Institution Building in Urban Education.* New York: Russell Sage Foundation.

_____. 1978. *The Last Half Century: Societal Change and Politics in America.* Chicago: University of Chicago Press.

Johnston, John. 1972. *Econometric Methods.* 2d ed. New York: McGraw-Hill.

Jones, E. L. 1981. *The European Miracle.* New York: Cambridge University Press.

Jubin, Brenda. 1968. *Program in the Arts, 1911–1967.* New York: Carnegie Corporation.

Kalberg, Steven. 1980. Max Weber's Types of Rationality: Cornerstones for the Analysis of Rationalization Processes in History. *American Journal of Sociology* 85:1145–79.

Kamm, Henry. 1987. With Prague, Glasnost Comes in a Fainter Echo. *New York Times,* November 7, p. 4.

Kanter, Rosabeth Moss. 1972. *Commitment and Community.* Cambridge: Harvard University Press.

_____. 1977. *Men and Women of the Corporation.* New York: Basic Books.

Karabel, Jerome. 1983. The Politics of Structural Change in American Higher Education: The Case of Open Admissions at the City University of New York. In *The Compleat University: Break from Tradition in Three Countries,* ed. H. Hermanns, U. Teichler, and H. Wasser, 21–58. Cambridge, Mass.: Schenkman Publishers.

_____. 1984. Status Group Struggle, Organizational Interests, and the Limits of Institutional Autonomy: The Transformation of Harvard, Yale and Princeton, 1918–1940. *Theory and Society* 13:1–40.

Katz, Michael B. 1975. *Class, Bureaucracy, and Schools: The Illusion of Educational Change in America.* New York: Praeger.

Katz, Michael C., and Carl Shapiro. 1985. Network Externalities, Competition, and Compatibility. *American Economic Review* 75(3):424–40.

_____. 1986. Technology Adoption in the Presence of Network Externalities. *Journal of Political Economy* 94(4):822–41.

Keim, Gerald D. 1978. Corporate Social Responsibility: An Assessment of the Enlightened Self-Interest Model. *Academy of Management Review* 3:32–39.

Kelley, Harold H. 1971. *Attribution in Social Interaction.* Morristown, N.J.: General Learning Press.

Kennedy, Peter. 1985. *A Guide to Econometrics.* 2d ed. Cambridge: MIT Press.

Keohane, Robert O. 1984. *After Hegemony.* Princeton: Princeton University Press.

_____. 1988. International Institutions: Two Research Programs. *International Studies Quarterly* 32:379–96.

Keppel, Frederick P. 1926. *Education for Adults and Other Essays.* New York: Columbia University Press.

_____. 1934. The Arts. In *Recent Social Trends in the United States,* ed. William F. Ogburn. New York: McGraw-Hill.

Keppel, Frederick P., and R. L. Duffus. 1933. *The Arts in American Life.* New York: McGraw-Hill.

Kestenbaum, Meyer, chair. 1955. *Final Report of the Commission on Intergovernmental Relations.* House Doc. 198, 84th Cong., 1st sess. Washington, D.C.: U.S. Government Printing Office.

Kiesler, Sara, and Lee Sproul. 1982. Managerial Responses to Changing Environments: Perspectives on Problem Sensing from Social Cognition. *Administrative Science Quarterly* 27(4):548–70.

Kimball, Fiske. 1929. Report of the Director of the Museum. In *Fifty-third Annual Report of the Pennsylvania Museum and School of Industrial Art.* Philadelphia.

_____. 1933. Kimball Reviews Museum Study by Rea. *Museum News* 1:4–5.

Kimberly, John R. 1975. Environmental Constraints and Organizational Structure: A Comparative Analysis of Rehabilitation Organizations. *Administrative Science Quarterly* 20:1–9.

_____. 1980. Initiation, Innovation and Institutionalization in the Creation Process. In *The Organizational Life Cycle,* ed. J. Kimberly Miles and B. Miles, 18–43. San Francisco: Jossey-Bass.

Kingdon, Frank. 1948. *John Cotton Dana: A Life.* Newark, N.J.: Public Library and Museum.

Kinzer, David M. 1977. *Health Controls out of Control: Warning to the Nation from Massachusetts.* Chicago: Teach 'em.

Klahr, David, P. Langley, and R. Neches, eds. 1987. *Production System Models of Learning and Development.* Cambridge: MIT Press.

Kmenta, Jan. 1971. *Elements of Econometrics.* New York: Macmillan.

Knoke, David. 1981. Power Structures. In *Handbook of Political Behavior,* ed. Samuel L. Long, 3:275–332. New York: Plenum.

_____. 1982. The Spread of Municipal Reform: Temporal, Spatial, and Social Dynamics. *American Journal of Sociology* 87:1314–39.

_____. 1986. Associations and Interest Groups. *Annual Review of Sociology* 12:1–21.

Knoke, David, and Edward O. Laumann. 1982. The Social Organization of National Policy Domains. In *Social Structure and Network Analysis,* ed. P. Marsden and N. Lin. Beverly Hills, Calif.: Sage.

Kobayashi, Yoshihiro. 1980. Kigyo no gurupu no bunseki hoko: Kotorii jimukyoku *Kigyo shudan no jittai chosa ni tsuite o yonde* (A trend in the analysis of business groups: A comment on *About the research on the state of affairs in the business groups*). *Tokyo:* Bureau of Fair Trade Commission.

Kochan, Thomas, Harry Katz, and Robert McKersie. 1986. *The Transformation of American Industrial Relations.* New York: Basic Books.

Kohn, Melvin L. 1969. *Class and Conformity.* Homewood, Ill.: Dorsey.

Konrad, George, and Iven Szelenyi. 1979. *Intellectuals on the Road to Class Power.* New York: Harcourt Brace.

Koo, Hagen. 1984. The Political Economy of Income Distribution in South Korea: The Impact of the State's Industrialization Policies. *World Development* 12:1029–37.

Kosei Torihiki Iinkai Jimukyoku (Fair Trade Commission). 1983. *Kigyo shudan no jittai ni tsuite* (About the state of affairs in business groups). Tokyo: Bureau of Fair Trade Commission.

Kramer, Ralph M. 1981. *Voluntary Agencies in the Welfare State.* Berkeley: University of California Press.

Krasner, Stephen D., ed. 1983. *International Regimes.* Ithaca: Cornell University Press.

_____. 1988. Sovereignty: An Institutional Perspective. *Comparative Political Studies* 21(1):66–94.

Kratochwil, Frederich, and J. G. Ruggie. 1986. International Organization: A State of the Art on the Art of the State. *International Organization* 40(4):753–76.

Kretch, D., and R. S. Crutchfield. 1962. *Individual in Society.* New York: McGrawHill.

Kulik, Carol. 1989. The Effects of Job Categorization on Judgments of the Motivating Potential of Jobs. *Administrative Science Quarterly* 34(1):68–90.

Kuran, Timur, 1988. The Tenacious Past: Theories of Personal and Collective Conservativism. *Journal of Economic Behavior and Organization* 10:143–71.

Lachmann, L. M. 1971. *The Legacy of Max Weber.* Berkeley, Calif.: Glendessary Press.

Lagemann, Ellen Condliffe. 1983. *Private Power for the Public Good: A History of the Carnegie Foundation for the Advancement of Teaching.* Middletown, Conn.: Wesleyan University Press.

Lammers, Cornelis J., and David J. Hickson. 1979. A Cross-national and Cross-institutional Typology of Organizations. In *Organizations Alike and Unlike,* ed. C. J. Lammers and D. J. Hickson, 420–34. London: Routledge and Kegan Paul.

Landau, Martin. 1969. Redundancy, Rationality, and the Problem of Duplications and Overlap. *Public Administration Review* 29:346–58.

Langlois, Richard, ed. 1986. *Economics as Process.* New York: Cambridge University Press.

Larson, Magali Sarfatti. 1977. *The Rise of Professionalism: A Sociological Analysis.* Berkeley: University of California Press.

Laumann, Edward O., Joseph Galaskiewicz, and Peter Marsden. 1978. Community Structure as Interorganizational Linkage. *Annual Review of Sociology* 4:455–84.

Laurent, André. 1983. The Cultural Diversity of Western Conceptions of Management. *International Studies of Management and Organization* 8:75–96.

Lawrence, Paul R., and Lorsch, Jay W. 1967. *Organization and Environment.* Boston: Harvard Business School Press.

Leblebici, Huseyin, and Gerald R. Salancik. 1982. Stability in Interorganizational Exchanges: Rulemaking Processes of the Chicago Board of Trade. *Administrative Science Quarterly* 27:227–42.

Lee, M. L. 1971. A Conspicuous Production Theory of Hospital Behavior. *Southern Economic Journal* 38:48–58.

Lee, Sang M. 1986. Management Style and Practice of Korean Chaebols. Decision Sciences Institute Meetings, Honolulu, Hawaii.

Lehman, Edward W. 1975. *Coordinating Health Services.* Beverly Hills, Calif.: Sage.

Lester, Robert S. 1940. The Corporation and Operating Agencies. In Frederick P. Keppel and and R. S. Lester, *Report of the President and of the Treasurer,* 37–49. New York: Carnegie Corporation.

Levine, Andrew, Elliot Sober, and Erik Olin Wright. 1987. Marxism and Methodological Individualism. *New Left Review* 162:67–84.

Levi-Strauss, Claude. 1966. *The Savage Mind.* London: Weidenfeld and Nicholson.

Levitt, Barbara, and James G. March. 1988. Organizational Learning. *Annual Review of Sociology* 14:319–40.

Levy, R. I. 1973. *Tahitians: Mind and Experience in the Society Islands.* Chicago: University of Chicago Press.

Lindblom, Charles E. 1968. *The Policy-Making Process.* Englewood Cliffs, N.J.: Prentice-Hall.

_____. 1977. *Politics and Markets.* New York: Basic Books.

Litwak, Eugene, and Lydia F. Hylton. 1962. Interorganizational Analysis: A Hypothesis on Coordinating Agencies. *Administrative Science Quarterly* 6:395–420.

Lombardi, John. 1978. The Resurgence of Occupational Education. Topical Paper No. 65. Los Angeles: ERIC Clearing House for Junior Colleges.

_____. 1979. The Decline of Transfer Education. Topical Paper No. 70. Los Angeles: ERIC Clearing House for Junior Colleges.

Loney, Martin. 1977. The Political Economy of Citizen Participation. In *The Canadian State: Political Economy and Political Power,* ed. Leo Panitch, 346–72. Toronto: University of Toronto Press.

Lowi, Theodore J. 1964. American Business, Public Policy, Case Studies and Political Theory. *World Politics* 16:675–715.

_____. 1969. *The End of Liberalism.* New York: Norton.

_____. 1970. Decision Making vs. Policy Making: Toward an Antidote for Technocracy. *Public Administration Review* 30:298–310.

_____. 1972. Four Systems of Policy, Politics and Choice. *Public Administration Review* 32:314–25.

Lukes, Steven. 1972. *Emile Durkheim, His Life and Work.* New York: Harper and Row.

_____. 1974. *Power: A Radical View.* London: Macmillan.

Lynd, Robert, and Helen Lynd. 1929. *Middletown.* New York: Harcourt Brace and Jovanovich.

_____. 1937. *Middletown in Transition.* New York: Harcourt Brace.

McCarthy, John, and Mayer Zald. 1977. Resource Mobilization and Social Movements: A Partial Theory. *American Journal of Sociology* 82:121–41.

McDonnell, Lorrain M., and Milbrey W. McLaughlin. 1982. *Education Policy and the Role of the States.* Santa Monica, Calif.: Rand.

McGuire, Joseph W. 1963. *Business and Society.* New York: McGraw-Hill.

MacIver, Robert M. 1931. *Society, Its Structure and Changes.* New York: Ray Long and Richard R. Smith.

McKelvey, William. 1982. *Organizational Systematics.* Berkeley: University of California Press.

McKeough, W. D. 1975. *Ontario Budget 1975.* Toronto: Ministry of Treasury, Economics and Intergovernmental Affairs.

_____. 1976. *Ontario Budget 1976.* Toronto: Ministry of Treasury, Economics and Intergovernmental Affairs.

McNeil, William H. 1982. *The Pursuit of Power: Technology, Armed Force, and Society since A.D. 1000.* Chicago: University of Chicago Press

Majone, Giandomenico. 1980. Professionalism and Non-Profit Organizations. Working Paper No. 24. New Haven: Yale Program on Non-Profit Organizations.

Mann, Michael. 1973. *Consciousness and Action in the Western Working Class.* London: Macmillan.

_____. 1986. *The Sources of Social Power. Vol. 1.* New York: Cambridge University Press.

Marceau, Jane. 1989. *A Family Business? The Making of an International Business Elite.* New York: Cambridge University Press.

March, James C., and James G. March. 1977. Almost Random Careers: The Wisconsin School Superintendency, 1940–72. *Administrative Science Quarterly* 22:378–409.

March, James G. 1981. Decisions in Organizations and Theories of Choice. In *Perspectives on Organization Design and Behavior,* ed. A. H. Van de Van and W. F. Joyce, 205–44. New York: Wiley.

March, James G. and Michael Cohen. 1974. *Leadership and Ambiguity: The American College President.* New York: McGraw-Hill.

March, James G., and Johan P. Olsen. 1976. *Ambiguity and Choice in Organizations.* Bergen: Universitetsforlaget.

_____. 1984. The New Institutionalism: Organizational Factors in Political Life. *American Political Science Review* 78:734–49.

March, James G., and Herbert A. Simon. 1958. *Organizations.* New York: Wiley.

March, James G., and Roger Weissinger-Baylon, eds. 1986. *Ambiguity and Command.* Cambridge, Mass.: Ballinger.

Marrett, Cora Bagley. 1980. Influences on the Rise of New Organizations: The Formation of Women's Medical Associations. *Administrative Science Quarterly* 25:189–99.

Marshall, J. E. 1966. Eye Movements and the Visual Autokinetic Phenomenon. *Perceptual and Motor Skills* 22:319–26.

Marshall, T. H. 1964. *Class, Citizenship, and Social Development.* New York: Doubleday.

Matthews, R. C. O. 1986. The Economics of Institutions and the Sources of Growth. *Economic Journal* 96:903–18.

Maurice, Marc, F. Sellier, and J. J. Silvestre. 1982. *Politique d'éducation et organization industrielle en France et en Allemagne.* Paris: Presses Universitaires de France.

Mauss, Marcel. 1985. A Category of the Human Mind: The Notion of Person; The Notion of Self. In *The Category of the Person,* ed. M. Carrithers et al., 1-25. New York: Cambridge University Press.

Mayhew, Bruce H. 1980. Structuralism versus Individualism. *Social Forces* 59:335–575, 627–48.

Mayhew, Leon. 1984. In Defense of Modernity: Talcott Parsons and the Utilitarian Tradition. *American Journal of Sociology* 89(6):1273–1305.

Mazur, P. 1928. Diversification in Industry. *Review of Reviews,* June, 631–34.

Mead, George Herbert. [1934] 1972. *Mind, Self, and Society.* Chicago: University of Chicago Press.

Meier, Norman Charles. 1926. *Aesthetic Judgment as a Measure of Art Talent.* Iowa City: University of Iowa.

Meiksins, Peter F. 1984. Scientific Management and Class Relations: A Dissenting View. *Theory and Society* 13:177–209.

Melton, Arthur. 1935. *Problems of Installation in Museums of Art.* Washington, D.C.: American Association of Museums.

Merkle, Judith. 1980. *Management and Ideology: The Legacy of the International Scientific Management Movement.* Berkeley: University of California Press.

Merton, Robert K. 1940. Bureaucratic Structure and Personality. *Social Forces* 18:560–68.

_____. 1949. Patterns of Influence: A Study of Interpersonal Influence and of Communications Behavior in a Local Community. In *Communication Research, 1948–49,* ed. P. F. Lazarsfeld and F. Stanton, 16–22. New York: Harper.

Merton, Robert K., L. Brown, and L. S. Cottrell, Jr. 1959. *Sociology Today: Problems and Prospects.* New York: Basic Books.

Messinger, Sheldon. 1955. Organizational Transformation: A Case Study of a Declining Social Movement. *American Sociological Review* 20:3–10.

Meyer, John W. 1968. Collective Disturbances and Staff Organizations on Psychiatric Wards: A Formalization. *Sociometry* 31:180.

_____. 1970. The Charter: Conditions of Diffuse Socialization in Schools. In *Social Processes and Social Structure,* ed. W. R. Scott, 564–78. New York: Holt, Rinehart, and Winston.

_____. 1971. Institutionalization. Manuscript. Stanford University.

_____. 1977. The Effects of Education as an Institution. *American Journal of Sociology* 83:53–77.

_____. 1980. The World Polity and the Authority of the Nation State. In *Studies of the Modern World System,* ed. A. J. Bergesen. New York: Academic.

_____. 1981. Remarks at ASA session: The Present Crisis and the Decline in World Hegemony. Toronto, Canada.

_____. 1983a. Innovation and Knowledge Use in American Public Education. In *Organizational Environments,* ed. J. W. Meyer and W. R. Scott, 233–60. Beverly Hills, Calif.: Sage.

_____. 1983b. Institutionalization and the Rationality of Formal Organizational Structure. In *Organizational Environments: Ritual and Rationality,* ed. J. W. Meyer and W. R. Scott, 261–82. Beverly Hills, Calif.: Sage.

_____. 1986. Social Environments and Organizational Accounting. *Accounting, Organizations, and Society* 11:345–56.

_____. 1987. The World Polity and the Authority of the Nation-State. In *Institutional Structure,* ed. George Thomas et al., 41–70. Newbury Park, Calif.: Sage.

_____. 1988a. Conceptions of Christendom: Notes on the Distinctiveness of the West. In *Cross-National Research in Sociology,* ed. M. Kohn. Newbury Park, Calif.: Sage.

_____. 1988b. Society without Culture: A Nineteenth-Century Legacy. In *Rethinking the Nineteenth Century: Contradictions and Movements,* ed. F. O. Ramirez, 193–202. Westport, Conn.: Greenwood Press.

Meyer, John W., John Boli, and George Thomas. 1987. Ontology and Rationalization in the Western Cultural Account. In *Institutional Structure,* ed. George Thomas et al., 12–37. Newbury Park, Calif.: Sage.

Meyer, John W., and Michael Hannan. 1979. *National Development and the World System.* Chicago: University of Chicago Press.

Meyer, John W., and Brian Rowan. 1977. Institutionalized Organizations: Formal Structure as Myth and Ceremony. *American Journal of Sociology* 83:340–63.

_____. 1978. The Structure of Educational Organizations. In *Environments and Organizations,* ed. Marshall W. Meyer et al., 78–109. San Francisco: Jossey-Bass.

Meyer, John W., and W. Richard Scott. 1983a. Centralization and the Legitimacy Problems of Local Government. In *Organizational Environments: Ritual and Rationality,* ed. J. W. Meyer and W. R. Scott, 199–215. Beverly Hills, Calif.: Sage.

_____. with the assistance of B. Rowan and T. Deal. 1983b. *Organizational Environments: Ritual and Rationality.* Beverly Hills, Calif.: Sage.

Meyer, John W., W. Richard Scott, Sally Cole, and Jo-Ann Intili. 1978. Instructional Dissensus and Institutional Consensus in Schools. In *Environments and Organizations,* ed. Marshall W. Meyer, 233–63. San Francisco: Jossey-Bass.

Meyer, John W., W. R. Scott, and T. E. Deal. 1981. Institutional and Technical Sources of Organizational Structure. In *Organization and the Human Services,* ed. H. D. Stein, 151–78. Philadelphia: Temple University Press.

Meyer, John W., W. Richard Scott, and David Strang. 1987. Centralization, Fragmentation, and School District Complexity. *Administrative Science Quarterly* 32:186–201.

Meyer, John W., W. Richard Scott, David Strang, and Andrew Creighton. 1988. Bureaucratization without Centralization: Changes in the Organizational System of American Public Education, 1940–1980. In *Institutional Patterns and Organizations,* ed. L. G. Zucker, 139–67. Cambridge, Mass.: Ballinger.

Meyer, John W., David Tyack, Joane Nagel, and Audri Gordon. 1979. Public Education as Nation-Building in America: Enrollments and Bureaucratization, 1870–1930. *American Journal of Sociology* 85:591–613.

Meyer, Marshall, and M. Craig Brown. 1977. The Process of Bureaucratization. *American Journal of Sociology* 83:364–85.

Meyer, Marshall, W. Stevenson, and S. Webster. 1985. *Limits to Bureaucratic Growth.* Berlin: Walter de Gruyter.

Meyer, Marshall, and Lynne G. Zucker. 1988. *Permanently Failing Organizations.* Huntington Park, Calif.: Sage.

Mezias, Stephen J. 1990. An Institutional Model of Organizational Practice: Financial Reporting at the Fortune 200. *Administrative Science Quarterly* 35(3):431–57.

Michels, Robert. [1915] 1962. *Political Parties.* Trans. from the German by Eden Paul and Cedar Paul. New York: Collier Press.

Milgram, Stanley. 1974. *Obedience to Authority: An Experimental View.* New York: Harper and Row.

Mills, C. Wright. 1940. Situated Actions and Vocabularies of Motive. *American Sociological Review* 5:904–13.

Milofsky, Carl. 1981. Structure and Process in Community Self-Help Organizations. Working Paper No. 17. New Haven: Yale Program on Non-Profit Organizations.

Miyazawa, Setsuo. 1986. Legal Departments of Japanese Corporations in the United States: A Study of Organizational Adaptation to Multiple Environments. *Kobe University Law Review* 20:99–162.

Moe, Terry. 1984. The New Economics of Organization. *American Journal of Political Science* 28(4):739–77.

_____. 1987. Interests, Institutions, and Positive Theory: The Politics of the NLRB. In *Studies in American Political Development,* 2:236–99. New Haven: Yale University Press.

Molotch, Harvey L. 1976. The City as a Growth Machine: Toward a Political Economy of Place. *American Journal of Sociology* 82:309–32.

Molotch, Harvey L., and John R. Logan. 1987. *Urban Fortunes: The Political Economy of Place.* Berkeley: University of California Press.

Momigliano, Arnoldo. 1985. Marcel Mauss and the Quest for the Person in Greek Biography and Autobiography. In *The Category of the Person,* ed. M. Carrithers et al., 83–92. New York: Cambridge University Press.

Moody's Manuals of Industrials. 1920, 1930, 1940, 1950, 1970, 1980. New York: Moody's.

Moore, Wilbert E. 1979. *World Modernization.* New York: Elsevier.

Morris, Robert, and Ilana H. Lescohier. 1978. Service Integration: Real versus Illusory Solutions to Welfare Dilemmas. In *The Management of Human Services,* ed. R. C. Sam and Y. Hasenfeld, 21–50. New York: Columbia University Press.

Morrissey, Joseph P., Richard H. Hall, and Michael L. Lindsey. 1982. *Interorganizational Relations: A Sourcebook of Measures for Mental Health Programs.* Washington, D.C.: National Institute of Mental Health.

Mott, Paul. 1970. The Role of the Absentee Owned Corporation in the Changing Community. In *The Structure of Community Power,* ed. M. Aiken and P. Mott, 170–80. New York: Random House.

Moynihan, Daniel P. 1969. *Maximum Feasible Misunderstanding.* New York: Free Press.

Mueller, W. 1979. The Celler-Kefauver Act: The First 27 Years. Washington, D. C.: U.S. Government Printing Office.

Münch, Richard. 1986. The American Creed in Sociological Theory: Exchange, Negotiated Order, Accommodated Individualism, and Contingency. *Sociological Theory* 4:41–60.

Murphy, Jerome T. 1981. The Paradox of State Government Reform. *Public Interest* 64:124–39.

Musto, David A. 1975. Whatever Happened to "Community Mental Health"? *Public Interest* 29:53–79.

Nadel, S. F. 1953. Social Control and Self-Regulation. *Social Forces* 31:265–73.

Nakatani, Iwao. 1982. Risuku shearingu kara mita nihon keizai: Kigyo shudan no keizai gorisei ni kansuru ichikosatsu (Japanese economy viewed from risk-sharing: A perspective on economic rationality in the business groups). *Osaka Daigaku Keizaigaku* 32:219–45.

_____. 1984. The Economic Role of Financial Corporate Grouping. In *The Economic Analysis of the Japanese Firm,* ed. M. Aoki, 227–58. Amsterdam: Elsevier.

Nasaw, David. 1979. *Schooled to Order.* New York: Oxford University Press.

Nelson, Richard, and Sidney Winter. 1982. *An Evolutionary Theory of Economic Change.* Cambridge: Harvard University Press.

Neuhauser, Duncan. 1972. The Hospital as a Matrix Organization. *Hospital Administration* 17:8–25.

Neustadt, Richard, and Harvey Fineberg. 1978. *The Swine Flu Affair: Decision Making on a Slippery Disease.* Washington, D.C.: U.S. Government Printing Office.

Nishiyama, Tadonori. 1984. The Structure of Managerial Control: Who Owns and Controls Japanese Business. In *The Anatomy of Japanese Business,* ed. Kazuo Sato and Yasuo Hoshino. Armonk, N.Y.: M. E. Sharpe.

Noll, Roger G. 1971. *Reforming Regulation.* Washington, D.C.: Brookings Institution.

North, Douglass C. 1981. *Structure and Change in Economic History.* New York: Norton.

_____. 1983. A Theory of Institutional Change and the Economic History of the Western World. In *The Microfoundations of Macrosociology,* ed. M. Hechter, 190–215. Philadelphia: Temple University Press.

_____. 1984. Government and the Cost of Exchange in History. *Journal of Economic History* 44:255–64.

_____. 1986. The New Institutional Economics. *Journal of Institutional and Theoretical Economics* 142:230–37.

_____. 1987. Institutions and Economic Growth: An Historical Introduction. Paper presented at Conference on Knowledge and Institutional Change, University of Minnesota.

_____. 1990. *Institutions, Institutional Change and Economic Performance.* New York: Cambridge University Press.

North, Douglass C., and Robert Thomas. 1973. *The Rise of the Western World: A New Economic History.* New York: Cambridge University Press.

Numazaki, Ichiro. 1986. Networks of Taiwanese Big Business. *Modern China* 12:487–534.

Nystrom, N. C., and William H. Starbuck. 1984. To Avoid Organizational Crisis, Unlearn. *Organizational Dynamics,* Spring, 53–65.

Offe, Claus. 1984. *Contradictions of the Welfare State.* Cambridge: MIT Press.

Office of Management and Budget. 1972. *Standard Industrial Classification Manual.* Washington, D.C.: U.S. Government Printing Office.

Okumura, Hiroshi. 1982. Interfirm Relations in an Enterprise Group: The Case of Mitsubishi. *Japanese Economic Studies* 10:53–82.

_____. 1984. Enterprise Groups in Japan. *Shoken Keizai* 147:169–89.

_____. 1985. *Shin ni/ion no rokudai kigyo shudan* (Japan's six major business groups). Rev. ed. Tokyo: Daiyamondo Sha.

Olson, Mancur. 1965. *The Logic of Collective Action.* Cambridge: Harvard University Press.

Orloff, Ann, and Theda Skocpol. 1984. Why Not Equal Protection? Explaining the Politics of Public Social Spending in Britain and the United States. *American Sociological Review* 49(6):726–50.

Orrù, Marco, 1991. The Institutional Logic of Small-Firm Economies in Italy and Taiwan. *Studies in Comparative International Development* 26(1):3–28.

Orrùù, Marco, Gary G. Hamilton, and Mariko Suzuki. 1989. Patterns of Inter-Firm Control in Japanese Business. *Organizational Studies* 10:549–74.

Ostrom, Elinor, 1986. An Agenda for the Study of Institutions. *Public Choice* 48:3–25.

Ouchi, William G. 1980. Markets, Bureaucracies, and Clans. *Administrative Science Quarterly* 25:129–41.

_____. 1984. *The M-Form Society.* Reading, Mass.: Addison-Wesley.

Ouchi, William, and Mary Ann Maguire. 1975. Organizational Control: Two Functions. *Administrative Science Quarterly* 20:559–69.

Paradis, Lenora Finn, and Scott Cummings. 1986. The Evolution of Hospice in America toward Organizational Homogeneity. *Journal of Health and Social Behavior* 27:370–86.

Paris, Edna. 1972. Are There Really Any Opportunities for Youth? *MacLean's,* 34.

Parsons, Talcott. 1937. *The Structure of Social Action.* New York: McGraw-Hill.

_____. 1938. The Professions and the Social Structure. *Social Forces* 17:29–37.

_____. 1940. The Motivation of Economic Activities. In *Essays in Sociological Theory Pure and Applied.* Glencoe, Ill.: Free Press.

_____. 1945. The Present Position and Prospects of Systematic Theory in Sociology. In *Twentieth Century Sociology,* ed. G. Gurvitch and W. E. Moore. New York: Philosophical Library.

_____. 1951. *The Social System.* Glencoe, Ill.: Free Press.

_____. 1956. Suggestions for a Sociological Approach to the Theory of Organizations, Parts I and II. *Administrative Science Quarterly* 1:63–85, 225–39.

_____. 1960. *Structure and Process in Modern Societies.* Glencoe, Ill.: Free Press.

_____. 1971. *The System of Modern Societies.* Englewood Cliffs, N.J.: Prentice-Hall.

_____. 1977. *The Evolution of Societies.* Englewood Cliffs, N.J.: Prentice-Hall.

_____. 1982. *On Institutions and Social Evolution.* Ed. Leon H. Mayhew. Chicago: University of Chicago Press.

_____. 1990. Prologomena to a Theory of Social Institutions. *American Sociological Review* 55(3):319–33.

Parsons, Talcott, and Robert F. Bales. 1960. *Family Socialization and Interaction Process.* Glencoe, Ill.: Free Press.

Parsons, Talcott, and Edward A. Shils, eds. 1951. *Towards a General Theory of Action.* Cambridge: Harvard University Press.

Perrow, Charles. 1963. Goals and Power Structures. In *The Hospital in Modern Society,* ed. Eliot Freidson, 112–46. New York: Free Press.

_____. 1967. A Framework for the Comparative Analysis of Organizations. *American Sociological Review* 32:194–208.

_____. 1970. *Organizational Analysis: A Sociological View.* Belmont, Calif.: Wadsworth.

_____. 1974. Is Business Really Changing? *Organizational Dynamics,* Summer, 31–44.

_____. 1976. Control in Organizations. Paper presented at American Sociological Association annual meetings, New York, N.Y.

_____. 1977. The Bureaucratic Paradox: The Efficient Organization Centralizes in Order to Decentralize. *Organizational Dynamics* 5:2–14.

_____. 1985a. Comments on Langton's Ecological Theory of Bureaucracy. *Administrative Science Quarterly* 30:278–83.

_____. 1985b. Overboard with Myth and Symbols. *American Journal of Sociology* 91:151–55.

_____. 1986. *Complex Organizations: A Critical Essay.* 3rd ed. New York: Random House.

Perrucci, Carolyn C., Robert Perrucci, Dana B. Targ, and Harry R. Targ. 1988. *Plant Closing: International Context and Social Costs.* New York: Aldine de Gruyter.

Perrucci, Robert, and Joel E. Gerstl. 1969. *Profession without Community: Engineers in American Society.* New York: Random House.

Peterson, Paul E. 1981. *City Limits.* Chicago: University of Chicago Press.

Pfeffer, Jeffrey. 1974. Administrative Regulation and Licensing: Social Problem or Solution? *Social Problems* 21:468–79.

_____. 1981. *Power in Organizations.* Marshfield, Mass.: Pitman Press.

_____. 1982. *Organizations and Organization Theory.* Marshfield, Mass.: Pitman Press.

Pfeffer, Jeffrey, and Gerald Salancik. 1978. *The External Control of Organizations: A Resource Dependence Perspective.* New York: Harper and Row.

Piore, Michael, and Charles Sable. 1984. *The Second Industrial Divide.* New York: Basic Books.

Piven, Frances Fox, and Richard A. Cloward. 1971. *Regulating the Poor: The Functions of Public Welfare.* New York: Pantheon.

_____. 1977. *Poor People's Movements.* New York: Pantheon.

_____. 1980. Social Policy and the Formation of Political Consciousness. In *Political Power and Social Theory,* ed. M. Zeitlin, 1:117–52. Greenwich, Conn.: JAI Press.

Posner, Richard A. 1981. *The Economics of Justice.* Cambridge: Harvard University Press.

Powell, Walter W. 1983. New Solutions to Perennial Problems of Bookselling: Whither the Local Bookstore? *Daedalus* 112(1):51–64.

_____. 1985a. *Getting into Print: The Decision-Making Process in Scholarly Publishing.* Chicago: University of Chicago Press.

_____. 1985b. The Institutionalization of Rational Organization: Review of *Organiza*tional *Environments.* Contemporary Sociology 14(5):564–66.

_____. 1986. How the Past Informs the Present: The Uses and Liabilities of Organizational Memory. Paper presented at conference on Communication and Collective Memory, Annenberg School, University of Southern California.

_____. 1988. Institutional Effects on Organizational Structure and Performance. In *Institutional Patterns and Organization,* ed. L. Zucker, 115–36. Cambridge, Mass.: Ballinger.

_____. 1990. Neither Market nor Hierarchy: Network Forms of Organization. In *Research in Organizational Behavior,* ed. B. Staw and L. L. Cummings, 12:295–336. Greenwich, Conn.: JAI Press.

Powell, Walter W., and Rebecca Friedkin. 1986. Politics and Programs: Organizational Factors in Public Television Decision-Making. In *Nonprofit Enterprise in the Arts,* ed. P. J. DiMaggio, 245–69. New York: Oxford University Press.

Pressman, Jeffrey L., and Aaron Wildavsky. 1973. *Implementation.* Berkeley: University of California Press.

Przeworski, Adam. 1974. Contextual Models of Political Behavior. *Political Methodology* 1:27–61.

Przeworski, Adam, and John Sprague. 1971. Concepts in Search of Explicit Formulation. *Midwest Journal of Political Science* 15:183–218.

Przeworski, Adam, and Michael Wallerstein. 1986. Popular Sovereignty, State Autonomy, and Private Property. *Archives European Sociology* 27:215–59.

Puckett, Tom, and David J. Thucker. 1976. Hard Times for Ontario's Social Services. *Canadian Welfare* 52:8–11.

Pugh, D. S. 1976. The Aston Approach to the Study of Organizations. In *European Contributions to Organization Theory,* ed. G. Hofstede and M. S. Kassem. Assen, Netherlands: Van Gorcum.

Putnam, Robert D. 1976. *The Comparative Study of Political Elites.* Englewood Cliffs, N.J.: Prentice-Hall.

Putterman, Louis, ed. 1986. *The Economic Nature of the Firm.* New York: Cambridge University Press.

Radfoni, Neil A. 1984. *The Carnegie Corporation and the Development of American College Libraries, 1928–1941.* New York: American Library Association.

Ramsey, Grace Fisher. 1938. *Educational Work in Museums of the United States: Development. Methods and Trends.* New York: H. W. Wilson.

Ravitch, Diane. 1978. *The Revisionists Revised.* New York: Basic Books.

Rea, Paul Marshall. 1932. *The Museum and the Community: A Study of Social Laws and Consequences.* Lancaster, Pa.: Science Press.

Rechtschaffen, A., and O. Mednick. 1955. The Autokinetic Word Technique. *Journal of Abnormal and Social Psychology* 51:346–48.

Redding, Gordon, and Simon Tam. 1986. Networks and Molecular Organizations: An Exploratory View of Chinese Firms in Hong Kong. In *Proceedings of the Inaugural Meeting of the Southeast Asia Region Academy of International Business,* ed. K. C. Mun and T. S. Chan, 129–44. Chinese University of Hong Kong.

Reddy, William. 1987. *Money and Liberty in Modern Europe.* New York: Cambridge University Press.

Regier, Darrel A., Irving D. Goldberg, and Carl A. Taube. 1978. The De Facto U.S. Mental Health Services System: A Public Health Perspective. *Archives of General Psychiatry* 35:685–93.

Reid, William J. 1969. Inter-organizational Coordination in Social Welfare: A Theoretical Approach to Analysis and Intervention. In *Readings in Community Organization Practice,* ed. R. M. Kramer and H. Spect, 188–200. Englewood Cliffs, N.J.: Prentice-Hall.

Reynolds, Lloyd G., and Joseph Shister. 1949. *Job Horizons: A Study of Job Satisfaction and Labor Mobility.* New York: Harper.

Riesman, David. 1958. *Constraint and Variety in American Education.* Garden City, N.Y.: Anchor Books.

Riesman, David, and Ruell Denney. 1951. Football in America: Study in Culture Diffusion. *American Quarterly* 4:309–25.

Riker, William H. 1980. Implications from the Disequilibrium of Majority Rule for the Study of Institutions. *American Political Science Review* 74:432–446.

Ritti, R., R., and Fred H. Goldner. 1979. Professional Pluralism in an Industrial Organization. *Management Science* 16:233–46.

Roberts, George, and Mary Roberts. 1959. *Triumph on Fairmount: Fiske Kimball and the Philadelphia Museum of Art.* Philadelphia: J. B. Lippincott.

Robertson, A. F., Forthcoming. Reproduction and the Making of History: Time, the Family, and Modern Society. In Roger Friedland and Deirdre Boden, eds., *Nowhere: Time, Space and Modernity.*

Robinson, Edward S. 1928. *The Behavior of the Museum Visitor.* Washington, D. C.: American Association of Museums.

Rogers, David L., and David A. Whetten, eds. 1981. *Interorganizational Coordination.* Ames: Iowa State University Press.

Rogers, Everett M. 1962. *Diffusion of Innovations.* New York: Free Press.

Rokkan, Stein, with Agnus Campbell, Per Torsvik, and Henry Valen. 1970. *Citizens, Elections and Parties.* New York: McKay.

Rosaldo, Michelle Z. 1980. *Knowledge and Passion.* Cambridge: Cambridge University Press.

Rosch, Eleanor. 1978. Principle of Categorization. In *Cognition and Categorization,* ed. E. Rosch and B. B. Lloyd, 27–48. Hillsdale, N.J.: Erlbaum.

Rosch, Eleanor, Carolyn B. Mervis, Wayne D. Gray, David M. Johnson, and Penny Boyes-Braem. 1976. Basic Objects in Natural Categories. *Cognitive Psychology* 8:382–439.

Rose, Michael. 1985. Universalism, Culturalism, and the Aix Group: Promises and Problems of a Societal Approach to Economic Institutions. *European Sociological Review* 1:65–83.

Rosengren, William R., and Mark Lefton, eds. 1970. *Organizations and Clients.* Columbus, Ohio: Charles E. Merrill.

Rothman, David J. 1971. *The Discovery of the Asylum: The Social Order and Disorder in the New Republic.* Boston: Little, Brown.

Rothman, Mitchell. 1980. The Evolution of Forms of Legal Education. Manuscript. Department of Sociology, Yale University.

Rothschild-Whitt, Joyce. 1979. The Collectivist Organization: An Alternative to Rational Bureaucratic Models. *American Sociological Review* 44:509–27.

Rowan, Brian. 1981. The Effects of Institutionalized Rules on Administrators. In *Organizational Behavior in Schools and School Districts,* ed. S. B. Bacharach, 47–75. New York: Praeger.

_____. 1982. Organizational Structure and the Institutional Environment: The Case of Public Schools. *Administrative Science Quarterly* 27:259–79.

Roy, William. 1986. Functional and Historical Logics: Explaining the Relationship between the Capitalist Class and the Rise of the Industrial Corporation. Manuscript.

Ruggie, John G., ed. 1983. *The Antinomies of Interdependence.* New York: Columbia University Press.

Rumelt, Richard. 1974. *Strategy, Structure, and Economic Performance.* Boston: Harvard Business School.

Sabatier, Paul. 1975. Social Movements and Regulatory Agencies: Toward a More Adequate—and Less Pessimistic—Theory of Clientele Capture. *Policy Sciences* 6:301–42.

Sahlins, Marshall. 1976. *Culture and Practical Reason.* Chicago: University of Chicago Press.

Salancik, Gerald R., and Jeffrey Pfeffer. 1974. The Bases and Use of Power in Organizational Decision Making. *Administrative Science Quarterly* 19:453–73.

Salisbury, Robert, and John Heinz. 1970. A Theory of Policy Analysis and Some Preliminary Applications. In *Policy Analysis in Political Science,* ed. I. Sharkansky, 39–60. Chicago: Markham.

Sartori, Giovanni. 1984. Guidelines for Concept Analysis. In *Social Science Concepts,* ed. G. Sartori, 15–85. Beverly Hills, Calif.: Sage.

Schank, Roger, and Robert Abelson. 1977. *Scripts, Plans, Goals and Understanding.* Hillsdale, N.J.: Erlbaum.

Schelling, Thomas. 1978. *Micromotives and Macrobehavior.* New York: Norton.

Schmidt, William E. 1987. For Displaced Farmers, More Than Sympathy. *New York Times,* December 8, p. 10.

Schmitter, Philippe C. 1974. Still the Century of Corporatism? In *The New Corporatism*, ed. F. B. Pike and T. Stritch, 85–131. Notre Dame: University of Notre Dame Press.

_____. 1979. Modes of Interest Intermediation and Models of Societal Change in Western Europe. In *Trends toward Corporatist Intermediation*, ed. P. C. Schmitter and G. Lehmbruch, 63–95. Beverly Hills, Calif.: Sage.

Schneider, Mark A. 1987. Culture-as-Text in the Work of Clifford Geertz. *Theory and Society* 16:809–39.

Schotter, Andrew. I 981. *The Economic Theory of Social Institutions*. New York: Cambridge University Press.

Schulze, Robert. 1961. The Bifurcation of Power in a Satellite City. In *Community Political Systems*, ed. M. Janowitz, 19–80. New York: Free Press.

Schutz, Alfred. 1962. *Collected Paper I: The Problem of Social Reality*, ed. Maurice Natanson. The Hague: Martinus Nijhoff.

_____. 1967. *The Phenomenology of the Social World*. Trans. G. Walsh and F. Lehnert. Evanston, Ill.: Northwestern University Press.

Scitovsky, Tibor. 1985. Economic Development in Taiwan and South Korea, 1965–81. *Food Research Institute Studies* 19(3):215–64.

Scott, Joan Wallace. 1984. Men and Women in the Parisian Garment Trades. In *The Power of the Past*, ed. P. Thane, G. Crossick, and R. Cloud, 67–93. Cambridge: Cambridge University Press.

Scott, Marvin B., and Stanford M. Lyman. 1968. Accounts. *American Sociological Review* 33:46–62.

Scott, W. Richard. 1975. Organizational Structure. *Annual Review of Sociology* 1:1–25.

_____. 1977. Effectiveness of Organizational Effectiveness Studies. In *New Perspectives on Organizational Effectiveness*, ed. P. S. Goodman and J. M. Pennings, 63–95. San Francisco: Jossey-Bass.

_____. 1981a. *Organizations: Rational, Natural, and Open Systems*. Englewood Cliffs, N.J.: Prentice Hall.

_____. 1981b. Reform Movements and Organizations: The Case of Aging. In *Aging: Social Change*, ed. S. B. Kiesler et al., 331–45. New York: Academic Press.

_____. 1982a. Health Care Organizations in the 1980s: The Convergence of Public and Professional Control Systems. In *Contemporary Health Services: Social Science Perspectives*, ed. A. W. Johnson et al., 177–95. Boston: Auburn House.

_____. 1982b. Managing Professional Work: Three Models of Control for Health Organizations. *Health Services Research* 17:213–40.

_____. 1983. The Organization of Environments: Network, Cultural, and Historical Elements. In *Organizational Environments*, ed. J. W. Meyer and W. R. Scott, 155–75. Beverly Hills, Calif.: Sage.

_____. 1985. Conflicting Levels of Rationality: Regulators, Managers and Professionals in the Medical Care Sector. *Journal of Health Administration Education* 3, pt. 2:113–31.

_____. 1986. Systems within Systems: The Mental Health Sector. In *The Organization of Mental Health Services: Societal and Community Systems*, ed. W. R. Scott and B. L. Black, 31–52. Beverly Hills, Calif.: Sage.

_____. 1987a. The Adolescence of Institutional Theory. *Administrative Science Quarterly* 32:493–511.

_____. 1987b. *Organizations: Rational, Natural and Open Systems*. 2d ed. Englewood Cliffs, N.J.: Prentice-Hall.

_____. 1990. Symbols and Organizations: From Barnard to the Institutionalists. In *Organization Theory: From Chester Barnard to the Present and Beyond*, ed. O. E. Williams, 38–55. New York: Oxford University Press.

Scott, W. Richard, and Bruce L. Black, eds. 1986. *The Organization of Mental Health Services: Societal and Community Systems*. Beverly Hills, Calif.: Sage.

Scott, W. Richard, and John C. Lammers. 1985. Trends in Occupations and Organizations in the Medical Care and Mental Health Sectors. *Medical Care Review* 42:37–76.

Scott, W. Richard, and John W. Meyer. 1983. The Organization of Societal Sectors. In *Organizational Environments: Ritual and Rationality*, ed. J. W. Meyer and W. R. Scott, 129–53. Beverly Hills, Calif.: Sage.

_____. 1988. Environmental Linkages and Organizational Complexity: Public and Private Schools. In *Comparing Public and Private Schools*, ed. H. M. Levin and T. James, 128–60. New York: Falmer Press.

Sedlak, Michael W. 1981. Youth Policy and Young Women, 1950–1972: The Impact of Private-Sector Programs for Pregnant and Wayward Girls on Public Policy. Paper presented at National Institute for Education Youth Policy Research Conference, Washington, D.C.

Selznick, Philip. 1949. TVA and the Grass Roots. Berkeley: University of California Press.

_____. 1957. *Leadership in Administration*. Evanston, Ill · Row, Peterson.

Sergiovanni, Thomas J., Martin Burlingame, Fred D. Coombs, and Paul Thurston. 1980. *Educational Governance and Administration.* Englewood Cliffs, N.J.: Prentice-Hall.

Sewell, William H., Jr. 1987. Theory of Action, Dialectic, and History. *American Journal of Sociology* 93(1):166-72.

Sharpe, L. J. 1973a. American Democracy Reconsidered: Part I. *British Journal of Political Science* 3:1–28.

_____. 1973b. American Democracy Reconsidered: Part I. *British Journal of Political Science* 3:129–67.

Shaw, Clifford. 1940. The Chicago Area Project. In *Criminal Behavior,* ed. W. C. Reckless, 508–16. New York: McGraw-Hill.

Shefter, Martin, and Benjamin Ginsberg. 1985. Institutionalizing the Reagan Regime. Paper presented at the annual meeting of the American Political Science Association.

Shepsle, Kenneth A. 1986. Institutional Equilibrium and Equilibrium Institutions. In *Political Science: The Science of Politics,* ed. H. Weisburg, 51–82. New York: Agathon.

_____. 1989. Studying Institutions: Some Lessons from the Rational Choice Approach. *Journal of Theoretical Politics* 1:131–47.

Shepsle, Kenneth A., and Barry Weingast. 1981. Structure-Induced Equilibria and Legislative Choice. *Public Choice* 37:503–19.

_____. 1987. The Institutional Foundations of Committee Power. *American Political Science Review* 81:85–104.

Sherif, M. 1935. A Study of Some Social Factors in Perception. *Archives of Psychology* 187:45.

_____. 1967. *Social Interaction: Process or Product.* Chicago: Aldine.

Sherman, Roger. 1974. *The Economics of Industry.* Boston: Little, Brown.

Shibutani, Tamotsu. 1986. *Social Processes.* Berkeley: University of California Press.

Shils, Edward. 1975. *Center and Periphery.* Chicago: University of Chicago Press.

Shimokawa, Koichi. 1982. Nihon ni okeru jidosha meka, buhin meka kankei to sono bungyo kozo no rekishiteki hatten to gendaiteki igi: Sono gijyutsu kakushin to seisan no junansei ni kanrenshite (The relationship between automobile manufacturers and parts producers, historical development and contemporary significance of such a division of labor: Issues of technological innovation and flexible production). *Keiei Shirin* 19:23–47.

_____. 1985. Japan's Keiretsu System: The Case of the Automobile Industry. *Japanese Economic Studies* 12(4):3–31.

Shweder, Richard A., and Edmund J. Bourne. 1984. Does the Concept of the Person Vary Cross-Culturally? In *Culture Theory: Essays on Mind, Self, and Emotion,* ed. R. A. Shweder and R. A. Levine, 158–199. New York: Cambridge University Press.

Shweder, Richard, and Robert LeVine. 1984. *Culture Theory: Essays on Mind, Self, and Emotion.* Chicago: University of Chicago Press.

Siegfried, A. 1956. Stable Instability in France. *Foreign Affairs* 34:394–404.

Sills, David L. 1957. *The Volunteers: Means and Ends in a National Organization.* Glencoe, Ill.: Free Press.

Simon, Herbert A. 1945. *Administrative Behavior.* New York: Free Press.

_____. 1962. The Architecture of Complexity. *Proceedings of the American Philosophical Society* 106:467–82.

Singh, Jitendra V., Robert J. House, and David J. Tucker. 1986. Organizational Change and Organizational Mortality. *Administrative Science Quarterly* 31:587–611.

Singh, Jitendra V., and Charles J. Lumsden. 1990. Theory and Research in Organizational Ecology. *Annual Review of Sociology* 16:161–95.

Singh, Jitendra V., David J. Tucker, and Robert J. House. 1986. Organizational Legitimacy and the Liability of Newness. *Administrative Science Quarterly* 31:171–93.

Singh, Jitendra V., David J. Tucker, and Agnes G. Meinhard. 1988. Are Voluntary Organizations Structurally Inert? Exploring an Assumption in Organizational Ecology. Paper presented at Academy of Management meetings, Anaheim, Calif.

Skocpol, Theda. 1979. *States and Social Revolution.* New York: Cambridge University Press.

_____. 1985. Bringing the State Back In: Strategies of Analysis in Current Research. In *Bringing the State Back In,* ed. P. Evans et al., 3–43. New York: Cambridge University Press.

Skowronek, Stephen. 1981. *Building a New American State.* New York: Cambridge University Press.

Smelser, Neil. 1959. *Social Change in the Industrial Revolution.* Chicago: University of Chicago Press.

Smith, Lee. 1981. The Unsentimental Corporate Giver. *Fortune Magazine,* September 21, pp. 121ff.

Snell, Bruno. 1960. *The Discovery of the Mind.* New York: Harper and Row.

Social Planning Council of Metropolitan Toronto. 1976. *In Search of a Framework.* Toronto: Social Planning Council of Metropolitan Toronto.

Somers, Anne R. 1969. *Hospital Regulation: The Dilemma of Public Policy.* Princeton: Industrial Relations Section, Princeton University.

Spencer, Herbert. 1897. *Principles of Sociology.* New York: Appleton.

Splane, Richard. 1965. *Social Welfare in Ontario, 1791–1893.* Toronto: University of Toronto Press.

Sproull, Lee S. 1981. Response to Regulation: An Organizational Process Framework. *Administration and Society* 12:447-70.

Stackhouse, E. Ann. 1982. The Effects of State Centralization on Administrative and Macrotechnical Structure in Contemporary Secondary Schools. Project Report No. 82–A24. Stanford: Institute for Research on Educational Finance and Governance, Stanford University.

Starbuck, William H. 1976. Organizations and Their Environments. In *Handbook of Industrial and Organizational Psychology,* ed. Marvin D. Dunnette, 1069-1123. New York: Rand McNally.

Stark, David. 1980. Class Struggle and the Transformation of the Labor Process. *Theory and Society* 9:101–52.

_____. 1986. Rethinking Internal Labor Markets: New Insights from a Comparative Perspective. *American Sociological Review* 51:492–504.

Starr, Paul. 1980. Medical Care and the Boundaries of Capitalist Organization. Manuscript. Program on Non-Profit Organizations, Yale University.

_____. 1982. *The Social Transformation of American Medicine.* New York: Basic Books.

Staw, B. M. 1981. The Escalation of Commitment: A Review and Analysis. *Academy of Management* 6:577–87.

Staw, B. M., B. J. Calder, R. K. Hess, and L. E. Sandelands. 1980. Intrinsic Motivation and Norms about Payment. *Journal of Personality* 48:1-14.

Staw, B. M., and Ross, J. 1987. Behavior in Escalation Situations: Antecedents, Prototypes, and Solutions. In *Research in Organizational Behavior,* ed. B. M. Staw and L. L. Cummings, 9:39–78. Greenwich, Conn.: JAI Press.

Stein, Maurice. 1960. *The Eclipse of Community: An Interpretation of American Studies.* New York: Harper and Row.

Stenbeck, M. J. E. 1986. The Quality of Work Measurement. M. A. thesis, Department of Sociology, University of California, Santa Barbara.

Stepan, Alfred. 1978. *The State and Society: Peru in Comparative Perspective.* Princeton: Princeton University Press.

Stigler, George J. 1971. The Theory of Economic Regulation. *Bell Journal of Economics* 5:1–13.

Stinchcombe, Arthur L. 1965. Social Structure and Organizations. In *Handbook of Organizations,* ed. J. G. March, 142-93. Chicago: Rand McNally.

_____. 1968. *Constructing Social Theories.* New York: Haitourt Brace.

_____. 1973. Formal Organization. In *Sociology: An Introduction,* ed. Neil J. Smelser, 23–65. New York: Wiley.

_____. 1986a. Milieu and Structure Updated. *Theory and Society* 15:901–13.

_____. 1986b. Reason and Rationality. *Sociological Theory* 4:167–85.

Storer, N. W. 1973. *Focus on Society: An Introduction to* Sociology. Reading, Mass.: Addison-Wesley.

Streeck, Wolfgang, and Philippe C. Schmitter. 1985. Community, Market, State—and Associations?: The Prospective Contribution of Interest Governance to Social Order. In *Private Interest Government: Beyond Market and State,* 1–29. London: Sage Publications.

Suchman, Edward A. 1967. *Evaluative Research.* New York: Russell Sage Foundation.

Sudnow, David. 1964. Normal Crimes. *Social Problems* 12:255–75.

Sumiya, Toshio. 1986. *Gendai nihon shihon shugi no shihai kozo: Ni/ion kenzai to rokudai kigyo shudan* (The structure of domination in modern Japanese capitalism: Japanese economy and six major business groups). Tokyo: Shimpyoron.

Sumner, William G. 1906. *Folkways.* Boston: Ginn.

Sundquist, James L. 1969. *Making Federalism Work.* Washington, D.C.: Brookings Institution.

Sundstrom, William. 1988. Institutional Isomorphism: The Standardization of Rules and Contracts in Business Firms. Paper presented at Western Economic Association International Conference.

Suttles, Gerald D. 1984. The Cumulative Texture of Local Urban Culture. *American Journal of Sociology* 90:283–304.

Swanson, Guy. 1971. An Organizational Analysis of Collectivities. *American Sociological Review* 36:607–623.

———. 1986. Phobias and Related Symptoms: Some Social Sources. *Sociological Forum* 1:103–30.

Swidler, Ann. 1979. *Organization without Authority: Dilemmas of Social Control of Free Schools.* Cambridge: Harvard University Press.

———. 1986. Culture in Action: Symbols and Strategies. *American Sociological Review* 51:273–86.

Tamuz, Michal. 1982. Organizational Changes within the Mental Health Sector in California, 1940-1980. In *Institutional Sectors and Organizational Consequences: Schools and Other Public Organizations in a Federalist System,* ed. J. W. Meyer and W. R. Scott. Final report to the National Institute of Education. Stanford: Institute for Research on Educational Finance and Governance, Stanford University.

Taub, Richard P. 1988. *Community Capitalism.* Boston: Harvard Business School Press.

Taylor, Shelley E., and Jennifer C. Crocker. 1980. Schematic Bases of Social Information Processing. In *The Ontario Symposium on Personality and Social Psychology,* ed. E. T. Higgins, P. Herman, and M. P. Zanna, 1:89–134. Hillsdale, NJ.: Erlbaum.

Terreberry, Shirley. 1968. The Evolution of Organizational Environments. *Administrative Science Quarterly* 12:590–613.

Thévenot, Laurent. 1984. Rules and Implements: Investment in Forms. *Social Science Information* 23:1–45.

Thomas, George M. 1989. *Revivalism and Cultural Change: Christianity. Nation Building, and the Market in the Nineteenth-Century United States.* Chicago: University of Chicago Press.

Thomas, George M., and John W. Meyer. 1984. The Expansion of the State. *Annual Review of Sociology* 10:461–82.

Thomas, George M., John Meyer, Francisco Ramirez, and John Boli. 1987. *Institutional Structure: Constituting Stoic, Society and the Individual.* Newbury Park, Calif.: Sage.

Thompson, E. P. 1963. *The Making of the English Working Class.* New York: Random House.

Thompson, James D. 1967. *Organizations in Action.* New York: McGraw-Hill.

Tilly, Charles, ed. 1975, *The Formation of National States in Western Europe.* Princeton: Princeton University Press.

Tocqueville, Alexis de. [1856] 1955. *The Old Regime and the French Revolution.* Garden City. N.Y.: Doubleday.

Tolbert, Pamela S. 1985. Resource Dependence and Institutional Environments: Sources of Administrative Structure in Institutions of Higher Education. *Administrative Science Quarterly* 30:1–13

———. 1988. Institutional Sources of Organizational Culture in Major Law Finns. In *Institutional Patterns and Organizations,* ed. L. G. Zucker, 101–13. Cambridge: Ballinger.

Tolbert, Pamela S., and Robert N. Stern. 1989. Organizations and Professions: Governance Structures in Large Law Firms. Manuscript. Cornell University.

Tolbert, Pamela S., and Lynne G. Zucker. 1983. Institutional Sources of Change in the Formal Structure of Organizations: The Diffusion of Civil Service Reform, 1880–1935. *Administrative Science Quarterly* 28:22–39.

Tomkins, Calvin. 1970. *Merchants and Masterpieces: The Story of the Metropolitan Museum of Art.* New York: Moon.

Toyo Keizai Shimposha. 1986a. *Kigyo keiretsu soran* (Overview of firm alignments). Tokyo.

———. 1986b. *Nihon no kigyo gurupu.* (Business groups in Japan). Tokyo.

Troy, Kathryn. 1982. *The Corporate Contributions Function.* New York: The Conference Board.

Tucker, David J. 1981. Voluntary Auspices and the Behavior of Social Service Organizations. *Social Service Review* 55:603–27.

Tucker, David J.. Jitendra V. Singh, and Robert J. House. 1984. The Liability of Newness in a Population of Voluntary Social Service Organizations. Paper presented at the 49th American Sociological Association Annual Meeting. San Antonio, Tex.

Tucker, David J., Jitendra V. Singh, and Agnes G. Meinhard. 1987. Founding Conditions, Environmental Change and Organizational Mortality. Manuscript. School of Social Work, McMaster University.

———. 1990. Organizational Form, Population Dynamics and Institutional Change: A Study of Birth Selection Processes. *Academy of Management Journal* 33:151–78.

Tucker, David, Jitendra Singh, Agucs Meinhard, and Robert House. 1988. Ecological and Institutional Sources of Change in Organizational Populations. In *Ecological Models of Organizations,* ed. G. R. Carroll, 127–51. Cambridge, Mass.: Ballinger.

Tuma, Nancy B. 1980. *Invoking Rate.* Menlo Park, Calif.: SRI International.

Tuma, Nancy B., and Andrew J. Grimes. 1981. A Comparison of Models of Role Orientations of Professionals in a Research-Oriented University. *Administrative Science Quarterly* 26:187–206.

Tuma, Nancy B., Michael T. Harman, and Lyle P. Groeneveld. 1979. Dynamic Analysis of Event Histories. *American Journal of Sociology* 84:820–54.

Turk, Herman. 1977. *Organizations in Modern Life*. San Francisco: Jossey-Bass.

Tyack, David. 1974. *The One Best System: A History of American Urban Education*. Cambridge: Harvard University Press.

Tyack, David, and Elizabeth Hansot. 1982. *Managers of Virtue*. New York: Basic Books.

Udy, Stanley, H., Jr. 1970. *Work in Traditional and Modern Society*. Englewood Cliffs, N.J.: Prentice-Hall.

Ueda, Yoshiaki. 1983. Kigyo shudan ni okeru yakuin ken-nin no keiryo bunseki: Kigyo-kan kankei no sokutei (The mathematical analysis of interlocking directorates in enterprise groups: Measurement of interfirm relationships). *Shoken Keizai* 146:25–48.

_____. 1986. Intercorporate Networks in Japan: A Study of Interlocking Directorates in Modern Large Corporations. *Shoken Keizai* 151:236–54.

Useem, Michael. 1979. The Social Organization of the American Business Elite and Participation of Corporation Directors in the Governance of American Institutions. *American Sociological Review* 44:553–72.

_____. 1987. Corporate Philanthropy. In *The Nonprofit Sector: A Research Handbook*. ed. W W. Powell, 340–59. New Haven: Yale University Press.

Veblen, Thorstein. 1918. *The Higher Learning in America: A Memorandum on the Conduct of Universities by Business Men*. New York: B. W. Heubsch.

Walker, Jack. 1969. Diffusion of Innovations among the American States. *American Political Science Review* 63:880–99.

Wall, Wendy L. 1984, Companies Change the Ways They Make Charitable Donations. *Wall Street Journal*, June 21, pp. 1ff.

Wallerstein, Immanuel. 1974. *The Modern World System*. New York: Academic.

Wallich, H., and J. J. McGowan. 1970. Stockholder Interest and the Corporation's Role in Social Policy. In *A New Rationale for Corporate Social Policy*, 39–59. New York: Committee for Economic Development.

Wallis, K. 1972. Testing for Fourth Order Autocorrelation in Quarterly Regression Equations. *Econometrica* 40:617–36.

Warner, R. Stephen. 1978. Toward a Redefinition of Action Theory: Paying the Cognitive Element Its Due. *American Journal of Sociology* 83(6):1317–49.

Warner, W. Lloyd, and J. O. Low. 1947. *The Social System of the Modern Factory*. New Haven: Yale University Press.

Warren, Roland L. 1963. *The Community in America*. Chicago: Rand McNally.

_____. 1967. The Interorganizational Field as a Focus for Investigation. *Administrative Science Quarterly* 12:396–419.

_____. 1972. *The Community in America*. Rev. ed. Chicago: Rand McNally.

Warren, Roland L., Stephen Rose, and Ann Bergunder. 1974. *The Structure of Urban Reform*. Lexington, Mass.: D. C. Heath.

Weatherly, Richard A. 1979. *Reforming Special Education: Policy Implementation from State Level to Street Level*. Cambridge: MIT Press.

Webb, Eugene, D. T. Campbell, R. D. Schwartz, and L. Seechrest. 1966. *Unobtrusive Measures*. Chicago: Rand NcNally.

Webb, Eugene, and Karl E. Weick. 1979. Unobtrusive Measures in Organizational Theory: A Reminder. *Administrative Science Quarterly* 24:650–59.

Webb, Sidney, and Beatrice Webb. 1912. *The Prevention of Destitution*. London: Longmans, Green.

Weber, Max. [1919] 1946. Science as a Vocation. In *From Max Weber: Essays in Sociology*, ed. H. H. Gerth and C. W. Mills, 129–56. New York: Oxford University Press.

_____. [1922] 1963. *The Sociology of Religion*. Boston: Beacon Press.

_____. [1922] 1978. *Economy and Society*. Berkeley: University of California Press.

_____. [1927] 1950. *General Economic History*. Glencoe, Ill.: Free Press.

_____. 1947. *The Theory of Social and Economic Organization*. New York: Oxford University Press.

_____. 1952. *The Protestant Ethic and the Spirit of Capitalism*. New York: Scribner.

Weick, Karl E. 1969. *The Social Psychology of Organizing*. Reading, Mass.: Addison-Wesley.

_____. 1976. Educational Organizations as Loosely Coupled Systems. *Administrative Science Quarterly* 21:1–19.

Weick, Karl, and D. P. Gilfillan. 1971. Fate of Arbitrary Traditions in a Laboratory Microculture. *Journal of Personality and Social Psychology* 17:179–91.

Weingast, Barry, and William Marshall. 1988. The Industrial Organization of Congress; or, Why Legislatures, Like Firms, Are Not Organized as Markets. *Journal of Political Economy* 96:132–64.

Weinstein, James. 1968. *The Corporate Ideal in the Liberal State, 1900–1918*. Boston: Beacon Press.

Weiss, Janet. 1981. Substance versus Symbol in Administrative Reform: The Case of Human Service Coordination. *Policy Analysis* 7:21–46.

Welfling, Mary B. 1973. *Political Institutionalization: A Comparative Analysis of African Political Systems*. Beverly Hills, Calif.: Sage.

Westney, D. Eleanor. 1987. *Imitation and Innovation: The Transfer of Western Organizational Patterns to Meiji Japan*. Cambridge: Harvard University Press.

_____. 1989. Institutionalization Theory and the Organizational Dilemma of Multinational Enterprise. Working paper. Sloan School of Management, MIT.

Wharf, Brian, and Novia Carter. 1972. *Planning for Social Services: Canadian Experiences*. Ottawa: Canadian Council on Social Development.

White, Harrison, C. 1981. Where Do Markets Come From? *American Journal of Sociology* 87:517–47.

White, Harrison C., Scott A. Boorman, and Ronald L. Breiger. 1976. Social Structure from Multiple Networks, I: Blockmodels of Roles and Positions. *American Journal of Sociology* 81:730–80.

White, Morton G. 1949. *Social Thought in America*. New York: McGraw-Hill.

Wiebe, Robert. 1967. *The Search for Order, 1877–1920*. New York: Hill and Wang.

Wiewel, Wim, and Albert Hunter. 1986. The Interorganizational Network as a Resource: A Comparative Case Study on Organizational Genesis. *Administrative Science Quarterly* 30:482–96.

Wildavsky, Aaron. 1964. *The Politics of the Budgetary Process*. Boston: Little, Brown.

_____. 1979. *Speaking Truth to Power: The Art and Craft of Policy Analysis*. Boston: Little, Brown.

Wilensky, Harold L. 1964. The Professionalization of Everyone. *American Journal of Sociology* 70:137–58.

Wilensky, Harold L., and Charles Lebeaux. 1958. *Industrial Society and Social Welfare*. New York: Free Press.

Williamson, Oliver, E. 1975. *Markets and Hierarchies*. New York: Free Press.

_____. 1979. Transaction-Cost Economics: The Governance of Contractual Relations. *Journal of Law and Economics* 22:233–61.

_____. 1981. The Economics of Organization: The Transactions Cost Approach. *American Journal of Sociology* 87:548–77.

_____. 1985. *The Economic Institutions of Capitalism*. New York: Free Press.

Wilson, James Q., ed. 1980. *The Politics of Regulation*. New York: Basic Books.

Winer, B. J. 1962. *Statistical Principles in Experimental Design*. New York: McGraw-Hill.

Winter, Sidney G. 1964. Economic "Natural Selection" and the Theory of the Firm. *Yale Economic Essays* 4:224–72.

_____. 1975. Optimization and Evolution in the Theory of the Firm. In *Adaptive Economic Models*, ed. R. H. Day and T. Graves, 73–118. New York: Academic.

Wong, Siu-lun. 1985. The Chinese Family Firm: A Model. *British Journal of Sociology* 36:58–72.

_____. Forthcoming. *Emigrant Entrepreneurs: Shanghai Industrialists in Hong Kong*. Hong Kong: Oxford University Press.

Woodward, C. Vann. 1957. *The Strange Career of Jim Crow*. New York: Oxford University Press.

Woodward, Joan. 1965. *Industrial Organization, Theory and Practice*. London: Oxford University Press.

Wright, Erik Olin. 1979. *Class Structure and Income Determination*. New York: Academic.

_____. 1985. *Classes*. London: Verso.

Wrigley, Julia. 1982. *Class, Politics and Public Schools: Chicago, 1900–1950*. New Brunswick, N.J.: Rutgers University Press.

Wuthnow, Robert. 1980. The World-Economy and the Institutionalization of Science in Seventeenth-Century Europe. In *Studies of the Modern World System*, ed. A. Bergesen, 25–56. New York: Academic.

_____. 1987. *Meaning and Moral Order*. Berkeley: University of California Press.

Wuthnow, Robert, J. D. Hunter, A. Bergesen, and E. Kurzweil. 1984. *Cultural Analysis*. Boston: Routledge and Kegan Paul.

Wuthnow, Robert, and Marsha Witten. 1988. New Directions in the Study of Culture. *Annual Review of Sociology* 14:49–67.

Yang, Mayfair Mei-hui. 1989. The Gift Economy and State Power in China. *Comparative Studies in Society and History.* 31:25–54.

Young, Oran R. 1986. International Regimes: Toward a New Theory of Institutions. *World Politics* 39:104–22.

Youtz, Philip Newell. 1931. A Museum of the Twentieth Century. Paper presented at the May 21 meeting of the American Association of Museums, Pittsburgh, Pa. Manuscript in Philadelphia Museum of Art Archives, Record Group 6, PMA: 69th Street Branch—pamphlets, publications.

_____. 1932. The Sixty-ninth Street Branch of the Pennsylvania Museum of Art. Paper presented at the May 13 meeting of the American Association of Museums, Boston, Mass. Carnegie Corporation Archives, filed under Pennsylvania Museum of Art.

Zaid, Mayer N., and Patricia Denton. 1963. From Evangelism to General Service: The Transformation of the YMCA. *Administrative Science Quarterly* 8:214–34.

Zhonghua Zhengxinso, comp. 1985. *Taiwan diqu jituan qiye yanjiu* (Research on business groups in Taiwan). Taipei: China Credit Information Service.

Zimmerman, D. H., and M. Pollner. 1970. The Everyday World as a Phenomenon. In *Understanding Everyday Life,* ed. J. Douglas, 33–65. Chicago: Aldine.

Znaniecki, Florian. 1945. Social Organization and Institutions. In *Twentieth Century* Sociology, ed. O. Gurvitch and W. E. Moore, 172-217. New York: Philosophical Library.

Zo, Ki-zun. 1970. Development and Behavioral Patterns of Korean Entrepreneurs. *Korea Journal* 10:9–14.

Zolberg, Vera L. 1974. The Art Institute of Chicago: The Sociology of a Cultural Institution. Ph.D. diss., Department of Sociology, University of Chicago.

_____. 1986. Tensions of Mission in American Art Museums. In *Nonprofit Enterprise in the Arts: Studies in Mission and Constraint,* ed. P. J. DiMaggio, 184–98. New York: Oxford University Press.

Zucker, Lynne G. 1977. The Role of Institutionalization in Cultural Persistence. *American Sociological Review* 42:726–43.

_____. 1983. Organizations as Institutions. In *Research in the Sociology of Organizations,* ed. S. B. Bacharach, 1-42. Greenwich, Conn.: JAI Press.

_____. 1986. Production of Trust: Institutional Sources of Economic Structure, 1840–1920. In *Research in Organizational Behavior,* 8:53–111. Greenwich, Conn.: JAI Press.

_____. 1987. Institutional Theories of Organizations. *Annual Review of Sociology* 13:443–64.

_____. ed. 1988a. *Institutional Patterns and Organizations: Culture and Environment.* Cambridge, Mass.: Ballinger.

_____. 1988b. Where Do Institutional Patterns Come From? Organizations as Actors in Social Systems. In *Institutional Patterns and Organizations,* ed. L. G. Zucker, 23–52. Cambridge, Mass.: Ballinger.

_____. 1989. Combining Institutional Theory and Population Ecology: No Legitimacy, No History. *American Sociological Review* 54(4):542–45.Zwerling, L. Steven. 1976. Second Best. New York: McGraw-Hill.

THE COMMONS: A MULTIDISCIPLINARY APPROACH TO NONPROFIT ORGANIZATIONS, VOLUNTARY ACTION, AND PHILANTHROPY

ROGER A. LOHMANN

The task of identifying nonprofit organizations, voluntary action, and philanthropy as the principal constituents of a single "sector" within the larger economy, society, and polity has been a central challenge for the multidisciplinary paradigm that seems to be emerging in this field. The concepts of the commons and common goods are presented in this article as having important multidisciplinary implications. The commons is characterized by uncoerced participation, shared purposes and resources, mutuality, and fairness; the derivative concept of common goods is characterized as desirable ends that are universal and indivisible within a commons but not necessarily beyond. Taken together, the concepts of the commons and common goods offer the basis for a shared paradigm that can resolve the sector problem.

A primary task of any science is to identify the phenomena it seeks to describe and explain and to define them in terms that facilitate investigation and application. With respect to the current agenda of scientific interests among nonprofit, voluntary, and philanthropic researchers, significant portions of this basic scientific yeomanry took place long ago within several separate academic disciplines and scientific fields. Voluntary organizations (in sociology), charity and later community organization (in social work), and nonprofit organization (in public administration and cooperative extension), as well as fund accounting and trust law, were until quite recently minuscule subspecialties within existing disciplinary frameworks. They were in no position to compete with or challenge entrenched disciplinary paradigms. Other nonprofit and voluntary action topics, such as managing volunteers and fundraising, appear to have emerged entirely outside the organized knowledge industry of the universities, with its order of disciplines and sciences.

Since the origins of the Association for Voluntary Action Scholars in the early 1970s, different groups of specialists have been discovering and building upon mutual, overlapping, and at times competing interests under various ad hoc umbrellas. Recently, a profusion of new programs, institutes, associations, sciences, curricula, and even professions have been proclaimed in voluntary and nonprofit studies. In fact, it appears that nonprofit and voluntary studies are currently undergoing one of those unpredictable but recognizable crises of opportunity that occasionally come along to shake up the established order.

One of the clearest indicators that something is happening is the number of book publishers currently out trolling for manuscripts in this field. Publishers' representatives are seldom found among the crusaders for lost causes and moribund interests. Suddenly many are not just willing but downright eager to expand their lists in this area. As a result, the published work in this area is growing dramatically. Once, anyone with interests in this area could reasonably expect to rather easily keep abreast of everything published in a particular subspecialty, but this practice is becoming increasingly difficult with each passing year.

The sudden upsurge of interest in "the sector" has exposed the apparent lack of a general theoretical framework—a general paradigm, if you will—to encompass the entire subject and to relate specific interests and topics to one another. Smith and Freedman (1972, p. 1) concluded more than two decades ago that "the term theory has to be applied to the study of voluntary associations with care, since very little theory, in any strict sense of the word, has yet been developed in the field. There is no grand, all encompassing, and generally accepted theory of voluntarism, or even a respectable middle range theory." Several of the authors writing in the 1987 collection of research on nonprofit organizations make exactly the same point (Douglas, 1987; Salamon, 1987; Simon, 1987). Regrettably, this assessment is still accurate today, although the number of provocative and insightful premises, definitions, and propositions is considerably larger than it was two decades ago.

Although Alexis de Tocqueville provided a natural and durable starting point and offered great depth of insight on the nature of democratic society, his comments about "the sector" are rather sparse and by now somewhat threadbare. In sociology, David Horton Smith has done much to articulate the nature of the "voluntary sector," and Smith and Freedman's review of the voluntary literature remains interesting and useful (Smith, 1974; Smith and Freedman, 1972). In social work, Ralph Kramer (1981) has in recent years led a small cadre of those interested in voluntary agencies. Burton Weisbrod (1988) has summarized and synthesized the remarkable distillation of a bona fide nonprofit economics, which seems to have taken place in less than a decade. A great many other individual and collective contributions worthy of note could be identified.

Yet none of these disciplinary approaches appears to offer core concepts or theory capable of sustaining a coherent interdisciplinary view of what remains a vast collection of vaguely related topics and issues. What is still needed is a general paradigm or theoretical model to unify and bring some conceptual order to the whole. Several years ago, Jon Van Til (1988) proposed the French "social economy" approach as a possible paradigm. Others have identified facets of the relative advantages of the nonprofit sector in comparisons with commercial/market and public/government sectors (Hansmann, 1987).

The interdisciplinary nature of recent scholarly work on the "third sector" has disturbed and seriously eroded established patterns of disciplinary consensus over "the nature of the nonprofit beast" without offering any genuinely new overviews. The phenomenon brings to mind the repeated disturbances of normal science that are said to precede a paradigm shift in the Kuhnian model of scientific revolutions (Bernstein, 1983, pp. 68–70). The organization of an international and interdisciplinary community of practitioners, researchers, and scholars began with the formation of the Association for Voluntary Action Scholars and continues through the formation in March 1991 of the International Research Society for Voluntary Associations, Nonprofit Organizations, and Philanthropy. Creation of a multidisciplinary research community has loosened shackles that formerly constrained interests, narrowed possibilities for recognition and support, and limited opportunities for publication and community.

Meanwhile, nonprofit and voluntary action studies have also become a genuinely international interest. This is no longer a parochial Anglo-American topic. We are witnessing an extraordinary international outburst of creativity and energy in the study of nonprofit organizations, voluntary associations, philanthropy, volunteering, fundraising, and all related topics. As a result, we have a stronger and more vibrant base of information and empirical data than has ever previously existed. Yet the sheer creativity of the moment is further exacerbating the question of a central paradigm.

Behind all the enthusiasm, a certain malaise is associated with our collective inability to resolve the central paradigm question. Unquestionably, many bold hypotheses and typologies have been put forward in recent years. Virtually every issue of the journals and every research conference is bristling with interesting new data and provocative new hypotheses. However, mountains of statistics and separate, uncoordinated hypotheses do not add up to sound theory. Typologies like the Independent Sector (1987) classification scheme have important uses, but typologies alone cannot settle underlying theoretical questions.

The emergent national and international interdisciplinary community of nonprofit and voluntary action scholars has yet to find its vital center. The lack of a center is why so much recent work presented at meetings and conferences has been aimed at "relocating the core" of the field. Yet the problem remains and grows more perplexing. The problem is not that we lack a paradigm of nonprofit, voluntary, and philanthropic studies. It is that we have too many. Each of the disciplines and professions with a historical interest in nonprofit and voluntary studies seeks to promote its own legacy of key concepts, problems, and methods of research or intervention. Yet none of these disciplinary and professional paradigms speaks to the full range of interests and concerns of the field. In addition, they do not articulate or "interface" particularly well, representing as they do most of the major social science controversies of the past three centuries. Is a nonprofit organization different from a voluntary association? Do religious organizations, political parties, and fraternal orders produce public goods? Are the individualistic motivational paradigms of fundraising and volunteer management at odds with the utilitarian individualism of nonprofit economics and the social structuralism of nonprofit organizations?

The absence of a solid theoretical core for nonprofit, voluntary, and philanthropic studies leaves us all uncertain as to when differences reflect significant variations in meaning and intent and when they reflect simple disciplinary or theoretical colloquialisms. Until we find a conceptual center, we can all expect to continue being inundated with competing models and conceptions of all manner of sectors. Like other proposals before it, this article will either contribute further to the clutter or add bristles to the broom needed to tidy up the mess.

Missing at present is a set of central terms and concepts that embrace the diverse conceptions noted previously and that place specific issues and questions within a larger schema. To avoid as many of the contentious disciplinary questions as possible, we may want to employ some new terminology not overloaded with narrow disciplinary connotations. However, at the same time, it appears desirable to avoid the terminological excesses often associated with the social sciences.

In this article I will concentrate on two conventional terms of longstanding usage: the *commons*, an organizational/structural term for naming "the sector," and *common goods*, an associated term for labeling the goals, objectives, purposes, outputs, outcomes, products, and results of the sector. Together, these two terms form the conceptual core of an emerging theory of the commons that relocates and identifies the central (or common) interdisciplinary core of the study of nonprofit organizations, voluntary action, and philanthropy and distinguishes it from the study of markets, states, and households.

What results from adoption of these terms is an important shift in focus and perspective. We should not be too quick to assign paradigmatic roles to nonprofit, voluntary and philanthropic action in large, revenue-driven, or professionally staffed nonprofit organizations. Such organizations, along with displays of oligarchic leadership by wealthy and influential national organizations and entrepreneurial behavior by nonprofit managers, hardly represent definitive cases. They might better be seen as selections from a broader continuum of theoretical possibilities ranging from pure altruism through total self-interest. The same applies equally well to the "true" volunteer and the "civic-minded" foundation. Before such points can be explored more fully, however, it is necessary to clarify the central terms of the commons paradigm.

Overlapping Conceptions or Different Sectors?

A major intersection of mutual interests in nonprofit, voluntary, and philanthropic research and practice is probably to be found in the vicinity of that confusing group of terms that continue to attract so much attention. At present, no one may be completely sure whether the "nonprofit sector" is the same thing as or something quite different from the "voluntary sector" or the "independent sector" or the "nongovernment sector." It is not even altogether clear whether references to "not-for-profit" whatevers are intended to apply to "nonprofits" as well. This confusion offers a target of opportunity for zeroing in on the paradigm problem in nonprofit and voluntary studies: What exactly is it that represents the irreducible core of our mutual interests?

It may be possible to reach a higher level of interdisciplinary consensus by recognizing that each of these sector terms conveys important nuances of meaning and a core of common understandings. Each of the most frequently used sector terms—*nonprofit, "not-for-profit," voluntary, nongovernmental, third, independent, philanthropic,* and (reaching a bit) *eleemosynary, prosocial,* and *sodality*—points to important phenomena and makes critical distinctions. However, none denotes the core around which the field as a whole has rallied. The key question is whether any of these terms points to central, shared phenomena of concern throughout the field.

The *nonprofit sector* is usefully defined as an economic network of corporations characterized by "nondistribution constraints," or legal and ethical restrictions on the distribution of any operating surpluses incidental to the corporation's activities (that is, "profits") to shareholders, stockholders, or stakeholders (Hansmann, 1987). The concept has been of greatest interest in economic, legal, and management studies (some of which insist on the alternate term "not-for-profit"). Once *nonprofit* is defined as Hansmann does, rather than by the theoretically threadbare notion of a "profit motive," the question raised by the growing popularity of *not-for-profit* as a substitute term is answered. If one accepts the central significance of the nondistribution constraint, "not-for-profit" is merely a slightly convoluted way of saying "nonprofit."

Regardless of preferred terms, the issue is not so much whether a sector of corporations bound by the nondistribution constraint exists. Surely it does. The critical issue is whether corporations legally bound by the nondistribution constraint exhaust the limits of our mutual interests. Just as surely, they do not. However, the entire topic of social organizations bounded by ethical rather than legal nondistribution constraints has yet to attract the attention it deserves. (We will return later to the question of whether a nonprofit corporation is the same as a nonprofit organization, as current usage seems to imply.)

Similarly close examination of other sector terms is equally revealing. *Voluntarism* is most typically used to connote lack of coercion or restraint in participation. Thus, the *voluntary sector* can be defined as a system of clubs, associations, and groups characterized largely or exclusively by non-coercive membership or free and unconstrained participation. This concept has been of empirical interest to sociologists, of normative interest to democratic political theorists, and of practical interest to social workers, among others. (See Smith and Freedman, 1972, for a dated but still interesting review.)

Again, there is little doubt that such a voluntary sector exists in American, British, German, and other European societies (Bauer, 1990). But how does such a voluntary sector relate theoretically to a nonprofit sector? We may be able to accept that a nonprofit sector is equivalent to a not-for-profit sector, but can we accept that a sector of constrained corporations is identical to a sector of noncoercive and unconstrained clubs, associations, and groups? We can in the special case where the latter are all legally incorporated nonprofits bound by the nondistribution constraint. These two sector conceptions might also be equated if we assume that an ethical nondistribution constraint is the equivalent of a legal one and that voluntary clubs, associations, and groups are uniformly bound by such ethical constraints. However, this condition seems unlikely. Thus we are left with two partially overlapping conceptions.

Looking in another direction, we can define a *nongovernmental sector* as a network of organizations or institutions outside the formal apparatus of the political state and functioning independently of state oversight or direction, albeit capable of interacting with the state. This has proved to be a useful distinction for public administrators accustomed to distinguishing nongovernmental organizations from various public entities. The modern welfare state in the United States and elsewhere routinely incorporates such a nongovernmental sector (Kramer, 1981). In fact, the term may be most commonly used in international social welfare discussions. The critical issue in defining nongovernmental organizations appears to be neither distribution constraints nor participation.

The closely related notion of a *third sector* (O'Neill, 1989) distinguishes between commercial/market and public/government (first and second) sectors and nonprofit, nongovernmental organizations (which are, presumably, also nonmarket organizations). The third sector in this sense is simply the nonbusiness (or nonmarket) side of society outside the family. The third sector may thus be the last sector, or the third of four (adding the family or household sector) or even of five (adding what Smith, 1991, calls the "informal" sector). (The theory of the commons concurs with Smith that retaining the membership sector is essential to presenting a complete picture of nonprofit, voluntary, and philanthropic action.)

The market/state/nonprofit distinction arises from the ideas of Thomas Hobbes, through John Locke, John Stuart Mill, and the general heritage of utilitarian social and political theory. In light of previous distinctions, the current one raises interesting issues of the degree to which nongovernmental and noncommercial organizations are also noncoercive and unconstrained. Perhaps the greatest weakness of the concept of nongovernmental organizations is that it appears to be a content-empty negation. (For comments on the accumulation and utility of negative terms in nonprofit and voluntary action terminology, see Lohmann, 1989.)

An *independent sector* would presumably be able to function autonomously without untoward external interference or involvement (INDEPENDENT SECTOR, 1987). Whether independence also implies lack of coercion or constraint, disinterest in profit, and ethical and legal distribution constraints remains an open question. A *philanthropic sector* has been construed as consisting of individuals and organizations devoted to private action for the public good (Indiana University Center of Philanthropy, 1991). As an organization, INDEPENDENT SECTOR has produced an interesting and useful typology of "the independent sector." And the widespread reintroduction of *philanthropy* as an umbrella term breathes new life into a word with an ancient and honorable heritage in both English and its original Greek (INDEPENDENT SECTOR, 1987). Yet each term has attracted minimal conceptual justification, definition, or classification to date. Such issues as whether nondistribution constraints and uncoerced participation are essential characteristics of private action for the public good have not been closely examined.

As if the present welter of sector terms is not enough, we might even go so far as to suggest at least three more candidates. For example, we might suggest that an *eleemosynary sector* is one based on donations. Donative behavior is at least as characteristic of segments of "the sector" as other forms of volunteer labor are. Eleemosynary behavior is not uniquely characteristic of the Judeo-Christian tradition, as sometimes suggested. All the world's major religious systems are built at least partially on an eleemosynary base. Distinctive eleemosynary institutions (*kanjin*) are evident in Japanese Buddhism as early as the eighth century (Goodwin, 1987; Lohmann and Bracken, 1991). Similar eleemosynary behavior has been a characteristic of the Islamic charitable tradition of *zakat*, which is one of the five pillars of Islam, and a characteristic of the distinctive Islamic foundations, or *waqfs* (Hourarii, 1991). Even so, although the term *eleemosynary* appears in a good bit of legal terminology in the United States, it is probably little more than an anachronism. However, if we conclude that donation is the central characteristic of "the sector," then it must be an eleemosynary sector. Still, the connections among donative behavior, nondistribution constraints, uncoerced participation, and independent action for the public good have yet to be clearly spelled out in theory.

In a large and growing body of psychological literature dealing with altruism, disaster responses, learning of unselfish behavior, and related topics, the concept of prosocial behavior figures centrally (see Brief and Motowidlo, 1986, for example). From this vantage point, we might speak of the *prosocial sector. Prosocial*, in this sense, seems to express at an individual level much the same intent as *philanthropic* at the institutional level.

Likewise, the growing international dimensions of nonprofit and voluntary action research may eventually bump into the anthropological term for primitive forms of association, or *sodalities*, leading perhaps to the suggestion of an international *sodality sector* (Hill, 1970, pp. 42–45; Smith and Freedman, 1972, pp. 16–17). The sodality concept seems to embrace many of the implications of distribution, participation, and shared purpose without the particular institutional lens of a single culture.

This cursory review of sector terms reveals a consistent pattern behind various attempts to label "the" sector. In each case, an adjective highlighting a single characteristic is used to modify the term *sector*, with the implication that this modifier (and the characteristic it signifies) represents the central or critical characteristic. The idea that a sector requiring such a label actually exists appears to be taken for granted. In conventional usage, a *sector* may be a category, division, genre, or section of some larger unit. In this case, the larger something of which the sector is a part may be an economy, polity, society, or culture, depending on which disciplines are sectoring.

For interdisciplinary purposes, it seems useful to propose that any meaningful sector of this type must simultaneously be construed as an economic, social, political, and cultural unit. The notion of the sector as a unit of analysis defined by a single characteristic (distribution constraints, uncoerced participation, independence, donations, or private action for public good) fits easily within settled disciplinary perspectives. Consequently, the entire issue of using an unexamined, theoretical, primitive term is noncontroversial.

In the interdisciplinary context of nonprofit and voluntary studies, however, no discipline should blithely take its own primitive terms too much for granted. In this case, a host of questions—including whether that larger unit is an economy, polity, community, society, nation, class, or some overarching, combination "social system"—are also at issue. However, we need not immediately choose up disciplinary teams and have at one another in a Hobbesian war of each against all.

The immediate question is whether any unifying themes or constructs tie together these modifiers and what they signify in some larger synthesis. Would an impartial observer conclude that contemporary nonprofit, voluntary action, and philanthropy studies are addressing one or nine or more distinct sets of phenomena? Is this one science or many? In response to several who reviewed drafts of this article, it should be said that the multiple paradigm solution should not be quickly or easily dismissed. We may well be dealing with different sets of unrelated phenomena. On the other hand, it is not necessary to blithely assume that every nuance of terminology or usage indicates a separate theoretical universe of discourse. The possibility of a single, common universe of theoretical discourse can be explored here without completely dismissing a multiple paradigm solution.

The theoretical problem presented by the sector talk of the past decade assumes the possibility of one paradigm, however vague or distant perception or understanding of it may be at the moment. There seems to be no good reason to reject that premise at present. Indeed, even the changes in names of the society, from Association for Voluntary Action Scholars to Association for Research on Nonprofit Organizations and Voluntary Action, and the journal, from *Journal of Voluntary Action Research* to *Nonprofit and Voluntary Sector Quarterly*, indicate increasing interest in a single paradigm. The recent creation of an international organization for the study of nonprofit organizations, voluntary associations, and philanthropy is perhaps the most inclusive synthesis to date.

Further Synthesis: Commons and Common Goods

Yet this synthesis remains synthesis by listing. The question of the defining characteristics of the voluntary, independent, private, nongovernment, nonprofit, not-for-profit, eleemosynary, philanthropic, charitable, third-fourth-fifth, prosocial, sodality sector remains. The effort here is to move beyond labeling and to suggest that the concept of the commons, suitably defined, together with the closely associated concept of common goods, offers central unifying concepts with multidisciplinary implications of the type needed. To begin with, "the commons" is an appropriate and parsimonious label. Yet it embraces key aspects of each of the single-label terms listed above.

The concept of a commons also offers a suitable basis for both linking and distinguishing such difficult to reconcile concepts as nonprofit organization, volunteerism, charity, philanthropy, and altruism. The commons is a genuinely interdisciplinary concept with a pedigree reaching back to ancient Greece, but it has enough currency of use to escape sounding archaic. It may also prove suitable for linking the divergent scholarly interests of sociologists, political scientists, economists, social workers, philosophers, historians, and other researchers with those of practitioners interested in the area.

Commons Defined

The concept of the commons has explicit historical Greek, English, and American connotations. It can readily be traced to Aristotle, who said that "the good in the sphere of politics is justice; and justice consists in what tends to promote the common interest" (Barker, 1968; Ford Foundation, 1989; Jordan, 1989; and Sherover, 1989). Centuries later, St. Augustine also wrote of common goods (Udoidem, 1988). A large cluster of core concepts and practices linking participation in associations, philanthropic donation, common purpose, and shared resources are traceable to the beliefs and practices of the Athenian Greeks as filtered through the classicism of the Renaissance and the Age of Reason.

The main characteristics of a plausible modern concept of commons are encompassed by Aristotle's concept of *koinonia politiké* (usually translated as "civil society"). According to M. I. Finlay (1974), a scholar of ancient history, *koinonia* involves five related dimensions: free and uncoerced participation; common (or shared) purpose, whether major or minor, long-term or short-term; common holdings (such as a fund of jointly held resources, a collection of precious objects, or a repertory of shared actions); participation involving *philia* (a sense of mutuality, often inadequately translated as "friendship"); and social relations characterized by *dikiaon* (fairness or justice). Collectively, these five dimensions summarize in a single concept (denoted as *the commons*) what appear to be the central characteristics most frequently attributed to "the sector."

The English House of Commons—where the accent is more on discussion, debate, and political theater than on the American-style production of legislative outputs—is also an important point of reference here (Ryle and Richards, 1988). So also is English common law, grown out of precedent and practice rather than deduced from transcendent principle. Finally, the village commons—by turns pasture, recreation area, green space, public forum, and assembly point for voluntary militias—is an equally important reference point.

The American connotations of the commons are mostly associated with the experience of a democratic, pluralistic civil society and federal state, which Tocqueville first observed, and with an almost unimaginable variety of groups and communities devoted to peaceful pursuit of their own ends without external authority, control, or interference. The scale of the commons in American life is extensive. Even the most cautious observers note upwards of a million nonprofit organizations in the United States today (Weisbrod, 1988). If one also incorporates "the informal sector," toward which concepts of voluntary association point, the number of organized commons would undoubtedly increase several times, even as the significance of an exact count would decline.

A major consequence of this five-part definition of the commons is to relocate the vital center as well as the boundaries between the market, the state, and the world of nonprofit, voluntary, and philanthropic concerns. The sector defined by a nondistribution constraint on resources can also be interpreted more ideally, as the common sector of participation, joint purposes and resources, mutuality, and fairness. To the extent that non-profits display coercive or surplus-maximizing behavior, they can thus be interpreted as theoretically marginal—at the boundary between state or market. The existence of coercive or maximizing behavior in the contemporary commons is not at issue. Its defining character is. No one should doubt that "free riding," for example, exists. But it should be equally clear that free riding does not define nonprofit, voluntary, or philanthropic behavior; rather, it helps to locate the boundary between self-interested, profit-oriented market behavior and "common" behavior (see Sugden, 1984).

Public Goods

If the commons is seen as a sector characterized by participation, shared purposes and resources, mutuality, and concern for fairness, what are the implications for interpreting the outcomes or results of common effort? The term *common* is sometimes used in political theory as a synonym for *public* (as in the previous reference to Aristotle). Thus, *common good, public good, public interest,* and *general will* are often used to represent closely related ideas (see recent works by Daly and Cobb, 1989; Raskin, 1986). In this context, it is possible to set forth a conception of common good that is consistent with the major conclusions of this literature and yet useful for distinguishing the "products," outcomes, or results of common action from those of the marketplace or state.

The concept of goods as a way of focusing on the positive or desirable qualities of an object and on the outputs of particular social, economic, or political processes has definite interdisciplinary possibilities. These possibilities are explored, for example, in John Rawls's discussion of "the full theory of goods" in his theory of justice (1971, pp. 433–439). The key question is what we might say about the nature of the goods expected or resulting from common action.

Perhaps the single most common resolution of the goods problem in contemporary nonprofit, voluntary action, and philanthropic studies is the suggestion that the sector is characterized by private production of public goods (Austin, 1983; Sugden, 1984; Weisbrod, 1988). But the public goods formulation is, at best, only a partial solution. The concept of public good has a precise and exact definition to which many forms of nonprofit, voluntary, and philanthropic action simply do not adhere. Public goods are, by definition, universal and indivisible. But in no meaningful sense, for example, can associations of bird watchers, antique car collectors, charismatic cultists, or volunteers counting whales be considered engaged in the private production of public goods. Yet these groups are as characteristic of the sector as are hospitals, nursing homes, and government-subsidized social service "firms."

The shared purposes and outcomes of most types of commons fail to correspond to any precise definition of public goods. Common purposes need not be universally perceived as good or indivisible in their impact. But when common purposes are perceived as universally good and indivisible in their impact, the theoretical result is virtually the convergence of the commons and the state in a kind of "general will," as proposed by Jean-Jacques Rousseau. Short of this result, one can look to neither political nor economic theory to justify the idea of the private production of public goods. Udoidem (1988) suggested a way out of that box; contrasting *the* common (or public) good with *a* common good, the former being a unitary concept characterized by universality and indivisibility, like public goods and the public interest. The latter notion of a common good is of greater immediate interest here.

Common Goods

By loading all these connotations of the noun *commons* into an adjective, we can suggest the principal characteristics of the principal outcomes of nonprofit, voluntary, and philanthropic effort. Common goods are, in other words, desirable or preferred outcomes that are uncoerced, that are associated with shared purposes and pooled resources, and that engender a sense of mutuality (we often say community) and fairness (or justice).

Each sector, in other words, is theoretically associated with a distinctive type of good. Markets produce private goods, states produce public goods, and commons produce common goods. (The distinction of these ideal types also allows us to consider the marginal cases in which, for example, markets produce common goods and commons produce private or public goods.) In contrast with both private and public goods, common goods involve purposes, goals, objectives, and outcomes shared by a particular group, interest, faction, or party, whether in agreement with or in opposition to other ("outside") interests or simply indifferent to them. Thus, common goods may have limited appeal and need not be held up as universally desirable. Within a particular reference group, they may share with public goods the qualities of indivisibility and universality. Yet, outside that reference group, any common good may be a matter of indifference or may even be considered a "bad."

Many of the best examples of common goods involve religious ritual and beliefs. Attending mass is central to the meaning of being a Roman Catholic. It is, in that sense, universal within the Catholic commons. The mass is also indivisible. One does not receive "partial credit" for attending part of a mass. Like ceremonies and rituals of all types, the mass is, for its adherents, an indivisible and universal good. Yet, to non-Catholics the mass is not a good. It may be a matter of indifference or, as in the case of several Protestant reform movements, a source of antagonism and outright opposition (a "bad" rather than a good). It is, in other words, a clear example of a common good. The same may be said for Christian baptism and communion. Jewish Passover, Islamic observance of Ramadan or the pilgrimage to Mecca, and other religious ceremonies, rituals, and observances. Indivisibility arises out of the inherent unity of the observance, but the observance as a good is understood, accepted, and valued only within a recognized community of believers whose recognition of the good and recognition of one another are intimately connected.

The distinction between multiple common goods and *the* common (or public) good is useful for reconciling external, or community, conditions of plurality with the internal, or organizational, striving for solidarity, which is one of the essential characteristics of commons. Treating the purposes and outcomes of commons as common goods, therefore, can do much to resolve the paradoxical, confusing, and inconsistent applications of the concept of public goods to the analysis of nonprofit and voluntary action.

Conclusion

The concept of the commons as an environment of uncoerced participation, shared purposes, shared resources, mutuality, and fairness—and the closely related concept of common goods as the purposes and outputs of common effort—appears to be a promising base on which to build an interdisciplinary approach to the whole field of nonprofit and voluntary action studies.

The five theoretical dimensions of the commons give meaning to the nondistribution constraint and transform it beyond an empty legal formalism into a potentially powerful normative idea. These characteristics are also many, if not most, of the characteristics frequently ascribed to voluntary action. Emphasizing the "thirdness" of the nonprofit, voluntary, and philanthropic sector has made it possible to translate a jumble of competing and overlapping institutional perspectives into the unity whose characteristics the concept of the commons describes. Likewise, such negations as "nonprofit" and "nongovernmental" locate the third sector outside market and state, still without identifying any of its salient characteristics. The independence that comes from shared purposes and resources is surely one of those characteristics, but the concept of the commons allows us to remember that others exist as well. It is a small linguistic step from construing philanthropy as "private action for the public good" to "private action for common goods," but such a move has the potential of restructuring some of the most controversial questions in the field. Eleemosynary or donative behavior is an obviously important element in a sector in which sharing and mutuality are central characteristics. The idea of prosocial behavior speaks very clearly to all manner of individual participation and sharing in pursuit of common goods.

Perhaps most important of all in view of heightened international interest in nonprofit organizations, voluntary action, and philanthropy, the sodality concept serves as a constant reminder that most studies in this field have concentrated on late twentieth century American cases. Clearly, many of the basic concepts of the field extend beyond the U.S. context. But no one is completely clear on exactly how far these concepts extend and what transformations will occur as a result Commons and common goods may describe cultural universals, near-universals, or institutions unique to an emerging world culture, or they may relate only more narrowly to the West, to Anglo-American culture or to some more limited subset of nations, societies, or cultures.

The concepts of commons and common goods also bring together many different disciplinary perspectives. Free labor, which is also committed to shared purposes and resources, mutuality, and fairness in the pursuit of common goods, should be the central concern of nonprofit economics. Voluntary action with shared resources in pursuit of mutual objectives not only produces the solidarity based on mutuality and fairness; it also yields a unique solution to the Hobbesian problem of order, which has been of central concern to sociologists. Psychologists exploring prosocial behavior and anthropologists studying mutual aid and the primitive associations of sodality can help broaden and deepen our understandings of commons and common goods. At the same time, the concepts of commons and common goods have the potential for helping us understand the legal, administrative, and organizational problems in the contemporary world of foundations, public agencies, nonprofit organizations, fundraising, volunteering, and coproduction.

Together, the concepts of commons and common goods offer the conceptual anchor for a genuine synthesis of the many different paradigms defining the present interests of those working on nonprofit and voluntary studies.

References

Austin, D. M. (1983). The Political Economy of Human Services. *Policy and Politics,* 11 (3), 343–359.

Barker, E. (1968). *The Politics of Aristotle.* London: Oxford University Press.

Bauer, R. (1990). Voluntary Welfare Associations in Germany and the United States: Theses on the Historical Development of Intermediary Systems. *Voluntas, 1* (1), 97–111.

Bernstein, R. (1983). *Beyond Objectivism and Relativism: Science, Hermeneutics, and Praxis.* Philadelphia: University of Pennsylvania Press.

Brief, A. P., and S.J. Motowidlo. (1986). Prosocial Organizational Behaviors. *Academy of Management Review,* 11 (4), 710–725.

Daly, H. E., and J. B. Cobb. *For the Common Good: Redirecting the Economy Toward Community, the Environment, and a Sustainable Future.* Boston: Beacon Press.

Douglas, J. (1987). Political Theories of Nonprofit Organizations, in W. W. Powell (ed.), *The Nonprofit Sector: A Research Handbook*. New Haven, CT: Yale University Press.

Finlay, M. I. (1974). *The Ancient Economy*. Berkeley, CA: University of California Press.

Ford Foundation. (1989). *The Common Good: Social Welfare and the American Future Policy* (Recommendations of the Executive Panel). New York: Author.

Goodwin. J. R. (1987). Alms for Kasagi Temple. *Journal of Asian Studies, 46* (4), 827–840.

Hansmann, H. (1987). Economic Theories of Nonprofit Organization. In W. W. Powell (ed.), *The Nonprofit Sector: A Research Handbook*. New Haven, CT: Yale University Press.

Hill, J. N. (1970). Prehistoric Social Organization in the American Southwest: Theory and Method. In W. A. Longacre (ed.), *Reconstructing Prehistoric Pueblo Societies*. Albuquerque: University of New Mexico Press.

Hourani, A. (1991). *A History of the Arab Peoples*, Cambridge, MA: Harvard University Press.

INDEPENDENT SECTOR, (1987). *National Taxonomy of Exempt Entities: A System for Classifying Nonbusiness, Tax-exempt Organizations in the U.S. with a Focus on IRS Section 501(c)(3) Philanthropic Organizations*. Washington, DC: Author.

Indiana University Center of Philanthropy. (1991). *Research Grants in the Study of Philanthropy*. Indianapolis: Indiana University-Purdue University.

Jordan, B. (1989). *The Common Good: Citizenship, Morality, and Self-Interest*. New York: Basil Blackwell.

Kramer, R. (1981). *Voluntary Agencies in the Welfare State*. Berkeley: University of California Press.

Lohmann, R. (1989). And Lettuce Is Nonanimal. *Nonprofit and Voluntary Sector Quarterly*, 18 (4), 367–383.

Lohmann, R. and M. Bracken. (1991). *The Buddhist Commons in Japan and Asia*. Paper presented at the annual conference of the Association for Research on Nonprofit Organizations and Voluntary Associations, Chicago, Illinois.

O'Neill, M. (1989). *The Third America: The Emergence of the Nonprofit Sector in the United States*. San Francisco: Jossey-Bass.

Raskin, M. (1986). *The Common Good: Its Politics, Policies, and Philosophy*. New York: Routledge & Kegan Paul.

Rawls, John. (1971). *The Theory of Justice*. Cambridge, MA: Harvard University Press.

Ryle, M., and P. G. Richards. (1988). *The Commons Under Scrutiny*. London: Routledge.

Salamon, L (1987). Partners in Public Service: The Scope and Theory of Government-Nonprofit Relations. In W. W. Powell (ed.), *The Nonprofit Sector: A Research Handbook*. New Haven, CT: Yale University Press.

Sherover, C. M. (1989). *Time, Freedom, and the Common Good*. New York: State University of New York Press.

Simon, J. G. (1987). The Tax Treatment of Nonprofit Organizations: A Review of Federal and State Policies. In W. W. Powell (ed.), *The Nonprofit Sector: A Research Handbook*. New Haven, CT: Yale University Press.

Smith, C., and A. Freedman. (1972). *Voluntary Associations: Perspectives on the Literature, Cambridge, MA*: Harvard University Press.

Smith, David Horton. (1974). *Voluntary Action Research: 1974*. Lexington, MA: Heath.

Smith, David Horton. (1991). Four Sectors or Five? Retaining the Membership Sector. *Nonprofit and Voluntary Sector Quarterly*, 20 (2), 137–150.

Sugden, R. (1984). Reciprocity: The Supply of Public Goods Through Voluntary Contributions. *Economic Journal, 94*, 772–787.

Udoidem, S. I. (1988). *Authority and the Common Good in Social and Political Philosophy*. Lanham, MD: University Press of America.

Van Til, Jon. (1988). *Mapping the Third Sector: Voluntarism in a Changing Social Economy*. New York: Foundation Center.

Welsbrod, Burton A. (1988). *The Nonprofit Economy*. Cambridge, MA: Harvard University Press.

MAPPING THE BOUNDARIES

JON VAN TIL

In the scholarly literature, the boundaries between the major institutional sectors are usually spoken of as being "blurred," "overlapping," or "indistinct." Perhaps the best way to get a grip on these boundary relations is to review some of the most influential maps that have been drawn suggesting how the major institutional sectors in society relate to each other. Such maps have recently been drawn showing three (Mertens, 1998), four (Van Til, 1988), five (Smith, 1991), six (Paton, 1991), and even seven sectors (Schuppert, 1991).

Two-Sector Maps

The concept of "sector" provides a useful way of visualizing society's institutions. The traditional map of society's key institutions simply distinguishes between market and state. It is clearly inadequate to the realities of our times because it ignores the vast organizational terrain of society's third sector, as well as the important core institutions of family, kin, and neighborhood.[1]

Three-Sector Maps

Three-sector models are increasingly being used by scholars whose work focuses on voluntarism and nonprofit organizations. In such conceptions, business usually takes its place as the first sector (because it is largest); government is the second sector; and the voluntary nonprofit is the third sector.[2] Much of the scholarship of the nonprofit field uses this tripartite model. Seeing the third sector as composed of a special category of organizations, those that are both non-state and non-capitalist, is the basic insight of those who construct three-sector maps of society. Increasingly, contemporary social theorists refer to the distinctive nature of each of three sectors (government, business, voluntary) when they seek to represent the structure of a modern society.

Among the most compelling of the three-sector conceptions are two that developed in the shadows of the spreading fascism, communism, and militarism of their times. The central European social theorists Karl Polanyi (1944) and Karl Mannheim (1940) sought in their work to understand the ways in which business, government, and social institutions related to each other. Both aimed to develop a theory of the proper relation between the sectors, hoping thereby to contribute to a world in which the maladies of their era could be permanently banished.

To Polanyi, the key to peaceful development involved the creation of a balanced role for the three sectors of market, state, and society. The danger he saw was that the market would come to be seen as the essential institution, and its basis in contract would give rise to a misleading and incomplete vision of human freedom. There are limits to what such "free" enterprise can provide, he argued: markets fragment human relations and render important social relations invisible. They also tend to relegate the state to a position of insignificance.

In Polanyi's view, it is only when we come to recognize that the free market alone will not solve our problems that we come face to face with how freedom can be maintained in society. A line dividing liberalism, on the one hand, from fascism and communism, on the other, begins to appear. And we also begin to see that the difference between freedom and oppression is not primarily economic, but is rather moral and religious (1957: 258; cf. also Wolch, 1990). Polanyi's work suggests a vital role for what would later be called the "third sector": to play a leading role in the struggle for justice and freedom.

To Mannheim, the key to social reconstruction was to be found in applying knowledge to the resolution of problems and in learning how to do social planning. He introduced powerful distinctions between ideology (the interest of the status quo) and utopia (the vision of what ought to be), and between functional (what appears to work, however misguided it may be) and substantive rationality (what undergirds the resolution of genuine human needs).

Mannheim observed that modern "society is faced, not with brief unrest, but with a radical change of structure; . . . this realization is the only guarantee of preventive measures. Only if we know why Western society in the crisis zone is passing through a phase of disintegration is there any hope that the countries which still enjoy comparative peace will learn to control the future trend of events by democratic planning, and so to avoid the negative aspects of the process: dictatorship, conformity, and barbarism" (1940: 6).

Planner John Friedmann extended Mannheim's vision in the development of a full-blown social theory. Friedmann developed Mannheim's concern that we learn to plan for an increasingly democratic and interdependent world. Friedmann identifies productive roles for civil society (or voluntary sector) to play in modern society (1987: 355–56). The world, he observed, is best seen as a "common" (p. 383; cf. also Lohmann, 1992) in which varying institutional interests meet and contest with each other. Third-sector organizations, Friedmann asserts, play important roles in helping individuals and groups build societies that will meet their needs to work together productively.

Four-Sector Maps

In an earlier book I authored, *Mapping the Third Sector* (1988), a four-sector model of society is presented. The household, or informal sector, is added to the conventional three of business, government, and nonprofit sectors. A dynamic aspect is added to the model by a description of sector interdependence, with the household sector serving as the keystone. Households (or individual members of households) earn money and buy products and services in the business sector, form foundations, volunteer, and become members of associations in the nonprofit sector, and support government through voting and paying taxes.

In *Mapping the Third Sector*, I contended that each of the major sectors conduct transactions with each other across the various boundaries between them, and I showed how these transactions affect the third sector. Government, for example, both "legitimizes" and regulates third-sector organizations when it awards IRS certification of "501(c)" standing. Business provides resources through donations and the support of employee volunteering, while government reduces the tax burden of individual donors who support appropriately certified organizations. Figure 2 illustrates how the four major sectors routinely interact with each other.

GOVERNMENT regulates, subsidizes, and contracts with voluntary sector organizations.	BUSINESS provides philanthropy (through federated giving. corporate giving, and the establishment of foundations) and encourages worker volunteering.
(Some) THIRD-SECTOR organizations are certified by GOVERNMENT as eligible for tax-deductible contributions of income earned in BUSINESS, provide services contracted by GOVERNMENT, employ volunteer time and effort donated from the INFORMAL SECTOR.	INFORMAL organizations (family and neighborhood) provide many services as volunteers, often coordinated by THIRD-SECTOR organizations.

Figure 2. Transactions between the Sectors

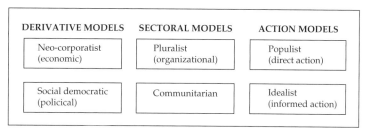

Figure 3. Van Til's Map of Models, Extended by Scott

Mapping the Third Sector sought to develop theoretical maps to aid in the understanding of the role of voluntarism in modern life. One map was metaphorical, the other conceptual.

The metaphorical map identified factors as pertaining to "climate," "topography," and deep "tectonic" structures. Climatic factors were depicted as dominant values in society: self-absorbed privatism and voluntaristic concern for others. Topographic factors were the familiar four sectors: private economic, government, voluntary, and informal. Underlying tectonic factors were linked to the key problems identified by major social theorists: the problem of solidarity of association identified by Alexis de Tocqueville and Emile Durkheim, the problem of bureaucratic control centrally addressed by Max Weber, the problem of economic hegemony that preoccupied Karl Marx, and the problem of oligarchical control posed by Robert Michels. My argument was that each level of analysis—values, institutional form, and deep social structure—had to be taken into account in understanding the role of the third sector in modern life.

Finally, *Mapping the Third Sector* distinguished between five principal theoretical approaches taken by scholars in their attempt to understand voluntary action and nonprofit organizations in modern society. These models were identified as being either "essentially" derivative, sectoral, or action oriented. Jacquelyn Thayer Scott (1992) built on this theory to make room for communitarian theory. Scott notes that third-sector organizations can play a critical role in building and supporting community at all levels of modern society (Figure 3).

More Than Four Sectors

David Horton Smith (1991) subdivides the third sector into two, distinguishing a "public benefit" from a "private benefit" third sector. But like Mannheim and Friedmann, Smith sees both variants of the third sector as manifesting society's "fundamental value-based concerns."

A more functional model has been developed by the British educator Rob Paton (1992), who focuses on two major dimensions: the formality-informality of organization and the social or economic nature of goals sought. Paton's model (Figure 4) identifies a range of economic styles of organization, and clusters them in sectors.

Finally, a seven-sector map has been presented by German legal scholar G. F. Schuppert (1991). The sectors he identifies are:

1. Market
2. State
3. Self-administered organizations
4. Self-organized groups
5. Associations
6. Organized interests
7. Private governmental organizations

What Schuppert essentially does in his representation is divide the third sector into five constituent parts, continuing the sub-structuring of this diverse societal arena that Smith began by dividing into two.

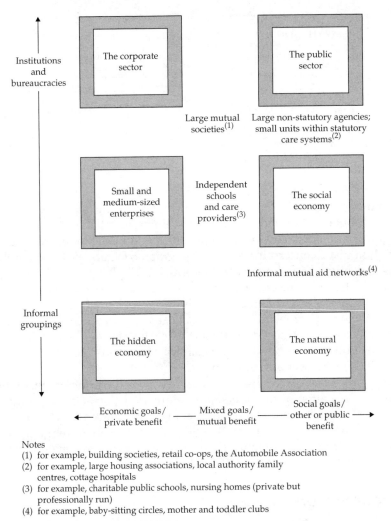

Notes
(1) for example, building societies, retail co-ops, the Automobile Association
(2) for example, large housing associations, local authority family
    centres, cottage hospitals
(3) for example, charitable public schools, nursing homes (private but
    professionally run)
(4) for example, baby-sitting circles, mother and toddler clubs

Figure 4. Paton's Map of the Organizational World

Of the drawing of social maps there will surely be no end. But a number of recent representations have introduced a more dynamic set of conceptions of size, scale, and boundary. They seek to depict the sectors in vital interaction with each other.

Interacting Sectors

Interactive sectoral models have been developed by several prominent European scholars of the third sector. Building on the observations of earlier writers that sectoral boundaries are themselves blurred, David Billis, Victor Pestoff, and Rudolph Bauer have presented models that combine multiple dimensions into fruitful representations.[3] Pestoff's triangle (1991), later elaborated by Evers and Svetlik, offers a compelling representation which places the third sector at the core of interactions anchored by market state, and family (Figure 5).

British organizational scholar Billis (1993) focuses on the blurring of the sectors (Figure 6).

In several far-reaching recent presentations, German social policy specialist Rudolph Bauer (1993, 1998) extends Billis's point that the nonprofit sector takes on major characteristics of the other sectors. Bauer suggests that volunteers tend to treat nonprofit organizations as though they were providers of charitable service, while board members tend to see them as though they were political organizations. Meanwhile, staff behaves as though the same organization is a business. In this

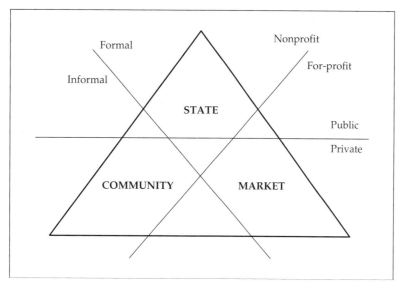

Figure 5. Pestoff's Triangle

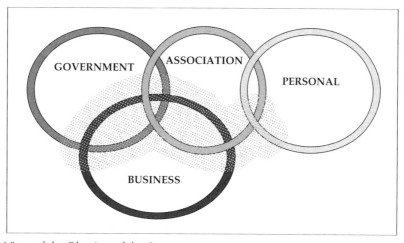

Figure 6. Billis's View of the Blurring of the Sectors

way, Bauer observes, a third-sector organization tends to take on the coloration of business (first sector), politics (second sector), and community (fourth sector). Figure 7 shows this representation.

Bauer (1998) sees the third sector as an intermediate realm between the market, state, and informal networks—a realm composed of a variety of different organizational types. Closest in structure and interest to market organizations are cooperatives and "communal economic corporations." Closest in interest to the state are "public benefit organizations," "federations," and "associations." Closest to informal networks are "societies," "self-help groups," and "small co-operatives."

Bauer's theory of the third sector goes a long way to advance understanding of why organizations in this category so often resemble governmental agencies, business corporations, or informal groups. Third-sector organizations take on the coloration of the other sectors, he indicates, and themselves contain organizational themes that closely resemble those of the other sectors.

If the third-sector is seen as an intermediary social construction, it follows that it can play a crucial bridging role in society. The linking potential of the third sector is one that is increasingly recognized in modern life, and the exploration of its expansion forms a central theme of this book.

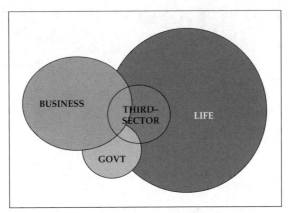

Figure 7. Rudolph Bauer's View of the Third Sector as a Coat of Many Colors

An Alternative View: Action Rather Than Sector

An alternative approach tends not to begin with the identification of sectors, but rather with a distinction between public and private action (cf. Dewey, 1927). This dichotomous approach introduces tension between the two forms of action, implicitly introducing a relationship of power or exchange into the discussion. Gamwell (1984), for instance, uses a two-sector modle, distinguishing between governmental and non-governmental organizations and then dividing the latter into "private-regarding and public-regarding" agencies. "Public-regarding" agencies are further split on the basis of exclusivity into "less inclusive" and "more inclusive" groupings, which latter are then divided into "nonpolitical regarding" and "political regarding." Sumariwalla (1983) visualizes two principal sectoral divisions also, and classifies nonprofit organizations as private-sector "non-business" entities, operating either in the public interest or as part of an "all other" sub-category.

An important contribution of these simple two sector models is that they focus less on boundaries (what fits inside) and more on relations across boundaries. As was discovered by Lord Beveridge (1948) in his pioneering study of voluntary action in Britain, the state and voluntary associations are partners in cooperation for social advance. As Ostrander, Langton, and Van Til (1987) would later demonstrate, the government, voluntary association, and business are more often interdependent with each other than independent of each other.

In much the same way, Kramer (1984) focuses his three-sector model on relationships for the delivery of personal and social services. He adds the element of power relationships, laying the foundation for a fuller understanding of nonprofits. In looking at the interrelationships among profit-making, governmental, and voluntary organizations, he examines the activities involved and identifies the five possible relationships among sectors as reprivatization, empowerment, pragmatic partnership, governmental operation, and nationalization.

Even our manner of naming the sectors (first, second, third) implies a power order. To gain perspective on this implied order it is helpful to look at the work of Peter Dobkin Hall (1992). Hall's historical analyses invite an interesting exercise about naming the order of the sectors. The nonprofit sector is, as we have seen, most often identified as the third sector. However, at any point in history, if we were to stop and try to put order to the sectors as we viewed them from the perspective of that time and place, we might call our first, second, and third sectors differently (cf. also Young, 1988). For example, why not call the family the first sector? It was here first. Would voluntary organizations, or government, be the second in order of time? The labels become very dependent on where one stands to do the labeling.

Part of the problem with understanding the sector issue comes from jumping into the parade in the middle of it. Salamon and Anheier (1992: 126) have noted that discussion of sectors is a relatively recent academic discovery. "[T]he emergence of the large-scale profit-making form and of public administration represented the major institutional innovations of the eighteenth and nineteenth centuries, and the results have been institutional complexes of enormous social and economic power." The nonprofit sector, as Hall (1992) indicates, is an even more recent invention, emerging only over the last twenty years in academic discourse.

Smith (1997) and Kramer (1998) take the critique of sector further in recent work. Like Hall, they view the concept of sector with suspicion, noting the vast diversity of purposes and structures contained within the third sector, and the lack of solidarity among its many varied participants. These themes will figure strongly in the argument of the present volume as well.

Beyond Prince and Merchant

A recent reader on third-sector organizations sports the intriguing title, *Beyond Prince and Merchant*. The realms of prince and merchant have traditionally been explored from separate disciplinary perspectives, with their interactions primarily concerning historians and social theorists. With the rise of a distinctive scholarship of voluntarism and nonprofit organization, the space between the two has begun to be filled.

Voluntary action has been described as "private action for the public good" (Payton, 1984) and "private organization serving a public purpose" (O'Neill, 1989). Voluntary action fulfills a variety of societal roles: 1) supporting society's ability to act for the common good (the communitarian model, a social role); 2) partnering with government to provide collective goods and services (the shadow state model, an economic role); 3) speaking for the minorities and serving as an advocate for pluralism and diversity (the loyal opposition model, a political role).

These perspectives each give rise to their own approaches to understanding what has been called the "third-sector elephant" (recalling the old story of the manifold observations of blindfolded experts trying to identify an elephant by touch). The economic approach argues that providing public goods which cannot be provided profitably in the market is a major task for voluntary action.[4] The political approach argues that voluntary organizations should advocate minority opinions, argue for change, and serve as a watchdog for government.[5] The communitarian approach argues that voluntary action provides a vehicle for individuals to join in common action for the common good. Additionally, legal[6] and organizational[7] perspectives have been developed and elaborated for third-sector definitions and organizations.

Two Influential Definitions

Two of the most influential and thoughtful definitions of the third sector have been offered by Lester M. Salamon and Helmut K. Anheier (1992) and Roger Lohmann (1992: 58–60), respectively. The definition provided by Salamon and Anheier is formal and operational, providing a way to distinguish nonprofit from other organizations in society. The defining structural/functional characteristics of third-sector organizations, Salamon and Anheier assert, are that they are formal, private, non-profit-distributing, self-governing, and voluntary (1992: 6). Lohmann, on the other hand, focuses in his definition on the processes and purposes common to third-sector organizations (Figure 8).

LOHMANN	SALAMON
PARTICIPATION IS UNCOERCED	VOLUNTARY
PURPOSE IS TO ADVANCE COMMON GOOD	PRIVATE (NON-GOVERNMENTAL)
RESOURCES ARE COMMON	NONPROFIT DISTRIBUTING
PARTICIPATION INVOLVES MUTUALITY	SELF-GOVERNING
SOCIAL RELATIONS ARE FAIR	FORMAL

Figure 8. Comparing the Lohmann and Salamon Definitions

In another effort, Salamon (1992) moves closer to Lohmann's definition; there he adds the point that the purpose of a nonprofit organization must address the building of a public good. As such, he recognizes the greatest strength of Lohmann's definition: its ability to capture the sense that a great aim of many third-sector organizations is the building of something distinctive from the collective action of many, gathered in a variety of places that allow for creation and construction.

Notes

1. Two-sector maps see the third sector simply as a residual organizational category, lacking both the clarity and the power of the two primary sectors of state and market. Belgian economist Sybille Mertens (1998) describes such renditions as belonging to the "old scheme of things," and maps the third sector as simply serving as background to the first two sectors.
2. This ordering has been presented by Bruce Hopkins in his influential book *Law of Tax-Exempt Organizations* (1997).
3. For a number of other visual representations of the sectors, see Kramer (1998), Appendix.
4. Economic definitions of the third sector are based on the concept of exchange (cf. Dewey, 1927). Among the most influential economic approaches are those of Mancur Olson (1971), Kenneth Boulding (1973), Henry Hansmann (1987a), and Burton Weisbrod (1988). Olson defines the problem of the "free rider" as endemic to voluntary organization; Boulding posits the existence of a "grants economy"; Hansmann posits market failure as a basic force behind voluntary organization development; and Weisbrod brings these elements together in an integrated theory. A weakness of the economic perspective, which lends itself well to the charting of national accounts of productivity, involves the underestimation of voluntary action. Much of what third-sector organizations do is not easily or appropriately valued in dollars (cf. Hodgkinson et al., 1992).
5. Nonprofits caught Tocqueville's eye as he looked at America because he was looking at democracy. In a sense, the third sector exists in relation to the concept of democracy in a society (cf. Bellah et al., 1985). More recently, Jennifer Wolch (1990) argues that one of the most significant roles of nonprofits involves advocacy, social innovation, and to "watch government." If nonprofits are perceived as intermediaries in society, then it is in their capacity as mediators that nonprofits act as advocates for the values, issues, and rights that are part of the interests of the sector. More importantly, they are a voice for the common good. They come to serve as a non-governmental way of expressing the power of the people. Etzioni (1993; cf. also Etzioni 1976) proposes that the political role of voluntary organizations be extended to provide a forum where the community vision can develop. He sees voluntary associations functioning as agents to build a sense of "common good," rather than as representatives of special interests in the political debate.
6. In *The Law of Tax-Exempt Organizations* (1997), Bruce Hopkins proposes a methodology for "defining" charitable organizations, which resembles the child's game: "I will tell you what it is not, you guess what it is." According to Hopkins, the best way to understand is to contrast. Not surprisingly, a negative definition of nonprofits surfaces. One positive factor for inclusion in the sector is, however, provided. According to Hopkins, the "private inurement" doctrine is currently the substantial dividing line adhered to in many recent tax court decisions. Clearly a "nonprofit" is fundamentally not meant to enrich anyone.
7. David Billis (1993) writes that organization theory has been insufficiently applied to understanding the managerial and organizational issues in the third sector. He formulates a third-sector definition from the organizational perspective. On the organizational culture of these public and private worlds, Billis reminds us that these organizations develop clearly understood rules of the game, bureaucratic structures, managerial command systems, membership and voting structures, and are based on ideas of commitment, love, and affection. In examining organizations this way, Billis raises the question of how third-sector organizations represent or advocate the interests of their stakeholders and members.

References

Abdelrahman, Maha M. 1998. "Civil Society . . . Second Best Option." Paper presented to the Third International Conference of the International Society for Third Sector Research, Geneva, July.

Alexander, George A. 1998. *Swarthmore by the Numbers.* Swarthmore, Pa.: Mind-Meetings Press.

Alexander, Lamar, et al. 1997. *Giving Better, Giving Smarter: The Report of the National Commission on Philanthropy and Civic Renewal.*

American Assembly. 1998. *Trust, Service, and the Common Purpose: Philanthropy and the Nonprofit Sector in a Changing America*. Indianapolis: Indiana University Center on Philanthropy.

Anderson, Elijah. 1999. *Code of the Street*. New York: W. W. Norton.

Anthony, Robert, and David Young. 1988. "The Role of the Nonprofit Sector." In David Gies, J. Steven Ott, and Jay M. Shafritz, eds., *Nonprofit Organization: Essential Readings*. Pacific Grove, Calif.: Brooks/Cole.

Barber, Benjamin R. 1984. *Strong Democracy: Participatory Politics for a New Age*. Berkeley: University of California Press.

———. 1995. *Jihad vs. McWorld*. New York: Random House.

———. 1998. *A Place for Us: How to Make Society Civil and Democracy Strong*. New York: Hill and Wang.

Barber, Benjamin R., and Richard M. Battistoni. 1993. *Education for Democracy: Citizenship, Community, Service*. Dubuque, Iowa: Kendall-Hunt.

Bates, Stephen. 1996. *National Service: Getting Things Done?* Chicago: Cantigny Conference Report, Robert McCormick Tribune Foundation.

Bauer, Rudolph. 1993. Plenary presentation at CIES Conference, Barcelona, June.

———. 1998. "Intermediarity: A Theoretical Paradigm for Third Sector Research." Paper presented to the Third International Conference of the International Society for Third Sector Research, Geneva, July.

Bellah, Robert N., Richard Madsen, Steven M. Tipton, William M. Sullivan, and Ann Swindler. 1985. *Habits of the Heart: Individualism and Commitment in American Life*. New York: Harper and Row.

Bennett, James T., and Thomas J. DiLorenzo. 1989. *Unfair Competition: The Profits of Nonprofits*. Lanham, Md.: Hamilton Press.

Bennett, William J., and Senator Sam Nunn. 1998. *A Nation of Spectators: How Civic Disengagement Weakens America and What We Can Do about It*. College Park, Md.: National Commission on Civic Renewal.

Berger, Peter L., and Richard J. Neuhaus. 1977. *To Empower People: The Role of Mediating Structures in Public Policy*. Washington, D.C.: American Enterprise Institute for Public Policy Research.

Beveridge, Lord. 1948. *Voluntary Action: A Report on Methods of Social Advance*. London: Allen and Unwin.

Billis, David. 1992. "Sector Blurring and Nonprofit Centres: The Case of the UK." A Paper prepared for Presentation to the Annual Meeting of ARNOVA. Yale University; New Haven.

———. 1993. *Organising Public and Voluntary Agencies*. London: Routledge.

Boris, Elizabeth T. 1998. "Myths about the Nonprofit Sector." *Charting Civil Society*, no. 4 (July). Washington, D.C.: The Urban Institute Center on Non-profits and Philanthropy.

Boris, Elizabeth, and Rachel Mosher-Williams. 1998. "Nonprofit Advocacy Organizations: Assessing the Definitions, Classifications, and Data." *Nonprofit and Voluntary Sector Quarterly* 27, no. 4 (December), 488–506.

Boschee, Jerr. N.d. "What Does It Take to be a 'Social Entrepreneur?'" Minneapolis: National Center for Social Entrepreneurs.

Boulding, Kenneth. 1973. *The Economy of Love and Fear*. Belmont, Calif.: Wads-worth.

Bradley, Bill. 1996. *Time Present, Time Past: A Memoir*. New York: A. A. Knopf.

Bramson, Leon. 1961. *The Political Context of Sociology*. Princeton: Princeton University Press.

Brudney, Jeffrey L. 1999. "The Perils of Practice: Reaching the Summit." *Nonprofit Management and Leadership* 9, no. 4 (Summer), 385–98.

Buckley, William F. 1990. *Gratitude: Reflections on What We Owe to Our Country*. New York: Randon House.

Burbidge, John, ed. 1998. *Beyond Prince and Merchant: Citizen Participation and the Rise of Civil Society*. New York: PACT Publications.

Cahn, Edgar, and Jonathan Rowe. 1992. *Time Dollars: The New Currency That Enables Americans to Turn Their Hidden Resource—Time—into Personal Security and Community Renewal*. Emmaus, Pa.: Rodale Press.

Canino, Maria Josefa, and Eugenia R. Echols. 1996. "Latinos and Community Based Nonprofit Organizations: A New Jersey Needs Assessment." Paper presented to the *Nonprofit Management Education 1996 Conference*, Berkeley, Calif. (University of San Francisco).

Carothers, Edward. 1970. *The Churches and Cruelty Systems*. New York: Friendship Press.

Carter, Stephen L. 1998. *Civility: Manners, Morals, and the Etiquette of Democracy*. New York: Basic Books.

Cnaan, Ram A., with Robert J. Wineburg and Stephanie C. Boddie. 1999. *The Newer Deal*. New York: Columbia University Press.

Coleman, James S. 1994. *Foundations of Social Theory*. Cambridge: Harvard University Press.

Connolly, William E. 1995. *The Ethos of Pluralization*. Minneapolis: University of Minnesota Press.

Corporation for National Service. 1997. *Strategic Plan*. Washington, D.C.

Council on Civil Society. 1998. *A Call to Civil Society: Why Democracy Needs Moral Truths*. New York: Institute for American Values.

Countryman, Matthew, and Lisa Sullivan. 1993. "National Service: 'Don't Do For, Do With.'" *Social Policy* (Fall), 29–34.

Covington, Sally. 1997. *Moving a Public Policy Agenda: The Strategic Philanthropy of Conservative Foundations*. Washington, D.C.: National Committee for Responsive Philanthropy.

Cunningham, Jill K. 1993. "Adrift in Utopia: Summer of Service Takes on Baltimore." *Philanthropy, Culture and Society* (November), 1ff.

Dahrendorf, Ralf. 1997. *After 1989: Morals, Revolution and Civil Society*. New York: St. Martin's Press.

Davidson, Greg, and Paul Davidson. 1988. *Economics for a Civilized Society*. Basingstoke: Macmillan.

DeMott, Benjamin. 1995. *The Trouble with Friendship: Why Americans Can't Think Straight about Race*. New York: Atlantic Monthly Press.

De Oliviera, Miguel Darcy, and Rajesh Tandon. 1994. *Citizens: Strengthening Global Civil Society*. Washington, D.C.: CIVICUS.

Dewey, John. 1927. *The Public and Its Problems*. New York: Swallow.

Dilulio, John J., Jr. 1998. "Beyond Ideology: Have Faith in Inner-City Youth." *Penn Arts and Sciences*, University of Pennsylvania (Fall), 7.

DiMaggio, Paul J., and Walter W. Powell. 1983. "The Iron Cage Revisited: Institutional Isomorphism and Collective Rationality in Organizational Fields." *American Sociological Review* 48, 147–60.

Duhl, Leonard. 1990. *The Social Entrepreneurship of Change*. New York: Pace University Press.

Dundjerski, Marina, and Susan Gray. 1998. "A Lesson in Mandatory Service." *Chronicle of Philanthropy* (September 10).

Eberly, Don E. 1998. *America's Promise: Civil Society and the Renewal of American Culture*. Lanham, Md.: Rowman and Littlefield.

Eberly, Don E., ed. 1994. *Building a Community of Citizens: Civil Society in the 21st Century*. Lanham, Md.: University Press of America.

Eberly, Donald J. 1988. *National Service: A Promise to Keep*. Rochester, N.Y.: John Alden Books.

——. 1991. *National Youth Service: A Democratic Institution for the 21st Century*. Washington, D.C.: National Service Secretariat.

Eberly, Donald J., ed. 1992. *National Youth Service: A Global Perspective*. Washington, D.C.: National Service Secretariat.

Ethiel, Nancy, ed. 1993. *Building a Consensus on National Service*. Wheaton, Ill.: Robert R. McCormick Tribune Foundations.

——. 1997. *National Service: Getting It Right*. Wheaton, Ill.: Robert R. McCormick Tribune Foundations.

Etzioni, Amitai. 1968. *The Active Society*. New York: Free Press.

——. 1976. *Social Problems*. New York: Free Press.

——. 1991. *A Responsive Society: Collected Essays on Guiding Deliberate Social Change*. San Francisco: Jossey-Bass.

——. 1993. *The Spirit of Community: Rights, Responsibilities and the Communitarian Agenda*. New York: Crown.

Evans, Sara M., and Harry C. Boyte. 1992. *Free Spaces: The Sources of Democratic Change in America*. Chicago: University of Chicago Press.

Evers, Adalbert. 1995. "Part of the Welfare Mix: The Third Sector as an Intermediate Area between Market Economy, State and Community." *Voluntas* 6, no. 2, 159–82.

Ferris, James M. 1998. "The Role of the Nonprofit Sector in a Self-Governing Society: A View from the United States." *Voluntas* 9 (June), 137–52.

Freud, Sigmund. 1930. *Civilization and Its Discontents*. New York: J. Cape and H. Smith.

Friedmann, John. 1987. *Planning in the Public Domain: From Knowledge to Action*. Princeton: Princeton University Press.

Fromm, Erich. 1955. *The Sane Society*. New York: Holt, Rinehart, and Winston.

Fukuyama, Francis. 1995. *Trust: The Social Virtues and the Creation of prosperity*. New York: The Free Press.

Galston, William. 1998. "Political Economy and the Politics of Virtue: U.S. Public Philosophy at Century's End." *The Good Society: A PEGS Journal* 8, no. 1 (Winter), 1ff.

Gamwell, Franklin I. 1984. *Beyond Preference: Liberal Theories of Independent Association*. Chicago: University of Chicago Press.

Gardner, Deborah S. 1997. *A Family Foundation: Looking to the Future, Honoring the Past*. New York: The Nathan Cummings Foundation.

Gartner, Audrey, and Frank Riessman. 1993. "Making Sure Helping Helps." *Social Policy* (Fall), 35–36.

Garton Ash, Timothy. 1990. *The Magic Lantern: The Revolution of '89 Witnessed in Warsaw, Budapest, Berlin, and Prague*. New York: Random House.

Gaul, Gilbert M., and Neill A. Borowski. 1993. *Free Ride: The Tax-Exempt Economy*. Kansas City: Andrews and McMeel.

George H. Gallup International Institute. 1993a. *America's Youth in the 1990s*. Princeton, N.J.: Gallup Institute.

——. 1993b. *Perspectives on National Service*. 2 vols. Princeton, N.J.: Gallup Institute.

Gilder, George. 1981. *Wealth and Poverty*. New York: Basic Books.

Glaser, John S. 1994. *The United Way Scandal: An Insider's Account of What Went Wrong and Why*. New York: Wiley.

Gross, Bertram. 1980. *Friendly Fascism: The New Face of Power in America*. Boston; South End Press.

Hall, Peter Dobkin. 1992. *Inventing the Nonprofit Sector and Other Essays on Philanthropy, Voluntarism and Nonprofit Organizations*. Baltimore: Johns Hopkins University Press.

Hammack, David C., and Dennis R. Young, eds. 1993. *Nonprofit Organizations in a Market Economy: Understanding New Roles, Issues, and Trends*. San Francisco: Jossey-Bass.

Hansmann, Henry. 1987a. "Economic Theories of Nonprofit Organization." In W. W. Powell, ed., *The Nonprofit Sector; A Research Handbook*. New Haven: Yale University Press.

——. 1987b. "The Evolution of the Law of Nonprofit Organizations." Paper presented to Spring Research Forum of Independent Sector, March.

——. 1996. *The Ownership of Enterprise*. Cambridge, Mass.: Harvard University Press.

Harbeson, John, Raymond Hopkins, and David G. Smith, eds. 1994. *Responsible Governance: The Global Challenge. Essays in Honor of Charles E. Gilbert*. Lanham, Md.: University Press of America.

Harris, Zellig S. 1997. *The Transformation of Capitalist Society*. Lanham, Md.: Rowman and Littlefield.

Havel, Vaclav. 1990. *Disturbing the Peace: A Conversation with Karel Hvizdala*. Translated from the Czech and with an introduction by Paul Wilson. New York: Knopf.

Haynes, Charles C., ed. 1996. *Finding Common Ground: A First Amendment Guide to Religion and Public Education*. Nashville: Vanderbilt University.

Hirschman, Albert. 1970. *Exit, Voice, and Loyalty*. Cambridge, Mass.: Harvard University Press.

Hirst, Paul. 1994. *Associative Democracy: New Forms of Economic and Social Governance*, Amherst: University of Massachusetts Press.

Hodgkinson, Virginia Ann, Richard W. Lyman, et al., eds. 1989. *The Future of the Nonprofit Sector: Challenges, Changes, and Policy Considerations*. San Francisco: Jossey-Bass.

Hodgkinson, Virginia A., Murray S. Weitzman, Christopher M. Toppe, and Stephen M. Noga. 1992. *The Nonprofit Almanac, 1992–1993: Dimensions of the Independent Sector*. San Francisco: Jossey-Bass.

Hoefer, Richard. N. d. "Nonprofit Group Influence on Social Welfare Program Regulation." Washington, D.C.: Aspen Institute Nonprofit Sector Research Fund.

Hopkins, Bruce R. 1997. *The Law of Tax-Exempt Organizations*. 7th ed. New York: Wiley.

Horwitz, Claudia. 1993. "What Is Wrong with National Service." *Social Policy* (Fall), 37–44.

Hyden, Goran. 1997. "Building Civil Society at the Turn of the Millennium." In John Burbidge, ed., *Beyond Prince and Merchant: Citizen Participation and the Rise of Civil Society*, 17–46. New York: PACT Publications.

James, William. 1968. "The Moral Equivalent of War" (1910). In *The Writings of William James*, ed. John J. McDermott. New York: Modern Library.

Jeavons, Thomas H. 1994. *When the Bottom Line Is Faithfulness: Management of Christian Service Organizations*. Bloomington: Indiana University Press.

——. 1998. "Is Friends' Faith Reflected in Their Economic Lives?" Philadelphia: PYM News, January–February, 2.

Kallick, David. 1993. "National Service: How to Make It Work." *Social Policy* (Fall), 2–7.

Kendall, Jane C., et al. 1990. *Combining Service and Learning: A Resource Book for Community and Public Service*. 2 vols. Raleigh, N.C.: National Society for Internships and Experiential Education.

Kramer, Ralph M. 1981. *Voluntary Agencies in the Welfare State*. Berkeley: University of California Press.

——. 1998. "Nonprofit Organizations in the 21st Century: Will Sector Matter?" Working Paper Series of the Nonprofit Sector Research Fund. Washington, D.C.: The Aspen Institute.

Kuhnle, Stein, and Per Selle, eds. 1992. *Government and Voluntary Organizations*. Aldershot: Avebury.

Kuttner, Robert. 1997. *Everything for Sale: The Virtues and Limits of Markets*. New York: Knopf.

Leland, Pamela. 1996. "Emerging Challenges to Tax-Exempt Status: Responding to a Challenge at the State or Local Level." Chapter 34-A in Tracy Connors, ed., *The Nonprofit Management Handbook*. New York: Wiley.

Levitt, Theodore. 1973. *The Third Sector: New Tactics for a Responsive Society*. New York: Amacom.

Lippitt, Ronald, and Jon Van Til. 1980. "Can We Achieve a Collaborative Community? Issues, Imperatives, Potentials." *Journal of Voluntary Action Research* 10, nos. 3–4, 7–17.

Lohmann, Roger. 1992. *The Commons: New Perspectives on Nonprofit Organizations and Voluntary Action*. San Francisco: Jossey-Bass.

Long, Robert F., and Joel J. Orosz. 1997. "Preparing Future Social Enterprise Leaders." Second Underwood Lecture at the University of Houston, April 23.

Lowi, Theodore. 1979. *The End of Liberalism: The Second Republic of the United States*. New York: Norton.

MacIntyre, Gertrude Anne. 1995. *Active Partners: Education and Local Development*. Sydney, Nova Scotia: University of Cape Breton Press.

MacIntyre, Gertrude Anne, ed. 1998. *Perspectives on Communities: A Community Economic Development Roundtable*. Sydney, Nova Scotia: University of Cape Breton Press.

McLaughlin, Thomas A. 1999. "Social Enterprise: Everyone Can and Should Learn from It." *The NonProfit Times* (February), 18.

Madison, G. B. 1998. *The Political Economy of Civil Society and Human Rights*. London: Routledge.

Magat, Richard. 1988. *Prospective Views of Research on Philanthropy and the Voluntary Sector*. New York: The Foundation Center.

Mannheim, Karl. 1949a. *Ideology and Utopia*. New York: Harcourt, Brace. (Originally published in 1929.)

——. 1949b. *Man and Society in an Age of Transformation*. New York: Harcourt, Brace. (Originally published in 1940.)

Margalit, Avishai. 1996. *The Decent Society*. Cambridge, Mass.: Harvard University Press.

Mertens, Sybille. 1998. "Nonprofit Organizations and Social Economy: Variations on a Same Theme." Paper presented to the Third International Conference of the International Society for Third Sector Research, Geneva, July.

Milofsky, Carl, and Stephen Blades. 1991. "Issues of Accountability in Health Charities: A Case Study of Accountability Problems among Nonprofit Organizations." *Nonprofit and Voluntary Sector Quarterly* 20, 371–93.

Monsma, Stephen V. 1996. *When Sacred and Secular Mix: Religious Nonprofit Organizations and Public Money*. Lanham, Md.: Rowman and Littlefield.

Morris, David. 1999. "Rooted Business." *Co-Op America Quarterly* (Summer), 11.

Moskos, Charles C. 1988. *A Call to Civic Service: National Service for Country and Community*. New York: Free Press.

National Commission on Civic Renewal. 1998. *A Nation of Spectators: How Civic Disengagement Weakens America and What We Can Do about It*. College Park, Md.: University of Maryland.

National Commission on Philanthropy and Civic Renewal. 1997. *Living Better, Giving Smarter*.

Nonprofit Sector Research Fund. 1997. *Competing Visions: The Nonprofit Sector in the Twenty-first Century*. Washington, D.C.: The Aspen Institute.

Odendahl, Teresa Jean. 1990. *Charity Begins at Home: Generosity and Self-Interest among the Philanthropic Elite*. New York: Basic Books.

Odendahl, Teresa Jean, ed. 1987. *America's Wealthy and the Future of Foundations*. New York: The Foundation Center.

Olson, Mancur. 1971. *The Logic of Collective Action*. Cambridge: Harvard University Press.

O'Neill, Michael. 1989. *The Third America: The Emergence of the Nonprofit Sector in the United States*. San Francisco: Jossey-Bass.

O'Neill, Michael, and Dennis R. Young. 1988. *Educating Managers of Nonprofit Organizations*. New York: Praeger.

Osborne, David, and Ted Gaebler. 1993. *Reinventing Government: How the Entrepreneurial Spirit is Transforming the Public Sector*. New York: Penguin.

Ostrander, Susan, Stuart Langton, and Jon Van Til, eds. 1987. *Shifting the Debate: Public/Private Sector Relations in the Modern Welfare State.* New Brunswick, N.J.: Transaction Press.

Parsons, Talcott. 1966. "On the Concept of Political Power." In R. Bendix and S. M. Lipset, eds., *Class, Status and Power*, 2nd ed., 1240–65. New York: Free Press.

Partnering Initiative on Education and Civil Society. 1998. "Declaration: Weaving a Seamless Web between School and Community." Washington, D.C.

Paton, Rob. 1991. "The Social Economy: Value-Based Organizations in the Wider Society." In Julian Batsleer et al., eds., *Issues in Voluntary and Non-Profit Management*, Chapter 1. Wokingham (U.K.): Addison-Wesley.

Payton, Robert. 1984. "Major Challenges to Philanthropy." In the proceedings of the 1984 Independent Sector Meeting and Spring Forum, ed. Virginia Hodgkinson. New York: Independent Sector.

——. 1988. *Philanthropy: Voluntary Action for the Public Good.* New York: American Council on Education, Macmillan Press.

Pestoff, Victor. 1991. "Cooperatization of Social Services—An Alternative to Privatization?" Paper presented at 10th EGOS Colloquium on "Societal Change between Market and Organization," Vienna. Summarized in Ivan Svetlik, "The Voluntary Sector in a Post-Communist Country: The Case of Slovenia," in Kuhnle and Selle, 1992, p. 200, and Kramer, 1998.

Polanyi, Karl. 1957. *The Great Transformation.* Boston: Beacon Press. (Originally published in 1944.)

Poppendieck, Janet. 1998. *Sweet Charity? Emergency Food and the End of Entitlement.* New York: Viking.

Putnam, Robert D. 1993. "The Prosperous Community: Social Capital and Public Life." *The American Prospect*, no. 13 (Spring), 35–42.

——. 1996. "The Strange Disappearance of Civic America." *The American Prospect* (Winter), 34–48.

——. 2000. *Bowling Alone: Civic Disengagement in America.* New York: Simon and Schuster.

Putnam, Robert D., with Robert Leonardi and Raffaella Y. Nanetti. 1993. *Making Democracy Work: Civic Traditions in Modern Italy.* Princeton: Princeton University Press.

Riesman, David, and Nathan Glazer. 1950. "Criteria for Political Apathy." In Alvin Gouldner, ed., *Studies in Leadership: Leadership and Democratic Action*, 505–59. New York: Harper and Brothers.

Rifkin, Jeremy. 1995. *The End of Work: The Decline of the Global Labor Force and the Dawn of the Post-Market Era.* New York: Tarcher/Putnam.

Robelen, Erik W. 1998. "Reengaging Young People." *Infobrief: An Information Brief.* Washington, D.C.: Association for Supervision and Curriculum Development, 13 (June).

Salamon, Lester M. 1992. *America's Nonprofit Sector: A Primer.* New York: The Foundation Center.

——. 1993. "The Nonprofit Sector and Democracy: Prerequisite, Impediment, or Irrelevance?" Paper presented to the Aspen Institute Nonprofit Sector Research Fund Symposium, Wye, Md.

——. 1994. "The Rise of the Nonprofit Sector." *Foreign Affairs* 74, no. 3 (July/August).

——. 1995. *Partners in Public Service: Government-Nonprofit Relations in the Modern Welfare State.* Baltimore: Johns Hopkins University Press.

——. 1997. *Holding the Center: America's Nonprofit Sector at a Crossroads.* New York: The Nathan Cummings Foundation.

——. 1999. *America's Nonprofit Sector: A Primer.* 2nd ed. New York: The Foundation Center.

Salamon, Lester M., and Helmut K. Anheier. 1992. "In Search of the Nonprofit Sector; I: The Question of Definition." *Voluntas, The International Journal of Voluntary and Non-Profit Organizations* (March).

——. 1994. *The Emerging Sector: An Overview.* Baltimore: Johns Hopkins University Press.

——. 1997. *Defining the Nonprofit Sector: A Cross-National Analysis.* Manchester: Manchester University Press.

Salamon, Lester M., Helmut K. Anheier, et al. 1998. "The Emerging Sector Revisited: A Summary." Baltimore: Johns Hopkins University Press.

Schattschneider, E. E. 1960. *The Semisovereign People: A Realist's View of Democracy in America.* New York: Holt, Rinehart, and Winston.

Schene, Patricia. 1992. "Accountability in Nonprofit Organizations: A Framework for Addressing the Public Interest." Thesis submitted to the Graduate School of Public Affairs, University of Colorado, Denver.

Schiff, Jerald. 1990. *Charitable Giving and Government Policy: An Economic Analysis.* Westport, Conn.: Greenwood Press.

Schudson, Michael. 1998. *The Good Citizen: A History of American Civic Life.* New York: The Free Press.

Schumpeter, Joseph Alois. 1947. *Capitalism, Socialism, and Democracy.* 2nd ed. New York and London: Harper and Brothers.

Schuppert, G. F. 1991. "State, Market, Third Sector: Problems of Organizational Choice in the Delivery of Public Services." *Nonprofit and Voluntary Sector Quarterly* 20, 123–36.

Scott, Jacquelyn Thayer. 1992. "Voluntary Sector in Crisis: Canada's Changing Public Philosophy of the State and Its Impact on Voluntary, Charitable Organizations." Thesis submitted to the Graduate School of Public Affairs, University of Colorado, Denver.

———. 1998. "Leveraging the Future: A Case Example of University-Community Collaboration When Hope and Resources Are Constrained." Sydney, Nova Scotia: Office of the President of the University College of Cape Breton.

Sherraden, Michael, and Donald Eberly. 1982. *National Service: Social, Economic, and Military Impacts*. New York, Pergamon.

Shils, Edward. 1997. *The Virtue of Civility: Selected Essays on Liberalism, Tradition, and Civil Society*. Indianapolis: Liberty Fund.

Smith, David Horton. 1973. "The Impact of the Voluntary Sector on Society." In David Horton Smith, ed., *Voluntary Action Research: 1973*, 387–400. Lexington, Mass.: D. C. Heath.

———. 1991. "Four Sectors or Five? Retaining the Member-Benefit Sector." *Nonprofit and Voluntary Sector Quarterly* 20, no. 2, 137–50.

———. 1997a. "The Rest of the Nonprofit Sector: Grassroots Associations and the Dark Matter Ignored in Prevailing 'Flat Earth' Maps of the Sector." *Nonprofit and Voluntary Sector Quarterly* 26, no. 2 (June), 114–31.

———. 1997b. "Grassroots Associations Are Important: Some Theory and a Review of the Impact Literature." *Nonprofit and Voluntary Sector Quarterly* 26, no. 3 (September), 269–306.

Smith, David Horton, Richard Reddy, and Bert Baldwin, eds. 1972. *Voluntary Action Research 1972*. Lexington, Mass.: D. C. Heath.

Stone, Robert. 1998. *Damascus Gate*. Boston: Houghton Mifflin.

Sumariwalla, Russy. 1983. "Preliminary Observations in Scope, Size and Classification of the Sector." In Virginia Hodgkinson, ed., *Working Papers for the Spring Research Forum: Since the Filer Commission*, 433–49. Washington, D.C.: Independent Sector, 1983.

Thompson, Ann Marie, and James L. Perry. 1998. "Can AmeriCorps Build Communities?" *Nonprofit and Voluntary Sector Quarterly* 27, no. 4 (December), 399–420.

Turner, Jonathan H., and Charles E. Starnes. 1976. *Inequality: Privilege and Poverty in America*. Pacific Palisades, Calif.: Goodyear Publishing Co.

Van Til, Jon. 1988. *Mapping the Third Sector: Voluntarism in a Changing Social Economy*. New York: The Foundation Center.

———. 1993. "Here Comes National Service." In Benjamin R. Barber and Richard M. Battistoni, *Education for Democracy: Citizenship, Community, Service*, 184–86. Dubuque, Iowa: Kendall-Hunt.

———. 1994. "Toward Responsible Volunteerism: An Exploration of Operative Doctrines." In Harbeson, Hopkins, and Smith, 1994, 433–49.

———. 1996a. "In the Third Space: On Civil Society and Other Popular Buzzwords." *NonProfit Times* (March).

———. 1996b. "So Many Answers, So Few Solutions." *NonProfit Times* (October).

———. 1997a. "Of America's Promise: Summit Was Grand, but Issues Remain." *NonProfit Times* (June), 20.

———. 1997b. "Making Their Commission." *The American Benefactor* (Fall), 11–12.

———. 1999. "NCRP: A Qualitative Assessment." Paper presented to ARNOVA, November.

Van Til, Jon, et al. 1990. *Critical Issues in Philanthropy*. San Francisco: Jossey-Bass.

Van Til, William. 1996. *My Way of Looking at It*. 2nd ed. San Francisco: Caddo Gap Press.

Verba, Sidney, Kay L. Schlozman, and Henry E. Brady. 1995. *Voice and Equality: Civic Voluntarism in American Politics*. Cambridge, Mass.: Harvard University Press.

Waldman, Steven. 1995. *The Bill: How the Adventures of Clinton's National Service Bill Reveal What Is Corrupt, Comic, Cynical—and Noble—about Washington*. New York: Viking.

Walzer, Michael. 1983. *Spheres of Justice: A Defense of Pluralism and Equality*. New York: Basic Books.

Walzer, Michael, ed. 1995. *Toward a Global Society*. Providence, R.I.: Bergham.

Weisbrod, Burton. 1988. *The Nonprofit Economy*. Cambridge, Mass.: Harvard University Press.

Wernet, Stephen P., and Sandra A. Jones. 1992. "Merger and Acquisition Activity between Nonprofit Social Service Organizations: A Case Study." *Nonprofit and Voluntary Sector Quarterly* 21, no. 4 (Winter), 367–80.

Wilson, William Julius. 1996. *When Work Disappears: The World of the New Urban Poor*. New York: Knopf.

Wish, Naomi B., and Roseanne M. Mirabella. 1998. "Nonprofit Management Education: Current Offerings and Practices in University-Based Programs." In *Nonprofit Management Education: U.S. and World Perspectives*, ed. Michael O'Neill and Kathleen Fletcher. Westport, Conn.: Praeger.

Wolch, Jennifer R. 1990. *The Shadow State: Government and Voluntary Sector in Transition*. New York: The Foundation Center.

Wolf, Maura. 1993. "Involving the Community in National Service." *Social Policy* (Fall), 14–20.

Wolf, T. 1984. *The Nonprofit Organization*. Englewood Cliffs, N.J.: Prentice-Hall.

Young, Dennis R. 1988. "The Nonprofit Sector as the First Sector: Policy Implications." Part 2, no. 3 of *Looking Forward to the Year 2000: Public Policy and Philanthropy*. Spring Research Forum Working Papers. Washington, D.C.: Independent Sector.

THE UNIVERSITY AS CITIZEN: INSTITUTIONAL IDENTITY AND SOCIAL RESPONSIBILITY

A SPECIAL REPORT
WILLIAM M. SULLIVAN

To act responsibly, we must know who we are. If higher education today is uncertain about its social responsibilities, as seems manifestly the case, then this suggests that the American academy is unsure about its institutional identity. For organizations as for individuals, responsibility follows from relationships. But relationships grow out of our purposes even as how we relate to others helps to shape our aims. Vital and successful institutions stand out by their ability to maintain their direction and sense of meaning even amid significant shifts in the social landscape. Indeed, they can aid in providing direction for other institutions, keeping them true to their purposes. Now, however, as major economic and social change shakes American society, higher education is facing serious tests of its resourcefulness: Can the academy reinvigorate its central mission amid difficult and confusing conditions?

Higher education has shown such resourcefulness in the past, reshaping itself in response to new challenges and opportunities. A century ago, the academy reinvented itself through the creation of an innovative group of new universities such as Cornell and Chicago, along with the metamorphosis of some older private and state colleges, such as Harvard and Yale, the Universities of Wisconsin and California. These new institutions attempted to combine the European idea of research with the traditional American collegiate emphasis on teaching and the formation of citizens. The most creative among them would try to mediate the inherent tension between disciplinary specialization and curricular coherence by emphasizing the integrating nature of their public mission.

Higher education entered the new twentieth century by announcing its dedication to bringing the powers of cultivated intellect to bear on the economic, social, and cultural life of American democracy. Its sense of mission was often rooted in a reform-minded liberal Protestantism, yet its best aspirations soared beyond the sectarian as well as the purely national. The universities proclaimed themselves in service to great, panhuman ideals. Those aims were almost immediately compromised by the prejudices of class, race, sex, and religion, as well as by the imperious patronage of "captains of industry." Still, in the popular mind the mission of the academy has remained distinctly public and philanthropic. To reinterpret this earlier sense of public purpose for our time could start a recovery of the academy's identity, sparking renewed efforts to clarify what higher education is responsible for and to whom.

During the past half-century, higher education has cooperated with national initiatives to provide educational opportunity to a larger segment of the population than has been true in other industrial nations. At its best, today's academy, diverse in form and descending from many traditions, Illustrates the American ability to derive collective strength from social diversity and institutional pluralism. For example, the liberal arts institutions continue to have a distinctive and vital mission: to bring the tradition of the humane and civic arts to bear on the problems and concerns of the present. The religious traditions of service and prophecy go on spurring new forms of engaged learning and scholarship in many institutions. Community colleges are showing new vitality by reclaiming their role as innovators in expanding educational opportunity and as sites for civic development. As advocates of civic engagement remind us, campuses educate their students for citizenship most effectively to the degree that they become places for constructive exchange and cooperation among diverse groups of citizens from the larger community. All these traditions have importance. Moreover, by engaging with the needs of the communities that often lie just beyond the campus, institutions formed by the values of their past often are able to gain new energy from the creative sparks of fresh dedication to their defining mission.

Yet, at the same time it is far from evident that the historic defining purposes of higher education remain sufficiently alive to guide the academy through the difficult time of reorganization that it is entering. When the issue of purpose is raised within higher education, it is as often a source of division as a rallying point. Conflicting influences from various external patrons such as business, philanthropy, and government, as well as dissension within, have pushed academic leadership to simply shelve the whole issue of identity and purpose, relying instead on a bland managerialism to get by. But that strategy seems less and less viable. The academy has come under a good deal of skeptical scrutiny of late, to say nothing of serious attack from hostile critics. But we also get a powerful clue that something is importantly wrong from the sense of drift and demoralization that seems all too common in the world of higher education.

Despite its great size and prestige, much of American higher education today suffers from a sense of demoralization and decline. In part this problem is political and financial, as critics within state governments and elsewhere have mounted serious attacks on the integrity of the enterprise as a whole. Higher education is today a "mature industry," rather than the growing sector it was for most of this century. It is also a remarkably diversified and decentralized sector, ranging from elite research universities, both private and public, through private liberal arts colleges, religious schools, state comprehensive systems, and two-year institutions. This makes generalization risky. Fundamentally, however, there is a common problem afflicting this "mature industry." This is the question of identity. Higher education seems to have lost an animating sense of mission. There is much talk of reform, but mostly of an administrative and financial nature, with little attention to content and purpose. Yet, it is precisely the neglect of the question of purpose that has robbed the academy of collective self-confidence at just the moment it most needs to defend itself in increasingly bitter arguments about educational policy and finance.

In the absence of an updated version of its founding conception of itself as a participant in the life of civil society, as a citizen of American democracy, much of higher education has come to operate on a sort of default program of instrumental individualism. This is the familiar notion that the academy exists to research and disseminate knowledge and skills as tools for economic development and the upward mobility of individuals. This "default program" of instrumental individualism leaves the larger questions of social, political, and moral purpose out of explicit consideration. These things, if considered at all, are simply assumed to follow from the "real" business of the higher education "industry." So, for example, the nation's leading research universities are touted as the "best in the world" as evidenced by the number of foreign students flocking to them. It's noteworthy, however, that this is a market measure—i.e., the "value added" by U.S. degrees to internationally competitive professionals.

The consequences of the default program are indirectly evident in the type and quality of social leadership in the United States today. The leaders in business, government, the professions, the media, and religious and cultural institutions are, nearly without exception, graduates of higher education and, usually, of the most prestigious institutions. Moreover, the academy can count as its alumni and alumnae most of the top socioeconomic stratum in America, the upper 20 percent whom Robert Reich has dubbed symbolic analytic workers and whose outlook J. K. Galbraith has described as a "culture of contentment." This is the leadership core of the middle class. It is also the class that continues to benefit, as most Americans have not, from the current period of economic change sometimes called "globalization."

The most successful of this fortunate fifth of the American population have joined the wealthy in increasingly separating themselves from their fellow citizens by where they live, where they educate their children, the medical care they receive, the retirement they can expect. They have helped guide, or at least acquiesced in, the development of an increasingly divided and unequal society during the current period of self-proclaimed national economic success. Collectively, this comfortable minority has in fact if not in intent abdicated social responsibility for a narrow careerism and private self-interest. It is as if they have forgotten that they are members, and highly privileged ones at that, of the national society. In the absence of a sense of belonging to a larger moral entity, the most successful of Americans have in effect declared secession from the shared responsibilities of citizenship. Far from serving as a counterbalance, higher education, in the grip of the default program of instrumental individualism, has often promoted or colluded with this socially destructive process.

There are even more direct indications of the implications of the default paradigm of instrumental individualism for the future of academe itself. One might think of the University of Phoenix as the purest example to date of such a model of academe: a for-profit, expanding educational institution that grants degrees to adult learners in a variety of fields, all of immediate value to business and business careers. It is successful. And, notably, it operates without the expensive overhead "frills" of traditional academic institutions. The University of Phoenix has no permanent campus, no organized student life, and no permanent faculty.

How has the American academy arrived at this juncture? Ironically, perhaps, today's default program is the direct descendant of the celebrated post-World War II expansion of higher education. During the postwar decades, as Derek Bok has pointed out, American higher education came to enjoy an unprecedented level of prestige—and public support. This was because of the key roles higher education came to play during the era of the Cold War. In effect, higher education took responsibility, with government help, for advancing two major tasks then seen as essential to the national interest: technological progress, especially in defense-related areas such as the silicon chip and the Internet, and the skill and status upgrading of an expanding middle class. Higher education became an important partner with government and industry in the shaping of the postwar American order.

This second objective, the upgrading and expanding of the middle class, became the rationale for a series of federal initiatives, beginning with the G.I. Bill and continuing through Affirmative Action for women and minorities. These programs greatly expanded higher education while helping to make American society more democratic and inclusive than it had been before World War II. However, these efforts were as much a part of the logic of waging Cold War as the rapid development of military technology. If the United States was to compete ideologically with the appeal of communism abroad, so ran the rationale, its prosperity had to be visibly spread throughout the population, if only to refute the Communist claims that capitalism inevitably bred sharp inequalities and class tyranny.

With the end of the Cold War, the pursuit of greater social and economic equality no longer carries the same strategic importance. In the absence of ideological competition and external strategic threat, political support for increased economic and social equality has waned, especially among the already successful. As the political fortunes of concerns about social equality, already under attack from powerful social groups, have declined, so has government involvement in promoting access to higher education. As government effort has receded, the values of the market have assumed a larger role in determining the shape of the American academy, with the result that wealth has come to ever more completely determine both educational access and priorities. Business and industry, after all, are often the direct beneficiaries, as well as patrons, of much academic research and training.

It is important to note then, as Bok does not, that the postwar projects of higher education were heavily tilted toward instrumentalism from the start. They aimed at particular strategic outcomes thought critical to winning the geopolitical struggle with the Soviet Union. The relation of the means chosen to the purposes of higher education as an institution was a much less important issue. By focusing so relentlessly on contributing to external goals, the academy gradually lost the inclination to address these ends from the point of view of its own intrinsic responsibilities. In its most generous aspects, the postwar spirit imagined an academy that would take a creative role in improving the quality of democratic life in the American polity, including more open access to higher education. The aim was both to foster greater economic and social equality and to enlist for the nation previously ignored talents. Actual practice, however, emphasized immediate individual—and institutional—self-interest at the expense of both long-term democratic values and the academy's distinctive contribution to society's self-reflective capacities. Science was emphasized because it had proved to be the indispensable source of that technological advance that conferred military superiority, while access to higher education was promoted to spur economic growth by providing a skilled, more socially integrated professional work force. Federal interventions ensured that academic institutions structured themselves to facilitate this strategic program. These governmental efforts simultaneously provided a massive push toward increasing disciplinary specialization as the lion's share of resources poured into scientific and engineering fields. For their part, academic institutions were often quick to seize these often extravagant opportunities to advance their wealth and prestige, even changing their own identities and character in the process.

Just as federal largesse underwrote vast enterprises of research, so subsidies, grants, and loans promoted college degree programs that allowed individuals to grasp their opportunity by learning the skills currently in demand. Any other aims of higher education became peripheral. The long-term result was the withering within the academy of certain habits of thought crucial for its own integrity as well as for the wider good of democracy. Academic leaders stopped what effects the new purposes were having on the character and identity of their faculties, their students, or on their institutions themselves. In the drive for Cold War supremacy, virtually anything could be exploited to serve the ends of national security and economic growth. Even at the time, this could seem a troubling maxim to guide public policy in a democracy. After all, this was the principle that underlay the unprincipled use of propaganda by totalitarian regimes. Its adoption by the United States threatened to undermine public trust in government—a threat that was finally realized in the 1960s, with continuing consequences, The widespread use of these tools of expedience, given intellectual structure in the form of instrumental rationality, shaped not only state propaganda but much of commercial advertising and entertainment, even the public relations of the academy itself. It is hardly surprising, then, that within higher education, as throughout the nation, little thought was applied to inquiry into what institutional structures would be needed to ensure that the technologies—and the newly credentialed middle class professionals—would contribute to the goals of democratic life.

Under the pressure of Cold War imperatives there seemed little need to make conscious efforts at weaving these developments into the requirements for a self-reflective and mutually responsive nation. With the Cold War now over, higher education lacks even this instrumental rationale for connecting its functions of research and credentialing to larger public purposes. Academic spokespeople increasingly describe their enterprise in purely market terms, depicting it as a business much like any other, as they worry out loud about how to cultivate and expand their "customer base," especially business and consumers of educational services. They seem to assume that a kind of invisible hand will ensure that their single-minded pursuit of institutional growth and prestige will enhance the general welfare. However, the consequence of this embrace of the totems of the marketplace is that the American academy is losing its public mandate. It is thus no accident that despite the nation's manifest needs for investing in knowledge and skills in many areas of social importance, the academy has done so little to take the lead in proposing new public purposes to address these needs.

Various public figures have imagined candidates for such public efforts, such as the needs of the young and the poor in education, health care, and employment. We might add the strengthening of the nonprofit sector that provides so much essential social infrastructure, to say nothing of attention to improvement of democratic skills of public discussion. But these goals only make sense if one has first recognized the university as serving some larger public purpose as a citizen within civil society rather than simply a self-aggrandizing creature of the market. This is the perspective that is currently missing from the frequently anguished debates about what to do about higher education.

The malaise in the academy finds resonance in the sense of decline and drift within the ranks of the professions as a whole. The professions, after all, have grown out of the academy. The teachers of all professionals are themselves members of the professoriate. The professions remain further linked to the academy through in the common value of professionalism, the guiding ideal throughout higher education as well as professional fields of all kinds. Moreover, both the professions as a whole and higher education in particular have been relatively privileged and successful institutions in the United States during the past half-century. It is note-worthy, then, that many professional fields have, like the academy, come to accent the marketability of their technical skills while de-emphasizing their contribution to civic life. In other words, the professions today do not typically seek to gain legitimacy by stressing the social importance of the knowledge they provide and the functions they perform for the community. Rather, they emphasize the specialized, expert knowledge and skills they provide in the market.

The importance of their social contribution is increasingly measured, in the world of both the professions and higher education, by the market value of their specialized skills, without serious reference to how these functions relate to any broader social well-being. Movement in this direction has greatly intensified in recent decades, further eclipsing the civic as opposed to the purely technical understanding of professionalism. The dominant view of professional knowledge has accordingly shed aspects of a more socially embedded conception of knowledge, with its concomitant ideas of social authority accruing on the basis of social responsibility, while displaying an increasingly instrumental and detached understanding of professional expertise.

This shift in perspective has accompanied and helped to justify an increasing degree of specialization in professional fields. But this development has also so separated knowledge from social purpose that expertise and skill appear as simply neutral tools to be appropriated by successful competitors in the service of their particular ends. This is, of course, an instrumental view of knowledge. It finds its natural complement in an individualistic and libertarian moral attitude that favors laissez-faire in most areas of social life. Since the professions have continued to importantly define middle-class aspirations, however, this emphasis has had important effects beyond the professional ranks. These developments in the culture of professionalism not only reflect but have helped foster an aggressively individualistic understanding of society. An important corollary to this conception of knowledge, however, has been the narrowing of the idea of responsibility, both individual and collective.

This perspective of instrumental individualism has become dominant in much professional and academic opinion. On the one hand, it has seemed to release individuals and institutions from unwanted moral responsibility. All they need do is obey the impersonal dictates of market forces. And, in fact, the change in attitude has progressed along with a shift in the allocation of rewards, talent, and vocational interest during the past 25 years. That is, there has been a conspicuous movement within the educated work force away from teaching and public and social service occupations toward more market-oriented, private-sector professional employment. Within the professional ranks, moreover, the past two decades have seen the ominous growth of increasing gaps in prestige and income between a few "stars" at the top of the heap over against their erstwhile peers. However, this retreat from social responsibility has not produced enhanced freedom or fulfillment, even for most professionals. Nor has it much improved the moral quality of American life. Rather, the consequences could be said to have been widespread vocational demoralization on the part of professionals—a demoralization evident in a need to compensate through getting as much material reward as possible in the short term, within a society grown meaner, fiercer toward losers, and less hopeful about its collective future.

For higher education, the consequence of these developments has been a diffusion of identity, a loss of direction and defining purposes amid the pull of extraneous but enticing lures to professional and institutional self-interest. Academic institutions have followed market trends unreflectively—much as they have followed government-funding trends—with often negative consequences for their long-term commitments and defining values and purposes. The results have been growing divisions of all kinds within and among institutions of higher learning as well as within professional ranks. With this has come the weakening of concern with public responsibility. Perhaps these trends explain the paradox of finding so many of the "world's best universities" amid conditions of urban decay and social neglect. This is indeed an instance of the detachment of knowledge from responsibility carried to an extreme degree.

These unhappy outcomes reflect a profound tension within the academic enterprise, a tension that can be healthy for the enterprise but which, if unnoticed or ignored, can wreak havoc, as it now threatens to do. Consider an analogy from a related, though very different, professional enterprise: journalism. Like higher education, journalism is in the business of shaping its public as well as responding to it. Both institutions play crucial roles in making democratic societies viable: their activities are critical if public deliberation is to work at all under modern conditions. The way journalism and higher education conceive and carry out their purposes—the way they understand themselves—is integral to their ability to function as responsible institutions.

Today, journalism, especially in the traditional core institution of the metropolitan newspapers, finds itself under heavy pressure to reshape itself into an adjunct of a strictly commercial enterprise, to become one more part of the emerging global "info-tainment" industry. Yet, as Tom Rosenstiel of Columbia University's Project for Excellence in Journalism argues, this remains, as it has proven in the past, a self-defeating strategy for newspapers. It is worth considering Rostenstiel's argument since it provides an illuminating analogy to the current controversies in higher education.

Newspapers have often wanted to turn their reporting into directly profit-driven functions. The problem, according to Rosenstiel, has always been that readers resist and resent news reporting that they suspect has been concocted to please or manipulate them. As a result, papers—and television as well—have repeatedly found that the route to economic survival leads, paradoxically, toward investing heavily in news gathering and editorial independence. Building audience loyalty takes years. It also requires giving people information that may at first attract only a small following, just because it is new. "What journalism companies are selling," writes Rosenstiel, "is their authority as a public asset. And that depends, especially with an ever more skeptical public, on proving you're in it for more than a buck."

In other words, journalism succeeds commercially only when it actually acts as a citizen, when it places public service and concern for the integrity of its professional standards ahead of immediate profit. But it is equally important that the "professional standards" as well as the identity of both academe and journalism have been historically publicly focused in a strong sense. The identity of these occupations and their institutional homes only make sense in reference to what is common to a whole community, to a general, diverse, pluralistic constituency all of whom must nonetheless manage to cooperate. For both professions, truth must be publicly arrived at and publicly argued, while the most important truths under investigation concern not just what is happening or how things work but how we are to live as a nation.

The movement for public or civic journalism has galvanized much attention while also serving as a rallying point for efforts at reform in the media. The movement contends that journalism can find its full significance only by seeing itself as a critical partner in the "public sphere" of opinion and acting accordingly. The public sphere refers to the diffuse set of connections through which members of a democratic society try to understand and guide their affairs by active participation. Part of the appeal of the public journalism perspective derives from recognition on the part of important segments of the newspaper industry that its future depends on cultivating a readership interested in its product. That readership turns out to have a peculiar configuration, as compared with other "market segments." Newspaper readers turn out to be overwhelmingly persons who describe themselves as concerned with public affairs, not just consumers of news. They are also disproportionately active in the life of the larger society and likely to want a share in shaping the news as well as reading it. Thus, material interests bolster the ideal aim of building a more active and cooperative relationship between journalists and the public.

Something similar describes higher education in relation to its "market." Support for the academy in its integrity also depends on persons who see themselves not just as consumers of services but as participants in a larger public realm. These are persons, often themselves graduates of higher education, who are interested in it not just for its instrumental value in enhancing their own and their offspring's economic marketability, but because they respect the contribution higher education makes to the society through promoting intellectual activity and making it more available to citizens generally. There is a naturally reciprocal relationship between academic institutions and this public. This public values higher education as a force for improvement and democracy, while the academy finds its meaning through trying to expand and build up this public. The big question is whether it is possible to give this understanding of higher education a formulation that is at once intellectually sound and generally comprehensible. To attempt this today is to enter an important debate.

This debate is an ongoing national process of sorting out not only intellectual differences but rival principles of cultural authority and social organization as well.

The default program of instrumental individualism rests on a conception of rationality variously denominated as technocratic or scientistic. This conception in its several forms has assumed dominance within much of the academy. Its core tradition and values are those of Positivist empiricism, a cultural movement descending from the nineteenth century that generalizes a certain interpretation of the natural sciences into a total cultural program. Positivism insists that because natural scientific research succeeds by straining evaluative judgement out of observation of phenomena, therefore the larger truth must be that facts can be understood independently of value. The conclusion Positivists have drawn is that while factual knowledge can be objectively verified, all questions of ethics and meaning are merely matters of taste and subjective judgment. Hence the affinity of positivistic understandings of research for "applying" knowledge to the social world on the model of the way engineers "apply" expert understanding to the problems of structure, logistics, or communication. While increasingly outdated as an interpretation of how natural science in fact has developed, this epistemology is firmly entrenched as the operating system of much of the American university. It provides an important intellectual warrant for the legitimacy of the instrumental individualism of the default paradigm.

Just as the currently ascendant default program contains at its core an epistemology—a conception of knowledge and its purpose—so the alternative of socially responsive higher education grows out of a counter ideal of knowledge and its purposes, together with the kind of social relationships this ideal entails. The alternative to the socially detached, Positivist conception of knowledge and learning emphasizes the fusion of fact and value in practical experience, the interconnection of means and ends. Without denying individual talent or insight, this alternative model insists that knowledge grows out of the activities of a "community of inquirers," in the terminology of American Pragmatist C.S. Peirce. For this alternative understanding of the life of the mind, the common core of all processes of investigation is a kind of reasoning that is essentially social and in which there is always a purpose at work. Grasping and articulating this purpose is crucial because, whether acknowledged or not, such purposes in fact shape the practices of investigation and teaching. These purposes are themselves fundamentally rooted in the identity of the inquirers and their community, expressive of their common commitments and relationships.

The animating idea of this alternative conception of investigation and learning is that rationality is finally always practical, rooted in the practices of some social group. Knowing is an aspect of the overall effort by members of a society to orient themselves within the world. At its root, that is, reason is essentially "communicative," as knowledge is part of an ongoing conversation among inquirers about their world. Though not simply something manufactured by social processes, even knowledge of nonhuman nature is always mediated by the norms and aims of some social group. In modern societies, that group, or rather groups, has become institutionalized in the professional inquirers who staff the academy. As distinguishing aspects of human historical existence, rationality and knowing necessarily have moral and ethical dimensions. Knowledge and the process of inquiry bear on the quality of life and the nature of relationships among people. So, knowledge is finally a public value and concern, while those institutions that specialize in its discovery and interpretation necessarily exist within the framework of a modern society's overall goals and values.

This alternative understanding has in recent years begun to make significant impact on opinion within higher education. This has been due in part to the efforts of its contemporary spokespersons. Donald Schön's notion of "reflective practice," for example, has brought home the insufficiency of the received Positivist model of "applied science" in a variety of fields, both professional and academic. There is also the growing body of largely academic criticism of Positivism sometimes called the post-Positivist philosophy of science. Interestingly, these recent developments echo the founding ideas and program of the one indigenous American philosophical school, the classic Pragmatism of Peirce, James, Royce, and Dewey.

The significance of this tradition of thought for higher education and its contemporary problems has been worked out by Charles W. Anderson in such books as *Pragmatic Liberalism and Prescribing the Life of the Mind: An Essay on the Purpose of the University, the Aims of Liberal Education, the Competence of Citizens, and the Cultivation of Practical Reason.* Anderson has provided the useful clue that Pragmatism can provide a needed coherence in discussion of these issues through its approach. This might be called an inductive synthesis by means of critique. It is critical in the sense that it traces out the assumptions of the dominant model while also showing its, often unintended, consequences. It is an inductive method because it begins inquiry with the practices at hand and then directs that inquiry toward comparing those actual methods of the disciplines with their aims as these have been revealed and interpreted over time. By asking what particular practices are good for, this approach is also synthetic and integrative. It points beyond the current state of professional fields and institutions toward possibilities for cooperation often only half-recognized by practitioners. Very importantly, it is an approach that reveals the public significance of the intellectual enterprises.

The kind of inquiry through practical reasoning urged by Anderson articulates a strong alternative to the presently dominant default program. The perspective opened up by the Pragmatist account of practical reasoning suggests a way to rethink and, ultimately, to reconstruct all three aspects of the identity of the American university: its aims as a setting for inquiry; its formative educational function; and the social responsibilities that follow from its civic identity.

The way in which social relationships are conceived and lived out importantly influences how knowledge develops. This is because every intellectual enterprise, as it develops its distinctive practices and lore, shapes its participants' sense of identity and their notions of what is important in the field. While the internal life of a field is the most basic determinant of the values of its practitioners, the worlds of professional activity remain, to varying degrees, importantly open to influence from other institutions, not least their patrons and critics. Who the members of a field imagine the audience or supporters of their enterprise to be matters significantly when it comes to deciding what sorts of questions will gain priority and who will be recognized as significant partners in the process of learning.

The development of postwar science and technology, for example, was significantly shaped by the imperatives first of national defense and then of corporate profitability. These social influences pushed research in the direction of devices that are increasingly complicated (and expensive) to design, build, and maintain. In contrast, other dimensions of technical and engineering excellence such as ease of use, repair, and replicability, or simplicity of design, received far less attention. This largely tacit process of purpose-driven inquiry has had fateful consequences in many areas. Think of the growth of the huge institutional research and engineering complex, much of it university based, which has been developed at enormous expense to support today's high-tech, acute care medicine. Yet, this form of health care mostly benefits the affluent. There has been far less support for research and applications in public health, advances that benefit the public more broadly and that experience in Europe and elsewhere suggest may be as effective, if not more effective, in improving the overall well-being of the population as the more expensive developments of medical high-technology.

By this standard, the record of the postwar university has been a very mixed report. As we have seen, the postwar era saw higher education deliver prodigious advances in scientific knowledge and its applications while opening professional status to wider segments of the population. At the same time, however, higher education has allowed external patrons to set priorities without engaging in much scrutiny of the larger point and value of these priorities. And the academy has rashly embarked on projects out of an unreflective self-interest. Neither has higher education typically been self-reflective about its own organization and the effects on its identity and aims of the practices of the disciplines. Despite protestations of its dedication to disinterested research, the positivistic separation of the rationality of technique from thought about value and purpose has made such omissions academic matters of course.

It is precisely this narrowness of aim that a focus on practical reason promises to overcome. Practical reason views epistemic practices, like those of every human institution, as ultimately guided by partly implicit ideal aims. So understood, inquiry becomes a self-reflective process of investigating and appraising the quality of the performance, measured against some interpretation of its fundamental purpose. Of course, conceptions of purpose are always themselves open to question and challenge, and indeed the glory of the academy is that it is an institution that has tried to find ways to sustain just this process of ongoing scrutiny of practice and its aims. Yet, the academy has been as embarrassingly resistant as any other organization to applying its skills of inquiry to its own activities. The turn to practical reasoning is motivated by the desire to do just that.

Once this process of inquiry develops, however, new implications emerge. The questioning and appraising of specific practices within disciplines requires practitioners to become more self-aware about their function within their "community of inquirers." They typically come to adopt a stance toward their field that is at once critical and yet loyal to the basic aims of the enterprise, seeking to improve its aim at its essential purposes as they come to see them. Such a stance toward one's field obviously has strong affinities with the responsibilities of participation in an ongoing social enterprise. It becomes, as Charles Anderson has reminded us, an enhanced kind of citizenship, pertaining "not just to public affairs but to our performance in every realm of life." Once seriously involved in such inquiry Anderson suggests, the inquirers become progressively more aware of the importance of quality of performance, of how crucial self-reflective loyalty to purpose is in more and more areas of the life of their institutions, including how the disciplines and practices mesh or fail to mesh with each other in promoting the larger aims of knowledge that lead into the public realm.

Inquiry, properly understood, leads its participants into questions about the overall coherence and mutual import of their many specialized endeavors. It awakens responsibility by revealing how participants are already engaged in matters of public import and bearing. In this way, citizenship enters ever more seriously into the "job description" of academic professionals, not as an externally imposed "add-on" but as a defining feature of the very activities of inquiry and discourse themselves. Practical reason leads toward a collaborative search for practices that meet common purposes reliably and well. While this does not mean that the university loses its distinctive aims and organization, it does entail a more self-aware and deliberate relationship between the specialized concerns of academe and the problems and controversies of societies, such as our own, which are struggling to institute a fully democratic way of living.

We can only speculate what difference it might have made to the evolution of higher education during the postwar decades had such a conception of practical reason played a major role in academic thinking and administration. But the postwar record certainly confirms, even if ambiguously, that the link between the way knowledge is organized and institutional identity is real and important. Today's default program certainly fits much of the present organization of the academy. Yet, other efforts are under way to connect higher education with the society in ways consistent with the democratic implications inherent in the notion of inquiry as practical reason.

The notable upsurge of interest among students in social service volunteer programs, as well as the growth in institutional support for such efforts at every level of higher education, is testimony to the breadth of the sense that there is need for a change of direction, that academe must do more to educate for civic leadership and service. This movement is now very widespread, ranging from the national organization, Campus Compact, founded by university presidents in the 1980s, to a plethora of indigenous efforts in rural as well as metropolitan institutions. Within the curriculum, the appearance of the movement for "service learning" or "experiential learning," while not uncontroversial, has opened up discussion and sometimes fierce debate on the place of social service in academic practice, as well as the question of the nature of investigation and its relation to practical experience and self-reflection.

There are other experiments even more directly engaged in the task of reorienting the focus of the academy, in its research as well as its educational function. These have been projects to connect the intellectual and technical resources of higher education with the problems of surrounding communities, sometimes conceived as whole metropolitan regions and sometimes as the immediate, often poor, urban neighbors of the academy. This is a more complex movement, still very much in process. Some have developed as interinstitutional partnerships, sometimes with philanthropic support. These projects have built linkages among schools, including whole school systems, and various academic institutions from community colleges to research universities. Others have proceeded in a more "grassroots" way relying on the initiative of groups of faculty, students, and administrators working with groups outside the academy.

It is noteworthy that the more successful efforts to redefine university identity around service and citizenship share a certain family resemblance. This similarity is rooted in the practice of inquiry as practical reason. First, such efforts consciously conceive their purpose to be changing the university's understanding of research and teaching, along the lines of critical practical reason, toward a much greater focus on social service and improvement. "Participatory action research" is one such methodological innovation. Second, these efforts have typically sought to develop this change in attitude by establishing enduring partnerships with institutions, such as schools, social service agencies or businesses, and health care providers, with which the academy already shares aims, practices, and often personnel, at least in the form of apprentice teachers and health care professionals. Third, such projects seem to succeed best in actually becoming institutionalized as standard academic procedure when they develop as genuine partnerships in which knowledge and practices evolve cooperatively rather than proceeding in a one-directional way from experts to outsiders.

The success of these efforts at changing the dominant tendencies within the American academy depends in important part on how clearly the participants understand what they are doing—and how effective they can become at persuading others of the significance of what they are engaged in. To become more self-aware is the first step toward awakening one's responsibility. The second step is to recognize that serious self-scrutiny often leads to changes in identity, to growth in self-discovery, and a broadening of one's aims and loyalties. Identity, that is, receives important shape from social relationships and the way they are organized. In the Positivist scheme, researchers "produce" knowledge, which is then "applied" to problems, and problematic populations, by varying forms of design and engineering. On the other hand, if knowledge is developed through inquiry, the identity of the participants in the process will have bearing on the kind of knowledge discovered. These experiments suggest that academic institutions, like professionals, can realize their public responsibilities by becoming self-aware partners in addressing the needs of the nation's shredding social fabric. Once established over time by good faith on both sides, however, cooperation becomes self-sustaining as it manifestly produces an enlarged sense of identity and purpose for both the academy and its partners.

These practical experiments, and the theory of practical reason, also have important bearing on the directly educational mission of higher education. Today, as for some time, higher education remains a powerful formative institution. It exerts profound social and cultural influences in shaping expectations about what skills and knowledge are valuable, what career aspirations are reasonable and admirable, what kind of society Americans want to have, what kind of people they want to be. Much of college experience, the "hidden curriculum," consists in "anticipatory socialization." That is, universities and colleges link vocational preparation with personal aspirations by creating the social and cultural context within which individuals choose and shape their goals and skills. The environment and ethos of higher education, the values and purposes that are seen by students to matter among faculty, staff, alumni, and administrators are among the most powerful shaping forces in American society. To the degree that this environment reflects only or mostly the values of the current default program, higher education will simply reinforce the tendencies toward social disengagement so evident among successful Americans.

Because of its great influence not only as a source of innovation but as shaper of outlooks, higher education is a preeminently public—though nongovernmental—institution. Everyone has a stake and an interest in what it does. It is a critical participant in the democratic public sphere. We in the academy need to connect seriously with our actual social position, both as an institutional sector within the national society and as particular organizations living with often very different neighbors in our local communities. But we cannot do this without serious reflection and discussion about our identity and purposes. And this requires social vision. A more responsible and connected institutional life requires that we think of our institutions as distinctive participants in a public sphere, a member of democratic civil society, with important responsibilities to the nation and to the wider world. And not just as knowledge-producing entities or service providers (the industrial-market conception), but as important shapers of identity (including our own), as explorers and conservators as well as critics of values and goals.

This is not a wholly novel approach in American life. Within the tradition of what could be called developmental democracy earlier leaders, such as the philosopher John Dewey, warned of the perpetual American tendency to collapse the aspirations to democracy into the straight jacket of what

I have called the default program of individualism and instrumentalism. The price for this, these pioneers warned, is not more freedom but diminished possibilities for us all. On the other hand, democracy promises associated living. This means a fuller life for individuals as well as a more just and cohesive society. Individuals can develop a strong and confident sense of selfhood only as members of a society in which they can believe and invest their energies, one in which they can trust and know they are trusted. Higher education, too, finds its best self through contributing to such a society. This civic perspective can provide the leaders in academe with direction for developing a democratic yet reflective public. Such a public is the best guarantee that higher education will have a future in which it will be worthwhile to participate.

Bibliography

Chapter 2 Interpretative Frameworks and Concepts Relevant to Educating Professions and Institutions

Anheier, Helmut K. "Studying Nonprofit Organizations." In *Nonprofit Organizations: Theory, Management, Policy.* London and New York, 2005, pp. 3–19.

Dewey, John. "Search for the Great Community," Chapter Five of *The Public and Its Problem.* (See also Chapter One, "The Search for the Public") New York: H. Holt Company, 1927.

Foley, Michael and Virginia A. Hodgkinson. "Introduction," in *The Civil Society Readers.* Medford, MA: Tufts University Press, 2003.

Hall, Peter Dobkin. "Teaching and Research on Philanthropy, Voluntarism, and Nonprofit Organizations: A Case Study of Academic Innovation." *Teachers College Record.* Vol. 93, Spring 1992, pp. 403–433.

Kay, Lila E. "Rethinking Institutions: Philanthropy as an Historiographic Problem of Knowledge and Power," *Minerva: A Review of Science, Learning, and Policy.* Autumn 1997, pp. 283–293.

Roelofs, Joan. *Foundations and Public Policy: the Mask of Pluralism.* Albany: State University of New York Press, 2003.

Schneider, John C. "Philanthropic Styles in the United States: Toward a Theory of Regional Differences," *Nonprofit and Voluntary Sector Quarterly.* Vol. 25, No. 2, June 1996, pp. 190–210.

Warren, Mark E. *Democracy and Association.* Princeton and Oxford: Oxford University Press, 2001.

CHAPTER 3

INDIVIDUAL DONATIONS AND PATRONAGE

AMERICAN MILLIONAIRES AND
THEIR PUBLIC GIFTS

Several months ago there was compiled and published by the New York *Tribune* a directory of American millionaires. The list fills nearly a hundred large pages, and includes a grand total of 4,047 names. It is an extremely interesting publication, and the student of our social economics a hundred years hence will find it invaluable as a part of his material for the study of our condition in the last decade of the nineteenth century.

It would be instructive to have for comparison with this one a catalogue of the American millionaires of forty years ago. The list at that time could probably have been put into one or two pages of the kind of which the present directory requires nearly a hundred. At the outbreak of the war not only were great fortunes few in number, but the amount of property which in those, days was accounted great wealth would now be deemed a very moderate fortune.

Great Fortunes Arise From Great Opportunities

The stupendous development of the country has given opportunities never known in the history of the world before for the accumulation of immense private holdings, and our social life, our political methods, and our democratic institutions are all profoundly affected by the existence among us to-day of a recognized class of great capitalists who command congeries of agencies and forces which had no practical existence among us as recently as the election of Abraham Lincoln to the Presidency of the United States. The career of the late Jay Gould, so graphically recounted by Mr. Stead elsewhere in the REVIEW, is representative of the circumstances under which these colossal fortunes have been amassed by men who had the energy and the discernment to take advantage of their opportunities. The story of Mr. Andrew Carnegie, who, like Mr. Gould, began life as a poor boy not so very long ago, and whose wealth is now counted by the tens of millions, is in its own way not less typical. Even more remarkable than Mr. Gould's or Mr. Carnegie's, as measured by results, is the career of Mr. John D. Rockefeller, who is said to be so rich that he might transform a hundred paupers into a hundred millionaires and still remain the master of tens or scores of millions.

Mr. Rockefeller's accumulations are thoroughly typical of the fortunes made by hundreds of men listed in the *Tribune's* catalogue, in the fact that they represent the relentless, aggressive, irresistible seizure of a particular opportunity, the magnitude of which opportunity was due simply to the magnitude of this country and the immensity of the stream of its prosperous industrial life. The magnificent creative faculties and business abilities of Mr. George M. Pullman must perforce have brought profit to himself and to others, even if his sphere of operations had been restricted to some pent-up Utica. But the vastness of the fortune he has won is due to the vastness of the railroad system of the United States upon which his palace car service is employed. Mr. Pullman's hotels on wheels are to-day in motion over more than one hundred and twenty-five thousand miles of railways. The same tremendous development of the nation in the past quarter century which has peopled the wilderness, doubled the number of States in the Union, doubled the population of the country and created a series of magnificent new cities, has given us, along with a large increase in the average wealth of all those who belong to the property-holding classes, an immense increase also in the number of the men who are very rich.

Should the State Limit Private Wealth?

The large fortunes, for the most part, have been won through the same kind of honorable and legitimate adaptation of means to ends that has produced the smaller fortunes. As a matter of theory, it is perfectly legitimate to discuss the advantages and disadvantages that would arise from a legal limitation of the size of men's fortunes. As a matter of practice, moreover, the State may, whenever it chooses, arrange any system that in its sovereignty it may please to try, for the better equalization of wealth by progressive inheritance taxes, or by any of the other methods that statesmen, economists and socialist writers have suggested. But the phenomenon of the multi-millionaire is in fact too new to be ripe for any special legal treatment as yet.

In the nature of the case, there seems no logical reason why a man who is permitted to own one hundred thousand dollars should not also be permitted to own one hundred millions. There may, however, be good and sufficient reasons why the man who owns one hundred millions may be debarred from saying who shall hold and enjoy that vast accumulation of wealth when he himself is dead and gone. There is, indeed, much reason to believe that we shall, within a quarter of a century, witness some new and radical experiments in the direction of laws regulating the transmission of property.

"Social Wealth" Makes Millionaires

One thing about millionaires is sufficiently clear. Those very conditions which have made the accumulation of wealth in a rapidly expanding country comparatively easy, afford the most inviting opportunities for the expenditure of wealth in behalf of social objects. This proposition is too obvious to be gainsaid. Our great American fortunes are the product of social opportunities rather than of the mere creative power of their holders; and, while the possession of any superior gift or power entails responsibilities towards those less richly gifted which every true and thoughtful man must realize, it would seem especially true and plain that these new American millionaires, with fortunes amassed out of wealth produced by the sturdy and hopeful toil of men who have gathered here from all countries, should be keenly alive to the duty of holding themselves at the liberal service of their communities.

The time may come when our system of production and our system of taxation may be so arranged that what we term "social wealth"—the unearned increment in expanding land values, the productive value of railway and other franchises, and the other forms of wealth that arise out of conditions which society itself creates—will all accrue to the State for the benefit of the whole people. But thus far, while individual men have toiled at good wages for what their individual efforts could directly produce, the large bulk of the social wealth which they were unconsciously creating by the very fact of their living and working in communities has gone to make up the fortunes of the rich.

And Therefore Society Has Claims

This social wealth—accruing from the control of mines, of lands, of patented monopolies, of railway and local franchises, and so on—is the wealth which, if it could have been diverted into the treasury of the state or the municipality, would have provided our young nation with the libraries, the hospitals, the provisions for the aged and helpless, the kindergartens, the practical training schools, the universities, the parks and gardens, the art galleries, the public baths, the statues and fountains, the music halls and endowed places of refined and instructive entertainment, and the various other common possessions, accessible to poor and rich alike, which ought to exist throughout the entire land to minister to the progress of the nation.

It should not be as a work of charity or supererogation arising from good will, but rather from the sense of obligation, that these public institutions should be provided out of the surplus accumulation of our millionaires. As we have already said, it is the wealth created by the whole people, and not by themselves, which our conditions of production and industrial development have diverted into the coffers of the millionaires. It is, therefore, perfectly sound and demonstrable as an economic proposition that the people of the United States have a right to look to these millions for the provision of the class of institutions we have specified.

The Public Debts of Private Riches

The socialists demand that our modes of taxation shall be so radically changed that the State shall turn the stream of social wealth directly into its own coffers, without the intervention of the millionaire at all. Certain tax reformers, on the other hand, would not interfere with the operations of the millionaire, whom they regard as highly beneficial in his ability to seize and utilize wealth-yielding opportunities which might otherwise lie undeveloped. They would allow the bee to gather the honey, and subsequently they would lay hands upon a considerable part of the accumulated sweetness for the general benefit.

But whatever may come in the future from the demands of the socialist or the arguments of the progressive inheritance-tax reformer, it would be well if every millionaire should of his own accord begin to make use of his wealth as a fund which he is under heavy moral obligation to draw upon for the welfare of his fellow-men in general, and for the welfare in particular of those in his own community whose efforts have furnished the groundwork upon which his fortune was built up.

The Case of Mr. Yerkes

Thus Mr. Yerkes, in Chicago, has just recognized this principle by giving half a million dollars to the Chicago University for an observatory with the largest telescope in the world. Mr. Yerkes has made a great fortune by the operation of street railways in Chicago. He paid little or nothing for franchises which are worth many millions. If the municipality of Chicago had chosen to own and conduct its own street railway system, the wealth which these franchises earn would have accrued to the public treasury, and would have been available for educational and other social objects. Since these great values, created by the people themselves, have for the most part been absorbed into great private fortunes, it is only right that a community like Chicago should look to the holders of such fortunes for the public institutions without which, though seemingly rich, it would really be a poor and mean and unworthy community.

A Catalogue of Converted Millionaires

It would be highly interesting if the *Tribune* catalogue of millionaires could be checked off from beginning to end, in order to separate those who have shown some considerable measure of recognition of their obligation to use their wealth for the social well-being from those unfortunate and unpatriotic men who hold to the doctrine that what they have is theirs, to use as selfishly and narrowly as if they had no neighbors. The *Tribune's* lists have been compiled with very great pains; and while they cannot, in the nature of the case, be free from errors, including, doubtless, some fortunes which are not worth as much as one million dollars and omitting others which would be justly entitled to a place, they are sufficiently correct and representative for all practical purposes.

Jay Gould as One Type

It would be a difficult task that would confront a supposititious "Mission for the Conversion of Millionaires to a Sense of their Social Obligations," if it should attempt a reclassification of this catalogue with a view to dividing the redeemed from the unregenerate. Yet, in a tentative way, such a classification might be accomplished. Mr. Stead, in his character sketch, while not disposed to sit as a judge upon Mr. Gould's motives, has clearly chosen to use Mr. Gould as a type of the millionaires who do not recognize their obligation to use their wealth for the good of the community which created that wealth. If Mr. Gould's opportunities to gather for himself scores of millions—through the telegraph monopoly of North America, through the elevated railway monopoly of New York and through several great railway systems which were in a position to exact tribute from Western producers—were of the most extraordinary magnitude, so were also his opportunities to use his wealth for the benefit of the people of New York City, of St. Louis, of Texas and of the nation at large no less magnificent. And these opportunities entailed obligations, but apparently he did not recognize them.

Cooper, Peabody and Pratt as Other Types

On the other hand, we have in this country men who for years have recognized this obligation fully and have acted upon it systematically, with results so useful that no words can do them justice. The value of Peter Cooper's ministrations to the people of New York can never be fully appreciated, because there is no measuring rule that can be applied to meet the case. Long before his death the various agencies—the night schools, the art schools, the great reading room, the public meeting places and the other facilities for popular instruction—that are gathered under the roof of the Cooper Union, had repaid the cost a hundredfold. But now that the noble philanthropist has gone to his rest, his work lives on; and thousands of young people every year are the gainers for what one man saw fit to do with his wealth in the city where he had obtained it. In Brooklyn, the great Institute for popular instruction, founded and developed by the late Charles Pratt, will in like manner live on to testify to the wisdom and true sense of social obligation of the lamented citizen whose name it bears. The history of our earlier philanthropy is enriched by the name of Peabody, whose great library in Baltimore, with its accompaniment of endowed lecture courses, music schools and art classes, is an essential part of the life of that city; while his fund for the aid of education in the South and his fund for the building of tenement houses in London are accomplishing good results, the volume of which is increased from year to year.

Mr. Carnegie and His Gospel

Among the men of colossal fortune who are now practical exponents of the doctrine that great wealth imposes imperative obligations, no man has taken a more pronounced position than Mr. Andrew Carnegie. There has been an attempt in some quarters to disparage Mr. Carnegie's benefactions because the manufacturing establishments of which he is the largest owner have had serious disagreements with the labor unions. But the two matters have no necessary connection. The organization of industry and the adjustment of disputes between capital and labor present distinct problems, which cannot be discussed to good advantage in connection with the question of a millionaire's responsibility for the use of his realized wealth. Mr. Carnegie recognizes that responsibility in the fullest measure; and the methods he has chosen have been altogether admirable. His example cannot be too strongly commended. Public libraries, music halls, art galleries and similar institutions should be regarded as among the necessities rather than the luxuries of modern enlightened towns and cities, and it should be deemed the business of men of wealth to provide such institutions.

Mr. Rockefeller and Chicago University

No rich man's recognition of his opportunity to serve society in his own lifetime has ever produced results so mature and so extensive in so very short a time as Mr. John D. Rockefeller's recent gifts to the Chicago University. Upon the new seal adopted within a month or two by the institution are engraved the words "The University of Chicago, founded by John D. Rockefeller." It was certainly not longer ago than 1886 when it was announced that Mr. Rockefeller would give $600,000 towards the resuscitation of the defunct Chicago University, if others, under the auspices of the Baptist Educational Society of the United States, would bring the sum up to a million. The task was undertaken and the million was in due time secured, chiefly through the gifts of citizens of Chicago.

By this time Mr. Rockefeller's ideas about the University had considerably expanded, as had those of the people of Chicago. Prof. William R. Harper was not the man to assume charge of an institution that should begin with small things and feel its way to larger ones. He had seen the Johns Hopkins University created and placed in fully as high a rank as Harvard and Yale in a shorter time than has usually been thought necessary for the development of an ordinary business enterprise. Moreover, he had witnessed the seeming audacity of the proposal of Mr. Leland Stanford to create a vast university in California in the same business-like fashion that Mr. Stanford had created the great stock farm, where his fast horses are bred. There was contagion in President Harper's large views, and there was a good staying quality in Mr. Rockefeller's sense of social obligation. Possibly he had in mind the fact that his Standard Oil interests had gone steadily on increasing his wealth, and that the gaps made by his benevolences from time to time were quickly filled up by those accretions which every great fortune in active use almost inevitably gathers. In September, 1890, Mr. Rockefeller gave another million in cash; in February, 1892, he gave still another million, and his recent Christmas present to the University was yet another million in gold bonds.

The Infection of Liberality

Such giving has had an infectious quality, so that around Mr. Rockefeller's original offer of six hundred thousand dollars, there has accumulated like magic a total of seven millions, and there is now in full operation, with a body of more than one hundred professors and instructors gathered from all parts of America and Europe, a university doing work of the highest character and instructing six hundred students. Mr. Marshall Field gave the University grounds, worth a quarter of a million dollars, and joined with other Chicago citizens in giving a million dollars in cash for the new buildings. About a half million dollars has been given by the estate of William B. Ogden for the School of Science, the Reynolds estate has given a quarter of a million, Mr. C. T. Yerkes has, within a few months, given half a million for the telescope and observatory, and President Harper announces that the funds will soon reach ten million dollars, which he declares to be only the beginning of what the University will need and will expect.

The creation of this institution has a deep significance. It is to be made the centre for university extension work which shall to the largest possible extent distribute some degree of acquaintance with the higher education among as many as possible of the people of Chicago and vicinity. At the same time, it will minister to the most advanced learning and scientific research. And all this magnificent plant for the popular diffusion of learning and for the making of individual scholars and thinkers, has been evolved in an incredibly short space, through a slight levy upon the surplus millions of men who are no more conscious of the lack of the money they have given than they are conscious of being poorer when they pay a five-cent car fare. The Chicago University will have done more, perchance, to educate millionaires to an appreciation of what they might easily do for their communities than it will ever have accomplished in any other way. The gentlemen who have contributed the seven million dollars now in hand have merely made a beginning. They will go on from year to year to add to the equipment of this institution, and to provide other means for the public instruction and benefit which their increasing power of discernment will show them to be sadly needed. Mr. Rockefeller certainly can be relied upon, in his own ways, to continue thus to administer upon his own wealth in his lifetime.

Philip Armour's Gift to Chicago

Chicago has been announced also as the recipient of another princely benefaction from a millionaire still in the vigor of business life. Some years ago one of the Armour Brothers left at his death one hundred thousand dollars to be used for erecting a building for mission purposes to benefit the poor children of Chicago. It devolved upon Mr. Philip D. Armour to carry out the idea, and it has grown upon his hands into an institution of diversified purposes adapted precisely to the needs of the young people of the poorer and working classes. The Armour Institute is not simply a mission Sunday school, although a huge Sunday school is connected with it. There has been developed the plan of a series of trade schools; and the Armour Institute will do for Chicago a work similar to that so nobly done by the Polytechnic in London—a work like that of the Pratt Institute in Brooklyn, the Cooper Union in New York, and Mr. Drexel's magnificent new institution in Philadelphia, only that it will be still broader and more diversified, and will rest upon a basis distinctly religious, although undenominational. It is said that the carrying out of the full idea, including the new building for the manual training and practical classes, just completed, will have involved an expenditure by Mr. Armour of about three millions of dollars, including the large amount of productive property surrounding the institution which Mr. Armour has wisely given for purposes of perpetual endowment.

With the new University, the Armour Institute and the two magnificent libraries—the Newbury and the Crerar—which private beneficence has endowed, Chicago millionaires will have some good examples before their eyes. So much of the nation's wealth has been diverted into the coffers of rich men whose prosperity is identified with the development of Chicago, that the city ought within the coming decade or two to be the recipient of scores of splendid establishments for the public use and behoof, freely given and well endowed by millionaires.

Giving in Life Versus Giving at Death

We have had numerous enough warnings, in the breaking of wills and the disregard of accurate instructions left behind them by dying millionaires, to make it clear that, whenever their circumstances will permit, these gentlemen of wealth should themselves give practical effect to their benefactions while in the enjoyment of health and strength. A more lamentable miscarriage of justice, and a more pedantic perversion of law to work wrong, has seldom occurred than the defeat of Mr. Tilden's intention to give New York a great free library endowed with all his millions. Mr. Tilden fully recognized the obligations of wealth, and proposed most completely and nobly to meet those obligations; but he chose to have his trusted friends carry out his plans of beneficence after his death. Rather than be parties to so deep an offense as to prevent this money from reaching the ends it was designed to serve, the judges who were responsible for its diversion should have resigned their seats in order to make room for men whose legal consciences would have permitted them to render simple justice.

It does not follow when a man of wealth holds on to his millions through his lifetime and gives them to public uses after he can himself use them no longer, that his social obligations are less fully recognized by him than if he had built hospitals or colleges while alive. But he misses much of the satisfaction he might have found in life if he leaves his beneficences to be carried out by executors.

Thus Mr. Erioch Pratt, of Baltimore, who has built and endowed a great free library, has found infinite pleasure and satisfaction in giving his thought and energy to the working out of that noble enterprise. The late Johns Hopkins, on the other hand, bore the reputation of a man of limited benevolence and comparatively small public spirit during his lifetime, leaving his whole fortune of some seven millions of dollars for the creation of the famous university and the magnificent hospital which will make his name immortal. But after all Mr. Hopkins was no miser who at the close of life as a mere whim devised his wealth to public objects because it must of necessity go somewhere. He had deliberately, through long years, accumulated money with the intention that it should be used for the advance of learning and the relief of suffering. It was his judgment that his personal function was to accumulate the property rather than to attend to the details of its use for these public ends, and that it could be used to better effect after his death than before.

Classifying the Givers and Non-Givers

To revert once more to the idea of a checking off from the *Tribune's* lists of those millionaires who recognize wealth's responsibilities and account themselves as in some sense stewards to administer what is not their own for selfish uses—some such classification is practically made from time to time in almost every one of our large communities. The promoters of local charities thus classify their wealthy neighbors. The anxious managers of struggling colleges, and the leaders in movements designed to supply to any given city the public establishments which testify to Christian humanity or liberal culture or æsthetic development—all such workers make their lists, classifying their neighbors, and separating the givers from the non-givers.

Of course, many of the most truly liberal benefactors of their respective communities are not to be found in the *Tribune's* list, for the simple reason that their fortunes may be adjudged less than one million dollars. It need hardly be said that the half-millionaires are many times as numerous as the whole millionaires. But, making allowances for the fact that the larger part of the volume of benefaction that flows from rich men's purses comes from those whose wealth lies somewhere between one hundred thousand and one million dollars, it is none the less true that some very interesting conclusions might be drawn from even a casual checking off of the *Tribune's* millionaire list if the checking were done for each community by persons well informed as to the principal public benefactions and the general reputation for liberality of their wealthiest neighbors.

How the Cleveland List Checks Up

As a matter of experiment—not for statistical purposes but in order to gather up certain impressions—such a checking off has been attempted for a selected list of cities within the past month, for the use of this magazine. Let us, for example, turn to the list for the city of Cleveland. Sixty-eight fortunes are listed by the *Tribune's* compilers as making up the total of Cleveland's millionaires. The lists are returned to us checked in such fashion as to show that the persons who passed upon them considered twenty-eight of the sixty-eight fortunes as in the hands of owners who were, to a moderate extent atleast, mindful of their public opportunities and duties.

It is interesting to observe how many of these have rallied about Cleveland's principal educational institution, the Western Reserve University, which includes Adelbert College, the Case Scientific School and other departments. Mr. Leonard Case was a representative Cleveland philanthropist, whose name is perpetuated by the Case Library and the Case School of Applied Science. Mr. James F. Clark gave one hundred thousand dollars to the Woman's College of the Western Reserve University. Mr. W. J. Gordon will also be remembered as the giver to his city of the Gordon Park, valued at one million dollars. Mrs. Samuel Mather and her late husband have been large givers to local institutions. Mr. John L. Wood has within a few weeks given one-quarter of a million dollars for the medical college of the Western Reserve University, this bringing his total offerings to that institution up to some four hundred thousand dollars. Doubtless Cleveland's millionaires have done very meagre things for their city compared with what they might easily have done if fully alive to their obligations. But it is evident from a glance at the notes on the margin of the lists returned from Cleveland that very much which ministers to the best welfare of the people of the city would be blotted out if the gifts made by people of wealth were to be annihilated.

Cincinnati's Benefactors

The Cincinnati list enumerates some seventy fortunes worth one million dollars, and is returned with twenty-one checked as belonging to comparatively liberal givers for beneficent public purposes. It is well worth while to note in connection with Cincinnati the extent to which a few generous and broad-minded men of wealth may affect, by the character of their benefactions, the nature of the social and educational development of their community and the distinctiveness of its reputation. Thus Cincinnati has come to be famous as a musical and an art centre, and its advancement in these directions is largely due to the gifts that its public-spirited citizens have made. Mr. Charles West, of Cincinnati, during his lifetime gave three hundred thousand dollars to found the Art Museum, and this has been largely supplemented by the well-known Longworth family and their descendants.

The largest gifts ever made to the city, perhaps, were those of Reuben Springer, who gave Cincinnati its famous Music Hall, its College of Music, and the allied enterprises, which include schools of practical art. The Cincinnati Exposition, opened two decades ago, and continuing from year to year, was a most fruitful factor in the industrial and artistic development of the city, and was an enterprise closely allied with the development of the College of Music, the Art Museum and other beneficent institutions. The Cincinnati University was the gift of Mr. McMicken, who left it nearly a million dollars. Henry Probasco's gift of the magnificent "Tyler Davidson Fountain" gave a distinct impulse to public spirit among the rich men of Cincinnati. To Mr. Andrew Erkenbreckter, another generous millionaire, is due Cincinnati's famous Zoological Garden. Mr. Groesbeck has given a large endowment to secure free music of a high order in the Burnett Woods Park. Mr. Emory has built and endowed a hospital for children. And so the specifications might be continued.

Public Spirit in St. Louis

St. Louis is credited in the *Tribune's* list with some forty-five millionaires, and only ten of these are checked off by our correspondent as men of pronounced and well-known liberality. But St. Louis, nevertheless, owes much to the gifts of its men of wealth. The most conspicuous philanthropist of St. Louis was the late Henry Shaw, who twenty years before his death gave to the city the beautiful Tower Grove Park, which he himself laid out and cared for. He founded the world-famed "Shaw's Garden"—undoubtedly the finest botanical garden in America—which, upon his death at the age of eighty-six, two years ago, he left to the city together with his fortune of two or three million dollars for its maintenance. He founded a chair of botany in the Washington University at St. Louis, the incumbent of which is the superintendent of the garden. Nowhere else in the world is there such a university foundation for work in the field of botanical study. The beneficence of St. Louis has rallied largely about the Washington University, and Mr. George E. Leighton, President of the Board of Trustees, has done noble work in his efforts, personal and financial, for that institution.

Detroit's Good Millionaires

Detroit is credited with forty-two millionaires, of whom at least a dozen are counted by our Detroit informant as men who are making public-spirited use of their wealth. At the head of the Detroit list is General R. A. Alger, who is reported as having just now completed his annual distribution of gifts to city institutions and hospitals and other worthy objects of charity. It is said that ever since his business has been at all profitable he has annually devoted at least 20 percent of his entire income to worthy benefactions. Mr. D. M. Ferry is accounted a very large and generous giver, and his name is ranked with that of General Alger among the benevolent millionaires of Detroit. Senator James McMillan is also credited with having made several large endowments to educational and charitable institutions within the past few years. Mrs. Thomas W. Palmer, whose husband is President of the World's Fair Commission, is a Detroit lady of large benefactions, and her husband has recently given very valuable property to the city for park purposes, and is said to be about to build and endow, at a cost of at least half a million dollars, an Industrial Home for Women.

Late in January, Mr. Hiram Walker's gift of $125,000 to the Children's Free Hospital of Detroit is announced, and Colonel Hecker, another millionaire, makes a liberal gift to the Harper Hospital.

Among Detroit men worth less than a million, though very rich, was ex-Senator Baldwin, of Detroit, who died a few years ago and whose practice it had been to give away large sums in charity each year. Another Detroit man who gives with an unstinted hand is Mr. James E. Scripps, the well-known owner of newspapers, who is proprietor of the Detroit *Tribune* and the Detroit *Evening News*, and of afternoon newspapers in Cincinnati, Cleveland and St. Louis. He has just completed Trinity Reformed Episcopal Church in Detroit entirely at his own expense, and it cost him not less than one hundred thousand dollars. He gave seventy-five thousand dollars towards the establishment of the Detroit Museum of Art, and it is known that he has in hand other public benefactions in the nature of parks and various institutions. Detroit evidently has benefited very materially from the gifts of her millionaire citizens, and probably even more from her rich citizens who rank below the million line.

St. Paul at Least Has James J. Hill

"Our millionaire record," says the fully competent correspondent who checked off the St. Paul list, "is not good. Those I have checked and have not specially noted are simply less stingy than the rest." The *Tribune* list credits St. Paul with twenty-eight millionaires, and our correspondent checks nine names as distinctly better than the remaining nineteen. It is only fair to say as regards the young cities of the West that their rich men are so deeply involved in enterprises upon which they have not as yet fully "realized," that their largest benefactions must necessarily be somewhat deferred. St. Paul, however, has several millionaires of long standing whose lack of public spirit is a deplorable misfortune for the community in which they live.

Mr. James J. Hill, President of the Great Northern Railway, is probably the richest man in the Northwest. His means have, however, been largely absorbed in the development of his vast undertakings. Nevertheless, he has managed to make his liberal disposition fully manifest, his largest gift being approximately one million dollars for a Catholic Theological Seminary now in process of erection under the eye and auspices of his warm friend, Archbishop Ireland. Mr. Hill has also been a liberal giver to Protestant institutions, and he has shown his good will towards the neighboring city of Minneapolis by placing in its public library a number of very valuable paintings by modern European masters, at a cost of perhaps fifty thousand dollars. Such a graceful act has value, as an example to other rich men, far beyond the amount of money actually involved. Mr. Hill is a man from whom the "Twin Cities" and the Northwest may yet expect much well placed benefaction.

How Minneapolis Men Pull Together

Minneapolis carries in the *Tribune's* directory the names of forty-four men who are credited with having accumulated more than a million dollars. Our Minneapolis correspondent checks off fourteen names. In Minneapolis there has been a marked disposition on the part of men of wealth to contribute from their private pockets to the promotion of official or semi-official institutions for the welfare of the community. Thus the State University has, among the group of buildings erected with the tax-payers' money, its handsome Pillsbury Science Hall, which is the gift of ex-Governor John S. Pillsbury, and which cost one hundred and fifty thousand dollars. The State University has been the recipient of some other gifts, and has reason to expect that the rich men of Minneapolis will, in the future, do still more for it. The Pillsbury family have shown a strong benevolent impulse, Mr. George A. Pillsbury having contributed to the Pillsbury Academy at Owatonna (Minn.) gifts aggregating perhaps one hundred and fifty thousand dollars, besides his gift of a soldiers' monument to South Sutton, New Hampshire, the Free Library he built and endowed at his old home, Warren, New Hampshire, and the Margaret Pillsbury Hospital at Concord, New Hampshire. Mr. Charles A. Pillsbury is a general and constant contributor to various deserving objects, his large-mindedness being well shown by the profit-sharing plan which he pursues in his great milling enterprises.

The Minneapolis Public Library building, which represents an investment of about half a million dollars, well illustrates the good Minneapolis practice of joining public and private contributions. Thus the Library building has been paid for in about equal parts by local taxation and by the large gifts of men of wealth, conspicuous among whom are Mr. T. B. Walker, Mr. Thomas Lowry and Mr. Samuel C. Gale. The Harrison family of Minneapolis have been large givers, and Hamline University, the Methodist college of the vicinity, has received from them probably more than two hundred thousand dollars. The late Richard Martin left half a million dollars to the Sheltering Arms Hospital and some other benevolent institutions. Mr. L. F. Manage, some two years ago, sent, at his own expense, an elaborately equipped exploring expedition to the Philippine Islands. The late C. C. Washburn, who built the astronomical observatory at Madison, Wisconsin, during his lifetime, and made many other public gifts of large amount in that State, left some four hundred thousand dollars for the Washburn Memorial Home for Orphan Children in Minneapolis. Generally speaking, the Minneapolis men of wealth nearly all expect, sooner or later, to even their accounts with their fellow-men by some generous public gift.

California's Millionaire Philanthropists

California not only has a long list of men whose wealth is counted by millions, but its rich men are, in an unusually high proportion, the multi-millionaires. Most of them are accredited to San Francisco; although their possessions are scattered lavishly up and down the Pacific Coast, and many of them live as much in New York or Europe as in California. In view of the ease with which most of their fortunes were made by the appropriation of the gifts and wealth of nature, and in further view of the necessity of public institutions in that new region which has attracted population so rapidly, the California millionaires have not been reasonably mindful of their clear obligations. Some notable exceptions, however, are to be recorded.

The name of James Lick is known and honored wherever Knowledge and Charity are valued. He gave away his entire great fortune upon works of public benefit for his fellow Californians. His gifts included, besides various smaller ones, the world-famed Lick Observatory with its mammoth telescope on Mount Hamilton, and its great endowments; the Lick Public Baths of San Francisco, and the Academy of Science building, which forms the centre for the cultivation of scientific tastes in that city.

In Mr. Adolph Sutro, also, San Francisco possesses a millionaire of the type for whose multiplication the whole country might well make prayer and supplication. Mr. Sutro, among other things, built the famous Sutro Heights, a public garden containing statuary and many artistic adornments, besides a fine building which houses an art gallery and a marine museum. His philanthropy is systematic and thorough-going.

The Leland Stanford, Jr., University

The largest and now the most widely-famed of California millionaires' gifts to the public is the Leland Stanford, Jr., University, which a few short years ago was a mere conception, but which to-day is a working reality. The value of Senator Stanford's gifts and endowments for this University is variously estimated at from ten millions to twenty millions of dollars. The power of wealth has perhaps never been so vividly illustrated in all the history of mankind as in this magical creation of a great university on the broad California fruit-ranch. The wise men declared that the thing could not be done. Some were sure that money could never make a true University at that distance from Oxford and Harvard, short of a hundred years for the development of the country. Leland Stanford, the plain and unpretentious man of affairs, thought otherwise. He has created an institution which will minister in countless ways to the civilization of the Pacific Coast. Far from injuring the University of California by its nearness and its superior wealth, the Stanford University will be of the greatest benefit to its neighbor—stimulating, as it is sure to do, a more generous public and private support for the older institution at Berkeley, and joining with it to give a greater prominence to California as a new world's centre for the higher education.

Gifts to San Francisco and the State University

Among the benefactors of California should be mentioned Dr. Coggswell, who has given San Francisco a school for polytechnic teaching at a cost for building and endowments of perhaps a million dollars, the whole of which he has deeded in trust to the City of San Francisco. Dr. Coggswell has also erected public drinking fountains in San Francisco and in other large cities.

The State University at Berkeley has been so fortunate as to have received a number of important gifts from San Francisco millionaires, among them Mr. Michel Reese, who gave $30,000 to the University Library, and has given much other money to public charities and institutions. Mr. D. O. Mills, a well-known Californian, gave $75,000 to found a Chair of Philosophy in the University, and has spent several hundred thousands of dollars in founding an art gallery in the City of Sacramento, the capital of the State.

One of the most important recent gifts is that of Mr. Edwin F. Searles of one million dollars to the San Francisco Art Association for a new building, which, while serving the æsthetic interests of the metropolis, will also be an adjunct to the State University in the neighboring town of Berkeley. The location of several departments of the State University in San Francisco may in the course of time have the result of placing the larger half of the institution there rather than at Berkeley. Thus Mr. S. C. Hastings has given $100,000 to found the Hastings College of Law in San Francisco, as an adjunct department to the State University. Mrs. Phœbe Hurst has recently made large provisions in the form of scholarships for women in the State University; and, in short, the disposition to maintain that prominent institution at a high point of efficiency has never manifested itself so strongly as since Mr. Stanford made his endowment at Palo Alto.

Other California Benefactions

The City of Oakland, San Francisco's great residence suburb, owes much to the benefactions of Mr. Anthony Chabot, who has given it the Chabot Observatory at the cost of a quarter of a million, the Fabiola Hospital, some free kindergartens and a Home for Incurables, all of which he has freely endowed, and who has also given generously to many religious and philanthropic causes. Mr. Henry D. Bacon and Mr. A. K. P. Harmon are San Francisco men who have made large gifts to the State University. Dr. R. H. McDonald has given large sums for the promotion of temperance and various religious interests. Capt. Chas. Goodall has made extensive endowments of minor California educational institutions. Mr. Samuel Merritt has not only given about half a million dollars to an Eastern college, but has bestowed a similar sum upon the Samuel Merritt Hospital in Oakland. Miss Virginia Fair has endowed hospitals and Catholic institutions. The late Michael J. Kelley gave large bequests also to the Catholic Church and to orphan asylums both Protestant and Catholic. There are doubtless other large and generous gifts which might readily be added to those here specifically mentioned.

Thus if the institutions which the gifts of Californian millionaires have created for the benefit of the people of California were to be eliminated, there would disappear a great aggregation of admirable public establishments, beginning with the notable free kindergartens so generously maintained by the rich women of San Francisco, and including manual training schools, art schools and galleries, scientific museums, hospitals and orphanages, and practically all the college and university facilities that exist in the State. Where so much has been accomplished so easily, what might not California possess and become if all her millionaires should show the diposition of a Lick, a Sutro or a Stanford?

What Baltimore's Rich Men Have Done

To return from the Pacific to the Atlantic Coast, we find about fifty-five large Baltimore fortunes listed as equal to a million or more. The Baltimore millionaires, generally speaking, are not multi-million-aires, and their wealth has been accumulated slowly by old-fashioned business care and sagacity. The large endowments at Baltimore of a Peabody, a Johns Hopkins and an Enoch Pratt, have already been mentioned. The Baltimore list is returned from competent advisers in that city with just one-half of the names checked off as belonging to men of a recognized disposition to be generous, whether they have actually made very large gifts or not. The most noteworthy of recent benefactions at Baltimore is Miss Mary E. Garrett's check for $850,000 to the trustees of the Johns Hopkins University, to complete the sum which was stipulated as necessary to open the Medical College of the University to women. The Garrett family have made other public gifts in the line of hospitals, public monuments and education.

One of the most beautiful public gifts ever made to Baltimore came from Mr. W. T. Walters, the famous art collector, who gave the Barye bronzes in Mount Vernon place, and whose magnificent collection of paintings—the finest private collection in America, it is commonly said—may not improbably be made over by him, either in his lifetime or at his death, to the city of which he is a foremost citizen.

It is not, in the long run, the money value of a public gift which precisely measures its usefulness. The spirit, purpose, and timeliness of a gift count for much. Thus the Baltimore merchants, who came to the relief of the Johns Hopkins University to tide it over the period when the Baltimore and Ohio railway's financial troubles out off the University's income, rendered to the cause of the higher education in America a service which, at some other time, ten or twenty times the amount they paid could not have equaled in value. A few men of the spirit of Mr. Eugene Levering, of Baltimore, would suffice to save the credit of the rich contingent in any community.

The Practical Side of "Brotherly Love"

The City of Brotherly Love has much wealth, more of which is in family estates which have been steadily accumulating for a long time than in the form of very recent acquisitions, made by speculation or the rapid expansion of values. Philadelphia's quiet, unostentatious character is reflected in the forms of its philanthropy. A strong and steady stream of systematic benevolence for public causes in all parts of the world has always flown from the pockets of the rich people of the Quaker City. The large gifts for the relief of the famine-stricken Russians last year which emanated from Philadelphia were characteristic of the place, while it was equally characteristic that Philadelphia should have desired to send along with these gifts a protest to the Czar against the persecution of the Jews. Philadelphia is the home of the Indian Rights Association, and Mr. Herbert Welsh, possessing a large inherited fortune, gives his whole time and much of his money to the cause of the red man on the frontier. Great sums have also gone out of Philadelphia for the education of the colored race in the South. It was Philadelphia money that equipped the recent Peary Arctic Expedition.

Thus Philadelphia's bounty loves to search out the dark and hidden places of the earth, and the more remote these places are, the stronger is their hold upon the sympathy of the professional and traditional philanthrophy of William Penn's descendants and successors. But next to Indians, Africans, Esquimaux and starving Russian Jews beyond the Volga, Philadelphians love their own city and they do not altogether neglect it. The best and wisest of the Philadelphia philanthropies is the noble Drexel Institute, which will afford a centre of instruction for the sons and daughters of the plain people of Philadelphia. Other Philadelphians besides Mr. Drexel have given much for local educational purposes, and the various departments of the University of Pennsylvania have a long list of benefactors on their roll of honor. Mr. Charles C. Harrison, Chairman of the Ways and Means Committee of the University, is particularly to be commended for his gifts of money and of effort. Mr. Wharton, founder of the Wharton School of Finance and Economics of the University, should not be overlooked. Mr. Lenning's three-quarters of a million for the scientific department of the University was a notable gift. Mr. Henry C. Lea is another representative Philadelphian who has given largely for local library and University purposes. The late George Pepper left more than a million dollars to libraries, schools and charities, as also did the late Calvin Pardee. Mr. John B. Stetson has founded the useful Stetson Institute; another rich man has built the Wagner Institute. Mr. I. Z. Williamson founded the Williamson Free School of Mechanical Trades and numerous rich Philadelphians have built up and are generously adding to the endowment of such local institutions as the Academy of Fine Arts, the Academy of Natural Sciences, the Philadelphia Library, the Apprentices' Library and the Franklin Institute. The Ridgeway branch of the Philadelphia Library has an estate of about one million dollars, the bequest of the late John Rush.

As Baltimore has, in the Abell family, its millionaire newspaper proprietors of generous proclivities, so Philadelphia has in its best-known citizen, Mr. George W. Childs, a wealthy philanthropist who is honored everywhere, and in William M. Singerly, another newspaper millionaire of pronounced public spirit. It must suffice merely to mention Mrs. Matthew Baird's gifts to the Academy of Fine Arts, Colonel Bennett's to the Women's College of the University and to the Methodist Hospital, Mr. George Burnham's large gifts for religious objects, Mr. Bucknell's endowment of the institution which bears his name, Mr. Coxe's gifts to Lehigh and to various schools and churches, Mr. Clothier's to Swarthmore College, and Mr. Wanamaker's to various local objects. When these names are mentioned, there remain others probably as well entitled to a place in the roll of honor for philanthropy and public spirit.

Has Boston Not One Great Public Benefactor?

Our Boston correspondent is not complimentary to the rich men who breathe the atmosphere of that favored and superior locality. "This city," he declares, "will never sustain your thesis as to the generally liberal disposition of American millionaires of the present day. Our Boston millionaires give money when it is solicited (properly), and they all include in their wills some bequests to Harvard and to the Massachusetts General Hospital. That is all. Of great public benefactions we have none in Boston. The only large public gift in this vicinity has been made by a millionaire citizen of Cambridge, Mr. Rindge, who gave that city a magnificent city hall, a public library complete, and an industrial school."

This correspondent does not fail, however, to mention with warmth the gratitude that is due to Mrs. Hemmenway for her almost countless charities and broad and wise benefactions for the encouragement of science and the promotion of diverse public enterprises. He commends Mr. H. L. Higginson for having instituted the Boston Symphony Orchestra, but adds that the orchestra is now a very lucrative investment rather than a public benefaction. There was once a generous man named Lowell in Boston who endowed the Lowell Institute with a great scheme of free courses and lectures. His good work still lives on. Mrs. Quiney A. Shaw has founded and maintains a number of free kindergartens, and Mr. Daniel S. Forbes, who publishes the *Youth's Companion*, is very generous to Baptist churches and causes. Our correspondent mentions as a typical case a Bostonian who "occasionally gives his distinguished ancestor's autograph to the Massachusetts Historical Society."

Elsewhere in Massachusetts

Massachusetts is charged with a long list of millionaires in the *Tribune's* catalogue—some three hundred in all—and considerably more than two hundred of them are in the Boston list. It is to be regretted that they cannot give a better account of themselves. The rich men of the smaller Massachusetts cities would doubtless make a more commendable showing for philanthropy. Thus the newspapers of January 19, reporting the death of Mr. Horace Smith, of Springfield, add that his entire great fortune has been left to a class of charitable and philanthropic objects which he fostered in his lifetime. Mr. Jonas G. Clark, of Worcester, several years ago founded, and now maintains unaided, the Clark University; and other Worcester millionaires have made creditable gifts. However badly the millionaire list of

Massachusetts may seem to check off, it is not to be forgotten that among people of smaller means there is in New England a constant, systematic appropriation of money out of current income for educational, religious and benevolent causes, at home and abroad, such as no other part of the world can equal.

Gotham's Eleven Hundred Millionaires

The State of New York, exclusive of New York City, is credited with 405 millionaires, of whom about one hundred and seventy-five are assigned to the Brooklyn list. The New York City list is compiled separately and contains 1103 names. Manifestly it would not be an easy task, nor indeed would it be either encouraging or advantageous, to attempt a sifting of the liberal from the selfish millionaires of Gotham. A few names stand out in brilliant contrast with the great majority by reason of unfailing philanthropy.

Of the largest New York fortunes it can only be hoped that ultimately they may fall into the hands of men who will have both the purpose and the intelligence to use them as levers for the development and the progress of the country, and particularly of New York City. For of all the great world-centres of our age, New York City is at once the richest as regards private purses and the meanest and poorest in its educational and æsthetic facilities and its possession of notable and serviceable institutions for the popular benefit. There are in New York colossal estates, accumulated by the simple process of sitting still and permitting the toilers of the metropolis to enhance the value of real property. Obviously, of all the great fortunes of America, these are the ones which morally owe most to the promotion of public causes. The Vanderbilt fortunes have in different directions exercised a large and intelligent beneficence, and there is reason for the hope that they will, with more and more system and purpose, be devoted to the service of the metropolis and the country. Mr. George Vanderbilt, than whom perhaps no man could be less desirous to pose as a philanthropist, is in quiet ways exercising extensive and wise beneficences.

Mr. Cornelius Vanderbilt's great gift to Yale has been announced within the past month. Vanderbilt University in Tennessee has been largely endowed by the family.

The rapid development of the Metropolitan Museum of Art to the point where it is really a magnificent and instructive collection of art objects shows how easily the rich men and women of New York can provide an institution for the instruction and delight of the people when once the disposition is aroused. The Natural History Museum is another such object lesson. The beneficence which has recently given enlargement to Colonel Auchmuty's Trade Schools ought to incite fifty rich men to found as many educational institutions of a similar kind for the boys and girls of the metropolis. If only the millionaires of New York would give back to their city and country a small fraction of the wealth which the city and the country have poured into their inflated coffers, many of the darkest problems that now confront and alarm thoughtful and observing men and women would already be half solved.

When, at the day of judgment, these multi-millionaires of Gotham stand up to be questioned as to what use their lives ever were to their fellow-men, it is just possible that some cross-questioning archangel may remark to each one in turn: "There were more than ten thousand liquor saloons in New York City in the days when you lived there, and there were many hundreds of still more harmful places of resort. Why did you not see to it that there were at least as many free kindergartens as drinking saloons in your city?" There ought, within the next five years, to be established in New York not a few dozen more kindergartens, but ten thousand of them—free as the air to every child whose parents can be induced to send it. And these kindergartens ought not to be established by the taxation of the people, but out of the surplus holdings of New York's thousand millionaires. They possess an aggregate of perhaps ten thousand millions of dollars. This sum has been taken from the social wealth produced by the united efforts of the mechanics, the farmers, the laborers and the toilers of every calling in all parts of the country, of which New York is the commercial metropolis. And when the ten thousand free kindergartens are established and fully endowed, there will be thousands of other institutions and objects of public benefit, which the millionaires of New York ought to find it their pleasure and privilege, as well as their duty, to provide.

RETHINKING BOUNDARIES: THE HISTORY OF WOMEN, PHILANTHROPY, AND HIGHER EDUCATION

ANDREA WALTON

By virtue of the lens they adopt, historians illuminate different aspects of the university's relationship to society and offer varied perspectives on the forces and actors that shape the university's character and borders. This study of Grace Hoadley Dodge (1856–1915), a founding trustee and treasurer of Teachers College, Columbia University and Elsie Clews Parsons (1874–1941), a patron-scholar of Columbia anthropology, uses the lens of philanthropy to provide new perspectives on the permeable nature of the university's boundaries. Blending institutional history and biography, the study examines the ways benefaction and service became avenues for women's meaningful participation in institution- and discipline-building at a paradigm-setting university.

By virtue of the lens they adopt, historians illuminate different aspects of the university's relationship to society and offer varied perspectives on the forces and actors that shape the university's character and borders. To illustrate, scholars of higher education have generally depicted the history of the university as a story bounded by the campus gates. Much historical writing in higher education has focused heavily on internal dynamics—organizational structure, presidential leadership, faculty careers, and student activities. By contrast, historians of philanthropy have emphasized the role of external factors in shaping the university. Philanthropic studies have documented and analyzed the influence of large national foundations and the sway of great institution-builders, the likes of donors John D. Rockefeller, Leland and Jane Stanford, and Ezra Cornell. Finally, historians of women's experience have depicted the university as an institution of power and privilege that has often excluded or marginalized women. Historians of women in education have explored the ways women challenged the boundaries of the male-dominated university by fighting for opportunities as students and scholars.[1]

This study contributes to the existing literature in three areas: the history of higher education, the history of philanthropy, and the history of women in education. It seeks to broaden our understanding of the university and its boundaries by studying the enduring and meaningful ties women were able to achieve and sustain to institutions of higher learning through philanthropy.

Understanding the ways philanthropy enabled women to cross certain boundaries—to participate in the life of the university and to transcend or enlarge upon certain expectations of "womanhood"—combines institutional history and biography.[2] The focus is an elite, eastern institution, Columbia University, and the motivations and achievements of two women who were affiliated with it during the pre–World War II years—Grace Hoadley Dodge (1856–1914) and Elsie Clews Parsons (1875–1941). The former was a founder and trustee of Columbia's graduate school of education, Teachers College; the latter was a scholar-patron who figured prominently in developing the study of anthropology at Columbia. These women were well known in their lifetimes, and a good deal has been written about them individually. But their careers have not been considered together as educators and philanthropists. Their juxtaposition in these roles provides insights into the motivations of women's educational philanthropy and deeper understanding of the permeability of the university's departmental and institutional boundaries.

As will be evident in the biographies of Grace Hoadley Dodge and Elsie Clews Parsons, philanthropy has more dimensions than the tally of gifts or the writing of cheques. Indeed, there is a personal element in philanthropy that warrants greater attention.[3] Philanthropy is a relationship of power or exchange; perhaps even a process of education, between giver and receiver. It is a relationship that holds meaning for both parties.[4] From the founding of this country, philanthropy and education have been deeply interwoven. Giving and serving have been a culturally acceptable way for women to contribute to civic and intellectual life by supporting educational enterprises. Moreover, education has often been the philanthropist's method of reform and uplift. For Dodge and Parsons, and indeed for many women, engaging in philanthropy itself was educative and liberating; it enabled them to invest personal meaning, including gender-specific concerns, into giving. Educational philanthropy was an avenue by which women might pursue and promote personal, intellectual, and social goals.[5]

The study of educational philanthropy, when refracted through the lens of individual lives intersecting with institutions, provides a valuable tool for examining the relationship among the history of philanthropy, the history of higher education, and the history of women in education. An understanding of how these three strands of history help situate the story of the university in the study of American culture is best captured by the work of Merle Curti. In fact, Curti's writing inspired this study of Dodge and Parsons and their ties to Columbia University.

In the late 1950s Curti hoped to open up scholarly research on philanthropy, which he identified as "one of the major aspects of and keys to understanding American social, cultural, and intellectual development."[6] Curti's interest in the cultural phenomenon of philanthropy dated back to his 1927 doctoral study of the American Peace Crusade.[7] But it was only later, in the post-World War II period of his career, that Curti's thinking about the patterns of giving in the U.S. crystallized. Indeed, he played a pivotal role in defining and stimulating the study of philanthropy as a field of historical research.[8] To Curti, the study of philanthropy was a way of seeing the familiar world of American history and culture, including education, in a fundamentally new light. In two path breaking articles, both appearing in the 1950s, Curti set forth an ambitious research agenda (a rationale for a large-scale history project at the University of Wisconsin) that sought to relate the scholarly study of philanthropy to diverse aspects of the nation's history—among them, religious traditions, "national character," taxation, social reform, voluntary associations, and the development of colleges and universities.[9]

Curti's history project at Wisconsin never addressed the entirety of his vast agenda, but the network of scholars linked with it produced a substantial body of well-grounded literature, including several studies related to education.[10] One volume in particular, *Philanthropy in the Shaping of American Higher Education* which Curti co-authored with his student Roderick Nash, remains a useful guide to anyone studying the field.[11] Now over thirty-five years old, the Curti-Nash study is dated by its abiding belief in educational progress and American exceptionalism, but the work merits reconsideration on at least three counts. First, it resonates with themes about the politics and influence of external support, and hence considers issues that are relevant today given higher education's increased reliance on philanthropic funding. Second, the Curti-Nash text offers a broad view of the scope and influence of philanthropy. Its analysis enlarges upon what might have been a narrowly-defined, straightforward account of endowments, fundraising, or "bricks and mortar" donations by probing the motivations of giving and offering insights into the impact, whether conservative or innovative, of philanthropy on different types of institutions, people, and ideas.[12] Third, and most important here, the text provides a lens for situating the study of philanthropy and the study of higher education within the study of American culture.

By documenting not only large financial gifts from men, but also smaller benefactions, like Lady Mowlson's endowment to Harvard or the funds raised for colleges by women's sewing circles and church baazars, Curti and Nash illustrated the historic importance of women's giving to institutions of higher education, even before women had access to formal higher education themselves.[13] By focusing not only on men's education but on colleges for women, Curti and

Nash began to tell the story of how philanthropy affected the educational experience of different social groups, including those who had been marginalized or had been excluded from the earliest institutions of higher learning in this country.[14] Further, the authors were not unaware of the ambiguities raised by private support for institutions nor unquestioning of the nature of benevolence. Indeed, Curti and many of his students had begun to conceptualize and write what many historians call for today—a more inclusive and contextualized history of higher education.[15]

Curti's substantive work on philanthropy has received uneven attention from scholars over the years, and thus has never fostered the type of collaborative inquiry or intellectual cross-fertilization he envisioned.[16] In the 1990s, though, a number of scholars working in women's history to explore female traditions of philanthropy, which had been relatively neglected since Curti's efforts.[17] In particular, Kathleen McCarthy's edited volume *Lady Bountiful Revisited* and Anne Firor Scott's *Natural Allies* generated new interpretations in the history of philanthropy by demonstrating how women often responded to their exclusion from men's philanthropic activities through the establishment of parallel structures of female institutions and networks. These separate activities allowed women to appropriate the cultural traditions of giving and serving and enabled women to bring private values to the public realm without stepping beyond the culturally sanctioned boundaries of "womanhood."

Like Curti in his era, contemporary scholars of women's philanthropy have been innovative in their approach to familiar aspects of U.S. history. Women's clubs and voluntary organizations, as well as women's leadership in the abolition and temperance movements, have been documented as part of the larger task of "recovering" women's past.[18] The significance of these female activities, though, has been understood primarily within the framework of the history of nineteenth-century reform or the woman's movement and its intellectual and social antecedents. By bringing a different lens, that of philanthropy, to women's history, McCarthy, Nancy Hewitt, Suzanne Lebsock, Lori Ginzberg, and others have contributed new perspectives that are informed by and contribute to the literature in philanthropic studies and women's history. As McCarthy observed, recent studies in women's philanthropy have questioned the assumptions and emphases of earlier studies of separatism and sisterhood, thereby illuminating the complex ways that philanthropy has given women social status and at times accentuated and reinforced the differences among women.[19] Indeed, the philanthropic lens can shed new light on the types of power that were available to women and how women used these avenues to pursue personal and social goals.[20]

The scholarship on women's philanthropy to date has not dealt centrally with formal education, but this literature can, like Curti's work in the 1950s, provide a "touchstone" for advancing our understanding of the dimensions and significance of women's philanthropic ties to institutions of higher learning.[21] Further inspiration for such study can be found in Margaret Rossiter's classic study of women in science.[22] Rossiter has identified two types of giving—"creative" and "coercive"—that have provided leverage and aided women in their efforts to challenge the university's boundaries, namely to secure women's access to higher education and professional opportunities. (One recalls wealthy Mary Garrett's successful efforts to open Johns Hopkins Medical School to women.)

But what remains to be explored more fully is the range and influence of women's sustained commitments to institutions of higher education—especially the research university, the apex of the educational hierarchy—and the meaning such giving held for the developing university and for the individual women who gave or served. Systematic study of women's educational philanthropy will portray women as "radicals" and "conservators," and it will challenge stereotypes depicting women as inheritors and transmitters of knowledge rather than as original, creative thinkers or stewards of institutions devoted to innovation and discovery.[23] The lives of Dodge, a Christian steward, and Parsons, an independent-minded, university-trained scholar and disciplinary patron, provide historical examples of how educational philanthropy became an avenue for women's meaningful participation in institution- and discipline-building and a source of both intellectual engagement and personal satisfaction.

A Steward: Grace Dodge and Her Vision of Education for Women and Girls

When she died in 1915, Grace Dodge left nearly one-half million dollars and another portion of her estate to Teachers College [TC], Columbia University.[24] Her longstanding involvement with Teachers College came about by her earlier role as a funder and leader in TC's eleemosynary antecedents— the Kitchen Garden Association, the Industrial Education Association, and the New York College for the Training of Teachers. These enterprises had sought to introduce industrial education into public schooling and teaching training in New York City. As a founding trustee and treasurer of Teachers College, Dodge through her own benefaction, active fund raising, and commitment to certain social values helped shape the character of the Teachers College community and the institution's standing at Columbia University. Dodge's philanthropic commitment to Teachers College can best be understood within the context of her life.

Born in 1856, Grace Hoadley Dodge, the eldest of six children of William E. Dodge, Jr., and his wife Sarah Hoadley, grew up in an affluent Madison Avenue home, but hers was not a life of leisure. She was raised in an extended family of civic-minded men and women whose daily example and biblical teachings imbued her with the evangelical ideals of Christian service and duty. From these adults, and by extension from the guests their household welcomed—passionate reformers like Dwight Moody and Daniel Coit Gilman—Grace Dodge learned about giving and developed an appreciation of wealth as a trust.

Such lessons about giving and serving learned from family and religion were in fact more important in shaping Dodge's thinking and ambitions than formal education. Tutored privately at home during her childhood years, Dodge was sent as a teen to complete her studies at Miss Porter's School in Connecticut. By all accounts, her time studying away from home was unsettling. Dodge spent only two years, from 1872 to 1874, at Miss Porter's before getting her parents' permission to leave school and return home to New York City. She did so not to follow the life of a leisured "lady," but to pursue what she described as "loving God through work."[25] Her decision reflected cultural notions that affirmed female benevolence and was made possible by her family's financial circumstances.[26] Dodge, in fact, was carrying forth a family tradition of service and voluntarism that was rooted in evangelical Christianity. Passed from generation to generation, the ethos of giving touched the aspirations of male and female members of the extended Dodge family, strengthening familial bonds and ties between the family and an array of institutions in metropolitan New York, including the YMCA and Columbia University.[27]

Hoping to encourage and enable his daughter's philanthropic inclinations, William Dodge introduced Grace to two distinguished women who had devoted themselves to a public, philanthropic career: Josephine Shaw Lowell and Louise Lee Schuyler. Lowell was the founder of the Charity Organization Society, known as the COS. Schuyler had served in the U.S. Sanitary Commission and the State Charities Aid Association. Through these acquaintances, Grace Dodge became involved in the COS's Committee on the Elevation of the Poor in Their Homes, but it soon became apparent that her talents lent themselves to education rather than charity. Dodge was as comfortable conducting Sunday School classes at the Madison Square Chapel as teaching in the industrial schools sponsored by the Children's Aid Society.

Many young Christian women of Dodge's generation, resisting what Jane Addams described as the "family claim," moved to the settlement houses where they sought to test their beliefs and to apply their education to public service and social amelioration.[28] A single woman, Dodge assumed responsibility for the Dodge household and cared for her ill mother. Though she lacked the physical independence and college background that buoyed the career of settlement workers, she achieved an independent and spiritually meaningful identity for herself by drawing upon her family's traditions of giving. Whereas her male relatives were active supporters of civic and religious organizations for men, notably the YMCA, Grace Dodge translated and carried forth this tradition through her devotion to the YWCA, and to an array of organizations promoting the education of girls and women. In fact, she would be elected to unify the YWCA as the first president of its national board in 1906.

Dodge's embrace of a life of service to others through education in its many forms rested partly in the lessons she learned from her family's Social Gospel activities and partly in her elevated vision of Christian womanhood. Like many men and women of the middle or upper-classes, Dodge affirmed women's distinctive, and ostensibly superior, moral qualities. The ideals were to be cultivated, and women such as Dodge were in a position to devote time and money to this cause. Thus it was not surprising that Dodge did not hesitate and, in fact readily agreed, when she was approached by a group of female silk workers for her guidance and assistance in forming their own club.

Her concern with these particular young women, which gave rise to a lifelong commitment to the education and welfare of "working girls," was shaped by religious conviction and influenced by the nineteenth century's deep-seated ambivalence toward urban life. Many social hygiene reformers, Dodge among them, were concerned that harsh economic realities and living conditions of the city might ruin women and jeopardize middle-class standards of purity.[29] What little we know from Dodge's interaction with the working girls suggests that she believed the relationship was one of mutual education.[30] From her vantage point, the female workers challenged any facile sense of noblesse oblige on her part, forcing her as a "giver" to think about the impact of her philanthropy on the "receiver"—or as she put it, to consider the class politics of working "with" rather than "for."[31] In Dodge's view working girls' education linked women's growing self-reliance and social reform. It thus was as worthy and vital to building and sustaining community life as was the role of formal higher education. She regarded her voluntary club work as a career and described herself as a wage-earner whose salary was "paid in advance."[32]

Steward of an Idea: From the Kitchen Garden Association to Teachers College

By the early 1880s, Dodge was a well-regarded leader in working girls' education and industrial education. In 1886 she acquired another avenue of influence when she became one of two women commissioners appointed by Mayor Grace to the Board of Education. Dodge's family background, her own education, and her focus on practical education and knowledge as the fulcrum of social reform help explain why she became so deeply identified with the privately-funded Kitchen Garden Association and the Industrial Education Association (known as the KGA and IEA respectively), which sponsored classes for children and teachers in hopes of eventually introducing industrial education into the New York City public schools. The events that shaped the KGA and IEA's reorganization first as the New York College of Teaching, and then as Teachers College in 1892, and its affiliation a year later with Columbia University shed light on the ties between private, civic initiatives in urban education—philanthropic activities to which women contributed significantly—and the ad-hoc process of university building.[33]

Dodge was one of the few individuals whose personal circumstances and sustained commitment to the ideas and values for which the KGA and the IEA stood enabled her to oversee this institutional evolution and to guide Teachers College's entrance into the university. Dodge's involvement dated back to the 1880 founding of the all-female Kitchen Garden Association, which was inspired by reformer Emily Huntington's efforts to teach household skills to young female immigrants and working girls. According to Huntington, the tenement conditions and pauperism that were a concern to citizens like Dodge were educational problems that could be ameliorated by fostering a "love of work."[34] Huntington's approach, which appealed to Dodge's sensibilities, aimed to blend Froebelian philosophy and the methods of kindergarteners.

In 1884 the KGA broadened its philanthropic mission to include the education of young boys and the group reorganized as the coeducational Industrial Education Association. The IEA's guiding principles, outlined in the "Articles of Faith," asserted that education as generally conceptualized "trains the memory too largely, the reasoning powers less, the eye and hand too little." According to the IEA, manual training was "not a form of specialized training, but an essential aspect of general education."[35] Though Alexander Webb, President of City College, was the new group's titular head, Dodge was in actuality responsible for daily affairs. Dodge thus played a role in 1887 when the IEA was chartered as the New York College for the Training of Teachers (soon to be renamed Teachers College) with the Columbia-trained philosopher Nicholas Murray Butler as president.[36] More important, Dodge's stewardship continued after 1893 when Teachers College became affiliated with Columbia as the university's professional school of education.[37]

An Advantageous Affiliation: Teachers College Enters Columbia University

The Teachers College-Columbia University affiliation, though not without difficulties, was perceived to be mutually beneficial. Dodge and the reformers who had carried forth the core mission of the Kitchen Garden Association understood that achieving the types of reforms they advocated for New York City public schools required inroads into teacher training and that this goal could best be fostered by establishing ties to a university. From its vantage point, Columbia regarded bringing Teachers College into affiliation as consonant with efforts to modernize the university. Columbia's tenth president, Frederick A. P. Barnard, who in fact was an honorary member of the IEA, had advocated the scientific study of education as early as his annual report of 1881. But earlier attempts to introduce the university study of education at Columbia had been tabled by trustees for financial reasons and because they feared the possibility of coeducation.[38] By contrast, an affiliation with an established institution such as Teachers College meant that boundaries would preserve Columbia's prestige and all-male status. Columbia gained "an annex or adjunct to [its] theoretical and historical work in psychology and education" without financial expenditure or threat of feminization.[39]

This example of philanthropy's contributions to shaping the contours of the university is neither insignificant nor an isolated case. Only a few years earlier Columbia had responded to growing civic demands for women's liberal arts education by adopting this same strategy—i.e., by bringing an existing, philanthropically-funded institution, Barnard College, into the university's configuration. Like its association with Barnard, Columbia's affiliation with Teachers College represented a "fit" between the demands of its host city and the university's ambitious agenda for expansion and development. As part of Columbia University, Teachers College would be well situated to further the goal of reforming public schools—a goal that Grace Dodge and Nicholas Murray Butler, now Columbia's president, shared. Yet the status-conscious university would be able to keep women, "special" preparatory students, normal school graduates, and coursework in less prestigious applied fields at a distance from the arts and sciences—psychically, organizationally, and physically.[40]

The possibility of strong and enduring ties between Teachers College and Columbia was not always certain. Informal ties between the two institutions lost ground when Butler resigned the TC presidency in 1891 to become dean of Columbia's newly-formed Faculty of Philosophy. Immersed in administrative and professorial duties at Columbia, Butler would in fact resign from the TC board in 1894.[41] And, Butler's relationship to Teachers College would change once again in 1901, when he succeeded Seth Low as president of Columbia University.

Despite the brevity of his TC association, Butler's recollections of the founding and early years of Teachers College were invested not only with a sense of the enterprise's importance, but of his importance to the enterprise. Butler's emphasis and interpretation in recounting TC's early years reflected the values and priorities of a university man vested in developing a professional school of education and in promoting the university study of education. In his descriptions of Teachers College's rise from earlier organizations—the KGA, IEA, and the New York College for Training of Teachers—Butler distanced TC's character and mission from that of its philanthropic antecedents. He defined the study of education as a field of expertise—a body of knowledge that was to be developed by university scholars—and, hence, drew distinctions between "philanthropic" and "educational" motives and enterprises. While such distinctions were vital to professionalizers, who believed in the science of education, they excluded certain groups of people and made less sense to individuals of Dodge's sensibilities, for whom philanthropy, religion, and education were fused.[42]

Though Butler's view of the founding of Teachers College became the standard account, one that ironically drew the boundaries of history in such a way as to eclipse the philanthropist Grace Dodge's role, Dodge's contemporaries did in fact recognize her crucial part in creating Teachers College, in fostering the institution's connection to the city, and in sustaining the institution during its early years. James Earl Russell, dean of TC from 1898 to 1927, with whom Dodge worked closely, incisively wrote, "Teachers College is the product of two confluent streams. One originated with President Barnard. . . . This is the idea of professional training for teachers as part of the work of a great University. The other stream started with Miss Dodge's interest in the girls and boys in the New York public schools . . . Teachers College came into existence, an institution which President Barnard had foreseen with prophetic vision but which awaited the time when Grace H. Dodge should energize it with her dynamic power."[43]

Trustee as Fundraiser, Donor, and Teacher[44]

More recently scholars like Esther Katz and Ellen Condliffe Lagemann (whose studies published in the 1970s and 1980s brought the concerns of women's history to the study of education) looked beyond Butler's recollections and recognized Dodge's hand in the formative years at Teachers College.[45] The translation of the philanthropic sensibilities and ideals of the KGA and IEA at some level into Teachers College's campus life, even as the study of education was becoming increasingly secularized, psychologized, and dominated by professional men, was a direct result of Dodge's unwavering commitment to certain social and religious values. Though Dodge was not in a position to participate in the intellectual framing of the academic study of education, she was able to advance TC as an institution. She worked tirelessly as a fund raiser and trustee to assure Teachers College's intellectual vigor, stability, and prominence against the pressures of competition from other institutions and worrisome deficits, even during the financial downturn of 1893.[46]

Her concern with intellectual standards and her efforts to sustain spiritual values and religious activities in the university's community became the hallmark of Dodge's efforts as a TC trustee.[47] Though few women served on boards of trustees, Dodge served with distinction as a TC board member and the College's treasurer. She spoke eloquently and passionately to educate her board colleagues about the need to assure the intellectual and fiscal health of an institution held in trust: "We want Brains—more strong and clever men and women. We should have chairs endowed; but while waiting for this, we should be able to say to President Hervey, 'We will be responsible for ten or more thousands of dollars next year.'"[48]

Dodge's skill in offsetting debt, year after year, and her uncanny ability to interest prominent women and New York families—the Dodges, the Macys, the Thompsons, the Milbanks—in the work of Teachers College did not go unrecognized by colleagues and civic-minded New Yorkers.[49] J.P. Morgan, a tough-minded Wall Street financier who was not easily impressed, in fact once called Grace Dodge "the finest business brain in the United States."[50] But Dodge regarded her efforts to bring stability to Teachers College less as an obligation or a managerial responsibility, than as a heartfelt mission. Grace Dodge, in the spirit of stewardship, worked tenaciously through fund-raising letters, receptions, and personal solicitations to build a top-caliber faculty and to provide well-equipped facilities as well as to gain respect and cooperation for Teachers College within Columbia University. Her own generosity addressed the needs of students, such as funding scholarships for foreign students or paying for the tasteful appointment of meeting rooms for the university women. As a donor, she built the Household Arts Building, in her mother's memory (at a cost of nearly a half a million dollars) and through her own generosity and fund raising efforts gained substantial support for the domestic science and nursing programs that distinguished Teachers College in its scope and curricular diversity from many other early schools of education.[51]

Over the years, Dodge worked with Teachers College's first president Walter Hervey and his successor dean James Earl Russell (the change in the executive head's title reflects TC's ties to Columbia University), to build Teachers College's campus and curriculum.[52] Reflecting the emphases of her life experiences—her involvement in church, working girls' clubs, and the YWCA—Dodge brought concerns about developing the "religious and spiritual side of life" to the attention of decision-makers at Teachers College and, equally important, to members of the broader Columbia University community.[53] She cultivated these priorities through her attentiveness to chapel service and her interest in the curriculum. For example, she explored the ways ties between Teachers College and Union Theological Seminary might provide a foothold for nationally-recognized work in Bible study and religious education.[54] Her concern with the spirit and mind was at a variance with the prevailing trends of secularization, but her daily involvement with the college allowed her to keep the questions alive. In 1907 she wrote, "I realize that our students are going out as great leaders in the educational world in the future, and that they should have the impress of this spiritual power, as well as so much else."[55]

Dodge's efforts in building Teachers College can only be more fully understood within the broader framework of the many interconnected social commitments she balanced with her university responsibilities. Dodge was not interested in a self-aggrandizing legacy; she viewed her service and support of Columbia's professional school of education as the institutionalization of an idea, of certain values carried forth by the KGA and the IEA. Her philanthropic contributions to Teachers College were related to her ongoing club work with immigrant and working girls and were consonant with her involvement in a host of educational enterprises that promoted self-reliance and civic uplift. Her actions reflected her belief in an elevated feminine morality and, hence, women's distinct contribution to the public good. While faithfully serving Teachers College, Dodge also assumed national leadership in the YWCA, served as chair of the board of trustees of a women's college in Constantinople, and continued her personal involvement in her original working girls' club.

Increasingly, though, Dodge felt the forces of professionalization working against the values that she and others in the KGA and IEA had embraced. Dean Russell hoped to encourage her by underscoring that the "missionary fervor" and "human element," indeed the "heart and soul," were as important as "intellect and business acumen," but increasingly professionalizing forces within the College and more sharply delineated roles for trustees, administrators, and faculty prevailed.[56] This tension was most evident in Dodge's concern that "psychology with its clean cut critical spirit" was displacing the Froebelian approach to the education of kindergarteners at Teachers College.[57] Dodge realized that "several of us in the old regime will either have to go out or change methods."[58] When she died in 1915, the religiously-suffused philanthropic values that she embraced, and which had animated her entire career, may have been losing or had lost ground in the academy. But Dodge's contribution, as a woman who was a steward over the institution she helped to found and who cared deeply for the intellectual, spiritual, and social needs of women of the college, left an impress.

Scholar-Patron: Elsie Clews Parsons—A "New" Woman and a Professional Social Scientist Without a Formal Academic Appointment[59]

As a member of the Women's Graduate Club at Columbia University in the 1890s, Elsie Clews Parsons had observed first-hand Grace Dodge's trusteeship and her acts of generosity and kindness to women across the university divisions.[60] Parsons's own philanthropy, though, took a different tack. As a young woman she was involved in settlement work, but her notable contributions as a philanthropist and educator came through her patronage of anthropological scholarship and her crucial role in cultivating the academic study of anthropology at Columbia. With a sustained pattern of timely gifts to Columbia's anthropology department (widely considered the nation's premier department) and to the larger profession—e.g., $200 for a doctoral student's fieldwork, $2,000 for a publication effort, and $1500 to provide a department secretary at Columbia—Parsons created research and publication opportunities for Franz Boas and his students, and for herself.[61]

Born in 1874, Elsie Clews Parsons, like Grace Dodge, was the child of a prominent New York City family. Her father, Henry Clews, a Wall Street banker, was proud of his daughter's "intellectual capacity" but nonetheless believed in the Victorian ideology of separate spheres, which assigned sexually-differentiated roles to men and women.[62] Her mother, Lucy Madison Worthington Clews, hailed from an aristocratic Southern family. A woman who supposedly was allowed $10,000 a year for "fashion mistakes," she valued fashion more highly than books. Although willing to join upper-crust New Yorkers in lending her name to support Barnard College, New York City's "experiment" in women's education, Mrs. Clews frowned upon her own daughter's intellectual ambitions.[63] Schooling, she believed, cultivated a daughter's manners but higher education was meant only for those girls of lower social standing who might need to support their way in life by teaching. Whereas the Dodge household reflected the ethos of Social Gospel reform, one that allowed for women's Christian-minded public service, the Clews household embraced the strict gender conventions and status quo of fashionable late-nineteenth-century New York society.

Unlike Grace Hoadley Dodge for whom religion brought coherence to life, Parsons, who counted religion among the conventions she rejected, did not conceptualize wealth as a trust. But neither did Parsons embrace her parents' view of wealth as status.[64] For her, wealth was a key to independence and an avenue for achieving what she described, echoing Nietzche, as "the will to power." Impressed by her father's tenacity and perseverance in business affairs, Elsie Clews Parsons with similar zeal pursued quite different ends; she veered away from parental values and leisure-class expectations, away from prescribed "feminine" roles, and instead pursued the life of intellect and reason. The combination of her personal finances, social connections, and her intellectual and social ties to Columbia University, enabled Parsons to defy convention and customs and to craft her career as a freelance social scientist. As both a scholar and a patron, she supported a university department and a field of modern social science inquiry that promised to challenge the ideological underpinnings of established gender roles and the status quo.

Elsie Clews Parsons's "rebellion" against the rigid codes of Manhattan's fashionable society and the expectations her family set for her was reflected and enabled by her pursuit of higher education.[65] Parsons's decision to matriculate at Barnard in 1892 was daring and auspicious. Then located in a rented brownstone at 345 Madison Avenue (nearby Columbia at 49th Street), Barnard, though only three years old, was gaining a fine reputation. Barnard students were steeped in the ethos of classical learning in their daily studies, while their extracurricular activities brought them into contact with the city's reform and settlement efforts. Beginning what biographer Desley Deacon described as a "ten-year association with the settlement movement," Parsons served as the student elector of the Barnard Chapter of the College Settlement Association.[66] This student organization was sponsored by Dean Emily James Smith (later Putnam) and Dr. Emily Gregory, Barnard's only female faculty member. College-level academics provided Parsons with a framework for studying the social questions she was already formulating on her own and for understanding the causes of social conditions she observed directly. Studying the new social sciences, in particular, offered her an affirming, intellectual sense of "self-preservation against family and environment."[67] Parsons could now anchor her social views with theory and, through her developing grasp of history, reach a more mature understanding of women's social status.

Parsons graduated from Barnard College in 1896. After earning her master's degree at Columbia in sociology, she embarked upon doctoral studies. She was one of the first women to benefit from Barnard Dean Smith's negotiations with Columbia's President Seth Low and the Columbia trustees to provide women with opportunities for graduate education. Though Parsons could not study in the Faculty of Political Science, which refused to admit women (succumbing to pressure by Dean John Burgess, a staunch opponent of coeducation), Parsons's interests were pursued instead in the Faculty of Philosophy. Her ideas were influenced by Nicholas Murray Butler's commanding grasp of educational philosophy and his civic interest in improving public education, by Herbert Osgood's knowledge of colonial history, and by the sociologist Franklin Giddings's concept of the "consciousness of kind."[68] Influenced by these professors, Parsons undertook a dissertation that combined her interests in education, legal systems, and women's history. She received her doctorate in 1899, with the publication of *The Educational Legislation and Administration of the Colonies*.

In the early phase of her career, from her Columbia graduate school days until 1905, Parsons was a lecturer at Barnard, where she taught courses on the family and guided students in settlement work. She combined her academic career with married family life, settlement work, municipal reform, and school board activities. (Her husband, Herbert Parsons, was a prominent Republican and an active participant in good government and settlement efforts.) Her early writings, several of which appeared in *Charities and the Commons*, drew from the familiar progressive idioms of education, economy, and efficiency. The pattern of her reform activities enabled Parsons to examine some questions that had preoccupied her since youth and brought her into professional contact with some of New York City's leading figures in social reform-among them, Lillian Wald, Mary Simkhovitch, and Florence Kelley, all of whom had in their own ways challenged traditional gender norms and committed themselves to working toward social change.[69]

Parsons's personal and public writings often reflected her concern with the lives of individuals and the proper relationship between the individual and the state. In her 1897 Columbia master's thesis on "Poor Relief in New York City," she elevated the "personal devotion" of private charity over public intervention and government determination of individual "worthiness" or "helpableness."[70] Within a decade, her articles appearing in *Charities* argued for a progressive "cooperation between public and private agents of education," more private day nurseries, voucher system school restaurants near public primary schools, and enlarged responsibilities for the school nurse and the school board.[71]

Parsons's genuine concern with aiding the city's poor and with developing the autonomy of city neighborhoods was coupled with concern for what was an unrecognized, and therefore unmet, vocational need among middle- and upper-middle-class women. She gained notoriety—and, notably, the praise of the philanthropist Olivia Sage—for her promotion of settlement work as a useful endeavor to lend some purposefulness to women's lives.[72] It was, as she put it, a plan "for girls with nothing to do."[73] Such young women, Parsons argued, needed a sense of direction, an avenue for becoming productive and for acquiring altruistic social values: "Girls are realizing more and more that the ability and freedom to work are indispensable to a talent for life."[74] By the mid-1910s, Parsons had appropriated the economic theory of competition developed by Thorstein Veblen and Ellen Key to help explain the customs and practices that created different work and different social roles for men and women. Increased leisure had "thwarted" women's achievements and made them an unproductive "economic caste," Parsons argued. "Parasitical women," she wrote in 1913, are "our greatest menace."[75]

Fortunately for her, Parsons's scholarly endeavors—the avenue she chose to achieve self-worth and identity—were not thwarted by the prejudices facing women who had to seek the security of academic positions. Parsons was financially and psychologically removed from the material concerns and competitive pressures that her generation, especially her colleagues in anthropology, experienced in vying for academic appointments, promotion, and security.[76] In the pre-World War I years, she applied her university training and personal finances to promoting what she openly described as social propaganda, "program books." Parsons's freelance sociology, which she published until the 1910s, provided her the opportunity, by now less accessible to university academics, to intertwine social science and social criticism. "Propaganda is certainly as justified as ethnology, and perhaps worth infinitely more . . . ," wrote her friend Berkeley anthropologist Alfred Kroeber, who added, "I wish I were one of the fortunate ones endowed with free choice of profession."[77]

Settlement work was an early avenue that Parsons pursued to effect social change, as were her sociological critiques of the strictures of marriage, the family, and religion. By 1910 she had become interested in Franz Boas's study of culture and had turned seriously to anthropology and folklore. She became a noted scholar of black folklore and culture. Parsons's social views and intellectual commitments coincided through her own scholarship and her patronage of Columbia anthropology. For her part, Parsons viewed anthropology as a way to extricate the study of culture from the moral, philosophical realm and to analyze social and cultural power in a systematic, rational, and empirical way. If the ideas themselves were liberating to Parsons, so too was the possibility of crafting the terms of one's engagement with Columbia University and the anthropological profession.

The Patron-Scholar: Becoming Part of the Inner Circle

For a university outsider and a woman to achieve such influence in the "inner circle" of a university department and discipline may be attributable to the inchoate nature of anthropological study during the interwar years. However, the well-known tensions between the anthropology department chair Franz Boas, a German-born Jew and pacifist during World War I, and Columbia's autocratic President Nicholas Murray Butler also played a role. Boas's political stance and allegiance to his homeland deeply angered Butler. While Boas weathered the controversies that brought the much publicized departures of professors James McKeen Cattell and Henry Wadsworth Dana, Butler withdrew administrative support and cut funding for the anthropology department. This action was a serious threat to plans to develop anthropology as a university discipline. Boas's efforts to build and sustain a rigorous program of university training and anthropological field work thus, by necessity, relied variously and somewhat tenuously upon the personal generosity of several New York City bankers and philanthropists—Jacob Schiff, Felix Warburg, and Paul Warburg, among them. These men were prominent figures among New York City's Jewish community and longstanding benefactors of Columbia University. While their support was valued, Boas's connection to Parsons had other dimensions and brought other benefits. Boas recognized Parsons as a Columbia-trained social scientist and ally, with access to finances and social networks. She was a woman of social pedigree and the wife of a prominent Republican reformer. She had ties to Barnard College and was on good terms with Nicholas Murray Butler. But Boas's relationship with Elsie Clews Parsons also differed at another fundamental and crucial level. She became an important figure in departmental life and, moreover, in the intellectual advancement of the discipline. She was Boas's colleague, his confidente, his scholarly executor, and his enabler.

Scholars interested in the history of anthropology and women's history have documented the importance of Parsons's ability to provide funding for travel and publication to young anthropologists at Columbia and at other major centers of research, particularly Chicago, Yale, and Berkeley.[78] She supported men as well as women, but was known as an advocate for women in the discipline, and similarly, her alumnae activities at Barnard proved her a friend to the cause of women's higher education.[79]

Parsons was accepted, in both intellectual and social terms, by the "inner circle" of Columbia anthropology. Her absence during her fieldwork expeditions and other activities was felt. As her friend Alfred Kroeber wrote, "We need you back. The lunches—they come on Tuesdays again—have degenerated into shop gossip and swapping yarns."[80] It was her working relationship with Franz Boas, though, that enabled Parsons, sans an academic appointment, to function as an intellectual and contributing member of the Columbia department. Known as "Papa Franz" to a circle of younger female students at Columbia and Barnard, Boas's relationship with Parsons, a mature, married woman was intellectually open and collegial, rather than paternal. It was a close relationship but one that at some level was mediated by the dynamics between donor and recipient. Generously acknowledging his debt to his benefactor and, hence, cultivating future support, Boas used their conversations to appraise student potential and interest Parsons in research projects. He facilitated her funding of research projects under the auspices of the university's Social Science Research Council and her personal philanthropy, the "Southwest Society."[81] And, as university politics and friction with Butler further marginalized Columbia's anthropology department, Boas increasingly relied on Parsons's financial help to maintain the department secretary's salary (Parsons in fact became known as the department's "angel").[82]

In Boas's eyes, Parsons was a kindred, politically-minded individual. As Deacon notes, Parsons "came to the defense of Franz Boas" when he became embroiled in controversy for challenging the Columbia administration's efforts to document "unpatriot" expressions and behavior by faculty members. In a letter to the *New York Times*, Parsons openly criticized Columbia officials, "That the trustees of a great American university should thus desire to violate the principle of academic freedom is tragic; that they should seek to check in the university the kind of political reference or discussion which may occur in any legislature, in any newspaper, at any public meeting, is grotesque, a bit of almost incredible buffoonery."[83]

Boas, therefore, felt comfortable during his conversations with Parsons airing his concerns about politics threatening academic freedom and, on occasion, asked her to intercede on his behalf in matters outside of the university (for instance, the immigration status of a relative or a violation of intellectual freedom in government scientific institutions).[84] Indeed, the relationship, which overcame the divide of "professional" and "amateur," had mutual benefits, and was more complex than financial support.[85]

Parsons's influential role at the Columbia anthropology department did not stem from the amount of money that Parsons gave, but from the targeted, timely nature of her giving (given the department and discipline's pressing needs) and her intellectual engagement with Franz Boas.[86] Discretionary money enabled her to create her own scholarly career, on her own terms. Beyond that, wealth enabled her, in a time of few teaching positions and limited foundation interest in anthropology, to provide career-enabling opportunities for Columbia's Ruth Benedict, Barnard's Gladys Reichard, the American Museum of Natural History's Margaret Mead, and others among the second generation of Boas's students—including two department secretaries turned anthropologists.[87]

Unlike Dodge who found deep satisfaction and affirmation in a connection with the recipients of her giving, Parsons, as Margaret Mead recalled, remained somewhat distanced from the younger generation of Columbia women, even while financially supporting their work.[88] This may be explained partly by intellectual differences, but also by generational and personality differences. Parsons rejected any notion of "women's culture" or feminist arguments emphasizing women's differences from men. She did not see herself either as a "female iconoclast" or a "lady scientist," nor did she limit her anthropological thinking to women as a social group. In this respect, her orientation was similar to that of many early women social scientists in the new research universities who, as Rosalind Rosenberg's work showed, rejected the "separate but equal" doctrine and distanced themselves from traditionally female activities.[89]

Like Dodge, Parsons built a career that was multi-faceted and involved interactions with both university colleagues and different social groups; her career's many dimensions were fostered by the varied opportunities of the metropolitan life. She stood with one foot in the professional worlds of the Columbia University community and the American Anthropological Association (she was elected its first female president in 1941) and the other foot in the popular world of Manhattan's social and reform clubs. Just as Dodge achieved a sense of identity and continuity through her work at Teachers College and with the YWCA, Parsons comfortably moved from explaining folklore traditions before an American Anthropological Association audience to espousing feminism at a Greenwich Village meeting. But whereas Dodge's philanthropy aimed to forge connections between the organizations and people she valued, Parsons used wealth to move in different spheres while compartmentalizing her various endeavors and preserving the independence she cherished.

Parsons was more an intellectual radical than a grass roots activist. She mixed freely among a circle of New York reformers, journalists, and intellectuals, including many who were privileged by birth and education but felt disaffected from their middle- and upper-middle-class backgrounds. Their careers reflected an eclectic fusion of Greenwich Village bohemianism, feminism, socialism, and twentieth-century progressivism.[90] At Mabel Dodge Luhan's Greenwich Village salon, she engaged in discussion and debate with such vibrant, influential personalities as Margaret Sanger, Randolph Bourne, Max Eastman, and Walter Lippmann. Views were exchanged on American politics and culture, socialism, feminism, birth control, progressive education, and psychoanalysis.[91] As a member of New York City's Heterodoxy, a women's luncheon club for iconoclastic thinkers, Parsons shared her ethnographic insights on social organizations with women. Her audience included women whose social views might differ but who nonetheless shared her desire for social change: among them, Charlotte Perkins Gilman, Fola LaFollette, Henrietta Rodman, and her dearest friend, Barnard alumna Alice Duer Miller. She also attended the Liberal Club and encouraged her friend the journalist Randolph Bourne to join her at New York's Heretics Club, whose members included Alyse Gregory, Henrietta Rodman, Freda Kirchway, and several Columbia affiliates, among them, Pliny Goddard, Alexander Goldenweiser, Leta Hollingworth, Harry Hollingworth, Helen Parkhurst, and William Montague.[92] As Parsons once explained to Bourne, whom she admired as a fellow "renegade Anglo-Saxon," these intellectual gatherings provided an alternative more radical and cross-disciplinary than the university's academic culture.[93] They offered a mixture of academics and radicals, men and women, that was synergistic and potentially enlightening: "I go places where two cultures are gathered together only because of the individuals I may be lucky enough to chance on."[94]

Parsons had the financial, social, and cultural resources needed to circumvent the financial hardships and other uncertainties of scholarly life faced by all academics (particularly radicals and women) during the early twentieth century. Beyond that, Parsons's creative use of her personal wealth enabled her to negotiate on her own terms the boundaries between personal and public life, and to balance her diverse, and at times opposing, responsibilities as propagandist, scholar, daughter, wife, and mother—roles her close friend Alfred Kroeber, in fact, once described as her "several careers."[95]

Conclusion

Both Dodge and Parsons had special ties to and, therefore, reasons to support Columbia University, but their stories should not be reduced to instances of rich women—"ladies bountiful"—seeking and gaining prominence and gratitude by responding to fund-raising solicitations or by writing cheques in support of the local institution. Their goals were more transcendent and purposeful, their personal engagement with the recipients of their philanthropy more sustained, and the influence of their decision-making and financial support more widely significant.

Dodge's stewardship of the philanthropic KGA and IEA and her later role in helping to institutionalize the study of pedagogy at Columbia University sheds light on the ways educational philanthropy was often linked to broader currents of reform and the ways the philanthropic relationship established meaningful ties between the university and women as givers. Further, the story of Grace Dodge's involvement in educational reform first outside the university and then as a central figure at Teachers College provides a window for understanding women's contributions to the ad-hoc nature of university building at Columbia. As the story of Teachers College illustrates, Columbia grew and bolstered its standing as a center of advanced study and research by drawing a privately-funded institution into its configuration. This process of changing and redefining the boundaries of the university had ramifications for women. As historian Douglas Sloan showed with respect to science, the "enclosure" of once popular fields of study or private enterprises within the emerging university changed the locus of intellectual life and the dynamics of participation.[96] Although Sloan's analysis did not consider the variable of gender, the model of university building he documented meant that Columbia could enhance its intellectual authority and standing in New York City's intellectual landscape, and not insignificantly its enrollments, while guarding its all-male status. It did so by delineating roles for women, by clarifying divisional boundaries, and by keeping the less prestigious service professions and the possibility of feminization at a distance.[97] But even within this context of university building and rising professionalism, philanthropy remained an avenue for women's participation and influence in university affairs, as Dodge's experience as a donor and trustee at Teachers College testifies.

Quite different in her sensibilities and career from Dodge, Parsons fashioned an intellectual role, as an iconoclast and scholar. Confident in her standing as a university-trained social scientist, Parsons used her wealth to build and sustain a career that allowed her to participate in university and professional life, yet enabled her to remain independent, combining on her own terms the roles of scholar, patron, and social critic. The university-generated research to which she contributed financially and intellectually would, she believed, provide the empirical basis to debunk the myths of race and gender. In-depth knowledge of culture would be the fulcrum of social change that would liberate the individual and cast off superstition and archaic custom.

The lives of these two women and the patterns of their career reflect the intricacies of their personalities but also suggest broad generational differences in the goals, underpinnings, and approaches of women's educational philanthropy—from Christian evangelicalism to faith in the expertise of social science—as the Victorian era gave rise to the modern era.[98] Though their preoccupations, sensibilities, social ideals, and perspectives on modernity differed greatly, the purposefulness Dodge and Parsons as philanthropists displayed in negotiating their relationship to the university enterprise was strikingly similar. Both women enjoyed the privileges of race, class, and family background that enabled them to overcome obstacles of gender, even defying conventions for women of their class. Both saw education and philanthropy as dual methods through which they, and indeed other women, might contribute to the university's ideals of service and participate, even as "amateurs," in the world of ideas and learning that was being professionalized and increasingly associated with the male-dominated university's rising intellectual authority.

Beyond suggesting the diversity among women and the varied motivations underlying their philanthropy, the examples of Dodge and Parsons shed further light on women's roles in forging

Columbia's ties to the metropolis and reveal how these two women, through their financial support and service, created careers for themselves. These two lives, considered together in relation to Columbia's history, suggest dimensions of women's educational philanthropy that historians have not fully appreciated and explored. In addition to their well-documented roles and contributions to campus life as students, faculty, and administrators, through the vehicle of philanthropy, particularly through the sustained relationships that can be fostered between giver and receiver, these women made a tangible contribution to intellectual and social life on campus. This was accomplished even at elite institutions, even during the tenure of powerful presidents, and even as large foundations devoted to scientific philanthropy and to supporting the "best men" began to hold sway, militating against women's participation.[99]

The pivotal connections that Grace Dodge and Elsie Clews Parsons had to Columbia's academic community offer a valuable perspective on the boundaries between the academy and society. Moreover, they point to contributions that are eclipsed by the facile distinctions historians often draw between "amateurs" on the outside of the university and the inner circle of university "professionals." Not to consider Elsie Clews Parsons as part of Columbia's anthropological community—as a veritable contributor to department life—would be myopic and inaccurate.

The study of philanthropy and higher education thus opens up some methodological questions about ways to further our understanding of the development of universities. Shifting the lens away from the focus of the academic department or the role of the president toward the formative and influential ties of benefaction and trusteeship—for example, relationships that connect individuals, ideas, and intellectual communities across institutional boundaries—will further understanding of the place of the academy and its reach in the entire intellectual landscape. The philanthropic lens might help us further situate the study of higher education within the broader culture, as Curti had hoped.

Even a cursory look at other institutions suggests that the case of Columbia was not an isolated instance of this type of philanthropic activity for women. Women contributed to developments at some of the country's most prestigious universities. Sara Yorke Stevenson, a member of the Philadelphia Civic Club-cum-museum curator, was instrumental in securing the funding for the University of Pennsylvania Museum's archaeological expedition to Nippur, from 1889 to 1900.[100] Helen Culver, Ethel Sturges Dummer, and Anita Blaine McCormick were important patrons of education and social science research in Chicago.[101] Mary Copley Shaw supported Alice Fletcher's anthropological research at Harvard.[102] Phoebe Hearst, through her wealth and service as the first female Regent of the University of California, promoted anthropological work at Berkeley and tried to improve the status of women students and scholars on campus.[103]

The list could go on, but would only underscore the salience of this phenomenon. The levels at which philanthropic women interacted with their university recipients no doubt varied. Moreover, studies are needed to ascertain whether the phenomenon is particular to a certain time period, to particular types of institutions and disciplines, to stages of development, or to metropolitan settings. In the case of Columbia, we find that women like Dodge and Parsons were able to capitalize on their personal resources and those of the city to traverse the university's boundaries, and that the city in a real sense expanded the gates of the university. As journalist Edwin Slosson observed in 1910, "Columbia University is willing to lose somewhat of its identity and distinctiveness through merging itself with the city in order that it may most fully share its life." Simply put, from Slosson's vantage point, one could no more trace the boundaries of Columbia than define the "limits of the metropolis itself."[104]

This study shows that no single motivation underlies women's actions. Nor is there a distinctly "feminine" approach that is restricted to women's philanthropy. To write a comprehensive history of women's philanthropy in higher education, one would have to consider the range of institutions in the landscape of higher learning and fully address the differences among women—such as race, class, ethnicity, religion, and region.[105] Such a history would deepen understanding of the intellectual and social connections linking education, philanthropy, and culture—a theme that Curti outlined over forty years ago. One could imagine that the systematic study of philanthropy might provide a new framework for considering women's contributions, not only to the research university but to a variety of educational institutions. Or, further study might inform revisionist considerations in both the history of philanthropy and the history of higher education, eventually pointing to a new periodization in these fields. Encouraging such study is consonant with the revisionist goals of writing histories of higher education that are more attentive to context and that integrate the experience of women.[106] And, finally, studies in the history and dimensions of women's educational philanthropy would provide boards of trustees and fund raisers, as well as students and researchers in higher education, with a usable history. Such study would consider not only the role of foundations, the annual gains in campus coffers or the Andrew Carnegies who have shaped institutions of higher education, but would consider the range of individual philanthropists—among them, prominent women like Dodge and Parsons as well as lesser known figures—who gave and served and, consequently, played a role in campus and intellectual life and in creating ties between the university and its environs.

Notes

1. I have drawn these characterizations in broad terms for the purposes of illustrating what I consider to be the major orientation of studies in each field. There are, of course, historical studies and historians that challenge these boundaries and blur these distinctions—and, as my title suggests, it is such an approach that I have in mind in undertaking the study of women's educational philanthropy and the university.

2. Literally the "love of mankind," the definition of "philanthropy" is historically-specific and has changed over time. Kathleen D. McCarthy notes that "from the seventeenth century until the last third of the nineteenth century, 'philanthropy,' encompassed both giving and voluntarism, with an emphasis on social reform." Kathleen D. McCarthy, ed., *Women and Philanthropy in the United States, 1790–1990* (New York: Center for the Study of Philanthropy, Curriculum Guide, #1, spring 1998), 2. Contemporary scholars writing from a variety of perspectives have conceptualized philanthropy to include time, service, and voluntary association. In terms of education, for instance, one can study the philanthropic contributions of donors, patrons, and trustees. See Robert L. Payton, *Philanthropy: Four Views* (New Brunswick: Transaction, 1988); Brian O'Connell, ed., *America's Voluntary Spirit: A Book of Readings* (New York: Foundation Center, 1983). My working definition—giving and serving in the public interest—embraces both financial giving and giving of one's time through service and association is more useful for considering the variety of women's contributions.

3. The need for biographical studies of philanthropy in order to explore the role of the family and religion is explored in Andrea Walton, "With Strength to Reason and Warmth to Feel: Clementine Miller Tangeman (1905–1996), Philanthropist and Educator," Working Paper No. 1 (The Center for the Study of American Culture and Education, New York University School of Education, 1998).

4. For a discussion of philanthropy in relational terms, see Susan Ostrander and Paul G. Schervish, "Giving and Getting: Philanthropy as a Social Relation," in *Critical Issues in American Philanthropy: Strengthening Theory and Practice*, Jon Van Til and Associates (San Francisco: Jossey-Bass, 1990), 67–98. For educational aspects of philanthropy, see Ellen Condliffe Lagemann, *Jane Addams on Education* (New York: Teachers College Press, 1985), Introduction.

   In a 1999 essay, Ellen Condliffe Lagemann observed that new theoretical frameworks in the social sciences, particularly the rise of the "new institutionalism"—which moves beyond depicting institutions as either "passive" or totally rational and efficient entities—have generated and facilitated research interest in the history of foundations, the disciplines, and the professions, particularly science and medicine. See Ellen Condliffe Lagemann, *Foundations in History: New Possibilities for Scholarship and Practice*, "Introduction" (Bloomington: Indiana University Press, 1999), ix–xviii. See also Walter W. Powell and Paul J. DiMaggio, *The New Institutionalism in Organizational Analysis* (Chicago: University of Chicago Press, 1991). See Barry D. Karl, "Philanthropy and the Maintenance of Democratic Elites," *Minerva* 35 (fall 1997): 207–20 and Lily E. Kay, "Rethinking Institutions: Philanthropy as an Historiographic Problem of Knowledge and Power," *Minerva* 35 (fall 1997): 283–93.

5. The systematic study of women's educational philanthropy, particularly in the higher education arena, might complement and inform our studies of women students, faculty, and administrators or the leadership of women in the social settlements and support of the arts. See Helen Lefkowitz Horowitz, *Culture and the City: Cultural Philanthropy in Chicago from the 1880s to 1917* (Lexington: University of Kentucky Press, 1976); Mina Carson, *Settlement Folks: Social Thought in the American Settlement Movement: 1885–1930* (Chicago: University of Chicago Press, 1990); Kathleen D. McCarthy, *Women's Culture: American Philanthropy and Art, 1830–1930* (Chicago: University of Chicago Press, 1991).

6.   Merle Curti, "The History of American Philanthropy as a Field of Research," *American Historical Review* 62 (January 1957): 352.

7.   Allen F. Davis, "Memorial to Merle E. Curti," *American Studies Association Newsletter* 19 (June 1996), 15.

8.   Curti's focus on philanthropy came about largely because of his prominent involvement in a 1956 conference, which F. Emerson Andrews orchestrated with funding from the Russell Sage and Ford foundations. Popular criticisms and Congressional hearings on foundation activities in the 1950s sparked interest among foundation heads to support scholarship documenting philanthropic activities, motivations, and outcomes. The Merle Curti Papers at the Wisconsin Historical Society contain information on the Princeton conference and foundation efforts to stimulate historical assessment of philanthropic initiatives. See Margaret W. Otto, *Report of the Princeton Conference on the History of Philanthropy in the United States* (New York: Russell Sage Foundation, 1956); Merle Curti and Roderick Nash, *Philanthropy in the Shaping of Higher Education* (New Brunswick, Rutgers University Press, 1965); and Merle Curti, "The History of American Philanthropy as a Field of Research," *American Historical Review* 62 (January 1957): 352–63.

9.   See note 7.

10. See Otto, *Report of the Princeton Conference*, passim; and Davis, "Memorial to Merle E. Curti," 15. The Wisconsin Project, started in 1958, influenced the careers of a number of scholars of educational history. David Allmendinger and Paul Mattingly, for instance, are recognized for their contributions as research assistants and critics in the preface to *Philanthropy and the Shaping of American Higher Education*, vi. Peter Dobkin Hall provides details of the network scholars who studied with or were influenced by Curti. See Peter Dobkin Hall, "The Work of Many Hands: A Response to Stanley N. Katz on the Origins of the 'Serious Study' of Philanthropy," *Nonprofit and Voluntary Sector Quarterly* 28 (December 1999): 522–36, esp. 524.

11. The Curti-Nash text in many respects remains the most useful full-length overview of the philanthropic matrix that guided the rise of colleges and universities—a topic that had been neglected since earlier works by Jesse Sears and Ernest Hollis. See Jesse Brundage Sears, *Philanthropy in the History of American Higher Education*; with a new introduction by Roger Geiger (New Brunswick: Transaction Publishing, 1990; c1919). Sears, who studied with Paul Monroe at Teachers College, Columbia University, also wrote the entry on "philanthropy" in the *Cyclopedia of Education* (1913). Sears's dissertation was notable for its use of quantitative analysis and its consideration of women. By contrast, Ernest Victor Hollis's 365-page study indexes only two references to women. See Ernest Victor Hollis, *Philanthropic Foundations and Higher Education* (New York: Columbia University Press, 1938), 86, 153.

12. A recent forum on possibilities for revisionism in the history of higher education notes these standard categories of analysis. See, for example, Linda Eisenmann, Philo A. Hutcheson, and Jana Nidiffer, "A Conversation: Historiographic Issues in American Higher Education," *History of Education Quarterly* 39 (fall 1999): 291–336.

13. See also Jesse Brundage Sears, *Philanthropy*, passim.

14. This inclusiveness was evident earlier in Curti's work. See also Merle Curti, *The Social Ideas of Educators* (New York: C. Scribner's Sons, 1935), which includes material relevant to the education of women and African Americans.

15. See note 11, as well as Eisenmann, "Reconsidering a Classic," 689–717.

16. That Curti's work has received uneven attention from scholars writing about institutions of higher education is, I believe, a function of the field's traditional emphasis on public, government funding. For the dynamics of the field, see Stanley N. Katz, "Where Did the Serious Study of Philanthropy Come From, Anyway?" *Nonprofit and Voluntary Sector Quarterly* 28 (March 1999): 74–82; and Hall, "The Work of Many Hands."

17. The work of a few scholars influenced by Curti's work did address women. See, for example, Keith E. Melder, "Ladies Bountiful: Organized Women's Benevolence in Early Nineteenth-Century America," *New York History* 48 (July 1967): 231–54. The two most important books in opening up the study of women's philanthropy have been Kathleen D. McCarthy, ed., *Lady Bountiful Revisited: Women, Philanthropy and Power* (New Brunswick, N.J.: Rutgers University Press, 1990) and Anne Firor Scott, *Natural Allies: Women's Associations in American History* (Urbana: University of Illinois Press, 1991). See particularly McCarthy's introduction; Kathryn Kish Skar, "Who Funded Hull House," 94–115; and Darlene Clark Hine, "'We Specialize in the Wholly Impossible,' The Philanthropic Work of Black Women," 70–93, in *Lady Bountiful Revisited*, ed. McCarthy. See also Kathryn Kish Sklar, *Florence Kelley and the Nation's Work* (New Haven: Yale University Press, 1995); Margaret W. Rossiter, *Women Scientists in America: Struggle and Strategies to 1940* (Baltimore: Johns Hopkins Press, 1982); and Ellen Condliffe Lagemann, ed., *Jane Addams On Education* (Piscataway: Transaction Press, 1994; c1985).

18. See McCarthy, *Lady Bountiful*, "Introduction"; and also idem, "The History of Women in Nonprofits," in *Women and Power in the Nonprofit Sector*, eds. Teresa Odendahl and Michael O'Neill (San Franscisco: Jossey-Bass, 2000), 23–24.

19. McCarthy, "The History of Women in Nonprofits," 23–24.

20. The study of women's educational philanthropy, particularly in the higher education arena, might complement and inform our studies of women students, faculty, and administrators, or the leadership of women in the social settlements and support of the arts. See Helen Lefkowitz Horowitz, *Culture and the City: Cultural Philanthropy in Chicago from the 1880s to 1917* (Lexington: University of Kentucky Press, 1976); Mina Carson, *Settlement Folks: Social Thought in the American Settlement Movement: 1885–1930* (Chicago: University of Chicago Press, 1990); Kathleen D. McCarthy, *Women's Culture: American Philanthropy and Art, 1830–1930* (Chicago: University of Chicago, 1991).

21. Closer examination of women's philanthropic involvement with educational institutions might uncover more examples of women's agency and influence through giving and serving. For instance, in her 1994 essay, McCarthy writes, "crusades that succeeded by dint of numbers often proved impotent in changing the policies of the kinds of heavily endowed 'legitimating institutions' created by such wealthy male patrons as John D. Rockefeller and Andrew Carnegie. . . . Women played a limited role in these legitimating institutions, often handling over significant donations to the stewardship of male trustees." McCarthy, "The History of Women in Nonprofits," 23–24.

22. See note 2.

23. See Joyce Antler and Sari Knopp Biklen, eds., *Changing Education: Women as Radicals and Conservators* (Albany: State University Press, 1990). Florence Howe illustrated this point by quoting sociologist David Riesman's introduction to Jessie Bernard's *Academic Women* in 1964: "Women," he says, "prefer to be teachers, passing on a received heritage and responsively concerning themselves with their students while men of equivalent or even lesser ability prefer to be men-of-knowledge, breaking the accustomed mold and remaining responsive not to students but to the structure of the disciplines and their colleagues in the invisible university." Florence Howe, "Feminism and the Education of Women," in *Myths of Coeducation: Selected Essays 1964–1983* (Bloomington: Indiana University Press, 1984), 184.

24. My account of Dodge's early days draws from a biographical chapter in Ellen Condliffe Lagemann, *A Generation of Women* (Cambridge, Mass.: Harvard University Press, 1979), 9–31; see Esther Katz, "Grace Hoadley Dodge: Women the Emerging Metropolis, 1856–1914" (Ph.D. diss., New York University, 1981); Abbie Graham, *Grace H. Dodge: Merchant of Dreams* (New York: The Woman's Press, 1926); s.v. "Dodge, Grace Hoadley," in *Notable American Women, 1607–1950*, ed. Edward T. James (Cambridge, Mass.: Belknap Press, 1971), hereafter cited as *NAW*; and Lucetta Daniel, "Impressions of Miss Dodge," *Association Monthly* 9 (March 1915): 9. A useful discussion of the broader context for philanthropic efforts such as Dodge's is Jane Allen Shikoh, "The 'higher life' in the American City of the 1890's: A Study of Its Leaders and Their Activities in New York, Chicago, Philadelphia, St. Louis, Boston, and Buffalo" (Ph.D. diss., New York University, 1973). Esther Katz's study provides a good account of Dodge's financial support and fundraising efforts. According to Katz, in the period from 1892 to 1897 donations and gifts to TC, thanks largely to Dodge's skilled fund raising as a trustee, reached one and quarter million dollars. Annual deficits, which Katz estimates at $60,000 to $100,00 per year, were cleared by Dodge's fund raising or personal generosity. See Katz, "Grace Hoadley Dodge," 152–55. Abbie Graham offers additional information on Dodge's fund raising. In 1892 Dodge raised $55,000; in 1893 she helped secure Mrs. Macy's gift of $225,000 for the Mechanical Arts Building and an additional $55,000; and between March and July of 1894, she raised $100,000 for a college building. See Graham, *Grace H. Dodge*, 179. Dodge herself gave nearly half a million dollars in 1915 to build the College's Household Arts Building.

25. Graham, *Grace H. Dodge*, 57.

26. Lori Ginzberg, *Women and the Work of Benevolence: Morality and Politics in Nineteenth-Century United States* (New Haven: Yale University Press, 1990); Anne Boylan, "Timid Girls, Venerable Widows and Dignified Matrons: Life Cycle Patterns Among Organized Women in New York and Boston, 1797–1840," *American Quarterly* 38 (winter 1986): 779–97.

27. Her great-grandfather, David Low Dodge, was the son of a noted leader of the YMCA and himself a founder of the New York Peace Society. Her grandfather, William E. Dodge, made his wealth in mining (Phelps, Dodge & Co.) and contributed financially to civic causes. Her father, William Dodge, Jr., was a highly-regarded benefactor and trustee of a number of New York's charitable and educational institutions. He had been a supporter of Columbia's Earl Hall, a student activities center devoted to religious activities. Her mother, though limited by poor health, supported a number of philanthropic causes, including the visiting committee of the State Charities Aid Association to New York's Bellevue Hospital. Dodge's cousins Olivia Egleston Phelps and Caroline Phelps-Stokes were active supporters of social

reform and benefactors of a number of educational institutions, including Columbia University. The sisters funded the building of St. Paul's Chapel in the early 1900s. *NAW*, s.v. "Dodge," Grace; Ginzberg, *Women and the Work of Benevolence*, 199–200.

28. Jane Addams, "The College Woman and the Family Claim," in *Jane Addams on Education*, ed. Ellen Condliffe Lagemann (New York: Teachers College Press, 1985), 64–73.

29. An analysis of the motivations and class politics of initiatives in vocationally-oriented working girls' education merits greater attention than can be offered here. Dodge was active in social hygiene. See, for example, James Bronson Reynolds, "Miss Dodge's Contribution to the Moral Protection of Women," *Association Monthly* 9 (March 1915): 82–90.

30. Dodge's writings to working girls' clubs are still available. See Grace Hoadley Dodge, *A Bundle of Letters To Busy Girls on Practical Matters* (New York: Funk & Wagnalls, 1887).

31. *NAW*, s.v. "Dodge," 490. Grace Hoadley Dodge, "Preface," in *Wage-Earning Women*, Annie Marion MacLean (New York: McMillan, 1910), vi

32. *NAW*, s.v. "Dodge," 490. See also Mabel Cratty, "The Fine Profession of Being a Laywoman," *Association Monthly* 9 (March 1915): 171

33. Like other affiliates, Teachers College entered into a series of agreements that clarified and amended its relationship to Columbia. A second agreement of affiliation was signed in 1898. Teachers College maintained its financial and legal independence.

34. *NAW*, s.v. "Dodge"; MacLean, *Wage-Earning Women*, vi; Dodge, *A Bundle of Letters*.

35. As Esther Katz noted, in 1886 the IEA was instructing 1,904 students. Only one year later, its roster had grown to 4,383. The IEA aligned itself with civic leaders. Katz lists IEA's honorary members as including: William E. Dodge, Jr., Charles Loring Brace, Frederick A. P. Barnard, General John Eaton (Commissioner of Education), Abraham Hewitt, Seth Low, and the Reverend Henry C. Potter. See Katz, "Grace Hoadley Dodge," 123, 121.

36. Dodge in fact raised the $10,000 that helped pay for Butler's salary from George Vanderbilt. See Katz, "Grace Hoadley Dodge," 141–42. Butler was a loyal Columbia alumnus. He earned his A.B. in 1882, his A.M. in 1883, and his Ph.D. in 1884.

37. Teachers College's first agreement of affiliation came in 1893. An 1898 agreement brought the College into the university more fully. A dean would now head Teachers College and represent TC on Columbia's University Council.

38. See Nicholas Murray Butler, *Across the Busy Years: Recollections and Reflections*, vol. I (New York: Charles Scribner's Son, 1935), 72–75. Butler's account emphasizes Barnard and his realization that "it would probably be easier to build up a teachers' college outside the University, and to bring it later into organic relations with the University, than to undertake its establishment under the control and at the expense of the Trustees." See Nicholas Murray Butler, "The Beginnings of Teachers College," *Columbia University Quarterly* I (September 1899): 344. See also, Katz, "Grace Dodge," 143.

39. Nicolas Murray Butler to Seth Low, 11 April 1894, Central Files Collection, Columbia University.

40. Roger L. Geiger identified Columbia's unusual configuration in comparison to other research universities: "Columbia University almost defies characterization. . . . Columbia tried to be all things to all people and somehow managed to bring it off. This was largely accomplished through compartmentalization. Columbia went about its many tasks, and related to its numerous constituencies, through separate units that were either completely self-contained (Barnard and Teachers College) or nearly so." "After the Emergence: Voluntary Support and the Building of American Research Universities," *History of Education Quarterly* 25 (fall 1985): 379. For a discussion of resistance to the study of education in universities, see Ellen Condliffe Lagemann, *An Elusive Science: The Troubling History of Education Research* (Chicago: University of Chicago Press, 2000), 16.

41. See Katz, "Grace Hoadley Dodge," 161.

42. Butler writes of the philanthropists, "[they] were strangers to the educational ideas involved in the new departure. Gradually, however, the force of the argument which was constantly kept before them was sufficient to overcome prejudices that were the natural outgrowth of the habit of viewing the introduction of manual training in the light of philanthropy, rather than in the light of education, and the problem was solved." See Nicholas Murray Butler, "The Beginnings of Teachers College," 345–46. In his autobiography, Butler noted the problems that arose from the concerns of the philanthropists "who feared that the philanthropy for which they cared so much would be over-shadowed by academic interests and ideals." See Nicholas Murray Butler, *Across the Busy Years*, 181. For a sense of how philanthropic women like Dodge might have viewed the unity of education and philanthropy, refer to Frances Goodale's report on women's philanthropic activities for the 1893 Chicago Exposition: "Philanthropy

cannot be divorced from Education nor from Religion. The three are one." Frances Abigail Rockefeller Goodale, *Literature of Philanthropy* (New York: Harpers, 1893), 2.

43. James Earl Russell, "Miss Dodge and Teachers College," *Association Monthly* 9 (March 1915): 68.

44. Grace Hoadley Dodge (GHD) to James Earl Russell (JER), 9 July 1899, 99B, Box 7, James Earl Russell Papers, Special Collections, Teachers College, Columbia University; hereafter cited as JER.

45. See Lawrence A. Cremin, David A. Shannon and Mary Evelyn Townsend, *A History of Teachers College, Columbia University* (New York: Columbia University, 1954); Lagemann, *A Generation of Women*, 26–27; Katz, "Grace Hoadley Dodge," 144, 181; and Bette Weneck, "The Average Teacher Need Not Apply: Women Educators at Teachers College, 1887–1927" (Ph.D. diss., Columbia University, 1996). Though his work does not address women's educational philanthropy, Thomas Bender's study of New York City offers a good discussion of the tensions between civic and academic culture that relates here, and more important, Bender offers another instance of Butler's self-aggrandizing view of his role in Columbia's history. Butler accorded very little credit to his predecessor, Seth Low. See Thomas Bender, *New York Intellect: A History of Intellectual Life in New York City, from 1750 to the Beginnings of Our Own Time* (Baltimore: Johns Hopkins University Press, 1987), 279.

46. When TC affiliated with Columbia in 1893, it achieved a distinctive place among institutions in New York City that educated women—namely, Hunter, the public female normal school (a counterpart to City College), New York University's School of Pedagogy, and the newly opened Barnard College. Teachers College might collaborate with Barnard, also a Columbia affiliate, and might compete successfully with NYU, but in Dodge's view, Hunter lacked the resources needed to make the transition to collegiate standards. Dodge's stance, shared by her co-commissioner of education, Mary Nash Agnew, drew controversy. As Katherine Grunfeld notes in her study of Hunter College, Dodge and Agnew, both having well-known Columbia affiliations, were criticized by city teachers. They were accused of class politics and for being guided by their loyalty to elite institutions over public interest, for lobbying at the state capital against awarding Normal collegiate status. See Katherina Kroo Grunfeld, "Purpose and Ambiguity: The Feminine World of Hunter College" (Ed.D. diss., Teachers College, Columbia University, 1991), 68–69.

47. Because there was no dean of women, Dean Russell relied on Dodge to ascertain the needs of women students. See JER to GHD, 24 December 1898, Box 6, 97A, JER.

48. Grace Hoadley Dodge, Comments at Opening Ceremony of Teachers College, n.d. (likely about 1895), Record Book, Teachers College Special Collections; Katz, "Grace Hoadley Dodge," 154. There has been little historical study of the role of trustees, particularly female trustees. See Mariam K Chamberlain, "Women as Trustees," in *Women in Academe: Progress and Prospects* (New York: Russell Sage Foundation, 1988), 333–56.

49. Merle Curti and Roderick Nash note Grace Dodge's ability to successfully raise funds from these families. See Curti and Nash, *Philanthropy and the Shaping*, 142. Among those whose interests Dodge helped to assure were Caroline Choate (Mrs. Joseph Choate), Mrs. Josiah Macy, and Mrs. Peter Bryson. For a discussion of the local nature of philanthropy that provided important support to urban universities, and Columbia's reliance on the great families of New York City, see Roger Geiger, *To Advance Knowledge: The Growth of American Research Universities, 1900–1940* (New York: Oxford University Press, 1986), 47–53.

50. "Tribute to Grace Hoadley Dodge," *Teachers College Record* 15 (January 1915): 72.

51. GHD to JER, 20 November 1908, Box 7, 106B, JER.

52. JER to GHD, 24 December 1898, Box 6, 97A, JER. Grace Dodge also worked closely with three other women who had sustained ties to Teachers College—Mrs. Peter Bryson, who founded the library, and Mrs. Josiah Macy and Edith Macy (wife of V. Everit Macy), both of whom contributed to campus building.

53. GDH to JER, 16 December 1906, Box 7, 106A; GDH to JER, 19 December 1907, Box 7, 106A, JER.

54. Raymond C. Knox, "Miss Dodge and Religious Education," *Association Monthly* 9 (March 1915): 70–71.

55. GHD to JER, 21 December 1907, Box 7, 106A, JER.

56. GHD to JER, 11 January 1910, Box 6, 97A, JER. The scholarship on professionalization and professionalism is extensive and varied. The most crucial elements determining professional status are related to having formal, expert knowledge related to certain sets of problems. This knowledge is certified by training, credentials, and membership in a community that is guided by its self-regulating ethics and standards. See, for example, Eliot Friedson, *Professional Powers: A Study of the Institutionalization of Formal Knowledge* (Chicago: University of Chicago Press, 1986). According to Andrew Abbott, the process of professionalization involves competition and jostling between groups, i.e., professions, for jurisdiction over a particular field. See Andrew Abbott, *The System of Professions: An Essay on the Division of Expert Labor* (Chicago: University of Chicago Press, 1988). In terms of the disciplines, the importance of the university as the site of training, intellectual community, and employment has been paramount. The

study of education being institutionalized in new professional schools of education like Teachers College was guided by psychology rather than the social values and philosophy that Dodge and her KGA colleagues embraced. Within this framework, Grace Dodge, though an educator, was not an "expert." She was an "amateur." Relating these terms to Parsons is a bit more difficult, which is, in fact, my point. Like Dodge, Parsons was written out of Columbia's history until interest in women's history developed. Through her philanthropy (e.g., funding fieldwork, supporting the publications of the American Folklore Society) Parsons created her own career, forged ties to the university, and helped to professionalize anthropology. For a discussion of anthropology's move from being an avocation of travelers and a museum study to a university study, see George Stocking, *Race, Culture, and Evolution: Essays in the History of Anthropology* (New York: Macmillan Free Press, 1968). Parsons had a Ph.D., a professional credential, but no professional position. Like Dodge, she stands less prominent in history written by "insiders."

57. See "Dodge, Grace," in *NAW*, 491. For a discussion of the tensions between Susan Blow, a Froebelian, and Patty Smith Hill, an advocate of psychological approaches to early childhood education and Hill's displacement of the Froebelian influence at Teachers College, see also Barbara Beatty, *Pre-school Education in America: The Culture of Young Children from the Colonial Era to the Present* (New Haven: Yale University Press, 1995), 116–18.

58. JER to GHD, 18 October 1900, Box 6, 97A, JER; quote in Katz, "Grace Hoadley Dodge," 164.

59. A.L. Kroeber, "Elsie Clews Parsons," *American Anthropologist* 45 (April-June 1943): 252; Rosemary Zumwalt, *Wealth and Rebellion: Elsie Clews Parsons, Anthropologist and Folklorist* (Urbana: University of Illinois, 1992); Desley Deacon, *Elsie Clews Parsons: Inventing Modern Life* (Chicago: University of Chicago Press, 1997).

60. After receiving her master's degree in 1897, Parsons taught at the Horace Mann School, Teachers College's model school.

61. The contributions that Parsons made to Columbia and to anthropological associations over the years were sizable. For example, from 1916 to 1941, Parsons contributed over $30,000 to the American Folklore Society. Information on the variety of publications and ventures that Parsons funded is found in Zumwalt, *Wealth and Rebellion*, 313–26. Parsons often gave her funding through a vehicle such as Columbia's Social Science Research Council or the Southwest Society. See Deacon, *Elsie Clews Parsons*, 244, 452n5.

62. Elsie Worthington Clews married Herbert Parsons in September 1900 and retained her maiden name as her middle name. For clarity's sake, I refer to her as Parsons through this discussion. Henry Clews was adamant in his belief in women's proper sphere and spoke publically in opposition to suffrage. See Zumwalt, *Wealth and Rebellion*, 36.

63. Desley Deacon, *Elsie Clews Parsons: Inventing Modern Life* (Chicago: University of Chicago Press, 1997), 19.

64. Parsons described her childhood and her goal for achieving a "personal morality" that would "triumph over status morality" in an unpublished manuscript, "Journal of a Feminist" (circa 1913–1914), 13, Parsons Papers.

65. Zumwalt, *Wealth and Rebellion*, 32–54.

66. Deacon, *Elsie Clews Parsons*, 31.

67. Kroeber, "Elsie Clews Parsons," 252.

68. According to Rosalind Rosenberg, Giddings courses attracted women interested in philanthropy. His theory of "consciousness of kind" described "a state of consciousness in which any being, whether low or high in the scale of life, recognizes another conscious being as like kind with itself." This theory provided a framework for fostering civic connectedness and both individual and social transformation. See Rosalind Rosenberg, *Beyond Separate Spheres: Intellectual Roots of Modern Feminism* (New Haven: Yale University Press, 1982), 151–52.

69. See Ellen Fitzpatrick, *Endless Crusade: Women Social Scientists and Progressive Reforms: The Social Settlements and Progressive Reforms* (New York: Oxford University Press, 1990); Allen F. Davis, *Spearheads for Reform: The Social Settlements and the Progressive Movement* (New Brunswick: Rutgers University Press, 1984).

70. Quoted in Hare, 37. A copy of Elsie Clews's master's thesis is in Box 3, Franklin Giddings Papers, Rare Book and Manuscripts Collection, Columbia University, New York City.

71. Elsie Clews Parsons, "Divisions of Labor in the Tenement House," *Charities and the Commons* 15 (December 1905): 443–44; idem, "The School Child, the School Nurse, and the Local School Board," *Charities and the Commons* 14 (1905): 1102; idem, "Penalizing Marriage and Childbearing," *Independent* 60 (January 1906): 146–47.

72. Margaret Olivia Sage, "Opportunities and Responsibilities of Leisured Women," *North American Review* 181 (November 1905): 712–21.

73. Ibid. See also Parsons's comment regarding reactions to her plans in *Charities and the Commons* 16 (March 1906): 1080–81. In 1907 Sage founded the Russell Sage Foundation, which funded developments in social work. Ruth Crocker, "The History of Philanthropy as Life-History: A Biographer's View of Mrs.

Russell Sage," in *Philanthropic Foundations: New Scholarship, New Possibilities,* ed. Ellen Condliffe Lagemann (Bloomington: Indiana University Press, 1999), 318–28.

74. Elsie Clews Parsons, "A Plan for Girls With Nothing to Do," *Charities and the Commons* 14 (May 1905): 3–7; idem, "Girls with Nothing to Do," *Charities and the Commons* 15 (October 1905): 124; and "Aim of Productive Efficiency," 503.

75. Elsie Clews Parsons, *Old-Fashioned Woman: Primitive Fancies About the Sex* (New York: Putnam, 1913), 6.

76. E.g., her Columbia classmate Alfred Kroeber.

77. Alfred Kroeber to Elsie Clews Parsons, 5 May 1916, Parsons Papers. See also Elsie Clews Parsons, "American 'Society' I," *New Republic* 16 (December 1916): 184.

78. See Zumwalt, *Wealth and Rebellion;* Deacon, *Elsie Clews Parsons,* Peter H. Hare, *A Woman's Quest for Science: Portrait of Anthropologist Elsie Clews Parsons* (Buffalo: Prometheus Books, 1985).

79. Parsons, for example, provided some funding to support Melville Herskovits's research in Africa. Parsons served as an alumnae trustee at Barnard. She took an active interest in naming the new dean after Laura Gill's forced resignation in 1906 (Parsons nominated Alice Miller, Mary Simikhovich and Emily James Putnam—all three were married women) and in 1915 was the head of the trustee committee launching the Million Dollar Campaign to commemorate Barnard's Silver Anniversary.

80. Quoted in Deacon, *Elsie Clews Parsons,* 201–02.

81. Esther S. Goldfrank, *Notes on an Undirected Life: As One Anthropologist Sees It* (New York: Queens College Press, 1978), 21–35. Franz Boas to Elsie Clews Parsons, 12 June 1924; 28 September 1932; 2 April 1936, all in Parsons Papers.

82. Goldfrank, *Notes on an Undirected Life,* 21–35. Zumwalt notes that Parsons "felt the economic necessity to reduce the amount of her support for anthropological work in 1932 and 1933." This included "cutting her annual contribution to his secretarial fund to $1500." Zumwalt, *Wealth and Rebellion,* 316.

83. Quoted in Deacon, *Elsie Clews Parsons,* 179.

84. As Desley Deacon noted in her biography of Parsons, Parsons once asserted to Helen Gurley Flynn that she had personal income of only $2500 a year, "an allowance from my father." Parsons underscored the point, by adding, "To many of my acquaintances my circumstances are misleading." Whether the comment was meant to deflect a request for financial assistance or was an accurate picture of Parsons's personal finances is difficult to assess. See Desley Deacon, *Elsie Clews Parsons: Inventing Modern Life* (Chicago: University of Chicago Press, 1997), 198.

85. See note 55.

86. Goldfrank, *Notes,* 5.

87. Ibid.

88. Margaret Mead, *An Anthropologist at Work* (New York: Houghton Mifflin, 1959), 318.

89. Ruth Bunzel and Margaret Mead, eds., *The Golden Age of Anthropology* (New York: George Braziller, 1960), 5; see also Rosalind Rosenberg, *Beyond Separate Spheres,* passim.

90. Rosalind Rosenberg, "The Academic Prism: The New View of American Women," in *Women of America,* ed. Carol Berkin (Boston: Houghton Mifflin, 1979), 319.

91. Parsons served as president of the American Folklore Society from 1918 to 1920, the American Ethnological Association from 1923 to 1925, and the American Anthropological Society from 1940 to 1941.

92. "Heretics" list, Parsons Papers.

93. Parsons was particularly close to Bourne. She uses the phrase in an undated letter to Bourne, in Parsons-Bourne Papers, Columbia University Rare Book and Manuscript Room; see also Eric Sandeen, "Born Again: The Correspondence Between Randolph Bourne and Elsie Clews Parsons," *American Literary History* 1 (fall 1989): 489–509.

94. There has been much writing about New York City's rebels, Robert E. Humphrey, *Children of Fantasy: The First Rebels of Greenwich Village* (New York: Wiley, 1978); Judith Schartz, *The Radical Feminist of Heterodoxy: Greenwich Village, 1912–1940* (Norwich, Vt.: New Victoria Publishers, 1986).

95. Kroeber to Parsons, n.d., Parsons Papers.

96. My thinking about universities and their boundaries and ties to civic life has been influenced by Douglas Sloan, "Science in New York City, 1867–1907," *ISIS* 71 (March 1980): 35–76. For use of the concept of "enclosure," see, for example, Robert A. McCaughey, *International Studies and Academic Enterprise: A Chapter in the Enclosure in American Learning* (New York: Columbia University Press, 1984).

97. Examples of this strategy are found in the history of Columbia's affiliation with Teachers College and Barnard College and the disbanding of its School of Library Service at the turn of the century and even Columbia's connection to the New York School of Civics and Philanthropy (later known as the School of Social Work).

98. Revision of the major themes and periodization to guide the historical study of philanthropy is underway. The standard account, which describes a shift from the personal, religiously-based notions of charity to modern foundation philanthropy is Robert Bremner, *American Philanthropy* (Chicago: University of Chicago Press, 1960).

99. Women's patronage merits further investigation. See "The Most Available and Suitable Man: Columbia's Miller Chair and Salo Baron," in *Jewish Learning in the American University: The First Century*, Paul Ritterband and Harold S. Wechsler (Bloomington: Indiana University Press, 1994), 150–81. Linda Eisenmann notes that Florence Anderson, Secretary of the Carnegie Corporation, was instrumental in women's programming, but her role and this area of the foundation's funding has not been addressed in its scholarly history, Ellen Condliffe Lagemann's *The Politics of Knowledge*. See Linda Eisenmann, "Befuddling the 'Feminine Mystique': Academic Women and the Creation of the Radcliffe Institute, 1950–1965," *Educational Foundations* 10 (summer 1996): 5–26; particularly note 29.

100. Nippur is in modern day Iraq. In 1894 Stevenson was recognized as the first woman to receive a honorary doctorate from the University of Pennsylvania, Martin Meyerson, *And Gladly Teach: Franklin and His Heirs at the University of Pennsylvania, 1740–1976* (Philadelphia: University of Pennsylvania Press, 1978), 117–21.

101. For Helen Culver, see Rudolf K. Haerle, Jr., "William Isaac Thomas and the Helen Culver Fund for Race Psychology: The Beginnings of Scientific Sociology at the University of Chicago, 1910–1913," *Journal of the History of the Behavioral Sciences* 27 (January 1991): 21–41. For Ethel Sturges Dummer, see Flora Lazar, "From Social Science to Psychosomatic Research: The Failure of An Alliance, 1908–1935" (Ph.D. diss., Columbia University, 1994). For Anita Blaine McCormack, see Kathleen D. McCarthy, *Noblesse Oblige: Charity and Cultural Philanthropy in Chicago, 1849–1929* (Chicago: University of Chicago Press, 1980), 56–60.

102. Christine Moon Van Ness, "Sara Yorke Stevenson," in *Women Anthropologists: A Biographical Dictionary*, eds. Ute Gacs et al. (New York: Greenwood Press, 1988), 344–49.

103. Lynn D. Gordon, *Gender and Higher Education in the Progressive Era*, 56–60.

104. Edwin E. Slosson, *Great American Universities* (New York: Arno, 1977, c1910), 446–47.

105. Writings in the history of women's philanthropy have been invigorated and advanced from its initial middle-class preoccupations by theoretical debates centered on diversity. The best overview of the recent literature is a 1994 review by Kathleen D. McCarthy. She notes that works by Nancy Hewitt, Suzanne Lebsock, and others have challenged earlier collectivist interpretations of "sisterhood" and encouraged greater recognition of possible "fissures" in the aims and impact of women's contributions in the voluntary sphere. See Kathleen D. McCarthy, "The History of Women in the Nonprofit Sector: Changing Interpretations," in *Women and Power in the Nonprofit Sector*, eds. Teresa Odendahl and Michael O'Neill (San Francisco: Jossey Bass, 1994), 17–38.

106. Julie A. Reuben, *The Making of the Modern University: Intellectual Transformation and the Marginalization of Morality* (Chicago: University of Chicago Press, 1996); George W. Marsden, *The Soul of the University: From Protestant Establishment to Established Nonbelief* (New York: Oxford University Press, 1994). Marsden and Reuben, for instance, have offered nuanced and provocative reconsiderations of secularization. Other scholars have sought to broaden the types of educational sites and clientele that are studied—e.g., academies, community colleges, normal schools, students of color, and the poor. See, for example, Eisenmann, Hutcheson, and Nidiffer, "A Conversation," 291–336.

* Special thanks to Hamid Mubarak for his helpful comments on the draft manuscript and to the Indiana University Center on Philanthropy for a Lilly Faculty Research Grant to complete this study.

"THE MOST AVAILABLE AND SUITABLE MAN": COLUMBIA'S MILLER CHAIR AND SALO BARON

PAUL RITTERBAND & HAROLD S. WECHSLER

We have searched the heavens, the earth, and the waters under the earth, on three continents, and finally the unanimous judgment of our advisers rested upon Professor Baron as the most available and suitable man.

—NICHOLAS MURRAY BUTLER[1]

In spring 1928, Linda Miller, a Temple Emanu-El congregant and recent widow of Nathan L. Miller, a prominent New York businessman, endowed a professorship of Jewish History, Literature, and Institutions at Columbia University in her husband's memory. President Nicholas Murray Butler thereupon appointed a committee to find the most suitable occupant. In the case of the Littauer endowment, Harvard chose a scholar already on the faculty. Columbia's 1928 roster yielded no candidate, and the committee looked outside the institution. The scarcity of positions in Jewish learning, especially at prestigious universities, and the number of potential candidates educated in American Semitics departments or abroad suggested that the committee would not conduct a lengthy or difficult search. But Columbia's optimism dissipated as interested parties exerted an array of communal and scholarly pressures concerning the appointment.

This chapter analyzes the diverse definitions of "suitability" that emerged during the committee's 15-month search—definitions offered by the donor, search committee members, and other practitioners. The eventual appointment of Salo Baron was an attempt to mediate between communal and institutional expectations for a position that could influence the growth of Jewish scholarship in universities for the rest of the century.

The committee confronted two difficult problems. What weight should it accord to a candidate's personality, religiosity, and denominational preference? Academic norms had supposedly made these factors irrelevant. Second, where did the chair best fit into the university? An earlier generation had favored inclusion of Jewish learning in Semitics departments. With the waning of interest in Semitics, would another discipline be more hospitable to—and profit more from—the chair? Practitioners understood that in answering these questions the committee would consider the dearth of university-based Jewish scholarship, diminution of communal support, loss of presidential interest, and failure to achieve recognition.

Many observers noted that Jewish Semitists often strayed from the Jewish aspects of their discipline. They hoped that the Miller chairholder would focus primarily on Jewish topics and also speak to the general concerns of the parent discipline. No one argued that the chair should become the base of a separate department, the solution particularists later termed most conducive to retaining a Judaic scholarly focus. But which discipline would provide the most congenial environment?

Answers to these questions proved critical for the field's subsequent history. Indeed, Salo Baron, the most available and suitable man, permanently moved the university-based study of Judaism past Semitics and philology, opened the study of history in American universities to Judaic insight, placed his students in academic positions that advanced the study of Jewish history, and promoted the development of Jewish learning in universities.

The Endowment

By 1928, activity on behalf of Judaica chairs in major American universities again accelerated. Henry Hurwitz's Menorah Association shifted from nurturing student Menorah groups to advocating endowments for Jewish scholarship. In 1927, the B'hai B'rith announced that it too sought to endow Judaica chairs. But only Hyman Enelow, still the junior rabbi at Temple Emanu-El, actually succeeded in securing an endowment.[2]

Enelow's fortunes at Emanu-El worsened after he arranged the Littauer gift. Rival Nathan Krass held a commanding position, and Enelow was consigned to directing Emanu-El's Sunday School. In 1933, the temple would release him, and he died soon after, a broken man.[3] In the midst of his professional troubles, Enelow found refuge in the home of Nathan and Linda Miller. "There," wrote a friend of the Millers,

> he found true friendship, understanding, admiration, spiritual community. There he could expand, give full reign to his trenchant wit, pour out his versatile knowledge, lose the acerbity and harshness he seemed to present to an unsympathetic world, and express his true self in a native kindliness that answered spontaneously and joyously to the like quality in his hosts.[4]

The Millers had moved to New York City about a decade before the arrival of the young rabbi from Kentucky. Each spouse attained considerable stature, Nathan as a Wall Street businessman, Linda as a philanthropist and connoisseur of the arts. A deep, affectionate relationship developed between Enelow and the Millers. Shortly before his death, Nathan Miller wrote Enelow that he was "personally under many more obligations to you than I will ever be able to repay, even if I live to be as old as Methuselah."[5] Enelow's weekly Emanu-El sermons, his Monday morning lectures on Jewish topics, and his informal conversations intensified the Millers' interest in their Reform Jewish background. Enelow gradually impressed upon them the importance of Jewish scholarship, not as an end in itself, but as a method of deepening one's devotion to Judaism. "Jewish knowledge suffused with *kawanna*, soul," in the words of Linda Miller's biographer.[6]

Linda Miller's endowment was not her first gift to advance Jewish scholarship. At Enelow's suggestion, for instance, she subsidized Israel Davidson's *Ozar ha-Shirah ve-ha-Piyyut* (*Thesaurus of Medieval Hebrew Poetry*). The thesaurus contained detailed information about 35,000 poems and prayers from post-Biblical times to the beginning of the *Haskalah* movement.[7] Enelow convinced Miller that an endowed chair—similar to the chair Lucius Littauer, her New Rochelle neighbor, gave to Harvard—would be the logical culmination of her philanthropy and an appropriate memorial to her husband. He then convinced Columbia authorities to accept the gift.

The endowment carried a stipulation: the chairholder should emphasize the "spiritual and intellectual aspects of Jewish life," not "the nationalist ideas which have recently become popular in some quarters." Sharing the anti-Zionism of Reform Judaism, and probably warned that Richard Gottheil would participate in the appointment process, Miller alerted Columbia to her wishes.[8]

The Littauer and Miller endowments occurred less than three years apart, but the difference in benefactorial expectations reflects the changes in communal thinking about university-based Jewish learning. Lucius Littauer endowed a research professorship, but Linda Miller was equally concerned with "spirituality," teaching, and scholarship. The Jewish undergraduate influx into American universities over the previous 20 years—Jews made up about 40 percent of the Columbia College student body just after World War I—turned communal interest toward maintaining or enhancing Jewish student identity. Linda Miller's concern led Columbia to consider the candidate's "personality" if not his "spirituality." So, too, the candidate's Jewish orientation. "There are, both within and without the Jewish group," Miller wrote Butler, "scholarly individuals who put an interpretation of Judaism that seems, to me, subversive of all that is finest in Jewish tradition. I feel that I might get a good measure of unhappiness out of certain conceivable appointments."[9] Miller knew of Enelow's unhappiness at Emanu-El and of his "spiritually" and "religiously" oriented scholarship. She assumed that a donor's wishes would have considerable weight and nominated her not unwilling mentor for the chair. She then listed his qualifications and inferred that she would supply the necessary funds "if I could put aside any uneasiness as to the personality of the professor in charge."[10]

Butler now understood that he was dealing with an earnest woman unwilling to settle for the mere honor of naming a professorship. American higher education had matured (and most faculties had been "professionalized") considerably since the days of Richard Gottheil's appointment. Columbia had accorded the benefactors of Gottheil's position the right of "presentation" but had reserved for itself the right of "acceptance." Butler now insisted that Columbia was responsible for its own appointments. "You will, I am sure," he replied to Miller, "see the embarrassment that would result from naming a professor at the insistence of a generous benefactor. No matter what the comperence of such a man might be, his colleagues would regard him as one apart, and his power for the University service would be gravely diminished, if not destroyed."[11] Butler promised to send Enelow's credentials to the search committee but offered no assurances about the outcome of the committee's deliberations.

Miller accepted Butler's logic but added: "For me it reduces itself to the ever vexatious question of squaring practice with principle."[12] She asked to select the chairholder from a short list that Columbia provided. Butler only offered to submit the names of finalists "in confidence to you for your suggestions and criticism before any final steps were taken."[13] Miller thanked Butler for exhibiting "such a sympathetic understanding." She authorized her financial agent to transfer the necessary securities[14] and Columbia received the funds two months later.[15]

The Committee and Its Mandate

Butler then turned to recruitment. Perceiving the appointment's "vexatious" nature, he asked Graduate Faculties dean Frederick J. E. Woodbridge to chair the search committee and to choose "an outstanding scholar who will not be a factionalist but who will command respect both within and without the University."[16] Thinking that the chair might support growth in comparative history of religions, Butler suggested Joseph H. Hertz, London's Chief Rabbi. Hertz was a Columbia Ph.D. whose dissertation had analyzed the philosophy of James Martineau, a nineteenth-century English Unitarian clergyman and defender of theism against the challenges of the physical sciences.

Butler's suggestion, given Miller's strictures, reveals his paucity of information about Jews and Jewish scholarship. Hertz's writings, apart from his thesis, were popular, but not scholarly, and Hertz, an Orthodox Jew, battled Reform Judaism in England. He was also a Zionist who played a key role in the events that led to the 1917 Balfour Declaration. Miller would have identified him immediately as a "factionalist" who emphasized Judaism's "political" rather than "spiritual" or "intellectual" aspects.[17]

Fortunately for Butler, the composition of the committee precluded mistakes of the sort Columbia would make when replacing Richard Gottheil.[18] The presence of professors Gottheil, A. V. Williams Jackson (philology), James T. Shotwell (history), William Westerman (ancient history), and Herbert W. Schneider (philosophy) insured appointment of a recognized scholar. The presence of social science professor Robert M. MacIver (an authority on intergroup relations), university chaplain Raymond D. Knox, and Union Theological Seminary president Henry Sloane Coffin assured that the successful candidate would address issues that also interested non-Jews. Columbia College dean Herbert Hawkes, Barnard College dean Virginia Gildersleeve (an anti-Zionist), associate Graduate Faculty dean Robert Fife, and Woodbridge represented divisions likely to work with the new appointee.[19] The committee contained two Jews, Gottheil and philosophy professor Irwin Edman, an associate of the Menorah movement. Edman conducted much of the committee's legwork despite his lack of knowledge of the field of Jewish learning and thereby gained considerable influence—especially during Gottheil's lengthy residence in France while on leave of absence.

Edman and Gottheil agreed on the importance of the appointee's personality. Gottheil believed that appointing someone with a difficult personality would exacerbate anti-Semitism at Columbia for many years. "So much—in the U.S. especially," he wrote, "depends upon a man's outward bearing that this has great influence upon the students and upon the community at large."[20] Edman sought a man with "culture," someone whose demeanor and scholarship reflected taste and refinement. Butler respected Linda Miller's wishes and sent Enelow's name and qualifications to the committee, but he reminded committee members that they, not the donor, would make a final recommendation to the president and trustees.[21]

Gottheil would naturally have an important say in the appointment, and viewed the endowment as a major addition to his severely understaffed department. Learning while in Paris that Butler had appointed a committee, he asked its members to delay their first meeting until he returned to campus. His wife's illness kept him in France for most of the 1928/29 academic year, but Gottheil's written suggestions served as the committee's initial agenda. His influence waned when these suggestions failed to bear fruit. The committee then set out on its own to define the chair's domain and to find an occupant.

Columbia could locate a chair of Jewish history, literature, and institutions in any of a half dozen departments. Gottheil assumed the chair would go to Semitics, but it could also go to Religion, English and Comparative Literature, History, or Philosophy, or become the basis for a new department. Should the committee seek out the scholar and then determine the location, or should it define the scope and then locate the scholar? The vested interests of possible consultants impeded the committee's ability to find answers and progress in filling the chair came slowly.[22]

In fall 1928, Gottheil's influence was at its peak. Enelow and Gottheil had known each other since Enelow's arrival in New York more than 15 years earlier. Gottheil wrote that Enelow had been "treated in our home—not only as a spiritual guide, but as a friend of the closest character."[23] In 1923, Gottheil suggested to Stephen Wise, then recruiting faculty members for the Jewish Institute of Religion, that Enelow would be an excellent professor of theology. He called Enelow "the best instructed of all the Rabbis here."[24] But Gottheil was cool to Enelow's candidacy for the Miller chair. Perhaps he objected to Enelow's intellectual orientation, which emphasized the study and criticism of texts and the suffusion of knowledge with "soul." Gottheil had waited too many years for the introduction of Jewish history and *kulturgeschichte* at Columbia to lose this opportunity, and he likely resented learning about the Miller chair from Butler rather than from Enelow.[25] Gottheil took serious offense at any slight to a family member, and he noted that "Enelow, who, certainly, must know about Mrs. Gottheil's illness, has not sent a word of spiritual encouragement."[26] Finally, Gottheil had settled upon another candidate—Michael Saul Ginsberg.

That Gottheil would sponsor a holder of the Doctor of Letters from the University of Paris came as no surprise to those who knew him. A long-time Francophile, and recipient of the Legion of Honor, Gottheil had married into a prominent French family and usually spent his summers in his wife's native land. Ginsberg was born in 1899 in Moscow, and after holding two minor university posts and a professorship at the Institute of Jewish Sciences in Petrograd, migrated to France. By the time of his nomination, he had received the *diplome* from the École du Louvre and the D. Litt. from the Sorbonne. Ginsberg applied for a professorship at the Jewish Institute of Religion, but Wise turned him down in 1927.[27] He renewed his application in August of 1928, stating that since his last letter he had received his doctorate and published a book on the history of political relations between Rome and Judea.[28] Wise took his candidacy somewhat more seriously this time, and his right-hand man at the institute, George A. Kohut, interviewed Ginsberg in Europe in late September.

Ginsberg convinced Kohut that his interest in the Institute stemmed from more than his poor prospects in Europe—his field and his Judaism worked against him—and from his family's desperate financial plight: he had applied to only one other American institution, apparently Jewish Theological Seminary. But President Cyrus Adler and trustee chairman Louis Marshall treated Ginsberg "cavalierly" (Kohut's word). His inability to speak Hebrew was a major liability since the Institute offered instruction in that language. "I think he knows a little Bible," wrote Kohut, "but nothing more, so that this constitutes a serious drawback to his efficiency as a teacher of Jewish history."[29] Gottheil, who chaired the Institute's board of trustees, heartily endorsed Ginsberg.[30] But Wise concluded that "it would be a great mistake to take a man in the History Department or in any other department who is not a good Hebrew scholar—and Ginsberg is not."[31] Wise expressed his regrets to Ginsberg and held out little hope for an appointment for some time to come.[32]

Gottheil then suggested Ginsberg to the Miller chair committee. With the venerable Semitics professor abroad, and with no other member familiar with Jewish scholarship, the committee tried to compile an acceptable short list. Enelow's name was ranked prominently. Other candidates included: Herbert Danby, an English Hebraist and canon of Jerusalem's Anglican Cathedral of St. George; Bernard Drachman, an orthodox rabbi in New York City and former instructor at Jewish Theological Seminary; Louis Ginzberg, a member of the Jewish Theological Seminary faculty, and Julian Obermann, then of the Jewish Institute of Religion and later of Yale University.[33] Relying heavily on Gottheil's recommendation, Woodbridge informed Butler that Michael Ginsberg "appears to me the most promising of the men suggested."[34]

Butler informed Linda Miller of the committee's first choice. Two months earlier, Stephen Wise had questioned Ginsberg's experience, but Butler told Miller that the committee believed he was "the best living scholar for the newly endowed chair," that "there is no other scholar of his standing," and that "he would be a great ornament to this new chair and to American scholarship in his chosen field." Butler suggested an initial three-year appointment so that "he might have the opportunity to display his qualities and his personality to his American colleagues."[35]

Miller cast a skeptical eye on the proposed appointment. She asked three men, "two of whom are amongst the most distinguished and learned professors at the Jewish Theological Seminary . . . and all of them say they had never heard of the man."[36] She reminded Butler of his promise and asked him to list the other candidates. Butler, easily deducing that Hyman Enelow was the "third man," elicited a memorandum from Woodbridge certifying Michael Ginsberg's competence. He forwarded the memorandum, over his signature, to Miller along with the remainder of the committee's short list, adding Hertz's name, which the committee had omitted.[37] This presentation did not heighten Miller's enthusiasm. "My impression [of Ginsberg]," she wrote, "is that of a promising young man who is just beginning his career." She had added an extra $50,000 to her endowment "so as to enable Columbia to secure the service of the most prominent scholar available," she reminded Butler.

She then criticized the other names on the short list—Hertz: "I am surprised that his name should be mentioned in this connection"; Drachman: "I can't imagine how any responsible person should drag his name into such a matter. . . . I don't see how anybody could ever dream of him as a University professor"; and Obermann: "I believe his specialty is in Semitic Languages or Comparative Religion rather than in Jewish History and Literature."

Louis Ginzberg met Miller's definition of prominence, but she understood "that he is opposed to liberal Judaism, and I, for one, would rather see a man appointed whose sympathies would embrace all types of Judaism." Henry Danby was not Jewish, and while most academic searches at this time of heightened anti-Semitism excluded Jewish candidates, the nature of the subject matter and Miller's wishes here dictated the appointment of a Jew. That left Hyman Enelow, about whom "your committee could easily find out . . . if they cared to consider his name."[38]

Miller's letter, with its astute characterizations, stung Butler and the committee. Perhaps she went too far in suggesting that the appointee be a Reform Jew. Reform Jews, she believed, were the only Jews that tolerated all major forms of Judaism, since Orthodox and Conservative Jews as a class opposed major portions of Reform doctrine. But, in truth, the committee could not justify a full professorship at a premium salary to an unproven scholar like Ginsberg. Butler sent Miller's letter to the committee and tried to disabuse Miller "as to the undesirability of choosing a young and promising scholar." Only a junior scholar "has a real chance to succeed and distinguish himself and the chair," he wrote. "Scholars of middle or mature age rarely bear transplanting without losing their productivity."[39]

Without Richard Gottheil to maintain enthusiasm for Ginsberg,[40] the committee meanwhile convinced itself that Ginsberg "is not a Hebrew scholar, but rather a classicist" and dropped his name.[41] Linda Miller had exercised a de facto veto, even if she did not have the right of "presentation," and Butler and the committee had learned the cost of bad homework. Butler lost the battle, but not his conviction that a young scholar might best fill the chair. Other confrontations lay ahead, and he invoked this belief again a year later.

Jockeying for Position

Richard Gottheil's frustration was no match for Hyman Enelow's. Most interested parties assumed that Columbia would soon appoint Enelow. "I earnestly hope," George Kohut wrote to Enelow, "that having inspired this gift, it may become your privilege to become the first occupant of the newly created Chair."[42] When rumors spread that Columbia would offer the position to someone else, many observers assumed that Enelow had removed himself from consideration. Dr. Wise "regretted to learn from me that you would not be available for appointment," Kohut told Enelow. "He agreed that your retirement from the ministry would mean a very great loss to the American Jewish pulpit."[43]

Others advanced claims—or enlisted friends to act on their behalf—upon learning that Enelow's appointment was not automatic. Felix Warburg, benefactor of the new Hebrew University in Jerusalem, wrote: "My brother in Hamburg has asked me to state that, as far as he can judge, Mr. Julian Obermann, who is in this country and is a man of high character, is well qualified for this field."[44] Kohut and Wise feared that Columbia would take this opportunity to replace the aging Gottheil with the new chair's occupant. Gottheil, however, reassured them that he had known of the endowment for months but that Butler had pledged him to secrecy. Feeling free to back a candidate, Wise and Kohut settled on Louis Ginzberg.[45]

Rumors abounded. "I hear all sorts of wild rumors as to who is to have it," Wise wrote Gottheil, "Enelow himself or Ginzberg of the Seminary, but those rumors mean nothing."[46] "Just at present," he wrote a few weeks later, "the rumor is that either Buttenweiser or Mann will be called."[47] (Moses Buttenweiser was professor of Biblical Exegesis at Hebrew Union College. Jacob Mann was Hebrew Union's professor of Jewish History and Talmud.) Speculation persisted, but most observers concluded that Columbia would turn to Hyman Enelow after a diligent search.

The Emanu-El rabbi was in an awkward position. He cherished hopes of receiving the call but confusion about his candidacy and Gottheil's hostility hampered his ability to mount an indirect campaign. Some influential Jews thought Enelow's personality a major hindrance. Kohut wished he might be "more of a *Mensch*."[48] Wise thought him "a good student, but he is a sour, embittered truly cynical person, and the fact is that he has not the power of teaching and interesting young people."[49]

Learning that the committee was still considering his name, Enelow attempted to appear before it. He asked Julius A. Bewer, a professor at Union Theological Seminary, to arrange for a committee member (perhaps the Seminary's president, Henry Sloane Coffin) to hear his endorsement of Jacob Mann's candidacy. Bewer declined, noting that Miller had just urged Enelow's candidacy.[50] Enelow then enlisted Lucius Littauer. Still devoted to the rabbi who induced him to endow Harry Wolfson's position, Littauer was "prepared to do everything under heaven to get the place for [Enelow]."[51] His physician told Wise that Littauer wanted the Jewish Institute of Religion head to speak to the committee on Enelow's behalf. "The Institute," the emissary promised, "would be the beneficiary if I would do what I could." Wise said he declined the offer because Enelow "is not a great and outstanding scholar of Jewish civilization" and "lacks altogether the power of conveying, in an attractive way, the things he knows."[52]

Wise, and almost everyone else, still assumed that Enelow would ultimately receive the appointment. He asked Gottheil, as a last-ditch maneuver, whether he could approach Butler or Woodbridge "about some real and outstanding personality, such as [Ismar] Elbogen [of the *Hochschule für die Wissenschaft des Judentums* in Berlin] or, as I believe [Mordecai] Kaplan." Kaplan, founder of the Reconstructionist movement, taught at Jewish Theological Seminary. Wise twice entreated him to join the Jewish Institute of Religion faculty and actually succeeded on the second occasion only to learn that Kaplan had changed his mind. "Kaplan is not a Spinoza," Wise concluded, "but he is a Jewish teacher and a gentleman, and Enelow is one of these in a limited degree."[53] Gottheil authorized Wise to speak for him about Kaplan, but Wise hesitated, reasoning that since the chair appeared within Enelow's grasp, there was virtue in silence.[54]

When a Columbia delegation unexpectedly called upon Wise a few days later, he surveyed some possible candidates: Umberto Cassuto of Florence, "a fine representative of the Sephardic side of Jewish life"; Ismar Elbogen, "a good Hebrew scholar and a fine person"; Cecil Roth; and Mordecai Kaplan, "a sound scholar [with] a great gift for teaching and . . . a larger body of disciples than almost any Jew I know in this country." Wise, after learning that "the donor's wishes . . . were by no means binding," said about Enelow: "I merely raised the question that may be raised regarding him [presumably his personality]." Wise and other consultants apparently persuaded the committee to reject Enelow, but when committee members went further afield, they soon concluded that every name precipitated controversy.[55]

A Time of Assessment

Columbia's 1928/29 intersession came at an opportune moment. Needing to mount a full-scale search, committee members used the hiatus to evaluate potential candidates and to assess the academic and communal pressures facing them. Eliminating the Enelow and Ginsberg candidacies did little to define the scope of the chair—Jewish "history, literature, and institutions" encompassed an enormous amount of intellectual territory. From the academic sidelines, members of the Menorah movement, earnest if ineffective advocates of Jewish studies in universities, urged the committee to identify someone with the breadth that the chair's title suggested. Do not, urged Menorah's Herbert Solow, appoint a mere compiler and textual commentator. A century earlier, *Wissenschaft des Judentums* marked a significant intellectual milestone, but, Solow noted, by the 1920s, "the rationalistic, anti-medieval, assimilationist, reformist theological interests of [the] founders have become permanent restrictions on the thought of all their followers." A scholar in the *Wissenschaft* tradition might produce a catalogue or a compendium—never an intellectual synthesis—and would appeal to no one who defined history to include social and economic trends.[56]

Irwin Edman's presence on the committee assured the representation of this viewpoint. A frequent contributor to *Menorah Journal*, his emphasis on gentility and general education resonated with Menorah's stance. The committee concluded that the occupant should devote attention both to Jews and Judaism. This tendency, already present when the committee considered Michael Ginsberg's candidacy, came to the fore in the ensuing months. The sentiment arose from eclectic sources, including Gottheil's interest in *kulturgeschichte*, Menorah's ideology, and the presence on the committee of non-Jewish historians.

But would such an appointment please Linda Miller? Miller continued to express no interest in Jewish "peoplehood." Some, without citing Enelow by name, argued that Columbia must refrain from appointing a rabbi, since university scientific traditions placed a clergyman in an untenable situation. But Miller hoped the chair's occupant "would try to reach the student body along spiritual lines."[57] Some urged the committee to ignore the personal factional beliefs of any candidate, but Miller constantly pressed for a Reform Jew. "I personally prefer a scholar belonging to the liberal school," she frequently reminded Butler, since he "would be more likely to do justice to the various aspects of Jewish life." And while some urged that a young scholar receive the appointment since it would permit him to develop within a university environment, Miller had other ideas. At every turn, the committee confronted the desires of the benefactress. With no available member expert in Jewish history, literature, and institutions, and after the awkward encounter with Miller over Michael Ginsberg, the committee concluded that it must consider her wishes, but the effort failed.

During intensive deliberations in February of 1929, the committee concluded that Louis Ginzberg, professor of Talmud at Jewish Theological Seminary, merited the call. A preeminent Judaica scholar whose *Legends of the Jews* had received general acclaim, Ginzberg probably *believed* in little, save the importance of modern Jewish scholarship. However, he *observed* enough of Jewish tradition and felt enough empathy to work out his ambivalences within a Jewish framework.[58] He opposed Reform Judaism and Reconstructionism because he believed that significant changes in Jewish tradition would not lead to a major "return to religion" among American Jews and might further undermine Jewish religiosity. These views compounded the committee's difficulties.

Ginzberg, an established, imaginative scholar with an international reputation, was an excellent candidate, and Gottheil remained silent on the Katz incident. Knowing that Miller would object to a permanent appointment for Ginzberg, the committee recommended that Columbia use the endowment "to invite distinguished scholars here from time to time to lend their prestige to the enterprise and to devote a portion of the income from the fund to fellowships to encourage study and research on the part of younger men." It recommended Ginzberg's appointment as visiting lecturer for the 1929/30 academic year.

The committee recommended the religion department for the chair's home and the consideration of Ralph Marcus and Henry Rosenthal for fellowships.[59] Rosenthal, who had studied at Columbia, continued his education at Jewish Theological Seminary and became a rabbi, mainly because academic Judaica positions were scarce.[60] Butler sent the committee report to Miller, gave instructions to open negotiations with Ginzberg, and left for his annual vacation believing that he had solved a knotty problem.[61]

Dean Woodbridge had not contacted Ginzberg when Miller's reply arrived. While reiterating her preference for a Reform scholar, she took the university to task primarily for changing the endowment's terms unilaterally through the appointment of visiting professors. She reminded Butler about his promise "to secure the most eminent scholar available for this chair" and asked that their mutually agreed upon plan be executed.[62] Woodbridge, however, urged the Columbia president to move cautiously given the unprecedented nature of the appointment and "a difference of opinion regarding emphasis" among the interested parties. Universal recognition of Ginzberg's scholarship dictated his call, while its temporary nature indicated "that the University was not committed to an orthodox as over a liberal position." In fact, Woodbridge revealed, Miller's allegiance to the "liberal school" and the committee's desire not to prejudice its interests were strong reasons for its failure to recommend Ginzberg for permanent appointment.[63]

Several considerations prompted Butler to back his committee. First, the Columbia president had probably become exasperated with a benefactress who constantly refused attempts at accommodation. In addition, Butler evinced concern that considerations of scholarly competence had become entangled in sectarian rivalries within the Jewish community. Whereas Woodbridge viewed the endowment as "the really first great opportunity to give to Jewish studies the university significance they ought to have," Miller gave high priority to the spiritual inspiration of students. The result of Columbia's difficulty in "finding a man who will look at the development of the subject as a university enterprise as distinct from a sectarian one" was a resort to a solution all knew to be "makeshift."[64] Anticipating Ginzberg's unacceptability in Miller's eyes, the committee declined to recommend his permanent appointment.

To cover all bases, the committee sent Irwin Edman to interview Linda Miller's other Reform candidate, Jacob Mann of Hebrew Union College. Initially attracted by the prospect of moving to an institution where his scholarship would be appreciated, Mann's conversation with Edman rapidly disenchanted him. "Edman talked of a chair of Jewish culture," he recounted, "requiring the occupant to be a sort of jack of all trades who, in addition to advising graduate students on all sorts of Jewish culture (from Biblical times to 1929!) is also to give a three-hour per week course to undergraduates (Jewish and Gentile), which means a most elementary course on Judaism to people with no previous knowledge whatever of Jewish studies, not being even familiar with the Hebrew alphabet." Edman and Mann conceived of the chair in opposing terms: the former saw it as important for the propagation and advancement of culture, the latter for the advancement of scholarship. The interview did not change the committee's resolve.[65]

Butler approved negotiations for Ginzberg's temporary appointment, but a deal was never struck.[66] Indeed, there is no evidence that the committee contacted Ginzberg, who was on sabbatical in Palestine for the 1928/29 academic year. The committee probably failed to implement its earlier decision because just at this time its members became aware of a candidate who might merit permanent appointment. This candidate did not entail "local difficulties" and might prove more attractive to Linda Miller. The committee again turned to the European Jewish scholarly community.[67]

Ismar Elbogen

The *Hochschule für die Wissenschaft des Judentums* (opened in 1872) and located near the University of Berlin, was a response to, and benefitted from, the refusal of nineteenth-century German universities to welcome Jewish learning. In the summer of 1929, however, this major center for European

Jewish scholarship faced an anxious future. One faculty member, Julius Guttmann, a historian of philosophy, accepted a visiting professorship at Hebrew Union College and eventually went to The Hebrew University in Jerusalem. Two colleagues departed soon after: Chanoch Albeck to Hebrew University in Jerusalem and Chaim Torczyner to the Jewish Institute of Religion, leaving Ismar Elbogen, professor of Jewish history and literature, among the small remaining senior staff.[68]

The appointment of Elbogen, a Reform Jew and a recognized senior scholar, Woodbridge and the committee concluded, "would be more agreeable to the donor than the appointment of anyone here with the exception of Rabbi Enelow whom the committee does not feel justified in recommending."[69] Elbogen, who had garnered considerable respect from his American colleagues while a visiting lecturer at the Jewish Institute of Religion, received strong testimonials from Wise and George Foot Moore.[70] Only Menorah members dissented from his candidacy. They acknowledged Elbogen's erudition but regarded him as "a typical product of the Germanic school of Jewish scholars, with no more of a humanistic approach, no more broadness of vision or depth of thought than any of a dozen competent textual scholars now professing in seminaries in Cincinnati, New York, London and Breslau." Calling Elbogen "an orthodox, theological-minded and dull scholar," the Menorah faction concluded that he would have few students and little general influence.[71]

The committee, decidedly rejecting these criticisms, recommended a permanent appointment at a premium salary, but Butler suggested an initial three-year term "with appropriate explanation that this is not an unusual method in the case of men from other institutions."[72] James Gutmann, a young Columbia philosophy professor, extended a "feeler" to Elbogen, and the committee asked Irwin Edman to conduct more extensive negotiations while in Europe for the summer.[73] Edman sent Columbia authorities guardedly optimistic reports. Elbogen found New York's research facilities tempting.[74] But he—like Paul Haupt 40 years earlier—emphasized salary and pension. Edman was authorized to offer a $7,500 salary, but when Elbogen requested $10,000 and a pension comparable to his German entitlement, Butler met the salary request and offered him a removal allowance.[75] He added: "It is the well-established tradition of Columbia University to permit none of its distinguished servants to suffer if old age or disability should overtake them."[76]

The detailed nature of the negotiations gave committee members cause for optimism. But on September 19, 1929, just before he received Butler's final offer, Elbogen cabled that he could not accept the call, and receipt of Butler's letter did not change his mind.[77] The Berlin Jewish community, students, and colleagues pressured Elbogen to remain at the *Hochschule*. Alluding to faculty attrition, he wrote, "the Trustees have urged me and placed the responsibility of the continuance of the college upon my shoulders."[78] Elbogen also declined offers of temporary appointments.[79] Contemporaries understood Elbogen's resolve to remain at the *Hochschule*.[80] No one envisioned that he would live out his years on Morningside Heights, a refugee from Nazism, with joint appointments at Hebrew Union College, the Jewish Institute of Religion, Jewish Theological Seminary, and Dropsie College.[81]

Butler thereafter communicated with Linda Miller on an *ex post facto* basis Only after receiving Elbogen's cable declining the offer did he inform her that Columbia had embarked upon serious negotiations and that all hoped for a favorable reply. Miller responded that she had followed the negotiations through the newspapers and only regretted "that the committee seemed to find it impossible to find an American who, I think might have reached the student body in a spiritual way in addition to the pursuits of scholarly research." By the fall of 1929, Linda Miller was relegated to an insignificant role in the selection process. Her candidate out of the running, she merely acknowledged Butler's letters.[82]

While pondering the Columbia offer, Ismar Elbogen travelled to St. Moritz. There he encountered David S. Blondheim, professor of romance philology at Johns Hopkins. Elbogen said that he was still considering the offer but asked whether he could suggest Blondheim's name should he decline Columbia's invitation.[83] Blondheim, taken aback, replied in the affirmative, though he urged Elbogen to accept the call. A specialist in medieval Judeo-Romance dialects, Blondheim had studied at Johns Hopkins and later at the École des Hautes Études in Paris. He taught first at the University of Illinois and then at Johns Hopkins.

Blondheim's work differed from the research of most contemporaries. His research on the connections between certain Judeo-Romance texts and the earliest Latin Bible translation was reminiscent of Harry Wolfson's efforts to move between Jewish and non-Jewish scholarship, but his analyses of Old French glosses on Rashi's Talmudic commentaries were virtually unparalleled in secular institutions. Blondheim viewed an opportunity to teach a graduate course on French literary criticism at the University of Illinois as a burden, not an opportunity. The subject was "about as far from the one I am chiefly concerned with as anything could be." On the whole, however, the Illinois position initially satisfied him, and he turned down an assistant professorship at the University of California when Illinois met the California offer. Urbana was closer to the east, he noted, and Illinois had superior research facilities.[84] But Blondheim, unable to live comfortably as a Jew in Urbana, accepted a 1917 call from Johns Hopkins that brought him closer to the "Jewish center."[85] At Johns Hopkins, promotions and salary increases came more slowly than expected, and after a few research trips to Europe, Baltimore appeared to be "an abominable provincial town."[86] Europe's sophistication intoxicated other American scholars, but few colleagues readjusted so poorly to America.

Personal factors compounded matters. In the mid-1920s, Blondheim divorced his Orthodox wife and began an affair in Europe with Eleanor Dulles, sister of John Foster and Allen Dulles.[87] Conduct acceptable in Europe—Blondheim and his mistress lived together openly in Paris for a year—was condemned in America. The couple met covertly on weekends after their return to the U.S.[88]

Elbogen's proposition came as an attractive surprise to Blondheim. Blondheim believed that Edman was the committee's only Jewish member and was unsympathetic to his type of research.[89] George Kohut, an old acquaintance, told Blondheim that Gottheil sat on the committee. Kohut mounted an elaborate campaign on Blondheim's behalf and easily enlisted Wise.[90] Gottheil, finally back at his post, was more difficult—and not only because his relationship with Kohut had its testy side.[91] The Columbia professor thought of Blondheim as "an accomplished writer on subjects dealing with Jewish life in past and present," primarily from a linguistic point of view, not as a historian.[92] Blondheim's supporters never could overcome this crucial determination.

For Gottheil, and for the committee, the distinction between literary and historical approaches had become decisive. The heterogeneous composition of the committee—deans, theologians, Jewish faculty members, and disciplinary representatives—reflected the original, vague mandate to include Jewish history, literature, and institutions; but between the fall of 1928 and the fall of 1929, the committee made progress in defining the chair's scope, credentials suitable for its occupant, and its departmental location.

Committee members from the outset preferred a cultivated, engaging scholar who lacked strong feelings on Zionism. Michael Ginsberg's candidacy led them to comprehend the wishes of the chair's donor. Hyman Enelow's candidacy reinforced their caution on questions of personality and the eligibility of a rabbi, while Jacob Mann's candidacy prompted them to decide against a philologist or a textual critic. Consideration of Louis Ginzberg led committee members to prefer scholars who lacked strong ties to Orthodoxy or Conservatism. Ismar Elbogen's candidacy—he would update Graetz's history of the Jews—heightened interest in historians, preferably with breadth. Along the way, the members came to prefer a European—to avoid domestic difficulties—with foreign training, though it is unclear whether committee members believed this education enhanced the candidate's scholarship or cultivation. The committee arrived at a consensus under the counsel of Gottheil—and of the historian Salo Baron from the Jewish Institute of Religion.

Baron on History

Goddess, if I began at the beginning,
If there were time to detail our tribulations,
Evening would fall on Olympus before I had finished. . . .

Achates, is there a place
Left in the world not full of our miseries?[93]

—Aeneas

Salo (Shalom) Wittmayer Baron was born in Tarnow, located in Galicia, in 1895, and came to Vienna during World War I. He earned doctorates in philosophy (1917), political science (1922), and law (1923) from the University of Vienna, and was ordained at the Jewish Theological Seminary of Vienna in 1920. Baron taught at the Jewish Teachers College (*Jüdisches Pädagogium*) in Vienna until 1926.[94] Stephen Wise took interest in Baron in 1925 and invited him to teach at the Jewish Institute of Religion on a "trial" basis.[95] The Institute's dean, Harry Slonimsky, did not at first favor Baron's retention since "he thinks we might get a bigger and stronger man," but Baron's teaching ability and personality impressed Wise. "He is not a genius," Wise noted, "but in some ways he is better than a genius, for he is solid, and substantial, and dependable, and, the Lord be praised, untemperamental."[96] Kohut shared Wise's enthusiasm and called Baron "a man of uncommon ability, not only in the field of learning, but in practical affairs as well." Baron, Kohut predicted, "will be heard of as a leader in many directions, and I am indeed proud of the fact of having persuaded our dear and lamented friend, Chajes, to release him for service in America."[97]

Baron came off probation within a year, and Kohut held out his productivity as a model for other J.I.R. faculty members: "[Baron] is writing many books and has nevertheless time to write minor articles of no mean importance, while all the others are conspicuous by their quiescence," he noted. "All of them have literary gifts, and if they cultivated the art of expression in public print it would go far toward stimulating interest in our work."[98] In 1928, Baron declined a call to the chair in modern history at the Breslau seminary, a chair that Heinrich Graetz once occupied.[99]

During the 1920s, Richard Gottheil secured inclusion of a course on Judaism among Columbia's offerings, to be taught in turn by scholars of different theological leanings. He retained Baron—then at J.I.R.—to teach the course, and the young historian established a reputation for excellent teaching. Baron's life's work was a multi-volume social and economic history of the Jews, but he also demonstrated knowledge of rabbinic literature and told the committee of his interest in the interaction between Persian and Hebrew culture.[100]

Baron apparently met with the committee to discuss Jewish history during the negotiations with Elbogen, a meeting that also permitted the committee to evaluate Baron if the Elbogen talks collapsed. We know little about the encounter save that Baron argued—apparently persuasively—that, with Wolfson at Harvard, university-based Jewish learning next needed a historian, located in a history department. But within weeks of this meeting, Baron published articles on "Research in Jewish History" and "The Study of Jewish History" that resembled criticisms offered by other contemporary Jewish historians and that suggest the tone and substance of his meeting with the committee. The articles examined American university precedents in the field of Jewish history, criticisms of scholarship in that field, and the congruence of university based Jewish history and the "New History," the predominant historical outlook in American universities.

In one sense, "Jewish history" was frequently taught in courses on ancient history or in connection with the Bible, but ancient history courses primarily surveyed the powerful neighbors of the Jews. Jewish history was a prolegomenon to the study of Christianity in university Bible courses, at least until publication of George Foot Moore's *Judaism*, and post-Biblical Jewish history remained largely unstudied even after the book's appearance. Semitists occasionally attempted to introduce Jewish history courses, just as some nineteenth-century classicists supplemented linguistic work with Greek and Roman history courses.[101] But university-based Jewish history courses required more resources and greater specialization than Semitists commanded. If history departments had been more hospitable to Jews—who were most likely to be interested and qualified to offer Jewish history— the appointees might have emulated the Jewish Semitists who neglected pertinent Jewish questions. Scholarly attention to Jewish history remained low, a condition the Miller endowment could redress.[102]

Including Jewish history in the university's subject pantheon, Baron probably told the committee, might reduce or eliminate partisanship, parochialism, pedantry, and preservationism or antiquarianism. Jewish interest in history arose in the nineteenth century, historiographies often noted, along with Jewish emancipation. Jews traditionally extolled their indifference to history and invidiously compared Gentile "activity" to their observance of timeless commandments. Jewish participation in general cultural life after emancipation awakened an interest in a more sophisticated understanding of the past. Practitioners of *Wissenschaft des Judentums*, such as Isaac Martin Jost and Leopold Zunz, were motivated by respect for a bygone era, while filiopietism inspired Heinrich Graetz.[103]

Subsequent generations of historians acknowledged the extraordinary grasp of disparate types of literature that Graetz displayed in his history of the Jews but criticized his subjectivity, especially his anti-Catholicism, ultra-rationalism, and bias against East European Jewry. "All persons who have favored the Jews inevitably figure as saints and heroes," Cecil Roth noted, "while whoever opposed or oppressed them automatically become ruffians and hypocrites."[104] Despite its faults and obsolescence, no one superseded the Graetz synthesis until Baron began publishing his opus. Graetz's partisanship probably appealed to assimilated German and American Jews who faced increased anti-Semitism and an influx of East European coreligionists.[105]

The American Jewish Historical Society spurred the study of American Jewish history—American Jews did not venture into other aspects of Jewish history for several decades—but critics charged that the Society, too, harbored partisanship. One detractor, for example, held the Society responsible for "a tendency to write American Jewish history in order to plead the Jews' case as citizens and human beings"—a tactic that failed to forestall the rise in anti-Semitism, or to improve the quality of scholarship.[106]

Parochialism, the second shortcoming of non-university based Jewish history, implied the sacrifice of contextual and comparative elements. "Our stock Histories are too much self-centered," a critic wrote. "We are not shown what our ancestors did learn from the rest of mankind, and what they did return, stamped with the genius of our race. For, unique as our History is, we are still a people made up of human beings, to whom nothing human is strange."[107] Some historians chastised Graetz's disciples for emphasizing minuscule events that pertained to German Jewry while ignoring important questions about other Jews that their master raised.[108] Methodologies, Baron and other advocates of university inclusion argued, also had to be universal, and categories that applied to other groups must explain Jewish motivations and actions. "God's will" was an unacceptable explanation for an event.[109] Within the university, Jewish scholarship suffered not from parochialism but from extreme universalism. Advocates of university-based Jewish scholarship believed universalism, in reasonable doses, was a salutary corrective to the writings of historians of the Jews who worked in other settings.

Baron disagreed with scholars who insisted that mastery of the Talmud was the inescapable prerequisite for all historical scholarship that involved Jews. Extant methodologies, not command of rabbinical texts, should determine the canons of historical Jewish scholarship.[110] Baron agreed with Jewish Theological Seminary bibliographer Alexander Marx that the Talmudic emphasis resulted from a need to insert a positive theme into the long, dreary period of Jewish history that began with the fall of the Second Temple. Historians could not employ Jewish political history as a viable organizational theme and the period was otherwise noted for the monotonous recitation of Jewish sufferings and martyrdoms. Marx employed the term "literary history" to denote the analysis of Jewish spiritual activity.[111] Cecil Roth termed it "the irreparable disaster of becoming almost a branch of theology."[112] Resulting historical scholarship neglected contextual elements and even neglected to ask the correct questions of the assembled data.

Critics suggested that socio-economic analysis replace the literary-theological emphasis. "The description of the ordinary life of the people, their legal status and their economic activities will not only relieve the dreary picture of the periodically recurring persecutions, but also help to explain the causes of these persecutions and contribute towards a better understanding of the course of events."[113] As long as aphorisms such as "history is past politics, and politics present history" determined scholarly agendas, the history of a people in diaspora was a poor candidate for university inclusion. But the eclipse of political history and a broadened conception of Jewish history facilitated entry. The committee had to identify an individual with a broad understanding of social and economic history, a command of Jewish source material—documenting the socio-economic history of a people required examination of more than the obvious sources—and the ability to employ the theoretical and methodological advances made since the emergence of *Wissenschaft des Judentums*.

Critics frequently denounced historians of the Jews for pedantry: finding a "broad" scholar would be difficult. Scholars, noted Cecil Roth, devoted "oceans of ink" to "the exact sequence and habitat of the various medieval German rabbis."[114] Historians of American Jewry were also charged with repetitiveness, pedantry, and myopia: "They were assiduous in the collection of such facts as would determine the first occurrence of this or that Jewish event or the initial appearance of a Jew in a certain locale, but they seemed incapable of doing more than that. They were interested in results, not causes or trends."[115] Historians, another critic wrote, "have now proceeded far enough in the prosecution of their researches to pause and objectively to contemplate the body of facts which they have accumulated thus far." Collection, preservation, and publication inadequately described the historian's domain. A "philosophy of Jewish history" giving due weight to material, as opposed to spiritual, motivation was within reach.[116]

Some observers questioned whether extant sources permitted the scholars to generalize. These observers called for examination of non-Jewish sources: documents and deeds, chronicles, letters, inscriptions, and references in non-Jewish literature and legislation. This necessary and painstaking process, Baron cautioned, was not an excuse to forego tentative scholarly syntheses.[117] Broader goals and strategies determine tactics, critics insisted, not the other way around. Jewish history, when studied at all, suffered from filiopietism, a tendency to chronicle rather than to interpret, lack of a political dimension, and a neglect of source material and methodology.[118] Its failure to conform to Christian or western periodization pointed to the subject's inability to draw upon general history or contribute to "general" historical scholarship.

Salo Baron indicted the prevalent lachrymose conception of Jewish history, that is, as "a history of scholars and persecutions (Gelehrten- und Leidens-geschichte)."[119] An emphasis upon great individuals, events, texts, and sufferings, and a myopic idealism flawed the historical study of Jews. Baron criticized the tendency in the *Wissenschaft des Judentums* movement to see "in Jewish history the gradual progression of the Jewish religious or national spirit in its various vicissitudes and adjustments to the changing environments," a secularized equivalent to the earlier theocratic attribution of the Jewish destiny to "God's will."[120] Lacking a university base, he asserted, the field still suffered from the dominance of theologians and philologists rather than trained historians.[121] The "official" historical outlook was a form of social control—a Jewish scholarly equivalent to the "bloody shirt" that traditional Jewish communal leadership tirelessly invoked. Academization of Jewish history would result in a new periodization scheme, based upon general history, to replace "the otherwise noteworthy Krochmal-Graetzian scheme of the successive cycles of growth and decay in Jewish history."[122] Locating the subject in a university would also allow for historical explanation based upon universal categories. "There is a growing feeling that the historical explanations of the Jewish past must not fundamentally deviate from the general patterns of history which we accept for mankind at large or for any other particular national group," Baron wrote.[123] University access, finally, would rectify the imbalance between sociological and religious emphases in historical analysis. "It is consequently but the unavoidable and intrinsically justified adaptation of the general method of sociological interpretation to the peculiar problems of Jewish history," Baron noted, "when the element of religious experience is given its due share within the totality of the social forces."[124] Baron thus emphasized general historical—rather than uniquely Jewish—methodologies.[125] He sought out Jewish topics with general implications—not issues deemed of intrinsic worth because they were "Jewish" or general issues that had possible Jewish implications.[126]

What did Columbia see, intellectually, in Jewish history? As Baron addressed the search committee, Carlton J. H. Hayes, chairman of the history department, also wrote about "landmarks" in the development of historical scholarship during the previous quarter century. Hayes cited the relative decline in the study of political history and the "rising vogue of *Kulturgeschichte*," the importance of archaeological excavations for understanding ancient history and ancient religion, and "the effort to reconcile the science of historical investigation with the art of presenting its results."[127] Hayes continued, "In the realm of material culture, economic factors in man's past provide nowadays the topics for innumerable monographs and the central theme for many a great coöperative publication."[128]

By 1928, "the New History," which accorded social, economic, and religious activities equal status with political behavior, stressed the contextual and expressed affinity with the social sciences, had been ascendant for almost two decades.[129] A stateless people that nonetheless had an important history in the Common Era, the Jews were now ripe for historical investigation. By applying new concepts and techniques to Jewish history, a broadly trained historian could reformulate old subjects for other historians while refuting the contention that mastery of the sacred corpus took precedence over methodological sophistication. When he assumed his Columbia post, Baron offered a lecture series on "the interrelation of social and religious forces, as exemplified in the long historic evolution of the Jewish people"—a Jewish topic with universal implications, not a general topic with Jewish implications, or a topic of supposedly intrinsic Jewish worth.[130] This outlook governed his next half century of scholarship.

Dénouement

Baron's ideas were sympathetically received by the committee's historians, especially Westerman, who needed a better knowledge of Jewish history to conduct his own research on the ancient world. With Elbogen out of the picture, the committee settled the question of scope and tried to answer a single question: was David Blondheim a historian? Kohut concluded that Gottheil knew nothing of Blondheim's works save for their titles, and slowly changed Gottheil's conviction that Blondheim was primarily a philologist.[131] Kohut then told Edman that American and foreign Judaica scholars preferred Blondheim's candidacy because of his distinguished scholarship (specifically the Rashi volume), his teaching experience, and his cultivation.[132] Blondheim's chances further improved when Elbogen informed Edman of his enthusiastic support.[133] Butler's request for immediate action once the Elbogen correspondence ended led the committee to send Edman and Herbert Schneider to Baltimore to interview Blondheim.[134]

The meeting went well, but Blondheim's referees destroyed his chances. The committee concluded that Blondheim's true expertise lay in medieval philology, although it recognized his interest in Jewish history. Whether the committee knew of Blondheim's divorce and love affair is not clear. But given the importance that key committee members attributed to personal traits, these "shortcomings" would have been fatal to his candidacy.[135] The news of the committee's decision shocked Blondheim, and the disappointment increased the frustrations in his tortured life—frustrations that culminated in his suicide in 1934.[136]

In retrospect, it appears that Salo Baron had always been the most available and suitable man for the Miller chair.[137] In fact, one not cognizant of the chair's history might assume that Linda Miller endowed it with him—not Enelow—in mind. The committee, after an exhaustive, two-continent search, reported that it chose Baron over Blondheim "because of his constant identification with Jewish studies and also because of his more historical and philosophical interests."[138]

Baron's youth was his major liability because Linda Miller still envisioned appointment of a mature scholar. Butler had conceded the point in the case of Michael Ginsberg but remained firm in Baron's case. Miller also asked about Baron's partisanship. "I do hope he will pay deference to my wishes on the subject of the so-called ethnic Jew," she wrote. "Of course Zionism is dead," she continued, but the "ethnic Jew" doctrine still endangered Judaism as a spiritual force.[139] Butler reassured her "that Dr. Baron is without any partisanship in reference to the matters which he will have to undertake to present" and that Baron impressed him academically and personally when they met.[140]

Baron has recounted his negotiations with Butler. Impressed that Butler had a feel for Jewish learning, Baron expressed two concerns—first that he have some graduate students, second, that Columbia assign the chair to the history department. He believed that Jewish history could not yet be taught on the graduate level at a secular university since qualified students enrolled only in Jewish teachers colleges or in seminaries. The quality of students enrolled in his Columbia extension course further discouraged him. Baron added that his students at the Jewish Institute of Religion put his lectures to immediate use—often in their next Friday night sermons.[141] Neither Butler nor the committee could assuage him completely on this point. For these and financial reasons, Baron continued to teach at the Institute for a number of years after his Columbia appointment. But upon his arrival at Columbia, he found that his well-attended classes included many students who took his courses for general, rather than specialized purposes.

Agreeing that the chair belonged in the history department, Butler and Hayes secured the department's assent. Butler asked Baron to offer an undergraduate course, not for the spiritual edification of students as Linda Miller would have wanted, but "with a view of interesting them in this general field of study and so leading them forward, at least in some number, to become scholars in the branches of knowledge which will be under your direction."[142] Baron received a $7,500 salary, not as much as Columbia offered Elbogen but more than he received at the Jewish Institute of Religion.[143] George Kohut called the appointment "providential."[144] Rabbi Arthur Hertzberg years later noted that Baron was the first member of a history department at an American university to teach Jewish history. He concluded that "the many such chairs that now exist owe much to his example, and a substantial number of his former students are among their occupants."[145] The true significance of the Nathan Miller chair lies in Columbia's survey of the field of Jewish learning and its definition of work of university quality and spirit. Jewish studies in secular universities could thenceforth transcend philological and archaeological investigations and embark upon *kulturgeschichte*—to use Richard Gottheil's term. The endowment breathed life into university-based Jewish learning at a time when universities kept other chairs vacant after their occupants departed from the scene. Salo Baron's appointment assured the survival of Jewish studies in universities and opened new directions for research.

Conclusion

The history of Jewish scholarship in American colleges and universities mirrors thinking about modern Jewish history. Jewish history is often discussed in dualistic terms—revolving around such dichotomies as universalism and particularism, tradition and modernity, the individual and the Jewish community, and ethnicity and religion. Similar dichotomies characterize discussions of Jewish learning: universal and particular, seminaries (including *yeshivot*) and university (as centers of learning), piety and professionalization (as motivating forces), and theological and "scientific" (as modes of interpreting the Jewish experience) Jewish historical writing contains many titles that begin with the preposition "from," suggesting a linear progression along an important axis, and progress to a "to." Jewish emancipation, which brought rapid, visible changes to European Jewry, may explain the emphasis upon linear, dualistic analyses. The realities of Jewish life and the history of Jewish learning are more subtle. The creation of new institutions and norms did not immediately doom old structures, indeed, there were historical and scholarly Jewish counter-reformations. And individual Jews and Jewish scholars are subject to many "dualisms" at once, each demanding resolution, yet all interdependent.

Salo Baron's availability and suitability stemmed from his ability to straddle dualisms. Baron studied and taught in both universities and seminaries; communicated with academic and communal audiences; and successfully related Jewish history to general themes, while focusing on Jews and Judaism. Between 1930 and 1970—a period in which pluralism increasingly dominated American social thought—Jewish learning subfields and practitioners were most likely to gain access to universities when they displayed the ability to effect similar balances.

Notes

1. Butler to Julian Mack, December 21, 1929, CUF, "N" file.
2. On Menorah, see Joselit, "Without Ghettoism," 133–54. On B'nai B'rith, see "Plan Chairs of Hebrew," *New York Times* (January 21, 1927), 17:1.
3. See the protest against his dismissal offered by several key members of the Jewish Theological Seminary faculty in the Marx Papers, JTS, "Hyman Enelow" file.
4. See Ruth S. Hurwitz, "Linda R. Miller: A Memoir," *Menorah Journal* 25 (October–December, 1937), 360.
5. Miller to Enelow, March 20, 1925, Enelow Papers, AJA, box 573, "General Correspondence 1924–1925" file.
6. Hurwitz, "Linda R. Miller," 361.

7. Davidson to Enelow, August 7, 1925, and Enelow to Davidson, September 15, 1925, Enelow Papers, AJA, General Correspondence, box 574, "D-E" file.

8. Miller to Butler, May 9, 1928, CUF, "Mi-My" file.

9. Miller to Butler, June 2, 1928, ibid.

10. Miller to Butler, May 15, 1928, ibid.

11. Butler to Miller, May 28, 1928, ibid. Compare Butler's reasoning with that of Max Weber in "The Bernhard Affair," in Edward Shils, ed. and tr., *Max Weber on Universities: The Power of the State and the Dignity of the Academic Calling in Imperial Germany* (Chicago: University of Chicago Press, 1974).

12. Miller to Butler, June 2, 1928, CUF, "Mi-My" file.

13. Butler to Miller, June 4, 1928, ibid.

14. Miller to Butler, June 6, 1928, ibid. Enelow envisioned a $200,000 endowment that would provide for a $9,000 to $10,000 salary at prevailing interest rates. Butler suggested $250,000, arguing that "it is very desirable in order to make the work of such a chair as useful as possible that the incumbent have at his disposal a small fund for those forms of assistance and items of equipment which make his work so much more productive. He frequently needs scholarly assistance for a longer or shorter time and various illustrative material, books and other, which are always available for his service" (Butler to Miller, May 11, 1928, ibid.). Mrs. Miller concurred, contingent upon a satisfactory agreement concerning the chair's occupant.

15. The trustees accepted the gift at the beginning of the 1928–29 academic year. See Frederick A. Goetze to Butler, August 28, 1928, CUF, "Frederick Goetze" file; Columbia University, *Trustees' Minutes 49: 26–27*, and Columbia University, *Charters, Acts of the Legislature and Official Documents and Records* (New York: Printed for the University, 1933), 319–20.

16. Butler to Woodbridge, June 7, 1928, CUF, "Frederick Woodbridge" file.

17. See *Encyclopaedia Judaica*, s.v. "Joseph Herman Hertz."

18. In fact, one might speculate that Butler took precipitous action in 1936 to avoid the morass in which the Miller committee soon found itself.

19. Butler to Woodbridge, June 20, 1928, CUG, "Frederick Woodbridge" file.

20. Gottheil to Wise, June 29, 1925, JIR Papers, AJA, no. 19, 16/18, "Richard Gottheil" file.

21. Butler to Woodbridge, September 27, 1928, CUF, "Frederick Woodbridge" file. Mrs. Miller, in acknowledging receipt of a list of committee members, called the list "impressive," but added: "The fact that no final selection can be made without the sanction of the President, etc., is nevertheless an especial source of satisfaction" (Linda Miller to Butler, September 28, 1928, CUF, "Mrs. Nathan Miller" file).

22. Gottheil to Butler, July 9, 1928, CUG, "Gi-Gu" file. "Of course," he wrote, "the Chair will be in the Department of Oriental languages and literatures."

23. Gottheil to Wise, October 24, 1928, Wise Papers, AJA, box 947, "Correspondence with Richard J. H. Gottheil, 1923–1929" file. For one example of their relationship, see James F. Carr to Gottheil, October 2, 1915, Gottheil Papers, AJA, Correspondence 2, 1898–1919, "Misc. and unidentified" file.

24. "R. G." memo, attached to Gottheil to Wise, November 2, 1923, Wise Papers, AJA, box 947, "Correspondence with Richard Gottheil, 1923–1929" file.

25. In an interview, Salo Baron commented that Gottheil had desired a philologist, but the latter's avid backing of historian Michael Ginsberg indicates otherwise (Baron interview, New Canaan, Conn., August 30, 1978). "What has become of the matter about which you and I spoke when we last met?" Gottheil wrote Enelow. "Do you not think that it is proper and fitting that I should know? On your account, I am ashamed to ask at this end of the line" (Gottheil to Enelow, May 30, 1928, Enelow Papers, AJA, box 8, file 7: "Gottheil, Richard J. H., 1913–1932").

26. Gottheil to Wise, October 24, 1928, and November 11, 1928, Wise Papers, AJA, box 947, "Correspondence with Richard J. H. Gottheil, 1923–1929" file. Gottheil demonstrated his sensitivity on family matters when he reproached Stephen Wise for failing to include his father in the pantheon of American Reform Jewish leaders in an article; see Gottheil to Wise, April 13, 1927, ibid.

27. Wise to Ginsberg, September 20, 1927, JIR Papers, AJA, no. 19, 9/3, "Faculty—Candidates for" file.

28. Ginsberg to Wise, August 9, 1928, ibid.

29. Kohut to Wise, October 3, 1928, George Kohut–Stephen S. Wise Correspondence (hereafter Kohut-Wise), AJA, box 2308.

30. Gottheil to Wise, September 27, 1928, JIR Papers, AJA, no. 19, 9/3, "Faculty—Candidates for" file.

31. Wise to Kohut, October 10, 1928, ibid.

32. Ibid. See also Wise to Salo Baron, August 27, 1928, and October 8, 1928, and Ginsberg to Wise, October 2, 1928, ibid.

33. Woodbridge to Butler, November 28, 1928, CUF, "Frederick J. Woodbridge" file. Danby translated the Mishnah and Tosefta of the tractate *Sanhedrin* (1919) and Joseph Klausner's *Jesus of Nazareth: His Life,*

Times, and Teaching (New York: Macmillan, 1925) and published *The Jew and Christianity* (1927). One of the first Christian Hebraists to see modern Hebrew as a serious academic medium, Danby would accept an appointment as professor of Hebrew at Oxford in 1936 (*Encyclopaedia Judaica*, s.v. "Danby, Herbert"). Drachman severed his Seminary connection when it began to deviate from Orthodoxy; he later taught at Yeshiva College. Best known for his autobiography, *The Unfailing Light: Memoirs of an American Rabbi* (New York: Rabbinical Council of America, 1948), Drachman was not a prolific scholar. (See *Encyclopaedia Judaica*, s.v. "Drachman, Bernard," and Jeffrey S. Gurock, "From Exception to Role Model: Bernard Drachman and the Evolution of Jewish Religious Life in America, 1880–1920," *American Jewish History* 76 (1987), 166–81.) Obermann taught Semitic languages at Hamburg and came to the Jewish Institute of Religion shortly after publishing his study of Al-Ghazali's philosophy (*Der philosophische und religiöse Subjekrivismus Ghazalis*). At Yale, he edited the Yale Judaica Series (*Encyclopaedia Judaica*, s.v. "Obermann, Julian Joel"). Louis Ginzberg is discussed below.

34. Woodbridge to Butler, November 21, 1928, CUF, "Frederick J. Woodbridge" file.
35. Butler to Miller, November 22, 1928, CUF, "Mrs. Nathan J. Miller" file.
36. Israel Davidson almost certainly was one consultant. The other consultant may have been Alexander Marx (Miller to Butler, November 25, 1928, ibid.). Columbia's looser formal relations with the Jewish Theological Seminary help explain why the search committee had a Union Theological but not a Jewish Theological Seminary representative.
37. Butler to Woodbridge, November 26, 1928, CUF, "Frederick J. Woodbridge" file; Woodbridge to Butler, November 2, 1928, ibid., and Butler to Miller December 3, 1928, CUF, "Mrs. Nathan J. Miller" file.
38. Miller to Butler, December 5, 1928, ibid.
39. Butler to Miller, December 7, 1928, ibid. See also Butler to Woodbridge, December 7, 1928, CUF, "F. Woodbridge" file.
40. "About the professorship at Columbia, I can know little at this distance," a frustrated Gottheil wrote Wise. He later lamented: "It is most unfortunate that I cannot be at my post at so important a moment" (Gottheil to Wise, November 25, 1928, ibid., and Gottheil to Wise, February 9, 1929, JIR Papers, AJA, no. 19, 16/19, "Richard Gottheil" file). "I was told," Wise wrote Gottheil a month after Miller's final letter, "that your own candidate, the young French Jew, was not in the running" (Wise to Gottheil, January 10, 1929, Wise Papers, AJA, box 947, "Correspondence with Richard J. H. Gottheil, 1923–1929" file). A year later, Gottheil renewed his suggestion that Wise call Ginsberg to the Jewish Institute of Religion. Wise again declined. See Gottheil to Wise, August 22, 1930, and Wise to Gottheil, September 2, 1930, JIR Papers, AJA, no. 19, 16/19, "Richard Gottheil" file.
41. Wise to Gottheil, February 1, 1929, Wise Papers, AJA, box 947, "Correspondence with Richard J. H. Gottheil, 1923–1929" file. Wise privately agreed with the committee but did not wish to offend his mentor. He wrote: "I don't know how they got that information, but in any event the opinion does obtain that he is not a [Judaica] text man at all."
42. Kohut to Enelow, October 18, 1928, Enelow Papers, AJA, box 582, "K" file.
43. Kohut to Enelow, November 7, 1928. Kohut apparently misinterpreted a sentence that Enelow wrote in reply to his earlier letter. Enelow had stated: "As to who will be appointed to the chair endowed by Mrs. Miller, I really haven't the least notion, and I am quite sure that no outsider will be allowed to say anything about it" (Enelow to Kohut, October 23, 1928, ibid.). Kohut assumed that Miller did not proffer a nomination because Enelow preferred to remain at Emanu-El. See Kohut to Wise, October 26, 1928, Kohut-Wise, AJA, box 2308, "1928–1929" file.
44. Warburg to Butler, December 3, 1928, CUF, "Wa-Wh" file.
45. Kohut to Wise, October 26, 1928, Wise to Kohut, October 31, 1928, JIR Papers, AJA, no. 19, 16/19, "Richard Gottheil" file, and Gottheil to Wise, October 24, 1928 and November 11, 1928, Wise Papers, AJA, box 947, "Correspondence with Richard J. H. Gottheil, 1923–1929" file.
46. Wise to Gottheil, November 12, 1928, ibid.
47. Wise to Gottheil, December 7, 1928, ibid.
48. Kohut to Wise, October 22, 1928, Kohut-Wise, AJA, box 2308, "1928–1929" file.
49. Wise to Gottheil, March 18, 1929, Wise Papers, AJA, box 947, "Correspondence with Richard J. H. Gottheil, 1923–1929" file.
50. Bewer to Enelow, December 4, 1928, and Enelow to Bewer, December 6, 1928, Enelow Papers, AJA, General Correspondence 1928–1929, box 582, "S" file. Mann had experienced increased dissatisfaction with Hebrew Union following his arrival from Baltimore several years earlier. "Our Rabbinical Schools are turning out Rabbis, but not scholars," he wrote Enelow. "How often at our own faculty meetings, when I insist on raising the standard, is this Pontifical argument hurled at me:—'But we need Rabbis and not specialists!' Whatever hopes I may have had when I came here, of raising some disciples, they

are now gone. I have to find some consolation in my own research work. Our 'Nachwuchs' will not come from the Rabbinical schools in America, and certainly not from the HUC with all its millions, buildings, largest Faculty and student body, etc., etc." (See Mann to Enelow, March 26, 1929, ibid., box 583, "M" file).

51. Wise to Gottheil, February 7, 1929, Wise Papers, AJA, box 947, "Correspondence with Richard J. H. Gottheil, 1923–1929" file.

52. Wise to Julian Mack, January 29, 1929, Wise Papers, AJHS, box 119, "Julian Mack" file.

53. Wise to Gottheil, January 10, 1929, Wise Papers, AJA, box 947, "Correspondence with Richard J. H. Gottheil, 1923–1929" file. Linda Miller endorsed Enelow's anti-Zionism, but Wise considered these beliefs another liability. Referring to Enelow's allusion to the serious situation the Jewish Agency for Palestine faced that year, Wise wrote: "It is terrible for a Russian Jew, such as he is, to deal in that bitterly hostile way with what he sneeringly and contemptuously calls 'the Palestinian Movement'" (Wise to Gottheil, July 1, 1929, ibid.).

54. Gottheil to Wise (telegram), January 21, 1929, JIR Papers, AJA no. 19, 16/19, "Richard Gottheil" file. Gottheil considered Kaplan's personality a greater selling point than his erudition. "Religion and life to him are identical," he told Wise in another context, "and his influence upon the students will be tremendous. They are attracted by his personality; they are charmed by his depth of thought and of feeling; they are ready to go through fire and flame in order to carry out the ideals that he implants in them" (Gottheil to Wise, July 14, 1923, Wise Papers, AJA, box 947, "Correspondence with Richard Gottheil, 1923–1929" file).

55. Ralph Marcus apparently arranged the meeting. See Wise to Gottheil, February 1, 1929, ibid. Littauer, perhaps realizing that his indirect tactics failed, telephoned Butler on February 19, ostensibly to register his disappointment that Columbia had yet to make an appointment. (See Butler to Miller, February 19, 1929, CUF, "Mrs. Nathan Miller" file.) A rumor subsequently circulated that Enelow met with search committee members including Woodbridge and that "he had made himself utterly impossible at and for Columbia by reason of his arrogance and the acrimonious way in which he had talked" (Wise to Gottheil, July 1, 1929, Wise Papers, AJA, box 947, "Correspondence with Richard J. H. Gottheil, 1923–1929" file). For a sympathetic description of Enelow, see Davidson to Miller, April 24, 1929, Davidson Archives, JTS, "Mrs. N. Miller" file.

56. Herbert Solow to Irwin Edman, June 15, 1929, Menorah Collection, AJA, box 9, file 15.

57. Miller to Butler, March 4, 1929, CUF, "Mrs. Nathan J. Miller" file.

58. See Ginzberg, *Keeper of the Law*, 82.

59. Woodbridge to Butler, February 28, 1929, CUF, "Frederick Woodbridge" file.

60. The committee subsequently reaffirmed its fellowship recommendations. "Dr. Ralph Marcus of the Semitics Department, and of the Jewish Institute of Religion," it reported, "should be encouraged to intensify his researches in the field of Hellenistic Judaism. He is unusually competent in the field and promises soon to become an authority on Philo." The committee called Rosenthal "the most promising young man in New York for the kind of work we need." His publications portended "significant contributions to the field of Talmudic scholarship." Rosenthal planned to resume the history of the Talmud where George Foot Moore had left off. See "Memorandum to the Committee on the Appointment of Professor of Jewish Institutions, Dean Woodbridge, Chairman," undated (accepted as a report of the Committee, May 29, 1929), William L. Westerman Papers (hereafter Westerman Papers), CU-RBML, "W" file.

61. Butler to Woodbridge, March 1, 1929, CUF, "Frederick Woodbridge" file; Butler to Miller, March 1, 1929, CUF, "Mrs. Nathan J. Miller" file; and Philip Hayden to Woodbridge, March 22, 1929, CUF, "Frederick Woodbridge" file.

62. Miller to Butler, March 4, 1929, CUF, "Mrs. Nathan J. Miller" file.

63. Woodbridge to Butler, March 25, 1929, CUF, "Frederick Woodbridge" file.

64. Woodbridge to Butler, April 11, 1929, ibid.; "Memorandum to the Committee."

65. Mann was also indignant at Edman's discussion of salary. He told Edman that the committee should decide on the chair's scope and then consider likely candidates. He concluded that a call from Columbia would be unlikely (Mann to Enelow, April 11, 1929, Enelow Papers, AJA, General Correspondence 1928–1929, box 583, "M" file). Enelow concurred: "I can see now that if that is what the committee wants, you are out of the question. There is no sense in jumping from the frying pan into the fire, however disagreeable the former might be" (Enelow to Mann, April 17, 1929, ibid.). Enelow did not encourage Mann's aspirations. Edman may have eliminated Mann on the grounds of personality: "He is no gentleman; a horrible person," Israel Abrahams once said of him. "He is a great scholar, but I understand, not a gentleman," wrote George Kohut. Stephen Wise concurred. In 1926 Wise offered a position at the Jewish Institute of Religion to Salo Baron instead of to Mann. See Wise to Kohut, October 24, 1928, and Kohut to Wise, October 26, 1928, Kohut–Wise, AJA, box 2308, "1928–1929" file.

66. Butler to Woodbridge, April 13, 1929, CUF, "Frederick Woodbridge" file.

67. Woodbridge to Butler, June 1, 1929, ibid.

68. Salo Baron to Wise, July 23, 1929, JIR Papers, AJA, box 1467, "Dr. Salo W. Baron" file. See Richard Fuchs, "The Hochschule fur die Wissenschaft des Judentums in the Period of Nazi Rule," Leo Baeck Institute, *Yearbook* 12 (1967), 3–31, and Isi Jacob Eisner, "Reminiscences of the Berlin Rabbinical Seminary," ibid., 32–52. Elbogen subsequently co-edited the *Encyclopaedia Judaica* (10 vols., 1928–1934), and wrote *A Century of Jewish Life* (Philadelphia: Jewish Publication Society of America, 1944) to update Graetz.

69. The committee ascertained that Elbogen could perform his work effectively in English. See Woodbridge to Butler, June 1, 1929, CUF, "Frederick J. Woodbridge" file.

70. Wise told Julian Mack, whom the committee also consulted, that "Columbia could not find a better person in all the world than Elbogen, and that Elbogen is not only a great Jewish scholar but a rare teacher; that he knows how to deal with non-Jews as well as with Jews and that he is the embodiment of Jewish culture" (quoted in Wise to Kohut, June 6, 1929, Kohut-Wise, AJA, box 2308, "1928–1929" file).

71. Herbert Solow to Irwin Edman, June 5, 1929, Menorah Collection, AJA, box 9, file 15: "Irwin Edman."

72. Butler to Woodbridge, June 4, 1929, CUF, "Frederick J. Woodbridge" file.

73. The committee reaffirmed its fellowship suggestions and added Beryl Levy's name to its list. Levy, an academically distinguished Columbia College senior, planned graduate work in Jewish learning at Columbia ("Memorandum to the Committee"). The report stated: "On the basis of our own experience in this matter, that finding an effective personnel to supplement the individual work of the occupant of the chair, involves considerable familiarity with the student body, with local conditions, with other departments of the University, and with the general mode of procedure here; that therefore it would be an almost impossible task for an outsider (like Dr. Elbogen) to face such a problem immediately; and that therefore this Committee ought to assume some responsibility in this matter, in order to prevent further delay or rasher decisions."

74. Elbogen's interest in New York's manuscripts suggests the field's maturation. Forty years earlier, Richard Gottheil spent much time and effort acquiring the first such manuscripts, and most American Semitists were still obliged to cross the Atlantic to visit European archives.

75. Edman to Woodbridge, July 11, 1929, attached to Fackenthal to Edman, July 25, 1929, CUF, "E" file.

76. Butler to Elbogen, September 12, 1929, ibid. Elbogen would have begun service at Columbia at a relatively advanced age, and the statutory pension was admittedly inadequate; hence Butler's reassurance. See Fackenthal to Elbogen, September 19, 1929, ibid.

77. Elbogen to Butler, September 19, 1929; Fackenthal to Butler, September 23, 1929; and Edman to Elbogen, September 19, 1929, ibid.

78. Elbogen to Butler, September 28, 1929, ibid.

79. Butler to Elbogen, October 24, 1929, and November 15, 1929; Elbogen to Butler, October 28, 1929, and November 13, 1929, ibid. We do not know whether Butler's failure to spell his first name correctly in any of his correspondence affected Elbogen.

80. See for example Wise to William Rosenau, September 20, 1929, JIR Papers, AJA, no. 19, 9/3, "Faculty—Candidates for" file.

81. See Adler to Warburg, June 24, 1937, in Robinson, ed., *Cyrus Adler: Selected Letters*, 2:331–32.

82. Butler to Miller, September 30, 1929, and Miller to Butler, October 2, 1929, CUF, "Mrs. Nathan J. Miller" file.

83. Blondheim to Alexander Marx, September 8, 1929, Marx Papers, JTS, "D. S. Blondheim, 1925–1930" file.

84. See *Encyclopaedia Judaica*, s.v. "Blondheim, David Simon." "You seem to be the only man in the country really interested in the Jewish side of what I have tried to do," he wrote Marx in 1913 (Blondheim to Marx, March 21, 1913, Marx Papers, JTS, "David S. Blondheim" file). He favorably compared the Illinois facilities to those at the University of Wisconsin. Wisconsin, he noted, had a Semitics department and Illinois had none. But "we are much better off for Judaica and Hebraica than they are" (Blondheim to Marx, April 26, 1916, ibid.).

85. Blondheim to Marx, March 18, 1917, ibid.

86. Kohut to Enelow, October 18, 1928, Enelow Papers, AJA, box 582, "K" file; Blondheim to Marx, April 14, 1923, and September 8, 1929, Marx Papers, JTS, "D. S. Blondheim" file.

87. Blondheim to Marx, March 29, 1923, ibid. See also Mordecai Kaplan Diary, JTS, August 11, 1929.

88. On the Blondheim–Dulles relationship, see Leonard O. Mosley, *Dulles* (New York: Dial, 1978), and Eleanor Lansing Dulles, *Eleanor Lansing Dulles, Chances of a Lifetime: A Memoir* (Englewood Cliffs: Prentice-Hall, 1980).

89. Mordecai Kaplan shared Blondheim's uneasiness about Edman: "Edman, like Morris R. Cohen, is or had been poisoning the minds of the Jewish boys against Judaism. Again I am basing my inference in the case of Edman nor upon direct but only upon circumstantial evidence" (Mordecai Kaplan Diary, JTS, September 18, 1929).

90. See Blondheim to Wise, October 12, 1929, and Wise to Blondheim, October 16, 1929, JIR Papers, AJA, no. 19, 5/8, "Columbia University" file.

91. "[Kohut] is a man without any backbone whatever. . . . I have no use for the whole K. family. . . . I am extremely surprised to see that this particular member of it is so closely connected with your Institute," Gottheil told Wise (Gottheil to Wise, January 20, 1923, Wise Papers, AJA, box 947, "Correspondence with Richard J. H. Gottheil, 1923–1929" file). For Kohut's attitude, see Kohut to Marx, October 30, 1929, Marx Papers, JTS, "George A. Kohut, June–December, 1929" file.

92. Kohut to Marx, October, 19, 1929, ibid.

93. Vergil, *The Aeneid*, Patric Dickinson, tr. (New York: New American Library, 1961), 17, 19.

94. *Encyclopaedia Judaica*, s.v. "Baron, Salo (Shalom) Wittmayer."

95. Gottheil to Wise, July 29, 1925, JIR Papers, AJA, no. 19, 16/18, "Richard Gottheil" file; Wise to Elbogen, June 2, 1926, Wise Papers, AJHS, box 35, "I. Elbogen" file.

96. Wise to Kohut, December 1, 1926, JIR Papers, AJA, "Salo Baron" file; Wise to Elbogen, June 2, 1926, Wise Papers, AJHS, box 35, "I. Elbogen" file.

97. Kohut to Marx, January 7, 1928, Marx Papers, JTS, "G. A. Kohut, January–March, 1929" file.

98. Kohut to Wise, October 29, 1928, Kohut–Wise, AJA, box 2308, "1928–29" file; Wise to Gottheil, September 22, 1929, JIR Papers, AJA, no. 19, 16/19, "Richard Gottheil" file.

99. Wise to Kohut, April 18, 1928, and Baron to Wise, April 20, 1928, JIR Papers, AJA, box 1467, "Dr. Salo W. Baron" file.

100. Irwin Edman and Herbert W. Schneider, "Report to the Chairman of the Committee on the Appointment of a Professor of Jewish Institutions," December 6, 1929, attached to Woodbridge to Butler, December 12, 1929, CUF, "Frederick Woodbridge" file.

101. See, for example, Herbert Weir Smyth, "The Classics, 1867–1929" in Morison, *Development of Harvard University*, 60–61. By the end of the nineteenth century, many classicists had shifted their arguments for curricular predominance from the ability to train the mental faculties to an emphasis on Greek and Roman culture as antecedents to modern Western civilization (see Rudolph, *Curriculum*, 183. Cf. Daniel Bell, *The Reforming of General Education: The Columbia College Experience in the National Setting* [Garden City, N.Y.: Anchor Books, 1966], 223–24). Just as Tenny Frank and William L. Westerman undertook research on ancient history after advanced study of Latin literature, James H. Breasted and other scholars who wrote the history of the ancient Near East were trained in Semitics. See John Higham with Leonard Krieger and Felix Gilbert, *History: Professional Scholarship in America* (New York: Harper, 1973 [1965]), 37–38.

102. Charles Gross, a Jewish professor of history at Harvard, specialized in medieval history and the British constitution. Gross, an exceptional case, published several articles with Jewish themes, notably in the *Publications of the American Jewish Historical Society*. See Morison, *Three Centuries*, 375–76; Feuer, "Stages in the Social History of Jewish Professors"; and Novick, *That Noble Dream*, 172.

103. See Heinrich Hirsch Graetz, *The Structure of Jewish History and Other Essays*, Ismar Schorsch, tr. and ed. (New York: Jewish Theological Seminary of America, 1975).

104. Roth, "Jewish History," 422–23.

105. Sarna, *J.P.S.*, 34–39.

106. Jonas, "Writing American Jewish History," 142.

107. George Jeshurun, "Wanted—A Modern Reader's Jewish History," *The Jewish Forum* 4 (January, 1921), 681.

108. "A man may busy himself with every country on the surface of the globe," Cecil Roth wrote, "but until he touch upon the Jews of Germany he is regarded as a pure antiquarian. On the other hand, the young native who presents his doctorate thesis on the vicissitudes of the community of his township is reckoned at once a universal authority" (see Roth, "Jewish History," 424).

109. If a scholar "declares that the Jews came here and prospered in America because God, blessed be He, willed they should," wrote a critic, "his crusading piety and energy are scarcely likely to convince a critic who has drunk deep at the materialistic spring." See Albert M. Friedenberg, "Thoughts on the Philosophy of American Jewish History," *Publications of the American Jewish Historical Society* 28 (1922), 234.

110. "The professional world looks down with scorn upon any neophyte who has not served his apprenticeship over the folios of the Talmud," wrote Cecil Roth. "Now a profound knowledge of the Talmud is a useful adjunct to any student of Jewish history. But it is by no means indispensable. The only indispensable

requirement for research in Jewish history or any period or from any angle—as for any branch of scholarship—is a knowledge of the principles and methods of research. . . . Jewish history is written and taught today by persons whose education may qualify them to deal with Rabbinical texts, but who have not mastered even the elements of the historian's craft." Roth urged scholars to view the Talmud as "a highly interesting theological and psychological phenomenon" not as "the substance of Jewish history" (Roth, "Jewish History," 426, 428).

111. Alexander Marx, "Aims and Tasks of Jewish Historiography," *Publications of the American Jewish Historical Society* 26 (1918), 14–15.

112. Roth, "Jewish History," 426.

113. Alexander Marx, "Aims and Tasks," 15. See also Roth, "Jewish History," 428.

114. Roth, "Jewish History," 428.

115. Jonas, "Writing American Jewish History," 143, 147, quotation from 147.

116. Friedenberg, "Thoughts," 234, 236.

117. See Marx, "Aims and Tasks," 29; Wolfson, "The Needs of Jewish Scholarship," 28–32; and Salo Baron, "Research in Jewish History," *The Jewish Institute Quarterly* 4 (May, 1928), 1–8.

118. "We see God in each ethical action, but not in the finished whole, in history; for why would we need a God, if history were divine?" wrote Franz Rosenzweig in a modern restatement of the antihistorical position. Quoted in Lionel Kochan, *The Jew and His History* (New York: Macmillan Press, 1977), 99.

119. Salo W. Baron, "The Study of Jewish History," *The Jewish Institute Quarterly* 4 (January 1928), 9. This denunciation became closely identified with Baron. See Arthur Hertzberg and Leon A. Feldman, "Foreword" in Salo W. Baron, *History and Jewish Historians: Essays and Addresses by Salo W. Baron*, Arthur Hertzberg and Leon A. Feldman, comps. (Philadelphia: Jewish Publication Society of America, 1964), ix, and Jeanette Meisel Baron, "A Bibliography of the Printed Writings of Salo Wittmayer Baron" in *Salo Wittmayer Baron Jubilee Volume on the Occasion of His Eightieth Birthday* (Jerusalem: American Academy of Jewish Research and Columbia University Press, 1975), 3.

120. Baron, "Emphases in Jewish History" in Baron, *History and Jewish Historians*, 76.

121. Baron, "Study of Jewish History," 8.

122. Baron, "Emphases in Jewish History," 69. "Not accepting the periodization of post-exilic Jewish history by Zunz and his 19th century successors into literary epochs with its implication that literature was the be-all of Jewish history," wrote Lloyd P. Gartner, a Baron student, "Baron orients it to the dynamic of general history." (See Lloyd P. Gartner, "A Successor to Graetz," *Midstream* 16 [November, 1970], 71).

123. Baron, "Emphases in Jewish History," 77–78.

124. Ibid., 86.

125. "Some Talmudists have cavilled at alleged inadequacies of Baron's rabbinic learning," wrote Gartner, "but no Talmudist has yet attempted these fundamental topics—a social history of Talmudic times and the analytic, unhomiletic study of the social teachings of Talmudic Judaism" (Gartner, "Successor," 69).

126. Baron echoed Cyrus Adler's contention that Jewish scholarship, properly undertaken, might also help to unify a Jewish community that fragmented during emancipation. See Baron, "Emphases in Jewish History," 89.

127. Carleton J. H. Hayes, "History" in Dixon Ryan Fox, ed., *A Quarter Century of Learning 1904–1929* (New York: Columbia University Press, 1931), 19, 25.

128. Ibid., 19.

129. See James Harvey Robinson, *The New History: Essays Illustrating the Modern Historical Outlook* (New York: Macmillan, 1912), and Higham, *History*, 104–16. "How silly it is," Hayes quotes Robinson, his mentor, and the movement's ideologue as saying, "for historians to waste time in determining 'whether Charles the Fat was in Ingelheim or Lustnau on July 1, 887,' when they should be contemplating the jaw of the Heidelberg Man." See Hayes, "History," 11.

130. See Salo W. Baron, "Preface," *A Social and Religious History of the Jews* (New York: Columbia University Press, 1937), l:v, and Gartner, "Successor," 68.

131. Kohut to Marx, October 8, October 9, October 30, and November 11, 1929; Marx to Kohut, October 11, 1929, Marx Papers, JTS, "George A. Kohut, June–December, 1929" file; Marx to Blondheim, October 13, 1929, Blondheim to Marx, October 27, 1929, Marx Papers, JTS, "D. S. Blondheim, 1925–1930" file.

132. Kohut to Edman, October 11, 1929, Marx Papers, JTS, "George A. Kohut, June–December, 1929" file.

133. Kohut to Marx, October 9, 1929, ibid., Blondheim to Marx, October 11 and October 14, 1929; Marx to Blondheim, October 13, 1929, Marx Papers, JTS, "D. S. Blondheim" file. Elbogen also mentioned Jacob R. Marcus of Hebrew Union College, Julian Obermann of the Jewish Institute of Religion, and Cecil Roth. Kohut dismissed Marcus as too young, Obermann as not a historian, and Roth as unavailable. When Elbogen subsequently endorsed Fritz Baer's candidacy, Kohut expressed little surprise since he knew

of prior judgment reversals and attributed them "to [Elbogen's] anxiety to be kind to everyone." Kohut added that Elbogen "overplays his generosity and gives the impression that he is all things to all men," thus reducing the importance of his endorsement. See Kohut to Blondheim, November 11, 1929, Marx Papers, JTS, "George A. Kohut, June–December 1929" file.

134. Fackenthal to Woodbridge, November 15, 1929, CUF, "Frederick J. E. Woodbridge" file.

135. Blondheim to Marx, November 19, 1929, Marx Papers, JTS, "D. S. Blondheim" file. Harry Wolfson and Cyrus Adler endorsed him "with [unspecified] reservations," and Kohut concluded that Wolfson's "interference . . . completely nullified Blondheim's chances" (Kohut to Marx, December 17, 1929, Marx Papers, JTS, "George A. Kohut, July–December, 1929" file). See also Edman and Schneider, "Report. . . . " Ironically, about 15 years later, Schneider, a professor of religion, was forced to resign from Columbia when the university administration learned of his recent divorce. Blondheim's subsequent marriage to Dulles led to demands for his resignation from Jewish scholarly organizations, including the JPS and the American Academy of Jewish Research. Louis Ginzberg spearheaded the drive against Blondheim, according to his son. See Eli Ginzberg, *My Brother's Keeper* (New Brunswick, N.J.: Transaction Publishers, 1989), 25.

136. Kohut to Marx, December 27, 1929, and January 6, 1930; Marx to Kohut, January 3, 1930, Marx Papers, JTS, "George A. Kohut, July–December, 1929" file; Kohut to Blondheim, February 3, 1930, Marx Papers, JTS, "G. A. Kohut, January–March, 1930" file; Marx to Blondheim, February 17, 1930, Marx Papers, JTS, "D. S. Blondheim, 1925–1930" file.

137. The committee also considered Isaac Husik, professor of philosophy at the University of Pennsylvania, and Louis I. Finkelstein, professor of theology at the Jewish Theological Seminary. Husik received warm recommendations, but the committee desired a historian, not a medieval Jewish philosopher. It eliminated Finkelstein because of his sectarianism and his domestic training. See Woodbridge to Butler, December 12, 1929, CUF, "Frederick J. Woodbridge" file. Finkelstein's prior scholarship included studies of Jewish self-government in the Middle Ages and of the conflict between the Sadducees and Pharisees. He succeeded Alder as president of the Jewish Theological Seminary.

138. Woodbridge to Butler, December 12, 1929, CUF, "Frederick J. Woodbridge" file. Elbogen, Wolfson, Wise, and Ralph Marcus would enthusiastically endorse Baron's candidacy for the Miller chair.

139. Miller to Butler, December 20, 1929, CUF, "Mrs. Nathan Miller" file.

140. Butler to Miller, December 16, December 19 and December 23, 1929, ibid.

141. When he expressed these concerns at a meeting with committee members, Herbert Schneider replied that he should then go home and write books. Baron replied that he wasn't ready to retire.

142. The university also retained Baron's assistant and promised to build up its library collection (Butler to Baron, December 14 and December 19, 1929; Baron to Butler, December 16 and 21, 1929, CUF, "Ba" file).

143. "It will be a great loss to the Institute, as there is no one, so far as I know who can adequately replace him," Kohut told Marx. "Baron covers such a wide field and his range of knowledge is so remarkable that we would have to get three or four people to take over the subjects which he has been teaching, quite apart from his directorship of the School of Advanced Studies and his Librarianship, which was by no means a negligible part of his activities." (See Kohut to Marx, December 17, 1929, Marx Papers, JTS, "George A. Kohut, July–December, 1929" file.)

144. Kohut to Marx, January 6, 1920, ibid., "January–March, 1930" file.

145. *Encyclopaedia Judaica*, s.v. "Baron, Salo (Shalom) Wittmayer."

THE RICH GIVETH, AND THEY TAKETH AWAY

SARAH LACY

**Larry Ellison's recent withdrawal of a gift to Harvard made headlines,
but he's not alone in wanting control over his charitable gifts**

There's no controlling or predicting Larry Ellison, the maverick chief executive of Oracle (ORCL). To that, investors, competitors, and industry watchers can attest. Announcements of meetings with, and even public appearances by, the executive ought to be accompanied by a disclaimer, as he's known for showing up late or not at all. So when the world learned that Ellison wouldn't be delivering on a $115 million pledge to Harvard University, many onlookers weren't shocked.

But if Ellison's side of the story is true, his about-face isn't unique among strong-minded, results-driven businesspeople-turned-philanthropists. According to Oracle, it boiled down to Ellison wanting to know he'd get good results from his investment—a hallmark of philanthropic efforts by self-made entrepreneurs, particularly in the tech world. Ellison plans to announce a new gift later this summer, most likely to a health-care or disease-research foundation.

Second Thoughts

Ellison pledged the money to Harvard following a meeting with former University President Larry Summers, says Oracle Spokesman Bob Wynne. The two discussed Summers' theory of using an economic model to rate the quality of government health-care programs around the world. Ellison was intrigued and agreed on a handshake to donate the money. Later, Summers came under fire for comments made in January, 2005, suggesting that the lack of women in science and engineering is because of men's "intrinsic aptitude" for these jobs. In March of last year, Harvard's faculty passed a lack-of-confidence vote, and about a year later Summers said he'd resign.

While it's true that talks broke off before the resignation, Ellison started to rethink the donation as Summers' problems deepened, Wynne says. Now that Summers is out, he has officially rescinded the commitment. The University and other skeptics counter that not only University institutions but often its professors and staff stay in place regardless of who's president. Still, Ellison was concerned that with the biggest advocate for the program gone, it wouldn't have the same effect. "It was his brainchild and he was going to oversee it," Wynne says of Summers. "If the president of the university is going to sponsor your initiative and he's gone, how do you know your giving is going to be effective?" (Ellison would not comment directly for the story.)

That question is at the heart of several withdrawn contributions over the years, although few are on the scale of Ellison's. In 2001, Netscape founder Jim Clark withdrew $60 million of his $150 million pledge for a biomedical research center at Stanford University in protest against federal restrictions on stem-cell research. In 2002, philanthropist Robert Thompson withdrew a $200 million pledge to build Detroit-area charter schools amid the city's political infighting. Also in 2002, Washington (D.C.) businesswoman Catherine B. Reynolds reneged on a $38 million deal that would have gone to the Smithsonian Institution because she wanted more control over how the money would be spent.

A Question of Control

There's a difficult balance of power between an institution and a philanthropist. The philanthropist holds the money and ostensibly much sway. But a large gift to an institution can give wealthy businesspeople an image boost—or do damage if a gift is revoked. That trade-off has become starker in recent years as media and the public have paid more attention to the philanthropic efforts of the rich and famous, says Melissa A. Berman, president and CEO of Rockefeller Philanthropy Advisors.

Donors increasingly want a say in how money is used, and more and more in the business world are funding solutions to specific problems, rather than writing blank checks to well-heeled institutions. Institutions that publicly criticize donors—even when they renege on commitments—risk alienating others and jeopardizing current lucrative ties. "I think these are not conversations that should be conducted through the media," Berman says. "By the time it gets to this level, it doesn't seem like there's a lot of hope of repairing the relationship."

But social pressure does play a role: Consider the megabillionaires who've grabbed recent headlines. Bill Gates is curtailing his day-to-day role at Microsoft to focus on his philanthropic efforts with the Bill & Melinda Gates Foundation, and Warren Buffett recently announced he would leave most of his $42 billion fortune to the Foundation (see BusinessWeek.com, 6/27/06, "Buffett's Mega-Gift").

Competitive Giving

Such announcements create pressure on the rest of the billionaire set, says Leslie Lenkowsky, professor of public affairs and philanthropic studies at Indiana University. "This is conspicuous philanthropy," he says. "Now to be a member of the billionaires' club, you not only have to play in business and go to Davos, you have to be philanthropic." That may play to Ellison's competitive nature.

Ellison's philanthropic profile has been rising over the last few years. He ranked No. 27 in *BusinessWeek*'s Philanthropy Ranking last year, his first appearance on the list. He was estimated to have given or pledged 4% of his net worth, about $690 million. Ellison has said he'll make a donation elsewhere, and the smart money says it will be connected to health care and medical research on aging and disease. On June 27, he made the first installment of a $100 million donation to the Ellison Medical Foundation, an organization he started in 1998 with an annual $20 million commitment.

That payment was the result of an unconventional settlement to an insider-trading lawsuit, so in some minds, Ellison's track record is still mixed. His late summer announcement should prove how hard he wants to compete in the game of world-class philanthropy.

Lacy is a reporter for BusinessWeek Online in Silicon Valley.

Bibliography

Chapter 3 Individual Donations and Patronage

Curti. Merle, "Anatomy of Giving: Millionaires in the Late 19th Century." *American Quarterly*, Vol. 15 (1963), pp. 416–35.

————. "Philanthropy, Patronage, Politics." *Daedalus*, Winter 1987.

Foster, Margery Somers. Chapter V of *"Out of Smalle Beginnings . . . ": An Economic History of Harvard College in the Puritan Period*. Cambridge, MA: Belknap Press of Harvard University Press, 1962, pp. 128–155.

Pugh, Walter. "'A Curious Working of Cross Purpose," in the Founding of the University of Chicago." *History of Higher Education Annual*, 1995, pp. 93–121.

Rudolph, Frederick. "Financing the College." *American College and University: A History*. New York: Alfred Knopf, 1962, 176–200.

Walton, Andrea, ed. *Women and Philanthropy in Education*. Bloomington, IN: Indiana University Press, 2005.

CHAPTER 4

FOUNDATIONS, CORPORATE PHILANTHROPY, AND VOLUNTARY ASSOCIATIONS: PERSPECTIVES ON THEIR INFLUENCES IN ORGANIZING KNOWLEDGE, SETTING STANDARDS AND SHAPING ACCESS AND EQUITY

THE AMERICAN PRIVATE PHILANTHROPIC FOUNDATION AND THE PUBLIC SPHERE 1890–1930

BARRY D. KARL & STANLEY N. KATZ

The growing use of the term "public policy" to describe programmes planned, supported, and administered by the federal government may conceal one of the most profound social revolutions in American history. The power of the federal government to command compliance with the aims of social reform, which vast majorities of Americans may agree are noble, rests on a legal authority that those same majorities, even a few years ago, would not have believed existed. Federal administrators, backed by federal courts, are able now not only to withhold money appropriated by Congress for support of local schools, transportation, and police and fire protection, but also to take private business firms to court to enforce social changes which may have played little or no part in the legislation which authorised the original programmes. Even those who supported the need for social reform can be puzzled by the size and shape of the federal authority which has emerged to bring it about.

The fact that the issues involved are part of a peculiarly American historical problem which has evolved over the last century tends to be obscured in the hail of bureaucratic decisions, court orders, and *ad hoc* agreements based on the very realistic belief that if equality and justice are the objectives, this is the most efficient way of attaining them. The new methods have an effectiveness which is undeniable. They do, indeed, achieve changes. It is, however, difficult for historians to believe that change which transforms centuries-old patterns of political practice and conduct can take place without some more explicit and thoughtful commentary. One might then be able to defend the revolution on grounds more philosophically attractive than efficiency.

In some respects, the peculiarly American aspects of the problem offer us the best historical point of departure. The major political debates of the first century of American government centred on the issue of the power of the federal government to control national policy. The hard-fought battles which ultimately produced a measure of agreement on such issues as banking, currency, and the tariff, also produced a civil war which abolished slavery. Underneath what we now acknowledge as the limited success of such national crusades, however, was the commitment to government which began at home—in state legislatures, in traditional county and town systems, and in the growing urban governments. The compromises which followed the Civil War affirmed the limitations of the federal government where the making of policy was concerned, but most of all in the formulation of policy on social issues. This was an important affirmation for the South in particular where "social issues" meant not only the treatment of Negroes, but the whole problem of poverty in what was, in effect, an under-industrialised and a recently defeated colony with relatively little industry.[1] State and local governments were perceived as independent entities pursuing locally determined "public" aims of their own, aims which might in fact conflict with aims pursued by other "publics" in other communities and regions. The term "public" itself was loosely applied, stretched to include the interests of business and professional groups whose concern with the health and well-being of the community, as well as its moral and charitable needs, could be defined by many different organisations and associations which no one would have called governmental.

The Formation of a National Society

Awareness of the need for some kind of national institutions and procedures for influencing the quality of the lives of all citizens came basically from two sources, one quite traditional and the other quite new. The older of the two, the charitable and religious beliefs and institutions which had served as the organisational base for national, educational and social reform since the Jacksonian era, no longer appeared to be effective, even though for many the benevolent motive remained unchanged. The Civil War had taught a lot of lessons, among them the divisiveness of denominational interests and transience of religious enthusiasm.[2] At the same time, however, the growing consciousness of the needs of the technological revolution under way had led some entrepreneurs and managers engaged in the building of national industry in the nineteenth century to see a new range of national needs in education, in scientific research, and in the relation of the two to human welfare more generally.[3]

The combination of the religious and the technological objectives was by no means uniquely American. It is an outlook which existed in Great Britain and Germany, and among groups much like those interested in such problems in America. In America, Great Britain and Germany, enlightened members of the middle and upper classes joined reform movements designed to modernise and bureaucratise modes of welfare which the new social scientists were proposing.[4] While the threat of a socialist revolution served more successfully and much earlier as a spur to reform in Europe than it did in America, the consciousness of vast technological changes in medicine, in industrial methods and in techniques of education and social management may have been more important. The proponents of socialism and capitalism alike were interested in the technological revolution and the knowledge it entailed.

What made the combination of charity and technology unique in American society was the tradition of federalism—the unwillingness of Americans to give their national government the authority to set national standards of social well-being, let alone to enforce them. Part of the problem lay in the diversity of ethnic, racial and cultural groups which had been affected dramatically by the successive waves of late nineteenth-century immigration and the unprecedentedly rapid expansion and settlement of the western lands. The traditional American idea of equality did not reflect a national standard according to which communities could measure the quality of education, medical care, treatment of the aged or the unemployed, even from neighbourhood to neighbourhood in the growing cities, let alone from state to state. For better or for worse, federalism in the nineteenth century had become a way of making pluralism palatable by confining unresolvable differences and accepting them. While few methods were as open and as obvious as the establishment of the Indian reservations—or as much supported by federal policy—local communities were free to find ways of containing conflicts resolvable otherwise only by periodic outbreaks of brutality.

From the vantage point of historical distance, one can see the problem more clearly than it was perceived at the time. Among a national élite of modern industrial reformers, a growing consciousness of the desirability of national programmes of social welfare collided with a general political culture which could not accept a national government bent on such reform. It was a culture which would have been threatened down to its partisan and regional roots by any attempt to create a nationally unified conception of social policy. Into the gap created by this impasse stepped the modern foundation, a system of national philanthropy—privately devoted to increasing the welfare of mankind. Not until the New Deal would the federal government move into areas dominated by private philanthropy and local government, and then only in a very limited form engendered by the Great Depression and accomplished by emergency measures that many believed would not become permanent changes. Even Americans who looked upon the social programmes of the New Deal as the origins of the American welfare state still accepted the fact that such national problems as compensation for the unemployed, the children of the poor, or the indigent and disabled elderly would vary widely according to the resources provided by state and local governments as much as regional traditions.[5]

Federal financial support was always deemed to be supplementary, encouraging rather than controlling state and local policies. Private organisations supported by associations of well-to-do citizens and religious groups worked jointly with agencies managed by local communities and bore the major responsibility for dealing with the condition of those unable to care for themselves. Schools run by various local committees and boards would continue to hold a widely differing range of powers to tax citizens within their jurisdictions and to distribute educational services the quality of which depended largely on the willingness and financial ability of citizens to supply the necessary funds. Wealthier communities would educate their children differently from less wealthy communities, while ethnic and racial distinctions would play their traditional roles in determining balances of quality.

The emergence of the federal government as the controlling presence in the management of national social policy is a remarkably recent phenomenon: historians have scarcely seemed to notice how recent it is. Familiar with federal management of banking and currency, and observant of the slowly developing culmination of battles over the federal government's power to determine who could vote and under what circumstances, they have accepted such extraordinary innovations as the Civil Rights Act of 1964, the Elementary and Secondary School Act of 1965, and the subsequent legislation of programmes for support of the arts and humanities, for the requirement of occupational safety and for control of the environment as though they were simply predictable extensions of New Deal and Fair Deal reforms. By the end of the decade of the 1970s, the federal government had become the country's main arbiter in the establishment of policies affecting the social status of Americans. To the familiar policies for the promotion of equality of economic opportunity and political equality had been added policies to promote social equality; the latter intruded in spheres of life previously governed by custom and individual preference and interest.

The growth in the activities and powers of the central government, and the revenues it has collected to pursue its new objectives have had profound consequences for the philanthropic foundations. The relative decline in power of the traditional foundation in the face of increased federal management of reform has produced puzzlement and defensiveness on both sides.[6] Alternately the targets of attack from those who accused them of fomenting radical social reform and those who saw them as protectors of conservative powers and beliefs, foundations have continued to insist that they are private organisations engaged in appropriately private efforts to improve the condition of life. The vastly enlarged role of the federal government in supporting and managing the same kinds of projects, even at times with foundation support and borrowed foundation staffs, has not changed the defence. "Private philanthropy" remains the distinctive phrase it has always been. "Private" began as a legitimating modifier, but as the meaning of the term was changed so has its political force.

Any effort to disentangle the history of foundations depends, then, not simply on providing a story that traces the formation of the first great foundations in the first two decades of the twentieth century, but some understanding as well of the relation of such organisations to national government and politics. That relation, in turn, rests on a history of debate over the appropriate role of the federal government in achieving the reforms at which it aimed. Such questions might lead to a sounder historical understanding of the process whereby a national welfare state was legitimated against two centuries of opposition.

As early as 1854 when the Jacksonian reformer, Dorothea Dix succeeded in having her proposal for federal support of mental hospitals passed by both houses of Congress, President Franklin Pierce's veto stated the historical opposition in its starkest terms. "I cannot but repeat what I have before expressed," he wrote,

> that if the several States, many of which have already laid the foundation of munificent establishments of local beneficence, and nearly all of which are proceeding to establish them, shall be led to suppose, as they will be, should this bill become a law, that Congress is to make provision for such objects, the fountains of charity will be dried up at home, and the several States, instead of bestowing their own means on the social wants of their own people, may themselves, through the strong temptation, which appeals to States as to individuals, become humble suppliants for the bounty of the Federal Government, reversing their true relation to this Union.[7]

The same year Henry Barnard submitted a proposal to create an "agent for education" whose office would be part of the Smithsonian Institution, but opposition from Joseph Henry of the Smithsonian helped to justify a generalised opposition that raised such issues as parochial and private education, as well as the argument that individual citizens should educate their own children and not be required to educate the children of others. A strong movement for the creation of a national system of education was part of the general furore about reform that followed in the immediate aftermath of the Civil War. While it was initially part of the argument for the creation of the Freedman's Bureau, educators like Emerson White saw it as a wider alternative. He called for the creation of a national system which would require states to maintain systems of public schools. In his argument, a National Bureau of Education would provide inspection and encouragement. Despite a fair amount of support for some kind of national programme, the opposition could still argue effectively that Congress could not take over state prerogatives or threaten local control of schools. Even though the bill involved asked only for the collection and distribution of information, opponents could see behind the veil.[8]

While the work of the United States Sanitary Commission during the Civil War undoubtedly affected the post-war interest in public health boards and hospital facilities in the states, the wartime Commission had been a privately financed and privately managed agency. Efforts to press wartime enthusiasm for reform on the post-war government succeeded, finally, in the establishment in 1879 of a National Board of Health; but its life was brief and unhappy. Hedged about with restrictions on its activities intended to assure states that they would do little more than attempt to control entry and spread of yellow fever in port cities (one of the oldest and most accepted aims of the sanitarians), the Board none the less ran into opposition from its friends, who thought it weak and ineffective, as well as from its enemies, who thought it an infringement on the local practice of medicine.[9]

The resolution by the Civil War of the battle over states' rights did not herald a conversion of federal power into a national instrument of social reform. Indeed, one could argue that the war and the political settlement that followed it effectively blunted the pressure of Jacksonian reform. Federal support for civil rights, an aim at least some reformers believed had been a major purpose of the country's agony, was still a century away. Within a generation, Progressive reformers intent on forcing their society to face the damage and dislocation produced by advancing industrialisation and urbanisation were still content to press their revolution on state and local governments rather than Congress.

Although the move toward increased federal involvement in action to deal with social problems was slow and cautious, usually involving merely the provision of statistical information, the mood created by the more rapidly expanding demand for federal regulation of business had unexpected repercussions. The United States Supreme Court, apparently concerned over increased use of federal authority to regulate, took the opportunity in *Lochner* v. *New York* (1905) to declare a *state* law regulating the hours of bakers unconstitutional.[10] Since control of labour conditions was the entering wedge of reformers seeking federal rather than state redress, the future of national social reform looked ominous.

The confining of social reform to state and local government was part of a tradition of local and private initiative that accepted differences in customs, racial and religious attitudes and regional resources of personal wealth and industrial development. The line between private and public was loosely drawn and scarcely perceived by community leaders who viewed property taxes as money out of their pockets, the use of which they wanted to superintend as carefully as they watched the money they donated to churches and charitable organisations. Even after they and their wives ceased personal management of the hospitals, schools, and havens for the poor they had founded, they continued to sit on boards and committees that oversaw the government of such social institutions. Until the turn of the century, they still ran for political office in cities like New York, Boston, and Chicago, fighting corruption and calling for more efficient uses of public money.[11] They continued to support the welfare agencies and the various programmes to supervise housing, safety and health they themselves had founded long after such agencies had become "public" in the sense of looking to municipal revenues for part of their financial resources. Smaller communities, many without formal government of any kind, looked to county and state boards in similar fashion. Where state and local government were concerned, the line between public and private was bridged by a sense of personal association and community action underscored by an almost universal familiarity with local and regional church organisation. Westward expansion and settlement had moved on a network of

Protestant sectarian organisations that provided various kinds of community services. Such organisations preceded the establishment of governments and courts and some, like the Y.M.C.A., were explicitly charged with maintaining order by providing wholesome living conditions for the country's itinerant labour force.[12] None the less, the inability of Americans to accept the idea of a national social order was not an objection to the fact of social control but to its location in the central government. Nineteenth-century Americans controlled social organisation and social behaviour in states and local communities in accordance with their Victorian social beliefs, their racial, religious, and ethnic attachments, and their sense of compassion for the poor, the aged, the sick and the unemployed. It was a system that worked so effectively that its breakdown in the depression of the 1930s came as a shock to those who had supported it. Neither Herbert Hoover nor Franklin D. Roosevelt was prepared to abandon it and the slow consciousness within the New Deal that federal responsibility would ultimately have to be the answer is a mark of the reluctance to admit the ending of an era.[13]

To define the era that ended thus poses problems of what might be called historical consciousness. The awareness on the part of a small but significant group of Americans that the older system of local charitable support and local reform might not continue to work, at least if left in its traditional form, is where the transition begins. The creation of the modern foundation and its legitimation as a national system of social reform—a privately supported system operating in lieu of a governmental system—carried the United States through a crucial period of its development: the first third of the twentieth century. While other western societies facing similar problems moved towards national systems of governmentally supported programmes, American society evolved a private method of producing many of the same results.[14] The method was destined to have consequences not only for the period when foundations reigned supreme in the field of research bearing on social policy, but for the later and more recent period as well. The role the federal government was ultimately forced to accept was shaped and continues to be shaped by the presence of private philanthropy.

From Charity to Philanthropy

By the last decade of the nineteenth century, the traditional institutions and goals of American charitable action no longer sufficed to achieve the aims and satisfy the ambitions of an emerging philanthropic class, whose values changed from "charity" to "philanthropy".[15] The philanthropists as a group were newly minted captains of industry, self-made men riding the crest of America's surge to industrial prosperity in the last third of the nineteenth century. They were not well assimilated into the institutions and patterns of élite charitable activity, although they were mostly committed to sectarian religious traditions. And they were making money faster than they could give it away. For a generation still imbued with the notion of the stewardship of wealth, this fact alone posed problems and created an incentive to establish new modes of charitable action.

They were modern businessmen committed to notions of rationality, organisation and efficiency. They saw no reason why their charitable action should not be guided by the same principles as their business concerns, and indeed the task of giving away large sums of money almost necessitated the rationalisation of charity. These new men were also imbued with the ethic of modern science, which taught, at a minimum, the distinction between causes and results, between pathology and symptomatology.[16] The new generation of philanthropists therefore came to perceive the inefficiency of the general goal of charity, which was the alleviation of the immediate effects of "social dysfunction": poverty, sickness and the various gross forms of social disorder. A more scientific and business-like approach, they thought, was to attack the root causes of social dysfunction directly, when one could determine what they were. And how did one find out? The answer, it seemed clear by the turn of the twentieth century, lay in the scientific investigation of social and physical well-being. The answers lay in research, and in precisely that sort of investigation which characterised the work of scientists and the new social scientists in the emerging American university system. Economically, philosophically and politically, then, philanthropy and the modern university with its emphasis on research are the products of the same era and the same impulses.[17]

Captains of industry such as John D. Rockefeller and Andrew Carnegie, towards the end of their active business careers, wholeheartedly accepted the ambitions of the modern spirit of philanthropy. They understood that their wealth could best be used to investigate the underlying causes of human and social evil, but of course it was not obvious to them or their contemporaries how such a goal could most readily be achieved.[18] One solution, clearly, was simply to contribute material resources to the new universities, or to help found them, as Rockefeller did with the University of Chicago in 1892. But it was not yet clear how scientifically ambitious the universities would become, especially since it was not until after 1910 that the intellectual aspirations of the universities would clearly separate the graduate schools of the university from the college, with its primary commitment to the education of undergraduates.[19] Moreover, to give to the universities, it became clear—although it was always clear to Rockefeller—was to lose control over the use of the funds which they contributed. In any case, the universities were new and untried.

What alternative institutions were there? By and large, traditional charitable institutions were narrowly focused on particular problems and committed to cautious and well-tried courses of action. They were directed by quasi-professionals and élite trustees who were not likely to change their goals or patterns of behaviour radically. Although a good deal of effort went into the rationalisation of such traditional and charitable activity, under the guidance of the "charity organisation" movement, this was clearly a rationalisation of tradition. Radically new approaches would require new institutional forms, and at least one type began to seem fairly obvious and attractive by the latter part of the nineteenth century. This was the endowment, generally organised legally as a trust, with a specific yet untraditional goal.[20]

These new charitable trusts were mainly founded in response to the dilemmas concerning the status of Negroes in the "New South". The most important of these was founded by George Peabody, an American businessman then resident in England, and was devoted to the improvement of Negro education.[21] Peabody recruited to his board of trustees a distinguished group of eastern businessmen-philanthropists, and spurred the creation of parallel efforts, all of which were more or less co-ordinated, ultimately under the guidance of the Southern Education Board. John D. Rockefeller, who had been earlier attracted to the movement, responded to this stimulus by the creation in 1902 of the General Education Board, the primary mission of which was to address itself to southern education, but its immense financial resources gave it new scope, power and potentiality.[22]

The Welfare of Mankind as an Objective

At just about this time comparable institutions began to emerge, on the apparently simultaneous and unexamined assumption that the philanthropic trust could best be organised with very general terms of reference. In this way, the donor could make a substantial gift in trust, that is in perpetuity, to be managed by a self-perpetuating board of trustees, its use limited only by the most general statement of purpose imaginable—ordinarily, to promote the "well-being of mankind". Although the philanthropic trust seems obvious in retrospect, it was both unlawful—given the standards of British and American trust law—and unforeseen at the moment it sprang into a multiple existence in the first decade of the twentieth century. The philanthropic foundation thus represents the fusion of traditional charitable organisation, ancient methods for the perpetuation of family wealth and novel social, legal and intellectual ideas.

In the earliest period of foundation-founding, philanthropists established a number of different models before they settled on a preference for the philanthropic foundation with general purposes. The university itself was one such form, and probably Johns Hopkins and the University of Chicago were its most perfect embodiments.[23] A second possible form was the research institute, along the lines of the Rockefeller Institute of Medical Research and the Carnegie Institution of Washington. These were, essentially, universities without students in which carefully selected investigators could pursue scientific inquiry unhindered by the obligations of teaching and administered in a manner which avoided the politics, goals and traditions of educational institutions. The research institute, a form with obvious European antecedents, was destined for a long and successful career in the United States, although, as the history of Rockefeller University indicates, Americans have always viewed institutions of pure research with a sceptical eye.[24] Third, the reform trust with a single purpose proliferated. The tradition begun by Peabody was carried on under a variety of different labels: the Rockefeller Sanitary Commission for the Eradication of Hookworm Disease, the Carnegie Foundation for the Advancement of Teaching and the like. These trusts were all more or less closely devoted to the solution of particular social problems, and in some cases they were restricted in time, either for a designated number of years or to that period of time sufficient to solve the designated problems. Fourth, the tradition of social work itself spawned a number of institutions intended to carry on the newly professionalised conduct of social work, and which proved to be a sort of mid-point between charitable and philanthropic action. The best exemplar of such an institution was fittingly entitled the (Chicago) School of Civics and Philanthropy. Such institutions were closely aligned with the new national and international associations of social workers, and also with state and local agencies charged with social welfare tasks.[25]

The most adventurous of the philanthropists, however, preferred not to limit themselves or their philanthropic successors. Thus, beginning with the creation of The Carnegie Corporation in 1911 and the Rockefeller Foundation in 1913, the modern philanthropic foundation came into existence. This is not to suggest that the foundation came into existence full-blown, although its legal form has remained unchanged to this day. Rather, what has persisted has been the notion of large economic resources devoted in perpetuity to the advancement of the general welfare of society, and distributed according to the changing wishes of the trustees—and later, staff—who were the legal custodians of the fund. Moreover, from the very start it seemed clear that a substantial proportion of the annual income of these institutions was to be devoted to scientific and social research, much of it done through grants to universities, but substantial proportions performed by scientists employed by the foundations themselves.[26]

The philanthropic foundation was, then, a noble and heroic endeavour, and it was also unique to the United States. The reasons for this are not altogether clear, although of course there were few countries, even in Europe, in which so many large fortunes were created so quickly, and in which, therefore, so much readily disposable capital was in the hands of so many new men.[27] Equally important, there was in the sectarian United States no national Church with a tradition of charitable action and with strong links to schemes of public welfare of all kinds. There was, that is, a huge field of opportunity for privately controlled charitable investment at just that moment when modern reform, professionalisation and reorganisation were taking hold of American society. There was thus an opportunity for the philanthropists to align themselves with the reformers and the new professional classes on the basis of a common commitment to humanitarian, democratic and generally acceptable political and social goals.

There was also an opportunity, as a society of corporations gave way to the corporate state, for the foundation, the corporate form of charity, to play a major role in preparing the way for the modern state. For by supporting research and thereby influencing the choice of social policies, the philanthropists were capable of exercising the function of shaping governmental actions in what was increasingly identified as the private sector, especially once the associational ethos of the first decade of the century gave way to the new emphasis on the value of private action of the 1920s.[28] Some of this was consciously striven for, some of it came into existence seemingly unperceived, but by the late 1920s it had become clear that the foundations and their allies had played an important role in forming a national policy for American society quite different from that of the explicitly rejected welfare capitalism of Great Britain and the Continent.

The immediate ancestors of all modern philanthropic foundations are the Russell Sage Foundation, the Carnegie Corporation and the Rockefeller Foundation. The Russell Sage Foundation, founded in 1907 by Olivia Sage with the inheritance from her despised financier-husband, employed the form and rhetoric of the foundation with a general purpose but in fact it represented a continuation and modernisation of the tradition of social work. The foundation was conceived of and managed by Robert DeForest, a wealthy lawyer and proponent of the "charity organisation movement".[29] It drew its staff and its projects, most of which were carried on by the foundation itself, from the network of social work organisations, and most of all its long-term director John Glenn, a lawyer-social worker from Baltimore.[30] More modern, in the sense that it drew its purposes more generally from the views of its trustees and staff, and distributed its funds more widely, was the Carnegie Corporation. After an early period characterised by the commanding presence of Andrew Carnegie, the Corporation invested fairly widely in American universities and research projects, as did the Rockefeller Foundation following the First World War.

For all three foundations, but especially for Carnegie and Rockefeller, there was begun the process of awarding grants which developed links between the philanthropic organisations, research workers, social reformers and government. The lines between government and private action, through financial support, were blurred when they were recognised at all, as evidenced by investment of the General Education Board in "public" education of Negroes[31] or the Rockefeller Foundation's investment in the United States Department of Agriculture experimental stations in the south.[32] The foundations also supported private and public institutions of a novel character, designed to stimulate the research upon which the making of public policy depended. Among such efforts were the Brookings Institution, the National Academy of Sciences–National Research Council, the Social Science Research Council and the National Bureau of Economic Research.[33] They thus had a hand in creating a complex system of institutions devoted to the generation, communication and control of research with a bearing on public policy, and they quickly came to play a significant role in the determination of the membership of the interlocking staffs which came to dominate the major national organisations concerned with the promotion of research. To argue that this occurred by 1930 is certainly not, however, to argue that it was the deliberate intention of the philanthropists.

Populistic and Anti-Capitalistic Distrust of Foundations

One cannot exaggerate the extent to which contemporaries perceived the potential of the foundation movement, both for good and ill. Almost from the moment of the creation of the first foundation, there came into being a body of criticism which has not significantly altered over the past 75 years. The criticism was, on the whole, populistic and was based on the assumption that the foundations represented the investment of ill-gotten gains in a manner which threatened to subvert the democratic process by giving philanthropists a determining role in the conduct of American public life. As one reads through the hostile literature, originating in the protest against congressional incorporation of the Rockefeller Foundation[34] and the Walsh Commission hearings on industrial relations of 1915–16,[35] following through bitter attacks of Harold Laski[36] and others in the late 1920s and early 1930s to the twin attacks on conservative congressmen and political radicals in the 1950s[37] and 1960s,[38] similar themes recur: money which ought to be in the hands of the public is being retained by aristocrats for purposes beyond the control of democratic institutions; the academic freedom of universities is being subverted by control of academic budgets by the foundations; public policy is being determined by private groups; the scientific and scholarly research and the artistic creativity of individuals are being stifled by the emphasis of foundations on group-research; smallness and individual effort are thwarted by materialistic and business-oriented demands of foundation management; foundations are bastions of an élite of white, Anglo-Saxon, Protestant managers holding out against the normal development of a pluralistic and ethnic society; and so on. These criticisms, and their counterparts, are founded generally in the half-examined premise that foundations pose an intellectual and financial threat to the democratic constitution of the national intellectual life. More important, there exists the almost totally unexamined view that an intellectual conspiracy threatens the health of the body politic. The foundations have learned to live with this criticism, although it accounts for their perennially defensive political and intellectual attitude, but what matters to the present argument is the way in which the foundations overcame political challenges to their legitimacy in the first years of their existence.

The first assault was directed primarily at the philanthropical activities of John D. Rockefeller. It arose out of Rockefeller's attempt to secure a congressional charter of incorporation for his foundation in 1910, when, as he knew, he would have no difficulty whatsoever in achieving precisely the same legal result in the state legislature in Albany. Congress had already granted corporate charters to the General Education Board,[39] the Carnegie Institution of Washington[40] and the Carnegie Foundation for the Advancement of Teaching,[41] but sensitivity to special acts of incorporation had increased at the same time that Rockefeller's reputation had declined. Rockefeller sought federal authorisation precisely at the time that his Standard Oil empire was in the last stages of its unsuccessful struggle against dismemberment on grounds of violation of anti-trust regulations, and when his reputation as a "robber baron" was a standing offence to public opinion.[42] He undoubtedly thought that congressional recognition of his remarkable generosity would convey to the public his own sense of moral rectitude, but of course the result was just the opposite, and his failure to win over the Senate seemed to confirm the official condemnation of his business conduct.

Matters were exacerbated in the hearings of the Walsh Commission in 1915 which produced at the same time devastatingly negative information on Rockefeller's sense of social responsibility in the management of industrial relations and the showcase for a broad range of liberal disapproval of the very concept of philanthropy. Under the leadership of the progressive lawyer, Senator Frank Walsh, the United States Commission on Industrial Relations conducted a wide-ranging inquiry into the impact of the modern industrial system on labour relations in the United States. The Commission quickly identified the new philanthropic foundations as thinly disguised capitalist manipulation of the social order, and interrogated most of the leading creators of foundations of the era: Rockefeller, Carnegie, and Daniel Guggenheim. The Rockefellers were hardest hit, since the "Ludlow Massacre" which had just occurred at their Colorado Fuel and Iron subsidiary revealed even young John D. Rockefeller, Jr. as implicated in ruthlessly oppressive policies of the most appalling character against labouring men, and caught him in a bare-faced lie when he denied participation in the management of the affairs of the Colorado Fuel and Iron Company. The message was not lost on Walsh, who pointed out that John D. Rockefeller, Sr.'s "philosophy" sought "to justify our existing economic and industrial regime, and the relation of the great foundations thereto". Walsh contended that the Commission hearings had led him to "challenge the wisdom of giving public sanction and approval to the spending of a huge fortune thru such philanthropies as that of the Rockefeller Foundation," since "the huge philanthropic trusts, known as foundations, appear to be a menace to the welfare of society." The problem was that the enormous leverage of industrial wealth enabled the philanthropists "to become molders of public thought. . . ."

> Even if the great charitable and philanthropic trusts should confine their work to the field of science, where temperament, point of view, and economic theory cannot enter, many of us should still feel that this was work for the state, and that even in the power to do good, no one man, or group of men should hold the monopoly.[43]

Walsh's sentiments have been repeated many times during the ensuing 65 years.

Hostility to the idea of the foundation was thus intense in the period up to American entry into the First World War, but of course with the single exception of the rejection of the Rockefeller charter, which was meaningless in view of the ready availability of state authorisation, there was really nothing the opponents of foundations could do to eliminate them. And in any case the tide of opinion with respect to foundations began to change rapidly after 1916.[44] Perhaps the most significant reason for this shift in opinion was the extraordinary effort of the Rockefeller philanthropy in support of European relief, but perhaps even more important was the widespread penetration of the expanded government by businessmen in connection with the multifarious tasks required for the conduct of war.[45] Many of the young members of philanthropic staffs and trustees of foundations were themselves active in the war in civilian and military capacities, and returned with a new understanding of and acceptance in the public sphere after 1918.

A number of factors contributes to the legitimation of the foundations following the War. Perhaps most important was the quick maturation of the foundations themselves. By this we mean the death or removal of the original donor from the management of the foundation, and the emergence of foundation staff as the predominant determiners of the actions of the foundations. This was true in all the major foundations, even at Rockefeller where John D. Rockefeller, Jr. survived his father to symbolise family presence in the foundation, but he deferred to the newly professionalised staff in the management of the foundation's affairs. The process was speeded by the emergence of strong personalities who devoted all their time to their work at the major foundations: John Glenn at Russell Sage, George Vincent at Rockefeller and Frederick Keppel at Carnegie. These professionals and their staffs were supported by trustees who, increasingly, were not drawn from among the personal and business associates of the donors, but rather represented a selection from the business and social élite of the north-eastern United States, and thus helped to broaden support of the foundations within that élite.[46]

The acceptance of foundations was also promoted by the activities of the foundations during the period from 1918 until the Great Depression. Money carefully given sometimes makes friends among its recipients, and that was certainly the case with the foundations. The universities were quickly won over, as were numerous private and public agencies which had been helped by the philanthropists. The foundations encouraged the development of intermediary organisations, such as the Social Science Research Council, to mediate between themselves and competitors for the support proffered by the foundations and they thus succeeded in creating a belief that they were not permanently aligned with any one set of individual research workers or with particular institutional recipients of their awards. They also shrewdly supported a wide variety of recipients, individual and corporate, and they also carefully selected the objects of their largesse in order to avoid public controversy. Medicine was always safe as well as any number of subjects within the ordinary and accepted range of social welfare. What was to be avoided was the appearance of investment in research which touched on controversial political questions even when that was in fact the objective of foundations and research workers. The result of ten years of effort was the creation of a network of institutions— mainly but not entirely universities—and individuals, in education, government and social work, who came to know and depend upon one another, and who frequently exchanged places.[47] Since they numbered amongst themselves a good many of the leaders of public opinion, it is not surprising that the new institutions received a generally favourable press.

The acceptance of the foundations was most importantly reinforced by their dramatic successes. It could be claimed that the grants and initiative of the foundations had eliminated pellagra, hookworm, typhoid, yellow fever, malaria, and numerous other physical ailments which had throughout history damaged and shortened life.[48] They had contributed to the search for international peace following the First World War, contributed to the improvement of the techniques of the social survey on which so much reform was based, and pointed a way toward schemes of social reform, especially in the urban areas.[49] In the 1920s it was generally accepted that the foundations were doing good and it was not really until the very different years following the Second World War that they encountered a new wave of public suspicion.[50] Nothing succeeds like longevity, and by 1929 the foundations had come to appear traditional, inevitable and acceptable.

The Convergence of the Progressive Movement and the Aspirations of the Foundation

The emergence of the modern foundation at that special point in American history generally defined as the "Progressive era" suggests some important questions both about philanthropy and "Progressivism." The creators of the great foundations were not "Progressives," either politically or intellectually. It is inconceivable that either Carnegie or Rockefeller could have supported all of Theodore Roosevelt's policies as president, although Carnegie had been sympathetic to Theodore Roosevelt in 1912. Rockefeller feared Bryan and enthusiastically supported McKinley. Both men fought against organised labour with the kind of brutality many in their position considered appropriate.[51]

At the same time, the activities of the new foundations, like those of their donors before they created the foundations, continued to support issues and institutions which were espoused by the Progressive movement. This included not only the concerns with medicine and social welfare, but universities and other research institutions directly concerned with governmental economic policy. Some kind of bureau of governmental research interested John D. Rockefeller as early as 1915; and while a national institution of that kind was not clearly envisaged until after the First World War he had already contributed to the New York Bureau of Municipal Research.[52] Indeed, both Carnegie and Rockefeller had supported local reform groups which were later designated "progressive" for at least a decade before the term had been given any political significance.

Part of the problem of defining their relation to the era lies in the distinction, once again, between local and national reform. Wealthy local leaders in cities like Boston and New York had long engaged in campaigns for reforms of various kinds to which they contributed time and money. They joined a growing group of influential leaders in universities and of publishers associated with national newspapers and periodicals to support reformers drawn from the social and intellectual élite which included Seth Low, president of Columbia University and mayor of New York, Charles Eliot of Harvard and William Rainey Harper of the University of Chicago. They visited clubs like the Lotos in New York, the Cosmos in Washington, and the City Club of Chicago to discuss local and national problems in convivial and opulent surroundings. Woodrow Wilson attended club dinners and spoke on programmes with Andrew Carnegie and other influential New Yorkers long before he gave up the presidency of Princeton and entered politics. If some, like James Jackson Storrow of Boston, were losing political campaigns to new leaders in partisan local politics like "Honey-Fitz" Fitzgerald, men against whom they now felt themselves arrayed, the national scene could well have seemed more inviting and encouraging, particularly after Wilson's nomination by the Democratic convention of 1912 and his election to the presidency.

The new industrial élite had all taken part in the national development of more effective collaboration between the federal government and industry. Some, like Rockefeller, were advocating national charters for business corporations to enable them to deal more directly with Washington and with those aspects of regulation and rationalisation they were finding useful.[53] Industrial firms like Standard Oil and the steel manufacturers who had recently come together to create United States Steel were national enterprises. Relations with and among the states were incidental to the national scale of their industries and therefore inefficient. Some of those who had sought to introduce systems of budgeting and uniform methods of accounting in their local governments were now looking hopefully towards similar transformations in federal economic management.[54] Even progressives who joined with populists in decrying the evils of the trusts and seeking either their regulation or their dissolution were attracted to the same conceptions of efficient management that many who had built the trusts were seeking.

When philanthropists like Rockefeller and Carnegie sought to apply similar and familiar governmental and legal standards to the national corporations they believed their foundations to be, they ran into political opposition which puzzled them. Local urban reform movements had tended to be anti-political, attacking corruption in the management of tax revenues. Locally, the issues of schools, charity and welfare, protective services of various kinds, and the rapidly growing problems of housing and land-use control had all entangled the charitable interests of philanthropic reformers with the political aims of partisan organisations. Philanthropic reform had always been a tangled skein, several threads of which always led to local political parties and their leaders. The alliances that could be struck between local reform groups, industrial leaders, and party leaders could be struck most effectively when there existed leaders who could maintain ties with all three groups, or at least with any two of the three. Theodore Roosevelt of New York and Carter Harrison in Chicago were two of the more remarkable examples. Roosevelt, like his younger cousin Franklin at a later date, was in fact a professional politician throughout his career, yet none even among their closest followers would have defined them as "pols" or linked them with the rabble of political hacks which their reform literature denigrated. Yet the Roosevelts were among the classic philanthropic families of New York, members of the merchant banking élite that had also produced the Mellons of Pittsburgh and would eventually produce the Kennedys of Boston. Some became politicians, some did not, but all could be classed with the wealthy philanthropists.

The attempt on the part of the new foundations to conduct their activities on a national scale and to win national political recognition for so doing raised the issue of whether or not the traditional relationships between philanthropists and government which were acceptable in dealing with local issues and issues in the states could be transferred to the federal government. This seemed to them a reasonable extension of an experience they had helped modernise, one which should, by the turn of the century, have been able to override the opposition the Jacksonians had faced from Pierce and other traditionalists in 1854. The fact that John D. Rockefeller in his submission of a revised foundation charter after its first defeat in Congress was willing to make concessions to governmental supervision which dwarf even the most recent efforts at governmental regulation of foundations indicates, perhaps, the extent of his desire for an acknowledgement of the Rockefeller Foundation's legitimacy in the eyes of a national public. Congress could "impose such limitations upon the objects of the corporation as the public interest may demand," the new charter was to read. Congress could direct the dissolution of the foundation after 100 years. Election of new trustees would be subject to disapproval within 60 days by a majority of a group which would consist of the President of the United States, the chief justice of the Supreme Court, the president of the Senate, the speaker of the House of Representatives, and the presidents of Harvard, Yale, Columbia and the Johns Hopkins Universities and the University of Chicago.[55]

The proposed new charter also raises two additional problems which are essential to understanding the character of the modern foundation. One is the question of whether such a charter would have made the corporation public or private. The second is the question of whether social concerns, even so broadly defined as "the well-being of mankind," can be separated from the political and economic interests of the federal government. The two problems are inextricably intertwined in ways which, once again, appear to be peculiar to the situation in the United States.

The relation between public and private was part of the dilemma of Progressivism as well. From what one can tell, the Progressive generation—indeed, reformers back into the Jacksonian era—did not look on the institutions of state and local government as institutions that raised the issue of privacy. State and local governments still came under the rubrics of self-government and all that implied to those for whom local and state citizenship was the primary source of political legitimacy. Local and state government and politics responded to the commands of the interest groups, special élites, and traditional religious organisations which controlled political power. The federal government had no generally and widely esteemed traditions and, in the minds of those satisfied with the systems of local politics that gave them their sense of governing themselves, it did not need one. Only wars required such a sense of nationality and every war before the Spanish-American war could be taken as proof that there were many obstacles to the formation of such a national culture.

When Progressivism was transformed from a reform movement into a political movement, it raised the issues of a national culture in ways that would continue to be threatening to the local and regional bases of American politics. Yet, urbanisation and industrialisation had pushed the country to a point where fundamental inequities in living conditions and economic opportunities could be described as national issues rather than as matters to be dealt with, if they were to be dealt with at all, by local or regional action.[56] Whether or not the frontier had served as the relief valve that made such a national consensus unnecessary, Americans of the turn of the century were being pressed to believe that they needed such a sense of nationality. The arguments for a national viewpoint and for national institutions were being put forth by national publications and the national network of local élites who travelled to the various city reform clubs to speak, the growing numbers of academics who moved from university to university carrying their interests in social reforms with them, and now the philanthropists who were being persuaded by their advisers to support scientific research. Whatever they thought scientific research meant, they agreed on the ideal of universality embedded in the search for the "root causes" of the evils they had once been content to attack, instance by instance. Universality and nationality were bound, ultimately, to encounter the particularity and localism on which the fervent individualism Americans identified as their common birthright was based.

The failure of Progressivism as a political movement for social reform left a large scope for philanthropy.[57] That failure stemmed in part from the refusal of Americans to make the federal government a centre of national social reform. One can explain that refusal in a variety of ways. Localism and individualism were among the ideals preserved by those who remembered President Pierce's concerns with the fountains of charity; but one could cite a harder and more politically realistic set of reasons by the turn of the century. Southern politicians had their own historical recollections of the consequences of national reform movements. Reconstruction had taught unforgettable lessons about the power of the federal government when it set out on a reforming crusade. Western agrarian interests had reason to be concerned about the effects of federal regulatory powers even on subjects like banking and railroad rates where they had pressed for expanded authority but discovered in the aftermath that they would still have to fight to ensure that centralised power would be exercised in their interests. Industrial leaders like Rockefeller and Carnegie were aware, even as they argued for federal acceptance of their philanthropic endeavours, that they wanted to limit federal intervention in their industrial interests. The fact that they chose not to confuse the profits they expected with their philanthropy distinguishes them sharply from the tradition of philanthropy which had sought to humanise the industrial system by engaging industries themselves in the social lives of workers.[58] Neither Carnegie nor Rockefeller ever seemed to think of themselves as doing anything for workers through their philanthropy, except only through paternalistic gifts of pensions, although Carnegie did endow libraries for some of his workers. Indeed, they had for years taken an unyielding position about the discontent and the unionisation of their workers; and they continued to do so, even after the formation of their foundations. Their business interests were effectively separated from their obligations to society; the former required one attitude towards the federal government, the latter another.

Yet Rockefeller, at least, sought some kind of federal support for his philanthropic activities through his request for a charter. It is by no means easy to see what he actually thought he was doing, what changes in the attitude and direction of federal policy toward social welfare he thought he was advancing. It is not known whether he asked himself whether success in his request for a federal charter would lead other philanthropists to look to the federal government for charters; or whether all national philanthropy should be federally chartered.[59]

That rejection may be more important than the confused debates which surrounded it. Both Progressivism and the move toward a national system of philanthropy implied that there had to be some national standard for dealing with social reforms. The very limited successes of Progressivism as a national movement certainly suggest that the American voters were not prepared to accept ideas that a group of its leaders in reform were pressing on it. As reformers on a national scale back as far as the Jacksonian era were aware, efforts to establish national programmes would be interpreted as efforts to enforce compliance with national programmes. In that sense, the Civil War had been a grotesque example of the logic of compliance with a reform movement on a national scale. Despite the fact that reformers would continue to argue that their aim was primarily one of educating the public to an understanding of its own best interests and not forcing them to comply with commands from Washington, the threat was there.

In any case, the great accretion of power in Washington and the creation of a national system of philanthropy were crucial steps in the sharpening of the line between public and private in ways that would have been startlingly unfamiliar to men like Rockefeller and Carnegie, if not to American public opinion in general. Foundations were "private" now in what might be called a new sense of the term. "Private," a term which once designated a form of behaviour that could be distinguished from actions performed by the public or under public scrutiny, could not be restricted to sources of financial support and methods of control, regardless of the substantive content of the actions. The term "public" had always had a somewhat ambiguous meaning in that regard, and it continued to do so in local affairs. Public agencies continued to depend on private donors without worrying about the distinction. Public utilities, public schools, and a whole range of social services provided to and by hospitals and courts amalgamated private and public financial support and management. The complex process of enfranchising private companies to operate "public" transportation or provide "public" services continued to raise questions of corruption and periodic cries for governmental ownership; but the relation between public and private could be flexibly redrawn as circumstances required. Where the federal government was concerned that kind of accommodation appeared to be impossible.

Yet the modern foundation, from the very beginning, was engaged in a process of influencing the formulation of policies which affected the public and in which the public had an interest. Government could be called upon to support, or to continue, or even to try to prevent the carrying out of programmes designed by private groups. The federal government's rejection in principle of a process that was locally acceptable did not change matters, particularly after presidents began looking to private sources to provide the funds for their own in promoting research bearing on policies the government was pursuing or considering. What that rejection did, however, was to change the terms in which the periodic debates over influence and direction were to be argued. Private philanthropy was forced to accept the fluctuations of public opinion which swung from periodic praise for the goods resulting from the research which foundations had supported and even initiated, and denunciations of foundations as part of a conspiracy to take over the government and as efforts to impose on the entire society ideas which were repugnant to significant sections of society. The officers of the foundation could respond to the swings by optimistic moments of camaraderie in which they advised and cajoled federal officials to do things government had not before been doing and episodes of flight in which they sought to restrict themselves to issues that could not possibly get them into trouble. The curing of sick children was always at the top of the list.[60]

The Private Foundation and the Public Sphere

It is possible that in the process of developing the modern foundation, both defenders and critics gave the term "private" a special and deceptive meaning. The right to refuse disclosure, once part of any dictionary definition of the term, could scarcely be given the full defence it had always had. The various "tax-benefits" conferred on donors became the instrument which justified public investigation; but the truth of the matter was far more serious than the questionable idea that foundations were spending money that, somehow, rightfully belonged in the public treasury. Whatever the source of the money and its relation to the public treasury, the programmes it was supporting were intended to influence the situations and actions of part or all of the public. "The welfare of mankind" which appeared in various forms in the initiating documents of the foundations was being interpreted and used far more explicitly than the "general welfare" clause of the constitution of the United States.[61]

The federal government's rejection of responsibility for changing society was tied to a tradition that still defined the causes of social disorder and misery as local. The growing consciousness of the country as a whole as a single system of causes and effects, without regard to the traditional boundaries of locality, was in part a product of the growth of national industry and of the national economy; this went hand in hand with the growing consciousness of scientific propositions about "root causes" and "scientific cures." Science was not only national but international. It transcended state as well as national boundaries and made obsolete the politics that confined observations of problems and experiments that promised their solution.

The fact that national foundations came into being at the moment they did might well have been an historical accident; but they served purposes which could be recognised in every language but that of politics. The relation between public, and private became, in the process, a heuristic device that concealed the truth only from those on both sides who wanted it concealed. Rockefeller's openness in seeking a federal charter may have been politically naïve, but there was also a more realistic argument for it.

In any case, the creation of the private foundation in an era of attacks on "invisible governments" was and would remain something of an anomaly. Americans had found a way of doing "privately" what governments in other advanced industrial societies were beginning to do. Despite the periodic investigations through which the United States Congress expressed its uneasiness, governmental executive agencies at all levels looked to private donors, among them foundations, for the research on which they sought to base new social and economic policies.[62] Although the First World War appeared on the scene as the kind of accidental event no one would have predicted, American entry helped establish patterns to be followed over the next three decades.

The First World War transformed the role of philanthropy in American society in several distinctive ways. First of all, from the outbreak of the war in Europe in August 1914 until American entry in April 1917, American philanthropists and American philanthropy set about aiding the victims of the war through a massive outpouring of money and material, through an *ad hoc* administrative system privately created but operating under the watchful, if not always totally supporting eye of the Department of State.[63] The Rockefeller group alone gave $22,000,000 and served as liaison between the various groups who competed with one another in the delivery of American benefactions.[64] Herbert Hoover headed the Belgian Relief Commission. His own interests were influenced by principles that were destined to characterise his career in the public service over the next two decades, particularly the belief that the governments being aided abroad should also be prepared to match the contributions being made to them, lest they become dependent upon American gifts, and damaged somehow by that dependence.[65] That idea, the need to assure benefactors that the communities being helped were willing to take action in their own support, had been part of the American philanthropic tradition. Carnegie had invoked it in his gifts of libraries, but not books.[66] Carnegie agreements contained a clause requiring communities to provide the site and 10 per cent. of the amount of the gift for annual maintenance. Rockefeller had supported it in his insistence that local boards be established to receive such grants as his contributions to the University of Chicago, and to raise additional funds on their own. The issue of matching governmental support had not been raised so baldly on the domestic scene as it was abroad, but it had been there when the occasion made it appear to be appropriate. Local philanthropists in cities like Boston, New York and Chicago had grown accustomed to expecting that the specialised services they provided for public use—social workers for the courts, advisers for the schools, and boards to test and certify milk—be taken over by governmental institutions once they had proved their utility.[67]

Equally important, however, was a second and related effect of the war. Woodrow Wilson's decision to administer the government's arrangements through *ad hoc* boards and agencies jointly staffed by private citizens and public officials set a pattern of what was called, somewhat deceptively, "voluntarism," or "volunteerism," depending, in a sense, on whether the system was perceived as one willingly obeyed by patriotic citizens or managed by volunteer administrators given unprecedented power to act in the public interest. While the method was looked upon as part of a special effort justified by the emergence of the war and destined for dismantling at its end, it did in fact reflect patterns of philanthropic public service which had their origins in the recent history of philanthropy.[68] In the depression of the 1930s, the wartime experience was looked to, a bit romantically at times, as a model of voluntary public assistance, community self-help put to the country's service. The expansion of the American Red Cross during the war from an agency which expended roughly $5,000,000 a year, to one which could raise and distribute $100,000,000 in a single campaign and $400,000,000 during the war itself was not viewed as a temporary exigency, necessarily, but as an experience that could be repeated when required; and the scale of operations changed.[69] To be sure, in the immediate aftermath of the war, the insistence on getting the federal government out of direct engagement with the lives of citizens was strong, even among Progressives who had once viewed the intervention as an opportunity to achieve their aims. But the recollection of the experience remained. The memory of it as a national triumph frequently obscured its repressive and coercive side.

In some respects the role which foundations sought for themselves during the war was no more prescient and no further advanced than the roles sought by knowledgeable and intelligent Americans of the period. Even the Carnegie Endowment for International Peace was puzzled to define its appropriate position in the three years before American entry, attempting to remain neutral even after reports of supposed anti-German statements by Mr. Carnegie had generated a certain amount of confusion. With American entry into the war, the Endowment seemed to shift its interests and began worrying about shifting American academic interest to things French, rather than German, setting up methods of a new approach to international education which they would probably not have insisted was anti-German, even though such an implication was clearly there.[70]

The Rockefeller medical interests were suited to wartime specialisation, and they provided the funds for the building of a hospital in New York City, the purpose of which was to investigate new treatments for wounds, burns, and the effects of poison gas.[71] John D. Rockefeller, Jr. himself served on the War Labor Board in an effort to foster a consensus between labour, management and government. But while he was seeking more friendly relations, his father's hostility to government was growing.[72] While his response was, in some respects, the hard-bitten reply of a man who still considered taxation a threat to his independence of action and judgement, it was also a statement of a generational difference that would continue to affect the philanthropic world. For the older man's generation, philanthropy did things government did not, or could not, or should not do. When the federal government decided to do them, philanthropy stepped out. The war was teaching a different lesson. Co-operation looked more promising, at least for the moment. The relation between a strict separation of functions and some kinds of co-operative effort continued to shape the relation between philanthropy and government. The battles between them and the attempts of one to influence the other continued to suggest at the same time that their separation was at least partly illusory.

The foundations, too, took part in the issues which troubled the domestic wartime scene. The creation of the National Civic Federation in 1900 had been part of a privately supported effort to establish more informative communication between management and labour in a form more acceptable to industrial leaders than was union hostility. It had been a favourite interest of Andrew Carnegie and it had attracted support from the elder Rockefeller. During the war its nationalist attacks on the alleged radical attack on American society had been part of the wartime furore which had, by the end of the war, begun to trouble liberals and moderates concerned over the then new issue of civil liberties. Its director, Ralph C. Easley, had become a patriotic zealot and sought to make the Federation the leading anti-radical agency in the years after the war. By 1920 he and his agency had become an embarrassment to both the Carnegie Corporation and the Rockefeller Foundation. They reduced their contributions or tried to maintain them at their lowest pre-war level in response to his pleas, while they discussed among themselves and their advisers the appropriateness of continuing to support an organisation they believed to be headed in a totally wrong direction. While later critics of philanthropy saw their interest in the National Civic Federation as proof of their preoccupation with anti-radical and anti-labour activities, their correspondence suggests a far more sophisticated understanding of the condition of labour and the attitudes of American society. They saw little urgency in the threat of radicalism.[73]

The war had transformed the country's sense of the role of American philanthropy in ways no one anticipated. Part of that transformation was simply a function of the size of the national effort to allay suffering in Europe before America's entry into the war, to develop the armed forces, to arouse the spirit which the war effort required after the years of doubts and indecision and to define war aims in ways that were consistent with a popular view of the national interest in a world setting. The war bond drives to finance the war by what appeared, at least, to be individual subscription, the American Red Cross drives which greatly multiplied that organisation's scale of operation and the enlistment of the services of private citizens for voluntary effort, from the "dollar-a-year men" who actually ran the civil side of the military operation and the ladies who gathered together to roll bandages, knit sweaters, or provide coffee and doughnuts at railway stopovers, were all examples of a national voluntary effort that obscured for a time the sanctions applied to those who refused to volunteer because they found that particular war or all war unacceptable.[74] None the less, the model of citizen philanthropy moved into the 1920s intact. The formation of groups of citizens to organise local charities more efficiently went on at a quickened pace, as did the effort to popularise small contributions by handing out little envelopes to school children limiting the gift to one penny.[75] (Franklin Roosevelt's later establishment of the March of Dimes was built on the same idea: philanthropy was not and should not be simply a responsibility of the rich.)

Foundations after the Life-time of their Founders

Within the new situation of the older foundations, another transformation was taking place as the new foundations began to face the consequences of their perpetuity. The death of Andrew Carnegie in 1919 followed several years of inactivity during which one can see the beginnings of the realignments of power and management which were destined to become the focus of reorganisations in the 1920s. John D. Rockefeller Jr.'s decision to retire as president of the Foundation in 1918 and to become chairman of the board, and the naming of George Vincent as president, suggests a similar transition. John D. Rockefeller Jr.'s struggle to overcome his shyness had been tested severely by the appearance before the Industrial Relations Commission several years earlier when he had been forced to acknowledge a fact, the significance of which struck him at the time, namely, that the work of the foundation and the management of the response to the strike in Colorado had both been carried on from the same small suite of offices at 26 Broadway in New York City. The obvious proximity had generated the kind of beliefs which the critics of the Rockefeller Foundation had always feared and it seemed to establish an ostensible pattern of insidious influence the foundation world would continue to have to bear as part of the burden of doing good. Friends of the family like Charles W. Eliot, retired from his presidency of Harvard for a decade but still looked to for advice, urged him to give up the strenuous responsibility of management, and he did.[76]

The transition of the Carnegie philanthropies was complex in a somewhat different way. The Carnegie Corporation of New York was Andrew Carnegie's last and biggest philanthropic corporation. He had never made its purpose clear, particularly to the extent of defining its relation to the other Carnegie philanthropic bodies. The fact that its board included the presidents of the other corporations tended to confirm, at least in the minds of the men who ran such institutions as the Carnegie Institution of Washington, the Carnegie Endowment for International Peace, and the Carnegie Institute for Technology in Pittsburgh, the possibility that Carnegie had intended the Corporation in New York as a holding company of sorts to manage and supply the others, not as an independent fund with an independent set of purposes. The battle lines were drawn—and the conclusion quite possibly determined—by Carnegie's own selection of a former president of the Massachusetts Institute of Technology, Henry S. Pritchett, as president of the Carnegie Foundation for the Advancement of Teaching.[77] Pritchett had assumed that Carnegie would leave all of his remaining money to the Foundation. The creation of the Corporation was a blow.

The first of the former college presidents to be drawn into foundation management, rather than as advisers or as board members, Pritchett began simply as the officer in charge of the programme of college and university teachers' pensions which the Carnegie Foundation for the Advancement of Teaching administered; but his location in New York in the office of the Corporation, his proximity to Carnegie, and his influence in the selection of staff were crucial.[78] The Corporation itself was, during Carnegie's lifetime, little more than an agency for his own benefactions. He ruled as president and delegated such interests as libraries, church organs, and the extraordinary system of simplified spelling he wanted everyone in the organisation to employ to his initial staff which consisted of James Bertram and Robert Franks, his personal secretaries and aides. Pritchett sometimes referred to them as "Mr. Carnegie's clerks."[79]

The selection of James B. Angell as the first president of the Corporation after Andrew Carnegie's death gave the Corporation the beginning of a brief, independent life. It was brief, relatively speaking, only because Angell committed about six years of available funds to various projects before he left, after serving less than a year, to become president of Yale, but independent because the grants were not in support of the other Carnegie enterprises. Pritchett, during Carnegie's last illness, had established a close working relation with the chairman of the board, Elihu Root, and the two of them became the managers of the Carnegie philanthropic enterprise. It was a relationship which made them not only managers of the future, but its prophets. It is unlikely that Pritchett alone could have battled such powers as Nicholas Murray Butler and John Campbell Merriam; but with Root at his side and with a stern and unshakeable patience, he triumphed. As acting-president of the Corporation, he was crucial in the appointment of Frederick Keppel as Angell's successor. The two of them, based in New York, one determined in the paternalism of his endeavour, the other a wise and shrewd filial politician, created the independent course of the Carnegie Corporation of New York.[80] Butler and his associates on the board could argue the violation of Carnegie's intention, but to no avail.[81] However correct they may have been about Carnegie's original plan—and he had used his own presidency of the Corporation of New York as they thought his successors should have used it—he had left the money in such a way as to avoid tying the hands of his successors. Root, Pritchett, and Keppel remained untied.

Although the Rockefeller family was bound to remain very much in evidence in the direction of the foundation's interests, the same problems of reorganisation there suggest that relationships of the donors to the planning of the activities of the foundation were perhaps not so important as the much more pervasive consciousness of the need to plan, to create direction and purpose, to construct a system for the administrative management of plans and purposes and to establish the board of trustees as the body through which perpetuity would be achieved.[82] In the large foundations in the 1920s one can find the pattern which was to persist in the development of all foundations large enough to be forced to face the problem. Successive presidents would have to assemble professional staffs to manage the activities of the foundation. Successive boards of trustees would have to respond to policies, determine new directions, appoint—or dismiss—presidents, and manage as, in effect, surrogate donors. Even where donors were present as board members, and obviously deferred to as such, the principle of perpetuity and the responsibility of acting as a community of trustees was clear.

In Rockefeller and in Carnegie what had begun as a small group of secretaries, friends, trusted lawyers, and, later, a few acceptable presidents of acceptable universities had become, by the end of the 1920s, an administrative system which still included many of the same types, but with a clear sense now of their own independence as a community or group of communities from the intentions of one wealthy man. In both cases, efforts were made to interpret the intentions of "the Founder" in a tone which at times seems somewhat mystical; but those intentions were, quite rapidly, transformed into ideas of preferred policies: education, in the case of Rockefeller. Where Carnegie's interest in libraries is concerned, the transformation of that in the 1920s is a good example. From the construction of library buildings, the Carnegie Corporation moved to the creation of academic schools to train professional librarians. The University of Chicago, initially the somewhat reluctant and puzzled recipient of the offer of money, became the first university to create a "graduate school of library science." The Carnegie Corporation clearly took the initiative, supported surveys to determine the need for such a school, following the model which had been created a decade earlier to carry out the reforms proposed by Abraham Flexner for medical education, decided where such a school would best be located, and enticed the administration of the University of Chicago to establish the school.[83]

Social Improvement through Social Science

One can see a similar initiative in the Rockefeller Foundation's support of projects in the social sciences where the problem is complicated by the fact that social science can come dangerously close to politics and hence to political criticism. The staff of the foundation had been divided internally on the subject since the beginning. Medicine was safe philanthropy in the days when medical policy was considered public only when it affected the poor or the military. Most medical research was private and most provision of medical care was private, local or religious in its support. The decision by the Rockefeller Foundation to support social science had earlier roots in John D. Rockefeller Sr.'s interest in research in economics; but such expansions in the 1920s and the support of the Social Science Research Council, the National Bureau of Economic Research, and the Institute for Government Research (later renamed the Brookings Institution in honour of its philanthropic founder) were all Rockefeller entries in the field of research on social science with practical intentions.[84]

The expansion of research in social policy by foundations in the 1920s raised a number of complex issues. The creation of research corporations which did not bear the foundation name was one way of coming to grips with the problem of political criticism. The establishment of the Spelman Fund of New York in 1928 was certainly an example of a compromise bordering on subterfuge, since the funds came from the Laura Spelman Rockefeller Memorial (1918). Beardsley Ruml had been active in social science and public administration. The growing opposition of officers of the Rockefeller Foundation led to the separation of such interests into organisations less identifiable with the Rockefeller name. The Spelman Fund was explicitly directed toward problems in public administration and social science, and Ruml eventually left Rockefeller to pursue his interests more directly.

Yet in the 1920s the investment of the Rockefeller and the Carnegie foundations in social problems grew. Rockefeller entered the field of low-cost housing, and both foundations enlarged their concern with race relations.[85] The entry of the Commonwealth Fund into the field immediately after the war put the wealth of Edward S. Harkness and his mother to similar purposes, even though their initial interest in economic and legal research was ultimately dropped in favour of medical care.[86] The "New Era" of the 1920s meant, for foundations, a new social-scientific utopianism and the development of voluntary, non-governmental systems of bringing about desired changes in American society.

When, in the first months of his presidency, Herbert Hoover assembled a group of the country's most prominent social scientists to study the state of American society, he approached foundations himself and received the support he had requested.[87] Although *Recent Social Trends in the United States* did not finally appear until 1933, it was intended as a document of "policy research" which the President could use as the basis for a major programme of social reform. No such massive social survey had been done before, nor has one been done since. A privately financed effort which utilised the support of government staffs and agencies as well as staffs from public and private research institutions, it remains a unique model of the kind of co-operative public-private effort of which the founders of the major foundations had dreamed. Indeed, improving the "welfare of mankind" may even have faded beside the assurance that social science research could lead to governmental policies which would in turn create a society without poverty and without war.

Even the hostility towards private business that ultimately came to dominate the New Deal did nothing to stop the expansion of influence by privately supported research on the making of governmental policy. If Franklin Roosevelt preferred to conceal the fact that so many of his major advisers on policy and some of his major programmes in social reform were the result of support by one or more of the private foundations, it was because he had no choice when he needed the outside aid; and he depended upon it willingly, if not gratefully. Not until 1939 when the creation of the Executive Office of the President gave him funds to commission and conduct such research was he even relatively independent of the reluctance of Congress to support such endeavours. The programme which led to the establishment of the Executive Office of the President had been prepared by a group supported in part by the Rockefeller Foundation, indirectly, to be sure, through the Social Science Research Council, but supported by it none the less.

New foundations continued to emerge, even amidst the criticisms of the 1930s. Ford in 1936 and Lilly in 1937, although originally inactive measures of tax-avoidance, were destined to become important factors in the next 25 years.[88] In the period after the Second World War, the relations between foundations and the makers of national policy grew even closer as foundations provided government with international research opportunities which would have run into opposition from Congress, while government agencies looked to foundations for ways of supplying money for covert activities some of the research workers themselves did not perceive. It was an era that would ultimately come under a great deal of criticism from virtually everyone involved, but at least from the perspective of a kind of organisational pattern developed over half a century, the inter-relations and interpenetrations reflected a triumph of *ad hoc* procedure. Administratively, foundations became one of the crucial foci in the training of the country's managerial élite and the creation of the research techniques and the data that the élite needed. They were part of a system which provided governments and universities with advice and staff, in turn drawing their own staffs from universities and government. The course of careers from foundation to university to government and back again became the track which the United States depended upon to develop staff and leadership for its system of government, as well as ideas. The careers of Dean Rusk, McGeorge Bundy, and John Gardner, to name only the most obvious, illustrate the pattern.

Private Foundations, Pluralism and Collectivistic Liberalism

The seeming breakdown of the system during the war in Vietnam is far more complex than simple notions about the "best and the brightest" or the rebellion of the intellectuals would suggest. The attack on foundations that began in the election battles of 1968 and focused on such matters as voter-registration in the South and the Ford Foundation's support for the close associates of the assassinated Robert Kennedy were again striking events which obscured an historical past in which foundations traditionally worked to do for southern Negroes what their white neighbours would not do for them, and in which foundation officers found ways of sustaining the temporarily displaced members of an élite they had helped create.[89] Both actions were traditional parts of the pattern of action of American foundations. Both were products of the fact that for over half a century, foundations had been bridging the hitherto unbridged gap which Americans had created between public and private, between state and nation, and between social and political, between traditional American ideas and the urgent problems of the time.

Even so, the discussion of the problem in terms of the old polarities persisted. Defenders of the public from interference by foundations continued to assume that government alone could do, or prevent the doing of, things which regional majorities or local interests rejected. Foundations defended themselves as "private" despite the special benefits which they received from the tax law or moved to a new level of linguistic fabrication by defining themselves as members of a "third sector," despite the fact that such language only sustains an historical illusion.[90]

Foundations came into existence because American society was unable to maintain a social order which corresponded to its passionately held localist ideals. The ideals are as real as the political history which prevented their fulfilment. In the process, however, foundations helped create a voice which transcended politics, even when they were engaged in influencing them. As the battles of 1968 and 1969 showed, their voice had been critical in raising issues effectively and with organisational skill and sensitivity.

The transformation of federal approaches to social problems in the 1970s raises as many historical questions as it answers and poses as many threats.[91] So does the emergence of corporate philanthropy and new foundations with mandates to criticise and reform government policy. The historical argument, once again, has been transformed. Whether or not it has been changed is another matter.

Notes

1. Wilson, Woodrow, *Division and Reunion, 1829–1889* (New York: Longmans, Green, 1893).
2. Bremner, Robert H., *The Public Good: Philanthropy and Welfare in the Civil War Era* (New York: Knopf, 1980).
3. Hays, Samuel P., *The Response to Industrialism, 1885–1915* (Chicago: University of Chicago Press, 1957).
4. Owen, David, *English Philanthropy 1600–1900* (Cambridge, Mass.: Harvard University Press, 1964).
5. U.S. National Resources Planning Board, *Security Work and Relief Policies*, Report of the Committee on Long-Range Work and Relief Policies to the National Resources Planning Board (Washington, D.C.: U.S. Government Printing Office, 1942).
6. Commission on Private Philanthropy and Public Needs, *Giving in America: Toward a Stronger Voluntary Sector*, Report of the Commission on Private Philanthropy and Public Needs (Washington, D.C.: The Commission, 1978).
7. *Congressional Globe*, XXVIII, 2 (1854), p. 1,062.
8. Bremner, R. H., *op. cit.*, pp. 171–207.
9. Dupree, A. Hunter, *Science in the Federal Government* (Cambridge, Mass.: Belknap Press of Harvard University Press, 1957), pp. 256–270.
10. 198 U.S. 45.
11. See Diner, Steven J., "A City and its University: Chicago Professors and Elite Reform, 1892–1919," unpublished Ph.D. dissertation. The University of Chicago, 1972; see also Buenker, John D., *Urban Liberalism and Progressive Reform* (New York: Scribner's, 1973).
12. Hopkins, C. Howard, *History of the Y.M.C.A. in North America* (New York: Association Press, 1951), pp. 227–239, 455–458, 594–604.
13. See Romasco, Albert U., *The Poverty of Abundance: Hoover, the Nation and the Depression* (New York: Oxford University Press, 1965). Harry Hopkins, when appointed by Franklin D. Roosevelt as director of the New York State Temporary Emergency Relief Administration, was head of the New York Association for Improving the Condition of the Poor, a private charitable organisation.
14. A valuable treatment of a private philanthropic system developing in the shadow of a welfare state is to be found in Owen, D., *op. cit.*; see also Clough, Shephard B., "Philanthropy and the Welfare State in Europe," *Political Science Quarterly*, LXXV (March 1960), pp. 87–93.
15. See, for example, Allen, William H., *Modern Philanthropy: A Study of Efficient and Appealing Giving* (New York: Dodd, Mead, 1912).
16. Rosenberg, Charles, *No Other Gods* (Baltimore: Johns Hopkins University Press, 1976).
17. Veysey, Laurence R., *The Emergence of the American University* (Chicago: University of Chicago Press, 1965).
18. Carnegie, Andrew, "The Best Fields for Philanthropy," *North American Review*, CXLIX (December 1889), pp. 682–698; Rockefeller, John D., *Random Reminiscences of Men and Events* (New York: Doubleday Page, 1909), pp. 130–188; Gates, Frederick T., "Memo by Mr. Gates," 7 October, 1908, *Frederick T. Gates Papers*, Rockefeller Archive Center, Hillcrest, Pocantico Hills, New York, Box II, File 27 (hereafter *Gates Papers*).

19. Veysey, L. R., *op. cit.*, pp. 22–57.
20. Lowell, Josephine S., "True Aim of Charity Organization Societies," *Forum*, XXI (June 1896), pp. 494–500.
21. Curry, J. L. M., *Brief Sketch of George Peabody and a History of the Peabody Education Fund Through Thirty Years* (Cambridge: John Wilson, 1898); Ware, Louise, *George Foster Peabody: Banker, Philanthropist, Publicist* (Athens, Georgia: University of Georgia Press, 1951).
22. Fosdick, Raymond B. and Pringle, Henry, *Adventures in Giving* (New York: Harper, 1962).
23. Hawkins, Hugh, *Pioneer: A History of the Johns Hopkins University 1874–89* (Ithaca: Cornell University Press, 1969); Storr, Richard, *Harper's University: The Beginnings* (Chicago: University of Chicago Press, 1966).
24. Corner, George W., *A History of the Rockefeller Institute, 1901–1953: Origins and Growth* (New York: Rockefeller Institute Press, 1964), pp. 1–55.
25. Trattner, Walter and Klein, Philip, *From Philanthropy to Social Welfare* (San Francisco: Jossey-Bass, 1968).
26. Jerome D. Greene to Trustees of The Rockefeller Foundation, 21 January, 1914, *Files of The Rockefeller Foundation*, Rockefeller Archive Center, Record Group 3, Series 900, Box XVIII, Folder 129 (hereafter cited in this fashion: RF 3.900.XVIII.129).
27. See, for example, Giovanni Agnelli Foundation, *Guide to European Foundations* (New York: Columbia University Press, 1973).
28. Hawley, Ellis W., "Herbert Hoover, the Commerce Secretariat, and the Vision of an 'Associative State', 1921–1928," *Journal of American History*, LXXXI (June 1974), pp. 116–140.
29. "Suggestions for a Possible Sage Foundation. Memorandum made by R. W. deForest for Mrs. Sage," 10 December, 1906, Russell Sage Foundation Files, New York.
30. Glenn, John M., "Personal Reminiscences," *The Sight-Saving Review*, X (September 1940); Glenn, John M., Brandt, Lillian and Andrews, F. Emerson, *The Russell Sage Foundation, 1907–1946* (New York: Russell Sage Foundation, 1947).
31. See Harlan, Louis R., *Separate and Unequal: Public School Campaigns and Racism in the Southern Seaboard States, 1901–1915* (Chapel Hill: University of North Carolina Press, 1953), pp. 75–101.
32. McConnell, Grant, *Private Power and American Democracy* (New York: Knopf, 1966).
33. Oswald W. Knauth to Beardsley Ruml, 2 December, 1920, Carnegie Corporation of New York Files, New York.
34. U.S. Senate, 62nd Congress, 3rd session, *The Rockefeller Foundation*, Report No. 1258 (Washington, D.C.: U.S. Government Printing Office, 1913); U.S. House of Representatives, 62nd Congress, 2nd session, *The Rockefeller Foundation*, Report No. 529 (Washington, D.C.: U.S. Government Printing Office, 1912); U.S. Senate, 61st Congress, 2nd session, *Incorporation of the Rockefeller Foundation*, Report No. 405 (Washington, D.C.: U.S. Government Printing Office, 1910); *Congressional Record*, LI (1913), pp. 1,109–1,113, 1,808–1,811, appendix pp. 74–75.
35. U.S. Senate, 64th Congress, 1st session, *Industrial Relations: Final Report and Testimony Submitted to Congress by the Commission on Industrial Relations*, Document No. 415 (Washington, D.C.: U.S. Government Printing Office, 1916).
36. Laski, Harold J., *Dangers of Obedience* (New York: Harper, 1930).
37. U.S. House of Representatives, Select Committee to Investigate Tax-Exempt Foundations, 82nd Congress, 2nd session, *Final Report*, House Report 3514 (Washington, D.C.: U.S. Government Printing Office, 1954); U.S. House of Representatives, Select Committee to Investigate Tax-Exempt Foundations, 82nd Congress, 2nd session, *Hearings* (Washington, D.C.: U.S. Government Printing Office, 1954); U.S. House of Representatives, Select Committee to Investigate Tax-Exempt Foundations, 83rd Congress, 2nd session, *Final Report*, House Report 2681 (Washington, D.C.: U.S. Government Printing Office, 1954); U.S. House of Representatives, Select Committee to Investigate Tax-Exempt Foundations, 83rd Congress, 2nd session, *Hearings* (Washington, D.C.: U.S. Government Printing Office, 1955).
38. U.S. House of Representatives, Committee on Ways and Means, 91st Congress, 1st session, *Hearings on the Subject of Tax Reform* (Washington, D.C.: U.S. Government Printing Office, 1969); U.S. Senate, Committee on Finance, 91st Congress, 1st session, *Hearings on House Report 13270* (Washington, D.C.: U.S. Government Printing Office, 1969).
39. 32 U.S. Statutes: 768–769, 12 January, 1903.
40. 33 U.S. Statutes: 575–577, 28 April, 1904.
41. 34 U.S. Statutes: 59–61, 10 March 1906.
42. See Nevins, A. F., *Study in Power: John D. Rockefeller, Industrialist and Philanthropist* (New York: Scribner's, 1953), vol. II, pp. 356–385; Pringle, Henry F., *The Life and Times of William Howard Taft: A Biography* (New York: Farrar and Rinehart, 1939), vol. II pp. 659–667.
43. Walsh, Frank P., "Perilous Philanthropy," *The Independent*, LXXXIII (August 1915), p. 262.

44. Nevins, A. F., *op. cit.*, vol, II, p. 420.

45. Cuff, Robert, *The War Industries Board: Business-Government Relations during World War I* (Baltimore: Johns Hopkins University Press, 1973).

46. George E. Vincent to Jerome D. Greene, 13 September 1928, RF 3.903. I.1; H. S. Pritchett to the trustees of the Carnegie Corporation of New York, 13 February, 1922, Carnegie Corporation of New York Files; F. P. Keppel to Nicholas Murray Butler, 28 November, 1938, Carnegie Endowment for International Peace Archives, Department of Special Collections, Butler Library, Columbia University, New York.

47. Kusmer, Kenneth L., "The Functions of Organized Charity in the Progressive Era: Chicago as a Case Study," *Journal of American History*, LX (December 1973), pp. 657–678.

48. See U.S. House of Representatives, 62nd Congress, 2nd session, *The Rockefeller Foundation*, Report No. 529, pp. 2–3; see also Benison, Saul, "Poliomyelitis and the Rockefeller Institute: Social Effects and Institutional Response," *Journal of the History of Medicine and Allied Sciences*, XXIX (January 1974), pp. 74–92.

49. McClymer, John F., "The Pittsburgh Survey, 1907–1914; Forging an Ideology in the Steel District," *Pennsylvania History*, XLI (April 1974), pp. 169–186.

50. See editorial, "Scientific Philanthropy," *The New York Times*, 5 January, 1929.

51. McCloskey, Robert G., *American Conservatism in the Age of Enterprise* (Cambridge, Mass.: Harvard University Press; 1951); Carnegie, Andrew, *Problems of Today: Wealth-Labor-Socialism* (New York: Doubleday, Page 1908); Fitch, John A., "Ludlow, Chrome, Homestead and Wall Street in the Melting Pot," *Survey*, XXX (13 February, 1915), pp. 531–534.

52. See Dahlberg, Jane S., *The New York Bureau of Municipal Research: Pioneer in Government Administration* (New York: New York University Press, 1966); Grossman, David M., "Professors and Public Service, 1885–1925: A Chapter in the Professionalization of the Social Sciences," unpublished Ph.D. dissertation, Washington University, St. Louis, 1973; Saunders, Charles B., Jr., *The Brookings Institution: A Fifty-Year History* (Washington, D.C.: Brookings Institution, 1966); Critchlow, Donald T., "The Brookings Institution: The Early History 1916–1952," unpublished Ph.D. dissertation, University of California, 1976.

53. Rockefeller, J. D., *op. cit.*, pp. 68–69.

54. Message of the President of the United States transmitting report of the Commission on Economy and Efficiency on the subject of the need for a national budget, 27 June, 1912, 62nd Congress, 2nd session, *The Need for a National Budget*, House Report No. 854 (Washington, D.C.: U.S. Government Printing Office, 1912).

55. U.S. Senate, 62nd Congress, 3rd session, *The Proposed Incorporation of the Rockefeller Foundation in the District of Columbia* (Washington, D.C.: U.S. Government Printing Office, 1910).

56. Croly, Herbert, *Promise of American Life* (New York: Macmillan, 1909); Wiebe, Robert, *The Search for Order* (New York: Hill and Wang, 1964).

57. Link, Arthur S., "What Happened to the Progressive Movement in the 1920s?," *American Historical Review*, XLIV (July 1959). pp. 833–851.

58. Brandes, Stuart D., *American Welfare Capitalism, 1880–1940* (Chicago: University of Chicago Press, 1970) calls John D. Rockefeller, Jr. a "welfare capitalist". While that description may have had some relevance after Ludlow, his father could never have been accused of sharing those sentiments.

59. See U.S. Senate, 62nd Congress, 3rd session, *The Rockefeller Foundation*, Report No. 1258; U.S. House of Representatives, 62nd Congress, 2nd session, *The Rockefeller Foundation*, Report No. 529; U.S. Senate, 61st Congress, 2nd session, *Incorporation of the Rockefeller Foundation*, Report No. 405; *Congressional Record*, LI (1913).

60. Frederick T. Gates to John D. Rockefeller, Sr., 19 March, 1914, *Gates Papers*, Box III, File 58.

61. Chambers, Merrit M., *Charters of Philanthropies* (New York: Carnegie Foundation for the Advancement of Teaching, 1948).

62. Karl, Barry D., "Presidential Planning and Social Science Research: Mr. Hoover's Experts," *Perspectives in American History*, III (1969), pp. 347–412; Herbert Hoover to F. P. Keppel, 26 October, 1927, Carnegie Corporation of New York Files.

63. Jerome D. Greene to William J. Bryan, 24 April, 1915, RF 1.100. LVII. 567; William Phillips to Jerome D. Greene, 28 April, 1915, *loc. cit.*

64. Fosdick, Raymond B., *The Story of the Rockefeller Foundation* (New York: Harper, 1952).

65. Herbert Hoover to Wickliffe Rose, 21 November, 1914, RF 1.100. LXVI. 653.

66. Wall, Joseph F., *Andrew Carnegie* (New York: Oxford University Press, 1970), pp. 815–819; see also Dunne, Finley P., "The Carnegie Libraries," *Dissertations by Mr. Dooley* (New York: Harper, 1906), pp. 177–182.

67. Lubove, Roy, *The Professional Altruist: The Emergence of Social Work as a Career, 1880–1930* (New York: Atheneum, 1972), pp. 1–55.

68. Cuff, R. D., *op. cit.*; Fosdick, Raymond B., *Chronicle of a Generation* (New York: Harper, 1958).

69. Cutlip, Scott M., *Fund Raising in the U.S.: Its Role in American Philanthropy* (New Brunswick, N.J.: Rutgers University Press, 1965); Davison, Henry P., *The American Red Cross in the Great War* (New York: Macmillan, 1919).

70. Henry S. Pritchett to John B. Clark, 30 June, 1915, Carnegie Corporation of New York Files.

71. T. Mitchell Prudden to George F. Vincent, 15 November, 1918, RF 1.100. LXIV. 642.

72. John D. Rockefeller, Sr. to John D. Rockefeller, Jr., 25 April, 1917, Rockefeller Family Archives, Rockefeller Center, New York, Record Group 2, Box LVII (hereafter RFA).

73. Weinstein, James, *The Corporate Ideal in the Liberal State* (Boston: Beacon Press, 1968); Memorandum of interview with General Carty, 11 June, 1926, Carnegie Corporation of New York Files.

74. Cutlip, S. M., *op. cit.*

75. Kingsley, Sherman C., "Reconstruction of the War Chest," *Proceedings of the National Conference of Social Work*, XLVI (1919), pp. 697–702.

76. Charles W. Eliot to Jerome D. Greene, 20 September, 1915, RF 3.903. I.1.

77. *A Manual of the Public Benefactions of Andrew Carnegie* (Washington, D.C.: Carnegie Endowment for International Peace, 1919).

78. Flexner, Abraham, *Henry S. Pritchett* (New York: Columbia University Press, 1943); an autobiographical sketch is contained in Henry S. Pritchett to Floyd C. Shoemaker, 1 May, 1923, Carnegie Corporation of New York Files.

79. "Confidential Memorandum for the Trustees," 1922, Carnegie Corporation of New York Files; Henry S. Pritchett to Elihu Root, Jr., 19 November, 1921, Carnegie Corporation of New York Files.

80. See Henry S. Pritchett to Elihu Root, Jr., 29 March, 1918, 19 November, 1921, Carnegie Corporation of New York Files.

81. Nicholas M. Butler to Walter A. Jessup, 11 October, 1937; Nicholas M. Butler to F. P. Keppel, 18 October, 1937; Samuel H. Church to Walter A. Jessup, 8 January, 1942; F. P. Keppel, memorandum of interview with Elihu Root, Jr., 13 October, 1926, Carnegie Corporation of New York Archives.

82. Kohler, Robert E., "A Policy for the Advancement of Science: The Rockefeller Foundation, 1924–29," *Minerva*, XVI (Winter 1978), pp. 480–515; George E. Vincent, "Memorandum on Policies and Organization of Rockefeller Boards," 29 January, 1927, RF 3.900.XIX.138.

83. "Memorandum of Conversation with President Burton Regarding his Letter of 17 March, 1925," Carnegie Corporation of New York Files.

84. Raymond B. Fosdick to John D. Rockefeller, Jr., 3 December, 1921, RFA, Record Group 2, Box LVII; Lawrence B. Dunham to Thomas M. Debevoise, 20 June, 1927, *loc. cit.*

85. John D. Rockefeller, Jr. to Charles O. Heydt, 13 July, 1925, RFA, Record Group 2, Box X; memorandum from Henry James to F. P. Keppel, 11 July, 1932, Carnegie Corporation of New York Files.

86. Commonwealth Fund, *The Commonwealth Fund: Historical Sketch, 1918–1962* (New York: Commonwealth Fund, 1963).

87. Karl, B. D., *op. cit.*

88. See Greenleaf, William, *From These Beginnings: The Early Philanthropies of Henry and Edsel Ford, 1911–1936* (Detroit: Wayne State University Press, 1964), esp. ch. 7; Nielsen, Waldemar A., *The Big Foundations* (New York: Columbia University Press, 1972), pp. 78–98, 170–176.

89. U.S. House of Representatives, Committee on Ways and Means, 91st Congress, 1st session, *Hearings on the subject of Tax Reform*; U.S. Senate, Committee on Finance, 91st Congress, 1st session, *Hearings on House Report 13270.*

90. Commission on Private Philanthropy and Public Needs, *op. cit.*

91. Karl, Barry D., "Philanthropy, Policy Planning and the Bureaucratisation of the Democratic Ideal," *Daedalus*, CV (Fall 1976).

EARLY CONFLICTS IN SOCIAL WORK EDUCATION

LINDA M. SHOEMAKER

* This article explores early conflicts in the creation of professional education for social workers in the nation's first three schools of social work—the New York School of Philanthropy, the Boston School for Social Workers, and the Chicago School of Civics and Philanthropy. As social workers advocated a shift from on-the-job training to systematic professional preparation in the early twentieth century, leaders in the nation's charity, social science, and reform communities sought to shape the emerging schools. Their multiple visions of social work raised fundamental questions about the mission and direction of the nascent social work profession.

In 1897, Mary Richmond sent out a clarion call for the creation of what she called a "training school in applied philanthropy." Speaking to an audience of some of the nation's most powerful leaders of public and private charitable relief organizations at the annual meeting of the National Conference of Charities and Correction, Richmond proposed systematic training and education in a shared body of knowledge for the growing numbers of young workers entering the field. The time had come, she argued, to put an end to haphazard, on-the-job, trial-and-error training for positions in the nation's myriad organizations serving the poor and "dependent." Speaking with the experience of many years leading the Baltimore Charity Organization Society, Richmond insisted, "We owe it to those who come after us that they be spared the groping and blundering by which we have acquired our own stock of experience."[1] Richmond anticipated little resistance to her idea for a school; hers was not, in fact, the first such exhortation. She did expect, however, considerable "discussion" about "what the practitioner in [the] field is expected to know and to be."[2]

I consider some of these early discussions about what social workers should know and should be within the context of the creation of the nation's first schools of social work in New York, Chicago, and Boston. An exceedingly diverse cast of characters was involved in the development of social work education, and their debates about what social workers should know and be all highlight the multiple roots and competing visions of social work in the early twentieth century. Particularly illuminating are their debates about the knowledge base of social work; the sexual division of labor within social work; and the connections between and among social work, social reform, social policy, and the emerging welfare state.

The Early Breadth of Social Work Education

Richmond's vision found its first expression in the summer following her catalytic speech. The New York Charity Organization Society (COS) pioneered in social work education with a 6-week "Summer School in Philanthropic Work," led by Philip Ayres, the assistant director of the COS. Ayres assembled a group of 27 pioneering students (20 women and 7 men) from as far away as Colorado and Minnesota. They were put through their paces with a blistering 6-day-a-week schedule of lectures, classroom discussions, visits to institutions, social research, and practical training. A typical day's schedule was as follows: "June 29: Institutional and placing-out methods in the care of children, an address by Mr. Homer Folks. Provision for babies and for mothers and babies, an address by Miss M. V. Clark. Visits to the home for the friendless and the foundling asylum." That was just the morning's work. In the span of 6 weeks, students visited over 40 institutions; in the days following the visit to the foundling asylum, for example, students visited the College Settlement on Rivington Street, Blackwell's Island, a county poor house, the University Settlement, and so on. They heard 39 lectures by prominent figures in the social work, social science, and reform communities of New York and the nation. For practical experience, students worked in the district offices of the COS. The summer school ended with students' presentations of original research projects, "suitable for publication," the school hoped, on topics ranging from recent immigration, to tenement house and sweatshop conditions, to day nurseries and foster care.[3]

After several years of the summer school, the New York COS launched the year-long New York School of Philanthropy in 1904, under the direction of Edward Devine. New York was not alone in its pioneering efforts in social work education. The Chicago School of Civics and Philanthropy was founded in 1903 by Graham Taylor, a social gospel minister and the head of the Chicago Commons Settlement House.[4] Meanwhile, in Boston, Harvard University and Simmons Female College joined forces with the Boston Associated Charities and founded the Boston School for Social Workers in 1904, under the direction of Jeffrey Richardson Brackett, who had long ties to the charity organization movement in Baltimore.

Although these schools were hardly identical, their early shared characteristics are striking, especially the broad range of people involved and the diversity of issues and approaches they brought to the first social work classrooms. Lecturers in the schools included representatives of a wide range of Progressive Era academics, reformers, and charity workers. Social scientists and reformers, including John Graham Brooks, Charles Henderson, and John Commons; leaders of the nation's settlement houses, such as Jane Addams, Lillian Wald, and Robert Woods; directors of the leading Charity Organization Societies, such as Josephine Shaw Lowell, John Glenn, and Richmond; plus hundreds of lesser-known municipal leaders, institution directors, and trade union organizers, all contributed to this heady mix, creating an ethos that made the schools, in the memory of one early faculty member, "center[s] of the most lively social thought."[5] "Lively" is an apt description, as there was considerable disagreement over the aims and directions of social work and social welfare. Passing through these schools, for example, were advocates of European-style social insurance and speakers on the "evils of relief." Students might hear from an advocate for social justice for immigrants on one day and an immigration restrictionist on the next.

As guest lectures gradually gave way to more regimented course work, the diversity in approaches to social work remained. Curricula at all of the schools included highly theoretical and historical courses in economics and sociology; deeply personal and even religious discussions of social ethics; practical, nuts-and-bolts coverage of relief work with families, the mechanics of institutions, and child welfare work; reform-oriented courses on labor and housing legislation; and even plumbing.[6] From social theory to lead pipes, a cacophony of voices and visions worked to construct the meanings of social work in the early twentieth century. In these years, schools of social work well reflected the amorphous, chaotic, and often contradictory world of Progressive reform swirling around them.

Not all social work educators were comfortable with the amorphous nature of their emerging profession. In 1909, for example, Brackett, of the Boston School, was complaining that the meaning of social work was so imprecise that the American public could not distinguish between "social work, sociology, and socialism."[7] Although Brackett's words well illustrate the fluid nature of social work at this time, his concern was certainly more than semantic. His evident desire to separate social work from the academic realm of sociology and the state-building politics of socialism points to some of the deepest divisions in and conflicting visions of the emerging profession.

There are three pivotal moments of conflict in the histories of the New York, Boston, and Chicago schools that serve to illuminate some of these divisions. The 1912 resignation of Samuel McCune Lindsay from the directorship of the New York School highlights debates about the knowledge base of social work and tensions between advocates of university- and agency-based training for social workers. The 1916 disassociation of Harvard University from the Boston School reveals constricting ideas about the appropriate sexual division of labor in social work. Finally, the celebrated 1920 "coup" in Chicago, when Edith Abbott and Sophonisba Breckinridge wrested control of the

Chicago School away from Graham Taylor and brought it under the auspices of the University of Chicago, creating the School of Social Service Administration, speaks not only to questions about the knowledge base and gendered contours of social work, but also to the connections between social work, social policy, and social reform, which were in the process of formation.

Conflicts in Social Work Education

Questioning the Knowledge Base of Social Work in New York

One of immediate questions to confront social work educators was what to teach and where to teach it. What constituted the appropriate knowledge base of their profession, and should their schools be affiliated with universities or with social agencies? In 1897, Richmond had argued against a university connection, fearing that too "academic" or theoretical an orientation would ill serve practitioners in training. Others, though, contended that only a university with a strong social science curriculum could equip social workers for the professional paths ahead of them.

When Lindsay was hired to direct the New York School in 1907, a university connection and a strong social-science-based curriculum seemed assured. Lindsay, a professor of economics and sociology who had formerly directed the American Academy of Political and Social Science and the National Child Labor Committee, had a vision of social work that linked social science and social policy. He took the New York School on an immediate sociological and policy-oriented turn, teaching courses in social theory and labor legislation, and registering social work students in sociology and economics courses at Columbia University.

The New York School's Committee on Philanthropic Education was alarmed by Lindsay's approach and rather unceremoniously rejected his vision for the school within a few years. Glenn, who sat on the school's board and was the director of the Russell Sage Foundation, spelled out his objections to Lindsay's curriculum. "The required courses," Glenn wrote, "consist merely of lectures on economics and social economy. . . . The courses impress me as academic—I use the word respectfully—rather than technical." Glenn and the committee believed that social workers in training most needed a technical, skill-based education that would prepare them to be the child welfare workers, relief agents, and institution attendants that were in such demand by public and private agencies in the city and around the country.[8]

His vision rebuffed, Lindsay submitted his resignation in 1912. Without social science, and without the university, Lindsay predicted, the New York School would never be "a great national institution for the training of leaders in all branches of social work." It would be nothing more than "a training school, much more limited in scope, devoted to the development of a finer technique in a few lines of work."[9] Lindsay resigned his post but did not surrender his vision. He transported his courses wholesale into the Department of Political Science at Columbia University, where he continued to embody his vision of the social worker as scholar.

After Lindsay's departure, the New York School led the field toward a more narrowly focused and skill-based definition of social work, with casework theory and practice at the center of the profession's knowledge base. A key motivator behind this transition was Porter Lee, former director of the Philadelphia Charity Organization Society, who had been hired as an instructor in casework the year Lindsay resigned. Working closely with New York's social agencies, the New York School developed highly specialized tracks in family, child, medical, and, eventually, psychiatric casework.[10]

The ultimate rise of the technique-based casework curriculum under Lee represents more than social work's conflicted relationship with academia. At root in this struggle are competing explanations of poverty and other social ills. Lindsay, the social scientist, understood social problems to be primarily structural and environmental and thus emphasized sociology and economics as the intellectual foundations on which social workers would create ever more effective social policy. Lee sought the answers to individual distress in individual and psychological, rather than structural, explanations. New York's turn toward casework was important in molding the emerging profession. Long recognized as the leader in social work education (at least in the East), New York's shift away from the social sciences and toward casework set the tone for much of social work education in the 1920s.

The Gendered Contours of Social Work Education in Boston

Another telling moment of conflict occurred in Boston in 1916. After 12 years of apparently peaceful and productive cooperation, Harvard University withdrew from the Boston School, leaving Simmons College, a vocationally oriented women's college, the lone affiliate of the school. In some ways the Boston story reflects some of the same university versus agency, sociology versus casework tensions that played out in New York. However, there is an additional layer of analysis as well. The history of the Harvard-Simmons relationship reveals social workers' preconceptions about gender-appropriate work, which led to two separate educational tracks in Boston and codified a very definite sexual division of labor in the Boston training programs for social workers.

From the start, Boston school founders expressed the traditional nineteenth-century notion that women's participation in social work was a reflection and extension of their domesticity. Woods, head resident at Boston's South End House and who helped shape the Boston School's mission and curriculum, wrote that social work was "a perfectly natural extension of the interest and duties of the woman in her own home and in normal neighborhood society."[11] Consistent with this domestic justification was an underlying assumption that women would be willing to accept the lowest-paid and lowest-status jobs in the new profession. Simmons College President Henry Lefavour, during the planning stages of the Boston School, claimed that "there are various inferior grades of work that women will be willing to occupy while men may not."[12] Director Brackett concurred, asserting that women accepted lower salaries in social work "because many women work with something of a missionary spirit, and are ready to take what can be paid."[13]

The construction of a male social worker identity within the Boston School shared little with the low-status, low-paid, altruistic, and domestic conceptualization of social work for women. Woods argued consistently that young men were not interested in work "which centers in the needy family and individual."[14] Harvard President Charles Eliot added that many men were not temperamentally well suited to work with the "defectives" and the "unattractive mass of human beings" who, he thought, made up the social worker's usual clientele. Most men, he observed, preferred to work with "the normal human being." Work with "defectives," he thought, "requires a missionary spirit," which he, as Brackett, apparently viewed as a female trait.[15] In constructing a masculine form of social work, Woods emphasized public service and leadership. Defining social work for men as a form of "unofficial statesmanship," Woods argued that the field "calls upon young men to enter upon a definite and absorbing career of public service" and "opens the way in some cases to political action and political office."[16]

The institutionalization of gendered paths for female and male social workers was reflected in the direction of the post-1916 curricula at Simmons and Harvard. The newly independent Simmons College School of Social Work increasingly emphasized a technical, skill-based, and specialized curriculum. Women at Simmons concentrated on "acquiring knowledge about the causation and intricacies of human behavior, in mastering the details of [their casework specialization] . . . and especially in developing skills in individual relationships."[17] Simmons's shift was more than a simple turn away from sociology, as in New York. It was the beginning of the codification of a sexual division of labor among social work students in Boston, which is readily apparent in the path Harvard chose after the 1916 split. After a few years of drift, Harvard hired Richard C. Cabot, a leader in the development of medical social work, to revive its Department of Social Ethics. This program offered Harvard's male undergraduates courses in the social sciences, research methods, and social problems. Such education undergirded what its organizers viewed as a "masculine" version of social work. Harvard's social ethics department was preparing male social workers for careers in social research, social reform, and government, not careers in casework. Cabot did include casework in the curriculum until 1929; however, this was a casework education that placed an "emphasis on social theory." Cabot's explicit goal in teaching professional technique and methods was to "train men to become *executives* in public or private agencies of social welfare."[18]

Although the sexual division of labor was very clear-cut in Boston, it was not a given. Others envisioned social work as a realm within which women could, and indeed should, be the executives and policy makers. No social work leaders better represent this position than Abbott and Breckinridge, whose efforts to shape social work in Chicago are discussed below.

Social Work and State Building in Chicago

Until 1920, the Chicago School was under the direction of its founder, Graham Taylor. While he was away on vacation in 1920, Abbott and Breckinridge, both Chicago-trained Ph.D.s and frequent Hull House residents who had worked for Taylor in the research department of the school since 1907, achieved what has been likened to a palace coup. They wrested control of the school from Taylor and transformed the former School of Civics and Philanthropy into a graduate school at the University of Chicago, the School of Social Service Administration (SSA). Infused with the values of Chicago's progressive white women's reform network, and long-standing advocates of broad social science training for social workers, Abbott and Breckinridge sought to put their school at the service of Progressive Era reform and state building.

As in Boston and New York, the Chicago coup in some ways reflected the now familiar conflict between academic and technical education. Abbott was outspoken in her disdain for narrowly focused casework training. "The student too often becomes a routine technician," she complained, "sometimes a clever technician—but still a technician."[19] For Abbott, no social worker should be a routine technician. All social workers should be prepared to evaluate and formulate social policy, to administer social agencies, and to lead. This included women as well as men.

Abbott and Breckinridge's decisions for preparing leaders in social work shared much with the visions of Lindsay and the Harvard social ethics department. The SSA emphasized broad social science education and research. Over the course of the 1920s, Abbott argued not only that social workers needed the social sciences, but that social work was a social science, which she called "the social science of social welfare." This social science of social welfare linked Abbott and Breckinridge's academic, professional, and reform goals. Although it remains in many ways an appealing formulation, it was also the result of restrictive gender codes.

As much of social work was making the casework turn, Abbott and Breckinridge could not leave the emerging profession behind and follow Lindsay's example by heading for the nearest university social science department. As women, even as women with impressive intellectual achievements, their only hope for academic careers was to build their own field. Indeed, as Linda Gordon has noted, "It is arguable that the development of the entire modern field of social work . . . was shaped by the refusal of the University of Chicago sociology department to hire Edith Abbott or Sophonisba Breckinridge."[20]

Despite all their criticism of the "vocational" approach to social work education, Abbott and Breckinridge built up a casework curriculum in the 1920s and published a series of casebooks designed for classroom use in courses on casework practice.[21] This might seem unexpected given their reformist and social science orientation. Perhaps they could do little else as the field increasingly embraced casework as its intellectual and professional center. But more than that, Abbott and Breckinridge were contesting the very nature and meaning of casework at SSA. Theirs was a reformist and state-building vision of casework, which differed from the merely individualizing and often stigmatizing approach of their contemporaries. Breckinridge argued, for example, that the study of casework records, an in-depth examination of the experiences of families in distress, would reveal, "the extent to which our older social machinery fails and needs to be rearranged and adjusted to modern conditions of family and community life." One underlying aim of teaching casework, she wrote, was to "develop in the student a quickened sense of the responsibility of the caseworker for necessary community action."[22] In Breckinridge's hands, then, the study of social work practice with individuals need not preclude the discussion and pursuit of social welfare policy and social reform. Abbott's writings on social research make a similar point. Casework was the best forum for evaluating the success or failure of social policy; casework should guide the creation of new social legislation.[23]

For Abbott and Breckinridge, it was through casework, through intimate contact with human beings in need, that social workers and social reformers could learn most about the human consequences of modern industrial capitalism and the impact and effectiveness of social policy. Only through this kind of direct "evidence," only through linking practice and policy, could "the social science of social welfare" lead to effective and just social policy. Ultimately, for Abbott and Breckinridge, the creation of just social policy was the overriding goal of social work. Above all, Abbott wrote, "we are social reformers and we look to the reconstruction of this world in which we live."[24]

Conclusion

In the opening decades of the twentieth century, schools of social work were vital centers of thought and debate about the nature, mission, and direction of the emerging profession. From the first experimental steps of the New York Summer School of Philanthropy in 1898 to the establishment of the first graduate school of social work in Chicago in 1920, social workers, social scientists, policy makers, and social reformers all sought to shape the growing field. Their multiple, overlapping, and often competing visions of social work demonstrate that the nature and mission of social work are neither static nor monolithic. Social work's meanings were—and continue to be—contested terrain.

Notes

1. Mary Richmond, "The Need of a Training School in Applied Philanthropy," *Proceedings of the National Conference of Charities and Correction,* 1897 (Boston: Geo. H. Ellis, 1898). pp. 181–88.
2. Ibid., p. 182.
3. Philip Ayres, "A Training Class in Applied Philanthropy." *Charities Review* 8 (September 1898): 315–20, "Summer Class in Philanthropic Work, 1899," *Charities Review* 9 (March 1899): 12–14, "A School of Philanthropy," *Charities Review* 9 (August 1899): 250–54; Alice Higgins, "The Summer School of Philanthropy," *Charities* 9 (July 12, 1902): 45–47, "Summer School in Philanthropy," *Charities* 9 (July 19, 1902): 61–63: Paul Kellogg. "The Summer School in Philanthropic Work," *Charities* 9 (July 26, 1902): 90–92.
4. The Chicago School underwent several name changes before Taylor and his assistant, Julia Lathrop, agreed on the name. Chicago School of Civics and Philanthropy, when the school was incorporated in 1908.
5. Eduard C. Lindeman, "The New York School of Social Work: An Interpretive History," 1952, Box 14, file "History of the NY School by ECL," p. 9, Eduard C. Lindeman Collection, Columbia University Archives, New York (hereafter CUA).
6. The Boston School's course in plumbing left an enduring impression on one student, who remembered many years later how she had "learned to read plans and talk the lingo about joists and stresses and pipes—lead pipes versus galvanized versus iron." Years later, she still remembered the power of this knowledge, claiming proudly, "I could put the fear of God into a Boston housing inspector." See "Alumnae Achievement Award winner," *Simmons Review* (Summer 1961), p. 31.
7. Jeffrey Brackett, "Social Work," 1909, Jeffrey Richardson Brackett Papers: Simmons College Archives, Boston (hereafter SCA).
8. Letter from John M. Glenn to Samuel McCune Lindsay, March 19, 1912, box 107, file "New York School of Philanthropy," Samuel McCune Lindsay Papers. CUA.
9. Samuel McCune Lindsay to Robert W. deForest, March 27, 1912. Reprinted in Saul Bernstein, *The New York School of Social Work, 1898–1941* (New York: Institute of Welfare Research, Community Service of New York, 1942), pp. 25–28.
10. Lindeman (n. 5 above), pp. 5–7.
11. Robert A. Woods, "Social Work: A New Profession" (1905), reprinted in *The Neighborhood in Nation-Building* (New York: Arno, 1970), pp. 88–104.
12. Henry Lefavour, quoted in Alice Channing, "The Early Years of a Pioneering School," *Social Service Review* 28 (December 1954): 430–40.
13. Boston School for Social Workers Administrative Board Meeting Minutes, January 20, 1908, box 1, file 4, SCA.
14. Boston School for Social Workers Administrative Board Meeting Minutes, April 30, 1906, box 1, file 4, SCA.
15. Ibid.
16. Woods (n. 11 above), p. 96.
17. Channing (n. 12 above), p. 440.
18. James Ford, "Social Ethics 1905–1929," in *The Development of Harvard University since the Inauguration of President Eliot,* ed. Samuel Eliot Morison (Cambridge, Mass.: Harvard University Press, 1930), pp. 223–30 (emphasis added).
19. Edith Abbott, "The University and Social Welfare," *Social Welfare and Professional Education* (Chicago: University of Chicago Press, 1931), p. 13.

20. Linda Gordon, *Pitied but Not Entitled: Single Mothers and the History of Welfare* (Cambridge, Mass.: Harvard University Press, 1994), p. 169. See also Robyn Muncy, *Creating a Female Dominion in American Reform, 1890–1935* (New York: Oxford University Press, 1991).

21. Edith Abbott, *Immigration: Select Documents and Case Records* (Chicago: University of Chicago Press, 1924); Sophonisba Breckinridge, *Family Welfare Work in a Metropolitan Community: Selected Case Records* (Chicago: University of Chicago Press, 1924).

22. Breckinridge (n. 21 above), pp. 3–4, 13–15.

23. Edith Abbott, "Some Basic Principles in Professional Education for Social Work," *Social Welfare and Professional Education* (n. 19 above), and "Research in the Program of Social Worker and Agency," Grace and Edith Abbott Papers, box 5, file 3, Regenstein Library Special Collections, University of Chicago.

24. Abbott, "Research in the Program of Social Worker" (n. 23 above), p. 15.

 * This article was presented at the Charlotte Towle Conference, "Exploring the Development of Social Work Practice," University of Chicago, School of Social Service Administration, May 30–31, 1996.

Science, Foundations, and American Universities in the 1920s

Robert E. Kohler

The partnership between private philanthropy and the university is one of the most distinctive features of American science between 1920 and 1940. Except in agriculture, federal and state governments played a minor role in supporting academic science. Industry was an important source of funds for sciences such as chemistry, but it was the more directly philanthropic support of private foundations that supported graduate training and research in the period when the United States began to rival Europe as a scientific power. Foundation investment in scientific manpower, facilities, and community organization—on the order of $100 million—had much to do with this westward shift of world science between the wars.[1]

Before 1920: Philanthropic Reluctance

Scientists had dreamed of tapping philanthropic fortunes since the 1890s and since about 1910 had been knocking regularly on foundation doors. But neither individual entrepreneurs nor institutions like the National Academy of Sciences and the American Association for the Advancement of Science (AAAS) could persuade foundation leaders that academic science was a legitimate philanthropic concern. In 1918 no major foundation supported university science; by 1925 a dozen did, including some of the largest. Foundation perceptions of academic science changed dramatically in the years following World War I. Symbolic of this change are the negotiations between the National Research Council (NRC) and the Rockefeller Foundation in 1918–1919, which began with the foundation's proposal to endow a research institute in physical science and ended with a large national program of research fellowships to be used in universities.[2]

When individual philanthropists supported science before 1920, they did so by creating independent research institutes in which research was separated from teaching. Precisely because research seemed to them essential to national progress, philanthropists felt it was best pursued by full-time professional investigators who were not distracted by teaching or other service roles. The Rockefeller Institute for Medical Research (1901) and the Carnegie Institution of Washington (1902) were created to undertake research on large, fundamental problems that university or government scientists could not and should not tackle.[3]

Between 1910 and 1920 it became quite fashionable for philanthropists to establish research institutes, especially in medicine. A 1921 survey identified sixteen such institutes, with combined annual expenditures of nearly $600,000.[4] Many of these institutes were affiliated with medical schools to take advantage of existing facilities and research talent. But research and teaching were generally kept separate. Philanthropists were not antiacademic: they just believed that a functional division of labor was best for all.

University scientists' individualistic habits deepened philanthropists' skepticism about supporting academic science. In many colleges, research was regarded primarily as a way to improve teaching. Grant seekers assumed that funds would be more or less evenly distributed among the disciplines, as small grants-in-aid to individuals. For them the purpose of grants was to broaden participation in research by the deserving rank and file, especially those in institutions too poor to provide time and funds intramurally.[5] This demand-side strategy for increasing research was ill suited to foundation ideals. It left little room for foundations to concentrate selectively on large problems or centers of excellence; grants-in-aid smacked of old-fashioned individual relief. Not surprisingly, philanthropists showed no interest in a partnership on those terms.

National scientific organizations were unable to act as intermediaries. The National Academy of Sciences was dominated by laissez-faire purists who feared the strings attached to outside grants.[6] Not even the master promoter George Ellery Hale could attract philanthropic money to the Academy. In 1920 the Academy's research endowment yielded only $10,000 per year, which was dispersed in small individual grants. The AAAS was no more effective in finding patrons and spread its meager income ($4,000 in 1921) among the deserving poor of science.[7]

The large foundations created between 1900 and 1920 also proved resistant to scientists' overtures. Growing out of nineteenth-century traditions of voluntary activism in health, education, and social welfare, foundations had much larger social ambitions than furthering science per se. Their purpose was community organization, propaganda, and consciousness raising on a mass scale, not aiding individual research. Scientists were not objects of charity, nor was the research they did relevant to social improvement. Voluntary agencies were concerned with diffusing knowledge, not creating it. They did not doubt that ultimate cures for diseases of the body corporeal and the body politic would come from research, but the greatest opportunities for immediate results seemed to lie in more efficient use of existing knowledge.

Foundations' organizational style clashed with scientists' habits of individualistic laissez-faire. Foundations were part of the movement toward consolidation of large national institutions, the same movement that was creating business oligopolies and trusts.[8] Foundation leaders saw their unique role in history as applying methods of big business to community activities—education, health, welfare—that had traditionally been regarded as expressions of individual virtue. For them, direct aid to individuals was retrogressive; their aim was to coordinate individual and local activities into collective programs directed by national institutions.[9] Foundations favored causes that displayed collective purpose and modern business organization. Few academic scientists displayed those qualities in 1915.

In order for a partnership to develop between foundations and university science, a rationale had to be devised that served the institutional purposes of both parties. Not surprisingly, it was the endowed research institutes, not the foundations, that took the first steps toward a working relationship. Both the Carnegie Institution of Washington and the Rockefeller Institute had research grant programs. The Carnegie Institution was by far the largest extramural source of funds for academic scientists before 1920—over $100,000 per year. However, the experiment was by no means an unqualified success, either for the Institution's president, Robert S. Woodward, or for his academic clients. The use of student research assistants was especially divisive. Woodward saw this practice as a diversion of research funds to teaching; professors complained that Woodward did not appreciate the importance of linking research and training. Embittered, Woodward lost no opportunity to express his conviction that universities were no place for real research. Simon Flexner, the director of the Rockefeller Institute, also became an articulate and well-placed advocate of an institutional separation of research and teaching.

Observing the unhappy experiences of the Carnegie and Rockefeller grants programs, foundation leaders avoided entanglements with university scientists. In 1915, for example, the veteran grant getter Edward C. Pickering asked the Rockefeller Foundation to give $50,000 for a program of small grants-in-aid to be administered by a committee of the AAAS. Rockefeller secretary Jerome Greene politely but firmly declined, for fear of "diverting a great Foundation from its true function of experiment, discovery, initiative, and demonstration, to being a mere bag of money."[10] Greene and others were not indifferent to science: quite the contrary, they were sympathetic and even eager to support science in some way. But what way? No foundation could risk becoming a passive partner in routine research by rank-and-file teachers: such a role would betray its most cherished institutional mission. Philanthropists and academic scientists alike assumed that the measure of a successful grant was the output of research papers by an individual, not the training of new talents or the building of a departmental program.

The parties could not agree on procedures that would ensure success, however, and the lack of a broader basis of common interest in improving the research community made a meeting of minds difficult.

What broke the impasse was the linkage of research to the expansion of graduate training. Communities of scientists, rather than individuals per se, became the common cause of university and foundation leaders. This supply-side strategy satisfied philanthropists that they were developing a community vital to the nation's well-being. As the sole producers of scientists, universities finally had a strategic advantage over research institutes. In 1916 Thomas Hunt Morgan hatched a scheme for the Rockefeller Foundation involving grants for training researchers. Significantly, Pickering misunderstood its novelty and force, perceiving it merely as an aid to education instead of to research, and thus a competitor to his own scheme.[11] Morgan's proposal never reached the Rockefeller Foundation. Within a few years, however, the idea that informed it became the basis of a new partnership between foundations and university scientists.

Led by the Rockefeller and Carnegie groups, foundation grants for research in universities increased a hundredfold by the mid 1920s, dwarfing the Carnegie Institution's grant program (see Table 1). No less important, programs of research fellowships and grants to specific departments or projects replaced gifts of general endowment and individual grants-in-aid. The prewar pattern of scattered aid to the rank and file gave way to programs concentrating on specific scientific communities and institutions. Philanthropists became active partners in training researchers and improving opportunities for research in universities.

This trend was not immediately apparent to academic observers, who worried that philanthropists still seemed to favor research institutes. There was some reason for alarm. The Rockefeller Foundation and the Carnegie Corporation gave large sums to endow half a dozen institutes, including the Phipps Institute and the Marine Biological Laboratory at Woods Hole. The Corporation established the Food Research Institute in 1921 and the Brookings Institute in 1922. Philanthropists endowed new research institutes in botany and physics: the Boyce Thompson Institute for Plant Research (1924), the Tropical Plant Research Foundation (1924), and the Henry W. Bartol Research Foundation (1918). In 1918 the Rockefeller Foundation proposed to establish a national institute for research in physics and chemistry, analogous to the Rockefeller Institute for Medical Research. Such institutes competed directly with universities for the best research staff and foundation funds.[12]

By 1925 or so, however, it was clear that academic fears were exaggerated. The new sense of an active partnership was evident at a 1925 conference of university administrators and foundation

TABLE 1

Funds for Support of University Research in 1920 (Over $1,000)

Institution	Annual Expenditure ($)	Field	Date Established
American Academy of Arts and Sciences	1,500	Physical	1892
American Association for the Advancement of Science	4,000	General	1800s
American Medical Association	3,500	Medical	1902
Carnegie Institution	117,000	General	1902
Elizabeth Thompson Science Fund	1,200	General	1885
Engineering Foundation	2,000	Engineering	1816
National Academy of Sciences	10,500	Physical	1800s
National Geographic Society	100,000	Exploration	1888
Smithsonian Institution	6,000	Meteorology	1891

Source: Callie Hull and Clarence J. West, "Funds Available in the United States for the Support and Encouragement of Research in Science and Its Technologies," *Bulletin of the National Research Council*, 1928, No. 6; 1934, No. 95.

heads. Frederick Keppel, president of the Carnegie Corporation, was as always a bellwether of philanthropic fashion:

> The conventional view of the relation between the university and the foundation is that the university is the active and the foundation the passive element. . . . While there is a certain element of truth in the conventional picture, . . . foundation grants are coming more and more to be in support of specific projects, and the initiative for these projects may come from anywhere—from an individual, from a foundation, from a university, or perhaps most often from one of the national organizations of scholars. . . . I do not think it an exaggeration to say that any important research project which has the endorsement of a representative group of scholars can find support from one or another of the foundations.[13]

Keppel noted that foundations were investing large sums in graduate and post-graduate training: no fewer than 1,500 fellowships a year, he estimated. Also, foundations were drawing on universities for their program managers and for advice in selecting grants. They in turn aided interdisciplinary projects and publicized news of research trends. Foundations and universities were partners "in the same great enterprise, the advancement of human knowledge."[14]

Keppel put his finger on some of the chief reasons for the new sense of trust and partnership between foundations and university scientists. The ability of the National Research Council to plan and manage collective research projects allayed philanthropists' fears of academic individualism. Participation in such co-operative projects also lessened academic fears of outside interference. Most important, research was perceived by both parties, not just as an end in itself, but as an essential element in educating socially progressive elites. It was the organizational and cultural implications of science, more than its purely intellectual or even practical benefits, that appealed to philanthropists.

Community Development in Science

Scientific and philanthropic purposes were united by a shared conception of "community development." Although this phrase was not common usage at the time, it expresses the essence of the larger social system of which science patronage was a part. Foundations had always been concerned with social institutions in education, public health, charity, and social welfare; in the 1920s they began to treat scientists in the same fashion. The strategy of community development can be seen in every aspect of philanthropic work in the 1920s. Programs in public health, education, housing, social work, parks and playgrounds, child welfare agencies, health care centers, and so on all aimed at developing the structure and collective spirit of some community of people. Groups suffering from particular handicaps or diseases or exposed to particular risks and members of particular age groups each became the object of a specialized philanthropy.[15] The few programs aimed at the sciences were part of this larger social movement and must be understood in that context.

Historians of philanthropy have emphasized the individual character of foundation fellowship and grant programs.[16] But it is the collective, communitarian character of foundation programs in the 1920s that sets them apart from the truly individualistic prewar style of science patronage. Foundation leaders did speak the language of individual merit, of course, and grants were generally made to individuals rather than institutions. However, such grants were made to individuals in their capacity as leaders of research communities and as institution builders. The purpose of foundation programs was to develop the institutional infrastructure of science; to promote a programmatic style of research, and to encourage cooperation among scientists. Programs of fellowships and project grants were designed to produce a new generation of elite scientists and to create a system of centers for scientific development. Foundation leaders were system builders and turned to science in the same systematic way that they had to the nation's colleges, medical schools, or public health agencies. Wickliffe Rose's slogan "make the peaks higher" captures the meritocratic collectivist spirit of science patronage in the 1920s.

The emerging partnership between foundations and university science grew out of a shared concern with the supply of scientific manpower, which became a cause for alarm in the early 1920s. World War I dramatically and permanently expanded nonacademic markets for scientists at the same time that mobilization temporarily reduced the supply. Business mistrust of ivory-tower scientists had begun to erode before 1916, when wartime military research and development programs gave academics the chance to display their practical problem-solving skills. Their success sharpened manufacturers' desire to get the best researchers for their laboratories. Meanwhile, the supply of science graduates was cut off. War projects had emptied universities of their teaching faculty in 1916, and the draft obliged young scientists to postpone professional training. These demographic disruptions gave rise to a manpower bottleneck. Though temporary, this bottleneck was a good opportunity for scientists to press their claims for more public support. University leaders were especially alert to the opportunities for a monopoly on the production of certified professional researchers.

The war also spawned new institutions for mobilizing science for national service. The most important of these was the National Research Council. Created by the activist minority of the conservative National Academy of Sciences, the Council was designed to expand and improve private science by linking it more closely to public purposes. The NRC enjoyed a degree of independence from the Academy, and an endowment of $5 million from the Carnegie Corporation in 1919 gave it an independent income to pursue its (moderately) collectivist ends.[17] Among the chief goals of NRC activists George Ellery Hale, Arthur Noyes, Vernon Kellogg, and Robert Millikan was to tap foundation endowments for university research.

Heads of foundations and health agencies had made many personal contacts with scientists during the war. The experience of working together on great and pressing problems gave both parties a sense of mutual trust. The NRC's activist spirit persuaded philanthropists that scientists too had purposes transcending their parochial disciplinary interests. Foundations had paid for many of the NRC's general administrative activities during the war, and as demobilization dried up government support of its military projects, foundations were under some pressure from NRC leaders to continue their support. For the first time, philanthropists perceived scientists as an activist, public-spirited elite, sharing many of their own social ideals.

The NRC's organization and style were very much in keeping with the "associational state" of the early 1920s, in which trade associations and other voluntary agencies did what in Europe was done by government agencies.[18] In fact, the NRC was essentially a trade association for science: part interest group and lobby, part scientific parliament and communications center, and part service agency. Lacking any formal authority and distrusted by scientific individualists, the NRC used the language of cooperation and the methods of persuasion and cooption. Its committees served as clearing houses for research news, employment bureaus, public relations offices, and places where academics, industrialists, and philanthropists could consort. Many NRC committees organized cooperative research projects, and a few raised funds and carried them out. The Council published surveys of scientific personnel, research and fellowship funds, and industrial research facilities. Elite but open to merit, activist but voluntaristic, problem-oriented, and nationalistic, the NRC was strikingly close in spirit to the large foundations and voluntary health associations.

The NRC played a crucial role in the accommodation between foundations and university science in the early 1920s (this may indeed have been its most significant achievement). The Council's activist style reassured philanthropists that grants would be devoted to strategic, not routine, academic purposes. NRC leaders were recognizably of the same political persuasion as foundation heads and their industrial allies. More practically, NRC committees took on the burden of selecting and administering fellowship and grants programs. These committees insulated foundations from random supplications by the rank and file and gave some assurance that funds would be spent for collective, rather than merely individual, purposes. Peer committees likewise reassured individual recipients that they would not be directly pressured by foundation bureaucrats or forced to do applied research. The mutual mistrust of the prewar years was dispelled in large part because the NRC was able to play a mediating role between patrons and their academic clients.

Between 1916 and 1940 foundations channeled nearly $12 million through the NRC (see Table 2). Almost all (97.5%) of these funds came from the Carnegie Corporation and the four Rockefeller boards. The Corporation supported mainly the organizational activities of NRC divisions and general committees. Most Rockefeller funds went to specific projects. The largest projects by far were the NRC fellowships, but substantial sums were also invested in committee-sponsored cooperative research

TABLE 2

National Research Council Expenditure of Foundation Funds, 1916–1940

Institution	Sum Expended (in $1,000s)
Carnegie Corporation	
General	2,714
Projects	353
Rockefeller boards (RF, IEB, GEB)	
Fellowships (RF, IEB, GEB)	4,431
Grants-in-aid (RF)	449
General (RF)	370
Publications (RF)	856
Sex Research Committee (RF)	1,177
Drug Research Committee (RF)	532
Radiation Biology Committee (RF)	143
Miscellaneous (IEB, GEB)	114
Laura Spelman Rockefeller Memorial	286
Other foundations	315
Total	11,740

Source: National Research Council, *Annual Reports*, 1918–1939.

NOTE: RF = Rockefeller Foundation, IEB = International Education Board, and GEB = General Education Board.

projects on endocrine and sex biology, drug addiction, and radiation biology. Subsidies for research tools like *Biological Abstracts* and *International Critical Tables* and fluid funds for individual research grants also appealed to philanthropists as ways of improving communication and the quality of research. NRC leaders had also hoped to attract funds from smaller foundations and industries, but these hopes were not realized. Community development on the grand scale was a game only for the foundation elite.

The Social Science Research Council (SSRC), created in 1923, played a role in the social sciences analogous to that of the NRC. Even more than the NRC, the SSRC was an operating arm of foundations. The Laura Spelman Rockefeller Memorial contributed $3.9 million, or 92% of the $4.2 million spent by the SSRC in its first decade; seven other foundations provided the rest.[19] Expenditures followed the pattern set by the NRC: fellowships, cooperative research projects, and aids to publication and conferences. Although Beardsley Ruml of the Memorial took a more direct and active role in selecting projects than did the Rockefeller and Carnegie leaders, the SSRC played as crucial a role as the NRC in mediating between foundations and professional communities. Together, the SSRC and the Spelman Memorial may best be regarded as an endowed trade association for the social sciences.

Another sign of the evolving partnership between philanthropy and universities was the shift from general support to grants earmarked for research and training. This trend is evident in Eduard Lindemann's tabulations of the expenditures of a hundred large foundations and community trusts in the 1920s (see Table 3). Gifts to university endowment funds declined in fits and starts from over half the total to less than a quarter. Gifts for fellowships increased sharply in the first half of the decade, and grants to particular departments of learning rose sharply in the second half. Funds for specific research projects tripled.[20]

Similar patterns can be seen in foundation gifts to medicine and public health, with minor differences in timing (see Table 4). Gifts of general endowment to medical schools declined markedly only after 1929, reflecting the later peaking of philanthropic interest in medical education. Support of medical research also lagged behind that of the basic sciences but began to rise in 1929, as gifts of endowment were phased out. This trend continued in the 1930s, when foundation support for medical research outstripped grants for the natural sciences.

TABLE 3

Expenditures on Higher and Professional Education (Excluding Health) by One Hundred Foundations, 1921–1930 (in $1,000s)

Year	Research	Scholarships	General	Special Departments	Associations	Total
1921	2,050	105	4,731	54	815	7,755
1922	2,196	180	5,532	78	810	8,796
1923	2,841	264	2,965	279	679	7,028
1924	4,297	397	10,526	1,040	616	16,876
1925	2,887	623	1,713	395	612	6,230
1926	4,164	923	2,610	749	631	9,077
1927	6,942	1,285	5,069	4,835	605	18,735
1928	5,524	1,301	2,858	4,610	230	14,523
1929	5,745	1,301	7,500	2,660	43	17,249
1930	7,303	1,486	3,318	4,008	22	16,137
Total	43,949	7,865	46,822	18,708	5,063	122,406

Source: Eduard Lindemann, *Wealth and Culture* (New York: Harcourt Brace, 1938), pp. 20–21, 70–111. Lindemann lumps together college and graduate fellowships. His totals for research include the Carnegie Institution of Washington's annual budget of over $1 million.

TABLE 4

Expenditures on Medicine by One Hundred Foundations, 1921–1930 (in $1,000s)

Year	Research	Education	Fellowships	Associations	Hospitals	Total
1921	221	7,050	45	239	1,321	8,876
1922	132	7,992	61	238	1,542	9,965
1923	146	7,552	116	389	1,398	9,601
1924	115	4,627	279	253	1,521	6,795
1925	110	5,725	424	476	2,197	8,932
1926	113	6,786	371	1,321	2,810	11,401
1927	380	7,528	306	354	2,354	10,922
1928	184	5,814	345	752	4,827	11,922
1929	719	5,950	411	653	3,731	11,464
1930	1,205	2,294	315	381	3,817	8,012
Total	3,325	61,318	2,673	5,056	25,518	97,890

Source: Lindemann, *Wealth and Culture*, pp. 100–105.

The four Rockefeller boards were by far the largest single source of fellowships. To those in chemistry and physics (1919) were added medicine (1921), mathematics and biology (1923), and the social sciences (1924). Over 1,100 natural scientists held NRC fellowships between 1919 and 1938, one quarter of whom studied in Europe. The Rockefeller Foundation invested $3.93 million in NRC fellowships through 1940, and the General Education and International Education Boards channeled $0.47 million more to fellowships through NRC committees. In the social sciences, the Laura Spelman Rockefeller Memorial put $1.4 million into fellowships.[21]

Unlike general educational fellowships, the NRC research fellowships had a strong directive effect on scientific communities. They were aimed at specific disciplines and attracted the best young talent to fashionable lines of research. They provided a pool of highly trained and mobile manpower for emerging centers like Stanford, Princeton, Michigan, and Caltech, as well as expanding graduate programs of older elite universities. Programmatic, selective, and efficiently administered, these fellowships played a major role in creating or importing new scientific specialties: for example, theoretical physics and general physiology.[22]

Many foundations followed the Rockefeller Foundation into the fellowship field (see Table 5), but only a few had programs as systematic and expertly managed: the Guggenheim Foundation, for example. The vast majority were local charities that included a fellowship or two among their diverse activities because it was fashionable. Frank Aydelotte recalled (disapprovingly) the flurry of small, often short-lived fellowship programs established just after the war, many on "very slender financial and intellectual foundations."[23]

The intentions behind these fellowship programs reflect the diverse ideals of postwar reconstruction. Many were devoted to improving international relations through cultural exchange and were supported by communities of hyphenated Americans. Such programs multiplied rapidly after the war, fed by strong feelings of solidarity with wartime allies, fear of revolutions and resurgent autocracies, hatred of German cultural imperialism, and ambition to take Germany's place at the center of world culture.[24] These programs were not aimed at scientists; but with their strong internationalist ideology and European networks, scientists were well placed to take advantage of them.

Manufacturers also set up more or less systematic fellowship programs, led by Du Pont and the food-processing industries. These programs were intended mainly to ensure privileged access to the supply of trained experts for industrial R & D departments.[25] Hospitals and research institutes likewise used restricted fellowships to compete for scarce manpower.

Graduate fellowships also appealed to educational foundations faced with the enormous expansion of college enrollment in the 1920s. Borrowing techniques of professional fund-raisers, universities undertook large and highly successful endowment drives—an "epidemic," Frederick Keppel called it.[26] With their fixed incomes, educational foundations realized that they must specialize if they were to serve "some distinctive purpose, and not merely add to the sum total of the great volume of expense."[27] Graduate schools were a strategic leverage point for influencing the quality of higher education and were small enough for foundations to make an impact. The training of professionals had long been a subsidiary part of foundation programs in education, public health, and social work. As the need for services outgrew philanthropic means, training of academic research elites became an available and appealing next step for educational foundations looking for a vital but affordable mission.

Research grants were a more problematic means of supporting science than fellowships, because selecting projects involved technical know-how and direct dealing with individual researchers. Memory of past experience with small grants, plus real administrative difficulties, inhibited foundations from organizing such programs during the 1920s. It was mainly the largest, most progressive foundations that led the way. The Carnegie Corporation and Carnegie Institution, the International and General Education Boards, and the Laura Spelman Rockefeller Memorial accounted for nine tenths of all research grant funds in the 1920s (see Table 6). Much of the rest came from small, specialized foundations, run by scientists, engineers, or physicians. It was not until the 1930s and 1940s that individual grants became a common way for middling foundations to invest in science.

The large foundations' research grant programs were not, strictly speaking, individual grants-in-aid but hybrids of individual and institutional grants. It was this hybrid character, in fact, that

TABLE 5

Graduate or Postdoctoral Fellowship Programs Active in the 1920s (SelectedM)

Institution	Program Founded	No. (Approx.)	Fields and Limits
American Association of University Women	1908	15	General
American Field Service	1919	12	General (France)
American Scandinavian Foundation	1911	42	General
Anthropology Lab–Rockefeller Foundation	1929	13	Anthropology
Bartol Foundation	1923	10	Physics (in-house)
Belgian American Educational Foundation	1920	6	General (Belgium)
Coffin Fund	1922	8	Physical engineering
Commonwealth Fund	1918	32	General (Britain-U.S.)
Du Pont Company	1922	24	Chemistry
John Simon Guggenheim Foundation	1925	50	General
Kosciuszko Foundation	1925	6	Technology (Poland)
Mellon Institute	1913	55	Technology (in-house)
National Committee for Mental Hygiene[1]	1926	11	Behavioral science
National Research Council–Rockefeller Foundation	1919	40	Medicine
	1919	40	Physical sciences
	1923	40	Biology
Rhodes Scholarship Trust	1904	32	General (Oxford)
Sigma Xi	1921	10	General
Social Science Research Council–Laura Spelman Rockefeller Memorial	1925	20	Social science
Textile Foundation	1930	30	Technology

Source: Callie Hull and Clarence J. West, "Fellowships and Scholarships for Advanced Work in Science and Technology," *Bulletin of the National Research Council*, 1923, No. 38; 1929, No. 72; 1934, No. 94. These surveys were not exhaustive, and the resulting data are only indicative of the trend.

1 Funded by the Rockefeller Foundation and the Commonwealth Fund.

allayed foundation fears of research grants. Most commonly, funds were provided in the form of three- to seven-year block grants to departments or research groups led by productive and charismatic individuals. These block grants might be supplemented by personal grants-in-aid or by capital grants for facilities and equipment, but the goal was to develop local communities of scientific workers, not to aid any particular researcher or to support universities in general. It was the capacity of the system to expand and improve itself that mattered to foundations. They concentrated on a few institutions with the idea of building up centers of scientific achievement that would then serve as a demonstration and inspiration for the rank and file. The linkage of research and training was essential. NRC fellows gravitated to these centers, serving as vectors of the best practice when they went on to teaching careers. Like the fellowship programs, project grants were seen as long-term investments in formal and informal institutions of scientific communities.

The strategy of community development in preference to individual aid made it possible for foundations to become patrons of science on a grand scale. Block grants delegated technical judg-

TABLE 6

Philanthropic Expenditures for University Science Circa 1927

Institution	Sum Expended (in $1,000s)	Fields
Laura Spelman Rockefeller Memorial	8,142	Social sciences
General Education Board	4,209 (appropriations)	General
International Education Board	2,816 (average 1923–1933)	General
Rockefeller Foundation	1,387	General
Carnegie Corporation	558	General
Daniel Guggenheim Fund	374 (average 1926–1930)	Aeronautics
Carnegie Institution	191	General
Chemical Foundation	181 (estimated)	Chemistry
National Geographic Society	100	Exploration
National Tuberculosis Association	45	Medicine, chemistry
Herman Frasch Foundation	40	Chemistry
Charles A. Coffin Foundation	20	Engineering, science
American Medical Association	13	Medicine
Ella Sachs Plotz Foundation	10 (approximately)	Medicine
National Academy of Science	8	General
Smithsonian Institution	6	Meteorology
American Association for the Advancement of Science	4	General
American Academy of Arts and Sciences	3	General
American Society for Industrial Engineering	1	Engineering
Elizabeth Thompson Science Fund	1	General

Source: Hull and West, "Funds Available in the United States for the Support and Encouragement of Research in Science and Its Technologies" (cit. Table 1).

ments of research priorities to scientific authorities, leaving philanthropists to assess entrepreneurial capacities, organizational needs, and the quality of institutions: matters that they, as professional organizers, were accustomed to decide on.

The Carnegie and Rockefeller Programs

The big five—the International and General Education Boards (IEB and GEB), the Laura Spelman Rockefeller Memorial, the Rockefeller Foundation, and the Carnegie Corporation—became patrons of science about the same time, but in ways that reflected their different histories. Educational foundations accommodated most easily to the idea of community development. The IEB was a new organization; so its president, Wickliffe Rose, easily gave it a new mission in science. Bringing the GEB into line was more difficult, however, owing to the burden of its past commitments to general education. Competing internal interests in general-purpose foundations like the Rockefeller Foundation and the Carnegie Corporation made the process of change more complex and uncertain. There was little opposition to Beardsley Ruml's plans to turn the focus of the Spelman Memorial from traditional charity to the social sciences. James Angell began to turn the Carnegie Corporation toward science, but his departure left the field open to people with different priorities. Internal politics in the Rockefeller Foundation effectively blocked the initiatives of Edwin Embree and others on behalf of science.

A common element in all five cases is the character and experience of the individuals most centrally involved, especially Rose, Ruml, and Angell. These individuals represent a new generation of professional philanthropists eager to transform older, more personal organizations into well-managed and programmatic agents of social reconstruction. They shared an enthusiasm for science as an agency for social progress, and a belief that universities would play a central role in social change. These shared beliefs reflected a common background in academic administration, and in organizing relief and public health work during and after World War I. The new patrons of science all had previous experience in manpower or community development; they were all connected in some way with emerging science lobbies like the NRC.

Beardsley Ruml and the Spelman Memorial

Beardsley Ruml came to the Spelman Memorial in 1923 from a career in personnel management and applied psychology. He had directed the massive occupational testing and manpower selection programs for the army during the war and in 1919 was associated with Walter Scott's industrial personnel consulting firm. After serving as James Angell's assistant for a year at the Carnegie Corporation, Ruml brought to the Memorial the ideals and organizational techniques of scientific personnel management.[28] He shared the belief, pervasive in his circle after the war, that social scientists should play a central role in reconstructing national institutions, and that the chief bottleneck was the shortage of social scientists who possessed both knowledge and practical skills. The big chance for private philanthropy, as Ruml saw it, was to take the lead in training a new generation of social scientists of that sort.

Taking a cue from the University of Pennsylvania's Department of Industrial Research (a spin-off of wartime experiments in "scientific" labor relations), Ruml envisioned a national system of similar centers of research, training, and service in social work, public administration, and so on. Social scientists had long favored research institutes as the best way of integrating research and practice, and Ruml steered large sums to the Brookings Institute and the National Bureau of Economic Research. For the core of his program, however, he relied on university departments. In 1923 the manpower problem seemed most pressing, and universities were the sole producers of social scientists.

Some centers specialized in particular problems, and Ruml made efforts to engineer an intellectual division of labor. (Being a scientist himself, he was better able than most philanthropists to take an active role.) However, the main purpose of the Memorial-sponsored centers was to develop all social science communities together. For example, Spelman Memorial grants to universities were managed by local research councils, which were supposed to integrate the social science disciplines and provide programmatic guidance for research and training.

About half the departments Ruml selected for support were in research universities; many, however, were in smaller institutions that he hoped would become centers of social activism in under-developed regions.[29] This was community development on a truly vast scale. Ruml relied mainly on departmental block grants but supplemented these with a large program of fellowships, comparable to the NRC programs, and maintained the Social Science Research Council as an agency of planning and communication. The Memorial invested about $21 million in the social sciences between 1923 and 1930. It did what the Carnegie and Rockefeller boards together were to do for the natural sciences and may have served as a model for Rose's plans for the IEB.

Wickliffe Rose, the GEB, and the IEB

Rose's plans for the natural sciences grew out of experiences and ideals similar to Ruml's. As director of the International Health Board (IHB), Rose had been engaged since 1914 in setting up systems of public health agencies. The shortage of professional public health administrators, he found, was the main impediment to the growth of the system. More precisely, Rose *created* a shortage, by expanding the demand and raising the standards for professional public health officers. Around 1914 he began to use the IHB to build up schools of public health in strategically placed universities around the world. To stimulate the supply of talent, he also began a program of public health fellowships.[30] Rose had been developing professional communities for a decade when he was unexpectedly asked by John D. Rockefeller, Jr., to take charge of the General Education Board. Accustomed to an international reach, Rose asked that a new international board be created to give him a scope in education comparable to that he had in public health.

But why did Rose devote the International Education Board to scientific research? He had no previous experience in sponsoring research and had scrupulously avoided getting the IHB into the business of research grants, leaving that to the Rockefeller Institute. A division of labor had developed between Rose and Simon Flexner, with Rose administering field operations and Flexner taking responsibility for research and selection of IHB fellows. However, Rose's close relation with Flexner and the Rockefeller Institute circle exposed him to their views of science, which he evidently absorbed. Simon Flexner was a prominent advocate of the view that medical research was best done by chemists, physicists, and biologists. Rose shared Flexner's idealistic beliefs about the role of science in medical and social improvement—he probably learned them at Flexner's knee. Obliged to devise a program for the IEB in short order in 1923, Rose drew on the ideological resources at hand.

Rose's experiences in organizing war relief and emergency public health programs in postwar Europe broadened his interest in science as a social force. Like many active in postwar Europe, Rose felt he was witnessing the imminent collapse of Western civilization. He saw industries idle and currencies in ruin, rampant malnutrition and epidemics, governments paralyzed, and extremist politics on the rise. For Rose, these were the great challenges for private philanthropy. He was well aware that foundations could not begin to meet the need for mass relief and economic recovery; they could, however, ensure the survival of universities and professional communities, from which the leadership for recovery would come.

Rose's long-term goals for the IEB were to build systems of agricultural and industrial education and to promote the use of scientists in agriculture, industry, and social welfare. In the short term, his goal was to put resources in the hands of those who would train the next generation of scientists. To Rose, science exemplified the central values of Western civilization. He looked to scientists as culture bearers, exemplars of reason and enlightened community activism.[31]

Such views were commonplace in the reform circles in which Rose moved. He had close connections with the NRC activists, especially Vernon Kellogg and Robert Millikan. One of Hoover's chief lieutenants in European food relief, Kellogg had come close to becoming a philanthropist himself. As NRC secretary and a Rockefeller trustee, he maintained close contacts between the NRC and the Rockefeller boards. In 1919 Millikan had made an eloquent appeal to philanthropists to develop university centers of scientific research and training which had deeply moved Rose.[32] This speech was, in effect, the plan for direct aid to university science that Millikan had proposed to the Rockefeller Foundation. Rejected by George Vincent, the idea resonated with Rose and contributed to what eventually became the program of the IEB. Rose was also connected with scientific reform circles in Britain, Spain, and Scandinavia comparable to that around the NRC. He had discovered these groups through his work with the IHB during the war and as the Rockefeller Foundation's informal medical envoy in 1918–1920. A few years later, they became advisers and recipients of grants from the IEB.[33]

Like Ruml, Rose adopted a strategy of concentrating resources in a few centers of research and training—making the peaks higher, to use his own slogan. His mode of operation was to identify productive, inspiring teachers and provide the material means to expand their programs into regional or national centers of scientific development.[34] In practice, Rose operated in a rather more traditional way than Ruml, making more capital grants for buildings and equipment and fewer for group research in specific problem areas. Rose was not scientifically trained, and though he enjoyed talking shop with eminent scientists, he left scientific decisions to the experts. The IEB's programs were also less comprehensive in execution than in conception (see Table 7). The vast scope of his plans, plus local political and financial impediments, obliged Rose to seize opportunities as they arose.

In the United States, GEB programs were gradually brought into line with IEB ideals, but there too Rose was obliged to trim his sails to fit practical realities. The GEB's practice of pledging large sums contingent on matching funds meant that actual expenditures lagged years behind appropriations. The GEB had $9.4 million in outstanding commitments in 1919, one third of total appropriations since 1902.[35] It was risky to initiate projects. GEB leaders in the early 1920s emphasized the need to phase out programs in general education, but even Rose found it difficult to do much in the five years before his retirement in 1928.

The distribution of GEB projects reveals a strategy of regional centers operating within an existing hierarchy of universities (see Table 8). Established graduate universities like Harvard and Chicago did well, but Rose especially favored up-and-coming institutions like Caltech, Princeton, and Stanford: elite teaching colleges that were building up graduate training and research. Potential new centers of graduate training in the South and West, such as Vanderbilt and Texas, also caught his eye. Rose envisioned a comprehensive scheme of regional development comparable to the Spelman Memorial's. By 1927–1928 GEB circuit rider Halston J.

TABLE 7

International Education Board, Major Expenditures, 1923–1933

Field and Recipient	Sum Expended (in $1,000s)
Natural and agricultural sciences	
Mt. Palomar Observatory	5,572
Harvard University	2,360
Cambridge University	1,920
Edinburgh University	507
Madrid Institute of Physics and Chemistry	429
Göttingen University	357
Paris University	322
Copenhagen University	284
Paris Botanical Garden	197
University of Virginia	172
Bulgarian College of Agriculture	117
Leiden University	80
Tromsö Institute (Norway)	75
Stockholm University	68
Naples Zoological Station	55
Jungfrau High Altitude Institute	36
Miscellaneous	142
Publications and abstracts	115
Fellowships	956
Total natural and agricultural sciences	13,764
Agricultural education and demonstration	
Projects and miscellaneous	475
Fellowships	540
Total agricultural education	1,015
Humanities	9,933
General education	3,443
Total nonscience	14,391
Total expenditures	28,155

Source: George W. Gray, *Education on an International Scale: A History of the International Education Board 1923–1938* (New York: Harcourt Brace, 1941). Some small grants for equipment and supplies are omitted.

Thorkelson was discreetly but systematically surveying scientific talent in a wide range of American colleges and universities.[36]

Rose's grand ambitions for science were modified in practice by political and economic realities. Populist antipathy to private foundations frustrated his plans for centers in land-grant universities like Wisconsin. Cornell failed to raise matching funds to secure a pledge of $1.5 million for biology and agriculture. In several cases, aid to basic science departments followed from previous GEB investment in medical schools; at the University of Rochester, for example. Rose's old-fashioned cultural tastes also diverted him from the GEB's main purpose of building up graduate training. His two greatest projects were the Mt. Palomar Observatory and the Oriental Institute at Chicago: both more research institutes than training centers, and in areas closer to the cultural priorities of the 1880s than the 1920s.

In its multidisciplinary range and continental scope, Rose's ambition was, admittedly, not just grand but grandiose. The early 1920s were a time for utopian visions, however. Without the grand ideal of community development and social reconstruction, visionaries like Ruml and Rose would probably not have been able to steer traditional institutions like the GEB and the Spelman Memorial to the support of scientific training and research.

James Angell and the Carnegie Corporation

In the Carnegie Corporation, James R. Angell played, briefly, a role comparable to that of Ruml and Rose. One of the founders of the University of Chicago's school of psychology, Angell had turned to administration around 1908, first as dean and then as acting president (1918–1919). Like many academic psychologists, Angell got involved in personnel management through work for the army in World War I. He served on the Committees on Classification of Personnel and on Education and Special Training. The latter was responsible for coordinating civilian and military training and setting up the Student Army Training Corps.[37] His interest in industrial manpower continued for a time after

TABLE 8

General Education Board Appropriations for Natural and Biomedical Sciences, 1923–1931

Recipient	Sum expended (in $1,000s)
National Research Council	503
California Institute of Technology	3,079
Vanderbilt University	1,550
Princeton University	1,000
Rochester University and Medical School	1,750
Woods Hole Marine Biology Laboratory	500
Harvard University	675
University of Chicago	1,798
University of Chicago Medical School	1,000
Cornell University	1,500
Stanford University	990
University of Texas	65
University of Pennsylvania Medical School	280
Columbia University Medical School	24
Yale University Medical School	24
Yale Institute for Human Relations	500
Washington University Medical School	200
Richmond University	167
Total appropriations	15,605
Paid by 1940	14,481

Source: General Education Board, *Annual Reports*, 1923–1930.

the war. Angell was also active in the organization of scientific work, serving as chairman of the NRC in 1919–1920.[38] Organization and training of scientific manpower remained his chief concerns as president of the Carnegie Corporation in the years 1920–1921.

In his brief tenure as president, Angell initiated several large programs in the sciences, which ultimately brought total expenditures to $16 million (see Table 9). However, he did not succeed in attaching the Corporation permanently to the cause of science. After he resigned in 1921 to become president of Yale University, his successors turned to new causes, and the nascent program in science was gradually discontinued.

That program reflected Angell's previous experiences as an academic administrator and head of the NRC. Defining education as the Corporation's overarching purpose, Angell saw the greatest organizational need in education in the areas of research and graduate training:

> The graduate school, so-called, in our great American universities has not as yet fully found itself, and its attempt on the one hand to produce creative scientists and scholars has landed it in certain difficulties. . . . There is at this point a real possibility for an agency like the Corporation to do a constructive and significant piece of work. . . . The intrinsic needs of our time, as well as the deep rooted interests of the founder, would lead me to urge that the Corporation commit itself as a matter of permanent policy to the furtherance of research.[39]

University departments were the key to Angell's program. He was less interested in sponsoring particular researches than in building an organized infrastructure for research. Improvement of scientific research was inextricably linked in his mind with the production of a new generation of elite researchers.

Despite his invocation of Carnegie's interest in education, Angell was in fact boldly departing from the Corporation's traditionally eclectic interests. The Corporation had been primarily a purse for Carnegie's other institutions and had relied on the Carnegie Institution to distribute its annual allocation for small grants-in-aid. Angell intended to take charge of allocation himself and to concentrate on large programmatic grants to institutions at the expense of specific researches and fellowships. He therefore initiated a series of grants to Caltech to develop research schools in physics, chemistry, and geology. These grants were continued, if without much enthusiasm, even after his

TABLE 9

Carnegie Corporation Expenditures on Sciences, 1916–1931

Recipient	Sum Expended (in $1,000s)
Carnegie Institution of Washington Endowment	6,350
Research grants	270
National Research Council Endowment	6,890
Research grants	66
California Institute of Technology	
Endowment	600
Departmental grants	345
Phipps Institute (University of Pennsylvania)	200
University of Pennsylvania Medical School	250
Woods Hole Marine Biology Laboratory	127
Diabetes research grants	114
Nutrition research grants	90
Stomatology group research	105
Medical sciences grants	113
Biological sciences grants	30
Physical sciences grants	85
Conferences, publications, etc.	98
Total	15,733

Source: Robert M. Lester, *Summary of Grants Primarily for Research in Biological and Physical Sciences* (New York: Carnegie Corporation, 1932), pp. 7–18. The period covered by Lester is 1911–1931.

departure. Angell also administered a grant of $5 million to the National Academy of Sciences. Part of this went to support the NRC's programs for developing science: to draw attention to new research fields, to improve scientists' communications among themselves and with the general public, and to raise funds from industry. Some members of the board disapproved of the new direction exemplified by these grants, but apparently the reform minority had caught them off guard.

But despite Angell's innovations and his sharing the same ambitions for science as the NRC activists and their Rockefeller patrons, the pattern of Corporation gifts was distinctly its own, even during his tenure. The grants to Caltech were the closest in spirit to the Rockefeller community development programs: these were middle-range project grants to centers of advanced training and research. Much more prominent, however, among the Corporation's disbursements are two large grants of endowment: the one to the NRC, engineered by Angell, and another to the Carnegie Institution, made by Keppel in 1925. Although large, Angell's NRC grant, like the Caltech grants, was at least designed to support programs in community development. No such ideal can be seen in the later grant to the Institution. Also striking, and totally unlike the Rockefeller programs, is the large number of small grants for specific medical researches. After Angell left, the Corporation settled into a pattern of small, scattered grants-in-aid to individual research that for one reason or another—usually newsworthiness—appealed to the trustees. The Caltech project was never to become the prototype of a program of project grants to other departments.

The distinctive style of the Corporation's program in science was the result of complex internal politics. Its board was divided from the beginning. Between 1911 and 1919 it was little more than a vehicle for Andrew Carnegie's personal charities. Dominated by the founder and his friends, the board simply had picked favorites from a flood of petitioners. A few progressive members of the board seized the occasion of Carnegie's death in 1919 to give the Corporation a professional management and programmatic purpose. One key actor was Henry Pritchett, former president of MIT and president of the Carnegie Foundation. Another was Elihu Root, former secretary of state, an ardent believer in the role of science in national development and a close ally of the NRC leadership. As acting president in 1919–1920, Root was responsible for the grant to the NRC; he also engineered Angell's appointment as the Corporation's first full-time administrative head.[40] Despite the disapproval of the board traditionalists, Root gave Angell carte blanche to give the Corporation a purpose appropriate to the times; for both of them, that purpose was science.

Had Angell stayed on as president, he and Root together could probably have succeeded in making the Corporation an endowment fund for the development of science. However, Angell's abrupt departure fatally weakened the power of the NRC's friends on the Corporation's board. Root tried to get someone like Angell to succeed him: Edwin G. Conklin and John C. Merriam, both scientists and NRC activists, were considered. Merriam, president of the Carnegie Institution, was the obvious choice, but he had been runner-up to Angell in 1920, and Root felt that an offer now would be embarrassing. Both Root and Henry Pritchett feared that Carnegie's friends on the board would not be so easily outmaneuvered again.[41] Evidently they were right, for Pritchett was made acting president until a suitable outside candidate could be found. Corporation policy was once more up for grabs.

Oddly enough, moderate trustees like Pritchett and Robert S. Woodward were in some ways more of a problem than the conservative faction of the board. Although both Pritchett himself and Woodward were strongly proscience, they were also confirmed skeptics about the role of universities in programmatic research. Just retired from the Carnegie Institution, Woodward was a powerful voice for investing in research institutes. Since joining the board in 1916, Pritchett had opposed relying on universities for important national research.[42] Unlike Angell, Pritchett was less interested in graduate schools than in restoring the traditional moral purposes of undergraduate teaching, an interest reinforced by his role as president of the Carnegie Foundation for the Advancement of Teaching. Thus while Woodward and Pritchett were Root's chief allies in his efforts to modernize the Corporation's management, they were not wholly sympathetic with what Root and Angell specifically proposed to do. Pritchett's 1922 plans resembled Carnegie's more than Angell's, emphasizing libraries, adult education, the arts, and aid to other Carnegie institutions. Research was mentioned only in connection with teaching methods.[43]

Pritchett's successor, Frederick Keppel, was a humanistic educator with no real interest in science and little desire to take an active role in formulating programs. He settled down to the tasks of liquidating the accumulated debts of the Carnegie Foundation's troubled pension program and of restoring the Carnegie Institution's inflation-eroded endowment.[44] Keppel also settled down to undoing Angell's initiatives in science: he kept a few group research grants going to demonstrate the method of collective research, but the moral vision that drew Ruml, Angell, and Rose to science was missing.[45] As a humanist, he moved in circles that did not intersect with the NRC. The last grant for scientific research was finally terminated in 1932. The early grants to the NRC and Caltech remain as vestigial evidence of the pervasive influence of the NRC activists and their ideals on philanthropy in the early postwar years.

The Rockefeller Foundation

The Rockefeller Foundation was similarly hampered by internal politics from realizing the ideals of community development. The Foundation remained almost exclusively a silent partner, channeling funds for fellowships and research grants through committees of the NRC (see Table 10). This symbiotic relationship permitted philanthropists to aid specific research communities without creating an internal administrative bureaucracy, and without running the risk of making particular institutions dependent on outside patronage. Foundation president George Vincent was almost obsessively concerned in the early 1920s to avoid such entanglements.

Vincent's background resembled Angell's in many ways: the Midwest, academic social science, and a strong drift from scholarship to administration. However, the two moved in somewhat different social circles and had had different roles during the war. Vincent was not closely connected with the NRC crowd, and owing to the Rockefeller Foundation's leading role in public health, he moved most easily among leaders of reform movements in public health and social welfare. Like Angell, he was the first professional head of a major philanthropy, but he lacked Angell's concern with developing graduate schools. He too had to cope with powerful vested interests.

Vincent's chief problem was not with his trustees, as Angell's was—the Rockefeller Foundation was never the instrument of its founder and had always been more professionally managed than the Carnegie Corporation—but with entrenched and expansionist operating agencies like the International Health Board and the China Medical Board. Vincent's greatest problem was preventing these agencies from coopting the Foundation's income and blocking initiatives in areas where he and his staff wanted to take a leading role. Vincent was in a double bind: large new projects might break the monopoly of vested interests like Rose's IHB, but they might also break the bank by creating more expensive baronies. The pattern of Vincent's presidency (1917–1928) was one of tentative ini-

TABLE 10

Rockefeller Foundation Expenditures on Science, 1915–1918

Recipient	Sum Expended (in $1,000s)
Rockefeller Institute (1915–1922)	
Endowment and projects	9,859
National Research Council	
Medical Committee (1918–1919)	20
Fellowships, physical sciences	833
Fellowships, medical sciences	1,500
Fellowships, biological sciences	321
Division of Studies (1924–1928)	
Research projects	550
Biological stations	600
Fellowships and miscellaneous	79
Total exclusive of Institute	3,903
Total	13,762

Source: Rockefeller Foundation, *Annual Reports*, 1914–1928.

tiatives followed by retrenchment, of grand schemes left unfulfilled. This pattern is evident in the Foundation's dependence on the NRC.

The Foundation had a clear opportunity to take the lead in the medical and behavioral sciences, given its preeminence in medicine and public health and the Rockefeller family's patronage of mental health and social behavior through the Bureau of Social Hygiene and the National Committee for Mental Hygiene. Raymond Fosdick, a trustee and an influential lawyer-reformer, played a role in the Rockefeller circles analogous to Root's in the Carnegie network. Like Root, Fosdick was politically well-connected and had a lively interest in science as a force for social progress.[46] He pressed Vincent constantly to be bolder, but rivalries among internal interests effectively crippled Vincent and left the initiative to Ruml and Rose, who were quick to seize it.[47] Before the reorganization of the Rockefeller boards in 1928, the Foundation itself undertook no general program in support of science.

The Rockefeller Foundation did make one experiment in developing a research community; however, it was short-lived. This scheme was the brainchild of Edwin Embree, secretary of the Foundation and, in 1924, the first director of a "Division of Studies." This new division was designed by Vincent and Embree to strengthen the authority of the Foundation president's office in its constant competition with the entrenched operating divisions. But whereas Vincent was concerned mainly to gain some control so as to change the programs of existing divisions, Embree was ambitious to emulate the grand divisional chiefs like Flexner and Rose, to hatch large new programs that might grow to rival those in public health and medical education.[48]

After discussion of various appropriate purposes for the division, Vincent and Embree settled on "human biology," a somewhat fashionable but ill-defined rubric for the sciences of human heredity, growth and development, psychology, and behavior. There were precedents for such a program in the Foundation's grant to the Marine Biology Station at Woods Hole and in its ongoing support of the National Committee for Mental Hygiene. Embree's idea was to develop the biological sciences underlying human behavior.[49] He envisioned his program as complementing Ruml's in the social sciences. The two even discussed an integrated program in human growth, inheritance, and psychology, with Ruml taking on the social aspects and Embree the biological side of human behavior.[50] Embree conceived of his program as one in the biological sciences, but what gave his conception its distinctive character was its connection to social movements. He sought programmatic themes in social issues that were arousing wide popular interest in the early and mid 1920s: race relations, ethnic conflict, crime, mental hygiene, and eugenics. By making this connection Embree sought not only to locate his biological program within the Foundation's traditional interest in medicine and public health, but also to distinguish it from Rose's program in general biology.[51]

Embree self-consciously emulated Ruml and Rose's grand entrepreneurial style and adopted their strategies of community development. He proposed to establish regional centers of research and training to serve as nurseries for a new generation of leaders who would give coherence to an important but misunderstood and controversial field.[52] With much hustle and bustle, he undertook a survey of scientific institutions in countries around the Pacific Basin. Grants were made to research projects at half a dozen universities, including Raymond Pearl's research on the biology of lifespan, Robert Yerkes's research on anthropoid apes, and Charles B. Davenport's work on human heredity. It was an eclectic assembly that included anthropological research on Australian aborigines, general physiology, racial mixing in Hawaii, and brain physiology. Embree designed a fellowship program, developed contacts with the Australian NRC, and planned to develop regional university centers in cooperation with the National and Canadian National Committees for Mental Hygiene. He managed to spend over half a million dollars before the Division of Studies was dissolved and absorbed by the Division of Medical Education in 1927.[53]

The failure of Embree's program was overdetermined. Despite his best efforts, he never won the support of crucial trustees, like Simon Flexner and Raymond Fosdick: not surprisingly, he never persuaded Flexner that "human biology" had any real scientific value; nor did he persuade Raymond Fosdick that it was anything but an entering wedge to a vast program in general biology. The officers were split by jurisdictional disputes: "Rose claimed that his program of the natural sciences included biology as well as physics and chemistry. Russell took the attitude that public health was the only aspect of human biology worth considering. Vincent took no stand at all. Pearce was sympathetic and helpful but politics and lack of leadership were too much for any new work to survive." Ever wary of large new programs, Vincent gave little support, and Embree's flirtation with the politically hot issues of eugenics and behavior made everyone at 61 Broadway nervous.[54] The Rockefeller family had created the Bureau of Social Hygiene as a separate entity from the Foundation precisely to protect the latter from such controversy.

Embree also blamed himself: "For three years I sweat blood on the job in New York. On the whole I think the results were those that would be expected from a very immature person. The things I got done were not bad, but I did not get the philosophy of the thing for years and years and was therefore unable to formulate a really statesmanlike program."[55] It is true that Embree lacked Ruml's scientific knowledge of the field he proposed to develop; nor did he have Rose's long experience and skill in administration. His ambitions were too obvious, and he moved too fast, unaware that he did not have the full confidence of key people in the Foundation. But one considerable problem was the inherent weakness of "human biology." As a scientific program, it had no more coherence and focus than the disparate social movements, designed to extend public health methods from infectious diseases to maladies of the environment, home, workplace, and social inequalities, that gave it its appeal. There was no well-defined community of practitioners, no definite constituency. There was no clear record of scientific achievement and no definite agenda for research. Embree probably blamed himself too much. It seems unlikely, given the inherent difficulties, that an officer with more political experience could have succeeded with such an ill-defined and controversial field.

The failure of Embree's program illustrates how difficult it was for general-purpose foundations to orchestrate systematic development of specific fields of science. In the 1920s these succeeded best when managed by committees of experts under the aegis of the NRC. General programs of support proved a better vehicle for developing relations between foundations and universities. Programs supporting postgraduate training and demonstration centers of organized research were an ideal arrangement for both parties, fulfilling their institutional missions while protecting traditional prerogatives.

Other Foundations

A few smaller foundations also mounted programs to aid specialized research communities associated with new, research-intensive technologies. The Daniel Guggenheim Fund, for example, specialized in aeronautics. Between 1926 and 1930 the Fund invested some $2.2 million in seven universities to build wind tunnels and to develop programs of research and graduate training. Almost $1.2 million more was spent on public information and promotion, applied research and development, and commercialization.[56] It is a classic example of the strategy of community development. Development of the domestic organic chemical industry was the aim of the Chemical Foundation, organized in 1919 to disburse the income from German properties and patents seized by the U.S. government in 1917. Led by the feisty patent attorney and lobbyist Francis P. Garvan, the Chemical Foundation acted more like a traditional family charity, scattering its funds in small doses rather than concentrating on strategic centers. Garvan had idiosyncratic enthusiasms and a strong will: it was very much a one-man show.[57] Among the voluntary health agencies, the National Tuberculosis Society's program of cooperative research on TB exemplifies the style of community development.[58] Its expenditures were not large by IEB standards ($560,000 between 1921 and 1940), but it set the pattern for the much larger grant programs of the National Foundation for Infantile Paralysis and the American Cancer Society in the late 1930s.

The End of Community Development

Large programs aimed at developing whole communities of science reached a high-water mark about 1927 and were already receding when the Depression hit. The Carnegie Corporation's program had long been in decline, and the IEB, GEB, and Spelman Memorial programs were formally terminated in the 1928 reorganization of the Rockefeller boards. The Foundation's new divisions of natural, social, and medical sciences continued the programs of the 1920s, but with smaller budgets and without Rose and Ruml's freewheeling style. NRC fellowship programs were phased out or absorbed by divisional programs in experimental biology, psychosomatic medicine, and other special fields.[59]

In the 1930s foundation strategies reverted to a style more reminiscent of the 1910s than the 1920s. Individual research grants replaced block grants to departments. Long-term expansion of research capacity gave way to specific, short-term research projects. The language of relief again began to be heard, as industrial markets for researchers dried up and young scientists hung on desperately in graduate schools. The linkage of research and training, so compelling in the 1920s, lost its magic. Plummeting income from foundation endowments forced foundations to reassess the actual results of programs aimed at expanding the capacity of the research system.

The Depression accelerated a cycle of change that had already begun to turn by 1928. The war-born enthusiasm for social and moral reconstruction had begun to cool, perhaps because reality had not quite lived up to utopian expectations. Collective research projects proved interesting additions to the scientific scene, but had habits of cooperation percolated down into the daily life of individual investigators? Investment in regional centers had added a few universities to the top elite, but had the leaven worked in society at large? Grand plans like Rose's began to seem grandiose to realists like Raymond Fosdick. The sciences were essential to particular aspects of modern civilization but were not the magic key to progress that they had seemed in 1919. The ideal of community development in science was an expression of the special circumstances and mood of 1919–1928, and it did not outlast them.

The 1920s style of community development came midway between the evangelical style of Progressive reform movements and the managerial, bureaucratic social engineering of the New Deal, and it combined elements of both.[60] Much has been written about the disappearance of Progressive reform in the 1920s.[61] The reform impulse did not disappear, however; it was expressed in different ways as reformers' strategies changed. Prewar political and propaganda campaigns to legislate a new social and moral order were largely abandoned (with the notable exception of Prohibition). They were succeeded in the 1920s by numerous specialized reform movements aimed at particular local or occupational communities. The overtly moralistic character of prewar reform gave way to a more managerial rhetoric; but the language of cooperation was infused with moral import, suggesting again that older habits of thought had simply taken new forms. The large foundations and voluntary health agencies took responsibility for social services that had once been wholly private and would soon become largely public. They were quasi-public agencies for social development.

The ideals of community development are exemplified in another way by trade associations, which acted as quasi-public agencies for industrial development.[62] Private and voluntary, these associations assumed public responsibilities for developing specialized industrial communities. They undertook promotion and political lobbying; disseminated information about markets and technological innovations; engaged, in a limited way, in research and development; and kept up relations with universities and the NRC. Advocates of such associations hoped to reap the benefits of collective action without giving up traditional habits of laissez faire. The similarity to the scientific research councils is striking—hence my suggestion that the NRC was a trade association for science.

The idea of community development is useful for historical analysis because of the consistency of organization, ideals, and behavior of social welfare foundations, voluntary health agencies, the NRC and SSRC, and the trade associations. Like any such concept, however, it is useful only within its proper limits. We should not presume that there was *a* community of science in the 1920s; there was not. What united NRC activists like Hale, Millikan, and Noyes with patrons like Ruml, Angell, Embree, and Rose was a vision of cooperative, self-regulating research communities. The ideal was imperfectly realized, of course, but it makes sense of what was done by those who strove to make it real.

Lasting Effects

What then were the effects of foundation programs on the organization and practice of science? Of course, the effects were far greater in some sciences than in others. For obvious reasons, private foundations steered clear of sciences that were amply supported by government or industries. Rooted in nineteenth-century traditions of voluntary public health, education, and social control, foundations naturally favored areas of science that were related in some way to such concerns. This pattern is clear from Eduard Lindemann's analysis of foundation expenditures (see Table 11). Large expenditures on astronomy and physics suggest the continuing appeal to philanthropists of traditionally elite academic disciplines, despite all the rhetoric of the economic benefits of science. Low expenditures on chemistry, geology, agriculture, and forestry point historians of those disciplines to the richer connections with industry and government established between 1880 and 1910. Strong support of neurology, psychiatry, and mental hygiene reminds us of the moral and behavioral aspects of nineteenth-century reform. American leadership in the biobehavioral sciences after 1920 owes much to the conjunction of the postwar enthusiasm for basic science with older philanthropic interests in behavior and social control.

The effects of foundation grants on practice within the biobehavioral sciences are more difficult to discern, because the foundations' role cannot be considered apart from the role of other patrons and of contending interests within the sciences. For example, some historians lay the responsibility for a reductionist, scientistic bias in the social and behavioral sciences at the door of foundations. This one-sided view neglects the many other reasons, social and intellectual, for scientists to adopt such values.[63]

The obvious place to look for direct effects of foundation programs is the organization of scientific institutions. Organizing is what philanthropists knew how to do, after all, and what they set out to do in science. By providing development funds to university departments, foundations made it possible for universities to preserve a research role, tilting the balance against those who favored a separation of research from teaching. Foundation support of the research councils was instrumental in creating a strong national scientific elite in a geographically widely dispersed system in which localism and individualism were still a habit for many scientists. Foundation participation was crucial to the new social networks of communication and influence that shaped science between the wars.

Foundations also altered the pecking order of universities. The large foundations' policy of concentration on regional centers gave up-and-coming universities the leverage to join the elite research universities.[64] The role of Carnegie and Rockefeller grants in the spectacular rise of Caltech is well documented, but the rise of Vanderbilt, Duke, and other universities in the South and Southwest is no less a result of a philanthropic tradition that had its roots in the reconstruction of the South. State and technical universities too turned to foundations in the 1930s.[65]

The alliance of large foundations, elite research universities, and the NRC constituted a distinct region or subsector of the science system, comparable to the alliances of land-grant universities and federal

TABLE 11

Expenditures on Science by a Hundred Foundations, 1920–1929

Field	Sum Expended (in $1,000s)	Field	Sum Expended (in $1,000s)
Natural science, general	9,744	Biology	4,386
Physics	4,478	Botany and forestry	247
Astronomy	2,794	Psychology	1,187
Chemistry	324	Mental hygiene	1,120
Geology	288	Anthropology	971
Mathematics	24	Economics	3,691
Medicine	5,998	Political science, history	1,455
Public health	2,245	Engineering	316

Source: Lindemann, *Wealth and Culture* (cit. Table 3), pp. 72–85. I have combined funds for departments, fellowships, associations, research, and unclassified in both U.S. and foreign institutions. Unclassified is less than 10% of the total.

bureaus, and of R & D-intensive industries and elite engineering schools. In each of these subsystems, institutionalized channels for exchanging resources, manpower, and services structured opportunities for growth and innovation in particular fields of science, in ways that have just begun to be explored.

Notes

1. Shelby M. Harrison and F. Emerson Andrews, *American Foundations for Social Welfare* (New York: Russell Sage Foundation, 1946); Raymond B. Fosdick, *Adventure in Giving: The Story of the General Education Board* (New York: Harper & Row, 1962); Fosdick, *The Story of the Rockefeller Foundation* (New York: Harper, 1952); and Roger L. Geiger, *To Advance Knowledge: The Growth of American Research Universities, 1900–1940* (New York/Oxford: Oxford Univ. Press, 1986), esp. Ch. 4.

2. Nathan Reingold, "The Case of the Disappearing Laboratory," *American Quarterly*, 1977, 29:79–101.

3. George W. Corner, *A History of the Rockefeller Institute, 1901–1953* (New York: Rockefeller Institute Press, 1964); Nathan Reingold, "National Science Policy in a Private Foundation: The Carnegie Institution of Washington," in *The Organization of Knowledge in Modern America, 1860–1920*, ed. Alexandra Oleson and John Voss (Baltimore: Johns Hopkins Univ. Press, 1979), pp. 313–341; Starr J. Murphey to John D. Rockefeller, Jr., 13 Feb. 1902, in "Papers Concerning the Proposed New Buildings and Endowment of the Medical School," C. W. Eliot Papers, Box 104, Folder 47, Harvard University Archives, Cambridge, Mass.

4. Callie Hull, "Funds Available in 1920 in the United States of America for the Encouragement of Scientific Research," *Bulletin of the National Research Council*, 1921, No. 9.

5. Howard Plotkin, "Edward C. Pickering and the Endowment of Scientific Research in America, 1877–1918," *Isis*, 1978, 69:44–57.

6. A. Hunter Dupree, *Science in the Federal Government* (Cambridge, Mass.: Harvard Univ. Press, 1959); and Rexmond C. Cochrane, *The National Academy of Sciences: The First Hundred Years, 1863–1963* (Washington, D.C.: National Academy of Sciences, 1978).

7. Hull, "Funds Available in 1920" (cit. n. 4).

8. Louis Galambos, "The Emerging Organizational Synthesis in Modern American History," *Business History Review*, 1970, 44:279–290.

9. Paul M. Limbert, *Denominational Policies in the Support of and Supervision of Higher Education* (New York: Columbia Teachers College, 1929); Verl S. Lewis, "The Development of the Charity Organization Movement in the United States, 1875–1900" (Ph.D. diss., Western Reserve Univ., 1954); Selskar Gunn and Philip S. Platt, *Voluntary Health Agencies* (New York: Ronald, 1945); Harold Cavins, *National Health Agencies* (Washington, D.C.: Public Affairs Press, 1945); Richard H. Shryock, *National Tuberculosis Association, 1904–1954* (New York: National Tuberculosis Association, 1957); and Ernest V. Hollis, *Philanthropic Foundations and Higher Education* (New York: Columbia Univ. Press, 1938).

10. Nathan Reingold, "The Disappearing Laboratory" (cit. n. 2), p. 89; Plotkin, "Edward C. Pickering" (cit. n. 5), pp. 52–56.

11. T. H. Morgan to E. C. Pickering, 23 Oct. 1916; Pickering to Morgan, 13 Oct., 25 Oct., 1 Nov. 1916; and Morgan to Clyde Furst, 17 and 23 Oct. 1916; Edward C. Pickering Papers, Harvard University Archives.

12. Ray L. Wilbur, "The Advantages of Distribution of Research Funds to Universities Rather Than to Independent Research Institutes," and discussion, *Journal of the Proceedings of the Association of American Universities*, 1923, 25:60–70; "A Preliminary Conference on University Research," *Science*, 1923, 63:518; and Carnegie Corporation, *Annual Report of the President, 1921/22* (New York, 1922), pp. 21–22, 31–42.

13. Frederick Keppel, "Opportunities and Dangers of Educational Foundations," *J. Proc. Assoc. Amer. Univ.*, 1925, 27:64–72, quoting from pp. 65–66. The conference proceedings are published in this volume.

14. *Ibid.*, pp. 65–67.

15. Clarke A. Chambers, *Seedtime of Reform: American Social Service and Social Action, 1918–1933* (Minneapolis: Univ. Minnesota Press, 1963); and Walter Trattner, *From Poor Law to Welfare State: A History of Social Welfare in America* (2nd ed., New York: Free Press, 1979).

16. Stanley Coben, "American Foundations as Patrons of Science: The Commitment to Individual Research," in *The Sciences in the American Context: New Perspectives*, ed. Nathan Reingold (Washington, D.C.: Smithsonian Institution Press, 1979), pp. 229–248.

17. Daniel J. Kevles, "George Ellery Hale, the First World War, and the Advancement of Science in America," *Isis*, 1968, 59:427–437; and Cochrane, *The National Academy of Sciences* (cit. n. 6), Chs. 9, 10.

18. Ellis W. Hawley, *The Great War and the Search for a Modern Order* (New York: St. Martin's Press, 1979), Chs. 5, 6.

19. Social Science Research Council, *Decennial Report, 1923–1933* (New York, 1934), pp. 104–105.

20. Eduard Lindemann, *Wealth and Culture* (New York: Harcourt Brace, 1938).

21. *National Research Council Fellowships, 1919–1938* (Washington, D.C.: National Research Council, 1938); National Research Council, *Annual Reports* (Washington, D.C., 1920–1938); and Martin Bulmer and Joan Bulmer, "Philanthropy and Social Science in the 1920s: Beardsley Ruml and the Laura Spelman Rockefeller Memorial, 1922–1929," *Minerva*, 1981, *19*:347–407, on p. 387.

22. Stanley Coben, "The Scientific Establishment and the Transmission of Quantum Mechanics to the United States, 1919–1932," *American Historical Review*, 1971, *76*:442–466; and Myron J. Rand, "The National Research Fellowships," *Scientific Monthly*, 1951, *73*:71–90.

23. Frank Aydelotte, "Opportunities and Dangers of Educational Foundations," *J. Proc. Assoc. Amer. Univ.*, 1925, *27*:60–64, on p. 62.

24. Merle Curti, *American Philanthropy Abroad: A History* (New Brunswick, N.J.: Rutgers Univ. Press, 1963); and Emily S. Rosenberg, *Spreading the American Dream* (New York: Hill & Wang, 1982).

25. Callie Hull and M. Mico, "Research Supported by Industries through Scholarships, Fellowships, and Grants," *Journal of Chemical Education*, 1944, *21*:180–190.

26. Carnegie Corporation, *Annual Report of the President, 1923/24* (New York, 1924), p. 9; and Geiger, *To Advance Knowledge* (cit. n. 1), Ch. 3.

27. Carnegie Corporation, *Report of the President* [Henry Pritchett], *1921/22* (cit. n. 12), p. 10.

28. Bulmer and Bulmer, "Philanthropy and Social Science in the 1920s" (cit. n. 21); and Geiger, *To Advance Knowledge* (cit. n. 1), pp. 149–160.

29. Bulmer and Bulmer, "Philanthropy and Social Science in the 1920s," Tables 2, 4, pp. 373, 387.

30. Fosdick, *The Story of the Rockefeller Foundation* (cit. n. 1), Ch. 4.

31. Robert E. Kohler, "Science and Philanthropy: Wickliffe Rose and the International Education Board," *Minerva*, 1985, *23*:75–95.

32. Robert A. Millikan, "The New Opportunity in Science," *Science*, 1919, 50:285–297; and Wickliffe Rose to Simon Flexner, 15 Nov. 1919, Simon Flexner Papers, American Philosophical Society Library, Philadelphia.

33. Kohler, "Science and Philanthropy" (cit. n. 31).

34. George W. Gray, *Education on an International Scale: A History of the International Education Board, 1923–1938* (New York: Harcourt Brace, 1941), pp. 16–17.

35. General Education Board, *Annual Report. 1918119* (New York, 1919), pp. 68–69.

36. General Education Board, *Annual Report, 1924/25* (New York, 1925), pp. 7–8. For Thorkelson's reports to Rose see correspondence in GEB project files, Rockefeller Archive Center, Pocantico Hills, North Tarrytown, N.Y.

37. W. S. Hunter, "James Rowland Angell, 1869–1949," *Biographical Memoirs of the National Academy of Sciences*, 1951, 26:191–208, on p. 195.

38. James R. Angell, "The Organization of Research," *Sci. Mon.*, 1920, 11:26–42; Angell, "Reasons and Plans for Research Relating to Industrial Personnel," *Journal of Personnel Research*, 1922, 1:1–6.

39. James R. Angell, "Proposals with Reference to General Policy," 9 May 1921, Folder Program & Policy, pp. 4–5, Carnegie Corporation Archives, New York.

40. Henry Pritchett to Elihu Root, 21 Feb. 1921, Carnegie Corporation Archives, Folder Root-Pritchett.

41. Pritchett to Root, 21 Feb., 1 Apr., 13 Aug. 1921, *ibid.*

42. Henry Pritchett, "Fields of Activity Open to the Carnegie Corporation," 15 Apr. 1916; "The Administration of the Carnegie Corporation," 1 Mar. 1918; "Memorandum," n.d., Jan. 1920; and "Memorandum for the Use of the Trustees of the Carnegie Corporation," 5 Nov. 1921; *ibid.*

43. Henry Pritchett, "A Policy for the Carnegie Corporation," 16 May 1922, *ibid.*

44. Policy Committee report, "To the Carnegie Corporation of New York," 15 Nov. 1922; and Frederick Keppel, "Summary of Unpaid Obligations," 30 Sept. 1928; both *ibid.*; and Carnegie Corporation, *Annual Reports* (New York, 1922–1930).

45. [Frederick Keppel], "Memorandum Concerning Grants to Research," 24 Oct. 1927, Carnegie Corporation Archives, Folder Program & Policy.

46. Raymond B. Fosdick, *Chronicle of a Generation* (New York: Harper, 1958); and Fosdick, *The Old Savage in the New Civilization* (Garden City, N.Y.: Doubleday Doran, 1928).

47. Kohler, "Science and Philanthropy" (cit. n. 31).

48. Edwin Embree to George Vincent, 4 May 1923; and Rockefeller Foundation board minutes, 5 Dec. 1923; both in Rockefeller Archive Center.

49. "Conference of Members and Officers, Princeton," 23–24 Feb. 1925, Rockefeller Foundation (RF) 900.22.165, Rockefeller Archive Center.

50. Embree to Raymond Fosdick, 26 Aug. 1925; Embree to Vincent, 27 April 1925; RF 915.4.33, Rockefeller Archive Center.

51. Edwin Embree, "Studies in Human Biology," pp. 11–14, on p. 11, and "Conferences Concerning Human Biology," exhibit D, 23–24 Feb. 1925; both in "Conference of Members and Officers, Princeton, February 23–24, 1925," RF 900.22.165, Rockefeller Archive Center.

52. Embree, "Studies in Human Biology" (cit. n. 51), pp. 11–14; and Embree to Fosdick, 26 Aug. 1925, and Embree to R. L. Wilbur, 11 July 1927; both RF 915.4.33, Rockefeller Archive Center.

53. "Division of Studies," Jan. 1926, RF 900.22.166; and board minutes, 23 Feb. 1927, RF 913.1.1; both Rockefeller Archive Center.

54. Edwin Embree, "Rockefeller Foundation," n.d. (c. 1930), quoting p. 12, Embree Papers, Box 1; S. Flexner to G. Vincent, 27 Jan. 1925, RF 900.21.159; R. Fosdick to S. Flexner, 12 Jan. 1927, RF 100.4.35; and "Conference of Members and Officers, Princeton," 23–24 Feb. 1925, p. 3, RF 900.22.165; all Rockefeller Archive Center. F. F. Russell was head of the International Health Board; Richard Pearce was head of the Division of Medical Education.

55. Embree, "Rockefeller Foundation."

56. Richard P. Hallion, *Legacy of Flight: The Guggenheim Contribution to American Aviation* (Seattle: Univ. Washington Press, 1977), pp. 171–172.

57. Williams Haynes, *American Chemical Industry: A History*, 5 vols. (New York: Van Nostrand, 1945), Vol. III.

58. Virginia Cameron and Esmond R. Long, *Tuberculosis Medical Research* (New York: National Tuberculosis Association, 1959); and Dorothy White Nicholson, *Twenty Years of Medical Research* (New York: National Tuberculosis Association, 1943).

59. Robert E. Kohler, "A Policy for the Advancement of Science: The Rockefeller Foundation, 1924–29," *Minerva*, 1978, 16:480–515.

60. Paul Boyer, *Urban Masses and Moral Order in America, 1820–1920* (Cambridge, Mass.: Harvard Univ. Press, 1978); and Otis L. Graham, Jr., *An Encore for Reform* (New York: Oxford Univ. Press, 1967).

61. Arthur S. Link, "What Happened to the Progressive Movement in the 1920s?" *Amer. Hist. Rev.*, 1959, 64:833–851.

62. Hawley, *The Great War and the Modern Order* (cit. n. 18).

63. See Pnina Abir-Am, "The Discourse of Physical Power and Biological Knowledge in the 1930s: A Reappraisal of the Rockefeller Foundation's 'Policy' in Molecular Biology," *Social Studies in Science*, 1982, 12:341–382; see also esp. the replies to that article, *ibid.*, 1984, 14:225–264.

64. Callie Hull and Clarence J. West, "Funds Available in the United States for the Support and Encouragement of Research in Science and Its Technologies," *Bull. Nat. Res. Council*, 1934, No. 95.

65. On Caltech see Robert H. Kargon, "Temple to Science: Cooperative Research and the Birth of the California Institute of Technology," *Historical Studies in the Physical Sciences*, 1977, 8:3–31; and John W. Servos, "The Knowledge Corporation: A. A. Noyes and Chemistry at Cal-Tech, 1915–1930," *Ambix*, 1976, 23:175–186. On state and technical universities see Alan H. Jones, *Philanthropic Foundations and the University of Michigan, 1922–1965* (Ann Arbor: Univ. Michigan School of Education, 1972); and John W. Servos, "The Industrial Relations of Science: Chemical Engineering and MIT, 1900–1939," *Isis*, 1980, 71:531–549. See Geiger, *To Advance Knowledge* (cit. n. 1), for a good survey of the university scene.

AFTER THE EMERGENCE: VOLUNTARY SUPPORT AND THE BUILDING OF AMERICAN RESEARCH UNIVERSITIES

ROGER GEIGER

The Standard American University

In 1908 and 1909 the science journalist Edwin E. Slosson visited and described fourteen of what he called "The Great American Universities." The volume of that title which he published still deserves a place among the most interesting books of this century on higher education. The members of his select group—California, Illinois, Michigan, Minnesota, and Wisconsin among the state universities; Columbia, Harvard, Pennsylvania, Princeton, and Yale from the descendents of the colonial colleges; and Cornell, Johns Hopkins, Stanford, and Chicago from the "new" endowed universities— these schools for the most part led other institutions of higher education in numbers of students, the size of their budgets, and the scholarly achievements of their faculties.[1]

More than a half-century later roughly the same group of institutions became the focus for another significant study, this time from an historical perspective: Laurence Veysey's *Emergence of the American University*.[2] The endpoint of Veysey's analysis occurs at the same juncture as Slosson's observations. And both authors agree about one fundamental characteristic of these institutions by that date: they largely seemed to have evolved into a single type that Slosson called "the standard American university . . . [a] peculiar combination which has evolved in the United States of instruction and research, graduate and undergraduate students, letters and technology" (382–83). Slosson was by far the more sanguine about this development. Veysey felt that competitive emulation between universities had produced "a dull standardization for the whole" (331); compartmentalization, which made the coexistence of these varied tasks possible, he described as a type of "ignorance"—"the patterned isolation of [the university's] component parts" (337–38); and Veysey seemed particularly dismayed that the themes of utility, research, and culture that he had so artfully tracked by this date had become homogenized into the standard pabulum of presidential addresses.

Regardless of what one makes of it, the evidence seems clear that by 1910 the major universities had grown much alike. The state universities and the largest of the privates were already discernible forerunners of the contemporary multiversity. As for the others, Stanford and Yale would shed many of their remaining idiosyncracies in the ensuing decade; Princeton had already built Dean Andrew Fleming West's notorious Graduate School, which had the ironic effect of anchoring Princeton permanently within the academic mainstream; and Johns Hopkins . . . well, it was the course of development there that prompted Slosson to discourse on standardization in the first place.

To a large extent the 'standard American university' of Slosson and Veysey constitutes the starting point for my own study of research universities in the first forty years of the century.[3] I have added MIT and (after 1920) Caltech to Slosson's list because of the undeniable importance of those two institutions for the development of American science. If this group of institutions was at the top of the academic heap in 1910, it was even more clearly so by 1940—and indeed, with minor adjustments, remains so today. I have preferred to employ the later coinage, *research* universities, because it accurately describes their distinctive position relative to the rest of American higher education even as early as 1910. Finally, I have departed in spirit from Veysey—but not from Slosson— by carrying the study of the research universities beyond the first decade of the century.

Slosson was told at all fourteen universities that he had arrived "at a critical moment"; that they were "in a transition stage" (75). Indeed, his whole enterprise was predicated upon explaining the vast changes that had occurred, and were still occurring, in America's most dynamic universities. For Veysey, however, the evolution of the American university had by 1910 reached a "stopping place." The tasks for the future were merely those of maintenance and duplication (338). The intellectual history of higher education, which Veysey himself relished, seemed to have drawn to a close; the destiny of research universities he would consign to the arcane history of bureaucracy.[4]

Obviously, I do not share this viewpoint. Veysey takes for granted a realization of the American university that was only dimly foreshadowed in the structures that had emerged by 1910. At that date, for example, American universities were little more than provincial outposts of European science. Twenty years later these same institutions could legitimately claim world leadership in many scientific fields. By then, too, they existed within a new and complex structure of philanthropic and coordinating agencies that transcended the organizational boundaries of individual universities. Closer to Veysey's central point, it is not clear to me why the ideas that inspired the creation of Caltech were any less novel or less interesting than those behind William Rainey Harper's Chicago. Caltech was, in fact, an embodiment of the research ideal that was, according to Veysey, hopelessly diluted by 1910. Caltech, in addition, even lacked a president and an athletic stadium! (cf. 340). Finally, and most pertinent to the subject of this paper, the process of standardization that Veysey depicted did not continue unabated after 1910: the direction of change actually reversed itself. Before long the research universities began to become differentiated from one another and, to a still greater extent, differentiated from the rest of American higher education. Clearly this is a history that should not be too readily dismissed.

In this essay it is only possible at best to indicate the logic behind this evolution—the forces that made these universities become more alike in years prior to 1910 (and indeed until 1920) and then less alike thereafter. This can be done most succinctly by examining the resources that research universities required for their continued development. Basically, these were three: students, faculty, and money.

The emphasis on students may seem incongruous here. After all, research purists like Daniel Coit Gilman, G. Stanley Hall, or Abraham Flexner had viewed students, especially American undergraduates, as the chief impediment to the advancement of knowledge. Even as late as the first half of the 1920s, it appeared that the locus of American science was destined to be in studentless independent research institutes, not universities. It turned out, however, that American society in this era was only willing to support consistently those knowledge-bearing institutions that also educated the young. For the research universities undergraduates were at first an unavoidable burden, but eventually they became an asset.

In the undertaking of fruitful research, the most critical and scarcest input is unquestionably the individuals who have the dedication and talent to produce valuable findings. Moreover, such individuals are relatively mobile. They consequently tend to gravitate toward those institutions that offer them the greatest scope for their science and the highest appreciation of their performance. Thus, the existence of physical facilities for research, the presence of like-minded colleagues, and—last and probably least—the offer of above-market salaries will tend to determine where productive scholars reside. Filthy lucre, in other words, entered the sacred groves of academe. How much a school could get, and how much of that it was willing to commit toward the general ends of research, were key issues in the development of research universities. Finances, in fact, explain something about the nature of the standard American university, circa 1910.

In the fall of 1909 the comprehensive private universities and the state universities covered by Slosson for the most part had enrollments in the four thousand range (see table 1). (The universities that appear to have fewer students in the table—California, Chicago, and Columbia—in fact contained other units that have not been counted here to maintain consistency.) These ten institutions

TABLE 1

Full-time Fall Enrollments in Research Universities, 1909 to 1939.

Small Private Universities	*1909*	*1914*	*1919*	*1924*	*1929*	*1934*	*1939*
Johns Hopkins	725	1058	1300[d]	1380	1468	1798	1653
MIT[a]	1530	1893	2884	2949	3066	2606[f]	3100
Princeton	1400	1641	1850	2392	2459	2622	2694
Stanford	1747	1888	2441	2949	3535	3670	4345
Yale	3297	3289	3326	4731	5084	5036	5367
SUBTOTAL	8699	9769	11081	14401	15612	15732	17159
National %	3.3	3.2	2.6	2.0	1.7	1.6	1.3
Comprehensive Private Universities							
Chicago	2690	3887	4682	4989	5867	5950	6011
Columbia[b]	3664	5248	5331	7640	8886	7981	8008
Cornell	4103	5078	5718	5232	5500	5717	6949
Harvard	4054	4534	5273	7035	8377	7671	8209
Pennsylvania	4599	5736	7094	7626	7119	6115	7347
SUBTOTAL	19110	24483	28098	32522	35749	33434	36524
National %	7.2	8.1	6.1	4.5	3.9	3.4	2.8
State Research Universities							
Cal-Berkeley[e]	3352	5848	9967	10476	11383	13218	17744
Illinois	4783	5137	8052	10089	12413	10747	13510
Michigan	4755	5522	8255	8856	9688	9005	12098
Minnesota	4121	3940	7451	9417	10657	12188	15301
Wisconsin	4295	4874	6875	7643	9468	8053	11268
SUBTOTAL	21306	25321	40600	46481	53609	53211	69921
National %	8.0	8.4	8.8	6.5	5.8	5.5	5.3
NATIONAL TOTAL:	266654	303223	462445	716000[d]	924275	975000[d]	1317158

Source: Edwin E. Slosson, *Great American Universities* (New York: Macmillan, 1910), (1909 unless otherwise noted); *Science* 65(1915):92; *School and Society* 12(1920):110–13; 21(1925):154; 30(1929):794–95; 40(1934):793–94; 50(1939):778–79. Totals from *Report of the Commisioner of Education* (1915); and, *Biennial Surveys of Education.*

[a]From *Biennial Survey of Education.*

[b]Not including Barnard College and Teachers College; from Columbia University, *President's Reports.*

[c]From Verne A. Stadtman, ed. *The Centennial Record of the University of California* (Berkeley: University of California, 1967).

[d]Estimated.

[e]1923–24.

[f]1933–34.

were the largest universities in the country. From the turn of the century until World War I they enrolled one-sixth of American college students. In these years bigger was better for American universities: the three biggest by Slosson's accounting—Columbia, Harvard, and Chicago—were in fact the best. The dynamics behind this situation largely account for the phenomenon of standardization. At least three factors seem to have been at work.

First was the pattern of financing private universities. According to Trevor Arnett, the expert on college finance for the Rockefeller philanthropies, an endowed university should ideally receive about half of its income from student tuition and half from its invested funds.[5] In addition, the faculty payroll would typically consume about half of a university budget. Thus, a rough equation was implicitly advanced: students ought to pay the immediate cost of their instruction, meaning the salaries of their teachers, while the university's other assets would absorb the overhead costs. By

1910 Chicago, Columbia, Harvard, and Yale slightly exceeded this standard, while Cornell, Penn, and Princeton were close to this mark.[6] Given this standard, then, more students meant more faculty. The natural means for building departments sufficiently large to keep pace with the expansion of knowledge was by increasing the student body.

Arnett's standard required that universities have a means of attracting capital as well in order to provide for their remaining financial needs: it is here that the second factor, philanthropy, comes in. During this era colleges and universities basically found voluntary support locally. "When Harvard needs money she seeks it on State Street,"[7] was a dictum that held true until the beginning of this century. The dependence of private universities upon local benefactors created an implicit obligation to fulfill the needs of a local or regional constituency. In this respect they scarcely differed from the state universities of the West, which justified their public support through the services they rendered to the populations of their respective states. The nature of those services is the third factor behind the growth and standardization of these universities.

Although there was a gradual secular expansion of traditional college departments, the spectacular growth rates of this period were caused by the creation and expansion of additional units. The undergraduate arts college comprised only a fraction of the emergent research universities: Columbia College students comprised only 19 percent of the Columbia University enrollment; the comparable figure for Penn was just 9 percent; for Michigan 34 percent; for Illinois, 20 percent. For all fourteen of Slosson's universities the arts college averaged 31 percent of total enrollments.[8] The new compartments of the research universities—engineering, commerce, education, dentistry, pharmacy, art, and music—as well as the traditional professional schools of law and medicine were more direct embodiments of university service. They were, in fact, often begun through the initiative of outsiders with major gifts.

The exceptions to this type of growth—the smaller research universities—tend to validate the pattern. Princeton, and to a lesser extent Yale, had weak local ties and thus never accepted the obligation for local service. Stanford and Johns Hopkins, on the other hand, were at this juncture still trying to live on their original endowments. Stanford, in addition, had a donor constituency of one—Jane Lathrop Stanford—who among other things insisted upon limiting the size of the university. Hopkins, however, was just beginning to provide services to the Baltimore area and also beginning to seek to augment its endowment.

It should be emphasized that the three kinds of resources needed by universities had to be consistent with one another. In this era a greater number of students and schools allowed universities to hire more faculty while also demonstrating service to their communities. Service encouraged capital gifts that augmented the facilities and general research capabilities of the university. And that, in turn, fulfilled the principal wishes of a research-minded faculty. For each university the formula was slightly different; but it was sufficiently similar for the ten large research universities to propel a process of isomorphism, or standardization.

Voluntary Support and the Differentiation of Universities

The obvious question, then, is—what happened to change this pattern? Although these factors were to a large extent interdependent, I believe that the crucial change occurred in the most exogenous of them—in the nature of voluntary support.

The history of higher education philanthropy remains largely uncharted, despite the valuable pioneering effort by Merle Curti and Roderick Nash.[9] By that I mean that not even a tentative sense of chronology or periodization yet exists. Consequently, in order to facilitate my own history, I propose that one slight seam be recognized in this otherwise seamless web: 1905. That year was a turning point for fund-raising at both Harvard and Yale, and those two institutions were the vanguard of American higher education in this respect. In general, one could say that fund-raising was a difficult business even for these universities before that date. The principal form of major gifts—bequests—could not be arranged to suit the needs of the university; and most of the giving of living donors tended to be restricted to specific uses (prizes, scholarships, memorials, subscriptions, etc.) while the university's chief need was for more unrestricted income. After 1905 the number of living donors increased, the frequency of major donations rose, and more gifts became available for unrestricted use. For a few fortunate institutions the money began to pour in; and most fortunate of all were Harvard and Yale.

The Yale Alumni Fund was created independently in 1891 to allow loyal graduates able to spare only small sums to aid their alma mater collectively. For the next ten years the Fund annually collected and turned over to Yale about $10,000 of current income. By 1905, however, donations were coming into the Fund at such a rate that a portion began to be set aside in a Principal Fund. The rapid growth of the alumni contributions to current expenses and to endowment symbolize a transformation in Yale's outlook and Yale's fortunes. About this time Yale perceived its reliance upon its alumni to be its "distinctive position." It would soon boast that its endowment was the most "democratic" in American higher education. Moreover, these contributions made a difference. Within five years it appeared to President Arthur Twining Hadley that Yale's persistent financial woes were lifted for the first time within living memory.

Meanwhile at Harvard, whose voluntary support already vastly out-distanced all rivals, significant changes were also taking place. For a 1904–05 fund-raising drive Harvard went beyond State Street to New York City in order to tap prosperous graduates for substantial contributions. The same year, 1905, the class of 1880 gave the university $100,000 for unrestricted endowment. The significance of this act was that every ensuing class followed this precedent on the occasion of their twenty-fifth anniversary. In a short time these gifts alone roughly equaled the Principal Fund of the Yale Alumni.

The new pattern of giving was enormously lucrative. In the decade from 1905 to 1915 both schools added about $10 million to their endowments. But that was just the beginning. During the decade of the 1920s Yale received $91 million in voluntary support, while Harvard trailed slightly with receipts of $83 million. It took some time, however, for perceptions and actions to become reoriented toward this new, magnanimous constituency of donors. A new pattern of development for the private research universities only crystallized after the war.

War conditions unsettled both the finances and the attendance patterns of American higher education. The severe inflation that accompanied the war struck colleges at a time when they could do little to enhance their revenues. Faculty salaries, in particular, suffered severe losses in terms of purchasing power, and fears were widespread that professors would seek more lucrative salaries in industry. Virtually all the private universities undertook fund-raising drives immediately after the war with the avowed purpose of raising faculty salaries. At the same time, the postwar years saw an unexpected surge in enrollments all across higher education. The universities found their facilities strained to the limit, while their budgets were deeply in the red.

In time the financial side of this dual problem was resolved quite satisfactorily. The postwar endowment drives were entirely successful for the research universities. Higher salaries seemed to stabilize the faculty crisis (if there had in fact been one). These achievements were then, in effect, magnified by a period of economic deflation. By the early years of the 1920s the outlook had brightened considerably for the research universities. But the enrollment surge in American higher education continued unabated after the effects of demobilization had long passed. This phenomenon was greeted first by surprise, then by alarm within the leading sectors of private higher education.

The logic of the situation was clear, even though a course of action was not. While the universities were basically trying to restore their capital assets to something like their prewar values, further expansion would only create additional capital needs. Instead, it appeared that a period of consolidation was in order. The presidents of both Harvard and Columbia said after the war that the proliferation of university functions had gone far enough, that it was time to perfect and intensify the university's work. Perhaps more significantly, the foundations changed their minds. After a prodigious effort at building university endowments immediately after the war, the General Education Board soon realized that enrollment growth had made its goals chimerical. Soon Trevor Arnett was saying that undergraduates should pay the full cost of their education and that the task of private philanthropy should henceforth be to encourage research and graduate education.[10] Moreover, there was a pervasive disillusionment caused by the exuberance of the collegiate culture. Too many people, it began to be said, were going to college. In this atmosphere it was easy for the private research universities to reach the decision to place limitations on their enrollments. In 1919 an effective ceiling was placed on the Columbia College entering class; in 1920 the Cornell faculty voted to limit enrollment; Stanford adopted a fixed class size in 1921, followed by Princeton, Yale (1922), Harvard (1923), and Chicago (1928).

The reasons for this step were not solely financial; they were also social and pedagogical. Any attempt to separate these tangled motives would be futile. Rather, one should see how they interpenetrated one another and reinforced the interests of the principle constituencies involved.

It was easy to persuade private college alumni that too many people were going to college. Their alma maters had grown enormously since their day; and perceived changes in the social and ethnic composition of students, minor though they were, were scarcely welcomed in an age of rampant nativism. Alumni in general were readily sold on the theme that the time had come to enhance the quality of their university, especially when they were assured, as at Yale, that no qualified graduate's son would be denied admission.

Administrators of the eastern universities realized how vital it was to retain the loyalties of the prep school crowd, who set the social tone for the campus as a whole. Admission schemes were already in place to provide them ready access, so it was merely a matter of raising the bar a bit for the others. Limitation also held the appealing prospect of raising academic standards in the undergraduate college. In addition, there were so many things that the university genuinely needed, or thought it needed, more than facilities for additional students.

Finally, the attraction of no-growth was probably greatest for faculty. Fewer students to teach (given some additional appointments); better students to teach: it promised to be a solution to the traditional teaching/research dilemma of the American university![11]

The Divergence of Public and Private Research Universities

The establishment of enrollment ceilings at the leading private universities in the 1920s essentially placed the public and private research universities on two different developmental tracks. "A state university," President Marion L. Burton of Michigan emphasized at the beginning of the 1920s, "must accept happily the conclusion that it is destined to be large" and should use the advantages of size to attain a distinctive form of excellence.[12] For the private universities, however, bigger was no longer better. Henceforth they would try to be better rather than bigger.

The enrollment figures bear out this divergence (see table). From 1909 to 1924 the small private research universities grew by almost two-thirds, but in the next fifteen years (1924–39) they expanded by less than 20 percent. During the same intervals the comprehensive privates grew by close to 70 percent, and then just 12 percent. The state research universities, however, more than doubled (+118 percent), and then rose by another 50 percent. By 1939 the average size of these state universities was 14,000 full-time students, while the comprehensive privates averaged 7300. (The small privates ranged from 900 at Caltech to 5000 at Yale.) During these same years the research universities were a shrinking segment of American higher education. From 20 percent of total enrollments in 1914, they declined to 14 percent in 1924, and to less than 10 percent by 1939. These quantitative trends are superficial indications of fundamental developments within the research universities.

Perhaps most striking is the coherence of the research universities as a group during the twenties and thirties. Caltech managed to join this elite, but no institution dropped out, even though these two decades witnessed far-reaching changes in university research. A variety of things happened within this group, however. The "big three" remained at the top of the prestige hierarchy for the entire period. The conspicuous winners in terms of prestige enhancement were undoubtedly Caltech, Princeton, and California—Berkeley three radically different types of institution. Wisconsin and Penn probably declined. Nevertheless, by the late 1930s these sixteen institutions all had more distinguished scientists on their faculties by a considerable margin than any other university.

Two factors were probably paramount in stimulating the strong academic development of these sixteen schools. First was the competitive structure of American higher education. These universities had to offer above-market salaries to their top researchers, had to provide them with the time and facilities for research, and had to subsidize their graduate students—or face losing them to other institutions that would do such things. But something additional was needed to assure that these universities would be motivated to compete with one another in just this way. That something was largely provided by the foundations.

The major foundations did not begin to pour large sums into university research until the mid-twenties. They then began making large capital grants for the establishment and maintainance of research facilities, as well as providing "fluid research funds" in given areas that universities could allocate themselves to faculty research projects. Major grants were largely confined to the research universities, and research capital was given almost exclusively to private institutions. Foundation preferences in grant-making strongly encouraged these universities to make research a high institutional priority. Wickliffe Rose, head of both the General Education Board and the International Education Board, advocated a policy of "making the peaks higher"—that is, supporting the strongest scientific centers. In addition, universities were often asked to match foundation capital grants with funds raised from their own donors. These policies assured that a significant portion of the substantial amounts of voluntary support received during these years would be devoted to academic strengthening and research. By the late 1920s it became apparent that no private university could remain in the ranks of the research universities without the aid of foundation support. At MIT, for one, this realization caused a major reorientation of research policies. In the 1930s foundation support for research was increasingly given in the form of project grants. Here too, grants were made to the most capable scientists at institutions possessing the necessary facilities. They consequently went predominantly to the research universities, public and private. Nevertheless, while foundation support for research tended to produce uniform academic aspirations within the university research system, considerable diversity existed in the means employed to attain this end.

Institutional Patterns

As voluntary support came to loom large in the destiny of research universities, their character tended to be shaped by the amounts that they received and the sources from which it came. The set of programs that each university offered, the number and type of students it considered optimal, the institutional outlook and priorities—all these things were not determined by its donors but were part of a coherent and consistent institutional personality to which the sources of voluntary support were an integral component. The divergent tendencies of the top three research universities should be sufficient to illustrate this.

By 1910 it was abundantly evident that the great strength of Harvard University was made possible by the generosity of the Harvard College alumni. The general feeling was that the College had been neglected during the long presidency of Charles Eliot (1869–1909); however, the collegiate experience of Harvard undergraduates was uppermost in the mind of his successor, A. Lawrence Lowell (1909–1933). Freshman dormitories, the tutorial system, the fortuitous creation of the Harvard houses, *and* selective admissions are the distinctive policies associated with his tenure. All this was possible without any attenuation of research or graduate education. The extraordinary affluence of Harvard permitted it to sustain the most prestigious faculty in the country. Further help from the foundations naturally followed. Harvard was ultimately able to offer virtually optimal conditions to both its future college alumni and its research-minded faculty. The weight of alumni giving produced essentially the same orientation toward undergraduate teaching at both Princeton and Yale, but with rather different consequences for scientific research. Princeton made a concerted effort at developing the natural sciences in the 1920s, and as a result it improved its scientific standing more than any other private university in this era. Yale, with its rather tardy integration of the Sheffield Scientific School, was reluctant to make such a commitment and consequently had difficulty sustaining its previously strong position in the sciences.

The University of Chicago practically invented the role of urban service university by instituting such novelties as summer school and extension study and by establishing practical curricula like commerce or household administration. Accordingly, the growth of the university was supported by local Chicago philanthropists in addition to the major benefactions of John D. Rockefeller, Sr. It is interesting, then, that by the 1920s Chicago was turning into an ivory tower among research universities—the most single-mindedly academic institution in this group. This seems to have been possible because of the special relationship the university continued to have with the Rockefeller wealth. The Laura Spelman Rockefeller Memorial, the General Education and International Education boards and the Rockefeller Foundation itself—all found reason to make frequent and substantial capital grants to Chicago. These funds largely assured the academic preeminence of the university. In the meantime wealthy Chicagoans continued to give, but chiefly to support the professional side of the university. Thus, it developed great strength on the graduate level—graduate training and research in the academic disciplines, and more locally oriented professional schools. Unlike all other research universities (save Johns Hopkins), the undergraduate college carried little weight. Its alumni for the most part were neither wealthy nor devoted to the university. The college could thus become the object of internal discord, and collegiate loyalties were held in such disdain that Chicago became the only major university to abandon football.

Columbia University almost defies characterization. While the elite colleges of Columbia and Barnard were shielded from the masses through restricted admissions, the university sponsored Seth Low Junior College in Brooklyn and aggressively promoted extension courses. It served its urban community further through Teachers College and the summer school. At the same time its professional schools maintained links with New York's professional/business elite. Lodged within this edifice, holding various overlapping affiliations, was one of the country's most distinguished academic faculties. Columbia tried to be all things to all people and somehow managed to bring it off. This was largely accomplished through compartmentalization. Columbia went about its many tasks, and related to its numerous constituencies, through separate units that were either completely self-contained (Barnard, Teachers College) or nearly so. When all these units are taken into account, Columbia was twice as large at the end of the 1920s as the other private comprehensive research universities. Columbia's many commitments produced an insatiable need for capital. Its alumni support was comparatively weak, and grants from foundations were never overwhelming. Columbia consequently depended chiefly upon New York City millionaires. Such benefactors, however, also tended to have giving agendas of their own. It was always a struggle to harness such giving to the immediate needs of the university. Inevitably, some of these gifts imparted additional responsibilities. When President Nicholas Murray Butler took the reins of Columbia in 1901 he characterized the institution as a "giant in chains" because of its many needs and inadequate means. Ironically, his leadership largely assured that Columbia's needs would grow at least as rapidly as its endowment.

A separate story could be told about each of the private research universities concerning the nature of its voluntary support and its academic development during the interwar years. For the sake of completeness, however, it is more important to indicate how the state research universities kept pace with their private sector rivals during this era of private financing of university research.

State-supported universities basically prospered during the 1920s. For the five public research universities enrollments grew 44 percent during the decade, while legislative appropriations for current expenses increased by 130 percent.[13] Like their private counterparts, then, the state research universities were able to concentrate their resources and enhance their research capabilities. In particular, they all were able to set aside a part of their growing budgets explicitly for research, something that had not been possible before the war. The most conspicuous success among this group was the University of California, which forged into the front ranks of research universities during this period. Less obviously, the University of Michigan enhanced an already solid standing. In both cases something more than legislative apropriations were needed.

California and Michigan enlarged their faculties more than other state universities during the 1920s, thus continuing the basic prewar course of development. The consequent youth and dynamism of their faculties proved particularly valuable during the years of retrenchment that followed. During both decades Michigan and California consistently enlarged their graduate enrollments, thus effectively drawing teaching responsibilities closer to faculty research. Both institutions had presidents who favored science and academic development generally. More significantly, though, the faculties of both schools gained considerably greater administrative authority in this period. Finally, these two universities were the leading recipients of voluntary support in the public sector. Michigan was particularly fortunate in receiving a multi-million dollar gift from the Rackham Fund that was entirely devoted to graduate education and research. Under this combination of circumstances growth was entirely compatible with academic excellence.

In sum, by the end of the 1920s the standard American university of Slosson and Veysey had been transcended by a new pattern of professional uniformity and institutional diversity. The faculty of research universities belonged to national disciplinary communities. Their professional activities in their subject matter reflected the thinking of these wider communities, and their treatment as professionals by their own institution conformed to a wider system of norms regarding rank, promotion, compensation, and opportunities for research. The institutions to which they belonged, however, related to the extra-academic world in strikingly different ways. These differences were manifested in the kinds of teaching responsibilities they assumed, the services they rendered, and the resources they were capable of devoting to research.

This cross-cutting of discipline and institution has been described by Burton R. Clark as the "master-matrix of higher education."[14] In the university research system of the United States these cross-cutting strands have contributed to both the strength and the pluralism of American science. The pervasive influence of the national scientific community has been a force guiding the research universities within the academic mainstream, while established channels of voluntary support have shaped the character of particularly the private research universities. The importance of both these considerations—of pleasing the scientists and scholars on whom the institution's academic reputation depends and satisfying an external constituency on whom the flow of resources depends—created a tension that determined the orientation of each university. This tension has prevented the institutes of technology from neglecting basic science in favor of applied work; it has restrained the state universities from sacrificing quality to quantity; it has mitigated the social exclusiveness of the eastern private schools; and it has moderated the inescapable service commitments of urban research universities. At the same time, the association of these diverse particular roles with fundamental academic inquiry has bolstered their effectiveness and prestige. Institutional pluralism has been an important component in the extraordinary success of American research universities. Over the years they have proven to be more dynamic and more adaptable than the "standard American university," had it persisted, is likely ever to have been.

Notes

1. Edwin E. Slosson. *Great American Universities* (N.Y., 1910).
2. Laurence R. Veysey, *The Emergence of the American University* (Chicago. 1965).
3. Roger L. Geiger, *American Research Universities in the Twentieth Century* (N.Y., forthcoming). This volume contains more complete documentation for the material used in this paper.
4. Laurence R. Veysey, "The History of Education," *Reviews in American History*, 10, 4(Dec. 1982):281–91.
5. Trevor Arnett, *College and University Finance* (N.Y., 1922). pp. 10–12; also. U.S. Bureau of Education, *Bulletin*, No. 30(1918):44.
6. Data from Geiger.
7. Bishop William Lawrence, *Memories of a Happy Life* (N.Y., 1926), pp. 215–16; Seymour E. Harris, *The Economics of Harvard* (N.Y., 1970). p. 78.
8. Data from Slosson.
9. Merle Curti & Roderick Nash, *Philanthropy and the Shaping of American Higher Education* (New Brunswick, 1965).
10. Trevor Arnett, "To What Extent Should College Students Pay the Cost of Education?" Association of University and College Business Officers of the Eastern States, *Minutes of the Eighth Annual Meeting*, (1927). pp. 18–29.
11. Hugh Hawkins, "University Identity: The Teaching and Research Functions" in *The Organization of Knowledge in Modern America. 1860–1920*. Alexandra Oleson & John Voss. eds. (Baltimore. 1979). pp. 285–312.
12. Quoted in Howard H. Peckham, *The Making of the University of Michigan, 1817–1967* (Ann Arbor, 1967). p. 140.
13. Data from Geiger.
14. Burton R. Clark, "Perspectives on Higher Education. The Organizational View" in *Perspectives on Higher Education: Eight Disciplinary and Comparative Views*. Burton R. Clark, ed. (Los Angeles. 1984).

FOUNDATIONS, UNIVERSITIES, AND RESEARCH

HAROLD J. LASKI

It seems fated that the social sciences should take over their methodology from sister-disciplines which aim at, and achieve, results which are not open to those who study human relations. In the eighteenth century the achievements of Newton led students of politics to find in physical analogies the sovereign key to their problems; in the nineteenth century the discoveries of Darwin made the pursuit of biological metaphor the favorite sport of almost every thinker with a book to write. In our own day the symbols are drawn from another field. It has become fashionable for the observer to apply to the social process the latest discoveries of psychology; and the complexes of the statesman, the listed impulses of the man in the street, the unreasoning instincts of men acting as a crowd are all joyously scrutinized as the home of the final secret. Somehow, it seems to be thought, psychology at least will give us a social law of gravitation.

But a new technic has appeared, the votaries of which are as ardent in their faith as ever were the followers of a religious creed. In the past, for the most part, men analyzed in solitude the facts before them; and they put down, without much mutual discussion, such vision as was vouchsafed to them. This procedure, it appears, was an error of high magnitude. "We risk waste effort," writes Professor Wesley Mitchell, "when we use our narrowly limited individual resources in attacking problems which might yield to joint endeavors. The mathematical, physical, and biological sciences were first in this country to organize an effort to see their problems whole and to facilitate co-operation among specialists concerned with clusters of problems. But shortly after the National Research Council was formed several representatives of political science, economics, sociology, and statistics came together for a similar purpose. Out of this informal beginning the Social Science Research Council developed in 1923. It was presently strengthened and broadened by the accession of psychologists, anthropologists, and historians." And out of these small beginnings there has developed an organization of considerable magnitude, with its executive, its conferences, its committees on problems and policy, its advisory committees on method, agriculture, corporate relations, crime, cultural areas, migration, industrial relations, and the rest, its grants-in-aid to the established, and its fellowships to the immature. We need, it seems to affirm, to proceed upon the principles of mass-production: division of labor at the base, scientific assembling of the material prepared at the top. When this is done in each department of social science we shall have—at least we may hope—laws of political behavior the exactitude of which will be comparable to those of chemistry or of physics. The work now afoot may, a generation from now, come to mark an epoch in the development of social science.

And Professor Mitchell would, I think, agree that the universities have gone to work with a stout heart and an iron will. No university to-day is complete without its research institute; no foundation is worthy of the name unless its directors are anxiously scanning the horizon for suitable universities which can be endowed with such institutes. There are few universities where the movement is not away from the discussion of principle to the description and tabulation of fact. Everything is being turned into material for quantitative expression since this best yields to co-operative effort. We investigate output per man per hour per machine in every industry and in every country. We study the movement of prices in every century and every continent. We describe the tax system, or the method of railroad regulation, or the promotion system in the civil service in India and China, in

Italy and Albania and Japan. Research associations in the different social sciences are passionately at work, devising methods, comparing methods, holding conferences "for consecutive thinking and planning not feasible at other seasons." We have bibliographies of special subjects and bibliographies of bibliographies. We have brief abstracts of papers, and long abstracts of papers; soon we are to have a whole journal composed of nothing but abstracts.

And, of course, we study what we do. The research institutes report to the universities; the universities report to the directors of foundations; the directors of foundations report to their trustees; the trustees seek reports from detached outsiders upon the reports they have received. Conferences are held for the reception of reports; and men are judged by the impression of them the reports convey. Trustees look to university presidents to pick the professors likely to attract endowments from the foundations; university presidents look for professors who can produce the kind of research in which the foundations are interested; professors search for healthy young graduates who can provide the basis for the ultimate generalizations. There are endless committees to co-ordinate or correlate or integrate. There are new executive positions for men who do not themselves research but judge whether other people are suitable for the task of research. These are formidable people, widely traveled, gracious, but firm in manner, as befits men who have vast benefactions to dispense. There are interim reports, special reports, confidential reports, final reports. There are programs for the development of every theme. There are surveys for the dissection of every problem, industrial, racial, national, international. There are experimental centers, statistical centers, analytical centers. More energy, I venture to believe, has gone this last five years into the systematization of research in this field than in any previous generation of intellectual effort.

II

If I suggest here certain skepticisms as to the policy involved, it is with no feeling except one of admiration for the ardor and enthusiasm which has gone into the effort. My doubts center about three aspects of the situation. I doubt whether the results to be achieved are likely to be proportionate to the labor involved. I doubt, in the second place, whether the effect upon university institutions is likely, in the long run, to be healthy; and I doubt, in the third place, whether the result of the policy will not be to give to the foundations a dominating control over university life which they quite emphatically ought not to have.

Let me take each of these aspects separately. In the social sciences every investigator has two great problems. He has first of all to find his facts, and secondly, he has to assign a scheme of values to them. They are not, as William James said, born free and equal. They have to be weighed. They have to be given a significance most of which depends upon the personal philosophy of the individual investigator. If, for instance, I tabulate the membership of the English Cabinet since 1801, and discover that some sixty per cent were born of immediately aristocratic parentage, I have merely provided a basis for interpretations of the most diverse kind. I may take the result to mean the fine determination of the English peerage to devote itself to public service; I may take it to measure the differential advantage an English aristocrat possesses when he embarks upon a political career; or I may take it as a criterion of the degree to which the English social system puts barriers in the way of the common man who desires to distinguish himself in political life. Obviously enough, my interpretation will largely depend upon my personal scheme of values. The latter has no validity until it has the facts upon which to work. It becomes of intense importance as soon as the facts are at its disposal.

Now my own argument is that co-operative research is of high value once it has been determined to find a body of facts; it is of dubious value in determining what body of facts would be significant when found, and of still more dubious value in assigning values to them after their discovery. For the proof of these things I appeal to anyone who has ever engaged seriously in the business of research. One finds a problem which clamors for solution. One begins to dig, and the mere process of digging by oneself is a definite means of illumination. One gets material, broods upon it, arranges it, dissects it, discusses it. It becomes a part of one's personality. It becomes absorbed into the whole scheme of one's philosophy. It gives point and color to the whole. It is intimately a part of oneself.

The revelation of what it seems to imply is borne in upon one almost unconsciously by living with it. And the generalization is made, usually in a difficult solitude, and in a mood which, if it is akin to anything, is essentially allied to artistic inspiration. That is why, I would add, the great scientist, the great philosopher, the great historian have always been in their essence great artists.

If it is the thesis of co-operative research that it can replace the process I have just described, my answer is that it is simply untrue; and that it is untrue even in the mathematical, physical, and biological sciences which are adduced in proof of the proposition. If that is not the claim, then my argument is that the place for co-operative research is in aiding the thinker to secure the best possible materials in the easiest possible way for his thought. Co-operative research, in other words, stands to the social sciences in the same relation as computing to the astronomer or as the making of slides or the provision of animals for dissection to the biologist. He indicates what he wants, and the materials are placed at his disposal. His eyes, his time, his energy have been saved. But the really vital task is still his, and no amount of co-operation can ever replace his vital duty to do it himself. Co-operation can suggest questions to be asked, difficulties to be considered, material to be searched. It cannot replace, and it has never adequately replaced, the vision and the insight of the individual thinker.

It is, of course, all to the good that men engaged in these disciplines should meet and talk over their common problems. It is all to the good, also, that they should pool their common knowledge and suggest lines of inquiry which their experience as investigators indicates to them as desirable. Every university teacher who is worth his salt is doing that every day as a matter of normal routine. It does not need any elaborate organization to make it possible; indeed, it is likely to be the more fruitful the less it assumes a formal shape. And so far as aid in the collection of material is concerned, and its reduction to usable form, that is either a matter for the trained computer, or else for the young graduate student who is learning the business of serious research. If the latter has real ability he will not do it for long; the call to original investigation of a superior kind is too insistent to be stifled. Here, again, it is extraordinarily difficult to see why there is need for elaborate institutes of research, with executive staffs and growing hordes of faded underlings. Anyone who has done investigation knows that their aid at the critical point is essentially a *pis aller*. Once the stage has been reached where judgments have to be made, the investigator, like the soldier at headquarters, must make his own decisions and stand or fall by them. He will never see clearly if he is content to see through other men's eyes.

All this applies with especial force to the immense apparatus of bibliography and abstraction now being prepared for his assistance. A fairly long experience has taught me that if of the listing of titles there is no end, most of them are not worth listing and do not repay investigation. What one wants is the critical bibliography—like those, for instance, of Charles Gross—which warn as well as encourage. Essentially the same is true of abstracts. Either a paper is worth reading as a whole, in which case one merely wants its title, or it is not worth reading at all, in which case to make an abstract is a waste of time and money. Yet thousands of dollars are being spent annually in America on bibliographies which are a snare and a delusion; and one of the greatest foundations has just devoted half a million dollars to a journal which is simply to contain abstracts of articles in the social sciences. It is not, I think, going beyond the mark to describe most of this expenditure as simply wasted. I can have confidence in, say, a book on American history recommended to me by Professor Turner, or in one on economics recommended to me by Professor Allyn Young; but if I have merely a title from an unknown bibliographer who has probably not examined the book, in the absence of other information, I save my eyes and my time.

It is, indeed, an excellent side of this co-operative research that it should lead to the award of fellowships to young men of promise in the hope that their leisure may bear fruit in research. But here it is imperative to award the fellowship essentially on promise and not because a student proposes to examine some subject in a list of which the research institute or committee has approved. Anyone who reads the output of books on this side of the problem cannot help but doubt whether it is promise that comes first. So many of the themes chosen are hackneyed; so many of them are really matter for an article rather than a book. Few of them deserve to be printed, and fewer still are ever reprinted. Let the reader take the long lists of doctoral dissertations published by the Library of Congress and he will observe, on any careful examination, that most of them were intellectually dead before they were born. And the trouble is, further, that under the blessing of a planning committee, a young man who has been assigned a fellowship for a given theme must continue his researches in that surrounding field unless he desires a reputation for instability of mental temper. A young professor who had investigated a small subject as it exists in America and had come to England for a year to investigate the same theme here paid me a visit. All that he could want to know about it, he could have learned in six weeks. But what with his bibliographies and card-indexes, he was able quite without effort to spend his full quota of time upon material unworthy of his powers. Some of my colleagues and I tried vainly to tempt him into alien paths; but he seemed to feel that it was not the part of academic wisdom to venture upon the unexpected.

On this head, then, I venture the guess that, compared to the results attainable, the money spent on the collection and preparation of material is enormously disproportionate. I know, on incontrovertible authority, of an American foundation which has produced a single volume at a cost of eighty thousand dollars; and I do not think that volume could be regarded as epoch-making. I know of another foundation each of whose efforts has cost some eight or nine thousand dollars; all of them have had a largely temporary value, and few of them have done other than summarize, often with admirable vigor and accuracy, material easily available elsewhere. Even where the valuable work is being done of giving grants-in-aid to deserving scholars, the cost of the panoply of investigating the claim, deciding upon its merits, and allocating the sum decided upon is greatly in excess of anything necessary. Most of it could quite easily be unpaid work, done by other scholars for love of their subject; and this method would usually save many a scholar many heart-burnings as he seeks to explain his purposes to a bright young, or pompous old, executive of some foundation, to whom the very meaning of research is, in any effectively creative sense, entirely unknown.

III

I turn to the second aspect of the problem: the effect of the system upon the universities. Here, the controlling fact is that the great foundations have immense sums to disburse. It is the inevitable result that an energetic university president or an ambitious university teacher should think out his plans in terms of what the foundation is likely to approve. Certain obvious consequences follow. "Dangerous" problems are not likely to be investigated, especially not by "dangerous" men; that would not win the esteem of the trustees who can be counted upon to dislike disturbing themes. I know, for instance, of an important project, brought to a point after long and difficult negotiation, which was killed by a foundation in the belief that its completion would be displeasing to Signor Mussolini. And it must be remembered that the system, as it works, is all to the disadvantage of the scholar whose results, however important, come slowly. The president wants material for a formidable annual report which will obtain a renewal of the grant. Other things being equal, his blessing goes to the members of the staff who can give him material for such a report; and, where vacancies occur, search will be made for men of a similar stamp elsewhere. The personnel of the university, in a word, comes to be dominated by the "executive" type of professor, who is active in putting its goods into the shop-window. The university with a big grant has its place in the press. The president is marked out as a man able to do things. The enthusiasm for quantity—the most insidious of all academic diseases—grows by what it feeds on. Those who cannot aid the development of the new tendencies find themselves without influence and discouraged. Men, only too often, are judged by their output; and, as soon as that point is reached, they spend their time, not in reflection upon ultimate principle, but in the description of social machinery or the collection of materials. It is the business of a university to breed great scholars; and in such an atmosphere great scholars will hardly be bred.

Nor must we neglect the effect of this upon the teaching in the university itself. Anyone who analyzes in this regard the tendencies in social science will, I think, be struck by two things. There is an increasing drift away from the study of basic principles and towards the study of concrete facts; and there is an increasing disposition to give the student practical field-work of some kind.

I speak here, of course, of the undergraduate period. Of that stage, whether in England or America, I can only say this: it is all that a teacher can hope to do, even with an able student, in the time at his disposal, to make the student aware of the fundamental problems in his subject. His main urgency must be the attempt to clear away the bewildering mass of detail and to make the student see a few big general principles in firm outline. I taught in American universities for four years; and I have had many American students since my return to London. My difficulty with them has always been that, though they have been taught to assimilate masses of fact, they have rarely learned to reflect upon the scheme of values they ought to read into those facts. Still more rarely do they attempt that integration of the social sciences which Professor Mitchell declares it is one of the purposes of co-operative research to attain. They keep their principles of economics in one compartment, and their principles of politics in another. They even more rarely relate the social sciences to philosophy, or glimpse the significance of that totality of vision which Professor Whitehead has set out with such magistral nobility. Only principles at this stage will cause them the intellectual excitement which is the main business of him who teaches undergraduates; and the passion for pouring upon him masses of concrete description prevents him from penetrating beyond them to their real significance.

One of the universities most noted for its adherence to this method of research tells us with enthusiasm of how the new technic has vivified its methods of teaching. Students are enabled to embark upon "field-work" in their courses; they gain a living sense of the concrete material. They learn, we are to assume, that "pungent sense of effective reality" which tears through the miasma of dialectic. But here, surely, there are many things to be said. If a student grapples with a big body of material, seeks to arrange it, and to discover its significance, no one can doubt that the experience will be of high value to him. Probably what he has to report about it will not be very valuable; but he will experience something of the excitement that comes to a young lawyer who handles his first case in court. That, however, is not what is meant by "field-work" in the new sense of the word. It means that the student goes out and collects a body of facts for his teacher, that he co-operates with the latter in some part of an investigation. Now if that is done on any considerable scale it is taking the student's mind away from essentials; it is teaching him not to inquire and to evaluate, but to describe. It is computer's work made better only to the degree that the teacher later explains what meaning he attaches to the result.

The real value of the method lies there; and the process of collecting the material bears the same relation to the task of teaching the student to think clearly as a visit to a precinct station to an explanation of the police-power. And if any considerable time is spent on the task there is loss we can ill afford of the opportunity we have to make the student see the great problems we confront and give him awareness of how great men, ancient or modern, have sought to solve them. I still dare to believe that an undergraduate who had glimpsed the reason why the mind of man still echoes the thought Plato uttered two thousand years ago would be fitter for the task of research than one who had co-operated in a house-to-house inquiry into non-voting in Keokuk and assisted in tabulating the results.

The truth is that we are in danger of becoming over-interested in the collection of material for its own sake and under-interested in the problem of the philosophy the material implies. We are getting absorbed in method, to the exclusion of an anxiety about the results our methods attain. That is being reflected in the teaching-work in social science to an amazing degree. It is shown in the innumerable conferences held and books published thereon. It is demonstrated by the increasing number of vast treatises in which the text is drowned in a terrifying apparatus of notes and bibliographies and excursuses and appendices through which the reader bores his way with a sense that neither he nor the author has seen the wood for the trees. It is seen in the passion for the *inédit* however insignificant; and in the yearning to publish something somewhere at all costs. We have got to remember that one takes a journey for the sake of the destination. The end of social science is the better understanding of the world; and that will come not from the mere multiplication of men able to collect more facts, but from the increase of those who know, first, what facts need to be collected, and, second, what value those facts have when assembled.

IV

Nor is it easy to be satisfied with the position of the foundations themselves. Here, let me say at once that some of them are blessed indeed in their personnel; when one thinks of a man like Abraham Flexner, with his insight, his wisdom, his humility, one wonders why, long ago, one of the great universities had not implored him to lend it the aid, as its president, of his creative imagination. But a man like Abraham Flexner is rare indeed among the executives of a foundation. Usually the director gives the impression of considerable complacency and a keen sense of the power at his disposal. He has not often himself engaged in the serious business of research. He has dipped into an immense number of subjects; he is usually captivated by the latest fashion in each. He travels luxuriously, is amply entertained wherever he goes (he has so much to give), and he speaks always to hearers keenly alert to sense the direction of his own interests in order that they may explain that this is the one thing they are anxious to develop in their own university. When you see him at a college, it is like nothing so much as the vision of an important customer in a department store. Deferential salesmen surround him on every hand, anticipating his every wish, alive to the importance of his good opinion, fearful lest he be dissatisfied and go to their rival across the way. The effect on him is to make him feel that he in fact is shaping the future of the social sciences. Only a very big man can do that. From which it follows that he is a very big man.

He has no desire—let it be admitted in the fullest possible degree—to control the universities he seeks to benefit. The gifts are made; and it is, I believe, only in the most exceptional instances that any conditions of any kind are attached to them. But, with all the good will in the world, he cannot help controlling them. A university principal who wants his institution to expand has no alternative except to see it expand in the directions of which one or other of the foundations happens to approve. There may be doubt, or even dissent among the teachers in the institution; but what possible chance has doubt or dissent against a possible gift of, say, a hundred thousand dollars? And how, conceivably, can the teacher whose work fits in with the scheme of the prospective endowment fail to appear more important in the eyes of the principal or his trustees than the teacher for whose subject, or whose views, the foundation has neither interest nor liking? What possible chance has the teacher of an "un-endowed" subject to pull an equal weight in his institution with the teacher of one that is "endowed"? How can he avoid the embarrassment that may come when he is asked, as he has been asked, to put his own work on one side and co-operate in the particular piece of research the foundation has adopted and upon the report about which the standing of his own institution may depend? What are his chances of promotion if he pursues a path of solitary inquiry in a world of colleges competing for the substantial crumbs which fall from the foundation's table? And, observe, there is not a single point here in which there is the slightest control from, or interference by, the foundation itself. It is merely the fact that a fund is within reach which permeates everything and alters everything. The college develops along the lines the foundation approves. The dependence is merely implicit, but it is in fact quite final. If a foundation is interested in international affairs the college will develop a zeal for its study, or for anthropology, or the negro problem, or questions of population. But it would also, whatever the cost, develop a passion for ballistics or the Bantu languages if these were the subjects upon which the foundation was prepared to smile.

I remember vividly a summer school in a European city which was visited by the director of an important foundation. Its organizers were hard pressed for funds and hopeful that some manna might fall from the particular heaven in which this director dwelt. I was invited to meet him at dinner, and instructions were offered to me about the kind of reception he was to have. Though none of us felt that what he has written possessed any special importance, we were to treat him as a high authority upon his subject. We were to elicit his frank views about the school, and explain that his hopes and fears coincided with our own. We were to discuss—of course in an impersonal way—the great achievements to the credit of his foundation, and the high influence it had exerted in the promotion of international good will. We were to refer delicately to our sense of the fitness of things which had led a foreign government to decorate him for his services. We were to indicate our faint hope that the light of his countenance might be pleased to shine upon so humble an effort as the summer school. In so delicately perfumed an atmosphere it was indeed comforting to watch the expansion of his personality.

I think we almost convinced him that he was a great man; certainly he was pleased to indicate that he believed a distinguished future lay before "some of your group." And in due time the school made its formal application, and the appropriate manna fell from heaven.

As a rule, of course, the environment, on both sides, is manipulated with a finesse more exquisitely molded and more subtly staged. But that it is recognized where the real control lies no one who has watched the operation in process can possibly doubt. The man who pays the piper knows perfectly well that he can call the tune. He can shut down, at a moment's notice, one of the most promising graduate schools in the United States by the simple process of deciding to spend its wonted subsidy in another direction. He can close an activity for which his foundation was famous all over the world, to which, also, men of international reputation have given years of devoted service, merely by deciding that there is not room for its activities in his next year's budget; and the unfortunate subjects of his decision are without opportunity either of appeal or protest. Those who have access to him among the universities become important merely by the influence they exert. Let him select a scholar to travel among the colleges and report upon the teaching and organization of a particular subject, and the scholar will be received with the same breathless reverence as a Jacobin representative on mission. The foundations do not control, simply because, in the direct and simple sense of the word, there is no need for them to do so. They have only to indicate the immediate direction of their minds for the whole university world to discover that it always meant to gravitate swiftly to that angle of the intellectual compass.

V

No one, I suppose, has ever undertaken research, however humble, without feeling that the business of discovering facts is grim and necessary and infinitely laborious. But it is one thing to find them for the purpose of an end beyond themselves, and it is another thing, and a dangerous thing, to elevate the mere process of their discovery into a religious rhapsody. For immediately the second road is followed, a body of vital consequences follows. Immense sums of money become necessary; and the essential factor in the situation becomes the man or the institution with money to give. The laborers in the vine-yard set themselves to cultivate his good will. And because scientific "impartiality" is important—for the donors must not be accused of subsidizing a particular point of view—the emphasis of research moves away from values and ends to materials and methods.

The men who used to be architects of ideas and systems become builders' laborers. They are rated not for what they think and its value, but for how they can organize and its extent. The man who dominates the field is the man who knows how to "run" committees and conferences, who has influence with, and access to, a trustee here and a director there. The governing bodies of universities are naturally impressed by imposing buildings, long lists of publications, reports of committees with high-sounding names; how, for them, shall such activities not be important upon which foundations born of the grim, material success they understand, are prepared to lavish millions? The directors are content enough, for their esteem is flattered and they have the assurance of innumerable committees that, one day, results of the first importance will be born. And if somewhere a faint doubt obtrudes, a reference to the technic of the natural sciences and the immense results secured there is usually sufficient to stifle skepticism.

Yet if we look at the history of scientific research, the great discoveries do not, somehow, seem to have come in this way. They have been rather a matter of some lonely thinker brooding in solitude upon the meaning of facts from the significance of which he cannot escape. He gets a sudden moment of illumination, and he proceeds to test the hypothesis by finding whether it will fit the facts at his disposal. So, at least, inspiration seems to have come to Newton, to Darwin, to Clerk-Maxwell, to Einstein. And, in the vast majority of cases, the material which has given birth to the great idea, the apparatus of experiment that has proved its value have been simple alike in conception and execution.

So, too, in the social sciences. The great inventive minds, Plato, Hobbes, Rousseau, Hegel, Bentham, do not seem to have been natural members of committees. They found their ideas in a body of factual experience which impressed them so overwhelmingly that they could not avoid the effort to discover its meaning. One could, I imagine, have helped Adam Smith a little with books and references. One can help to-day a great medievalist like Haskins by copying out the charter he wants, or a great jurist like Mr. Justice Holmes by finding the references to the cases he requires. No one suffers from discussion with his fellows. The partnerships of Maitland and Sir Frederick Pollock, of Bertrand Russell and Professor Whitehead receive no emphasis now from anyone's eulogies.

Where co-operative research means these things, or others kindred to them; where, as Maitland once said, it may lead the great man, when he comes along, to fling us a footnote of gratitude for having saved his eyes and his time, I protest its value as eagerly as any. But, in its newer forms, it seems to me to raise hopes unlikely of fulfilment. It is an immense superstructure without due bed rock in the facts of intellectual creativeness. We are in danger of paying a price for its erection that we are ill able to afford.

W.E.B. DU BOIS AND CHARLES S. JOHNSON: DIFFERING VIEWS ON THE ROLE OF PHILANTHROPY IN HIGHER EDUCATION

MARYBETH GASMAN

Introduction

Philanthropy is typically defined as a charitable act, a gift, or an organization that dispenses such gifts. Rarely do we think negatively about gifts. However, as the literature in this area tells us, there is much mistrust of philanthropy and those behind it. Some critics have pointed toward the ulterior motives underlying the gifts of philanthropists.[1] Is it really a gift or does it serve the philanthropist more than the recipient? Others have drawn attention to the unethical business practices of the corporations behind the philanthropies.[2] How can "tainted" money promote good? Still others have questioned the amount of control that many philanthropists gain once their beneficiaries become dependent on them.[3] Are philanthropists giving money just to extend the reach of their power? Despite these criticisms, philanthropy, in the words of Robert Bremner, "has been one of the principal methods of social advance."[4]

The history of black colleges is interwoven with that of philanthropy. Since the post-Civil War era, northern industrialists have been actively providing financial support to black colleges. Initially, they supported primarily industrial education, which provided blacks with manual training and skills. This lack of wholehearted support for the liberal arts aroused the ire of W.E.B. Du Bois and led to his well known, and often misunderstood, debate with Booker T. Washington. Du Bois advocated a liberal arts education for at least a "Talented Tenth" of the black population—in order to create an intellectual elite that could advance the civil rights of all black people.[5] Washington urged the majority of blacks to "cast down your bucket where you are" and work within the system of segregation in the South.[6] He believed that blacks should be committed to economic improvement and eventually civil rights would follow. Economic improvement would come through a steadfast commitment to hard work and the ownership of property.[7] Du Bois was not opposed to industrial education; he "believed that we should seek to educate a mass of [Negroes] in the three R's and the technique . . . and duty of good work." But, he also thought that the "race must have thinkers and leaders" who possess a liberal arts education.[8] In Du Bois's opinion, what was most unsettling about Washington was his willingness to be a pawn to the northern philanthropists and southern whites.[9] Louis Harlan notes that Washington ". . . frequently played upon the desire of southern whites to have a docile, subordinate black population and the desire of northern capitalists to have a skilled, tractable, and hard-working black laboring class."[10] This fundamental difference between Du Bois and Washington caused a rift between the two black leaders.[11]

In the second decade of the twentieth century, the industrial philanthropists shifted their emphasis toward higher education for African Americans and decided to concentrate their efforts on a few elite institutions such as Fisk and Dillard.[12] Despite this change in philosophy, Du Bois continued to be hesitant about philanthropic support of black higher education. He had witnessed the impact of philanthropy on curriculum at his alma mater, Fisk, in 1908[13] and was not convinced that the "enlightened philanthropists" would change their ways.[14] As late as 1946, he wrote, "Education is not and should not be a private philanthropy: it is a public service and whenever it becomes a gift of the rich it is in danger."[15] According to Du Bois, philanthropy stood in the way of the African American's "truthful" education.[16] However, not all African-American intellectuals agreed with him. One who did not was Charles S. Johnson, and Du Bois would later criticize Johnson just as he had Washington thirty years earlier. An analysis of the disagreement between these two men exposes a new and more complex layer of issues concerning higher education for African Americans and philanthropy.

Unlike Du Bois, sociologist and educator Charles S. Johnson worked closely with white philanthropists beginning in the early 1920s and continued to do so until his death in 1956. He saw the foundations as a means for making advances for African Americans—a way of cultivating scholars and leaders. This essay will examine the views of both Du Bois and Johnson with regard to philanthropy. It will not attempt to provide a comprehensive treatment of either figure but will instead compare and contrast their views and experiences with respect to philanthropy. It will illustrate why Du Bois thought that philanthropy was, and would remain, an obstacle to higher education even though it was being used to support many of the goals he had advocated. The paper will also examine Johnson's belief in philanthropy as a pragmatic route with which to create opportunities for African Americans. Through an exploration of Johnson's background, it will uncover the experiences that led to this belief. Finally, it will point to some of the difficulties and limitations of both men's perspectives.

To assess the views of both scholars, this research draws upon their papers, available at Fisk University (Charles S. Johnson Papers, Special Collections) and the University of Massachusetts (W.E.B. Du Bois Special Collections). The author reviewed speeches, letters, unpublished autobiographies, and reports. This essay incorporates material from the large number of publications authored by both Du Bois and Johnson. Information was gathered from interviews conducted by both the author and historian Patrick J. Gilpin.[17] Further, the research draws upon secondary sources written about both Du Bois and Johnson.

Understanding Du Bois—Radical Intellectual

Born in 1868 in Great Barrington, Massachusetts, W.E.B. Du Bois grew up in a mostly white community in the Northeast. He had his first encounter with "southern" segregation only after enrolling at Fisk University in Nashville, Tennessee, in 1885. Although Jim Crow laws had not yet appeared on the books in Nashville, Du Bois experienced the discriminatory "social norms" and separation of the races upon arrival in the community.[18] It was at this point that he began to understand his purpose and developed his sense of activism. In his words, "So I came to this region where the world was split into white and black halves, and where the darker half was held back by race prejudice and legal bonds, as well as by deep ignorance and dire poverty. But facing this was not a lost group, but at Fisk a microcosm of a world and a civilization in potentiality. Into this world I leapt with enthusiasm. A new loyalty and allegiance replaced my Americanism: henceforward I was a Negro."[19] Du Bois graduated from Fisk and moved on to earn multiple degrees from Harvard—culminating in a Ph.D. in history in 1895. While at Harvard, Du Bois received a research grant for study in Europe from the Slater Fund.[20] This was his first "hands-on" interaction with industrial philanthropists. The Slater Fund had claimed in national newspapers that it was looking for "colored" men worth educating.[21] To obtain the grant, Du Bois had worked diligently, writing letter after letter to former United States President Rutherford B. Hayes, the head of the Fund. Despite the fund's national call and Du Bois's excellent credentials, Hayes replied, upon receiving Du Bois's application, that scholarships were no longer available. After two years of writing to Hayes, Du Bois finally persuaded the fund to give him a scholarship. As if to deny that Du Bois had beaten them, the fund made him pay back half of the scholarship upon completion of his studies in Europe.

After graduating from Harvard, Du Bois worked as an instructor at Wilberforce College in Ohio. Eventually, he moved to Atlanta University. There, Du Bois's outrage over racism grew—fed by the increasing discrimination and the horrible practice of lynching taking place throughout the South. At this point, "legalized" Jim Crow had become commonplace and the gains of Reconstruction were all but reversed.[22] No longer able to remain a "detached scientist," Du Bois began to wield his intellect and voice. With the publication of the landmark book, *The Souls of Black Folk*, he identified for the American people the century's most pressing problem—that of "the color line."[23]

Du Bois's experience at Atlanta University fueled his frustration with white philanthropy. He appealed to railroad baron Jacob Schiff and steel magnate Andrew Carnegie for financial backing for a scholarly journal and social science center at Atlanta University. Both journal and center would aim at the black intelligentsia and would focus on race issues in the United States. Both philanthropists refused, and Du Bois attributed this to their connections with Booker T. Washington's Tuskegee "machine."[24] In many cases, Washington had final authority over which black colleges and scholars received philanthropic funds. At this point, Du Bois felt that Atlanta University was suffering the loss of potential philanthropic contributions due to his presence. He noted, "Young President Ware had received almost categorical promise that under certain circumstances increased contributions from the General Education Board and other sources might be expected, which would make the University secure. . . . I was sure that I was at least one of these 'circumstances,' and so my work in Atlanta . . . faded."[25]

As a result of his frustration and desire for change, Du Bois began the Niagara Movement in 1905 and helped found the National Association for the Advancement of Colored People (NAACP) in 1909.[26] Initially, the NAACP's board of directors hoped that Du Bois would use his prominent stature to raise funds for the organization. He refused that role. In a frank admission, he stated, "I knew that raising money was not a job for which I was fitted. It called for a friendliness of approach and knowledge of human nature, and an adaptability which I did not have."[27] Instead of being a fundraiser, Du Bois became the director of publications and research. In this position, he acted as a social critic and provided opportunities for many of the Harlem Renaissance artists, writers, and poets.

While at the NAACP, Du Bois, once again, clashed with white philanthropists. Of note were his dealings with NAACP board member Oswald Garrison Villard, the owner of the *New York Evening Post* and grandson of noted abolitionist William Lloyd Garrison. Du Bois felt that Villard expected blacks to be humble and thankful—to be respectful of his wealth and willingness to share it.[28] Du Bois, of course, would neither acquiesce to racist social norms nor bow down to riches—his personality would not allow it. Not long after Du Bois started to edit the *Crisis*, Villard clamped down on its content. In an effort to draw attention to the horrors of mob violence against blacks, Du Bois frequently published a list of lynchings in *The Crisis*, sometimes accompanied by graphic photographs. Villard suggested that he also include a list of black crimes. Du Bois refused, noting the ridiculous nature of this request.[29] When there was a clear situation in which to stand up and say, "enough is enough," Du Bois showed courage and resolve.[30]

In 1911, a frustrated Du Bois took aim at white philanthropy and its role in the education of blacks. With the publication of his literary piece *The Quest of the Silver Fleece*, he caricatured the members of the General Education Board as arrogant, conniving, and unconcerned about the "higher" education of African Americans. For example, John D. Rockefeller appeared as John Taylor, a northern businessman whose bank accounts increased daily and whose promise to southern whites was "We'll see that . . . you Southerners get what you want—control of Negro education."[31] Through the farcical style of the novel, Du Bois showed his contempt for the northern industrial philanthropists and their manipulation of African-American education during the early part of the twentieth century.[32]

In 1917, the publication of a particularly critical report on black education by the Phelps Stokes Fund, with the support of the General Education Board, infuriated Du Bois. Written by Thomas Jesse Jones *Negro Education: A Study of the Private and Higher Schools for Colored People in the United States* called for the elimination and consolidation of the majority of black institutions of higher education.[33] White sociologists and philanthropists lauded the report's findings. In 1918, Du Bois fired back at Jones and the philanthropists in a *Crisis* article entitled "Negro Education." "Here, then, is the weakness and sinister danger of Mr. Jones' report. It calls for a union of philanthropic effort with no attempt to make sure of the proper and just lines along which this united effort should work. It calls for cooperation with the white South without insisting on the Negro being represented by voice and vote in such 'cooperation,' and it calls for a recasting of the educational program for Negroes without insisting on leaving the door of opportunity open for the development of a thoroughly trained class of leaders at the bottom, in the very beginnings of education, as well as the top."[34] According to Eric Anderson and Alfred Moss, Jr., Du Bois' critique "permanently marked Jones' reputation."[35] Du Bois's scathing but insightful portrait of the northern philanthropists' actions did not earn him their favor.

W.E.B. Du Bois's willingness to speak out on issues and his unpopularity with white northerners contributed to his rocky relationship with many in the NAACP, in particular its executive secretary Walter White. Frustrated by the constant battles with that organization, Du Bois left in 1934. A quiet offer from friend and Atlanta University President John Hope was the sanctuary Du Bois needed. This institution proved to be an inspirational setting for Du Bois. It was here that he began *Phylon*, published *Black Reconstruction in America*, completed important sociological studies, and wrote several autobiographical pieces.

However, it was also at Atlanta University that Du Bois had one of his most frustrating experiences with philanthropy.[36] This experience would be a thorn in his side for many years and would eventually lead him to give up any hope that philanthropy could make significant change in society.[37] From the age of twenty-nine, Du Bois had longed to publish an Encyclopedia of the Negro. He first mentioned his idea publicly at the Academy of Political and Social Science meeting in Philadelphia in 1897 but was unable to find any support for it. In 1906, he wrote to Andrew Carnegie to request funds for the encyclopedia—again, to no avail. Determined to realize his goal, he continued to contact foundations, including Rockefeller's General Education Board. Although his efforts were commended by the GEB, sponsorship could not be found. When the Phelps-Stokes Fund finally held a conference on the issue in 1931, Charles S. Johnson and Walter White were included but Du Bois was not. Thus, "the most important group scholarship enterprise of the twentieth century was convened without Du Bois being invited" or even credited for his idea.[38] Thomas Jesse Jones, the Phelps-Stokes's education director, saw Du Bois as "the definition of radicalism, a brilliant troublemaker bloated with racial pride and devoid of political common sense."[39] On the day of the conference, the blacks present noted Du Bois's absence and, under pressure, the Fund promised to include him in future meetings. At the second meeting, Du Bois expressed his anger over the Phelps-Stokes Fund's suggestion that the editor of the encyclopedia be white: he did not think it was possible for white editors to express the black point of view. The Fund countered with the rather twisted idea that in true social science the one who knows everything about a topic (as Du Bois did about the Negro) cannot be objective.[40] In his typically conciliatory manner, Charles S. Johnson suggested joint editors—one black and one white. Eventually Du Bois and sociologist Robert E. Park were chosen for the project.

In 1934, the Phelps Stokes Fund presented the encyclopedia project to the GEB in an attempt to secure funding. They were confident that the GEB would support the project and that their approval would lead to the Carnegie Corporation's backing as well. However, the GEB turned them down. According to David Levering Lewis, "Du Bois' involvement . . . would preclude favorable foundation action for an indefinite period."[41] Although the idea was revived when he moved to Ghana, Du Bois' Encyclopedia of the Negro was never published. To "dodge the credibility of Du Bois' proposal for the encyclopedia," the philanthropists commissioned what they thought would be an equally interesting project—a psychological study of race that would become Gunnar Myrdal's *American Dilemma*.[42] The failure of this lifelong pursuit cemented Du Bois's mistrust of philanthropy.

Under John Hope's presidency, Du Bois had flourished at Atlanta University. However, when Rufus Clement became president, Du Bois began to have difficulty and was soon dismissed from his position. Despite receiving offers, in 1944, from the sociology departments of both Howard and Fisk Universities, Du Bois was persuaded to return to the NAACP.[43] But only four years later, he would have another disagreement with the leadership, this time over his public support of 1948 Progressive Party presidential candidate Henry Wallace. He left the NAACP and spent the remainder of his life writing, speaking, and traveling internationally. Despite his lack of affiliation with a university or the NAACP, Du Bois maintained his influence among blacks in the United States and abroad.[44] His work was interrupted briefly, in 1951, when the United States Department of Justice indicted him on charges of failing to register as a foreign agent. Du Bois was eventually acquitted of this Cold War smear. In 1961, Du Bois left the United States to live in Ghana where he died in 1963 at age 95.[45] Du Bois had spent a lifetime criticizing racial injustice in the United States. Initially he made attempts to work against racial discrimination and ignorance with the support the power elites—attempting to garner funds from major philanthropists. With repeated failures on this front, however, Du Bois may have become convinced that the American capitalist system was in and of itself the engine of racism. Hence it is no surprise he spent his last years in exile.

Understanding Johnson: Liberal Educator and Race Relations Pioneer

Twenty-five years after W.E.B. Du Bois's birth and just a few years prior to *Plessy v. Ferguson's* "separate but equal" ruling, Charles S. Johnson was born in Bristol, Virginia. In contrast to Du Bois, Johnson experienced southern segregation and discrimination from an early age. As the Jim Crow laws went into effect, many of the places that Johnson's family frequented suddenly became unavailable to blacks. In particular, Johnson recalled an incident in an ice cream parlor that "was the beginning of a new self-consciousness that burned."[46] After newspapers carried a short statement about new legislation pertaining to "Negros," Johnson and his mother were suddenly refused a seat at the counter where they had sat each Sunday. According to Johnson, incidents like this from his youth spurred his commitment to alleviating racial problems.[47]

After graduating from high school in 1913, Johnson enrolled in Virginia Union College and earned a bachelor's degree in sociology in 1916. He then moved north to the University of Chicago to study with Robert E. Park who became Johnson's mentor and the two remained close friends until Park's death in 1944. Johnson interrupted his studies at the University of Chicago to enlist in the military during World War I.[48] Upon returning to Chicago in 1919, he found himself in the midst of a race riot caused by the stoning of a young man who accidentally swam into the "White side" of a Chicago beach. According to Martin Bulmer, this incident led Johnson to a deeper interest in "interpreting 'colored people to whites and white people to Negroes.'"[49] Further, that riot sparked his involvement with the Chicago Race Relations Commission as associate executive secretary. The Commission published *The Negro in Chicago: A Study of Race Relations and a Race Riot*; Johnson received national acclaim for his involvement with the study and the commission. It was at this time that Johnson became acquainted with Sears and Roebuck tycoon Julius Rosenwald. Both Rosenwald and Edwin Embree, the president of the Rosenwald's philanthropic foundation, admired Johnson.

Embree and Johnson had a close professional relationship throughout their careers. It was well-known among the black and white liberal communities that Embree relied on Johnson to make recommendations as to what the Rosenwald Fund should support.[50] Embree provided most of the financial backing for Johnson's ideas, including the internationally known social science department that he would later establish at Fisk.[51] Not only did Embree steadfastly endorse Johnson, but Johnson acted as a conduit to the black community for Embree. Embree was greatly concerned with race relations ("the Negro problem") and saw Johnson as the type of black leader who offered a solution. This is evident in Embree's book *Thirteen Against the Odds* (1946), in which he highlights the influence and accomplishments of prominent African Americans and greatly lauds Johnson.[52] In 1934, Johnson and Embree collaborated with Will W. Alexander to produce a study entitled *The Collapse of the Cotton Tenancy*, which challenged the federal government to intervene in the southern situation: "buy up huge acreages of farm lands now in the hands of insurance companies, land banks, and others, and distribute this land in small plots of minimum size required to support farm families."[53] Johnson's work with Embree, which began in the 1920s, would lead to a lifetime of working with the nation's leading philanthropists.

In 1921, Johnson moved to New York to work as the director of research and investigations at the National Urban League. Much like Du Bois, Johnson was offering a forum to Harlem Renaissance luminaries through his editorial position at *Opportunity*, the Urban League's literary magazine.[54] While in New York, Johnson began to "rub elbows" with the city's white philanthropists. According to Harlem Renaissance artist Aaron Douglas, [Johnson's] "subtle sort of scheming mind had arrived at the feeling that literature was a soft spot of the arts and in the armor of the nation, and he set out to exploit it."[55] This strategy would become a hallmark of Johnson's approach to creating opportunities for African Americans. Sociologist and Johnson contemporary Blyden Jackson portrayed the Renaissance as a stage on which Johnson thought "America [would be] utterly emancipated from the color caste." Jackson points to a dinner hosted by Johnson at the Civic Club in New York on March 21, 1924, as his most significant contribution to the Harlem Renaissance: "It was a dinner at the 'white' Civic Club, one of the very few places in downtown Manhattan where an interracial group, be it ever so elite, in the 1920s could have broken bread together undisturbed."[56] Johnson invited over 300 people—white and black—who identified themselves with the Renaissance. The guests included: Alain Locke, James Weldon Johnson, W.E.B. Du Bois, William Baldwin III, Jessie Fauset, Albert Barnes, and many influential white publishers. Before the event many black writers and poets had to entrust their manuscripts to unscrupulous agents, but with the success of the evening came interest from prominent American publishers.

Near the close of the Harlem Renaissance in 1928, Charles S. Johnson returned to the South to take a position as director of the social science department at Fisk University. The Julius Rosenwald Fund and the Laura Spelman Rockefeller Memorial handpicked him for that position. These foundations granted Fisk money to support the social science department and made clear their interest in Johnson.[57] While at Fisk, he propelled the department to national prominence and created an internationally known race relations institute. He was a prolific writer and published *Shadow of the Plantation* (1934), *The Negro College Graduate* (1938), and *Patterns of Negro Segregation* (1943) among others. Throughout his work, Johnson focused on the study of racial oppression through the eyes of those who were experiencing it rather than those who were responsible for causing it. He spent years developing ethnographic case studies through the use of "human documents" and identifying "vectors of social change."[58] Johnson thought that by gauging people's attitudes and ideas, it was possible to reveal the information that would lead to political emancipation. He believed in cooperation along racial lines and looked for allies within the white community. For Johnson, cooperation met working within the power structure—specifically national government and philanthropy—and using his connections within these institutions to bolster his public stature on issues of race relations. He favored a steady "chipping away" at segregation and inequality rather than large-scale protest or "radical" attacks. In Johnson's words, "No strategy is sound that does not envisage the total picture in such a way that a person can be helped in deciding, in some smaller individual cases, what is soundest and most important to stress and what on the whole, is of minor consequence."[59] This less confrontational approach has made Johnson the subject of much criticism by both black scholars such as E. Franklin Frazier and white liberals such as August Meier.[60] In addition to his work on race relations within the academic setting, Johnson served as a trustee for the Julius Rosenwald Fund from 1934 to 1948, working specifically as the codirector of the race relations program. From 1944 to 1950 he served as the director of the race relations division of the American Missionary Association. In addition, Johnson served on various international committees, including the United Nations Educational, Scientific, and Cultural Organization (UNESCO) and was an advisor to the Supreme Commander for the Allied Powers in Japan after World War II.

In 1946, after a heated national debate led by Fisk alumni, Johnson became the first black president of the institution. At the request of a vocal group of alumni, W.E.B. Du Bois publicly opposed his appointment and, in a September 7, 1946: *Nation* article, suggested that Johnson might be a pawn of philanthropy: ". . . here can be no doubt as to the present situation; the Northern white trustees [philanthropists] hesitate to put a Negro into the presidency; they would prefer a complacent, even second class, white man. The white Southern trustees would consent to a Negro president provided he was a Negro amenable to their guidance and not "radical" that is, not an advocate of the FEPC, the abolition of the poll tax, or any New Deal policies. It is rumored that they are in partial agreement on a man of this sort."[61] It was clear to Fisk alumni and all involved that Du Bois was talking about Johnson.[62] However, Du Bois was mistaken in his assessment of Johnson and the situation at Fisk. As part of an informal network of advisors to the Roosevelt administration, Johnson did much to support the very New Deal policies that Du Bois mentioned.[63] Further, Johnson was not the favorite candidate of the white northern philanthropists on the Fisk board. They saw him as much more valuable in the field of sociology. In the end, it was the actions of several black board members, who recognized Johnson's skill in dealing with philanthropy, which led to his selection. The university needed to meet an endowment challenge set forth by the Rockefeller Foundation, and the board knew that Johnson was better situated to accomplish this task than the other contender, Charles H. Wesley (Du Bois's candidate of choice). According to John Hope Franklin, a Fisk board member during Johnson's presidency, "Charles Wesley's world was a black world. Johnson's world was a white world. Wesley would not have been able to attract funds as Johnson did."[64]

In less than a decade under Johnson's leadership, Fisk built five major buildings, acquired a world-class fine art collection compliments of artist Georgia O'Keefe, and was awarded chapters of *Phi Beta Kappa*, the *American Association of University Women*, and the *Association of Schools of Music*.[65] Under Johnson, Fisk's budget was doubled and over a million dollars was added to its endowment. Always looking to the future, Johnson was cognizant that Rockefeller and Rosenwald monies for black education were dwindling. Thus, he eagerly cultivated new relationships with Clarence Faust of the Ford Foundation and New York socialite John Hay Whitney, securing money from both men to begin the Basic College program—an early college entrance program for Du Bois's "Talented Tenth" at Fisk. That program nurtured scholars and leaders such as Johnnetta B. Cole, David Levering Lewis, and Hazel O'Leary. The Basic College was the culmination of both Johnson's efforts to promote racial equality and his relationships with white philanthropy.[66] However, his work was cut short in 1956 when, on the way to a Fisk board meeting in New York, he died of a heart attack.

Uncovering their Goals

Despite their different backgrounds and perspectives, W.E.B. Du Bois and Charles S. Johnson shared several goals in their pursuit of quality black higher education. Du Bois believed in the need for black colleges and their ability to acclimate students to the larger society: [The student] "may adjust himself, he may through the help of his own social group in the neighborhood of this school successfully achieve an education. . . ." Further, in discussing the needs of black students, Du Bois stressed "individual attention, close acquaintanceship with their fellows and that skilled guidance that only can be gotten in the small college."[67] Johnson not only agreed with these goals but also worked toward their accomplishment in many of his programs.

Du Bois differed from Johnson over the funding of black colleges. In 1946, he proclaimed that to provide the most benefit to black students, a college president must "be not a financier and collector of funds but an educational administrator capable of laying down an education program and selecting the people who will carry it out."[68] He believed that any use of philanthropy in this regard interfered with the search for "truth" in the educational process. According to Du Bois, if "colleges are going to depend on the gifts of the rich for support they cannot teach the truth. . . . [The] impoverishment of the truth seekers can only be avoided by eventually making the state bear the burden of education and this is socialism."[69] Du Bois believed that support and leadership by the state would provide for the growth of strong and secure black colleges. "The state must in the future support and control higher education because of its large and increasing cost."[70] Black colleges could rely on neither unstable church support nor "undesirable" philanthropic support.[71] Stability and consistency, according to Du Bois, would lead to a college experience that nurtured the black student.

While Johnson would not have opposed the use of government funds for black colleges, he clearly believed that there was a role for philanthropy. In some ways, Johnson's career shows the drawbacks of philanthropic support for education. The control given to him by the foundations lent an authoritarian tendency to his leadership style.[72] He determined how much funding was allocated, and in many cases, what types of projects were funded. Johnson did much to support black higher education; however, he tended to squelch ideas that were different from his own. According to Butler Jones, Johnson controlled "the race relations research territory available to blacks [and] exercised suzerainty over fellowships and grants."[73] Likewise, Patrick J. Gilpin notes that Johnson, "had the last word on foundation and other philanthropic grants. Academic, social, and economic leaders relied heavily, sometimes exclusively, upon his judgment, recommendation, or disapproval. Often it was only with his blessing that the South could get needed funds from outside the area."[74] Johnson's connections created a "power base" that stretched far and wide. He had the funding, respect, and support of white liberals in both the North and South.

But, unlike Booker T. Washington, Johnson worked to create a liberal arts program that was identical to the one favored by Du Bois. Throughout his career, Johnson held a great interest in the welfare of black college students. Not only did his research relate to this area, but his philanthropic service and affiliations coincided with the advancement of African Americans. Johnson helped direct Rosenwald money toward scholarships for black students and later went on to create the Basic College with foundation monies. This program is perhaps the best example of Johnson's overall philosophy pertaining to students and student learning. Unsure of the possibility of integrated black education in the South, Johnson created the Basic College early entrant program, to give promising black students the opportunity to learn in a nurturing, stimulating environment. Students were taught in cohesive learning groups and benefited from the presence of artistic, literary, and political figures whom Johnson invited to the Fisk campus. They studied, ate, and lived together in small cohorts that provided support within the academic setting. According to Peggy Alsup, one of the Basic College students, "Charles Johnson believed in the whole concept of identifying young Black bright kids who thrive in an environment where they have good teachers and encouragement. He was trying to demonstrate too that it did not matter what your color was as long as you have the potential."[75] Johnson was providing students with exactly the college environment prescribed by Du Bois. However, he was doing it in a way that was ideologically opposed to Du Bois's perspective. In fact, according to Basic College graduate David Levering Lewis, "The two sociologists could not have been temperamentally and ideologically more dissimilar."[76]

Philanthropy: Obstacle or Avenue?

If Johnson was able to achieve success, one might expect Du Bois to soften his views on the use of philanthropy and perhaps be more cordial toward Johnson himself. However, the opposite was true. Long after the foundations ceased to meddle in the curriculum and even after they began to embrace a more pro-civil rights agenda, Du Bois continued to oppose them. His hard line perspective on white philanthropy was based on two essential elements. One was personal experience, and in particular, a seemingly purposeful repression of his research agenda. The other was an ideology that was highly complex and distinctly to the left of most of his peers.[77]

Among the most vexing of Du Bois's negative experiences with philanthropy were those that involved Booker T. Washington. In Washington, Du Bois saw a man who had been corrupted by philanthropy and whose work undermined the pursuit of black progress. And to Du Bois, Johnson looked a lot like Washington. Certain connections between the two men were quite compelling. As demonstrated, Johnson was the "golden child" of the Rosenwald Fund. During the early years of that Fund, Washington had played a similar role—assisting Julius Rosenwald with his school-building projects by deciding which counties would receive one.[78] Another connection between Washington and Johnson was their close relationship with Robert E. Park. Park had served as a ghostwriter and advisor to Washington and said of this experience, "I think I probably learned more about human nature and society, in the South under Booker Washington, than I learned elsewhere in all my previous studies."[79] Of course, Johnson studied under Park at the University of Chicago and considered him one of the greatest influences on his career, thought process, and life. Lastly, there was Johnson's involvement with the Urban League. This organization was founded in part by Ruth S. Baldwin, the widow of William H. Baldwin, Jr.—a close friend of Washington, a Tuskegee trustee, and a major industrial philanthropist. Washington gave his support to Baldwin's widow when she started the Urban League. He felt that the League was much more in line with his ideas than the NAACP. Because of these similarities between Johnson and Washington, it is likely that Du Bois viewed the Fisk sociologist as being in the mold of the "Wizard of Tuskegee." This view persisted in spite of Johnson's accomplishments in the area of liberal education.[80]

But Du Bois's views were more than just a matter of personal bias. As shown, his work was unfairly rejected on numerous occasions because of meddling by the foundations. His negative experiences and leftist views reinforced one another over the course of his life. In Du Bois's words, "philanthropy [was a force] which organized vast schemes of relief to stop at least the flow of blood in the vaster wounds which industry was making."[81] Thus, in his mind, philanthropy was merely interested in Band-Aid solutions rather than attacking the root causes of social ills.[82] According to historian Sterling Stuckey, "Du Bois was struck by the essential vulgarity of the Andrew Carnegies and was opposed to any alliance of black workers with a system responsible for the enslavement of their fathers."[83]

The philanthropists had shown time and time again that they were not willing to support the kind of scholarship that Du Bois thought was crucial to the future of the United States. The fact that only Johnson's more mainstream type of research was funded was to Du Bois evidence that the philanthropies were not fully ready to cooperate in the advancement of blacks. Du Bois thought that Johnson "split the difference endlessly and that what passed for wisdom was cliché with the apparatus of scholarship behind it."[84] He was, in Du Bois' words, "if not reactionary, certainly very cautious."[85]

Johnson shared Du Bois's sense of outrage over the injustices black students faced, but his experiences led him to take a much different approach. From Johnson's perspective, the philanthropists seemed more enlightened—they valued his opinions and trusted him. The Rosenwald Fund and the Laura Spelman Rockefeller Memorial made Du Bois's vision of a center for social science research possible at Fisk, under the direction of Johnson. The Fisk sociologist was convinced that through cooperation across racial lines, blacks would benefit and succeed.[86] In fact, students on the Fisk campus left the insulated environment fostered by Johnson with the notion that "the only thing wrong with [this] country was that it was a little slow at embracing [blacks]. And it soon would. [Students] were persuaded that [they] could compete, and to use race as an excuse was really quite demeaning."[87] This attitude toward racial issues was also prevalent in Johnson's writings and speeches. While addressing the Southern Sociological Society, in Atlanta, Georgia, in 1944, Johnson said, "There is fairly widespread agreement that race relations in the South have deteriorated in character since the beginning of the war. [However, it is my] thesis [that] the emotional disturbances of the present period, involving racial issues, are symptoms of accelerated social changes, and that these changes are wholesome, even if their temporary racial effects are bad."[88] Thus, Johnson's essentially optimistic view of the American system explains his faith in the ability of American institutions to ameliorate the racial climate. In a *New York Times* article written after the *Brown* decision, Johnson affirmed his whole-hearted support of the American way of life: "Basically, this is a struggle today not between North and South, or whites and Negroes, or between the national and international points of view. It is a struggle between those who believe in democracy and those who do not."[89] For Johnson a solution to the racial problems he had experienced throughout his life was possible through democracy and through the free enterprise system that included industrial philanthropy.

For Du Bois, the final rejection of his *Encyclopedia of the Negro* was an equally strong denial that United States's style democracy and capitalism offered a solution to race problems. Du Bois would offer other proposals for racial uplift including a black self-tax to support education. He proposed such a plan in a speech given in 1946 entitled, "The Future and Function of the Negro College." In the spirit of black self-determination, he called on the black college alumni and local constituency to "tax themselves. . . . I say 'tax' and I mean tax: a payment as regular and recognized as just as compulsory as any tax. I believe it would be possible but only possible if this kind of contribution was lifted out of the class of ordinary miscellaneous giving to which we are so used and stressed throughout the college course as an absolute necessity for the maintenance of independent methods of education."[90]

Only a few months after his "self taxation" speech, Du Bois conceded that fundraising and associations with philanthropy might just be needed in the educational process. Upon hearing of Johnson's selection for the presidency of Fisk, Du Bois reluctantly wrote to a trustee who was also aligned against Johnson's candidacy: "He has the ear of the foundations and he will probably get the money that Fisk sorely needs. He will probably rebuild the university physically and may be able to get a faculty about him of the sort of teachers that Fisk needs. At any rate, the only thing that we can do now, it seems to me, is to keep still and give him a chance."[91] Despite his shaky admission that philanthropy may be necessary to the education of blacks, Du Bois himself would not work in this way. Although he had brief interactions with philanthropists in his early years, he was true to his words and convictions. In a 1958 statement to historian Merle Curti, Du Bois wrote, "During my whole career, I have tried not to be put in a position where collecting money from philanthropists would be any considerable part of my work. For that reason I have always declined to [be a] candidate for the presidency of any college or organization where I had to raise funds. Philanthropy is being guided by Big Business to ward off Socialism and Communism, to control labor unions, and to curb all sorts of 'radical' thought."[92] In light of this continuing commitment to a leftist perspective, it is not surprising that Du Bois left the United States to spend his last years in Ghana.[93]

Conclusion

According to historian David Levering Lewis, W.E.B. Du Bois had "influence, not power." Du Bois himself was aware of his situation, noting in 1932 that one who agitates must be willing to pay the price.[94] He was an agitator—one who was skilled at bringing attention to issues. He did not need philanthropy to accomplish this task.[95] He was stubborn and fought vehemently for his ideas. Because this put him in conflict with the powerbrokers of his time, he often acted from the position of "respected outsider."[96]

Charles S. Johnson, on the other hand, has been described as "one of the race's foremost diplomats, whose hands were on the purse strings of numerous foundations."[97] Johnson was a builder who needed monetary support to realize his goals. He worked hard to gain the trust of white philanthropists and eventually was able to make independent decisions in his roles as director of the social science department and president of Fisk University. He studied the ways of philanthropists and acted upon this knowledge. He took the lead by bringing ideas to the philanthropists and seeking their funding. According to Richard Robbins, "The foundations had the money, and they allocated it. They had confidence in Johnson. He needed their resources to get the work done; he went to them. . . . Nowhere is there any record of Johnson being compelled to submit his work to censorship imposed by the foundations. In the milieu of his time, in an era of extreme racism, he managed to obtain the grants, get the studies done, and conceivably, advance the understanding of racial oppression and what strategies could be deployed against it."[98] This is a much different relationship than that of earlier black college presidents who were sometimes manipulated by white philanthropists. The level of independence that Johnson had achieved allowed him to accomplish many of the goals set forth by Du Bois—an African-American social science center, a race relations institute, and the education of the "Talented Tenth." Johnson, however, was not able to be an agitator. Unlike Du Bois, he would sometimes back down from direct confrontation if it meant losing funds for a key program or a position of power.[99] His personality was quieter and he was a firm believer in working across racial lines.

Although Johnson was accused of compromising in some situations, he did so with a strategy in mind.[100] Johnson was cognizant of the political situation in the United States. He was willing to seek funding from the sources Du Bois favored (i.e., alumni and government), but as a realist, he knew these groups had their limitations. The major drawback to Johnson's approach was his inability to make his innovative programs flourish after his death. While this criticism has been applied to other African-American leaders, the fact that Johnson was working within an educational context makes it particularly severe. Responding to ad hoc concerns, political leaders often expect that their influence will fade after the agenda has been accomplished. Educational leaders like Johnson, however, put programs in place to deal with ongoing concerns—student learning, research, etc. This usually allows for the continuation of those programs after their term in office. In Johnson's case, however, the programs disappeared, and he was virtually forgotten for a long period of time. As a result of his tight hold on power, he entrusted no one with his strategies for working with philanthropists. Only after the processing of his presidential and personal papers many years later, were we made aware of these strategies.

What makes it worthwhile to revisit Johnson is the example he provides in his interactions with the philanthropists. Johnson brought a global awareness to his work in education and race relations.

His understanding of changes in the social and economic conditions at mid century, coupled with his shrewd knowledge of the ways of the philanthropists, allowed him to direct funds toward programs that advanced the situation of African Americans in the South. Because he had done extensive writing and research on the southern economic structure, Johnson was well aware of the possibilities for the social changes that were emerging. The collapse of cotton tenancy meant that segregation was no longer a linchpin in the southern economic system. Therefore, northern industrial philanthropy did not have to be as cautious about programs that challenged segregated norms. As a result of Johnson's participation on international committees, including UNESCO, he was also cognizant of the impact of global events at home. In fact, he understood that the defeat of fascism in Europe and the developing Cold War made segregation an embarrassment to the capitalist system. Johnson was aware of these changes and used them to his advantage.[101] He inserted himself in situations—such as United Nations' committees, foundation boards, and governmental advisory committees—that gave him access to prominent personalities. He came to virtually every foundation meeting with a proposal tucked into his briefcase, allowing him more control of the agenda and use of funds.[102] During face-to-face interactions with philanthropists, Johnson was a master of the spoken word. Thus, he was able, through the use of white monetary support, to help students find the "truth" that Du Bois sought on the college campus. He was a strong advocate of research and under his auspices many academic careers were spawned.

In Du Bois's eyes, however, the fact that industrial philanthropy wanted to give African Americans access to education as part of its Cold War agenda was no great victory for blacks.[103] It is important to note that his later criticisms of philanthropy no longer focus on the curtailment of academic freedom and acquiescence in southern segregation, but on the problem of capitalism in general and its complicity in racism. Although supportive of and involved in civil rights efforts,[104] Du Bois realized that a victory against segregation might come at the expense of the global emancipation of people of color—that the end of legal segregation might be a propaganda tool for international capitalism.[105] And this led him to support socialist governments abroad.

At first glance, the fact that Du Bois is reluctant to recognize Johnson's accomplishments in educating the "Talented Tenth" seems like a change in his position on black education. However, when examined in the context of his overall worldview this position is quite consistent.[106] Of many of his fellow black intellectuals, Du Bois wrote in *Dusk of Dawn*, "[They] were deeply American with the old theory of individualism, with a desire to be rich or at least well-to-do, with suspicion of organized labor and labor programs; with a horror of racial segregation."[107] Of their approach, he held, "The bulk of my colleagues saw no essential change in the world. It was the same world with the problems to be attacked with the same methods as before the war. All we needed to do was continue to attack lynching, to bring more cases before the courts, and to insist upon our full citizenship rights."[108] Du Bois believed that as mid century approached, the problems of the world were quite different and that the old liberal solutions would no longer work. Whereas the debate between Du Bois and Washington focused mainly on the narrowing of curricula through the influence of philanthropy, the Du Bois/Johnson disagreement came to encompass questions of the use of capital in the larger society and its impact on issues of race and power. The fact that the latter debate took place, in large part, during the Cold War era made it different in nature and scope from the former. According to Du Bois, few in the race relations circles, including white philanthropists, "moved from [the] undisturbed belief in the capitalist system toward the left, toward a conception of a new democratic control of industry."[109] Du Bois believed that this restructuring of power was critical to worldwide racial emancipation.

When these beliefs got him into trouble during the McCarthy Era, who came to his defense but Johnson. Of this, Du Bois said, "[Of the] 50 presidents of Negro colleges, every one of which I had known and visited—of these only one, Charles S. Johnson of Fisk University, publicly professed belief in my integrity before the trial. . . ."[110] Given Johnson's views and experience with Du Bois, it is likely that he did this not as a gesture of friendship, but as a part of his commitment to the ideal of free speech. In spite of this support, Du Bois continued to shun Johnson. Thus each man was true to his own beliefs—Johnson, to his belief that the freedoms promised by the American system would bring advancement to blacks and Du Bois, to his belief that they would not.

Notes

1. James D. Anderson, *The Education of Blacks in the South, 1860–1935* (Chapel Hill: University of North Carolina Press, 1988); Edward Berman, *The Influence of the Carnegie, Ford, and Rockefeller Foundations on American Foreign Policy: The Ideology of Philanthropy* (Albany: State University of New York Press, 1983); Stephen J. Peeps, "Northern Philanthropy and the Emergence of Black Higher Education—Do-gooders, Compromisers, or Co-conspirators?" *Journal of Negro Education* 50:3 (Summer 1981): 251–269; John Stanfield, *Philanthropy and Jim Crow in American Social Science* (Westport, CT: Greenwood Press, 1985); Teresa J. Odendahl, *Charity Begins at Home: Generosity and Self-interest Among the Philanthropic Elite* (New York: Basic Books, 1990).

2. Washington Gladden, "Tainted Money," *Outlook* 52 (1895): 886–87; William H. Rudy, *The Foundations. Their Use and Abuse* (Washington, D.C.: Public Affairs Press, 1970).

3. Anderson, *Education of Blacks in the South*; Berman, *Influence of the Carnegie, Ford and Rockefeller Foundations*; Stanfield, *Philanthropy and Jim Crow*; E. Franklin Frazier, *Black Bourgeoisie* (Glencoe, IL: Free Press, 1957); Vincent P. Franklin and James D. Anderson, eds. *New Perspectives on Black Educational History* (Boston: G. K. Hall & Co., 1978); Harold J. Laski, *The Dangers of Obedience and Other Essays* (New York: Harper and Brothers, 1930).

4. Robert Bremner, *American Philanthropy* (Chicago: University of Chicago Press, 1988), 2. Eric Anderson and Alfred A. Moss, *Dangerous Donations: Northern Philanthropy and Southern Black Education, 1902–1930* (Columbia: University of Missouri Press, 1999).

5. W.E.B. Du Bois, "The Talented Tenth, "*The Negro Problem: A Series of Articles by Representative American Negroes of Today* (New York: J. Pott & Company, 1903), 33–75.

6. Washington was not opposed to a liberal arts education and in fact, he sent his children to liberal arts colleges. However, for the majority of the freedmen, he advocated industrial education.

7. Booker T. Washington, *Up From Slavery* (New York: A.L. Burt, 1901); Booker T. Washington, "Atlanta Compromise," Cotton States and International Exposition, September 1895, Atlanta, Georgia; Louis R. Harlan, *Booker T. Washington, 1, The Making of a Black Leader, 1856–1901* (New York: Oxford University Press, 1972); Louis R. Harlan, *Booker T. Washington, II, The Wizard of Tuskegee, 1901–1915* (New York: Oxford University Press, 1983).

8. W.E.B. Du Bois, "The Hampton Idea," *The Education of Black People, Ten Critiques, 1906–1960* ed. Herbert Aptheker (New York: Monthly Review Press, 1973): 5–15, 5.

9. Of course, Washington was not wholly a pawn. He, in many cases, manipulated white philanthropists and used their money to support progressive causes such as voting rights. See Harlan, *Booker T. Washington: The Wizard*, 144.

10. Harlan, *Booker T. Washington: The Wizard*.

11. Sterling Stuckey, *Slave Culture. Nationalist Theory and the Foundations of Black America* (New York: Oxford University Press, 1987). As Du Bois's influence grew stronger, Washington grew paranoid and spied on him. In some cases, Washington's meddling curtailed Du Bois' potential successes. For example, in 1903, after the "Boston Riot," Washington became angry with Du Bois and his colleagues for disturbing his public speech. From this point on, Du Bois was on Washington's black list. See Harlan, *Booker T. Washington: The Wizard*, 47–49 for more information. Of course, Du Bois was also constantly trying to stay one step ahead of Washington. In many cases, Du Bois blamed him for difficulties with publishers and funders.

12. Anderson, *The Education of Blacks*. For more information, please see Derrick P. Aldridge, "Conceptualizing a Du Boisian Philosophy of Education: Toward a Model for African American Education," *Educational Theory* 49:3 (Summer 1999): 359–379.

13. W.E.B. Du Bois, "Galileo Galilei," (1908) *The Education of Black People, Ten Critiques, 1906–1960*, ed. Herbert Aptheker. (New York: Monthly Review Press, 1973): 17–30.

14. In 1906, Du Bois discovered that money from the Slater Fund supported an "applied science" Department at Fisk. He was outraged that Fisk, a traditionally liberal arts institution, would succumb to such a request from a northern philanthropist. For more information see, Joe M. Richardson, *The History of Fisk University* (Alabama: The University of Alabama, 1980). In actuality, the Slater Fund grant was only used for the secondary and normal school students who attended Fisk. The college students did not participate in the department of applied sciences.

15. W.E. B. Du Bois, "The Future and Function of the Private Negro College," *The Education of Black People*, 142.

16. W.E.B. Du Bois, *A Soliloquy on Viewing My Life from the Last Decade of Its First Century. The Autobiography of W.E.B. Du Bois* (New York: International Publishers, 1968).

17. Interviews conducted by Patrick J. Gilpin are located in the Fisk University Special Collections (in vault) and were conducted in the 1970s.

18. C. Vann Woodward, *The Strange Career of Jim Crow* (New York: Oxford University Press, 1966).

19. Du Bois, *A Soliloquy*, 108.

20. The Slater Fund was created with monies from John Fox Slater's textile manufacturing business in Norwich, Connecticut. The Fund supported industrial education at black colleges during the nineteenth century.

21. Du Bois, *A Soliloquy*, 151

22. Woodward, *The Strange Career of Jim Crow*.

23. Du Bois, *The Souls of Black Folk*.

24. Du Bois, *A Soliloquy*.

25. W.E.B. Du Bois, *Dusk of Dawn. An Essay Toward an Autobiography of a Race Concept* (New York: Harcourt, Brace, and Company, 1940): 94.

26. The Niagara Movement was a short-lived attempt to secure full civil rights and political participation for African Americans. The NAACP is an interracial organization, which called for integration and an end to lynching. It also supported much of the artistic talent present during the Harlem Renaissance.

27. Du Bois, *A Soliloquy*, 257–258.

28. Ibid. Despite their squabbles, Du Bois gave Villard credit for changing his believe in the capitalist system to a more leftist perspective which supported a more democratic control of industry. (See also Du Bois, *Dusk of Down*, 290).

29. Du Bois, *A Soliloquy*. Du Bois may have also resented Villard for pushing for cooperation between he and Booker T. Washington. Despite leaning toward Du Bois's side philosophically, Villard thought that Washington and Du Bois could work together—this would accomplish more. According to Louis Harlan, "Oswald Garrison Villard "dreamed of joining the forces of Washington, whose work at Tuskegee he admired and supported, and W.E.B. Du Bois, the champion of human rights ... he was virtually alone in his belief that the two leaders could be reconciled." Harlan, *Booker T. Washington: The Wizard*, 360.

30. Manning Marable, *W.E.B. DuBois. Black Radical Democrat* (Massachusetts: G.K. Hall & Co., 1986).

31. W.E.B. Du Bois, *The Quest for the Silver Fleece* (Miami, Florida: Mnemosyne Lewis, 1969), 161; Lewis, *W.E.B. Du Bois. Biography of a Race*, 447.

32. Anderson, *Education of Blacks in the South*.

33. Thomas Jesse Jones, ed. *Negro Education: A Study of the Private and Higher Schools for Colored People in the United States* [1917] (New York: Arno Press and the New York Times, 1969).

34. W.E.B. Du Bois, "Negro Education," reprinted in David Levering Lewis, *W.E.B. Du Bois. A Reader* (New York: Henry Holt Publishers, 1995): 261–269:269.

35. Anderson and Moss, *Dangerous Donations*, 204.

36. This controversy began while Du Bois was at the *Crisis* but came to a head during his tenure at Atlanta University.

37. Lewis, interview with author, 3 August 2001.

38. Ibid. According to David Levering Lewis, Thomas Jesse Jones, the education director for Phelps-Stokes, said that the foundation's idea was sparked by Monroe Work's *Negro Year Book*. Work's book was published by Tuskegee the same year. For a detailed explanation of the situation, see Lewis, *W.E.B. Du Bois. The Fight for Equality*, 426–433.

39. Thomas Jesse Jones quoted in David Levering Lewis, *W.E.B. Du Bois. The Fight for Equality*, 427.

40. David Levering Lewis, interview with author, 3 August 2001.

41. Lewis, *W.E.B. Du Bois. The Fight for Equality*, 434.

42. David Levering Lewis, interview with author, 3 August 2001.

43. It was Charles S. Johnson who persuaded then president of Fisk University, Thomas Elsa Jones, to make an offer to W.E.B. Du Bois. Charles S. Johnson to W.E.B. Du Bois, 26 May 1944, located in Charles S. Johnson Papers [hereafter Johnson Papers], Special Collections, Fisk University, Nashville, Tennessee.

44. Gerald Horne, *Black and Red. W.E.B. Du Bois and the Afro-American Response to the Cold War, 1944–1963* (Albany: SUNY Press, 1986).

45. Du Bois, *A Soliloquy*, 391.

46. Charles S. Johnson, "A Spiritual Autobiography," n.d. [1947], 4, Johnson Papers.

47. Ibid.

48. Although often referred to as "Dr. Johnson," Johnson did not have a Ph.D. He was awarded a Ph. B (Bachelor of Philosophy) from the University of Chicago in 1919. (See University of Chicago Registrar).

49. Martin Bulmer, "Charles S. Johnson, Robert E. Park, and the Research Methods of the Chicago Commission on Race Relations, 1919–22: An Early Experiment in Applied Social Research," *Ethical and Racial Studies* 4:3 (1981): 2899.

50. Patrick J. Gilpin, "Charles S. Johnson. An Intellectual Biograpy," (Ph.D. diss., Vanderbilt University, 1973).

51. Patrick J. Gilpin and Marybeth Gasman, "Charles S. Johnson: Sociologist, Race Relations Diplomat, and Educator during the Age of Jim Crow," (Albany: State University of New York Press, forthcoming).

52. Edwin R. Embree, *Thirteen Against the Odds* (New York: The Viking Press, 1946).

53. Charles S. Johnson, Edwin R. Embree, and W. W. Alexander, *The Collapse of Cotton Tenancy: Summary of Field Studies & Statistical Surveys, 1933–35* (Chapel Hill: University of North Carolina Press, 1935): 65.

54. Perhaps it is indicative of their contrasting personalities that Johnson's journal was entitled *Opportunity* while Du Bois' was entitled *Crisis*.

55. David Levering Lewis, *When Harlem was in Vogue* (New York: Oxford University Press, 1981): 125.

56. Blyden Jackson, "A Postlude to a Renaissance," *Southern Review* 25, 4 (1990): 746–765, 753.

57. Gilpin and Gasman, *Charles S. Johnson*.

58. Charles S. Johnson, *Shadow of a Plantation* (Chicago: The University of Chicago, 1934); idem., *Patterns of Negro Segregation* (New York: Harper & Row, 1943); and idem., *The Negro College Graduate* (New York: Negro Universities Press, 1969). Richard Robbins, *Sidelines Activist: Charles S. Johnson and the Struggle for Civil Rights* (Jackson: University of Mississippi Press, 1996), 179.

59. Charles S. Johnson, "Famous Sociologist Asks, Answers Some Key Questions for Negroes," *The Chicago Defender* (September 26, 1942): 32.

60. For more information see, August Meier, *A White Scholar in the Black Community* (Amherst: University of Massachusetts Press, 1993); Anthony Platt, *E. Franklin Frazier Reconsidered* (New Brunswick, New Jersey: Rutgers University Press, 1991).

61. W.E.B. Du Bois to Ernest Alexander 11 July 1946; Carter Wesley to Ernest Alexander, 15 July 1946; James Stamps to Ernest Alexander, 18 July 1946; James Stamps to Ernest Alexander, 26 June 1946; Confidential memo to the president of the alumni association and alumni representatives on the Fisk board of trustees, 12 July 1946; Ernest Alexander to W.E.B. Du Bois, 20 July 1946; Sadie St. Clair Daniels to Ernest Alexander, 23 July 1946; W.E.B. Du Bois to Ms. Freda Kirchway, editor of *Nation* Magazine, 26 July 1946, all located on Reel 58 in the W.E.B. Du Bois Papers [hereafter Du Bois Papers], University of Massachusetts, Amherst. W.E.B. Du Bois, "A Crisis at Fisk," *Nation* (September 7, 1946): 269–270, 270.

62. W.E.B. Du Bois to Ernest Alexander 11 July 1946; Carter Wesley to Ernest Alexander, 15 July 1946; James Stamps to Ernest Alexander, 18 July 1946; James Stamps to Ernest Alexander, 26 June 1946; Confidential memo to the president of the alumni association and alumni representatives on the Fisk board of trustees, 12 July 1946; Ernest Alexander to W.E.B. Du Bois, 20 July 1946; Sadie St. Clair Daniels to Ernest Alexander, 23 July 1946; W.E.B. Du Bois to Ms. Freda Kirchway, editor of *Nation* Magazine, 26 July 1946, all located on Reel 58 in the Du Bois Papers. W.E.B. Du Bois, "A Crisis at Fisk," *Nation* (September 7, 1946): 269–270, 270.

63. Robbins, *Sidelines Activist*; Katrina Sanders, "Building Racial Tolerance Through Education: The Fisk University Race Relations Institute, 1944–1969," (Ph.D. diss., University of Illinois, 1997).

64. John Hope Franklin, interview with author, 5 June 1999.

65. For more information on these programs, see Charles S. Johnson Papers, 1955–56 clipping file, located in the Fisk Archives. Specifically, Charles S. Johnson to Marie Johnson, July 25, 1956, box 144, folder 8, Johnson Papers. In this letter, Johnson notes the growth of the university. See also, Gilpin, "Charles S. Johnson. An Intellectual Biography."

66. Marybeth Gasman and Edward Epstein, "Modern Art in the Old South: The Role of the Arts in Fisk University's Campus Curriculum," *Educational Researcher* 4:2 (March 2002): 13–20.

67. Du Bois, "The Future and Function of the Private Black College, (1946)" *The Education of Black People*, 144, 146. For more information on Du Bois' views on higher education, please see Aldridge. "Conceptualizing a Du Boisian Philosophy;" Frederick Dunn, "The Educational Philosophies of Washington, Du Bois, and Houston: Laying the Foundations for Afrocentrism and Multiculturalism," *Journal of Negro Education* 62, 1 (Winter 1993): 24–34; James B. Stewart, "The Legacy of W.E.B. Du Bois for Contemporary Black Studies," *Journal of Negro Education* 53, 3 (Summer 1984): 296–312.

68. Du Bois, "The Future and Function of the Private Black College (1946)," *The Education of Black People*, 144. This speech was given at the commencement of Knoxville College, in Tennessee on June 10, 1946. Charles S. Johnson became president of Fisk University in July the same year—much to Du Bois' dismay. Du Bois' opposition to Johnson's selection is evident in the continual theme in the speech of presidents not being a financier or someone who solicits monetary gifts.

69. Du Bois, "The Future and Function of the Private Black College, 157.

70. Ibid., 140.

71. One of the reasons Du Bois, at one point, called for the elimination or consolidation of the weaker black college is their lack of stable financial support. State funding would, in Du Bois's mind, lead to security for black colleges.

72. Marybeth Gasman, "A Renaissance in Nashville: Charles S. Johnson's Use of Philanthropy to Build Fisk Univeristy in the Post-War Period," (Ph.D. diss., Indiana University, 2000). Gilpin and Gasman, "Charles S. Johnson."

73. Butler Jones, "The Tradition of Sociology Teaching," in John Bracey, August Meier, and Elliot Rudwick, eds. *The Black Sociologists: The First Half Century* (Belmont, CA: Wadsworth Publishing Company, 1971): 137.

74. Gilpin, "Charles S. Johnson," 631.

75. Peggy Alsup, interview by author, 31 March 1999.

76. Lewis, *W.E.B. Du Bois. The Fight for Equality*, 157.

77. Ibid.; Adolph Reed, *W.E.B. Du Bois and American Political Thought* (New York: Oxford University Press, 1997); Hugh Murray, "Review Essay. Du Bois and the Cold War." *The Journal of Ethnic Studies* 15:3 (Fall 1986): 115–124; Dan S. Green and Earl Smith, "W.E.B. Du Bois and the Concepts of Race and Class," *Phylon* XLIV 4 (December 1983): 262–272.

78. Harlan. *Booker T. Washington. The Wizard.*

79. Ibid., 291.

80. Ironically, Charles S. Johnson wrote an article entitled "The Social Philosophy of Booker T. Washington," in the April 1928 issue of *Opportunity*. His ability to see the best of Washington's ideas may have contributed to Du Bois' mistrust of Johnson.

81. W.E.B. Du Bois, *Darkwater. Voices from Within the Veil* (New York: AMS Press, 1920, reprinted 1969): 136.

82. Lewis, interview with author, 3 August 2001.

83. Stuckey, *Slave Culture*, 272.

84. Lewis, interview with author, 3 August 2001.

85. W.E.B. Du Bois to George Padmore, 17 March 1950 in Herbert Aptheker ed. *W.E.B. Du Bois, The Correspondence of W.E.B. Du Bois, Volume III, Selections, 1944–1963* (Amherst: University of Massachusetts Press, 1978), 281.

86. Gasman, "A Renaissance in Nashville."

87. Lewis, interview with author, 3 August 2001. Lewis was a student at Fisk University during Johnson's presidency. Other students have corroborated his statements including: Richard Thornell, interview with author, 23 August, 2001, Peggy Alsup interview with author, 31 March 1999, Prince Rivers, interview with author, 25 March 1999, Vivian Norton, interview with author, 11 May 1999, Earl Daily, interview with author, 22 April 1999, Jane Forde, interview with author, 27 April 1999, Richard Thornell, interview with author, August 24, 2001.

88. Charles S. Johnson, "The Present Status of Race Relations in the South," *Social Forces*. 23, 1, October 1944: 27–32, 27. For similar rhetoric, see idem., "The Negro in Post-War Reconstruction: his Hopes, Fears and Possibilities," *Journal of Negro Education* 11:4 (October 1942): 343–348; idem., "Social Changes and Their Effects on Race Relations in the South," *Social Forces* 23:5 (March 1945): 343–348; and idem., "The Decade in Race Relations," *Journal of Negro Education*, 13:3 (Summer 1944): 441–446.

89. Charles S. Johnson. "A Southern Negro's View of the South," *New York Times Magazine* (September 23, 1956): 15, 64–67, 65.

90. Du Bois, *Education of Black People*, 145–146.

91. W.E.B. Du Bois to Ernest Alexander, 9 November 1946, Reel 58, W.E.B. Du Bois Papers.

92. W.E.B. Du Bois to Professor Merle Curti, 4 June 1958, Herbert Aptheker, ed. *The correspondence of W.E.B. Du Bois. Volume III Selections, 1944–1963* (Amherst: University of Massachusetts Press, 1976), 430.

93. Lewis, *W.E.B. Du Bois. The Fight for Equality*.

94. Ibid., 431.

95. Cornel West, "W.E.B. Du Bois: An Interpretation," Africana: An Encyclopedia of the African and African American Experience," eds. Kwame Anthony Appiah and Henry Louis Gates (New York: Basic Civitas Books, 1999).

96. Lewis, interview with author, 3 August 2001.

97. Richard Bardolph, *The Negro Vanguard*. (New York: Vintage Books, 1959): 327.

98. Robbins, *Sidelines Activist*, 9.

99. Gilpin and Gasman, "Charles S. Johnson." In 1945, Johnson was selected to be the first black president of the Southern Sociological Society. The following year he presided over the society's annual meeting in Atlanta, Georgia. The conference announcement included information about housing at the Biltmore Hotel. However, when Juliette V. Phifer, a black member of the society, sent in her hotel reservation she was told, by Johnson, that accommodations were not available for black participants. Alternative housing was made available for black participants at Atlanta University. Rather than risk his position in the society, Johnson acquiesed in southern norms. Charles S. Johnson to Juliette V. Phifer, May 7, 1946, Charles S. Johnson Papers.

100. Gilpin, "Charles S. Johnson," 635.
101. Marybeth Gasman, "Passport to the Front of the Bus: The Impact of Fisk University's International Program on Segregation in Nashville Tennessee," *49th Parallel: An Interdisciplinary Journal of North American Studies*, 7 (Winter 2001): online journal at: artsweb.bham.ac.uk/49th parallel/backissues/issue7/Frontpg7.htm
102. Prince Rivers, interview with author, 25 March 1999.
103. Lewis, interview with author, 3 August 2001.
104. Horne, *Black and Red*.
105. Lewis, interview with author, 3 August 2001; Lewis, *W.E.B. Du Bois, The Fight for Equality*.
106. Reed, *W.E.B. Du Bois and American Political Thought*.
107. Du Bois, *Dusk of Dawn*, 290.
108. Ibid.
109. Ibid.

THE PHILANTHROPIC AEGIS

HUGH HAWKINS

Autonomy was not claimed by the institutional associations. They did as their members directed, or so leaders declared. Another source of control, less often mentioned, was agencies that contributed financial support, notably philanthropic foundations, those new social institutions of immense potential that were an American innovation of the early twentieth century. Foundation influence over certain of the associations ultimately became a principal route for foundation-inspired changes in colleges and universities themselves.

Around 1910 the institutional associations sometimes provided the setting for principled opposition to foundations. When the effort to win a federal charter for the Rockefeller Foundation heightened worries about the expanding power of these private bodies, Schurman of Cornell addressed the issue before his assembled presidential colleagues. He warned of the foundations' meddlesome tendencies and their freedom from public accountability. In general, however, the establishment of foundations stirred lively anticipations of funding for association members. Only after World War I did it become clear that the associations themselves could benefit from foundation grants, through both direct support and subvention for specific projects. Apart from funding, the foundations influenced the associations as models of successful "third-sector" ventures, which could claim to be neither governmental nor profit seeking. In structure and ideology the two types of organization found much to share. Both developed central bureaucracies, claimed to be "above politics," and faced accusations of asserting illegitimate power.[1]

Early Encounters

In seeking to understand the foundations, it is misleading to dwell on priorities between the ventures of Andrew Carnegie and those of John D. Rockefeller. Carnegie, with his essays, elaborated a theory of stewardship for the age of gigantic industrial fortunes, whereas Rockefeller said little on the subject. As Roger Geiger has pointed out, however, the two men's philanthropies developed in parallel. First came aid to single great educational institutions (the University of Chicago, Carnegie Tech), then research institutes (the Rockefeller Institute for Medical Research, the Carnegie Institution of Washington), then broad educational aid through a philanthropic trust (the General Education Board [GEB], the Carnegie Foundation for the Advancement of Teaching [CFAT]), climaxing in general-purpose foundations to which the bulk of the two men's benefactions was assigned (the Rockefeller Foundation, the Carnegie Corporation of New York).[2]

Rockefeller's religiously motivated giving had begun in his youth. Less religious and disinclined to aid religious institutions, Carnegie in his early charities aimed at stimulating self-help and local initiative. In both cases, the men they chose to administer their educational trusts were not mere dispensers of charity. Rather, as representatives of a new species that later evoked the name *phitanthropoid*, they launched drives for standardization that suited the current "gospel of efficiency." Admirers of "system," they wanted society to move away from laissez-faire toward greater cooperation. Rockefeller's chief advisor in philanthropic matters, the minister Frederick T. Gates, had caught the oil magnate's eye as head of the American Baptist Education Society, founded in 1888. Gates, who had sought to limit the multiplication of impecunious Baptist colleges, claimed to have introduced "the principles of scientific giving" into Rockefeller's charities. Henry S. Pritchett, having recently assumed the presidency of MIT, began cultivating Carnegie's friendship in 1901 and strongly influenced the shaping of the Carnegie Foundation, which he headed for twenty-five years. Disdaining mere alms giving, both Gates and Pritchett were determined that these philanthropic programs for education would bring order to what they considered a chaotic situation.[3]

Having originally directed its attention to the South, the General Education Board (founded 1902, chartered by Congress 1903) launched in 1905 a program of aid to higher education throughout the nation. According to Rockefeller's directive, drafted by Gates, the income from additional endowment was to be used "to promote a comprehensive system of higher education in the United States." Of the various things "system" might involve, Gates, who headed the GEB from 1907 to 1917, was particularly attentive to institutional distribution. Were colleges too close to each other to be well supported? Were some ill-placed in relation to population? The earliest report of the board, covering the period 1902–14, contains information on colleges that were poor, scantily attended, and limited to narrow curricula, information meant to demonstrate an oversupply. Gates did not want any grants to go to the "no less than nine so-called Christian colleges" in Nebraska, which had sprung, he argued, from real estate speculation and local pride. In Gates's opinion, the institutions of higher education in the country could well be reduced in number by three-fourths and "formed by careful selection into a system of higher education." Arguments that weaker institutions met important needs in sustaining a religious tradition or providing access to education for young people nearby or that they promised future usefulness if college attendance increased, were not given much credence in the years when the idea of system dominated the new foundations. In their formative period, the great foundations, like the institutional associations, stressed the twin ideas of the need for educational order and the unreliability of democratic government as a source for such order.[4]

In the long run, the GEB lost its more extreme ambitions for reordering higher education. Its grants in the early 1920s to bolster inflation-ravaged faculty salaries had more to do with the need to keep teachers teaching than with a master plan for selective institutional survival. But the desire for central coordination continued—in not only the GEB's historic grants to medical schools, but also its less conspicuous efforts to promote regularization of financial records. Reasoning that accurate knowledge about an institution's needs and likelihood of survival required the capacity to decipher its accounts, the board enlisted Trevor Arnett, a University of Chicago administrator with a genius for accounting, and sent him into the field. (He claimed to find one college president who kept receipts and bills in his hat.) The institutional associations, having themselves urged standard statistics as early as a NASU discussion of 1904, welcomed Arnett's work, particularly his guidebook *College and University Finance* (1922). If those at the center saw standard accounting methods as a source of control, local administrators saw them as easing the rising burden of questionnaires and offering financial benefits. An AAU delegate expressed thanks for an address by Arnett which showed how "in large industrial concerns . . . great sums of money are saved by proper accounting systems." In 1928, the year Arnett became president of the GEB, he also served as president of the AAC, a post usually reserved for the head of a college. His AAC presidential address advocated higher faculty salaries, a cause he believed might be advanced by waiving the right of permanent tenure.[5]

Although the ACE had used foundation funds in its early ventures in international educational exchange, it was not until 1921 that it received major foundation funding for a project. In a process often to be repeated, informal discussions among foundation officials, representatives of associations, and college administrators led to a conference that drew up a proposal for an investigation with an overseeing board and a staff to carry out the research. The investigation of college revenues and expenditures recommended in this case was to be much broader than Arnett's inquiry for the GEB. Four foundations, including the GEB and the Carnegie Corporation, supported the plan with $170,000, a figure that dwarfed the ACE's earlier expenditures. The ACE set up a commission on the Educational Finance Inquiry headed by George D. Strayer of Teachers College, Columbia. It issued a thirteen-volume report in 1924 comparing educational and other public expenses and examining the effect on education of different systems of taxation.[6]

The Carnegie Foundation and the Associations

Although the GEB's matching grants to colleges exceeded $10 million by 1914, the Carnegie Foundation (incorporated 1905, chartered by Congress 1906) figured more prominently in the deliberations of the institutional associations. Developing in part because of expectations for widespread Carnegie pension benefits, this salience also owed much to the determination of Pritchett to make the foundation a "great agency" in the unification of American higher education. A figure representative of the Progressive Era's quest for system, Pritchett had been a professor of astronomy, the head of the U.S. Coast and Geodetic Survey, and a promoter of an independent National Bureau of Standards. He scarcely expected Newtonian relationships in the educational universe, but he was determined that it be mapped and standardized. Carnegie's idea of awarding pensions to professors, whom he regarded as underpaid altruists, sustained considerable reshaping under Pritchett's influence. After initial reluctance, the founder himself took pride in the foundation's "good work . . . in raising the standards of education." With the pension program absorbing more and more of the CFAT's resources, Carnegie in 1913 gave it additional endowment for a "Division of Educational Enquiry" to continue the investigations for which it was already famous.[7]

Aiding Pritchett in his undertaking were the trustees of the new foundation, nearly all college or university presidents, some of them leaders in the institutional associations. Since Carnegie's gift specified pensions for teachers in "higher educational institutions," Prichett declared it his duty to define the type and identify legitimate exemplars through careful investigation. Of the 627 initial questionnaires sent out to putative institutions of higher education, 421 were returned. Building on standards set earlier by the New York Board of Regents, the CFAT's pioneering national list ranked as institutions of higher education only those employing at least six full-time professors, offering four years of liberal studies, and requiring for admission four years of high school preparation (a minimum of fourteen "units"). These standards meant many exclusions. No college in the South was eligible, although Tulane raised its admission requirements in time to be on the initial list of fifty-two "accepted institutions." There was nothing particularly new in the complaint that the terms *college* and *university* lacked fixed meaning. Daniel C. Gilman had talked that way a quarter of a century earlier. But Pritchett's amassing of data about institutions that claimed to purvey higher education helped make him for two decades one of the most powerful figures in the academic world.[8]

Pritchett showed no hesitation in exerting his influence on the institutional associations. His second annual report included a rather acerbic history of the AAU, which he criticized as inconsistent in its membership standards and remiss in not defining *university* and *graduate study*. At its next meeting the AAU elected the CFAT to membership and appointed Pritchett to its Committee on Aim and Scope. President Schurman greeted the appointment with barbed wit, saying Pritchett was being asked "to assist in doing a very small piece of work which he can easily throw off, standardizing the colleges of the United States." Soon AAU committees took to meeting in the CFAT's offices.[9]

Two institutional associations promptly confronted the foundation over its decision to deny pensions to professors at tax-supported institutions, an exclusion implied but not clearly required by Carnegie's letter of gift. State universities and land-grant colleges seized the occasion to make use of their respective associations. In a series of meetings and letters, Pritchett defended his position, and he used the first CFAT *Bulletin* to discuss the controversy. Without the authority conferred on spokesmen by the existence of the NASU and the AAACES, it is doubtful that public institutions would have received so full a hearing. These two associations acted as pressure groups, sending representatives to argue before the CFAT trustees. The AAU played a different role. It provided neutral ground on which both Van Hise of Wisconsin, with the state university perspective, and Eliot of Harvard, chair of the Carnegie trustees, could explore the issues, and the discussion was broadened to include long-term effects.[10]

The controversy dragged on. Van Hise and his allies often had sympathy with Pritchett's hope to restructure American higher education, but they contended that the CFAT would gain more leverage on public institutions if they were included among candidates for the pension program. What seemed the climax came in January 1908, when Pritchett addressed a special meeting of the NASU. Shortly thereafter, he and Van Hise worked out a compromise for temporary participation by some state universities, while those institutions launched efforts to develop state-supported pension programs.[11]

At this juncture, Carnegie himself intervened, adding to the original endowment so that tax-supported universities could be admitted without time limitation. Delighted members of the NASU sent an engraved resolution of appreciation to Carnegie and elected Pritchett to honorary membership. But Pritchett, still determined to elevate and regularize academic standards, managed to apply strict eligibility requirements to the public institutions. Besides meeting the entrance and graduation criteria already set, they must have an annual income of $100,000 and demonstrate that politicians did not control their governing boards. Partly because of these standards, but also because of the trustees' growing awareness that even their expanded funds might not cover the commitments already made to private institutions, only nine public institutions were admitted to the pension program before the shift to a contributory system in 1919. The NASU nevertheless took satisfaction in its accomplishment, with one member irenically suggesting that, even if all were not included, it was still a gain that some of the state universities were deemed equal to the private.[12]

Effective in dealing with Congress, the land-grant association was not well positioned to attract private philanthropy for its members. After Carnegie's intervention but before specific tax-supported beneficiaries had been named, Pritchett addressed the AAACES. Noting that the foundation would aid only colleges limiting admission to candidates with four years of high school education, he expressed doubt that it would be wise for many of the agricultural colleges to break with their constituencies by setting requirements that high. Even as he gave such advice, unusually localistic for him, he criticized the agricultural colleges for failing to become part of a system: "You have not yet brought about in your own conception . . . any uniformity as to what your mission is, as to what your work is, as to what your relations to education are to be. This is exactly what the Carnegie Foundation desires to know." The association thereupon wishfully voted to acknowledge the foundation's "sympathetic and helpful consideration of the land-grant colleges."[13]

Debate at the next year's convention featured reactions to Pritchett's challenge, with renewed efforts made to specify the function of land-grant colleges and to reconsider their entrance and graduation requirements. There were also some sour grapes. One speaker called the CFAT's endowment "pitiful" compared to the vast public wealth on which the land-grant colleges drew. The 1910 presidential address was devoted to answering the "unwarranted disparagement" to which Pritchett had subjected the land-grant institutions in his latest annual report. Of the members of the AAACES which were not also state universities, only one, Purdue, was added to the Carnegie program after the donor's second gift. Perhaps this was a minimal gesture toward the pleas made by the association, but it was more probably intended to reward the coordination recently worked out between that land-grant institution and Indiana University, a triumph of system on the state level.[14]

Although recognizing that many colleges had begun under religious auspices, Carnegie had made clear his wish that the pension program not include "sectarian institutions," those "under the control of a sect or [requiring] Trustees (or a majority thereof), Officers, Faculty or Students, to belong to any specified sect, or which impose any theological test." Excluded institutions often protested to the foundation, leaving what one CFAT insider branded an ugly record of special pleading and sharp dealings. Reaction to this discrimination helps explain the formation of the Council of Church Boards of Education and its offspring, the AAC. If the much-touted pension program barred church colleges, then they had better begin to counsel together about their position in American education. Perhaps even more influential in the creation of the AAC were the comments in CFAT publications on the oversupply of small colleges, animadversions echoed in the first report of the GEB (1914). As discussed in chapter 4, the originators of the AAC, sharing the foundations' concern about standards, set minimum qualifications for membership and defined a "minimum college"; nevertheless, the AAC hoped to encourage weaker institutions that seemed on the right track.[15]

Threatened with bankruptcy, the CFAT in 1916 launched a study of possibilities for a contributory pension plan as an alternative to its original policy. In meeting the crisis, Pritchett took pains to involve the institutional associations. A special commission included representatives of the AAC, the AAU, and the NASU, as well as the newly formed American Association of University Professors.

While the president-dominated institutional associations proved largely acquiescent in the CFAT's plans for the Teachers Insurance and Annuity Association (TIAA), the AAUP raised strong objections. Resulting changes included the addition of professors to the governing board of the new organizations, and the episode forecast a long record of AAUP challenges to positions taken by institutional associations.[16]

Foundations and Associations in the Interwar Period

The Carnegie Foundation's much wealthier sibling, the Carnegie Corporation (established 1911), had assisted the beleaguered noncontributory pension program. Although the two continued to work together, the corporation began to have an independent role in education. After Carnegie's death in 1919, the corporation gradually paid off the backlog of commitments to his favorite causes and instituted programs far more socially directive than those embraced by the founder, a quintessential nineteenth-century liberal. In 1919 the corporation gave $5 million to the National Academy of Sciences and its activist offshoot the National Research Council, soon followed by other grants to encourage development of science and scholarship. Under the presidency of James Rowland Angell, who left to head Yale University, and the acting presidency of Pritchett, the Carnegie Corporation sought to coordinate research and centralize policy formation through entities "accessible to the federal government but not controlled by it." The institutional associations, with their limited-government ideology and their position as national networks, were potential beneficiaries of this approach.[17]

The Carnegie Corporation's president from 1923 to 1941, Frederick P. Keppel, knew the workings of one institutional association well. As an assistant to Butler at Columbia he had performed administrative chores for the AAU. As an Assistant Secretary of War during World War I he had worked closely with training programs and won the intense admiration of Samuel Capen. In 1925 the board of regents of the University of Wisconsin showed its antipathy toward both the origins of foundations' wealth and their reformist pretensions by forbidding the university to accept their grants. Keppel reacted with a landmark address before the AAU. Muting the language of system, he praised the breadth of view possible for foundations and their role as clearinghouses for educational ideas. He predicted that thenceforth foundations would channel their funds less to individual institutions than to projects of general applicability, a change that promised enhanced importance for institutional associations as sponsors of foundation-funded undertakings.[18]

Unlike the other associations, the ACE and the AAC drew often and heavily on foundation largesse—and wisdom, as their leaders tended diplomatically to add. Beginning in 1921, when it won the grant for an investigation of educational finance, the ACE usually received at least twice as much yearly income from foundations as from members' dues. The grants to the AAC were relatively small when compared to those received by the ACE and were almost always less than income from dues (Table 3). Still, at times the AAC seemed a captive of the Carnegie Corporation, from which it received its first grant in 1925 and in whose headquarters the AAC executive committee often met, with corporation officials present. In keeping with Keppel's special interest in advancing the fine arts, the AAC accepted Carnegie Corporation grants to conduct studies of campus architecture and of visual arts teaching, as well as grants to allow brief campus stays, including concerts and other performances, by visiting artists.[19]

Even while citing gifts from foundations as evidence that the ACE was a responsible and permanent body, Capen used the dues support from members to justify an extravagant claim that the council was "absolutely democratic, absolutely representative." Arguing that an endowment would be unhealthy for the council, he saw nothing wrong in continuing to seek project support from endowed philanthropic foundations. In fact, although it failed in efforts to get building funds from the Carnegie Corporation, the ACE quickly became the greatest beneficiary of foundation aid among the institutional associations. At the apex of other associations, it was a credible locus for foundation efforts to reform the whole of American higher education. Grants came from various Rockefeller philanthropies, the Carnegie Corporation, and the Commonwealth Fund, created in 1918 by Edward S. Harkness and his mother, widow of one of John D. Rockefeller's Standard Oil partners. The ACE

TABLE 3

Financial Receipts of the AAC and the ACE, 1918–1950

Association of American Colleges

Fiscal Year Ending in:	From Dues	% of Receipts from Dues	From Foundation Grants	% of Receipts from Foundation Grants	Total Receipts
1918	$2,350	96.7	0	0	$2,430
1920	5,730	100.0	0	0	5,730
1922		(not available)			8,070
1924	7,000	94.0	0	0	7,450
1926	7,880	61.2	$5,000	38.8	12,880
1928	9,950	59.7	0	0	16,670
1930	20,750	79.7	2,000	7.7	26,020
1932	21,660	32.1	39,870	59.1	67,470
1934	23,620	80.6	1,500	5.1	29,290
1936	25,340	54.2	14,530	31.1	46,750
1938	26,400	32.1	10,500	12.8	82,190
1940	27,680	34.7	6,750	8.5	79,680
1942	29,010	42.9	19,300	28.5	67,700
1944	29,550	37.5	26,250	33.3	78,860
1946	30,710	54.0	2,000	3.5	56,820
1948	47,950	59.2	0	0	80,930
1950	49,490	63.0	0	0	78,560

American Council on Education

Fiscal Year Ending in:	From Dues	% of Receipts from Dues	From Foundation Grants	% of Receipts from Foundation Grants	Total Receipts	Receipts for General Fund	Receipts for Special Funds
1918				(not available)			
1920	$23,540	98.2	0	0	$23,970		
1922	23,910	29.1	$57,500	70.0	82,190		
1924	25,270	25.3	49,720	49.7	99,960		
1926	32,780	15.3	142,390	66.3	214,890		
1928	34,070	20.3	114,450	68.3	167,460		
1930	36,240	34.1	50,870	47.8	106,410		
1932	34,650	49.6	17,190	24.6	69,830		
1934	22,670	28.5	38,510	48.5	79,450		
1936	21,590	10.1	158,560	64.3	212,930		
1938	20,980	8.5	173,700	70.5	246,510		
1940	24,110					$102.580	$854,570
1942	30,840					92,870	649,620
1944	36,240					88,180	728,990
1946	45,990					105,430	850,590
1948	84,500					140,530	758,100
1950	113,120					151,300	880,080

Source: For the AAC, Treasurer's Report appearing in *AAC Bulletin* and, for the ACE. Auditor's Report. Treasurer's Report, or "Financial Statements of the American Council of Education" appearing in *Educational Record*, for fiscal years ending in even numbers. Notes: I have substracted the opening "cash on hand" in figuring total receipts for each year. To avoid double-counting I have deleted AAC dues allocations in 1948 and 1950 to the Arts Program and the Commission on Christian Higher Education. After 1938 the ACE Financial Statement did not separately identify receipts from foundations.

The creation in 1939–40 of an ACE Publications Revolving Fund prevents continuing a consistent series and heightens the likelihood of double-counting. I have chosen from 1940–30 to list receipts for the General Fund (which included all dues), spent mostly for central office expenses, and receipts for Special Funds, spent mostly for special projects but including such standing programs as the Cooperative Test Service. Because the central

TABLE 3 (Continued)

office received payments from special projects for administrative services, these two figures cannot be added together without double counting. It might be possible from archival records to determine the changing proportion of Special Funds income from Foundation grants and from fees paid by governments and private bodies. I have not undertaken that chore. Note also that the Publications Fund does not appear above.

 ACE receipts for special funds in 1938 were $134,620. The sharp increase in 1940 traces mostly to receipts for the American Youth Commission, the Cooperative Test Service, and the Commission on Teacher Education, the three amounting to approximately $500,000.

 The ACE fiscal year shifted in 1936–37 from May 1–April 30 to July 1–June 30. The fourteen-month figures for that year do not appear in this table.

 Direct contributions from John D. Rockefeller, Jr., usually from his Benevolent Fund, are counted as receipts from foundations.

benefited (as did the AAC to some extent) from having a central staff that could draw up projects and negotiate with foundation officers, sharing with them an emerging style and language.[20]

 Specially created committees rather than central office staffs usually conducted foundation-supported projects, such as the ACE's programs to improve the teaching of modern languages, which the Carnegie Corporation supported, and others to promote "personnel methods" (testing, record keeping, and counseling), which had Rockefeller backing. But after 1924 the ACE sought and sometimes obtained a percentage of grants to cover "the cost of executive work." With no fellowship program for scholarly research, such as those foundations provided through the NRC and the SSRC, the ACE did little for small-scale investigations and in 1936 explicitly denied any role as "middleman between persons who have projects and foundations or other sources of financial support." A few months later, however, Zook was advising the president of New Mexico State College on which members of foundation staffs would be most likely to favor a program to improve rural life.[21]

 Many avenues could turn money into influence in educational affairs. Foundations could carry out their own research projects, such as the CFAT's studies of teacher education, or action projects, such as the GEB's program to coordinate the black colleges of Atlanta. One alternative was to create new organizations, technically independent but designed to accept foundation grants, such as the Institute of Economics and the American Association for Adult Education, both established in the 1920s under Carnegie Corporation sponsorship. But sometimes foundations chose institutional associations as their vehicles. If the ACE sponsored a study, it could be "distinctly understood that the Foundations have no control of the investigation or of the publication of the results." Such an arrangement appealed to foundations in the face of persisting questions about their exercise of power without public supervision (in short, about their legitimacy), but only the naive imagined the foundations to be neutral benefactors of other organizations' programs. The highly courteous correspondence between foundations and associations demonstrated the influence that accompanied the power to give or withhold grants, to insist on redefinition of goals before a project was financed, or to fund a project in stages. In 1927 a professor warned of the threat to university autonomy if foundations were allowed to develop into a "general staff." Similar questions were raised in a statistically meticulous examination of the foundations published in 1936. Such studies, it need hardly be said, were not supported by the institutional associations.[22]

 Its foundation-supported study of educational finance helped establish the ACE's viability as a national instrument for analyzing educational problems. During the 1920s foundations came to regard the council as a highly respectable donee. It was based in education, their favorite benefaction, and as an association of associations was well placed to perform a sifting function. The head of social science programs for the GEB and the Rockefeller Foundation let it be known in 1936 that the ACE "will probably have to prepare the way before any national association of school officials is likely to get a grant from any of the foundations with which I am acquainted."[23]

 While performing mediatorial work in getting grants for other organizations, the ACE itself grew increasingly dependent on foundation aid. The failure of the GEB to approve successive plans at the ACE for a study of the teaching of English effectively killed the undertaking. Support for the ACE was in doubt during the early years of the Great Depression when leaders of the Rockefeller philanthropies undertook searching reconsiderations that led them to express dissatisfaction with projects that were "often unrelated to human aspiration or need." From such reappraisal grew opposition to continued support of the ACE so long as it kept to the course Mann had charted. As Associate Director John H. MacCracken had foreseen, the views of Rockefeller and Carnegie officials were controlling in decisions of 1933–34 to restructure the ACE. (See table 3 for the changing percentage of ACE receipts from foundations.)[24]

Mann's vision of American education, with its principled objections to direct federal aid, was ill-adapted to times of economic crisis. Beyond that, he did not, in the foundations' view, have the administrative talents necessary for a greatly expanded program. It was more than a personnel change that the foundations sought. They encouraged the ACE to broaden its field to all of American education, judging its traditional focus on higher education unduly elitist. With the collaboration of Dean William F. Russell of Teachers College, Columbia, who was ACE chairman, the New York—based foundation executives had their way, and the ACE expanded its responsibilities to include "all phases" of American education. George F. Zook became the new ACE director, and the GEB granted $300,000 for "general expenses and cooperative enterprises" during the next five years. The council thereupon began helping the Federal Emergency Relief Administration in a student-aid program that went directly counter to Mann's antigovernment pronouncements.[25]

A second grant of a half million dollars, also from the GEB, directed the council into youth problems broadly conceived. Through its new American Youth Commission, the ACE launched studies far beyond its traditional province, dealing with lower schools and venturing into questions of unemployment and crime. Notable publications resulted, including *Youth Tell Their Story* and *Children of Bondage*. Other GEB grants to the ACE supported programs for education through film and teacher training, from the latter of which the American Association of Colleges of Teacher Education (AACTE) ultimately sprang. Both projects reflected the GEB's new interest in what it labeled "general education." In response to foundation wishes, the ACE had radically shifted course.[26]

In 1940–41 the GEB grant was up for renewal. The Problems and Plans and Executive Committees began in 1939 to devote much of their attention to the impending end of the GEB's subvention for general purposes, which had averaged roughly $50,000 a year. Zook observed that, although certain services, such as surveys, financial advising, and tests, might be partly covered by user fees, continued foundation support for even these programs would usually be needed. As to nonproject expenses, dues, which had reached approximately $22,500 a year, could cover part but not all. Zook noted with pride that among the "four comprehensive councils" created during and after World War I (all heavily reliant on foundation support), the ACE alone had drawn significantly on membership dues. (He had in mind the National Research Council, the American Council of Learned Societies, and the Social Science Research Council.) A special ACE committee under Mark A. May of Yale's Institute of Human Relations began reconsidering programs and seeking funds. The upshot was a request to the GEB for an endowment of one and a half million dollars to provide a building and annual endowment income. Less ambitious requests for term grants were also presented. The GEB opted for a two-year grant of $95,000 and set up its own committee under George A. Works of the University of Chicago to review the functioning of the ACE.[27]

A frequent appraiser of institutions, the ACE was now itself the object of inspection. The Works report urged an even stronger role for the Problems and Plans Committee, making it a source of major policy pronouncements, and called for the ACE to become yet more representative of the public elementary and secondary schools. On the whole, the report supported the ACE's standard arguments for its importance as an identifier of major educational problems and a center for coordination.[28]

In response the ACE formed a broadly representative special committee, which gathered in July 1941 in Skytop, Pennsylvania. Not surprisingly, the five-day conference produced a statement of general approval for the ACE, emphasizing its need for a strong central office. More daring was the conference's proposal to add ACE representatives to the elite Educational Policies Commission (EPC), created in 1935 by the NEA and the American Association of School Administrators (AASA). Although this proposed "National Education Policies Commission" appeared to respond appropriately to the Works committee's call for greater ACE involvement in the public schools, the plan did not meet GEB approval. This failure eroded ACE prestige, as did the NEA's successful insistence that it become joint sponsor with the ACE of a new National Committee on Education and Defense.

With the merged policy commission plan scuttled, the ACE proceeded in keeping with the Works report recommendations to elevate the policy role of its own Committee on Problems and Plans, in 1944 renaming it the Committee on Problems and Policies. More important than its rejection of the new commission, however, was the GEB's agreement to provide general support for the ACE—$300,000 over a period of six or seven years. The GEB made clear that it would not extend this grant and that the ACE must develop other funding sources. The episode demonstrated once again the power of foundations over the nation's apex organization of higher education.[29]

War changed matters in ways that increased the council's autonomy. It gained a quasi-governmental role and a greater chance to aid institutions confused by federal actions. Even larger than its grant from the Carnegie Corporation to help coordinate educationally related defense programs was a payment from the War Department for development of examinations for officer candidates. There were indications that the ACE would never again be so dependent on the foundations. But foundation grants coinciding with the arrival of new ACE presidents in 1951 and 1961 indicated a continued wish to influence the ACE's direction at crucial turning points.[30]

As they took form in the early years of the twentieth century, both philanthropic trusts and institutional associations faced uncertainties about role, power, and survival. Often the foundations and associations shared common aims, such as that of systematizing and standardizing American education. Between World Wars I and II the greater power unquestionably lay with the foundations because of their ability to give or withhold money. But the associations provided the foundations with a valuable source of ideas and personnel, besides offering some insulation from public criticism. After World War II, increases in other sources of funds, especially tax support and tuition, lessened foundation influence over higher education, including the associations, which were able to raise dues sharply. The emergence in 1947 of the giant Ford Foundation, with particular concern for education, heightened the stakes but did not essentially change the relationships with foundations which the associations had already worked out. By then they were old hands at the game.[31]

Notes

1. J. G. Schurman. "Some Problems of Our Universities—State and Endowed." *NASU Proc.* 7 (1909): 30–31: H. S. Pritchett, "Remarks on the Carnegie Foundation," ibid., 60–62; Schurman. ibid. 8 (1910): 275, 286; William J. Kerr, "Some Land Grant College Problems," *AAACES Proc.* 24 (1910), 37–51: P. D. Hall, "Historical Overview," in Powell. *Nonprofit Sector* (see ch. 2. n. 4), 8–17. See also James Douglas, *Why Charity? The Case for a Third Sector* (Beverly Hills. Calif., 1983): Michael O'Neill. *The Third America: The Emergence of the Nonprofit Sector in the United States* (San Francisco, 1989).

2. Roger L. Geiger, *To Advance Knowledge: The Growth of American Research Universities. 1900–1940* (New York, 1986), 45. For an elaborate comparative analysis of Carnegie and Rockefeller's philanthropies, see Steven C. Wheatley, *The Politics of Philanthropy: Abraham Flexner and Medical Education* (Madison, Wis., 1988). ch. 1. For evidence that the public saw the two philanthropists in competition, see Joseph Wall, *Andrew Carnegie* (New York, 1970), 884. For Canegie's role as advisor to other philanthropists, see ibid., 881. For an analysis of the Commission on Industrial Relations hearings in 1915, where both Rockefeller and Carnegie appeared, see Barbara Howe, "The Emergence of Scientific Philanthropy, 1900–1920: Origins, Issues, and Outcomes," in Robert F. Arnove (ed.), *Philanthropy and Cultural Imperialism: The Foundations at Home and Abroad* (Boston, 1980), 25–54.

3. Wheatley, *Politics of Philanthropy*, 36–37; Allan Nevins, *John D. Rockefeller: The Heroic Age of American Enterprise* (New York, 1940), 1:120, 226, 2:210–11; Raymond B. Fosdick, *The Story of the Rockefeller Foundation* (New York, 1952), 7 ("principles"); Storr, *Harper's University* (see ch. 1. n. 26). 9–11; Lagemann. *Private Power for Public Good*, ch. 2. The term *philanthropoid* was coined by the second generation of foundation managers (Wheatley, *Politics of Philauthropy*, 141).

4. Raymond B. Fosdick, *Adventure in Giving: The Story of the General Education Board, a Foundation Established by John D. Rockefeller* (New York, 1962), 127 ("promote"), 131 ("no less," "formed"), 327; Nevins, *John D. Rockefeller.* 2:496; *The General Education Board: An Account of Its Activities, 1902–1914* (New York, 1915), ch. 5; Burke, *American Collegiate Populations* (see ch. 1, n. 4). 82–89; D. B. Potts, "American Colleges in

the Nineteenth Century," *HEQ* 11:363–80. See also Merle Curti and Roderick Nash, *Philanthropy in the Shaping of American Higher Education* (New Brunswick, N.J., 1965).

5. Fosdick, *Adventure in Giving*, 148, 137–39; *NASU Proc.* 2 (1904): 20; *AAU Proc.* 24 (1922): 77 ("industrial"); Trevor Arnett. "Teachers' Salaries." *AAC Bul.* 15 (1929): 9–19. For the GEB's medical school program, see Fosdick, *Adventure in Giving*, ch. 12; Wheatley, *Politics of Philanthropy*, esp. ch. 3.

6. AR, *Ed. Rec.* 3 (1922): 183–84; "Report of the Commission in Charge of the Educational Finance Inquiry," ibid., 202–5; Dobbins. *ACE Leadership*, 11.

7. "The Carnegie Foundation Not a Charity But an Educational Agency," CFAT AR 2 (1907): 63–65; Lagemann, *Private Power for Public Good*, 23–29: Abraham Flexner, *Henry S. Pritchett: A Biography* (New York, 1943), 24–66: Andrew Carnegie to Charles W. Eliot. June 16, 1910, quoted in Lagemann, *Private Power for Public Good*, 52 ("good work"). Part I of this book revealingly contrasts the ideas and personalities of Carnegie and Pritchett.

8. Wall, *Andrew Carnegie*, 873; CFAT AR 1 (1906): 38–39, 21–22: Savage, *Fruit of an Impulse*, 100–103.

9. CFAT AR 2 (1907): 89–92; *AAU Proc.* 9 (1908): 11, 73 ("to assist"); Savage, *Fruit of an Impulse*, 134.

10. Andrew Carnegie to CFAT trustees. Apr. 16. 1905, printed in CFAT AR 1 (1906): 7–8; *Papers Relating to the Admission of State Institutions to the System of Retiring Allowances of the Carnegie Foundation* (CFAT, Bul. 1, New York, 1907): *AAU Proc.* 8 (1906): 65–73. In Theron F. Schlabach. *Pensions for Professors* (Madison, Wis., 1963), a meticulous work focused on this controversy, see esp. pp. 40–42.

11. Charles R. Van Hise to James B. Angell. Dec. 13, 1907, Jan. 31, 1908. JBA, box 7.

12. *NASU Proc.* 5 (1907): 214–40. 6 (1908): 49–59, Schlabach, *Pensions for Professors*, 63–66, 77–79, 83, 87; Savage, *Fruit of an Impulse*, 74–77. Although the ground for the NASU's existence was members' shared identity as public universities, in this case the association had been eager to show the ambiguities of the public-private distinction and had in large measure succeeded. By contrast, the AAACES did include at least two institutions—Cornell and MIT—which, though receiving Morrill grants, were largely private.

13. H. S. Pritchett, *AAACES Proc.* 22 (1908): 51 ("you"); ibid., 52 ("sympathetic").

14. D. W. Working, *AAACES Proc.* 23 (1909): 70 ("pitiful"); William J. Kerr, "Some Land Grant College Problems," ibid. 24 (1910): 37–52, 38 ("unwarranted"); ECR. ibid., 112; "Indiana University and Purdue University," CFAT AR 5 (1910): 23–26. See also the discussion of agricultural education in ibid. 4 (1909): 97–107.

15. Andrew Carnegie 10 trustees, Apr. 16, 1905, in CFAT AR 1:8 ("control"): Savage, *Fruit of an Impulse*, 77–78, 90.

16. CFAT AR 12 (1917): 5; Schlabach, *Pensions for Professors*, 91; Savage, *Fruit of an Impulse*, 116–18, 138–40; William Graebner. *A History of Retirement: The Meaning and Function of an American Institution*, 1885–1978 (New Haven, 1980), 117. The NASU held a rare executive session to discuss the suggested shift to a contributory plan (*NASU Proc.* 14 [1916]: 131).

17. Ellen Condliffe Lagemann, *The Politics of Knowledge: The Carnegie Corporation. Philauthropy, and Public Policy* (Middletown, Conn., 1989), 27–31, 29 ("accessible").

18. "The University of Wisconsin and Subsidies from Foundations," *S&S* 22 (1925): 459–61: Frederick P. Keppel. "Opportunities and Dangers of Educational Foundations." *AAU Proc.* 27 (1925): 65, 67; Lagemann. *Politics of Knowledge*, 100–103.

19. Enec. emte. min., 1924–26. passim. AAC Ar.: Savage, *Fruit of an Impulse*. 135; R. L. Kelly, "The Teaching of the Fine Arts," *AAC Bul.* 13 (1927): 209; Lura Beam. "The Place of Art in the Liberal College," ibid., 265–88; Snavely, *Search for Excellence*, 126; Lagemann. *Politics of Knowledge*, 108–9.

20. AR. *Ed. Rec.* 3 (1922): 191–92 ("absolutely"): D. J. Cowling to C. R. Mann, May 26, 1926, ACE Ar., 7-14-8; ECR, *Ed. Rec.* 6 (1925): 173–74; Waldemar A. Nielsen, *The Big Foundations* (New York. 1972), 254. See Table 3.

21. Raymond A. Kent, chairman of the ACE, "The Program of the ACE," *Ed. Rec.* 17 (1936), suppl. 10, p. 62 ("middleman"); Ray Fyle to G. F. Zook. Mar. 2. 19. 1937: Zook to Fyfe. Mar. 9. 1937. ACE Ar., 9-3-3. For the Committee on Personnel Methods, supported by John D. Rockefeller. Jr.'s Benevolent Fund, see *Ed. Rec.* 8 (1927): 186: "The Committee on Personnel Methods," ibid. 9 (1928). suppl. 8. pp. 4.5. For Carnegie and Rockefeller connections with the testing movement, including the role of the ACE, see Lagemann, *Private Power for Public Good*. ch. 5. On central office reimbursement for administering grants, see exec. comemiu., Feb. 27, 1924, copy in M1.B. box 13 ("cost"); "Treasurer's Report," *Ed. Rec.* 9 (1928): 170.

22. Lagemann, *Private Power for Public Good*, 85–89: Fosdick, *Adventure in Giving*, 196–205; Donald T. Critchlow, *The Brookings Institution, 1916–1952: Expertise and the Public Interest in a Democratic Society* (DeKalb. Ill., (1985), 56: David W. Eakins, "The Origins of Corporate Liberal Policy Research, 1916–1922: The Political-Economic Expert and the Decline of Public Debate," in Israel, *Building the Organizational Society* (ch. 1.

n. 43). 174; Lagemann. *Politics of Knowledge*, 65, 105–6; Barry D. Karl and Stanley N. Katz. "The American Private Philanthropic Foundation and the Public Sphere, 1890–1930," *Minerva* 19 (1981): 267: Geiger, *To Advance Knowledge*, ch. 4; AR. *Ed. Rec.* 3 (1922): 183 ("distinctly"); Hans Zinsser, "The Perils of Magnanioity: A problem in American Education," *Atlantic Monthly* 139 (1927): 248–49; Eduard C. Lindeman, *Wealth and Culture* (New York, 1936), esp. 52–54. On the legitimacy question, see Lagemann, *Private Power for Public Good.* esp. preface and ch. 8; Curti and Nash. *Philanthropy in American Higher Education*, 221–22, 227. See also J. McKeen Cattell. "Life Insurance and Annuities for Academic Teachers," *S&S* 8 (1918): 541–49, and the moderately approving R. E. Vinson. "What Foundations Are Doing," *NASU Proc.* 21 (1923): 91–97.

23. AR. *Ed. Rec.* 3 (1922): 183; Lindeman, *Wealth and Culture*, 20; Edmund E. Day 10 G. F. Zook, Dec. 28, 1936, ACE Ar., 9-3-5 ("probably").

24. ECR, *Ed. Rec.* 6 (1925): 174; Nielsen; *Big Foundations*, 57, 60 ("often"); Fosdick, *Story of the Rockefeller Foundation*, 207–9; J. H. MacCracken to Donald J. Cowling, Apr. 6, 1933. ACF. Ar., 7-17-12.

25. On the restructuring, see above, ch. 3 under "The ACE Central Office under Capen and Mann."

26. *Activities of the American Youth Commission* (Washington, D.C., 1937); AR, *Ed. Rec.* 20 (1939): 336–39; ibid. 21 (1940): 279–86; Fosdick, *Adventure in Giving*, 240–44, 253–55: Dobbins, *ACE Leadership*, 25–26, 28, 142.

27. AR, *Ed. Rec.* 20 (1939): 362–66; ibid. 21 (1940): 262–65.

28. Ibid. 22 (1941): 241–43: "Report of the Committee on the Place of a National Organization in American Education [Works Committee]." typescript, ACE. Ar., 10-17-4.

29. Min. of joint meeting, ACE exec. emte. and P&P emte., Sept. 6, 1941, ACE Ar., 10-19-7; ibid., Dec. 19, 1941, Apr. 30. 1942, ACE Ar., 10-20-2: AR. *Ed. Rec*, 22 (1941): 292; ibid 23 (1942): 325, 330–31: George F. Zook to A. M. Schwitalla, Jan. 22, 1941. ACE. Ar., 10-19-7; *NEA Proc.* 79 (1941): 749. As president of the ACE. Zook was already an advisory member of the EPC. Apparently, the GEB concluded that higher education's role in the EPC could be increased without formal restructuring. In 1941 James B. Conant became a member of the EPC: thenceforth, university administrators were increasingly included. In 1951 the *executive* committee of the ACE and the EPC jointly published *Education and National Security* (Washington, D.C.).

30. AR, *Ed. Rec.* 23 (1942): 330–34: P&P emte. min., Nov. 7–8, 1950, ACE Ar., 10-65-2; Logan Wilson to Everett N. Case, Sept. 19, 1962. ACE. Ar., 16-12-26; AR, *Ed. Rec.* 32 (1951): 247; Dobbins, *ACE Leadership*, 101.

31. The Ford Foundation gave the ACE a $2 million general support grant in 1962 and $3.7 million for programs over the next five years (Dobbins. *ACE Leadership*, 121). See also Dennis C. Buss, "The Ford Foundation in Public Education: Emergent Patterns," in Arnove. *Philanthropy and Cultural Imperialism*, 331–62.

Appendix

Manuscript Collections Cited

AAC Ar.	Association of American Colleges Archives. AAC national headquarters, Washington, D.C.
AAU Ar.	Association of American Universities Archives, consulted at AAU national headquarters, now in the Milton S. Eisenhower Library, Johns Hopkins University
ACE Ar.	American Council on Education Archives, consulted at ACE national headquarters, now in the Hoover Institution Archives, Stanford University
ACIA	President's Office Records: Institutional Associations, 1934–76, Amherst College Archives
AGR	Alexander G. Ruthven Papers, Bentley Library. University of Michigan
AHR	Aurelia Henry Reinhardl Papers. Mills College Archives
AM	Alexander Meiklejohn Papers, Amherst College Archives
AOL	Armin O. Leuschner Papers, Bancroft Library, University of California, Berkeley
ASD	Andrew S. Draper Papers, University of Illinois Archives, Urbana-Champaign
CCL	Clarence C. Little Papers, Bentley Library. University of Michigan
CWE	Charles W. Eliot Papers, Harvard University Archives
DBT	Donald B. Tresidder Papers, Stanford University Archives
DK	David Kinley Papers, University of Illinois Archives

exec. cone.	executive committee
GEB	General Education Board
HEQ	*History of Education Quarterly*
HUAC	House Un-American Activities Committee
IAU	International Association of Universities
IIE	Institute of International Education
IWM	lnterchurch World Movement
JCA	Joint Committee on Accrediting
LACM	Liberal Arts College Movement
Lib. Ed.	*Liberal Education* (1959–)
mimeo.	mimeographed document
min.	minutes
MIT	Massachusetts Institute of Technology
NACE	National Advisory Committee on Education
NAICU	National Association of Independent Colleges and Universities
NASULGC	National Association of State Universities and Land-Grant Colleges
NASULGC Proc.	*Proceedings of the National Association of State Universities and Land-Grant Colleges* (1964–)
NASU Proc.	*National Association of State Universities Transactions and Proceedings* (1903–63)
NCAA	National Collegiate Athletic Association
NCA	National Commission on Accrediting
NEA	National Education Association
NEA Proc.	*National Education Association of the United Stales Addresses and Proceedings*
NRA	National Recovery Administration
NRG	National Research Council
NSF	National Science Foundation
NYA	National Youth Administration
NYU	New York University
PCHE	President's Commission on Higher Education
P&P cmte.	Problems and Plans Committee, ACE (beginning 1944, Problems and Policies)
ROTC	Reserve Officer Training Corp
S&S	*School and Society*
SATC	Students' Array Training Corps
SSRC	Social Science Research Council
SPEE	Society for the Promotion of Engineering Education
SUA	State Universities Association
TCR	*Teachers College Record*
UMT	Universal Military Training
USAFI	United States Armed Farces Institute
USBE	United States Bureau of Education
USDA	United States Department of Agriculture
USOE	United States Office of Education
VA	Veterans Administration

HIGHER EDUCATION AS A NATIONAL RESOURCE

A RETROSPECTIVE ON THE INFLUENCE OF THE CARNEGIE COMMISSION AND COUNCIL ON HIGHER EDUCATION

JOHN AUBREY DOUGLASS

"Dr. Kerr; I realize it's a little premature for you to announce any plans, but I would like to ask if you have any idea what you might like to do. Would you like to head another university?" Kerr: "Well, I really have to think about that. I've had a number of opportunities over these years: I'm not without opportunities at the moment. And I am going to want to give consideration to them. I don't expect to be unemployed very long."

—1967 press conference following the University of California Board of Regents' decision to fire Clark Kerr as its president.

It is one of the more famous chapters in the history of American higher education. In late 1966, Ronald Reagan won the governorship of California, beating a self-proclaimed "pragmatic liberal" who supported California's pioneering public higher education system. Reagan's campaign focused much of its rhetorical energy on the need to "clean up the mess at Berkeley." And when he was elected governor, one of his first actions was to successfully pressure the University of California's (UC) Board of Regents to end Clark Kerr's tenure as the university's president.

After nearly nine years of leading the UC system in an era of rapid enrollment and program expansion, including a significant hand in guiding the state's famed Master Plan for Higher Education and the opening of three new campuses, Kerr was one of the great stars of American higher education. He had proven an extremely adept leader of the nation's largest public research university—and more. Kerr was a significant thinker on the role of universities and colleges in the modern world. His 1963 Godkin Lectures on what he termed the "multiversity" were a *tour de force*—an acute observation on the condition, strengths, and weaknesses of America's burgeoning universities.

By 1967, however, he also was the subject of vitriolic attacks both from the left and the right—from the left for being a part of the military-industrial complex, from the right for being an appeaser of radical protesters and communist sympathizers.

Despite pressure from a significant contingent of regents that Kerr resign—to appease the new governor and for some regents, to settle old scores with Kerr—he refused. On January 20, 1967, the board voted 14 to 8 to terminate Kerr's presidency, essentially ending his 38-year affiliation with the university, first as an economics graduate student, then as a faculty member, then as chancellor at Berkeley (1952–1958), and finally as university president (1958–1967). Kerr retained a faculty position at Berkeley, but that seemed small comfort.

In a press conference only hours after the regents' vote, Kerr was gracious but also pointed. "I do not believe in the principle that because there is a new governor there needs to be a new president of the university," he stated. Later he famously quipped, "I leave the university as I entered it, fired with enthusiasm."

Kerr had not given much thought to his fate after the regents' vote. But others had. The evening of his dismissal as president, Kerr received a number of phone calls offering condolences, encouragement, and jobs. The most important came from Alan Pifer, the president of the Carnegie Corporation and the Carnegie Foundation for the Advancement of Teaching (CFAT). Pifer asked Kerr to help establish and direct what became the Carnegie Commission on Higher Education, which would promote research and reflection on higher education and its role in society.

The Commission and the Council

Pifer had become president of the Carnegie Corporation and the CFAT in 1965 after serving as the corporation's vice president. He had succeeded John W. Gardner, who had accepted a position as President Johnson's head of Health, Education, and Welfare (HEW). Pifer, Gardner, and the board of the Corporation had considered closing down the Foundation, since, in Pifer's view, it had not done much since the early 1950s. The idea of Kerr's leading an expansive study of higher education justified the CFAT's continuation. The commission (1967 to 1973) and then its successor, the Carnegie Council on Higher Education (1973–1979) became the sole activity of the Foundation between 1967 and 1979.

The commission was to be a national effort, unprecedented in its scope and in the freedom of its director—Kerr—to guide its research. Pifer promised substantial funding for five years or more, with no need to find other sources of support. And Kerr would be allowed to direct the effort from Berkeley, establish an office near the campus, hire staff, and draw scholars and practitioners into the commission's fold. Pifer would serve as its chairman.

Kerr worked with Pifer and with Alden Dunham and David Robinson, both at the Carnegie Corporation, to shape the commission's agenda. They planned to investigate and provide recommendations on the most vital issues facing American higher education in the latter part of the 20th century. In doing so, the commission would not speak for the higher education community, "but rather *about* higher education and its needs and contributions."

Kerr and his compatriots set out a research agenda that eventually produced 37 policy reports and 137 sponsored research and technical reports. Most of the major reports were not published until 1970, almost three years after the establishment of the commission, reflecting the deliberate process and careful research devoted to each. A flurry of reports came out in the very early 1970s, reflecting Kerr's and the commission's goal of informing and influencing the 1972 reauthorization of the Higher Education Act.

Allen Pifer had initially offered the commission a five- to six-year lifespan, which turned into seven. At the end of that period, much had changed. The enthusiasm for national solutions to the problems of the Great Society had vanished, funding for education had dissipated, and enrollment projections indicated a long-term flattening of demand for higher education.

When the commission's lifespan under the original agreement with Pifer ended, Kerr requested to maintain the momentum in a new form—as the Carnegie Council on Policy Studies in Higher Education. He wanted to sponsor a new round of studies on the "steady state" of American higher education and follow up on many of the key reports of the commission. The council took form in 1973 and lasted until 1979, when Kerr decided that he would "retire." At that time, Pifer also retired as president of the Carnegie Corporation and the CFAT. Ernest Boyer then became the CFAT's—although not the corporation's—new president. Boyer chose not to continue the council, instead seeking to make his own mark on American education.

Sample Listing of Carnegie Commission and Council Reports

- *Quality and Equality: New Levels of Federal Responsibility for Higher Education*, 1968, Revised Recommendations, 1970
- *A Chance to Learn: An Action Agenda for Equal Opportunity in Higher Education*, 1970
- *The Open-Door Colleges: Policies for Community Colleges*, 1971
- *Higher Education and the Nation's Health: Policies for Medical and Dental Education*, 1971
- *Less Time, More Options: Education Beyond the High School*, 1970
- *The Capitol and the Campus: State Responsibilities for Postsecondary Education*, 1971

- *Institutional Aid: Federal Support to Colleges and Universities*, 1972
- *The More Effective Use of Resources: An Imperative for Higher Education*, 1972
- *The Purposes and Performance of Higher Education in the United States: Approaching the Year 2000*, 1973
- *Higher Education: Who Pays? Who Benefits? Who Should Pay? 1973*
- *The Federal Role in Postsecondary Education: Unfinished Business*, 1975–1980, 1975
- *More than Survival: Prospects for Higher Education in Period of Uncertainty*, 1975
- *Making Affirmative Action Work in Higher Education: An Analysis of Institutional and Federal Policies with Recommendations*, 1975
- *Selective Admission in Higher Education*, 1977
- *Federal Reorganization: Education and Scholarship*, 1977
- *Next Steps for the 1980s in Student Financial Aid: A Fourth Alternative*, 1979
- *Three Thousand Futures: The Next Twenty Years for Higher Education*, 1980

Assessing Influence

Higher education as a field of study has grown substantially since the work of Kerr's commission and council. But since that time, there has been no similarly concerted and systematic effort to address the operation, funding, and role of America's universities and colleges. Many of the Carnegie reports and studies remain salient, and they offer contemporary policymakers and observers of American higher education a benchmark on our progress and remarkably fresh solutions to the problems we face today.

The sheer volume and quality of the commission's and council's sponsored studies and published material was astonishing. One critical factor in the productivity of the commission and the council was their financial independence. In total, the Carnegie Corporation provided approximately $1.8 million for the commission—a large sum in that era. The Ford Foundation and the Commonwealth Fund also supported a number of commission and council projects in the area of education for health-related professions, and the American Council on Education cooperated in a collection of surveys intended to gauge institutional change.

A second factor that accounts for the commission's and the council's productivity was Kerr's recruitment of a new generation of higher education leaders and practitioners who had the opportunity—indeed the mandate—to think creatively. Kerr welcomed old and new friends to the 19-member commission, including current and former university and college presidents Nathan M. Pusey (Harvard), Eric Ashby (Cambridge University), William Friday (North Carolina), Katherine McBride (Bryn Mawr). David Henry (University of Illinois) and Theodore M. Hesburgh (Notre Dame), as well as academics such as Carl Kaysen (Institute for Advanced Studies, Princeton) and David Riesman (Harvard).

In a number of instances, the influence of the commission, the council, and their bevy of affiliated scholars was substantial: in other areas, it is hard to find any direct outcomes. Yet the sheer existence and breadth of the work by Kerr and his many colleagues produced beneficial effects even when it didn't change policy and practice.

The commission and council created a wealth of detailed knowledge and adventuresome ideas that altered and accelerated the way Americans think about higher education. The breadth of the commission's and council's work helped to build a higher education community more habituated to self-reflection and discourse. Only a few major scholarly journals existed prior to the work of the commission, including *The Journal of Higher Education*, established in 1930. By the 1970s, however, new organizations and publications had emerged. The American Association for Higher Education (AAHE) was established in 1969 and in 1984 began to edit *Change*. The Association for the Study of Higher Education (ASHE) broke off from AAHE in 1976 and subsequently published *The Review of Higher Education*.

At the end of the commission's six-year lifespan, and after 21 special reports and 80 sponsored studies had been published by McGraw-Hill and then Jossey-Bass, Kerr and his colleagues faced criticism—a natural outcome for such an expansive effort to evaluate and reshape American higher education. Kerr and the various incarnations of his board were not timid, and they took risks in making controversial recommendations in a world of shrinking higher education resources and, arguably, a hardening within the academy against new experiments and notions of reform.

Sample Listing of Studies Sponsored by The Carnegie Commission and Council

- Howard R. Bowen, *The Finance of Higher Education*, 1968
- William G. Bowen, *The Economics of Major Private Universities*, 1968
- E. Alden Dunham, *A Profile of State Colleges and Regional Universities*, 1969
- Lewis B. Mayhew, *Graduate and Professional Education, 1980: A Survey of Institutional Plans*, 1970
- Eric Ashby, *Any Person, Any Study: An Essay on American Higher Education*, 1971
- Eugene C. Lee and Frank M. Bowen, *The Multicampus University: A Study of Academic Governance*, 1971
- Symour E. Harris, *A Statistical Portrait of Higher Education*, 1972
- Alexander W. Astin and Calvin B.T. Lee, *The Invisible Colleges: A Profile of Small, Private Colleges with Limited Resources*, 1972
- James A. Perkins, *The University as an Organization*, 1973
- Margaret S. Gordon (ed), *Higher Education and the Labor Market*, 1974
- S.M. Lipset and David Riesman, *Education and Politics at Harvard*, 1975
- Martin Trow et al, *Teachers and Students: Aspects of American Higher Education*, 1975
- Lyman Glenny et al, *Presidents Confront Reality: From Edifice Complex to University Without Walls*, 1976
- Howard R. Bowen, *Investment in Learning: The Individual and Social Value of American Higher Education*, 1977
- Frederick Rudolph, *Curriculum: A History of the American Undergraduate Course of Study Since 1636*, 1977
- Charlotte V. Kuh, *Market Conditions and Tenure for Ph.D.S in U.S. Higher Education*, 1978
- Arthur Levine, *When Dreams and Heroes Died: A Portrait of Today's College Student*, 1980
- *Three Thousand Futures: The Next Twenty Years for Higher Education*, Carnegie Council, 1980

Yet many within the higher education community understood the great value and unsurpassed breadth of the effort, even if they disagreed with many of the commission's recommendations. Harold Enarson wrote in *The Journal of Higher Education* in 1973 that in all the Carnegie reports and studies, "the commission is pragmatic to the core. Start with the system, the changing needs of our time, the visible problems that plague us, and then propose steps and solutions at the edge of the possible."

An Ambitious Research Agenda

Fundamental to the world-view of Kerr, Pifer, and their colleagues was the belief that mass higher education and the expansion of America's vast public and private mix of colleges and universities was vital to the nation's social and economic future. They also professed that an increased federal role was essential for adequately supporting the nation's higher education venture.

This led to studies on a variety of related issues, including the financing of higher education and the intertwined issues of equity, financial aid, and affordability. Their recommendations in this area often pitted Kerr and his colleagues against powerful political and institutional interests.

Paying for higher education. The first sponsored studies were brilliant: they included Howard R. Bowen's *The Finance of Higher Education* and *The Economics of Major Private Universities* by William G. Bowen (no relation), both published in 1968. Howard Bowen, an economist, made a famous observation in his study that came to be known as the "revenue theory of costs": In their search for quality and excellence, he noted, colleges and universities will spend every dollar they get—so higher education will always cost as much as institutions can raise. At the same time, Earl Cheit authored a study that pointed to the precarious fiscal position of many colleges and universities, stating that American higher education was entering a "new depression," characterized by sustained decreases in revenue.

Despite Cheit's predictions, the flow of federal funds to states and institutions for higher education grew steadily in the eight years after Sputnik—funds to support scholarships, basic research, and, for a period, capital construction. How those funds were dispersed created disgrutlement, however. Some Washington lawmakers wanted to allocate a portion of or all federal research and financial aid funds on a proportional basis to states or directly to institutions based on their enrollment size or other similar calculations. Instead, specific states and institutions, usually the privates and elite public institutions, gained the most resources from the federal coffers.

The federal financial-aid pattern initiated under the GI Bill had been to enable students to make their own choices by giving them, and not institutions, the bulk of federal grants and loans. In its first report offering formal recommendations. *Quality and Equality: New levels of Federal Responsibility for Higher Education* (1968: revised and expanded in 1970), the Carnegie Commission argued fervently against block funding and maintained that federal financing by and large needed to take the form of grants and loans given directly to needy students. One of the "most urgent national priorities," argued Kerr and his compatriots, "is the removal of financial barriers for youth who enroll in our diverse colleges and universities, whether in academic or occupational programs."

Moving toward block funding, Kerr believed, would pit states and institutions against each other, making federal funding of financial aid an overtly political process steeped in special-interest advocacy. Funding students and not institutions avoided or mitigated this possibility while empowering students to choose whichever institution best met their needs. These Carnegie recommendations eventually led to the Basic Educational Opportunity Grant (BEOG) and the State Student Incentive Grants (SSIG), which later became Pell Grants and Perkins Loans.

While proposing that the federal government concentrate most of its financial aid funding on need-based grants, the commission also advocated supplementary federal "matching grants" to institutions to "encourage commitment" of funds from private, state, and local government sources. If a student with a federal educational opportunity grant went to a particular institution, for example, the commission recommended that the institution gain an additional 10 percent of the total sum of the grant to use at its discretion for needy students.

Keeping college affordable also drove the commission's 1971 report *The Open Door Colleges*, which focused on the need for expanded federal, state, and local support of the inexpensive community colleges, as well as the colleges' need for curricular improvements, better governance, and higher standards for faculty. Many states subsequently gave greater attention to the pivotal role of these local colleges.

These were just some of the many proposals put forth by the commission to leverage resources for needy students and to expand access. But few found sufficient support in Washington to blossom into specific policies at that time. For example, the 1970 supplementary report to *Quality and Equality* proposed a National Student Loan Bank as a federally chartered, nonprofit private corporation financed by the sale of government-guaranteed securities to replace the indirect loan system in which private banks acted as the intermediary—essentially skimming off profits while the federal government assumed all the risks of potential defaults. Savings under the direct loan program would allow for expanding eligibility for such loans and establishing more lenient repayment schedules.

Private financial institutions vehemently opposed the proposal, and it went nowhere. Undaunted, a 1979 Carnegie Council report. *Next Steps for the 1980s in Student Financial Aid*, again suggested a nonprofit direct-loan agency that would "replace the existing inadequate, costly, and inequitable loan programs by a National Student Bank." The report also asked the federal government to avoid "tuition tax credits, which are regressive and self-defeating."

Ten years later, the Bush administration finally established a "direct loan" program on an experimental basis. But it was President Clinton who championed the scheme (while ignoring the council's recommendation against tuition tax credits). His administration attempted to rebut arguments by banks and supporters on Capitol Hill that a government-chartered agency could not be as efficient as the private sector.

Today, powerful political opposition has failed to kill the program. But direct loans represent only about one-fourth of all federally subsidized loans, even as evidence mounts that a complete move to direct loans could save billions of dollars that could be reinvested in financial aid programs. Using OMB numbers, a recent study by Student Loan Watch calculates that government-guaranteed loans cost taxpayers 12 cents, while direct loans cost less than one cent for every federal dollar spent.

Despite its preference that the federal government's support of higher education come largely in the form of financial aid, the Carnegie Foundation affirmed the historical practice of direct state funding of public institutions. But the 1973 report *Higher Education: Who Pays? Who Benefits? Who Should Pay?* claimed that not only was the era of high levels of state subsidization for public higher education coming to an end, the traditional mode of low or no tuition was inequitable *and* insufficient.

Taxpayers across all income segments supported the education of, in general, the children of the privileged. "A low tuition policy by itself." concluded the study, "tends to channel more subsidies to higher-income groups." The commission recommended that while fees for the first two years at community colleges should be extremely low or non-existent, at four-year public institutions they should be increased.

At the time, undergraduate students and their families paid for less than a quarter of a student's education in the four-year public sector; in the private sector, they paid approximately 62 percent of the costs. Within public institutions, the commission argued that the student and family contribution should increase to a third, state governments should subsidize another third, and the federal government should fund the remaining share—figures derived not by a careful analysis but in large part by what might be politically acceptable.

Why burden students and their families with greater cost sharing? One reason was equity. Another reason was the need to raise revenue. Public higher education faced a projected decline in state government investment and only limited additional federal subsidies (although the commission and council consistently argued for a larger federal contribution). Moreover, at that time there was no major expectation of substantial increases in endowment funds for the operational costs of publics. The key was to target student aid policy toward low-income and, to a lesser degree, middle-income families.

In the early 1970s, the public sector enrolled seven of every 10 students. That share was projected to grow—and it did. The commission proposed that a modest tuition/high financial aid model needed to replace the low tuition/low financial aid model, such as the one that had characterized the California Master Plan, for the long-term health of four-year public institutions. The higher price would help defray the operational costs of institutions and help fund more robust financial aid program. Increasing tuition would thus rebalance who paid, help maintain quality and institutional capacity, and theoretically help expand access for needy groups. The commission recommended that the increase in tuition in public institutions be "modest and gradual." It also proposed that states and the federal government provide greater subsidies to private institutions to help slow and possibly contain fee increases.

In an age dominated by projections of enrollment declines and a devotion to the long-honored concept that lower tuition rates translated into improved access for disadvantaged groups, the Carnegie model had little political traction. Public colleges and universities generally saw it as an excuse for state governments to reduce their subsidization of higher education in favor of increasing tuition.

Yet the commission's work has remarkable currency today. Over the past couple of decades, public institutions have experienced long-term declines in public investment—as a percentage of state budgets and in real dollars per student for many major public universities. In many states the publics delayed raising fees but finally did so in earnest in the early 1990s—the consequence of the severe national recession and state budget shortfalls, tax cuts, and structural deficits. But tuition increases have created substantial political problems for public institutions, fee increases tend to come in brief spurts, and often they do not make up for long-term declines in state funding.

Meanwhile privates have been able to raise their tuition rates substantially, possibly over-pricing their product but funneling the largess into financial aid and into improving their undergraduate programs and services. As operating budgets rose faster in the elite privates than they did in the elite publics, arguably one consequence is that the quality of undergraduate programs at flagship public institutions has declined relative to their private peers.

Today, students and their families pay approximately one quarter of the cost of their education at public four-year institution, on average and not counting financial aid—depending on the type of institution, how you count, and noting that costs have risen substantially above the rate of inflation, about what it was when Carnegie did its analysis.

In addressing the funding dilemma, the commission did not ignore the institutional responsibility to keep costs down. One way in which institutions could increase what later came to be called their "learning productivity" related to time-to-degree. In the 1970 report *Less Time, More Options*, the commission advocated a three-year bachelor's degree and a PhD program shortened by a year or two—depending on the field. Similarly, the commission advocated shortening the program and residency period for health professionals. However, since then degree time has lengthened, especially in graduate education.

The 1972 report *The More Effective Use of Resources* also claimed that colleges and universities should "greatly reduce" the number of degrees offered, maintaining that their proliferation not only was costly but eroded the coherence of undergraduate education, a negative aspect of the multiversity. This recommendation was destined to be ignored. Reflecting the ever-expanding nature of academic research, growing specialization, and the internal politics of institutions, the number of degree programs continues to grow. Another familiar proposed solution was year-round operation. In the intervening decades, many institutions have moved to something like full-year operation, depending on how one defines it, but most campus facilities have yet to be used to their full capacity.

Curriculum reform. Curriculum reform was another major emphasis of the commission, fostered by the realization that while America hosted a great array of academically strong institutions, it also included a group of relatively weak colleges and universities. There was also indirect evidence that the quality of undergraduate education had suffered, as public colleges and universities rapidly expanded during the 1960s. Student-to-faculty ratios, for example, had climbed—particularly within the large public universities—and there appeared to be greater disparities in the resources available to the different disciplines.

How to inspire and invigorate the undergraduate experience? One route was to offer ideas on curricular reform, including "stop-out" programs for life-long learning. Money was another answer. With the hope of a growing, although circumscribed, federal role, one of the commission's first recommendations in the arena of curriculum reform was a National Foundation for the Development of Higher Education to fund institutional programs that established "new directions in curricula" while strengthening "essential areas that have fallen behind or never been adequately developed."

Under the aegis of the proposed National Foundation, the commission argued, an annual federal allocation of $200 million could help improve undergraduate education, support university and college outreach efforts to improve the curricula of local schools, help fund regional arts centers operated by consortia of postsecondary institutions, and integrate service-learning into academic programs.

The commission, with remarkable prescience, also thought the proposed foundation could investigate the "effective use of modern technology" (video and cable TV broadcasts and limited forms of computer-based instruction in the era before the PC) for teaching. A report authored by Eric Ashby and Ralph Besse, *The Fourth Revolution: Instructional Technology in Higher Education*, stated that universities and colleges "now face the first great technological revolution in five centuries in the potential impact of the new electronics." They estimated that by the year 2000, perhaps 10-to-20 percent of instruction "may be carried on through informational technology." They doubted that this would happen by way of a paradigm shift. Rather, they thought change would come slowly, "costing more money" and "adding [to] rather than replacing older approaches."

344 Philanthropy, Volunteerism & Fundraising in Higher Education

A federally funded foundation with sizable resources, of course, never came about. The 1972 reauthorization of the federal Higher Education Act did establish the Fund for the Improvement of Postsecondary Education (FIPSE), but it became a unit of the U.S. Office of Education. While for several decades it had a remarkable effect on higher education, given its modest funding, it is now increasingly dedicated to the distribution of federal earmarks.

The commission and the council also sought to improve the curricula and degree production of professional programs, especially those related to health. Margaret S. Gordon provided much of the work that led the commission to recommend, in *Higher Education and the Nation's Health* (1970), a more active federal role in expanding the capacity of medical schools, providing grants to residents and interns, and supporting community-based health programs organized by universities. The work of the commission in this area influenced the subsequent passage of the Health Manpower Act of 1971. intended to support a 50-percent increase in medical school students.

The classification of colleges and universities. To help with the collection of data on higher education enrollments, budgets, and degrees, in 1968 the federal government established the Higher Education General Information Survey (HEGIS, which later became IPEDS). But HEGIS had significant limitations. At that time, most efforts at categorizing colleges and universities simply noted their status as a public or private institutions, the degrees they offered (two-year, four-year master's, etc.), and whether they were accredited. But lumping together a broad range of institutions hindered analysis. Creating a more nuanced classification framework, thought Kerr and his associates, would be an important step in more fully understanding the world of American higher education.

The development of the Carnegie Classification of Institutions was one of the Carnegic Commission's most influential projects. After years of study and debate, in 1973 the Carnegie Classification was unveiled, and it continues to influence the way we view American higher education, (For a thorough discussion of the Carnegie Classification, see Alex McCormick's and Chunmei Zhao's article in this issue.)

Again, the Commission faced formidable opposition. Many institutions disliked being categorized—particularly those with ambitions to expand their degree programs or those that feared such classification might jeopardize their state and federal funding.

Nearly four decades later, the Carnegie Classification (like the Carnegie unit) remains a valuable, yet often-criticized, tool. A recent critique called it "a great leap forward in describing the diversity of higher education in the United States." while observing that its "wide acceptance may be its greatest liability, as its present uses have far exceeded its original purpose." As some feared, it grew from a way to describe American higher education into a powerful influence on how states approached the governance and financial support of public institutions.

And in an age increasingly fascinated with rankings of any type, the public and institutions themselves appeared to view it as a hierarchical prestige and quality scheme. In his recent volume on the history of American higher education, John Thelin observes that the classification "set off a competitive rush by institutions to meet the operational criteria" to move up the ladder that it seemed to have created. For this and other reasons, the Carnegie Foundation for the Advancement of Teaching is now substantially revising the classification system's categories and methodology.

Funding and leadership. To implement all of its proposals, the Carnegie Commission estimated that the federal government would need to invest, over an eight-year period, an additional $12.6 billion above its existing commitments for financial aid and other programs. And it proposed that the federal government reorganize itself to more adroitly influence American higher education.

Beginning in the 1930s, the Carnegie Foundation for the Advancement of Teaching had argued for a cabinet-level position devoted to education. In 1972, the commission revived the idea, since "higher education is today a basic national resource." Later, a revised proposal advocated an "undersecretary or secretary of Education, Research, and Advanced Studies" within the Department of Health, Education, and Welfare (HEW). The Carter administration did reorganize HEW, elevating the commissioner of education to a cabinet post. Yet the appointment has, thus far, had only a minor influence on federal policy related to higher education.

Kerr's Final Reflections

The work of Kerr and his many colleagues generated a new wave of analysis and reflection on the growing role of higher education in society. Kerr believed that colleges and universities, the states, and the federal government all needed to work together to continue America's great adventure as the world's first mass higher education system. But it was clearly the federal government for which Kerr and his colleagues saw a special and new role.

In the halls of government and on campuses, the work of the commission and council contributed to the ongoing discussion of the purposes of higher education. "Their reports galvanized discussions on campuses across the country," notes Scott Wren, who authored several self-assessments by the commission and council. "They were read by Presidents and Chancellors (even students and faculty) and got them to re-examine and discuss a broad range of issues."

In its final 1979 report, *Three Thousand Futures*, the Carnegie Council noted that many of its most dismal predictions had not come to pass. Total enrollment between 1970 and 1979 had increased 24.3 percent rather than declining as predicted. Earl Cheit's "new depression" had not arrived. State governments had actually increased their share of institutional expenditures for public colleges and universities from 36.6 percent to 41.6 percent. And tuition levels had not increased but had declined as a percentage of personal income, from 10.5 percent to 9.6 percent for those attending public institutions and from 50.3 percent to 44.5 percent at privates. American higher education, the report noted, was "generally in good shape." Surveys sponsored by the council indicated that confidence in higher education had grown.

So Kerr, the primary author of the final report, was generally optimistic. However, a number of worries remained. The federal contribution to higher education (not including research) had not grown as urged by the commission and council; instead it had dropped 23 percent. The rising operational costs of higher education, a weakening economy hyper-inflation sparked by the OPEC oil crisis, the specter of declining state investment in higher education, and the political problems of increasing tuition fees in public institutions all seemed to indicate that the financial analysis and models offered by the Carnegie Commission and Council remained relevant.

The general rigidity of colleges and universities and the corresponding lack of curricular innovation also worried Kerr. Government mandates and controls, along with "aging faculties, the emergence of veto groups, and the spread of collective bargaining" appeared to him as significant barriers to innovation.

Three Thousand Futures argued that America's vast and highly differentiated network of public and private institutions (the 3,125 institutions in existence by 1979) was one of America's greatest strengths. The nation needed to preserve that diversity and avoid convergence or decline.

Higher Education as a National Resource Revisited

At the time of the commission's and council's great work, American higher education's participation rates, affordability, and degree attainment—as well as the vast size and quality of its research enterprise—were the envy of the world. Europe and many other countries looked to higher education in the United States as a model for adoption on their own cultural and political terms.

Things have changed, America is still generally unconcerned about the competition in what is now a global economy, and our world-class research infrastructure remains healthy. But in some important ways, there are growing problems.

American participation rates in tertiary education have leveled off and show indications of declining. Among younger students, many EU countries have approached, and in a few cases exceeded, the participation rates found in the United States. Among OECD members, America now ranks only 13th in the percentage of the population that enters postsecondary education and then completes a bachelor's degree or enters a postgraduate program. One reason among many: the United States is the only OECD country with a significant long-term drop in secondary graduation rates. Another reason: increased fees at public universities, while arguably moderate, have not been accompanied by an adequate growth in national and state financial-aid programs or in significant increases in institutional productivity. It is not that America's higher education system is not still relatively vibrant, but the trajectory is worrisome.

Many of the Carnegie Commission's dire predictions did not come true—until the 1990s. We now have clearly significant problems with access and financing—particularly among the publics, which enroll and will continue to enroll the vast majority of students. And there is no one calling attention to the problems we face with the authority Kerr mustered in the 1970s. In the United States, these are second-or third-tier national policy issues. In many EU countries—with their concerted efforts to, in the words of the Bologna Agreement, "increase the international competitiveness of a European system of higher education"—they are first-tier issues.

In this context, the leadership of Clark Kerr and the commission and council he headed seem both prophetic and badly needed.

Arguably, the federal government has a greater role to play in supporting American higher education than ever before. Although such a suggestion cuts against the current political ethos of free markets and less government and raises the danger of another stifling round of bureaucracy, one might reconsider how a national strategy could strengthen American higher education.

Kerr and his associates imagined ways in which federal support might enhance access and quality while also empowering students and institutions. Herein lies a formula well worth revisiting.

Philanthropy and the Emergence of Women's Studies

Mariam K. Chamberlain & Alison Bernstein

One of the major achievements of women in higher education over the last two decades is the initiation and growth of women's studies as a formal area of teaching and research. Although women's studies as such did not come into being until the late 1960s, there had been a stream of research on women since at least the early nineteenth century. Historical works on the condition of women and their contributions to society, for example, were published in the 1830s, a period that coincides with the rise of the women's movement in America.[1] Social science research about women dates from the latter part of the nineteenth century when female social scientists launched the modern study of sex differences.[2] In the early decades of the twentieth century there was a further expansion of scholarly research on women under the impetus of the suffrage movement. In addition to the efforts of individuals on campus, a series of studies about working women was initiated in 1910 by the Russell Sage Foundation, which had been established three years earlier as a private organization funding social science research.[3] These important precursors to women's studies suggest that the academy historically turned its attention to women when the struggles for women's rights gained center stage in the broader society. This phenomenon was especially true in the late 1960s and early 1970s.

The idea of women's studies emerged in the late 1960s as feminist scholars on campus, reflecting the concerns of the women's movement, began to question the portrayal of women and their underrepresentation in the college curriculum. In 1969 a group of faculty members at Cornell University organized a conference that was concerned with issues raised by the women's movement and their implications for higher education. One of the outcomes of the conference was the formation of a faculty seminar to examine to what extent and how women and their role in society were reflected in the curriculum, particularly in the social and behavioral sciences. What they found was a pattern of neglect and often distortion that clearly called for a remedy. The action taken was to establish at Cornell an interdisciplinary course on women, which was followed in 1970 by a coordinated female studies program consisting of six courses from different departments of the university. At about the same time a similar effort was under way on the West Coast, where a women's studies program was started at San Diego State University.

From these beginnings women's studies courses and programs spread rapidly, both in the United States and abroad. By the end of the 1970s more than 100 women's studies courses had been created and by December 1971 there were more than 600. Today, according to a recent survey of campus trends conducted by the American Council on Education, over two-thirds of all universities, nearly half of all four-year colleges, and about one-fourth of all two-year institutions offer women's studies courses. Roughly, this means that some form of women's studies curriculum exists at over 2,000 of the more than 3,000 accredited colleges and universities in the country. Moreover, the world of feminist scholarship in the United States now includes over 60 centers or institutes for research on women, numerous professional journals for the publication of the new knowledge, and more than 100 feminist bookstores across the country. Women's studies are also well along in other countries, not only in Europe but also in developing countries, notably India.

Philanthropy has played a key role in the growth and institutionalization of women's studies as a scholarly activity. This early support for women's studies came from a relatively small number of foundations, mainly those that were active across a broader spectrum of programs encompassing civil rights, education, and the women's movement. In the case of the Ford Foundation, at least, support for women's studies was undertaken in a context that included not only a concerted foundation-wide grant program but also an examination of Ford's own internal processes and external relations as they affected women. When the foundation established formal programs relating to the rights and opportunities for women in 1972, it stated:

> This new concern for programming in women's rights stemmed from internal as well as external forces and events. In 1970 a staff committee undertook to investigate the opportunities available to women working in the Foundation. Actions growing out of that committee's recommendations include adoption of an affirmative action program to increase the number of minority and women professionals on the Foundation staff, appointment of women to the Board of Trustees, adjustment of salary differentials between male and female professionals, establishment of a child-care compensation program for lower salaried employees, and broadening of maternity medical and leave benefits.[4]

The main avenue of support for women was, however, grant-making and in the Education Division support for women's studies was available, but never a large part of the total effort.

At first women's studies were not recognized by the academic community as the intellectual revolution they turned out to be. Rather, they were generally perceived as a passing fad, political in origin and not to be taken seriously. The pioneers were a small group of committed feminist scholars who risked their tenure possibilities and careers to develop the new courses, often without compensation. The early years of the women's studies movement coincided with the formation of women's caucuses and commissions for the advancement of women within the professional associations, and these served as mutual support groups for the feminist scholars.[5] They also served as vehicles for rapid communication and exchange of information about new course material.

It was at this stage that the Ford Foundation entered the picture. Several of the leading women's studies advocates approached the foundation with a case for support and were given a sympathetic reception. The foundation already had a history of supporting major programs of curriculum change, including foreign area studies during the 1950s and black studies beginning in the 1960s. As a first step in support of women's studies, the foundation announced a national fellowship program in 1972 for faculty and doctoral dissertation research on the role of women in society and women's studies broadly construed. The fellowships were open to both women and men in the humanities, social sciences, and related professional fields, providing stipends and research expenses for an academic year. Beyond the significant financial support that this program represented was the recognition it gave to women's studies as a legitimate field of academic endeavor. Indeed, at the time some feminists expressed the view that the recognition was at least as important as the funding. A further fallout of the program came from the volume of applications received and the wide range of topics proposed for research, which served to raise awareness both inside and outside the foundation of the potential importance of the field. Later, fellowship support for women's studies became increasingly available from other foundations, such as the Rockefeller Foundation, and government agencies, such as the National Endowment for the Humanities (NEH), as part of their general support of the humanities. In addition to its humanities fellowships, the Rockefeller Foundation offered awards during the period 1983–1989 under a research grants competition on changing gender roles.

As women's studies evolved and grew, the Ford Foundation continued to play a strategic role throughout the 1970s and 1980s.[6] In 1973 a grant to the Feminist Press enabled Florence Howe and her associates to compile and publish a directory, *Who's Who and Where in Women's Studies*.[7] Howe, founder and director of the Feminist Press, was and continues to be one of the most influential advocates of women's studies. *Who's Who and Where* listed nearly 3,000 feminist teachers, female and male, teaching approximately 5,000 women's studies courses in over 2,000 colleges and universities across the country. This landmark volume served two purposes: It facilitated communication among women's studies practitioners and it demonstrated to the broader academic and philanthropic community the growth and dimensions of the new field.

Progress and Institutionalization

By the middle of the 1970s women's studies, which had started as a marginal and fragile academic endeavor, became increasingly institutionalized on campus. In a 1976 survey carried out for the federal government's National Advisory Council on Women's Educational Programs, Florence Howe reported that there were more than 270 organized degree-granting programs in women's studies in institutions of higher education.[8]

The next stage in the development of women's studies was the establishment of research centers on campus to provide institutional resources for the efforts of scholars. In 1974 the Center for Research on Women was established at Wellesley College with initial support from the Carnegie Corporation. In the same year, the Center for Research on Women was organized at Stanford University with support from the Ford Foundation. These centers provided models for the rapid expansion of campus-based research centers that followed.

The Ford Foundation had earlier supported other centers for research on women apart from those directly related to the advancement of women's studies. One of the first was the Center for the American Woman and Politics, a unit of the Eagleton Institute of Politics at Rutgers University. The center was founded in 1971 to conduct research, develop educational programs, and provide information services relating to women's participation in the political process. The foundation also provided funding to the Center for Women Policy Studies, organized in 1972 in Washington, D.C., to conduct studies relating to public policy issues affecting women. Over the years the center has played an influential role in shaping policies in several areas, such as sex discrimination in the granting of credit, educational opportunities for women, and domestic violence. Both of these centers were supported for specific purposes relating to the foundation's interests in public policy and national affairs. The grant to Stanford was the first of a sustained series of grants designed to strengthen the academic base of women's studies by providing on-campus institutional resources. Since that time more than fifteen colleges and universities have received grants to develop campus-based research centers.

In building a network of women's studies research centers, the foundation sought to meet the needs of different parts of the country as well as particular areas of research. For example, the Southwest Institute for Research on Women (SIROW) at the University of Arizona was formed in 1979 to serve as a research and resource center for scholars in a four-state region (Colorado, New Mexico, and Utah in addition to Arizona). Subsequently, a similar regional center was established at the University of Washington for the Northwest and at Duke University for a joint center with the University of North Carolina serving a tri-state region including South Carolina and Virginia. A prime example of a center based on the needs of a particular area of research is the Center for Research on Women at Memphis State University, which is concerned primarily with research at the intersection of gender, race, and socioeconomic class.[9]

The number of research centers continued to grow throughout the 1970s and 1980s, with and without outside foundation support for start-up expenses. Initial expenses were more likely to be provided by the home institution with the expectation that external funds for research projects and other activities would be forthcoming, as in fact they were. In 1982, the Charles Stewart Mott Foundation and the Ford Foundation helped to establish the Spelman College Women's Center, the first women's studies institute on a historically black college campus. The Rockefeller Foundation has, since 1988, provided large-scale support to several of the research centers for resident fellowships relating to women's issues in the humanities. Similarly, the Andrew W. Mellon Foundation has provided substantial funding for research and social change at the Murray Research Center and the Schlesinger Library, both located at Radcliffe College.

In addition to the formation of women's studies teaching programs and research centers, other steps in the process of institutionalization were taken during the seventies, again with foundation support. One was the formation of the National Women's Studies Association (NWSA) in 1977. To help launch the association, the Ford Foundation made a small but strategic grant to the organizing group, enabling them to meet and prepare working papers and plans for the founding convention. The purpose of the association, as stated in the preamble to its constitution, was "to further the social, political, and professional development of women's studies throughout the country and the world, at every educational level and in every educational setting." The association drew a large and diverse membership consisting not only of scholars but also administrators, community activists, and other women's studies practitioners as well as schoolteachers. As of 1990 its membership had reached 3,500.

Another essential element in the development of a new field is the availability of pertinent scholarly journals and textbooks. The growth in the volume of publications in women's studies since its inception has been phenomenal. New journals such as *Women's Studies* and *Feminist Studies* appeared in 1972 and *SIGNS: Journal of Women in Culture and Society* made its debut in 1975. *SIGNS*, published by the University of Chicago Press with Catharine Stimpson as its founding editor, has become the most widely known of the new journals in the United States and abroad. Recognizing its potential, the Ford Foundation provided modest support to help launch *SIGNS* and other foundations, notably Carnegie, Rockefeller, and the Lilly Endowment, have subsequently funded special issues.

New presses were also created to serve the needs of various women's studies constituencies. The largest and most successful of these, as well as the first, is the Feminist Press, which was established in 1970 and is now located at the City University of New York. It has grown with the women's studies movement, reflected its concerns, and contributed to its growth. It has published curricular material for the school and college level; has reprinted fiction, autobiography, and other works by women authors to restore the lost history, culture, and literature of women; has produced texts and anthologies for curriculum use; and has served as a resource for reference material relating to women. Its activities have been supported by a number of foundations and government agencies, among them the Ford Foundation, the Carnegie Corporation, the Rockefeller Family Fund, the National Endowment for the Humanities, and the Fund for Improvement of Postsecondary Education and the Women's Educational Equity Act Program of the U.S. Department of Education.

Curriculum Integration

The widespread introduction of women's studies courses and programs as part of the curriculum of higher education, important as it is, does not fully represent the impact of the new scholarship on the academy. By their nature, women's studies are cross-disciplinary and feminist perspectives have a bearing on the mainstream curriculum and its core disciplines, particularly in the humanities and social sciences. The work of feminist scholars not only enlarged but also began to challenge the assumptions of the traditional disciplines. An early attempt to measure the impact of women's studies on the general college curriculum was undertaken by a group of faculty members at Princeton University in 1976. The project, funded by the Ford Foundation, was limited to an examination of introductory courses in four disciplines that were perceived to be among the most active in women's studies—history, sociology, psychology, and English. The staff of the project collected and analyzed 355 course syllabi from 172 departments in a variety of institutions. Supplementary information was gathered through questionnaires sent to department heads, directors of women's studies programs, and publishers of textbooks. The overall conclusion was that, with few exceptions, little or no attention was being given to women in the mainstream curriculum. Department heads reported that the presence of women in their departments and the existence of women's studies program on campus were important factors in determining whether faculty members were taking heed of the new scholarship and incorporating it into their courses. Yet unless they did so, as the report noted, most undergraduate men and many undergraduate women would continue to leave college without considering the role of women in history, the implications of sex discrimination in the labor market, or the influence of sex stereotyping on their daily lives. As a result, the men and women who would be among those most likely to be making policy and shaping society would be doing so without benefit of this knowledge. It was concluded, therefore, that special efforts were called for to introduce faculty members to the new scholarship on women and its implications for curriculum.[10]

Since that time, there have been numerous projects, called integration or mainstreaming projects, designed to do just that. A variety of approaches have been used, including the preparation of monographs and guides to relevant topics and source material, workshops, summer institutes, conferences, faculty development grants, consultations, and curriculum-revision programs. One of the earliest and most extensive of these programs was a four-year cross-disciplinary project at the

University of Arizona carried out with funding from the National Endowment for the Humanities. This program, which began in 1981, was a forerunner of what became a movement to integrate material about women into the core curriculum. Since that time there have been some 200 mainstreaming or integration projects, sponsored by internal and external grants.[11] External funding has been provided directly or indirectly by various foundations, including in this instance the Andrew W. Mellon Foundation, and by state education agencies as well as federal sources. The most outstanding of the state-supported programs is the New Jersey Project, a statewide attempt to foster the integration of gender scholarship into the curriculum. Since 1986 the New Jersey Department of Higher Education has provided a total of over $1.5 million in forty grants to nineteen institutions for support of campus-based curriculum integration projects.[12]

These projects have resulted in a flood of publications about mainstreaming. Some notable examples are: *Changing Our Minds*, edited by Susan Hardy Aiken et al.; *The Impact of Feminist Research in the Academy*, edited by Christie Farnham; *Feminist Scholarship: Kindling in the Groves of Academe*, edited by Ellen Carol DuBois et al.; *A Feminist Perspective in the Academy*, edited by Elizabeth Langland and Walter Gove; and *Transforming Knowledge*, by Elizabeth Kamarck Minnich.[13]

Mainstreaming Minority Women's Studies

In March 1985, the Ford Foundation hosted a meeting of some thirty-eight academics interested in the movement to integrate women's studies into the curriculum. The meeting was designed to examine the triumphs and failures of the past decade of curriculum reform as it developed in response to the new scholarship on women. An important theme that emerged from the meeting and was underscored by Beverly Guy-Sheftall, the director of the Spelman College Resource and Research Center on Women, was the inadequate attention to the roles, contributions, and perspectives of women of color in most curriculum integration efforts. Moreover, Guy-Sheftall urged that funders of historically black colleges and black studies programs pay more attention to gender issues since, in her experience, there was resistance to curriculum integration and women's studies at these institutions and in these programs. Other scholars of black women's studies argued that faculty members—particularly minority males—at such institutions typically regard women's studies as a divisive influence; minority faculty and students alike are often hostile to the feminist movement itself, which they traditionally (and understandably) view as a white women's preserve.[14]

These comments led Ford Foundation staff to underwrite an evaluation of several externally funded curriculum integration projects in 1987. These projects included those that had received support from federal agencies like the Fund for the Improvement of Postsecondary Education (FIPSE) and the National Endowment for the Humanities (NEH) as well as projects that had received funding from Ford, Rockefeller, and smaller, less well known philanthropies. The evaluation reinforced the conclusions of the 1985 meeting and convinced the foundation to turn its attention more specifically to the growing body of scholarship on women of color and the increasing number of women scholars active in its production. Grants in the mid-1980s to Spelman College and Memphis State University, which are the locations for two of the principal centers for research on black women, had laid the ground-work for a comprehensive program to mainstream minority women's studies, but in 1988 a broader program for Centers for Research on Women was launched. The program was designed to enable these centers to collaborate with minority scholars and racial-ethnic studies programs in planning and implementing projects to incorporate research and teaching about women of color into the undergraduate curriculum. The foundation committed a total of nearly $1.7 million to this program and, through it, supported thirteen projects at a highly diverse set of institutions including the University of California at Los Angeles, Barnard College, Metropolitan State College in Minnesota, and the University of Puerto Rico/Cayey Campus.

While the formal evaluation of these projects has not yet been completed, there is early evidence that this program has identified a number of key issues facing women's studies scholars and teachers as they move to greater levels of contact with a broad range of academics. As Liza Fiol-Matta, the coordinator of the program, has written, "at a time when cultural diversity has become more of a concern" and, one might add, a focus of controversy on American campuses, "[mainstreaming minority women's studies] acknowledges that understanding and properly valuing that diversity comes from education and acceptance of the need to reformulate our own knowledge."[15] Women's studies in the 1990s will be increasingly called on to reexamine and expand its own theoretical base and scholarly interest in issues of race and class, as well as defend the need for a more inclusive curriculum. Also, mainstreaming minority women's studies projects has broken new ground for women's studies by recognizing the importance of appointing women of color to central roles in the projects. It is unfortunately still true that, of the more than sixty organized Centers for Research on Women, only three have been headed or founded by women of color. This is a reflection largely of the proportion of doctorates awarded to minority women thus far. The development of a new generation of women's studies scholars is inextricably linked to the advancement of minority women scholars with an appreciation of the role gender analysis plays in their own work.

The Global Reach of Women's Studies

Prior to 1980, women's studies as such were little known outside the United States. Although research about women was carried out to some extent by individual scholars or government agencies, teaching programs were all but nonexistent except in Canada, the United Kingdom, and a few places on the European Continent. Foreign scholars were eager to learn about the new developments in the United States, and the Ford Foundation was ready to offer assistance for this purpose by providing travel and study awards to key individuals in other countries. The participation of foreign scholars in annual meetings of the National Women's Studies Association became a major vehicle for the spread of ideas and organized programs abroad.

In 1979, UNESCO also sent representatives to attend the NWSA meeting, which was held that year at the University of Kansas. Their participation clearly impressed them with the potential importance of women's studies for achieving equality for women. On their return they convened the Committee of Experts in Paris, which, after several days of deliberation, recommended that UNESCO cooperate in the creation and development of women's studies programs and research as part of university curricula and in other relevant institutions integral to their Plan for the Development of Human Rights Teaching.[16] Although this recommendation was not followed by any large-scale action program, UNESCO did respond in a limited way by supporting regional meetings and seminars. In Latin America these meetings were instrumental in the formation of the Latin American Women's Studies Association.

A more substantial impetus to the spread of women's studies to countries throughout the world was provided by the U.N. Mid-Decade Conference for Women in Copenhagen in July 1980. At that time, as part of the Forum of Non-Governmental Organizations, a series of women's studies seminars and workshops was organized by the Feminist Press and the National Women's Studies Association in the United States, the Simone de Beauvoir Institute in Canada, and the Shreemati Nathibai Damodar Thackersey Women's University in India. These sessions were attended by more than 500 representatives from fifty-five countries. Many learned about women's studies for the first time. Others had an opportunity to exchange views on issues of theory, pedagogy, research methodology, and policy analysis. The result was the formation of a worldwide network of women's studies scholars and practitioners. Following the Copenhagen conference, women's studies moved ahead rapidly in some parts of the world, such as India. Elsewhere, a beginning was made. Five years later, at the U.N. End of Decade Conference held in Nairobi, the program of women's studies held in conjunction with the conference was co-sponsored by twenty-six organizations and institutions representing fifteen countries. There were over one thousand participants in the sessions, all of them active in some way in women's studies.

In the interim, women's studies scholars and activists organized a series of international congresses for communication and exchange of knowledge on issues of common concern. The first International Interdisciplinary Congress on Women took place in Israel at the University of Haifa in 1981. This was followed by a second congress, held in the Netherlands at the University of Groningen in 1984. Subsequent congresses were held every three years—the third in Ireland at Trinity College of the University of Dublin in 1987, and the fourth at Hunter College in New York in 1990. The number of participants grew from six hundred representing thirty-five countries in 1981 to more than two thousand women from over sixty countries in 1990. Although these congresses were primarily by and for women, a few men participated.

Throughout the 1980s the Ford Foundation continued to support the development of women's studies not only in the United States but internationally as well. It was in a strategic position to play an important role in the international sphere not only because of its long-term support of women's studies and women's programs more broadly, but also because of the presence of a network of field offices overseas. The foundation subsidized the participation of key individuals in the women's studies seminars and the workshops at the U.N. meetings in Copenhagen and Nairobi. It also provided planning support for the first International Interdisciplinary Congress at Haifa and continued to provide for individuals participating in the subsequent congresses. Ford field offices in India, Bangladesh, and Latin America support local women's studies centers and research and documentation programs. New programs of women's studies are now emerging in Africa and in Eastern Europe, including the Soviet Union, sometimes aided by new funding sources such as the Global Fund for Women or, as in the case of Eastern Europe, the Soros Foundation. While there are other foundations and national and international aid agencies that are concerned with the roles and status of women in developing countries, most have concentrated attention on women's role in production and reproduction and their status in the family. By and large, their program priorities and interests do not include women's studies. Increasingly, however, support is coming from indigenous educational sources, which in the long run is as it should be.

Conclusion

It is virtually impossible to know with assurance the role philanthropic dollars played in the growth and development of women's studies over the last two decades. The simple fact that there are thousands of courses and hundreds of women's studies programs suggests that this academic effort has a life of its own that is not wholly dependent on outside sources of funding. In fact, if one were to calculate the total amount of philanthropic dollars spent on women's studies projects in the last twenty years, it would reach perhaps $36 million, or a little over $1.8 million per year. The Ford Foundation was clearly the source of much of this funding, perhaps two-thirds of the total. But it did not function as the only national foundation giving encouragement and financial assistance to women's studies scholars. One is struck by the range of foundations that have made far more modest contributions to the enterprise, but whose willingness to legitimize this activity with small grants for special publications, conferences, and research studies of gender roles helped secure a place for women's studies in the academy. Moreover, these philanthropic dollars had the effect of stimulating private donors to make contributions to women's studies in the form of endowed professorships at institutions like the University of Oregon, Brown, Rutgers, and Princeton. (There is no evidence that foundations have underwritten endowed chairs in women's studies, although they do fund chairs in other fields.)

Perhaps the best way to understand philanthropy's role in building women's studies as a cross-disciplinary field is by looking at the types of projects that were funded and the types of institutions that received support. It is interesting to note that women's studies funding at Ford went through four distinct stages: (1) dissertation awards to individuals; (2) grants to institutions to establish more permanent organized centers for research; (3) grants to support a range of corollary activities such as *Signs*, and the establishment of two national associations—the National Women's Studies Association and the National Council for Research on Women; and (4) project-level support for curriculum integration and mainstreaming minority women's studies. The striking thing about the first three stages is their similarity to other philanthropic approaches to establishing a new scholarly field, whether management education or Latin American Studies. A similar pattern is also discernible in efforts to support women's studies abroad. The fourth-stage curriculum projects chart a more ambitious course, since the goal goes beyond establishing a space for women's studies in the academy. Instead, these projects are focused on transforming the ways we think about women, men, and gender relations in the relevant disciplines. In this way, philanthropic support for women's studies has broken new ground.

Finally, it could be argued that philanthropy's role in the emergence of women's studies was less one of stimulating scholars to pay attention to gender (they were doing that already), and more akin to accelerating the process of change. The metaphor that FIPSE staff members often used to describe its role was based on the image of a car climbing a steep mountain. The car, or in this case women's studies, was already on its journey, but outside funding gave it the extra power to get to the top. Philanthropy helped women's studies gain both momentum and legitimacy in the last twenty years. Whether it can help women's studies become more inclusive of race, ethnicity, and class and whether philanthropy will continue to help women's studies scholars influence the direction of curriculum change remain challenging and unanswered questions for future grant-makers and women's studies faculty alike.

Notes

1. Gerda Lerner, *Teaching Women's History* (Washington, D.C.: American Historical Association, 1981), pp. 6–7.
2. For an excellent account of the lives and achievements of these women, see Rosalind Rosenberg, *Beyond Separate Spheres* (New Haven and London: Yale University Press, 1982).
3. The studies were carried out under the direction of Mary van Kleeck, who joined the foundation as head of its Committee on Women's Work in 1910 and then served as director of the Department of Industrial Studies until 1947. Her work is documented in John M. Glenn, Lilian Brandt, and F. Emerson Andrews, *Russell Sage Foundation, 1907–1946* (New York: Russell Sage Foundation, 1947).
4. *That 51 Per Cent: Ford Foundation Activities Related to Opportunities for Women* (New York: The Ford Foundation, 1947), pp. 3–4.
5. During the period 1969–1971 about fifty such groups were formed in associations such as the American Anthropological Association, the American Economic Association, the American Historical Association, the American Political Science Association, the American Psychological Association, and the Modern Language Association. For more on the early history of these groups, see Kay Klotzberger, "Political Action by Academic Women," in *Academic Women on the Move*, ed. Alice Rossi and Ann Calderwood (New York: Russell Sage Foundation 1973).
6. For a monograph on the development of women's studies and the role of the Ford Foundation, see Catharine R. Stimpson with Nina Kressner Cobb, *Women's Studies in the United States* (New York: Ford Foundation, 1986).
7. *Who's Who and Where in Women's Studies*, ed. Tamar Berkowitz, Jean Mangi, and Jane Williamson, with an Introduction by Florence Howe (Old Westbury, N.Y.: The Feminist Press, 1974).
8. Florence Howe, *Seven Years Later: Women's Studies Programs in 1976* (Report of the National Advisory Council on Women's Educational Programs, Washington, D.C., 1977). The National Advisory Council was established by Congress as part of the Women's Educational Equity Act in the Educational Amendments of 1974.
9. For a complete picture of the network of research centers, see "Research Centers," in *Women in Academe*, ed. Mariam K. Chamberlain (New York: Russell Sage Foundation, 1988), ch. 13.
10. Princeton Project on Women in the College Curriculum, Final Report, March 1, 1977 (unpublished).
11. *Liberal Learning and the Women's Studies Major* (College Park, Md.: National Women's Studies Association, 1991).
12. *Transformations* 2, no. 1 (Winter 1991): 1.
13. Susan Hardy Aiken et al., eds., *Changing Our Minds* (Albany: State University of New York Press, 1988); Christine Farnham, ed., *The Impact of Feminist Research in the Academy* (Bloomington: University of Indiana Press, 1987); Ellen Carol DuBois et al., eds., *Feminist Scholarship: Kindling in the Groves of Academe* (Urbana and Chicago: University of Illinois Press, 1985); Elizabeth Langland and Walter Gove, eds., *A Feminist Perspective in the Academy* (Chicago: University of Chicago Press, 1983); and Elizabeth Kamarck Minnich, *Transforming Knowledge* (Philadelphia: Temple University Press, 1990).
14. For a full report on this meeting see Margot C. Finn, "Incorporating Perspectives on Women into the Undergraduate Curriculum: A Ford Foundation Workshop," *Women's Studies Quarterly* 13, no. 2 (Summer 1985): 15–17.
15. Liza Fiol-Matta, Introduction to *Mainstreaming Minority Women's Studies Program* (New York: National Council for Research on Women, 1991) (pamphlet), p. 5.
16. UNESCO, Final Report and Recommendations, Document SS-80/Conf. 626.9, Research and Teaching Related to Women: Evaluation and Prospects Meeting (Paris, May 20, 1980).

THE SCHOLARSHIP OF TEACHING:
NEW ELABORATIONS, NEW DEVELOPMENTS

PAT HUTCHINGS & LEE S. SHULMAN

It's the middle of June as we begin this article, and our writing faces serious competition from the spirited company of 43 faculty in residence here at The Carnegie Foundation. Members of the Carnegie Academy for the Scholarship of Teaching and Learning (CASTL), these "Carnegie Scholars"—selected through the Pew National Fellowship Program, one of CASTL's components—examine teaching and learning issues in their fields in order, as our program materials say, to 1) foster significant, long-lasting learning for all students, 2) advance the practice and profession of teaching, and 3) bring to teaching the recognition afforded to other forms of scholarly work. One Scholar is studying "moments of difficulty" as opportunities for student learning; another is pilot-testing a new model for teaching accounting; several have focused their work on ways to make students more purposeful, self-directed learners. CASTL is only a piece of the larger picture, but work such as this opens useful windows on what is happening in this fourth of the four scholarships, the "scholarship of teaching": what it is, its contributions and conundrums, and, especially, how notions about it have evolved since its initial appearance in work by Ernest Boyer and Eugene Rice at the beginning of this decade.

For starters, it's now safe to say—as many in higher education predicted—that the scholarship of teaching has been a catalyst for thought and action. True, some faculty find the term off-putting or confusing. At a recent event for campuses, one participant reported that there was a readiness among her colleagues for many of the ideas behind the scholarship of teaching but that the phrase itself was divisive and simply could not be used. In general, however, the scholarship of teaching and the vision it embodies—albeit sometimes fuzzily—have generated significant interest and activity in the last few years. Within the context of the Carnegie program, for instance, we would point not only to the 43 faculty selected to participate (representing nine fields and diverse campuses), but to the much larger pool of applicants the program attracts. There are, in short, now faculty—lots of them—who are eager to engage in sustained inquiry into their teaching practice and their students' learning and who are well positioned to do so in ways that contribute to practice beyond their own classrooms.

We would point, as well, to the growing list of campuses (about 120 as we write this, ranging from Augustana College to Xavier University of Louisiana, from Brown University to Birmingham-Southern, from Middlesex Community College to the University of Minnesota) that have made a public commitment to the scholarship of teaching through CASTL's Campus Program. Coordinated by Carnegie's partner, the American Association for Higher Education (AAHE), the Campus Program invites campuses to undertake a public process of stock-taking and planning for ways they can support knowledge-building about teaching and learning. Our hope is that many of these campus conversations will evolve into what we are calling campus "teaching academies," new entities that can serve as support systems, sanctuaries, and learning centers for scholars across the disciplines, interdisciplines, and professions pursuing the scholarship of teaching seriously. Scholarly and professional societies, too, are part of the action, working as partners with Carnegie and AAHE to advance the development of the scholarship of teaching.

But there is, as they say, more: witness the growing literature on the topic in just the last few years. In 1996, K. Patricia Cross (long-time champion of faculty members' study of their students' learning) and her colleague Mimi Harris Steadman gave us Classroom Research: Implementing the Scholarship of Teaching. Two years later it was Scholarship Assessed, the sequel to Scholarship Reconsidered, in which Charles Glassick, Mary Taylor Huber, and Eugene Maeroff set forth standards for assessing the full range of scholarly work in which faculty engage, including teaching and the scholarship of teaching. Last spring saw the release of a special issue of Indiana University's journal Research and Creative Activity, dedicated wholly to the scholarship of teaching as practiced by faculty in that system (and introduced in a terrific essay by Eileen Bender and Donald Gray). Meanwhile, Jossey-Bass is planning a new volume on the subject, drawing on an international study by Carolin Kreber of the University of Alberta. And of course, this article in Change should be mentioned, drawing as it does on all this earlier work and on current work through the Carnegie Academy. Also notable are the many events and gatherings focused on the scholarship of teaching. AAHE's National Conference last March featured a special Campus Colloquium on the scholarship of teaching, at which interest far exceeded the 250-person capacity. Marquette University recently posted a call for proposals for a "Scholarship of Teaching" conference to be held this fall in conjunction with its Preparing Future Faculty program. This summer's Academy of Management meeting includes an invited symposium on the scholarship of teaching; next year's American Chemical Society meeting will do the same. In addition, AAHE's conference on faculty roles and rewards next February will have as its theme "Scholarship Reconsidered Reconsidered," with a major strand of sessions focused on the scholarship of teaching.

Finally, we now see the beginnings of an infrastructure to support the scholarship of teaching: "teaching academies" and other entities established on campuses to help sustain such work; Web-based resources, such as the Crossroads Project of the American Studies Association, through which faculty can make their teaching and scholarship of teaching "community property" available for peer review and commentary; and new online journals focused on the scholarship of teaching, such as the one at George Mason University (www.doiiit.gmu.edu/inventio). Our colleague at Carnegie, Mary Huber, recently began a study of forums in which the exchange of information and ideas about teaching and learning in higher education takes place. "What has been surprising to me," Huber reported in her presentation at AAHE's National Conference last March, "is not only how many forums there are right now for this exchange, but how surprised people seem to be to find this out." From where we sit, it seems that the character of that exchange may be shifting, too, with growing numbers of folks looking for ways to turn a corner toward this thing called the scholarship of teaching.

What does one find around that corner? What is this thing we're calling "the scholarship of teaching"? This is not, it turns out, merely a routine question but a marker of how this topic has evolved over the past several years. Five years ago, say, the scholarship of teaching was typically used as a term of general approbation, as a way of saying that teaching—good teaching—was serious intellectual work and should be rewarded. This was, after all, the powerful message most readers took from Scholarship Reconsidered. We must, Boyer wrote, "move beyond the tired old 'teaching versus research' debate and give the familiar and honorable term 'scholarship' a broader, more capacious meaning," one that includes four distinct but interrelated dimensions: discovery, integration, application, and teaching. Boyer thus sought to bring greater recognition and reward to teaching, suggesting that excellent teaching is marked by the same habits of mind that characterize other types of scholarly work.

What Boyer did not do was to draw a sharp line between excellent teaching and the scholarship of teaching. Now, however, we've reached a stage at which more precise distinctions seem to be wanted. Indeed, we sense a kind of crankiness among colleagues who are frustrated by the ambiguities of the phrase. How, they're asking, is excellent teaching different from the scholarship of teaching? If it is, why should anyone care about it? Is there a useful distinction to be made between the scholarship of teaching and "scholarly teaching"? Where does student learning fit in? These, in fact, are the very questions that campuses in the Campus Program are responding to as part of their process of stock-taking. They're important questions—to be taken up not in the name of creating yet another set of terms but as a way of being clear about our ends and the strategies necessary to reach them.

In this spirit, we would propose that all faculty have an obligation to teach well, to engage students, and to foster important forms of student learning—not that this is easily done. Such teaching is a good fully sufficient unto itself. When it entails, as well, certain practices of classroom assessment and evidence gathering, when it is informed not only by the latest ideas in the field but by current ideas about teaching the field, when it invites peer collaboration and review, then that teaching might rightly be called scholarly, or reflective, or informed. But in addition to all of this, yet another good is needed, one called a scholarship of teaching, which in another essay, we have described as having the three additional central features of being public ("community property"), open to critique and evaluation, and in a form that others can build on: A scholarship of teaching will entail a public account of some or all of the full act of teaching—vision, design, enactment, outcomes, and analysis—in a manner susceptible to critical review by the teacher's professional peers and amenable to productive employment in future work by members of that same community (Shulman, in The Course Portfolio, 1998, p. 6).

A fourth attribute of a scholarship of teaching, implied by the other three, is that it involves question-asking, inquiry, and investigation, particularly around issues of student learning. Thus, though we have been referring here to the scholarship of teaching, our work is with the Carnegie Academy for the Scholarship of Teaching and Learning. Indeed, our guidelines for the Carnegie Scholars program call for projects that investigate "not only teacher practice but the character and depth of student learning that results (or does not) from that practice."

And with this, we believe, the circle comes full round. A scholarship of teaching is not synonymous with excellent teaching. It requires a kind of "going meta," in which faculty frame and systematically investigate questions related to student learning—the conditions under which it occurs, what it looks like, how to deepen it, and so forth—and do so with an eye not only to improving their own classroom but to advancing practice beyond it. This conception of the scholarship of teaching is not something we presume all faculty (even the most excellent and scholarly teachers among them) will or should do—though it would be good to see that more of them have the opportunity to do so if they wish. But the scholarship of teaching is a condition—as yet a mostly absent condition—for excellent teaching. It is the mechanism through which the profession of teaching itself advances, through which teaching can be something other than a seat-of-the-pants operation, with each of us out there making it up as we go. As such, the scholarship of teaching has the potential to serve all teachers—and students.

This vision will not be easily reached. And it will not be achieved except over the long haul. It is important to stress that faculty in most fields are not, after all, in the habit of—nor do most have the training for—framing questions about their teaching and students' learning and designing the systematic inquiry that will open up those questions. Indeed, one of the fundamental hurdles to such work lies in the assumption that only bad teachers have questions or problems with their practice. Randy Bass, a faculty member in American Studies at Georgetown University, and a Carnegie Scholar, writes, in scholarship and research, having a problem is at the heart of the investigative process; it is the compound of the generative questions around which all creative and productive activity revolves. But in one's teaching, a "problem" is something you don't want to have, and if you have one, you probably want to fix it. . . . Changing the status of the problem in teaching from terminal remediation to ongoing investigation is precisely what the movement for a scholarship of teaching is all about ("The Scholarship of Teaching: What's the Problem?" Inventio, 1998–99, online journal at www.doiiit.gmu.edu/inventio/randybass.htm).

Even faculty like Bass, who identify "problems" they want to explore and have the intellectual tools for doing so, face the reality that they live and work in a culture (on their campus and/or in their scholarly or professional community) that is only beginning to be receptive to such work. Doing it is a risk, both in terms of tenure and promotion and in terms of wider impact on the field, since there are as yet few channels for other faculty to come upon and engage with this work in ways that will make a lasting difference. And, of course, there's the issue of time. In short, the scholarship of teaching runs against the grain in big ways.

Moreover, there are hard intellectual questions yet to be hashed out. One is suggested by a recent e-mail we received from one of the Carnegie Scholars. "Personally," he says, "I can be perfectly content in my own world to continue doing this kind of work because it helps me develop pedagogical expertise and I think students will benefit from that. But I wonder whether this work and the knowledge it 'creates' will be credible with others. Presently I believe that it will not be well received by those in my discipline because it does not use 'credible' methods of inquiry." At issue here, as readers will see, is not only this individual's motivation to do the scholarship of teaching, but also a larger set of issues related to methods and rules of evidence, and therefore to issues of rigor and credibility. Put simply: Will this work "make it" as "scholarship"?

One of the things we have learned from the work of the Carnegie Scholars is how hard it is for faculty, regardless of their own field and its rules of evidence, not to assume that credibility means a traditional social science model of inquiry. Part of the attractiveness of the social sciences comes from the fact that they cover a lot of methodological ground these days, having been extended and transformed over the years through the influence of fields such as anthropology, linguistics, and hermeneutics. They have been transformed, too, by the fact that most of the questions about human behavior we most want answered are not, in the end, "science" questions, ones that lend themselves to immutable general truth, but rather questions about phenomena as they occur in local, particular contexts (like classrooms!). But to get at the fullest, deepest questions about teaching, faculty will have to learn and borrow from a wider array of fields and put a larger repertoire of methods behind the scholarship of teaching.

Which brings us to a second challenge: the need to keep the scholarship of teaching open to a wide set of inquiries. One of the things we have observed thus far is that many faculty gravitate to questions that might be described as "instrumental": Does this new method I'm trying lead to more or better learning than the traditional one?

Such questions are eminently sensible, the very ones, we suspect, for which there is a real audience on campuses, where faculty (and their deans) want to know whether a given approach is likely to be more powerful than another and whether it is therefore worth the time and resources to make the change. But the scholarship of teaching can also make a place for "what" questions—questions in which the task is not to "prove" but to describe and understand an important phenomenon more fully: What does it look like when a student begins to think with a concept rather than simply about it? How can we describe the character of learning in a service-learning site? There must be a place, too, for questions that allow for more theory-building forms of inquiry, and for the development of new conceptual frameworks.

Indeed, if the scholarship of teaching is to advance as a field, there must be inquiry into the process of inquiry itself. We think here of a wonderful paper by Deborah Ball and Magdalene Lampert in which they discuss their teaching in an elementary school classroom, not "to highlight our practice" (which others wanted them to do) but to draw on "our knowledge of investigating practice." Understanding their topic as a problem of representation and communication, they "realized that if we could represent practice, then the possibilities for investigating and communicating about teaching and learning—by different communities—would be enhanced" ("Multiples of Evidence, Time, and Perspective: Revising the Study of Teaching and Learning," in Issues in Education Research, ed. Ellen Condliffe Lagemann and Lee S. Shulman, 1999). Third, there are issues about the most appropriate forms, media, and "genres" for making the scholarship of teaching available to the field. The word "scholarship," for many academics, conjures up the image of a traditional published article, monograph, or book. But as illustrated by the selection of examples in a "baseline" (that is, "where-we-started") bibliography on the scholarship of teaching developed for CASTL (and available to readers on the Carnegie Web site: www.carnegiefoundation.org), a much wider variety of forms is now emerging.

Thus, the bibliography includes a book-length study of student errors in writing; a public pedagogical colloquium given by a faculty job candidate during the hiring process; a course portfolio with evidence about the effects of technology in the course; an online resource for exchanging and commenting on course materials and case studies; a protocol for ongoing collaborative inquiry; and a textbook. But it remains to be seen which of these will most advance the goals of the scholarship of teaching, which will be most useful for review and for building on. Technology, for instance, would seem to have special promise as a vehicle for the scholarship of teaching, but much remains to be learned about how to tap its potential.

Finally, there is the issue of sustainability, which matters since the impacts of a scholarship of teaching will be achieved only over the long haul. It is heartening to see individual faculty developing examples of the scholarship of teaching; these will become prompts for a next set of efforts (just as they built on work from the several traditions that converge in the scholarship of teaching). But what's needed as well is a culture and infrastructure that will allow such work to flourish.

Among the many infrastructures that might be imagined, we end this article by focusing on just one possibility—a possibility appropriate to the need and available to many of the campus leaders who read this magazine. It is this: that campuses should think about redefining the work of their institutional research offices. Traditionally, these offices have been treated as a kind of company audit, sitting outside the organization's inner workings but keeping track of its of its "effectiveness" as witnessed by graduation rates, student credit hours, faculty workloads, and so forth.

Imagine, instead, a kind of institutional research that asks much tougher, more central questions: What are our students really learning? What do they understand deeply? What kinds of human beings are they becoming—intellectually, morally, in terms of civic responsibility? How does our teaching affect that learning, and how might it do so more effectively? These are, in fact, questions that the assessment movement (at its best a kind of cousin to the scholarship of teaching) put into the picture on some campuses, but they're hardly questions we've finished with. If we reconceived "institutional research" to be about such questions, in the service of its faculties, led by faculty members, then the scholarship of teaching would not be some newly conceived arena of work, or a new route to tenure, but a characteristic of the institution that took learning seriously.

The scholarship of teaching draws synthetically from the other scholarships. It begins in scholarly teaching itself. It is a special case of the scholarship of application and engagement, and frequently entails the discovery of new findings and principles. At its best, it creates new meanings through integrating across other inquiries, negotiating understanding between theory and practice. Where discovery, engagement, and application intersect, there you will find teaching among the scholarships.

Added Material

Pat Hutchings is a Senior Scholar at The Carnegie Foundation for the Advancement of Teaching. Lee S. Shulman is President of The Carnegie Foundation, and is Professor of Education at Stanford University.

Bibliography

Chapter 4 Foundations and Corporate Philanthropy: Organizing Knowledge and Shaping Access and Equity

Anderson, Eric and Alfred A. Moss, Jr. *Dangerous Donations: Northern Philanthropy and Southern Black Education.* University of Missouri Press, 1999.

Anderson, James D. *The Education of Blacks in the South, 1860–1935.* Chapel Hill: University of North Carolina Press, 1985.

Arnove, Robert F, ed. *Philanthropy and Cultural Imperialism: The Foundations at Home and Abroad.* Boston: G.K. Hall, 1980.

Ascoli, Peter Max. *Julius Rosenwald: The Man Who Built Sears, Roebuck and Advanced the Cause of Black Education in the American South.* Bloomington: Indiana University Press, 2006.

Bender, Eileen. "The SOTL 'Movement' in Mid-Flight." *Change,* Vol. 37, September/October, 2005.

Beresford, Susan V. "Taking a Long View: The Roots and Mission of the Ford Foundation" available at www.fordfoundation.org (includes information on the Gaither Report).

Bonner, Thomas. *Iconoclast: Abraham Flexner and a Life in Learning.* Baltimore: Johns Hopkins, 2002.

Boyer, Ernest. *Scholarship Reconsidered: Priorities of the Professoriate.* Princeton, NJ: Carnegie Foundation for the Advancement of Teaching, 1990.

College: The Undergraduate Experience in America. New York: HarperCollins, 1987.

Covington, Sally. *Moving a Public Policy Agenda: The Strategic Philanthropy of Conservative Foundations.* Washington, DC: National Committee for Responsive Philanthropy, 1997.

Critchlow, Donald. *The Brookings Institute: Expertise and the Public Interest in a Democratic Society.* Dekalb, Ill: Northern Illinois University Press, 1985.

Cueto, Marcos. *Missionaries of Science: The Rockefeller Foundation and Medical Science in Latin America.* Bloomington, IN: Indiana University Press, 1994.

Keppel, Francis. *The Foundation: Its Place in American Life,* 1930. Reprint with an introduction by Ellen Condliffe Lagemann, New Brunswick, NJ: Transaction, 1989.

Kevles, Daniel J. "Foundations, Universities, and Trends in Support for the Physical and Biological Sciences, 1900–1992," *Daedalus,* (Fall 1992), pp. 195–235.

Kiger, Joseph. *Historiographic Review of Foundation Literature: Motivations and Perceptions.* New York: Foundation Center, 1987.

McCaughey, Robert. *International Studies and Academic Enterprise: A Chapter in the Enclosure of American Learning.* New York: Columbia University Press, 1984.

Nielsen, Waldemar A. *The Big Foundations.* New York: Columbia University Press, 1972.

"Philanthropy, the State, and the Development of Historically Black Public Colleges: the Case of Mississippi," *Minerva: A Review of Science, Learning, and Policy,* Vol. 35, No. 3, pp. 295–309.

Priest, Douglas M. *Privatization and Public Universities.* Bloomington, IN: Indiana University Press, 2006.

Richardson, Theresa and Donald Fisher, *The Development of the Social Sciences in the United States and Canada: The Role of Philanthropy.* Stanford, CT: Ablex, 1999.

Rose, Kenneth W. and Darwin H. Stapleton, "Toward a 'Universal Heritage': Education and the Development of Rockefeller Philanthropy, 1884–1913," *Teachers College Record,* Vol. 93, No. 3 (Spring 1992), pp. 536–555.

Silva, Edward and Sheila A. Slaughter. *Serving Power: The Making of the Academic Social Science Expert.* Westport, CT: Greenwood, 1984.

Schlossman, Steven Michael Sedlak and Harold Wechsler. "The 'New Look': The Ford Foundation and the Revolution in Business Education," *Selection,* Vol. 14, No. 3 (Spring 1998), pp. 8–28

Schneider, William H. ed. *Rockefeller Philanthropy and Modern Biomedicine: International Initiatives From World War I to the Cold War.* Bloomington, IN: Indiana University Press, 2002.

Scott, Anne Firor. *Natural Allies: Women's Associations in American History.* Urbana: University of Illinois Press, 1991.

Stanfield, John H. *Philanthropy and Jim Crow in American Social Science.* Westport, CT: Greenwood Press, 1985.

Wisely, Susan. "Parting Thoughts on Foundation Evaluation." *American Journal of Education,* Vol. 23, No. 2 (Spring 2002), pp. 159–64.

PART II

VOLUNTEERISM

VOLUNTEERISM:
SERVICE TO CAMPUS AND SOCIETY

ANDREA WALTON & MARYBETH GASMAN

Part II of this Reader enlarges our discussion of the philanthropic traditions in higher education with a focus on volunteerism. The term is used here to identify another aspect of the multi-faceted tradition of philanthropy, which has influenced institutions of higher learning in the U.S. The non-paid giving of time and energy on behalf of others in an effort to better society—what we have considered under the umbrella of volunteerism—is too often overshadowed in our public discourse and scholarship about philanthropy by the record of financial giving to higher education and its highly tangible and quantifiable outcomes (among them, for example, endowments, capital campaigns, annual giving, and the endowing of chairs and scholarships). Although we often speak, in common parlance, about philanthropy as the giving of "time, talent, and treasure," we frequently tend to focus on the last component of that trio: treasure—that is, finances.

The discussion of volunteerism that follows expands our notions of philanthropy, shifting the Reader's focus from a consideration of monetary and institutional forms of giving to higher education (considered at length in Part I), to the "people side" of giving. In doing so, we hope to bring to the foreground the giving of time and talent, thereby more accurately capturing the historic and contemporary connections between philanthropy and higher education, from the leadership of students in social movements and campus activism, to contemporary service learning innovations, to discussions of civic engagement, and last, but hardly least important, to the service of board members to the institutions whose interests, traditions, and assets they hold in "trust."

By shifting the lens from the uses of wealth to collective action aimed at social improvement and community building and similarly from donations to voluntary service for the "public good," our vision of the pervasiveness of philanthropic action in higher education and who counts as a philanthropist broadens. Of course, the definition and pursuit of "the public good," in the context of a plural democratic society, involves the element of competition—among ideas and groups.[1] Moreover, questions about who is serving and who is being served, and about the power dynamics between giver and recipient still arise. However, we hope to open up in the selections about volunteerism that follow greater complexity and nuance as well as historical consciousness in what is often a narrow and polarizing discussion about the topic of philanthropy

✳✳✳

Chapter 5 focuses on students and their volunteerism and activism. By their nature, colleges and universities are places where students are exposed to both conservative and innovative forces. Part of higher education's traditional aim has been to perpetuate certain values and transmit certain ideas and cultural beliefs and traditions from one generation to the next. Yet higher education has also been the lever of social and culture change; it provides a forum for testing, challenging, and refining both old beliefs and new ideas, and for cultivating new generations of creative thinkers and leaders. In considering the moments and figures that have shaped higher education, we often focus narrowly on aspects of a "high" history (the leadership of presidents and faculty or the generosity of donors, for example). Consequently, we often overlook the ways students also have influenced the character and direction of academic institutions and have carried the knowledge and ideas generated by the academy beyond its gates. Most relevant here, it is useful to recognize that students not only have benefited from but have participated in and helped to perpetuate the tradition of educational philanthropy.

In fact, the student traditions of volunteerism and service have helped forge ties between campus and the locale, as well as broader social movements. Consider, for example, the ideal of service embedded in the founding charters of many Greek letter organizations, the work of college social settlement workers in the city slums, the fight for economic justice by student protesters in the 1930s, students sit-ins in the 1960s for campus policy changes in housing, the participation of college students in voter registration drives and Freedom Schools during the Civil Rights Movement, the anti-apartheid movement in the 1980s, and more recently anti-sweatshop organizing, calls for socially responsible investing and socially conscious class reunions, curriculum reform, greater diversity among faculty, administration, and governing boards, and efforts to address human rights and peace issues, poverty, and racial injustice both here and abroad.

Notably, too, while examples of the impact of student radicalism and liberal activism are more familiar in the public imagination, the efforts of conservative student groups also have been part of the student philanthropic tradition. The activities and programs of conservative students have tapped into currents of conservative thought outside the academy and have offered a competing vision of the "public good" to the one championed by their liberal counterparts. For example, conservative students have organized on campuses to generate debate about a number of issues. They have worked to preserve their sense of the university's mission by opposing affirmative action policies, critiquing political correctness, and arguing for certain assurances of balance in the classroom. Involvement in voluntary activities sponsored by conservative students on campus has helped many of these individuals segue into careers and leadership positions in government service, journalism, at think-tanks, and in politics.[2]

In considering student activism, we turn first to the voices of young Chicano students who organized in the late 1960s to uplift their status on campuses and in the political realm. "El Plan de Santa Barbara," a 155-page plan, was written in 1969 by the Chicano Coordinating Council on Higher Education (during a meeting at the University of California, Santa Barbara). This manifesto called for the implementation of Chicano Studies programs throughout California's public colleges and universities. In addition to calling for increased Chicano Studies programs, the document outlined curricula and called for Chicano political independence. Moreover, El Plan de Santa Barbara was the founding document of the influential Chicano student group MEChA (Movimiento Estudiantil Chicano de Aztlán). This document, much like other student manifestos of the era, such as the Port Huron Statement of Students for a Democratic Society (1962), underscores the role of the student as citizen and highlights the connections among education and empowerment and community building.

In his article, "Southern Black Student Activism: Assimilation or Nationalism," Joel Rosenthal provides a complex, nuanced overview of African American student involvement in the Civil Rights and Black freedom movements. His critical stance examines activism in multiple areas of the country, making sure to explain the distinct nature of the South and how Jim Crow politics influenced the actions of Black college students. Rosenthal is particularly good at explaining the various approaches to Black student activism, including the Black Power Movement and non-violent strategies.

In "Long-term Effects of Volunteerism During the Undergraduate Years," Alexander W. Astin, Linda J. Sax, and Juan Avalos draw upon data from a national study of the effects of then-President Bill Clinton's Learn and Serve America Higher Education Program. Significantly, Astin et al., show that the short-term effects of participation in service activities persist well beyond the college years. Moreover, the authors demonstrate that increased involvement in service activities during college leads to increased monetary donations to alma mater after graduation. Researchers in the field of philanthropic studies are only beginning to examine the ways participation in service or giving affects an individual through the lifecycle.

In "Democratic Citizenship and Student Activism," Florence A. Hamrick uses democratic political theory to advance the idea that well thought-out student activism on college and university campuses provides an opportunity for future "hands-on" citizenships for students (thus the learning outcomes of activism are consistent with the values of the student affairs profession, as captured, for example, in the Student Personnel Point of View statements of 1937 and 1949). Of particular interest is Hamrick's description of "dissenters." Rather than dismissing these students as troublemakers, she notes that they are typically students of color, or are members of underrepresented groups that they are willing to take risks and to assume a citizenship role on campus. Of importance for practitioners, Hamrick urges student affairs leaders at colleges and universities not only to be tolerant of student activism and dissent but to respect and support it.

Robert Rhoads, in his article entitled "In the Service of Citizenship: A Study of Student Involvement in Community Service," advances community service as a strategy for citizenship education. Based on students' community-service experiences at several large universities, Rhoads argues that civic and intellectual growth takes place when participating in community service, including increased self-exploration, understanding of others, and interest in a common or social good. As Rhoads notes, there is a convergence of the outcomes and the concern of "caring" associated with Deweyan approaches or contemporary feminist pedagogies. Participation in community service that makes students feel good about themselves and their actions leads to increased activism and participation.

In recent years, funders who are interested in the contours of civic life and higher education scholars have been attentive to attitudinal trends and generational characteristics of college students. In "Undergraduates in Transition: A New Wave of Activism on American College Campus," Arthur Levine and Deborah Hirsch survey student attitudes toward activism at five colleges and universities. Writing in 1991, they found that students, compared to those in the past, were less selfish and enjoyed greater participation in social action. Levine and Hirsch also found that colleges and universities are creating more opportunities for student volunteerism and that increased volunteerism leads to more activism. Like Hamrick above, Levine and Hirsch urge college and university officials to embrace volunteerism as well as activism. Moreover, the authors ask administrators to see activism as part of civic education, a primary goal of higher education.

The next selection in Chapter 5 underscores that even as the notion of civic decline has galvanized educational reforms and influenced funding priorities of foundations, there is still scholarly debate about the phenomenon. Michael Schudson's essay "What if Civic Life Didn't Die?" pushes against those scholars who have argued that civic participation is on the decline—an argument popularized by Harvard sociologist Robert Putnam's *Bowling Alone* (2000).[3] Schudson calls into question the ways that scholars define civic decline. Yes, Schudson argues, in today's society people may be involved in fewer organizations, but research shows that the quality of the involvement is greater. Moreover, he argues that civic participation is episodic and issue-oriented; there have been increases and decreases throughout the course of American history. Lastly, Schudson argues that civic participation may now be more passive; today, people are more inclined to sign their names to petitions or to give money to support causes rather than acting publicly on their interests, convictions, and passions.

The final selection in Chapter 5 responds to the up-swell of criticism of the university in the 1980s and 1990s and considers the need to reconstruct the university. Ira Harkavy and John L. Puckett's "Lessons from Hull House for the Contemporary Urban University" considers the work of Jane Addams and her colleagues at Chicago's Hull House. The authors find in the history of Addams's settlement work insight into the current culture and structure of the university—the separation of research and reform, the privileging of pure over applied research, the split between teaching and research, and the tendency to study problems in isolation rather than holistically. In their view, these structures impede the ability of the university—especially social science research—to help solve pressing social problems. The authors recount how they have implemented an academically based community-service program at the University of Pennsylvania, conceptualizing this reform as an effort to embrace the historic ideal of university service.

***

Chapter 6 considers the widespread innovation of service learning. The ideal of service goes back in the history of higher education in the U.S. It is embedded in the land grant ideal and the ideal of the research university's connections to local communities through the work of faculty experts.[4] The ideal is also embedded in the character-building tradition of the liberal arts college (for example, one is reminded of Wellesley College's motto, "to serve rather than be served"), as well as the moment in the past when scholarship and reform were more intimately connected. For example, well before the vogue of service learning, innovative professors like Wellesley professor Vida Scudder introduced students to ideas about social classes through literary study and settlement work.[5]

Interest in service learning has grown dramatically since the 1980s. Today, the literature on service learning is burgeoning and the range of programs and innovations on campuses nationwide is vast. In 2006 Campus Compact had over 950 members. An efflorescence of articles and books and a series of Wingspread declarations have helped to focus public attention on the uncertainty, some might argue "crisis," in the public sphere as political participation has declined, perhaps most worrisome among the nation's youth. Some observers have questioned whether higher education might better meet the challenges of the era by introducing innovations such as service learning and other reforms designed to help reinvigorate the university's historic civic mission. The intellectual foment centered on these issues is reflected in the founding of higher education institutions such as Tuft's University College of Citizenship and Public Service in 1999 (now known as the Jonathan M. Tisch College of Citizenship and Public Service), in government programs such as Learn and Serve, and the actions of individual donors and foundations.

Importantly, service learning is a reform that, as its name suggests, addresses both civic and instructional goals. It resonates with many of the concerns that have long preoccupied educators—one recalls John Dewey's writings on discovery and experience in education and the value of associated living. Some advocates of service learning today are interested in the power of experiential education and are looking for pedagogical strategies to enhance student learning. Others see participation in service learning as a type of socialization for students in philanthropic traditions. Still others embrace service learning because of its social justice concerns and the growing political interest in civic engagement that has directed attention, positive and negative, to campuses. The selections that follow provide an introduction to the literature on service learning from both civic and pedagogical angles.

Thomas D. Bordelon and Iris Phillips study 500 randomly selected students at a mid-sized American Midwestern metropolitan university to look at what characteristics influence student participation in service learning and student perspectives on the quality of the experience. The study suggests that students tend to view service learning favorably, regardless of whether they actually participate, but are more engaged in talking about the value of service learning than "engaging in its activities" (p. 152). Interestingly, the authors point to a gender difference in student interest in service learning, with women students, who may well already carry care-related social roles being less interested than their male counterparts. The study points to the need for more research on the attributes that led to participation and the perspectives students have on the service learning experience.

Robert G. Bringle and Julie A. Hatcher in "Reflection in Service Learning: Making Meaning of Experience" remind us that service learning helps meet the goal of achieving active, meaningful instruction. The authors point to the idea of reciprocity—between campus and community—which provides the under-girding of service learning and emphasize reflection as an integral part of the service learning experience. This article provides practical information about how to foster and assess reflection as an aid to developing critical thinking skills. As they note, "the structure of a reflection activity can influence the results of a service experience: whether they will be educative and lead to new ways of thinking and acting, or miseducative and reinforce existing schemata and stereotypes" (p. 185).

Dan W. Butin's discussion of "The Limits of Service-Learning in Higher Education" situates service learning within the landscape of the broader general reconsideration of scholarship that the late Ernest Boyer (of the Carnegie Foundation for the Advancement of Teaching) hoped to spawn. Affirming the success of this "scholarship of engagement," Butin nevertheless points to the difficulties of institutionalizing service-learning in higher education in order to ensure the longevity of the reform. He analyzes Andrew Furco's work and the Wingspread statement "Calling the Question: Is Higher Education Ready to Commit to Community Engagement?" and identifies two fundamentally different approaches to institutionalizing service learning: the incremental and the transformative. Butin argues that service learning might best learn from the institutionalization of women's studies, which made the transition from a political, activist movement to an academic enterprise that asks critical questions about the gendered nature of social structures and beliefs.

Matthew Hartley, Ira Harkavy, and Lee Benson also consider the question of institutionalizing service learning. They examine service learning at four different types of institutions: the University of Pennsylvania (an urban research university), Tufts University (as mentioned above, a university with a college devoted to citizenship and public service), Swarthmore (a selective liberal arts college), and Widener University (a regional comprehensive institution). Providing a nuanced discussion of the challenges of institutionalization at different stages, they note the importance of change on two levels, structural and ideological, if service-learning's longevity is to be ensured.

The next several selections are oriented toward questions of particular interest to practitioners. E. Gil Clary, Mark Synder, and Arthur Stukas in "Service-Learning and Psychology: Lessons from the Psychology of Volunteers' Motivations" stress the importance of finding ways to focus on the internalization of pro-social values on the part of students and see service learning, like volunteer work, as one vehicle to achieve this goal. They question whether altruism exists or should be the goal and argue that the most productive and mutual beneficial helping process is established when the giver, acting in enlightened self interest, is also receiving a benefit from the service.

Mary Kirlin provides an overview of research on service learning, volunteerism, and community service and argues that many programs do not realize their potential contribution to the goal of achieving more engaged citizens because they lack any purposeful civic skills component. Kirlin asserts that students need to use the types of civic skills that programs hope to foster by identifying problems and experiencing collective decision-making in their volunteer activities. Further, she discusses the critical role of adolescence to increase civic-minded behavior in college and beyond.

Richard M. Battistoni's discussion of "What is Good Citizenship? Conceptual Contributions from Other Disciplines" is taken from a resource book published by Campus Compact. In an earlier chapter having outlined ways to implement service learning in connection with social science course work, Battistoni outlines a number of conceptual frameworks—views of citizenship—that can inform the theory and practice of service learning in fields such as literature, the performing arts, and even business and computer science. The discussion here focuses on civic professionalism, social justice, connected knowing (the "ethic of care"), public leadership, the public intellectual, and the scholarship of engagement.

Andrew Furco in "Service-Learning: A Balanced Approach to Experiential Education" looks at service learning on a continuum of a wide variety of innovations. He analyzes the balance of the weight given to pedagogical and philanthropic goals and the balance between benefits to giver and recipient in various service-oriented educational approaches.

❋❋❋

Chapter 7 in Part II focuses on trusteeship. The reliance on a lay board is a distinguishing feature of higher education in this country, going back to Harvard's external board of overseers. The current literature on trustees in educational settings is largely directed to legal issues and practice-related topics. It is also important, however, to conceptualize academic trusteeship as a form of philanthropic service and an integral part of the larger discussion of the civic mission of the university and the university's relationship to society.[6] The cluster of readings in this chapter open up some discussion of the composition of boards, a topic that Eduard Lindeman explored in depth in his classic *Wealth and Culture* (1936), and about which far more research is needed; these readings are a first step toward considering the types of discussions from history, leadership studies, and the world of practice that might provide the type of reflective education needed to help prepare individuals for the responsibilities and opportunities of trusteeship.

In his remarks entitled "Current Challenges to Foundation Board Governance: A Worst Case Scenario or The Perfect Storm?" Emmett Carson brings his perspective on the current context for foundations garnered from his work as president of the Minneapolis Foundation (one of the nation's oldest community foundations) and from his membership on several non-profit boards. Carson's reflections delivered at the Council on Foundations Board Trustee Dinner in April 2003 remind us that the nonprofit world is influenced by events in the business sector and that because of certain widely publicized business scandals, "board governance is receiving its highest level of public scrutiny in years." As Carson notes, the Sarbanes-Oxley legislation calling for greater accountability, the nonprofit world's uneven response to 9/11, and a period of economic downturn placed substantial and unforeseen pressures on foundations and nonprofits in recent years. Carson explains that in responding to these challenges, foundation boards must "judge...individual and collective actions by whether they will improve or erode the public trust." Although Carson does not address higher education directly, the challenges he outlines are relevant for academic institutions and their governing boards.

The commentary by historians John S. Whitehead and Jurgen Herbst looks back at the Dartmouth Case of 1819. The controversy arose when John Wheelock succeeded his father as president of Dartmouth (founded under a royal charter in 1769), and a disagreement arose with the trustees over certain conditions at the college, ending with Wheelock's dismissal. The New Hampshire legislature intervened and amended the charter, reorganizing the institution as Dartmouth University. The state courts found that the legislature's action was warranted since Dartmouth was a public corporation. Represented by Daniel Webster (Dartmouth College 1801) the trustees won their case on appeal to the U.S. Supreme Court. Historians still debate the significance of the case. Some see the ruling as solidifying the distinctions between "public" and "private," asserting that the case affirmed the sanctity of the private corporation and gave impetus to the efflorescence of private denominational college building in the 19th century. Other scholars assert that the lines between "public" and "private" were still blurred at the Dartmouth Case and that such modern distinctions emerged only at the Civil War. The Whitehead-Herbst article is included here because the Dartmouth Case figures so prominently in both the history of philanthropy and of higher education in the U.S.

Mariam Chamberlain, former Ford Foundation officer and founding president of the National Council for Research on Women, points to the dearth of women on academic governing boards compared to their numbers in higher education, as well as the frequent channeling of women trustees into stereotypical committee assignments. Chamberlain's call for greater female representation on boards and more sustained efforts to identity and mentor women for trustee service is as relevant today as it was when she wrote the article.

The title "Black Trustees Abound at America's Major Colleges and Universities" for this brief item from *The Journal of Blacks in Higher Education* is misleading. The succinct discussion reveals that the representation of African Americans on boards of colleges and universities is still not comparable to the demographics in society but that "black trustees are increasingly part of the normal governance of institutions of higher education" (p. 35). Substantially more research needs to be done on the role of Black trustees in higher education historically and today.

Larry C. Spears discusses the attributes that Robert Greenleaf outlined in his concept of servant leader and describes the growing interest in Greenleaf's work since the 1990s. As Spears notes (much like Chait, Ryan, and Taylor's discussion of governance and leadership that follows), "the words *servant* and *leader* are often thought of as being opposites" (p. 1). As Spears observes, the concept of servant-leader is consonant with an interest in less hierarchical and more participational forms of decision-making and governing, including feminist approaches. Further, servant leadership can be useful to service learning initiatives and the education and training of not-for-profit trustees.

Richard P. Chait, William P. Ryan, and Barbara E. Taylor, in a chapter from their award-winning *Governance as Leadership: Reframing the Work of Nonprofit Boards* (2005), draw attention to growing interest in trusteeship, given recent scandals in the corporate sphere and fiascos in academic governance. They underscore the importance of the selection of new trustees and planning ways to tap the most significant and creative contributions from the current board members. The work illuminates different types of power and resources that a board has and usefully connects the ideas of governance and leadership.

"Why College Trustees?" provides a glimpse into past discussions about trusteeship. Dana talks about the ways institutions should provide trustees with opportunities for service, rather than having trustees be mere figureheads, and discusses the qualities of character and intellect needed to perform the trustee function well. The author calls for the need for a theory of trusteeship. This document from 1947, the beginning of the post-World War era, provides an interesting context in which to read Chait, Ryan, and Taylor's assessment of our current thinking about needing to think about trustees as leaders.

Finally, the "Role of Community College Trustees" considers the circumstances of a type of institution that is far too often overlooked in the higher education literature and yet it fulfils an important educational role. This article highlights the role of trustees as donors to institutions and reminds us that people are more likely to give to higher education—or other causes—when they are asked. It is the importance of reaching out to donors and finding a good fit between donor interests and institutional needs that provides the focus of Part III: Fundraising.

Notes

1. Jane Mansbridge, "On the Contested Nature of the Public Good," in *The Non-Profit Handbook*, edited by Walter Powell and Elizabeth Clemens (New Haven: Yale University Press, 1998). See also, Andrea Walton, "Teaching Philanthropy in the History of Higher Education: Values and the Public Good," *Journal of College and Character*, Vol. 2, available at www.collegecharacter.org.
2. A useful literature on conservative philanthropy is just emerging. See Leslie Lenkowsky and James Piereson, "Education and the Conservative Foundations," in *Reconnecting Education and Foundations*, edited by Ray Bacchetti and Thomas Ehrlich (San Francisco: Jossey-Bass, 2007), pp. 347–378. See also Ellen Condliffe Lagemann and Jennifer de Forest, "What Might Andrew Carnegie Want to Tell Bill Gates," pp. 47–67, especially 61–62 in the same volume.
3. Robert D. Putnam, *Bowling Alone: The Collapse and Revival of American Community* (New York: Simon Schuster, 2000).
4. Stephen J. Dinner, *A City and Its Universities: Public Policy in Chicago, 1892–1910.* (Chapel Hill: North Carolina Press, 1980).
5. Julia Garbus, "Service-Learning, 1902," *College English*, Vol. 64, No. 5 (May, 2002), pp. 547–565.
6. R. Novak and Susan Whealler Johnston, "Trusteeship and the Public Good," in *Higher Education for the Public Good* edited by Adriana J. Kezar, T.C. Chambers, and J.C. Burkhardt. (San Francisco: Jossey-Bass, 2005).

CHAPTER 5

STUDENT VOLUNTEERISM AND ACTIVISM

EL PLAN DE SANTA BARBARA, 1969

In 1969 Latino students from several California universities came together at the University of California at Santa Barbara to organize their goals for higher education reform. Emerging from this conference was "El Plan de Santa Barbara"—a clear and detailed articulation of the needs and demands of Latino college students. In addition, under the leadership of the Chicano Coordinating Council on Higher Education (CCHE), student groups at the Santa Barbara conference agreed to forego their individual names and become the Movimiento Estudiantil Chicano de Aztlán (MEChA).

From: Appendix, Carlos Muñoz Jr., *Youth, Identity, Power: The Chicano Movement* (New York: Verso, 1989), pp. 191–202. Original owned by Armando Valdez.

Manifesto

For all peoples, as with individuals, the time comes when they must reckon with their history. For the Chicano the present is a time of renaissance, of *renacimiento*. Our people and our community, *el barrio* and *la colonia*, are expressing a new consciousness and a new resolve. Recognizing the historical tasks confronting our people and fully aware of the cost of human progress, we pledge our will to move. We will move forward toward our destiny as a people. We will move against those forces which have denied us freedom of expression and human dignity. Throughout history the quest for cultural expression and freedom has taken the form of a struggle. Our struggle, tempered by the lessons of the American past, is an historical reality.

For decades Mexican people in the United States struggled to realize the "American Dream." And some—a few—have. But the cost, the ultimate cost of assimilation, required turning away from *el barrio* and *la colonia*. In the meantime, due to the racist structure of this society, to our essentially different life style, and to the socioeconomic functions assigned to our community by Anglo-American society—as suppliers of cheap labor and a dumping ground for the small-time capitalist entrepreneur—the *barrio* and *colonia* remained exploited, impoverished, and marginal.

As a result, the self-determination of our community is now the only acceptable mandate for social and political action; it is the essence of Chicano commitment. Culturally, the word *Chicano*, in the past a pejorative and class-bound adjective, has now become the root idea of a new cultural identity for our people. It also reveals a growing solidarity and the development of a common social praxis. The widespread use of the term *Chicano* today signals a rebirth of pride and confidence. *Chicanismo* simply embodies an ancient truth: that man is never closer to his true self as when he is close to his community.

Chicanismo draws its faith and strength from two main sources: from the just struggle of our people and from an objective analysis of our community's strategic needs. We recognize that without a strategic use of education, an education that places value on what we value, we will not realize our destiny. Chicanos recognize the central importance of institutions of higher learning to modern progress, in this case, to the development of our community. But we go further: we believe that higher education must contribute to the information of a complete man who truly values life and freedom.

The destiny of our people will be fulfilled. To that end, we pledge our efforts and take as our credo what José Vasconcelos once said at a time of crisis and hope: "At this moment we do not come to work for the university, but to demand that the university work for our people."

Political Action

Introduction

For the Movement, political action essentially means influencing the decision-making process of those institutions which affect Chicanos, the university, community organizations, and non-community institutions. Political action encompasses three elements which function in a progression: political consciousness, political mobilization, and tactics. Each part breaks down into further subdivisions. Before continuing with specific discussions of these three categories, a brief historical analysis must be formulated.

Historical Perspective

The political activity of the Chicano Movement at colleges and universities to date has been specifically directed toward establishing Chicano student organizations (UMAS, MAYA, MASC, MEChA, etc.) and institutionalizing Chicano Studies programs. A variety of organizational forms and tactics have characterized these student organizations.

One of the major factors which led to political awareness in the 60s was the clash between Anglo-American educational institutions and Chicanos who maintained their cultural identity. Another factor was the increasing number of Chicano students who became aware of the extent to which colonial conditions characterized their communities. The result of this domestic colonialism is that the *barrios* and *colonias* are dependent communities with no institutional power base of their own. Historically, Chicanos have been prevented from establishing a power base and significantly influencing decision-making. Within the last decade, a limited degree of progress has taken place in securing a base of power within educational institutions.

Other factors which affected the political awareness of the Chicano youth were: the heritage of Chicano youth movements of the 30s and 40s; the failures of Chicano political efforts of the 40s and 50s; the bankruptcy of Mexican-American pseudo-political associations, and the disillusionment of Chicano participants in the Kennedy campaigns. Among the strongest influences on Chicano youth today have been the National Farm Workers Association, the Crusade for Justice, and the Alianza Federal de Pueblos Libres. The Civil Rights, the Black Power, and the Anti-war movements were other influences.

As political consciousness increased, there occurred simultaneously a renewed cultural awareness which, along with social and economic factors, led to the proliferation of Chicano youth organizations. By the mid 1960s, MASC, MAYA, UMAS, La Vida Nueva, and MEChA appeared on campus, while the Brown Berets, Black Berets, ALMA, and La Junta organized in the *barrios* and *colonias*. These groups differed from one another depending on local conditions, and their varying state of political development. Despite differences in name and organizational experience, a basic unity evolved.

These groups have had a significant impact on the awareness of large numbers of people, both Chicano and non-Chicano. Within the communities, some public agencies have been sensitized, and others have been exposed. On campuses, articulation of demands and related political efforts have dramatized NUESTRA CAUSA. Concrete results are visible in both the increased number of Chicano students on campuses and the establishment of corresponding supportive services. The institutionalization of Chicano Studies marks the present stage of activity; the next stage will involve the strategic application of university and college resources to the community. One immediate result will be the elimination of artificial distinctions which exist between the students and the community. Rather than being its victims, the community will benefit from the resources of the institutions of higher learning.

Political Consciousness

Commitment to the struggle for Chicano liberation is the operative definition of the ideology used here. *Chicanismo* involves a crucial distinction in political consciousness between a Mexican American and a Chicano mentality. The Mexican American is a person who lacks respect for his cultural and ethnic heritage. Unsure of himself, he seeks assimilation as a way out of his "degraded" social status. Consequently, he remains politically ineffective. In contrast, *Chicanismo* reflects self-respect and pride in one's ethnic and cultural background. Thus, the Chicano acts with confidence and with a range or alternatives in the political world. He is capable of developing an effective ideology through action.

Mexican Americans must be viewed as potential Chicanos. *Chicanismo* is flexible enough to relate to the varying levels of consciousness within La Raza. Regional variations must always be kept in mind as well as the different levels of development, composition, maturity, achievement, and experience in political action. Cultural nationalism is a means of total Chicano liberation.

There are definite advantages to cultural nationalism, but no inherent limitations. A Chicano ideology, especially as it involves cultural nationalism, should be positively phrased in the form of propositions to the Movement. *Chicanismo* is a concept that integrates self-awareness with cultural identity, a necessary step in developing political consciousness. As such, it serves as a basis for political action, flexible enough to include the possibility of coalitions. The related concept of La Raza provides an internationalist scope of *Chicanismo*, and La Raza Cósmica furnishes a philosophical precedent. Within this framework, the Third World Concept merits consideration.

Political Mobilization

Political mobilization is directly dependent on political consciousness. As political consciousness develops, the potential for political action increases.

The Chicano student organization in institutions of higher learning is central to all effective political mobilization. Effective mobilization presupposes precise definition of political goals and of the tactical interrelationships of roles. Political goals in any given situation must encompass the totality of Chicano interests in higher education. The differentiation of roles required by a given situation must be defined on the basis of mutual accountability and equal sharing of responsibility. Furthermore, the mobilization of community support not only legitimizes the activities of Chicano student organizations but also maximizes political power. The principle of solidarity is axiomatic in all aspects of political action.

Since the movement is definitely of national significance and scope, all student organizations should adopt one identical name throughout the state and eventually the nation to characterize the common struggle of La Raza de Aztlán. The net gain is a step toward greater national unity which enhances the power in mobilizing local campus organizations.

When advantageous, political coalitions and alliances with non-Chicano groups may be considered. A careful analysis must precede the decision to enter into a coalition. One significant factor is the community's attitude towards coalitions. Another factor is the formulation of a mechanism for the distribution of power that ensures maximum participation in decision making: i.e., formulation of demands and planning of tactics. When no longer politically advantageous, Chicano participation in the coalition ends.

Campus Organizing: Notes on MEChA

Introduction

MEChA is a first step to tying the student groups throughout the Southwest into a vibrant and responsive network of activists who will respond as a unit to oppression and racism and will work in harmony when initiating and carrying out campaigns of liberation for our people.

As of present, wherever one travels throughout the Southwest, one finds that there are different levels of awareness on different campuses. The student movement is to a large degree a political movement and as such must not elicit from our people the negative responses that we have experienced so often in the past in relation to politics, and often with good reason. To this end, then, we must re-define [sic] politics for our people to be a means of liberation. The political sophistication of our Raza must be raised so that they do not fall prey to apologists and *vendidos* whose whole interest is their personal career or fortune. In addition, the student movement is more than a political movement, it is cultural and social as well. The spirit of MEChA must be one of "hermandad" and cultural awareness. The ethic of profit and competition, of greed and intolerance, which the Anglo society offers must be replaced by our ancestral communalism and love for beauty and justice. MEChA must bring to the mind of every young Chicano that the liberation of his people from prejudice and oppression is in his hands and this responsibility is greater than personal achievement and more meaningful than degrees, especially if they are earned at the expense of his identity and cultural integrity.

MEChA, then, is more than a name; it is a spirit of unity, of brotherhood, and a resolve to undertake a struggle for liberation in a society where justice is but a word. MEChA is a means to an end.

The Function of MEChA—To the Campus Community

Other students can be important to MEChA in supportive roles; hence, the question of coalitions. Although it is understood and quite obvious that the viability and amenability of coalition varies from campus to campus, some guidelines might be kept in mind. These questions should be asked before entering into any binding agreement. Is it beneficial to tie oneself to another group in coalition which will carry one into conflicts for which one is ill-prepared or involve one with issues on which one is ill-advised? Can one safely go into a coalition where one group is markedly stronger than another? Does MEChA have an equal voice in leadership and planning in the coalition group? Is it perhaps better to enter into a loose alliance for a given issue? How does the leadership of each group view coalitions? How does the membership? Can MEChA hold up its end of the bargain? Will MEChA carry dead weight in a coalition? All of these and many more questions must be asked and answered before one can safely say that he will benefit from and contribute to a strong coalition effort.

Supportive groups. When moving on campus it is often well-advised to have groups who are willing to act in supportive roles. For example, there are usually any number of faculty members who are sympathetic, but limited as to the number of activities they will engage in. These faculty members often serve on academic councils and senates and can be instrumental in academic policy. They also provide another channel to the academic power structure and can be used as leverage in negotiation. However, these groups are only as responsive as the ties with them are nurtured. This does not mean, compromise MEChA's integrity; it merely means laying good groundwork before an issue is brought up, touching bases with your allies before hand.

Sympathetic administrators. This is a delicate area since administrators are most interested in not jeopardizing their positions and often will try to act as buffers or liaison between the administration and the student group. In the case of Chicano administrators, it should not a priori be assumed that because he is Raza he is to be blindly trusted. If he is not known to the membership, he must be given a chance to prove his allegiance to La Causa. As such, he should be the Chicano's man in the power structure instead of the administration's Mexican-American. It is from the administrator that information can be obtained as to the actual feasibility of demands or programs to go beyond the platitudes and pleas of unreasonableness with which the administration usually answers proposals and demands. The words of the administrator should never be the deciding factor in students' actions. The students must at all times make their own decisions. It is very human for people to establish self-interest. Therefore, students must constantly remind the Chicano administrators and faculty where their loyalty and allegiance lie. It is very easy for administrators to begin looking for promotions just as it is very natural for faculty members to seek positions of academic prominence.

In short, it is the students who must keep after Chicano and non-Chicano administrators and faculty to see that they do not compromise the position of the student and the community. By the same token, it is the student who must come to the support of these individuals if they are threatened for their support of the students. Students must be careful not to become a political lever for others.

Function of MEChA—Education

It is a fact that the Chicano has not often enough written his own history, his own anthropology, his own sociology, his own literature. He must do this if he is to survive as a cultural entity in this melting pot society which seeks to dilute varied cultures into a grey upon grey pseudo-culture of technology and materialism. The Chicano student is doing most of the work in the establishment of study programs, centers, curriculum development, entrance programs to get more Chicanos into college. This is good and must continue, but students must be careful not to be co-opted in their fervor for establishing relevance on the campus. Much of what is being offered by college systems and administrators is too little too late. MEChA must not compromise programs and curriculum which are essential for the total education of the Chicano for the sake of expediency. The students must not become so engrossed in programs and centers created along established academic guidelines that they forget the needs of the people which these institutions are meant to serve. To this end, *Barrio* input most always be given full and open hearing when designing these programs, when creating them and in running them. The jobs created by these projects must be filled by competent Chicanos, not only the Chicano who has the traditional credentials required for the position, but one who has the credentials of the Raza. Too often in the past the dedicated pushed for a program only to have a *vendido* sharp-talker come in and take over and start working for his Anglo administrator. Therefore, students must demand a say in the recruitment and selections of all directors and assistant directors of student-initiated programs. To further insure strong if not complete control of the direction and running of programs, all advisory and steering committees should have both student and community components as well as sympathetic Chicano faculty as members.

Tying the campus to the *Barrio*. The colleges and universities in the past have existed in an aura of omnipotence and infallibility. It is time that they be made responsible and responsive to the communities in which they are located or whose members they serve. As has already been mentioned, community members should serve on all programs related to Chicano interests. In addition to this, all attempts must be made to take the college and university to the *Barrio*, whether it be in form of classes giving college credit or community centers financed by the school for the use of community organizations and groups. Also, the *Barrio* must be brought to the campus, whether it be for special programs or ongoing services which the school provides for the people of the *Barrio*. The idea must be made clear to the people of the *Barrio* that they own the schools and the schools and all their resources are at their disposal. The student group must utilize the resources open to the school for the benefit of the *Barrio* at every opportunity. This can be done by hiring more Chicanos to work as academic and non-academic personnel on the campus; this often requires exposure of racist hiring practices now in operation in many college [sic] and universities. When functions, social or otherwise, are held in the *Barrio* under the sponsorship of the college and university, monies should be spent in the *Barrio*. This applies to hiring Chicano contractors to build on campus, etc. Many colleges and universities have publishing operations which could be forced to accept *Barrio* works for publication. Many other things could be considered in using the resources of the school to the *Barrio*. There are possibilities for using the physical plant and facilities not mentioned here, but this is an area which has great potential.

MEChA in the Barrio

Most colleges in the Southwest are located near or in the same town as a *Barrio*. Therefore, it is the responsibility of MEChA members to establish close working relationships with organizations in that *Barrio*. The MEChA people must be able to take the pulse of the *Barrio* and be able to respond to it. However, MEChA must be careful not to overstep its authority or duplicate the efforts of another organization already in the *Barrio*. MEChA must be able to relate to all segments of the *Barrio*, from the middle-class assimilationists to the *batos locos*.

Obviously, every *Barrio* has its particular needs, and MEChA people must determine with the help of those in the *Barrio* where they can be most effective. There are, however, some general areas which MEChA can involve itself. Some of these are: 1) policing social and governmental agencies to make them more responsive in a humane and dignified way to the people of the *Barrio*; 2) carrying out research on the economic and credit policies of merchants in the *Barrio* and exposing fraudulent and exorbitant establishments; 3) speaking and communicating with junior high and other high school students, helping with their projects, teaching them organizational techniques, supporting their actions; 4) spreading the message of the movement by any media available—this means speaking, radio, television, local newspaper, underground papers, posters, art, theatres; in short, spreading propaganda of the Movement; 5) exposing discrimination in hiring and renting practices and many other areas which the student because of his mobility, his articulation, and his vigor should take as his responsibility. It may mean at times having to work in conjunction with other organizations. If this is the case and the project is one begun by the other organization, realize that MEChA is there as a supporter and should accept the direction of the group involved. Do not let loyalty to an organization cloud responsibility to a greater force—*la Causa*.

Working in the *Barrio* is an honor, but is also a right because we come from these people, and, as such, mutual respect between the *Barrio* and the college group should be the rule. Understand at the same time, however, that there will initially be mistrust and often envy on the part of some in the *Barrio* for the college student. This mistrust must be broken down by a demonstration of affection for the *Barrio* and La Raza through hard work and dedication. If the approach is one of a dilettante or of a Peace Corps volunteer, the people will know it and react accordingly. If it is merely a cathartic experience to work among the unfortunate in the *Barrio*—stay out.

Of the community, for the community. *Por la Raza habla el espiritú.*

SOUTHERN BLACK STUDENT ACTIVISM: ASSIMILATION VS. NATIONALISM

JOEL ROSENTHAL

Introduction

American society is complicated by the intermeshing of class and ethnic differences. Not only do persons differ in regards to the traditional dimensions of income, power, and prestige, but they are also of different races, religions, and nationalities. For those tens of millions of Americans who fall outside the purview of WASP America there is the persistent problem, both social and personal, of self-identification. Each ethnic group has been faced with models which variously de-emphasize and glorify their group's ethnicity.[1] There has been considerable ambivalence about the virtues of ethnic diversity by members of the WASP majority and among hyphenated Americans as well.[2] No one has felt this ambivalence more acutely than the Negro. In the words of W. E. B. Du Bois, "One ever feels his twoness,—an American, a Negro; two souls, two thoughts, two unreconciled stirrings; two warring ideals in one dark body, whose dogged strength alone keeps it from being torn asunder."[3] The implications of this bifurcated nature have been profound, indeed. As Blacks have fought to alter their inferior status in American society, they have chosen models which have alternately emphasized and de-emphasized their group's ethnicity. These competing strains are nowhere more evident than among the nation's Southern Black students whose presence was thrust upon the public consciousness with the advent of the sit-ins. Their activities, neglected by public and scholarly concern, have taken place against the backdrop of the nation's Southern Negro colleges and universities.

Student Discontent Before the Sixties

Basic Characteristics

In the South there exist somewhat in excess of one hundred institutions whose presence is unknown to the public at large. Most of these schools predate the twentieth century although several of the larger public institutions were born in more recent times. Whether private sectarian schools or state-supported ones, the central fact surrounding the evolution of the nation's historically Negro colleges and universities is that their emergence was "in all essential features a response to racism."[4] In terms of both power and philosophy, the Black colleges have developed primarily in response to the needs and demands of the dominant white majority.

Founded, financed, and originally administered by whites, these schools encouraged an exaggerated middle class style of life rather than developed a type of cultural nationalism among their students.[5] Existing in a hostile environment, the leaders of the Negro colleges frequently chose to cater to the prejudices of the racist majority. In response to the demands of the Southern segregated style of life, Negro higher education evolved a highly authoritarian structure which minimized potentially explosive contacts with the surrounding white world.[6] The Southern Black colleges and universities socialized a Negro middle class destined for a life of relative financial attainment but without fundamentally challenging the group's subordinate social position.

Structurally, these institutions were authoritarian in nature with strict regulation of student and faculty expression. However, there always existed a group of student and faculty critics basically dissatisfied with the nature and direction of Black higher education. The substance of their criticism was the futility of the Negro pursuing an exclusively assimilationist philosophy of education.[7] The irony of the Black college in this view was that its assimilationist philosophy was inappropriate for the segregated outside world.

Focusing upon this inherent conflict, these early critics developed an analysis of Black higher education which emphasized not only the inequities of Black education but also called for an education rooted in the particularity of the Negro experience.[8] A growing number of Black intellectuals proposed the development of a militant Black university which would speak more genuinely to the needs and aspirations of the black community. Among the more articulate spokesmen of this New Negro Movement were Horace Mann Bond, a leading scholar of Negro education, and James Weldon Johnson, an executive secretary of the NAACP in the 1920s. The Movement was primarily a cultural renaissance with relatively minor support among the black masses and black middle class students. The NAACP, the largest Negro organization, was then as now both interracial and committed to working through traditional mechanisms of change.[9]

Active Discontent

During the nineteenth century, there were isolated incidents of direct action by students at the nation's Negro colleges.[10] However, it was not until the 1920s that large numbers of Negro institutions found their students protesting a variety of inequities. Not surprising was the fact that widespread direct action took place at the so-called "elite" institutions whose students had the greatest interracial contact with white society. There the aspirations to enter into middle-class American life were the greatest and the disparities between black and white cut most deeply. Strikes and boycotts took place protesting the confining moral codes and deplorable physical conditions at the Negro colleges and the fact that whites were in control of Negro higher education. During those years strikes took place at such venerable Negro institutions as Fisk,[11] Hampton,[12] and Howard.[13] The 1930s saw the development of the first mass student movement in the country's history.[14] And, although the majority of colleges were unaffected by the decade's activities, the Negro institutions were not immune. No longer was protest by black students limited to the "elite" institutions or to the issues of black control and student power. Discontent struck a number of state controlled institutions on a wide variety of issues. But perhaps the most distinguishing characteristic of Southern black student dissent during the thirties was the impetus provided by white liberal and radical students.

White radical concern was reflected in such journals of the student left as *Student Review*, the monthly organ of the National Student League (NSL) between 1931 and 1935. The NSL was the agent of the Communist party and the Young Communist League on American campuses during the thirties. Contributors looked favorably upon the growing discontent at the Southern Negro colleges over such issues as the Scottsboro Trial which brought displays of support at private schools such as Fisk and state controlled institutions like South Carolina College for Negroes at Chapel Hill.[15] The lesson, according to the radical left was clear:

> Just as the Negro miners in the South are forming locals in their mines and uniting with the white workers to protest their class interest, so also must the Negro students in their various colleges form social problems clubs and affiliate with the revolutionary students movement under the leadership of the National Student League.[16]

NSL representatives travelled the South in an effort to promote Negro affiliation and report on activities at the Negro colleges.[17] They also held a Conference on Negro Student Problems.[18]

Southern Negro student discontent did not require the encouragement of NSL representatives during these years, and much of the student activity was not attributable to the latters' efforts. In 1934, white students from the University of Virginia and Negroes from Virginia Union went to the state legislature and demanded increased appropriations for their respective schools.[19] The same year brought a strike against the alleged "Victorian atmosphere and the convent-like restrictions" imposed by President John M. Gardy at Virginia State College.[20] The Denmark Vesey Forum for the discussion of economic and sociological questions was organized at Fisk University. Its members organized a campus protest under the leadership of Ishmael Flory when a Negro was lynched at the edge of campus. They also led protests and picketing of a local theater which was segregated and prevented a group of school singers from appearing. Fisk President, Dr. Thomas E. Jones, expelled Flory for his activities which were deemed "detrimental to the best interests of the University."[21]

By 1935, the student movement turned its attention toward the issues of war and facism. Anti-war conferences were held at universities throughout the United States, including Howard and Virginia Union. Students took the Oxford Pledge "not to support the government of the United States in any war it may conduct."[22] On April 12, 1935, an estimated 150,000 students struck for an hour against war and facism. Among them were 3,000 Negro students from Howard University, Virginia Union, Virginia State and Morgan College.[23] At Howard University, 250 students marched against war and facism and more than 600 refused to attend classes.[24] Another strike, held on April 22, 1935, drew an estimated 500,000 students; and according to one enthusiastic observer, "For the first time the majority of students in the Negro colleges participated: Hampton Institute, Morehouse College, Virginia Union as well as the veteran Howard. . . ."[25]

World War II and the depression undermined the movement of the thirties but did not eliminate the structural and psychological dissatisfactions underlying Southern Negro college student protest. Negro involvement in the war merely made participants more aware of the disparities between American ideals and realities. Returning veterans provided the impetus for a desegregation drive at historically Negro Lincoln University in Oxford, Pennsylvania.[26] This movement which spanned the middle and later forties was important not only for its achievements but also as a harbinger of the sit-in movement of the sixties. The mode of protest was a prototype for the disciplined, nonviolent protests of ten and fifteen years ahead. The students appealed to the "sympathy and goodwill" of the citizenry by careful dress and speech, negotiated with the manager of the local coffee shop, conducted a poll among the citizens regarding their feelings towards eating in restaurants with Negroes and sitting beside Negroes in theaters, and finally held another conference with the manager to discuss the results of the poll. Students followed this course of action during several school years but were not successful until 1954 when the students who had sued the Oxford Theatre were awarded $600 damages and court costs together with an injunction against the theatre forbidding segregation of patrons and an injunction against the police authority in Oxford forbidding the use of its powers to support discrimination in public places. During this period, the school's "hands-off" policy was characterized by President Horace Mann Bond's formal endorsement of the students' nonviolent approach: "Resist evil; resist it without violence. Resist evil without hatred and malice. This is the highest and hardest duty of the true Christian."[27]

Following the Supreme Court's *Brown* decision in 1954, the pressures for desegregation increased. Students at the Southern Negro colleges played an increasingly important role in applying pressure. They found themselves, however, caught in a bind between their respective administrations and direct outside pressure. The administration at South Carolina College for Negroes (SCCN) expelled the Student Council President for his role in the petitioning by Negro parents of Orangeburg to apply the Supreme Court desegregation decision to the local schools. The expulsion touched off a student protest. At the end of the 1955–56 academic year, fifteen students, three teachers, and two other staff members were banned from the campus.[28] At the same time SCCN students protested the South Carolina legislature's resolution to probe NAACP activity on the campus.[29] During October, 1956, students at Alcorn Agricultural and Mechanical College in Lorman, Mississippi, "attempted a protest strike against the general conditions under which they suffered, but the administration effectively broke it up."[30] A more serious incident took place the following year when Dr. Clennon King, an Alcorn professor, wrote a series of articles in the Mississippi *State-Times* purportedly supporting segregation.[31] The State Board of Education expelled the student protesters and removed President J. R. Otis for his stand in favor of the students.[32] The State College Board ordered the students to return to classes or find their school closed.[33] Students also played central roles in the Tallahassee Bus Protest[34] and the desegregation of public facilities in Baltimore, Maryland.[35]

The Sit-in Era

Events

By 1960 the groundwork for mass student participation in direct action had been established. The structural bases for Southern Black student dissatisfaction were as old as the history of relations between the races. The philosophy of nonviolence was deeply rooted in the expanding Negro movement and had been employed already by students at Lincoln University in the forties and fifties. All that was required now was the spark that would ignite the smoldering discontent and that spark was provided by four freshmen students at North Carolina A & T when they sat down one day at the "whites only" section of a local drug store.[36] The age of the sit-ins was born as thousands of students from North and South sat-in, slept-in, and waded-in throughout the South and Southwest. At the center of the storm were thousands of students from the nation's historically Negro colleges, an estimated twenty-four percent of whom took some part in the sit-in movement.[37] During the early stages of the movement, the sit-ins were concentrated in the larger Southern cities, a majority taking place in cities of over 100,000 population.[38] In over half of these urban centers, the presence of a college or university was decisive.[39] The sit-in movement had relatively little impact, however, upon race relations in the rural Black Belt where Blacks constituted a higher proportion of the population.

Middle Class Goals/Means

The middle-class nature of the sit-in movement was evident in the goals and tactics of its participants.[40] The objective was not rejection of middle-class American life but rather inclusion in it. On this goal there was almost complete unanimity during the early sixties. The issue for debate was the means to be employed. The choice was nonviolence, not only because it was commensurate with the religious roots of Southern Negroes but also because it was more likely to gain allies among a section of the dominant white majority. In the words of two close students of the sit-in era, ". . . these students have selected nonviolent protest as an acceptable means of demonstrating their anger at barriers to first-class citizenship. Far from being alienated, the students appear to be committed to the society and its middle-class leaders."[41]

It was no mere accident that the protest movement would select nonviolent means of gaining acceptance into white middle-class society for it was the perfect tool for a movement with assimilationist objectives. It emphasized respectability and decorum and sought to convert members of the dominant white majority. For example, a set of instructions widely circulated among sit-in participants throughout the South contained the following exhortation:

Don't strike back or curse aloud if abused.
Don't laugh out.
Don't hold conversations with floor walkers.
Don't leave your seats until your leader has given you instructions to do so.
Don't block entrances to the store and aisles.
Show yourself friendly and courteous at all times.
Sit straight and always face the counter.
Report all serious incidents to your leader.
Refer all information to your leader in a polite manner.
Remember the teachings of Jesus Christ, Mohandas K. Gandhi, and Martin Luther King.[42]

Fundamentally there was little difference between these instructions and those given to Lincoln University students fifteen years earlier.

Administrative Response

One unintended consequence of the early sit-ins was the exposure to public view of the vulnerability of the Negro institutions. Their susceptibility to external pressure was evident in the administrative treatment of students and faculty involved in the protests. In general, there was a distinction between the public and private administrative responses. According to Dorothy Dunbar Bromley and Susan McCabe,

> Presidents of privately-supported Negro colleges . . . were freer to abstain from disciplining the "sit-in" students than those responsible for tax-supported Negro colleges, which felt the full force of threatened reprisals from segregation-consecrated governors, legislators and trustees.[43]

The students themselves perceived this distinction—students perceiving "administrators at state-run institutions as less supportive of the sit-ins than administrators at the private institutions."[44] Student protestors were expelled from Alabama State College,[45] Southern University,[46] Florida A & M,[47] Albany State College,[48] and other state supported institutions. Large numbers of faculty also lost their jobs. One chronicler of this period said: "It must be reported as one of the bitter ironies in the civil rights movement in the South that the administrations of some Negro institutions have exercised autocratic control over the actions and utterances of their faculties and students."[49]

The private Negro institutions were not unaffected by external pressures. Like their public counterparts, these institutions normally chose their presidents for "their acquiescent ability to work well with the white power structure. . . ."[50] Financial dependence characterized the private schools whose reliance was on private philanthropy rather than on state legislatures. Consequently, the discouragement of direct student action was not lacking but only more indirect. Southern states were not left without means of dissuading students and faculty from attempting to alter the traditional Southern mode of race relations. A classic case was provided by two private institutions, Allen University and Benedict College, located in Columbia, South Carolina. Students and faculty at these institutions were dismissed under pressure from Governor George B. Timmerman, Jr., Chairman of the State Board of Education. The mechanism was the removal of certification of graduates for teaching in the state's public schools. Such action, in effect, would have meant the destruction of these institutions whose primary function was the provision of teachers for South Carolina's segregated school system.[51]

The New Negro

Articulated as the objective of the sit-in movement was the desire to alter the South's segregated social system. However, at the center of the movement was the need on the part of increasing numbers of Negro youth to redefine themselves. Among this new generation of students there were those dissatisfied with the stereotype of the passive Negro male. In contrast, Martin Luther King became the model of an "assertive Negro male" who dared confront directly through action the forces of Southern white power. King and his tactics provided a constructive social outlet for "the evolution of a new social character in Negro youth."[52] In the words of one of the four original protestors at North Carolina A & T College: "At the end of that first sit-in, I didn't feel nearly as guilty as [I] had felt prior to it. . . . Before the sit-ins, I felt kinda lousy, like I was useless."[53]

That feeling of uselessness was now gone, for the sit-ins provided a mechanism whereby large numbers of Negroes could "express publicly the frustration and resentment that [had] been hidden for so long."[54] Thousands of young black students experienced the affirmativeness of being black. Although many never doubted this, countless others echoed the sentiment expressed by Diana Nash, an early leader of the Nashville sit-ins: "Within the movement . . . we came to a realization of our worth."[55]

The Limits of Nonviolence

A coalition of Negroes and whites, students and nonstudents, participated in the sit-ins; its members pushed forward faster than either the federal government or the more established civil rights organizations. In May of 1961 the Congress of Racial Equality (CORE) with the aid of the Student Nonviolent Coordinating Committee (SNCC), the student arm of the movement, organized "freedom rides" to insure desegregation of interstate bus terminals. Considerable white violence ensued and while Martin Luther King agreed to postpone the freedom rides, the SNCC students continued. By August of 1961, SNCC had extended its goals to include voter registration with the help and encouragement of the Taconic and the Marshall Field Foundations. Many SNCC workers took a year off from school. The opposition was so great that King requested federal intervention, but with no success. By 1961, the leading adult civil rights groups joined forces with SNCC under the banner of the Council of Freedom Organizations (COFO). COFO's major effort took place during the summer of 1964, the Mississippi Freedom Summer, and brought hundreds of black and white SNCC workers, NAACP lawyers, college professors, and clergy to Mississippi. The response was rape, church bombings, murder, and culminated in the death of James Chaney, Andrew Goodman, and Michael Schwerner.[56]

The summer made the members of SNCC painfully aware of the limits of the liberal coalition on civil rights. Although Lyndon Baines Johnson, then President, would do more than any of his predecessors in the area of civil rights, he was unwilling to directly confront the Southern wing of the Democratic Party. Turning to politics in 1965, SNCC organized political structures in Mississippi (The Mississippi Freedom Democratic Party) and Alabama (The Black Panther Party). As the Johnson Administration made an increasing commitment to Viet Nam, the more militant black students pushed for a new strategy. The first major break with the old liberal coalition came when SNCC, during January, 1966, publicly condemned the Administration's Southeast Asian policy.[57]

The Black Power Era

As the Civil Rights Movement encountered obstacles in both the North and the Black Belt South, the black-white liberal coalition of the early sixties became strained, and the turn toward a type of black nationalism predicted by some became a reality.[58] The rallying cry for this development was black power, and one of its more articulate advocates was Stokely Carmichael who found a ready audience among Southern Negro college students. In Carmichael's view, the integration movement:

> [was] based on the assumption that there was nothing of value in the Negro community and that little of value could be created among Negroes, so the thing to do was to siphon off the "acceptable" Negroes into the surrounding middle-class white community. . . . The goals of . . . integration. . . . are quite simply middle-class goals, articulated by a tiny group of Negroes who had middle-class aspirations.[59]

Carmichael's perspective called for the preservation of the "racial and cultural personality of the Negro community" while simultaneously carrying on the fight for freedom. In the words of one observer, the students were "calling for the goal of integration to be tempered by the pursuit of a form of cultural pluralism. . . ."[60]

Dissident Faculty

Faculty members played a much more crucial role in protests on black campuses than did their counterparts at white institutions.[61] It made little difference whether the dissident faculty members were white or black. However, the turn toward black nationalism raised the issue of the role of the white liberal in the movement for black liberation. Whites were admonished to return to their own communities to fight white racism at its source.[62] Ironically, at the very moment that black nationalism was raising its head there was an influx of young white faculty members from the nation's most prestigous graduate and professional schools. The three major programs bringing young liberal whites to the Southern Negro colleges were the Southern Teaching Program, the Recruitment of Southern Teachers, and the Woodrow Wilson Internship Program.[63] Given the growing restiveness of the students and the structural problems of the institutions themselves, the presence of these individuals added an additional disquieting element to an already volatile setting.

The first serious incident took place during the summer of 1966 when President Milton K. Curry, Jr., of Bishop College in Dallas, Texas, dismissed a large group of white instructors for purportedly "stirring up students" on issues of civil rights and academic freedom.[64] In Curry's view, "They seem to have the idea they came down here for a social revolution. Some of them must be sick, frustrated young fellows."[65] At South Carolina State College the non-retention of several Woodrow Wilson interns with doctorates precipitated a student boycott which broadened into a general protest concerning the state's educational policies.[66] Similarly, three Woodrow Willson instructors were not retained following the 1966–67 academic year at Southern University in Baton Rouge, Louisiana, where there had been considerable anti-administration activity on the part of the students.[67]

At other institutions, the growing student dissatisfaction was encouraged by the more independent members of the black faculty. Like their white counterparts, these teachers were usually trained at the nation's more prestigous graduate schools and, consequently, possessed perspectives far broader than those faculty members whose lives had been spent within the confines of the Negro educational world. In many instances, the young black faculty members had returned to the Black colleges at great personal sacrifice but with a genuine dedication to changing the traditional mold of these colleges. Because of the traditionally autocratic nature of the administrations of these schools, the young militant black faculty frequently found hope only among the growing army of discontented students. At Texas Southern University, Professor Mack Jones, who as a student had been the institution's first Woodrow Wilson scholar, was fired at the end of the 1967 academic year due to his role as faculty advisor to a SNCC affiliated chapter which had struggled the entire year to gain official recognition on the TSU campus.[68] Similarly, Howard University rid itself of a number of faculty members who were either supportive of student dissenters or sympathetic to their grievances. Most famous of these was Professor Nathan Hare who had written several articles strongly critical of Negro higher education.[69] At Grambling College three faculty members were fired.[70]

The Black University

Contemporaneous with the emergence of black nationalism there arose a critique of Negro higher education from within the Negro community. The seeds of this struggle were at least as old as the famous controversy between W. E. B. Du Bois and Booker T. Washington. The alternative of black nationalism had surfaced during the New Negro Movement of the twenties. However, the thread of black nationalism running through the history of Negro higher education was now pushed to its extreme. Unlike its precursors, the new version of black nationalism was linked to an emerging brand of mass student activism. While some students and faculty participated in direct action, others wrote about the deficiences of Negro higher education and the place of the black man in America. The issue of the Negro college, a mere side issue during the sit-in era, became a focal point of student and faculty dissent.

It was argued, both in the streets and in scholarly publications, that the Negro colleges were structured to produce black skins with white masks, in the phrase of Franz Fanon who was one of the heroes of the period.[71] In this view, the Negro college represented an institution of dependency; it had emerged because of white racism and not because of any affirmative commitment to things black. The need was to develop a black university. Although there were a multitude of views concerning the specifics of such an institution, there was considerable agreement about its general outlines. There was general philosophical agreement that the black university should be structured "to serve the Black masses."[72] This would mean not only the establishment of a black curriculum but also a commitment to deal with the intractable problems of the black communities.[73] To some, this would require the purging of white faculty and administrators; to others, the purging of mediocrity regardless of race. To some, the black university would emerge from the ashes of the Negro college; to others, there was a belief in the possibility of restructuring existing schools. Some fought for changes with pen and ink; others took to the street.

With the movement away from assimilation and the rejection of a primarily moral appeal, there was no longer a place for a mass of highly disciplined students trained in the tactics of non-violence. Gone was the rational link between goals and means which had existed during the time that the nonviolent philosophy of Martin Luther King was ascendant. The moral commitment of Martin Luther King was merely a tactical expediency for many students.[74] The use of force was symbolized in Stokely Carmichael's phrase "by any means necessary" in answer to the question of how Blacks intended to achieve their goals.[75] During the middle and late sixties, two philosophies of goals and means (violence and nonviolence, cultural nationalism and assimilation) were in constant competition for the hearts and souls of the thousands of Southern Negro college students. While there was broad support for the sentiment that the Negro colleges were "unresponsive to student complaints" and grievances, there was great disagreement over tactics.[76] Most Negro colleges experienced organized boycotting of classes by students, one-third experienced serious property damages.[77] However, at no institution did more than a small minority of students engage in more violent forms of confrontations with authorities.

The Response

Black institutions experienced a higher proportion of violent and obstructive protests than did white institutions during the late sixties.[78] At the same time, a higher proportion of off-campus police were employed in confrontations on black campuses.[79] In some instances, requests for police came from Negro administrators themselves, as in the cases of Grambling and Lane colleges.[80] While most of these confrontations did not result in death or destruction, the Negro colleges had more than their share of "Kent States." Most destructive confrontations between students and civilian authorities took place at the larger state-supported schools. At Alcorn A & M, highway patrol used tear gas and clubs to prevent a student protest against the institution's head in 1966, and two years later these same forces wounded three students by gunfire while clearing a burning dormitory.[81] In May 1967, an officer was killed and several students were wounded following the discharge of approximately 500 rounds of ammunition by police at Texas Southern University in Houston.[82] Three students were shot to death by police at South Carolina State College in Columbia, South Carolina, in February 1968.[83] An honor student was killed during a shootout between students and police in May 1969, at North Carolina A & T in Greensboro.[84] A year later, two Blacks (one university and one high school student) were killed when Mississippi highway patrolmen fired into a crowd of students at Jackson State College in Mississippi.[85] Finally, two students were killed when sheriff's deputies re-took the Southern University administration building in Baton Rouge, Louisiana, on November 16, 1972.[86]

Conclusion

The deaths at Southern University temporarily marked the end of the era of violent confrontations on the Negro college campuses. They did not, however, still the battle between the forces of integration and black nationalism among the Southern Negro college students. Today, there is a more reflective mood among discontented students and faculty. Changing patterns of dress, speech, and curriculum symbolize the successes of the new emphasis on ethnicity, and yet the powerful pull of assimilation has not abated. The enticements of the historically white colleges are drawing sizable numbers of the nation's most talented black students and faculty away from the Southern Negro colleges. A series of annexations and mergers and an influx of whites has reduced the number of all-black state colleges. The Race Relations Information Center, an independent Nashville-based organization that investigates and analyzes racial problems, concluded in a 1971 study that, "The Negro public colleges are in imminent danger of losing their identity through integration, merger, reduced status or outright abolition."[87]

Whether the vision of the black university will become a reality or whether forces beyond the control of the black community will merely absorb the historically Negro colleges are issues which remain unanswered. In the meantime, the same structural problems of inadequate funds and facilities, white control of Black education, stifling of student and faculty nonconformity, and the essentially assimilationist nature of Black higher education which have joined in varying degrees in the past to produce direct forms of student protest remain beneath the surface with the potential for erupting once again.

Notes

1. Milton M. Gordon, *Assimilation in American Life: The Role of Race, Religion and National Origin* (London: Oxford University Press, 1961).
2. Andrew Greeley, "The Rediscovery of Cultural Diversity." *The Antioch Review*, XXXI (Fall 1971), 343–365, 350.
3. W. E. B. Du Bois, *The Souls of Black Folk: Essays and Sketches* (Chicago: A. C. McClurg & Co., 1903), p. 3.

4. Christopher Jencks and Davis Reisman, "The American Negro College," *Harvard Educational Review*, XXXVII (1967), 3–60, 29; Edward Brown, "The Black University," in Gary R. Weaver and James H. Weaver (eds.) *The University and Revolution* (Englewood Cliffs, N.J.: Prentice-Hall, Inc., 1969). pp. 141–151, 142.

5. Robert P. Stuckert, "The Negro College—A Pawn of White Domination," *The Wisconsin Sociologist*, III (January 1964), 1–8, 1.

6. E. Franklin Frazier, *The Negro in the United States* (Rev. ed.; New York: The MacMillan Co., 1957), p. 479.

7. Michael Miles, *The Radical Probe; The Logic of Student Rebellion* (New York: Atheneum, 1971), pp. 194–197.

8. *Ibid.*

9. *Ibid.*

10. Cf. George Cunningham, "The Negro Fights for Freedom; II. Alcorn College, Miss.," *Anvil and Student Partisan*, VII (Fall 1957). 5–7, 5.

11. Marcia Lynn Johnson, "Student Protest at Fisk University," *Negro History Bulletin*, (October 1970), 137–140.

12. W. E. Burghardt DuBois, "The Hampton Strike," *Nation*, CXXV (November 2,1927), 471–472.

13. Rayford W. Logan, *Howard University; The First Hundred Years, 1867–1967* (New York: New York University Press, 1968), pp. 120–122.

14. A brief overview of pre-Berkeley student activism is found in Philip G. Altbach and Patti Peterson, "Before Berkeley: Historical Perspectives on American Student Activism," *The Annals*, CCCXCV (May 1971), 1–14.

15. Everett L. Beans, "The Negro Student," *Student Review*, I (March 1932), 8–9.

16. *Ibid.* p. 9.

17. Edmund Stevens and Gabriel Carritt, "The Southern Student Stirs," *Student Review*, II (October 1932), 18–19; Maurice Gates, "South Revisited," *Student Review*, IV. (March 1935), 15.

18. *Student Review*, II (February 1933), 9.

19. James Wechsler, *Revolt on the Campus* (New York: Covici & Friede, 1935), p. 370; Lyonel Florant, "Youth Exhibits a New Spirit," *The Crisis*, XLIII (August 1936), 237; Maurice Gates, "Negro Students Challenge Social Forces," *The Crisis*, XLII (August 1935), 233.

20. Gates, *op. cit, p.* 233; Wechsler, *op. cit.*, p. 370; Florant, *op. cit.*, p. 237.

21. Gates, *op. cit.*, p. 233; Florant, *op. cit.*, p. 238.

22. Gates, *op. cit.*, p. 233.

23. *Ibid.*

24. Florant, *op. cit.*, p. 238.

25. Joseph P. Lash, "500,000 Strike for Peace: An Appraisal," *Student Advocate*, I (May 1936), 3.

26. Lewis Jones, "The Student Demonstrations as a Social Movement; Prototype—A Case Study," in *The Influence of Student Demonstrations on Southern Negro Colleges; Part II; The Negro Student Movement*, A Report from the Department of Race Relations of Fisk University to the Field Foundation, Inc. (October 1962), pp. 37–50.

27. *Ibid.*

28. *New York Times* (June 25, 1956).

29. *New York Times* (April 13, 1956).

30. Cunningham, *op. cit.*, p. 5–7.

31. *New York Times* (March 9, 1957).

32. *Ibid.*

33. Nashville *Tennessean* (March 9, 1957).

34. Lewis M. Killian, *The Tallahassee Bus Protest* (New York: Anti-Defamation League of B'nai B'rith, 1958).

35. August Meier, "The Successful Sit-In in a Border City," *Journal of Intergroup Relations*, II (Summer 1961), 230–232.

36. Fredric Solomon and Jacob R. Fishman, "Youth and Social Action: II.; Action and Identity Formation in the First Student Sit-In Demonstration," *J. of Social Issues*, XX (April 1964) 36–45.

37. Donald R. Matthews and James W. Prothro, *Negroes and the New Southern Politics* (New York: Harcourt, Brace & World, 1966), p. 412.

38. Martin Oppenheimer, "Institutions of Higher Learning and the 1960 Sit-Ins: Some Clues for Social Action," *Journal of Negro Education*, XXXII (1963), 286–288, 286.

39. *Ibid*, p. 287.

40. Ruth Searles and J. Allen Williams, Jr., "Negro College Students' Participation in Sit-Ins," *Social Forces*, XL, (March 1962), 215, 216; James W. Vander Zander, "The Non-Violent Resistance Movememt Against Segregation," *American Journal of Sociology*, LXVIII (March 1963), 544–550, 549.

41. *Ibid*, 219.

42. *New York Times* (March 2, 1960).
43. Dorothy Dunbar Bromley and Susan McCabe, "Impact of the 'Sit-In' Movement on Academic Freedom," *Negro Education Review*, XII (April 1961), 63–71, 64.
44. John McLeod Orbell, *Social Protest and Social Structure: Southern Negro College Student Participation in the Protest Movement* (Unpub. Ph.D. Dissertation, Chapel Hill, University of North Carolina, 1962), p. 80.
45. Bromley and McCabe, *op. cit.*, pp. 64–65.
46. *Ibid.*, pp. 66–67.
47. *Ibid.*, p. 69.
48. C. Van Woodward, "The Unreported Crisis in the Southern Colleges," *Harper's Magazine*, CCXXV (October 1962), 86.
49. William P. Fidler, "Academic Freedom in the South Today." *AAUP Bulletin* (Winter 1965), 415.
50. Samuel P. Wiggins, *Higher Education in the South* (Berkeley: McCutchan Publishing Corporation, 1966), p. 283.
51. Academic Freedom and Tenure: Allen University and Benedict College," *AAUP Bulletin* (Spring 1960), 87–104.
52. Frederic Solomon and J. R. Fishman, "The Psychosocial Meaning of Nonviolence in Student Civil Rights Activities," *Psychiatry*, XXVIII (May 1964), 91–99, 99.
53. Solomon and Fishman, "Youth and Social Action: II; . . .," *op. cit.*
54. Solomon and Fishman, "Meaning," p. 92.
55. Diana Nash, "Inside the Sit-Ins and Freedom Rides: Testimony of a Southern Student," in Mathew H. Ahmann (ed.), *The New Negro* (Notre Dame: Fedes Publishers, 1961), pp. 43–60, 49.
56. This overview is taken from Helene Hanff, *The Movers and Shakers; The Young Activists of the Sixties* (New York: S. G. Phillips, 1970), pp. 19–63.
57. Reprinted in Joanne Grant (ed.), *Black Protest*, (Greenwich, Conn., 1968), pp. 416–418.
58. James W. Vander Zander, *op. cit.*, p. 549.
59. Speech delivered to the Howard University School of Law student body and faculty on October 14, 1966.
60. Mack Jones, "Some Observations on Student Rebellion on Black Campuses," *Journal of Social and Behavioral Sciences*, XV (Fall 1969), 61–65, 64.
61. Durward Long, "Black Protest," in Julian Foster and Durward Long, (eds.), *Protest: Student Activism in America* (New York: William Morrow & Company, Inc., 1970), pp. 459–482, 467.
62. Carmichael, *op. cit.*
63. The experience of two Woodrow Wilson instructors is found in Andress Taylor and John A. Sekora, "The Woodrow Wilson Internship Program: A Case Study," *Journal of General Education*, XIX (October 1967), 202–215.
64. Paul M. Gaston, "The Bishop College Debacle," in Southern Teaching Program, 1965: An Evaluation Prepared for the Southern Regional Council, pp. 29–32.
65. *New York Times* (August 20, 1965), p. 15.
66. Paul Clancy, "The Fight for Quality on Two Negro Campuses," *Reporter* XXXVII. (July 13, 1967), 37–39.
67. "Academic Freedom and Tenure; Southern University and Agricultural and Mechanical College," *AAUP Bulletin*, LIV (Spring 1968), 14–24.
68. Joel Rosenthal, "The TSU 'Riot'" (Unpublished manuscript, 1968).
69. Cf. Nathan Hare, "Behind the Black College Student Revolt," *Ebony*, XXII (August 1967), 58–61.
70. "Academic Freedom and Tenure: Grambling College," *AAUP Bulletin*, LVII (March 1971), 50–52, 52.
71. Aristide and Vera Zolberg, "The Americanization of Franz Fanon," *The Public Interest* (Fall 1967), pp. 49–63.
72. Cf. Keith Lowe, "Towards a Black University," Southern Student Organizing Committee, Nashville, Tennessee, undated.
73. Ernest Stephens, "The Black University in America Today," *Freedomways*, VII (Spring 1967), 131 137.
74. Cf. Prathia Hall, "The American South," in Marjorie Hope, *Youth Against the World* (Boston: Little, Brown & Co., 1965), pp. 137–155, 144.
75. Robert L. Terrill, "Up from Uncle Tomism," *Commonweal*, XCII (April 3, 1970), 87–88ff., 87.
76. Cf. Sophia F. McDowell, Gilbert A. Lowe, Jr., and Doris A. Docketts, "Howard University's Student Protest Movement," *Public Opinion Quarterly*, XXXIV (Fall 1970), 383–388, 388.
77. E.C. Harrison, "Student Unrest on the Black College Campus," *The Journal of Negro Education*, XLI (Spring 1972), 113–120.
78. Long, *op. cit.*, p. 467.
79. *Ibid.*
80. Cf. Robert Deitz, "Grambling? A Football Factory Is in an Educational Uproar," *National Observer* (November 6, 1967); Terrell, p. 87 ff.

81. *The Clarion-Ledger* (February 22, 1968); *New York Times* (February 22, 1968).

82. Bernard Friedberg, "Houston and the TSU Riot," in William McCord, John Howard, Bernard Friedberg, and Edwin Harwood (eds.), *Life Styles in the Black Ghetto* (New York: W. W. Morton & Company, Inc., 1969), pp. 36–51; Blair Justice, *Violence in the City* (Texas Christian University Press, 1969).

83. Jack Nelson and Jack Bass, *The Orangeburg Massacre* (Cleveland, Ohio: The World Publishing Co., 1970); Warren Marr II, "Death on the Campus; the Orangeburg Story," *The Crisis*, LXXV (March 1968), 88–901.

84. "The Seige of Greensboro," *Newsweek*, LXXIII (June 2, 1969), 38; "Changing Greensboro: Black Protest," *Time*, XCIII (May 30, 1969), 22.

85. President's Commission on Campus Unrest, *The Killings at Jackson State* (Washington, D.C.: U.S. Government Printing Office, 1970); Ed William, "Jackson State College," in *Augusta, Georgia and Jackson State University; Southern Episodes in a National Tragedy*, Southern Regional Council, Inc., Atlanta, Georgia, June 1970.

86. Milwaukee *Sentinel* (November 17, 1972.)

87. *New York Times* (November 26, 1971).

Long-Term Effects of Volunteerism During the Undergraduate Years

Alexander W. Astin, Linda J. Sax, & Juan Avalos

A growing number of colleges and universities in the United States have become actively engaged in encouraging their undergraduate students to participate in some form of volunteer service (Cohen & Kinsey, 1994; Levine, 1994; Markus, Howard, & King, 1993; O'Brien, 1993). Further, service is increasingly being incorporated into the curriculums of major and general education courses (Cohen & Kinsey, 1994; Levine, 1994). While relatively few colleges include service learning or volunteer service as a curricular requirement, the number is growing and such a requirement has become an increasingly frequent topic of debate (Markus, Howard, & King, 1993). That the top leadership in higher education, has become increasingly supportive of service as part of the undergraduate experience is reflected in the phenomenal growth of the Campus Compact, a consortium of colleges and universities dedicated to promoting service among students and faculty. The Campus Compact now numbers well over 500 institutions.

One of the issues frequently raised by faculty and others who might be skeptical about the value of a service or volunteer experience is the one of efficacy: How is the student's educational and personal development affected by service participation? To date, empirical studies on the impact of service are quite scarce although evidence of the benefits of "involvement" in college is certainly abundant (Astin, 1993; Pascarella & Terenzini, 1991). While recent studies provide some evidence that service is associated with civic involvement and cognitive development, such research is generally limited because it relies on small samples of students from a single institution (Batchelder & Root, 1994; Giles & Eyler, 1994; Markus, Howard, & King, 1993). Although such studies have opened the door by providing a useful framework for the study of service, a consensus has indeed emerged about the urgency of collecting longitudinal, multi-institutional data on how students are affected by the service experience (Batchelder & Root, 1994; Cohen & Kinsey, 1994; Giles & Eyler, 1994; Giles, Honnet, & Migliore, 1991; Markus, Howard, & King, 1993; O'Brien, 1993).

Recently, the Higher Education Research Institute at UCLA completed a national study of the effects of President Bill Clinton's Learn and Serve America Higher Education Program, an activity of the Corporation for National Service, which is designed to facilitate the development of volunteer service programs for college students. This longitudinal multi-institutional study allowed for the examination of the effects of service participation *after* controlling for students' precollege propensity to engage in service. Findings suggested that service participation is positively associated with a number of short-term cognitive and affective outcomes during the undergraduate years (Astin & Sax, 1998). Among other things, the study found that service participation positively affects students' commitment to their communities, to helping others in difficulty, to promoting racial understanding, and to influencing social values. In addition, service participation directly influences the development of important life skills, such as leadership ability, social self-confidence, critical thinking skills, and conflict resolution skills. Service participation also has unique positive effects on academic development, including knowledge gained, grades earned, degrees sought after, and time devoted to academic endeavors.

While the Astin and Sax (1998) study examined the short-term effects of service participation, the purpose of the study reported here is to determine whether service participation during the undergraduate years has any *lasting* effects on students once they leave college. Among the questions to be explored are: Does undergraduate service participation continue to affect the student's educational development after college? How are other postcollege behaviors influenced? Do the value changes that have been associated with service participation during college persist after the student leaves college?

Context for the Study

The long-term effects of college can be looked at from two different perspectives: First, how students in general develop once they leave college (the generic "impact of college"); and second, how post-college development is affected by particular college *experiences*. The study reported here is of the latter type. While most studies of the long-term impact of college tend to focus on whether college attendance or degree attainment makes a difference (see Pascarella & Terenzini, 1991), few studies have been carried out to assess the long-term impact of particular college experiences such as community service.

To place this study in the larger context of the higher education research literature, we propose that our principal independent variable—participating in community service during the undergraduate years—be regarded as a form of student *involvement* (Astin, 1975, 1984, 1985). Briefly stated, the theory of involvement postulates that the benefits (i.e., "value-added") that students enjoy as a result of the college experience will be directly proportional to the time and effort that they invest in that experience. A large body of research shows that diverse forms of involvement are associated with a wide variety of positive student outcomes (Astin, 1977, 1993; Pascarella & Terenzini, 1991). The most potent forms of student involvement appear to be academic involvement (e.g., time spent studying and carrying out class assignments), interaction with peers, and interaction with faculty. While community service has so far received relatively little attention in student development research, it clearly qualifies as a substantial "investment of time and energy," and it ordinarily involves interaction with peers. In the case of course-based service, it would also be likely to increase both student-faculty interaction as well as the amount of time and energy that the students devote to the course.

Method

An opportunity to explore this topic was afforded by the availability of a national sample of former college students that included longitudinal data collected at three time points: at the time of initial entry to college in the fall of 1985, four years later in 1989, and nine years after college entry during 1994–1995. These data were collected as part of the Cooperative Institutional Research Program (CIRP), which is sponsored by the American Council on Education and the Higher Education Research Institute (HERI) at the University of California, Los Angeles. The CIRP annually collects a broad array of student background information using the Student Information Form (SIF), and is designed to serve as a pretest for longitudinal assessments of the impact of college on students.

The Surveys

The Student Information Form. The SIF was mailed to campuses in the spring and summer of 1985 for distribution to first-year college students during orientation programs and in the first few weeks of fall classes. The 1985 SIF includes information on students' personal and demographic characteristics, high school experiences, and expectations about college, as well as values, life goals, self-concepts, and career aspirations. A total of 279,985 students at 546 participating colleges and universities completed the SIF.

The 1989 Follow-up Survey. In 1989, HERI conducted a four-year longitudinal follow-up of students at four-year institutions who had completed the first-year survey in 1985. The 1989 follow-up survey includes information on students' college experience, their perceptions of college, and post tests of many of the items that appeared on the 1985 freshman student survey. The follow-up sample of 93,463 of the original 279,985 first-year students was selected in three different ways. A initial sample of 16,658 students from 309 institutions was selected through stratified random sampling. This procedure was designed to best reflect the national distribution of students across different institutional types. A second follow-up sample of 34,323 students at 52 institutions was afforded through a grant from the Exxon Education Foundation for the purpose of studying general education outcomes. Finally, we surveyed an additional 42,482 students at 100 institutions through a grant from the National Science Foundation designed to study undergraduate science education. Ultimately, we had responses from 27,064 students from 388 colleges and universities, resulting in an overall response rate of 29.0 percent. (See Astin, 1993, for more details on this sample.)

The Nine-Year Follow-up Survey. We conducted a second longitudinal follow-up survey in 1994–1995. This nine-year follow-up survey provides information on graduate school and early career experiences, as well as post-test data on many of the attitudinal and behavioral items appearing on the 1985 and 1989 surveys. This survey was sent to a sample of 24,057 students who had completed both the 1985 first-year and the 1989 follow-up surveys. A response rate of 51.4 percent was obtained, yielding a final sample of 12,376 from 209 institutions that had data at all three time points.[1]

Primary Independent Variable

The principal independent variable used in this study comes from the first (1989) longitudinal follow-up survey conducted four years after the student entered college. Students were asked, "During your last year in college, how much time did you spend during a typical week in volunteer work?" Students could respond along an eight-point continuum ranging from "none" to "over 20." After inspecting the distribution of responses to this question, we decided to collapse the top categories to create a five-category measure: (1) none, (2) less than 1 hour per week, (3) 1–2 hours per week, (4) 3–5 hours per week, and (5) 6 or more hours per week. The weighted percentage distribution of students' responses on this collapsed scale are as follows: 61.3, 13.3, 13.3, 7.0, 5.1. Thus, more than three students in five reported no involvement in volunteer service work during their last year of college, whereas only about one in twenty reported volunteering for six or more hours per week.

Dependent Variables

The nine-year follow-up survey (1994–1995) provided a number of opportunities to assess the impact of volunteer service participation during college on postcollege outcomes. Our selection of dependent variables was guided by two considerations: First, the short-term outcomes (e.g., satisfaction, academic performance, interest in graduate school, and sense of personal empowerment) that recent research has shown to be affected by service participation (Sax, Astin, & Astin, 1996); and second, the theory underlying the concepts of volunteerism and service learning, which argues, among other things, that service participation deepens students' understanding of social problems such as environmental degradation, poverty, and racial tension, and strengthens their commitment to civic values. (See, for example, Barber, 1993; Newman, 1985). We were also interested in testing the argument, sometimes advanced by opponents of service-learning, that participation in community service "politicizes" students. Finally, although no previous research or theory suggests that service participation should enhance the student's earnings, preparation for graduate school, or sense of commitment or loyalty to the alma mater, we included such outcomes on a purely exploratory basis.

With these guidelines in mind, we selected 18 outcome measures comprising a diverse array of academic and nonacademic behaviors, attitudes, and goals. The majority of these items had been pretested when the students entered college and post-tested four years later in the first follow-up conducted in 1989. Dependent variables include: five *behavioral* outcomes (attended graduate school, highest degree earned, donated money to the undergraduate college, frequency of socializing with persons from other racial/ethnic groups, and hours per week spent in volunteer/community service work during the past year); five measures of *values* (the student's degree of commitment to participate in community action programs, help others in difficulty, participate in programs to clean up the environment, promote racial understanding, and develop a meaningful philosophy of life); two *ratings of the undergraduate college* (adequacy of preparation for graduate work and for job); and two *satisfaction* measures (with graduate school, with job). Additional dependent measures included: political leaning (five-point scale from far right to far left), degree aspirations, income, and agreement with the statement, "Realistically, an individual person can do little to bring about changes in our society." This last measure is included as a "negative" outcome measure; that is, one would expect that involvement in service work would tend to empower students with the conviction that they can indeed make a difference in the society.

Additional Independent Variables

Following the CAMBRA approach to causal modeling (Astin & Dey, 1996), we included a number of first-year student "input" variables as control variables. These included pretests on 12 of the 18 dependent variables. Such pretests were available on all outcomes except the two satisfaction measures, the two undergraduate college ratings, income, and donating money to the undergraduate college. Input variables also included a set of 13 variables that we found through exploratory analyses to predict students' precollege propensity to engage in service. These include: four *behavioral* measures (performed volunteer work, tutored another student, attended religious services, and smoked cigarettes); three measures of *values* (the student's degree of commitment to participate in community action programs, help others in difficulty, and be very well off financially); two *reasons for attending college* (to make more money and improve reading and study skills); self rating on leadership ability, and measures of racial background and religious preference. Student's gender, socioeconomic status, and high school grades are additional inputs included in this study.

Analysis Design

The principal purpose of the data analysis was to estimate the effects of volunteer participation during the undergraduate years on each of the eighteen postcollege outcomes. For this purpose, we employed the CAMBRA method of causal modeling, which utilizes blocked, stepwise linear multiple regression analysis to focus on changes in the partial regression coefficients for all variables at each step in the analysis (Astin & Dey, 1996). CAMBRA provides a powerful means of decomposing and comprehending multicollinearity in a complex multivariate data set.

The basic approach in CAMBRA is to view each step (or block) in stepwise regression as a new model, differentiated from the model defined by the previous step (or block) by the newly added variable (or block of variables). The power of CAMBRA resides in its ability to demonstrate how the addition of a new variable (or block of variables) affects the relationship between *every other* variable—both in *and* out of the model—and the dependent variable. Identifying changes in the "effect" of variables that are not part of the variables currently defining the model is possible because of a novel feature of SPSS regression that computes the "beta in" for each such variable. "Beta in" shows what the standardized regression coefficient for a nonentered variable would be if it were the one entered on the *next step*. By following step-by-step changes in betas (for variables in the model) and "beta ins" (for variables not yet in the model), the investigator can get a comprehensive picture of how multicollinearity is affecting the entire data set.

CAMBRA also allows the investigator to conduct a series of path analyses by observing how the coefficients for variables already entered are changed when later variables are entered. When an entering variable significantly diminishes the coefficient for an earlier variable, an "indirect" path has been identified. When an earlier variable's coefficient remains significant through the final step, a "direct" path has been identified. The unique situation that occurs when an entering variable *strengthens* the coefficient for an earlier variable (a condition not covered in most writings on path analysis) is called a "suppressor effect" (i.e., the entering variable has been "suppressing" the observed effect of the earlier variable on the dependent variable) (Astin, 1991; Astin & Dey, 1996).

Each CAMBRA analysis had four blocks: (a) entering first-year student (input) variables; (b) hours spent volunteering during the last year in college (the principal independent variable); (c) the first (1989) posttest; and (d) hours spent in volunteer/community service work during the past year (i.e., 1994–1995). We included all entering first-year student or input variables in the first block, not only to control for initial differences in the students' pretest performance on each outcome measure, but also to control for possible self-selection bias (i.e., the student's predisposition to engage in volunteer service work during college).

We included the third block—the initial (1989) posttest on the dependent variable—to determine the extent to which the long-term effects of undergraduate service participation could be explained by its short-term effect on the first posttest measure obtained four years after entering college. In other words, does undergraduate service participation have any effect on the student nine years after college entry (1994), above and beyond its short-term effect as assessed only four years after entering college (1989)?

We included hours per week spent in volunteer or community service work in 1994 as the fourth and final block to determine if the effects of volunteering during college could be explained by its effect on volunteering after college. In other words, do students develop a "habit" of volunteering which persists after college, and can this continuing involvement help to explain the effect of undergraduate service participation on other long-term outcomes?

In short, we included these final two blocks of variables to learn something about the factors that *mediate* the long-term effects of service participation during the undergraduate years. (Note that the fourth block obviously had to be excluded from the one regression in which hours per week spent in volunteer/community service work was the dependent variable.)

We conducted a separate CAMBRA analysis for each of the 18 dependent variables. We confined regressions involving income and job satisfaction to students who were employed full-time at the time of the follow-up. Similarly, we limited the two regressions involving graduate school to students who had either completed their graduate work or were enrolled in graduate work at the time of the follow-up. We also excluded subjects who were missing data on either the dependent variable or the principal independent variable (volunteer participation during the undergraduate years) from any analysis. The sample sizes thus ranged between 5,604 cases (the student's rating of how well the undergraduate college prepared him or her for graduate work) to 11,478 (the frequency with which students socialized with persons from other racial/ethnic groups). Because of these very large sample sizes, we used a very stringent confidence level ($p < .001$) to select input variables into each regression. However, to provide as comprehensive a picture of the findings as possible, we report all results that show effects of service participation (after controlling for inputs) at the $p < .05$ level.

Results

Before discussing the results of the multivariate analyses, it is useful to examine our principal independent variable in somewhat more detail. Table 1 shows a simple cross-tabulation between this variable and its counterpart, hours per week spent in volunteer/community service work at the time of the second follow-up in 1994–1995. Although the simple correlation between these two variables is quite modest ($r = .22$), how much a student volunteers during college can clearly have a substantial effect on how much that student volunteers after college. Thus, spending six or more hours per week in volunteer work during the last year of college, as compared to not participating in volunteer work, nearly doubles the student's chances of being engaged in volunteer work in the years after college, and more than doubles his or her chances of spending either one, three, or six plus hours per week in postcollege volunteer/community service work. For example, 44 percent of those who spent six or more hours per week volunteering during their last year in college were spending at least one hour per week volunteering after college, contrasted to only 19 percent of those who did not volunteer during their last year of college.

To what extent does the student's engagement in service during high school relate to involvement during college and in the years after college? To explore this question we have performed a three-way cross-tabulation using the "pretest" measure of volunteer engagement, which comes from an item in the 1985 first-year student questionnaire that reads: "Performed volunteer work" (students were asked to indicate whether, during the past year, they had performed this activity "frequently," "occasionally," or "not at all"). Though this first-year student input variable showed very modest correlations with hours spent volunteering during college ($r = .18$) and five years after college ($r = .16$), it is associated with substantial differences on the other two measures. (See Table 2.) Of particular

TABLE 1

Engagement in Volunteer/Community Service Work Nine Years After Entering College as a Function of Volunteering During the Undergraduate Years (Percentages)

Hours Per Week Spent in Volunteering During Last Year of College (1989)	Hours Per Week Spent in Volunteer/Community Service in 1994–1995				
	None	Any	1 or More	3 or More	6 or More
6 or more	38	62	44	20	9
3 or more	42	58	41	22	7
1 or more	40	60	40	19	5
Any	37	53	26	12	4
None	63	37	19	9	4
Total	55	45	21	12	4

TABLE 2

Engagement in Volunteer/Community Service Work Nine Years After Entering College as a Function of Volunteering During High School and College

Hours Per Week Spent Volunteering During Last Year of College	Volunteered During High School	Hours Per Week Spent in Volunteer/Community Service Nine Years After Entering College in (1994–1995) (Percentages)	
		Less than 1	1 or More
One or more	frequently	67	49
	occasionally	59	38
	not at all	48	38
Less than one	frequently	64	33
	occasionally	57	27
	not at all	30	16
None	frequently	43	27
	occasionally	38	19
	not at all	31	13

interest is the fact that, even after controlling for hours per week spent volunteering during college, the frequency of volunteer participation during high school *still* correlates with hours spent volunteering nine years later. This is especially true among students who engaged in volunteer work for less than one hour per week during college: Those who volunteered "frequently" in high school were more than twice as likely to devote at least some time to volunteer/community service work nine years later than those who did no volunteer work during high school (64% versus 30%). Table 2 thus shows that the "habit" of volunteering persists over a relatively long period of time.

For example, among those who did no volunteer work during either high school or college, only 13 percent were spending one hour or more per week in volunteer work nine years after entering college. This figure more than triples, to 49 percent, among those who volunteered frequently during high school *and* averaged one or more hours of volunteer work during college.

Despite these consistencies, Table 2 also indicates that a good deal of volunteer engagement is situationally determined. Thus, among those students who were frequent volunteers in high school and who devoted one or more hours per week to volunteer work during college, fully one-third (33 percent) were not engaged in *any* volunteer or community service work nine years after entering college. At the same time, among those who did no volunteer work in either high school or college, nearly one-third (31 percent) devoted at least some time to volunteer or community service work nine years after entering college.

Thirteen of the 18 dependent variables showed significant effects from service participation during the undergraduate years. These findings are summarized in Table 3. The first column of coefficients indicates the effect of volunteering during college on each long-term outcome after all significant input variables have been controlled. All of the effects are in the expected direction, including the expected negative effect on the "disempowerment" measure, "Realistically, an individual person can do little to bring about changes in our society." Being a volunteer during college, in other words, is associated with a greater sense of empowerment in the years after college.

In the behavioral realm, participating in volunteer service during college is associated with attending graduate school, earning higher degrees, donating money to one's alma mater, socializing with persons from different racial/ethnic groups, and participating in volunteer/community service work in the years after college. In the value realm, volunteering during college is positively associated with five values measured in the postcollege years: helping others in difficulty, participating in community action programs, participating in environmental cleanup programs, promoting racial understanding, and developing a meaningful philosophy of life. Clearly, the positive short-term effects of volunteering during college on civic and social values observed in earlier studies (Markus, Howard, & King, 1993; Sax, Astin, & Astin, 1996) persist beyond college. Volunteering during college is also associated with higher degree aspirations as measured nine years after college entry and with the student's perception that his or her undergraduate college provided good preparation for work. This latter finding is consistent with the notion that participating in service work gives the stunt important practical experience in the "real world."

The second column of coefficients in Table 3 shows the effects of undergraduate service participation after controlling for the immediate postcollege measures obtained in 1989. What these coefficients tell us is whether undergraduate service participation continues to affect the nine-year outcome measures (the second posttest) once its effects on the immediate postcollege outcomes (the first posttest) are controlled. The fact that every single partial beta coefficient shown in the second column is smaller than its corresponding coefficient shown in the first column suggests that most of the effects of undergraduate service participation are at least *partially* mediated by its short-term effects on the four-year outcomes. One of these effects appears to be entirely mediated in this fashion—the belief that individuals can do little to change society. Thus, in the regression, the highly significant ($p < .0001$) partial beta shown in column 1 is reduced to nonsignificance ($p > .05$) after controlling for the immediate postcollege outcomes. Not surprisingly, the largest reductions occur with value outcomes, all of which were posttested immediately after college as well as nine years after entering college.

The last column of coefficients in Table 3 shows the long-term effects of undergraduate service participation after controlling for involvement in volunteer work nine years after college. Controlling for the last variable has little effect, suggesting that few of the long-term effects of volunteerism during college can be explained by volunteerism after college. Only three additional outcomes—donating money to one's alma mater, participating in environmental cleanup, and developing a meaningful philosophy of life—are reduced to nonsignificance by controlling for postcollege volunteerism; and in all three instances, the changes in the coefficients are trivial. Indeed, these three outcome measures had beta coefficients that were only marginally significant ($p < .05$) after controlling for immediate postcollege outcomes. In short, these findings show that

TABLE 3

**Thirteen Postcollege Outcomes Showing Significant Effects From Service
Participation During the Undergraduate Years**

	Beta After Controlling for:		
94–95 Outcome Measures	*1985 Inputs*	*1989 Outcomes*	*Hours Spent Volunteering in 1994–1995*
Behavioral:			
Highest degree earned	.05****	.04****	.04***
Attended graduate school	.03***	.02*	.02*
Donated money to alma mater	.03**	.02*	.01
Socialized with someone from a different racial/ethnic group	.06****	.03***	.03**
Hours spent volunteering in 1994–95	.15****	.13****	N/A
Values: Commitment to			
Helping other in difficulty	.09****	.04****	.03**
Participating in community action programs	.11****	.05****	.05****
Participating in environmental cleanup	.05****	.02*	.01
Promoting racial understanding	.08****	.03***	.02**
Developing a meaningful philosophy of life	.05****	.02*	.01
Atitude: Individuals can do little to change society	-.05****	-.02	-.01
Degree Aspirations	.06****	.04***	.03**
How well college prepared students for work	.04***	.03*	.02*

**** p < .0001
*** p < .001
** p < .01
* p < .05

the long-term effects of undergraduate service participation cannot be explained simply in terms of its effects on postcollege volunteer engagement. This finding was perhaps to be expected, given that the simple correlation between undergraduate and postcollege volunteerism is only .22. Once again, these results suggest that the "habit" of volunteering is not the main determinant of who will get involved at any point in time but rather that much engagement in volunteerism is situationally determined.

Discussion

This study makes it clear that the short-term effects of volunteer service participation during the undergraduate years persist beyond college and are not simply short-term artifacts. While it is true that these longer-term effects are indeed mediated to some extent by the shorterm effects measured at the time of college completion (especially in the area of values and attitudes), undergraduate service participation continues to have direct effects at least through the first five years following the completion of college. In the parlance of path analysis, we would say that undergraduate service participation has both "direct" nd "indirect" effects on postcollege outcomes. Of equal importance is. The finding that undergraduate volunteer participation affects students n both the affective and cognitive realms, including direct effects on educational outcomes, such as attendance at graduate school and the acquisition of higher degrees.

While service participation during the undergraduate years did not result in any significant effects on satisfaction with graduate school or on the student's perception of how well the undergraduate college preared him or her for graduate work, it did show a significant positive effect on the student's perception of how well the undergraduate college prepared the student for work. And, while undergraduate service participation showed no measurable effect on either income or overall job satisfaction, it did show a significant positive effect on the student's spiration for advanced degrees.

That undergraduate service participation should increase the likelihood that the student will actually donate money to the alma mater would be of particular interest to college officials and trustees. Most of the debate about including a "service requirement" in the undergraduate curriculum has focused on the *educational* efficacy of volunteer participation or service learning. While our earlier work shows clearly that service participation does indeed have beneficial effects in the academic area (Astin & Sax, 1998), this study suggests that there may be a considerable institutional self-interest in encouraging more students participate in service work.

It is also important to point out that the long-term effects of undergraduate service participation are very consistent with the rationale underlying many service learning and volunteer programs in academia. Volunteering encourages students to become more socially responsible, are committed to serving their communities, more empowered, and are committed to education. That volunteering encourages socialization across racial lines and increases commitment to promoting racial understanding in the years after college is consistent with our recent short-term study (Astin & Sax, 1998) showing that undergraduate service participation strengthens the student's interest in issues relating to multiculturalism and diversity.

Although service had favorable effects on 13 of 18 outcome measures, it is important to address those five outcomes which appear to be unaffected by service work during college. First, the fact that service participation does *not* appear to affect the student's political leanings seems to refute the argument that service participation "politicizes" students. Second, although we expected that participation in service during college might have a positive effect on satisfaction with graduate school and employment, even if only indirectly through its positive effects on satisfaction with college (Astin & Sax, 1998), service in fact had no effect on these two outcomes. It may be that job satisfaction and satisfaction with graduate school are both heavily dependent on situational factors such as pay and working conditions (in the case of employment), or financial aid and accessibility of faculty (in the case of graduate school). Finally, the two remaining outcomes with nonsignificant effects (income and preparation for graduate school) were included solely on an exploratory basis, with no previous research suggesting that they should be affected by service participation.

Several limitations of the current study should be noted. First, although the results are highly significant statistically, the coefficients shown in Table 3 are quite small. This is perhaps to be expected, given that our measures were relatively simple self-report questionnaire items and given that we were dealing with longitudinal changes over a relatively long span of time. Even so, it is important to recognize that even small coefficients such as these can be associated with important practical differences, especially when one looks at effects over the entire range of the variable. (See, for example, Tables 1 and 2, which are based on relatively weak correlations between the variables displayed.)

A potentially more important limitation is the nature of our independent variable, which is simply a generic assessment of the amount of time that students devoted to volunteer service work during the last year in college. We did not obtain specific information, for example, on service learning experiences (as opposed to simple volunteer work) or on the *type* of service performed or the location of the service. All of these issues are being addressed in studies of volunteer service we are currently conducting.

References

Astin, A. W. (1975). *Preventing students from dropping out*. San Francisco: Jossey-Bass.

Astin, A. W. (1977). *Four critical years*. San Francisco: Jossey-Bass.

Astin, A. W. (1984). Student involvement: A developmental theory for higher education. *Journal of College Student Personnel*, 25, 297–308.

Astin, A. W. (1985). *Achieving educational excellence*. San Francisco: Jossey-Bass.

Astin, A. W. (1991). *Assessment for excellence*. New York: Macmillan Publishing Company.

Astin, A. W. (1993). *What matters in college? Four critical years revisited*. San Francisco: Jossey-Bass.

Astin, A. W., & Dey, E. L. (1996). *Causal analytical modeling via blocked regression analysis (CAMBRA): An introduction with examples*. Los Angeles: Higher Education Research Institute, UCLA.

Astin, A. W., & Molm, L. D. (1972). Correcting for nonresponse bias in followup surveys. Unpublished manuscript, Office of Research, American Council on Education, Washington, DC.

Astin, A. W., & Sax, L. J. (1998). How undergraduates are affected by service participation. *Journal of College Student Development*, 39(3): 251–263.

Barber, B. R. (1993). *An aristocracy of everyone*. New York: Ballantine Books.

Batchelder, T. H., & Root, S. (1994). Effects of an undergraduate program to integrate academic learning and service: Cognitive, prosocial cognitive, and identity outcomes. *Journal of Adolescence*, 17, 341–355.

Cohen, J., & Kinsey, D. (1994). "Doing good" and scholarship: A service-learning study. *Journalism Educator*, 48, 4–14.

Dey, E. L. (1997). Working with low survey response rates: The efficacy of weighting adjustments. *Research in Higher Education*, 38, 215–227.

Giles, D. E., & Eyler, J. (1994). The impact of a college community service laboratory on students' personal, social, and cognitive outcomes. *Journal of Adolescence*, 17, 327–339.

Giles, D. E., Honnet, E., & Migliore, S. (Eds.). (1991). *Research agenda for combining service and learning in the 1990s*. Raleigh, NC: National Society for Internships and Experiential Education.

Levine, A. (1994, July/August). Service on campus. *Change*, 26, 4–5.

Markus, G. B., Howard, J. P. F., & King, D. C. (1993). Integrating community service and classroom instruction enhances learning: Results from an experiment. *Educational Evaluation and Policy Analysis*, 15, 410–419.

Newman, F. (1985). *Higher Education and the American Resurgence*, 31. Princeton, NJ: Carnegie Foundation for the Advancement of Teaching.

O'Brien, E. M. (1993). Outside the classroom: Students as employees, volunteers and interns. *Research Briefs*, 4. Washington, DC: American Council on Education.

Pascarella, E. T., & Terenzini, P. T. (1991). *How college affects students*. San Francisco: Jossey-Bass.

DEMOCRATIC CITIZENSHIP AND STUDENT ACTIVISM

FLORENCE A. HAMRICK

Elements of democratic political theory are presented to advance an interpretation of principled student activism on campuses as citizen-engagement and an opportunity for hands-on citizenship education. A brief scenario of campus dissent is described as an illustration of democratic aims, processes, and underlying principles. Finally, implications for student affairs practice are offered.

College and university campuses increasingly reflect the racial, cultural, and socioeconomic heterogeneity of American society. For example, the proportion of college students from minority backgrounds grew from 18.9% to 23.4% between 1991 and 1995, and the proportion of women college students increased from 54.3% to 55.1% ("The Nation," 1991, 1995). At many campuses, increased diversity has coincided with bold and vocal student challenges to institutional policies and decisions identified as indifferent or hostile to underrepresented students. Underrepresented students and coalitions formed by these students are certainly not the first or only student groups to challenge administrative decisions, but such challenges publicly call into question the genuineness of higher education's espoused welcome for those with diverse voices and perspectives (Hill, 1991). As dissenting students identify and frame issues for public deliberation and compel attention to their concerns, they assume vital citizenship roles through their engagement in principled dissent.

Conditions that surround students' efforts to effect change on campuses may provide educational and empowering citizenship experiences or may serve to frustrate and further marginalize student citizens. The purpose of this discussion is to add to the theory base in student affairs by presenting selected features of democratic political theory and examine its usefulness in helping student affairs professionals develop and sustain a campus environment that facilitates student exercise of democratic citizenship.

Educating for Citizenship

Preparing students for mature participation in the civic life of a democracy is consistently cited as a primary purpose of higher education. In a recently commissioned American Council on Education study, over 90% of Americans surveyed believed that a central task of colleges and universities is to develop contributing citizens (Harvey & Immerwahr, 1995). Additionally, three major statements that specify assumptions, values, and purposes of student affairs work over 50 years ("National Association," 1989) display a marked consistency on this issue as illustrated by the passages below:

> This conference also wishes to emphasize the necessity for conceiving of after-college adjustment as comprehending the total living of college graduates, including not only their occupational success but their active concern with the social, recreational, and cultural interests of the community. Such concern implies their willingness to assume those individual and social responsibilities which are essential to the common good. (1937 statement; "National Association," 1989, p. 58)

> As a responsible participant in the societal processes of our American democracy, his [sic] full and balanced maturity is viewed as a major end-goal of education and, as well, a necessary means to the fullest development of his [sic] fellow citizens. From the personnel point of view any lesser goals fall

short of the desired objectives of democratic educational processes and is a real drain and strain upon the self-realization of other developing individuals in our society. (1949 statement; "National Association," 1989, p. 22)

A democracy requires the informed involvement of citizens. Citizenship is complex; thus, students benefit from a practical as well as an academic understanding of civic responsibilities. Active participation in institutional governance, community service, and collective management of their own affairs contributes significantly to students' understanding and appreciation of civic responsibilities. (1987 statement; "National Association," 1989, p. 14)

Additionally, the preamble of the Student Learning Imperative (American College Personnel Association, 1994) included an expectation that college graduates be able to "deal effectively with such major societal challenges as poverty, illiteracy, crime, and environmental exploitation" (p. 1). These calls for civic commitment and action suggest that social problems cannot be addressed merely by applying academic knowledge of, for example, criminal justice, sociology, law, or biological sciences. Following the excerpts above, graduates must also be able to apprehend a problem as a social one, situate themselves as citizens with attendant responsibilities to identify and deal with social problems, and marshal attention and resources to address problems. Such engagement draws on leadership skills, social and political expertise, rhetorical persuasion, and perhaps most importantly on an inclination and commitment to use one's energies and abilities in service to a collective society. Finally, a shared assumption in the statements above is that students develop—or should have opportunities to develop—these skills and commitments during college.

At most colleges and universities, opportunities are provided for students to participate in the organized public life of the campus. On macro levels, students are elected to representative governance bodies or chosen to serve as student representatives to campus committees or advisory groups. In these capacities, students help determine funding priorities, make budgetary allocations to various campus units or organizations, review conduct codes and often preside over hearings, and review or propose institutional policies. At micro levels, students often collectively negotiate shared living arrangements on residence hall floors that reflect agreed-upon values (e.g., tolerance, respect) and operationalize these values into mutually binding agreements (e.g., guidelines for use of common spaces, suitemate contracts, quiet hour policies). In each of these instances, students participate as citizens engaged in the shared governance of collectives of which they are a part.

A variety of positive outcomes from student citizenship experiences has been studied. Ignelzi (1990) focused on the moral growth potentials for students participating in self-governing collectives, and Terenzini (1994) described a range of developmental domains that relate to maturity as citizens. Community service and volunteer programs are often structured to place students in leadership or service roles in economically or socially disadvantaged settings with the intention of encouraging a citizen-leader disposition in those participating students (e.g., Astin, 1995; Perreault, 1997; Whipple, 1996). These programs offer powerful experiences to students and encourage their development into responsible, concerned, and engaged citizens. In similar ways, students who engage in principled dissent and active protest on campus are participating in a different, yet equally valuable, democratic citizenship experience that is worthy of our attention and appreciation.

Chambers and Phelps (1993) provided a comprehensive discussion of the developmental impact of student activism. Although information on permissible legal parameters in dealing with student activism (e.g., Paterson, 1994) is certainly important, student affairs professionals should also be prepared to appreciate the exercise of citizenship that is increasingly occurring on campuses and work to ensure that these experiences are educationally meaningful with respect to democratic citizenship. To this end, political theories that describe collective political determination and action can complement the predominant theoretical literature on students' development as individuals. Specifically, attention to democratic political theory and practices can inform programmatic attempts to educate students for democratic citizenship as well as assist student affairs administrators to appreciate and discern the democratic actions already occurring on numerous campuses.

Democratic Theory and Diversity

In speaking of ethnic and cultural diversity in the United States, political theorist Benjamin Barber (1992) asserted that "diversity remains America's most prominent virtue and its most unsettling problem. . . . *E pluribus unum* is our brave boast, but we are neither very united nor very comfortable with our diversity" (p. 42). Furthermore, he noted that cultural and ethnic diversity is not a recent phenomenon:

> [A]s any careful reader of American history cannot help but notice, America has always been a tale of peoples trying to be a People, a tale of diversity and plurality in search of unity. . . . The purist view of a WASP nation was never more than the peremptory hope of one part of America's immigrant population. (p. 41)

Not surprisingly, then, our political legacy is a continuing search for "unity in diversity" (Bull, Fruehling, & Chattergy, 1992, p. 1), where respect for individual rights, including freedoms to pursue and honor various cultural traditions, shares center stage with collective social determination through democratic governance. This legacy of tension or balance is readily characterized by American political traditions of liberalism and democracy with emphases on, respectively, protection of individual freedoms and provisions for collective decision-making. Current developments on college campuses such as more frequent demonstrations and activist leadership among students of traditionally underrepresented groups suggest the need for a greater understanding of how autonomous and increasingly diverse individuals can and often do productively engage in collective deliberation and action.

The promise of such engagement, however, has not been consistently realized. Almost a century ago, W. E. B. DuBois (1903) presented his perspective on the American social and political climate of the time:

> [The African American] realizes at last that silently, resistlessly, the world about flows by him [*sic*] in two great streams: they ripple on in the same sunshine, they approach and mingle their waters in seeming carelessness—then they divide and flow wide apart. . . . Now if one notices carefully one will see that between these two worlds, despite much physical contact and daily intermingling, there is almost no community of intellectual life or point of transference where the thoughts and feelings of one race can come into direct contact and sympathy with the thoughts and feelings of the other. (p. 128)

Aims of Democracy

According to Dewey (1926), democracy is "more than a form of government; it is primarily a mode of associated living" (p. 101). In a democracy, individuals relinquish some measure of self-determination in favor of societal determination that will restrict, but presumably also enhance, individual well-being through social well-being (Dewey, 1926). Critically, democracy is self-governance. Authority in a democracy is vested not in an external power but in the same citizens who have relinquished individual authority. According to Gutmann (1987), democracy "authorizes citizens to influence how their society reproduces itself" (p. 15). Democracy allows for a society's "change in social habit—its continuous readjustment through meeting the new situations produced by various intercourse" (Dewey, 1926, p. 100). Education for democratic citizenship focuses on enabling students' participation in the democratic process of "conscious social reproduction" (Gutmann, 1987, p. 14), but this does not mean that students learn only to identify a preference, cast a ballot, and count yeas and nays. To ensure the fairness and continuity of democracy, democratic principles as well as processes must be safeguarded.

Principles of Democracy: Nonrepression and Nondiscrimination

Gutmann (1987) identified two principles essential to democracy: nonrepression and nondiscrimination. Nonrepression deals with ideas; specifically, the conceivable range of ideas and opinions must not be repressed or stifled. Nondiscrimination provides for individuals' equal access to democratic deliberations and processes unrestricted by bias or prejudice.

Further, a democratic society cannot support policies or decisions that are themselves repressive or discriminatory (Gutmann, 1987). The Reverend Martin Luther King, Jr. (1963) evoked both principles in his eloquent "Letter from the Birmingham Jail":

> A law is unjust if it is inflicted on a minority that, as a result of being denied the right to vote, had no part in enacting or devising the law. Who can say that the legislature of Alabama which set up that state's segregation laws was democratically elected? Throughout Alabama all sorts of devious methods are used to prevent Negroes from becoming registered voters, and there are some counties in which, even though Negroes constitute a majority of the population, not a single Negro is registered. Can any law enacted under such circumstances be considered democratically structured?
>
> Sometimes a law is just on its face and unjust in its application. For instance, I have been arrested on a charge of parading without a permit. Now, there is nothing wrong in having an ordinance which requires a permit for a parade. But such an ordinance becomes unjust when it is used to maintain segregation and to deny citizens the First Amendment privilege of peaceful assembly and protest. (unpaged)

In the first paragraph, King pointed out that decisions that will bind all members of a society cannot themselves be products of deliberations undertaken by only a subset of that society. Such a practice violates the democratic principle of nondiscrimination. In the second paragraph, King asserted that benign laws or regulations had been selectively applied to prevent the airing of unpopular ideas. Such a practice is illegitimate because it violates the principle of nonrepression. As King so clearly comprehended, democratic process in the absence of democratic principles had in effect curtailed democracy. To the extent that the presence of either repression or discrimination renders democratic process as well as decisions illegitimate, these two principles serve to enable democracy as well as provide grounds for contesting current practices.

Democracy and Dissent

The democratic aim of conscious social reproduction is accomplished through processes to determine the will of the majority. Citizens in a democracy are assumed to be participants in these processes through directly voicing input or preference (e.g., Barber, 1984) or through opportunities to influence representative bodies. The will of the majority is considered binding on all citizens within the collective, even on dissenters and nonparticipants.

However, principled dissenters play an especially critical role in a democracy. As Flacks (1996) concluded: "[M]ovements are inherently the primary framework for direct democracy, providing the moments in which ordinary people directly and consciously participate in the exercise of voice rather than allowing others to speak for them" (p. 104). In the absence of direct participation, Fraser (1989) warned of "passive citizenship" (p. 156) in a society that identifies needs, offers programs to address the identified needs, and evaluates client (not citizen) success through measures of conformity or compliance. Dissenting citizens form opposing forces in democratic societies that preserve ranges of opinions and commitments and provide bellwethers to herald changes in sentiment or collective will. For example, numerous participants in the civil rights movement of this century engaged in acts of civil disobedience, demonstrating their commitment to democracy through their disobedience of unjust laws. In this way, principled dissent serves to highlight aspects of a society and its governance that are falsely democratic. Principled dissent is a form of democratic citizenship at least as critical to democracies as citizens' routine, faithful participation in established processes. Indeed, Giroux (1987, 1996) cautioned against confusing patriotism—which he considered largely unexamined chauvinism—with citizenship, which is instead exemplified by critique and monitoring of the presumed democratic system and processes.

Democratic aims and principles are in all likelihood familiar notions in student affairs, since the above discussion evokes the professional values of autonomy, justice, and fidelity (Kitchener, 1985) and Boyer's (1990) descriptions of open and just campus communities. The two democratic principles are also consistent with widely espoused academic values of academic freedom and nondiscrimination in terms of admissions, access to services, and employment. Interpretations of repression and discrimination, however, differ widely on campuses and in society, as currently evidenced through dialogues on affirmative action programs, ethnic and cultural studies programs, and other issues recently accompanied by dissent and protest.

Narrative

The following narrative and analysis will demonstrate the application of democratic theory and principles to one episode of dissent. Although the facts in the narrative are based on occurrences over the past 3 years at Iowa State University, only selected elements that are most relevant to democratic theory and principles are summarized here. The comments following the narrative are not intended in any way to solve complex developments which continue to unfold. The analysis is offered instead to illustrate some practical insights that can be gained through application of democratic theoretical perspectives.

One of the aging buildings at Iowa State University, a public land-grant university, was recently renovated. The building and a center housed there (designed for the study of women and politics) were named in honor of a 19th century alumna whose work on behalf of women's suffrage is widely known. Extensive fund-raising secured major gifts as well as numerous small contributions from alumni and other sources. A well-attended week-long celebration featured historic reenactments, panel presentations, and speeches and ended with the formal rededication ceremony.

The distribution of a newsletter published by an African-American student group coincided with the dedication ceremonies. An article in the newsletter denounced the naming decision, charging that the honored alumna had made racist and xenophobic remarks during her suffrage work. A groundswell of concerned students and others coalesced into a movement aimed at changing the building's name. Movement members communicated their dissent through speeches as well as editorials and letters to the editor in the campus newspaper, maintaining that the honor was not deserved and that university officials had made the naming decision despite early knowledge of the questionable remarks. Further, they charged that educational presentations and dialogues about the honoree's career and legacy that were held as part of the dedication celebration had omitted or minimized public discussion of the honoree's controversial remarks.

Editorials and responses quickly appeared in campus and statewide media, and the movement's efforts attracted some national notice as well. Two controversies emerged from this dialogue. One question was whether the alumna's remarks—considering the context in which they were made—could defensibly or conclusively label her as racist or xenophobic. A second controversy was whether the university had attempted to orchestrate the event so that only remarks favorable to the honoree were aired. The building name controversy was a popular topic of informal discussion on campus, and a silent protest march sponsored by the movement attracted more than 100 students, faculty, and staff. Movement members subsequently revealed plans to write donors with appeals to withdraw their contributions to the building and the center.

Over the course of several weeks, the student senate hotly debated legislation calling on the university to reverse the naming decision. The bill passed but was vetoed by the student body president. Throughout the controversy, the university president publicly maintained that, although he heard and understood the movement's concerns, he would not support the name change. The student group announced plans for a weekday rally at the administration building, but were denied a permit on the grounds that their meeting would disrupt university functioning. The rally went on as planned, and organizers were informed that they would be charged with violating the student code of conduct.

Discussion

The above narrative provides much grist for discussion and could easily be analyzed using an assortment of conceptual lenses because developmental, administrative, legal, and other issues are evident. However, in this discussion, aspects of the narrative that are related to democratic aims, principles, and processes will be highlighted.

One may first question to what extent democratic notions should influence deliberation or decision-making at an institution that is not itself a democracy. Although the formal college or university is not typically organized as a representative or participatory democracy, colleges nonetheless are sites for learning about and experiencing democratic citizenship. Furthermore, exercises of citizenship can and sometimes do influence the formal organization through the attention or pressure brought about by dissenting opinions and actions. As Gutmann and Thompson (1996) clearly stated, educational institutions, interest groups, and civic associations comprise a valuable "middle democracy," (p. 12). That is,

> [In] the land of everyday politics, . . . legislators, executives, administrators, and judges make and apply policies and laws, sometimes arguing among themselves, sometimes explaining themselves and listening to citizens, other times not. . . . [This is also where] adults and children develop political understandings, sometimes arguing among themselves and listening to people with differing points of view, other times not. (1996, p. 40)

Colleges and universities represent institutions within which decisions are made by some established institutional processes. Those decisions as well as the manner in which decisions are reached subsequently become text for collective deliberations and evaluation in the campus's accompanying political arena.

Democratic Aims

As discussed earlier, democracy provides a means for conscious social reproduction. Through their focus on the controversial legacy of the honoree, the dissenting students contested what was being reproduced through the naming decision; they also questioned the level of consciousness employed by the makers of this particular decision.

Aims and symbols of aims are often interpreted in different ways. For example, selecting a woman—and one who was militant and radical in her time—may symbolize a progressive and enlightened university. Yet, because of the honoree's questionable remarks, the naming can also symbolize and tacitly affirm a climate of indifference or hostility to minority students. Through opening a public dialogue to air an alternate interpretation of the honoree's legacy, movement students sought to highlight the values (i.e., racism, xenophobia) that they felt the university was implicitly honoring through honoring this alumna. For many students in the movement, the naming decision provided tangible evidence of the ongoing racially indifferent campus climate. For these students, the building became a manifestation of minority students' perceptions of continuing marginalization, and the naming decision symbolized *unexamined* social reproduction—in other words, perpetuation of a racist climate on campus.

The cultural properties of symbols and heroes and heroines, and their importance for administrative leaders in invoking institutional priorities and values, have been widely discussed (Birnbaum, 1990; Tierney, 1988). An examination of democratic political theory adds an additional property of symbols as affirmation of the tacit values that are esteemed on a campus. In the above narrative, the same symbol may for some denote conscious social reproduction that is adaptive and pioneering and for others denote a largely unexamined perpetuation of negative or bigoted values.

Principles of Democracy

According to Gutmann (1987), nondiscrimination and nonrepression must be preserved to ensure the possibility of continuing democracy. Yet, because discussions leading to and surrounding administrative decisions are often not publicized, those not privy to the discussions can only infer rationales after decisions are made. However, attention to democratic principles helps to identify appropriate questions to ask about the case and about the climate for democracy on campus.

The naming of the building. The selection of the honoree was an administrative decision made by the university's governing board using administrative processes and procedures in which democratic processes may or may not have been modeled. However, the narrative demonstrates that administrators might be wise to adopt democratic values in their deliberations even if they are not formally required. In this case, broad participation at early deliberation stages and airing a wide range of opinions would have alerted administrative decision-makers to the range of opinions on this matter.

In terms of nonrepression of ideas, at least one set of unpopular ideas for early airing would be the honoree's controversial remarks. However, even if the honoree's questionable remarks had been known, as student activists suspected, this knowledge may not have been suppressed during official discussions leading to the decision. Decision-makers may indeed have been satisfied, for example, that the remarks were less troubling because of the historical context in which they were made. However, if public suppression efforts had been undertaken, this action would violate the principle of nonrepression.

The student protest. The student-led dissent emerged at the time of the building's dedication. In terms of nondiscrimination of participation, students employed a broad range of tactics to communicate their objections publicly. As long as student efforts to be heard publicly were not unjustly blocked, the principle of nondiscrimination was maintained. Although few of the initial decision-makers chose to respond publicly to the movement's charges and counterarguments, students apparently were not impeded in employing a variety of efforts at fostering public dialogue. As King (1963) discerned, otherwise impartial laws or policies can be discriminatory if they are applied selectively to block certain groups or unpopular opinions. The decision to deny a rally permit might have been the same, or perhaps had been the same in the past, regardless of the group requesting the permit. The decision to charge rally organizers with conduct code violations may have reflected an impartial policy that would be applied, or had been applied previously, in similar circumstances. Observers often do not have this type of information on which to base their analyses. Although universities can legally block protests that violate time, place, and manner restrictions (*Healy v. James*, 1972), administrators must take care that rules are not selectively enforced, for such enforcement would violate the principle of nondiscrimination. For example, if rallies by minority group students are judged to be disruptive of university business whereas similarly situated rallies by majority group students are not, minority students' participation in the campus political arena is selectively curtailed through what amounts to discrimination.

In terms of nonrepression of ideas, movement members aired a wide variety of opinions and used multiple outlets to articulate their positions and demands. In this sense, movement members' efforts to educate and persuade community members were not prohibited. However, members also charged that the educational presentations on the honoree's legacy, held during the dedication celebration, had not included multiple perspectives on her controversial remarks. Substituting celebration for an opportunity to dialogue is problematic with respect to nonrepression; in this case, movement members charged that only an officially sanctioned version of the honoree's legacy was aired. Indeed, Giroux (1987) views such events as serious threats to democracy, charging they represent a form of political illiteracy that "abandon[s] substantive information and debate for the glitter of the spectacle" (p. 109) and in a sense, substitutes unexamined patriotism for considered citizenship. Similar conclusions were reached, in fact, when television commentators described both the Democratic and Republican 1996 national political conventions as orchestrated "infomercials" rather than occasions for public debate and exchange of views. To uphold nonrepression of ideas, programmed celebrations should not be substituted for opportunities for dialogue. If dialogue is planned to accompany a celebration but time for such is compromised, scheduling a continuation of the event with sole emphasis on dialogue would appear to strengthen the university's commitment to open dialogue and nonrepression of ideas.

The student government actions. In terms of formal democratic action, the will of the student majority was determined by vote of the representative student government, which was in turn rejected by presidential veto. Since the student government president acted within constitutional powers, the veto did not subvert democracy but instead engaged and encouraged democratic mechanisms for redress. For example, the dissent may well serve as rationale for a recall election or appear as a campaign issue in the next election. Critically, democracy progresses through engagement of these formal mechanisms as well as through the monitoring and challenge from citizen-dissenters.

The unauthorized rally. Civil disobedience is a long and honored tradition in democracies, and movement members sustained this tradition by holding the unauthorized rally. However, university officials were not necessarily wrong to deny a permit. To honor the principle of nondiscrimination, dissenters should be accorded the same treatment as any other student group. Additionally, dissenting students should be subject to equal treatment under the conduct code that applies to all students. University representatives, through sharing information with students about rationales for policies and potential ranges of sanctions can, in a sense, partner with the dissenting students to ensure that students not only are able to disobey administrative policies but also are informed of the potential consequences of their planned disobedience. To uphold nondiscrimination, administrative representatives must ensure policies are impartially applied. Dissenters must not be subject to additional or more energetic scrutiny than is applied to students in general. Also to uphold non-repression of ideas, administrative decisions and possible sanctions must not preclude the students' continued airing of their ideas. One critical policy question to ask is whether the sanctions may curtail or prohibit students' subsequent freedom to participate in dissenting acts or to voice their ideas. Sanctions that compromise students' participation or expression are inconsistent with the democratic principles of nondiscrimination and nonrepression.

Conclusions and Implications for Practice

Gutmann (1987) cautioned that conflict, as the matter for democratic deliberations, is not something that a democratic society should seek to avoid. Indeed, minimizing conflict may serve to further marginalize those raising principled objections to decisions and processes. The goal of democracy is not the creation of artificial homogenization or false harmony, and movements play an important role through fostering dissent and conflict. As Jane Smiley remarked: "I used to think that conflict leads to violence as pink shades into red. . . . Now I think that violence occurs as an attempt to stop conflict, a stab at silencing the cacophony of differing opinions and divergent values" ("Melange," 1996, p. B3). Additionally, Fraser (1989) described the desirability of an "arena of conflict among rival interpretations of needs" (p. 170) as a way to better comprehend ranges of needs and strategies to meet these various needs. Thus, campus dialogue and disagreement can be interpreted as indicators of a vital and engaged community in which democratic learning and exercise of citizenship is not only permissible but nurtured.

At its best, democracy ensures that a common ground of deliberative processes and principles of fairness underpins the articulation, clarification, and dispute of controversial issues. Providing this common ground, as well as respect for deliberation, can foster students' development as democratic citizens. Parks Daloz, Keen, Keen, and Daloz Parks (1996) asserted: "The act of setting norms, tone, and boundaries that can hold conflicted discourse creates a shared culture with a teaching power of its own" (p. 15). In accordance, three conclusions regarding democratic education and student activism are offered, each with implications for student affairs practice.

Dissenters as Campus Citizens

Not all, but many dissenting students are from minority and traditionally underrepresented groups on predominantly white campuses that have been characterized as hostile or, perhaps worse, indifferent to their needs. In a sense, one might have difficulty imagining minority group students as desirous of citizenship in such communities. Yet as dissenters, these same students are willing to take risks of further marginalization or dismissal as "troublemakers" or "extremists" precisely to assume a citizenship role on campus. Interpreted within a democratic citizenship framework, principled dissenters are loyal citizens who make a supreme act of commitment to the campus and to its democratic arena. Instead of downplaying their concerns or quietly leaving the campus, dissenting students engage their concerns as democratic citizens who seek to participate in democratic self-determination. Although dealing with the discomforts surrounding campus dissent presents concerns for student affairs and other university administrators, students' unwillingness to commit to a community or to help shape and realize the public good of the community is indicative of citizen apathy—a far more threatening problem for democracies.

In many ways, campus dissent can be seen as service-learning or community improvement work. However, dissenting students have identified their own campuses as the underserved or under-privileged settings that warrant their leadership and attention. As service-learning participants engage in projects to better the selected programs or sites, improve their leadership skills, and commit to addressing problems of the broader society, activism offers dissenting students opportunities to hone a similar and equally necessary set of citizenship dispositions and skills. Student affairs administrators and counselors work to place students in service learning programs, and dissenting student-citizens are no less deserving of assistance and respect for their endeavors. Although student affairs administrators' dual roles as institutional representatives and educators sometimes present problems in dealing with campus dissent, the roles need not be unreconciled or unreconcilable. As campuses continue to frame diversity as an institutional priority and the fostering of multiculturalism as a responsibility of all (Stage & Hamrick, 1994), these dual roles will continue. As avowed proponents of democratic citizenship development, student affairs administrators may have much to learn from staff and faculty members who serve as formally appointed advocates for minority students and often find themselves balancing their responsibilities for supporting and encouraging students with their responsibilities as institutional representatives.

Campuses and Change

In many ways, dissenting students call institutional attention to discrepancies in intent and practice with respect to multiculturalism. Further, dissenting students often question if a campus is committed to change, if a campus is open to the possibility of change, and what is necessary to fulfill institutional promises or goals. Hill (1991) asserted that multiculturalism is achieved when a community can't imagine existing without everyone's presence and contributions. Through their resistance, dissenting students insist on contributing. They are unwilling to serve only as docile presences or as only recipients of the campus's offerings, thus rejecting Fraser's (1989) role of passive client in predetermined programs.

Dissenting students offer alternate opinions, conclusions, and judgments, allowing a broader range of perspectives and enriching subsequent dialogue. In terms of democratic political theory, the challenges to extant assumptions represented by this broader range of perspectives increases the potential that a campus can make considered, conscious decisions about what multiculturalism will mean on the campus. According to Dewey (1926), this potential represents the promise of democracy for an increasingly diverse society:

> The extension in space of the number of individuals who participate in an interest so that each has to refer his [sic] own action to that of others, and to consider the action of others to give point and direction to his [sic] own, is equivalent to the breaking down of those barriers of class, race, and national territory which kept men [sic] from perceiving the full import of their activity. . . . They secure a liberation of powers which remain suppressed as long as the invitations to action are partial, as they must be in a group which in its exclusiveness shuts out many interests. (p. 101)

Honoring the principles of democracy does not require capitulation to dissenters, but dissent must not be suppressed. Campuses committed to democratic education therefore welcome opportunities for dialogue and debate as signs that conditions for democratic education are present. In an interview, the award-winning jazz trumpeter and composer Wynton Marsalis offered a contemporary echo of Dewey when he characterized jazz performance as part and parcel of the democratic ideals of the nation from which jazz emerged:

> [In playing jazz,] you and I, we come together and have a conversation. I consider what you're saying. And I come away thinking "It could be true" or "It's definitely not true." Playing jazz means learning how to reconcile differences, even when they're opposites. . . . Jazz is a music of conversation, and that's what you need in a democracy. You have to be willing to hear another person's point of view and respond to it. Also, jazz requires that you have a lot of on-your-feet information, just like a democracy does. There are a lot of things you simply have to know. (Scherman, 1996, pp. 30, 35)

"Civic Life" on Campus

As the discussion above makes clear, conceptions of what makes up the civic life of students and the appropriate campus environments for learning democracy and citizenship must not be limited only to formal student governance bodies. However, in their work with elected student leaders, advisors must be careful to ensure that technical procedural tools intended to, for example, assure orderly meetings, are not selectively applied to avoid or preclude open participation or the expression of unpopular ideas. For many students, and particularly for minority group students, issues that subsequently emerge as political concerns may well have germinated elsewhere on the campus where support for and validation of student involvement (e.g., Rendon, 1994) already exist. Professionals concerned with educating for citizenship and supporting citizen participants should acknowledge the educational value of these alternate campus settings for citizen involvement and work to support students and advisors as they seek to engage the campus community as citizens. Administrators and advisors should also ensure that nonrepression and nondiscrimination are preserved for students who engage in institutionalized political expression as well as in public campus dissent.

In summary, the student affairs profession has consistently espoused via its major public statements a commitment to preparing students for democratic citizenship. Dissent, when interpreted as citizen involvement and a source of democratic learning experience, advances a community's search for mutual agreements while preserving and legitimating the expression of a broad range of perspectives and judgments. Although public campus dissent presents legal and administrative challenges for student affairs and other campus staff, dissent is also citizenship in action—worthy not only of tolerance but respect and support. Steiner (1994) emphasized the empowering potential of democratic education:

> Rather than trying to find a lowest common denominator on which to build consensus, democratic education should offer citizens a chance to wrestle with the complex and multifarious issues that confront their polity. Opposed to the assumptions that the majority are suited best for mindless productivity or a life of politically acquiescent technological contributions, an authentic democratic education implies that schooling provides citizens with the skills to question the basic assumptions of their society. . . . Rather than chasing a downward spiral toward ensuring that citizens are equipped to follow instructions, it points to an ascending set of challenges that assume a high potential to negotiate and shape a considered life. (pp. 23–24)

In the end, educating for democratic citizenship may not be an optional undertaking on campus. As members of Gutmann and Thompson's (1996) "middle democracy," student affairs staff educate through the principles and values they convey or fail to convey in policies and practices. Citizenship and civic education take many forms on campus, and campuses and democracies are each enriched by respecting dissent as a legitimate and necessary manifestation of democratic citizenship.

References

American College Personnel Association. (1994). *The student learning imperative: Implications for student affairs.* Washington, DC: Author.

Astin, A. W. (1995, October 6). The cause of citizenship. *Chronicle of Higher Education, 42,* pp. B1-B2.

Barber, B. R. (1984). *Strong democracy: Participatory politics for a new age.* Berkeley: University of California Press.

Barber, B. R. (1992). *An aristocracy of everyone: The politics of education and the future of America.* New York: Oxford University Press.

Birnbaum, R. (1990). *How colleges work: The cybernetics of academic organization and leadership.* San Francisco: Jossey-Bass.

Boyer, E. L. (1990). *Campus life: In search of community.* Princeton, NJ: Carnegie Foundation for the Advancement of Teaching.

Bull, B. L., Fruehling, R. T., & Chattergy, V. (1992). *The ethics of multicultural and bilingual education.* New York: Teachers College Press.

Chambers, T., & Phelps, C. E. (1993). Student activism as a form of leadership and student development. *NASPA Journal, 31,* 19-29.

Dewey, J. (1926). *Democracy and education.* New York: Macmillan.

Du Bois, W. E. B. (1903). *The souls of Black folk*. Chicago: A. C. McClurg & Co.

Flacks, R. (1996). Reviving democratic activism: Thoughts about strategy in a dark time. In D. Trend (Ed.), *Radical democracy: Identity, citizenship, and the state* (pp. 102–116). New York: Routledge. Fraser, N. (1989). *Unruly practices: Power, discourse and gender in contemporary social theory*. Minneapolis, MN: University of Minnesota Press.

Giroux, H. A. (1987). Citizenship, public philosophy, and the struggle for democracy. *Educational Theory, 37(2)*, 103–120.

Giroux, H. A. (1996). Pedagogy and radical democracy in the age of "political correctness." In D. Trend (Ed.), *Radical democracy: Identity, citizenship, and the state* (pp. 179–193). New York: Routledge.

Gutmann, A. (1987). *Democratic education*. Princeton, NJ: Princeton University Press.

Gutmann, A., & Thompson, D. (1996). *Democracy and disagreement*. Cambridge, MA: Belknap.

Harvey, J., & Immerwahr, J. (1995). *Goodwill and growing worry: Public perceptions of American higher education*. Washington, DC: American Council on Education.

Healy v. James, 408 U.S. 169 (1972).

Hill, P. J. (1991, July/August). Multiculturalism: The crucial philosophical and organizational issues. *Change, 23*, 38-47.

Ignelzi, M. G. (1990). Ethical education in a college environment: The just community approach. *NASPA Journal, 27*, 192–198.

King, M. L., Jr. (1963). Letter from the Birmingham Jail. Available: http://www-leland.stanford.edu:80/group/King/.

Kitchener, K. S. (1985). Ethical principles and ethical decisions in student affairs. In H. J. Canon & R. D. Brown (Eds.), *Applied ethics in student services* (pp. 17–29). San Francisco: Jossey-Bass.

Melange: Commencement 1996. (1996, June 7). *Chronicle of Higher Education*, p. B3.

The Nation. (1991, August 28). *The Chronicle of Higher Education, 38(1)*, 3.

The Nation. (1995, September 1). *The Chronicle of Higher Education, 42(1)*, 5.

National Association of Student Personnel Administrators. (1989). *Points of view*. Washington, DC: Author.

Parks Daloz, L. A., Keen, C. H., Keen, J. P., & Daloz Parks, S. (1996, May/June). Lives of commitment: Higher education in the life of the new commons. *Change, 28*, 10–15.

Paterson, B. G. (1994). Freedom of expression and campus dissent. *NASPA Journal, 31*, 186–194.

Perreault, G. E. (1997). Citizen leader: A community service option for college students. *NASPA Journal, 34*, 147–156.

Rendon, L. I. (1994). Validating culturally diverse students: Toward a new model of learning and student development. *Innovative Higher Education, 19(1)*, 33–42.

Scherman, T. (1996, March/April). The music of democracy: Wynton Marsalis puts jazz in its place. *Utne Reader*, 29–36.

Stage, F. K., & Hamrick, F. A. (1994). Diversity issues: Fostering campuswide development of multiculturalism. *Journal of College Student Development, 35*, 331–336.

Steiner, D. M. (1994). *Rethinking democratic education: The politics of reform*. Baltimore: Johns Hopkins Press.

Terenzini, P. T. (1994). Educating for citizenship: Freeing the mind and elevating the spirit. *Innovative Higher Education, 19(1)*, 7–21.

Tierney, W. G. (1988). Organizational culture in higher education: Defining the essentials. *Journal of Higher Education, 59(1)*, 2–21.

Whipple, E. G. (1996). Student activities. In A. L. Rentz & Associates (Eds.), *Student affairs practice in higher education* (2nd ed., pp. 298–333). Springfield, IL: Charles C. Thomas.

IN THE SERVICE OF CITIZENSHIP:

A STUDY OF STUDENT INVOLVEMENT IN COMMUNITY SERVICE

ROBERT A. RHOADS

Introduction

> I learn more through my volunteer work than I ever do in any of my classes at school. Talking to people from diverse backgrounds provides so much insight that people just can't imagine. I study all these different theories in political science and sociology, but until you get a chance to see how the social world influences people's everyday lives, it just doesn't have that much meaning.
>
> I have been involved in volunteer work ever since I was in high school, and I'll probably continue to do stuff like Habitat [for Humanity] until I'm old and gray. I get a lot out of working to serve others, and it's a good feeling to know that I have helped someone even if it's in some small way. It helps me to cherish people more and understand what life is all about.

The preceding comments are from college students who discussed their involvement in community service and the meaning they derive from such activities. Both of these students give voice to a form of learning that may be termed "citizenship education" in that a concern for the social good lies at the heart of the educational experience (Delve, Mintz, & Stewart, 1990). These students are reflective of others described throughout this article who through participation in community service explore their own identities and what it means to contribute to something larger than their individual lives.

In recent years, the role of higher education as a source of citizenship preparation has come to the forefront. In this regard, higher education reflects a rising tide of concern for national service and the common good, as programs such as AmeriCorps, Learn and Serve America, Habitat for Humanity, and Big Brothers and Big Sisters have evoked our most prominent leaders as well as citizens across the country to commit themselves to the service of others. The influence this national movement has had on the academy is most apparent in the growth of organizations such as Campus Compact and Campus Outreach Opportunity League (COOL) whose memberships and influence increased dramatically in the early 1990s (Markus, Howard, & King, 1993). Professional organizations associated with the academic enterprise also have added fuel to the growing concern over social responsibility and citizenship. For example, in 1997 the call for proposals from the American Association for Higher Education Conference on Faculty Roles and Rewards specifically identified an interest in how community service and service learning contribute to a more engaged faculty. The 1996 Annual Meeting of the American Educational Research Association was organized around the theme of "Research for Education in a Democratic Society," and at the 1995 American

College Personnel Association Annual Convention, one of the keynote speakers, Dr. Robert Coles, addressed the issue of moral education when he called for greater commitment to service learning and community service.

Although it is hard to argue with calls to foster social responsibility among our students, our future leaders, there also is a tremendous need for clarification. With this said, the following key questions offer a guide for addressing some of the confusion revolving around community service: (1) Are community service and service learning interchangeable concepts or are there important differences? (2) What is the role of community service in engaging students as democratic citizens in a culturally diverse society? (3) Are there variations in the structure of service activities which produce different experiences for students? The first question is examined as I explore the relevant literature on community service and service learning. The second and third questions are addressed primarily through discussions of the theoretical perspective, findings, and implications. Thus, the latter two questions form the heart of the theoretical and empirical analysis offered throughout this article. In weaving theoretical and empirical work together to address these questions, I follow the tradition of critical theory and support the argument that all research is theoretically rooted: Sometimes the perspective of the author is spelled out (as in this case), while at other times it must be interpreted based on the assumptions undergirding the work (Tierney & Rhoads, 1993). This is by no means a rejection of empiricism in favor of theory, but instead should be understood as an effort to bridge the gap separating the two.

Community Service and Service Learning

Over recent years there has been an incredible growth in attention paid to community service and service learning (Jacoby & Associates, 1996; Kendall, 1990; Kraft, 1996; Kraft & Swadener, 1994; Rhoads, 1997; Waterman, 1997; Zlotkowski, 1995). The increasing interest in service reflects to a large degree a concern that institutions of higher education be more responsive to society and that higher learning in general ought to have greater relevance to public life (Boyer 1987, 1994; Study Group 1984; Wingspread Group, 1993). A convincing argument could be made that for American colleges and universities a commitment to service "is a movement whose time has come" (Rhoads & Howard, 1998, p. 1).

The issue to be addressed in this brief review of the literature concerns distinguishing community service from service learning. The primary difference between these two concepts is the direct connection service learning has to the academic mission. Typically, service learning includes student participation in community service but with additional learning objectives often associated with a student's program of study. For example, a student majoring in social work may participate in service activities at a local homeless shelter in conjunction with a course of study on urban poverty. Specific activities designed to assist the student in processing his or her experience are included as part of the service learning project. The student, for example, may be expected to write a reflective paper describing the experience and/or there may be small-group interactions among students involved in similar kinds of experiences. The learning objective might be to help students interpret social and economic policies through a more advanced understanding of the lived experiences of homeless citizens. Seen in this light, service learning seeks to connect community service experiences with tangible learning outcomes. Assessing such outcomes becomes a central concern of research and evaluation (Boss, 1994; Giles & Eyler, 1994).

Although service learning often is specifically tied to classroom-related community service in which concrete learning objectives exist, some writers suggest that student involvement in community service may be tied to out-of-class learning objectives and thus constitute a form of service learning as well (Jacoby & Associates, 1996; Rhoads, 1997). From this perspective, student affairs professionals who involve students in community service activities may engage in the practice of service learning when there are clearly articulated strategies designed to bridge experiential and developmental learning. The confusion between "class-related" versus "out-of-class-related" service learning led Rhoads and Howard (1998) to adopt the term "academic service learning" to distinguish the formal curriculum (largely faculty initiated) from the informal curriculum (largely student affairs initiated). Howard (1998), for example, defined academic service learning as "a pedagogical model that intentionally integrates academic learning and relevant community service" (p. 22). For Howard there are four components of academic service learning. First, it is a pedagogical model and is therefore to be understood as a teaching methodology. Second, academic service learning is intentional; that is, there are specific goals and objectives tying the service experience to course work. Third, there is integration between experiential and academic learning. And finally, the service experience must be relevant to the course of study. As Howard explains, "Serving in a soup kitchen is relevant for a course on social issues, but probably not for a course on civil engineering" (p. 22).

From an educational standpoint, it makes sense to link community service activities with intentional learning objectives whenever possible. Obviously, when student participation in community service can be connected to specific learning activities involving reflection, group interaction, writing, and so on, the experience is likely to have a greater impact on student learning and move into the realm of service learning (Cooper, 1998; Eyler, Giles, & Schmiede, 1996).

In addition to varying degrees of connection community service may have to academic learning objectives, there are also differing opinions on which goals of higher education service ought to address. Whereas Howard stresses the role of service as a pedagogical model used to assist in course-related learning, others see service (community service and service learning) as a key strategy for fostering citizenship (Harkavy & Benson, 1998; Mendel-Reyes, 1998; Rhoads, 1998). This vision of community service and service learning is captured most pointedly in the philosophical work of John Dewey, in which education is fundamentally linked to the social good and what it means to exist in relation to others.

Theoretical Perspective: Dewey, Mead, and Gilligan

This article is grounded in the philosophical work of John Dewey and his contention that education has a vital role to play in a democratic society. In his classic work *Democracy and Education*, Dewey argued that a democratic society demands a type of relational living in which one's decisions and actions must be made with regard to their effect on others. "A democracy is more than a form of government; it is primarily a mode of associated living, of conjoint communicated experience. The extension in space of the number of individuals who participate in an interest so that each has to refer his own action to that of others, and to consider the action of others to give point and direction to his own" (1916, p. 93). Dewey's vision of democracy challenges all citizens to take part in a form of decision making that balances the interests of oneself with those of others. Democracy seen in this light demands that individuals understand the lives and experiences of other members of a society. How else can we weigh the effect of our actions if others remain distant and unknown?

Implied throughout Dewey's conception of democracy is an ethic-of-care philosophy akin to the work of feminist scholars such as Gilligan (1982) and Young (1990), in which caring for others forms a core component of identity (often discussed as the "relational self"). This is conveyed in Dewey's view of liberty: "Liberty is that secure release and fulfillment of personal potentialities which take place only in rich and manifold association with others" (1927, p. 150). Recent political theorists such as Battistoni (1985) also have recognized the importance of developing relational understandings of social life. For example, Battistoni supported Tocqueville's (1945) claim that American democracy is dependent upon "the reciprocal influence of men upon one another" (p. 117). For Battistoni, reciprocal influence is fostered through participatory forms of education, which he claimed are more likely to foster citizens who see themselves as active participants in the political process. Similarly, in discussing the relationship between citizenship and education, Barber argued that citizens must recognize their dependence upon one another and that "our identity is forged through a dialectical relationship with others" (1992, p. 4). Barber calls attention to the idea that citizenship is fundamentally tied to identity. Mead and Gilligan provide additional insight into the connection between citizenship and identity through their respective concepts of the "social self" and the "relational self."

Mead's (1934) idea of the social self derives in part from James (1890) and Cooley (1902), who both suggested that an individual's self-conception derives from the responses of others mirrored back to the individual. Mead argued that the self forms out of the interaction between the "I" and the "me." The "I" is the individual acting out some sort of behavior; the individual doing something such as talking, listening, interacting with others, expressing an idea. The "me" relates to the sense one has about the "I" who is acting out a behavior or set of behaviors. The sense we develop about the "I" derives from the interpretations we suspect that others have of us. We cannot develop an initial sense about ourselves without the help of others, who provide feedback and interact with the behaving "I." Through the imagined thoughts of others, we envision ourselves as a "me" as we become the object of our own thoughts. According to Mead, an individual cannot develop a sense of self without the interactive context of a social group or a community. Therefore, the other, either the particularized or generalized other, is essential to the development of the self.

Feminist theorists such as Gilligan also have developed a conception of the self strongly rooted in otherness. Gilligan (1979, 1982) was one of the first theorists to point out that women often make moral decisions based on a sense of connection with others. She argued that women's moral decision making reflected a fundamental identity difference based on gender. Whereas men tend to seek autonomy and make moral decisions founded on abstract principles such as justice, women, in general, seek connectedness and weigh moral decisions based on maintaining or building relationships.

As a result of early child-parent interactions and ongoing gender socialization (which arguably begins at birth), relationships become central to the social world of women (Chodorow, 1974, 1978). For men, the relational quality of social life is often displaced by a strong sense of individualism. The other is fundamentally a part of women's experience and kept at somewhat of a distance for men. The development of the self for females may be characterized by connectedness. Male development may be characterized by individuation. These general patterns (which obviously vary in degree from one individual to the next) have significant implications for how males and females relate to others and how they understand themselves in the context of the social world.

Based in part on early feminist work, various scholars have argued that regardless of gender differences, society is likely to benefit when its members develop a commitment to caring (Larrabee, 1993; Noddings, 1984, 1992, 1995; Oliner & Oliner, 1995). This is poignantly noted by Sampson (1989), who argued,

> The feminist perspective should no longer be understood as developing a psychology of women but, I believe, is better seen as developing a psychology of humanity tomorrow. The real issue, therefore, does not involve gender differences per se, as much as it speaks to an emerging theory of the person that is appropriate to the newly emerging shape of a globally linked world system. (p. 920)

Of course, Sampson's point about the "globally linked world" reminds us of an earlier issue raised in this article concerning how cultural diversity might influence citizenship education (recall key question Number 2: What is the role of community service in engaging students as democratic citizens in a culturally diverse society?). Arguably, as a society grows increasingly diverse, communications are likely to become more challenging. Cultural differences, though they may be understood as a source of community for learning and sharing among citizens (Tierney, 1993), nonetheless pose a significant challenge to social interaction and an individual's ability to connect with the other, who, in the case of a heterogeneous society, is likely to be a diverse other.

Woven together, Dewey, Mead, and Gilligan, among others, provide insight into how citizenship education might encompass learning about the self, the other, and the larger society in which one exists. The "caring self" is the term I use to capture the synthesis of their work. The caring self is intended to convey the idea of a socially oriented sense of self founded on an ethic of care and a commitment to the social good. Furthermore, it is reasonable to assume that community service, with its focus on caring for others, would offer excellent settings to explore the development of the caring self. But is this the case, and if so, in what kinds of service contexts are the qualities associated with the caring self likely to be forged?

This brings me to the crux of my argument and what I intend to shed light on through a study of student involvement in community service. Arguably, unless individuals have a deep sense of caring for others, it is less likely that they will engage in interactions with diverse others in a meaningful way. Caring may be seen as the solution to the challenge presented by a postmodern society characterized by difference. In essence, I contend that fostering a deep commitment to caring is the postmodern developmental dilemma all of education faces, including higher education. If we are to promote democratic citizenship in these challenging times, then we must foster in our citizens a commitment to caring. Higher education has a major part to play in this process, and involving students in community service may be one vehicle for meeting this challenge. The question that needs to be asked then, is, How and in what kinds of community service settings is caring to be fostered? Before addressing this question through a discussion of the findings, I first clarify the methodology used in conducting the study.

Methodology

The primary goal of this article is to advance understanding of community service as a strategy for citizenship education. Through a qualitative study of college students involved in community service, I shed light on various facets of the service context that may be most beneficial to challenging students as caring citizens. The focus is not on student learning per se; instead, I target the kind of meaning students construct about their service encounters as a means to identify important aspects of community service associated with caring. I need to be clear here. This article does not attempt to assess developmental change by examining student involvement in community service. Although such a strategy is important and falls in line with the tradition of student outcomes research (Astin, 1979, 1993; Feldman & Newcomb, 1970; Pascarella & Terenzini, 1991), this article takes more of a phenomenological direction in which the essence of community service is the primary concern. Hence, the kind of experiences students describe are important in this study, not as learning outcomes, but as indications of the nature of the service context.

The data for this article were derived from research and participation in community service projects conducted in conjunction with three universities: Pennsylvania State University, the University of South Carolina, and Michigan State University. Community service projects ranged from week-long intensive experiences requiring travel to distant out-of-state communities to ongoing student service projects in the local communities or states in which these universities are situated. I participated as a volunteer in many of the service projects described throughout this article. My role ranged from a staff supervisor in a few cases to that of a graduate student volunteer with limited responsibility in other instances. In every case, my primary role was as a volunteer and not as a researcher; the data I collected was more of an outgrowth of the community service experience and was not the central objective. The comments here are not meant to shortchange the research strategy employed, but instead are intended to clarify for the reader the context of my interactions and involvement with the student volunteers. In fact, my role as a volunteer may actually add strength to the naturalistic strategies used in collecting data as I was able to engage in ongoing and meaningful dialogue with the research participants (Denzin, 1989).

Based on the methodological strategies associated with naturalistic inquiry, data were collected using a variety of techniques, including formal and informal interviews, surveys, participant observation, and document analysis (Lincoln & Guba, 1985). The principal documents used as a source of data were journals students were asked to keep as part of their community service experience. The use of multiple data collection techniques provides a degree of triangulation and offers the researcher an opportunity to confirm or reject tentative interpretations (Denzin, 1989).

The early phase of the study was conducted in conjunction with Pennsylvania State University and the data obtained was part of a formal evaluation of community service activities by students. This phase of the project involved surveys of students' experiences and was considered program evaluation and as such did not require human subject approval at Penn State. The second phase, which primarily involved interviews and observations, necessitated gaining human subject approval. Students were informed of the study and given the opportunity to participate or decline. It was during this phase of the study that student journals were used, but only with student approval.

During the six year period (1991–1996) in which data were collected, 108 students participated in interviews, 66 students completed open-ended surveys, and more than 200 students were observed at various project sites in which participant observation was central. Approximately 90% of the students involved in the community service projects were undergraduates, and about 10% were graduate students. The vast majority (approximately 80%) of the undergraduates were traditional-age students in the range of 18 to 24 years old. Females represented approximately 60% of the sample, and in terms of race, the majority were Caucasian (roughly 85%), with African Americans constituting the largest minority group—about 8 to 10% of the overall group.

Interview transcripts (from both formal and informal interviews), open-ended surveys, field notes from participant observation, student journals, and documents collected in conjunction with various service projects form the entire data base for the study. Once collected, the data were read repeatedly in an effort to identify important and relevant themes. The process followed the kind of analytical strategy stressed in the work of cultural anthropologists and interpretivists (Geertz, 1973; Rosaldo, 1989). Specifically, themes were identified based on their contextual significance and relevance to the overall goal of the project: *to better understand the context of community service and how such activities might challenge students' understandings of citizenship and the social good*. In a procedure described by Lincoln and Guba (1985) as "member checks," themes and interpretations were shared with several students as part of a process to obtain feedback and incorporate student reactions into the final manuscripts.

Based on the data analysis, several themes were identified. Three of those themes—students' explorations of the self, understandings of others, and views of the social good—form the basis for this article. Other issues, such as "student motivation" for getting involved in community service and "attitudes toward community service," are examples of additional themes that emerged from the data analysis but are peripheral to this article and thus are not discussed in any substantive way.

Findings

In keeping with the theoretical concern of democratic citizenship and fostering more caring selves, the findings are organized around three general concerns suggested by students in discussing their participation in community service: self-exploration, understanding others, and the social good. These themes are highly interactive and, in general, students' exploration in all of these areas contributes to understanding what I describe as the caring self.

Self-Exploration

Participation in community service is an educational activity that lends itself to identity clarification. For example, a student who was part of an intensive week-long community service project in South Carolina talked about identity issues and her participation in the project: "I'm kind of in a search for my own identity, and this trip is part of that search. I just don't know quite who I am yet. I'm struggling to figure it all out. These kinds of experiences help. I'm most genuine in these kinds of settings." Another student added, "Getting involved in community service helps me to get back in touch with who I really am. It reminds me that I have more to live for than merely myself." A third student offered the following comments:

> I've always done service work. During my freshman year at USC [University of South Carolina] I worked on the City Year project and the Serv-a-thon. I believe service is an important part of leadership. It's important to give back to the community. The last four weeks I've been totally into myself, like running for vice president of the student body. I signed up for this project because I wanted to get outside myself for awhile.

This student saw the service project as an opportunity to connect with others and in her words "get outside" of herself. For her, the service project offered a chance to become more other-focused and to contribute to her community.

A second student described her involvement in community service as part of a journey to better understand herself: "My work as a volunteer has really helped me to see that I have so much more to understand about myself in order to grow. I'm still on the journey and have a long way to go." And a third student discussed what he learned about himself: "I got involved in volunteerism because I wanted to learn more about myself. I've learned how to love a wide range of people despite differences between us. I've learned not to be judgmental." A fourth offered insight into the kind of soul searching students often go through as a result of service work:

> Sometimes I feel like I'm only fooling myself and that I'm really only into service so that I can help myself. I list this stuff on my resume and I feel guilty because I know it will help me get a teaching job. Is that why I do this? I know it makes me feel better about what I do in my spare time, but who am I really serving?

This student recognized, like others, the positive returns of service, not only in terms of experience helpful for landing employment, but for the feelings reflected back to the self.

Self-exploration through community service often involved a kind of self-interrogation that helped students to think more seriously about their lives. Listen to the following student as she recalled her volunteer work with troubled youth:

> I got involved in a lot of self-esteem work, primarily with teenagers. It helped me to think more seriously about my understanding of myself and how others think of me. I began to wonder about what kind of person I was and was going to be. I began to ask questions of myself: "Am I too judgmental? Am I open to others? Am I sensitive to how other people see the world?"

Once again, the role of community service in challenging one's sense of self is clear. Equally clear is how one's sense of self is tied to the social context and the views others hold of us.

Understanding Others

A significant learning experience associated with community service was the opportunity to better understand the lives students worked to serve. Students were able to put faces and names with the alarming statistics and endless policy debates about homelessness as well as rural and urban poverty. As one student explained,

> Expressing what it has meant to me to actually have the chance to engage in conversations with people who used to be total strangers is next to impossible. It has been eye opening. My understanding of homeless people was based on what I'd see on the news, in magazines, or on TV shows. They were not real people and I could easily turn my back on them and the problem in general.

Similar comments were offered by Penn State and Michigan State students involved in community service projects working with homeless citizens in DC, Louisville, and New York City:

> Every homeless person has a name, a story.
> They just want to be recognized and treated as human beings. There are names behind the statistics.
> Working with the people of the streets has transformed "those people" into real faces, real lives, and real friends. I can no longer confront the issue without seeing the faces of my new friends. This has an incredible effect on my impetus to help.
> All the statistics about homeless people and the stories of people freezing to death in the winter never really sunk in until I made friends with Harry and Reggie. There are faces now.

Students who worked in rural areas with low-income families also derived benefit from personal interactions with those they worked to serve. One student commented on the general outcomes associated with having personal interactions in service settings: "The whole experience helps you to see that others are real people and have real problems and yet can come together to help one another. . . . When you work with the people on their houses or in their back yard it adds to the experience. You get a chance to know the people. You have a face or a personality to go with the work." A second student stated, "The fact that we were able to interact a great deal with the people in the community added so much to the overall experience. I've done volunteer work in the past where I never really got the chance to meet with the people who I was actually trying to help." A third student, who participated in a week-long service project in a low-income rural area, added, "This week has taught me so much about other people and the problems they face in life. You can read about growing up poor, but getting to share a conversation with someone who has overcome so much during their lifetime is quite a different matter. . . . It's made me much less judgmental of others and their place in life."

A common point made by students was the fact that community service work with people of diverse cultural backgrounds forced students to confront generalizations they had of the other. For example, students talked about various stereotypes they held about poor people and how such stereotypes were erased as a result of their service work. Several students noted how surprised they were to find so many intelligent and educated people without jobs or places to live. One student maintained that the only accurate stereotype relates to the amount of bad luck that most homeless people have experienced. A second added, "I learned that all people are innately afraid and that no one deserves to be without a voice and a safe place and that stereotypes can be more damaging than can be fathomed." A third student talked about how his preconceptions about homeless people had been shattered through his interactions with them. As he explained, "This experience gave my beliefs and convictions about the homeless a personal basis that I'll never forget."

Many of the preconceptions students had about the poor were rooted in their limited experience with cultural diversity. Although socioeconomic factors were the primary source of difference between students and community members, race was another factor. Interactions with a variety of low-income individuals and families often challenged students' conceptions of the diverse other. Because the vast majority of the student volunteers were Caucasians and many of the community members served by the students were African Americans, a number of racial issues emerged from time to time. A Penn State sophomore talked about the difference she felt between herself and the large number of homeless African Americans she encountered during her volunteer work in DC: "I definitely felt a major barrier between Blacks and Whites in this country. There were times working in the soup kitchens where I felt very uncomfortable." A college junior studying mathematics commented on a similar feeling: "It was an experience for me simply to be placed in the awkward environment of walking around in predominantly African American, poor neighborhoods. I want to remember that feeling of insecurity. It reminds me of the vast differences between races in our society."

Often, issues of race and class blended together and challenged students' prejudices in a multi-faceted way. Listen to the following two students discuss their experiences:

> There is something that I'm not proud of and I always considered myself open-minded and not prejudiced, but when I worked at Sharon's house [Sharon is an African-American woman who needed repairs done to her home] it reminded me that some of my previous thinking about the poor had been based on stereotypes. I mean I've always kind of thought in the back of my mind that people become poor or destitute because they are not motivated or not as intelligent. But Sharon has a master's degree and is very articulate. I see now that there may be many causes or barriers that people face that can limit them. It was an eye opener and I see now that I was carrying this misconception about them being to blame for their plight.
>
> Meeting homeless people and talking with them taught me that some of my stereotypes about the poor, about Blacks, have been rooted in my own life of White, middle-class privilege. I have never had to work that hard to get a college education, for example, yet I've bought into the idea that others who have less than me are somehow lazy because they are poor. Heck, they may have worked twice as hard as I have. I've never really had my views of the poor challenged until this experience working with homeless people.

The generalizations and stereotypes to which students referred were seen by several as the by-product of the media. As one student, a senior in geography, pointed out, "I learned that my perceptions of poverty, crime, and homelessness are influenced and perhaps shaped by misconstrued images that I see on television." Another student also talked about how television had played a major role in how she had come to envision African Americans. She pointed out that in her rural Pennsylvania community, "there wasn't a single African-American family. I never even met an African American until I attended college."

The Social Good

As one might expect, given the context of caring for others, issues related to the social good often surfaced. Community service is ripe for such discussions and offers a context conducive to serious thought about the larger social body. One student offered an example of the kind of serious thought that may evolve from community service work:

> There are a lot of people in this country who need help to make ends meet. You can choose to help them or you can turn your back on them. I want to help people, and I want those who choose not to help to know that there are consequences for walking away. There are children who will go hungry and people who will be living in the streets. I cannot live with that on my conscience.

For this student, the social good suggests a world in which no one starves or goes homeless. Giving up some of his own time and energy to help others "make it" is in line with his vision of social responsibility.

Other students offered similar remarks about the social good. For example, one student commented, "Intellectual exploration has been rewarding but also suffocating at times and so I find the desire to commit myself to experiential work. I found one way could be by working in a homeless shelter and understanding social issues from a political standpoint as well as from the perspective of those living and breathing poverty."

For another student, the common good included the role of education in assisting the poor. He saw service as important, but there were deeper issues underlying poverty. He explained,

> Service activities are important, but we also have to help teach people how to fish. You just can't give people food or build houses for them without also helping them develop the skills to take care of their own lives and their own families. . . . Part of my goal is to help others to develop their own abilities so that they can lead productive lives.

This student alludes to the idea that simply providing "bandages," though important and necessary, may not heal deeper wounds. In this case, the student highlights how sometimes the problems rest with the poor and their limited skills.

Other students also concerned with the deeper roots of economic inequities chose to focus on social structure instead of individuals as part of their effort to make sense of the social good. For example, one student saw community service as a stepping stone to larger work for social change: "I need to be in community with people who are interested in radical social change. Together we can work and witness all kinds of changes, and perhaps come closer to finding some answers." Another student alluded to the structural aspects of poverty as she discussed her learning experiences:

> Community service is something that I think everybody should get involved doing. You see a different side of our country when you see some of the struggles the poor face. You begin to understand the barriers to their economic situation and why it is so hard to get out of poverty. I talked to this one woman, and she explained to me how expensive day care is for her children and that in order for her to take a job she needs to make at least eight to ten dollars an hour. And no one will pay her that.

For the preceding student, community service experience helped her identify a structural problem that limits low-income workers—the lack of affordable day care.

Not everyone who participated in this study saw service as necessarily a positive force for improving society. Listen to the following student take issue with some of the general comments he heard about the positive aspects of service:

> To be honest, and it's hard to say this around all these "do gooders," I'm not sure all this volunteer stuff really does a whole lot of good. I know, I'm one of those volunteers too. But I keep asking myself a bunch of questions: "Am I doing this to help the homeless or am I doing this to help myself? Who really benefits?" Maybe I'm being too skeptical, but I think most of the students here are like me but won't admit it. It makes them feel good to help feed someone, and that way they can go back to living their happy little lives without feeling too guilty.

Despite the biting cynicism of the preceding student's comments, he makes an important point that turns our attention back to the theoretical thrust of this article: The idea that one often develops positive feelings about oneself as a result of involvement in service reminds us that our sense of self indeed is tied to others. When warm feelings are shared with a student engaged in service, then logically, that student may see him or herself in a more favorable manner. The interactional context is one reason why community service is so critical to forging more caring selves. Through acts designed to serve others, students learn to feel better about themselves. At the same time, their relationship to others and to the larger social body is strengthened. Hopefully, reaching out becomes a way of life and the diversity that offers the potential to divide one from another becomes instead a source of sharing. This is the essence of the caring self.

Implications for Structuring Community Service

As noted earlier, this study was phenomenological in nature. The study did not seek to determine whether students become more caring citizens as a result of their service. Instead, by approaching the subject phenomenologically, I was able to identify aspects of the community service context that might contribute to students' considerations of the self, others, and the social good. The underlying assumption of course is that such considerations are likely to contribute positively to one's ongoing development as a caring citizen. Thus, in thinking about the implications of the findings I was able to identify three structural components of community service that appear to be critical to advancing citizenship as defined in this article. These key components are *mutuality, reflection*, and *personalization*.

There are two aspects of mutuality I stress: One aspect relates to a recognition that both parties—the so called "doers" and the "done to," in Radest's (1993) terms—benefit from the service encounter. Students involved in service receive incredible rewards for their work in the form of personal satisfaction. And, if their work is effective, community members also receive rewards in the form of a service provided. Thus, one might say that the experience is mutual.

The gifts that students receive through their community service offerings are not without complications. Students frequently expressed a degree of guilt for feeling good about themselves as a result of their service to others. A line from the great American poet, Delmore Schwartz, comes to mind here: "Nothing is given which is not taken." Taking or "receiving" the gifts offered by community members is something students engaged in service must learn to do. In fact, effective leadership training for students ought to prepare them to be recipients of the rewards of service. "In giving, one must learn to receive," noted one student who worked with homeless citizens in Washington, DC.

The second aspect of mutuality relates to the structure of the relationship between service providers and community members who may receive a specific service. Too often we are guilty of determining the needs of those to be served with little to no involvement on their part. For community service to be most effective for the development of caring citizens, then, the planning of such activities ought to include those to be served in an equal and empowering manner. After all, Dewey's conception of democracy entails each person taking others into consideration when making decisions affecting the public realm.

A second key to making community service most effective for citizenship development is the inclusion of reflection as part of the service work. By the term "reflection" I refer to activities designed to help students process their service experiences in a manner involving serious thought. Small-group discussions and writing assignments are common tools used to foster student reflection. As is noted earlier in this article, community service that incorporates reflection moves closer to what is typically considered service learning in that the reflective activity helps to link service to an educational outcome.

Several of the service projects observed through this study did not involve structured reflection and the students' experiences suffered. One example occurred in New York City, where a young woman became so intimidated by her interactions with a homeless man who screamed profanities at her that she vowed to never again work with the homeless. The project she worked on was led entirely by students and there was no opportunity for guided reflection. In interviewing this student, I was left to ponder how her reaction might have been different had she been able to interact with an experienced facilitator. Would she have been able to work through her feelings and perhaps take something positive from the traumatic encounter?

Other examples from this study reveal the power of reflection. Recently, I accompanied a group of 23 students from Michigan State University to Merida in the Yucatan where we worked at a Salvation Army shelter for children, a low-income health facility, and a women's resource center. As part of helping MSU students process their experiences, staff volunteers facilitated reflection groups each evening after students returned from their work sites. At the end of the week, we evaluated the project and consistently students described the reflection activities as one of the highlights of their cross-cultural experience (despite the "educational" overtones such activities carried!).

Perhaps the most significant aspect of community service that I found to contribute to caring is what may be called the personalization of service. For community service to be challenging to a student's sense of self, it seems most beneficial for service to involve opportunities for meaningful interaction with those individuals to be served. Time and time again students discussed how significant it was for them to have the opportunity to interact with individuals and families on a personal basis.

Conclusion

The challenge of education to foster caring citizens has taken on enormous proportion in contemporary society as the struggle between individualism and social responsibility has taken on new meaning (Bellah, Sullivan, Swidler, & Tipton, 1985; Coles, 1993; Palmer, 1993; Parks Daloz, Keen, Keen, & Daloz Parks, 1996; Wuthnow, 1991, 1995). Community service is one option educators can select to enhance the development of citizens concerned with the social good. Caring is central to the effectiveness of community service, and thus students are challenged to give serious thought to what it means to care as they struggle to evaluate their commitment to the lives of others. Because the relationship between individuals and their obligation to one another is a cornerstone of democracy, community service may be seen to contribute to citizenship in a democratic society.

The students in this study highlight how cultural diversity poses additional challenges to one's development as a caring citizen. They described how community service often is an interaction between diverse others. This is the essence of Radest's (1993) argument when he maintained that community service may be seen as an "encounter with strangers" in which the challenge of service is that we each learn from the other and we each give as well as receive. From this perspective, community service represents a dialogical encounter with diverse others and serves as a bridge to build communal ties. Thus, community service offers one vehicle for preparing students to communicate in a culturally diverse world.

Finally, because service encourages students to see themselves as intimately connected to the other, a learning context is created in which the caring self is more likely to emerge. Fostering a sense of self grounded in an ethic of care is one of the central challenges of education and becomes increasingly important as our society grows more diverse. By fostering an ethic of care, higher education encourages the sense of otherness needed for democracy to survive and, indeed, thrive in a complex and fragmented social world.

References

Astin, A. W. (1979). *Four critical years: Effects of college on beliefs, attitudes and knowledge.* San Francisco: Jossey-Bass.

Astin, A. W. (1993). *What matters in college?: Four critical years revisited.* San Francisco: Jossey-Bass.

Barber, B. (1992). *An aristocracy of everyone: The politics of education and the future of America.* New York: Oxford University Press.

Battistoni, R. (1985). *Public schooling and the education of democratic citizens.* Jackson, MS: University Press of Mississippi.

Bellah, R. N., Sullivan, W. M., Swidler, A., & Tipton, S. M. (1985). *Habits of the heart: Individualism and commitment in American life.* New York: Harper & Row.

Boss, J. A. (1994). The effect of community service work on the moral development of college ethics students. *Journal of Moral Education, 23*(2), 183–198.

Boyer, E. L. (1987). *College: The undergraduate experience in America.* New York: Harper & Row.

Boyer, E. L. (1994, March 9). Creating the new American college. *Chronicle of Higher Education*, p. A 48.

Chodorow, N. (1974). Family structure and feminine personality. In M. Rosaldo & L. Lamphere (Eds.), *Women, culture and society* (pp. 43–66). Stanford, CA: Stanford University Press.

Chodorow, N. (1978). *The reproduction of mothering: Psychoanalysis and the sociology of gender.* Berkeley: University of California Press.

Coles, R. (1993). *The call of service: A witness to idealism.* Boston: Houghton Mifflin.

Cooley, C. H. (1902). *Human nature and the social order.* New York: Charles Scribner's Sons.

Cooper, D. (1998). Reading, writing, and reflection. In R. A. Rhoads & J. P. F. Howard (Eds.), *Academic service learning: A pedagogy of action and reflection.* New Directions for Teaching and Learning, no. 73 (pp. 47–56). San Francisco: Jossey-Bass.

Delve, C. I., Mintz, S. D., & Stewart, G. M. (1990). *Community service as values education.* New Directions for Student Services, no. 50. San Francisco: Jossey-Bass.

Denzin, N. (1989). *The research act* (3rd ed.). New York: Prentice-Hall.

Dewey, J. (1916). *Democracy and education.* New York: Macmillan.

Dewey, J. (1927). *The public and its problems.* New York: Henry Holt and Company.

Eyler, J., Giles, D. E., & Schmiede, A. (1996). *A practitioner's guide to reflection in service-learning: Student voices and reflections.* Washington, DC: Corporation for National Service.

Feldman, K. A., & Newcomb, T. M. (1970). *The impact of college on students.* San Francisco: Jossey-Bass.

Geertz, C. (1973). *The interpretation of cultures.* New York: Basic Books.

Giles, D. E., Jr., & Eyler, J. (1994). The impact of a college community service laboratory on students' personal, social, and cognitive outcomes. *Journal of Adolescence, 17,* 327–339.

Gilligan, C. (1979). Woman's place in man's life cycle. *Harvard Educational Review, 9*(4), 431–446.

Gilligan, C. (1982). *In a different voice: Psychological theory and women's development.* Cambridge, MA: Harvard University Press.

Harkavy, I., & Benson, L. (1998). De-Platonizing and democratizing education as the bases of service learning. In R. A. Rhoads & J. P. F. Howard (Eds.), *Academic service learning: A pedagogy of action and reflection.* New Directions for Teaching and Learning, no. 73 (pp. 11–20). San Francisco: Jossey-Bass.

Howard, J. P. F. (1998). Academic service learning: A counternormative pedagogy. In R. A. Rhoads & J. P. F. Howard (Eds.), *Academic service learning: A pedagogy of action and reflection.* New Directions for Teaching and Learning, no. 73 (pp. 21–29). San Francisco: Jossey-Bass.

Jacoby, B., & Associates. (Eds.), (1996). *Service-learning in higher education: Concepts and practices.* San Francisco: Jossey-Bass.

James, W. (1890). *Principles of psychology* (Vol. 1). New York: Holt.

Kendall, J. C. (Ed.). (1990). *Combining service and learning: A resource book for community and public service* (Vol. 1). Raleigh, NC: National Society for Experiential Education.

Kraft, R. J. (1996). Service learning. *Education and Urban Society, 28*(2), 131–159.

Kraft, R. J., & Swadener M. (Eds.). (1994). *Building community: Service learning in the academic disciplines.* Denver: Colorado Campus Compact.

Larrabee, M. J. (Ed.). (1993). *An ethic of care: Feminist and interdisciplinary perspectives.* New York: Routledge.

Lincoln, Y. S., & Guba, E. G. (1985). *Naturalistic inquiry.* Beverly Hills: Sage.

Markus, G. B., Howard, J. P. F., & King, D. C. (1993). Integrating community service and classroom instruction enhances learning: Results from an experiment. *Educational Evaluation and Policy Analysis, 15*(4), 410–419.

Mead, G. H. (1934). *Mind, self, & society* (Charles W. Morris, Ed.). Chicago: University of Chicago Press.

Mendel-Reyes, M. (1998). A pedagogy for citizenship: Service learning and democratic education. In R. A. Rhoads & J. P. F. Howard (Eds.), *Academic service learning: A pedagogy of action and reflection.* New Directions for Teaching and Learning, no. 73 (pp. 31–38). San Francisco: Jossey-Bass.

Noddings, N. (1984). *Caring: A feminine approach to ethics and moral education.* Berkeley: University of California Press.

Noddings, N. (1992). *The challenge to care in schools: An alternative approach to education.* New York: Teachers College Press.

Noddings, N. (1995). Teaching themes of care. *Phi Delta Kappan, 76*(9), 675–679.

Oliner, P. M., & Oliner, S. P. (1995). *Toward a caring society: Ideas into action.* Westport, CT: Praeger.

Palmer, P. (1993). *To know as we are known: Education as a spiritual journey*. San Francisco: Harper.

Parks Daloz, S., Keen, C. H., Keen, J. P., & Daloz Parks, L. A. (1996). *Common fire: Lives of commitment in a complex world*. Boston: Beacon Press.

Pascarella, E. T., & Terenzini, P. T. (1991). *How college affects students: Findings and insights from twenty years of research*. San Francisco: Jossey-Bass.

Radest, H. (1993). *Community service: Encounter with strangers*. Westport, CT: Praeger.

Rhoads, R. A. (1997). *Community service and higher learning: Explorations of the caring self*. Albany: SUNY Press.

Rhoads, R. A. (1998). Critical multiculturalism and service learning. In R. A. Rhoads & J. P. F. Howard (Eds.), *Academic service learning: A pedagogy of action and reflection*. New Directions for Teaching and Learning, no. 73 (pp. 39–46). San Francisco: Jossey-Bass.

Rhoads, R. A., & Howard, J. P. F. (1998). *Academic service learning: A pedagogy of action and reflection*. New Directions for Teaching and Learning, no. 73. San Francisco: Jossey-Bass.

Rosaldo, R. (1989). *Culture & truth: The remaking of social analysis*. Boston: Beacon.

Sampson, E. E. (1989). The challenge of social change for psychology: Globalization and psychology's theory of the person. *American Psychologist, 44*(6), 914–921.

Study Group on the Conditions of Excellence in American Higher Education. (1984). *Involvement in learning*. Washington, DC: National Institute of Education.

Tierney, W. G. (1993). *Building communities of difference: Higher education in the 21st century*. Westport, CT: Bergin & Garvey.

Tierney, W. G., & Rhoads, R. A. (1993). Postmodernism and critical theory in higher education: Implications for research and practice. In J. C. Smart (Ed.), *Higher education: Handbook of theory and research* (pp. 308–343). New York: Agathon.

Tocqueville, A., de (1945). *Democracy in America*. New York: Alfred A. Knopf.

Waterman, A. S. (Ed.). (1997). *Service learning: Applications from the research*, Mahwah, NJ: Lawrence Erlbaum Associates.

Wingspread Group on Higher Education. (1993). *An American imperative: Higher expectations for higher education*. Racine, WI: Johnson Foundation.

Wuthnow, R. (1991). *Acts of compassion: Caring for others and helping ourselves*. Princeton, NJ: Princeton University Press.

Wuthnow, R. (1995). *Learning to care: Elementary kindness in an age of indifference*. New York: Oxford University Press.

Young, I. M. (1990). The ideal of community and the politics of difference. In Linda J. Nicholson (Ed.), *Feminism/postmodernism* (pp. 300–323). New York: Routledge.

Zlotkowski, E. (1995). Does service learning have a future? *Michigan Journal of Community Service Learning, 2*(1), 123–133.

Undergraduates in Transition: A New Wave of Activism on American College Campuses

Arthur Levine & Deborah Hirsch

ABSTRACT. U.S. student attitudes are surveyed and attention drawn to evidence of recent changes displayed in a study of five colleges/universities undertaken by the authors in 1989/90. 'Collective optimism' appeared, heroes reappeared and what moved students most was the Challenger explosion rather than the political events which had been emphasised by their predecessors. Attitudes were less selfish and there was greater participation in social action. Examples are given of colleges which have responded by increasing opportunities for community service. The authors suggest that an analysis of past trends indicates that a rise in volunteerism leads to a period of student activism. The inverviews with students carried out by the authors provide evidence of such a development. The article concludes with a suggestion of points which colleges/universities should face in the light of these changes in student attitudes.

Changing Student Character

We tend to think of college students in generational stereotypes. The students of the 1920s were wet, wild and wicked. The students of the '30s were somber and radical. Students in the late '40s were mature and 'in a hurry.' The undergraduates of the 1950s were silent. The students of the late '60s and early '70s were angry and activists. The students of the 1980s were self-concerned, and career-driven. Such stereotypes are not particularly accurate ways of describing any generation of students. They conceal more than they reveal. But they do capture the direction of changes, providing a photograph of the trends in each era.

Indeed, Arthur Levine's research on undergraduates in 1980 found a national student body that was optimistic about their personal futures (91%) but very pessimistic about our collective future together (59%). Levine described their outlook as a 'Titanic Ethic.' They had the sense that the ship, call it the U.S. or the world, was going down. And if they were being forced to ride on a doomed vessel, students had decided to go first-class—seeking all the goodies to make the voyage as luxurious as possible for as long as the ship was still afloat.

When these students were asked who their heroes were, the most common response was no one. Less frequently they cited rock stars, athletes, and Hollywood types. Political leaders were almost entirely absent from their lists.

The college students of the 1980s were too young to remember the optimism of the New Frontier or Lyndon Johnson's Great Society. Traditional college students were only a year old when John Kennedy died. They were six when Martin Luther King and Robert Kennedy were assassinated. They were seven when men landed on the moon. They were twelve when Watergate reached its painful conclusion. And they were thirteen when the last U.S. troops left Vietnam. They said the social events that had the strongest impact on them were the Vietnam War, the Civil Rights movement, and Watergate. As one student put it, 'they seemed to be on television all the time when I was growing up.' For three out of four students, the effects of these events were distinctly negative. As a result, this group of students described themselves as cynical, expressing little confidence in politics, politicians, and government. A plurality believed that all social institutions were dishonest and that most people looked out only for number one.

Instead, these students were most concerned with getting a job and making money. As shown in the UCLA Higher Education Research Institute annual freshman surveys, more than three out of four students indicated that it was essential or very important not to be well off financially, but to be *very* well off financially. Students of the late '70s and '80s sought a college education to make more money and get a better job. In addition, involvement in campus organizations was down, as was the level of altruism and community participation on and off campus. Like their perception of the rest of the country, undergraduates were 'looking out for number one,' and were deeply concerned with obtaining the material rewards of life—'going first-class on the Titanic'. (Levine 1980)

These attitudes persisted throughout the 1980s with the exception of Watergate, Vietnam, and the Civil Rights Movement being dominant events in the lives of students. Throughout the decade of the 1980s the events receded in importance as student birth rates grew later. By 1989, college students were only four years old when the last of these three events occurred.

Yet even today, this stereotype of students appears to remain accurate. Current students continue to be apprehensive about their job prospects and are still interested in making money. Indeed, the chance to make more money and get a better job remain principal reasons for many students in choosing to go to college, according to the UCLA Higher Education Research Institute surveys of college freshmen.

However, our research indicates that a much more subtle change is occurring among college students. Over the past fourteen years, the authors have been carrying out 'focus group' interviews with students on campuses around the country. During the last two years, their answers to a series of questions have changed dramatically.

Students in Transition

This paper reports on a study of five colleges and universities carried out in 1989–90. The campuses were located in the east, midwest, south and west. They were Protestant, Catholic and nonsectarian. They were public and private. They were both four-year colleges and universities.

When we asked students on these campuses whether they were optimistic or pessimistic about the future, 90% said they were optimistic about their personal futures, which is comparable to the response of previous years. However, 83% said they were optimistic about our collective future together. This rise in collective optimism has occurred almost entirely in the past two years.

What is even more interesting is the way students describe their optimism. One young woman claimed to be 'cynically optimistic'. Another student caught the same spirit in saying he was 'pragmatically optimistic'. The optimism of current students is not well described by words like naive, innocent, or pollyannish. There is a hard edge to it, which seems somewhat surprising among young people.

When we asked these students whether they had any heroes, we also received a different answer. The majority of students—more than three out of four—named a hero. As usual a few cited historically important figures like John Kennedy or Martin Luther King. A small number also mentioned contemporary figures such as George Bush, Jesse Jackson and Alice Walker. (An interesting point is that minorities and older students were more likely to name contemporary and historical figures than the younger and majority students). However, the majority of students named local heroes—a relative, a neighbor, a teacher—people in their community they wanted to be like or admired.

Two changes stand out here. First is that students now have heroes. This would seem to go hand in hand with the rise in optimism. Second, it is interesting that the stage for heroes has shifted from the national level to the local. In many respects the country's agenda is more diffuse today. The two or three clear national issues of the 1960s and '70s have disappeared in favor of a multiplicity of local issues. There are very few widely popular national leaders in contrast to the many who make a difference at the local level.

This reality is made clear in a third question we asked students, 'What social or political event has had the greatest effect upon your life and your generation?' On each of the five campuses a

TABLE 1

Attitudes about Money and Work

	1971	1978	1983	1989
Reasons noted as very important in deciding to go to college:				
make more money	50%	60%	67%	72%
get better job	74%	75%	76%	76%
Essential or very important to be very well of financially	48%	53%	69%	75%

Source: UCLA Higher Education Research Institute.

majority of students gave the same answer: 'the Challenger explosion. This was for us a fascinating answer. In part what makes it interesting is how very different it is from the answers of their predecessors. Although a painful national tragedy, in contrast to Watergate, the Civil Rights Movement and the Vietnam War, this was an accident of technology without profound social disruption or very negative long-term consequences. Also notable is that when we asked students why this event stood out for them, they said they watched it together on television or heard it announced together at their school. The Challenger explosion was a shared tragedy in a generation that had no comparable experience.

This situation is very different from that of the students of the 1970s. Intriguing, too, is that current students did not cite the events of Tiananmen Square in China, the destruction of the Berlin Wall, or the unravelling of Eastern Europe which was beginning at the time. One wonders whether these events will be mentioned more frequently in the future. A point worth noting, however, is that, with the exception of the Vietnam War, the answers to this question have always emphasized domestic rather than international events.

To understand these responses, it may help to place them in context. This year's college freshmen were born in 1973, ten years later than the students of 1980. This means they were born ten years after the assassination of President Kennedy, after the cities burned, and after the promise of the Kennedy/ Johnson years ended. They were born the year after the Watergate break-in and were one when the last U.S. troops left Vietnam. They were seven when Ronald Reagan was elected president. They were eight when the hostages returned from Iran. They were nine when the double-digit inflation ceased and unemployment numbers started falling. They were 15 when George Bush became president. These events and the attendant disillusionment associated with each are not part of the life of this generation.

Current students know only two presidents—Ronald Reagan and George Bush. They have grown up in relatively good times, assuming they are not poor, in which case these were the worst times in a quarter century. (However, fewer poor people are going to college now than in 1980.) They say they have heard about the bad old days from parents and older siblings.

The changes we observed are particularly interesting when taken in combination with the recent surveys by the Higher Education Research Institute at UCLA of 1989 freshmen. First, this research shows that while almost three out of four (72%) of today's college freshmen are looking for careers which will yield high earnings, two out of three are also interested in a career which will allow them to make a contribution to society (66%). It appears that the 'me generation' which was so clearly apparent on campuses a few years ago is beginning to recede.

Second, today's freshmen are more activist than their predecessors. More than one out of every three report having participated in a demonstration the year before college. This is half again as many as the freshmen of 1971 (see Table 2).

TABLE 2

**Freshmen Reporting Participation in a
Demonstration the Year Before College**

1971	23%
1978	17%
1978	21%
1989	1989

Source: UCLA Higher Education Research Institute Surveys

TABLE 3

Participation of College Students in Volunteer Activities

Activity	*Percentage Participating*
Fundraising	47
Service activity	45
Church service project	41
Charity organization project	31
Election campaign	20
Elderly and retirees	19
Environmental project	17
Hospital service	12

Source: Boyer, Ernest L. *College: The Undergraduate Experience in America*, 187, p. 214

Third, this year's freshmen are constructively involved in social action. Almost two out of three freshmen (62%) in the UCLA survey reported having performed volunteer work in the year prior to college. This is continuing on campus.

The Carnegie Foundation for the Advancement of Teaching's National Survey (1987) found that about one-half of undergraduates surveyed participated in some form of service activity during their college years (Table 3).

As more and more students get involved in volunteerism, more colleges are developing programs to encourage students to become involved in community service. In 1985, 121 college presidents formed Campus Compact, a coalition of colleges and universities to create opportunities for students to learn more about, and experience, volunteerism. In 1989, the Campus Outreach Opportunity League (COOL) was founded by Wayne Meisel, a recent Harvard undergraduate who organized campus service programs in Cambridge, to stimulate and expand community service projects on college campuses. To date, the organization has enlisted the support of student leaders from over 450 colleges and universities across the country. And the National Association of Independent Schools reports that about half of its members offer some volunteer service and about one-quarter of them require it prior to graduation. Many colleges are establishing budget lines and creating offices staffed by professionals to oversee these projects. Several colleges are also offering course credit for community service.

A New Wave of Activism: Students Involved in Community Service

Our research finds a mushrooming of public service programs for college students. A sampling of programs on campuses around the country includes the following patterns of changes.

Birmingham Southern. Administrators have seen a sharp increase in the number of students who participate in volunteer organizations. Each fall, the college designates a day in which the entire community—faculty, administrators and students—participates in service projects. Two years ago, 10 students were involved, last year 250 students volunteered, and this year over 500 students joined with faculty and staff to donate more than 3,000 hours of service. In addition, 72% of the student body participated in ongoing community service programs that included among others: tutorial and adult literacy programs, support for area youngsters, environmental clean-up, and working with the homeless. Winter breaks and summer vacations have also become times for more concentrated volunteer efforts both in the U.S. and abroad.

Tulane University. The number of undergraduates involved in a student-run community service organization has increased by 50% in the past two years. They run tutoring programs for inner-city students, volunteer in area hospitals and nursing homes, prepare prison inmates for the GED, and serve meals in a soup kitchen. As in other colleges across the country, conservation and recycling movements are booming.

Oberlin College. Administrators have seen a dramatic increase in the number of students involved in community service. Two years ago, 59 students were volunteering in a variety of community settings; last semester over 300 were involved. The College has also begun offering credit-bearing community service courses in such settings as a shelter for the homeless, a battered women's home and a low-income Hispanic neighborhood.

Mount St. Mary's College in Maryland. Over one-third of the students volunteer their services through campus organizations that are battling real social problems. Like peers at other schools, the students spend spring breaks and summers working with the poor. They have painted apartments for low-income and disabled families in rundown urban areas. In rural Appalachia, they have taught teenage mothers and fathers basic child development skills and helped residents plant vegetable gardens.

California State University, Northridge. Campus officials estimate that more than 20% of the undergraduate student body participate in some form of community service. Students have become affiliated with local public schools to counsel at-risk students and to create after-school programs to help gang members stay out of trouble.

Tufts University. Membership in the student-run organization, which dropped to fewer than 20 students in the 1970s and early '80s, has grown to over 400 students. Some of the service projects include: working with battered women, pregnant teens and the disabled in shelters for the homeless, nursing homes, area hospices, and a battered women's residence. Some students also volunteer during winter and spring breaks in an intensive service experience in needy communities across the country. Tufts has also recently developed a community service option which allows students to defer admission in order to become involved in an intensive and sustained service project for one year. They believe this program will become a model for service learning.

Brown University. A leader in the field of student volunteering, over one-third of Brown students participate in some form of community service. Four years ago, Brown established the

Center for Public Service to formalize student participation in public service as a central part of their undergraduate experience. The Center complements the efforts of the twenty-year-old student community outreach organization which serves as a clearinghouse for volunteer service placements. The Center maintains a resource library, publishes a newsletter, administers community service fellowships, and sponsors several annual events which include: discussions and workshops showcasing alumni and guests who have made a commitment to careers in public service, and a program called a 'Taste of Service' where students participate in various service projects as a part of freshman and transfer orientation.

University of Minnesota. Over 500 students are involved in community service which includes programs for the homeless, environmental clean-up, a big buddy program for at-risk grade schoolers; community internships; and corporate internships which focus on issues of company ethics and social responsibility.

These programs differ from similar initiatives on other college campuses in that they include an education component. Volunteers meet weekly for discussion sessions which elicit reflection on the issues that arise in the course of service. Group facilitators work to help students build relationships with people from diverse backgrounds, develop skills, and explore values and personal growth using William Perry's developmental model for college students as a framework. Students who choose to do an internship take a mandatory five-credit course which uses group process and writing assignments to confront issues of ethics, leadership and power in organizations.

Stanford University. Student surveys indicate that 70% of undergraduates are involved in some form of public service. The Haas Center for Public Service serves as a clearinghouse for placements, sponsors conferences and workshops, and offers a number of programs for service such as: tutoring school children, working with the hungry and the homeless, aiding the elderly, and promoting conservation. Some students spend breaks and summers volunteering on reservations with Native Americans, planting trees for the National Forest Service, working with the homeless or mentally ill, and providing earthquake relief for the poor.

Other students spend a year in local government or in Washington learning about public policy and national service. Additionally, the Center offers fellowships to provide post-graduate opportunities in which students serve with a distinguished mentor in government or the nonprofit sector.

The Center's most recent focus is on working with faculty to develop courses that incorporate service in the classroom. In fact, a recent faculty retreat focused on developing a curricular service requirement.

Volunteerism: A Precursor to Student Unrest?

What strikes us about volunteerism on campuses today is not simply the rising numbers; it is that the activity is sustained and aimed at very real and intractable social issues. It is very different from the traditional pattern of student social participation, which is more short-term and tends to deal with benign community issues.

We believe this constellation of changes—rising optimism, the revival of heroes, increasing activism, and growing social involvement—marks a transition in college student character. Historically, student character has followed a cyclical pattern, oscillating back and forth between personal preoccupation and social engagement. In this century, there have been three cycles. Periods of student personal preoccupation have followed World War I, World War II and Vietnam. They lasted a little less than a decade and a half and were followed and preceded by times of social engagement, lasting about equally as long. Periods of personal preoccupation have been characterized by diminished student activism; more centrist politics; increased isolationism and reduced international concern; rising interest in social activity, Greek membership, and alcohol consumption; greater liberalism in matters of personal freedom; increased church participation; reduced intellectual orientation; and more concern with the material aspects of life. Periods of social engagement have had the opposite characteristics.

Our research indicates that every period of student unrest has been preceded by a rise in student volunteerism and social engagement. The seeds of future unrest were apparent in our interviews. Students told us that through their internships they were seeing real problems endured by real people that they had never been exposed to before; they were witnessing overwhelming need, and they were feeling the conflicting senses of accomplishment for what they were able to do and impotence in their inability (and in the unwillingness of others) to meet desperate social needs more need fully. The results, as explained by Keith Morton, Director of the University YMCA at the University of Minnesota, is that students typically experience a range of powerful and often overwhelming feelings of frustration and anger. These feelings generally vent themselves in accelerated political and social activism. As one Tufts student found, 'Every major push for improvement in our society . . . has been fueled by students like us. Real change has been made in the real world and more is needed.' The political side to volunteering lies in challenging the status quo by creating or urging others to respond to current events, social problems and community needs.

In short, our point is that college students appear to be making a transition to greater social activism. In the next few years, we would expect to see a revival on the part of students in political action, more interest in the 'relevance' of the college curriculum, more concern with international issues, and a greater emphasis on campus governance and societal concerns. Given the mood on campuses today, it would not be surprising if diversity and race relations became one of the early issues for activism. A recently completed, but yet unpublished study by one of the authors convinces us that there are very few campuses in America in which this issue is not heated. The recent experience of Wesleyan University would not represent an anomaly so much as a precursor of what could well occur throughout U.S. higher education.

We believe that it is critically important for colleges and universities to recognize these changes in students.

Historically, campuses have been slow to perceive such changes and even slower to respond. The result has been that higher education has had to contend not only with activist students, but also with a great deal of anger. Traditionally, the focus has been reactive rather than prospective, with a tendency to seek quick fixes rather than planning for long-term solutions.

Higher education has an opportunity now to lead, to use the current changes in student character as a basis for education, to prepare a generation of citizens who are socially engaged rather than socially estranged and institutionally alienated as occurred in the 1960s. We have a chance to think about students and engagement carefully, rather than being urgently pushed to stop campus unrest and end disruption. This is a luxury, an opportunity to seize upon.

In the short run, we believe that colleges and universities should develop or continue to build upon existing service programs which will provide students opportunities for constructive social involvement. Such opportunities might include service projects ranging from one-day experiences to ongoing semester or year-long volunteer placements to intensive projects during school breaks and summer vacations. Additional avenues for social action can be designed through credit-bearing internships, residence hall activities and student organizations. It would be useful to build instructional components into these service experiences as the University of Minnesota and others do. In addition, colleges should celebrate and honor constructive social engagement and accomplishments via speakers' series, institutional awards, and both curricular and co-curricular activities.

In the longer run, colleges will need to address even more basic issues. They will need to ask hard questions about their programs, practices and values. With respect to programs, colleges must ask whether, after a decade of drift toward vocational subjects, they are teaching the skills and knowledge that students need for civic engagement. Do their general education programs go beyond the sampling of disciplines to focus on the common human agenda, the historical purpose of a liberal education? Are college curricula relevant, not in the 1960s sense of letting a hundred flowers bloom, but rather in including newly emerging scholarship and focusing on the critical issues and challenges of the times?

With respect to practices, colleges might ask whether current policies and procedures permit the involvement of a generation of students who will be more eager to participate in governance. Do governance mechanisms reflect the values of an engaged campus community? Is the desired relationship with the off-campus community clear and reflected in practice?

With respect to values, are the academic community's standards of ethics and beliefs clearly spelled out and translated into action? Are they modeled to students by faculty, administration and staff?

To address these questions is a very large job. Most colleges and universities will feel little urgency to do so. But they really should. Because they can do so now without the politicization and pressure which may follow later.

References

Astin, Alexander W. *et al.* (1972). *The American Freshman: National Norms for Fall 1971*. Cooperative Institutional Research Program American Council on Education: University of California at Los Angeles.

Astin, Alexander W. *et al.* (1989). *The American Freshman: National Norms for Fall 1988*. Cooperative Institutional Research Program American Council on Education: University of California at Los Angeles.

Astin, Alexander W. *et al.* (1984). *The American Freshman: National Norms for Fall 1983*. Cooperative Institutional Research Program American Council on Education: University of California at Los Angeles.

Astin, Alexander W. *et al.* (1990). *The American Freshman: National Norms for Fall 1989*. Cooperative Institutional Research Program American Council on Education: University of California at Los Angeles.

Boyer, Ernest. L. (1989). *College: The Undergraduate Experience in America*. The Carnegie Foundation for the Advancement of Teaching. New York: Harper and Row.

Levine, Arthur (1980). *When Dreams and Heroes Died*. San Francisco: Jossey-Bass.

WHAT IF CIVIC LIFE DIDN'T DIE?

MICHAEL SCHUDSON

Robert Putnam's important and disturbing work on civic participation ("*The Strange Disappearance of Civic America.*" *TAP*, Winter 1996) has led him to conclude that television is the culprit behind civic decline. But lest we be *too* disturbed, we ought to consider carefully whether the data adequately measure participation and justify his conclusions and whether his conclusions fit much else that we know about recent history. I suggest that his work has missed some key contrary evidence. If we could measure civic participation better, the decline would be less striking and the puzzle less perplexing. If we looked more carefully at the history of civic participation and the differences among generations, we would have to abandon the rhetoric of decline. And if we examined television and recent history more closely, we could not convict TV of turning off civic involvement.

Consider, first, the problem of measuring whether there has been civic decline. Putnam has been ingenious in finding multiple measures of civic engagement, from voter turnout to opinion poll levels of trust in government to time-budget studies on how people allocate their time to associational membership. But could it be that even all of these measures together mask how civic energy is deployed?

Data collected by Sidney Verba, Kay Lehman Schlozman, and Henry Brady suggest the answer is yes. In 1987, 34 percent of their national sample reported active membership in a community problem-solving organization compared to 31 percent in 1967; in 1987, 34 percent reported working with others on a local problem compared to 30 percent in 1967. Self-reports should not be taken at face value, but why does this survey indicate a slight increase in local civic engagement? Does it capture something Putnam's data miss?

Putnam's measures may, in fact, overlook several types of civic activity. First, people may have left the middling commitment of the League of Women Voters or the PTA for organized activity both much less and much more involving. As for much more: Churches seem to be constantly reinventing themselves, adding a variety of groups and activities to engage members, from singles clubs to job training to organized social welfare services to preschools. An individual who reports only one associational membership—say, a church or synagogue—may be more involved in it and more "civic" through it than someone else who reports two or three memberships.

Second, people may have left traditional civic organizations that they used for personal and utilitarian ends for commercial organizations. If people who formerly joined the YMCA to use the gym now go to the local fitness center, Putnam's measures will show a decrease in civic participation when real civic activity is unchanged.

Third, people may be more episodically involved in political and civic activity as issue-oriented politics grows. For instance, in California, motorcycle riders have become influential political activists since the 1992 passage of a law requiring bikers to wear helmets. According to the *San Diego Union*, of 800,000 licensed motorcyclists, 10,000 are now members of the American Brotherhood Aimed Toward Education (ABATE), which has been credited as decisive in several races for the state legislature. Members do not meet on a regular basis, but they do periodically mobilize in local political contests to advance their one legislative purpose. Would Putnam's data pick up on this group? What about the intense but brief house-building activity for Habitat for Humanity?

Fourth, Putnam notes but leaves to the side the vast increase in Washington-based mailing list organizations over the past 30 years. He ignores them because they do not require members to do more than send in a check. This is not Tocquevillian democracy, but these organizations may be a highly efficient use of civic energy. The citizen who joins them may get the same civic payoff for less personal hassle. This is especially so if we conceive of politics as a set of public policies. The citizen may be able to influence government more satisfactorily with the annual membership in Sierra Club or the National Rifle Association than by attending the local club luncheons.

Of course, policy is a limited notion of government. Putnam assumes a broader view that makes personal investment part of the payoff of citizenship. Participation is its own reward. But even our greatest leaders—Jefferson, for one—complained about the demands of public life and, like Dorothy in liberating Oz, were forever trying to get back home. Getting government off our backs was a theme Patrick Henry evoked. And who is to say that getting back home is an unworthy desire?

The concept of politics has broadened enormously in 30 years. Not only is the personal political (the politics of male-female relations, the politics of smoking and not smoking), but the professional or occupational is also political. A woman physician or accountant can feel that she is doing politics—providing a role model and fighting for recognition of women's equality with men—every time she goes to work. The same is true for African American bank executives or gay and lesbian military officers.

The decline of the civic in its conventional forms, then, does not demonstrate the decline of civic-mindedness. The "political" does not necessarily depend on social connectedness: Those membership dues to the NRA are political. Nor does it even depend on organized groups at all: Wearing a "Thank you for not smoking" button is political. The political may be intense and transient: Think of the thousands of people who have joined class action suits against producers of silicone breast implants or Dalkon shields or asbestos insulation.

Let us assume, for argument's sake, that there has been a decrease in civic involvement. Still, the rhetoric of decline in American life should send up a red flag. For the socially concerned intellectual, this is as much off-the-rack rhetoric as its mirror opposite, the rhetoric of progress, is for the ebullient technocrat. Any notion of "decline" has to take for granted some often arbitrary baseline. Putnam's baseline is the 1940s and 1950s when the "long civic generation"—people born between 1910 and 1940—came into their own. But this generation shared the powerful and unusual experience of four years of national military mobilization on behalf of what nearly everyone came to accept as a good cause. If Putnam had selected, say, the 1920s as a baseline, would he have given us a similar picture of decline?

Unlikely. Intellectuals of the 1920s wrung their hands about the fate of democracy, the decline of voter turnout, the "eclipse of the public," as John Dewey put it or "the phantom public" in Walter Lippmann's terms. They had plenty of evidence, particularly in the record of voter turnout, so low in 1920 and 1924 (49 percent each year) that even our contemporary nadir of 1988 (50.3 percent) does not quite match it. Putnam himself reports that people born from 1910 to 1940 appear more civic than those born before as well as those born after. There is every reason to ask why this group was so civic rather than why later groups are not.

The most obvious answer is that this group fought in or came of age during World War II. This is also a group that voted overwhelmingly for Franklin D. Roosevelt and observed his leadership in office over a long period. Presidents exercise a form of moral leadership that sets a norm or standard about what kind of a life people should lead. A critic has complained that Ronald Reagan made all Americans a little more stupid in the 1980s—and I don't think this is a frivolous jibe. Reagan taught us that even the president can make a philosophy of the principle, "My mind's made up, don't confuse me with the facts." He taught us that millions will pay deference to someone who regularly and earnestly confuses films with lived experience.

The "long civic generation" had the advantages of a "good war" and a good president. Later generations had no wars or ones about which there was less massive mobilization and much less consensus—Korea and, more divisively, Vietnam. They had presidents of dubious moral leadership—notably Nixon, whom people judged even in the glow of his latter-day "rehabilitation" as the worst moral leader of all post-World War II presidents. So if there has been civic disengagement in the past decades, it may be not a decline but a return to normalcy.

If the rhetoric of decline raises one red flag, television as an explanation raises another. Some of the most widely heralded "media effects" have by now been thoroughly discredited. The yellow press had little or nothing to do with getting us into the Spanish-American War. Television news had little or nothing to do with turning Americans against the Vietnam War. Ronald Reagan's mastery of the media did not make him an unusually popular president in his first term (in fact, for his first 30 months in office he was unusually unpopular).

Indeed, the TV explanation doesn't fit Putnam's data very well. Putnam defines the long civic generation as the cohort born from 1910 to 1940, but then he also shows that the downturn in civic involvement began "rather abruptly" among people "born in the early 1930s." In other words, civic decline began with people too young to have served in World War II but too old to have seen TV growing up. If we take 1954 as a turning-point year–the first year when more than half of American households had TV sets—Americans born from 1930 to 1936 were in most cases already out of the home and the people born the next four years were already in high school by the time TV is likely to have become a significant part of their lives. Of course, TV may have influenced this group later, in the 1950s and early 1960s when they were in their twenties and thirties. But this was a time when Americans watched many fewer hours of television, averaging five hours a day rather than the current seven, and the relatively benign TV fare of that era was not likely to induce fearfulness of the outside world.

All of my speculations here and most of Putnam's assume that one person has about the same capacity for civic engagement as the next. But what if some people have decidedly more civic energy than others as a function of, say, personality? And what if these civic spark plugs have been increasingly recruited into situations where they are less civically engaged?

Putnam accords this kind of explanation some attention in asking whether women who had been most involved in civic activities were those most likely to take paying jobs, "thus lowering the average level of civic engagement among the remaining homemakers and raising the average among women in the workplace." Putnam says he "can find little evidence" to support this hypothesis, but it sounds plausible.

A similar hypothesis makes sense in other domains. Since World War II, higher education has mushroomed. Of people born from 1911 to 1920, 13.5 percent earned college or graduate degrees; of those born during the next decade, 18.8 percent; but of people born from 1931 to 1950, the figure grew to between 26 and 27 percent. A small but increasing number of these college students have been recruited away from their home communities to elite private colleges; some public universities also began after World War II to draw from a national pool of talent. Even colleges with local constituencies increasingly have recruited faculty nationally, and the faculty have shaped student ambitions toward national law, medical, and business schools and corporate traineeships. If students drawn to these programs are among the people likeliest in the past to have been civic spark plugs, we have an alternative explanation for civic decline.

Could there be a decline? Better to conceive the changes we find as a new environment of civic and political activity with altered institutional openings for engagement. Television is a part of the ecology, but in complex ways. It is a significant part of people's use of their waking hours, but it may be less a substitute for civic engagement than a new and perhaps insidious form of it. TV has been more politicized since the late 1960s than ever before. In 1968, *60 Minutes* began as the first money-making entertainment news program, spawning a dozen imitators. *All in the Family* in 1971 became the first prime-time sitcom to routinely take on controversial topics, from homosexuality to race to women's rights. *Donahue* was first syndicated in 1979, *Oprah* followed in 1984, and after them, the deluge.

If TV does nonetheless discourage civic engagement, what aspect of TV is at work? Is it the most "serious," civic-minded, and responsible part—the news? The latest blast at the news media, James Fallows's *Breaking the News*, picks up a familiar theme that the efforts of both print and broadcast journalists since the 1960s to get beneath the surface of events has led to a journalistic presumption that no politician can be trusted and that the story behind the story will be invariably sordid.

All of this talk needs to be tempered with the reminder that, amidst the many disappointments of politics between 1965 and 1995, this has been an era of unprecedented advances in women's rights, gay and lesbian liberation, African American opportunity, and financial security for the elderly. It has witnessed the first consumers' movement since the 1930s, the first environmental movement since the turn of the century, and public health movements of great range and achievement, especially in antismoking. It has also been a moment of grassroots activism on the right as well as on the left, with the pro-life movement and the broad-gauge political involvement both locally and nationally of the Christian right. Most of this activity was generated outside of political parties and state institutions. Most of this activity was built on substantial "grassroots" organizing. It is not easy to square all of this with an account of declining civic virtue.

Robert Putnam has offered us a lot to think about, with clarity and insight. Still, he has not yet established the decline in civic participation, let alone provided a satisfying explanation for it. What he has done is to reinvigorate inquiry on a topic that could scarcely be more important.

LESSONS FROM HULL HOUSE
FOR THE CONTEMPORARY URBAN UNIVERSITY

IRA HARKAVY & JOHN L. PUCKETT*

This article presents a rationale for reinventing the American university to become once again a mission-oriented institution. With particular attention to social work and the social sciences, we trace the origins of that rationale to Jane Addams and her colleagues in Chicago. Historical analysis not only indicates that progressive change can occur, but it also is useful in revealing and clarifying deeply embedded impediments to change. We also describe a general strategy of organizational structures, activities, and mechanisms being developed at the University of Pennsylvania to help enable the "neo-Progressive" reconstruction of the university through academically based community service.

Since 1981 and the publication of Ernest Boyer and Fred Hechinger's *Higher Learning in the Nation's Service*, there has been a growing criticism that "higher education in America is suffering from a loss of overall direction, a nagging feeling that it is no longer at the vital center of the nation's work."[1] With the publication of Derek Bok's 1990 book, *Universities and the Future of America*, that criticism reached a new level of urgency and significance. From the paramount insider position within the higher educational system, Harvard's president concluded that "most universities continue to do their least impressive work on the very subjects where society's need for greater knowledge and better education is most acute."[2] Bok's conclusion (reached near the end of his Harvard presidency) necessarily leads to the further conclusion that the American university has failed to do what it is supposed to do. In short, esotericism has triumphed over public philosophy, narrow scholasticism over humane scholarship.

Urban universities are now compelled to work with their neighbors for their own immediate and long-term self-interest. There are four reasons why universities should be involved in urban revitalization efforts. The first reason is institutional self-interest, including the safety, cleanliness, and attractiveness of the physical setting. Each of these contributes to the campus ambience and to the recruitment and retention of faculty, students, and staff. Needless to say, high walls and imposing gates cannot shield students, faculty members, or administrators from the disturbing reality that surrounds the urban campus.

The second reason involves a more indirect effect on institutional self-interest. It includes the costs (financial, public relations, and political) to the institution that result from a retreat from the community, as well as the benefits that accrue from active, effective engagement. As Lee Benson and Ira Harkavy have noted:

> As conditions in society continue to deteriorate, universities will face increased public scrutiny (witness the Congressional hearings chaired by Representative John Dingell of Michigan last year). The scrutiny is bound to intensify as America focuses on resolving its deep and pervasive societal problems amid continuously expanding global competition. Institutions of higher education will increasingly be held to new and demanding standards that evaluate performance on the basis of direct and short-run societal benefit. In addition, public, private, and foundation support will be more than ever based on that standard, and it will become increasingly clear to colleges and universities that "altruism pays"—in fact, that altruism is practically an imperative for institutional development and improvement.[3]

The third reason involves the advancement of knowledge, teaching, and human welfare through academically based community service focused on improving the quality of life in the local community. The benefits that can emerge from this approach are the integration of research, teaching, and service; the interaction of faculty members and graduate and undergraduate students from across the campus; the connection of projects involving participatory action research with student and staff volunteer activities; and the promotion of civic consciousness, value-oriented thinking, and a moral approach to issues of public concern among undergraduates. Historically, universities have missed an extraordinary opportunity to work with their communities and to engage in better research, teaching, and service. The separation of universities from society, their aloofness from real-world problems, has deprived universities of contact with a necessary source of genuine creativity and academic vitality.

Promoting civic consciousness, we believe, is the core component of the fourth reason for significant university involvement with the community. Sheldon Hackney has described this as the "institution's obligation to be a good citizen, and its pedagogic duty to provide models of responsible citizenship for its students."[4] In other words, universities and colleges have, along with schools and religious institutions, a special responsibility to be moral institutions, exemplifying the highest civic and character-building values of society. At the heart of civic responsibility is the concept of neighborliness—caring about and assisting those living in close proximity to us. As an institution, a university's actions and inactions express morality; a university's indifference or civic engagement teaches lessons to its students and to society. This citizenship and character-building role, of course, was at the very center of the American college. However, the didactic approach to citizenship education and morality employed by its predecessors would today be both off-putting and at odds with the openness of the modern university.

Collectively, these arguments indicate that it is now both necessary and mutually beneficial for urban universities to work to revitalize their local communities. The complex problems of urban society necessitate a radical reorientation and reinvention of the urban American university to become, once again, a mission-oriented institution devoted to the use of reason to improve the human condition. That mission was the driving force behind the organization of the modern research university in the late nineteenth century. University presidents of the Progressive Era worked to transform the American university into a major national institution capable of meeting the needs of a rapidly changing and increasingly complex society. Imbued with a boundless optimism and a belief that scientific and social-scientific knowledge could change the world for the better, they saw universities as leading the way toward an effective and humane reorganization of society. Progressive academics viewed the city as their arena for study and action. The city was the site of significant societal transformations; the center of political corruption, poverty, crime, and cultural conflict; and a ready source of data and information. It was, according to Richmond Mayo-Smith of Columbia University, "the national laboratory of social science, just as hospitals are of medical science."[5] As Jane Addams and her colleagues in Chicago illustrated, the city was also the place in which academics could combine social science and social reform.

Social Science and Social Work: The Progressive Tradition

Social work as a field of social scientific inquiry gained impetus from Hull House, the social settlement founded by Jane Addams and Ellen Starr on Chicago's West Side in 1889.[6] The philosophy and programs of Hull House were modeled after Toynbee Hall, the first settlement house, established in 1884 by the Anglican vicar Samuel A. Barnett in London's East End. Adopting a multifaceted institutional approach to the social problems of the immigrant groups in the Nineteenth Ward, the Hull House residents offered activities and services along four lines, designated by Addams as the social, educational, humanitarian, and civic. The residents' programs included college extension classes, clubs and literary programs, ethnic festivals, art exhibits, recreational activities and neighborhood shower baths, a summer camp program, a cooperative boarding house for working women, and kindergarten, visiting-nurse, and legal services. Moreover, Hull House was a site for labor union activities; a forum for social, political, and economic reform; and a center for social science research.

Regarding its research function, as Addams once noted, "The settlements antedated by three years the first sociology departments in universities and by ten years the establishment of the first foundations for social research."[7]

In *Twenty Years at Hull-House*, Addams emphasized the benefits that accrued to the activist social worker from engagement with the community and its problems. She wrote of "a fast-growing number of cultivated young people who have no recognized outlet for their active faculties. They hear constantly of the great social maladjustment, but no way is provided for them to change it, and their uselessness hangs upon them heavily. . . . 'There is nothing after disease, indigence and guilt so fatal to life itself as the want of a proper outlet for active faculties.'"[8] For women, the problem of lacking constructive social outlets for their reform impulses was acutely felt, constricted as they were by Victorian gender roles. Viewed as an expression of "social motherhood," settlement work provided a satisfactory professional outlet for women that was not incommensurate with established gender roles and practices, particularly the idea of the "woman's sphere." Addams acknowledged this when she remarked that "many women today are failing properly to discharge their duties to their own families and households simply because they fail to see that as society grows more complicated, it is necessary that woman shall extend her sense of responsibility to many things outside of her home, if only in order to preserve the home in its entirety."[9]

For activist-oriented young men and women of Addams's generation, settlement work constituted, in Addams's apt phrase, a "subjective necessity." In 1889, Starr told a friend that "Jane's idea, which she puts very much to the front and on no account will give up, is that [the settlement] is more for the people who do it than for the other class."[10] Addams herself later wrote, "I hope it will never be forgotten in Chicago, at least where Hull House feels somewhat responsible for the Toynbee Hall idea, that Toynbee Hall was first projected as an aid and outlet to educated young men. The benefit to East Londoners was then regarded as almost secondary, and the benefit has always been held as strictly mutual."[11]

In 1895, Addams and the residents of Hull House—notably, Florence Kelley, Agnes Holbrook, and Julia Lathrop—published *Hull-House Maps and Papers*, a sociological investigation of the neighborhood immediately to the east of Hull House; in Addams's words, it was a record of "certain phases of neighborhood life with which the writers have been familiar."[12] Inspired by Charles Booth's *Life and Labour of the People in London*, the Hull House residents compiled detailed maps of demographic and social characteristics and produced richly descriptive accounts of life and work in a poor immigrant neighborhood.[13] Theirs was not dispassionate scholarship, as evidenced by Kelley's poignant advocacy of sweatshop laborers, whose "reward of work at their trade is grinding poverty, ending only in death or escape to some more hopeful occupation. Within the trade there has been and can be no improvement in wages while tenement-house manufacture is tolerated. On the contrary, there seems to be no limit to the deterioration now in progress."[14]

Closely associated with Hull House in its early years were the male sociologists at the University of Chicago, who acknowledged that "it was Addams and Hull-House who were the leader and leading institution in Chicago in the 1890s, not the University of Chicago."[15] Indeed, *Hull-House Maps and Papers* oriented the Chicago School of Sociology to urban studies and strongly influenced the direction taken by that department for the next 40 years.[16] The changing relationship of Addams and her Hull House colleagues with the Chicago sociologists from the 1890s to the late 1910s mirrored the American university's transition from an outwardly directed, service-centered institution to an inwardly directed, discipline-centered institution. It was also a marker of the separation of knowledge production from knowledge use, indeed, of social science from social reform, by the end of the Progressive Era.

In its early years, the University of Chicago demonstrated that by doing good, a research university could do very well. When Chicago's first president, William Rainey Harper, described the mission of his newly minted university as "service for mankind wherever mankind is, whether within scholastic walls or without those walls and in the world at large,"[17] he expressed a pervasive attitude of Progressive Era academics that "scholarship, teaching, and public service were fully compatible."[18] As Steven Diner has written, Harper and his Progressive colleagues also realized that the university's funding was contingent on the public's goodwill:

> When the University of Chicago opened in 1892, universities were still quite new and were just beginning to explore the possibilities of service to their society. This was not a time for introspection or self-criticism, but an era of growth and experimentation. Nothing in the experience of American universities thus far indicated that public service might harm the university; but the experience of the antebellum college suggested the shortcomings of a remote seminary of learning for its own sake. Its detachment from public service had resulted in neither solid scholarship, sound teaching, nor popular support. Indeed, most university presidents of the early twentieth century concluded that service was the only way to win support for the advancement and dissemination of knowledge on the highest level.[19]

The Chicago School of Sociology was created in this nexus of "serving society by advancing intellectual inquiry."[20] In the early years of the Chicago School, no invidious distinctions were made between the applied sociology pursued by Addams and the Hull House residents and the academic research of the first generation of University of Chicago sociologists. Indeed, the two groups had a close working relationship, grounded in personal friendships, mutual respect, and shared social philosophy. Four men of the early Chicago School—Albion Small, Charles Henderson, Charles Zeublin, and George Vincent—were ministers or ministers manqué, intellectual Social Gospelers with strong civic commitments. (The exceptions, with limited theological proclivities, were George Herbert Mead and William I. Thomas.) Like the women of Hull House, the Chicago sociologists were "social activists *and* social scientists."[21] Action social research, Chicago style, encompassed scholarly documentation of a social problem and lobbying of politicians and local community groups to obtain action.[22]

Recent feminist scholarship takes issue with the charge that the social science of Hull House and the early Chicago School was unscientific. Mary Jo Deegan, for example, argues that *Hull-House Maps and Papers* "established the Chicago tradition of studying the city and its inhabitants" and provided "the major substantive interests of Chicago sociologists": a focus on immigrants, poverty, and occupational structure. She asserts that Robert Park and Ernest W. Burgess, leaders of the Chicago School's second generation, adopted the research concerns and methods of Addams and her colleagues even as they staked their own prior claim as the founders of urban sociology.[23]

After 1915, Chicago Sociology increasingly distanced itself from social reform, notwithstanding the continued focus on the form, structure, and problems of city living. Increasingly, that focus was circumscribed by a natural science model and an underlying commitment to "the detached and objective study of society," which "allowed no room for an ameliorative approach."[24] Park and Burgess emphasized "urban studies . . . within a scientific framework."[25]

The career of Sophonisba Breckinridge is indicative of the attenuation of action-oriented, reformist social science in Chicago in the decades before America's entry into World War I. When Breckinridge enrolled in the University of Chicago's Department of Political Science in 1894, she entered a Progressive world where scientific rigor was deemed compatible with social problem solving.[26] According to Ellen Fitzpatrick, "All accepted the notion that scholars had a duty to address contemporary problems in their work. All agreed on the importance of empirical research. And all shared the belief that careful scientific investigation was a *sine qua non* for intelligent reform."[27] Unequal gender relations, however, stymied the entry of women with doctoral degrees (in Breckinridge's case, a doctor of philosophy awarded in 1902, a doctor of jurisprudence awarded in 1904) into the social science professoriat at the University of Chicago. The new feminist historiography has documented an emerging nexus of gender, social reform, and social science at the beginning of the twentieth century: after 1904, women would be relegated to the margins of the university, the confines of the newly opened Department of Household Administration, "a special intellectual province for women," where Breckinridge would find a home as an assistant professor. Yet, her training had prepared her for a headier challenge: "While the political scientist pursued research that resulted in an essay entitled 'Industrial Conditions of Women Workers in Chicago Illustrated by the Packing Houses' in 1905–06, her colleagues in the household administration department wrote papers such as 'The Relative Digestibility of Animal and Vegetable Albumen,' 'Loss of Nutrients in Beans Due to Soaking,' 'Comparative Richness of Gelatin-Yielding Material in Old and Young Animals,' and 'Pectin Bodies in Fruit Juices and the Effect of Temperatures and Density in the Setting of Fruit Jelly.' Such concerns were far afield from the principles of law, political science, and political economy."[28]

In 1909, Breckinridge was appointed dean of the Chicago School of Civics and Philanthropy, an independent social work and research training center funded by the Russell Sage Foundation. Over the next decade she and her colleague Edith Abbott, both of whom took up residence in Hull House, directed extensive surveys in such areas as housing, stockyards, juvenile court, and public-school truancy and nonattendance. The merger of the School of Civics and Philanthropy with the University of Chicago in 1920 led to both women's appointment as associate professors of social economy in the newly created School of Social Service Administration. There, Breckinridge and Abbott "sought to create a new setting within the university that would permit them to address public issues and advance social research. In so doing, they helped professionalize social work, a field they first adopted and then worked to make their own."[29] Yet, theirs was a Pyrrhic victory. The feminization of professional social work marked it as the last enclave of social reform. As noted by Ellen Lagemann, the implications of the rift between social reform and social science at the University of Chicago were considerable:

> As a result, the new departmental lines drawn there created divisions, not just at Chicago, but also elsewhere, between theoretical, "objective," academic social research, on the one hand, and more reformist, political, and applied social work, on the other. The structural and intellectual divisions thus created were soon compounded by gender divisions that rapidly took on hierarchical status distinctions as well. Sociology, which came increasingly to be dominated by men, was more and more seen as a source for insights to be tested and applied by "social workers," most of whom were women; and settings for "social work," including social settlements like Hull House, were more and more seen as places to which (male) university sociologists might send students to collect data, which the sociologists and not the social workers would then analyze in a university laboratory and elaborate into theory.[30]

Applied social science largely vanished from the academy after 1918. World War I was the catalyst for a full-scale retreat from action-oriented, reformist social science. The brutality and horror of that conflict ended the buoyant optimism and faith in human progress and societal improvement that had marked the Progressive Era. American academics were not immune to the general disillusion with progress. One economist wrote that "it would perhaps be an exaggeration to say that the European war . . . has rendered every text in social science thus far published out of date, but it would not be a very great exaggeration."[31] Indeed, despair led many social scientists to retreat into a narrow scientistic approach: "They began to talk of the need for a harder science, a science of facts and numbers that could moderate or dispel the pervasive irrational conflicts of political life."[32] Scholarly inquiry directed toward creating a better society was increasingly deemed inappropriate. While faith in the expert and in expert knowledge was carried on from the Progressive Era, it was now divorced from its reformist roots. The dominant conception of science was clear and simple: it was what physical scientists and engineers did.[33] "Sociology as a science is not interested in making the world a better place in which to live, in encouraging beliefs, in spreading information, in dispensing news, in setting forth impressions of life, in leading the multitudes or in guiding the ship of state," Chicago sociologist William F. Ogburn declared. "Science is interested directly in one thing only, to wit, discovering new knowledge."[34] The retreat from applied social science in the 1920s crystallized a tendency that Addams had discerned at the turn of the century:

> We recall that the first colleges of the Anglo-Saxon race were established to educate religious teachers. For a long time it was considered the religious mission of the educated to prepare the mass of the people for life beyond the grave. Knowledge dealt largely in theology, but it was ultimately to be applied, and the test of the successful graduate, after all, was not his learning, but his power to save souls. As the college changed from teaching theology to teaching secular knowledge the test of its success should have shifted from the power to save men's souls to the power to adjust them in healthful relations to nature and their fellow men. But the college failed to do this, and made the test of its success the mere collecting and disseminating of knowledge, elevating the means into an end and falling in love with its own achievement.[35]

The Retreat from Social Reform: Structural Conflicts and Contradictions in the Academy

Throughout the American university, a strong tradition developed that separated scholarly research from the goal of helping to create a better society. The political and cultural dynamics of post–World

War I scientistic social science were reflected in the burgeoning field of psychiatric social work. In the 1920s, psychiatric social workers staked their claim to scientific legitimacy and professional status by defining their knowledge base as psychoanalytic theory and adopting a therapeutic, ostensibly scientific, approach that emphasized clients' social-psychological adjustment rather than social amelioration. Casework, if not Freudian psychology, also dominated other subspecialities of social work—for example, family casework and child guidance—and during the twenties, that approach became the raison d'être of the profession as a whole. University schools of social work, which numbered 28 by 1929, and social work education were unified "around the idea of generic casework."[36] Professional social work training did not include preparation for a career in settlement work. The local Community Chest, which gained control of settlement house budgets, dampened reform; only in non-Chest cities such as Chicago and New York were settlement workers able to sustain some reform activity. Not surprisingly, that activity was associated with the charismatic leadership of Addams of Hull House, Graham Taylor of Chicago Commons, and Lillian Wald of Henry Street Settlement, and it was not broadly institutionalized.[37]

Between the wars the reform impulse was further weakened by the fact that every major university formed similar and increasingly specialized departments, and a faculty member's primary source of identification and allegiance became his or her discipline, not the university. Since World War II, a steady infusion of federal funds allocated to individual researchers working under departmental auspices has accelerated the growth of a disciplinary-based reward system.[38] Departmental and disciplinary divisions have served to increase further the isolation of universities from society. A 1982 Organization for Economic Cooperation and Development report entitled *The University and the Community* noted, "Communities have problems, universities have departments."[39] Beyond being a criticism of universities, that statement neatly indicates why universities have not contributed as they should. Quite simply, their unintegrated structures work against understanding and helping to solve highly complex human and societal problems. This tendency has resulted in less effective research, teaching, and service. Indeed, all three missions have been impoverished by what might be termed a "false trichotomization." For example, that trichotomy has contributed to an enormous imbalance in the production of knowledge.

Dazzling advances have occurred in university-based research in science and technology. New ideas, concepts, technologies, approaches, and techniques are developed with ever-increasing rapidity. Although designed to improve human welfare, the application of scientific advances too frequently results in new and more forbidding problems. The wondrous possibilities of new medical technologies, for example, have become distorted, helping to create a health care "system" unresponsive to the "low-tech" preventive needs of the vast majority of citizens.[40]

How to make rational use of science and technology should be a primary focus of university research. It should be a primary focus because it is a primary problem facing human beings in the late twentieth century. If universities had an integrated mission—the creative, dynamic, and systemic integration of research, teaching, and service—intellectual resources would be significantly devoted to developing humane applications of scientific knowledge to help those living in conditions of profound poverty and neglect.

Integrating research, teaching, and service will be particularly difficult because of a fundamental contradiction in the structure of the American research university itself, a contradiction that occurred with its very creation. That is, the American research university was a product of a combination of the German research university and the American college. Daniel Coit Gilman, the founder of Johns Hopkins and central architect of the late nineteenth-century research university, in fact, claimed that one of his proudest accomplishments was "a school of science grafted on one of the oldest and most conservative classical colleges." Although referring specifically to the merger of the Sheffield Scientific School with Yale College, Gilman felt that this achievement exemplified his contribution to American higher education.[41]

Gilman did not make reference to the institutional contradiction that necessarily derived from a merger of two markedly different entities. The research university, on the one hand, was dedicated to specialized scholarship, and it was through the production of specialized inquiry and studies that the university provided service. For the American college, on the other hand, general education, character building, and civic education were the central purposes. The goal was to serve society by cultivating in young people, to use Benjamin Franklin's phrase, "an *Inclination* join'd with an *Ability* to serve."[42] The research university has, of course, dominated this merger, creating an ethos and culture that rewards specialized study rather than more general scholarship and the education of the next generation for moral, civic, and intellectual leadership.

Given the structural contradictions built into the American university, and nearly a century of increasing specialization, fragmentation of knowledge, and separation of scholarship from direct service to society, it will not be easy for higher educational institutions to effectively integrate research, teaching, and service and substantively increase their contributions to knowledge and human welfare. Certainly the significant problems facing American society and the pressures to change that are coming from a variety of constituents will mean that some new directions will have to be forged. But will they be the right directions, directions that enhance the university's ability to carry out its mission? And will these new directions be significant and basic enough to reduce the impediments to progress that hinder the creative, dynamic, systemic integration of research, teaching, and service?

Academically Based Community Service: Toward Revitalizing Universities and Communities

In three key respects, Hull House provides a model and inspiration for work being undertaken at the University of Pennsylvania. First, the Hull House residents emphasized amelioration and reform. Although they acted too frequently for rather than with their neighbors, they believed in and espoused the ideal of empowering community residents to address social problems.[43] Second, as indicated by *Hull-House Maps and Papers*, their ameliorative, reformist approach to social science integrated the production of new knowledge and the uses made of that knowledge.[44] Third, Addams and her Chicago colleagues recognized that the social problems of the city are complex, deeply rooted, interdependent phenomena that require holistic ameliorative strategies and support mechanisms if they are to be solved. The settlement house provided, albeit on a small neighborhood scale, a comprehensive institutional response to social problems.

Our approach has been to advance academically based community service—service rooted in and intrinsically tied to teaching and research. Among other things, it is an approach that seeks to integrate the research, teaching, and service missions of the university, while also spurring intellectual integration across disciplines. We have found that the very nature of concrete, real-world problems, particularly the problems of the university's immediate geographic community, encourages genuine interschool and interdisciplinary cooperation. No single component of the university can significantly help understand and reduce the complex, myriad, interrelated problems of the urban poor. In combination, however, advances can be made. And that combination must go beyond the various components of the university. It necessarily must also include other institutions, such as public schools, businesses, unions, community organizations, government, and voluntary associations.

Our goal is to develop an innovative model of how higher educational institutions can fruitfully and simultaneously work together to advance knowledge and human welfare. The work builds on John Dewey's proposition that knowledge and learning can be most effectively advanced through working to solve immediate, strategic societal problems. For Dewey, "Thinking begins in . . . a *forked-road* situation, a situation which is ambiguous, which presents a dilemma, which proposes alternatives."[45] In effect, our forked-road situation is the intellectual problem of what can be done to overcome the pervasive problems affecting the people of West Philadelphia.

To a significant extent, our work can be viewed as testing the validity of Dewey's proposition about how we learn and think. Even more fundamentally, it tests the validity of Francis Bacon's central proposition that knowledge advances most effectively when the "relief of man's estate" is made the true end of knowledge. In 1620, Bacon put the argument as follows: "Lastly, I would address a general admonition to all, that they consider what are the true ends of knowledge, and that they seek it not either for pleasure of the mind, or for contention, or for superiority to others, or for profit, or fame, or power, or for any of these inferior things; but for the benefit and use of life; and that they perfect and govern it in charity. For it was from lust of power that the angels fell, from lust of knowledge that men fell; but of charity there can be no excess, neither did angel or man ever come in danger by it."[46]

How are we to know whether a Deweyan-Baconian approach is indeed superior to the traditional, scholastic model that dominates the American university? For Bacon the test was simple: by their fruits shall we judge modes of inquiry and thought. In other words, to what extent does research change the world for the better? In *Reconstruction in Philosophy*, Dewey praised Bacon for his brilliant analysis of the sociology of knowledge and his call for cooperative research: "To Bacon, error had been produced and perpetuated by social influences, and trust must be discovered by social agencies organized for that purpose. . . . The great need [Bacon proclaimed] is the organization of co-operative research, whereby men attack nature collectively and the work of inquiry is carried on continuously from generation to generation."[47]

Since 1985, the University of Pennsylvania has been involved in a broadly based community project to help improve the quality of life in West Philadelphia. The project has two main organizational components. With staff offices in the West Philadelphia community, the West Philadelphia Improvement Corps (WEPIC) represents a coalition of university faculty, staff, undergraduate and graduate students, and West Philadelphia teachers, students, and school administrators. WEPIC provides a year-round program that currently involves over 2,000 children, their parents, and community members in education and cultural workshops, recreation, job training, and community improvement and service activities. The program is coordinated by the West Philadelphia Partnership, a mediating, nonprofit, community-based organization composed of major institutions (including the University of Pennsylvania) and local community groups, in conjunction with the Greater Philadelphia Urban Affairs Coalition and the Philadelphia School District. The recently established Center for Community Partnerships at the University of Pennsylvania coordinates and provides opportunities for participatory action research projects conducted under the aegis of WEPIC.

This approach is quite different from strategies undertaken in the 1960s, when escalating poverty, crime, violence, racial strife, and student protest demanded a response from urban universities. Federal and foundation-supported programs, notably, urban extension programs, urban studies centers, and urban observatories, were created to link university research and technical assistance to urban concerns. The goal, according to Paul Ylvisaker of the Ford Foundation, whose 1958 speech signaled the beginning of an era of reengagement, was to create urban equivalents to the Agricultural Extension Service. Typically, these efforts were not partnerships, that is, mutually beneficial relationships between the city and the university. For all the public and private funds expended, relatively little of substance was accomplished, and a genuine and acute disappointment about the level of university performance set in.[48] The development of a mediating organization that encourages partnerships and the pooling of institutional and community resources has helped the University of Pennsylvania to sustain and expand its contribution to the WEPIC coalition.[49]

WEPIC has reinvented and updated an old notion—that the neighborhood school can effectively serve as the core neighborhood institution, an institution that both provides comprehensive services and galvanizes other community institutions and groups. That idea motivated the early settlement workers, who recognized the centrality of the neighborhood school in community life and its potential as a catalytic site for community stabilization and improvement. At the turn of the century, settlement pioneers mediated the transfer of social, health, vocational, and recreational services to the public schools of major American cities.[50] Dewey's notion of "the school as social center" reflected the vision of Addams and other settlement workers that urban public schools would incorporate settlement ideas and functions.[51] The school and the curriculum would become, in effect, focal points of neighborhood development, improvement, and stabilization. Although Dewey did not make it explicit, this idea is consistent with his general theory that the community-centered school would help catalyze the development of a "cosmopolitan local community."[52] For the neighborhood school to be truly comprehensive, to function as a genuine community center, to help transform its catchment area into a cosmopolitan local community, however, it needs additional human resources and support.

In 1929, near the end of her extraordinary career, Addams wrote that the social settlement served the same function as the university, but the settlement's impact encompassed a broader and needier population:

> It was the function of the settlements to bring into the circle of knowledge and full life, men and women who might otherwise be left outside. Some of these men and women were outside simply because of their ignorance, some of them because they led lives of hard work that narrowed their interests, and others because they were unaware of the possibilities of life and needed a friendly touch to awaken them. The colleges and universities had made a little inner circle of illuminated space beyond which there stretched a region of darkness, and it was the duty of the settlements to draw into the light those who were out of it. It seemed to us that our mission was just as important as that of either the university or the college.[53]

The key challenge today, however, is not to have social settlements function as universities but rather to have universities function as perennial, deeply rooted settlements, providing illuminated space for their communities as they conduct their mission of producing and transmitting knowledge to advance human welfare and to develop theories that have broad utility and application. As comprehensive institutions, we would argue, universities are uniquely qualified to provide broadly based, sustained, comprehensive support. The community school project itself becomes the organizing catalyst enabling the university to function as a social settlement as one innovative, humanistic strategy to better perform its traditional mission, as well as to better perform its role as a cosmopolitan civic university.

Reports from the Field: Communal Participatory Action Research in West Philadelphia

As we noted previously, a broadly based coalition of agencies, organizations, and institutions today is a sine qua non for school and community revitalization in collapsing urban centers. If it is to be an effective partner in this coalition, the university must institutionalize a strategy that engages academic resources in ways that integrate and strengthen its missions of teaching, research, and service. The strategy we have chosen is to develop a permanent, humanistic natural laboratory in West Philadelphia. We do not treat West Philadelphia as a laboratory for experimentation on poor people, that is, as a site for study rather than assistance. Our approach emphasizes a mutually beneficial, democratic relationship between academics and nonacademics. In that relationship, academic researchers learn from and with the community, do research collaboratively with and not on people, and contribute to the solution of significant community problems. Put another way, we believe that West Philadelphia, and the community school in particular, should serve as a natural social and cultural laboratory in which communal participatory action research functions as a humanistic strategy for the advancement of knowledge and human welfare.[54]

Participatory action research is "a form of action research in which professional social researchers operate as full collaborators with members of organizations in studying and transforming those organizations. It is an on-going organizational learning process, a research approach that emphasizes co-learning, participation, and organizational transformation."[55] Both participatory action research and communal participatory action research are directed toward problems in the real world and are concerned with application. They differ in the degree to which they are continuous, comprehensive, and beneficial and necessary to the organization or community studied and the university. The participatory action research process is exemplified in the work of William Foote Whyte and his associates at Cornell University to advance industrial democracy in the worker cooperatives of Mondragón, Spain.[56] Its considerable utility and theoretical significance notwithstanding, the research at Mondragón is not an institutional necessity for Cornell. By contrast, the University of Pennsylvania's enlightened self-interest is directly tied to the success of its research efforts in the West Philadelphia community, hence its emphasis on communal participatory action research. In short, proximity and a focus on problems that are institutionally significant to the university encourage sustained, continuous research involvement. A crucial issue, of course, is the degree to which these locally based research projects result in general knowledge. We would argue that "local" does not mean "parochial" and that the solution to local problems necessarily requires an understanding of national and global issues as well as an effective use and development of theory. Two research projects in West Philadelphia, one conducted by a physical anthropologist, another by a graduate student in communication studies, illustrate these propositions.

Francis Johnston, chairperson of the University of Pennsylvania's Department of Anthropology, carries out research in the Turner Nutritional Awareness Project, a joint community/university-sponsored participatory action research project at the John P. Turner Middle School that is designed to improve the nutritional status of the community. "The Project is comprehensive in scope, with components dealing with nutritional assessment, with instruction in concepts of nutrition, and with the collection of a broad range of related information, including such areas as knowledge, preferences, and attitudes concerning food, food streams within the neighborhood, and other sources of information (merchants, media, etc.)."[57] Turner School teachers participate in the design and presentation of the intervention. Sixth-grade Turner students participate in the nutrition education program, and, as seventh graders, they teach elementary school students about basic nutrition and healthy habits.[58]

In a recent study, Johnston and his students in an undergraduate anthropology course on "Biomedical Science and Human Adaptability" collected measurements of physical growth status and dietary intakes from 11- to 15-year-old African-American youths. Data on growth were collected on 136 individuals; for both sets of indicators, data were collected on 113. A nutrition software package was used to calculate the nutrient values of students' dietary intakes, and individual records were merged into a single data set for computer statistical analysis. Tabulations of the data supported the following conclusion: "Overall, the data indicate a population with a very high prevalence of obesity, and diets high in saturated fat and low in polyunsaturated fat. Also of potential concern is the indication of low intakes of zinc and high intakes of sodium. Given the increased health risks of urban African-Americans, these findings on young adolescents suggest the development of programs designed to improve diets and enhance health in general in this age group."[59]

Johnston's work with undergraduates further distinguishes the University of Pennsylvania's approach from other varieties of action research. Communal participatory action research extends to creating or restructuring academic courses to include an explicit community focus and action component. The assumption is that embedding community service into courses, research, and general intellectual discourse will lead to positive changes in the institutional climate, providing a linkage between service and education.

A dissertation study in the Annenberg School for Communication provides a second illustration of communal participatory action research. For 2 years, Eleanor Novek, a former professional journalist and editor, was involved at West Philadelphia High School, a WEPIC site, as a coteacher and researcher in the development of "an educational demonstration project, an urban high school English/journalism class which uses production of a community-focused newspaper as a strategy for the self-determination of young African Americans."[60]

Novek's research on self-determination and student empowerment built on Jürgen Habermas's theory of communicative action, elements of reference group theory (e.g., Robert Merton), and superordinate goal theory (Muzafer Sherif and Caroline Sherif), not only to interpret and to theorize from ethnographic data, but also simultaneously to shape the intervention strategies, effecting an ebb and flow of theory and action. The specific vehicle for this work was QWest, a school-based community newspaper project, each component of which was adjudicated and carried out by students. In a recent report of her study, Novek has constructed several criteria of self-determination on the basis of her theoretical perspective, and she provides a summary of evidence from participant observations and student writing to indicate the progress made in each category. Her description of risk taking and the crossing of social boundaries is a case in point:

> A shy young woman who never spoke up in class, not only obtained an interview with Ramona Africa, the lone survivor of the world-infamous MOVE bombing in May 1985, but also brought her to the school to address the whole class. A taciturn young man interested in rap music visited one of the largest African American radio stations in the city and interviewed a popular disc jockey on the air.

Another student took it upon himself to develop and distribute an attitude survey about the QWest project to class members. Two students applied for and won admission to a minority workshop for high school journalists—the first time any students from their school had participated. Another began freelancing sports reports for a community newspaper.[61]

As our examples are designed to suggest, genuine thinking has occurred in the forked-road situation of West Philadelphia, engendering new approaches to school and community development. We believe that we have made a good start. The interaction of faculty, staff, and students working at the same site, attempting to solve immediate realworld problems, has fostered an unprecedented degree of academic integration at the University of Pennsylvania and spurred the development of new organizational structures and mechanisms to encourage and coordinate academically based public service. We want to emphasize, however, just how extraordinarily difficult it is to change the university and its community. Even after more than 8 years, our work is still in a developing phase.

Conclusion

In this article, we have presented a rationale for reinventing the American university to become once again a mission-oriented institution. With particular attention to social work and the social sciences, we have traced the origins of that rationale to Jane Addams, the women of Hull House, and other Progressive Era social scientists qua social reformers. Historical analysis not only indicates that progressive change can occur, but it also is useful in revealing and clarifying impediments to change, for example, the entrenchment and longstanding dominance of narrowly scholastic social science. We have also described a general strategy of organizational structures, activities, and mechanisms developed at the University of Pennsylvania to help enable the "neo-Progressive" reconstruction of the university through academically based community service.

It is our contention that American social science should be about the "relief of man's estate." These endeavors should be about overcoming the urban crisis and preventing urban chaos. In his studies of creativity, psychologist Howard E. Gruber has emphasized the connection between individual creativity and a desire to solve real-world problems. Gruber's concept of "creative altruism," which we think has relevance for universities, highlights that connection with particular clarity: "We can envisage and identify cases of 'creative altruism,' in which a person displays extraordinary moral responsibility, devoting a significant portion of time and energy to some project transcending immediate need and experience. Creative altruism, when it goes the limit, strives to eliminate the cause of suffering, to change the world, to change the fate of the earth."[62]

Creative altruism imbued the social work and social science of Addams and the women of Hull House at the turn of the twentieth century. As we have indicated, their ideals and practice provided exemplars for the development of social work and sociology at the University of Chicago. We have argued that their humanistic, real-world, problem-solving approach to social science has strong potential to produce better teaching, better research, and better service than conventional social science. The "settlement idea," which has inspired our collective efforts at the University of Pennsylvania and other campuses and communities, is a legacy of the early history of American social work.[63] If the American university is to fulfill its promise and help create a decent and just society, it must give full-hearted, full-minded attention to solving our complex interrelated problems. The benefits of doing so would, we are convinced, be considerable for the university, social science, and the American city.

Notes

1. Ernest L. Boyer and Fred M. Hechinger, *Higher Learning in the Nation's Service* (Washington, D.C.: Carnegie Foundation for the Advancement of Teaching, 1981), p. 3.
2. Derek Bok, *Universities and the Future of America* (Durham, N.C.: Duke University Press, 1990), p. 122.
3. Lee Benson and Ira Harkavy, "Universities, Schools, and the Welfare State," *Education Week* (April 29, 1992), p. 27. Representative George E. Brown, Jr., chairman of the House Committee on Science, Space,

and Technology, and Representative Rick Boucher, chairman of the Subcommittee on Science for that committee, have sharply criticized the priorities of contemporary scientists and the academic research community, which they view as detached from broad societal concerns; see Colleen Cordes, "As Chairman of Key House Committee Restates His Vision, Scientists Worry," *Chronicle of Higher Education* (September 8, 1993), pp. A26–A28; Rick Boucher, "A Science Policy for the 21st Century," *Chronicle of Higher Education* (September 1, 1993), pp. B1–B2. The Senate Committee on Appropriations voices a similar complaint about the National Science Foundation, admonishing that agency to address "specific national goals" or face curtailment of its funding; see 103d Congress, Senate Report 103–137 (September 9, 1993), pp. 165–69.

4. Sheldon Hackney, "Universities and Schools: Hanging Together or Hanging Separately?" (address at Bank Street College, New York, May 2, 1992), printed in the University of Pennsylvania *Almanac* (May 12, 1992), p. 6.

5. As quoted in Barry D. Karl, *Charles E. Merriam and the Study of Politics* (Chicago: University of Chicago Press, 1974), p. 31.

6. See Kathryn Kish Sklar, "*Hull-House Maps and Papers:* Social Science as Women's Work in the 1890s," in *The Social Survey in Historical Perspective, 1880–1940*, ed. Martin Bulmer, Kevin Bales, and Kathryn Kish Sklar (New York: Cambridge University Press, 1991), pp. 111–47.

7. Jane Addams, "The Objective Value of a Social Settlement" (1893), in *The Social Thought of Jane Addams*, ed. Christopher Lasch (Indianapolis: Bobbs-Merrill, 1965), pp. 44–61; quotation from Jane Addams, *The Second Twenty Years at Hull-House: September 1909 to September 1929, with a Record of a Growing World Consciousness* (New York: Macmillan, 1930), p. 405, cited in Lela B. Costin, *Two Sisters for Social Justice: A Biography of Grace and Edith Abbott* (Urbana: University of Illinois Press, 1983), p. 45.

8. Jane Addams, *Twenty Years at Hull-House* (New York: Macmillan, 1910), pp. 118, 120.

9. As quoted in John H. Ehrenreich, *The Altruistic Imagination: A History of Social Work and Social Policy in the United States* (Ithaca, N.Y.: Cornell University Press, 1985), p. 35. See also Kathryn Kish Sklar, "Hull House in the 1890s: A Community of Women Reformers," *Signs: Journal of Women in Culture and Society* 10, no. 4 (1985): 675–77; and Stanley Wenocur and Michael Reisch, *From Charity to Enterprise: The Development of American Social Work in a Market Economy* (Urbana: University of Illinois Press, 1989), pp. 26–29.

10. As quoted in Gertrude Himmelfarb, *Poverty and Compassion: The Moral Imagination of the Late Victorians* (New York: Knopf, 1991), p. 241.

11. As quoted in Allen F. Davis, *American Heroine: The Life and Legend of Jane Addams* (New York: Oxford University Press, 1973), p. 65.

12. Residents of Hull House, *Hull-House Maps and Papers* (Boston: Thomas Y. Crowell, 1895; reprint, New York: Arno, 1970), p. viii.

13. The key volume, which included Booth's "Descriptive Map of London Poverty," was Charles Booth, *Life and Labour of the People of London* (London: Williams & Northgate, 1891), vol. 2. See Sklar, "*Hull-House Maps and Papers:* Social Science as Women's Work in the 1890s," in Bulmer, Bales, and Sklar, eds. (n. 6 above), p. 122.

14. Residents of Hull House (n. 12 above), p. 41. This volume was published as part of a book series, Library on Economics and Politics, edited by Richard Ely of the University of Wisconsin.

15. Mary Jo Deegan, *Jane Addams and the Men of the Chicago School, 1892–1918* (New Brunswick, N.J.: Transaction, 1988), p. 5. Hull House provided a training ground for noted women reformers of the Progressive Era: Kelley, Lathrop, Alice Hamilton, Mary Kenny O'Sullivan, Sophonisba Breckinridge, Grace Abbott, and Edith Abbott. See Allen F. Davis, *Spearheads for Reform: The Social Settlements and the Progressive Movement, 1890–1914* (New Brunswick, N.J.: Rutgers University Press, 1967; rev. ed., 1984), pp. 103–47.

16. Deegan (n. 15 above), p. 24.

17. As quoted in Ellen Fitzpatrick, *Endless Crusade: Women Social Scientists and Progressive Reform* (New York: Oxford University Press, 1990), p. 33.

18. Steven J. Diner, *A City and Its Universities: Public Policy in Chicago, 1892–1919* (Chapel Hill: University of North Carolina Press, 1980), p. 50.

19. Ibid. This "public spiritedness" was evident in the "University Extension Division," which released professors into the city to provide instruction for the citizenry at large. Edward Shils notes that nearly a quarter of the University of Chicago faculty participated in municipal reform activities at the high watermark of the city's Progressive movement. See Edward Shils, "The University, the City, and the World: Chicago and the University of Chicago," in *The University and the City: From Medieval Origins to the Present*, ed. Thomas Bender (New York: Oxford University Press, 1988), pp. 210–30.

20. Fitzpatrick (n. 17 above), p. 39. As Fitzpatrick indicates, this commitment was also shared by the political science and political economy departments at Chicago: "They stressed the importance of using scholarship to advance both knowledge and civicmindedness" (p. 41).

21. The quotation appears in a different context in ibid., p. xv, but our research indicates that it aptly describes the first-generation Chicago sociologists. For discussion of Social Gospel influences in American social science in its formative period, see Arthur S. Link and Richard L. McCormick, *Progressivism* (Arlington Heights, Ill.: Harlan Davidson, 1983), pp. 23–24. In the early 1890s, Small, Vincent, and Edward Bemis (whom Harper would fire in 1895 because of Bemis's support of the 1894 Pullman strike) worked with Addams, Kelley, and community leaders to help secure legislation eliminating sweatshops and regulating child labor. In the winter of 1910, Henderson and Mead joined the women of Hull House in support of 40,000 striking garment industry workers; in 1915, Mead participated in another garment union strike.

22. The most important research study of the early Chicago School was *The Polish Peasant in Europe and America* (Chicago: University of Chicago Press, 1918), a 2,232-page study coauthored by Thomas Znaniecki and Florian Znaniecki. See Martin Bulmer, *The Chicago School of Sociology: Institutionalization, Diversity, and the Rise of Sociological Research* (Chicago: University of Chicago Press, 1984), pp. 45–63, p. 238, n. 1.

23. Deegan (n. 15 above), quotations from p. 55; see also chap. 6. *Hull-House Maps and Papers* helped inaugurate the Social Survey movement, of which the Pittsburgh Survey, 1907–9, was the largest and most prominent example. Sponsored by the Russell Sage Foundation, the Pittsburgh Survey was carried out by a combination of academics and nonacademics, including Kelley, formerly of Hull House. The survey was conceptually unified around the seminal role of the steel industry in shaping Pittsburgh's urban environment and growth. See Stephen R. Cohen, "The Pittsburgh Survey and the Social Survey Movement: A Sociological Road Not Taken," in Bulmer, Bales, and Sklar, eds. (n. 6 above), pp. 245–67.

24. Bulmer, *Chicago School of Sociology* (n. 22 above), p. 69.

25. Ibid., p. 89. Bulmer's study focuses on the period 1915–35. See also Fitzpatrick (n. 17 above), p. 200; Shils (n. 19 above); and David Ward, *Poverty, Ethnicity, and the American City, 1840–1925* (Cambridge: Cambridge University Press, 1989), pp. 151–79.

26. The University of Chicago was hardly a hothouse for radical social change, as evidenced by the trustees' firing of Bemis, who took the side of labor in the violent Pullman strike of 1894: "The scientific study of pressing social issues was one thing; openly advocating 'radical' causes without reference to scientific inquiry was another" (Fitzpatrick [n. 17 above], p. 40). Yet, according to Shils, "The trustees of the University of Chicago, despite assertions by critics such as Thorstein Veblen and Upton Sinclair, have an impressive history of self-restraint, for which there is ample evidence" (Shils [n. 19 above], p. 218).

27. Fitzpatrick (n. 17 above), p. 70.

28. Ibid., p. 86.

29. Ibid., pp. 20–25, 87–200 passim; quotation from p. 166. For more on Breckinridge and Abbott's collaboration and friendship, see Costin (n. 7 above), pp. 41–67.

30. Ellen C. Lagemann, introduction to *Jane Addams on Education*, ed. Ellen C. Lagemann (New York: Teachers College Press, 1985), p. 35.

31. Dorothy Ross, *The Origins of American Social Science* (New York: Cambridge University Press, 1991), p. 321.

32. Ibid.

33. Ibid., pp. 326–30; Dorothy Ross, "American Social Science and the Idea of Progress," in *The Authority of Experts*, ed. Thomas L. Haskell (Bloomington: Indiana University Press, 1984), pp. 157–71; Sheldon Hackney, "The University and Its Community: Past and Present," *Annals of the American Academy* 488 (1986): 135–47; Martin Bulmer and Joan Bulmer, "Philanthropy and Social Science in the 1920s: Beardsley Ruml and the Laura Spelman Rockefeller Memorial, 1922–29," *Minerva* 19 (1981): 347–407.

34. Ogburn's 1929 presidential address to the American Sociological Society, quoted in Bulmer, *Chicago School of Sociology* (n. 22 above), p. 182. For the role of private foundations such as the Carnegie Corporation, Russell Sage Foundation, and Laura Spelman Rockefeller Memorial in sustaining this representation of social science through funding programs, see Ellen C. Lagemann, *The Politics of Knowledge: The Carnegie Corporation, Philanthropy, and Public Policy* (Middletown, Conn.: Wesleyan University Press, 1987), chap. 3; Wenocur and Reisch (n. 9 above), pp. 55–58, 272, n. 8; Deegan (n. 15 above), pp. 96–97.

35. Jane Addams, "A Function of the Social Settlement" (1899), in Lagemann, ed. (n. 30 above), p. 90.

36. Wenocur and Reisch (n. 9 above), p. 137.

37. Ibid., pp. 77–106, 127–48; Judith Ann Trolander, *Professionalism and Social Change: From the Settlement House to Neighborhood Centers, 1886 to the Present* (New York: Columbia University Press, 1987), pp. 21–24. In the 1930s, although social workers and many social scientists helped to create a body of research and social planning that undergirded many New Deal reforms, their work was not rooted in sustained efforts to transform local environments; reflecting the norms of the American Association of Social Workers, as professional social workers gained a higher profile in the public sector, they adapted casework technologies to treat the unemployed. By 1936, as the Depression deepened, a rank-and-file movement

involving some 15,000 underpaid, radicalized social workers, most of whom lacked professional credentials and held jobs in heavily stressed public welfare agencies, had arisen to challenge the professional enterprise, organizing protective associations and trade unions and advocating a planned economy and income redistribution. Although social work unions remained viable until about 1950, the radical critique was not sustained after 1940. See Wenocur and Reisch (n. 9 above), pp. 151–207; Leslie Leighninger, *Social Work: Search for Identity* (New York: Greenwood, 1987), pp. 51–101.

38. For discussion of the strengthening of disciplinary communities, see David Alpert, "Performance and Paralysis: The Organized Context of the American Research University," *Journal of Higher Education* 56, no. 3 (1985): 241–81; and Christopher C. Jencks and David Riesman, *The Academic Revolution* (New York: Doubleday, 1968), pp. 523–31.

39. Center for Educational Research and Innovation, *The University and the Community: The Problems of Changing Relationships* (Paris: Organization for Economic Cooperation and Development, 1982), p. 127. For other critiques of university-community relationships, see Derek Bok, *Beyond the Ivory Tower: Social Responsibilities of the Modern University* (Cambridge, Mass.: Harvard University Press, 1982); Hackney, "University and Its Community" (n. 33 above); Clark Kerr, *The Uses of the University* (Cambridge, Mass.: Harvard University Press, 1982); and Peter L. Szanton, *Not Well Advised* (New York: Russell Sage Foundation and Ford Foundation, 1981).

40. For discussion of the environmental threats posed by science divorced from social, moral, and ethical concerns, in this case, quantum mechanics and molecular biology, see Herbert J. Bernstein, "Idols of Modern Science and the Reconstruction of Knowledge," in *New Ways of Knowing: The Sciences, Society, and Reconstructive Knowledge*, ed. Marcus G. Raskin and Herbert J. Bernstein (Totowa, N.J.: Rowman & Littlefield, 1987), pp. 37–68.

41. Daniel Coit Gilman, *University Problems in the United States* (1898; reprint, New York: Garret, 1969), foreword, p. iii.

42. Albert H. Smyth, ed., *The Writings of Benjamin Franklin* (New York: Macmillan, 1907), 2:396.

43. Wenocur and Reisch (n. 9 above), pp. 138–46.

44. Martin Bulmer speaks of "research done with a reformist and ameliorative purpose," in Martin Bulmer, "The Decline of the Social Survey Movement and the Rise of American Empirical Sociology," in Bulmer, Bales, and Sklar, eds. (n. 6 above), p. 305.

45. John Dewey, *How We Think* (New York: D. C. Heath, 1910), p. 11.

46. As quoted in Lee Benson and Ira Harkavy, "Progressing beyond the Welfare State: A Neo-Deweyan Strategy: University-assisted, Staff-controlled and Managed, Community-centered Community Schools as Comprehensive Community Centers to Help Construct and Organize Hardworking, Cohesive, Caring, Cosmopolitan Communities in a Democratic Welfare Society," *Universities and Community Schools* 2, nos. 1–2 (1991): 4–6. The National Academy of Sciences has stated in quintessentially Baconian terms, "The countries that best integrate the generation of new knowledge with the use of that knowledge will be positioned to be the leaders of the 21st century" (the Senate Committee on Appropriations [n. 3 above], p. 167). Referencing Bacon's vision, Bernstein writes, "We have . . . lost the original connection between scientific truth and social good; we have refined moral concerns out of the process" (Bernstein [n. 40 above], p. 52). For a useful discussion of Bacon's oeuvre, see Lee Benson, "Changing Social Science to Change the World: A Discussion Paper," *Social Science History* 2 (1978): 427–41.

47. John Dewey, *Reconstruction in Philosophy* (New York: Henry Holt & Co., 1920; enlarged ed., Boston: Beacon, 1948), pp. 36–37. Addams attributed the following Bacon-like statement to Dewey: "When a theory of knowledge forgets that its value rests in solving the problem out of which it has arisen, that of securing a method of action, knowledge begins to cumber the ground. It is a luxury, and becomes a social nuisance and disturber" (Addams, "Function of the Social Settlement" [n. 35 above], p. 76).

48. Hackney, "University and Its Community" (n. 33 above); Organization for Social and Technical Development, *Urban Universities: Rhetoric, Reality, and Conflict* (Washington, D.C.: Department of Health, Education, and Welfare, 1970); Peter M. Tobia, *The University in Urban Affairs: A Symposium* (New York: Editor, 1969); Szanton (n. 39 above); George Nash, *The University and the City: Eight Cases of Involvement* (New York: McGrawHill, 1973).

49. See Ira Harkavy and John L. Puckett, "The Role of Mediating Structures in University and Community Revitalization: The University of Pennsylvania and West Philadelphia as a Case Study," *Journal of Research and Development in Education* 25, no. 1 (1991): 10–25.

50. Vocational counseling and school social work were sui generis innovations of the settlement movement. See Marvin Lazerson, *Origins of the Urban School: Public Education in Massachusetts, 1870–1915* (Cambridge, Mass.: Harvard University Press, 1971), pp. 191–97; Murray Levine and Adeline Levine,

A Social History of Helping Services: Clinic, Court, School, and Community (New York: Appleton-Century Crofts, 1970), pp. 125–43. The settlement movement also provided a "practical testing ground" for social innovations that were not sui generis, for example, kindergartens, playgrounds, school nursing, vocational education, and vacation schools; in the 1910s, these programs were widely adopted by the public schools. See Morris I. Berger, *The Settlement, the Immigrant and the Public School: A Study of the Influence of the Settlement Movement and the New Migration upon Public Education: 1890–1924* (1956; reprint, New York: Arno, 1980); Davis, *Spearheads for Reform* (n. 15 above), esp. pp. 40–59, quotation from p. 57; Amalie Hofer, "The Social Settlement and the Kindergarten," *National Educational Association Proceedings* 34 (1895): 514–25; Isabel M. Stewart, "The Educational Value of the Nurse in the Public School," in *The Ninth Yearbook of the National Society for the Study of Education*, ed. Thomas Wood (Chicago: University of Chicago Press, 1910), 2:19–26.

51. John Dewey, "The School as Social Center," *National Educational Association Proceedings* 41 (1902): 373–83. As a case in point, Addams served on the board of managers of the National Society for the Promotion of Industrial Education, established in 1906, to help persuade the public schools to take over the settlements' manual training programs. See Davis, *Spearheads for Reform* (n. 15 above), p. 52; and Paul U. Kellogg, "The National Society for the Promotion of Industrial Education," *Charities and the Commons* 17 (1906–7): 363–71, cited in Davis, *Spearheads for Reform* (n. 15 above), p. 273, n. 24. The idea of public schools as social centers, or community schools, has persisted in a minor key throughout the twentieth century. For example, see Clarence A. Perry, *Wider Use of the School Plant* (New York: Russell Sage, 1911); Edward J. Ward, ed., *The Social Center* (New York: Appleton, 1913); Eleanor T. Glueck, *The Community Use of Schools* (Baltimore: Williams & Wilkens, 1927); Samuel Everett, ed., *The Community School* (New York: Appleton-Century, 1938); Elsie R. Clapp, *Community Schools in Action* (New York: Viking, 1939); Nelson B. Henry, *The Fifty-second Yearbook of the National Society for the Study of Education, Part 2: The Community School* (Chicago: University of Chicago Press, 1953); Edward G. Olsen, ed., *The Modern Community School* (New York: Appleton-Century Crofts, 1953); Leonard Covello, *The Heart Is the Teacher* (New York: McGrawHill, 1958); W. Fred Totten and Frank J. Manley, *The Community School: Basic Concepts, Function, and Organization* (Galien, Mich.: Allied Education Council, 1969); Maurice F. Seay and associates, *Community Education: A Developing Concept* (Midland, Mich.: Pendell, 1974).

52. Benson and Harkavy, "Progressing beyond the Welfare State" (n. 46 above), pp. 23–27.

53. Addams, *Second Twenty Years at Hull-House* (n. 7 above), pp. 404–5.

54. Benson and Harkavy, "Progressing beyond the Welfare State" (n. 46 above), pp. 2–28; Ira Harkavy, "The University and the Social Sciences in the Social Order: An Historical Overview and 'Where Do We Go from Here?'" *Virginia Social Science Journal* 27 (1992): 1–25.

55. Davydd J. Greenwood, William Foote Whyte, and Ira Harkavy, "Participatory Action Research as a Process and as a Goal," *Human Relations* ("International Dimensions of Action Research: Sources of New Thinking about Inquiry That Makes a Difference," ed. Max Elden and Rupe Chisholm) 46 (1993): 175–92. See also William Foote Whyte, Davydd J. Greenwood, and Peter Lazes, "Participatory Action Research: Through Practice to Science in Social Research," *American Behavioral Scientist* ("Action Research for the 21st Century: Participation, Reflection and Practice," ed. William Foote Whyte) 32, no. 5 (1989): 513–51; and William Foote Whyte, ed., *Participatory Action Research* (Newbury Park, Calif.: Sage, 1991).

56. William F. Whyte and Kathleen K. Whyte, *Making Mondragón: The Growth and Dynamics of the Worker Cooperative Complex* (Ithaca, N.Y.: ILR, 1988); Davydd J. Greenwood and José Luis González Santos, *Industrial Democracy as Process: Participatory Action Research in the Fagor Cooperative Group of Mondragón* (Assen/Maastricht: Van Gorcum, 1992).

57. Francis E. Johnston and Robert J. Hallock, "Physical Growth, Nutritional Status, and Dietary Intake of African-American Middle School Students from Philadelphia," *American Journal of Human Biology* (in press).

58. Ibid.

59. Ibid.

60. Eleanor M. Novek, "Buried Treasure: The Theory and Practice of Communicative Action in an Urban High School Newspaper" (paper presented to the Association for Education in Journalism and Mass Communication, Kansas City, Mo., August 1993), p. 1.

61. Ibid., p. 15. Other criteria, or markers, include "providing experiences of mastery, strengthening group bonds, and increasing their influence in social systems" (p. 21).

62. Howard E. Gruber, "Creativity and Human Survival," in *Creative People at Work*, ed. Doris B. Wallace and Howard E. Gruber (New York: Oxford University Press, 1989), p. 185. For Gruber's most recent development of the idea of creative altruism, see his essay, "Creativity in the Moral Domain: Ought Implies Can Implies Create," *Creativity Research Journal* ("Creativity in the Moral Domain," ed. Howard E. Gruber) 6, nos. 1–2 (1993): 3–15.

63. For example, the Committee on Inner City Initiatives of the Western New York Consortium of Higher Education (12 colleges and universities) has focused on the collaborative development of the Martin Luther King, Jr., Center, a community school and community center in East Buffalo. See Stephen C. Halpern, "University-Community Projects: Reflections on the Lessons Learned," *Universities and Community Schools* 3, nos. 1–2 (1992): 44–48.

* John Puckett's contribution to this article was supported by a Spencer Foundation Postdoctoral Fellowship. We are also grateful to Lee Benson and Ellen Lagemann for their superb advice and encouragement.

Bibliography

Chapter 5 Social Movements, Student Volunteerism, and Activism

Altbach, Phillip G. and Cohen, R. "American Student Activism: The Post-Sixties Transformation." *The Journal of Higher Education, Vol. 61*, No. 1 (1990), pp. 32–49.

Batstone, David and Eduardo Mendieta. *The Good Citizen*. New York: Routledge 1999.

Bellah, Robert. *Habits of the Heart: Individualism and Commitment in American Life*. New York: Harper and Row, 1985.

Bennett, Jr. Lerone. "SNCC: Rebels with a Cause." *Ebony*, Vol. 20 (January 1965), pp. 146–153.

Colby, Ann, Thomas Ehrlich, E. Beaumont, and J. Stephens, *Educating Citizens: Preparing Students for Lives of Moral and Civic Responsibility*. San Francisco: Jossey-Bass, 2003.

Ehrlich, Thomas. *Civic Responsibility and the University*, Phoenix: Oryx Press, 2000.

Eyler, Janet and Giles, Jr., Dwight E. "Citizenship." In Janet Eyler and Dwight E. Giles, Jr. (eds.). *Where's the Learning in Service-Learning?* (pp. 151–164). San Francisco: Jossey-Bass, 1999.

Foley, Michael and Virginia A. Hodgkinson, "Introduction," *The Civil Society Readers*. Medford, MA: Tufts University Press, 2003.

Gasman, Marybeth. "Sisters in Service: African American Sororities and Philanthropic Support of Education. In Andrea Walton (ed.), *Women and Philanthropy in Education*. Bloomington, IN: Indiana University, pp. 195–214.

Jenkins, Craig J. and Craig Eckert. "Channeling Black Insurgency: Elite Patronage and the Development of the Civil Rights Movement." *American Sociological Review*, Vol. 51 (1986), pp. 812–830.

Katz, Stanley N. "Excellence Is By No Means Enough," *Common Knowledge*, Vol. 8 (September 2002), pp. 427–438.

King, Helen H. "Eva Jefferson: Young Voice of Change: Associated Student Government of Northwestern University, Evanston, Illinois." *Ebony*, Vol. 26 (January 1971), pp. 71–74.

Skocpol, Theda and Morris P. Fiorina, eds. *Civic Engagement in American Democracy: What Has Higher Ed Done Creating Citizens*. Washington, DC: Brookings Institute, 1999.

Schudson, Michael. *The Good Citizen: A History of American Civic Life*. Cambridge:

Harvard University Press, 1999.

Sutherland, E. ed. (1965). *Letters from Mississippi*. New York: McGraw-Hill, Inc.

Tyack, David. "Civic Education—What Roles for Citizens?" *Educational Leadership*, Vol. 54 (February 1997), pp. 22–24.

Wellman, J. *Contributing to the Civic Good: Assessing and Accounting for the Civic Contributions of Higher Education*. Working Paper. Washington DC: The Institute for Higher Education Policy, 2002.

CHAPTER 6

Service Learning: A View of Philanthropic Action in Education

Service-Learning:

What Students Have to Say

Thomas D. Bordelon & Iris Phillips

ABSTRACT This exploratory study conducted at a mid-sized American Midwestern metropolitan university explores service-learning. The study describes the characteristics of students choosing service-learning and examines learning from the students' perspective. A survey instrument was used to assess the attitudes of 500 randomly selected students, some of whom participated in service-learning projects. Their responses were contrasted with students who did not participate in a service-learning opportunity. The results of this study create a profile of students' perception of service-learning.

Service-learning

Service-learning promotes its objectives to increase opportunities for students in the community, strengthen community relationships, and provides integrative learning experiences for students (Gray et al., 1999). Successful integration of learning hinges on the support of faculty members, community access to services, agencies' tradition of service, and the individuals in leadership roles exerting the power to affect organizational change.

The value of service-learning assumes that the learning environment extends from the classroom to the community, and that there are valuable resources fortifying student learning that cannot be obtained through participation in college alone. The precarious link between learning in formal settings provided by institutions of higher education and haphazard community volunteering is evidently not made by students. Out of the concern that students are less involved in community service, programs have emerged to reinforce what is learned in the classroom with strengthening students' sense of personal responsibility for improving their community (Root et al., 2003). Service-learning, therefore, is an attempt to bolster the importance of volunteerism in the community by formalizing the learning experience in college and university curriculums. The relationship between university and community agency is interdependency, both sympathetic to the other's growth and needs (Bringle and Hatcher, 2002).

Service-learning at a Community Level

Service-learning components are generally recognized as interplay between what students need to learn by participating in community organizations and initiatives that address specific community needs. Learning in the community directs students' energies towards practical efforts to resolve pressing social problems now, rather than wait until they graduate (Myers-Lipton, 2003). Successful collaborative relationships hinge on their ability to include a large representation of stakeholders, develop leadership, and demonstrate a willingness to compromise in order to achieve their goals (Selin et al., 2000). Weinreich (2003) observes that service-learning creates an environment that challenges students to use their time effectively, access resources needed to solve problems, and deal with a complex and dynamic environment. Although service-learning outcomes vary in relation to numerous variables, one attribute seems to hold true: service-learning succeeds in promoting personal satisfaction among students who select this type of learning experience. When remuneration is offered to students,

students' satisfaction with service-learning is diminished. Service-learning seems to be its own reward (Root et al., 2003). The environment conducive for learning is one that permits students structured experiences so that they talk, think, and perform tasks useful to the community organization. The community provides skills that support learning in a school setting, such as fostering a sense of caring for others in the community (Hinck and Brandell, 1999). Acting on concern for the community is likely to be realized at a neighborhood level, as a neighborhood is a well of resources for individuals and shapes the lives of its inhabitants (Kearns and Parkinson, 2001).

The benefits of service-learning are variously reported by Kerrigan et al. (2003), who studied 3000 students over a 5-year period. The authors determined that successful service-learning experiences depended on the adequate orientation of students to civic engagement and collaborative learning experiences, and engaging students in many opportunities to discuss and reflect on lessons learned. Batchelder and Root (1994) found that students gained confidence to resolve complex social problems when they received high quality classroom instruction and on-site supervision.

In other important ways, however, service-learning does not seem to demonstrate effectiveness in its encouragement to align students' long-term energies with participation in projects promoting the civic good. In some studies, civic engagement does not seem to promote in students a longlasting desire to engage in civic life more so than any other path (Daynes and Wygant, 2003). In other studies, such as conducted by Astin et al. (1999), students who participated in a service-learning experience constituting at least six hours a week in their senior year in college were twice as likely to perform voluntary community service when they graduated. Morgan and Streb (2003) point out that the quality rather than the quantity of service-learning experiences should be the focus of community-based learning. Students require a sense of ownership in the civic experience: engage in meaningful experiences, discuss their activities, and make decisions that influence the quality of their service. Without these attributes, service-learning can be counterproductive, causing students to devalue their civic experience.

Supporting service-learning on campus may come in the form of workshops that provide students, faculty, and community agency members to increase their awareness of social issues impacting their community, and sharing insights and practical solutions. These workshops are not meant to replace a firm infrastructure of support provided by cooperating agencies, but to augment the learning opportunities offered by service-learning (Checkoway, 1996). Workshops may be more likely to be supported by colleges with a defined mission of service. As indicated by Anonio et al. (2000), a study of faculty demonstrates that likely participants in community service are lower ranking faculty, female, African Americans, and those who teach in 4-year colleges.

Risks and Rewards of Service-Learning

Service-learning is not without its risk to students, community agencies, and universities. Ethical problems may arise as students may find themselves in learning situations where they do not have the skills and experience to recognize danger, for example. Rich (2003) notes that each discipline should turn to its ethical principles for guidance when facing ethical issues since problems tend to be bound to the context of a situation. Importantly, not all disciplines need to embrace service-learning as essential to the education of their students. Each course does not need to have a service-learning component to successfully educate students, nor should they. However, students who engaged in more than one service-learning experience reported possessing a stronger understanding of how civic engagement related to course materials (Corbett and Kendall, 1999).

Service-Learning from Students' Perspectives

An examination of attributes influencing students' participation in service-learning courses has not been studied. It is not understood how variables such as age, employment status, academic major, and child rearing influence students' interest in service-learning. If service-learning is a means by which faculty and students may participate in civic engagement, how do students perceive this type of learning opportunity? This study focused on collecting information designed to shed light on what influences students to participate in, and their perceptions of, service-learning. In addition, this study examines what student characteristics may influence their desire to participate in service-learning and what are student perceptions regarding service-learning.

Method

Design

A mid-sized Midwestern university in the United States was selected as it places a special emphasizes on community service. Five hundred students (five percent) were randomly sampled from a total student population of approximately 9800. In order to obtain a representative sample from the campus population, no selection criteria such as previous involvement in service-learning, grade point average, age, major, and year in school, for example, were specified. The institutional research office generated a random list of names and addresses for 500 students.

A self-administered, mail-back survey was used in this exploratory study to collect students' demographic characteristics and experiences with service-learning. Owing to time and funding constraints the recommended procedure for survey mailings that includes incentives, postcard reminders, and a final certified mailing was not complied with (Dillman, 1978). The study was conducted in one spring and summer semester. Sampled students received a covering letter and the survey at their permanent addresses with one follow-up mailing three weeks later.

The design of the instrument collected information relating to service-learning throughout the campus, such as student experiences with service-learning, student perception of service-learning depending on their participation in service-learning activities, disciplines participating in service-learning, and prevalence of service-learning on the campus. The instrument design elicited descriptive information about student attributes that may influence their participation in service-learning opportunities, such as age, academic major, employment status, gender, number of children, and volunteer activities outside of course related activities.

From the sample, the researchers received 110 usable responses; a 22 percent response rate of representatives of the university student body. The mean age of respondents was 29.87, with a median age of 25 and a range from 18–56. Females represented 73.6 percent of respondents (81) and males represented 25.5 percent of respondents. Of the 110 respondents, 93.6 percent reported their ethnicity as white (103) with the remaining respondents self-reporting as 4 African American, 2 Asian American, and 1 Hispanic. Respondents represented all grade levels within the university: 14 freshmen, 12 sophomores, 22 juniors, 28 seniors, and 28 graduate students. The university population has a mean age of 24, and is 93.7 percent white, 4 percent African American, and 2.3 percent 'other.' Sixty-five percent of the student population is female.

The research instrument used in this study was the Higher Education Service-Learning Surveys (HESLS from the Service-Learning Research and Development Center developed at The University of California-Berkeley Service-Learning Research & Development Center by Diaz-Gallegos, Furco and Yamada, 1999). The HESLS includes four subscales: academic (6 items), civic responsibility (9 items), career (6 items), empowerment (8 items), and open-ended questions. The instrument created for the student survey included two items from the HESLS academic subscale. The negatively worded item, 'I do not find courses in school relevant to my life outside of school' and the positively worded item, 'I learn more when courses contain hands-on activities' were selected.

Three items from the HESLS civic responsibility subscale were used in the developed instrument. The positive worded items, 'Being involved in a program to improve my community is important', 'I am concerned about local community issues', and the negatively worded item, 'It is not necessary to volunteer my time to help people in need', were chosen to represent student commitment to civic responsibility. Additionally, the item 'I am interested in doing something about problems in my school or neighborhood' was added to the civic responsibility subscale.

Based on the literature review and student input, ten additional items were added to the instrument. Three of these items were designed to measure student interest in service-learning opportunities: 'I am interested in my major incorporating a course involving community activities'; 'If a course including service-learning and a regular course were available, I would choose the service-learning course"; and 'I am interested in community activities developed and integrated into class time'.

Six items were added to the instrument to assess student perception of service-learning as follows. 'Service-learning is important to the obtainment of academic goals and education objectives', 'Service-learning empowers students and allows them to take control of the academic goals and education objectives', 'I believe I can learn more from service-learning than in the classroom alone', 'I believe service-learning can enhance life skills'; 'I believe I can understand myself better through service-learning', and 'I believe service-learning can provide meaningful activity that can benefit others and myself'.

The survey instrument used the 4-point Likert-type scale from the HESLS to allow variance among responses in each scale item (see Table 1). Each of the four points on the instrument is anchored as 1 = strongly disagree; 2 = disagree; 3 = agree; and 4 = strongly agree.

The HESLS included several open-ended questions such as 'During this academic year, have you performed community service not related to this course (for example, religious-affiliated activities, tutoring, and volunteer work for a local community agency)? If yes, what type of service did you perform?' and 'How often were you involved in this service?' Included in this survey was the question 'Have you ever participated in a service-learning component at this university?'

In addition to demographic information such as age, gender, ethnicity, year in school, and major, other demographic information was collected to explore student attributes that may influence their perceptions of service-learning. The items included the number of children students cared for at home, the number of hours employed outside the home, and travel distance in miles from the university. Respondents were given an opportunity to provide comments in an open area in the instrument.

Results

Student perceptions of service-learning appear favorable regardless of whether students had ever participated in service-learning. A t-test for dependent samples indicated no statistically significant differences between students' mean scores on the instrument regardless of their personal experience with service-learning courses.

Analysis of student attributes indicated that 66.4 percent of respondents (73) actively participated in volunteer community service apart from any university service-learning course. Of those 73 students reporting community activities, 18.2 percent (20) were involved in religious activities, and 17.3 percent (19) were active in some youth related activity. Other responses included community clean-up, humane society work, tutoring, and hospital and homelessness volunteering. These students reported the range of their volunteer times as daily to rarely. For example, 2.7 percent (2) reported daily service, 39.7 percent (29) weekly service, 23.3 percent (17) monthly service, 5.5 percent (4) reported 2–3 months or rarely, and 28.8 percent (21) reported yearly service. There were no statistically significant differences between gender and their involvement with community activities.

An ANOVA with the variable, 'If a course including service-learning and a regular course were available, I would choose the service-learning course' and ratio variables age, grade level, number of children, number of hours employed, and number of miles traveled demonstrated no statistically significant finding. Since 50.9 percent of respondents were 25 or younger, age was recoded into a dichotomous variable of 25 or younger and 26 and older. Chi-squared computed for a 2×2 table indicated no statistically significant differences in age and service. Chi-squared analysis indicated no statistically significant differences between students who would choose a service-learning course over a regular course compared to their community volunteer service, their past participation in a service-learning course at the university, or in their major area of study.

The analysis of gender indicated a statistically significant difference of $p < .007$ when compared to choosing a service-learning coure over a regular course. Of the 25 males who responded to the item. "If a course including service-learning and a regular course were available, I would choose the service-learning course', 12 responded yes (48.0 percent) and 13 responded no (52.0 percent). However, of the 78 female respondents, only 16 reported affirmatively (27.2 percent), while 72.8 percent responded negatively (62 percent). An ANOVA with gender as the nominal grouping variable and ratio variables of age, grade level, number of children, hours of employment, and number of miles traveled did not indicate statistically significant differences between males and females.

TABLE 1

Students' Mean Scores of Survey Instrument by Service-Learning Experience

	Service-Learning Experience	No Service-Learning Experience	Level of Significance
Being involved in a program to improve my community is important	3.36	3.23	0.297
I am concerned about local community issues	3.18	3.05	0.102
I do not find courses in school relevant to my life outside of school REVERSED	1.86	2.04	0.916
It is not necessary to volunteer my time to people in need REVERSED	1.48	1.73	0.952
I learn more when courses contain hands-on activities	3.43	3.29	0.994
I am interested in doing something about problems in my school or neighborhood	3.10	2.85	0.638
My schedule allows me to participate in a community activity outside of the classroom	2.29	2.39	0.766
I am interested in community activities developed and integrated into class time	3.19	2.89	0.909
I am interested in my major incorporating a course Involving community activities	2.95	2.88	0.906
Service-learning is important to the obtainment of academic goals and educational objectives	3.14	2.94	0.5325
Service-learning empowers students and allows them to take control of their academic goals and educational objectives	3.10	2.87	0.510
I believe I can learn more from service-learning than in the classroom alone	2.95	2.81	0.809
If a course including service-learning and a regular course were available at USI, I would choose the service-learning course	3.05	2.79	0.472
I believe service-learning can enhance life skills	3.33	3.20	0.074
I believe I can understand myself better through service-learning	3.19	2.90	0.473
I believe service-learning can provide meaningful activity that can benefit others and myself	3.48	3.19	0.200

The study's results indicated that 79.8 percent of respondents (87) reported they had not participated in a service-learning component and only 20.2 percent of the students (22) had experienced service-learning. Of the 22 respondents reporting having a service-learning experience, 21 students reported these experiences were in their majors. Students engaged in service-learning represented seven graduate students, two business students, seven enrolled in education and human services, four in health professions, and one liberal arts major.

Of the 110 respondents, 13 provided individual comments. Respondent comments centered on the two major themes of time constraints and the appropriateness of requiring service-learning in higher education. Addressing the issue of time constraints, one student stated:

> I am 49, married w/2 teenagers and a puppy. I am student teaching during the day and have two masters' level classes at night. As my husband's employer is relocating us this spring, I am also busy getting the house ready to sell. I have no time for service-learning now and therefore no interest. OK?

Most of the comments were made about the students' perception of appropriateness of service-learning. 'Service Learning is wasted on those without self-interest and not needed by those who are self-interested', and another wrote:

> I did not pay to learn for a professor not to teach anything. If I want to do service projects or had time, I'd join the Kiwanis for free. I believe service-learning is important to the obtainment of spiritual health and self-actualization. I am not sure this life achievement should be met through education. I feel it should be a personal choice.

Only one positive comment was made: 'I did a service-learning class my senior year in high school and found it so beneficial to the class I work with and myself'.

Discussion

Institutions of higher education are recognizing the potential for partnership with community agencies for their power to hone students' skills. These skills can be guided by academic discourse and applied to improving lives in the local community. The results of this study suggest that students perceive service-learning with appeal whether they have engaged in a service-learning experiences or not.

This study's findings are limited to a Midwestern university in the United States and thus have limited generalizability to other institutions of higher education. The university studied may not be representative of student diversity at other Midwestern universities in the United States. The sample size obtained is small, yet it is representative of the university population in demographic detail; however, it may not be representative of students who have engaged in service-learning experiences. The small number of respondents limits the use of statistical analysis of multiple variables such as age, gender, and service-learning experience. Only 13 respondents chose to provide open-ended comments. All but one comment were not supportive of service-learning, suggesting that students who responded to the open-ended questions expressed a strong viewpoint.

Although the American Midwestern university's mission indicates that service-learning experiences are a bedrock of its existence, less than a quarter of the students surveyed had engaged in such an opportunity. The disconnect between what the university says it does and what it actually delivers may be related to the lack of incentives to faculty and students that other universities have found necessary to support a program of service-learning. The findings of this study suggest that it is important to know how successful these universities are at recognizing the attributes of their student population to provide service-learning experiences to those students who might benefit, and whether they provide the services to the community as they claim. The findings also suggest that students find service-learning attractive on principle more so than in action, implying that talking about its virtues is a different matter from engaging in its activities.

There appears to be little difference between students who have engaged in service-learning experiences and those who have not. Curiously, women reported less interest in participating in a service-learning experience. It is speculated that women may fulfill social roles of elevated responsibilities for the lives of others. Therefore, women may perceive the addition of another service-related experience as unappealing or unnecessary. This study also raises the question of why women are less interested in participating in service-learning opportunities. Gender differences seem to be a factor that is yet to be explored in understanding the desire and lack of desire to participate in service-learning experiences. More research needs to be conducted on social roles and expectations beyond the classroom to understand gender difference as related to the desire to enrol in service-learning courses.

References

Antonio, A., Astin, H. & Cress, C. (2000) 'Community Service in Higher Education: A Look at the Nation's Faculty', *Review of Higher Education* 23(4): 373–97.

Astin, A., Sax, L. & Avalos, J. (1999) 'Long Term Effects of Volunteerism During the Undergraduate Years', *Review of Higher Education* 22(2): 187–202.

Batchelder, T. & Root, S. (1994) 'Effects of an Undergraduate Program to Integrate Academic Learning and Service: Cognitive, Prosocial Cognitive, and Identify Outcomes', *Journal of Adolescence* 17(August): 341–55.

Bringle, R. & Hatcher, J. (2002) 'Campus-community Partnerships: The Terms of Engagement', *Journal of Social Issues* 58(3): 503–16.

Checkoway, B. (1996) 'Combining Service and Learning on Campus and in the Community', *Phi Delta Kappa* 77(9): 600–9.

Corbett, J. & Kendall, A. (1999) 'Evaluating Service-learning in the Communication Discipline', *Journalism & Mass Communication Educator* 53(4): 66–76.

Daynes, G. & Wygant, S. (2003) 'Service-learning as a Pathway to Civic Engagement: A Comparative Study', *Metropolitan Universities—An International Forum* 14(3): 84–96.

Dillman, D. (1978) *Mail and Telephone Surveys: The Tailored Design Method*. New York: Wiley.

Gray, M., Ondaatje, E., Fricker, R., Jr. & Geschwind, S. (2000) 'Assessing Service-learning: Results From a Survey of "Learn and Serve American Higher Education"', *Change* 32: 30–9.

Hinck, S. & Brandell, M. (1999) 'Service-learning: Facilitating Academic Learning and Character Development', *National Association of Secondary School Principals* 83(609): 16–24.

Kearns, A. & Parkinson, M. (2001) 'The Significance of Neighbourhood', *Urban Studies* 38(12): 2103–10.

Kerrigan, S., Gelmon, S. & Spring, A. (2003) 'The Community as Classroom: Multiple Perspectives on Student Learning', *Metropolitan Universities—An International Forum* 14(3): 53–67.

Morgan, W. & Streb, M. (2003) 'First, Do No Harm: Student Ownership and Service-learning', *Metropolitan Universities—An International Forum* 14(3): 36–52.

Myers-Lipton, S. (2003) 'Developing a Service-learning Minor: Its Impact and Lessons for the Future', *Metropolitan Universities—An International Forum* 14(3): 68–83.

Rich, B. (2003) 'Ethical Issues and Questions for Service-learning Faculty and Administrators in Urban Universities', *Metropolitan Universities—An International Forum* 14(3): 111–22.

Root, S., Eyler, J. & Giles, D. (2003) 'The Bonnor Scholars Program: A Study of the Impact of Stipends on Indicators of Community Service Ethic', *Metropolitan Universities—An International Forum* 14(3): 15–110.

Selin, S. Schuett, M. & Carr, D. (2000) 'Modeling Stakeholder Perceptions of Collaborative Initiative Effectiveness', *Society & Natural Resources* 13(8): 735–47.

Weinreich, D. (2003) 'Service-learning at the Edge of Chaos', *Educational Gerontology* 29: 181–95.

Acknowledgements

The authors acknowledge the contributions of Melissa A. Baumgart and Lauren C. Lesher for collecting data used in this study. Their efforts were funded through a RISC Grant awarded by the University of Southern Indiana.

REFLECTION IN SERVICE LEARNING: MAKING MEANING OF EXPERIENCE

ROBERT G. BRINGLE & JULIE A. HATCHER

Traditional methods of instruction based on lectures and textbook readings can be effective in some instances and for some types of learning, yet many educators seek methods to enhance traditional student learning and to expand educational objectives beyond knowledge acquisition. Two related issues illustrate the limitations of traditional methods. The first is context-specific learning. Students are taught a particular module of content, they are provided examples of how to solve particular types of problems, and then they practice solving these types of problems. However, when the nature of the problem is varied, or when similar problems are encountered in different contexts, students fail to generalize prior learning to these new circumstances or situations. The second issue that frustrates educators is the shallow nature of the content learned through traditional instruction and the degree to which it does not promote personal understanding. That is, although students may demonstrate rote learning of a particular educational module, that new information does not always enlighten understanding of their own lives and the world outside the classroom. When knowledge acquisition is viewed as the most important goal of education, the educational system fails to develop intellectual habits that foster the desire and capacity for lifelong learning and the skills needed for active participation in a democracy.[1]

Recognizing these limits to traditional instructional methods, a Task Group on General Education, appointed by the American Association of Colleges in 1994, recommended that college instructors focus more attention on active learning strategies. Several types of active learning strategies identified in the report address these challenges (i.e., context-specific learning, personally relevant learning) and successfully expand the educational agenda beyond the acquisition of knowledge. Recommended active learning strategies include using electronic and interactive media; promoting undergraduate research; structuring collaborative learning experiences; and developing problem-based learning.[2] The benefits of these active learning strategies include the promise that students are more engaged in the learning process. As a result, students are more satisfied with the learning experience, which in turn fosters academic persistence and success. In addition, educational outcomes are enriched, deepened, and expanded when student learning is more engaged, active, and relevant. Another type of active learning that holds similar promise is service learning.

Service Learning

Service learning is defined as a "course-based, credit-bearing educational experience in which students (a) participate in an organized service activity that meets identified community needs and (b) reflect on the service activity in such a way as to gain further understanding of course content, a broader appreciation of the discipline, and an enhanced sense of civic responsibility."[3] According to this definition, service learning is an academic enterprise. Although other forms of community service (e.g., volunteering) can have educational benefits, service learning deliberately integrates community service activities with educational objectives. This means that not every community service activity is appropriate for a service learning class. Community service activities need to be selected for and coordinated with the educational objectives of the course. Furthermore, the community service should be meaningful not only for the student's educational outcomes but also to the community. Thus, well-executed service learning represents a coordinated partnership between the campus and the community, with the instructor tailoring the service experience to the educational agenda and community representatives ensuring that the students' community service is consistent with their goals.[4] Thus, high-quality service learning classes demonstrate *reciprocity* between the campus and the community, with each giving and receiving.

The definition of service learning also highlights the importance of **reflection**. Reflection is the "intentional consideration of an experience in light of particular learning objectives."[5] The presumption is that community service does not necessarily, in and of itself, produce learning. Reflection activities provide the bridge between the community service activities and the educational content of the course. Reflection activities direct the student's attention to new interpretations of events and provide a means through which the community service can be studied and interpreted, much as a text is read and studied for deeper understanding.

Philosophical Basis for Reflection

The extensive work of John Dewey offers a philosophical foundation for the role that reflection assumes in the learning process as a bridge between experience and theory. Indeed, personal experiences, such as those gained through community service, allow theory to take on meaning when reflection supports an analysis and critical examination of the experience. Dewey contends that experience is as important as theory.

> An ounce of experience is better than a ton of theory simply because it is *only in experience* that any theory has vital and verifiable significance. An experience, a very humble experience, is capable of generating and carrying any amount of theory (or intellectual content), but a theory apart from an experience cannot be definitely grasped even as theory. It tends to become a mere verbal formula, a set of catchwords used to render thinking.[6]

Too often, the presentation of a theory by an instructor or in a textbook is viewed by students as an empty, pedantic venture. It is through active learning and the interplay between abstract, remote content and personal, palatable experiences that student learning is deepened and strengthened.

According to Dewey, reflection is an "active, persistent, and careful consideration of any belief or supported form of knowledge in light of the grounds that support it."[7] Reflection consists of "turning a subject over in the mind and giving it serious and consecutive considerations."[8] Dewey acknowledges that experience by itself does not necessarily result in learning; experiences can be either "miseducative" or "educative." Experience becomes educative when critical reflective thought creates new meaning and leads to growth and the ability to take informed actions. In contrast, experiences are miseducative when they fail to stimulate critical thought and they more deeply entrench existing schemata. Dewey notes that communication, particularly face-to-face discourse, is a key to creating educative experiences. Communication with others leads not only to educational growth but also to social and moral development. Gouinlock is clear in identifying the moral dimensions of Dewey's educational philosophy. He notes, "The values, aims, and expected response of others play a critical role in stimulating revised interest in each participant. Accordingly, in a community where full and open communication exists, one finds an essential condition for the growth of new values and forms of behavior."[9]

Many forms of inquiry can produce reflection about the tensions between theory and application. Dewey specifies four conditions that maximize the potential for inquiry-based learning to be educative: (a) it must generate interest in the learner; (b) it must be intrinsically worthwhile to the learner; (c) it must present problems that awaken new curiosity and create a demand for information; and (d) it must cover a considerable time span and foster development over time.[10] Service learning classes structured to meet these four conditions can thereby create educative experiences for students. Because service learning extends the walls of the classroom into the community, students frequently encounter new circumstances and challenges. These experiences often create dissonance, doubt, and confusion. Dewey values such perplexity, for it is at that very point that reflection and thinking begin: "Thinking begins in what may fairly enough be called a forked-road situation, a situation that is ambiguous, that presents a dilemma, that proposes alternatives. . . . Demand for the solution of a perplexity is the steadying and guiding factor in the entire process of reflection."[11]

At the heart of Dewey's educational philosophy are three principles: (a) education must lead to personal growth; (b) education must contribute to humane conditions; and (c) education must engage citizens in association with one another.[12] When reflection activities engage the learner in dialogue and other forms of communication about the relationship between relevant, meaningful service and the interpretative template of a discipline, there is enormous potential for learning to broaden and deepen along academic, social, moral, and civic dimensions.[13] This occurs not only when reflection activities ask the learner to confront ambiguity and critically examine existing beliefs, but also when the retrospective analysis has prospective relevance that leads to informed future actions.[14]

Types of Reflection for Service Learning

There are many examples of reflection activities (e.g., reading, writing, doing, telling) that can be used in service learning classes.[15] We have chosen to highlight a few that we feel are particularly worthwhile to use when working with college students. Many of them are based upon written work. Writing is a special form of reflection through which new meaning can be created, new understanding of problems can become circumscribed, and new ways of organizing experiences can be developed. Analysis through writing helps to make challenging experiences less overwhelming, fosters problem solving, and facilitates the exploration of the relationships between past learning, current experiences, and future action.[16]

Journals. Student journals are common reflection activities in service learning courses because they are easy to assign and they provide a way for students to express their thoughts and feelings about the service experience throughout the semester. It is important that students know, at the beginning of the course, what is expected in a journal and how it is going to be used. Some journals, intended as personal documents, are never submitted for a grade. Journals may also be reviewed periodically by the instructor. Occasionally, journals are shared with other students or with community agency personnel. If journals are to be evaluated for a grade, then this policy should be made clear at the beginning of the semester and the criteria for grading the journal should be specified to the students.

Before assigning a journal, it is important to consider what learning objectives the journal is intended to meet. Journals can be an effective way to develop self-understanding and connect the service experience to the course content. Journals can also be used during the semester to record information that is used in more formal reflective activities, such as a paper or class presentation. Our experience is, and other instructors concur, that unstructured journals too often become mere logs of events rather than reflective activities in which students consider their service activities in light of the educational objectives of the course. Table 1 identifies some ways that journals can be structured to transcend mere description and promote connections between the course content and the service activities.

Experiential Research Paper. An experiential research paper is a formal paper based on the experiential learning theory.[17] Students are asked to identify a particular experience or set of events at a service site and to reflect upon and analyze the experience within a broader context in order to make recommendations for subsequent action. For example, in order to complete this assignment, students might be asked at mid-semester to identify and describe a perplexing, frustrating, or confusing experience at the service site. Students then identify an important social issue that may be underlying this circumstance (e.g., health care to homeless youth, eating disorders among adolescent girls, volunteer recruitment strategies). They identify the multiple perspectives from which the issue can be analyzed and how it might be the basis for making recommendations to influence community agency operations, policies, or procedures. Students then locate articles in professional journals and other relevant sources to provide a conceptual framework for the issue. During the second half of the semester, students use this research to write a formal paper that analyzes the social issue and includes recommendations.

TABLE 1
Types of Reflective Journals

Key Phrase Journal: Students are asked to integrate an identified list of terms and key phrases into their journal entries as they describe and discuss their community service activities. Students may be asked to underline or highlight the key phrases in order to identify their use.

Double-entry Journal: For this journal, students use a spiral notebook. On the left side of the journal students describe their service experiences, personal thoughts, and reactions to their service activities. On the right side of the journal, they discuss how the first set of entries relates to key concepts, class presentations, and readings. Students may be asked to draw arrows indicating the relationships between their personal experiences and the formal course content.

Critical Incident Journal: Students focus on a specific event that occurred at the service site. Students are then asked to respond to prompts designed to explore their thoughts, reactions, future action, and information from the course that might be relevant to the incident. For example,

Describe an incident or situation that created a dilemma for you because you did not know how to act or what to say.

Why was it such a confusing event?

How did you, or others around the event, feel about it?

What did you do, or what was the first thing that you considered doing?

List three actions that you might have taken, and evaluate each one.

How does the course material relate to this issue, help you analyze the choices, and suggest a course of action that might be advisable?

Three Part Journal: Students are asked to respond to three separate issues in each of their journal entries: (a) Describe what happened in the service experience, including what you accomplished, some of the events that puzzled or confused you, interactions you had, decisions you made, and plans you developed. (b) Analyze how the course content relates to the service experience, including key concepts that can be used to understand events and guide future behavior. (c) Apply the course materials and the service experience to you and your personal life, including your goals, values, attitudes, beliefs, and philosophy.

Directed Writings: Students are asked to consider how a particular aspect of course content from the readings or class presentations, including theories, concepts, quotes, statistics, and research findings, relate to their service experiences. Students write a journal entry based on key issues encountered at the service site.

Ethical Case Study. At the service site students frequently encounter events that raise not only intellectual and practical, but also moral and ethical, issues. In this reflection activity, students are asked to write case studies of an ethical dilemma they confronted at the service site, including a description of the context, the individuals involved, and the controversy or dilemma they observed. Case studies can be written to include course content, as appropriate. Once the case studies are developed, they can provide the bases for formal papers, class presentations, or structured group discussions. These case studies are particularly well suited to an exploration and clarification of values because their diverse perspectives allow students to discuss the issue from alternative points of view. Lisman's seven-step method for discussing case studies can be adapted to service learning classes.[18]

Directed Readings. Some textbooks might not adequately challenge students to consider how knowledge within a discipline can be applied to the service site. This may particularly be the case for civic, moral, or systemic issues that students encounter. Additional readings that effectively probe these issues and prompt consideration of the relevance and limitations of course content can be assigned. The directed readings might come from the discipline. Alternatively, books that contain selected readings or chapters might be appropriate, including *Service-learning Reader: Reflections and Perspectives on Service; Education for Democracy; The Call of Service; and Common Fire.*[19] Students can be asked to write a two-page summary of the reading and its relevance to their service experience.

Class Presentations. Students can share experiences, service accomplishments, or products created during their service in classroom presentations that use videos, PowerPoint, bulletin boards, panel discussions, or speeches. These presentations provide excellent opportunities for students to organize their experiences, develop creative displays, and publicly celebrate their accomplishments. Community agency personnel can be invited to these presentations.

Electronic Reflection. Reflective exercises and dialogue interactions can occur through various means. Service learning practitioners are currently exploring the manner in which electronic modalities can be used as replacements for or supplements to traditional reflection activities. The recent book edited by James-Deramo is an important resource for educators interested in using Web-based modes of communication (e.g., class home pages, chat rooms, on-line survey forms), electronic mail, and class listservs to present material; structure discussions; submit reflective journal entries; and deal with issues at the service site. This resource also highlights ways to build learning communities among students and instructors by using technology.[20]

Assessing Reflection

Selection and Design of Reflection Activities. Designing reflection activities for a service learning class requires careful thought about the nature, structure, and function of each component. These considerations must incorporate other class assignments, whether or not all students are involved in service learning. Optional service might limit the use of class discussion and the variety of forms and modalities of reflection. In addition, we have suggested that effective reflection should observe the following five guidelines: reflection activities should (a) clearly link the service experience to the course content and learning objectives; (b) be structured in terms of description, expectations, and the criteria for assessing the activity; (c) occur regularly during the semester so that students can practice reflection and develop the capacity to engage in deeper and broader reflection; (d) provide feedback from the instructor about at least some of the reflection activities so that students learn how to improve their critical analysis and develop from reflective practice, and (e) include the opportunity for students to explore, clarify, and alter their values.[21]

Outcome. Students differ in how easily they engage in reflection and how quickly they mature in ability to learn from reflection. Table 2 presents a set of criteria developed by Bradley to assess levels of reflection.[22] Presenting these criteria to students prior to reflection activities can be helpful in creating expectations about their own development as reflective learners. Students can also be asked to evaluate their reflection activities with the criteria prior to evaluation by the instructor. This exercise provides opportunities for self-evaluation by the students as well as occasions to compare student and instructor assessments.

Consequences of Reflection

Little research has been conducted on how the amount or type of reflection activity is related to student outcomes. Mabry conducted analyses across twenty-three different service learning classes. The results tabulated the responses of students who engaged in classroom reflection activities (e.g., discussion groups with other students, using experiences in class, being asked in class for examples from service experience) and participated in face-to-face discussions with site supervisors, course instructors, and other students attributed more learning to the service experience than did students who had not engaged in those reflection activities.[23] These effects were significant after controlling for demographic variables, pre-test variables, and other independent variables.

There may be other benefits for the learner who engages in reflection in addition to course-specific learning outcomes. Pennebaker, Kiecolt-Glaser, and Glaser's experimental study manipulated whether

---

TABLE 2
Bradley's Criteria for Assessing Levels of Reflection

Level One

1. Gives examples of observed behaviors or characteristics of the client or setting, but provides no insight into reasons behind the observation; observations tend to become dimensional and conventional or unassimilated repetitions of what has been heard in class or from peers.
2. Tends to focus on just one aspect of the situation.
3. Uses unsupported personal beliefs as frequently as "hard" evidence.
4. May acknowledge differences of perspective but does not discriminate effectively among them.

Level Two

1. Observations are fairly thorough and nuanced although they tend not to be placed in a broader context.
2. Provides a cogent critique from one perspective, but fails to see the broader system in which the aspect is embedded and other factors that may make change difficult.
3. Uses both unsupported personal belief and evidence but is beginning to be able to differentiate between them.
4. Perceives legitimate differences of viewpoint.
5. Demonstrates a beginning ability to interpret evidence.

Level Three

1. Views things from multiple perspectives; able to observe multiple aspects of the situation and place them in context.
2. Perceives conflicting goals within and among the individuals involved in a situation and recognizes that the differences can be evaluated.
3. Recognizes that actions must be situationally dependent and understands many of the factors that affect their choice.
4. Makes appropriate judgments based on reasoning and evidence.
5. Has a reasonable assessment of the importance of the decisions facing clients and of his or her responsibility as a part of the clients' lives.

---

college students wrote on four consecutive days about either traumatic experiences or superficial topics. Those who wrote about the traumatic event, compared to the other group, had more favorable immune-system responses, less-frequent health-center visits, and higher subjective well-being.[24] Similar effects have been found in other studies conducted by Pennebaker and colleagues.

Writing about emotional upheavals has been found to improve the physical and mental health of grade-school children and nursing home residents, arthritis sufferers, medical school students, maximum-security prisoners, new mothers, and rape victims. Not only are there benefits to health, but writing about emotional topics has been found to reduce anxiety and depression, improve grades in college, and . . . aid people in securing new jobs.[25]

Pennebaker also reports on analyses of the essay's content to determine if characteristics of the narratives were related to the writer's subsequent health and well-being. The most important factor that differentiated persons showing health improvements from those who did not was the improved ability to include causal thinking, insight, and self-reflection in their stories. Thus, reflection activities that promote personally meaningful as well as academically meaningful explorations of experiences encountered in service settings may yield health as well as intellectual benefits to students.

However, the instructors should keep in mind the risks associated with structured, ongoing reflection activities in a service learning course. Batson, Fultz, Schoenrade, and Paduano conducted studies that examined the effects that critical self-reflection can have on the perceived motives of someone who has helped others. Critical self-reflection is an honest attempt to answer the question, "Why *really* am I doing good?" Batson and his colleagues found that critical self-reflection caused a self-deprecating bias that eroded the attribution that helping was done for altruistic reasons.[26] The effect was particularly strong for individuals who valued honest self-knowledge and those who were cognizant of the personal gain they would receive by helping others. It is interesting that all three of these conditions? reflection on motives, promoting self-knowledge, and personal gains for helping (e.g., course credit)? can exist in service learning courses.

Conclusion

Higher education has experienced a tremendous growth in service learning courses during the 1990s. This growth has been supported by funds and technical assistance provided by the Corporation for National Service and Campus Compact to promote service learning. Through "Learn and Serve America: Higher Education" grants, the corporation has stimulated the creation of thousands of service-learning courses. Similarly, Campus Compact estimates that 11,800 service-learning courses are available to students on its member campuses. As service learning becomes a more integral part of the curriculum, the manner in which it can improve educational goals needs better understanding.

Altman describes three distinct types of knowledge: content knowledge (i.e., rote learning of content), process knowledge (e.g., skills), and socially relevant knowledge.[27] Traditional instructional methods may effectively produce content knowledge and possibly process knowledge. However, service learning can promote both content and process knowledge,[28] and it is particularly well-suited for developing socially relevant knowledge in students. How reflection activities are designed plays an important role in their capacity to yield learning, support personal growth, provide insight, develop skills, and promote civic responsibility.

Trosset found that students often view discussions with peers, particularly discussion about race, gender, and sexual preference, as primarily forums for advocacy and persuading others to accept new viewpoints on controversial issues.[29] Discussions were not viewed by students as ways to explore differences through dialogue. Droge and Heiss, however, found a contrasting picture: students endorsed discussions with peers as opportunities to learn from others, to have their views challenged, and to use materials other than their personal experiences to inform and change their views.[30] These contrasting cases in higher education should alert educators to the different assumptions that students may bring to experiential and educational activities. Differences such as these will be present among service learning students. Creating a classroom climate of trust and respect is an essential element in fostering reflective practice among students; students who are more skeptical of the process can be supported in taking personal risks in the learning process.

These differences also highlight how the structure of a reflection activity can influence the results of a service experience: whether they will be educative and lead to new ways of thinking and acting, or miseducative and reinforce existing schemata and stereotypes. For service learning to educate students toward a more active role in community, careful attention must be given to reflection. Reflection activities must allow students to discover the value of dialogue, embrace the importance of perplexity in the learning process, and develop the ability to make meaning of personal experience.

Notes

1. John Dewey, *Democracy and Education* (New York: Macmillan Inc., 1916).
2. Task Group on General Education, *Strong Foundations: Twelve Principles for Effective General Education Programs.* (Washington, D.C.: Association of American Colleges, 1994).
3. Robert G. Bringle and Julie A. Hatcher, "A Service-learning Curriculum for Faculty," *Michigan Journal of Community Service Learning* 2 (1995): 112.
4. Edward Zlotkowski, "Pedagogy and Engagement," in *Colleges and Universities as Citizens*, ed. Robert Bringle, Rich Games, and Edward Malloy (Boston: Allyn & Bacon, 1999) 96–120.
5. Julie A. Hatcher and Robert G. Bringle, "Reflections: Bridging the Gap between Service and Learning," *Journal of College Teaching* 45 (1997): 153.
6. Dewey, *Democracy and Education*, 144.

7. John Dewey, *How We Think A Restatement of the Relation of Reflective Thinking to the Educative Process* (Boston: D.C. Heath and Company, 1933), 146.

8. Ibid., 3.

9. James Gouinlock, ed., *The Moral Writings of John Dewey* (New York: Prometheus Books, 1994), xxxvi.

10. Dwight E. Giles and Janet Eyler, "The Theoretical Roots of Service-learning in John Dewey: Towards a Theory of Service-learning," *Michigan Journal of Community Service Learning* 1 (1994): 77–85.

11. Dewey, *How We Think*, 14.

12. Julie A. Hatcher, "The Moral Dimensions of John Dewey's Philosophy: Implications for Undergraduate Education," *Michigan Journal of Community Service Learning* 4 (1997): 22–29.

13. Giles and Eyler, "The Theoretical Roots of Service-learning."

14. Dewey, *How We Think*.

15. Janet Eyler, Dwight E. Giles, and Angela Schmiede, *A Practitioner's Guide to Reflection in Service-learning: Student Voices and Reflections* (Nashville: Vanderbilt University, 1996).

16. James W. Pennebaker, *Opening Up: The Healing Power of Expressing Emotions*. New York: Guilford Press, 1990), 40.

17. David A. Kolb, *Experiential Learning: Experience as the Source of Learning and Development* (Englewood Cliffs, N.J.: Prentice-Hall, 1984).

18. C. David Lisman, *The Curricular Integration of Ethics: Theory and Practice* (Westport: Praeger Publishing, 1995).

19. Gail Albert, ed., *Service-learning Reader: Reflections and Perspectives on Service* (Raleigh: National Society for Experiential Education, 1994); Benjamin R. Barber and Richard M. Battistoni, eds., *Education for Democracy* (Dubuque: Kendall/Hunt, 1993); Robert Coles, *The Call of Service: A Witness to Idealism* (New York: Houghton Mifflin, 1993); Laurent A. Daloz, et al., *Common Fire: Lives of Commitment in a Complex world* (Boston: Beacon Press, 1996).

20. Michele James-Deramo, ed., *Best Practices in Cyber-Serve: Integrating Technology with Service-Learning Instruction* (Virginia Tech Service-Learning Center: Corporation for National Service, 1999).

21. Hatcher and Bringle, "Reflections."

22. James Bradley, "A Model for Evaluating Student Learning in Academically Based Service," *Connecting Cognition and Action: Evaluation of Student Performance in Service Learning Course*, ed. Marie Troppe (Denver: Education Commission of the States/Campus Compact, 1995).

23. J. Beth Mabry, "Pedagogical Variations in Service-Learning and Student Outcomes: How Time, Contact, and Reflection Matter," *Michigan Journal of Community Service Learning* 5 (1998): 34.

24. James W. Pennebaker, Janice Kiecolt-Glaser, and Ronald Glaser, "Disclosure of Traumas and Immune Function: Health Implications for Psychotherapy," *Journal of Consulting and Clinical Psychology* 56.2 (1988): 239–45.

25. Pennebaker, *Opening Up*, 40.

26. C. Daniel Batson, et al., "Critical Self-Reflection and Self-Perceived Altruism: When Self-Reward Fails," *Journal of Personality and Social Psychology* 53 (1987): 594–602.

27. Irwin Altman, "Higher Education and Psychology in the Millennium," *American Psychologist* 51 (1996): 371–98.

28. Randall E. Osbome, Sharon Hammerich, and Chanin Hensley, "Student Effects of Service-learning: Tracking Change across a Semester," *Michigan Journal of Community Service Learning* 5 (1998): 5–13.

29. Carol Trosset, "Obstacles to Open Discussion and Critical Thinking: The Grinnell College Study," *Change* 30.5 (1998): 44–49.

30. David Droge and Janet Heiss, "Discussion and Critical Thinking among College Students: Are Grinnell Undergraduates Weird?" (Northwest Communication Association, Coeur d'Alene, ID, April 1999).

THE LIMITS OF SERVICE-LEARNING IN HIGHER EDUCATION

DAN W. BUTIN

Introduction

The service-learning movement has become a major presence within higher education. More than 950 colleges and universities are Campus Compact members, committed to the civic purposes of higher education. Tens of thousands of faculty engage millions of college students in some form of service-learning practice each and every year. Major federal and private funding sustains and expands an increasingly diverse K-16 service-learning movement.

The substantial spread of service-learning over the last ten years mirrors a larger development in the academy—namely, higher education has begun to embrace a "scholarship of engagement" (Boyer, 1990; Shulman, 2004), be it manifested as experiential education, service-learning, undergraduate research, community-based research, the scholarship of teaching and learning movement, or stronger relationships with local communities. A scholarship of engagement is seen to link theory and practice, cognitive and affective learning, and colleges with communities. Such a paradigm of teaching and learning seemingly breaches the bifurcation of lofty academics with the lived reality of everyday life to promote critical inquiry and reflective practice across complex and contested local, national, and international issues.

Yet even as the idea of service-learning moves into the academic mainstream, its actual institutional footprint appears uncertain. Service-learning is all too often positioned as a co-curricular practice, funded through "soft" short-term grants, and viewed by faculty as "just" an atheoretical (and time-consuming) pedagogy that may be detrimental for traditional tenure and promotion committees to take seriously. It is in this context that service-learning advocates have begun to devote intensive efforts to institutionalize service-learning within higher education. As service-learning practice and theory has reached a critical mass, attention has turned in the last few years to ensuring its institutional longevity.

In this article, I take a critical look at the attempted institutionalization of service-learning in higher education. I query whether service-learning can become deeply embedded within the academy; and, if so, what exactly it is that becomes embedded. Specifically, this article suggests that there are substantial pedagogical, political, and institutional limits to service-learning across the academy. These limits, moreover, are inherent to the service-learning movement as contemporarily theorized and enacted. As such, I argue, there may be a fundamental and unbridgeable gap between the rhetoric and reality of the aspirations of the present-day service-learning movement.

It should be noted that the goal of this article is not to dismiss, denigrate, or derail the immense work put in by two generations of service-learning scholars and advocates. Service-learning has immense transformational potential as a sustained, immersive, and consequential pedagogical practice (Butin, 2005a). Yet such potential, I suggest, can be fostered only by explicating the limits of present-day theoretical foundations and pedagogical practices that may inadvertently inhibit and constrain service-learning scholars and practitioners. As the concluding section makes clear, such an explication may in fact offer substantial alternative possibilities for institutionalizing service-learning in higher education.

This article situates the service-learning movement through an analysis of its drive towards institutionalization. Such an analysis reveals some of the fundamental and underlying assumptions of the service-learning field. I then show how these assumptions harbor significant pedagogical, political, and institutional impediments for the authentic institutionalization of service-learning. I conclude by suggesting how a reframing of such assumptions may allow service-learning to be repositioned as a disciplinary field more suitable for becoming deeply embedded in higher education.

Institutionalizing Service-Learning

After a heady decade of exponential growth, the service-learning movement appears ideally situated within higher education. It is used by a substantial number of faculty across an increasingly diverse range of academic courses; administrative offices and centers are devoted to promoting its use; and it is prominently cited in college and university presidents' speeches, on institutional homepages, and in marketing brochures.

Yet as the recent Wingspread statement (2004) put it: "The honeymoon period for engagement is over; the difficult task of creating a lasting commitment has begun" (p. 4). For underneath the surface, the service-learning movement has found its institutionalization within higher education far from secure. Fewer than half of all service-learning directors are full-time, and 46% of all service-learning offices have annual budgets below $20,000 (Campus Compact, 2004). While the idea of service-learning is given high support across the academy, it is infrequently "hard wired" into institutional practices and policies. Service-learning is overwhelmingly used by the least powerful and most marginalized faculty (e.g., people of color, women, and the untenured), by the "softest" and most "vocational" disciplines and fields (e.g., education, social work), and with minimal exchange value (e.g., tenure and promotion prioritization) (Antonio, Astin, & Cross, 2000; Campus Compact, 2004). Recent research (Bell et al., 2000) suggests that even institutions at the top of the "service-learning pyramid" consistently have to revisit and rework service-learning implementation and institutionalization.

More troubling still is that the academy's "buy in" to service-learning may be much easier said than done, with few political or institutional costs for failing to achieve substantial goals. Rhetoric may be winning over reality. It is thus that the Wingspread Statement "call[s] the question": "Is higher education ready to commit to engagement?" (Brukardt et al., 2004, p. ii). This can be framed in poker parlance of calling the bluff. Does higher education have the desire, the long-term fortitude, and the resources to remake itself? Is higher education able, for the sake of itself, its students, and American society more generally, to embrace a more engaged, democratic, and transformative vision of what it should be, should have been, and was before? (Benson, Harkavy, & Hartley, 2005). If so, then it had better ante up.

There is thus a burgeoning literature on the institutionalization of service-learning. I want to focus on Andy Furco's work (2001, 2002a, 2002b, 2003; Furco & Billig, 2002) and on the Wingspread statement because each takes a diametrically opposed stance on the *means* of institutionalizing service-learning; both, however, carry exactly the same assumptions of what the *outcomes* of such institutionalization should be. While the literature is ever-growing and far from singular in perspective (Bell et al., 2000; Benson, Harkavy, & Hartley, 2005; Bringle & Hatcher, 2000; Gray, Ondaatje, & Zakaras, 2000; Hartley, Harkavy, & Benson, 2005; Holland, 2001; Kramer, 2000), Furco's work and the Wingspread statement are emblematic of the dominant vision and goals for service-learning institutionalization and the two primary and divergent paths to achieving such goals.

Specifically, Furco's work offers a systematic rubric for gauging the *incremental* progress of service-learning institutionalization; the Wingspread statement, in contrast, promotes a *transformational* vision for service-learning in higher education. Educational historian Larry Cuban (1990, 1998) has cogently referred to this distinction as first- versus second-order change and has explored the historical contexts and conditions that support one form of educational reform over another. More interesting for this article is that, irrespective of the divergent means propounded, both perspectives have a vision of service-learning as a meta-text for the policies, practices, and philosophies of higher education. Thus, irrespective of how it is to be institutionalized, service-learning is seen as the skeleton key to unlock the power and potential of postsecondary education as a force for democracy and social justice. By further explicating the divergent means propounded by incrementalist and transformationalist perspectives, it becomes possible to grasp the overarching assumptions and implications of the service-learning movement.

Furco (2002b) has developed a rubric for viewing the institutionalization of service-learning. The rubric acts as a road map that individuals and institutions committed to embedding service-learning throughout their campuses may follow. It further works as a formal or informal assessment mechanism to gauge progress along the institutionalization path. Furco operationalizes institutionalization across five distinct dimensions "which are considered by most service-learning experts to be key factors for higher education service-learning institutionalization" (p. 1): (a) philosophy and mission, (b) faculty support and involvement, (c) student support and involvement, (d) community participation and partnerships, and (e) institutional support. While Furco argues elsewhere (2001, 2002a, 2003) that research identifies the key institutional factors as faculty and institutional support, the rubric makes clear that "What is most important is the overall status of the campus's institutionalization progress rather than the progress of individual components" (p. 3).

The real value and usefulness of the rubric is that it clearly and succinctly lays out the step-by-step increments by which a campus can institutionalize service-learning. Faculty support for and involvement in service-learning, for example, moves from "very few" to "an adequate number" to "a substantial number" of faculty who are knowledgeable about, involved in, and leaders of service-learning on a campus. Staffing moves from "no staff" to "an appropriate number . . . paid from soft money or external grant funds" to "an appropriate number of permanent staff members" (p. 13). The rubric does not suggest how such incremental progress is to be achieved; each campus culture and context is different. Instead, it lays out an explicit framework for (in Cuban's terminology) "tinkering" toward institutionalization.

The Wingspread participants (Brukardt et al., 2004) have a fundamentally different agenda: "Our goal in calling the question is nothing less than the transformation of our nation's colleges and universities" (p. ii). Six specific practices are articulated to institutionalize engagement and accomplish this goal: (a) integrate engagement into mission, (b) forge partnerships as the overarching framework, (c) renew and redefine discovery and scholarship, (d) integrate engagement into teaching and learning, (e) recruit and support new champions, and (f) create radical institutional change. Many of these practices mirror Furco's rubric and are possible to implement without radical transformation: integrating engagement into a mission statement, forging stronger partnerships, fostering more engaged pedagogy, and recruiting new voices to speak for engagement are all doable without fundamentally altering the structure and practices of higher education.[1]

What *is* radically different are the third and sixth practices. Redefining scholarship and creating radical institutional change by, for example, overturning higher education's "hierarchical, elitist and competitive environment" (p. 15) is a revolutionary call to arms. And the Wingspread participants are well aware of this. Each specific practice in the statement has a "What Is Needed" section that offers concrete action steps. For example, it recommends "expanded assessment and portfolio review options for faculty" (Brukardt et al., 2004, p. 14) to integrate engagement into teaching and learning. This seems eminently reasonable. Yet under the "Create Radical Institutional Change" section, what is needed is "Courage!", "New models", "Serious . . . funding", "New links between academic work and critical public issues", and "Institutional flexibility and willingness to experiment—and to fail." These are not action steps. They are a battle cry.

Thus, where Furco's rubric offers a deliberate and deliberative procession of rational increments, the *Wingspread Statement* provides a fiery manifesto for reinvention. Irrespective of which model is better (or whether, perhaps, both are necessary), of relevance is that both assume that, by whichever means necessary, service-learning should become an overarching framework for higher education. This framework, moreover, should be embedded both horizontally across departments and vertically throughout all levels of an institution's pronouncements, policies, and practices. Both presume that service-learning can and should be done from accounting to women's studies; that all students, faculty, administrators, and community partners can be involved; and that everything from line-item budgets to institutional webpages have the imprint of service-learning.

Such a scenario is nothing less than a grand narrative for higher-education-as-service-learning, for it positions service-learning *as a politics* to transform higher education and society. The implications are both prominent and problematic. Such a perspective presumes that service-learning is a universal, coherent, cohesive, amelioristic, and liberatory practice. It further presumes that service-learning is not somehow always already a part of the institutional practices and norms it is attempting to modify and overcome. Yet as the following sections clarify, such presumptions are unfounded.

The Limits of Institutionalization

In this section I question the notion of service-learning as an overarching and transformative agent of social change and social justice in higher education and society more generally by focusing on three specific claims made by the service-learning movement—that service-learning is a means (a) to transform pedagogy, (b) to usher in a more democratic and socially just politics in higher education, and (c) to redirect postsecondary institutions outward toward public work rather than inward toward academic elitism.

These claims, it should be noted, are premised on an inherent compatibility between service-learning and the academy. This seeming compatibility indexes assumptions that civic engagement and "real world" learning are hallmarks of the future of higher education. Yet such assumptions are, of course, open to contestation and critique, perhaps the most biting of which has come from Stanley Fish. Fish (2004) has opined that we should stick to questions about the truth and not bother with issues of morality, democracy, or social justice: "We should look to the practices in our own shop, narrowly conceived, before we set out to alter the entire world by forming moral character, or fashioning democratic citizens, or combating globalization, or embracing globalization, or anything else" (p. A23; see also Butin, 2005b, for a contextualization of this argument). Fish was responding directly to a publication from a group of scholars at the Carnegie Foundation's Higher Education and Development of Moral and Civic Responsibility Project (Colby et al., 2003), but his critique has general resonance for those who see the academy as primarily a site of knowledge production and dissemination rather than of something as nondefinable and potentially partisan as moral and civic betterment.

I am sympathetic to Fish's arguments and have elsewhere explicated the theoretical limits of service-learning as beholden to a teleological and ethical stage theory framework in which students and faculty are supposed to move from a perspective of "service-learning as charity" to "service-learning as social justice" (Butin, 2003, 2005b, in press-a). Yet such larger theoretical debates about the values and purposes of service-learning vis-à-vis higher education are ultimately beyond the scope of this article, for the question today is no longer *if* service-learning is to become a part of the academy so much as *how* it is already becoming a part of it and the resulting implications.

Pedagogical Limits to Service-Learning

Advocates see service-learning as a transformative pedagogy that links classrooms with the real world, the cognitive with the affective, and theory with practice, thereby disrupting a banking model of education premised on passive students, expert faculty, and the "simple" transfer of discrete and quantifiable knowledge (Freire, 1994; hooks, 1994). Service-learning is supposed to foster respect for and reciprocity with the communities that colleges and universities are all too often in but not of.

But is this possible? Campus Compact's (2004) annual membership survey shows the following departments with the highest offering of service-learning courses: education (69%), sociology (56%), English (55%), psychology (55%), business/accounting (46%), communications (46%), and health/health related (45%). In a now-classic formulation, Becher (Becher & Trowler, 2001) argued that academic disciplines can be differentiated along two spectra: hard/soft and pure/applied. Hard-pure fields (e.g., chemistry and physics) view knowledge as cumulative and are concerned with universals, simplification, and quantification. Hard-applied fields (e.g., engineering) make use of hard, pure knowledge to develop products and techniques. Soft-pure fields (e.g., English) view knowledge as iterative and are concerned with particularity and qualitative inquiry. Soft-applied fields (e.g., education, management) make use of soft, pure knowledge to develop protocols and heuristics. What becomes immediately clear is that service-learning is overwhelmingly used in the "soft" disciplines. Biology is the highest "hard" field (at number 10 with 37%), with the natural sciences next at number 18 (with 25%).

I, of course, acknowledge that the hard/soft and pure/applied distinctions are socially constructed typologies that carry longstanding ideological baggage and serve as proxies for contestations surrounding the power, legitimacy, and prestige of any particular discipline. Scholars in the sociology of knowledge and history of science have shown not simply the ambiguity and permeability of the boundaries between so-called "soft" and "hard" disciplines, but have fundamentally questioned the (to use Foucault's terminology) "scientificity" of claims to the objective and neutral practice of mapping reality (Hacking, 1999; Lather, 2005; Latour, 1979). Yet what is at issue here is not whether there is "really" a distinction between the hard and soft sciences, but how such a socially constructed distinction is ultimately determined and practiced in our day-to-day life. As Cornel West (1994) once wryly noted, taxicabs in Harlem still didn't stop for him even if race was a social construction. Likewise, there is a plethora of empirical evidence (Biglan, 1973; Lueddeke, 2003; NCES, 2002) that teaching practices differ significantly across disciplines; as such, these disciplinary distinctions serve as useful heuristics for understanding how service-learning may or may not be taken up across the academy.

The service-learning field acknowledges that soft disciplines are much more apt to make use of service-learning, yet proponents presume that this is simply a consequence of *either* poorly marketing what service-learning can offer the hard sciences (from an incrementalist perspective) or the inability of the hard sciences to transform themselves into useful public disciplines (from a transformational perspective). What both perspectives miss is that Becher's typology demonstrates that each grouping of disciplines manifests "its own epistemological characteristics . . . [of] curriculum, assessment and main cognitive purpose . . . [and] the group characteristics of teachers, the types of teaching methods involved and the learning requirements of students" (Neumann & Becher, 2002, p. 406).

Of most salience here are divergent concepts of teaching styles and assessment procedures between hard and soft disciplines. I will focus only on the hard disciplines here to make vivid their antipathy to service-learning assumptions. Given the sequential and factual nature of the hard disciplines, lecturing predominates as the teaching style. Moreover, the cumulative nature of knowledge makes moot any notion of student perspectives or "voice" in the field. It is simply not relevant how students "feel" about subatomic particles. As such, "in keeping with their atomistic structure [hard/pure knowledge fields] prefer specific and closely focused examination questions to broader, essay-type assignments" (Neumann & Becher, 2002, p. 408). "Objective" tests, norm-referenced grading, and lack of rubrics (given the right/wrong nature of what constitutes knowledge) are typical.

U.S. Department of Education statistics support these theoretical insights. The most recent available data (NCES, 2002, Table 16) show that the social sciences and humanities use apprenticeships and fieldwork much more often (10–15% depending on the discipline) than the natural sciences (2–3%). Humanities and social sciences faculty are almost twice as likely to use research papers than natural science faculty (70–85% versus 40–50%, respectively), and half as likely to grade on a curve (20–30% versus 40–50%) (Tables 18, 22). While some of these data are confounded by the type of institution (e.g., doctoral versus nondoctoral institutions), fairly distinct patterns and differences among disciplines are visible.

Above and beyond these disciplinary differences, though, emerges a more troubling realization. Fully 83% of all faculty use lecturing as the primary instructional method in college classrooms. This percentage does not drastically change across the type of institution, faculty rank or tenure status, or discipline (NCES, 2002, Tables 15, 16). Thus, irrespective of disciplinary and epistemological differences, the vast majority of faculty in higher education see themselves as embodying the normative (read: non service-learning-oriented) model of teaching and learning.[2] This dominant trend is further exacerbated by the reality that non-tenure track faculty by now constitute almost half of all teaching faculty in higher education (Snyder, Tan, & Hoffman, 2004). A normative model of teaching is thus reinforced by the marginal and transitory status of faculty. There thus appears to be a very low upper limit to the use of service-learning across higher education.

If faculty demographics do not conform to who should make use of service-learning, then student demographics do not align with the type of students supposedly doing service-learning. I have argued elsewhere that the service-learning field assumes an "ideal type" of service-learning student: one who volunteers her time, has high cultural capital, and gains from contact with the "other" (Butin, 2003). The service-learning literature is replete with discussions of how students come to better understand themselves, cultural differences, and social justice through service-learning. The overarching assumption is that the students doing the service-learning are White, sheltered, middle-class, single, without children, un-indebted, and between ages 18 and 24. But that is not the demographics of higher education today, and it will be even less so in 20 years.

NCES (Snyder, Tan, & Hoffman, 2004) data show that the largest growth in postsecondary enrollment will be in for-profit and two-year institutions; already today, fully 39% of all postsecondary enrollment is in two-year institutions (Table 178). Moreover, 34% of undergraduates are over 25 years of age; 40% of undergraduates are part-time. Even considering just full-time undergraduates, more than 18% are over 25 years of age (Tables 176, 177). Additionally, college completion rates continue to be low: fewer than half of all college entrants complete a baccalaureate degree, with graduation percentages dipping much lower for two-year institutions and among part-time, lower-class, and/or non-White students. Finally, U.S. census data forecast that White youth will become a numeric minority in our K-12 schools within a generation; this changing demographic wave is already impacting the makeup of higher education.

These statistics raise three serious pedagogical issues for the service-learning field. First, service-learning is premised on full-time, single, nonindebted, and childless students pursuing a "liberal arts education." Yet a large proportion of the postsecondary population of today, and increasingly of the future, views higher education as a part-time, instrumental, and pre-professional endeavor that must be juggled with children, family time, and earning a living wage. Service-learning may be a luxury that many students cannot afford, whether in terms of time, finances, or job future.

Second, service-learning is premised on fostering "border-crossing" across categories of race, ethnicity, class, (im)migrant status, language, and (dis)ability. Yet what happens when the postsecondary population *already* occupies those identity categories? The service-learning field is only now beginning to explore such theoretical and pragmatic dilemmas (e.g., Henry, 2005; Henry & Breyfogle, in press; Swaminathan, 2005, in press), and these investigations are already disrupting some of the most basic categories within the service-learning field (e.g., the server/served binary, student/teacher and classroom/community power dynamics and reciprocity).

Third, there is a distinct possibility that service-learning may ultimately come to be viewed as the "Whitest of the White" enclave of postsecondary education. Given changing demographics and the rise of the "client-centered" postsecondary institution, service-learning may come to signify a luxury available only to the privileged few. Educational research has clearly shown how inequities across K-12 academic tracks (in e.g., teacher quality, adequate resources, and engaging curricula) correlates to youth's skin color and socioeconomic status. Such hierarchies within service-learning in higher education are not unthinkable.

Arguments can, of course, be made from both incrementalist and transformationalist perspectives. The former will argue that these issues will simply take more time to work through while the latter will argue that, in transforming higher education, such issues will become irrelevant. Perhaps. The goal here is not to be defeatist, presentist, or conservative; it is not to argue that higher education is a static and unchangeable monolith. Rather, my goal is simply to map out the structures and norms that inhibit the institutionalization of a viable and powerful service-learning pedagogy.

Political Limits to Service-Learning

Even if service-learning succeeds in overcoming the pedagogical barriers just described, what exactly is it that will become institutionalized? By framing service-learning as a politics, advocates may in fact be undermining their most valued goal. Specifically, by viewing service-learning as a universal transformative practice, advocates may allow it to become misappropriated and drained of its transformative potential.

Service-learning has a progressive and liberal agenda under the guise of a universalistic practice. The *Presidents' Declaration on the Civic Responsibility of Higher Education* (Campus Compact, 2000), for example, declares:

> Higher education is uniquely positioned to help Americans understand the histories and contours of our present challenges as a diverse democracy. It is also uniquely positioned to help both students and our communities to explore new ways of fulfilling the promise of justice and dignity for all. . . . We know that pluralism is a source of strength and vitality that will enrich our students' education and help them learn both to respect difference and to work together for the common good. (p. 1)

This is a noble and neutral sounding statement. Who could be against "the common good"? Yet clearly, the "diversity" and "dignity" being spoken are not those belonging to political conservatives. Rather, the reference is to the multiple populations within the United States who have suffered historically (and many still do today) due to social, cultural, economic, and educational marginalization, degradation, and destruction.

This view has a certain natural-seeming quality within the academy, as higher education is supposed to expand its participants' perspectives about how to think and act differently in becoming a public citizen. Yet while this goal also has a deep resonance with the service-learning field (and, some might say, is at the heart of the service-learning field [see Stanton, Giles, & Cruz, 1999]), it is certainly not the norm in our highly divided red state/blue state America. The most obvious example of this division is David Horowitz's (n.d.) "academic bill of rights."

Horowitz, the president of the Center for Study of Popular Culture, has crafted a seemingly neutral policy declaration demanding that colleges and universities not discriminate against political or religious orientations, thus enabling "academic freedom and intellectual diversity" to flourish in the academy. "Academic freedom," the document states,

> consists in protecting the intellectual independence of professors, researchers and students in pursuit of knowledge and the expression of ideas from interference by legislatures or authorities within the institution itself. This means that no political, ideological or religious orthodoxy will be imposed on professors and researchers through the hiring or tenure or termination process, or through any other administrative means by the academic institution. (p. 1)

The document goes on to enumerate numerous principles and procedures that flow from this statement of principle. These include, among others, that a faculty member cannot be "hired or fired or denied promotion or tenure on the basis of his or her political or religious beliefs," that "students will be graded solely on the basis of their reasoned answers," and that "exposing students to the spectrum of significant scholarly viewpoints on the subjects examined in their courses is a major responsibility of faculty. Faculty will not use their courses for the purpose of political, ideological, religious or anti-religious indoctrination" (p. 2). These proposals sound eminently reasonable until one realizes that Horowitz is deliberately attempting to dismantle what he sees as the liberal orthodoxy permeating higher education.

Horowitz and Lehrer (n.d.) have shown, and social science research confirms (Lindholm et al., 2005; Klein & Stern, 2005; Rothman, Lichter, & Nevitte, 2005), that higher education faculty are overwhelming registered as Democrats, with (according to his data) an overall ratio of 10 to 1 across departments and upper-level administrations. On some campuses (e.g., Williams, Oberlin, Haverford), Horowitz could not find a single registered Republican faculty member. This, Horowitz (2003) argues, is not diversity:

> What is knowledge if it is thoroughly one-sided, or intellectual freedom if it is only freedom to conform? And what is a "liberal education," if one point of view is for all intents and purposes excluded from the classroom? How can students get a good education, if they are only being told one side of the story? The answer is they can't. (p. 1)

The attack on the liberal leanings of higher education is not new. What is new, though, are Horowitz's (2003) proposed strategies:

> I have undertaken the task of organizing conservative students myself and urging them to protest a situation that has become intolerable. *I encourage them to use the language that the left has deployed so effectively in behalf of its own agendas.* Radical professors have created a "hostile learning environment"

for conservative students. There is a lack of "intellectual diversity" on college faculties and in academic classrooms. The conservative viewpoint is "under-represented" in the curriculum and on its reading lists. The university should be an "inclusive" and intellectually "diverse" community. I have encouraged students to demand that their schools adopt an "academic bill of rights" that stresses intellectual diversity, that demands balance in their reading lists, that recognizes that political partisanship by professors in the classroom is an abuse of students' academic freedom, that the inequity in funding of student organizations and visiting speakers is unacceptable, and that a learning environment hostile to conservatives is unacceptable. (pp. 2–3; emphasis mine)

Service-learning is not explicitly on the list of Horowitz's grievances, but it very well could (and might) be. The service-learning literature is replete with students' resistance to the implicit and/or explicit social justice emphasis. Susan Jones (2002; Jones, Gilbride-Brown, & Gasorski, 2005), for example, has carefully shown how student resistance manifests itself in service-learning experiences and how instructors might—through a "critical developmental lens"—begin to overcome such resistance. Yet what is clear is that such resistance is not about liberals resisting a conservative agenda; as one resistant student wrote in Jones's end-of-semester evaluation: "I don't enjoy the preaching of a debatable agenda in the first hour. Perhaps teaching from a more balanced perspective would be better than 'isms [that] are keeping us down.' . . . More emphasis on community service. Less on ideologically driven readings and lessons" (qtd. in Jones, Gilbride-Brown, & Gasorski, 2005, p. 14).

The point is not that service-learning should stop having an ideological agenda, nor that service-learning should now embrace conservative service-learning to provide "balance." Rather, it is that service-learning embodies a liberal agenda under the guise of universalistic garb. As such, it is ripe for conservative appropriation; to date, close to two dozen states have either proposed or are about to propose legislation patterned on the academic bill of rights.[3] In Pennsylvania, where I teach, the state legislature has approved a committee to investigate potential bias in the academy. Leading higher education organizations have recently released their own responses of what constitutes academic freedom (AACU, 2005). An era of legislative and public scrutinizing of higher education's political practices has begun.

Horowitz (or any university president under public pressure) can thus very easily raise the specter of service-learning offices that are indoctrinating first-year students into biased, unscientific, and indefensible liberal groupthink practices through, for example, daylong conferences about capital punishment or women's rights. The solution? Horowitz would argue that either the entire service-learning office needs to be dismantled to avoid such blatant political abuse of public funds or that the university needs to completely rethink and redo how it helps students to think about such issues—by allowing undergraduates to work, for example, with a pro-life group to send out mailings or picketing with a retentionist organization committed to keeping the death penalty.

Service-learning is in a double-bind. If it attempts to be a truly radical and transformative (liberal) practice, it faces potential censure and sanction. If it attempts to be politically balanced to avoid such an attack, it risks losing any power to make a difference. At the root of this double-bind and the reason it cannot escape from this dilemma is that service-learning has positioned itself as a universalistic and thus neutral practice.

But as Stanley Fish (1999) has pointed out, there is no such thing.[4] "If, for example, I say 'Let's be fair,' you won't know what I mean unless I've specified the background conditions in relation to which fairness has an operational sense" (p.3). No statements or positions are value-free; they come saturated with particular historical, social, and cultural baggage. Thus, not only do genuinely neutral principles not exist, but when seemingly neutral principles *are* articulated, it is a blatantly political and strategic move. Fish continues:

Indeed, it is crucial that neutral principles not exist if they are to perform the function I have described, the function of facilitating the efforts of partisan agents to attach an honorific vocabulary to their agendas. For the effort to succeed, the vocabulary (of "fairness," "merit," "neutrality," "impartiality," "mutual respect," and so on) must be empty, have no traction or bite of its own, and thus be an unoccupied vessel waiting to be filled by whoever gets to it first or with the most persuasive force. (p. 7)

Seemingly neutral principles are thus used strategically to promote one's specific ideological agenda, irrespective of political orientation. This is exactly what Horowitz has done with "intellectual diversity" and what the service-learning movement is attempting to do with "civic engagement." But in attempting to hold the (imaginary) center, such strategizing in fact politicizes the term in question through binary extremism. In the former case, "intellectual diversity" becomes a stalking horse for right-wing conservatism; in the latter case, "civic engagement" becomes linked to radical left-wing demands for "social justice" (Butin, in press-a).

Service-learning thus finds itself positioned as attempting to deliver a very specific and highly political notion of the truth under the guise of neutral pedagogy. Its overarching stage theory of moving individuals and institutions from charity-based perspectives to justice-oriented ones, in fact, maps directly onto our folk theories of what constitutes Republican and Democratic political positions: Republicans believe in individual responsibility and charity while Democrats focus on institutional structures and social justice (Westheimer & Kahne, 2004).

To claim service-learning as a universalistic practice available to all political persuasions is thus to ignore its politically liberal trappings as presently conceptualized and enacted. To cite just one obvious counter-example, is it service-learning if Jerry Falwell's Liberty University requires as a graduation requirement that all undergraduates spend a certain amount of time helping to blockade abortion clinics and thus saving the lives of the unborn? What if this activity was linked to reflection groups and learning circles and students had to create portfolios showing how such community service was linked to their academic courses?

Few service-learning advocates, I suggest, would quickly or easily accept that this is service-learning, much less service-learning committed to social justice. But to not accept such a counter-example is to admit that service-learning is not a universalistic practice. It is to admit that service-learning is an ideologically driven practice. And in so doing, service-learning falls neatly into the "intellectual diversity" trap. Once trapped, there is no way out. Service-learning, in order to survive in higher education, will have to become "balanced."

Institutional Limits to Service-Learning

I have suggested so far that service-learning faces major pedagogical and political barriers to becoming institutionalized. Yet if service-learning could overcome these pedagogical and political barriers, would it then be the truly transformative movement envisioned? Again, sadly, I doubt it, for higher education works by very specific disciplinary rules about knowledge production, who has the academic legitimacy to produce such knowledge, and how (Messer-Davidow, Shumway, & Sylvan, 1993). The very institution that service-learning advocates are trying to storm, in other words, may drown them.

The clearest example of this already-ongoing process is what I'll term the "quantitative move" in the service-learning field. Put otherwise, service-learning scholarship is becoming adept at using the "statistically significant" nomenclature. The idea is to show that service-learning can, holding all other variables constant, positively impact student outcomes. Thus, a wide variety of scholarly studies has shown service-learning to be a statistically significant practice in impacting, among other things, students' personal and interpersonal development, stereotype reduction, sense of citizenship, and academic learning. (See Eyler et al., 2001, for a comprehensive summary.) Much of this research has very low betas (i.e., the actual impact is not, statistically speaking, profound); nevertheless, service-learning has been "proven" to make a measurable difference in a positive direction vis-à-vis other pedagogical and institutional variables.

The idea behind this quantitative move is obvious. Service-learning advocates want to show that service-learning is a legitimate practice with legitimate, consequential, and measurable outcomes in higher education. When in Rome, the thinking goes, do as the Romans. The problem is that Rome has burned. There are three distinct reasons why the quantitative move ultimately will not help to institutionalize the kind of service-learning hoped for.

The first reason is that quantifying the value-added of service-learning is methodologically impossible. There are simply too many variables commingling and interacting with each other to allow for valid and reliable conclusions. The number of variables, from type of sites to types of interactions to types of reflection to types of teaching styles, becomes too unmanageable to accurately quantify and measure. In this way service-learning is analogous to teaching and other "wickedly" complex problems defying quantitative solutions.

For example, educational researchers have for 30 years been trying to adequately quantify the most basic principle in the field: what makes a high-quality teacher. Yet as the research supporting the No Child Left Behind legislation and the push for alternative certification pathways shows, there are no such data (at least none that can be agreed upon).[5] While on its face such uncertainty is absurd, it is also the end result and consequence of a quixotic search for absolute and quantifiable surety. None exists, and attempts to find it quickly become beholden to political pressures about which variables are measured and how. I do not deny that the quantitative move offers some basic guidance on some basic proxy variables. This is an important development. But to pin the legitimacy of service-learning on its quantification is to misunderstand how legitimacy ultimately works.

This strategy of legitimization is, in fact, the second reason why the quantitative move falters in the academy—namely, the paradigms by which we see the world are inextricably linked to our value systems as legitimate scholars. Thomas Kuhn, in his classic *The Structure of Scientific Revolutions* (1996), posited that paradigms shift, not because of rational discourse among objective scientists but because the old guard dies away and is replaced by the young turks with their own particular paradigm. While the conservative status-quo nature of this view has been roundly critiqued, the underlying psychological framework seems sound (see, e.g., Gardner, 2004): the more contested and revolutionary an issue, the stronger our resistance to it.

To again use an example from teacher education, a recent review of the literature on teacher change argued: "What we see expressed in these current studies of teacher education is the difficulty in changing the type of tacit beliefs and understandings that lie buried in a person's being" (Richardson & Placier, 2001, p. 915). Thus after four years of coursework, field experiences, and self-selective dispositions toward becoming a good teacher, the vast majority of teacher candidates leave their programs believing pretty much what they came in with.

It is thus naive for service-learning advocates to believe that a large number of academics will be persuaded to accept service-learning simply because data show it to have a statistically significant impact on any particular student outcome. As I have argued elsewhere (Butin, 2005b), a simple thought experiment puts this lie to rest: If data showed that students' work with terminally ill AIDS patients negatively impacted student understanding of the social health system, would that be reason enough to stop the program? Probably not. Service-learning advocates would instead

> question the validity and reliability of such data: How is "understanding" being measured? Is success defined instrumentally (i.e., test grades) or holistically (i.e., emotional intelligence, long-term changes)? What was the timeframe of my assessment procedures? Did I use pre-and post-tests or interviews? Was there an adequate control group? (p. 102)

Of course, if such data were consistent and long-term there might be good reasons to desist or substantially modify the service-learning component. But not only are most data not rigorous enough to warrant immediate acceptance, they also function as only a small part of how we marshal evidence to support our views of the world. The quantitative move toward statistically significant measurement thus cannot, on its own, convince scholars to embrace or reject service-learning.

The third reason that the quantitative move in service-learning undermines, rather than promotes, the institutionalization of service-learning is because it *is* quantitative. David Labaree (2004) has used Becher's typology of academic disciplines to point out the decidedly problematic implications of a soft discipline (in this case educational research) in search of a hard disguise:

> In order to create a solid ground for making hard claims about education, you can try to drain the swamp of human action and political purpose that makes this institution what it is, but the result is a science of something other than education as it is experienced by teachers and students. As I have argued elsewhere [Labaree, 1997], such an effort may have more positive impact on the status of researchers (for whom hard science is the holy grail) than the quality of learning in schools, and it may lead us to reshape education in the image of our own hyper-rationalized and disembodied constructs rather than our visions of the good school. (p. 75)

The scientific quantification of any human practice is what Max Weber (Sica, 2000) termed "rationalization." It is the attempt to order and systematize, for the sake of efficiency and (thus supposedly) progress, practices that were formally intuitive, haphazard, and grounded in heuristics rather than science. The point again is not that we should avoid scientific inquiry; rather, simply put, the point is that this is not at the heart of service-learning, nor should it be. To promote service-learning in the academy through quantification is to buy into a paradigm not of its own making. The quantitative move may help service-learning scholars gain a certain legitimacy in the academy. What it will not do is expand the boundaries of how to think about the academy, and it will not provide a decidedly different discourse of how service-learning should be institutionalized.

Possibilities for Service-Learning in Higher Education

Thinking about service-learning as a form of politics has deep rhetorical resonance. Service-learning advocates argue that its practices and policies are uplifting and transformational for all involved. Yet as I have argued in the sections above, such rhetorical resonance also has limited and limiting possibilities for institutionalizing service-learning in the academy. Such an approach cannot overcome the deep and specific pedagogical, political, and institutional barriers.

It is beyond the scope of this article to provide a comprehensive alternative to the problematics just outlined. Rather, what I want to make clear is that the limits just outlined are fundamentally linked to the undergirding theoretical presuppositions of contemporary service-learning theory and practice. I want to thus briefly explicate such presuppositions in order to rethink and reframe how service-learning may be otherwise institutionalized.

Fundamentally, advocates presume service-learning to be a politics by which to transform higher education. As such, service-learning becomes positioned within the binary of an "oppositional social movement" embedded within the "status quo" academy. Moreover, this perspective reifies (and thus assumes) service-learning as a coherent and cohesive pedagogical strategy, able to see its own blind spots as it pursues liberal and always liberatory agendas.

But such is not the case. The service-learning movement is an amalgam of, among other things, experiential education, action research, critical theory, progressive education, adult education, social justice education, constructivism, community-based research, multicultural education, and undergraduate research. It is viewed as a form of community service, as a pedagogical methodology, as a strategy for cultural competence and awareness, as a social justice orientation, and as a philosophical worldview (see, e.g., Butin, 2003; Kendall, 1990; Lisman, 1998; Liu, 1995; Morton, 1995; Westheimer & Kahne, 2004). An immense diversity of ofttimes clashing perspectives thus cohabits under the service-learning umbrella.

Likewise, the service-learning movement has often downplayed or glossed over the minimal social justice outcomes of service-learning practices. For all of the human, fiscal, and institutional resources devoted to service-learning across higher education, there are, in fact, very minimal on-the-ground changes in the academy, in local communities, or in society more generally.

I do not dispute that, in isolated situations with unique circumstances, profound changes have occurred. What I am simply pointing out is that service-learning should not have to bear the burden (nor the brunt) of being the social justice standard-bearer. To do so would be to set up an impossible causal linkage between service-learning and social betterment. Much scholarship, for example, can be marshaled to show that the divisions in our society based on categories of race, class, ethnicity, and language have, in many cases, become worse, not better; that democracy for all intents and purposes has become a spectator sport as most of us (and particularly youth) have disengaged from the public sphere; and that the United States is the worst offender in the developed world of human principles and ethical norms for the treatment of its incarcerated population. Is this service-learning's fault? If service-learning succeeds as hoped in higher education and if these conditions continue to deteriorate, does this mean that service-learning is to blame? The issues cited have much more to do with a host of interconnected economic, social, political, and legal policies than they do with the percentage of faculty implementing service-learning on any particular campus.

What this realization makes clear is that thinking about service-learning as a politics to transform higher education is a theoretical cul-de-sac. I do not doubt that service-learning may in fact become deeply embedded within higher education. Yet I suggest that, service-learning scholars do not account for the pedagogical, political, and institutional limits enumerated, service-learning will have a minimal and unstable foundation for its long-term sustenance. Service-learning will become embedded only by giving up any analytic opportunity to understand how and why it is ultimately deeply limited.

All of the theoretical assumptions of the service-learning movement that I have just enumerated position it as a gleaming grand narrative. Service-learning scholars and activists want service-learning to be all things to all people. Service-learning wants to roam free across disciplines, across institutions, across society. It wants to change and transform any and all obstacles in its path. It wants freedom.

But that is not how things work in academia. Higher education is a disciplining mechanism, in all senses of the term. And that is a good thing. For to be disciplined is to carefully, systematically, and in a sustained fashion investigate whatever one is interested in doing, whether that is building bridges, changing communities, or understanding Kant. Positioning service-learning as a grand narrative is a set-up for implosion—from a vision to a mirage—for there is no mechanism by which a grand narrative can prevent itself from being questioned and critiqued once it has become a part of the academy. That is the basis of higher education and that is where, for better or worse, service-learning wants to be positioned.

The possibilities for service-learning, I thus suggest, lie in embracing rather than rejecting the very academy the service-learning movement is attempting to transform. More precisely, it is to speak about service-learning as akin to an academic discipline with the ability to control its knowledge production functions by internally debating and determining what issues are worthy of study, by what modes of inquiry, and to what ends. This approach assumes a plurality of perspectives of what service-learning is and should be. It assumes that the scholarship surrounding service-learning is not solely centripetal or convergent in focus.

Rather than continuing to think *about* service-learning as a politics to transform higher education and society, we might more fruitfully reverse the terminology and begin to think *through* service-learning about the politics of transforming higher education and society. (See Butin, in press-b, for a detailed explication of this argument.) I take this distinction from Robyn Wiegman's (2005; see also her 1999, 2002) analysis of the future of women's studies, specifically because I find the arc of institutionalization of women's studies in higher education instructive and applicable to the service-learning movement.

What women's studies has done over the last quarter century—through reasoned discourse and political pressure—has been to expand the academy's notion of what constitutes the "academic." Weigman argues that so long as women's studies and feminism were (and are) conflated with social activism, they risked being dismissed as yet another form of identitarian politics beholden to the unquestioned uplifting of an essentialized category (e.g., race, ethnicity, and gender). What makes women's studies an academic discipline and the gender(ed) subject the mode of inquiry is that its scholarship is able to both look outward (to examine an issue, such as education or the criminal justice system) and inward (to internally debate and determine what issues are worthy of study, by what modes of inquiry, and to what ends).

Women's studies, for example, was able to weather the storm of second-wave feminist critique (of being a White, middle-class and Western-centric enclave [see, e.g., DuBois, 1985; Moraga & Anzaldúa, 1981]) precisely *because* it could accommodate and appropriate such criticism within its academic purpose of teaching and research on the gendered subject. Wendy Brown (1997) could write an article entitled "The Impossibility of Women's Studies" only *because* such a critique was made possible by the academy's norms of what disciplines and the scholars within them are allowed to do.

There is no doubt that women's studies was disciplined in its institutionalization. It distanced itself from the "street" and from the fervent activism therein; it had to devote attention to bureaucratic maneuverings for funds and faculty rather than for institutional change and transformation; it had to settle for yearly conferences instead of round-the-clock activism. As Messer-Davidow (2002) phrases it, women's studies became routinized. Yet by becoming "disciplined," women's studies was able to produce the domains of objects and rituals of truth to be studied and recast. As such, I would argue, disciplinary institutionalization is not the negation of politics but the condition of its possibility. For it allows, in the safety of disciplinary parameters, scholars to debate and define themselves and their field.

Women's studies accomplished this goal by reversing its terminology to make the gender(ed) subject the mode of inquiry rather than using gender as the political project. I suggest that the service-learning field can do likewise by making community studies the mode of inquiry rather than using the community as a political project (Butin, in press-b). By reversing the terminology, by making community studies the disciplinary field, an entirely new model of practice becomes possible. It becomes possible to use all of the tools of the academy to analyze a very specific and bounded issue. Service-learning may no longer claim that it will change the face of higher education. But women's studies does not do that either anymore. Instead, women's studies scholars carefully and systematically elaborate how feminist perspectives are slowly infiltrating and modifying the ways specific disciplines and sub-disciplines work, think, and act (see, e.g., Stanton & Stewart, 1995). This is not radical and transformational change. This is disciplined change. It is the slow accretion, one arduous and deliberate step at a time, of contesting one worldview with another. Some of this contest is blatantly political. Some of it is deeply technical. Much of it is debatable, questionable, and modifiable—just like any good academic enterprise. And it is this process which is truly transformational.

At present, though, such heteroglossic analysis and critique is largely absent in the service-learning field. If service-learning is assumed to be "simply" a universal, coherent, and neutral pedagogical practice, then such an absence is understandable. But such is not the case, as this article makes clear. It thus becomes incumbent on scholars committed to a scholarship of engagement in general and to service-learning specifically to probe the limits of service-learning in higher education. For without an explicit articulation of its own limits, service-learning may be doomed to a limited and limiting model of transformation.

Notes

1. Of course such changes *shouldn't* be doable without fundamentally altering the structures and practices of higher education. The Wingspread statement is premised exactly on the notion that these practices would be taken up in "thick" ways. Unfortunately, these practices as articulated are all too easily mis-appropriated within the world of higher education. This is not to suggest that these practices are not important. In fact, they may actually be the most sustainable aspects of service-learning as presently conceived. The point here is simply that they are not at the heart of what the Wingspread statement really *means* when it talks about institutionalizing service-learning. What it really means, and what the third and sixth practices make vivid, is the desire to transform higher education through service-learning.
2. The NCES data have numerous methodological ambiguities. For example, the lack of a distinctive service-learning category may obscure its use, the lack of Likert-scales may distort actual use of instructional methods, and lecturing may be conflated with discussion. The primary point of the data, though, is the unambiguous marginality of non-lecturing pedagogical methods across higher education.
3. See the website of Students for Academic Freedom, <www.studentsforacademicfreedom.org>, for the most up-to-date tracking of these developments.
4. I am very well aware of the animosity of the service-learning field to Stanley Fish. Not many people have an entire Campus Compact website devoted exclusively to attacking them (http://www.compact.org/newscc/fish.html). Yet while I acknowledge the highly personal nature of some of Fish's attacks (Ira Harkavy, personal communication, 3/30/05), I suggest that his insights into this political dilemma are critical for understanding the issues at stake.
5. The data and debate around this issue are legion. See, for example, Cochran-Smith, 2001, 2003; Goldhaber & Brewer; 1999; NCDTF, 2004; NCTQ, 2004. The basic point, though, is this: If the educational field, after all this time and research, is still this stuck, woe to service-learning.

References

AACU. Association of American Colleges and Universities. (2005, December 21). *Academic freedom and educational responsibility*. Washington, DC: AACU.

ACE. American Council on Education. (2005, June 23). *Statement on academic rights and responsibilities*. Washington, DC: ACE.

Antonio, A. L., Astin, H. S., & Cross, C. (2000). Community Service in higher education: A look at the faculty. *The Review of Higher Education, 23*(4), 373–398.

Becher, T., & Trowler, P. (2001). *Academic tribes and territories: Intellectual enquiry and the culture of disciplines* (2nd ed.). Philadelphia: Open University Press.

Benson, L., Harkavy, I., & Hartley, M. (2005). Integrating a commitment to the public good into the institutional fabric. In A. Kezar, T. Chambers, & J. Burkhardt, J. (Eds.), *Higher education for the public good* (pp. 185–216). San Francisco: Jossey-Bass.

Bell, R., Furco, A., Ammon, M. S., Muller, P., & Sorgen, V. (2000). *Institutionalizing service-learning in higher education*. Berkeley, CA: University of California.

Biglan, A. (1973). Relationship between subject matter characteristics and the structure and output of university departments. *Journal of Applied Psychology, 57*, 204–213.

Bayer, E. L., (1990). *Scholarship reconsidered: Priorities of the professoriate*. Stanford, CA: Carnegie Foundation for the Advancement of Teaching.

Bringle, R. G., & Hatcher, J. A. (2000). Institutionalization of service learning in higher education. *Journal of Higher Education, 71*(3), 273–291.

Brown, W. (1997). The impossibility of women's studies. *Differences: A Journal of Feminist Cultural Studies, 9*(3), 79–102.

Brukardt, M. H., Holland, B., Percy, S. L., Simpher, N., on behalf of Wingspread Conference Participants. (2004). *Wingspread Statement: Calling the question: Is higher education ready to commit to community engagement*. Milwaukee: University of Wisconsin-Milwaukee.

Butin, D. W. (2003). Of what use is it? Multiple conceptualizations of service-learning in education. *Teachers College Record, 105*(9), 1674–1692.

Butin, D. W. (2005a). Preface: Disturbing normalizations of service-learning. In D. W. Butin, (Ed.), *Service-learning in higher education: Critical issues and directions* (pp. vii–xx). New York: Palgrave.

Butin, D. W. (2005b). Service-learning as postmodern pedagogy. In D. W. Butin (Ed.) *Service-learning in higher education: Critical issues and directions* (pp. 89–104). New York: Palgrave.

Butin, D. W. (in press-a). Anti-anti-social justice: Academic freedom and the future of justice-oriented pedagogy in teacher preparation. *Equity and Excellence in Education, 40*(2).

Butin, D. W. (in press-b). Disciplining service-learning: Institutionalization and the case for community studies. *International Journal of Teaching and Learning in Higher Education, 17*(3). Available at http://222.isetle.org/ijtlhe/index.cfm.

Campus Compact. (2000). *Presidents' declaration on the civic responsibility of higher education*. Providence, RI: Campus Compact.

Campus Compact. (2004). *2003 service statistics: Highlights of Campus Compact's annual membership survey*. Available at http://www.compact.org/newscc/2003_Statistics.pdf.

Cochran-Smith, M. (2001). Constructing outcomes in teacher education: Policy, practice and pitfalls. *Educational Policy Analysis Archives, 9*(11). Retrieved on February 3, 2004, from http://epaa.asu.edu/epaa/v9n11.html.

Cochran-Smith, M. (2003). Standing at the crossroads: Multicultural teacher education at the beginning of the 21st century. *Multicultural Perspectives, 5*(3), 3–11.

Colby, A., Ehrlich, T., Beaumont, E., & Stephens, J. (2003). *Educating citizens: Preparing America's undergraduates for lives of moral and civic responsibility*. San Francisco: Jossey-Bass.

Cuban, L. (1990). Reforming again, again, and again. *Educational Researcher, 19*(3), 3–13.

Cuban, L. (1998). How schools change reforms: Redefining reform success and failure. *Teachers College Record, 99*(3), 453–477.

DuBois, E. C. (1985). *Feminist scholarship: Kindling in the groves of academe*. Urbana: University of Illinois Press.

Eyler, J., Giles, D., Stenson, C., & Gray, C., (2001). *At a glance: What we know about the effects of service-learning on college students, faculty, institutions and communities, 1993–2000*. Washington, DC: Learn and Serve America National Service Learning Clearinghouse. Available at http://servicelearning.org.

Fish, S. E. (1999). *The trouble with principle*. Cambridge, MA: Harvard University Press.

Fish, S. E. (2004, February 13.). "Intellectual diversity": The Trojan horse of a dark design. *Chronicle of Higher Education*, pp. B13–B14.

Freire, P. (1994). *Pedagogy of the oppressed*. New York: Continuum.

Furco, A. (2001). Advancing service-learning at research universities. In M. Carada & B. W. Speck (Eds.), *Developing and implementing service-learning programs*. New Directions for Higher Education (No. 114, pp. 67–68). San Francisco: Jossey-Bass.

Furco, A. (2002a). Institutionalizing service-learning in higher education. *Journal of Public Affairs, 6,* 39–47.

Furco, A. (2002b). *Self-assessment rubric for the institutionalization of service-learning in higher education*. Berkeley, CA: University of California.

Furco, A. (2003). Issues of definition and program diversity in the study of service-learning. In S. H. Billig & A. S. Waterman, (Eds.), *Studying service-learning: innovations in educational research methodology* (pp. 13–34). Mahwah, NJ: Lawrence Erlbaum Associates.

Furco, A., & Billig, S. (2002). *Service-learning: The essence of the pedagogy*. Greenwich, CT: Information Age.

Gardner, H. (2004). *Changing minds: The art and science of changing our own and other people's minds*. Boston, MA: Harvard Business School Press.

Goldhaber, D. D., & Brewer, D. J. (1999). A three-way error components analysis of educational productivity. *Education Economics, 7*(3), 199–208.

Gray, M., Ondaatje, E., & Zakaras, L. (2000). *Combining service and learning in higher education*. Santa Monica, CA: RAND.

Hacking, I. (1999). *The social construction of what?* Cambridge, MA: Harvard University Press.

Hartley, M., Harkavy, I., & Benson, L. (2005). Putting down roots in the groves of academe: The challenges of institutionalizing service-learning. In D. W. Butin, (Ed.), *Service-learning in higher education: Critical issues and directions* (pp. 205–222). New York: Palgrave.

Henry, S. E. (2005). "I can never turn my back on that": Liminality and the impact of class on service-learning experiences. In D. W. Butin (Ed.) *Service-learning in higher education: Critical issues and directions* (pp. 45–66). New York: Palgrave.

Henry, S. E., & Brayfogle, M. L. (in press). Toward a new framework of "server" and "served": De(and re)constructing reciprocity in service-learning pedagogy. *International Journal of Teaching and Learning in Higher Education, 17*(3).

Holland, B. A. (2001). A comprehensive model for assessing service-learning and community-university partnerships. In M. Carada & B. W. Speck (Eds.), *Developing and implementing service-learning programs*. New Directions for Higher Education (No. 114, 51–60). San Francisco: Jossey-Bass.

hooks, b. (1994). *Teaching to transgress: Education as the practice of freedom*. New York: Routledge.

Horowitz, D. (n.d.). *Academic bill of rights*. Retrieved on January 7, 2005, from www.studentsforacademicfreedom.org/abor.html.

Horowitz, D. (2003). *The campus blacklist*. Retrieved on January 7, 2005, from www.studentsforacademicfreedom.org/essays/blacklist.html.

Horowitz, D., & Lehrer, E. (n.d.). Political bias in the administrations and faculties of 32 elite colleges and universities. Retrieved on January 7, 2005, from http://www.studentsforacademicfreedom.org/reports/lackdiversity.html.

Jones, S. R. (2002). The underside of service learning. *About Campus, 7*(4), 10–15.

Jones, S. R., Gilbride-Brown, J., & Gasorski, A. (2005). Getting inside the "underside" of service-learning: Student resistance and possibilities. In D. W. Butin (Ed.), *Service-learning in higher education: Critical issues and directions* (pp. 3–24). New York: Palgrave.

Kendall, J. (Ed.) (1990). *Combining service and learning: A resource book for community and public service*. Raleigh, NC: National Society for Internships and Experiential Education.

Klein, D. B., & Stern, C. (2005). Political diversity is six disciplines. *Academic Questions, 18*(1), 40–52.

Kramer, M. (2000). *Make it last forever: The institutionalization of service learning in America*. Washington DC: Corporation for National Service.

Kuhn, T. (1996). *The structure of scientific revolutions*. (3rd ed.) Chicago: University of Chicago Press.

Labaree, D. F. (1997). *How to succeed in school without really learning: The credentials race in American education*. New Haven, CT: Yale University Press.

Labaree, D. F. (2004). *The trouble with ed schools*. New Haven, CT: Yale University Press.

Lather, P. (2005). *Scientism and scientificity in the rage for accountability: A feminist deconstruction*. Paper presented at the American Educational Research Associates, April 14.

Latour, B. (1979) *Laboratory life: The social construction of scientific facts.* Los Angeles: Sage.

Lindholm, J. A., Szelényi, K., Hurtado, S., & Korn, W. S. (2005). *The American college teacher: National norms for the 2004–2005 HERI faculty survey.* Los Angeles: Higher Education Research Instititute, UCLA.

Lisman, C. D. (1998). *Toward a civil society: Civic literacy and service learning.* Westport, CT: Bergin & Garvey.

Liu, G. (1995). Knowledge, foundations, and discourse: Philosophical support for service-learning. *The Michigan Journal of Community Service-Learning, 2,* 5–18.

Lueddeke, G. (2003). Professionalising teaching practice in higher education: A study of disciplinary variation and "teaching-scholarship." *Studies in Higher Education, 28*(2), 213–228.

Messer-Davidow, E. D. (2002). *Disciplining feminism: From social activism to academic discourse.* Durham, NC: Duke University Press.

Messer-Davidow, E., Shumway, D., & Sylvan, D. J. (Eds.). (1993). *Knowledges: Historical and critical studies in disciplinarity.* Charlottesville, VA: University of Virginia Press.

Moraga, C., & Anzaldúa, G. (1981). *This bridge called my back: Writings by radical women of color.* Watertown, MA: Persephone Press.

Morton, K. (1995). The irony of service: Charity, project, and social change in service-learning. *The Michigan Journal of Community Service-Learning, 2,* 19–32.

NCES. National Center for Educational Statistics (2002). *Teaching undergraduates in U.S. postsecondary institutions: Fall 1998.* Washington, DC: U.S. Department of Education.

NCDTF. National Collaborative on Diversity in the Teaching Force. (2004). *Assessment of diversity in America's teaching force.* Washington, DC: DC: National Education Association. Retrieved on December 4, 2004, from http://www.nea.org/teacherquality/images/diversityreport.pdf.

NCTQ. National Council on Teacher Quality (2004). *Increasing the odds: How good policies can yield better teachers.* Washington, DC: NCTQ. Retrieved on December 4, 2004, from http://www.nctq.org/nctq/images/nctq_io.pdf.

Neumann, R., & Becher, T. (2002). Teaching and learning in their disciplinary contexts: A conceptual analysis. *Studies in Higher Education, 27*(4), 405–417.

Richardson, V. & Placier, P. (2001). Teacher change. In V. Richardson, & American Educational Research Association (Eds.), *Handbook of research on teaching* (4th ed., pp. 905–950). Washington, DC: American Educational Research Association.

Rothman, S., Lichter, S., & Nevitte, N. (2005). Politics and professional advancement among college faculty. *The Forum, 3*(1), 1–16.

Shulman, L. (2004). *Teaching as community property.* San Francisco: Jossey-Bass.

Sica, A. (2000). Rationalization and culture. In S. P. Turner, *The Cambridge companion to Weber* (pp. 42–58). New York: Cambridge University Press.

Snyder, T. D., Tan, A. G., and Hoffman, C. M. (2004). *Digest of education statistics 2003* (NCES 2005–025). U.S. Department of Education, National Center for Education Statistics. Washington, DC: Government Printing Office.

Stanton, D. C., & Stewart, A. J. (1995). *Feminisms in the academy.* Ann Arbor: University of Michigan Press.

Stanton, T., Giles, D., & Cruz, N. I. (1999). *Service-learning: A movement's pioneers reflect on its origins, practice, and future.* San Francisco: Jossey-Bass.

Swaminathan, R. (2005). "Whose school is it anyway?" Student voices in an urban classroom. In D. W. Butin (Ed.). *Service-learning in higher education: Critical issues and directions* (pp. 25–44). New York: Palgrave.

Swaminathan, R. (in press). Educating for the "real world": Perspectives from the community on youth, service-learning, and social justice. *Equity and Excellence in Education, 40*(2).

West, C. (1994). *Race matters.* New York: Vintage.

Westheimer, J. & Kahne, J. (2004). What kind of citizen? The politics of educating for democracy. *American Educational Research Journal, 41*(2): 237–269.

Wiegman, R. (1999). Feminism, institutionalism, and the idiom of failure. *Differences: A Journal of Feminist Cultural Studies, 11*(3), 107–136.

Wiegman, R. (2005). The possibility of women's studies. In E. L. Kennedy & A. Beins (Eds.), *Women's studies for the future: Foundations, interrogations, politics* (pp. 34–51). Piscataway, NJ: Rutgers University Press.

Wiegman, R. (2002). Academic feminism against itself *NWSA Journal, 14*(2), 18–34.

Acknowledgments: Thanks to Eric Bredo, Gitte Wernaa Butin, Sean Flaherty, Ira Harkavy, and two anonymous reviewers, whose very useful comments helped me clarify the arguments I was making.

Putting Down Roots in the Groves of Academe: The Challenges of Institutionalizing Service-Learning

Matthew Hartley, Ira Harkavy, & Lee Benson

Introduction

Service-learning, by almost any measure, has been an enormously successful academic innovation (Stanton, Giles, and Cruz 1999). A mere two decades ago Campus Compact was founded by three university presidents intent on making service an integral part of their students' experiences and aspiring someday to have 100 college and university presidents as members. Today, more than 900 presidents and their institutions have joined and 30 state offices provide training and technical assistance to students, faculty, and administrators in the areas of service-learning and civic engagement.[1]

However, service-learning has been embraced by institutions to varying degrees. On some campuses, proponents are located in "service enclaves" (Singleton, Burack, and Hirsch 1997)—isolated faculty members laboring with meager support. On other campuses, service-learning courses are found in only a few disciplinary areas—professional programs, the social sciences and a few environmental courses from the life sciences thrown in for good measure. However, some campuses have managed to embed service-learning into institutional life to a striking degree (Holland 1997). At these institutions, an influential group of faculty members, administrators, and board members have embraced the pedagogy and worked collectively to engage members of the larger institution in discussions about institutional priorities and purpose. Institutional support is evident in their annual operating budgets, the allocation of staff lines, and in some cases by the creation of a central office supporting these initiatives. A few colleges and universities have amended admissions requirements or redefined faculty roles and rewards and community-based research has gained some currency as a legitimate form of scholarship. But why the disparate levels of commitment? What are the factors that influence degrees of institutionalization and what are some of the strategies institutions have employed to promote service-learning?

The purpose of this chapter is to examine these questions by means of a review of the literature on institutionalization and by sharing the experiences of individuals at four campuses, Swarthmore College (Swarthmore, PA), Tufts University (Medford, MA), the University of Pennsylvania (Penn) (Philadelphia, PA), and Widener University (Chester, PA). The research and analysis reported here represent the pilot phase of a larger research project examining how colleges and universities embed civic engagement efforts into the lives of their institutions. What little quantitative data exists (e.g., Campus Compact's 1998 survey, discussed below) suggests that many—perhaps most—colleges and universities have enjoyed only partial success institutionalizing such initiatives. Although a few researchers have done important preliminary work identifying factors that promote or impede institutionalization (Holland 1997; Ostrander 2004; Ward 1996), we contend that for service-learning to firmly take root in the academy, advocates must learn to identify both the structural and ideological (or cultural) features of their own institutions if they wish to devise effective strategies for addressing them.

These four private institutions were chosen in part because they represent distinct institutional types: Swarthmore is a liberal arts college, Widener a regional comprehensive institution, Tufts a small research university and Penn a large research university. Although some students and faculty members have been involved in community-based learning for a decade or more at all of these institutions, comprehensive structural support for these efforts is more long-standing at Penn and Tufts and quite recent at Swarthmore and Widener. In short, these institutions represent different points on an institutionalization continuum.

Consistent with the practices of good research (Glesne and Peshkin 1992; Maxwell 1996; Rossman and Rallis 1997), it is important to note the relationship of the three authors of this study to Penn's Center for Community Partnerships (CCP) and to justify its selection as a site. Ira Harkavy directs CCP and has for years collaborated with Lee Benson in the classroom and on numerous articles and chapters. Benson and Hartley both serve on CCP's faculty advisory board. However, in order to mitigate bias, the decision was made to have Hartley, a second-year assistant professor whose relationship with CCP is quite recent and who knows none of the other participants (with the exception of Harkavy who was interviewed as the director of CCP), conduct the interviews. Two people were interviewed from each campus, the person responsible for day-to-day operations of the service-learning or community engagement initiative (e.g., director, dean, vice president) and a senior administrator or a senior faculty member. Their accounts were supplemented (and confirmed) through an analysis of institutional documents (e.g., reports, brochures, syllabi, Web pages.) Each interview was audiotaped and subsequently reviewed. Extensive interview notes were drafted and quotes that captured particularly important points were transcribed verbatim. The entire set of interview notes was coded, which resulted in the development of the key themes presented in section III.

We included CCP in the study for several reasons. First, it is one of the relatively few long-standing programs of its kind and two of the authors (Harkavy and Benson) have an intimate familiarity with the program and Penn. As such, it is an information rich source (Patton 1990) that seemed a shame not to use. Second, we had a professional interest in comparing and contrasting CCP's experience with that of other institutions. Third, the data drawn from this limited sample was intended primarily to illustrate the empirical and theoretical work found in the literature. Thus, the concerns we had about potential bias were mitigated by the fact that this is a pilot study and its findings are therefore tentative and exploratory. However, we now hold that the themes that emerged yield insights that not only are worthy of future exploration but that, because of their consistency across the interviews, are trustworthy and may prove useful to practitioners.

Description of the Four Institutions

Founded in 1992, Penn's CCP is a long-standing experiment in community-based learning and civic engagement.[2] CCP's director, Ira Harkavy, is associate vice president and reports to the vice president for Government, Community and Public Affairs with an indirect reporting relationship (a dotted line on the organizational chart) to the Provost. Harkavy manages a staff of 15. The Center has three advisory boards—community, faculty, student, and an external board that helps the Center's staff establish priorities and secure external support. Although Penn provides space and overhead, the university's budgetary strategy of "every tub on its own bottom" (Resource Center Management) means that the center is dependent upon grant money and fundraising to support many of its activities.

CCP helps to facilitate three kinds of activities: academically based community service, direct traditional service, and community development. Its projects include partnerships with West Philadelphia public schools, training programs for local school teachers around service-learning, a community arts initiative, among others. CCP also supports the many faculty members engaged in service-learning across the university. In 1992, 11 service-learning courses were offered. Today, over one hundred and twenty courses from a wide range of disciplines link Penn students to the community.

Tufts University's institutional commitment to civic engagement is underscored by the creation of the University College of Citizenship and Public Service in 1999 by the board of trustees thanks to the efforts of former president John DiBiaggio. University College provides a formal structure for coordinating the civic engagement efforts that have been occurring at Tufts for many years. Under the leadership of its dean, Robert Hollister, the stated goal of University College is to make "active citizenship a hallmark of a Tufts University education." University College sponsors a range of activities including voter registration drives and lectures and symposia on political issues and the presidential candidates. The Public Service Scholars program selects approximately fifty students each year whose role is to serve as catalysts for promoting service activities among students and faculty. The Faculty Fellows program awards two-year grants to a select group of tenured faculty members. "Fellows are selected because of their potential to engage other faculty and infuse Education for Active Citizenship throughout the University."[3]

Swarthmore College offers something of a contrast. Although senior administrators point to a long-standing ethos of service, community engagement efforts received little or no formal institutional support until relatively recently. In the late 1980s, a "Green" Dean—a recent Swarthmore alumnus/a—was hired to help coordinate student service efforts. However, faculty engaged in service-learning had to go it alone.

A series of events in the 1990s altered matters: the hiring of President Al Bloom in 1991 (whose scholarly work centers on "ethical intelligence"); an initially ill-fated effort to create a multicultural curriculum, which sparked a series of debates about Swarthmore's educational mission; and a new capital campaign all fed an emergent interest in civic engagement and service. In 2002, the Lang Center for Civic and Social Responsibility (conceived of and funded by former board chair Eugene Lang) was founded to provide a broad umbrella under which multiple efforts could be coordinated and supported.

Finally, Widener University is an institution poised on the brink of change. Its new president, James Harris, was hired by the board after his successful tenure at Defiance College where he led an institutional transformation revolving around civic engagement. Widener is a regional comprehensive institution with traditional disciplinary offerings as well as a number of professional programs. A series of presidential initiatives have recently been launched. A new Office for Community Engagement has also been instituted and its director reports directly to the president. Harris is also leading an effort to develop a closer working relationship with the wider Chester community. A small group of faculty had already been involved in service-learning and Harris is hoping to augment that group.

Institutionalizing Service-Learning: Lessons from the Literature

Service-learning has found its way into many, perhaps a majority of American college and university campuses. Data from a 1998 Campus Compact survey of 300 member campuses found that "99% of the respondents reported having at least one service-learning course, up from 66% in 1993. Of the 99%, 19% had 40 or more courses, 48% had between 10 and 39 courses, and just 33% had less than 10 courses" (http:www.compact.org/faculty/specialreport.html). Between 1998 and 2002, the overall percentage of faculty undertaking service-learning on member campuses grew from 13 percent to 22 percent (Hartley and Hollander 2005). Campus Compact describes this state of affairs with a three-tiered "service-learning pyramid." The vast majority of institutions, which form the foundation of the pyramid, have a small percentage of faculty (between 0 and 10 percent) engaged in service-learning, few institutional support mechanisms and the net result is sporadic and uncoordinated community engagement. A second (and smaller) group of institutions report that 10 to 24 percent of their faculty members are using service-learning in at least one class. These institutions tend to have offices dedicated to supporting service-learning or civic engagement (although Compact's report does not attempt to measure the adequacy of these structures by, say, comparing numbers of staff with the size of the faculty). Respondents report that the chief academic officers (e.g., provosts, vice presidents for academic affairs) at these institutions support service-learning through various incentives, encourage the development of new courses by offering stipends or a course release, but faculty roles and rewards remain unchanged. Fully engaged colleges and universities represent the tiny apex of the pyramid—institutions where service-learning is valued across all disciplines and specific policies have been adapted (e.g., faculty hiring and promotion and tenure guidelines) to support the efforts. In sum, though service-learning as a pedagogy is widespread, the extent to which it has been woven into institutional life varies considerably among Campus Compact member institutions.

Attributes of Higher Education that Impede Service-Learning

There are a number of factors mitigating these efforts. First, colleges and universities are "loosely coupled" organizations (Weick 1976). A college or university is divided into various schools, which are divided further into divisions and then again into departments. This academic specialization is the legacy of the German research university model and though it has historically proven to be a useful strategy for developing new bodies of knowledge, it has splintered the faculty. Further, power is diffused in loosely coupled systems. Because the units have specialized knowledge (the board isn't about to tell the economics department what to teach) change must occur through discussion and persuasion rather than command. Though the board of trustees has broad powers—the president serves at its pleasure and the board has the authority to create or close entire academic programs—it relies on the cooperation of administrators who understand the institution's inner workings and the faculty, whose expertise must be brought to bear if there is to be any curricular change.

A second factor impeding change is that people are busy with other things. Change requires additional time and effort and on any campus, people's attention is the scarcest resource (Hirschhorn and May 2000). This is particularly true of curricular initiatives. Faculty members teach, research, advise, serve on standing committees, write letters of recommendation, mentor young scholars, participate in peer review for academic journals and much more. It is therefore no surprise that faculty members see themselves as having precious little time to pursue any activity whose purpose may be construed as tangential to these core duties.

This brings us to the third mitigating factor, Platonization. Plato advocated the search for theoretical knowledge as the primary end of the academy and the dead hand of Plato is felt even today (Benson, Harkavy, and Hartley 2005). Academic disciplines tend to devalue research whose purpose is addressing local problems. The system of peer review tends to reward scholarship in familiar forms. Of course, Ernest Boyer's (1990) idea of a "scholarship of application"—using disciplinary knowledge to address particular community concerns—has sparked discussions at many institutions, but it has gained currency in comparatively few, particularly research universities. Given this rather limited definition of scholarship, small wonder that faculty members working toward promotion and tenure are reticent about becoming involved.

Finally, some scholars question the very propriety of promoting civic engagement. They argue that the primary purpose of higher education is to encourage the development of analytical skills, facility in written and oral communication, and knowledge of a particular field of inquiry. What students choose to do with this knowledge (or whether they do anything at all) is, from such a perspective, immaterial and beyond the scope of higher education. The idea of value neutrality is a potent inhibiting force. The German university model and its ethos of "value freedom" in research heavily influenced academic norms and helped to de-emphasize higher education's role in shaping students' values.[4]

Historians Lee Benson and Ira Harkavy (2002) note that

> [although] "value-free" advocates did not completely dominate American universities during the 1914–1989 period . . . they were numerous enough to strongly reinforce traditional academic opposition to real-world problem-solving activity, and they significantly helped bring about the rapid civic disengagement of American universities. (p. 13)

What Promotes or Impedes the Institutionalization of Service-Learning?

Several scholars have attempted to isolate the factors that promote or impede the institutionalization of service-learning. Kelly Ward (1996) examined five institutions whose institutional rhetoric asserted their commitment to service. She concludes that substantive commitment is indicated by: (1) the establishment and funding of a service-learning office; (2) broad-based discussions by faculty members about how to appropriately incorporate service into the curriculum; and (3) the tangible and symbolic support of institutional leaders. Barbara Holland's (1997) analysis of 23 institutional case studies supports and extends Ward's findings. Holland identifies seven distinct factors that indicate a commitment to service: (1) an institution's historic and currently stated mission; (2) promotion, tenure, hiring guidelines; (3) organizational structures (e.g., a campus unit dedicated to supporting service activities); (4) student involvement; (5) faculty involvement; (6) community involvement; and (7) campus publications. Holland goes one step further, however, and for each factor she differentiates between the activities of institutions for which commitment to service is of low relevance, medium relevance, high relevance, or those for whom service is fully integrated. The resulting matrix paints in broad brushstrokes a picture of what institutionalization entails. Holland underscores that the matrix is descriptive not prescriptive. "Without further research, the relationship, if any, among the levels of commitment to service is not clear, especially when one considers that movement could be in any direction on the matrix" (p. 40).

Although identifying such factors is an invaluable starting point for discussing the challenges and opportunities shared by service-learning proponents, Susan Ostrander's (2004) investigation of civic engagement efforts on five campuses underscores how particularistic the challenges can be from campus to campus. Ostrander argues four essential points. First, the emphasis of any given civic engagement initiative differs from institution to institution. One campus may see its central project as making curricular change while another may emphasize the importance of building equitable partnerships with community organizations. Second, certain "local factors" support or impede civic engagement—a distinctive mission, a consensus that the curriculum needs to be revitalized, a faculty that is actively involved in institutional decision-making—such unique elements must be identified and addressed for institutionalization to succeed. Third, a successful initiative requires the development of a convincing intellectual rationale that explains how the effort will result in better teaching and scholarship. Fourth, new organizational structures must be built to sustain the initiative and these structures not only must support the work within the campus (i.e., the faculty and students) but also serve community partners.

The findings of each of these researchers echo the earlier work of organizational theorists Paul S. Goodman and James W. Dean (1982). Goodman and Dean offer a framework for describing how any new organizational behavior comes to be institutionalized. They delineate five stages: The process begins when people become aware of a new activity or behavior—someone tells them about it and explains its value. In the second stage, a small group of individuals try the new behavior. Their experimentation yields important information about how valuable and viable it is in that specific organizational context (i.e., Does it work and do others find it acceptable or tolerable?). If the new behavior turns out to be more satisfying, effective, or enjoyable than its alternative (or if it attracts positive attention from valued peers or superiors), more people will try it and some individuals will begin *preferring* the behavior. If enough individuals, either a majority of people within the organization or the majority of influential people who control roles and rewards, come to prefer the behavior, then a new institutional norm is established. A consensus emerges that the behavior is appropriate and valuable. Institutionalization is complete when people within the organization view the behavior as an expression of the core purpose of an institution. "This is who we are."

Notice that what Goodman and Dean (and Ward, Holland, and Ostrander) are all alluding to is that institutionalization is the product of both structural and ideological change. Structural elements (more resources and more policies) are alone insufficient to alter the day-to-day behaviors of individuals, particularly those working in loosely coupled organizations like colleges and universities. Conversely, no band of zealous advocates for any idea will spur broad-based change if they cannot secure adequate resources. Structure and ideology are the twin drivers of institutionalized change.

The expansion of service-learning and the burgeoning emphasis on civic engagement at many colleges and universities has been likened to a social movement (Hollander and Hartley 2000; Maurasse 2001). What we argue here is that although social movement theorists have tended to stipulate that movements do not occur in bounded organizational contexts (Diani 1992), in fact, there appear to be striking similarities between social movements and organizational change at colleges and universities where, because they are loosely coupled organizations, hierarchical and bureaucratic constraints are of limited influence. Like a social movement, the idea of service-learning tends to be embraced by a small group of proponents. Some are "true believers"—individuals who are absolutely convinced of the efficacy (and even righteousness!) of their cause (Hoffer 1951). Others embrace the idea for pragmatic reasons (i.e., the new idea for a better way of doing things). These individuals form the ideological base of the movement—they are the ones who initially formulate the rationale for the innovation and energetically advocate for it. If influential organizational members form part of the group (e.g., members of the board, the president and administrators, senior faculty), this "guiding coalition" (Kotter 1996) also serves as a powerful political base. The success of the group is dependent on many things, but, broadly put, they must find a way to gather resources (as expressed in Resource Mobilization Theory, perhaps the dominant framework in social movement theory) but they must also secure the support of others—converting them to the cause or at a minimum convincing them not to oppose it.

Institutionalization of Service-Learning: Lessons from the Field

In this section, we compare and contrast the factors that have influenced the institutionalization of service-learning at four institutions. The subsections below to a degree correspond to Goodman and Dean's framework in that we are essentially describing how ideas spread, how behaviors proliferate and come to be preferred and eventually how an innovation achieves normative status. We make no claim that these findings (based on rather limited data collection at four private institutions) are generalizable to all institutions of higher learning. Our purpose is simply to underscore that structural and ideological elements both are required to produce deep institutional commitment and to examine some of the disparate challenges in achieving them.

Pre-change

The seeds of change can long lie dormant in an organization before innovation occurs (Kanter 1983). A concerted community engagement effort did not come to full flower for many years at these four institutions for a variety of reasons. At Widener, the concept of service to the community had been somewhat constrained. The institution sent its corps of cadets to march at city celebrations but over time, Chester's daunting crime and poverty resulted in the institution isolating itself. For example, the university routinely told its students never to cross the highway into the nearby neighborhoods. Penn's relationship to West Philadelphia several decades ago was strikingly similar. One trustee apparently suggested building a wall around campus to keep students safe.

Conversely, the beauty of Swarthmore's surroundings somewhat mitigated the urgency to serve, though Chester is only a few miles away from that campus. Further, as one participant noted: "Some people had gotten burned in Chester in the past." Creating service projects proved challenging and in a few instances there were uncomfortable interactions with members of the community who questioned the motives of faculty members from an elite, wealthy, private college.

Despite these challenges, there were a few early innovators and pioneers engaged in the community—faculty members who had found ways to incorporate this work into their teaching and scholarship and student volunteerism. For example, at Swarthmore several faculty members had successfully developed partnerships with community based organizations and schools, Also, student organizations had for decades organized service projects, some of them quite ambitious. Some twenty odd faculty members at Widener involved in service-learning began meeting to share ideas and promote the practice fully a year before President Harris was hired. The experience of these people provided a latent fund of knowledge about local community needs and the logistical and pedagogical imperatives of the work. Such individuals may also represent a potential coalition of proponents committed to such work. Certain values already have a degree of resonance within a community. A commitment to social justice stemming from its Quaker roots forms an essential part of Swarthmore's mission, for instance.

Introducing the Idea

Until an innovation is fully institutionalized (i.e., until the behavior is found throughout the organization, is supported by adequate structures, and is widely viewed as expressing core institutional values), a continual effort must be made by proponents to introduce the idea to others. Various venues of communication were used at these institutions—presidential speeches, town meetings, workshops, seminars, and committee meetings. Although it is certainly true that anyone has the potential to instruct or inform another person, his or her influence in the organization varies considerably. For example, a faculty member may draw a departmental colleague or students into a conversation about community engagement. A chair, because she controls the departmental agenda, may be able to facilitate a conversation among a larger group of faculty and a dean even more so. Senior administrators (both academic and administrative) have access to most if not all of the influential people on a campus. However, the person able to command the greatest number of people's attention is clearly the president (Schein 1985).

President Harris arrived from Defiance College intent on realigning the institutional mission to serve the community. One administrator remarked: "President Harris shared with me that when he was interviewing for the position he told the board 'don't hire me unless you are committed to transforming this institution around the idea of civic engagement.'" Once hired, Harris held a series of town meetings to discuss this vision and, more recently, has led an effort to redraft Widener's mission statement. The first sentence now states: "As a leading metropolitan university, we achieve our mission at Widener by creating a learning environment where curricula are connected to societal issues through civic engagement." Although presidents can lead conversations, they do not control them. At Swarthmore the emphasis on civic education came about in a more roundabout way. President Al Bloom arrived on Swarthmore's pristine suburban campus with an interest in promoting "ethical intelligence" in an increasingly global world. With his encouragement as well as the provost's, a group of faculty crafted a new multicultural curriculum that encountered fierce resistance. This setback, however, led the provost to invite faculty members to form seminar groups to discuss multiculturalism and the curriculum. These ultimately led to a range of discussions about the college's mission and a reaffirming of values constant since its founding by Quakers, a commitment to social justice and service to the community. Without the firm commitment of the senior leadership, including the president, engaging in a broad-based discussion of core issues such as curricular reform is difficult indeed.

Such conversations serve a number of purposes. At their most fundamental, as Goodman and Dean might note, they are a means of introducing ideas. Through collective debate and discussion, they allow ideas to be vetted and enable some to gain broad currency. Important distinctions need to be drawn: What do we mean by "service," who is our community, and what are the characteristics of civic or democratic behavior? Are we hoping to promote public service, participation in service-learning, community-based learning, or real-world problem solving (our preference)? At times these conversations were difficult and uncomfortable. One administrator at Swarthmore explained: "It's like having the sand inside the oyster—there's going to be a lot of itching and scratching, lots of reflection." Proponents of service-learning had to respond to a range of objections at each of these institutions. Faculty members unfamiliar with the pedagogy questioned its efficacy. Some raised concerns that service-learning might "dumb down" the curriculum. At Tufts, whose academic fortunes had clearly risen throughout the previous decade, innovative pedagogies were treated with particular suspicion. There were fears that widespread use of service-learning might be viewed as an emphasis unbefitting an elite research university. As one administrator observed: "For an aspiring institution, rigor is particularly important."

Institutions used several common strategies to promote service-learning. For example, the use of guest lecturers can enrich discussions by providing information about how other institutions have approached this task. A guest speaker can lend legitimacy to the project either symbolically (if he or she comes from a peer institution or better yet, an aspirational one) or by countering arguments with the growing body of research in civic engagement and service-learning. Specific workshops may be used to convey specific kinds of information, such as "service-learning 101." Public meetings also serve another important function. As the process moves from conveying an idea to jointly constructing a rationale for how it might be expressed in that specific context, public meetings are an occasion for proponents of the innovation to identify one another as a guiding coalition (Kotter 1996) and perhaps to reveal points of resistance. Over time, the conveyance of information shifts. For example, members of the organization will have marched sufficiently up the learning curve such that "how to" courses become less necessary or are targeted at certain groups, such as new students or faculty members. A different kind of communication occurs once the behavior becomes an institutional norm (as we discuss momentarily).

Encouraging the Behavior

Philosophical discussions of "service" and "social responsibility" are vitally important starting points. However, such lofty ideas must ultimately find expression in institutional behaviors and priorities. A primary goal must be supporting those *already* engaged in the behavior. Such individuals are an important resource about how service-learning fits into the organizational context, pedagogically (How does service-learning improve teaching and learning in my class?) and practically (What kinds of projects seem to suit our students best?). They can also be forceful advocates for this work. These institutions have also used a variety of strategies to encourage other individuals to move from thought to action.

First, they can lower the bar of participation by providing an easy way for those who show some interest to participate. Many individuals are initially unwilling to expend effort on something new because the activity doesn't yet seem important enough to supplant other professional tasks. Institutions can provide one-time service activities for students and often for faculty members. President Harris of Widener closed the university last year for Martin Luther King, Jr. Day and participated along with many faculty and staff members in planned service activities throughout the city of Chester.

Second, those willing to become more actively involved must also be encouraged and supported. Logistical support is vitally important for the success of service-learning initiatives. Swarthmore's director explains:

> If a faculty member wants to create a course, they can come here and we talk with them about what's involved and we create the community experience opportunity right down to arranging meeting with community partners—the professor is working with them from the beginning—what's best for the community *and* for the students? Eventually the professor will get a folder with the placements, [a staff member] will go to the class and talk to them about [the community] and if there's special training we provide that—talk to the students about how to enter a community, what is being arrogant and what is not. We can even help with reflection.

For decades Swarthmore offered little in the way of tangible support to faculty or students engaged in the community, with the exception of making grants to students for summer projects. In the 1980s, the Swarthmore Foundation was established and it began making more significant grants to faculty, staff, and students for community-based projects. In 1989, a "Green" Dean (recent alumnus/a) was hired to help students organize service activities. During President Bloom's administration, there were many conversations about how civic engagement efforts might be supported, spurred by Eugene Lang, chair of the board and a benefactor of the college. Early discussions about where to place the office led to the growing conviction that embedding it in any office would fail to provide a large enough umbrella for all the civic engagement activities (including service-learning). Such evolving support helps individuals to participate in service-learning in substantive and meaningful ways, which can lead to a greater sense of commitment on their part. Indeed, the experiences of these four institutions suggest that there is a close relationship between structural support and ideological support. Allocation of resources both symbolizes and is an essential element in producing support.

Third, institutions can encourage and reward individuals whose work supports the wider institutional effort. Last year Widener admitted its first group of Presidential Scholars. This group receives an education stipend, meets regularly as a cohort (often with the president in attendance), and, with the support of the special assistant to the president for Community Engagement, they are encouraged to develop a service project (Presidential Scholars are expected to perform 150 hours of community service each year). Swarthmore has for many years brought in a distinguished visiting professor whose work exemplifies community activism and engagement. Widener and Tufts are providing a course release to a group of tenured faculty members each year to enable them to develop new service-learning courses. Penn awards summer grants to faculty for curricular development as well.

The process of creating an environment conducive to the new behavior may require difficult decision-making. At one institution, it became evident that the provost, who had served the institution for some time, opposed the initiative. The provost had served the institution well for some time and had taken the lead on several curricular change efforts. He also enjoyed support from a group of influential faculty leaders. The incompatibility of the provost's curricular priorities and those of the service-learning proponents eventually led to the president asking him to resign.

Toward Normative Consensus

The position of any program or policy is ultimately tenuous—most can readily be wiped away at the whim of a new president. Institutionalization is more than a collection of administrative and curricular initiatives. As Goodman and Dean put it, it requires a normative consensus that the institutional behavior is not only acceptable but, in fact, it is an expression of the organization's core purpose. Some of this ideological groundwork is laid as people begin experiencing service-learning for themselves (or see how it adds value to their colleague's work). However, the perhaps unwelcome news for proponents of service-learning and civic engagement is that a true normative consensus must be formed one person at a time. Broad-based institutional efforts can bring the issue to the forefront and make it the subject of intense debate and conversation but ultimately individuals must conclude for themselves whether and how this work fits into their lives as scholars, teachers, administrators, and students. The good news is that if many individuals engage in this work, and normative consensus is achieved, it represents a powerful social contract among various constituencies that makes reversing the change extremely unlikely.

Ultimately, civic engagement and service-learning must be found to address important institutional imperatives: What is our unique institutional mission? What is the responsibility of our institution as part of this community? Who should we choose to join us in our effort—that is, which students should we admit and what faculty members should we hire? What should we expect of junior faculty members when they come up for promotion and tenure or merit raises? Responding to such questions requires long, careful, spirited, and at times even contentious, discussion. This is when the ideological battle is joined in earnest. Some of this may begin at the institutional level, for example, with the drafting of a new mission statement. But lofty statements must be translated into the nuts-and-bolts of daily life. It is therefore vitally important that the initiative be tied to larger institutional discussion of strategy and purpose. At Swarthmore, the decision to create a new center was arrived at during the planning of a capital campaign. To further highlight its importance, Jennie Keith, who had just returned to the faculty after two terms as provost, agreed to direct the center. The center director reports directly to the president. Departments must also individually decide for themselves how civic engagement may inform their work. This is where sufficient institutional support and sufficient number of proponents turns the tide.

As described earlier, there are numerous reasons why civic engagement efforts are resisted. Some academic norms rise to the level of conviction for certain faculty members. Many faculty members feel that the purpose of colleges and universities is to train the minds of students and that actually attempting to spur any sense of moral agency is either useless or a specious exercise: "Instruct students but don't try to encourage them to *do* anything to improve the world with that knowledge." There are also competing norms that may need to be addressed. For example, Swarthmore's long-standing ethos of service and the college's pride in the remarkable community-based projects initiated and led by students raised concerns that a more formal initiative might, as one administrator so eloquently put it, "pin the butterfly." The institutional value ("our students can achieve remarkable things all on their own") had to be amended to encourage greater participation by even more

TABLE 13.1

Examples of Structural and Ideological Elements

Structural Elements	Ideological Elements
Pre-change	
• Pioneer's fund of knowledge about the pedagogy and the community	• Pioneers' commitment to service-learning and their ability articulate how it fits into their work
	• The institution's history (or founding mission) may support ideas such as a service or responsibility to community
Introducing the idea	
• Meetings: A way to gauge support or resistance and to begin identifying member of a coalition	• President's speeches articulating a new direction for the institution
• Drafting a mission statement: establishing institutional priorities and goals	• Meetings: A way to discuss and debate the efficacy of the initiative, to identify shared values/priorities, and to surface objections
• Workshops to teach people how to engage in service-learning	• Drafting a mission statement: Jointly articulating a rationale of the value of the initiative
Encouraging the behavior	
• Allocating resource for logistical support (e.g., staff support)	• Making symbolic policy changes (e.g., closing Widener for a day or service on MLK, Jr. Day)
• Creating "low-cost" ways to try the behavior	• "Low-cost" service opportunities allow people to begin to experience the activity for themselves
• Offering logistical support for those who want to become more involved.	• Allocating resources to support those who want to become more involved enables people to see the value in it and to incorporate it more fully into their work
• Allocating resources to support more sustained service-learning efforts by faculty/staff/students who want to become more involved.	• Allocating significant resources signals that the idea is no "fad"
	• Rewarding those already involved
Toward normative consensus	
• Linking the idea to institutional planning processes (e.g., strategic planning, capital campaign planning)	• Addressing competing values (e.g., the fear of discouraging student ownership and initiative, "pinning the butterfly")
• Creating new structures that signal institutional support at the highest level (e.g., The Swarthmore board's new standing committee on civic engagement)	• New structures at the highest level signal a lasting institutional commitment to this value

students. On a more prosaic level, change survivors (Duck 2001) will tend to view any institutional change (including civic engagement) as just one more passing fad. At Widener, a few faculty members voice the fear that service-learning might become a requirement even though President Harris had explained in a "town meeting" that service-learning is but one way of contributing to a civic engagement mission. These individuals may, however, over time be won over with adequate evidence and sustained effort (Hartley 2003).

Consensus building is no easy task and it requires the involvement of many, many groups. Administrative functions (e.g., student affairs), with the strong support of a president, can readily change their policies. Other administrative functions (e.g., admission policies) require the advice and consent of the faculty. Certainly any curricular initiative entails securing faculty support. But faculty members need to be convinced and to this end, senior faculty members are in the best position to advocate forcefully for an initiative. Further, they are immune from retribution if the department ultimately concludes that such activities are faddish or otherwise inappropriate. Junior faculty members are in a far more tenuous position. (No surprise that Widener selected tenured faculty members for its service grants and Tufts faculty fellows are full professors).

Conclusion

For lasting change to occur, proponents of service-learning must pay close attention to both structural and ideological elements, which, as table 13.1 demonstrates, differ considerably from one stage of institutionalization to another. Further, service-learning may become embedded through a succession of efforts with some schools or programs serving as a vanguard and others joining later. Perhaps the most important implication of these findings is that institutionalization requires continual cultivation and tending. None of the individuals we spoke with at these institutions feels any sense of complacency. Most were able to point to members of an "old guard"—faculty members for whom new modes of scholarship and teaching are somewhat suspect—whose support was unlikely and whose influence needed to be taken into account. As one director put it, "There are some faculty for whom we're simply irrelevant and that's just the way it is." Success lies in a slow and deliberate cultivation of supporters who can attest to service-learning's efficacy. Swarthmore and Widener are beginning this process. Swarthmore's director explains:

> We're still moving out into groups of faculty that very much believe in what we're doing and wanted to do it but couldn't because they didn't have the resources. My hope is that as they talk about their experiences, we'll move out into the next ring of faculty members who haven't thought of this.

The more-established program at Penn and Tufts are already meeting the challenge of reaching into that "next ring" of faculty. However, the areas of scholarship and inclinations of these individuals in some cases make any connection to a broader civic engagement effort a more tenuous one than the early adopters. Each program faces considerable challenges. Hal Lawson (2002), in describing the ideal engaged campus notes: "All engaged universities are still evolving. All remain 'works in progress'" (p. 91).

The analysis presented here suggests that proponents of service-learning and civic engagement who seek institutionalization ought to approach their task like leaders of a grassroots movement—both structural and ideological issues must be addressed. It is insufficient to allocate institutional resources and staff lines for an innovation that has not gained widespread legitimacy within the organization. To do so is to build a Field of Dreams and hope "they" will come. Proponents must also seek to understand prevailing institutional norms and values: Is "service" or "responsibility to community" an important historic theme for the institution? If there are service-learning pioneers, how do they explain how their work fulfills their obligation to the institution and are there opportunities for larger conversation and dialogue? Conversely, an institution that eloquently redrafts its mission statement and publicly touts a renewed commitment to service but assumes that faculty and staff will carry the burden of sustaining the effort because of the intrinsic worth of the project has built a Potempkin Village—an elaborate façade that, while impressive, and apt to fool an outsider for a short time, will ultimately produce quite negligible results.

True institutionalization requires radical restructuring, the realigning of all the resources of the institution (structural and ideological) to a new and, in the current environment, somewhat contrarian purpose. Even at those institutions that have attempted to do both, significant challenges remain. It may be that total institutionalization by any institution is impossible in the current climate.

Too many external factors (e.g., disciplinary expectations, institutional competition, commodification) hamper it. Perhaps our best hope is for individual institutions to continue to struggle but also for them to recognize that they are part of a larger movement that must challenge the norms of the entire academy to ultimately achieve complete success at the local level.

Notes

1. See www.compact.org for additional information.
2. www.upenn.edu/ccp.
3. http://uccps.tufts.edu/05_Faculty/faculty/html.
4. A complete discussion of this process can be found in Julie Reuben's book, *The Making of the Modern University: Intellectual Transformation and the Marginalization of Morality.* Chicago: University of Chicago Press, 1996.

References

Benson, L. & Harkavy, I. (October 6–7, 2002). *Truly engaged and truly democratic cosmopolitan civic universities, community schools, and development of the democratic good of society in the 21st century.* Paper presented at the Seminar on the Research University as Local Citizen, University of California, San Diego.

Benson, L., Harkavy, I. & Hartley, M. (2005). Problem-solving service-learning in university-assisted schools as one practical means to develop democratic schools, democratic universities, and a democratic good society. In T. Chambers, J. Burkhardt, & A. Kezar (Eds.), *Higher education for the public good: Emerging voices from a national movement.* San Francisco: Jossey-Bass.

Boyer, E. (1990). *Scholarship reconsidered.* Princeton, NJ: The Carnegie Foundation for the Advancement of Teaching.

Diani, M. (1992). The concept of social movement. *The Sociological Review:* 1–25.

Duck, J. D. (2001). *The change monster: The human forces that fuel or foil corporate transformation and change.* New York, NY: Crown Business.

Glesne, C. & Peshkin, A. (1992). *Becoming qualitative researchers: An introduction.* New York: Longman.

Goodman, P. S. & Dean, J. W. (1982). Creating long-term organizational change. In P. S. Goodman (Ed.), *Change in organizations.* San Francisco, CA: Jossey-Bass.

Hartley, M. (2003). "There is no way without a because": Revitalization of purpose at three liberal arts colleges. *The Review of Higher Education,* 27(1): 75–102.

Hartley, M. & Hollander, E. (2005). The elusive ideal: Civic learning and higher education. In S. Fuhrman & M. Lazerson (Eds.), *Institutions of democracy: Public schools essay volume.* Oxford: Oxford University Press.

Hirschhorn, L. & May, L. (2000). The campaign approach to change: Targeting the university's scarcest resources. *Change,* 32(May/June): 30–37.

Hoffer, E. (1951). *The true believer: Thoughts on the nature of mass movements.* New York: Harper and Brothers.

Holland, B. (1997). Analyzing institutional commitment to service: A model of key organizational factors. *Michigan Journal of Community Service-learning* (Fall): 30–41.

Hollander, E. & Hartley, M. (2000). Civic renewal in higher education: The state of the movement and the need for a national network. In T. Ehrlich (Ed.), *Civic responsibility and higher education.* Phoenix, AZ: Orynx Press.

Kanter, R. M. (1983). *The change masters.* New York: Simon and Schuster.

Kotter, J. (1996). *Leading change.* Boston, MA: Harvard Business School Press.

Lawson, H. A. (2002). Beyond community involvement and service-learning to engaged universities. *Universities and Community Schools,* 7(1–2): 79–94.

Maurasse, D. (2001). *Beyond the campus: How colleges and universities form partnerships with their communities.* New York, NY: Routledge.

Maxwell, J. A. (1996). *Qualitative research design: An interactive approach.* Thousand Oaks, CA: Sage.

Ostrander, S. A. (2004). Democracy, civic participation, and the university: A comparative study of civic engagement on five campuses. *Nonprofit and Voluntary .*

Patton, M. Q. (1990). *Qualitative evaluation and research methods* (2nd ed.). Newbury Park, CA: Sage.

Rossman, G. B. & Rallis, S. F. (1997). *Learning in the field: An introduction to qualitative research:* Draft.

Schein, E. H. (1985). *Organizational culture and leadership* (2nd ed.). San Francisco: Jossey-Bass.

Singleton, S., Burack, C. A. & Hirsch, D. J. (1997). *Faculty service enclaves: A summary report*. Boston, MA: University of Massachusetts, Boston.

Stanton, T. K., Giles, D. E., Jr. & Cruz, N. I. (1999). *Service-learning: A movement's pioneers reflect on its origins, practice and future*. San Francisco, CA: Jossey-Bass.

Ward, K. (1996). Service-learning and student volunteerism: Reflections on institutional commitment. *Michigan Journal of Community Service-learning*, 3: 55–65.

Weick, K. E. (1976). Educational organizations as loosely coupled systems. *Administrative Science Quarterly*, 21: 1–19.

CIVIC SKILL BUILDING: THE MISSING COMPONENT IN SERVICE PROGRAMS?*

MARY KIRLIN

What are the best ways to instill democratic values and create civically engaged citizens? Much political, public, and scholarly attention has recently been paid to these and similar questions. Service learning and community service for adolescents and young adults have received the most attention (Perry and Katula 2001). Civic education has also been studied but does not draw the same attention as service learning (Niemi and Junn 1999). The September 2000 issue of *PS: Political Science & Politics* addressed service learning in higher education, but service for high school students is also receiving increasing amounts of attention. Estimates are that 83% of high schools nationally offer community service opportunities (Westheimer and Kahne 2000), that half of all community colleges have service learning courses and that nearly two million college students at four-year institutions participate in service learning (Hepburn, Niemi, and Chapman 2000). While specific articulated outcomes vary widely, researchers suggest that students who participate in service programs will become more civically engaged (Yates and Youniss 1998), understand and become more tolerant of our diverse society, and improve classroom learning (Hepburn, Niemi, and Chapman 2000). Empirical research suggests some positive outcomes from service learning relative to student cognition and classroom learning but little evidence supports expectations that service learning encourages civic behaviors such as voting, contacting elected officials, and being active in community affairs (Perry and Katula 2001).

This paper suggests one reason for the weak empirical results relative to civic engagement is that many service and volunteer programs have failed to sufficiently address development of fundamental civic skills such as expressing opinions and working collectively to achieve common interests as part of their design. As a result, while some studies of service learning participants show enhanced compassion and interest in social problems generally, those attitudinal changes do not consistently translate into behavioral changes (Eyler, Giles, and Braxton 1997; Perry and Katula 2001). This paper reviews recent empirical studies of community service, service learning, and volunteering, and then frames the consistently strong evidence that participation in clubs and organizations during adolescence leads to higher levels of civic engagement during adulthood within the political participation model developed by Verba, Schlozman, and Brady (1995). I suggest that the reason such participation is linked to later civic engagement is less related to civic identity development as suggested by some (Yates and Youniss 1998; Youniss, McLellan, and Yates 1997), than it is to development of fundamental civic skills necessary for civic engagement.

I am interested in how adolescents learn to become active adult members of their communities—to become "engaged," not only in political activities such as voting and campaign work, but also in community improvement activities via civic and volunteer associations (similar to Campbell 2000). I focus on how adolescents learn the *doing* of democracy, that is, active *participation*, not simply cognitive knowledge of political systems. Building upon the premise that adolescence is a critical time for socialization and development (Erikson 1968), I ask, "What activities during adolescence lead to long-term civic engagement?"

Community Service, Service Learning and Volunteering Impact Civic Engagement Weakly

Service learning, community service, and volunteering have been put forward as mechanisms to increase civic engagement of individuals (Yates and Youniss 1998). Community service programs typically consist of requirements for students to volunteer a given amount of time in their community. Hepburn, Niemi, and Chapman (2000) remind us that service learning is similar to community service in its volunteer component but has explicit links to classroom curricula.

Perry and Katula (2001) produce interesting results with their comprehensive review of 219 empirical studies of the relationship between service (including service learning and community service) and citizenship. After cautioning that limited empirical studies, small sample sizes, and differing objectives and methodologies affect the ability to draw concrete conclusions, they conclude that a) service appears to favorably influence citizenship related cognitive understanding; b) service and volunteering appear to positively influence later volunteering and giving; and c) the type of service that produces the most consistent positive results is service learning. However, they find that existing research does not address the relationship between citizenship skills and behaviors sufficiently to draw conclusions. While attitudinal changes were somewhat common there was no evidence of behavior changes. Perry and Katula (2001, 15) observe that "given the centrality of active citizenship in most theories and proposals for service, the paucity of research about citizenship outcomes, particularly behaviors, is noteworthy."

Hunter and Brisbin's (2000, 625) evaluation of college student's service-learning experiences in three locations is exemplary of the mixed findings common in empirical research in this area. Their study confirms that service-learning participants "learn about their community, further develop some academic skills and feel that they have helped members of their community." However, little to no change was indicated for self-reported attitudes towards political engagement.

Similarly, empirical evidence indicates volunteering has positive results for individuals on cognitive and attitudinal measures but weak results for increasing civic engagement of participants. A 1996 survey found approximately 60% of teens volunteered during the previous 12 months (Independent Sector 1997). Adolescent volunteers reported their experience helped them understand people who are different than themselves (48%) and to understand more about good citizenship (37%); but only 18% said they learned how to help solve community problems (Independent Sector 1997). A longitudinal study of the long-term effects of volunteering in college (Astin, Sax, and Avalos 1999) finds a positive—though tenuous—relationship between volunteering during college and later volunteering. Those who volunteered extensively in high school and college were twice as likely to be volunteering nine years later than those who did no volunteer work. However, among those that volunteered during high school and college, one-third were doing no volunteer work nine years later; of those who did no volunteer work in high school or college, 31% were volunteering nine years later.

Perry and Katula (2001, 27) ask why the relationship between attitudes and behavior in service programs does not appear to be strong. "Is the attenuation a result of service-learning pedagogy that does not translate into enough hands-on experience . . .? Or is it a function of institutions that do not reinforce service experiences?" Morgan and Streb (2001) suggest that students' voices in service learning projects are critical to achieving positive political engagement impacts. Other scholars suggest that service may not create an understanding of social interdependence or a sense of community responsibility (Raskoff and Sundeen 1998), or that motivations for service may be associated more with an individual's desire to help another rather than in a broader social or political understanding or commitment (Scrow 1991).

Civic Skill Development During Adolescence Is Critical

Basing their work on surveys of 15,000 adults, Verba, Schlozman, and Brady (1995) argue that adult participation in civic life requires three "participatory factors": desire to get involved (motivation); the ability to contribute something to the effort (capacity and skills); and some connection to the networks of individuals who ask others to become involved (networks). In a complex model, the authors trace "roots of participation" back to "initial characteristics" including gender, race and parent's education. They then identify three "pre-adult experiences" that affect later civic participation: education, discussion of politics at home, and participation in an extracurricular organization as an adolescent. The model continues with adult experiences that affect participation, but for purposes of this article, the "pre-adult" experiences are critical.

The pre-adult experiences affect the three participatory factors in the following manner. Education can lead to increased understanding of the importance of civic participation (motivation); provide money or time to contribute to civic endeavors (capacity); and introduce one to others concerned with civic life (networks). Discussion of politics at home can enhance the motivation to get involved. Finally, participation in organizations and clubs during adolescence can teach skills necessary for adult civic participation (capacity).

Verba, Schlozman, and Brady (1995) find that participation in high-school student government and other clubs was strongly associated with later civic engagement, and suggest that such membership teaches skills that are necessary for later involvement including "hands-on training in communication and organization skills." With the exception of sports, Verba, Schlozman, and Brady find this to be true regardless of the underlying nature and type of the club; participation in the chess or Spanish club is as effective for teaching civic skills as participation in student government.

Additional empirical research supports participation in organizations during adolescence as a predictor of future civic engagement. Like studies of service, the samples are sometimes small, but unlike service research, the five studies conducted between 1976 and 1995 came to similar conclusions, finding that individuals who were active in organizations during adolescence are two to four times more likely to be active in civic and political life than those who had not participated in organizations during adolescence (Beane et al. 1981; Hanks and Eckland 1978; Ladewig and Thomas 1987; Otto 1976; and Verba, Schlozman and Brady 1995). Adolescent participants were also two to four times as likely as their nonparticipating colleagues to be officers in organizations as adults. Adults were studied 12 to 30 years after their adolescent participation. In most studies, they were asked to recall their participation; although in two of the studies, participants were drawn from a pool of those known to be alumni from particular organizations (4-H and a school-based community planning project). Organizations that predicted future activity included participation in 4-H, student government, and school-based clubs such as yearbook, debate team, and a course where students helped the community with long-term planning efforts.

A more recent empirical study confirms and expands these findings. I analyzed a statewide California YMCA high school model-legislature program to find that the 1,069 alumni (ages 18 to 72) were statistically significantly more likely than the general population to be involved in several civic engagement behaviors. Specifically, 96% are registered voters, 87% voted in the 2000 presidential election, 47% have contacted an elected official about an issue, 45% have attended a local board or council meeting, 43% have gotten together with others informally to work on community problems, 35% have contributed to a campaign, and 36% have served on a board or been an officer in a group (Kirlin 2001). To control for income and education effects, I examined the civic engagement behaviors of three groups of alumni: those over 25 years of age who make less than $25,000 per year; those over 25 years of age who do not hold at least a bachelor's degree; and those whose parents held jobs that did not require a college degree (largely service or trades). All three groups of alumni were statistically significantly more involved than the general population on all measures of civic engagement except making campaign contributions. At least in this case, participation in extracurricular activities positively affected adult civic engagement, regardless of the income and education of the participants or their parents.

Glanville (1999) investigated whether individuals who were active in organizations as adolescents had "self-selected" into organizations based on preexisting personality characteristics or political attitudes. She finds that sociability, leadership attitudes, and interest in and awareness of political issues only partially account for the association between participation in organizations and later political and civic engagement. The remainder is attributed to the participation itself. Self-selection based on predisposition to politics did not seem to affect my (2001) study either. I asked 263 alumni why they became involved in the YMCA model legislature program; only 32% indicated they liked politics and government, while 65% said their friends got them involved.

Conrad and Hedin's (1982a, 1982b, 1989) research demonstrates the role experiential and participatory education play in preparing students to be active civic-minded citizens. School-based experiential learning has a positive impact when, among other things, student decision making is encouraged by teachers. Similarly, a recent international study finds that high school students who reported "an open classroom environment where they were encouraged to discuss issues and take part in shaping school life" showed greater civic knowledge and were more likely to indicate they expected to vote as adults (Tomey-Purta et al. 2001, 8).

These findings begin to knit together the consistent conclusions about the importance of adolescent participation. Involving students in many levels of the learning process may facilitate the development of civic skills important for later civic engagement.

Some researchers argue that these studies suggest enhanced civic identity among adolescents increases adult civic engagement. Yates and Youniss (1998, 496) argue that adolescent participation in organizations creates "reference points that aid in the formation of political understandings and engagement," norms of participation that become imbedded in identity, leading to engagement in civic life. Hepburn (2000) suggests that research linking adolescent participation in clubs and organizations to later civic engagement creates a rationale for community service in high school, agreeing with the Yates and Youniss premise of civic identity development as a key component.

However, research indicates that the impact of adolescent experiences is more plausibly attributable to enhanced civic skills. Adolescents' participation in organizations matters for later civic engagement not because it creates a civic identity but because it teaches concrete skills critical for civic engagement. Returning to the Verba-Schlozman-Brady model (1995), recall the three factors necessary for political participation: motivation, networks and capacity/skills. Because the types of organizations yielding future civic engagement were not always political or civic in nature, it does not appear that the primary benefit of adolescent participation in organizations is creating either the motivation for involvement (Verba's terminology) or civic identity development (Yates and Youniss's terminology). While network development is a plausible explanation for some of the relationship, and deserves research attention, the most logical explanation is that students are developing and practicing civic skills through their participation in organizations.

This argument is consistent with two additional findings from Verba, Schlozman, and Brady (1995). First, they find that participation in high school sports was negatively associated with later civic engagement. Conway and Damico (2001) have similar findings. While providing other benefits, organized sports provide little opportunity for civic skill development: the goal (winning) is predetermined, and adults undertake the planning for the season, organize the matches, and do most of the coaching. Opportunities for students to organize themselves, decide on objectives, and collectively make decisions are limited. The same may be increasingly true for service learning and community service; adults may have organized students too well, taking the fun (and civic skill learning) out of the effort.

The second important finding is that church participation, whether in adolescence or adulthood, is positively associated with civic engagement. Depending upon the particular institution, church can provide motivation and networks, and may also provide opportunities to learn and practice civic skills. Members have the opportunity to set goals (a new childcare program or building), organize fellow members (a picnic or bazaar), and negotiate with others to determine the common good. Verba, Schlozman, and Brady (1995) find church participation to be an equalizer for economic and education factors that would otherwise predict low levels of civic engagement.

Participants in Community Service and Service Learning Can Gain Civic Skills

Democratic society inherently demands collective decision making. Thus, young adults must practice the skills necessary for civic engagement; cognitive understanding of democracy is not sufficient. Adolescent participation in organizations provides the opportunity for hands-on development of foundational civic skills such as working in groups, organizing others to accomplish tasks, communicating, and working out differences of substance or process on the way to accomplishing a goal. Patrick (2000, 5) suggests participatory skills of citizenship in democracy include "interacting with other citizens to promote personal and common interests, monitoring public events and issues, deliberating about public policy issues, influencing policy decisions on public issues and implementing policy decisions on public issues." The list is particularly useful because it is based on actions that infer skills, not simply knowledge. However, to be competent in Patrick's civic skills, several very basic underlying skills must be mastered. Table 1 makes some preliminary suggestions as to what those skills might be. Some of these are cognitive in nature but many must be practiced in order to develop mastery. The premise that civic skill building can be important for later civic engagement has implications for program design and for research. Some relatively simple changes might greatly enhance the longterm civic-engagement effects of service and volunteer programs.

The most significant step is rethinking the front end of service and volunteer programs so that students have as much latitude as possible to learn and practice civic skills through the process of designing and organizing their activities themselves. This does not mean disengaging the service experience from the classroom content. Rather, it means facilitating students' discovery of what problems exist, whom they need to contact to address the issues, and what types of projects they will undertake. Giving students the opportunity to identify fellow students with similar concerns and then to decide what they will do about it is an important first step. Underlying this relatively simple step are several skills including voicing one's opinion, expressing interests, identifying like-minded individuals, and reaching consensus about action. Service and volunteer programs that provide preapproved lists of organizations ready to accept students for predetermined volunteer roles immediately remove several learning opportunities including understanding local events and identifying decision makers, stakeholders, and providers. Adults should facilitate learning by asking questions, and providing support and encouragement, but not prepackaged experiences.

Similar adaptations of classroom efforts may benefit civic learning in the classroom. I have begun testing this approach in an introductory undergraduate public affairs course. At the beginning of the term, students identify a public issue they would like to influence (by reading the local newspaper) and work in small (self-selected) groups to identify background, stakeholders, decision makers, and important timelines for the issue they have chosen. They then actively work to influence the outcome by writing letters, meeting with officials, attending and speaking at public meetings, and generating interest from others through media and other means. Requiring the students to practice civic skills led one student to observe, "Everyone thinks they know how to be involved but I didn't really know until I did it." Students have anecdotally reported increased understanding of the newspaper and local events, a much clearer understanding of who makes decisions and how to access them, and most importantly, confidence that they could get involved in an issue that interests them.

Important research questions arise from this argument. The identification of specific civic skills is crucial to understanding their roles in future civic engagement and to increasing our ability to build civic skill development into programs. Patrick's (2000) list is a starting point, and I have begun to identify some of the underlying skills, but further refinement is needed. Researchers can then fill the gaps in research on civic skill and behavior development in service programs by testing and identifying successful service programs.

Confirming the hypothesis that civic skill building can crosscut many types of organizations and lead to later civic engagement is fundamental. It is important to understand both the activities of current adolescents and the structure of programs intended to increase civic engagement. Currently there is inadequate information on the variety of possibly relevant programs offered by schools and nonprofit organizations, as well as the experiences individual students have. My efforts to collect information about programs, and attributes and numbers of participants from high schools in one Indiana county revealed very good data on numbers of students participating in sports but fragmented and incomplete information about students participating in nonsports activities. Some high schools had athletics directors with assistants while nonsports programs were assigned somewhat haphazardly to faculty and staff with no central coordination. Not surprisingly, schools reported

TABLE 1

Underlying Skills Necessary for Civic Skills

Civic Skill	Underlying Skills
Monitoring public events and issues	• Understand distinctions between three sectors of society (public, nonprofit and private) • Understand context for events and issues (what happened and why) • Capacity to acquire and thoughtfully review news (read the local newspaper)
Deliberating about public policy issues	• Think critically about issues • Understand multiple perspectives on issues
Interacting with other citizens to promote personal and common interests	• Understand democratic society (collective decision making as norm) • Capacity to articulate individual perspective and interests • Work with others to define common objective • Create and follow a work plan to accomplish a goal
Influencing policy decisions on public issues	• Identify decision makers and institutions • Understand appropriate vehicles for influencing decisions

approximately twice as many opportunities for sports participation as all clubs and organizations combined. Understanding what programs are available through schools and the broader community will help us to understand where civic engagement efforts may best be enhanced.

Additional research into the question of whether service and participation in organizations and clubs provide networks (as defined by Verba, Schlozman, and Brady 1995) will also be helpful. As people are increasingly mobile, networks developed during adolescence may be less important although practicing the skill of network development may still have importance for long-term civic engagement.

References

Astin, Alexander W., Linda J. Sax, and Juan Avalos. 1999. "The Long-Term Effects of Volunteerism During the Undergraduate Years." *The Review of Higher Education* 22:187–202.

Beane, J., J. Turner, D. Jones, and R. Lipka. 1981. "Long-Term Effects of Community Service Programs." *Curriculum Inquiry* 11:143–55.

Campbell, David. 2000. "Social Capital and Service Learning." *PS: Political Science & Politics* 33:641–45.

Conrad, Dan, and Diane Hedin, eds. 1982a. *Youth Participation and Experiential Education.* New York: Haworth Press.

—. 1982b. *Executive Summary of the Final Report of the Experiential Education Evaluation Project.* Minneapolis: University of Minnesota, Center for Youth Development and Research.

—. 1989. *High School Community Service: A Review of Research and Programs*. Madison, Wisconsin: National Center on Effective Secondary Schools.

Conway, Margaret, and Alfonso J. Damico. 2001. "Building Blocks: The Relationship Between High School and Adult Association Life." Presented at the Annual Meeting of the American Political Science Association, San Francisco.

Erikson, E.H. 1968. *Identity: Youth and Crisis*, New York: Norton.

Eyler, Janet, Dwight Giles, and John Braxton. 1997. "Report of a National Study Comparing the Impacts of Service-Learning Program Characteristics on Post Secondary Students." Presented at the Annual Meeting of the American Educational Research Association, Chicago.

Glanville, Jennifer L. 1999. "Political Socialization or Selection? Adolescent Extracurricular Participation and Political Activity in Early Adulthood." *Social Science Quarterly* 80:279–90.

Hanks, M., and Eckland, B.K. 1978. "Adult Voluntary Associations and Adolescent Socialization." *The Sociological Quarterly* 19:481–90.

Hepburn, Mary A. 2000. "Service Learning and Civic Education in the Schools: What Does Recent Research Tell Us?" In *Education for Civic Engagement in Democracy*, ed. Sheilah Mann and John J. Patrick. Bloomington: Indiana University, ERIC Clearinghouse for Social Studies/Social Science Education.

—, Richard G. Niemi, and Chris Chapman. 2000. "Service Learning in College Political Science: Queries and Commentary." *PS: Political Science & Politics* 33:617–22.

Hunter, Susan, and Richard A. Brisbin. 2000. "The Impact of Service Learning on Democratic and Civic Values." *PS: Political Science & Politics* 33:623–26.

Independent Sector. 1997. *Trends Emerging from the National Survey of Volunteering and Giving Among Teenagers*. Washington, DC.

Kirlin, Mary. 2001. "Adult Civic Engagement: Can Adolescent Extra-curricular Activities Overcome Income and Education Barriers?" Indiana University Purdue University Indianapolis. Typescript.

Ladewig, Howard, and John K. Thomas. 1987. "Assessing the Impact of 4-H on Former Members." College Station: Texas A&M University, Cooperative Extension Service.

Morgan, William, and Matthew Streb, 2001. "Building Citizenship: How Student Voice in Service-Learning Develops Civic Values." *Social Science Quarterly* 82:154–70.

Niemi, Richard, and Jane Junn. 1999. *Civic Edcuation: What Makes Students Learn?* New Haven, CT: Yale University Press.

Otto, L.B. 1976. "Social Integration and the Status Attainment Process." *American Journal of Sociology* 81:1360–83.

Patrick, John J. 2000. "Introduction to Education for Civic Engagement in Democracy" In *Education for Civic Engagement in Democracy: Service Learning and Other Promising Practices*, ed. Sheilah Mann and John J. Patrick. Bloomington: Indiana University, ERIC Clearinghouse for Social Studies/Social Science Education.

Perry, James, and Michael C. Katula. 2001. "Does Service Affect Citizenship?" *Administration and Society* 33:330–33.

Raskoff, Sally, and Richard A. Sundeen. 1998. "Youth Socialization and Civic Participation: The Role of Secondary Schools in Promoting Community Service in Southern California." *Nonprofit and Voluntary Sector Quarterly* 27:66–87.

Torney-Purta, Judith, Rainer Lehmann, Hans Oswald and Wilfram Schulz, 2001. *Executive Summary of Citizenship and Education in Twenty-eight Countries: Civic Knowledge and Engagement at Age Fourteen*. Amsterdam: International Association for the Evaluation of Educational Achievement.

Verba, Sidney, Kay Lehman Schlozman, and Henry E. Brady. 1995. *Voice and Equality, Civic Voluntarism in American Politics*. Cambridge, MA: Harvard University Press.

Westheimer, Joel, and Joseph Kahne. 2000. "Service Learning Required." *Education Week* 19 (20): 52.

Yates, Miranda, and James Youniss. 1998, "Community Service and Political Identity Development in Adolescents." *Journal of Social Issues* 54:495–512.

Youniss, James, Jeffrey A. McLellan, and Miranda Yates. 1997. "What We Know about Engendering Civic Identity." *American Behavioral Scientist* 40:620–32.

*This research was funded by a grant from the Indiana University Center on Philanthropy. The author wishes to thank Michael Leuthner and Jordan Olivetti for their research assistance.

WHAT IS GOOD CITIZENSHIP?

CONCEPTUAL CONTRIBUTIONS FROM OTHER DISCIPLINES

RICHARD M. BATTISTONI

The five conceptual frameworks I have just outlined give an example of how social scientists have answered the question of citizenship and how faculty might tie conceptions of citizenship to service-learning. If we want to engage all across campus in education for civic engagement, however, we need to go beyond the social sciences for conceptual frameworks that will inform the theory and practice of service-learning. While political and other social scientists have a rich tradition and language around concepts like democracy, citizenship, community, political participation, civil society, and public work, they obviously do not own these concepts, and given the evidence of declining political participation (especially among young people), they may not be communicating it very effectively or in a way that resonates with students. In fact, the more we engage in narrow or rhetorical definitions of service and citizenship, the more we may turn away both students and faculty—especially those outside the social science disciplines. This calls at once for all disciplines, which may have equally effective conceptual frameworks, to join into the discourse around a multidisciplinary civic education. To paraphrase a statement made by Vaclav Havel in one of his first New Year's Addresses as president of the Czech Republic, the public problems we face as a people are such that require the collaboration of "well-rounded people," those informed by a variety of perspectives and conceptual frameworks (Havel, 1997: 9).

In this spirit, more than a year ago I began a conversation with representatives from a number of different disciplinary associations about the language and conceptual frameworks that resonated with their own disciplines. Out of this initial conversation, I generated the following list of terms:

- social capital (or social trust)
- civic engagement
- civic responsibility
- citizenship
- "public intellectual"
- civic professionalism
- corporate/institutional citizenship
- social responsibility, social accountability (or public accountability)
- social issues
- social justice
- public agency, public capacity
- social ethics, civic ethics, public ethics
- democracy/democratic citizenship/democratic participation
- democratic practice
- public or community problem solving
- the creation of a public
- altruism
- prosocial behavior
- reciprocity
- civic or public leadership
- the creation of "public intellectuals"
- civic obligation
- public life
- other-regardingness

- public scholarship
- community identity
- community responsibility
- community building

- common ground

- creation of a more democratic society
- civil society
- the not-for-profit sector
- preparation for multicultural/intercultural citizenship
- community partnerships

The list was whittled down, based on positive faculty responses, to the following seven conceptual frameworks for civic engagement that come from theory and practice found in disciplines outside the social sciences. While certainly not exhaustive of the possibilities, these frameworks may better lend themselves to integrating service-learning into the civic engagement curriculum for many faculty than those found in the social sciences. As with the preceding chapter, a matrix comparing the answers each framework brings to the question of citizenship, civic education, the associated civic skills needed for effective public life, along with each framework's disciplinary affinities, follows the narrative summary (see Figure 2 on page 490).

Civic Professionalism

In discussing the concept of civic professionalism I draw primarily from the argument made by William Sullivan in his book *Work and Integrity* (Sullivan, 1995). Sullivan, a philosopher by discipline and one of the co-authors of *Habits of the Heart* and *The Good Society*, traces the ideal of professionalism and professional work to the social reformers writing at the turn of the twentieth century. Sullivan contends that under this ideal, professional work was characterized by three central features:

- specialized training in a field of codified knowledge usually acquired by formal education and apprenticeship,
- public recognition of a certain autonomy on the part of the community of practitioners to regulate their own standards of practice,
- and a commitment to provide service to the public which goes beyond the economic welfare of the practitioners.

—Sullivan, 2

In fact, the three features were originally thought to be intimately related to each other. The professional drew her social status, and the concomitant financial rewards, from her technical knowledge and expertise. This expertise also bought the professional autonomy in the workplace, something deemed critical to job satisfaction. In exchange, the professional was conceived as owing something back to the society from whom she drew this status and autonomy. So as a kind of *quid pro quo*, professionals were expected to contribute their knowledge to the public: indirectly, through their deliberations over matters of civic concern; and directly, through *pro bono* work with disadvantaged citizens. Originally referring to those working in the "classic honorific occupations of medicine, the bar, and the clergy," the status of professional was extended broadly to include fields such as business, education, engineering, governmental bureaucracy, health care (beyond physicians), architecture, and planning. But Sullivan asserts that while professionalization has grown tremendously over the past century, its connection to the "culture of civic democracy" emblematic of the third feature of professional work has weakened severely. While professional work has risen in social status and desirability, the civic responsibility that was originally understood as the price a professional paid for social and economic recognition and personal autonomy has declined. What we are witnessing today, according to Sullivan, is a professional ethic where technical expertise has become decoupled from civic purpose.

Sullivan argues that we must revitalize the civic orientation that originally stood at the foundation of the professions. In the United States, where the professions "pioneered and continue to model a socially attuned way to organize work," (Sullivan, 222), we need civically minded

Conceptual Framework	View of Citizenship	Understanding of Civic Education	Associated Civic Skills (see Ch.5)	Disciplinary Affinities
Civic Professionalism	Professional work with a civic purpose	Learning about the civic traditions and values of the professions	Public Problem Solving Civic Judgment	Progessional Disciplines
Social Responsibility	Responsibility to larger society	Learning about the public problems most closely associated with chosen field of work	Political Knowledge (Issues) Organizational Analysis	Health Professions Business Disciplines Computer Science
Social Justice	Bringing one's spiritual values to bear on social problems	Learning the principles of social justice and their application to public life	Civic Judgment Collective Action	Religious Studies Philosophy Faith-Based Institutions
Connected Knowing; Ethic of Care	Caring for the future of our public world	Learning about others and their perspectives on the world	Critical Thinking Coalition Building	Women's Studies Psychology Nursing
Public Leadership	Citizen as "servant-leader"	Learning the arts of collaborative leadership	Community Building Communication	Management Leadership Studies
Public Intellectual	Thinkers who contribute to the public discourse	Learning about the traditions of writers and artists who have served as public intellectuals	Civic Imagination & Creativity	Literature Visual & Performing Arts
Engaged/Public Scholarship	Participatory action researcher	Learning about how scholarly research might contribute to the needs and values of the community	Organizational Analysis Public Problem Solving	Journalism Communications Professional Disciplines Land Grant Instit.

Figure 2 Conceptual Frameworks in Other Disciplines

professionals more than ever. Clearly, the challenges that face our society today require even more professional expertise than those confronted by citizens during the Progressive era. "Few kinds of work would seem better fitted to these needs of the new era than professions with a civic orientation" (Sullivan, 237). In particular, Sullivan calls upon professional education to re-instill the civic dimension that seems lacking in contemporary discussions of professional ethics and integrity.

This concept of civic professionalism should have great resonance in a number of fields where service-learning has been used as a pedagogy. Professional school educators who already deploy community service as a method of teaching concepts and practices in disciplinary courses could expand service-learning to explore related civic themes. With this concept in mind, students engaged in curriculum-based community service in schools of business, education, engineering, the health professions, law, and planning could be encouraged to reflect on the civic dimensions of their anticipated work.

Social Responsibility

Where civic responsibility may be a concept that needs reviving, social responsibility is a well-established idea in a number of professions. We now see organizations devoted to connecting professional work with social responsibility in such fields as medicine, business, computer technology, architecture, and planning.

One of the first and most well-known organizations pushing this approach is Physicians for Social Responsibility (PSR). Begun during the Cold War in 1961, PSR originated with an understanding that all doctors have an ethical as well as a professional responsibility to work toward the elimination of violence—with an original emphasis on curbing nuclear weapons—global environmental degradation, and social and economic inequities. Part of this ethic of the physicians' social responsibility involves civic engagement: one of the central values of PSR is that "citizens have a right to informed participation in such decision-making processes made by both government and industry which affect their health, welfare, and environment" (www.psr.org/aboutpsr.htm).

Other organizations have followed the lead of PSR. Business for Social Responsibility has the mission of "providing members with innovative products and services that help companies be commercially successful in ways that demonstrate respect for ethical values, people, communities, and the environment" (www.bsr.org). Computer Professionals for Social Responsibility declares itself to be "a public interest alliance of computer scientists and others concerned about the impact of computer technology on society" (www.cpsr.org).

Faculty members—particularly those in disciplines which prepare students for professions with corresponding "social responsibility" arms—might see this idea of social responsibility as a natural pathway to a form of civic engagement. For example, as part of a service-learning course that's a required component of premedical education, students could be directed to the PSR literature and website as one of the tools for reflection on their service. A local representative from PSR could be invited in to discuss with students the social responsibilities of people entering the medical profession. And these connections would be enhanced even further if the community service connected to the course were in the specific areas addressed by PSR, such as peace and nonviolence, the environment, or public health. (See Placement Quality section that follows.)

Social Justice

Notions of social justice may also provide powerful connections to civic engagement for faculty, particularly those teaching in faith-based institutions of higher education. While numerous definitions of social justice exist, David Hollenbach offers one of the better ones, connecting social justice—as developed in the context of the social teachings of the Catholic Church—and civic engagement:

> It refers to the obligations of all citizens to aid in the creation of patterns of social organization and activity that are essential both for the protection of minimal human rights and for the creation of mutuality and participation by all in social life.
>
> —Hollenbach, 1988:27

A similar understanding can be found in the American Catholic bishops' pastoral letter on the economy:

> Social justice implies that persons have an obligation to be active and productive participants in the life of society and that society has a duty to enable them to participate in this way.
>
> —National Conference of Catholic Bishops, 1986: 36

The logic of this framework is that social justice moves individuals to work in active solidarity with fellow human beings to seek the common good of all who live in their community. Under this conception, then, a just individual is necessarily a good citizen.

A social justice framework has much to recommend itself. Not only does it offer a powerful nonpolitical path to civic engagement (important given the current student turnoff from traditional politics as documented at the outset of this book). Additionally, for faculty teaching service-learning courses at faith-based colleges and universities, this perspective can provide a seamless link between student service, the specific subject matter of their courses, the institution's mission, and civic engagement.

There exists a growing body of literature connecting faith, justice, and citizenship, usually tied to specific faith traditions and texts. To give just one example, the Catholic social justice tradition contains within it a principle known as "subsidiarity." Subsidiarity requires, on the one hand, that problems be solved and decisions be made at the smallest level of association, The assumption is that smaller communities—local not-for-profit organizations, churches, civic groups—can more effectively and compassionately address the needs of their people, and that a distant, often unresponsive federal government or multinational business enterprise should therefore not usurp or replace the authority of the smaller body to act on behalf of its members. But the principle of subsidiarity also holds that when "the demands of justice exceed the capacities" of the smaller/local units, then government has an affirmative duty to act in solving social problems (National Conference of Catholic Bishops, 1986:62). Teaching at Providence College, I have successfully introduced subsidiarity as a way of engaging my students who do community service from their faith backgrounds in conversations about politics and public problem solving. The principle of subsidiarity also fits nicely with discussions of mediating institutions and social capital formation (see discussion, page 16), and with basic principles of grass roots community organizing, especially the efforts sponsored by the Industrial Areas Foundation, a network of community-based organizations that teach citizens in local neighborhoods how to work together effectively to achieve public ends (see Rogers, 1990; Fischer, 1997).

More generally, social justice is a conceptual framework that can help faculty in terms of guiding students' reflection on their service. A social justice perspective can help move service-learners from the "personal" that often characterizes service to the "political," because a "foundation in social justice requires that community service from a faith perspective move beyond charity and address the root causes that create the need for service within our society and world" (Swezey, 1990: 78). It also allows faculty to ask the question, "How do/will you incorporate social justice and service into your daily lives?"—an opening to increased civic engagement. Social justice frameworks can provide ties between course-based service-learning and co-curricular efforts of campus ministry offices. And finally, a social justice perspective complements reciprocal approaches to community partnerships:

> Paramount to the quest for justice is the building of authentic relationships between students and the individuals and communities with whom they serve. These relationships affirm the reciprocal learning inherent in service. Service in this context is not a doing to or for but a service with a person or group; enabling and empowering disenfranchised individuals and communities to be "agents of their own development and not just the beneficiaries of someone else's efforts." Together, the student and the individuals or communities being served plan and carry out the community service experience. The task of the service becomes secondary to the relationships that develop within the service experience.
>
> —Swezey, 1990:87

Connected Knowing: "Ethic of Care"

Faculty coming into service-learning from a feminist perspective may find pathways to civic engagement through the literature on "connected knowing" or "caring" as a social ethic. Building on the work of Carol Gilligan (1982), Belenky, Clinchy, Goldberger, & Tarule (1986) developed the concept of "connected knowing" as a way of describing a "proclivity toward thinking" they found in undergraduate women, to be contrasted from the dominant understanding of how we ought to think, what they call "separate knowing." The critical distinction between the two kinds of thinking, they argue, lies in whether we see ourselves as dispassionately detached or empathetically connected to the object known (and by extension to other "knowing beings"):

The separate knower holds herself aloof from the object she is trying to analyze. She takes an impersonal stance. She follows certain rules or procedures to ensure that her judgments are unbiased. . . . Separate knowing often takes the form of an adversarial proceeding. The separate knower's primary mode of discourse is the argument.

Connected knowers are not dispassionate, unbiased observers. They deliberately bias themselves in favor of what they are examining. They try to get inside it and form an intimate attachment to it. The heart of connected knowing is imaginative attachment: trying to get behind the other person's eyes and "look at it from that person's point of view."

—Clinchy, 1989

Based upon the research into women's ways of knowing, feminist thinkers have called upon institutions of higher education to value connected knowing, to be places where "people are encouraged to think about the things that they care about and to care about the things they think about" (Clinchy, 1989).

Speaking of "care," there also abounds in the feminist literature discussions of an "ethic of care," not only to describe the way women's engagement with others has been characterized, but also as a political ethic to be embraced (Noddings, 1984). Joan Tronto (1993:103) defines "care" as human activity "that includes everything that we do to maintain, continue, and repair our 'world' so that we can live in it as well as possible. That world includes our bodies, our selves, and our environment, all of which we seek to interweave in a complex, life-sustaining web."

While the gendered origins or associations of connected knowing and/or caring can be contested, there should be no doubt that the feminist orientation toward knowledge and caring can be a powerful way of moving from personal to civic engagement. And this conceptual framework lends itself to the pedagogy of service-learning. Not only does much of community service work come out of the "caring professions," but a student's course-related service can be reflected through the conceptual lens of "caring." This even allows the community service connected to a course to be subjected to various critiques of "care" as a concept that may be oppressive to women particularly when service-learning programs or courses are disproportionately populated by women, as is the case on many campuses. (For an example of a service-learning course reflecting this conceptual framework, taught by a faculty member in philosophy, see Foos, 2000.)

Public Leadership

At first blush, concepts associated with "leadership" would not seem to be compatible with notions of democratic citizenship. After all, "leaders" usually produce "followers," and the characteristics of followers appear on the surface to be inconsistent with those of the engaged citizen. In the U.S. context, Benjamin Barber has gone so far as to argue that "strong leaders have on the whole made Americans weak citizens . . . the conditions and consequences of leadership often seem to undermine civic vigor" (Barber, 1999: 164–5).

There are, however, rich conceptions of public leadership that compliment understandings of engaged democratic citizenship. In fact, we can trace ideas about this kind of "transformational" democratic leadership at least as far back as Rousseau's *Social Contract*, with more contemporary versions found in the writings of John Dewey, James MacGregor Burns, and Saul Alinsky (see Dewey, 1916; Burns, 1979; Alinsky, 1969). Burns puts the reciprocal relationship between leaders and citizens in a democracy this way:

Leadership is not a surrogate for participation in a democracy, it is its necessary condition. Without leaders, a citizenry is unlikely to remain active; without active citizens, responsive leaders are unlikely to emerge, and leaders who do emerge are unlikely to remain responsive.

—Burns, 1979: 439

Viewed this way, then, a leadership framework can be yet another pathway to engaged citizenship. And given the emergence of "leadership studies" as a growing area on college campuses—not only in business disciplines but as an interdisciplinary field on its own—connecting the study of public leadership to civic engagement may make sense. Moreover, recent philosophies of "steward" or "servant" leadership have strong connections with service-learning, and can serve as bridges between leadership studies, community-based learning, and civic education (see Greenleaf, 1996; see also the Greenleaf Center for Servant-Leadership, at http://www.greenleaf.org. A good example of a university-based leadership program, one with strong service-learning connections, is the Jepson School of Leadership Studies at the University of Richmond; see: http://www.richmond.edu/academics/leadership).

The Public Intellectual

So far, the different conceptual models of citizenship offered tend heavily toward the social sciences and pre-professional disciplines. To the extent that we might find connections to the humanities, it would be primarily philosophers or theologians who see concepts that resonate with their disciplines. There may be little conceptually for those in literature of the arts to latch on to, leading to the question, "What does citizenship have to do with us?" My conversations with faculty in the literary, visual, and performing arts suggest that the tradition of the "public intellectual" or the artist inspired to contribute to a political vision may be a powerful pathway to civic engagement in these fields.

What is meant by the term "public intellectual?" Simply put, public intellectuals are writers, artists, and thinkers "who address a general and educated audience . . . who contribute to open discussions" (Jacoby, 1987: 5, 221). They are women and men of intellect or vision who are not content to share their work with a specialized, esoteric audience, but bring the power of their ideas to bear on the public problems or questions of the day. In a democracy particularly, where majorities and public opinion rule, it has been thought critical to society's growth and progress to have a class of people who can contribute their ideas and vision to general public discourse. Writing in the nineteenth century, Walt Whitman makes this case for such a contribution to democracy in the United States:

> Our fundamental want today in the United States, with closest, amplest reference to present conditions, and to the future, is of a class, and the clear idea of a class, of native authors, literatuses, far different, far higher in grade than any yet known, sacerdotal, modern, fit to cope with our occasions, lands, permeating the whole mass of American mentality, taste, belief, breathing into it a new breath of life, giving it decision, affecting politics far more than the popular superficial suffrage, with results inside and underneath the elections of Presidents or Congresses—radiating, begetting appropriate teachers, schools, manners, and, as its grandest result, accomplishing (what neither the schools nor the churches and their clergy have hitherto accomplish'd, and without which this nation will no more stand, permanently, soundly, than a house will stand without a substratum,) a religious and moral character beneath the political and productive and intellectual bases of the States.

> —Walt Whitman

Following Shelley, who called poets "the unacknowledged legislators of the world," Whitman believed that American poets, writers, artists, and thinkers had a duty to contribute to the public discourse, to "become the justification and reliance of American democracy" (Whitman, 1999: 49). This tradition of public intellectuals in the United States would carry from Whitman, Ralph Waldo Emerson, Herbert Melville, Margaret Fuller, and Mark Twain in the nineteenth century to such individuals as Herbert Croly, John Dewey, Langston Hughes, Walter Lippmann, and Frank Capra in the early decades of the twentieth century (for examples of modern artists who have served the function of public intellectual, see Barber & McGrath, 1982).

The concept of a public intellectual may seem antiquated to many today. Indeed, a number of scholars would argue that the public intellectual is a dying breed, owing to changes in the media and popular culture, university life and work, and the demands of modern science and technology (see Bender, 1993; Jacoby, 1987; Hollander, et al., 2001). Still, this is a conceptual framework that may resonate with faculty in the humanities (for an extension to economists, see Levine, 2001), offering a number of natural links to service-learning. Students engaged in literary or artistic service projects can be introduced to this tradition of civic engagement through written texts and other works of public or political art. This conceptual tradition can be tied to the skills of civic imagination and creativity, with course assignments designed to make explicit linkage between literature or art and public value.

The Scholarship of Engagement, Public Scholarship

As noted in the last section, the notion of the "public intellectual" may seem antiquated to many faculty, the product of a bygone era. In the past decade, many faculty, especially those involved in experiential or service-learning, resonate more deeply to notions of engaged or public scholarship. The idea of connecting academic scholarship to engagement owes much to Ernest Boyer. In a 1996 essay, Boyer claimed that higher education needed to "become a more vigorous partner in the search for answers to our most pressing social, civic, economic, and moral problems, and must reaffirm its historic commitment to what I call the scholarship of engagement." Building on his report for the Carnegie Foundation for the Advancement of Teaching, entitled *Scholarship Reconsidered*, Boyer argued that "the scholarship of engagement means connecting the rich resources of the university to our most pressing social, civic, and ethical problems" (Boyer, 1996: 11–20). A number of scholars have built upon Boyer's foundations, making the case for the civic purposes of academic research and scholarship (see Benson and Harkavy, 1997; Checkoway, 2001). The American Association for Higher Education's Forum on Faculty Roles and Rewards has advanced these notions of "engaged scholarship," and AAHE has published a number of resources for faculty interested in connecting advanced scholarship with public purposes (see their website, at: http://www.aahe.org/FFRR/).

As a variation on the theme of engaged scholarship, Jeremy Cohen has recently offered what he thinks is a more civically minded conceptual framework for the research work done by faculty and students: public scholarship. According to Cohen, public scholarship gives both faculty and students the opportunity to "imagine their academic capacity as a way to contribute as citizen participants, in a community structure where their intellectual decisions do make a difference." As Cohen defines it,

> public scholarship as an approach assumes a duty to make university scholarship public and to use our discoveries in the interest of the community. . . . The social act of public scholarship itself provides a laboratory in which students can view their work not as the isolated, self-indulged actions of a campus segregated from society, but as the contributions of citizens with membership in a larger community.
>
> —*Cohen, 2001: 15–16*

This conceptual approach lends itself to a different kind of community service: "participatory action research" conducted by students and their faculty in collaboration with their community partners. Under this model, community-based organizations identify research projects that would contribute to their work, and universities—through service-learning curricula—provide their research resources as a form of service. Seen this way, service-learning as engaged or public scholarship can be a vehicle for faculty and students to reflect upon the public purposes of academic research, and the civic responsibilities of academic institutions. At Stanford, for example, the Haas Center for Public Service offers a "Senior Honors Research in Public Service Seminar," a full-year course that "provides an organizational structure to encourage and support participants committed to developing a thesis that meets criteria for academic excellence and also realizes the program's theme and goal, 'research as a form of public service'" (Cruz, 1998). Academic programs at the institutions such as the University of Pennsylvania and the University of Illinois are grounded in this approach (see Harkavy, 2000; Reardon, 1997).

SERVICE-LEARNING AND PSYCHOLOGY: LESSONS FROM THE PSYCHOLOGY OF VOLUNTEERS' MOTIVATIONS

E. GIL CLARY, MARK SNYDER, & ARTHUR STUKAS

A critical task facing all societies is the transmission of important values, goals, and attitudes to successive generations. These values, goals, and attitudes are often regarded as essential to the group, providing order within the group and ensuring its long-term survival. Attitudes and values of a prosocial nature may be particularly valuable in achieving these ends. Prosocial attitudes and values underlie actions such as contributing to the betterment of the community and providing assistance to the less fortunate members of a society, such attitudes and values also promote inclinations toward humanitarian concern, community service, altruism, charitable giving, and voluntarism.

Societies, then, are faced with the task of promoting prosocial attitudes, values, and behaviors among their members, and developing these attitudes, values, and behaviors among successive generations. To ensure transmission, however, it is clear that the task is not simply to induce *compliance* by establishing mechanisms such as rewards for conformity and punishments for nonconformity, because such compliance leads people to adhere to standards only when under surveillance. Nor would it be sufficient to induce *identification*, by convincing individuals to act appropriately in order to have satisfying relationships with another person or group of people that is liked or respected. Instead, the best strategy for society's goal of value transmission may be to induce the *internalization* of prosocial attitudes and values. In other words, societies need individual members to adopt these socially important values, goals, and attitudes as their own, with the result that individuals will act in accord with these standards even in the absence of explicit rewards, punishments, or desirable relationships (for further discussion of compliance, identification, and internalization, see Kelman 1958).

The internalization of socially important attitudes and values is especially critical to the socialization of young people. Educational settings are often one venue for the introduction and advancement of society's central attitudes, values, and behaviors (for example, lessons in civic responsibility are common). Service-learning programs have been specifically designed to promote prosocial values and attitudes in an educational context (among other goals). In service-learning, students perform service to and in the community and do so within the context of an academic course. From the standpoint of "learning" in service-learning, the experiences of students participating in service-learning programs emphasize the educational importance of combining action with reflection: Students are asked both to engage in prosocial behaviors and to deliberate the merit and implications of those actions for themselves and for society as a whole. With respect to the "service" in service-learning, such programs stress that service to the community is not performed as charity but, rather, conducted in a spirit of reciprocity—students and service recipients both give and receive (Keith 1994; Kendall 1991).

With this description as a backdrop, it should be clear that service-learning activities have much in common with the phenomenon of voluntarism, in which individuals offer assistance to others on an unpaid basis. An understanding of voluntarism, then, promises to shed some light on the processes involved in service-learning experiences, some of the positive outcomes that may result, and some of the difficulties that may arise. In this chapter, we will discuss our program of research on voluntarism, focusing on the motivational dynamics underlying participation in volunteer service, and we will consider some of the implications of our research for service-learning experiences and programs.

Our examination of these issues is guided by two overall considerations drawn from our framework for understanding the motivations of volunteers. First, we will argue that it is critical that prosocial values and attitudes, which tend to emphasize the concerns and needs of others, are also linked to people's own self-interests and individual concerns. Our conceptualization of volunteers' motivation, thus, is compatible with, and indeed fleshes out, the service-learning notion that community service is a reciprocal arrangement that is beneficial for both the helper and recipient. Second, we will assert that prosocial values are most effectively established at the "back-end" (i.e., following action) rather than at the "front-end" (i.e., prior to action) of the transmission process; this is in keeping with the service-learning principle of action-reflection. Thus, our perspective should be directly applicable to classroom settings as it offers a conceptual map for students to reflect on and understand their own motivations and behaviors relevant to community service.

Motivations Underlying Community Service

Before considering questions about the development of prosocial values, attitudes, and actions, we turn first to the issue of the form that these values should take. Should society instill a principled approach to prosocial action or a more pragmatic one? In other words, should those engaged in the socialization of others stress that prosocial behavior that conforms to society's desires is wholly motivated by the goal of assisting others? Or should they emphasize that performing the prosocial behavior is most important and that the motivations underlying the behavior are merely secondary? In a nutshell, should a society such as our own strive to instill "pure altruism" in its young people or not? Within psychology, this question is part of the egoism versus altruism debate, an argument that centers on whether caring for, and helpfulness toward, others is based on a *selfless desire to assist others* or a *selfish desire to help oneself via assisting others* (Kohn 1990). For our purposes, there are two fundamental issues that deserve critical examination: (1) identifying the motivations that actually do underlie prosocial values and attitudes, and determining whether these ever take the form of pure altruism (assisting others out of concern for others and without regard for the self); and (2) determining whether pure altruism is a worthwhile goal for a society to pursue.

Does Pure Altruism Exist?

In the psychological literature on helping (see Batson 1987) and in the literature on volunteers' motivations (see Van Til 1988), the debate over the selflessness versus selfishness of a help giver's motives has been a hotly contested one. In these literatures, one can find theorists arguing for one extreme or the other; that is, either for the position that for some people and in some conditions help is altruistically motivated, or for the position that for all people regardless of circumstances help is egoistically motivated. Our reading of the literatures, as well as our own research, suggests an intermediate position that integrates features of both of these claims; we hold that people are motivated both by concern for others and by concern for the self.

According to our "functional" approach to volunteers' motivations (Clary and Snyder 1991, 1993; Clary, Snyder, and Ridge 1992), prosocial attitudes and actions can serve six psychological and social motivations or functions. Through participation, a volunteer may seek to satisfy an *understanding function* (to learn, to gain a greater understanding of people, to practice skills and abilities), a *career function* (to enhance one's job and career prospects, to gain experience and contacts), a *values function* (to act on important values such as humanitarian values, altruistic concerns, or desires to contribute to society), a *social function* (to fit into important reference groups, to gain social approval/avoid social disapproval), a *protective function* (to reduce feelings of guilt, to resolve or escape from one's own personal problems), and/or an *enhancement function* (to enhance self-worth, self-confidence, and expand one's social network). Moreover, the functional approach is multimotivational, in that an individual volunteer can seek to satisfy more than one function, and that in any given group different volunteers may be motivated by different sets of functions.

Given this multimotivational conceptualization, pure altruism is unlikely in that people can and do combine the values function (the most altruistic-like function) with other functions (which tend to involve concerns important to the self; see results reported by Clary, Snyder, and Stukas 1996). In addition, even the values function itself seems to incorporate other-concern and self-concern elements. That is, the values function includes both holding values related to caring and concern for others and the need to express and affirm the self as the kind of person who holds such values. Furthermore, those functions that appear to center on benefits to the self may also contain elements of concern for others. As an illustration, those motivated to volunteer by the social function may do so not only to fit into important reference groups but also out of a genuine respect for friends or family members with prosocial leanings.

Is there, however, empirical support for the proposition that prosocial activists actually possess both self- and other-oriented motivations? To address this question, and other questions about the motivations of people involved in community service activities, we have developed an inventory to measure volunteers' motivations. The Volunteer Functions Inventory, or VFI, consists of 30 motivations for volunteering, with each of the six functions identified above assessed by five items. In our research, we have found considerable evidence for the reliability and validity of the VFI. The scales of the VFI are internally consistent and temporally stable; factor analyses of responses to the VFI produced the predicted six factor solutions, with items loading on appropriate scales; examination of the VFI in a persuasion context indicated that the scales of the VFI possess predictive validity; discriminant validity was demonstrated by comparing the scales of the VFI against conceptually similar measures; and, in an actual volunteering context, satisfaction with the volunteer experience was associated with volunteers receiving feedback indicating that their own important motivational needs and goals (as measured by the VFI) were being met (Clary, Snyder, Ridge, Copeland et al. in press).

Based on our research with the VFI, the values function emerges as the most strongly endorsed motivation of volunteers, followed by the enhancement and understanding functions. In other words, our research with the VFI indicates the presence of both concern for the other and concern for the self in the motivations of volunteers. The research of other investigators has produced consistent results, although using different conceptualizations, different measures, and different items. Anderson and Moore's (1978) survey of volunteers' motivations found respondents reporting both self- and other-oriented motivations; Pearce (1983) observed that volunteer employees, relative to paid employees, possessed greater levels of both service and social motivations; and Callero, Howard, and Piliavin (1987) found that for some veteran blood donors, the altruistic role of blood donor merged with the self (i.e., the values of helping others and the need to identify oneself as one who expresses those values). Thus, it appears that the motivations of individual volunteers do combine other-oriented motivations with self-oriented motivations. Add to this the strong contention that individual motivational components themselves incorporate both self- and other-oriented features, and it seems that "pure altruism" is an altogether unlikely phenomenon.

Is Pure Altruism a Worthwhile Goal?

These considerations suggest that, in volunteer activity, community service, and the activities that occur as part of service-learning, pure altruism may rare (that is, it is more generally the case that people engage in these activities with a mixture of self-oriented and other-oriented motivations). Even so, the question remains of whether this form of prosocial values, goals, and attitudes is a goal that we, as a society, should strive to create. Should we, therefore, attempt to instill in our young people a motivational state where the interests of needy others take precedence over their own interests? Several considerations argue *against* this socialization goal.

A first concern arises as we reflect on the phenomenon of *burnout*, a condition sometimes found in helping professionals whereby helpers lose the ability to care about clients they once deeply cared about (Maslach 1978). According to Brickman (1987), burnout can be traced to people coming to feel that their actions are not meaningful and/or to believe that their actions cannot be effective in helping their clients. This latter aspect suggests that the "pure altruist" may be especially vulnerable, given that the task facing the helper involves a long and arduous process, with the problem often appearing to be insolvable. A mixture of self- and other-concern motives, however, may reduce the likelihood of burnout in that effectiveness can involve satisfying the client or satisfying one's own needs. That is, attempts to satisfy two (or more) motives increase the probability that at least one set of needs, at any point in time, will actually be met; one's motivational eggs, in other words, are placed in multiple baskets.

A second concern becomes evident when one takes the perspective of the recipient of help. As many have suspected, and research has confirmed, receiving help is a mixed blessing—recipients can achieve their goals with the help, but may also be left feeling somewhat helpless, relatively powerless, and generally inferior to the helper (Nadler and Fisher 1986). Even if recipients may not feel much gratitude toward helpers with ulterior (i.e., selfish) motives or whose help is not intentional, how do recipients feel about altruistic helpers? If such helpers are acting intentionally and helping out of concern for the needy other, recipients may feel indebted and may desire to repay the kindness. However, such circumstances create an inequitable relationship, and recipients may not know how to go about repaying helpers who are striving to be selfless in their helping. This kind of relationship may leave recipients with the feeling of an open-ended obligation and a sense of powerlessness. From this perspective, then, the "mixed-motive" helper (one with both self-concern and other-concern motives for helping) may be preferred in that each party's benefits and costs are explicit and the relationship can maintain a more equal footing, at least relative to that between a recipient and a purely egoistic or purely altruistic helper. Thus, the interaction between a mixed-motive helper and a recipient has considerable potential to involve a reciprocal relationship, and may therefore take on some of the features typically found in helping among families and friends; in other words, closer and more lasting psychological connections (see Hatfield and Sprecher 1983);

As a final point, let us consider the observations of Alexis de Tocqueville. In his advocacy of the doctrine of "self-interest properly understood," where individual citizens seek to combine their own interests with those of other citizens, Tocqueville speculates:

> If the doctrine of self-interest properly understood ever came to dominate all thought about morality, no doubt extraordinary virtues would be rarer. But I think that gross depravity would also be less common. Such teaching may stop some men from rising far above the common level of humanity, but many of those who fall below this standard grasp it and are restrained by it. Some individuals it lowers, but mankind it raises. (1969: 527)

Thus, to apply Tocqueville's doctrine to helping behavior, if society begins to socialize individuals to hold prosocial values and attitudes based on a mixture of motivations, some of which focus on themselves and some of which focus on others, then "pure altruism" will certainly become much rarer. However, those who might never have engaged in prosocial behavior, because "pure altruism" was upheld as the ideal (surely, a difficult ideal to reach given the evidence), and because they had not considered the possibility that they might combine their own self-interests with the interests of others, would now be enlightened. In other words, the rates of prosocial behavior should certainly go up if the doctrine of self-interest properly understood were in place, since the number of pure altruists who would be lost is far outweighed by the number of mixed-motive helpers who would be gained.

To summarize, our reading of the literature is that pure altruism, if it exists at all, is rare, and, more important, that pure altruism should not be the educational goal. Nor, we hasten to add, is the desired goal one of pure egoism (Tocqueville also wrote eloquently about the dangers of extreme individualism). Rather, we argue that the ideal for a society is one where there is a mixture of concern for self with concern for others; in the language of the functional approach, people combine the values functions with the understanding and/or enhancement functions, for example. Finally, let us note that this theme runs through discussions of service-learning, as evidenced by the emphasis on reciprocity and the goal that service-learning programs should stress that the student both serves and is served and the service recipient, in turn, is being served while serving (Keith 1994).

To return to our earlier discussion of burnout, we noted that this condition can be traced to caring people coming to believe that their helping behaviors are no longer effective. As mentioned earlier, a possible solution is helping helpers to see that multiple goals (both self-interested and other-interested) are being met by their prosocial action and that focusing on a different goal may help to stem any disillusionment they might feel about their effectiveness. But also recall that burnout has been tied to people coming to feel that their actions are not meaningful. We submit that values such as humanitarian concern, community service, and helping the less fortunate provide an important framework of meaning within which one's helpful actions are embedded (see also Jeavons 1993). Thus, just as the "pure altruist" may be susceptible to burnout, so, too, may be the "pure egoist." Having self-interested motivations alone is not the answer; instead, motivations of self-concern and other-concern each contributes its own advantages and serves to protect against the disadvantages of the other.

The Transmission of Prosocial Values and Attitudes

As we have argued above, prosocial attitudes and values are an important part of the process leading to prosocial action. The question then arises, what is the most effective way of transmitting these prosocial attitudes and values to younger generations? Our interest here is in exploring *when* values are best brought into the educational process in an explicit way. Generally speaking, the tendency is often to begin the transmission process with a focus on values, so that one strives to instill the values and then expects value-related actions to follow. But is this approach to values transmission actually the most effective? Research from several sources suggests that the answer may be no.

In a pair of studies, Clary, Snyder, Copeland, and French (1994) created different types of print advertisements promoting involvement in volunteer work. The advertisements took one of four approaches: (1) emphasized abstract reasons for volunteering (e.g., "people have a duty to help those in need, it's the humanitarian thing to do"), (2) emphasized concrete reasons for volunteering (e.g., "I could make a lot of new friends through a volunteer organization"), (3) counter-argued abstract reasons for not performing volunteer work (e.g., "volunteering is really someone else's responsibility" countered by "if everybody says that, nothing is going to get done"), or (4) counter-argued concrete reasons for not performing volunteer work (e.g., "I don't have the time" countered by "maybe I could rearrange my schedule to fit it in"). The key finding here concerns the first advertisement, the one that reminded people of their values about volunteering. In two separate studies, one using a sample composed largely of nonvolunteers and the other a sample recruited from an organization already using volunteers, that advertisement emphasizing values was judged to be the least effective; this held whether we asked for overall evaluations or for a more specific judgment of the ads' effectiveness in attracting new volunteers. The only circumstance in which there was some acceptance of the values ad was when we asked the sample of volunteers about each advertisement's effectiveness in retaining current volunteers: Here, the values advertisement was judged comparable to advertisements two and four, although one, two, and four all received lower ratings than advertisement three. Thus, these findings suggest that values such as humanitarian concern may play a less important role in the early stages of the volunteer process (i.e., recruitment) than in the later stages (i.e., retention).

A similar interpretation comes from Independent Sector's (1992) survey of Americans' patterns of giving and volunteering, in which a representative sample of American adults were queried about many aspects of their involvement in the nonprofit sector. Our analyzes of these responses, which included representative items from the VFI, revealed a tendency for nonvolunteers' motivations to cluster together and volunteers' motivations to spread out (Clary, Snyder, and Stukas 1996). That is, when reporting on the importance of the six motivations assessed by the VFI, the range of importance given to the motivations was greater for respondents reporting volunteer experience in the previous year, even though both groups reported that the values function was most important. This finding suggests that the process of volunteer action leads to a strong and clear values component, one that is distinct from other motivations for performing volunteer work. That is not to say that originally one's motivations are an amorphous mass, but rather that action serves to clarify and solidify the various psychological functions for performing volunteer work. We should note, however, that this hypothesis awaits further empirical confirmation, which can best come from an investigation in which a group of (previous) nonvolunteers are followed through the volunteer process to determine whether their values do indeed become more distinct through action.

Although these studies clearly speak to values related to voluntarism, community service, and service-learning activities, research from several other domains also argues for allowing attitudes and values to emerge from action. Much of this work comes from the social psychological literature concerning the conditions under which people are most likely to act on their attitudes. One line of research reports that people whose attitudes and values are formed on the basis of direct experience with the attitude/value domain are more likely to engage in behaviors consistent with the attitudes than those whose attitudes and values are traced to indirect experience, such as messages from others (Fazio and Zanna 1981). In addition, research on self-perception processes has also shown that people engaged in a particular type of action will come to see themselves as that type of person; for example, people induced to act helpfully come to see themselves as helpful people (e.g., Bem 1972; DeJong 1979). Thus, such research suggests that attitudes and values that come from action will be more likely to guide future action.

In sum, our research on voluntarism, as well as research on the relations between attitudes and actions, argues that prosocial attitudes and values are a critically important part of the creation of a prosocial society, but it may be more effective to include values later rather than earlier in the values transmission process. We believe that values transmission might be more fruitfully viewed as a *two-stage* process. In the first stage, involvement in volunteer work and community service is promoted by linking this action to the satisfaction of the individual's psychological functions and motivations. The second stage, however, is devoted to framing one's actions, which are now current actions, in the context of a broader, more abstract values system. This two-stage process, then, has much in common with the action-reflection model found in the service-learning literature: Students are encouraged to perceive their actions (in this case, service to individuals and the community) as a reflection of the kind of people they are (that is, as activists working for the "common good").

Creating a Prosocial and Activist Generation

Up to this point, our argument has been that the desired outcome of the internalization process is an individual whose prosocial attitudes, values, and behaviors are based on a mixture of concern for self and concern for others. Furthermore, we have argued that this outcome can most effectively be achieved if the process begins with promoting actions via appeals to self-interest, and then later embedding the actions within a framework of values. In this section, we wish to look more closely at the process of creating prosocial generations through the processes of socialization. An examination of these processes can inform our thinking about service-learning programs both as being mechanisms of socialization themselves and as providing opportunities for action related to already internalized values and attitudes.

From both the social psychological and developmental psychological literatures, many investigations have revealed that prosocial behaviors can be influenced by the presence of prosocial models. For example, people are more likely to donate money to sidewalk Salvation Army solicitors if they first observe a model making a donation (Bryan and Test 1972). More importantly for our purposes here, prosocial actions and values have been linked to these processes occurring within the family. And, as we see in the following discussion of three naturalistic studies, the influence of modeling helpfulness combines with a warm, nurturant relationship between model and recipient, in this case the parent and child.

In a retrospective study of participants in the civil rights movement, Rosenhan (1970) found that "fully committed" activists (who participated in the movement full-time for at least one year) reported that their parents had modeled helpfulness and established warm, nurturant relationships with them. On the other hand, the "partially committed" activists (who participated in one or two marches) reported negative relationships with parents who preached but did not practice helpfulness. These results were recently replicated in Clary and Miller's (1986) prospective study of crisis-counseling volunteers: Volunteers who reported a socialization experience of nurturant parental models of helpfulness were more likely to complete the expected length of service, while volunteers who reported an experience of more negative relationships with parents who did not model helpfulness were more likely to terminate their participation early. Finally, Oliner and Oliner's (1988) comparison of rescuers of Jews in Nazi-occupied Europe with nonrescuers also found modeling and identification processes to be important influences in the background of rescuers.

The findings of these studies are consistent with conceptual analyzes of the socialization process and with the results of many laboratory investigations. Specifically, one important way for the internalization of prosocial attitudes and values to occur is to provide children with nurturant relationships with parents and other care givers who model helpfulness. This socialization experience appears to have multiple effects, with children developing an intrinsic motivation to behave helpfully (in the language of the functional approach, the "values function"), empathic orientation to others in distress, and standards for action. Moreover, it seems highly unlikely that these parents (nurturant models) simply present a helpful episode in the same way as a television program does; rather the parents invite and expect their children to be active receivers of their message. That is, parents discuss the message with their children and most probably encourage their children to act helpfully. In fact, several of Rosenhan's fully committed activists recalled participating in helpful activities with their parents. Thus, consistent with our overall theme, the development and internalization of prosocial attitudes and values seem to be grounded in action.

Although this discussion has focused on the values transmission process when children are the target, research suggests that the same mechanism can also result in prosocial attitudes and values in adults. For example, Piliavin and her colleagues' studies of blood donors have observed two subgroups among "rookie" donors. One group of first-time donors appears to come to this activity with intrinsic motivation in hand, whereas the second group appears to be more extrinsically motivated. With repeated donations, there is a tendency for helpfulness-related values to gain in strength (the intrinsic group seems to be further along in this regard), and finally, for some donors, continued donations result in a "role-person" merger whereby the blood donor role becomes a central part of one's self (Callero, Howard, and Piliavin 1987; Piliavin, Evans, and Callero 1984).

To summarize, then, effective transmission of values, by which we mean here that prosocial attitudes and actions are internalized and provide the basis for later action, often appears to follow a course from extrinsic pressures to act helpfully (such as guidance from parents, teachers, and other adults) to intrinsic pressures to behave helpfully (see also Brickman 1987). Moreover, it seems to us that it is critical that the entire process be grounded in action. In other words, it is unlikely that simply being exhorted to feel and act in a prosocial manner will produce the desired result; rather, one must have direct behavioral experience in community service. Finally, it also appears that this goal of internalization of prosocial attitudes and values will be more likely to occur if people, and especially young people, are encouraged to explicitly link these actions to a values framework (i.e., they come to perceive community activism as an integral part of their selves).

Implications for Service-Learning Programs

In considering the process by which successive generations internalize values related to providing service to the community, two major points deserve emphasis. First, we have argued that these values and standards should combine concerns about the interests of other people with concerns about one's own interests; the mixture of self-interest and other-interest seems to be both more realistic and more effective than the alternatives of pure altruism and pure egoism. Second, we have proposed that the internalization of this state within individuals may best be accomplished by first encouraging prosocial action and then embedding the action within a framework of prosocial attitudes and values. These themes have clear implications for service-learning programs. We will consider two issues here: The first centers on the mandatory nature of many service-learning activities; the second involves the question of what is the most appropriate and effective relationship between helpers and recipients.

Mandatory Community Service

In discussions of service-learning programs and activities, it is important to consider that students are often *required* to offer service to the community. The question then arises as to the effects of this requirement, and in the context of our previous discussions, the question concerns the effect that mandatory service has on the internalization of community service values and attitudes. Although requiring students to participate in service activities may have some merit, we do have some concerns, based on our reading of relevant psychological theory and research, about this approach. Our first concern centers on those young people who have, through their socialization experiences, internalized prosocial attitudes and values. Research from several different domains has found an *undermining effect*: If someone with an intrinsic desire to perform some action has that action placed under external control, then the result is often a decrease in intrinsic interest (e.g., Thomas, Batson, and Coke 1981). To illustrate, people who are motivated by their values to help others may well become less motivated if they are exposed to external pressures to behave helpfully; in other words, they become convinced that their helpful behavior no longer comes from within but from without, and thus are less willing to help in the absence of external pressures.

And what about those who have not internalized prosocial attitudes and values? Although a mandatory program is quite likely to provoke action among those who would otherwise not act, it is doubtful that the action alone would necessarily result in internalized prosocial values. As we noted earlier, young people would probably benefit from receiving assistance with the task of framing their actions within a system of prosocial values (this is not to say that people cannot do so alone, but it seems risky to leave this to chance); or perhaps to put it more succinctly, programs should couple action with reflection. To illustrate this point with the functional perspective on volunteers' motivations, service-learning helpers might be encouraged to view their work as providing the opportunity to express values that are important to their selves, as well as offering opportunities to fulfill current needs and goals.

Mandatory programs, then, present some very real concerns with respect to the goals of, first, the internalization of prosocial attitudes and values and, second, the creation of citizens who will then act on these prosocial values over the course of their lifetimes (see also Switzer et al. 1995). From our perspective, a safer course may be one that brings people into prosocial action on the basis of the motivations and the functions important to the individual. For example, the student with an already developed values function should be involved on this basis, whereas the student with a more personal focus (e.g., career concerns) should be involved on that basis. Continuing our example, over the course of participation, both students should be encouraged to link their actions to other motivations, with the values person finding ways in which other, more personal needs are met and the career person finding that this work is also connected to important values. Multiply motivated prosocial actors will be beneficial both to themselves and to society.

The Experience of Receiving Aid

As we have already seen, research that has been devoted to people's reactions to receiving help from others has found that receiving help is a mixed blessing. With respect to the benefits of helping, the assistance of others can result in recipients having needs met that might otherwise go unmet. In terms of costs, receiving help can lower recipients' self-esteem (i.e., needing others' assistance suggests that one is incapable and/or incompetent), place recipients in a position of being relatively powerless, and may even create long-term dependency and helplessness.

Research on the experiences of the target or recipient of others' assistance, then, has illuminated this important aspect of the helping process. It should be pointed out that research on recipients' reactions to aid has, by and large, focused on helping that occurs in brief helping encounters. This is not to suggest that these reactions would not also occur in the long-term helping that occurs in voluntarism, service-learning activities, and other forms of community service, but rather to note that the benefits and costs to the recipient may well be greatly increased in these settings. That is, many of the problems addressed in community service settings are long-standing problems facing the least-advantaged members of a society (e.g., the many manifestations of poverty—hunger, homelessness, illiteracy, illness). Thus, in these kinds of settings, the needs of potential recipients are greatest and more accompanied by the dangers of helplessness and dependency.

Although much remains to be learned about the experiences and reactions of people who are receiving long-term aid, in the meantime we believe that a case can be made in favor of the "mixed-motive" helper. A long-term relationship between this kind of helper and a recipient should certainly be able to provide the same level of direct assistance as would any other kind of helper and would, at the same time, reduce the likelihood of the negative effects of receiving help. It seems to us that mixed-motive helpers, and especially helpers who are explicit about their own self-interests, would be better able to establish a relationship marked by the giving and receiving of both parties. That is, the obligations would be clear, the recipient would have the opportunity to reciprocate, and the result would be a relationship in which the power would be distributed more equitably; in effect, each party is both helper and recipient. Moreover, recipients should be less likely to have their self-esteem threatened, and should even have the opportunity to have experiences that will boost self-esteem. All in all, we expect that the mixed-motive helper may be better able to establish effective helping relationships with people in need. In doing so, both helper and recipient gain, which stands in contrast to the altruistic framework whereby one party sacrifices for the benefit of the other. Moreover, the mixed-motive helper seems more likely to create a relationship in which there is a psychological connection between the two people and one marked by closeness rather than distance.

In closing, let us note that the concerns we have been discussing are precisely ones that have been recognized by those involved in service-learning activities and programs. In service-learning, there is an emphasis on *reciprocity*, and a deemphasis on *charity* (see Keith 1994; Kendall 1991). Thus, according to Kendall, "[a] good service-learning program helps participants see their questions in the larger context of issues of social justice and social policy—rather than in the context of charity" (19). Similarly, service-learning programs have focused on the principle of action-reflection, suggesting that these larger issues and values involved are introduced after the activities have begun. In this way, internalization can best be conceived and the transmission of vital prosocial values, attitudes, and behaviors to successive generations successfully accomplished.

References

Anderson, J., and L. Moore. (1978). "The Motivation to Volunteer." *Journal of Voluntary Action Research* 7: 51–60.

Batson, C.D. (1987). "Prosocial Motivation: Is It Ever Truly Altruistic?" In *Advances in Experimental Social Psychology*, Vol. 20, edited by L. Berkowitz, pp. 65–122. New York: Academic Press.

Bem, D. (1972). "Self-Perception Theory." In *Advances in Experimental Social Psychology*, Vol. 6, edited by L. Berkowitz, pp. 1–62. New York: Academic Press.

Brickman, P. (1987). *Commitment, Conflict, and Caring*. Englewood Cliffs. NJ: Prentice-Hall.

Bryan, J. and M. Test. (1972). "Models and Helping: Naturalistic Studies in Aiding Behavior." *Journal of Personality and Social Psychology* 6: 400–407.

Callero, P., J. Howard, and J. Piliavin. (1987). "Helping Behavior as Role Behavior: Disclosing Social Structure and History in the Analysis of Prosocial Action." *Social Psychology Quarterly* 50: 247–256.

Clary, E., and J. Miller. (1986). "Socialization and Situational Influences on Sustained Altruism." *Child Development* 57: 1358–1369.

Clary, E., and M. Snyder. (1991). "A Functional Analysis of Altruism and Prosocial Behavior: The Case of Volunteerism." In *Review of Personality and Social Behavior*: Vol. 12. *Prosocial Behavior*, edited by M. Clark, pp. 119–148. Newbury Park, CA: Sage.

—. (1993). "Persuasive Communications Strategies for Recruiting Volunteers." In *Governing, Leading, and Managing Nonprofit Organizations*, edited by D. Young, R. Hollister, and V. Hodgkinson, pp. 121–137. San Francisco: Jossey-Bass.

—. J. Copeland, and S. French. (1994). "Promoting Volunteerism With Persuasive Messages: An Empirical Examination." *Nonprofit and Voluntary Sector Quarterly* 23: 265–280.

Clary, E., M. Snyder, and R. Ridge. (1992). "Volunteers' Motivations: A Functional Strategy for the Recruitment, Placement, and Retention of Volunteers." *Nonprofit Management and Leadership* 2: 333–350.

Clary, E., M. Snyder, and A. Stukas. (1996). "Volunteers' Motivations: Findings From a National Survey." *Nonprofit and Voluntary Sector Quarterly* 25: 485–505.

Clary, E., M. Snyder, R. Ridge, J. Copeland, A. Stukas, J. Haugen, and P. Meine. (In press). "Understanding and Assessing the Motivations of Volunteers: A Functional Approach." *Journal of Personality and Social Psychology*.

DeJong, W. (1979). "An Examination of Self-Perception Mediation of the Foot-in-the-Door Effect." *Journal of Personality and Social Psychology* 37: 221–239.

Fazio, R., and M. Zanna. (1981). "Direct Experience and Attitude-Behavior Consistency." In *Advances in Experimental Social Psychology*, Vol. 14, edited by L. Berkowitz, pp. 162–202. New York: Academic Press.

Hatfield, E., and S. Sprecher. (1983). "Equity Theory and Recipient Reactions to Aid." In *New Directions in Helping*, Vol. 1, edited by J. Fisher, A. Nadler, and B. DePaulo, pp. 113–141. New York: Academic Press.

Independent Sector. (1992). *Giving and Volunteering in the United States: Findings From a National Survey*, 1992. Washington, DC: Author.

Jeavons, T. (1993). "The Role of Values: Management in Religious Organizations." In *Governing, Leading, and Managing Nonprofit Organizations*, edited by D. Young, R. Hollister, and V. Hodgkinson, pp. 52–76. San Francisco: Jossey-Bass.

Keith, N.Z. (1994). "Introduction: School-Based Community Service: Answers and Some Questions." *Journal of Adolescence* 17: 311–320.

Kelman, H. (1958). "Compliance, Identification, and Internalization: Three Processes of Attitude Change." *Journal of Conflict Resolution* 2: 51–60.

Kendall, J.C. (1991). "Combining Service and Learning: An Introduction for Cooperative Education Professionals." *Journal of Cooperative Education* 27: 9–26.

Kohn, A. (1990). *The Brighter Side of Human Nature: Altruism and Empathy in Everyday Life*. New York: Basic Books.

Maslach, C. (1978). "The Client Role in Staff Burnout." *Journal of Social Issues* 34: 111–124.

Nadler, A., and J. Fisher. (1986). "The Role of Threat to Self-Esteem and Perceived Control in Recipient Reaction to Help: Theory Development and Empirical Validation." In *Advances in Experimental Social Psychology*, Vol. 19, edited by L. Berkowitz, pp. 81–122. New York: Academic Press.

Oliner, S., and P. Oliner. (1988). *The Altruistic Personality: Rescuers of Jews in Nazi Europe*. New York: Free Press.

Pearce, J. (1983). "Job Attitude and Motivation Differences Between Volunteers and Employees From Comparable Organizations." *Journal of Applied Psychology* 68: 646–652.

Piliavin, J., J. Evans, and P. Callero. (1984). "Learning to 'Give to Unnamed Strangers': The Process of Commitment to Regular Blood Donation," In *Development and Maintenance of Prosocial Behavior: International Perspectives on Positive Morality*, edited by E. Staub, D. Bar-Tal, J. Karylowski, and J. Reykowski, pp. 471–492. New York: Plenum.

Rosenhan, D. (1970). "The Natural Socialization of Altruistic Autonomy." In *Altruism and Helping Behavior*, edited by J. Macauley and L. Berkowitz, pp. 251–268. New York: Academic Press.

Switzer, G., R. Simmons, M. Dew, J. Regalski, and C. Wang. (1995). "The Effect of a School-Based Helper Program on Adolescent Self-Image, Attitudes, and Behavior." *Journal of Early Adolescence* 15: 429–455.

Thomas, G., C. Batson, and J. Coke. (1981). "Do Good Samaritans Discourage Helpfulness? Self-Perceived Altruism After Exposure to Highly Helpful Others." *Journal of Personality and Social Psychology* 40: 194–200.

Tocqueville, A., de. (1969). *Democracy in America*, Vol. 2, 1840. Translated by G. Lawrence and edited by J. Mayer. New York: Doubleday, Anchor Books.

Van Til, J. (1988). *Mapping the Third Sector: Voluntarism in a Changing Social Economy*. New York, Foundation Center.

Acknowledgements

Our research has been supported by grants from the Gannett Foundation and the Aspen Institute's Nonprofit Sector Research Fund to E. Gil Clary and Mark Synder, and grants from the National Science Foundation and the National Institute of Mental Health to Mark Synder.

SERVICE-LEARNING: A BALANCED APPROACH TO EXPERIENTIAL EDUCATION

ANDREW FURCO

The Service-Learning Struggle

For over a quarter of a century, education researchers and practitioners have struggled to determine how to best characterize service-learning. In 1979, Robert Sigmon defined service-learning as an experiential education approach that is premised on "reciprocal learning" (Sigmon, 1979). He suggested that because learning flows from service activities, both those who provide service and those who receive it "learn" from the experience. In Sigmon's view, service-learning occurs only when both the providers and recipients of service benefit from the activities.

Today, however, the term "service-learning" has been used to characterize a wide array of experiential education endeavors, from volunteer and community service projects to field studies and internship programs. By perusing schools' service program brochures, one realizes that the definitions for service-learning are as varied as the schools in which they operate. While some educators view "service-learning" as a new term that reveals a rich, innovative, pedagogical approach for more effective teaching, others view it as simply another term for well-established experiential education programs. As Timothy Stanton of the Haas Center for Public Service at Stanford University once asked, "What is service-learning anyway? . . . How do we distinguish service-learning from cooperative education, internship programs, field study and other forms of experiential education?" (Stanton, 1987). The National Society for Experiential Education, which for years has focused on various types of experiential education programs, broadly defines service-learning as "any carefully monitored service experience in which a student has intentional learning goals and reflects actively on what he or she is learning throughout the experience." (National Society for Experiential Education, 1994).

The Corporation for National Service provides a narrower definition that sees service-learning as a "method under which students learn and develop through active participation in thoughtfully organized service experiences that meet actual community needs, that [are] integrated into the students' academic curriculum of provide structured time for [reflection, and] that enhance what is taught in school by extending student learning beyond the classroom and into the community . . ." (Corporation for National and Community Service, 1990). The confounding use of the service-learning term may be one reason why research on the impacts of service-learning has been difficult to conduct.

In 1989, Honnet and Poulsen developed the Wingspread Principles of Good Practice for Combining Service and Learning (Honnet & Poulsen, 1989. Appendix B). While these guidelines offer a useful set of best practices for service oriented educational programs, they are not solely germane to service-learning and could easily serve as best practices for other types of experiential education programs (e.g., internships or apprenticeships). Similarly, the Association for Service-Learning in Education Reform (ASLER) has compiled a set of common characteristics of service-learning that help program directors determine whether their programs are meeting the overarching

service-LEARNING:	**Learning goals primary; service outcomes secondary**
SERVICE-learning:	**Service outcomes primary; learning goals secondary**
service learning:	**Service and learning goals completely separate**
SERVICE-LEARNING:	**Service and learning goals of equal weight and each enhances the other for all participants**

Figure 1 A Service and Learning Typology (Sigmon, 1994)

service-learning goals (ASLER, 1994 Appendix A). Again, while these characteristics are very useful in helping practitioners develop effective service-learning programs, they do not provide a definitive characterization of service-learning. ASLER characterizes service-learning as method of learning that enables school-based and community-based professionals "to employ a variety of effective teaching strategies that emphasize student-centered [sic.] or youth centered [sic.], interactive, experiential education . . . Service learning places curricular concepts in the context of real-life situations . . . Service-learning connects young people to the community, placing them in challenging situations . . . (ASLER, 1994). One could easily contend that other approaches to experiential education (i.e., internships or field education) purport to do the same. So then, how is service-learning different from other approaches to experiential education?

Developing a Definition

According to Sigmon, "If we are to establish clear goals [for service-learning] and work efficiently to meet them, we need to move toward a precise definition." (Sigmon, 1979). Recently, Sigmon attempted to provide a more precise definition of service-learning through a typology that compares different programs that combine service and learning. This typology broadened his earlier "reciprocal learning" definition to include the notion that "service-learning" occurs when there is a balance between learning goals and service outcomes. Herein lies the key to establishing a universal definition for service-learning (see Figure 1).

In this comparative form, the typology is helpful not only in establishing criteria for distinguishing service-learning from other types of service programs but also in providing a basis for clarifying distinctions among different types of service-oriented experiential education programs (e.g., school volunteer, community service, field education, and internship programs).

Distinguishing Among Service Programs

To represent the distinctions among various types of service programs, a pictorial is offered that presents an experiential education continuum upon which various service programs might lie. The pictorial is based on both Sigmon's earlier "reciprocal learning" principles and his most recent typology. Where each service program lies on the continuum is determined by its primary intended beneficiary and its overall balance between service and learning (see Figure 2).

As the pictorial suggests, different types of service programs can be distinguished by their primary intended purpose and focus. Each program type is defined by the intended beneficiary of the service activity and its degree of emphasis on service and/or learning. Rather than being located at a single point, each program type occupies a range of points on the continuum. Where one type begins and another ends is not as important as the idea that each service program type has unique characteristics that distinguish it from other types. It is that ability to distinguish among these service program types that allows us to move closer toward a universal definition of service-learning.

Using the pictorial as a foundation, the following definitions are offered for five types of service programs.

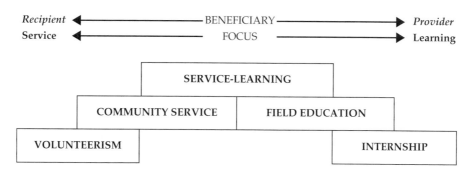

Figure 2 Distinctions Among Service Programs

Volunteerism

Volunteerism is the engagement of students in activities where the primary emphasis is on the service being provided and the primary intended beneficiary is clearly the service recipient.

According to James and Pamela Toole, the term volunteerism refers to "people who perform some service or good work of their own free will and without pay" (Toole & Toole, 1992). The inherent altruistic nature of volunteer programs renders them as service focused, designed to benefit the service recipient. A prime example is a school-based program in which student-volunteers occasionally or regularly visit the local hospital to sit with Alzheimer patients who need some company. The primary intended beneficiaries of the service are the Alzheimer patients (the service recipients), and the focus of the activity is on providing a service to them. Although the student-volunteers may receive some benefits from the experience (e.g., feeling pleased with themselves) as well as learn something in the process, these outcomes are clearly serendipitous and unintentional. As the hospital visits of the student volunteers become more regular, and as the students begin focusing more on learning about Alzheimer's disease, the program moves toward the center of the continuum to become more like community service (or even service-learning).

Community Service

Community service is the engagement of students in activities that primarily focus on the service being provided as well as the benefits the service activities have on the recipients (e.g., providing food to the homeless during the holidays). The students receive some benefits by learning more about how their service makes a difference in the lives of the service recipients.

As with volunteer programs, community service programs imply altruism and charity. However, community service programs involve more structure and student commitment than do volunteer programs. School-based community service programs might include semester-long or year-long activities in which students dedicate themselves to addressing a cause that meets a local community (or global) need. Recycling, hunger awareness, and environmental improvement are all forms of community service causes around which students have formed organizations to formally and actively address the issue. While the students' primary purpose for engaging in the service activity is to advance the cause, their engagement allows them to learn more about the cause and what is needed to be done to ensure the cause is dealt with effectively. As the service activities become more integrated with the academic course work of the students, and as the students begin to engage in formal intellectual discourse around the various issues relevant to the cause, the community service program moves closer to the center of the continuum to become more like service-learning.

On the opposite side of the continuum lie internship programs.

Internships

Internships programs engage students in service activities primarily for the purpose of providing students with hands-on experiences that enhance their learning or understanding of issues relevant to a particular area of study.

Clearly, in internship programs, the students are the primary intended beneficiary and the focus of the service activity is on student learning. Students are placed in internships to acquire skills and knowledge that will enhance their academic learning and/or vocational development. For many students, internships are performed in addition to regular course work often after a sequence of courses has been taken. Internships may be paid or unpaid and take place in either for-profit or nonprofit organizations. For example, a political science major might engage in an unpaid summer internship at a city hall to learn more about how local government works. Although the student is providing a service to the city hall office, the student engages in the internship primarily for his/her benefit and primarily for learning (rather than service) purposes. Similarly, a legal studies student may have a paid summer internship that allows that student to learn more about how a law firm operates. The student's primary motivations for partaking in the program—to learn legal skills and make some money—are clearly intended to benefit himself/herself. As both these students place greater emphasis on the service being provided and the ways in which the service recipients are benefiting, the closer the internship program moves toward the center of the continuum and becomes more like field education (and service-learning).

Field Education

Field Education programs provide students with co-curricular service opportunities that are related, but not fully integrated, with their formal academic studies. Students perform the service as part of a program that is designed primarily to enhance students' understanding of a field of study, while also providing substantial emphasis on the service being provided.

Field education plays an important role in many service oriented professional programs such as Social Welfare, Education, and Public Health. In some of the programs, students may spend up to two years providing a service to a social service agency, a school, or health agency. While strong intentions to benefit the recipients of the service are evident, the focus of field education programs tends to be on maximizing the student's learning of a field of study. For example, students in Education programs may spend up to one year as student teachers to hone their teaching skills and learn more about the teaching process. Because of their long-term commitment to the service field, students do consciously consider how their service benefits those who receive it. However, the program's primary focus is still on the student teachers' learning and their overall benefit.

Service-Learning

Service-learning programs are distinguished from other approaches to experiential education by their intention to equally benefit the provider and the recipient of the service as well as to ensure equal focus on both the service being provided and the learning that is occurring.

To do this, service-learning programs must have some academic context and be designed in such a way that ensures that both the service enhances the learning and the learning enhances the service. Unlike a field education program in which the service is performed in addition to a student's courses, a service-learning program integrates service into the course(s). For example, a pre-med student in a course on the Physiology of the Aging might apply the theories and skills learned in that course to providing mobility assistance to seniors at the local senior citizen center. While the program is intended to provide a much needed service to the seniors, the program is also intended to help the student better understand how men and women age differently, how the physical aging of the body affects mobility, and how seniors can learn to deal with diminishing range of motion and mobility. In such a program, the focus is both on providing a much-needed service and on student learning. Consequently, the program intentionally benefits both the student who provides the service and the seniors for whom the service is provided. It is this balance that distinguishes service learning from all other experiential education programs.

Conclusion

While conceptually, this pictorial can assist in bringing us closer to a more precise definition of service-learning, it is obvious that many gray areas still exist. What about the field education program or community service project that is located near the center of the experiential education continuum? How might we distinguish these programs from service-learning? I might argue that no experiential education approach is static; that is, throughout its life, every experiential education program moves, to some degree, along the continuum. Thus, at a particular point in time, a community service program may be farther left of center appearing to have greater focus on the service and its benefit to the recipient. At another point in time, the same program might appear to have an equal emphasis on service and learning, providing benefits to both the recipients and providers of the service. It is this mobility within program types that suggests that to fully distinguish service-learning programs from other forms of experiential education approaches, one must first determine a program's intended focus(es) and beneficiary(ies). From there, every service program's continuum range can be gauged to determine where it falls among the myriad of experiential education endeavors.

References

Alliance for Service Leaning in Education Reform (ASLER). Feb. 1994. Standards of Quality for School-Based and Community-Based Service-Learning.

Corporation for National and Community Service. 1990. National and Community Service Act of 1990.

Honnet, Ellen P, and Susan J. Poulsen. 1989. Principles of Good Practice for Combining Service and Learning. Wingspread Special Report. Racine, Wisconsin: The Johnson Foundation, Inc.

National Society for Experiential Education. 1994. Partial List of Experiential Learning Terms and Their Definitions, Raleigh. North Carolina.

Sigmon, Robert L. 1994. Serving to Learn, Learning to Serve. Linking Service with Learning. Council for Independent Colleges Report.

Sigmon, Robert L. Spring 1979. Service-learning: Three Principles. Synergist. National Center for Service-Learning, ACTION, 8(1): 9–11.

Stanton, Timothy. Jan.-Feb. 1987. Service Learning: Groping Toward a Definition. Experiential Education. National Society for Experiential Education, 12(1): 2–4.

Toole, James and Pamela Toole. 1992. Key Definitions: Commonly Used Terms in the Youth Service Field. Roseville, Minnesota: National Youth Leadership Council.

Andrew Furco. "Service-Learning: A Balanced Approach to Experiential Education." Expanding Boundaries: Serving and Learning. Washington, DC: Corporation for National Service, 1996. 2–6.

Bibliography
Chapter 6: Service Learning

Checkoway, Barry. "Renewing the Mission of the American Research University." *Journal of Higher Education*, Vol. 72, No. 2 (March/April 2001), pp. 125–147 in a special issue on the Social Role of Higher Education.

Dacheux, T. "Beyond a World of Binaries: My Views on Service-Learning." In D. W. Butin (Ed.), *Service Learning in Higher Education: Critical Issues and Directions*. New York: Palgrave Macmillan, 2005, pp. 67–70.

Henry, S. E. "I Can Never Turn My Back On That: Liminality and the Impact of Class on Service-Learning Experience." In D. W. Butin (Ed.), *Service-Learning in Higher Education: Critical Issues and Directions*. New York: Palgrave Macmillan, 2005, pp. 45–66.

Hodgkinson, Virginia. "Developing a Research Agenda on Civic Service." *Nonprofit and Voluntary Sector Quarterly*, Vol. 33, No. 4 (December 2004), pp. 184–197. This entire issue is focused on civic service.

Janowski, Thomas and John Wilson. "Pathways to Volunteerism: Family Socialization and Status Transmission Models." *Social Forces*, Vol. 74 (September 1995), pp. 271–292.

Kezar, Adriana and Robert A. Rhoads. "The Dynamic Tensions in Service Learning in Higher Education: A Philosophical Perspective," *Journal of Higher Education*, Vol. 72, No. 2 (March-April 2001), pp. 148–171.

Ostrander, Susan A. "Democracy, Civic Participation, and the University: A Comparative Study of Civic Engagement on Five Campuses," *Nonprofit and Voluntary Sector Quarterly*, Vol. 33, No 1 (March 2004), pp. 74–93.

Pascarella, Ernest T. "Colleges' Influence on Principled Moral Reasoning." *Educational Record* (Summer/Fall 1997), pp. 47–55.

Speck, Bruce. "Why Service-Learning?" *New Directions for Higher Education*, No. 114 (Summer 2001), pp. 3–13.

Wilson, John and Marc A. Musick. "Attachment to Volunteering." *Sociological Forum* Vol.14 (June 1999), pp. 243–272.

Selected Websites

A History of Student Activism www.actionforchange.org/getinformed/history.

Port Huron Statement of the Students for a Democratic Society, 1962, available at http: coursesa.matrix.msy.edu/~hst306/documents/huron

Primary Documents

Campus Compact. "The President's Declaration on the Civic Responsibility of Higher Education." Providence, RI: Campus Compact, 2000.

Charles R. Van Hise's Inaugural Address, June 7, 1904, in which he outlines the modern university commitment to public service, a concept later known as the "The Wisconsin Idea."

Wingspread Group. "An American Imperative: Higher Expectations for Higher Education" (1993).

Wingspread Group, "Renewing the Civic Mission of the American University" (1999).

CHAPTER 7

TRUSTEESHIP: SERVICE TO INSTITUTION AND COMMUNITY

WOMEN AS TRUSTEES

MARIAM K. CHAMBERLAIN

Scholars differ on the origins of lay boards of higher education. Some point to Harvard's first external board of overseers as a uniquely American governance structure.[1] Others cite prototypes of twelfth-century Italian city-states where boards of citizens served as liaisons between students and instructors. Educational policy in the Netherlands and Scotland following the Reformation in fact vested responsibility in lay leaders instead of the clergy.[2]

Whatever the colonists' precedents or innovation, however, Harvard's founding in 1636 eventually resulted in a lay governance structure that, with few challenges, became the model for American higher education. Oxford and Cambridge had been moving toward increasing lay control, but both they and their European counterparts, evolving from models of medieval master guilds, resisted the trend. They were, and with some modification still are, controlled by their senior faculties, at least in principle.[3] Critics of American higher education have been known to praise English and European systems as models of self-regulating control, but although we borrowed many Old World academic traditions, our governance structures *de jure* did not vest control in the hands of the faculty. Although we do have faculty governance systems that exercise power over academic matters, American colleges and universities are for better or for worse governed by lay boards, the ultimate sources of authority for the institutions whose assets they hold "in trust."[4]

Clergymen dominated governing boards of the early American colleges. With few experienced faculty members in the colonies, well-educated clergy provided both needed expertise and essential links between their colleges and the church and community. Experienced clergy also saw themselves as sources of vocational guidance—colonial colleges trained ministers.[5]

As higher education expanded in the late eighteenth and early nineteenth centuries, however, trustee selections diversified. With the rise of liberal arts colleges and professional and graduate schools, and especially with the founding of the land grant universities and state teachers' colleges, trustees began to include among their numbers representatives of the public-at-large, lay community leaders, business executives, and wealthy patrons who were expected to provide their institutions with one or more of the three Ws: "Work, Wealth, and Wisdom." Especially in the private sector, wealth played an increasingly important role, with the private sector trustee expected to "give, get, or get off." The history of universities in the late nineteenth century is fraught with tensions generated by wealthy, powerful donors—the Stanfords, for example—as their faculties struggled for academic freedom.[6]

Responsibilities and styles of boards have in fact varied considerably with the types of institutions governed; but although designated responsibilities have changed over the years, most noticeably reflecting the increasing complexity of higher education since World War II, the primary functions ascribed to boards have remained remarkably similar. In addition to fund-raising and institutional advocacy, a conventional summary includes responsibility for setting institutional policies and priorities; long-range planning; approving and monitoring budgets; and, judged by many to be the single most important role, selecting and evaluating the president.

Trustees are thus vested with considerable power and authority. They constitute the legal "body," the corporate presence of the institution. Reviewing both individual histories of institutions and the conventional body of trustee literature, however, it is apparent that trustee power, especially in the postwar decades, exists mostly as potential, power delegated but seldom exercised. Although critics such as Thorstein Veblen in an earlier day have contended that "boards are of no material use in any connection,"[7] the more common view among scholars and others is that that trustee power "could be a vital factor in strengthening and improving the operations of countless institutions."[8] One community college trustee observed that an effective board can counterbalance the teachers and administrators whom he sees as "notoriously conservative when it comes to change."[9]

This potential for implementing change, for "strengthening and improving," has for over a century sporadically caught the attention of women concerned with issues of women's education, but the attention paid to women on boards—their roles, their routes to and orientation on boards, even their potential for influence—is striking in its absence. There is little mention of women on boards in the scholarly literature—in the history of women's colleges or women's education, for example. Nor is there mention of women on boards in the most recent studies of women in higher education.[10] Even more curious, with several exceptions, little awareness of women's roles or potential as trustees has informed the shared strategies and programs of contemporary women activists in higher education. (See Appendix 15.1 for a summary and assessment of organized activities for women trustees during the last 20 years.)

Still more puzzling, however, is the surprising dearth of information about boards in general, information about board functioning or about those individuals who fill the roles of trustees and how they get to be who they are. One of the first attempts to describe and assess attitudes of a national sample of the trustee population was made in 1968 by Rodney Hartnett. A subsequent study in 1976 by Irene Gomberg and Frank Atelsek included a larger sample but a less comprehensive focus and analysis.[11] As Hartnett pointed out in the introduction to his study, ". . . it is somewhat remarkable that so little is known about who trustees are, what they do in their roles as trustees, and how they feel about current issues in American higher education."[12] The closer we get to describing board dynamics, in fact, the more elusive board functioning seems, and what little we know about the history and dynamics of women on boards offers one of the more depressing chapters in the history of women in higher education.

One noted scholar of boards points out that in colonial days "the collegiate boards had few (if any) members from the distaff side . . . [and] the aversion to women trustees and regents continued for a century."[13] One of the first official records we have of attention paid to women on governing boards of colleges and universities dates from April 1887. The occasion was an annual meeting of the American Association of University Women (AAUW), then known as the Association of Collegiate Alumnae (ACA). According to the official AAUW history, in a paper entitled 'The Relation of Women to the Governing Boards and Faculties of Colleges," an ACA leader concluded that "no active effort should be made to urge the appointment of women to professorships, but . . . the appointment of well-trained and qualified women as trustees was a measure worthy of hearty endorsement."[14]

Fortunately, as we have seen elsewhere in this volume, the speaker's suggestions to ignore the absence of women faculty were not heeded; almost a century later, however, her concern for women trustees reads like a progressive agenda for the 1990s. Boards remain bastions of white male privilege. The average trustee is white, male, Protestant, and Republican. In his late fifties, in business or a prestige profession, he personifies the traditional American definitions of success. Collectively, the network of higher education trustees in this country has access to the primary sources of wealth and power in our culture—a predominantly white male system of corporate and political influence. In spite of some attention paid to the need for more diverse representation on boards, the numbers of women and minority trustees have increased insignificantly, even in the last decade, and periodic efforts to raise issues of women in higher education to the board level, including the special concerns of women's own roles on boards, have met with little success.

A Theoretical Framework

Before pursuing in more detail the history and current issues of women on boards, however, it may be useful to describe a theoretical perspective that attempts to account for some of what we do know about board roles and functioning, especially as those roles relate to issues of institutional change and equal opportunity. Broadly sketched, higher education in America can be seen to have several contradictory strands: on the one hand, higher education has evolved as a heritage of the elite, a socialization process for the upper classes. The Ivy League institutions have for generations provided the imprimatur of success for the (male) children of the rich and the powerful. On the other hand, in a uniquely American tradition, colleges and universities have been expected to provide routes to upward mobility for the less privileged. As institutions, they have also been expected to serve as models of pluralism and collegial governance. With the evolution of the land grant universities and normal schools, the City University of New York and the California public college and university systems, for example, there has been an explicit tradition, an essential part of our national heritage and self-image, that colleges and universities provide not only access to the American dream, but themselves function as microcosms of egalitarian culture. And following the turmoil of the 1960s, even boards of elite institutions have been pressured to define as part of their institutional missions the role of fostering diversity and equal opportunity.

There are implicit contradictions here. Boards are by their very nature conservative. As one higher education scholar pointed out, it is a curious paradox that, for a democratic nation, we have evolved "a plan of university control which technically and legally does not show even a trace of democracy."[15] Yet board governance structures are not unique to higher education; and, perhaps more important, they are structures which, at least in broad outline, dominate the life of many social and political institutions, from corporations and government bureaucracies to churches and other community organizations.

A board is the corporate identity of its institution, the legal and symbolic structure which preserves institutional continuity through time. Faculty members, students, administrators, even alumni—all are transient, weaving in and out of the life of the institution. Constituent groups, traditions, buildings, and archives all shape a college's life and history, but only the board—the structural body of the institution—holds the "trust," both financial and symbolic. And as preservers of the trust, they engage in activities that, more often than not, are designed to preserve and extend their institutions in their own image. Among private boards, for example, selecting new trustees is the decision-making process trustees describe they are most directly involved in—an activity more frequently cited than fund-raising, long-range planning, even investment counsel.[16] Functional strategies for "conserving" the institution will obviously differ among boards in different types of institutions—in public institutions, for example, trustees are politically appointed or run for election—but the point is that boards, virtually by definition, are governing bodies which exist to perpetuate the institutions they represent. And few factional views survive this fundamental conserving force on boards. (Even student representatives soon take on both the dress and concerns of the institution "as a whole.")

Besides these structural constraints, however, there are also the inherent tensions generated by elites functioning in a democratic society.[17] Trusteeship offers a powerful reward/status position that marks success and power. While trustees "serve the public good"—in fact empowering and not infrequently financing much of the voluntary sector—board positions provide political rewards and a status system in the public sector, the epitome of club membership in the private sector. A marker of success and affiliation with "one's own kind," trusteeship offers connections and the best educated status money can buy. It is "what one does" in the professional, political, and social circles most private trustees and many public trustees move in.

This is not to deny the generosity of board members, their considerable volunteer support, and their contributions of both time and money. Yet this social perspective of status, privilege, and political and social affiliation is also essential for understanding the basic conserving function of boards.

Boards have little impulse to espouse diversity. Hence the conflict: Many of our institutions share at least the rhetoric of social mobility and an egalitarian society. The idea of the collegium is itself idealized as the model of a self-governing, learning community of scholar-teachers and students. Even elite institutions in the last decade have defined for themselves roles as leaders of diversity and have espoused, with and without government intervention, their roles in diversifying their student bodies, faculties, administrations, and boards. Yet the boards which govern these institutions, both the elite institutions and the colleges and universities of the American dream, are, with few exceptions, inclined to preserve and protect the status quo—both structurally, as the corporate actors of their institutions, and individually, as board members drawn from the ranks of the privileged and powerful. They tolerate diversity to the extent of opening the gates and letting in nonwhites and non-males, but only if they are "truly qualified," which is to say, "like us," individuals who will fit the expectations of existing social systems and hierarchies. Equal opportunity understood in all its implications is a radical challenge to the economic and governance structures of our institutions. Acknowledging the legitimacy of equal opportunity inevitably involves closer scrutiny of existing hierarchies and their functioning and requires closer scrutiny of the unexamined issues and assumptions affecting latent board functions. "Excellence" and other qualifications or "admissions" criteria are not objective systems of evaluation free of class or cultural bias.

Given these frames of reference and historical contexts, then, let us turn to a more detailed history and current assessment of women on boards—where they were and are and how they function. The objective of this chapter, finally, is to assess women's roles on boards as a microcosm of social change: how their experiences illuminate the bedrock of organizational structures and functioning which we must better understand if we are ever to evolve more equitable institutions capable of genuine diversity and equal opportunities. As Richard Lyman, president of the Rockefeller Foundation and former president of Stanford University, observed in taking on the leadership of Independent Sector, "The rhetoric of pluralism is cheap; learning, not just to tolerate diversity but to glory in it, is what counts."[18]

The History of Women on Boards

Limited data are available about the history of women on boards. A 1917 study of 143 colleges and universities found 75 women trustees, or 3 percent of the total of 2,470 trustees.[19] A 1947 study of 30 universities documents only 3.4 percent women.[20] With few exceptions, the only other sources of data available are archival records or published histories of individual institutions. Reviewing several published histories, it quickly becomes apparent that even those institutions which should have been more alert to the need for women on boards—the elite women's colleges, for example—reveal patterns strikingly similar to most other colleges of their day. Vassar, Smith, and Bryn Mawr, for example, were formed with all-male boards and, in Smith's case at least, they were "all men of superior ability, of sterling Christian character," all but one from Harvard, Yale, Brown, Amherst, or Williams.[21]

Unique among its sister institutions, Barnard was founded with a majority of women on its first board.[22] By 1889, however, attributed in part to the Association of Collegiate Alumnae's "hearty endorsement" cited earlier, "several positions of trust" had been opened to women in other ACA colleges. In 1889, seven ACA members served as trustees, representing four governing boards: Boston University, Smith, Vassar, and Wellesley. Responding to the association's mission to wield influence for women's education, they formed a Committee on Collegiate Administration which considered a range of issues affecting women's education, among them the organization of boards, methods of financial administration, the selection and appointment of teachers, relations of alumnae associations, and the status of special students.

The late 1890s and early 1900s saw a rapid increase in the numbers of students, men and women, attending colleges and universities. This influx, however beneficial for women at first, quickly became the excuse to prompt boards to adopt quotas, and policies of sex segregation in formerly integrated institutions became commonplace. Responding to "the seeming significance of this new movement toward the higher education of women," the ACA trustees committee established themselves as a group "watching and questioning tendencies in the higher education of women."[23] By 1909 the committee numbered 23 members serving on boards of six colleges and one university—Wisconsin; a woman had also been appointed to the Cornell board; and collectively, women trustees more rigorously focused on broader issues of concern to both women and to their institutions. By 1914 the committee had reconstituted itself as the Conference of Women Trustees and, until 1929, held meetings in conjunction with the biennial association conventions.

In 1914, however, they formalized their concerns as part of a national association resolution. Among broader institutional priorities identified—high academic standards and a "uniform and self-explanatory system of college accounting," for example—the resolution passed defined women trustees' responsibilities to include monitoring women faculty salaries "to see that the women teachers . . . receive salaries equal to those of men teachers of the same academic standing, and . . . are not assigned social and other non-academic duties not required of men scholars of equal rank. . . ." The women trustees' conference also owned as their responsibility the need "to take active measures to secure for all women teachers . . . the same opportunities of promotion in position and salary" that were afforded to men of comparable rank and standing. The committee also drafted what is most likely the first instance on record of availability pools. They resolved that women faculty be promoted "to head professorships in proportion to the relative numbers of men and women employed as instructors of higher grade in the colleges or universities which we represent. . . ."[24]

These explicit agendas must have provided some mutual support and resolve while they lasted but, then as now, a major issue confronting women on boards was the more fundamental reality of acceptance. Before women trustees could pursue the concerns they had outlined, they had to become active, functioning trustees. There is some evidence that then, as now, women were seen by at least some of their colleagues as active trustees and indeed took their board work seriously. One scholar commented on a decision the Smith board and others made in the 1920s to reduce life terms for trustees to renewable ten-year terms: "That the board would function better without these part-time members was a conception rapidly grasped by the livelier, especially the feminine, trustees."[25] In spite of commitment and liveliness, however, an earlier episode is probably more characteristic of the subtle and not so subtle barriers women trustees had to overcome. One of the first women trustees at Smith recalls:

> When I first became an alumna trustee, in 1906, it was the unwritten custom for the three women to sit in a demure row on the sofa, and the president, with his characteristic fine courtesy, always placed a footstool before each one of us. When Miss X. came on the board and attended the first meeting, she sat down in one of the chairs, with no perception that she was doing anything out of the ordinary. The president looked at her once or twice with a vague discomfort and finally said, "Miss X. would you not be more comfortable on the sofa with the other ladies?" Miss X. replying, "Oh no, I am quite comfortable here, thank you," he gave it up and thereafter the feminine three sat anywhere it happened to be convenient.[26]

The Current Status of Women on Boards

The Smith trustee who recalled the sofa incident also describes the "stately politeness" which distinguished trustee meetings. It is perhaps this disjuncture between perceived politeness and pervasive, albeit genteel, discrimination that accounts, at least in part, for the few cycles of attention paid to women on boards (see Appendix 15.1)—and accounts, at least in part, for women's own conflicting perceptions and self-images. For in describing the status and roles of women on boards, one is struck by profound contradictions. These are contradictions most likely endemic to any marginal group making a bid for acceptance and self-regard (it is difficult for anyone who is trying to work effectively in a group to acknowledge or confront directly the reality of marginal status), but in the case of women trustees—in most instances women of wealth and class—their energy, their often perceptive analyses of issues, and their self-images are riddled with contradictions. Women on school boards interviewed in 1973, for example, vigorously denied any problems with sex discrimination, yet went on to describe their routes to the board as "rough and narrow," with no room, for "a tough broad" or "a frilly female." And in spite of no perceptions of sex discrimination, they point out that a woman board member must have "a strong back, a thick skin, and an indomitable will" if she is successfully to withstand the pressures she will face.[27]

These contradictions run through many women trustees' perceptions. Although over 65 percent of women trustees responding to a 1978 Pennsylvania study disagreed—or strongly disagreed—with the observation that women belonged to less powerful board committees than their male peers, the largest groups of women trustees belong to committees which at least 94 percent of the same respondents did not view as most important. These contradictions notwithstanding, however, most women trustees responding to the Pennsylvania study also felt they were listened to, did not need to present a united front to be taken more seriously, and did not feel hampered by lack of access to informally shared information.[28]

In a series of interviews of New Jersey college and university board members conducted in 1982, the contradictions become more striking.[29] Women trustees often speak encouragingly about their institutions' commitments to affirmative action, for example. In one instance, a woman trustee comments that her president was actively supporting women on campus, yet she later observes that "he won't pull anything because he knows I'm here." These contradictions take their toll. To maintain what is essentially a split vision, women often blame themselves. Rather than criticize their boards for not setting up more effective orientation programs—a problem cited by both women and men trustees—they will protest that they did not know enough or were not able to find the time to catch up. In interview after interview, the women speak knowledgeably about board issues and dynamics—in authoritative tones of voice, in complex syntax—only to revert to stereotypically feminine, breathy responses and disjointed syntax riddled with pauses and hesitant interjections when they describe their own roles on their boards: classic symptoms of people who feel themselves not taken seriously.

In terms of numbers, there have been some gains in the representation of women on trustee boards, but the gains have not been large. The late 1960s saw numerous articles and stories in the popular media heralding "dramatic" institutional changes following in the wake of anti-war demonstrations and student unrest. Hartnett did a followup to his 1968 survey to measure the changes that a *New York Times* October 1969 editorial described as a "healthy tide . . . running toward reform of college boards of trustees to add diversity to their membership."[30] Twelve percent of the 376 boards responding to his followup had added one woman trustee; under 4 percent had added two, and less than 1 percent had added three. In a sense, the data suggest the reality of tokenism. Those institutions with few or no women were those which most often responded with additions or intentions of adding a woman trustee. Those boards with the highest representation of women on their boards in the 1968 study reported the fewest additions.

More recent data is provided by two studies conducted by the Association of Governing Boards of Universities and Colleges. The first was a survey of the composition of trustee boards in 1977, and the second was an update carried out in 1985. The studies concluded that the characteristics of the boards governing colleges and universities have not changed dramatically since 1977. There are estimated to be in all about 48,000 trustees and regents serving on 2,200 governing boards, of which about 200 are multi-campus boards. In 1985 the proportion of board members who were women was 20 percent compared with 15 percent in 1977. Six percent of board members were black in 1985 and that percentage was unchanged from 1977.[31] Table 15.1 provides a summary of the characteristics of governing board members in 1977 and 1985.

Women fare best on boards of women's colleges and in community and junior colleges. The 1976 survey conducted by Suzanne Howard for the American Association of University Women reported that women constituted 45 percent of the boards of women's colleges.[32]

In the 1978 Pennsylvania study, women trustees constituted 33 percent of the boards of women's colleges, and 5 of the 11 women's colleges responding to the study reported majority female boards.[33] The representation of women on community college boards in 1985 was 31 percent, according to a survey conducted under the auspices of the Association of Community College Trustees.[34]

Where women have made gains on trustee boards, the gains seem to have been a function of external pressures and legal mandates. The 1982 New Jersey data, for example, reflect the results of one of the only laws in the country mandating at least two women on each state and community college board: By 1982, 13.2 percent of state boards and 28.6 percent of community college boards were women. As in the Pennsylvania study, women do better on the boards of women's colleges, and because a relatively high proportion of private colleges in the state are Catholic women's colleges, the private and public sector figures in fact show remarkably similar proportions. Disaggregating the figures, however, it is clear that the gains show only in the public sector—with the impact of the state law—and in women's colleges.

Not only are women generally underrepresented on boards, but once on boards, women trustees are underutilized. The Pennsylvania study describes 75 percent of respondents citing the executive committee as one of the two most important committees of their boards. Only 25 percent, however, in fact served on executive committees, even though 37 percent felt qualified to do so. Over

TABLE 15.1

Characteristics of Governing Boards: 1977 and 1985

	1977	1985
Sex		
Men	84.9%	79.9%
Women	15.1	20.1
Total	100.0	100.0
Race		
White	93.0	90.1
Black	6.0	6.3
Hispanic	*	0.6
Other Minority	1.0	3.0
Total	100.0	100.0
Education		
Less Than High School	0.4	0.0
High School Diploma	6.5	4.4
AA, AS	2.8	22.9
BA, BS	38.8	40.2
MA, MS, MAT	19.4	22.8
MD, JD	21.2	18.9
PhD, EdD	11.0	10.7
Total	100.0	100.0
Age		
Under 30 Years	2.2	2.0
30–39 Years	7.3	6.8
40–49 Years	24.4	20.8
50–59 Years	35.0	38.1
60–69 Years	24.7	24.1
70 Years and Over	6.5	8.2
Total	100.0	100.0

Source: Association of Governing Boards, *Composition of Governing Boards*, 1985 (Washington, DC: AGB, 1986), p. 36.
*Not available.

45 percent also cited the finance or budget committee as one of the most important board committees, yet only 17 percent of women trustees served on finance and budget committees compared with the over 30 percent who reported they felt qualified to serve.[35] Clearly, these data also reveal an issue of women trustees' confidence and self-image: Given the demographic profiles of the trustees in the study, their educational background, their professional and volunteer experience, and their

other board service, they underestimate their qualifications. But considering the discrepancies between the competencies they do acknowledge and the opportunities they have for using those skills effectively, a strong case can be made for interpreting even their own assessment of their qualifications as evidence of stereotyping and feedback which the women themselves have internalized.

Women trustees' committee service echoes the conventional stereotypes of women's abilities and ambitions: service-oriented and concerned with the nurture and education of the young. Women "best" serve on those committees—student affairs and academic affairs, for example—that draw on those traditional female skills and experiences. And those are not the skills or the powerful committees which—at least on most boards—set institutional agendas and, in effect, control the "trust." But even where women's experience or self-images go beyond the stereotypes, they are still constrained and not given opportunities to use the skills they see themselves having to offer. Even though fewer women than their male peers in both the Pennsylvania and national samples have business-related professional experience, for example, most of those with business experience were not members of finance or budget committees.[36] And the third most-cited committee women felt qualified to serve on in the Pennsylvania study, for example—development, one of the traditionally more important committees in private institutions—ranks sixth among those on which women actually serve.

In positions of leadership on their boards, the situation is even bleaker for women trustees. Overall, 39 percent of respondents in the Pennsylvania study felt qualified to chair 258 committees. In fact, 18 percent chaired 67 committees. Even among those committees on which women trustees most often served—student affairs and academic affairs—women chaired 5 percent and 4 percent, respectively, compared with 23 percent and 18 percent who felt qualified to chair.[37] Clearly, as women generally in their fifties and more traditionally conservative, women trustees have internalized many of the role expectations and limitations imposed on women in our culture; what is striking, however, is that the data describing even their own expectations and qualifications document such limited opportunites for their abilities.

More implicit discrimination on boards, while harder to measure, is also rampant. A number of the New Jersey women trustees interviewed, for example, report being excluded from informal decision-making exchanges, interrupted or not recognized in group discussions, and generally not drawn into the mainstream of board activity. The standard behavior of dominant numbers of men in groups prevails: Behaviors described ranged from "stately politeness" on one board—with all the women seated around the periphery of the room, none at the main conference table—to elaborate apologies for off-color language and concern for the "ladies" present and, at the worst, sexist jokes.

A content analysis of several major national trustee publications reveals, at best, benign neglect. Not only do most articles ignore concerns of women's issues on campus, women trustees themselves do not figure in the informal culture reflected in the news items and photographs.

Clearly, women have not been integrated into "newsworthy" trustee activities—not even as part of the re-created descriptions of events which so often serve as opportunities to put forth a better public image. They may no longer be relegated to the sofa, but it is little wonder that women trustees manifest a sense of themselves as marginal.

The Contributions of Women on Boards

In spite of considerable odds operating against their effective trusteeship, however, women trustees constitute an important presence on boards—at least to those concerned with boards functioning as more flexible, liberal governance structures. In the one comprehensive survey of trustee attitudes available, women trustees reflect a significantly more liberal presence on boards than do their male peers.

Hartnett found, for example, that women trustees were more supportive than their male peers of free faculty expression of opinions and were more opposed to administrative control of the student newspaper and loyalty oaths for faculty members. Hartnett also documents women trustees' interest in their institutions' taking active roles in solving social problems and being "less enamored with organized fraternities and sororities as a positive influence for undergraduates." As Table 15.2

TABLE 15.2

Educational Attitudes of Male and Female Trustees at Four-Year Colleges and Universities: 1968

	Female Trustees				Male Trustees	
	Women's Institutions		Other Institutions			
	(N = 230)		(N = 289)		(N = 3,943)	
Educational Attitudes	Agree	Disagree	Agree	Disagree	Agree	Disagree
Academic Freedom						
Faculty members have right to free expression of opinions	83%	10%	78%	16%	66%	29%
Administration should control contents of student newspaper	16	77	21	69	42	50
Reasonable to require loyalty oath from faculty members	35	59	43	47	54	37
Who Should Be Served by Higher Education Attendance is a privilege, not a right	93	5	91	4	93	4
Academic aptitude should be the most important admissions criteria	76	19	69	24	74	21
Should be opportunities for higher education for anyone who wants it	91	6	89	6	84	12
Colleges should admit disadvantaged not meeting requirements	62	26	68	18	66	23
Others						
Institution should attempt to solve social problems	65	23	70	17	61	25
Students punished by local authorities for off-campus matters should also be disciplined by the college	33	52	43	45	50	38
A coeducational institution provides a better educational setting	31	54	69	19	67	20
Fraternities/sororities provide positive influence	27	66	36	43	47	34

Source: Rodney T. Hartnett, *The New College Trustee: Some Predictions for the 1970's* (Princeton, NJ: Educational Testing Service, 1970), p. 35.
Notes: Statements in table are abridged and modified.
Percentage "Agree" is a combination of those reponding "Strongly Agree" and "Agree." Percentage "Disagree" is a combination of those responding "Strongly Disagree" and "Disagree." Percentages do not add to 100 because of those responding "unable to say."

shows, women trustees of women's colleges were also somewhat more supportive of academic freedom. Hartnett points out that, overall, the women trustees in his sample more often held positions in "helping" professions (volunteer work, for example, or education)—and were more likely to be Democrats and liberal—but he concludes that using these background characteristics to explain the substantial differences in attitudes between men and women trustees is relatively unimportant: "What is important is that their appointment to trusteeships will probably contribute a more liberal viewpoint to most governing boards."[38]

The New Jersey interviews corroborate these findings. The women trustees interviewed generally tend to be more supportive of student concerns, especially of the needs of women students. Various women trustees (and few men trustees) express concern for and, at the least, awareness of such issues as part-time matriculation and the need to accommodate more flexible "rhythms" for women's education; student housing; role models for women students, especially in the sciences; and the need to foster leadership potential of students, especially women students. Women trustees are alert to issues such as day care and more flexible schedules for students, faculty, and staff. On one community college board interviewed, for example, several of the women trustees pointed to their responsibility for saving a day care program on campus that at least one trustee acknowledged would have been cut had it not been for women trustees' support. It is also the women trustees who pay attention to other "quality of life" issues on campuses which affect women and men students, faculty, and staff—adequate lounge space, food services, student centers, and dormitory accommodations, for example.

In addition to paying attention to these "soft" issues, women trustees are also more inclined to ask the "hard questions," requesting data on numbers of women and minorities on campus, for example, and questioning which numbers got collected and why. On the whole, women trustees are more alert than their male counterparts to their institution's legal mandates and responsibilities for affirmative action compliance.

Still another theme running through the interviews, however, is essentially a concern for more effective board functioning: on the need for consensus and the need to facilitate better group interaction by drawing out new trustees or trustees who do not participate; on the need for putting in place more efficient orientation programs and committee structures. It was a woman trustee on a liberal arts college board, for example, who developed a plan to rotate committee membership, giving all trustees more exposure, training them better in the process, and, as she described, eliminating the perceptual bias working which excluded women from such key committees as finance. Women trustees are also more likely to point to a necessary balance between social "grease" on a board and too much "in-group" socializing. On several boards, it was the women trustees who got the boards together for more structured informal socializing, using in at least one instance home entertainment as a strategy. This trustee was especially intent on drawing out members of the board who had not been participating and opening up other informal channels of communication in addition to the chairman's "touch base" network that had effectively cut out many of the women and men on the board. Time and again, it is also the women on boards who are most critical of elitism, of the narrower perspectives of, as one put it, "the corporation boys." More often than not, it is a woman trustee who describes the need to get more information, more diverse perspectives on issues coming before the board. While as aware as their male peers of the boundaries of governance and management, women trustees seem to assume more responsibility for soliciting information from other sources on campus, for being conduits to the board for information from various constituencies on campus.

Women trustees, generally, express preference for more direct involvement with campus activities. They take the time, in many instances, to get to know their institutions better than do their male counterparts. A number of male trustees in fact define their roles as better served with less involvement on campus—at all costs avoiding tripping over administrative boundaries. At least several of the women trustees, however, unobtrusively introduced themselves on campus and as a consequence seem to have evolved a more informed knowledge of the institutional styles and issues they are responsible for—without interfering with their presidents' prerogatives.

Conclusions

It is important to stress that the trustee activities and perspectives described as "women's contributions" are in fact issues of effective governance. The structural and social constraints defined earlier—the conserving nature of any "corporate actor" and the social pressures of status and power—often seem to operate against effective management. Coupled with the powerful constraints of stereotyping and perceptual bias, which women themselves often internalize, boards exhibit many of the dynamics which hamper opportunities for more vital, better-managed institutions.

Some of the tentative conclusions drawn from analysis of the New Jersey interviews corroborate these perspectives. Rauh observed in 1959 that trustees with more diverse backgrounds provide broader points of view and make for a more effective board.[39] In fact, the most diverse New Jersey board interviewed—with the broadest mix of age, gender, racial/ethnic heritage, and political affiliation—was the board which most successfully survived several major institutional crises. Of all boards interviewed, this group, operating as a "committee of the whole," paid the most attention to affirmative action at all levels of the institution. (The collective concerns did not evolve without some individual struggles to set the agenda, but concerns gradually were listened to and began to be articulated by most board members, eliminating the need of minorities and women to assume isolated advocacy roles.) Of all boards interviewed, this board also most effectively drew on the various strengths of all its members.

This is a public board, governing a relatively young institution, with change to some extent forced on it through external mandates, through political appointments and affirmative action pressures. At least two of the women on the board, for example, owe their appointments to other women on the board or on the state nominating committee. And it is a board quite different in tone and make-up from the boards that governed the first years of the institution. There are still considerable pressures to preserve the institutional status quo, and the college has barely survived several bitter power struggles, both within the institution itself and on the board. Yet, better than any of the other boards interviewed, they seem to have learned to work together and to listen to each other, and the women on the board have been instrumental, at least in several instances, in facilitating that exchange.

The status quo is all too often unnecessarily restrictive, a function of institutional structures blindly perpetuating themselves, a function of individuals preserving and protecting only partially understood prerogatives of status and class. Fresh energy brings new insights. Higher education needs all the resources it can attract in the coming decades, and drawing on pools of women and minorities with diverse experience and perspectives can offer valuable assets for institutional governance. Women have obviously made both gains and contributions as trustees, but they have yet to take places in numbers comparable to the talent available. And all of us—women and men, students, faculty, staff, and trustees—have paid too high a price for discrimination. As boards diversify to reflect more accurately the populations they serve, as they become more aware of the subtle biases at work countered by proven strategies for more effective governance, higher education may come closer to what we have demanded of it for at least 200 years: models of opportunity and collegial governance, diverse communities of learning.

Appendix 15.1

Organizing Women Trustees

At least three attempts to organize women trustees in the last 20 years have generated conferences, published conference proceedings, and a series of forums and workshops; but unlike the AAUW Conference on Women Trustees in 1887—which evolved over a 25-year period and, once organized, functioned for another 15—each contemporary effort has been short-lived. In 1964 the AAUW Committee on Standards in Higher Education held a conference in Washington which brought together trustees and administrators representing over 80 AAUW colleges and universities and national associations. The proceedings describe three questions addressed:

> How can the woman trustee best support the development plans of her institution in such areas as finance, high education quality, stimulating collegiate atmosphere, and preparation of the student for her life role?
>
> How can the trustee function in the area of women faculty recruitment, development, and promotion?
>
> What would help you to be a more effective trustee and assist you in working in the above-mentioned areas?[40]

In 1976, Cornell University, with funding from the Association of Governing Boards for publication of the proceedings, sponsored a two-day conference—Gateways and Barriers for Women in the University Community—for approximately 50 participants who were women trustees from ten colleges and universities, mostly Ivy League. The conference included presentations on affirmative action in the participating institutions; a panel, "Affirmative Action Today: An Interpretation"; a keynote address, "Role and Contributions of Woman Trustees and Administrators," by Judith Younger, deputy dean of the Cornell Law School; and workshops on women trustees and decision-making; trustee-administrator interaction; alumnae as future leaders; women administrators; and women faculty: recruitment, development, promotion, and remuneration. The published proceedings also included an annotated bibliography on women in higher education.[41]

In 1979 the North Carolina Planning Committee of the American Council on Education's National Identification Program for the Advancement of Women in Higher Education (ACE/NIP) sponsored a workshop for North Carolina women trustees which featured a speech by Anne Scott: "The Feminist Responsibilities of Women Trustees." The following year, the New Jersey ACE/NIP Planning Committee sponsored a forum for New Jersey women trustees, "Increasing the Effectiveness of Governing Boards," which raised a number of board/management issues directly or indirectly affecting women on boards and on campus: trustee selection, essentials of orientation and training, uses and limits of trustee power, the affirmative action advocacy roles of women and minority trustees, and the relationships of boards to constituencies in the Department of Education and Board of Higher Education. A gathering of women trustees in 1981 brought together a representative group of trustees who worked with the planning committee to develop and sponsor a finance workshop, one of several recommended information sessions trustees had identified as a need. Other activities included updated annual listings of all women trustees in the state; mailings to women trustees sharing newsletters, topical issues of concerns, and information about the nominations processes for all state and private colleges and universities; several rounds of active solicitation of trustee candidates; panel presentations and informal outreach to other professional women's networks in the process of soliciting nominations for boards; and the research project described in this chapter which interviewed women and men trustees on five representative college and university boards.

What is striking about all these efforts, however, is the difficulty of sustaining them, Meetings, workshops, and roundtables have been sponsored at national Association of Governing Boards conferences, initially drawing a number of interested participants. Other state ACE/NIP planning committees—Maryland and New York, for example—as well as the New York City metropolitan area have sponsored day-long conferences or forums. Unlike other professional women's networks, however, women trustee networks have not been ongoing or self-sustaining. Although goal-focused state, regional, and national programs seem to draw enthusiastic one-time audiences, other strategies are needed to reach larger numbers. At this juncture, it seems clear that the limited resources available for national and regional projects are best spent on developing resources women trustees can avail themselves of: updated state lists of women trustee names and addresses; information on representation of women on boards; bibliographies and lists of other resources; and strategies for increasing both the numbers of nominations and pools of potential trustees by facilitating more contacts among senior women in education, business, the professions, nonprofits, and government.

Notes

1. Lawrence A. Cremin, *American Education: The Colonial Experience, 1607–1783* (New York: Harper & Row, 1970), pp. 221–222.

2. J. L. Zwingle, "Evolution of Lay Governing Boards," in Richard T. Ingram, ed., *Handbook of College and University Trusteeship* (San Francisco: Jossey-Bass, 1980), p. 16.

3. Although in principle controlled by their faculties, these systems, more informally than are their American counterparts with lay boards, may also be de facto governed by elites, a ". . . small number of leading civil servants, government ministers, university vice-chancellors, and members of the University Grants Commission who shaped the face of the British university system for many years in small committee rooms or around tables at the Athenaeum Club." Martin Trow, *Problems in the Transition from Elite to Mass Higher Education* (Berkeley, CA: Carnegie Commission on Higher Education, 1973), p. 12.

4. See Cremin, *American Education*, p. 222; also Gerald P. Burns, *Trustees in Higher Education: Their Functions and Coordination* (Washington, DC: Independent College Funds of America, 1966), p. 5; Anne Gary Pannell, "Myth and Reality in Trustee-President-Dean Relationships," in *The Woman Trustee: A Report on a Conference for Women Members of Governing Boards, December 1, 1964* (Washington, DC: American Association of University Women, 1965), p. 23.

5. Burns, *Trustees in Higher Education*, p. 6. Trustee guidance continues to be a role defined by trustees, by corporate board members, for example, who offer expertise on the educated "manpower" most needed in coming decades.

6. See, for example, "Academic Freedom and Big Business," in Richard Hofstader and Walter P. Metzger, *The Development of Academic Freedom in the United States* (New York: Columbia University Press, 1955), pp. 413–467.

7. Thorstein Veblen, *The Higher Learning in America: A Memorandum on the Conduct of Universities by Business Men* (New York: Reprints of Economic Classics, Augustus M. Kelley, Bookseller, 1965; orig. ed., 1918).

8. Burns, *Trustees in Higher Education*, p. 15.

9. George E. Potter, "Responsibilities," in Victoria Dziuba and William Meardy, issue eds., *Enhancing Trustee Effectiveness: New Directions for Community Colleges* 15 (Autumn 1976):6.

10. See, for example, Alice S. Rossi and Ann Calderwood, eds., *Academic Women on the Move* (New York: Russell Sage Foundation, 1973); Carnegie Commission on Higher Education, *Opportunities for Women in Higher Education* (New York: McGraw-Hill, 1973); W. Todd Furniss and Patricia Albjerg Graham, eds., *Women in Higher Education* (Washington, DC: American Council on Education, 1974); and Carnegie Council on Policy Studies in Higher Education, *Making Affirmative Action Work in Higher Education* (San Francisco: Jossey-Bass, 1975).

11. Rodney T. Hartnett, *College and University Trustees: Their Background, Roles and Educational Attitudes* (Princeton, NJ: Educational Testing Service, 1969); Irene L. Gomberg and Frank J. Atelsek, *Composition of College and University Governing Boards*, Higher Education Panel Reports no. 35 (Washington, DC: American Council on Education, August 1977).

12. Hartnett, *College and University Trustees*, p. 12. Although, as noted, there is consensus on a range of legal and "prescriptive" responsibilities trustees *should* hold, there is in fact little data and less agreement in the trustee literature about what, in fact, boards *do*. A comprehensive overview of the literature synthesizes what the authors describe as the "somewhat pedestrian and largely descriptive literature in the field"; Robert E. Engel and Paul P. W. Achola, "Boards of Trustees and Academic Decisionmaking," *Review of Educational Research* 53 (Spring 1983):58. Engel and Achola observe in passing what is in fact a critical point: that, while several studies 'have attempted to document and analyze the actual trustee decision-making process by using content-analyses of board minutes, some of the most important decisions and issues affecting board decisions never reach the written record. These may be "non-decisions"—which "if brought into open debate, would seriously shred the social fabric," as Engel and Achola observe—or they might be the more implicit, often unexamined issues and assumptions affecting latent board functions—how assumed criteria for selection of new trustees, for example, perpetuate the board in its own image. No comprehensive board research has yet to tackle these more complex or subtle dimensions of trustee power and influence. This dearth of research is also true of research on boards in other sectors. One of the most recent studies of corporate boards, for example, describes as impetus for the study the authors' curiosity: "We were intrigued by this lack of information on director attitudes and behavior. . . ," Thomas J. Whisler, *Rules of the Game: Inside the Corporate Boardroom* (Homewood, IL: Dow Jones-Irwin, 1984).

13. Burns, *Trustees in Higher Education*, p. 7.

14. Marion Talbot and Lois Kimball Matthews Rosenberry, *The History of the American Association of University Women: 1881–1931* (Boston: Houghton Mifflin, 1931), p. 194.

15. Morton A. Rauh, *College and University Trusteeship* (Yellow Springs, OH: Antioch Press, 1959), p. 15.

16. Hartnett, *College and University Trustees*, p. 47.

17. These are also concepts apparently unresolved in the relevant social science literature. One strategy for reconciling the contradictions of democracy and elitism has been the concept of accountability, defining for the elite special fiduciary responsibilities and calling them accountable to the general population. Other scholars see trustee elites—especially given this concept of public accountability—as balancing the inherent elitism of the faculty (knowledge-based elitism) and the administration (information-controlling elitism); Engel and Achola, "Boards of Trustees," p. 57.

18. Richard W. Lyman, "Comments by the Incoming Chairperson," Independent Sector Annual Membership Meeting and Assembly, October 25, 1983.

19. Scott Nearing, "Who's Who Among College Trustees," *School and Society* 6 (September 1917):298.

20. Hubert Park Beck, *Men Who Control Our Universities* (New York: King's Crown Press, 1947), p. 92.

21. L. Clark Seelye, *The Early History of Smith College: 1871–1910* (Boston: Houghton Mifflin, 1923), p. 18.

22. Alice Duer Miller and Susan Myers, *Barnard College: The First Fifty Years* (New York: Columbia University Press, 1939).

23. Talbot and Rosenberry, *History of the AAUW*, pp. 196–197.

24. Talbot and Rosenberry, *History of the AAUW*, p. 200.

25. Margaret Farrand Thorp, *Neilson of Smith* (New York: Oxford University Press, 1956), p. 299.

26. Harriet Seelye Rhees, *Laurenus Clark Seelye: First President of Smith College* (Boston: Houghton Mifflin, 1929), p. 198.

27. Laura T. Doing, "Women on School Boards: Nine Winners Tell How They Play the Game," *American School Board Journal* 160 (March 1973):34–38.

28. Mona Norman Generett, "The Role of Women Trustees in Private Independent Colleges and Universities of Pennsylvania As Defined by Their Characteristics, Functions and Perceptions," unpublished doctoral dissertation, University of Pittsburgh, 1978, p. 52.

29. Mary Ellen S. Capek, "College and University Trusteeship in New Jersey," *Networking*, newsletter of the New Jersey Planning Committee of the American Council on Education National Identification Program, Spring 1983.

30. Rodney T. Hartnett, *The New College Trustee: Some Predictions for the 1970s* (Princeton, NJ: Educational Testing Service, 1970), p. 66.

31. Association of Governing Boards, *Composition of Governing Boards, 1985* (Washington, DC: AGB, 1986).

32. Suzanne Howard, *But We Will Persist: A Comparative Research Report on the Status of Women in Academe* (Washington, DC: American Association of University Women, 1978), pp. 56–57.

33. Generett, "Role of Women Trustees," p. 26.

34. Sheila Korhammer, "The Increasing Influence of Women on Community College Boards," *Trustee Quarterly*, Fall 1986, p. 22.

35. Generett, "Role of Women Trustees," pp. 52, 54.

36. Generett, "Role of Women Trustees," p. 60.

37. Generett, "Role of Women Trustees," p. 56.

38. Hartnett, *New College Trustee*, pp. 33–36. See also Helen Ruth Godrey, "A Profile of Female Trustees of Four-Year Public Colleges and Universities and a Comparison of Female and Male Trustee Perceptions of Selected Trustee Functions and University Issues," unpublished doctoral dissertation, Michigan State University, 1971.

39. Rauh, *College and University Trusteeship*, p. 37.

40. American Association of University Women, *The Woman Trustee: A Report on a Conference for Women Members of Governing Boards, December 1, 1964* (Washington, DC: AAUW, 1965), p. 5.

41. Cornell University, *Gateways and Barriers for Women in the University Community: Proceedings of the Mary Donlon Alger Conference for Trustees and Administrators*, sponsored by the Board of Trustees of Cornell University, September 10 and 11, 1976 (Ithaca, NY: Office of University Publications, Cornell University, 1977).

Current Challenges to Foundation Board Governance: A Worst Case Scenario or The Perfect Storm?

Emmett D. Carson

Introduction

It is a distinct honor to be asked to speak at the Council on Foundations' board trustee dinner. The issue of board governance has become a growing concern to the public, media, government officials and community groups due to a number of well-publicized scandals in both the private and nonprofit sectors. In addition, foundation boards are facing a number of other challenges that together amount to either a worst case scenario or a perfect storm.

The difference between a worst case scenario and the perfect storm is whether you survive the experience. Let me describe what I mean. There is a weekly television program called "Worst Case Scenario." In the show, an impossible situation is created in which survival seems unlikely. The show illustrates for viewers, step by step, how to live through the experience. Scenarios have included jumping from a burning boat through an oil slick filled with raging flames to surviving a head-on automobile collision.

By comparison, in the movie "The Perfect Storm," the characters face a storm of epic proportions. Unfortunately, at key steps along the way, the captain and the crew make a series of bad decisions that ultimately results in their demise. When the crew should initially turn back, they sail forward. When they should call for help, their captain destroys the radio. When they should wait in calm seas until the storm has subsided, they decide to try to make it back to port. It wasn't the severity of the storm that did them in. It was their poor decision making. Unlike a no-win situation in which there is no way to avoid the negative consequences, the difference between a perfect storm and the worst case scenario is whether you make the right decisions, at the right time, that will allow you to survive the experience. Today, foundation boards are finding themselves in just this situation and it will be largely our actions, and not those of others, that will determine the final outcome.

This evening, I want to talk about three things. First, I want to describe the multitude of difficult challenges that are facing foundation boards across the country. Second, I want to talk about how foundation boards should assess and address these challenges. Third, I want to talk about what foundation trustees and staff must ask, and expect, of the Council on Foundations in order that our field survives the current storm's onslaught.

I must confess to some degree of schizophrenia in preparing for this presentation. While I am vice chair of the Council on Foundations and chair its management committee as well as serve on several nonprofit boards, in my day job I am president and CEO of The Minneapolis Foundation. The Minneapolis Foundation is a community foundation that was started in 1915 and has total assets under management of $550 million. It is one of the oldest and largest community foundations in the country. The Foundation has a governing board of thirty trustees with six standing committees, 3 supporting organizations with a combined total of 27 trustees, and more than 735 separate charitable funds. I mention all of this to say that I have some small knowledge of foundation governance issues from both sides of the table.

Some of what I will say may trouble some of you. This is not my intention. I have a deep passion and love for our field and for what it has, and what it can, accomplish. My remarks reflect the concerns that I have about the future of philanthropy at this point in history. As a consequence, I have chosen to try to generate a healthy discussion of some difficult issues facing foundation boards at the risk of possibly making some of you uncomfortable. For this, I sincerely apologize.

Trouble Around Every Corner

It goes without saying that the issue of board governance is receiving its highest level of public scrutiny in decades. The accounting scandals in the private sector that engulfed Enron, WorldCom and Tyco, among others, have brought new attention to issues of corporate board governance. The widespread public concern resulting from fraud and ethical lapses by major corporations led to the passage of the Sarbanes-Oxley legislation in which Congress mandated new norms and standards for corporate governance. While the legislation focuses exclusively on corporations, its impact has been so profound that foundation and nonprofit boards across the United States are reassessing their governance practices based on this legislation.

Even before the Sarbanes-Oxley legislation, questions were being raised about the governance practices of foundations and nonprofit organizations following the charitable response to the 9/11 tragedy.[1] New York's attorney general has recently issued a white paper that recommends new legislation directed at nonprofit organizations based, in part, on the Sarbanes-Oxley law. He proposes that officers of nonprofit corporations certify the accuracy of the organization's financial statements and annual report. Minnesota's attorney general also has issued a white paper on his views about the best practices for governing boards of nonprofit organizations. We should expect and prepare for other states to take similar actions.

Added to this climate of changing expectations for board governance, the deteriorating investment environment over the last three years has caused foundation assets to plummet. The decrease in assets is requiring foundations to reassess their grantmaking priorities and to lay-off staff. While foundations have struggled to maintain their giving levels in the face of a falling market, a report by the Foundation Center indicates that two-fifths of foundations surveyed expected their giving to decline in 2003 and this sentiment was greater among larger foundations.[2] Similarly, a survey by *The Chronicle on Philanthropy* found that the assets of 6 of the 10 largest foundations declined for a combined loss of $10.6 billion and that more than 100 private foundations had planned to cut or freeze their grantmaking.[3] One foundation that has been very forthcoming about its budget challenges is the Hewlett-Packard Foundation that has seen its portfolio decline from a high of $13 billion in 1999 to $4.8 billion in 2002. The foundation has laid-off 60 of its 160 staff members including 39 program staff positions and has eliminated several grantmaking areas where it was the acknowledged leader.[4]

As if things weren't bad enough, the weak economy is also creating other problems. The poor national economy coupled with widespread budget deficits at the national, state and local levels has meant that there are increased social needs as it relates to job training, housing, and health care, among other needs. Moreover, many states, including my home state of Minnesota, are exacerbating the challenges faced by the poor and unemployed by proposing budget cuts that will drastically reduce or eliminate the very services that poor people rely on at the time when they need them most.[5] The budget shortfalls also mean fewer resources for arts and cultural organizations as well as transportation issues that affect growth/urban sprawl. All of this means that rather than being able to rely on state and local governments as partners in providing services, these entities are contributing to the problems. And, adding insult to injury, some elected officials are erroneously suggesting to the public that the greater social needs resulting from reduced government funding can be replaced with giving from foundations and nonprofit organizations.

How Should Foundations Respond?

It is imperative that in determining how we respond to these multiple crises, foundation boards recognize the unique role that foundations play in American society and judge our individual and collective actions by whether they will improve or erode the public trust. Foundations are unique institutions in that they hold resources in the public trust for the purpose of improving our society. As a result, foundation governance practices must now be completely transparent and beyond reproach.

Foundation board positions are no longer ceremonial positions. Board members must be fully engaged in the oversight of their foundations' operations and must actively seek to improve their skills. It is essential that foundations do everything they can to guard against both real and perceived abuses. In particular, foundation boards must provide careful oversight and documentation that compensation and benefits paid to foundation trustees and executives is fair and equitable; that foundation endowments are well managed; that the ratio of operating expenses to grants is reasonable; that conflict of interest policies have been developed and are adhered to; and that grant requests are fairly reviewed and judged against the same standards. Our field needs better tools and comparative data to help us meet these minimum standards.

For some foundations, it will be difficult to adjust to the new public norms for transparency and accountability. However, as we saw in the corporate arena, it only requires a few high profile actors to bring unwanted public scrutiny and increased legislative oversight. Doing the job right is different from doing the job well. Fundamentally, foundations exist to improve the quality of life in their communities. It is not enough for foundation boards to say they are following all of the best practices of board governance but doing little that they think has the potential to significantly improve some aspect of our society. Foundation boards should resist efforts to have their institutions replace government support for basic social services at the expense of funding experimentation and innovation because it suggests that philanthropic dollars are interchangeable with public tax dollars. If such a linkage is made by our actions, why should private individuals rather than elected representatives of government dispense such funds? Foundation boards must actively explain to legislators and the media that the role of foundations is not, and should not be, to fill funding gaps created by the government.

The increased social needs facing our communities provide a unique opportunity for foundations to show our true worth to the public. Now is the time for foundation boards to insist that staff consider and bring forward innovative solutions. Now is the time for foundations to experiment with new approaches. And, now is the time for each foundation to take risks consistent with their mission and values. Smaller foundation endowments along with reduced egos may make it easier for foundations to collaborate than in the past. However, it is important that the success of such collaborations not be judged by how many funding partners are involved or the total amount of funds contributed to a common cause but rather the value of what might be accomplished. Joint projects that rely on the least common denominator approach are not as useful as projects and initiatives that have the promise of changing how an issue is viewed or handled.

It is my belief that the times demand that foundations not only meet the highest standards of ethics and accountability but also show how we make a tangible difference in the lives of people. Unfortunately, notwithstanding the fact that foundations often state that we provide the risk capital for innovation, not enough of us can point to consistent, ongoing, examples in our grantmaking portfolios where we have taken risks. I use the word risk in this context to mean who is the foundation willing to offend to try something different, for example, its existing grantees, other funders or popular public opinion. Foundations must show the public, in every way, that the trust they place in foundations is justified and that they are engaged in the prudent risk-taking the public expects.

Foundation boards set the expectations for staff about what kinds of risks are acceptable. One tool that foundation boards should consider developing is a risk allocation model for their grantmaking portfolio in the same way that they use an asset allocation model for their investment portfolio. For each grantmaking area, foundation boards should specify what degree of risk is acceptable and what does that risk look like. In the same way that foundation boards determine the degree of diversification and risk within investment asset classes, boards can specify what percentage of each grantmaking area should be high risk, moderate risk and low risk. High risk grants carry the greater likelihood of failure and controversy. Such grants are likely to represent no more than 25 percent of the typical foundation's grantmaking, however, they should have the potential to make a significant difference if they are successful. I would note that high risk grantmaking doesn't require large grants.

At a time of increased needs and limited resources, it is equally important that foundation boards show that they are responsive to the needs of diverse communities. We should be concerned with statistics generated by the Council on Foundations that have consistently shown that 90 percent of the governing boards of foundations are white and that 79 percent of foundation professional staff are white.[6] Such statistics might suggest to policymakers, the media and the broader public that foundations may not equally serve all segments of the community and that there may be bias in our grantmaking practices. Foundation boards carry the responsibility to demonstrate through their words and actions that they take such concerns seriously and have initiated good faith efforts to address issues of diversity, consistent with their foundation's structure and grantmaking priorities. In this regard, the Council on Foundations has been very helpful in developing useful materials and guidance for its members on diversity issues.

A Changing Role for the Council on Foundations

As individual foundation boards examine what they can do to follow the best practices in the governance area as well as look for ways to ensure that their grantmaking exceeds the public's expectations, we must also assess whether the Council on Foundations must act differently as our advocate and principal spokesperson.

Historically, foundations have been fortunate to operate with only a minimum level of government oversight and regulation. This is due, in large part, to the high ethical standards that have been promoted by the Council on Foundations that have been embraced by most foundations and the resulting trust that has been cultivated in government officials and others in the ability of foundations to police themselves. To the extent that the public and government officials become aware of egregious examples of bad behavior by foundations, it is very likely that, as with the private sector, they will demand greater oversight of foundation activity. And, they should. In this regard, the Council's primary responsibility must always be to ensure that foundations act ethically, consistent with their higher purpose, as perceived by the broader public and elected officials.

The rise and fall of the once influential American Institute of Certified Public Accountants (Institute) is a good example of what can happen when a membership organization fails to understand and adjust to the rising bar of public expectations and accountability.[7] Before the Sarbanes-Oxley Act, the Institute enjoyed the right to set the regulatory standards for the entire accounting profession. However, during the height of public concerns about corporate accounting, the Institute remained steadfast against any efforts to reform accounting industry practices. In particular, the Institute fought against changing the rules that accountants should not perform both accounting and consulting services for the same clients. Rather than the Institute's viewing its most important role as protecting the ongoing integrity of the accounting profession, it acted as if its primary role was to protect the interests and actions of its individual members above the public interest. In making this strategic error, the Institute lost the public trust as well as its privilege to self-regulate its industry with a minimum of government oversight and regulations.

There is a powerful lesson in this for the Council on Foundations and its sister institution, Independent Sector. It is not enough to have standards of behavior if we are unwilling to criticize or sanction members and non-members alike who abuse those standards. Certainly, it is never easy for a membership organization to criticize its members and an appropriate balance must be struck between being an aggressive watchdog and a passive lapdog. However, failure to confront members who violate the established norms of best practices may threaten the rights and privileges enjoyed by all foundations.

It is important that as trustees, you not only maintain the ethical integrity of the foundations that you govern but also that you insist that the Council on Foundations sees its primary responsibility as maintaining the integrity of the field of philanthropy rather than the reputation of an individual member or non-member. This is a message that foundation trustees have yet to deliver. Similarly, it is important that the Council encourages its members to devote some portion of their grantmaking to providing the social risk capital that provides the rationale for our existence. The special award that the Council has established to highlight the public policy efforts of foundations is a good beginning and more must be done.

If I haven't been provocative enough, let me conclude with one final observation. Additional government regulation should not always be viewed as a negative development to be avoided. For an industry that relies on the strategies of partnering with government to provide services, influencing government to engage or not engage in particular activities, and encouraging government to adopt programs that have been successfully piloted by foundations, philanthropy's fear of any added government oversight or regulation seems somewhat counter-productive. We should be open to the possibility that, in some cases, reasonable government oversight could be beneficial and might help to clarify otherwise gray areas of accountability and minimally acceptable best practices. It also might help to standardize practices across states rather than leaving it to each state's attorney general to devise different rules and regulations with different interpretations. We should be equally prepared to think through how government might assist and strengthen our field in addition to thinking through strategies to ensure that government intervention does not unduly harm our field.

Conclusion

These are indeed challenging times for foundation boards. However, there is an enormous need, and opportunity, to improve the quality of life of people consistent with each foundation's mission, grantmaking priorities and the best practices of board governance. To achieve this promise, we must learn to accept that risk and public scrutiny are now routine elements of our work and not inconveniences to be ignored or avoided. Individual foundations must act, and expect that the Council will act, in ways that recognize that our most important asset is the public's trust. If we do so, our field will survive the current storm and emerge from the worst case scenario healthy and intact.

Notes

1. Emmett D. Carson, "Public Expectations and Nonprofit Sector Realities: A Growing Divide With Disastrous Consequences," Nonprofit and Voluntary Sector Quarterly, vol. 31, no. 3, September 2002, pp. 429–436.
2. The Foundation Center, "Foundation Growth and Giving Estimates," Foundation Today Series, 2003 Edition, p. 2.
3. Ian Wilhelm, "Foundation Assets Sag," Chronicle of Philanthropy, April 4, 2002.
4. Elizabeth Greene, "Cutting Its Losses: Plunge in Assets Forces Packard to Slash Programs," Chronicle of Philanthropy, March 20, 2003.
5. See *www.goodforminnesota.org*
6. Council on Foundations, Foundation Management Report (Washington, DC: Council on Foundations, 1996), p.73 and p. 156.
7. "Bloodied and Bowed, "by David Henry and Mike McNamee in BusinessWeek, January 20, 2003, pp.56–57.

HOW TO THINK ABOUT THE DARTMOUTH COLLEGE CASE

JOHN S. WHITEHEAD & JURGEN HERBST

Editor's note: The essays below are the product of an exchange between two scholars who have studied the impact of the Dartmouth College case on American higher education. The first essay is by John S. Whitehead, professor of history at the University of Alaska, Fairbanks; the second by Jurgen Herbst, professor of history and educational policy studies at the University of Wisconsin, Madison.

When I wrote *The Separation of College and State* almost fifteen years ago my goal was to trace the origins of the distinction between "public" and "private" higher education in the United States. In the 1960s the terms were well recognized; no historian of education argued with that. But when did the distinction first become well recognized by educators and the general public alike? I was suspicious of the claims sometimes bandied about at private institutions like my own Yale that the distinction dated to the very origins of American higher education. Even a cursory review of the existing literature revealed that in the colonial and early postrevolutionary periods there was at least a quasi-public relationship in terms of support and control between such institutions as Yale, Harvard, and Columbia and the colonial and early state governments of Connecticut, Massachusetts, and New York.

I concluded in *The Separation* that "a distinction between private and public or state institutions was not commonly recognized before the Civil War." After the war, particularly in the 1870s, people such as Harvard's Charles Eliot advocated that "private" colleges should be totally separate from any connection with state government. Dependence on the state, Eliot asserted, was "a most insidious and irresistible enemy of republicanism." About the same time university presidents in states such as Wisconsin and Michigan finally convinced their legislatures to make annual appropriations to the "state university" and accept some type of permanent responsibility for these institutions.

To make my case that the public/private distinction was a *postwar* phenomenon, I had a major obstacle to overcome—the Dartmouth College case of 1819. Almost every previous historian of higher education from Merle Curti to Frederick Rudolph to Lawrence Cremin had asserted in one form or another that the Supreme Court's decision in that case encouraged the development of "private" colleges by protecting them from state encroachment. Private donors were thus stimulated to found colleges. Public universities would have to be direct creations of the state, not state transformations of existing colleges. Most historians saw the spread of "private" or denominational colleges after 1819 as proof of the encouraging effects of the Dartmouth decision. They were, however, somewhat undecided whether or not public or state universities were retarded by the decision. These institutions did not appear to spring up with the same vigor as their private counterparts. The traditional interpretation portrayed the Dartmouth College case as a major watershed in educational history; it clearly affirmed the existence of the public/private distinction by 1819.

After a close observation of the available documents on the case, I revised the traditional interpretation. The case, I concluded, was not a watershed; it did not affirm a widely accepted public/private distinction. In fact, I could find few people except Justices Joseph Story and John Marshall who were particularly interested in such a distinction. Shortly after winning the case the Dartmouth trustees asked the New Hampshire legislature to pay for the legal fees they incurred in fighting the state. Throughout the 1820s Dartmouth continued to seek an alliance with New Hampshire, offering state representation on its board of trustees in exchange for financial support.

Looking beyond Dartmouth, I observed that the Supreme Court decision received scant attention after it was issued. I discovered no private college promoters who cited the case in sponsoring new institutions. In fact, some denominational colleges quite eagerly sought state aid and often received it. There was little evidence that the states paid any more attention or accepted any greater responsibility for the so-called state universities than for the denominational colleges in their boundaries. In many states, particularly in the West, the state legislature performed no other function in the prewar period than to transfer federal land grants designated for higher education to a group of state university trustees. Only in South Carolina and Virginia did I find a continuous state sponsorship of one university. In my revisionist view neither educators nor the general public saw denominational colleges and state universities in a particularly different light before the war. This is not to say that all institutions were viewed identically. It is to say that the public/private distinction so well known in the twentieth century was simply not on the minds of antebellum Americans.

Since the publication of *The Separation* in 1973, several historians have supported or accepted my revision, even while seeing further ramifications to the case. In 1974 the Dartmouth literature expanded with Steven Novak's article, "The College in the Dartmouth College Case: A Reinterpretation" in *The New England Quarterly*, Vol. 47, Novak noted that I offered "an elevated discussion of the implications of the case on the concepts of 'private' and 'public' education." However, he argued that the trustees were not really concerned with legislative control of the college. Their real concern was the religious direction of the institution. Would it be controlled by the evangelical, revivalist faith of the majority of the trustees or the liberal, Arminian-like theology of John Wheelock and his supporters? Novak concluded:

> To the participants in the college and the community, then, the significance of the Dartmouth College Case was not the political battle between Federalists and Republicans or the contest between the state legislature and the United States Supreme Court. It was, rather, the question who would control the religious future of Dartmouth and Hanover. The Supreme Court's 1819 decision in favor of the trustees was thus a major victory for the cause of evangelical education (p. 563).

Novak did not say whether Chief Justice Marshall or others outside the Dartmouth community shared the same religious, rather than political, concerns. Nor did he specifically confirm or refute my interpretation. However, his reinterpretation indicates that a public/private distinction was *not* on the minds of the Dartmouth trustees. This helps to explain why the trustees so readily interacted with the state after the case. They had never really objected to the state; only to its support of John Wheelock in their religious feud.

Further direct acceptance of my Dartmouth interpretation came in 1980 with the publication of Lawrence Cremin's masterful *American Education: The National Experience*. Here Cremin abandoned the traditional view he and Freeman Butts had espoused a quarter century earlier in their *History of Education in American Culture*. Instead he accepted my revision by name and concluded, "it is unlikely that it [Marshall's decision] had any significant effect one way or another upon the image of colleges as community institutions in the public mind." Throughout the same volume Cremin made repeated mention of the difficulty of defining private and public education at all levels, primary and collegiate, in the nineteenth century. "The distinctions," he noted, "were in process of becoming and therefore unclear and inconsistent."

With the imprimatur of Cremin it looked as if my revision was becoming the accepted view as *The Separation* approached its tenth birthday. Such was not to be the case. In 1982 Jurgen Herbst's *From Crisis to Crisis* appeared. With it the traditional version of the Dartmouth case reemerged along with a challenge to my postwar dating of the private/public distinction. "The Dartmouth College decision," proclaimed Herbst, "was the stimulus for American higher education as we have known it since 1819."

Herbst found in *From Crisis to Crisis* that America's colonial colleges, with one exception, were even more public than I had asserted in *The Separation*. He called them "provincial" colleges, public in nature not merely because of various evidences of public control and support, but also for the acknowledged monopoly function of training leaders in each of the respective colonies. The publicness started to break down in 1766 with the founding of Queen's College (Rutgers). By ending Princeton's monopoly as the provincial college of New Jersey, Queen's led the way for the creation of "private" colleges. Over the next half century the vast multiplication of colleges nationwide effectively de-monopolized higher education in most of the states. Herbst saw the Dartmouth decision as the Supreme Court's sanction of the de-monopolizing trend, hence affirming the privatizing movement in higher education that had been taking place since 1766.

In a review of *From Crisis to Crisis* for the Summer 1984 *History of Education Quarterly* I challenged Herbst's use of the term "private" in describing both Queen's and the host of local colleges that emerged prior to 1819 and said, "His definition rests on function and clientele rather than on the presence or absence of state officials on the governing boards. . . . Private now equals local; public equals statewide." It even seemed to me ironic that Queen's, Herbst's first private college, was the only colonial college to emerge as a state university in the twentieth century. I found no new evidence in *Crisis* suggesting that "private" college promoters cited the Dartmouth decision as a stimulus for their colleges and held to my revision that the decision at best "gave guidelines for and limits to the college-state relationship; it did not separate the two."

Since the appearance of my review, Jurgen Herbst and I have had a lively correspondence on these issues. Herbst now concedes that the term "private" may not be the best denominator for the local colleges, but he holds fast to the importance of the Dartmouth decision—particularly as it related to the numerous quarrels between legislatures and colleges that took place before 1819. I too have taken a long look at my previous work.

On dating the emergence of the private/public distinction I still hold that it was a postwar phenomenon. But Jurgen Herbst has convinced me that the de-monopolization or localizing of higher education which began with the founding of Queen's and which signaled the death of the provincial college requires even more study by historians of education. Clearly something of great consequence was happening here. But exactly what? How were colleges defining their educational function to the student bodies and communities they served? In this localizing phenomenon lie the origins of the diverse, pluralistic system that characterizes twentieth-century American higher education as much, if not more so, than the public/private distinction. What should we call this localizing process? We need a name for it.

Finding that name has caused considerable consternation for many historians. According to Herbst, "The appearance of *private* colleges thus came to signal the effectiveness of *local* efforts at development." Lawrence Cremin discovered the same colleges in *American Education*, but said, "They were essentially *local* institutions . . . seen primarily as community—and in that sense *public*—institutions." Daniel Boorstin disliked both terms and concluded in the second volume of *The Americans*, "The distinctly American college was *neither public nor private*, but a *community* institution." Public, private, neither public nor private—what is the real definition of the local or community college? Possibly we should abandon the terms public and private until we can define the local college without them. (The italics are mine.)

In searching for this elusive name we must also pay greater attention to the antebellum state universities. Most of the recent literature that I have read focuses on the prewar denominational colleges, probably because there were so many more of them. It has been my observation that the same localizing forces shaped the state universities of the period. If a distinction between public and private was emerging before the Civil War, we would expect to see the state universities developing differently. I don't see that they did. As Cremin claims in *American Education*, "Most state universities during the pre-Civil War period were no more public, or enlightened, or university-like in character than the dozens of denominational colleges that surrounded them and competed with them for students." So what should we call all these institutions that seem so indistinguishable? I intend to suggest a name. But first I want to look again at the Dartmouth decision in light of Jurgen Herbst's steadfast position.

The Dartmouth decision seems to mesmerize most historians of higher education. Even those who agree with my interpretation of the impact of the decision seem compelled to see the case as a milestone in American educational history. In 1983 Eldon Johnson expanded the Dartmouth literature once again with "The Dartmouth College Case: The Neglected Educational Meaning" in the *Journal of the Early Republic*. Writing a year after *Crisis* appeared, he still affirmed that I had shown with "convincing documentation" that the case had not "immediately severed the college-state alliance." Nonetheless, he concluded that the "Dartmouth episode . . . was an event in the formative years of American higher education which helped shape the future." The existence of a Supreme Court decision in antebellum college development must be too irresistible to dismiss. Possibly I de-emphasized it too much. Having reviewed the decision and the ever-growing literature on it, I am prepared to offer a slightly different interpretation. The decision still should be approached from two angles: (1) its effect on Dartmouth and (2) its wider implications for the development of American higher education.

Looking at the decision in terms of Dartmouth, I now find the issue even stranger than before. Jurgen Herbst and I both agree that Dartmouth was a quasi-public or provincial college when it was founded in 1769. It had not surrendered its monopoly role in New Hampshire higher education by 1819, nor did it lose it after 1819. Not only did the Dartmouth trustees seek new alliances with the New Hampshire legislature in the 1820s, they also successfully defeated an attempt in the same legislature to charter a competing state university. Dartmouth retained its monopoly role in New Hampshire, in contrast to neighboring Vermont and to every other state except Rhode Island in which a provincial college existed. If the Dartmouth decision allowed state and private institutions to exist side by side, it did so almost everywhere except in the state directly addressed in the case! I am inclined to agree with Steven Novak that the significance of the case for Dartmouth was a victory for piety rather than for privateness.

Still we must look beyond Dartmouth. To say that the case was not important because it did not directly affect New Hampshire would be like saying the Dred Scott decision was unimportant because Scott was manumitted the next year. In the wider arena I think there is a greater significance to the decision than I have previously acknowledged.

My previous contention has been that a public/private distinction was not *commonly recognized* before the Civil War. However, I must now make it clear that the public/private distinction had obviously been made. After all, that is what the Supreme Court's decision was all about. The court clearly declared there were two kinds of institutions—public and private. It made the distinction, placed Dartmouth in the private category, and indicated that the two kinds of colleges were entitled to different kinds of immunities. Clearly in the minds of *some* people the distinction existed.

What is puzzling to me about the decision, and in my mind unfortunate and downright pernicious, is the fact that the distinction bore little if any resemblance to the existing form and function of American colleges. No college in 1819, or I would assert in 1986, was or wanted to be a *public* institution in the Court's sense of an agency or branch of government. How quickly those of us who teach in state universities rise up today to beat off any assertion by governors and legislatures that our institutions are state agencies and should be so administered. Nor did any college want to be merely a *private* eleemosynary foundation whose primary function was to hold, safeguard, and distribute the *funds* of a donor. Such private institutions are more akin to today's Ford, Rockefeller, and Carnegie Foundations. They aid education by distributing funds, but they do not educate. Several historians have noted the exaggerations in the Court's decision. Eldon Johnson observed that the Dartmouth decision "went too far." But why was the Court willing to issue an opinion that was so at odds with reality?[1]

I would assert that even the justices of the Court were not really interested in making a public/private distinction. They wanted to protect educational institutions from legislative tampering. It is clear that men like Justices Marshall and Story along with other prominent Federalists found legislative influence, particularly by Republicans, dangerous to an orderly society. Story clearly stated in his concurring opinion that all educational institutions, public and private, should be immune from legislative interference. But the Court would have had difficulty in providing such blanket protection. The New Hampshire Supreme Court had upheld the legislature's action on the ground that Dartmouth was a public institution. The trustees had not challenged the right of the state to tamper with a public college. To overturn the New Hampshire decision the Court merely had to place Dartmouth in the private category.

If neither the Dartmouth trustees nor the U.S. Supreme Court were really interested in the public/private distinction, but only in the use that could be made of these terms to achieve a victory for piety or against the Republicans, then it is not surprising that little mention was made of the decision by college sponsors in the prewar period. Why should other people cite a decision that did not fit their specific needs? Nonetheless, the deed had been done. After 1819 things would never be the same. Even if for all the wrong reasons, the terms public and private, and the immunities that each implied, had now been proclaimed and sanctioned as the law of the land. If Americans ever felt a need to differentiate the vast multiplicity of institutions that surrounded them, the Court had pointed the way. It was just a matter of time.

By the 1860s the college scene was simply too confusing. The old clarity of the function of the provincial college was slipping out of anyone's memory, and the headiness of the college boom was no longer new. College leaders needed a distinguishing tool to create a new order. Public and private now had a use. Eliot and others could easily make their institutions private simply by reaching for the terms the Court had offered. The Dartmouth decision had not been challenged for almost a half-century. It provided a truly *ancient* precedent for postwar Americans.

If the terms private and public were not really appropriate to the form of American colleges in 1819, I would argue that they were equally unfortunate choices after the Civil War. Private or public—is that really what Americans wanted their colleges to be? Is that the order they wanted to place on the diversity? Americans have long claimed that the coexistence of such institutions distinguishes their university system from Europe where dependence on the state is the rule. But is that a distinction to be proud of? In some European countries (Denmark is the example I know best) the state supports so-called private schools because the people believe that everyone is entitled to a fair portion of the public wealth, not merely those who conform to majority views. Yet in America, in both schools and colleges, the public/private distinction has forced us to say that only those students who attend institutions attached to the state are entitled to an education supported by the common funds to which all have contributed. Is that a distinction Americans wanted to make or a cul-de-sac they backed themselves into by insisting that private and public are the terms that define their system?

At the same time that Eliot advocated privateness at Harvard and state universities began to receive annual appropriations, another kind of institution emerged which has tended to go by the wayside as an American norm. In *The Separation* I called it a hybrid institution; the prime example was Cornell. In founding Cornell, Andrew D. White blended the individual gifts of Ezra Cornell with the Morrill land grant for New York. Cornell was thus the manifestation of multiple forms of philanthropy—private and public. White thought he was doing the natural, the American thing in blending these gifts. I suggest that the Cornell example, which was duplicated in the West at Purdue, provides a clue to unraveling the localizing phenomenon in the antebellum period. Cornell was founded as an object of philanthropy. Possibly the one word that best describes the American college or university is philanthropic—not public or private. (Cornell has obviously not gone by the wayside. But one may well think what we try to call Cornell today. Is it public or private? Do we feel compelled to fit Cornell into terms that do not really describe it?)

American colleges and universities have been founded and sustained by multiple philanthropies ever since the blending of the funds of John Harvard and the Massachusetts General Court. Herbst's provincial colleges were philanthropic as were the multitude of denominational and civic colleges that took away the older institutions' monopoly. Colonial and early state support took on a philanthropic character with occasional gifts, land grants, bank bonuses, and refunds from the revolutionary war. The federal land grants in the Northwest Ordinance and the 1862 Morrill Act were also philanthropic in nature. Today state universities strive to receive "lump sum" legislative appropriations as much as private colleges long for unrestricted donations. Private and public universities receive generous contributions in their annual alumni appeals. Clearly the graduates see both kinds of institutions as philanthropic. Despite the IRS's willingness to accept voluntary contributions to reduce the national debt, how many of us want to direct our philanthropy to a branch of government—a truly public institution in John Marshall's view? Possibly the truly American quality of our colleges and universities has been the availability of vast, multiple sources of philanthropy in the United States and the ability of American institutions to blend those diverse contributions—in the same way that the American university blends so many diverse studies and disciplines in contrast to its European counterpart.

Private, public, philanthropic—where do these words now leave my discussion with Jurgen Herbst on the Dartmouth College case? I hope my meandering has been with some purpose. Both Herbst and I agree that the terms public and private may not be the best to describe the multiplicity of colleges emerging in the first two decades of the nineteenth century, or for the ensuing decades up to the Civil War. We also agree that the Dartmouth College decision sanctioned a distinction between public and private, though we may differ on when that sanction became important and why.

What is even more significant is the fact that we both agree that the words or terms we call American institutions are crucial, though Herbst is more concerned with the legal implications of the words while I place the emphasis on their descriptive use. The words we choose, be they *provincial, public, private,* or *philanthropic,* tend to shape our conception of the form, function, and even the Americanness of our colleges and universities. Educators have at times, I believe, even changed the function of their institutions to fit the meaning of the words rather than the educational desires of their clientele. It seems to me that educators have let the lawyers and the judges tell them what their institutions really are. And that may well be a reality I have trouble accepting. Once an institution is defined in law, its function may well change over time to fit that legal category. But that could be the topic for another paper!

Jurgen Herbst and I agree that the name game is serious business. Choosing the wrong word is more than a simple case of mislabeling. As historians we need to find the right words to describe our antebellum colleges if we are to understand their function in American society and in American law. This choice of words calls for the best thought and exchange of ideas we can give it.

Jurgen Herbst

In *From Crisis to Crisis* I questioned John Whitehead's denial that the significance of the Dartmouth College case lay in its legal implications for the separation of college and state. Instead, I reaffirmed that traditional interpretation, basing my case on a comprehensive survey of the college-state relations throughout the entire preceding period from the founding of Harvard in 1636 to the Dartmouth decision in 1819.

What had prompted me to take another look at the circumstances and significance of the Dartmouth College case? As I stated in the preface to *From Crisis to Crisis*, it was the unrest of the 1960s on college campuses and the request I received in 1967 to prepare a statement on the relationship between civil and academic jurisdiction for use in federal court that started me off on my inquiries into the legal history of American higher education. In that history, the Dartmouth College case loomed large as the first instance of a college dispute reaching the United States Supreme Court. That fact persuaded me to take the case as the closing point for my investigation. Consequently—and this will help to underline the difference in approach and conclusions between John Whitehead and me—I saw many of the major legal events concerning the American colonial college as stepping stones on the way to the Dartmouth decision. The decision itself, though of great significance for the establishment in this country of fairly unique traditions of both public and private higher education, appeared in my view as the capstone of a series of similar legal cases concerning the longstanding disputes over the relative rights of college corporations vis-à-vis the overriding powers of public government.

The decision to wend my way along the major points of crisis in colonial college history while trying to look at them, as it were, from the standpoint of contemporaries, yet, at the same time, explaining much of what I found in the language of our own day, led to some of the issues under dispute between Whitehead and me. The changing definitions of public and private is a case in point.

Whitehead quite rightly observes that the usual definitions of public and private rest on the presence or absence of state officials on governing boards or on the acceptance or rejection of state support and influence in the colleges. But for the years I considered in *Crisis*, these definitions, I contend, do not adequately fit the situation.

At Queen's College, the one "private" college of the colonial period, the governor, council president, chief justice, and attorney general of New Jersey served on the board of trustees. In some private colleges founded after the Revolution, such as Blount in Tennessee, public officials also served on governing boards; in others, such as Transylvania in Kentucky and Dickinson in Pennsylvania, they merely served in their private capacities, not representing their public office. Still other private colleges—Washington College, Jefferson College, and Allegheny College in Pennsylvania—received legislative appropriations. On the other hand, throughout the colonial period Yale, Connecticut's provincial college, was governed by a board of trustees made up entirely of ministers.

The difficulty stems from the fact that during the colonial period the terms "public" and "private" were not used with reference to colleges. Colleges were chartered by either crown or colony to serve the people of a province. Before Queen's College opened in New Jersey, there had never been more than one college in a colony. The colonists regarded this college as their provincial institution, granted it a monopoly over higher education, and subjected it to public oversight by the colony's authorities. It was the colony's public or provincial college. But as far as terminology was concerned, it was simply a college.

Things changed when, with the chartering of Queen's College, the provincial college monopoly was breached for the first time. Then an opportunity was given to regard a college as something other than a provincial, i.e. public, institution. To make that distinction evident I wrote of Queen's as a forerunner of our private colleges. That choice of term, it seems, has not been very felicitous.

As a parenthetical remark I should add that I do not use the term "provincial college" in the colloquial sense as an institution of low repute in the hinterlands, but in its technical or legal sense as a colony's or province's one chief institution of higher education. During the colonial period the provincial college enjoyed and jealously guarded its monopoly on higher education in the province. The 1762 fight of the Harvard overseers against the incorporation of Queen's College in western Massachusetts is a prime example.

When I moved into the early nineteenth century, matters got more complicated yet. I then spoke of the new degree-granting institutions sponsored by localities, churches, denominations, promotional settlement associations, and professional groups as private colleges. This raises the legitimate question why a college sponsored by a locality, whether city or region, should be a private rather than public institution? So Whitehead asks quite justifiably: Were all these institutions private "in the way we think of the term today?"

The answer, of course, is no. They were not private in the way we think of that term today. They were nonpublic or nonprovincial in the way the antebellum generation thought of them. That is to say, they neither belonged among the newly founded state universities, nor were they older institutions officially founded or taken over by a state legislature, nor could they be considered in any sense as descendants of the old provincial colleges. They were something different, something new.

How to explain the newness? Working on the book I became impressed with European and American tradition that, for generations, had seen colleges and universities as attributes of territorial or provincial sovereignty or establishment. That tradition came to be questioned toward the end of the eighteenth century. Ethnic and denominational diversity provided the first impulse for this questioning, the expansion of settlement after the Revolution the second. Thus something new came into being—colleges whose sponsors no longer desired that territorial, provincial, or public connection that would make them agencies of the state. As a group, no official name existed for these institutions. Thus they could not then have been known as private colleges in the way the later nineteenth century would use that term. I wrote of them as private because, whether their governors knew it or not, they were on their way toward just that destination.

Whitehead has persuaded me that for the colonial as well as for the early national period my choice of the term "private" college was not a happy one. He has told me that, working his way back from the present, he found the modern public/private distinction emerging in the late 1860s and 1870s. That makes good sense to me. The "privatization" of Harvard and David Pott's thesis of the emergence of the denominational college after the Civil War fit into this picture. So what, then, do we call the nonprovincial colleges that came into their own during the one hundred years following the 1766 founding of Queen's?

Various suggestions have been made. As Whitehead shows, the terms local and community college have been used. It is clear, however, that not all nonpublic colleges were local institutions. Those sponsored by denominational groups, settlement or proprietary professional associations, though always to be found in a given locality, were nonetheless not sponsored or supported by their locality. To refer to them as community institutions imparts to the term community so wide a meaning that I see no reason not to include state-sponsored colleges under that term as well. It then becomes impossible to distinguish public from nonpublic institutions altogether.

Now Whitehead recommends that we view these nonpublic institutions as philanthropic foundations. As he at the same time extends the use of the term philanthropic to colonial and early state support of the provincial colleges and to the Northwest Ordinance and the Morrill Act I do not see how that definition helps us. It brings us back to the dilemma I encountered in the use of the term community: both designations prevent us from distinguishing between public and nonpublic institutions.

Whitehead claims that that precisely is the advantage of the term philanthropic: it is closer to reality. His prime examples are Cornell and Purdue where public and private philanthropy exist side by side and do not permit the use of either an unqualified public or nonpublic designation.

Quite apart from the fact that we do not normally find it very difficult to distinguish the public and the nonpublic parts of the two institutions cited, Whitehead's suggestion does not address itself to the problem I encountered: is there a term we can use to distinguish the nonprovincial, nonstate institutions that in the one hundred years after the founding of Queen's College appeared as a historically new phenomenon in the United States? If, in our concern for descriptive accuracy we hesitate to employ the term used by the Supreme Court in 1819, then, I am afraid, we may have to settle for the not very elegant, but nonetheless descriptively more accurate "nonprovincial" or "nonstate."

Another observation of Whitehead's in his review of my book refers to the place of irony and logic in historical presentation. As I mentioned before, Whitehead wonders about my definitions of public and private and seems to think that the presence or absence of state officials on governing boards or the acceptance or rejection of state support and influence in the colleges might have made for a tighter, a more logical argument. Perhaps, but, as I pointed out above, it would not have worked.

We may well find this inconvenient, ironic, or illogical, but it is a fact we cannot well ignore. Somehow we have to cope with the illogicality of history and incorporate it into our interpretive structures without straining the logic of our presentation. For example, Whitehead finds it ironic that after the 1819 decision the Dartmouth trustees would again turn to the legislature for help. They even had the chutzpah to ask for state payment of the legal expenses incurred in their suit. He also finds it ironic that Queen's College, New Jersey, the institution to which I point as the first to demonstrate to us the beginnings of what became the private college in America, is today Rutgers, The State University. He could have added that it is ironic also that Harvard, our first provincial college, a little more than two centuries after its founding became a private university.

There is more that can be said on this point. It is, indeed, not logical that governing boards of nonstate colleges have again and again asked for state support. But, we should ask ourselves, what might have prevented them from doing so? Only the fear, I submit, that state support might carry with it certain obligations. As the case of Bowdoin College in 1820 shows, that fear was outweighed by the desire for cash and other privileges. Aren't we familiar with similar instances in the twentieth century as well? Colleges do not want legislative interference in their affairs, but they look for all sorts of government grants.

I find all this ironic, too, but I guess it disturbs me less than it bothers Whitehead. I tend to think that irony and illogicality are the stuff of history. As I tell my undergraduates in class, the history out there is not logic. Our history books and lectures, to be sure, had better be written and presented with excruciating care for logic if we expect anyone to read and comprehend them. But that's not the same as saying that history happens according to our rules of logic.

And finally, the meaning of the Dartmouth College case decision of the United States Supreme Court: Whitehead wrote in his book and repeats in his review that the Dartmouth decision did no more than give "guidelines for and limits to the college-state relationship. . . ." In the present discussion he says that the case was not a watershed and "did not affirm a widely accepted public-private distinction." I present the decision as the *magna carta* of the American system of higher education in which private and public institutions develop side by side, and the private colleges are protected against state violation of their charter without their consent.

Why do Whitehead and I differ? The reasons have much to do with our approaches to history. While Whitehead judges the major significance of the case to lie in what did or did not happen in the decades following the Supreme Court decision, I see it in the issues the decision had laid to rest in 1819 and in the avenues it had thereby opened for college development. As Whitehead fails to turn up any antebellum college sponsor who viewed or used the Dartmouth decision as a stimulus to private college development, he reports that he cannot find a "widely accepted" public/private distinction. I, on the other hand, see the decision as the terminus of a debate that had begun with Yale President Thomas Clap's dispute with the Connecticut Assembly, had found its climax in the struggles of the College of Philadelphia trustees with the Pennsylvania legislature, had then been revived again by the governors of Liberty Hall and Davidson academies, and had reached its definitive end in the Dartmouth decision. Thus, I evaluate that decision for its importance as a basis for the subsequent legal history of American higher education.

While Whitehead focuses on events and popular perceptions in the antebellum decades I, having traced legal antecedents in the colonial and early national period, write of long-range legal developments. From Whitehead's angle of vision, the Dartmouth decision revealed its *full* significance for the history of American higher education only after the Civil War; from my point of view it constituted a decisive *legal* turning point already in 1819.

Whitehead thinks it "unfortunate and downright pernicious" that the public/private distinction made by the Supreme Court in 1819 "bore little if any resemblance to the existing form and function of American colleges," that not even the justices of the Court "were really interested in making a public/private distinction," and that their purpose was "to protect educational institutions from legislative tampering." Admittedly, these are speculations, but I disagree with all three of them. I can see nothing unfortunate or pernicious in contemporary reality not then corresponding to a judicial view. Why should it? The Court's purpose was to set guidelines for the future, not to describe things as they then were. Given the long and technically highly complex history of the English law of corporations, the transformation of the legal distinction between English civil and charitable corporations into American public and private corporations was for the justices a challenging task. John Marshall and Joseph Story, as Whitehead himself writes, were indeed particularly interested in this subject. And, I submit, it may be doubted that the justices were any more interested in protecting educational institutions from government interference than they were in a far more important matter: to protect American business corporations under the contract clause of the Constitution from arbitrary legislative amendments or repeals of their charters.

How crucial is Whitehead's observation that few college founders referred to the Dartmouth decision as having encouraged the growth of private colleges? In a paper given at the April 1985 American Educational Research Association meeting in Chicago I countered with a question of my own: How often in the nineteenth century did the founders of turnpike and bridge companies, the entrepreneurs of railroads and canals, of iron smelters and lumber mills refer to the Dartmouth decision when they applied for charters for their enterprises? Whitehead responded that they did indeed quote from that decision, but not before the 1870s.

I have no quarrel with Whitehead on that point. I believe he is correct. But I was thinking of the decades between 1819 and 1870 when, due to Marshall's decision, the private corporation became *the* American way of doing business. That railroads and other private businesses prospered by happily accepting, even demanding, generous public subsidies may be illogical and ironic, indeed, but it did nothing to weaken the faith in free enterprise and private business as the nation's guardian angels.

As to whether there was a difference in the enthusiasm or lack of it shown by state legislatures in the chartering of public vis-à-vis private colleges in the period from 1829 to 1850, I am not prepared to go beyond impressions I gained from an admittedly cursory overview. I found that the chartering of private colleges in the state legislatures more often than not was routine business, done without much debate, unless the issue of denominational rivalry happened to be involved. It was otherwise with the promoters of public universities and colleges. They, like the promoters of public business corporations—public utilities, for example—required special pleading and extended legislative argument. In antebellum America it was cumbersome and frustrating to get support for chartering or maintaining a state university. It is hard to forget Philip Lindsley's poignant complaint when he, as president of the University of Nashville, found that he had no private sect or party "to praise, puff, glorify, and fight" for his institution. So why should college sponsors trot out the Dartmouth decision? At best they would have wasted their time; at worst they might have called a legislature's attention to the decision's reserve clause. So they were well advised to leave well enough alone.

The point I wanted to make is that after the Dartmouth decision we encounter no further serious challenge to the side-by-side existence of public and private colleges. The real significance of that arrangement—the essence of the American system of higher education—appears when one adopts a comparative perspective and looks to other countries. Almost everywhere else, public institutions are the rule, private the exception.

So, as I said, I'll stick to my guns and will say it once more: the Dartmouth decision laid the legal foundations on which our present public and private institutions and systems of higher education have been built. If the decision was not cited every time a new institution of higher education appeared in the United States, it only shows, I believe, how firmly entrenched the notion of the side-by-side existence of private and public institutions had become. In Whitehead's words, there may not have been a need for a *magna carta*. "College fever" could have spread without the decision. But, as we often say, it sure helped, and it remains the key to understanding that which is "American" about American higher education.

Notes

1. One article in the recent literature on the Dartmouth College case clearly challenges my position that the Court's decision was at odds with reality. Bruce A. Campbell revives the traditional interpretation of the beneficent effects of the decision with added emphasis in "Dartmouth College as a Civil Liberties Case: The Formation of Constitutional Policy," *Kentucky Law Journal* 70 (1981–82): 643–706.

    Campbell claims that the case was beneficial because it dealt with the reality of the "negative American experience with relations between colleges and governments from the late colonial into the early national periods." Looking at the college-state relation from 1740 to the Dartmouth case, Campbell asserts, "legislative threats to or attacks on colleges had produced at least stagnation in and often serious injury to the institutions and never any substantial permanent gain for education or government. In light of this record, the benign 'public' to whom Chief Justice Richardson thought colleges ought to be responsible was simply an unreal abstraction."

    With this background of college-state relations, Campbell argues that the Court stretched and imaginatively adapted the English common law on private eleemosynary corporations to protect Dartmouth from state encroachment because the English law "did not fit the American situation." To Campbell, John Marshall shaped constitutional policy to fit a real need to protect American colleges.

    Campbell's factual basis for the "negative experience" is highly questionable. He claims, "Functionally, Dartmouth had always been private, with only limited, sporadic contact with the state." This is at odds with both my work and Jurgen Herbst's. He calls the New Hampshire legislature's action an "attack." This is contrary to Eldon Johnson's perceptive analysis of the educational goals of New Hampshire governor William Plumer. He ignores the substantial financial aid given to such colleges as Yale and Harvard during this period.

    Given this problem with the facts of the issue, I do not see that the inclusion of Campbell's article in the text would advance the dialogue between Herbst and me. Herbst does not take issue with Campbell as strongly as I do but agrees that it is difficult to know exactly what Campbell means by "negative experience" and the injury that the colleges sustained. The article does deserve to be noted as a part of the recent Dartmouth literature.

BLACK TRUSTEES ABOUND AT AMERICA'S MAJOR COLLEGES AND UNIVERSITIES

At the highest-ranked universities and liberal arts colleges, black presidents are almost never found, and very few of these schools have more than a smattering of black faculty. But just as most major corporations have been diligent in appointing some blacks to their boards of directors, a large number of the nation's highest-ranked colleges and universities have named a politically correct number of black trustees.

During the late 1960s it became fashionable in corporate America to appoint one or two African Americans to a company's board of directors. In most cases these directors who were black were window dressing to deflect public criticism of the company's hiring and contracting policies. For banks and other financial institutions, the presence of black directors provided useful cover for redlining practices that denied credit to black neighborhoods. For the most part the opinions and wisdom of these early black corporate directors were solicited only on racial and social issues.

Today, nearly every major American corporation has enough blacks on its board of directors to roughly mirror the black percentage of the American population. Blacks appointed to corporate boards are usually distinguished black professionals, former politicians, academics, and business people who are well versed in the protocols of big business. They tend to be economic conservatives who will almost never publicly challenge a corporation's hiring policies or marketing practices in black communities.

The undisputed champion of African-American board members is attorney, Bill Clinton confidant, and consummate insider Vernon Jordan, a senior managing director at Lazard Freres in New York City. Jordan now sits on at least 10 corporate boards.

In the 1970s, too, American colleges and universities followed the lead of corporate America. Gradually they began to appoint African Americans to their boards of trustees. Once again, these trustees tended to produce racial cover. Issues such as South African investment, lily-white faculties, and an absence of black students were easier to defend when blacks served on the board of trustees of colleges and universities. Black trustees at institutions of higher education were held up as evidence that a college or university was serious about promoting racial diversity when in fact most were doing very little to achieve higher levels of black students, administrators, or faculty. In many cases black trustees were expected to explain shortfalls in a university's racial progress, to deal with disciplinary problems with black students, pacify radical tendencies among black faculty, and to validate established white opinion on the nature of social and economic problems in the inner city.

Political Correctness Invades the News Pages: Successful Blacks Are Held to Be "Inauthentic"

In a discussion of racial diversity in Internet-related companies, a recent article in *The Washington Post* (May 8, 2000) makes the following statement:

"General Colin Powell and Franklin D. Raines, chairman of Fannie Mac, are too prestigious to be considered representatives of racial diversity, and that is true of the people of color who serve on the boards of other local Internet companies."

Black Trustees at the Nation's Highest-Ranked Universities, 2000

(Listed According to the Highest Percentage of Black Trustees)

Institution	Total Trustees	Black Trustees	Percent Black
University of Michigan	8	2	25.0%
Univ. of N.C.-Chapel Hill	13	2	15.4
Brown University	40	6	15.0
Harvard University	7	1	14.3
Yale University	16	2	12.5
Princeton University	40	5	12.5
Stanford University	34	4	11.8
Cornell University	64	7	10.9
Emory University	38	4	10.5
University of Notre Dame	56	6	10.7
Georgetown University	42	4	9.5
Columbia University	24	2	8.3
Duke University	37	3	8.1
Washington University	54	4	7.4
Dartmouth College	16	1	6.2
University of Virginia	16	1	6.2
Johns Hopkins University	99	6	6.1
Northwestern University	70	4	5.7
Mass. Inst. of Technology	73	4	5.5
Rice University	20	1	5.0
University of Pennsylvania	91	3	3.3
Calif. Inst. of Technology	67	2	3.0
Carnegie Mellon Univ.	103	3	2.9
Univ. of Calif.-Los Angeles	36	1	2.8
Univ. of Calif.-Berkeley	114	3	2.6
University of Chicago	44	1	2.3
Vanderbilt University	55	1	1.8
TOTAL	**1,277**	**83**	**6.5**

Source: *Survey by IBHE RESEARCH DEPARTMENT.*

Black Trustees at the Nation's Highest-Ranked Liberal Arts Colleges, 2000

(Colleges Listed According to the Highest Percentage of Black Trustees)

Institution	Total Trustees	Black Trustees	Percent Black
Wesleyan University	30	6	20.0%
Amherst College	21	4	19.0
Mount Holyoke College	28	4	14.3
Williams College	22	3	13.6
Grinnell College	37	5	13.5
Obertin College	30	4	13.3
Haverford College	32	4	12.5
Bryn Mawr College	33	4	12.1
Smith College	25	3	12.0
Carleton College	44	5	11.4
Wellesley College	37	4	10.8
Swarthmore College	39	4	10.3
Trinity College	30	3	10.0
Vassar College	30	3	10.0
Bowdoin College	48	4	8.3
Bates College	38	3	7.9
Macalester College	28	2	7.1
Davidson College	50	3	6.0
Sewanee College	18	1	5.6
Pomona College	38	2	5.3
Middlebury College	28	1	3.6
Washington & Lee	29	1	3.4
Connecticut College	32	1	3.1
Colby College	32	1	3.1
Hamilton College	34	1	2.9
TOTAL	**813**	**76**	**9.3**

Note: Among the nation's 25 highest-ranked liberal arts colleges, Claremont McKenna College and Colgate University did not respond to the JBHE survey.

Source: JBHE Research Department.

Today black trustees of our major colleges and universities tend no longer to be treated as tokens. Institutions of higher education are confident that their racial policies are progressive. Even racially conservative faculty have come to realize that black students have better things to do than organize campus protests. Accordingly, black trustees are increasingly part of the normal governance of institutions of higher education.

Black Trustees at High-Ranking Universities

JBHE has conducted a survey on the racial makeup of the board of trustees of the nation's highest-ranking universities and the highest-ranking liberal arts colleges. All of the responding institutions had at least one black person on their board of trustees. For the 27 highest-ranked universities, we found a total of 83 blacks among the 1,277 trustees at these institutions. Thus, blacks make up 6.5 percent of all trustees at these high-ranking universities.

Cornell has the most black trustees with seven. Brown, Notre Dame, and Johns Hopkins each have six black trustees. Seven schools have only a single black trustee. They are Harvard, Dartmouth, Rice, the University of Virginia, the University of Chicago, UCLA, and Vanderbilt.

At 10 of the high-ranking universities, blacks make up 10 percent or more of all trustees. Leading the list is the University of Michigan at which two of the eight trustees, or 25 percent of the total, are black. Five of the schools at which 10 percent or more of the trustees are black are Ivy League institutions. They are Brown, Harvard, Yale, Princeton, and Cornell. This past spring, for the first time in the institution's 364-year history, Harvard appointed a black person to its eight-member board of overseers.

At the other end of the spectrum, five schools have a board of trustees that is less than 3 percent black. They are Carnegie Mellon, Berkeley, UCLA, Vanderbilt, and the University of Chicago.

Black Trustees at High-Ranking Liberal Arts Colleges

Blacks have a slightly better representation on the board of trustees of the 25 highest-ranking liberal arts colleges than on the board of high-ranking universities. Among the schools surveyed by JBHE, there are 76 blacks among the 81.3 trustees at these schools making up 9.3 percent of all trustees. Once again, all schools have at least one black trustee.

Wesleyan has the most black trustees in this group with six. There are five black trustees at Grinnell College in Iowa and Carleton College in Minnesota, two institutions located in areas with a very small black population. Six high-ranking liberal arts colleges have only one black trustee. They are Sewanee College, Middlebury College, Connecticut College, Colby College, Hamilton College, and Washington and Lee University.

On a percentage basis, Wesleyan again leads the list. Twenty percent of all Wesleyan trustees are black. Wesleyan is followed closely by Amherst College, where 19 percent of the trustees are black. Fourteen of the 25 high-ranking liberal arts colleges surveyed had boards of trustees that are at least 10 percent black. Only one board—at Hamilton College—was less than 3 percent black.

Tracing the Growing Impact of Servant-Leadership

Larry C. Spears

The servant-leader is servant first. It begins with the natural feeling that one wants to serve. Then conscious choice brings one to aspire to lead. The best test is: do those served grow as persons; do they, while being served, become healthier, wiser, freer, more autonomous, more likely themselves to become servants?

—Robert K. Greenleaf

The mightiest of rivers are first fed by many small trickles of water. This observation is also an apt way of conveying my belief that the growing number of practitioners of servant-leadership has increased from a trickle to a river. On a global scale it is not yet a mighty river. However, it is an expanding river, and one with a deep current.

The servant-leader concept continues to grow in its influence and impact. In fact, we have witnessed an unparalleled explosion of interest and practice of servant-leadership in the 1990s. In many ways, it can truly be said that the times are only now beginning to catch up with Robert Greenleaf's visionary call to servant-leadership.

Servant-leadership, now in its third decade as a specific leadership and management concept, continues to create a quiet revolution in workplaces around the world. Both this book and this introduction are intended to provide a broad overview of the growing influence this unique concept of servant-leadership is having on people and their workplaces.

As we near the end of the twentieth century, we are beginning to see that traditional, autocratic, and hierarchical modes of leadership are yielding to a newer model—one based on teamwork and community, one that seeks to involve others in decision making, one strongly based in ethical and caring behavior, and one that is attempting to enhance the personal growth of workers while improving the caring and quality of our many institutions. This emerging approach to leadership and service is called *servant-leadership*.

The words *servant* and *leader* are usually thought of as being opposites. When two opposites are brought together in a creative and meaningful way, a paradox emerges. And so the words *servant* and *leader* have been brought together to create the paradoxical idea of servant-leadership. The basic idea of servant-leadership is both logical and sensible. Since the time of the industrial revolution, managers have tended to view people as objects; institutions have considered workers as cogs within a machine. In the past few decades we have witnessed a shift in that long-held view. Standard practices are rapidly shifting toward the ideas put forward by Robert Greenleaf, Stephen Covey, Peter Senge, Max DePree, and many others who suggest that there is a better way to manage our organizations in the twenty-first century.

Today there is a much greater recognition of the need for a more team-oriented approach to leadership and management. Robert Greenleaf's writings on the subject of servant-leadership helped to get this movement started, and his views have had a profound and growing effect on many.

Robert K. Greenleaf

Despite all the buzz about modern leadership techniques, no one knows better than Greenleaf what really matters.

—*Working Woman* magazine

The term *servant-leadership* was first coined in a 1970 essay by Robert K. Greenleaf (1904–1990), entitled *The Servant as Leader*. Greenleaf, born in Terre Haute, Indiana, spent most of his organizational life in the field of management research, development, and education at AT&T. Following a 40-year career at AT&T, Greenleaf enjoyed a second career that lasted 25 years, during which time he served as an influential consultant to a number of major institutions, including Ohio University, MIT, Ford Foundation, R. K. Mellon Foundation, the Mead Corporation, the American Foundation for Management Research, and Lilly Endowment Inc. In 1964 Greenleaf also founded the Center for Applied Ethics, which was renamed the Robert K. Greenleaf Center in 1985 and is now headquartered in Indianapolis.

As a lifelong student of how things get done in organizations, Greenleaf distilled his observations in a series of essays and books on the theme of "The Servant as Leader"—the objective of which was to stimulate thought and action for building a better, more caring society.

The Servant-as-Leader Idea

The idea of the servant as leader came partly out of Greenleaf's half century of experience in working to shape large institutions. However, the event that crystallized Greenleaf's thinking came in the 1960s, when he read Hermann Hesse's short novel *Journey to the East*—an account of a mythical journey by a group of people on a spiritual quest.

After reading this story, Greenleaf concluded that the central meaning of it was that the great leader is first experienced as a servant to others, and that this simple fact is central to his or her greatness. True leadership emerges from those whose primary motivation is a deep desire to help others.

In 1970, at the age of 66, Greenleaf published *The Servant as Leader*, the first of a dozen essays and books on servant-leadership.[1] Since that time, more than 500,000 copies of his books and essays have been sold worldwide. Slowly but surely, Greenleaf's servant-leadership writings have made a deep, lasting impression on leaders, educators, and many others who are concerned with issues of leadership, management, service, and personal growth.

What Is Servant-Leadership?

In all of his works, Greenleaf discusses the need for a new kind of leadership model, a model that puts serving others—including employees, customers, and community—as the number one priority. Servant-leadership emphasizes increased service to others, a holistic approach to work, promoting a sense of community, and the sharing of power in decision making.

Who *is* a servant-leader? Greenleaf said that the servant-leader is one who is a servant first. In *The Servant as Leader* he wrote, "It begins with the natural feeling that one wants to serve, to serve first. Then conscious choice brings one to aspire to lead. The difference manifests itself in the care taken by the servant—first to make sure that other people's highest priority needs are being served. The best test is: Do those served grow as persons; do they, while being served, become healthier, wiser, freer, more autonomous, more likely themselves to become servants?"[2]

It is important to stress that servant-leadership is *not* a "quick-fix" approach. Nor is it something that can be quickly instilled within an institution. At its core, servant-leadership is a long-term, transformational approach to life and work—in essence, a way of being—that has the potential for creating positive change throughout our society.

Ten Characteristics of the Servant-Leader

Servant leadership deals with the reality of power in everyday life—its legitimacy, the ethical restraints upon it and the beneficial results that can be attained through the appropriate use of power.

—*The New York Times*

After some years of carefully considering Greenleaf's original writings, I have identified a set of 10 characteristics of the servant-leader that I view as being of critical importance. The following characteristics are central to the development of servant-leaders:

1. *Listening:* Leaders have traditionally been valued for their communication and decision-making skills. While these are also important skills for the servant-leader, they need to be reinforced by a deep commitment to listening intently to others. The servant-leader seeks to identify the will of a group and helps clarify that will. He or she seeks to listen receptively to what is being said (and not said!). Listening also encompasses getting in touch with one's own inner voice and seeking to understand what one's body, spirit, and mind are communicating. Listening, coupled with regular periods of reflection, is essential to the growth of the servant-leader.

2. *Empathy:* The servant-leader strives to understand and empathize with others. People need to be accepted and recognized for their special and unique spirits. One assumes the good intentions of coworkers and does not reject them as people, even while refusing to accept their behavior or performance. The most successful servant-leaders are those who have become skilled empathetic listeners. It is interesting to note that Robert Greenleaf developed a course in "receptive listening" in the 1950s for the Wainwright House in New York. This course continues to be offered to the present day.

3. *Healing:* Learning to heal is a powerful force for transformation and integration. One of the great strengths of servant-leadership is the potential for healing one's self and others. Many people have broken spirits and have suffered from a variety of emotional hurts. Although this is a part of being human, servant-leaders recognize that they have an opportunity to "help make whole" those with whom they come in contact. In *The Servant as Leader* Greenleaf writes: "There is something subtle communicated to one who is being served and led if, implicit in the compact between servant-leader and led, is the understanding that the search for wholeness is something they share."[3]

4. *Awareness:* General awareness, and especially self-awareness, strengthens the servant-leader. Making a commitment to foster awareness can be scary—you never know what you may discover!

   Awareness also aids one in understanding issues involving ethics and values. It lends itself to being able to view most situations from a more integrated, holistic position. As Greenleaf observed: "Awareness is not a giver of solace—it is just the opposite. It is a disturber and an awakener. Able leaders are usually sharply awake and reasonably disturbed. They are not seekers after solace. They have their own inner serenity."[4]

5. *Persuasion:* Another characteristic of servant-leaders is a reliance on persuasion, rather than using one's positional authority, in making decisions within an organization. The servant-leader seeks to convince others, rather than coerce compliance. This particular element offers one of the clearest distinctions between the traditional authoritarian model and that of servant-leadership. The servant-leader is effective at building consensus within groups. This emphasis on persuasion over coercion probably has its roots within the beliefs of The Religious Society of Friends (Quakers), the denomination with which Robert Greenleaf himself was most closely allied.

6. *Conceptualization:* Servant-leaders seek to nurture their abilities to "dream great dreams." The ability to look at a problem (or an organization) from a conceptualizing perspective means that one must think beyond day-to-day realities. For many managers this is a characteristic that requires discipline and practice. The traditional manager is consumed by the need to achieve short-term operational goals. The manager who wishes to also be a servant-leader must stretch his or her thinking to encompass broader-based conceptual thinking. Within organizations, conceptualization is, by its very nature, the proper role of boards of trustees or directors. Unfortunately, boards can sometimes become involved in the day-to-day operations (something that should always be discouraged!) and fail to provide the visionary concept for

an institution. Trustees need to be mostly conceptual in their orientation, staffs need to be mostly operational in their perspective, and the most effective CEOs and managers probably need to develop both perspectives. Servant-leaders are called to seek a delicate balance between conceptual thinking and a day-to-day focused approach.

7. *Foresight:* Closely related to conceptualization, the ability to foresee the likely outcome of a situation is hard to define, but easy to identify. One knows it when one sees it. Foresight is a characteristic that enables the servant-leader to understand the lessons from the past, the realities of the present, and the likely consequence of a decision for the future. It is also deeply rooted within the intuitive mind. As such, one can conjecture that foresight is the one servant-leader characteristic with which one may be born. All other characteristics can be consciously developed. There hasn't been a great deal written on foresight. It remains a largely unexplored area in leadership studies, but one most deserving of careful attention.

8. *Stewardship:* Peter Block (author of *Stewardship* and *The Empowered Manager*) has defined stewardship as "holding something in trust for another."[5] Robert Greenleaf's view of all institutions was one in which CEOs, staffs, and trustees all played significant roles in holding their institutions in trust for the greater good of society. Servant-leadership, like stewardship, assumes first and foremost a commitment to serving the needs of others. It also emphasizes the use of openness and persuasion rather than control.

9. *Commitment to the growth of people:* Servant-leaders believe that people have an intrinsic value beyond their tangible contributions as workers. As such, the servant-leader is deeply committed to the growth of each and every individual within his or her institution. The servant-leader recognizes the tremendous responsibility to do everything within his or her power to nurture the personal, professional, and spiritual growth of employees. In practice, this can include (but is not limited to) concrete actions such as making available funds for personal and professional development, taking a personal interest in the ideas and suggestions from everyone, encouraging worker involvement in decision making, and actively assisting laid-off workers to find other employment.

10. *Building community:* The servant-leader senses that much has been lost in recent human history as a result of the shift from local communities to large institutions as the primary shaper of human lives. This awareness causes the servant-leader to seek to identify some means for building community among those who work within a given institution. Servant-leadership suggests that true community can be created among those who work in businesses and other institutions. Greenleaf said: "All that is needed to rebuild community as a viable life form for large numbers of people is for enough servant-leaders to show the way, not by mass movements, but by each servant-leader demonstrating his own unlimited liability for a quite specific community-related group."[6]

These 10 characteristics of servant-leadership are by no means exhaustive. However, I believe that the ones listed serve to communicate the power and promise that this concept offers to those who are open to its invitation and challenge.

Tracing the Growing Impact of Servant-Leadership

Servant leadership has emerged as one of the dominant philosophies being discussed in the world today.

—Indianapolis Business Journal

Servant-Leadership as an Institutional Model

Servant-leadership principles are being applied in significant ways in a half-dozen major areas. The first area has to do with servant leadership as an institutional philosophy and model. Servant-leadership crosses all boundaries and is being applied by a wide variety of people working with for-profit businesses; not-for-profit corporations; and churches, universities, health care, and foundations.

In recent years, a number of institutions have jettisoned their old hierarchical models and replaced them with a servant-leader approach. Servant-leadership advocates a group-oriented approach to analysis and decision making as a means of strengthening institutions and improving society. It also emphasizes the power of persuasion and seeking consensus, over the old top-down form of leadership. Some people have likened this to turning the hierarchical pyramid upside down. Servant-leadership holds that the primary purpose of a business should be to create a positive impact on its employees and community, rather than using profit as the sole motive.

Many individuals within institutions have adopted servant-leadership as a guiding philosophy. An increasing number of companies have adopted servant-leadership as part of their corporate philosophy or as a foundation for their mission statement. Among these are the Sisters of St. Joseph's Health System (Ann Arbor, Michigan), The Toro Company (Minneapolis, Minnesota), Schneider Engineering Company (Indianapolis, Indiana), Townsend & Bottum Family of Companies (Ann Arbor, Michigan), and TDIndustries (Dallas, Texas).

TDIndustries, one of the earliest practitioners of servant-leadership in the corporate setting, is a Dallas-based heating and plumbing contracting firm that was recently profiled in Robert Levering and Milton Moskowitz's best-selling book, *The 100 Best Companies to Work for in America*. In their profile of TDIndustries, the authors discuss the longtime influence that servant-leadership has had on the company. TDI's founder, Jack Lowe Sr. stumbled upon *The Servant as Leader* essay in the early 1970s and began to distribute copies of it to his employees. They were invited to read through the essay and then to gather in small groups to discuss its meaning. The belief that managers should serve their employees became an important value for TDIndustries.

Twenty-five years later, Jack Lowe Jr. continues to use servant-leadership as the guiding philosophy for TDI. Levering and Moskowitz note: "Even today, any TDPartner who supervises at least one person must go through training in servant-leadership."[7] In addition, all new employees continue to receive a copy of *The Servant as Leader* essay.

Some businesses have begun to view servant-leadership as an important framework that is helpful (and necessary) for ensuring the long-term effects of related management and leadership approaches such as continuous quality improvement and systems thinking. Several of the authors represented in this book suggest that institutions which want to create meaningful change may be best served in starting with servant-leadership as the foundational understanding and then building on it through any number of related approaches.

Servant-leadership has influenced many noted writers, thinkers, and leaders. Max DePree, chairman of the Herman Miller Company and author of *Leadership Is an Art* and *Leadership Jazz* has said, "The servanthood of leadership needs to be felt, understood, believed, and practiced."[8] And Peter Senge, author of *The Fifth Discipline*, has said that he tells people "not to bother reading any other book about leadership until you first read Robert Greenleaf's book, *Servant-Leadership*. I believe it is the most singular and useful statement on leadership I've come across."[9] In recent years, a growing number of leaders and readers have "rediscovered" Robert Greenleaf's own writings through DePree and Senge's books.

Education and Training of Not-for-Profit Trustees

A second major application of servant-leadership is its pivotal role as the theoretical and ethical basis for "trustee education." Greenleaf wrote extensively on servant-leadership as it applies to the roles of boards of directors and trustees within institutions. His essays on these applications are widely distributed among directors of for-profit and nonprofit organizations. In his essay *Trustees as Servants* Greenleaf urged trustees to ask themselves two central questions: "Whom do you serve?" and "For what purpose?"[10]

Servant-leadership suggests that boards of trustees need to undergo a radical shift in how they approach their roles. Trustees who seek to act as servant-leaders can help to create institutions of great depth and quality. Over the past decade, two of America's largest grant-making foundations (Lilly Endowment Inc. and the W. K. Kellogg Foundation) have sought to encourage the development of programs designed to educate and train not-for-profit boards of trustees to function as servant-leaders.

Community Leadership Programs

The third application of servant-leadership concerns its deepening role in community leadership organizations across the country. A growing number of community leadership groups are using Greenleaf Center resources as part of their own education and training efforts. Some have been doing so for more than 15 years.

The National Association for Community Leadership (NACL) has adopted servant-leadership as a special focus. Recently, NACL named Robert Greenleaf as the posthumous recipient of its National Community Leadership Award. This award is given annually to honor an individual whose work has made a significant impact on the development of community leadership worldwide.

M. Scott Peck, who has written about the importance of building true community, says the following in *A World Waiting to Be Born:* "In his work on servant-leadership, Greenleaf posited that the world will be saved if it can develop just three truly well-managed, large institutions—one in the private sector, one in the public sector, and one in the nonprofit sector. He believed—and I know— that such excellence in management will be achieved through an organizational culture of civility routinely utilizing the mode of community."[11]

Service-Learning Programs

The fourth application involves servant-leadership and experiential education. During the past 20 years experiential education programs of all sorts have sprung up in virtually every college and university—and, increasingly, in secondary schools, too. Experiential education, or "learning by doing," is now a part of most students' educational experience.

Around 1980, a number of educators began to write about the linkage between the servant-leader concept and experiential learning under a new term called "service-learning." It is service-learning that has become a major focus for experiential education programs in the past few years.

The National Society for Experiential Education (NSEE) has adopted service-learning as one of its major program areas. NSEE has published a massive three-volume work called *Combining Service and Learning*, which brings together many articles and papers about service-learning—several dozen of which discuss servant-leadership as the philosophical basis for experiential learning programs.

Leadership Education

The fifth application of servant-leadership concerns its use in both formal and informal education and training programs. This is taking place through leadership and management courses in colleges and universities, as well as through corporate training programs. A number of undergraduate and graduate courses on management and leadership incorporate servant-leadership within their course curricula. Several colleges and universities now offer specific courses on servant-leadership. Also, a number of noted leadership authors, including Peter Block, Ken Blanchard, Max DePree, and Peter Senge, have all acclaimed the servant-leader concept as an overarching framework that is compatible with, and enhancing of, other leadership and management models such as total quality management, learning organizations, and community-building.

In the area of corporate education and training programs, dozens of management and leadership consultants now utilize servant-leadership materials as part of their ongoing work with corporations. Some of these companies have included AT&T, the Mead Corporation, Arthur Andersen, and Gulf Oil of Canada. A number of consultants and educators are now touting the benefits to be gained in building a total quality management approach upon a servant-leadership foundation. Through internal training and education, institutions are discovering that servant-leadership can truly improve how business is developed and conducted, while still successfully turning a profit.

Personal Transformation

The sixth application of servant-leadership involves its use in programs relating to personal growth and transformation. Servant-leadership operates at both the institutional and personal levels.

For individuals it offers a means to personal growth—spiritually, professionally, emotionally, and intellectually. It has ties to the ideas of M. Scott Peck (*The Road Less Traveled*), Parker Palmer (*The Active Life*), Ann McGee-Cooper (*You Don't Have to Go Home from Work Exhausted!*), and others who have written on expanding human potential. A particular strength of servant-leadership is that it encourages everyone to actively seek opportunities to both serve and lead others, thereby setting up the potential for raising the quality of life throughout society. A number of individuals are working to integrate the servant-leader concept into various programs involving both men's and women's self-awareness groups and 12-step programs like Alcoholics Anonymous. There is also a fledgling examination under way of the servant-leader as a previously unidentified Jungian archetype.

Servant-Leadership and Multiculturalism

For some people, the word *servant* prompts an immediate negative connotation, due to the oppression that many workers—particularly women and people of color—have historically endured. For some, it may take a while to accept the positive usage of this word *servant*. However, those who are willing to dig a little deeper come to understand the inherent spiritual nature of what is intended by the pairing of *servant* and *leader*. The startling paradox of the term *servant-leadership* serves to prompt new insights.

In an article titled, "Pluralistic Reflections on Servant-Leadership," Juana Bordas has written: "Many women, minorities and people of color have long traditions of servant-leadership in their cultures. Servant-leadership has very old roots in many of the indigenous cultures. Cultures that were holistic, cooperative, communal, intuitive and spiritual. These cultures centered on being guardians of the future and respecting the ancestors who walked before."[12]

Women leaders and authors are now writing and speaking about servant-leadership as a twenty-first century leadership philosophy that is most appropriate for both women and men to embrace. Patsy Sampson, who is former president of Stephens College in Columbia, Missouri, is one such person. In an essay on women and servant-leadership she writes: "So-called (service-oriented) feminine characteristics are exactly those which are consonant with the very best qualities of servant-leadership."[13]

A Growing Movement

Servant-leadership works like the consensus building that the Japanese are famous for. Yes, it takes a while on the front end; everyone's view is solicited, though everyone also understands that his view may not ultimately prevail. But once the consensus is forged, watch out: With everybody on board, your so called implementation proceeds wham-bam.

—*Fortune* magazine

Interest in the philosophy and practice of servant-leadership is now at an all-time high. Hundreds of articles on servant-leadership have appeared in various magazines, journals, and newspapers over the past few years. Many books on the general subject of leadership have been published that have referenced servant-leadership as the preeminent leadership model for the twenty-first century.

The Greenleaf Center for Servant-Leadership is an international, not-for-profit educational organization that seeks to encourage the understanding and practice of servant-leadership. The Center's mission is to fundamentally improve the caring and quality of all institutions through a new approach to leadership, structure, and decision making.

In recent years, the Greenleaf Center has experienced tremendous growth and expansion. Its growing programs include the following: the world-wide sales of more than 80 books, essays, and videotapes on servant-leadership; a membership program; workshops, retreats, institutes, and seminars; the Greenleaf Biography Project; a Reading-and-Dialogue Program; a Speakers Bureau; and an annual International Conference on Servant-Leadership. A number of notable Greenleaf Center members have spoken at our annual conferences, including: James Autry, Peter Block, Max DePree, Stephen Covey, Meg Wheatley, Ann McGee-Cooper, M. Scott Peck, Peter Senge, and Peter Vaill, to

name but a few. These and other conference speakers have spoken of the tremendous impact that the servant-leader concept has played in the development of his or her own understanding of what it means to be a leader.

Paradox and Pathway

The Greenleaf Center's logo is a variation on the geometrical figure called a "mobius strip." A mobius strip, pictured here, is a one-sided surface constructed from a rectangle by holding one end fixed, rotating the opposite end through 180 degrees, and applying it to the first end—thereby giving the appearance of a two-sided figure. It thus appears to have a front side that merges into a back side, and then back again into the front.

The mobius strip symbolizes, in visual terms, the servant-leader concept—a merging of servanthood into leadership and back into servanthood again, in a fluid and continuous pattern. It also reflects the Greenleaf Center's own role as an institution seeking to both serve and lead others who are interested in leadership and service issues.

Life is full of curious and meaningful paradoxes. Servant-leadership is one such paradox that has slowly but surely gained hundreds of thousands of adherents over the past quarter century. The seeds that have been planted have begun to sprout in many institutions, as well as in the hearts of many who long to improve the human condition. Servant-leadership is providing a framework from which many thousands of known and unknown individuals are helping to improve how we treat those who do the work within our many institutions. Servant-leadership truly offers hope and guidance for a new era in human development, and for the creation of better, more caring institutions.

WORKING CAPITAL THAT MAKES GOVERNANCE WORK

RICHARD P. CHAIT, WILLIAM P. RYAN, & BARBARA E. TAYLOR

Taken together, the fiduciary, strategic, and generative modes of governing provide a fresh view of nonprofit boards that accentuates the board as a source of leadership. A new perspective on boards leads naturally to new ideas about trustees. In fact, the implications are inescapable. When we redefine the nature of governance and modify expectations for boards, we inevitably rethink the requisites for trustees. What are the most beneficial assets that trustees can contribute to make governance as leadership work? How can the untapped potential of the board be unleashed?

For years, board members were selected on the basis of certain, desired traits. Because the board was a critical instrument of legitimacy, organizations usually favored trustees of social stature, moral integrity, and refined lineage. These characteristics were also a powerful predictor of another important attribute: wealth. To create a congenial and comfortable atmosphere, charitable organizations also preferred polite and proper board members. In 1971, Myles Mace described for-profit directors as "ornaments" on the corporate Christmas tree (Mace, as quoted in Lorsch and Maciver, 2000). And nonprofit boards were often no different.

With the advent of strategic planning and market-based competition, nonprofit organizations placed greater and greater emphasis on the recruitment of trustees with pertinent expertise. (See Chapter 3.) Worksheets developed by BoardSource, the Association of Governing Boards of Universities and Colleges and other umbrella organizations invariably included a checklist of professional skills or occupational backgrounds that might be represented on the "model" board, for example, accounting, government, law, marketing, real estate, strategy, and technology (Hughes, Lakey, and Bobowick, 2000). Although the principal selection criteria for trustees shifted from characteristics toward competencies, with increased attention to demographic diversity, one criterion remained constant: the capacity for substantial philanthropy relative to one's means.

Whether focused primarily on trustees' qualities or skills (or some combination), nonprofits generally acquire, rather than develop, these assets—almost like corporations that expand by takeovers rather than by product development, or universities that "steal" star professors from the competition rather than promote from within. On the whole, boards harvest, rather than cultivate, trustees with attractive traits and talents. Second, these assets appreciate modestly, if at all. An honest, polite trustee does not become more honest and more polite. An able lawyer or banker does not become markedly more proficient. And certainly, a male or female, or black or white trustee does not become more so over time. These trustee assets resemble an investment grade bond—a reliable, steady performer with virtually guaranteed dividends, but without significant upside potential. We know what we have, and we know, more or less, what this will yield.

The analogy to financial markets has relevance because trustees can be reframed as a source of multiple forms of capital, and not nerely as *pro bono* consultants to the organization. A board contributes various types of capital, and then invests those resources in the governance of the institution, ideally at a favorable rate of return to the organization. In the best cases, the capital represented by the board appreciates substantially over time. The most valuable boards contribute and invest more capital from more sources in more forms than other boards. The boards with the most capital provide the organization with a comparative edge, the ability to "outgovern" the competition, just as the most astute and industrious staff can outsmart and outwork the competition. The emphasis on capital underscores one other consideration to generate value capital must be deployed. Money under the mattress, or boards under anesthesia, are idle capital. For the purposes of governance as leadership, trustees must be working capital. (See Exhibit 1, which calculates the monetary value of a board's time when we convert voluntarism into real dollars.)

When boards are conceptualized as a source of capital, money leaps to mind, and we do not underestimate the importance of financial capital. Nonprofit organizations cannot do much without money, and much of this money flows directly or indirectly from trustees. However, trustee largesse and excellent governance are not synonymous, nor does institutional wealth negate the need for an effective board. Even the most affluent nonprofits require governance.

Board members and senior staff must learn to recognize, appreciate, and capture the value of four no less crucial forms of capital, beyond money, that trustees can provide. These are intellectual, reputational, political, and social capital (see Exhibit 2). Each form of capital can be generated by trustees and invested on the institution's behalf. And while every nonprofit board contributes some capital to the organization, sometimes unconsciously or passively (for example, the very existence of a board generates some legitimacy) and sometimes through gratis technical expertise, the strongest boards generate more capital more actively, purposefully, and productively.

The assets of a highly capitalized board should be balanced and diversified. Like a mixed-asset allocation model, the multiple forms of capital offer a template to analyze whether the board has an appropriate portfolio of capital to do governance as leadership in light of the organization's needs and aims. Because the model highlights the value of other assets (for example, resourcefulness, persuasiveness, and trustworthiness), the board's attention may be redirected from narrow fiduciary matters toward other less visible, but arguably more significant, priorities. As a result, different issues (and different trustees) may become important to the board.

We now turn to the four forms of capital that boards need to develop in order to govern on a higher plane. In this context, one might think about a "capital campaign" as an effort to acquire and deploy the resources that trustees must furnish for governance to become an act of leadership.

EXHIBIT 1

The Dollar Value of The Board's Time

Consider the board of a college, museum, school, symphony orchestra, hospital, or regional or national social service agency. There are perhaps 30 members on the board which typically meets five times a year for eight hours at a time. Now do the math.

Assume that the trustees, mostly successful professionals or executives, earn on average $200,000 a year. At that rate, the board "burns" about $120,000 a year. Many nonprofit boards have more members and meet more often, especially in committees, or for longer periods of time. In these cases, the "billable hours" can easily exceed $150,000 annually. On elite boards, where the average annual income might be twice as much, the board's contributed services could easily exceed $300,000. If the calculation were based on the trustees' net worth, the dollar value of the board's time would soar.

For that amount of money over the course of a year, trustees would expect a lot from lawyers, accountants, consultants, or other professionals the organization retained. In this sense, most nonprofit organizations leave a lot of money on the boardroom table. As fiduciaries, trustees strive to maximize the rate of return to the organization on facilities, endowment, personnel, technology, and other institutional assets. Ironically, few calibrate a rate of return on the board or even ask whether trustees represent an underutilized asset.

EXHIBIT 2
The Four Forms of Board Capital

Form of Capital	Resource Optimized	Traditional Use	Enhanced Value
Intellectual	Organizational learning	Individual trustees do technical work	Board as a whole does generative work
Reputational	Organization legitimacy	Organization trades on trustees' status	Board shapes organizational's status
Political	Organizational power	External heavyweight: Trustees exercise power on the outside	Internal fulcrum: Board balances power on the inside
Social	Efficacy of the board	Trustees strengthen relationships to gain personal advantage	Trustees strengthen relationships to bolster board's diligence

Intellectual Capital

All three modes of governance place a premium on intellectual attributes, whether technical expertise, strategic acumen, or generative ingenuity. (By contrast, affluence and pedigree are not essential to any mode.) Each mode suggests a different way to think about trusteeship and a different way to think as a trustee. In that sense, this entire book concerns intelligence. Since "wisdom" or "talent" have always been one of the trinities of trusteeship, one might reasonably ask "What's new about that?"[1]

We are not concerned here with the intellectual prowess of individual board members or a search for trustees with the most impressive IQs or SAT scores. Instead, we are concerned with intellectual capital: the "collective brainpower" that "can be put to use" (Stewart, 1997) to generate mission-critical resources. While regularly applied to both white- and blue-collar workers, the term has not been linked to boards of trustees (or corporate boards, for that matter).

Intellectual capital is *not* the sum of trustees' knowledge, any more than the intellectual capital of a law firm comprises the sum of what each attorney knows. Effective boards and successful companies require shared knowledge, or "organizational intelligence," defined by Thomas Stewart as "smart people working smart ways" (1997). A gulf between what individuals know and what the organization knows occurs so often that the syndrome has been condensed into a popular maxim: "If IBM only knew what IBM knows." The same could be said about boards of trustees. Each trustee has a storehouse, but the board as a whole often lacks common knowledge.

As we observed about the fiduciary and strategic modes, management frequently consults board members about technical matters such as audits, investment strategies, legal questions, real estate, marketing, and competitive positioning. Do we self-insure or purchase coverage? Invest abroad or only domestically? Renovate or raze? The organization "capitalizes" on the trustees' individual talents, skills, and experiences to answer such questions. So far, so good, but not good enough.

Governance as leadership requires more than individuals with various expertise, just as orchestras require more than musicians with mastery of various instruments. There must be a shared sense of the nature of the work and enough common knowledge to do the work together. Gover-

---

EXHIBIT 3

Communities of Practice

Leadership Transition. (Generative mode) Upon the appointment of a new president from outside the organization, the trustees of a large university considered how the board could be most helpful in the transition. Initial suggestions were to familiarize the president-designate with the organization's budget, personnel, and structure (Type I). Then, some trustees recommended that the Executive Committee meet with the new CEO to review the strategic plan and "backlogged" priorities (Type II). In the end, the board decided that the most useful step would be to have all trustees and the CEO meet for three hours to discuss, based on personal experience or secondhand accounts, the most (and least) effective ways for a new executive to enter an organization from the outside and "take charge." The Upshot was a well-advised new CEO and an entire board better acquainted with the meaning and constraints of a university presidency and more appreciative of the challenges of the office.

Development, (Strategic mode) The leadership of an organization that envisioned a capital campaign on the horizon was concerned that not all board members understood the elements of an effective program to engage stakeholders and promote philanthropic support. The Advancement Committee asked three trustees to serve on a panel, facilitated by a fourth, to talk with the board about their involvement in successful campaigns with other nonprofits. The topics included how their skills were put to use, the most valuable lesson or best practice they learned, what motivates giving, and the responsibilities they shouldered. The result was that a board, where trustees previously had different levels of familiarity and expertise with advancement, now had a shared understanding of building volunteer relationships, setting funding priorities, and conducting a campaign.

Financial Oversight. (Fiduciary mode) The board of a religiously sponsored nonprofit included many members without a financial background. As a result, relatively few trustees contributed to discussions about the organization's financial performance. In order to narrow the knowledge gap and expand participation, the trustees instituted a "Finances 101" refresher seminar, conducted by board members, just prior to receipt of the outside auditor's report. Now every member of the board, throughout the year, has a level of financial literacy sufficient to participate in fiduciary discussions about budgets, audits, and resource allocation.

nance as leadership flourishes when what the *board* knows informs what the *board* thinks—when the "collective brainpower" of the board enlightens the "collective mind" of the board.

This suggests that boards act as "communities of practice, creating multiple opportunities for the entire board or particular committees to pool usable knowledge and thereby learn together. (Exhibit 3 offers three examples of community of practice, each pegged to a particular governing mode.) Some knowledge is explicit, for instance, tactics to negotiate with a labor union or steps to accelerate construction projects. Other knowledge is tacit, like the intuition, instincts, and sixth sense that trustees access to assess people, opportunities, and trade-offs. Both "hard" and "soft" knowledge should be expressly communicated and collectively absorbed. For example, the entire board of an independent college, school, or hospital should understand why competition drives costs up, not down. The entire board of an orchestra or opera should know what motivates musicians. On every board, all trustees should know what some trustees know first-hand about the benefits and pitfalls of strategic planning. And every board should discover and discuss together the most important lessons the trustees have learned about governing over the past year.

Intellectual capital increases as more trustees understand more together. In turn, the organization profits far more from a knowledgeable board than from a loose federation of knowledgeable trustees. As a mental exercise, the board should periodically review an intellectual capital balance sheet that records what all trustees know now that some or all did not know—say, a year ago—about what the organization values and expresses, what constituents seek and experience; what the organization does and does not do, might or should do; and what works, what does not, and why. The threshold question then becomes not "What does *one* make of all this?" but "What do *all* make of this?"

Reputational Capital

Reputational capital, the ultimate intangible asset, can be converted into real value when "the power of a good reputation is harnessed to improve the relationships on which successful business depends" (Jackson, 2004).[2] Whether reflected in stock price or the premium offered to acquire a company, reputation enhances a company's power to price products, attract clients, and recruit personnel. A tarnished reputation, by comparison, can be lethal.

The same principles apply to nonprofits, only more so. The services and products nonprofits offer are purchased largely on faith rather than on empirical qualities or demonstrable outcomes. Consumers and donors depend heavily on the reputation of the college, clinic, or charity to make choices, whereas reputation has almost no effect on the purchase of commodities like light bulbs, eggs, and gasoline. This explains why these products frequently retail as generics or private labels. The brand name and, by extension, the reputation of the manufacturer barely matter. In contrast, it is virtually impossible to imagine a successful generic nonprofit. Armed with a strong reputation, a nonprofit will be favorably positioned to access capital markets recruit talented staff, attract capable trustees, and engender public support. Reputation may not be everything, but whatever occupies second place ranks far behind.

Mindful of the value of reputation, nonprofits employ various techniques to enhance relationships with critical constitues—for example, improve performance and quality, especially perceived by critical constituencies; obtain professional accreditation or certification; assure transparency; recruit noteworthy personnel; seek positive publicity; and mount image campaigns. However, remarkably few nonprofits leverage the board's reputational capital into substantial value for the organization.

The process starts with the selection of trustees. A board cannot accumulate or expend reputational capital through a hazard approach to recruitment. The organization should ask, What reputation do we want to advance (or repair) with what stakeholders?" For instance, an organization with a damaged reputation may require different trustees than one with a reputation intact. Or, a low-status organization may need high-status trustees, while a high-status organization may need more worker bees than queen bees.

Nonprofits attuned to the value of a board's reputation will intentionally make appointments that cultivate a particular reputation with a particular audience. Thus, the board of a New England college appointed several distinguished scholars to underscore to faculty and students the trustees' commitment to academic quality. The board of a midwestern hospital traditionally includes clergy to convey to patients and physicians an allegance to the precepts and ethics of the sponsoring order. (In the for-profit sector, various corporations, stained by scandal, have appointed outside directors of unassailable integrity in order to assure stockholders of the company's probity.) However adroitly accomplished, inspired appointments add only nominal value; far greater advantage arises when trustees are actively engaged on the organization's behalf. The relationships between trustee reputation and trustee engagement are illustrated in Exhibit 4.

Deadwood add no value; figureheads add token value. In the latter case, nonprofits exploit the "halo effect" as stakeholders transfer to the organization the legitimacy of prominent trustees. (The same principle applies in reverse: When the personal reputations of certain executives were tarnished by corporate misdeeds, many were encouraged or forced to resign from nonprofit boards to spare the organization taint by association.) The organization borrows board members' status at no cost to the trustees, a passive transaction for both parties. Of course, no-show, luminary trustees can also be a liability, especially when these "celebrities" confess to colleagues and acquain indifference or ignorance about the organization's purposes and performance.

Some nonprofits ask that trustees lend only a name but never a hand. Over the long run, however, a renowned roster of "nonplayers" records few victories. The rate of return on the board's reputational capital accelerates with trustee engagement. Therefore, nonprofits customarily seek 100 percent participation by trustees in the capital campaign or annual fund to symbolize the board's support for the organization and to strengthen the case to other development prospects. At a more advanced level, the worker bees and superstars publicly commend and promote the organization,

---

EXHIBIT 4

Brand Name Value of Board Members

Trustee Reputation and Name Recognition

Level of Trustee Engagement	High	Low
High	*Superstars* Marquee name, leadership role.	*Worker bees* Little or no name recognition, much sweat equity.
Low	*Figureheads* All hat, no horse. Brand equity without sweat equity.	*Deadwood* No hat, no horse, no value.

---

visibly volunteer, and enthusiastically use the organization's services. (I have a child enrolled here. I had surgery here. I attended a support group here.)

While helpful, these measures do not leverage the trustees' reputation. More resourceful and valuable examples include:

- Trustees of a private college contact the parents of the ablest high school seniors offered admission to tout the institution, answer questions, and express a personal interest in the student. Whenever possible, the college matches the trustee's background to the student's academic interests.

- At programs for parents of prospective students, trustees—not admissions officers or the headmaster—of an independent school explain the institution's strengths, values, and benefits, and answer parents' questions.

- The board of an eminent nonprofit, widely regarded as well-governed, parlayed that feature to "trade up in the applicant pool" for a new CEO.

In all of these cases, the trustees were not just dispatched by management on tactical missions to mend or fortify relationships with a particular constituency. Rather, the board consciously and strategically decided which stakeholders were sufficiently important to the organization's future to warrant the investment of a valuable resource: the trustees' reputational capital.

Boards are uniquely situated to generate and expend reputational capital. Trustees have credibility and stature as respected citizens, prestigious professionals, objective overseers, dedicated volunteers, and generous donors. These are truly distinctive attributes and assets, especially when taken together, that are not present anywhere else in the organization, no matter how gifted the executives or staff may be.

Furthermore, board members engaged in generative governance straddle the boundary between the organization and the larger environment. In other words, trustees operate exactly where reputations are forged. As with other competitive enterprises, the winners take advantage of location, while the also–rans do not. Trustees restricted to the boardroom and isolated from the intersections of influence contribute little or no reputational capital to fuel the organization's success. So life at the organization's boundaries promises at least two advantages: more grist for generative governance and more reputational capital for the institution.

Political Capital

All organizations, nonprofits no less than for–profits, are political systems where people, individually or in groups, attempt to acquire and retain control over various resources in order to pursue certain interests. In the process, conflicts arise, coalitions form, participants jockey for power, negotiations occur, compromises emerge, and decisions happen. Political capital connotes, in shorthand, the influence and leverage that people within an organization acquire and deploy to frame problems, to elevate one above others, and to promote one solution over another.

Despite noble missions, nonprofits are hardly above organizational politics. First, nonprofits are particularly pluralistic institutions with diverse parties, inside and outside the organization, that passionately pursue multiple, and often contradictory, goals. Without the common bond of a profit motive, interest groups arise, coalesce, and dissolve contingent on the issues under consideration. Second, nonprofits are not as hierarchical as corporations; most have an innate aversion to formal authority. Compared to business executives, nonprofit managers have noticeably less power. Not many can issue decrees, and far fewer can expect that any mandates will, in fact, be heeded. The autonomy of professionals (for example, physicians, musicians, professors, curators) neutralizes, or even trumps, the authority of management. Finally, participants vie over where and how decisions will be reached. Because process matters as much or more than substance, no one can easily assert the right to make a decision; authority and legitimacy are not one and the same.

To go a step further, we postulate that the political capital of the board matters most in the generative mode, where the consequences for the institution and the potential for conflict are both high. Therefore, a substantial expenditure of political capital will be necessary to encourage and prod the organization to confront generative questions many constituents would prefer to ignore. Questions of core values (Type III) will generally precipitate more intense discussion and dispute than questions of core competencies (Type II) or core budgets (Type I). Proposed departures from tradition (for example, the elimination of fraternities at a college, obstetrics at a hospital, or free admission at a museum) will almost certainly incite more ambivalence and disagreement than proposed departures from the operating budget or even the strategic plan. Granted, boards may have to expend political capital to nudge management to tackle fiduciary issues like deferred maintenance or inefficient energy systems, and strategic topics like targets of opportunity and competitive responses. On the whole, however, boards should carefully conserve political capital that can, when necessary, be judiciously deployed to frame, accentuate, and confront generative issues.

Nonprofit boards accumulate political capital principally in two ways. First, the potential to exert influence emerges from the trustees' eloquence, intelligence, expertise, prestige, and charisma. These are all means to have sway. In this sense, the board "buys" political capital through the recruitment of powerful trustees. Second, an openness to influence spawns influence and creates reciprocity of power. The board accumulates political capital when trustees are demonstrably susceptible to influence, for example, at executive sessions with the CEO, lunches with senior managers, open forums with clients, multiconstituency task forces with professional staff, focus groups with patrons, or attendance at organizational events. In this sense, the board "makes" political capital through the interplay of influence. Make or buy, the trustees' political capital enhances and balances the distribution of power available to the organization.

Traditionally, nonprofit executives harness the political capital of boards when constituents inside the organization want trustees to influence events and advocate positions outside the organization. Alert to the value of friends in high places, management may marshal the political capital of a well-connected board to lobby local or state government; to encourage favorable treatment from the media; to seek special considerations from the community or from corporations; or to persuade skeptical patrons, alumni, or donors that a controversial proposal or decision deserves support. These are the ordinary, and almost invariably fiduciary or strategic, external applications of the trustees' political capital.

Mobilization of the board's political capital inside the organization presents a somewhat different picture. Individual trustees, of course, spend political capital internally all the time, for instance, through a phone call or an aside to the CEO, a congent pledge, a special plea, a request for information—even an arched eyebrow. When trustees act alone, executives can become confused, frustrated, and whipsawed. On occasion, a single board member with ample political capital may prevail, regardless of the merits of the argument, which only further exasperates management. At worst, the board becomes little more than a horde of lobbyists for personal preferences and pet projects; in effect, the trustees start to look and act like every other constituency.

In order to achieve an attractive rate of return on the board's political capital, nonprofit organizations must avoid the extremes. At one end of the spectrum, some CEOs question the risk/reward ratio of a board internally influential beyond the fiduciary sphere. These executives favor and design structures that preclude all but the most cursory relationships between trustees and staff or stakeholders lest board members be unduly influenced by constituents or vice versa. At the other extreme, some boards plunge headlong into the internal fray, not merely to influence events but to unilaterally impose policies, programs, and even personnel. As described in the previous chapter, a board reluctant to assert influence internally invites governance by default, and a board hell-bent on exercising formal authority and veto power at every turn produces governance by fiat. Neither extreme has much to offer.

A more balanced approach that taps the board's political capital with little risk for management and substantial advantage for the organization adheres to three guidelines. First and foremost, the board expends political capital *as a board*—the outcome of collective determination, not the exercise of personal prerogative. While inherently desirable as a means to foster cohesiveness within the board, this approach promises an even more pragmatic advantage: preservation of capital. The more that trustees act independently, the faster the board's political capital dissipates; in nonprofit boardrooms as in capital markets, institutional investors have far greater leverage than individuals.

Second, the board asserts influence primarily through mainstream processes rather than back channels. Committed to transparency and accountability, nonprofit boards must rely on legitimate means to achieve legitimate ends. We do not expect boards, or board members, to peddle influence, pursue self-interest, or negotiate secret deals. In short, nonprofits, as a matter of principle, should invest political capital in "open markets."

Third, unique among all stakeholders, the board serves as the fulcrum of organizational politics, the counterbalance to the parochial interests of other constituencies. This may, from time to time, position the board as the "loyal opposition": independent-minded, impartial, and sufficiently dedicated to the *organization's* success to stake a contrary position or make an unpopular decision. At stressful and, one hopes, rare moments like these, when the trustees decide to withdraw political capital from the boards account, surely they will cherish the value of the political capital they methodically stockpiled in calmer times.

Social Capital

New concepts are more familiar or more misunderstood than "social capital," which sociologist Douglas Massey defines as the productive value that can be extracted from social networks and "organizations" (Massey, 2002). Confusion arises when people equate *relationships* with *social capital*; these are not synonymous terms. Relationships comprise the raw material that produces social capital. For instance, a close-knit neighborhood may create a safer environment for children, or a tightly integrated professional network may facilitate the exchange of valuable information about employment opportunities or best practices.

In an organizational context, certain characteristics (for example, a sense of inclusiveness, trust, shared values, and common purpose) enable people to extract productive value from their relationships. These attributes accelerate cooperation, commitment, cohesiveness, and efficient exchange of knowledge and information which, in turn, advance purposeful activity and common enterprise. As the group strengthens these qualities, the members' productivity increases and generates tangible benefits for the organization. By contrast, members of a group without social capital are far less motivated to act productively and achieve collectively.

Boards of trustees necessarily involve social relationships, but social relationships do not necessarily produce the kind of social capital that improves board performance. On some boards, most notably Type I boards, trustees are apt to have rather tenuous and distant relationships. The formal, compartmentalized nature of the work does not foster much interaction or induce much trust among board members. On other boards, where adaptive or strategic problems are tackled together, trustees may be closer and more intact as a team. And while the latter breed may enjoy a more sociable atmosphere, no advantage accrues unless and until the rapport and connections are converted into productive assets.

Typically, trustees convert the board's social relationships into social capital that serves their own personal, professional, commercial, or political interests. On prestigious boards, some members may seek social advancement through closer ties to social elites. Pursuit of self-interest does promote personal relationships; however, the social capital generated does not directly serve the organization or benefit the board. This advantage results when trustees ask, "What can social capital do to improve the board's performance or the organization's condition?"

Most important, boards can produce social capital by changing the dominant norms, the unspoken and unwritten rules that guide trustee behavior. The norm that boards most commonly reinforce through the mechanisms of social capital is congeniality. Trustees tend to be agreeable and like-minded colleagues, desirable qualities to a point. More than occasionally, the pendulum swings too far, and some or many trustees become reticent, acquiescent adherents of an unexamined consensus and few, if any, feel answerable for organizational performance. The compliant majority typically treats critics and skeptics as troublemakers and subtly sanctions the outliers with less air time, fewer important assignments, curtailed access to critical information, and social isolation. In the end, the board lacks both robust discourse and a sense of shared responsibility, essential ingredients of governance as leadership.

This creates problems in all three modes of governance. If no one feels "licensed" to raise questions about lavish expenditures or financial shenanigans, there can be massive fiduciary failure. If trustees lack "permission" to challenge dubious assumptions or questionable strategies included in a five-year plan, the organization may falter or even fold. Just as significantly, the trustees' ability to do generative governance will be impaired, or perhaps squelched, if the board's prevalent norms discourage inhibited conversations, alternative frames, and playful ideas.

There is an alternative. Like a top-notch management team, athletic squad, musical ensemble, or law firm, a board of trustees can translate personal relationships and mutual trust into social capital that stresses personal responsibility, collective industry, and improved performance.

Several mechanisms can lead to new norms of diligence. At a minimum, a board can develop a baseline statement of expectations for both individual trustees and the board as a whole. The value of a "code of conduct" should neither be dismissed nor overestimated. It is a point of departure. In one dramatic example, the trustees of a large nonprofit in metropolitan New York concluded at a retreat that the board's performance, based on an external evaluation and an internal self-assessment, was lackluster at best. Buoyed by the *esprit de corps* generated at the retreat; the trustees summoned the resolve to assume greater accountability and to articulate new, rigorous norms. The board then declared a sixty-day "open enrollment" period when incumbent trustees could either "re-up" under the new expectations or resign. About five of 30 members resigned, while the rest have adhered to a stiffer, self-imposed standard of performance and accountability. Attendance, engagement, and trustee satisfaction all increased significantly because the board parlayed a stronger group identity into more stringent norms and loftier internal expectations.

To further foster a norm of diligence, trustees can be placed in high-stakes environments where they may be held accountable for their performance and the organization's. These venues, as we have noted, are situated at organizational boundaries, where trustees—individually or, even better, as part of small groups—represent the board and the institution before various stakeholders. This tack recognizes an irony of governance: Boards act least like trustees when closeted together inside the boardroom and most like trustees when required to represent the organization outside the boardroom. To create and internalize a norm of diligence, trustees must leave the comfortable, secure atmosphere of the boardroom where laxity can go unremarked on, let alone challenged.

Thus, subgroups of trustees of a nationally prominent nonprofit personally visited with foundation officers to explain the organization's recent setbacks, to outline a course of action, and to request (ultimately, successfully) millions of dollars in additional support. Similarly, trustees of a state university in the Rockies arranged to meet with key legislators, donors, faculty, and citizens-at-large both to convey the board's ambitions for the institution and to better understand constituents' expectations. Interactions like these, which place trustees at the crossroads of the organization and stakeholders, cultivate a sense of responsible trusteeship and, at the same time, provide board members with firsthand knowledge that enriches the board's deliberations in all three modes. In these and similar situations, individual board members cannot, except at considerable personal embarrassment, simply plead ignorance about the organization's programs, finances, performance, and values.

A third approach relies on high-stakes issues, the hallmark of Type III governance, rather than high-stakes situations. In this scenario, the entire board works in breakout groups on the same crucial assignment, for example, "How do we learn to look at the organization through the eyes of key stakeholders?" or "How do we reconcile the tension between deeply-rooted traditions and contemporary relevance?" (Type II questions might be: "How do we reposition the organization in an ever more competitive environment?" or "What metrics best capture organizational performance?") In smaller groups, trustees are more likely to be prepared and productive; free riders have nowhere to hide. Since every group has the identical assignment (unlike regular committee work), when the board reconvenes all trustees are better positioned to judge the quality of each group's work. Substandard performance by one group will be instantly observable by the others. Colleagues will be disappointed, and the laggards may be tacitly sanctioned and stigmatized. Equally important, the nonperformers will exert little influence as crucial matters, like the institution's sense of self or the cornerstones of the next strategic plan, are vigorously debated. Both substantively and procedurally, this arrangement fosters consequential work and reinforces a common obligation to be diligent and to deliver quality.

Executive sessions without the CEO present (something now required of companies listed on the New York Stock Exchange) offer a fourth mechanism to convert the trust generated by social capital into constructively candid conversations. These are occasions for the trustees, as peers, to be self-aware and self-critical. "How have we performed as a group? Where have we lagged? How can we do better? Have we adhered to a norm of discourse and not a norm of consensus? Have we worked well in all three modes of governance?" Trustees are unlikely to address these questions as forthrightly in the presence of the CEO, at least until the board has become well-acclimated to a new norm of candor and self-reflection. But when trustworthiness permeates the social environment, trustees can more readily confront and correct subpar performance by the board.

Whatever the particular means to initiate and institutionalize self-regulated, self-enforced norms of diligence and rigor, social capital facilitates the process and offers boards a new and powerful resource to instill a keener sense of mutual obligation, a custom of critical inquiry, and a culture of accountability and productivity. These are desirable outcomes no matter what the mode of governance.

Without sufficient social capital, nonprofits are apt to focus on all manner of structural and technical devices—agendas, committees, bylaws, information systems, orientations, self-assessments—to improve board performance. Some incremental improvements will likely ensue. However, adjustments to board structure and operations will not resolve problems embedded in the board's values and culture. As Roger Raber, CEO and president of the National Association of Corporate Boards, observed at a seminar we convened, the most effective boards are "value-based, not rule based." Type III governance encourages and equips boards to frame and confront value-based questions and challenges throughout the organization. There is no place more appropriate for trustees to start than to attempt to make sense together of the board's purpose, persona, and performance, an admittedly tall task made markedly easier by a storehouse of social capital.

Capitalizing on Trustees

As responsible fiduciaries, trustees endeavor to conserve and enhance an organization's tangible assets like finances, facilities, endowment, and personnel. In the strategic mode, boards attempt to convert these same assets, as well as intangibles like organizational traditions, ethos, and image, into comparative advantage. Trustees have no less responsibility to extract maximum value from the board as from other organizational assets. And this value can be denominated in more currencies than financial capital.

In fact, if boards launched campaigns to cultivate and deploy the trustees' intellectual, reputational, political, and social capital that were roughly comparable to efforts to garner the trustees' financial resources, the results could yield substantial dividends. Both the organization and the board would be smarter, more respected, more influential, and better equipped to perceive and handle generative challenges. In short, the organization would be better governed.

Executives, too, might be tempted to go halfway with governance as leadership. Some will incline to engage in generative work but keep the board at bay. There might be a little generative discussion from time to time about how management frames issues, but there would be no robust exchanges and no searches for other frames. Management might provide some glimpses into the organization's culture, core competencies, and competitive advantage, but there would be few opportunities for the board, as a whole, to do an "independent study" at the boundaries of the organization. Skillful and persistent CEOs can dilute (or even thwart) governance as leadership, but as we cautioned in the previous chapter, to do so courts a significant risk. Halfway measures may authorize trustees to frame the organization's challenges and opportunities, but without adequate knowledge of the organization's values, beliefs, assumptions, and traditions. As a result, executives may get plenty of frames but very little framing. Far better, we believe, for executives to have partial control of a complete perspective than complete control of a partial perspective.

We believe that nonprofit boards face a problem of purpose, not a problem of performance. When organizations reframe governance as leadership, the board becomes more than a fiduciary of tangible assets and more than management's strategic partner, as vital as those functions are. The board also becomes a crucial and generative source of leadership for the organization. In short, the board learns to perform effectively in all three modes of governance. The better trustees do that, the more deeply the board will understand the purpose of governance. And the better the board understands governance, the better governed the organization will be. This is not a vicious circle; it is the cycle of successful governance.

References

Andrews, K. R. (1971). *The Concept of Corporate Strategy*. Homewood, IL Richard D. Irwin, Inc.

Baldridge, J. V., Curtis, D. V., Ecker, G., and Riley, G. L. (1978). *Policy Making and Effective Leadership*. San Francisco: Jossey-Bass.

Birnbaum, R. (1988a). *How Colleges Work: The Cybernetics of Academic Organization and Leadership* (1st ed.). San Francisco: Jossey-Bass.

Birnbaum, R. (1988b). Presidential Searches and the Discovery of Organizational Goals. *Journal of Higher Education*, 59(5), 489–509.

Birnbaum, R. (1992). *How Academic Leadership Works: Understanding Success and Failure in the College Presidency* (1st ed.). San Francisco: Jossey-Bass.

Birnbaum, R. (2000). *Management Fads in Higher Education*. San Francisco: Jossey-Bass.

Bolman, L. G., and Deal, T. E. (1997). *Reframing Organizations: Artistry, Choice, and Leadership* (2nd ed.). San Francisco: Jossey-Bass Publishers.

Brown, P. L. (2002, May 8). Megachurches as Minitowns. *New York Times*, pp. D1, D4.

Chait, R. P., Holland, T. P., and Taylor, B. E. (1993). *The Effective Board of Trustees*. Phoenix, AZ: American Council on Education and The Oryx Press.

Chait, R. P., Holland, T. P., and Taylor, B. E. (1996). *Improving the Performance of Governing Boards*. Phoenix, AZ: American Council on Education and The Oryx Press.

Chait, R. P., and Taylor, B. E. (1989). Charting the Territory of Nonprofit Boards. *Harvard Business Review*. (January–February).

Christensen, C. M. (1997). *The Innovator's Dilemma: When New Technologies Cause Great Firms to Fail*. Boston: Harvard Business School Press.

Clark, B. R. (1972). The Organizational Saga in Higher Education. *Administrative Science Quarterly*, 17(2).

Cohen, M. D., and March, J. G. (1974). *Leadership and Ambiguity: The American College President*. New York: McGraw-Hill Book Company.

Collins, J. (2001). *Good to Great: Why Some Companies Make the Leap . . . and Others Don't*. New York: Harper-Business.

Collins, J., and Porras, J. (1994). *Built to Last: Successful Habits of Visionary Companies*. New York: HarperBusiness.

Csikszentmihalyi, M. (2003). *Good Business: Leadership, Flow, and the Making of Meaning*. New York: Viking Penguin.

Deal, T. E., and Kennedy, A. A. (1982). *Corporate Cultures: The Rites and Rituals of Corporate Life*. Reading, MA: Addison-Wesley Publishing Company, Inc.

Deschamps, J. P., and Nayak, P. R. (1995). *Product Juggernauts: How Companies Mobilize to Generate a Stream of Market Winners*. Boston: Harvard Business School Press.

Dewan, S. K. (2004, April 28). New York's Gospel of Policing by Data Spreads Across U.S. *New York Times*, p. A1.

DiMaggio, P. J., and Powell, W. W. (1991). The Iron Cage Revisited: Institutional Isomorphism and Collective Rationality in Organizational Fields. In P.J. DiMaggio and W. W. Powell (Eds.), *The New Institutionalism in Organizational Analysis* (pp. 63–82). Chicago: University of Chicago Press.

Dubner, S. (2003, June 28). Calculating the Irrational in Economics. *New York Times*, p. B7.

Edgers, G. (2004, February 15). Art Fans Take a Vegas Vacation. *Boston Globe*, pp. N1, N4.

Fleishman, J. (1999). Public Trust in Not-for-Profit Organizations and the Need for Regulatory Reform. In C. T. Clotfelter and T. Ehrlich (Eds.), *Philanthropy and the Nonprofit Sector in a Changing America* (pp. 172–197). Bloomington, IN: Indiana University Press.

Fremont-Smith, M. R. (2004). *Governing Nonprofit Organizations: Federal and State Law and Regulation*. Cambridge, MA: Belknap Press of Harvard University Press.

Euerbringer, J. (1997, March 30). Why Both Bulls and Bears Can Act So Bird-Brained. *New York Times*, p. 1.

Gardner, H. (1983). *Frames of Mind: The Theory of Multiple Intelligences*. New York: Basic Books.

Gardner, H. (1993). *Creating Minds: An Anatomy of Creativity Seen Through the Lives of Freud, Einstein, Picasso, Stravinsky, Eliot, Graham, and Gandhi*. New York: Basic Books.

Gardner, H., collaboration with Emma Laskin. (1995). *Leading Minds: An Anatomy of Leadership*. New York: Basic Books.

Gergen, D., and Kellerman, B. (2000). Pain Management. *Compass: A Journal of Leadership*, 1(2), 40.

Golden, D. (2002, April 29). In Effort to Lift Their Rankings, Colleges Recruit Jewish Students. *Wall Street Journal*, pp. A1, A8.

Goleman, D. (1995). *Emotional Intelligence: Why It Can Matter More than IQ*. New York: Bantam.

Gonzalez, D. (2003, June 14). Holding On to Beliefs Despite the Insistence of Fact. *New York Times*, p. B1.

Hamel, G. (1996). Strategy as Revolution. *Harvard Business Review* (July–August).

Hamel, G., and Prahalad, C. K. (1997). *Competing for the Future*. Boston: Harvard Business School Press.

Heifetz, R. A. (1994). *Leadership without Easy Answers*. Cambridge, MA: Belknap Press of Harvard University Press.

Herzlinger, R. (1997). *Market Driven Health Care*. Cambridge, MA: Perseus Books.

Heskett, J. (1987). Lessons in the Service Sector. *Harvard Business Review* (March–April).

Houle, C. O. (1960). *The Effective Board*. New York: Association Press.

Houle, C. O. (1989). *Governing Boards: Their Nature and Nrture*. San Francisco: Jossey-Bass.

Hughes, S. R., Lakey, B. M., and Bobowick, M. J. (2000). *The Board Building Cycle: Nine Steps to Finding, Recruiting, and Engaging Nonprofit Board Members*. Washington, D.C.: BoardSource.

Jackson, K. T. (2004). *Building Reputational Capital—Strategies for Integrity and Fair Play That Improve the Bottom Line*. Oxford: Oxford University Press.

Janis, I. L. (1982). *Groupthink: Psychological Studies of Policy Decisions and Fiascoes*. Boston: Houghton Mifflin.

Julius, D., Baldridge, J. V., and Pfeffer, J. (1999). A Memo for Machiavelli. *Journal of Higher Education* (March–April), 113–133.

Kanter, R. M. (1983). *The Change Masters: Innovation & Entrepreneurship in the American Corporation*. New York: Simon & Schuster, Inc.

Kaplan, R. S., and Norton, D. P. (1996). *The Balanced Scorecard: Translating Strategy into Action.* Boston: Harvard Business School Press.

Kelling, G. L., and Coles, C. M. (1996). *Fixing Broken Windows: Restoring Order and Reducing Crime in Our Communities.* New York: Touchstone Press.

Kolata, G. (1996, April 12). The Long Shelf Life of Medical Myths. *New York Times*, p. 2.

Kotler, P., and Murphy, P. (1991). Strategic Planning for Higher Education. In M. Peterson (Ed.), *ASHE Reader on Organization and Governance in Higher Education* (4th ed.). Needham Heights, MA: Ginn.

Learning from Nonprofits. (1990, March 26). *Business Week*, 66–74.

Letts, C. W., Ryan, W. P., and Grossman, A. (1999). *High-Performance Nonprofit Organizations: Managing Upstream for Great Impact.* New York: John Wiley & Sons.

Lewontin, R. (2000). *The Triple Helix: Gene, Organism, and Environment.* Cambridge, MA: Harvard University Press.

Lorsch, J. W., and Maciver, E. (2000). *Pawns or Potentates: The Reality of America's Corporate Boards.* Cambridge, MA: Harvard Business School Press.

Mace, M. (1971). *Director: Myth and Reality.* Cambridge, MA: Harvard Business School Press.

Massey, D. (2002, July 12). What People Just Don't Understand About Academic Fields. *The Chronicle of Higher Education*, p. B4.

Mellado, J. (1991). "Willow Creek Community Church." Boston: Harvard Business School Publishing.

Mintzberg, H. (1994). *The Rise and Fall of Strategic Planning: Reconceiving Roles for Planning, Plans, Planners.* New York: Free Press.

Mintzberg, H. (1998). *Strategy Safari: A Guided Tour Through the Wilds of Strategic Planning.* New York: Free Press.

Morgan, G. (1997). *Images of Organization* (2nd ed.). Thousand Oaks, CA: Sage Publications.

Pfeffer, J. (1981). *Power in Organizations.* Boston: Pitman.

Pfeffer, J. (1992). *Managing with Power: Politics and Influence in Organizations.* Boston: Harvard Business School Press.

Polanyi, M. (1974). *Personal Knowledge.* Chicago: University of Chicago Press.

Porter, M. E. (1980). *Competitive Strategy: Techniques for Analyzing Industries and Competitors.* New York: The Free Press.

Porter, M. E. (1996). What Is Strategy? *Harvard Business. Review* (November–December), 61–78.

Robert III, S. C., Evans, W. J., Honemann, D. H., and Balch, T. J. (2000). *Robert's Rules of Order Newly Revised* (10th ed.). New York: Perseus Books.

Schein, E. H. (1992). *Organizational Culture and Leadership* (2nd ed.). San Francisco: Jossey-Bass Publishers.

Schein, E. H. (1993). How Can Organizations Learn Faster? The Challenge of Entering the Green Room. *Sloan Management Review* (Winter), 85–92.

Schmidtlein, F. (1988). College and University Planning: Perspectives from a Nationwide Study. *Planning for Higher Education*, 17(3).

Schon, D. A. (1983). *The Reflective Practitioner: How Professionals Think in Action.* London: Temple Smith.

Scott, W. R. (2003). *Organizations: Rational, Natural, and Open Systems* (5th ed.). Upper Saddle River, NJ: Prentice-Hall.

Senge, P. (1990). *The Fifth Discipline: The Art and Practice of the Learning Organization.* New York: Doubleday/Currency.

Shapiro, E. C. (1995). *Fad Surfing in the Boardroom.* Reading, MA: Addison-Wesley Publishing Company, Inc.

Smith, D. H. (1995). *Entrusted: The Moral Responsibilities of Trusteeship.* Bloomington, IN: Indiana University Press.

Spontaneous Generation. (2004). *Encyclopoedia Britannica Premium Service*, 2004.

Stacey, R. D. (1996). *Complexity and Creativity in Organizations.* San Francisco: Berrett-Koehler Publishers.

Stewart, T.A. (1997). *Intellectual Capital: The New Wealth of Organizations.* New York: Doubleday.

Taylor, B. E., Chait, R. P., and Holland, T. P. (1991). Trustee Motivation and Board Effectiveness. *Nonprofit and Voluntary Sector Quarterly*, 20(2), 207–224.

Taylor, B. E., Chait, R. P., and Holland, T. P. (1996). The New Work of the Nonprofit Board. *Harvard Business Review* (September–October).

Taylor, B. E., and Massy, W. F. (1996). *Strategic Indicators for Higher Education.* Princeton, NJ: Peterson's.

Volunteer Protection Act of 1997, Public Law 105–119 (1997).

Watson, G. H. (1993). *Strategic Benchmarking: How to Rate Your Company's Performance Against the World's Best*. New York: John Wiley & Sons.

Weick, K. E. (1976). Educational Organizations as Loosely Coupled Systems. *Administrative Science Quarterly*, 21, 1–19.

Weick, K. E. (1995). *Sensemaking in Organizations*. Thousand Oaks, CA: Sage Publications.

Zimmerman, B., Lindberg, C., and Plsek, P. (1998). *Edgeware: Insights from Complexity Science for Health Care Leaders*. Irving, TX: VHA Inc.

Notes

1. The standard versions of the trilogy are "work, wisdom, and wealth" and "time, talent, and treasure."
2. Corporate balance sheets assign tangible worth to goodwill as the market value of a company's shares beyond the liquidation value of its assets.

WHY COLLEGE TRUSTEES?

ELLIS HUNTINGTON DANA

Need for Organizational Adjustment and for More Modern Theory and Practice for Colleges

Trustees of colleges and universities vary in functions. Though by charter trustees legally control and hold a college or university, their functions are customarily limited to raising and investing funds, to holding and managing properties, to choosing a president, to helping to keep the educational program in touch with the times, to appointing faculty members, and to granting degrees.

If the trustee is to perform a real duty to the college, it, in turn, must offer him genuine opportunity for service. Only on the basis of such reciprocity can a relationship of mutual trust and understanding be maintained. A trustee, to be more than a figurehead, should have a genuine interest in education. He must be alert to the college's needs and opportunities. As a public-spirited, prominent citizen, he should cultivate a broad perspective on the educational needs of the community, state, and nation. He should try to interchange ideas with trustees from other colleges and universities as a means of acquiring breadth and perspective for his work. He should be available for counsel and tolerant of administrators. A trustee should grasp every opportunity to spread information about the college and increase its good will and prestige. To perform his functions effectively, he must be conversant with the history, aims, plans, programs, and needs of the college.

There should be a system by which a new trustee is given a full, though brief, summary of the important facts about the college he is to serve. These should include information, carefully presented and itemized, concerning the duties of a trustee, fellow trustees on the board, trustee or corporation traditions and procedures, bylaws, regulations, and college background, aims and purposes of the college, financial condition of the college, and the curriculum, program, and faculty of the college. With rotation in the office of trustee, a systematic plan of informing and cultivation is most important.

A definite plan of sharing information with trustees should include frequent personal and group cultivation, periodic letters of information, frequent luncheons and meetings, encouragement to view the significant workings of the college, careful preparation for all meetings, with a covering letter and agenda sent out in advance, a portfolio for each trustee, which should be kept by the college for use at each board meeting and should contain all materials bearing directly on points in the agenda, with background information on each point. The portfolios should be kept in order and up to date, from meeting to meeting.

Training trustees for leadership is just as important for a college as is training lay leadership in a church, a corporation, or a community fund. Education in leadership is even more important because so much now depends on the trustee.

Trustees must be informed that over the centuries a science of philanthropy has developed and grown as colleges and universities have grown. What seem to be new methods have been tried in one way or another before. The house-to-house canvass was used in 1552, when Henry VIII dissolved the monasteries. "Begging" letters, so called, were used in London one hundred years ago. The "benefit performance" is a method which goes back to the gala fairs and jousting tournaments of the twelfth century. The "financial agent" goes back one thousand years to such an officer in the medieval monastery. The "tithing method" has been adapted from its use since biblical times. There is the "dole" which goes back to early Grecian days. The "whirlwind campaign" used by Benjamin Franklin in advocating the interests of the University of Pennsylvania was broadened in conception and scope during World War I, yet it is not the last word on fund-raising technique, since conditions have greatly changed in two decades.

College trustees must be informed that a newer, more scientific method is now called for to meet the changing conditions. The older methods concentrated on the large givers, but today large givers are becoming increasingly less and less able to give. The emphasis is shifting more and more to the many. As a result, it is necessary to determine the modern place and function of a trustee; it is necessary to gauge the need for seeking still other laymen who can broaden the base of good will and who can cultivate new friends for new funds.

It is more and more recognized that a large board of trustees is preferable for the college, which is increasingly dependent upon financial gifts from groups and individuals. The wider the base of givers and potential friends, the more representative the board should be in its membership. Official connection often creates an interest on the part of a prominent person who might not be reached otherwise, and encourages large gifts or, at least, effective help in financial development. The larger the board, the larger the number of persons who may be expected to participate in giving, in offering names, or in cultivating prospective donors. For these reasons, large and small privately endowed colleges will find that it genuinely pays to have a large group of trustees or corporation members.

In most privately endowed American colleges and universities, the number of trustees or corporation members varies from as few as seven to as many as over fifty. The emphasis on larger boards occurs principally for reasons of financial support. Experience has demonstrated that a small board is sufficient for other than financial reasons. Large representative boards, however, are essential when financial support becomes indispensable. A board of trustees usually perpetuates itself, with the alumni nominating their representatives according to age, wealth, geographical distribution, and businesses and professions represented. Certain other standards developed from the experience of colleges and universities determine the selection of trustees or corporation members.

There should be a balanced representation of various age groups, with comparatively few older men or women, a majority of middle-aged members, and some relatively young trustees. This latter group is important to a board which must effectively propose and accept new ideas, and meet new trends courageously. Many colleges have a plan for automatic retirement of trustees at a certain age. Some have a provision placing them on an honorary status at seventy.

It must constantly be borne in mind, as Charles F. Thwing suggested, that "the future of a college is longer than its past" and that, therefore, trustees should be selected with a view to their probable contribution to the future welfare of the university. He also said that if a board is subject to constant renewal by an automatic process after a service of three or five years, men of any age may fittingly be elected; but if the place is regarded as permanent, only those who have not passed beyond mature middle life are to be selected.[1]

This is an important consideration in the selection of trustees, and in the building and rebuilding of a board to meet new needs and trends today.

Many colleges should have gradual changes made. In these extraordinary times, there should be a broader base of influential interest and support as the result of larger and more effective boards. Consequently, in general, the following organizational emphases are suggested for consideration:

More trustees and more younger trustees
More trustees from outside the city in which the college is located
More trustees representative of business and industry
More trustees representative of nationally known Americans
More flexibility and stimulation of organization as implied in the appointment of special-term trustees and in gradually doing away with life members
More honor to those who retire, and an automatic retirement age
More planned contacts and information for the purpose of actively stimulating more interest on the part of trustees
More challenging and specific jobs for trustees to do

Co-ordination of administration, trustees, alumni, faculty, and student representatives through an informal college council which can meet three times a year

This council will afford a wider understanding, more effective public relations, and, in the end, wider support.

The number of trustees' board meetings varies widely with different colleges and universities. Some meet only twice, some as often as six times, a year. However, board committees may hold bimonthly, or even monthly, meetings. During the academic year, the executive committee and also the finance committee may meet as often as once a month. There may be special meetings. All meetings should be purposeful, carefully planned, and made as interesting and as live as possible, both in content and conduct.

The following are some specific suggestions as to how trustees may become better informed and more effective, to be applied according to the needs of the individual college:

1. A strategy committee, composed of three members of the trustee committee on development and two prominent outside businessmen, may be formed for the purpose of making careful plans, and holding infrequent meetings, to attract new friends and funds.

2. A committee on development of trustees may be expanded to include other representative leaders. This enlarged committee from city and state may furnish a proving ground for prospective trustees. This will increase interest in the college, and will extend its influence.

3. Special-term trustees may be elected with special standing, privileges, and duties. The selection may be made from widely known persons who definitely represent other factors, not already covered by trustees, such as age, geographical distribution, wealth, position, and representation of business and professional groups. A special-term trustee may be elected to fill temporarily the vacancy of a regular trustee.

4. More emphasis on age may be important to assure a sufficient number of middle-aged and young trustees. The ages of the majority should be from thirty-five to sixty years.

5. Life membership for trustees may be gradually replaced by a rotating plan of six to ten years' service. Though life membership enhances prestige, it does not allow for sufficient new blood, new ideas, and the progressive growth needed by the smaller colleges.

6. More opportunities may be afforded trustees to meet administrative leaders, directors, and heads of departments and divisions in an informal way such as is suggested in the Informal College Council. This Council may meet several times each year.

7. Trustee members may be encouraged to attend the Trustees of Colleges and Universities Conference held each year in April at Lafayette College, or other similar meetings.

8. A trustees' day may be held each spring in April or early May. A special two-day period can be set aside for meetings, for visitation to classes, for conferences with administrative officers, and for a general get-together, with special discussions on college work, plans, and policies.

9. Trustees' breakfasts may be held periodically, perhaps bimonthly, for the purposes of getting better acquainted, of generating more information or enthusiasm about the college, or of inviting prominent college friends now and then as guests.

10. Special trustees' meetings may be held periodically to give students a chance to present and discuss certain phases of their work, and to provide an opportunity for faculty members to acquaint trustees more fully with what is going on and why, from a faculty viewpoint. This should improve knowledge, interest, and general morale.

11. More written information about the college may be made available to the trustees in more readable form.

12. Minutes of all meetings of trustees' committees and notices of important college happenings and events may be mailed to all trustees.

13. Trustees may be invited to disseminate information about the college, to suggest potential friends and, when possible, to cultivate new and old friends.

Today it may be important to enlist even a greater number of prominent persons. This may be achieved by way of "friends of the college." Claremont Colleges, consisting of three colleges in Southern California, organized a group of three hundred friends several years ago, who pay dues of $12.50 a year. California Institute of Technology has had a group of sustaining Associates who have contributed over $1,400,000 in a period of years. This "friends" or "associates" plan can be most successful. Usually these persons are selected apart from trustees. Such a group brings new blood into the organization and can stimulate and encourage the trustees. There are many persons who are interested in education and who want to be informed. In a friends' or associates' group, like-minded persons can be brought into closer relationship with each other and with the college. The friendship and support of such persons can become important influences in the development of a college.

It works both ways—advantages to the college and advantages to the friends or associates. Current information about the college, its affairs, and progress can be made available. Lecture privileges, college magazines, and research papers, especially for the group, can be offered to the associates by the college. Other college facilities can be placed at their disposal. Membership can and should be by invitation. Appointment should be a great honor. College friends and associates are primarily for the purpose of serving the highest and best interests of education through a college.

Never before in the history of privately endowed colleges has there been a greater need for the right kind and right number of trustees. This is one sure way to safeguard survival. What privately endowed colleges do now about obtaining an adequate number of properly qualified trustees, and what they do now in educating those trustees—other things in organization and administration being equal—will largely determine what these colleges can hope to expect in the future. [Vol. XVIII, No. 5]

Notes

1. The American College and University, pp. 17, 18.

Selected Website

Includes information about trustee selection and the importance of prospective trustees having demonstrated a commitment to public service.

www.usc.edu/dept/chepa/documents/publicationsw/selection.pdf

The Role of Community College Trustees in Supporting the Foundtion

Norm Nielsen, Wayne Newton, & Cheryle W. Mitvalsky

The role of the institutional trustees in supporting foundation efforts is explored. Four priorities are described: projecting a positive image for the college, overseeing and maintaining an institutional structure that supports the foundation, sustaining an engaged administration, and encouraging innovation.

With declining tax support for community colleges, creative methods of financing and fundraising are on the rise. These changes in revenue sources demand active, knowledgeable participation from institutional trustees. While not elected or appointed to be fundraisers, trustees often are called on to support fundraising efforts.

Kirkwood Community College, located in Cedar Rapids, Iowa, serves a seven-county area in eastern Iowa with a population of 400,000 and an immediate urban area of 140,000. Last year, approximately 20,000 students enrolled in college-credit classes, and another 49,000 enrolled in noncredit continuing education classes. The size of the college and scope of its mission, combined with declining tax support, makes fundraising a top priority.

The Board of Trustees at Kirkwood adheres to four principles for effectively supporting foundation efforts without neglecting other responsibilities to the college. Trustees should be aware of their responsibility to present a positive image for the college, which includes involvement at some level in college fundraising campaigns. Trustees should understand the importance of maintaining an institutional structure that supports and oversees the foundation. They should sustain a president and other college administrators who are active in the community to ensure trust between potential donors and the college. Finally, trustees should seek and support innovation from the foundation, the college, and the community.

Enhancing the Image

A primary role of the institutional trustee regarding fundraising is to maintain an environment in which the image of the college is enhanced for the members of the community. Trustees contribute to a positive image by presenting a cooperative spirit to the community; by offering visibility to various stages of fundraising; and by helping development staff and college administrators read the expressed needs, dreams, and abilities of the community.

The spirit with which institutional trustees do their work affects the community and sets the tone for the college. A board presenting a positive, cooperative, and, when possible, united front to the community helps activate potential donors. Regardless of how diligently the development staff cultivates and solicits donors, frequent split votes by the board or reports of divisiveness can negatively affect fundraising campaigns and efforts to pass or renew levies. Though healthy boards have meaningful disagreements when resolving difficult issues, institutional trustees should work toward a cohesive, team-building spirit that signals stability and trust to the community and potential donors. Longevity of institutional trustees also contributes to an enhanced image within the community. Kirkwood holds no limits on membership terms for institutional trustees as long as they are reelected. And, while the Board of Trustees has found value in retaining the same chair since 1984, new institutional trustee members who will contribute new ideas and energy are also welcomed.

Accurately reading the community's expressed needs and dreams can help institutional trustees enhance the college's image. Trustees who keep their eyes and ears open to the community can inform development staff and thus help gear fundraising efforts to the community's abilities and needs. Because of a softened local economy and stepped-up fundraising of other organizations, Kirkwood's current campaign is quieter this year, packaged in smaller bundles. Some companies currently prefer to give annually rather than commit to multiyear gifts, so we are putting a greater emphasis on annual giving efforts. Our institutional trustees, foundation board members, and development staff have been receptive to the signals from our community.

Awareness of how the board's presence, however informal, can facilitate fundraising is another important way that institutional trustees can positively affect the college's image. With each step in the fundraising process, such as identification, cultivation, solicitation, and recognition of donors, institutional trustees can contribute by being visible. Recently Kirkwood built two agricultural facilities—a swine confinement center and an equestrian center—with the help of institutional trustees who participated in identifying donors. A trustee was present at the college tours with potential donors, serving as a connector between the donors and the college. When the projects were completed, institutional trustees were present in support of donors enjoying public appreciation for their generosity.

Trustees should remember that fundraising is, first and foremost, *friendraising*. The visible presence of Kirkwood institutional trustees has been beneficial to the college, even at informal events. During Freedom Fest, a summer celebration in Cedar Rapids at which Kirkwood hosts musical events, institutional trustees intermingle with invited potential and past donors. Trustees also attend Jazz Under the Stars, a series of outdoor jazz and blues concerts co-sponsored by Kirkwood and held at various city parks. The potential influence of trustees on potential donors at these informal venues is immeasurable.

Institutional trustees also enhance the image of the college by being donors themselves. At Kirkwood, all institutional trustees and foundation board members are donors; the institution's stated goal is 100 percent participation from all college staff and faculty as well. With the prevailing philosophy that no gift is too small, all are encouraged to give within their means for the benefit of the students served by the college.

Overseeing and Supporting the Foundation

Institutional trustees should be instrumental in overseeing and maintaining an institutional structure that supports the foundation. A range of legal options is available in the relationships between the institutional trustees, the foundation, and the college. Different choices hold various strengths and weaknesses. Thomas Roha (1999) suggests that foundations that are too autonomous risk veering from their purpose, which is to serve the college. However, foundations not independent enough risk being viewed as mere legal entities of the institution.

The structure of Kirkwood Community College includes three boards that represent the seven-county area served by the college: the Board of Trustees, the Kirkwood Foundation, and the Facilities Foundation. (The Facilities Foundation oversees the use of campus vending-machine royalties for property procurement.) Although the Board of Trustees made the decision to keep the two foundations separately incorporated from the college, the foundations are not autonomous. Both are considered public and open to public scrutiny. Development staff members, who work for the Kirkwood Foundation, are paid out of the college's general fund rather than by monies raised by the foundation, to reinforce the idea that the Kirkwood Foundation and development staff answer to the college and its institutional trustees. Both foundations' board members are nominated by their own boards but approved by the Kirkwood Board of Trustees.

The college is fortunate to have an active, supportive Kirkwood Foundation board consisting of twenty-seven area leaders. The Kirkwood Foundation (hereafter "foundation") board members not only contribute financially on a personal level, but also are invaluable in assisting development staff in managing investments as well as soliciting and identifying potential donors. The foundation board members tend to be drawn from the immediate urban area, though the institutional trustees who oversee the foundation work to ensure that all of the college's constituents in the seven counties served by Kirkwood are considered in fundraising efforts.

Institutional trustees maintain visible relationships with the development staff and the foundation. The institutional trustees ratify all nominations to the foundation. Development staff and foundation members give semiannual reports to the Board of Trustees. In addition, two institutional trustees, as voting members, and the president, as an ex officio member, attend the foundation board's meetings held four times per year. The advice of the president and the institutional trustees is valued by the foundation regarding needs of the college and potential donor prospects. The presence of institutional trustees is a continual reminder of the core mission of the institution.

Because of their close working relationship with the foundation and development staff, institutional trustees understand the capacity for the development staff to contribute to the financial health of the college. The institutional trustees have been instrumental in advocating adequate development staffing for annual giving programs, large campaigns, and planned giving.

As Kirkwood's development staff has demonstrated success, the institutional trustees have hired more development personnel. Currently we have ten employees in our Resource Development Department, including three people in annual, major, and planned giving; three support staff; three grant writers; and an accounting specialist. We encourage innovative, creative thinking and results by our development staff in dealing with campaign proposals and potential donors, and we have not been disappointed.

The development staff is also instrumental in helping ensure effective communication between the institutional trustees and foundation board members. The staff organizes two social events a year at which the institutional trustees, senior administrators of the college, and the foundation board members gather to reinforce their shared commitment to the college. Foundation board members also recognize institutional trustees at every community event they organize to remind the public of the close working relationship with the institutional trustees.

While development staff members are skilled at identifying gifts that may be without charitable intent, the institutional trustees, accountable to the community, serve as another layer of checks and balances by being present and active on foundation boards. The message to the community is that the college operates at the highest code of ethics regarding the use of donations.

Sustaining an Engaged Administration

Choosing, sustaining, and standing behind an administrative staff that gets involved in the community is key priority for the institutional trustees. CEOs and other potentially large donors expect contact from the president and chief development officer. Private citizens and key leaders in business and industry need reassurance from college administrators that their donations will be used to reinforce and create educational programs, facilities, and student scholarships that truly make a difference.

At Kirkwood, the trustees encourage the president's and chief development officer's involvement in the community on bank, hospital, Chamber of Commerce, economic development, and social service boards, as well as country club memberships. Kirkwood administrators also work with other nonprofit organizations; our philosophy is that success in one campaign breeds success in other campaigns.

Development staff coordinates regular meetings on campus between Kirkwood administrators, community leaders, and private citizens. The staff plans lunches twice a month for the purpose of cultivating planned and endowed giving commitments. We invite people of the age and capacity for estate planning from throughout our seven-county area. The Kirkwood culinary arts students prepare the lunches and serve the guests and staff in the president's office, which has a panoramic view of the campus. Nearly all of our guests contribute to the college in some fashion. We anticipate future gifts totaling over $12 million because of these efforts to cultivate relationships with community members.

A high percentage of donations to Kirkwood are the result of connections made by these internal activities and through service, social, and philanthropic involvement in the community. The Board of Trustees supports the administration by ensuring enough support staff to help with its commitments. Being visible is challenging work for busy administrators; institutional trustees who understand the need for college leaders to be active outside the college will support them by maintaining the necessary support staff.

Encouraging Innovation

Fifteen years ago, Kirkwood Community College hired a new chief development officer and initiated a major fundraising campaign. No one could have predicted at the time how significantly this first campaign would galvanize various entities in the college and imprint future fundraising. Detailing the campaign will illustrate how Kirkwood institutional trustees rolled up their sleeves for an innovative fundraising effort.

Until 1990, Kirkwood's fundraising campaigns had been modest, yielding donations of $100,000 annually. With a newly hired chief development officer, the decision was made by the Board of Trustees, the president, and the foundation boards to hire a consultant to organize a large campaign effort. The consultant's preliminary interviews with nearly one hundred leaders of the community indicated a need to scale the college's $10 million wish list to $5 million and remove goals for facilities, focusing instead on student scholarships, faculty and staff development, and equipment upgrades. It was also clear that the campaign should be used to educate the public that the college was tax-assisted, not fully tax-supported. Critical issues and leadership were identified, as well as top dollar ranges to expect. Because of the interviews, community leaders were prepared for and excited about a Kirkwood campaign.

Various Kirkwood people were united for the campaign kickoff: the institutional trustees, the foundation boards, the development staff, and the president. Small organizational groups within the larger community and three hundred community volunteers were also trained for the campaign effort; each volunteer was asked to tell the Kirkwood story to five donors apiece. At the end of the two-year campaign, $6.5 million was raised—more than the initial goal of $5 million. The gain was substantial: the money had been raised; the Kirkwood story had been told many times; and relationships of trust and respect had been cemented in the community and within the college between the institutional trustees, the foundation trustees, and the development staff. Rolling up our sleeves together helped everyone appreciate each other's strengths and increased the bond of trust within the college. Before the campaign, lead gifts had been in the $50,000 range. When the campaign generated a lead gift of $1 million, institutional trustees more fully appreciated the importance and potential benefits of fundraising. They began to see more opportunities and have brought many partnerships and donors to the table since the campaign.

The institutional trustees also more fully understood the value of their geographical distribution. Because of their diverse constituents across the seven-county area served by Kirkwood, they convinced development staff that the campaign could not be one large campaign. The five rural counties had different leadership and issues from those of the two urban counties. The institutional trustees guided presentation styles in the rural counties and helped identify the key leadership there, as well as what gift levels could be expected from donors. Often, the institutional trustees accompanied development staff to county presentations. While initially the smaller counties yielded smaller gifts, estates from those smaller counties have evolved since that campaign, partially because of efforts by the institutional trustees.

With the success of the campaign, the way was paved for other innovative projects. A second large campaign was run five years later, raising $10.8 million. Smaller campaign efforts to build a swine confinement center drew a substantial $1 million—some of that funding came from sources identified by institutional trustees who accompanied development staff on visits to potential donors.

More recently, a new equestrian center has been completed. Initially planned as a $2 million educational facility, the center was upgraded to a $5 million educational and events center for horse shows on the weekends. The institutional trustees agreed to contribute $3 million, instead of the original $2 million, on the condition that the Kirkwood Foundation raise the other $2 million. This facility was built with significant funds from businesses and industries identified and cultivated by institutional trustees. The equestrian center is now completed and flourishing, with weekend bookings year-round already exceeding our projections; enrollment in the equestrian science program has also doubled.

Conclusion

An ongoing way that Kirkwood institutional trustees support fundraising efforts is simply by reminding ourselves and others of the Kirkwood story. Being clear and passionate about the mission and future of the college spreads excitement to others and helps create monetary support for the college from the community. At our institutional and foundation board meetings, we often invite students to tell their stories. All present are energized when a single mother shares how her scholarship, funded by the community, changed the direction of her life and the lives of her children. Stories like this remind us why we serve the college and increase our passion for sharing the Kirkwood story with the community. Elected or appointed institutional trustees may not see fundraising as a main priority, but it is naive not to understand that fundraising will be a condition of trusteeship. Institutional trustees who understand their crucial role in fundraising will most effectively help the communities that they are so fortunate to serve.

Reference

Roha, T. "Touchstones of Independence." *Trusteeship*, May-June 1999, pp. 28–31

Bibliography
Chapter 7: Trusteeship: Service to Institutions and Communities

Boyte, Harry C. & Kari, N. N. "Renewing the democratic spirit in American colleges and universities: Higher education as public work." In T. Ehrlich (Ed.), *Civic Responsibility and Higher Education.* Westport, CT: American Council on Education and Oryx, 2000, pp. 19–36.

Carnegie Commission on Higher Education. *Governance of Higher Education: Six Priority Problems.* Berkeley, CA: Carnegie Foundation for the Advancement of Teaching, 1973.

Cattell, James Mckeen. *University Control.* New York: The Science Press, 1913.

Chait, R. and B. Taylor. "Charting the Territory of Nonprofit Boards." *Harvard Business Review,* Vol. 67 (1989), pp. 44–54.

Chait, T. Holland, and B. Taylor. *The Effective Board of Trustees: Improving the Performance of Governing Boards.* New York: American Council on Education and Macmillan, 1996.

_____, T.P. Holland, and B. Taylor. *Improving the Performance of Governing Boards.* Phoenix: American Council on Education & The Oryx Press, 1996.

Corson, J. *Governance of Colleges and Universities.* New York: McGraw-Hill, 1960.

_____, J. "The Modernization of the University: The Impact of the Function of Governance." *Journal of Higher Education,* Vol. 42 (1971), pp. 430–441.

Davis, G. S. "Dissolution or Survival: The University of Bridgeport and the Unification Church." In M. M. Wood (Ed.), *Nonprofit Boards and Leadership: Cases on Governance, Change, and Board-Staff Dynamics.* San Francisco: Jossey-Bass, 1996, pp. 193–205.

Duryea, E.D. and Williams, D. *The Academic Corporation: A History of College and University Governing Boards.* New York: Falmer Press, 2000.

Fong, P. "A Trustee's Tale." *Community College Week*, (February 13, 2006), pp. 4–5.

Hall, P. D. *A History of Nonprofit Boards in the United States*. Washington, D.C.: National Center for Nonprofit Boards, 1997.

Hall, Peter Dobkin, *Cultures of Trusteeship Program on Nonprofit Organizations*. New Haven, CT: Institute for Social and Policy Studies, Yale University, 1990.

_____. *The Organization of American Culture, 1700–1900: Private Institutions, Elites, and the Origins of American Nationality*. New York: New York University Press, 1982.

Hines, E. R "The Governance of Higher Education". In J.C. Smart, ed., *Higher Education: Handbook of Theory and Research*, Vol. 15. New York: Agathon Press, 2000, pp. 105–156.

Lindeman, Eduard C. *Wealth and Culture: A Study of One Hundred Foundations and Community Trusts and Their Operations During the Decade 1921–1930*. New York: Harcourt Brace, 1936.

Ingram, R. T. "Rethinking the Criteria for Trusteeship." In T. J. MacTaggart (Ed.), *Seeking Excellence through Independence: Liberating Colleges and Universities from Excessive Regulation*. San Francisco: Jossey-Bass, 1998, pp. 29–146.

Michael, S. T., Schwartz, M., Cook, D.M., et al. "Trustee's Level of Satisfaction and Strategies for Improving Satisfaction: A Comparative Analysis of Higher Education Sectors." *Journal of Higher Education Policy and Management*, Vol. 21, No. 2 (1999), pp. 173–191.

Morrill, Justin L. "Servant to the People." In *The Ongoing State University*. Minneapolis: The University of Minnesota Press, 1960, pp. 24–37.

Novak, Richard and Susan Whealler Johnston, "Trusteeship and the Public Good," in Adriana J. Kezar, Tony C. Chambers, John C. Burkhardt, *Higher Education for the Public Good: Emerging Voices from a National Movement*. San Francisco: Jossey-Bass, 2005.

Ruml, Beardsley and Donald H. Morrison, *Memo to a College Trustee*. New York: McGraw-Hill, 1959.

Sullivan, William M. "Institutional Identity and Social Responsibility in Higher Education." In T. Ehrlich (Ed.), *Civic Responsibility and Higher Education*. Westport, CT: American Council on Education and Oryx, 2000, pp. 19–36.

Tierney, W.G. 1981. "Organizational Culture in Higher Education: Defining the Essentials." *The Journal of Higher Education*, Vol. 59, pp. 2–21.

_____. *The Responsive University: Restructuring for High Performance*. Baltimore, MD: The Johns Hopkins University Press, 1998.

Tierney, W.G., and J. Minor. *Challenges for Governance*. Los Angeles: The University of Southern California Press, 2002.

Turner, Richard C., ed. *Taking Trusteeship Seriously: Essays on the History, Dynamics, and Practice of Trusteeship*. Indianapolis: Indiana University Center on Philanthropy.

Wood, M. *Trusteeship in the Private College*. Baltimore: The Johns Hopkins University Press, 1985.

Zwingle, J. *Effective Trusteeship*. Washington, DC: Association of Governing Boards of Universities and Colleges, 1975.

PART III

FUNDRAISING

FUNDRAISING AS AN INTEGRAL PART OF HIGHER EDUCATION

MARYBETH GASMAN & NOAH D. DREZNER

From John Harvard's 1638 bequest to the colonies' first college through current billion-dollar-plus campaigns at private and public institutions throughout the country, fundraising has been an important aspect of American higher education. In "New England's First Fruits" (1693), a Harvard College document that many consider the first higher education fundraising brochure, the author describes citizens who "longed . . . to advance learning and to perpetuate it to prosterity." The early American economy was not able to create and sustain its colleges; as historian Frederick Rudolph expressed, this was left to the Old World: "Individual benevolence was nonetheless in the English tradition, and the colonial colleges therefore naturally looked to it for sustenance."[1]

Most of the contributors to the colonial colleges gave their gifts without restrictions as to how they could be used. Rather than investing for the future in endowments, the early colleges used the donations to erect buildings, buy books, provide scholarships, and pay faculty members' salaries. Merle Curti and Roderick Nash noted that these gifts were very significant to the future of higher education fundraising, not because of their size—in fact, they were small—but because "higher education and its philanthropic support were planted as ideas and actualities in American soil."[2]

With Harvard's Class of 1881 gift of $113,777 in 1906, the idea of class gifts became popular.[3] However, the regular solicitation of alumni for support of colleges and universities did not become commonplace until after World War I. As alumni contributions grew, so did the desire for alumni representation in institutional governing boards—with Cornell University leading the way in this regard. At first alumni donors favored mostly bricks and mortar projects such as residence halls, libraries, student centers, or athletic centers. However, alumni soon began to establish named scholarships as well.

According to Scott Cutlip, systematic and organized fundraising is a phenomenon of the American 20th century.[4] Harvard ushered in the era of professional fundraising in 1919 when it hired the firm of John Price Jones, to handle the institution's 15 million dollar endowment campaign.[5] Gradually, systematic fundraising moved from the elite colleges to institutions nationwide. The establishment of the Ohio State University Development Fund Association, in 1940, initiated alumni fundraising campaigns within state-supported institutions. And, in 1944, in response to a critical financial situation at the nation's private historically Black colleges, Frederick D. Patterson, the president of Tuskegee University, crafted the idea of a united appeal for private Black colleges. The formation of the United Negro College Fund pushed higher education giving in a new direction by reaching out to the average citizen for funds rather than focusing exclusively on a small number of wealthy donors.

According to Michael Worth, there are three main trends that have marked the development of higher educational fundraising since World War II. First, the field of fundraising became more professionalized.[6] Colleges and universities began to hire internal fundraisers rather than using only the well known fundraising firms, such as John Price Jones and Marts and Lundy. As a consequence of the higher profile that fundraising attained the chief development position rose to the most senior levels of college administration.[7] The second trend was the truly rapid growth of development programs. The third was the increased focus on the large gift—leading to a "narrowing of the fundraising pyramid."[8] More recently, as state support declined, more and more public two- and four-year colleges and universities began asking for gifts from individual donors. Fundraising staffs have been assiduously searching for all possible non-tax revenue sources to help meet institutional budget requirements.

As fundraising among both public and private colleges and universities grew, so did competition between them. Nearly 2,000 private institutions and more than 1,500 public two- and four-year colleges and universities compete with each other for the same donations. According to Duronion and Loession, "The competition for private dollars, both within the field of higher education and throughout the entire nonprofit world, is more vigorous now than ever before. For some institutions, doing well in this competition is no less than a matter of survival."[9]

Along with increased competition for funds and larger campaign goals, the higher education fundraising world has seen the growth of "mega gifts," beginning in the 1990s with the dot-com boom on the West coast. For example, in 1999, the Bill Gates and Melinda Gates Foundation gave $1 billion in support of scholarships for African American, Latino, and Native-American students. This donation is managed by the United Negro College Fund. In addition, in 2001, Stanford received the largest donation ever to a single institution—$400 million—from the Hewlett-Packard Foundation.[10] As noted, gifts such as these narrow the fundraising pyramid, "with a higher percentage of total support coming from fewer and fewer gifts at the very top."[11] According to a 1999 survey by the Council for the Advancement and Support of Education, 80 percent of donations came from the top 10 percent of the nation's donors. Moreover, 57 percent of gifts to higher education come from the top one percent of donors.[12]

Donating to colleges and universities is often viewed as a way to make change. According to Worth, donors give because they feel they can promote social justice, enhance "national economic competitiveness," and advance "technological and medical knowledge."[13] Fundraising has become the subject of much interest and some scholarship. Until recently, most of the scholarship has been written by working professionals and is thus highly practical in nature. However, some academics are also gaining an interest in the field and as such, both theoretical and empirical research are growing in the field.

Chapter 8 of the Reader looks at academic fundraising efforts of the past, placing a particular emphasis on how the profession developed. The first article here is Frank H. Oliver's "The Roots of Academic Fundraising." Oliver traces the origins of modern-day college and university fundraising, showing how the political, economic, and social forces of the 19th and early 20th centuries shaped current practice. He examines the approaches of Charles Summer Ward, who developed the time-bounded campaign fueled by intense publicity, and of Bishop William Lawrence, who insisted on viewing fundraising as a process rather than a campaign. Oliver argues that these two fundraising philosophies have fundamentally influenced the growth and development of the college fundraising office of today.

Samuel G. Cash, in an article entitled "Private Voluntary Support to Public Universities in the United States: An Early History," shows that fundraising is not new to public colleges and universities. Through historical research, he shows that the early state institutions, lacking a model for an "institution free from sectarian control and reliant on the state for support," followed the lead of the early colonial colleges. Contrary to popular belief, public institutions have always relied on both public and private support for their livelihood.

The last article in this chapter is W. Bruce Cook's "Fund Raising and the College Presidency in an Era of Uncertainty: From 1975 to the Present." Cook masterfully discusses the changing role that fundraising has played in the tenure of recent presidents. Through interviews with college and university presidents, including Derek Bok (Harvard University), Jim Duderstadt (University of Michigan), and Clark Kerr (Berkeley and the University of California System), as well as key researchers in the field of philanthropy, such as Robert Payton, Cook shows how presidents have difficulty adjusting to their role as fundraisers—especially now that this role includes familiarity with estate planning, tax laws, and planned giving. Cook also notes that boards of trustees consider fundraising skills, along with leadership, above all else when selecting new presidents.

We have included two chapters from Scott M. Cutlip's seminal work on the history of fundraising in the bibliography at the end of this chapter. The first chapter focuses on the professionalization of the fundraising field, while the second explores colleges and university fundraising during the 1920s. In addition, we have included "New England's First Fruits," considered to be the first fundraising publicity piece.

Chapter 9 focuses on alumni/ae giving and other relevant institutional constituencies. According to *Giving USA 2006*, individuals are responsible for the majority of giving to colleges and universities. Of these donors, the marjority are alumni/ae of the institution that they support. Alumni/ae giving is at the core of college and university advancement processes. Not only do these contributions support the day-to-day operations of an institution but they demonstrate to outside donors, such as foundations and corporations, that the alumni/ae has a commitment to the future success of the institution.

Understanding that currently 55 percent of college students are women and therefore women will eventually make up the majority of universities alumni, Peter Briechle asks, as his title suggests, "Does Institutional Type Affect Alumnae Donating Patterns in the United States?" Using surveys, Briechle finds that the blending of donor preferences and institutional needs is particularly important to alumnae when considering when and how much to give. This work adds to the philanthropic scholarship that examines female donors and complements Jeanie Lovell's article in the Fundraising in Diverse Communities chapter of the Reader.

In Charles Clotfelter's article, "Who Are the Alumni Donors? Giving by Two Generations of Alumni from Selective Colleges," we learn that a positive experience at college, involvement in co-curricular activities, and having a mentor all have positive effects on future alumni giving. He also shows that while a high proportion of alumni participate in campaigns, more than half of the dollars raised is given by one percent of alumni donors.

William Harrison, in his article entitled "College Relations and Fund-Raising Expenditures: Influencing the Probability of Alumni Giving to Higher Education," predicts the probability of alumni giving based on the amount of money spent on fundraising and alumni relationships. Using statistical modeling, Harrison shows that the old adage of "you have to spend money to make money" is true for alumni fundraising. He finds that an increase in alumni relations spending as little as $10 per current student can increase alumni participation from 25 to 26.4 percent.

Does a winning football season influence giving? Sarah Turner, Lauren Meserve, and William Bowen explore this question in their article, "Winning and Giving: Football Results and Alumni Giving at Selective Private Colleges and Universities." In fact, they find that there is no correlation between "winning and giving" at Division I and Ivy League schools, where athletic budgets are the largest. However, at Division III liberal arts colleges, where sports have a much lower profile, they find a modest increase in giving when there is a better win-loss ratio. This modest increase in giving is tied mostly to athletic-alumni.

While we do not include them in the Reader, we suggest, at the end of this chapter, articles that focus on the impact of econometrics on giving; student and alumni associations; and faculty and staff participation in annual funds.

Chapter 10 explores "The Mechanics of Fundraising." According to Thomas Broce, "fund raising as a professional process is best understood broadly . . . it must encompass the entire operation from goal identification to gift solicitation." In an effort to provide practitioners with well-rounded, hands-on information, this chapter speaks specifically to the day-to-day operations within the fundraising area. Understanding the mechanics of fundraising or how to successfully solicit gifts is of the utmost importance to all institutions of higher education, whether they be public colleges and universities that are facing decreases in state and federal funds or private ones that require increased dollars for scholarships in order to counteract increasing tuition. In this chapter, we bring together seminal literature that speaks to fundraising at different institutional types and donor levels.

While literature on fundraising and philanthropy in four-year higher education is limited in general, even less is known about giving to community colleges. The first article in this chapter, S. Renea Akin's "Institutional Advancement and Community Colleges: A Review of Literature" finds that in order for community colleges to be successful in their quest for funds beyond government support, they must integrate fundraising into the college's strategic planning; encourage politicians when they consider political appointments to the institution's board that the prospective member be able to solicit funds for the college; increase town-gown relations; and engage the president in fundraising efforts.

James Andreoni's "Toward a Theory of Charitable Fund-Raising" looks at the importance of seed-money to capital campaigns, whether these campaigns are for higher education or other non-profits. Rather than looking at the social and personal benefits of giving, Andreoni focuses on the economies of scale that are realized when leadership gifts allow for the creation of a greater public good.

Major gifts make up the majority of all funds raised in both capital and annual campaigns. In fact, research has shown that 89 percent of campaign dollars are raised by 10 percent of the donors. Bruce Cook's article "Surveying the Major Gifts Literature: Observations and Reflections" reminds us that giving is part of a relationship, in which both the donor and the organization have needs and that fundraising relationships must fulfill the needs of both donor and recipient. Likewise, Paul Schervish furthers our understanding of major gifts in his article, "Major Donors, Major Motives: The People and Purposes behind Major Gifts." Here he introduces us to the idea of "spirituality in the age of affluence." This spirituality, Schervish contends, adds to the complexity of wealthy donors' motivations and perceptions of the impact of their gift in society.

As donors and fundraisers have become more sophisticated, so has the profession of fundraising overall. Timothy Caboni's "Toward Professionalization: Fund Raising Norms and Their Implications for Practice" discusses the norms and practices of fundraisers. Building on his own prior work as a development officer, Caboni finds that fundraisers take into account both the welfare of their institution and that of the donor. He shows that these norms have been incorporated into professional associations and ethic statements.

As noted earlier, in the Origins of Fundraising chapter and in the work of Bruce Cook, the role of the president in fundraising has grown immensely over the past 50 years. In her article, "Charles S. Johnson and Johnnetta Cole: Successful Role Models for Fund-Raising at Historically Black Colleges and Universities," Marybeth Gasman gives us two poignant examples of Black college presidents who effectively raised money for their institutions. Their strategies took into account donor motivation, institutional needs, and proper stewardship. This article speaks both to Black colleges and predominantly White institutions alike.

At the end of this chapter, we suggest further readings that cover topics such as direct mail, prospect research, planned giving, pending wealth transfer, and public relations.

The term philanthropy has long been associated with a small number of White families and individuals, mostly men, "who enjoyed access to education, owned major businesses, held leadership positions in government, dominated the professions and inherited wealth". However, communities of color and women have had their own means for raising monies and resources for institutions tied to their communities. The changing demographics in the United States, which will soon put whites in the minority (and have already done so with males), will require fund raisers to reflect and devise creative strategies for maintaining balance within their services and attracting diverse funding constituencies.

Chapter 11 starts with Emmett D. Carson's "Black Philanthropy's Past, Present, and Future." In this piece, Carson skillfully examines the socioeconomic forces that have shaped African American philanthropy, including slavery, segregation, and notions of self-help. Carson also provides a working definition of Black philanthropy, noting that it means more than the giving of money, but instead the giving of time, talent, goods and services. Of particular importance are Carson's predictions for the future of Black philanthropy, including his practical suggestions for the nonprofit community.

Complementing Carson's article is Marybeth Gasman's "An Untapped Resource: Bringing African Americans into the College and University Giving Process." In this piece, Gasman reviews the rich history of African American philanthropy, including the contributions of the Black church, African American social and service organizations, and Black fraternities and sororities. Gasman also makes concrete, practical suggestions as to how college and university advancement and alumni staff can better include African Americans in college and university giving process.

In "Indians Giving: The New Philanthropy in Indian Country," Marjane Ambler describes the various and conflicting images of Native Americans and their philanthropic efforts. Of critical note, is her exploration of the impediments to effective fundraising within the Native American community. Ambler draws upon the philanthropic work of five Indian nations, providing examples of partnerships between national foundations and the Native American community.

Charles G. Rodriquez, in his piece "Education and Hispanic Philanthropy: Family, Sacrifice, and Community," urges the Hispanic community to see itself as philanthropic. In particular, he encourages support for efforts to increase retention and graduation rates at the nation's schools, colleges, and universities. As those with college degrees tend to be more philanthropic, Rodriguez shows that giving to education can be a self-perpetuating phenomenon for Hispanics. He calls on the leaders of the Hispanic community to foster a widespread culture of giving that supports their advancement as an ethnic group.

In "A Brief Examination of Institutional Advancement Activities at Hispanic Serving Institutions," Michael W. Mulnix, Randall G. Bowden, and Esther E. Lopez look at fundraising within the context of the nation's over 200 Hispanic Serving Institutions (HSIs). They provide a wide-reaching overview of HSIs and the challenges they face in the area of fundraising. In particular, the authors point out that the funding of most HSIs is intimately tied to both state and federal politics, making it essential that these institutions work to improve their advancement functions. Mulnix et al. suggest improvements in the support of alumni groups, public relations, and marketing.

Although the literature on African American and Hispanic philanthropy has been growing in recent years, there is little research on Asian-American philanthropy and even less on fundraising within the Asian or Asian-American community. We have included Jessica Chao's "What Is Chinese American Philanthropy?" in this chapter of the Reader to give a broad overview of one segment of Asian philanthropy in the United States. Interestingly, Chao refers to Chinese philanthropy as operating without a "unifying theme." Specifically, she says, "it is old and new, personal and institutional, extremely ethnic and paradoxically assimilated ." Chao argues that Chinese Americans practice a rich tradition of communal philanthropy that is assisted by the many social and civic organizations in the community. Although the focus of this article is on philanthropy, we have included it here because it offers insight into philanthropic approaches in the Chinese American community that can inform fundraising.

Noah Drezner's article, "Advancing Gallaudet: Alumni Support for the Nation's University for the Deaf and Hard-of-Hearing and Its Similarities to Black Colleges and Universities," is perhaps the first article on the topic of fundraising practices and traditions at Gallaudet University and within the deaf community. Comparing and contrasting these practices with the history of fundraising at the nation's Black colleges, Drezner traces the success and failures of both institutional types, and discovers compelling similarities.

The last article in this chapter is Jeanie Lovell's "Women's Philanthropy Programs at Coeducational Colleges and Universities." In order to identify effective models for fundraising among women in general, Lovell examines existing programs and initiatives to secure female donors at colleges and universities throughout the country. Lovell gives specific recommendations, noting how important institutional culture is to any successful plan for increasing philanthropic donations from women. In particular, she points to the need for colleges and universities to educate female donors in the ways of fundraising, while they are students and as young alumni.

In recent years, there has been a substantial increase in the quantity and quality of articles related to philanthropy and fundraising among people of color and women. We have incorporated many of the articles in the bibliography, including those that focus on fundraising within minority-serving institutions, diversity within the fundraising profession, and motivations for giving within specific racial, ethnic, and gender populations.

In Chapter 12, we provide articles that discuss the motivation behind giving. The first selection in this section of the Reader is Paul Schervish's "Inclination, Obligation, and Association: What We Know and What We Need to Learn about Donor Motivation." In this article, Schervish uses quantitative research to introduce us to the concept of donor motivation, or the "mobilizing factors" that enter into a person's decision to make a first gift and to increase the size of their subsequent donations. Building on Schervish's idea of "mobilizing factors" is Andrea Walton's "'To Bind the University to Nothing': The Giving of Clementine Miller Tangeman as a Case Study in Donor Motivation." In her historical case study, Walton provides an account of how donors draw on their personal experiences and beliefs when deciding how to make donations. She contends that historical biography can teach both prospective donors and development officers about the factors that influence donor motivation.

Additionally, in this chapter, we turn to a new form of giving that has emerged, that of venture philanthropy. There is virtually no scholarly literature on this topic and even less on its relationship to higher education giving. In her article, "When Venture Philanthropy Rocks the Ivory Tower," Luisa Boverini classifies the types of gifts in this new nomenclature, the social context that caused the creation of venture philanthropy, and the potential venture philanthropy has for higher education.

In the bibliography of this section, we have included Noah Drezner's "Recessions and Tax-cuts: The Impact of Economic Cycles on Individual Giving, Philanthropy, and Higher Education" to help the reader understand the interplay between societal forces and donor motivation.

Notes

1. Frederick Rudolph. *The American College and University. A History.* (New York: Vintage Books, 1962), 178.
2. Merle Curti & Roderick Nash. *Philanthropy in the Shaping of American Higher Education.* (New Brunswick, NJ: Rutgers University Press, 1965), 41.
3. Merle Curti & Roderick Nash. *Philanthropy in the Shaping of American Higher* Education. (New Brunswick, NJ: Rutgers University Press, 1965).
4. Scott Cutlip. *Fund Raising in the United States.* (New Brunswick, NJ: Rutgers University Press, 1965).
5. Scott Cutlip. *Fund Raising in the United States.* (New Brunswick, NJ: Rutgers University Press, 1965).
6. Michael Worth. *New Strategies for Educational Fundraising.* (New York: Praeger, 2002).
7. Michael Worth. *New Strategies for Educational Fundraising.* (New York: Praeger, 2002).
8. Michael Worth. *New Strategies for Educational Fundraising.* (New York: Praeger, 2002), 29.
9. Margaret Duronion & B. Loession. *Effective Fund Raising in Higher Education.* (San Francisco: Jossey-Bass, 1991), 1.
10. Michael Worth. *New Strategies for Educational Fundraising.* (New York: Praeger, 2002).
11. Michael Worth. *New Strategies for Educational Fundraising.* (New York: Praeger, 2002), 33.
12. Michael Worth. *New Strategies for Educational Fundraising.* (New York: Praeger, 2002).
13. Michael Worth. *New Strategies for Educational Fundraising.* (New York: Praeger, 2002), 33.

CHAPTER 8

ORIGINS OF FUNDRAISING

THE ROOTS OF ACADEMIC FUND RAISING

FRANK H. OLIVER

Abstract

The modern office of institutional advancement traces its roots to political, economic, and social currents of the late nineteenth and early twentieth centuries. Two men established distinct fund-raising philosophies during the period—Charles Sumner Ward, a paid YMCA executive, and Bishop William Lawrence, a Harvard alumnus and volunteer. This paper begins by exploring the differences in their approaches to large-scale fund raising. It then traces the growth and development of the fund-raising consulting industry. The origin of America's two most influential firms and their interactions on higher education is important because the first development officers for colleges and universities came from the ranks of (or were tutored by) executives of the fund-raising consulting firms. The firms still exist today as Brakeley, John Price Jones and Ketchum, Inc. The Brakeley/Jones company has historical ties that can be traced to Bishop William Lawrence, and the Ketchum firm traces its historical ties to Charles Sumner Ward. These two dominant firms demonstrated two different cultures and took dissimilar approaches to selecting and developing their personnel. Finally, the paper suggests that these historically different cultures may be the source of some conflict in academic fund-raising operations today.

Introduction

The roots of American higher educational fund raising grow back in two different directions. These roots were nurtured by the belief systems of two historically different approaches, and they were developed into commercial enterprises by two dissimilar personalities. This research explores the origins of academic fund raising, how the commercial firms influenced its development, and how distinct philosophies and approaches blended together to create current fund-raising culture in colleges and universities.

The paper begins with the presentation of two fathers of the art of fund raising and their distinct thinking about its processes. One school of thought came from the minds of executives of the Young Men's Christian Association (YMCA) led by Charles Sumner Ward. The second came from Bishop William Lawrence and his colleagues while working as volunteers for their alma mater, Harvard.

The commercial consulting firms, which began forming around the time of the First World War, predate development departments in higher education. Northwestern was the first institution to coin the term *development* in the 1920s.[1] That was more than a decade after the first consulting firm began operations.[2] Most academic development departments began forming after the Second World War. In the decades following the war, consultants either took positions in higher education or trained new appointees. The two most important and influential firms were Ketchum, Inc. and John Price Jones. The Ketchum brothers were University of Pittsburgh graduates trained by Charles Sumner Ward in a 1914 campaign for their alma mater. John Price Jones is a descendent of Bishop Lawrence. These two firms had unequalled influence on the development of higher educational fund raising.

The Ketchum and Jones firms practiced significantly different tactics in building their companies. For instance, Ketchum focused on staff training and progressing through a hierarchy of corporate responsibilities. The firm worked to create a Ketchum way of providing service. Jones, on the other hand, believed in on-the-job training. At John Price Jones, new consultants would work with a seasoned veteran and then manage a fund-raising program on their own. The two firms also sought different kinds of individuals as their consultants. Ketchum hired men from a traditional source of higher educational talent in the eighteenth and nineteenth centuries, namely, the ministry. Jones, in contrast, preferred to hire consultants from a relatively new profession, that of journalism. Both disciplines relied on communication acumen, but they attracted very different kinds of people to their ranks. Ketchum and Jones competed for business among colleges and universities for decades. Their descendant companies still do.

The thesis of this paper is that these two consulting firms, with their distinct work environments, employee selection, and training practices, created dissimilar organizational cultures, which imbued the academic advancement staff. Organizational cultures developing over time will be different if they begin with different attitudes, beliefs, values, techniques, and worldviews. Organizations that recruit journalists and those that recruit ministers *might* develop very differently. Organizations that insist on conformity in their approach and those who provide on-the-job training *are bound to* develop differently. While those who work in today's fund-raising world intuitively know elements of the two historic philosophies and approaches, few may know how they developed. The following traces the development of these two distinct philosophies and how they became corporate cultures. It then speculates on their possible effects on the field of academic fund raising today. Readers can consider the values and beliefs that sometimes separate experienced, intelligent professionals in style and approach. Some may also find the origin of many of their own value systems in fund-raising practice.

Research Methods

This paper is a historical study. The research for this paper included the writings of Charles Sumner Ward and Bishop William Lawrence, archival materials from the YMCA, the Brakeley, John Price Jones firm, the University of Pittsburgh, Elmira College, and newspaper accounts of fund-raising campaigns. It calls on several well-known volumes, namely Jencks and Reisman, Cutlip, Lucas, Duronio and Temple, and Worth and Asp.[3] It also cites some relatively obscure works, namely, Carter, Himmelstein, Lawrence, and Alberts.[4]

Research included personal interviews with leaders of the fund-raising industry from the late twentieth century and early twenty-first centuries. The individuals chosen for interviews were colleagues of the men who founded commercial fund-raising firms. To verify the paper's thesis, interviews were necessary to discuss the role Ketchum, Inc. and Brakeley, John Price Jones, Inc. played in training and supplying fund-raising practitioners to higher education, their choices of personnel, and the way they trained their consultants. George A. Brakely Jr., David S. Ketchum, Elliot S. Oshrey, C. L. Kirk, and Charles E. Lawson were interviewed between April 1997 and October 1998.

The paper begins with the philosophy and approach of Charles Sumner Ward, and his first campaign for higher education in 1914 at the University of Pittsburgh. It then explores the philosophy and approach of Ward's critic Bishop William Lawrence. These two men were the founding forces in the nascent practice of organizing fund-raising endeavors. They were contemporaries, but never competitors. The paper compares and contrasts their significantly different belief systems through their own writings. It then moves to two commercial fund-raising consulting firms during the economic boom years of the 1920s. It focuses on the John Price Jones firm, which was a direct descendant of Bishop Lawrence and on Carlton Ketchum who came from the YMCA school of fund raisers. The paper explores the corporate cultures created by these men during the period between the end of the First World War and the end of the Second World War.

George A. Brakeley Jr. enters the story via the John Price Jones firm as a young graduate of Princeton, and enjoys a meteoric rise in influence and prestige. Brakeley became the most influential force in academic fund raising, and eventually bought the John Price Jones company. The paper concludes with the argument that the products of these two corporate cultures affected higher educational fund raising in two ways. They helped form the applicant pools for development departments in post-war America and they conducted the overwhelming majority of campaigns and training programs for the new practitioners of fund development.

The Two Fathers of Fund Raising

Charles Sumner Ward

A YMCA executive, Charles Sumner Ward, has been generally credited with revolutionizing the techniques of organized fund raising.[5] Because of their compact time frame and the intensive use of public media, Ward's fund-raising methods became widely known as "the whirlwind campaign" one hundred years ago.

The whirlwind, intensive campaign was used to finance building construction for YMCAs in the late nineteenth century. YMCA records show that the occasional use of whirlwind campaign techniques date as far back as 1884, but they were rudimentary affairs, not yet possessing the characteristics of a full-fledged campaign.

Carter briefly described the concept after Ward and his colleague Lyman Pierce later refined it:

> Its method was to enlist the volunteer services of a hundred or more of the leading business and professional men of the city who would agree to solicit personally ten to twenty prospective contributors assigned to each of them. They agreed to do this within a period of one month, during which time the desired funds . . . would be subscribed.[6]

Officials of other charitable organizations took notice of these highly organized and intensive campaigns and eventually adopted their ways. For instance, organizers of federated fund raising for social agencies (the predecessor to Community Chests and United Ways) copied the YMCA's campaign model.[7]

Ward and Pierce collaborated for the first time in 1905 to raise funds for a new YMCA in Washington. According to undated YMCA archival material entitled *How to Raise Money*, the Washington campaign featured a number of fund-raising firsts. For the first time campaign headquarters were established for volunteers' convenience. Teams of workers chose names of prospective donors who were evaluated by their giving potential. Report meetings were initiated to share soliciting experiences. Another innovation was the campaign clock, which monitored the campaign's progress and put pressure on the volunteer solicitors.

Another campaign first was the use of a full-time publicity person.[8] The concept of public relations professionals came from the early part of the twentieth century, which created two important social and political currents. The first was the advent of yellow journalism and the muckrakers. The second current was the popularity of Theodore Roosevelt. Roosevelt's presidency came to represent a time known as the Progressive Era when the national mood yearned for a greater sense of fairness—a square deal. Americans and their federal government sought to break apart the great industrial trusts formed in the late nineteenth century. Eventually, the industrialists and the monopolies hired public relations experts to defend them from attacks by the journalists and the government.

Worth and Asp wrote about the importance of Ward and Pierce's approach: ". . . the first to demonstrate that fund raising success depended as much on method as on the personalities of the individuals involved . . . a significant change from earlier fund raising . . . for the first time fund raising was viewed as a systematic activity, based on a body of knowledge, applied by a professional specialist."[9]

Over the next decade the whirlwind campaign, which came to be known as "the Ward method," raised more than $60 million for capital projects, and its tactics became routine and standardized.

Ward's First Campaign for Higher Education

The Ward method was first applied to higher educational fund raising at the University of Pittsburgh. In 1914, Pittsburgh engaged Charles Sumner Ward to conduct a $3 million fund-raising campaign to help develop its new campus in Schenley Park. Chancellor Samuel Black McCormick, a Presbyterian minister and trained lawyer, had learned of Ward's work in raising $4 million to build a YMCA in New York.[10]

McCormick was in the process of changing the old Western University of Pennsylvania into a brand new institution. His problems with fund raising were massive. The geographic location of the university was McCormick's first problem. Many of Pittsburgh's town fathers questioned the need for a college or university in Pittsburgh. The eastern universities were well established by the early part of the twentieth century, and to the west of Pittsburgh the states had taken the responsibility of building universities for their constituents.

Adjacent to the property McCormick sought to develop was the Carnegie Institute, an educational and cultural complex, which was founded in 1895 by Andrew Carnegie. In 1903 Mr. Carnegie began to endow the development of technical schools at the Institute, which eventually became Carnegie Mellon University. Although Andrew Carnegie was a trustee of the University of Pittsburgh, he pointedly never supported it financially.[11] He believed that the city of Pittsburgh was well known for its technical expertise and did not see the need for another university with an out-of-touch, nineteenth century curriculum.

McCormick also faced a problem in the attitudes about higher education in the city. William Jacob Holland, a predecessor of McCormick, once called Pittsburgh a queer place, with narrow philanthropic interests. It seemed to Holland that people in Pittsburgh only wanted to build churches and hospitals.[12]

Nevertheless, Pitt's campaign engaged a remarkable number of volunteers. Businessmen, women, civic leaders, faculty, even students, were asked to volunteer and to pledge. On January 15, 1914, *The Pittsburgh Dispatch* reported on the campaign's organization when it announced:

> At 9 o'clock this morning the army of 200 workers who have enlisted for a period of ten days will make its first attack upon the fortress of Pittsburgh wealth, reassembling in its camp at noon to check up on what spoils shall have been taken, only to return to the fray again in the afternoon. The attack will be renewed each morning until January 26, when the commanders hope to be able to report a complete and decisive victory.[13]

The 200 volunteers were called privates. They comprised twenty teams, commanded by captains and lieutenants, in two divisions under one director general. The director general was appointed by an executive committee, which was chaired by E. V. Babcock. More than 7,000 prospects were carefully assigned, and each of the prospects was approached by only one solicitor.[14] When Ward completed his first campaign for higher education, *The Pitt Weekly* reported, "With all the fanfare, with careful organization, and with an extension of time, the campaign ended one million short of its goal."[15]

Chancellor McCormick provided two Pitt students, brothers Carlton and George Ketchum, to work as assistants to Charles Sumner Ward and Frederick Courtenay Barber, the campaign's publicity man.[16] Right after the Pitt campaign, Barber founded what is likely the first professional fund-raising company in America, Frederick Courtenay Barber & Associates, 1 Madison Avenue, New York. Carlton Ketchum went to work for Barber and was listed as the publicity manager for Elmira College.[17]

At the same time Charles Sumner Ward successfully applied his fund-raising experience to higher education—training men like Arnaud Martz, Lyman Pierce, and Carlton and George Ketchum— another fund raiser was finding success with a very different system of beliefs on how to raise money.[18] The following section presents an alternative philosophy and approach to the Ward method developed by Ward's contemporary Bishop William Lawrence.

Bishop William Lawrence

To say that Ward attracted critics would be an understatement. The intensity of the whirlwind campaign produced pressure on volunteers and pressure on donors. Potential donors were listed and categorized, which was considered offensive by many, particularly if the prospect had no personal interest in the charity. The Ward method approached philanthropy with the concept of obligation and duty. Those pressured often complained.[19]

One critic of the Ward method was also a pioneer in fund raising for higher education, Bishop William Lawrence. A researcher has no way to know for certain, but Lawrence's writings read like a critique of the Ward method. Holding back information from the public to stage a last-minute success would have been anathema to Lawrence:

> I have no use for those campaigners who hold back totals and then throw them on the public at strategic times. The public has come to distrust totals to the great loss of confidence in campaigns. Those who have given and those who are to be approached have a right to be treated honestly and will respond to honest treatment. . . . People when they have the facts are often finer than we think.[20]

Lawrence was an Episcopal priest who took a much less combative approach to raising money. Fund raising for Bishop Lawrence was an avocation. Born to aristocratic, privileged New England parents and educated at Harvard, class of 1871, Lawrence wrote: "I dislike the word 'campaign' in this connection almost as much as I abhor 'appeal.' Campaign suggests force or pressure, methods whereby people are dragooned to give. Appeal suggests a call upon the sympathies and emotions of the people, melting them to give. Both methods are weak and liable to bring reaction."[21]

Lawrence became an overseer of his alma mater, Harvard University, in 1894; in 1899 he was elected vice president of the alumni association, and in 1904 the association's president. As president, he called attention to the underpaid status of the university's faculty. He called on his fellow alumni to donate $2.5 million to increase the salaries of professors in the liberal arts. Lawrence wrote:

> My experience had been limited to the Hasty Pudding Club and the raising of one or two sums of one hundred thousand dollars. We therefore had to *feel our way* [emphasis added]. As the core of a committee of ten well-known alumni, three of us formed the working staff and later experience has shown me that three is enough . . . Our only central office was under my hat. Our only publicity consisted in a few syndicated articles on Harvard at a total cost of five hundred dollars, and such editorials and news as we could get into the papers . . .
>
> We were agreed as to certain principles. The friends of the University were to be given an opportunity to strengthen the College by the increase of the salaries of the teachers in liberal arts; for we could not cover all teachers in the university. There was to be no crowding or jamming for subscriptions. It were better not to complete the full amount. As a matter of fact, the total gift fell short only about one hundred thousand dollars. We could doubtless have gotten the whole by pressure, but it was worth the amount to close with the good will and confidence of the alumni.
>
> Our first duty was to get the facts into the heads of Harvard's friends.[22]

Bishop Lawrence's gift to improve the lot of the liberal arts faculty at Harvard broke new ground in fund raising. It was the first large-scale effort to systematically solicit support from alumni of a university for a specific program. Popular wisdom at the time held that donors would only give to build monuments, as in capital for new buildings. Lawrence proved that significant amounts of money could be raised for other purposes including professors' salaries. Lawrence was successful in his work without overt pressure. In addition to the editorials referenced above, the program consisted of a series of solicitation letters to Harvard's alumni, who numbered 10,000 at the time.[23]

Years later Bishop Lawrence was asked by his Episcopal Church to create a pension fund for its ministers. By raising more than $6 million for the pension fund, Bishop Lawrence proved again that large amounts of money were available for purposes other than constructing buildings. One of Lawrence's most trusted assistants during the ministers' pension fund-raising project was Guy Emerson, another Harvard graduate. Cutlip pointed out that "as Emerson was tutored by the Bishop in the art of money getting, so did Emerson, in turn, tutor John Price Jones, Robert F. Duncan and other fund raisers."[24]

Comparing and Contrasting the Two Fathers

There are important differences in the philosophies of Bishop Lawrence and the Ward method of raising money. In fact, the Bishop insisted on thinking of fund raising as a process or program rather than a campaign. Lawrence wrote of providing a *gift* for the purpose of helping professors, rather than the militaristic campaign jargon of Ward and Pierce. The *crowding and jamming* that Lawrence eschewed was a major strategic tenet of the Ward method. Last minute pressure to reach goal invigorated volunteers and coalesced public attention in the Ward method. Lawrence, on the other hand admonished:

> If you dominate or dragoon a man by your personality, you may get his money once, but not the next time. If, finding that the facts do not move him, you appeal to his emotions of sympathy and pity, and thereby get the money, you will find him cross the next time you call. You have taken undue advantage of him. My rule is never to allow a person to sign a pledge in my presence. If my facts do not convince him,—if the cause apart from the influence of my presence will not bring his contribution,— I do not want it. And if I should get it by undue personal pressure, I shall never succeed with that man a second time. . . .[25]

Personality mattered to Charles Sumner Ward. Ward warned against expecting publicity or public gatherings to raise money. According to Ward, ". . . the money is raised by personal solicitation of personally selected men and corporations. No subscriptions of money 'to be raised' by women's auxiliaries can be considered valid. Collections are not taken by newspapers, or in public meetings."[26]

The ministers' pension project uncovered another important difference in the philosophies of the Lawrence and the Ward Methods. The YMCA school of fund raisers preferred to publicize the names of large contributors. Bishop Lawrence did not believe in that practice. Instead, the Bishop carried a list of large donors with him on solicitation calls in case prospective donors wanted to know who had already given.[27]

On a few issues the two fund-raising philosophies agreed. Both thought it necessary to secure a few large gifts before asking others to participate. Lawrence wrote, "It also became clear to us that . . . we must first have some large gifts with which to stimulate the imagination of all and to give a thrust to later action."[28] Ward observed, "One or more large conditional gifts must be found prior to the opening of the campaign. . . . One strikingly large subscription . . . is much more effective than a group of smaller subscriptions."[29]

Both philosophies relied on a clearly articulated need, but differed significantly in the intensity of publicity necessary for success. For Lawrence, "Publicity demands quality, not quantity. Tons of paper and printer's ink are wasted every day."[30] Lawrence thought that information should be so clear and concise that a jogger could read it.

Also, both philosophies acknowledged the importance of the campaign's leadership. According to Lawrence: "The leaders of the campaign must be the leading alumni of the institution, . . . The people judge a cause by the kind of men who support it, and the kind of support they give . . . The leading business men of the city must be enlisted . . . real leaders in business, political, social and religious life have practically left their personal interests to give their time."[31]

To summarize these two fund-raising philosophies: the YMCA philosophy, with Charles Sumner Ward as leader, approached fund raising with all the finesse of a military invasion. Its proponents used intense publicity and high-pressure techniques on both volunteers and potential donors. They controlled information for the sake of the campaign. Personality, that is, who did the asking, made a difference in the YMCA school of thought.

Bishop William Lawrence would have none of that sort of behavior; the facts alone had to move an individual to philanthropy. If his own personality had to make the difference, Lawrence claimed that he did not want the money. Information in the Lawrence school of thought was minimal but had to be crystal-clear.

Both Charles Sumner Ward and Bishop Lawrence found remarkable fund-raising success. Ward established a commercial firm in New York in 1919, and Lawrence remained a fund-raising volunteer. Each of them then influenced two other men who came to dominate fund raising for higher education through commercial enterprises in the next decade—John Price Jones and Carlton Ketchum. The next section presents the dissimilar outlooks on the world and on the business of raising money held by Jones and Ketchum.

John Price Jones, a descendent of the Bishop Lawrence school of thought through Liberty Loan campaigns of the First World War, opened his firm in New York in 1919. Carlton and George Ketchum, descendents of the YMCA school of fund raisers, headquartered in the early 1920s in their hometown—Pittsburgh. These were two cities of remarkable wealth and influence at the time. Jones, a journalist by training, built his company with other journalists. Carlton Ketchum, a Presbyterian Sunday school teacher, saw fund raising as a calling, and liked to hire ministers. (George Ketchum left the fund-raising company to start a public relations firm shortly after Ketchum, Inc. began operations.) The values, approaches, selection of employees, and their subsequent training in these two companies created two very different cultures. The following section presents the growth and development of the Jones and Ketchum firms.

The Consulting Firms

John Price Jones, Inc.

In higher education John Price Jones became the leader of the profession. It is not possible to overestimate the impact Jones had on fund raising for colleges and universities. According to Cutlip, "a bright new star appeared in the World War I fund-raising constellation and started moving across that firmament in the immediate post war years bringing new light and brilliance to the field."[32] Jones was educated at Harvard, and then spent time in New York as a newspaper reporter and as a publicity man. During the First World War, Jones worked for an advertising agency and his employer donated his services to the Liberty Loan fund-raising campaign.

Jones put his journalistic instincts to good use in fund raising. He enjoyed researching potential donors and understood the value of keeping good campaign records. Jones carefully documented each of his Liberty Loan campaigns with information that could help the next one succeed.

In 1916, Harvard announced a campaign to raise $10 million for endowment, but the campaign stopped because of the country's entry into the First World War. Jones teamed with another Harvard alumnus, Robert F. Duncan, to resume the campaign after the war.

Jones applied the lessons he learned from Guy Emerson during the Liberty Loan campaigns of the First World War. There would be no rough and tumble methods of solicitation. Rather, the case for supporting Harvard was carefully and thoughtfully articulated; Harvard's needs were presented along with its greater opportunity for service (a manner that would have pleased their mentor Bishop William Lawrence). The strategy succeeded. Harvard's campaign oversubscribed its goal by November 1919 with more than $14 million raised for the University.

The Harvard campaign was an important turning point in the history of fund raising for American colleges and universities because the message sent from Cambridge was that the old ways of financing higher education were passé. Colleges would, from this campaign forward, organize and call on their alumni for *major* financial support.[33]

At the end of the campaign for Harvard, Mrs. Hanna Smith Andrews, a Smith alumna, asked if the group from Harvard might perform similar service for her alma mater. Duncan reported the request to Jones who wondered if there might be a business in this activity. There was. The John Price Jones Company was founded in November 1919.[34] Jones owned the company until the mid-1950s when he sold the controlling interest to Charles A. Anger.[35]

During Jones's time at the helm, his firm conducted some of the most important educational campaigns in America's history. Because of his success at Harvard, his new firm attracted the most prestigious clients in higher education. In turn, Jones was able to attract some of the most able executives and campaign directors. According to Carter, "He gathered a staff around him, many of whose names became widely known as consultants—Harold J. Seymour, Chester E. Tucker, George Brakeley, Sr., Robert Duncan, Carl Kersting . . .".[36] Many of these early Jones consultants were journalists trained in the art of communicating complex issues and programs to the world in understandable ways.

George A. Brakeley, Jr., who studied journalism at Penn and became the eventual successor to Jones, confirmed that Jones preferred hiring journalists as his campaign consultants.[37] Cutlip pointed out that Jones derogatorily referred to the YMCA fund raisers as *the Christers*.[38]

Preparation for becoming a campaign director at the Jones Company consisted of on-the-job training, which moved from working with a John Price Jones senior director, to directing a campaign on one's own. This training process was not dissimilar to Bishop Lawrence "feeling his way" through his first campaign for Harvard.[39]

While the John Price Jones culture was built by journalists and on-the-job training, another company successfully entered the fund-raising consulting business and found remarkable success. The next section explores the approach Carlton Ketchum, a protege of Charles Sumner Ward, took to building his firm.

The Ketchum Culture

Carlton Ketchum decided that in the post-Second World War period he would distinguish his firm through staff training. According to David S. Ketchum, who joined his father's company after service in the Second World War, the firm began summer staff conferences in Chautauqua, New York in 1950. After a few years, Ketchum moved the conferences to Penn State University where the firm was able to take advantage of the theoretical knowledge of the university's professors. The conferences were held during the last two weeks of August and spouses were invited to attend. Staff training was the pride of the Ketchum firm. The ultimate objective of Ketchum, Inc. was to provide a consistent product or service to each of its clients. Consistency came from training and supervision. According to David Ketchum:

> Our professionals started as assistant directors, and usually took three years before promotion to director. After several more years they might be promoted to senior director. The company established a separate supervisory department and designated three senior directors to serve as supervisors. These men did not have any direct campaign responsibilities. We tried very hard to keep our people, and we featured our directors in our sales presentations.

As our reputation grew, we were invited to make presentations to higher educational conferences. Then it became more and more difficult to retain people. The colleges and universities began to hire permanent staffs. Ketchum [Inc.] and the other AAFRC firms really trained many of their people.[40]

Ketchum, Inc. became the largest fundraising company in America, and their service included many campaigns for higher education. Its founder, Carlton Ketchum, used to say that they were not smarter than their competition, but they worked harder.[41] Carlton Ketchum created the culture of his organization by observing life through the lens of his own Protestant work ethic. He liked hiring men who saw campaigning as a ministerial calling. Meals at the summer conferences always began with a blessing. The Ketchum firm hired many former ministers and a few former priests.[42]

At the end of David Ketchum's time at the helm of the Pittsburgh firm in 1983, the company had more than 200 full-time employees. David Ketchum estimated that more than a third of the company's total revenue came from higher educational campaigns.

Ketchum, Inc. was sold to Ben Gill of Dallas, Texas, in 1994. Gill made his reputation directing campaigns for churches. One of the first strategies Gill pursued after the purchase was to re-institute the professional training conferences that were so important to Carlton Ketchum. According to Elliot S. Oshry, Executive Vice President of Ketchum, Inc. in charge of campaigning, the firm now conducts four conferences a year, which costs the company over $1 million. "You have to conduct a lot of campaigns to pay for that kind of training. Think about it: our directors do not collect a fee that week, we have to pay for their travel, lodging, meals . . ."[43]

Oshry began work for Ketchum, Inc. in 1974 and has observed remarkable change in campaigning and in the fund-raising profession during that time. The most important personal change for Oshrey was the impending merger of Ketchum, Inc. with its new owner from Texas. According to Oshry:

> Ketchum employees were worried about the blending of work cultures with Ben Gill's company. Many of our people were concerned about how they would be able to work with Southern Baptists. But we were wrong about the concerns; the transition was unbelievably smooth. When we got together, you could close your eyes and think you were at a Ketchum conference![44]

The Protestant work ethic of Carlton Ketchum was a good match for the culture created by church fund raiser Ben Gill.

George A. Brakeley, Jr.

George A. Brakeley, Jr. joined the John Price Jones firm in 1937 between his junior and senior years at the University of Pennsylvania where he studied journalism. The son and namesake of one of the original campaign executives in the Jones firm, George Archibald Brakeley, Jr. would become the next bright star in the constellation of fund raisers for higher education. At the end of his active career, Brakeley looked back on a career spanning fifty years during which he helped manage fund-raising programs totaling at least $7 billion in 1987 values.[45]

After the Second World War, Captain George A. Brakeley, Jr. rejoined the John Price Jones firm. After several years of successful fund-raising experiences in the United States, Brakeley's life changed forever when F. Cyril James, Principal and Vice Chancellor of McGill University in Montreal, chose him over two other candidates to direct a $9 million campaign. John Price Jones and Brakeley, Jr. quickly formed a new Canadian company, John Price Jones Company (Canada), which Brakeley, Jr. eventually bought.[46]

During his reign in Canada, Brakeley also recognized business opportunity where others had not—in America's west. Brakeley established a consulting company in the United States when he opened an office in San Francisco, the first fund-raising office west of the Mississippi River. Brakeley's first United States client was the Stanford University Medical Center. The University needed $6 million to move its medical campus from San Francisco to Palo Alto. By the mid-1950s, Brakeley had developed an excellent reputation in university consulting in Canada.

Stanford's president, Wallace Sterling, was a product of Canadian higher education. Sterling went to Stanford to take advantage of the rich collection of modern European historical documents at the Hoover Institute. After earning his Ph.D., Sterling taught history for approximately ten years at Cal Tech. Sterling also served for a short time as the Director of the Huntington Library and Gallery in Pasadena before he was appointed president of Stanford in 1948.[47] Sterling knew Brakeley's fund-raising reputation and opened the door for him to provide consultation on the Stanford Hospital and Medical School campaign.[48]

Fund raising did not play a significant role in the development of higher education in the western (or southern) United States before the Second World War. As America moved west, state legislators took more and more responsibility for developing colleges and universities. Leaders in America's western states were more likely than easterners to reach agreement on the importance of the public's role in developing higher educational institutions and systems. They were also quicker to tie public service and job development to higher education than many in the east.[49]

Brakeley, Jr. saw potential for fund raising in these large popular institutions. With his California company firmly established in the western United States, Brakeley sought and secured business in the public as well as the private sector of higher education. Brakeley was invited to become a consultant by many of the large public universities. For instance, for more than ten years he was the only consultant invited to the annual conventions of the American Land Grant Universities.[50]

A new day was dawning in America, and Brakeley knew how to take advantage of it. Several social, economic and political currents enabled fund-raising campaigns for higher education to evolve at an accelerated pace. The GI Bill swelled enrolments and placed further demands on higher education.[51] Money was increasingly available, and Americans understood the need to support higher education.[52] American corporations became major participants in fund-raising campaigns.[53] Philanthropic foundations grew in number and size.[54] America had become an economic super power and world leader in the decades after the Second World War.[55]

In 1962 Brakeley helped organize the centennial celebration of the Morrill Land Grant Act for the National Association of State and Land Grant Universities. Together with James Lewis Morrill, a direct descendant of the Land Grant Act's author, Justin Morrill, Brakeley helped establish the first foundation for a state university at the University of Minnesota. Brakeley served as a consultant to the University of Minnesota for more than eleven years and during the time of three presidents.[56]

In 1958, with John Price Jones now a gentleman farmer in eastern Pennsylvania, Brakeley opened offices on Madison Avenue in New York. Brakeley was then in direct competition with his former company, John Price Jones, Inc. The competition ended in 1974. Brakeley purchased the majority of the stock in John Price Jones, Inc. and renamed it Brakeley, John Price Jones, Inc.[57] Brakeley felt it was important to keep the Jones name in the fund-raising industry; Jones had earned his place in history.[58]

By the 1970s and 1980s Brakeley, Jr., became recognized as the national authority on philanthropy and fund raising for higher education in America and throughout the world. His personal ideas were always in demand during the period. Brakeley, Jr. had become the expert source of national media for comments on news or significant developments in philanthropy.[59]

Consulting Firms: Summary

The Jones and Ketchum firms flourished in the prosperity of the 1920s, then struggled to find ways to survive the difficult years between the Great Depression and end of the Second World War. After the war, the need for education captured America's attention, fund-raising techniques were refined, and consulting firms grew in influence. In the post-war era new working relationships were forged between higher education and the consultants. Colleges and universities now had the resources to employ their own fund-raising staffs. The Ketchum and John Price Jones companies developed human capital in the practices of raising money, which affected higher education in two ways—directly through consulting services or indirectly when the colleges hired consultants as employees. A new leader in fund raising for higher education emerged. George A. Brakeley, Jr., taking the most circuitous of routes, had replaced John Price Jones as the world's leading authority on educational fund raising.

Summary and Discussion

This paper explored the differences in belief systems, philosophies, and corporate development between the Lawrence/Jones/ Brakeley culture and the Ward/Ketchum culture, and proposed that these two distinctly different corporate cultures, which competed in the higher educational marketplace for decades, imbued the development staffs after the Second World War when colleges and universities added development officers to their administrations. The writer further suggests that differences in the training and backgrounds of today's practitioners may create tension in fund-raising academic operations. The approach to supporting this thesis has been inductive rather than deductive or propositional. In other words, it presents the story—the facts from several original and secondary sources—and suggests that readers draw their own conclusions.

This topic was chosen because it is fundamental information for thoughtful practitioners to consider. At the beginning of the twenty-first century, most people who work in what has come to be known as advancement think of the art of campaigning for money as simply a matter of individual opinion. In the distinct beginnings of the fund-raising industry, one is reasonably sure to find some meaningful places of disagreement on techniques, processes, and roles for today's advancement officers. *The CASE Journal of Educational Advancement* holds the promise to change that reality by publishing research and case studies on strategies, techniques, and ethics. The industry also needs academic programs to create, synthesize, and present information to people who want to work in what Harold J. Seymour once called the "vineyards of philanthropy." The fund-raising industry needs such a base of information.

Not surprisingly, this article has raised a number of other research questions. For instance, it would be interesting to conduct an ethnographic comparison of the Ketcham/Gill and the Brakeley, John Price Jones cultures today. There is no question that historically these two organizations provided higher education with the training and people to develop the academic fund-raising industry.

Researchers might also study successful academic programs, not in terms of dollars raised, but in terms of staff longevity. Turnover rates in institutional advancement are improving, but they are still highest in higher education compared to other divisions and departments.[60] This condition exists in spite of the belief that it is salutary for an institution's staff to maintain long-term relationships with donors. Understanding our differences (and understanding our own organizational cultures) might improve our institutional hiring practices and individual job searches. An individual who values humility and approaches fund development as a ministerial calling might not work well with someone who tracks and sometimes boasts of personal achievements.

Today, it is not unusual for colleges and universities to keep track of individual results of major gift officers for purposes of evaluation. Some colleges and universities have even compensated fund raisers with bonuses based on reaching goals. Do such practices motivate people, or do they lay the groundwork for ethical abuses? That is another important question, but a difficult one to research because institutions rarely publish ethical breaches in their alumni magazines.

The issue of institutional fit is important in choosing a consulting firm as well. Ketchum, Inc. got its most important break in the early-1920s when the University of Pittsburgh asked John Price Jones, Inc. to leave their campus.[61] One must conclude that the Pittsburgh culture (trustees, volunteers and faculty) felt Carlton Ketchum and his campaign methods were a more appropriate solution for their needs.

Individually, it might be interesting for practitioners to trace their own training back to its roots. Readers might consider who influenced them the most and where that person got his or her training. When we find disagreement it might be helpful to consider the cultural influences driving people (trustees, volunteers, co-workers) with whom there is conflict. People come from different schools of thought on fund-raising issues, and their belief systems have likely picked up elements from both explored here. Comprehending the differences might alleviate some stress, even help with a solution.

Notes

1. R. L. Stuhr (1977), *On Development*, Chicago, Gonser Gerber Tinker & Stuhr.
2. Elmira College (1914), *Elmira College, Mother of Colleges for Women 1855–1914: Its Past History, Its Present Work, Its Promise for the Future*, Elmira College, Elmira, NY.
3. C. Jencks and D. Riesman (1968), *The Academic Revolution*, Doubleday, Garden City, NY; S. M. Cutlip (1965/1990), *Fund Raising in the United States*, Transaction Publishers, New Brunswick, NJ and London; C. J. Lucas (1994), *American Higher Education: A History*, St. Martin's Press, New York; M. A. Duronio and E. R. Tempel (1997), *Fund Raisers: Their Careers, Stories, Concerns, and Accomplishments*, Jossey-Bass, San Francisco; M. J. Worth and J. W. Asp (1994), *The Development Officer in Higher Education: Toward an Understanding of the Role*, The George Washington University, Graduate School of Education and Human Development, Washington, DC.
4. P. C. Carter (1970); *Arnaud Cartwright Marts: A Winner in the American Tradition*, The Algonquin Press, New York; J. L. Himmelstein (1997), *Looking Good and Doing Good: Corporate Philanthropy and Corporate Power*, Indiana University Press, Bloomington and Indianapolis, IN; W. Lawrence (1926), *Memories of a Happy Life*, Houghton Mifflin, Boston; R. C. Alberts (1986), *Pitt: The Story of the University of Pittsburgh 1787–1987*, University of Pittsburgh Press, Pittsburgh.
5. Worth and Asp (1994), *The Development Officer in Higher Education* op. cit.
6. Carter (1970), *Arnaud Cartwright Marts* op. cit..
7. Cutlip (1965; 1990), *Fund Raising in the United States* op. cit.
8. Carter (1970), *Arnaud Cartwright Marts* op. cit..
9. Worth and Asp (1994), *The Development Officer in Higher Education* op. cit.
10. Alberts (1986), *Pitt: The Story of the University of Pittsburgh*; Cutlip (1965/1990), *Fund Raising in the United States* op. cit.
11. Alberts (1986), *Pitt: The Story of the University of Pittsburgh* op. cit.
12. Ibid.
13. "The $3,000,000 for Pitt starts gustily" (1914), *The Pittsburgh Dispatch*, January 15, p. 1.
14. Ibid.
15. "Campaign closes with two million dollars" (1914), *The Pitt Weekly*, January 30, p. 1.
16. Cutlip (1965/1990), *Fund Raising in the United States* op. cit.
17. Elmira College (1914), *Elmira College, Mother of Colleges for Women* op. cit.
18. Cutlip (1965/1990), *Fund Raising in the United States* op. cit.

19. Ibid.
20. W. Lawrence (1923), "An invigorating avocation," *Atlantic*, 132, pp. 317–23.
21. Ibid.
22. Lawrence (1926), *Memories of a Happy Life* op. cit.
23. Ibid.
24. Cutlip (1965; 1990), *Fund Raising in the United States* op. cit.
25. Lawrence (1923), "An invigorating avocation." op. cit.
26. C. S. Ward (1906), "The short-term building campaign," *Association Men*, 32, pp. 19–21.
27. Lawrence (1926), *Memories of a Happy Life* op. cit.
28. Ibid., p. 216.
29. Ward (1906), "The short-term building campaign." op. cit.
30. Lawrence (1923), "An invigorating avocation." op. cit.
31. Ibid.
32. Cutlip (1965;1990), *Fund Raising in the United States*, op. cit. p. 169.
33. Ibid.
34. Ibid.
35. G. A. Brakeley, Jr., personal communication, 1998.
36. Carter (1970), *Arnaud Cartwright Marts*, op. cit. p. 334.
37. G. A. Brakeley, Jr., personal communication, 1998.
38. Cutlip (1965/1990), *Fund Raising in the United States* op. cit.
39. Lawrence (1926), *Memories of a Happy Life*, op. cit. p. 215.
40. D. S. Ketchum, personal communication, October, 1998.
41. Ibid.
42. Ibid.
43. E. S. Oshry, personal communication, September, 1998.
44. Ibid.
45. G. A. Brakeley, Jr. (1987), "An historical approximation as to how the Brakeley Companies came to be and a professional history of the perpetrator" *Chairman's Letter*, October.
46. Ibid.
47. C. L. Kirk, Jr., personal communication, August, 1998.
48. G. A. Brakeley, Jr., personal communication, 1998.
49. Jencks and Riesman (1968), *The Academic Revolution*, op. cit.
50. G. A. Brakeley, Jr., personal communication, 1998.
51. Lucas (1994), *American Higher Education*; American Association of Fund Raising Counsel, Inc. Ad Hoc Committee on Publications (1966), *History of the AAFRC*, AAFRC, New York.
52. Lucas (1994), *American Higher Education*, op. cit.
53. Himmelstein (1997), *Looking Good and Doing Good*, op. cit.
54. G. Keller (1983), *Academic Strategy: The Management Revolution in American Higher Education*, The Johns Hopkins University Press, Baltimore and London.
55. Himmelstein (1997), *Looking Good and Doing Good*, op. cit.; H. Chua-Eoan (1998), "1948–1960: Affluence," *Time*, March 9, p. 128.
56. G. A. Brakeley, Jr., personal communication, 1998.
57. Brakeley (1987), "An historical approximation as to how the Brakeley Companies came to be.", op. cit.
58. C. A. Lawson, personal communication, April, 1997.
59. Duronio and Tempel (1997), *Fund Raisers*, op. cit.
60. Alberts (1986), *Pitt: The Story of the University of Pittsburgh*, op. cit.
61. Ibid.

Practitioner's Perspectives

This article traces the origins of pioneer fund-raising professionals and their impact on both academic fund-raising organizations and approaches to what we have come to know as formalized campaigns. The leaders of entrepreneurial fund raising ventures in the early twentieth century faced numerous challenges and opportunities. The author offers a historical context that can assist practitioners in development goals and associated processes and staff support required to successfully achieve established outcomes.

Approaches to institutional advancement and related fund-raising initiatives vary significantly across the spectrum of American higher education. The author provides a historical perspective and traces the roots of many established effective approaches to development. For example, the author's examination of Jones's approach to research, development of the case record keeping and ongoing evaluation of fund raising efforts provides evidence of early adaptation of many strategies currently utilized by practitioners in the field.

This article provides insight into the cyclic nature of fund raising and the impact of both internal and external variables. The onset of the Depression and the outbreak of the Second World War resulted in practitioners of the time identifying new approaches to outreach as well as developing standards for the profession. Further, the author provides a historical context for understanding the constant nature of change and the impact of unanticipated events such as "9/11." For practitioners' developing strategy, the article offers a historical argument for ongoing and effective review of vision, goal, objectives, and change management.

The author's examination of Ward's and Lawrence's early work in the field raise compelling questions for practitioners about the interrelationship between organizational culture and advancement practices. And the author expands on his review through an analysis of the John Price Jones approach to fund raising based in large part on the Lawrence school of thought. As practitioners we can gain valuable insights from both of these pioneers in the field and their approaches to staff development and the utilization of consultants. A central theme throughout the author's review of the literature is the critical link between staff development and performance. As leaders in our own institutions, it is essential to engage in the development of an ongoing collaborative, team-based staff development program embodied in institutional mission, guiding principles, goals and objectives. A determination of one's own strengths and weakness as a development unit within an academic institution is an essential step in the process of determining possible external resources to aid in the overall fund-raising effort at hand.

As leaders in the profession, we can learn from those who journeyed the development path prior to our tenure. History reveals a number of key strategies for success, which have remained crucial to this day. First, development organizations need to be fully integrated with the overall mission of the organization. Second, guiding principle must be clear to all so that organizational culture and values supports our fund-raising efforts. Third, a continuous improvement staff development program is essential for long-term personal retention and campaign success. And, fourth the determination of when and why to turn to external consulting resources need to be balanced with a clear and firm understanding of current internal staff strengths and value added objects that an external firm can bring to the campaign or fund-raising initiative at hand.

Linda S. Durant
Vice President for Institutional Advancement,
Dean College

Private Voluntary Support to Public Universities in the United States: Late Nineteenth-century Developments

Samuel G. Cash

Abstract

The early history of private support to state universities in the United States followed an inconsistent pattern. From the chartering of the first state university in 1785 through the antebellum period, state universities followed patterns of raising support established by the colonial colleges and relied on a combination of public and private support. This inconsistent pattern improved after the Civil War due to the intersection of powerful social and political forces. This study explores this second stage in the history of private voluntary support of public research universities in the United States during the latter part of the nineteenth century. During this period several factors affected the state institution's ability to attract private funds. These factors include changing social and educational aims, a redefinition of stewardship, and the changing Federal interest in higher education. The emergence of a more responsive American university in the late nineteenth century further stabilized levels of support and created a more consistent pattern of fund raising for state colleges and universities.

Introduction

As noted in an earlier article, inconsistency marked the patterns of support from the time of the chartering of the first state university in 1785 through much of the antebellum period in the United States.[1] Most of these early state universities struggled to obtain needed support from their states and resorted to various combinations of public and private support. This struggle revealed certain issues peculiar to the funding of higher education not unlike issues today. Institutional leaders attempted an understanding of the motives for giving; however, they were not able to focus on developing regular sources of private support probably due to regular conflicts with their states over funding. In terms of support, the early state institutions did little more than resemble the sectarian institutions of the day and, perhaps to a greater extent, the colonial colleges. As these institutions progressed, private support did not abate through periods of unstable state support. Private support through subscriptions and in-kind gifts stabilized an otherwise precarious fiscal status for these institutions as the forerunners of alumni associations, and "town-and-gown" relations gave state institutions a reasonable foundation in the realm of private fund raising.

After the Civil War, the patterns of support to state universities improved due to the intersection of powerful social and political forces. The rapid growth of industrial wealth, the move toward urbanization and westward expansion, the Protestant culture of American exceptionalism, and a secular understanding of the aims of education strengthened personal and state allegiances to the colleges and universities.[2] This was to be the age of the American university with its purposes of instruction, research, and service clarified through a utilitarian, or practical, education. As late nineteenth-century higher education became utilitarian some institutional leaders of the day began to see higher education as an equal partner in economic development with government and industry. Throughout this period the states increased their funding of higher education and its regularity while the pattern of voluntary support to the state institutions remained unstructured. The wealth to support private giving was available as entrepreneurial profits created personal fortunes that could support philanthropy. At this time, though, the changing social and educational aims, a redefinition of stewardship, and the changing Federal interest in higher education all may have affected the state institutions' ability to attract private funds. This paper explores these influences on raising private voluntary support at state universities after the Civil War and through the late nineteenth century.

Intersecting Social and Educational Aims

The changing educational aims of the time enabled the development of a more modern conception of a university in the United States. The emergence of the truly American university in the latter part of the nineteenth century was essentially one of assimilation to the changing environment of the time.[3] Institutional changes affected the levels and types of support needed to sustain these institutions. One such change was accessibility. The universities of this era became more accessible to the various segments of American society, resulting in an increased demand for higher education. The need for research in areas which would benefit industrial society produced an even greater demand for funds. The rise of science, engineering, and agricultural science and related research required funds to maintain the trend. Additionally, the professionalization of law, medicine, and business spurred the need for better equipped facilities and qualified instructors. Another change creating a need for funds was the addition of administrators at these institutions who had a more secular bent toward running an institution. Administrators characteristically thought in terms of institutional management; this included a concern for budgets, public relations, institutional statistics, and institutional standards. The administration's attention to organization planning had the effect of isolating the president from faculty ways of thinking. As a result, presidents focused on financial and organizational issues which provided growth and stability for the institution. Laurence Veysey suggests that the "progressive administrator . . . sought eagerly to broaden the base of his institution's support."[4] The administrators realized the importance of private support and for building coalitions at the statehouse for improving state funding. The rise of alumni groups, clubs, fraternities, and other campus groups created another avenue for private support. Additionally the rise of collegiate athletics contributed to the feverish need for adequate funds for facilities and staff.

The strengthening American economy of the latter part of the nineteenth century helped change American society and meet these new needs of the university. The economic expansion from the Civil War to the end of the nineteenth century enabled the expansion of higher education. One factor for this trend was significant increases in population. From the year 1850 to 1900 the total population of the United States increased from near 23 million to over 76 million.[5] The most dramatic increases in population during this period were located in the South, where the population increased from 8.9 million to 24.5 million, and in the North Central states which increased from 5.4 to 26.3 million.[6] A trend toward urbanization was evident in that the number of incorporated towns and cities of over 2,500 increased from 392 in 1860 to 1,737 in 1900.[7] Despite the economic setbacks of the Civil War, which drew capital away from industry, industrial production soared and the number of nonfarm business concerns grew from near 204,000 in 1857 to 427,000 by 1870 and 1,174,000 by 1900.[8] Despite certain economic declines throughout some of the years of the latter half of the nineteenth century, industrial and agricultural production increased through most of these years. Other important economic influences on social and educational change during this period include the growth of railroads, the growth of a petroleum industry, and advances in technology and innovation. Additionally through these years the federal government, due to the foresight of certain political leaders, began to see its economic role as a nonmarket influence to help control growth.

The Redefinition of Stewardship

The creation of wealth in the late 1800s, a result of the economic expansion of the time, enabled a level of giving to higher education never before achieved; however, it would appear that the state universities were not poised to obtain a great portion of these great fortunes. Although one might blame the leaders of the state universities for not having clearly articulated ideas about financial support at this time, focusing more on increasing legislative support instead, there were some changing cultural values and a redefinition of stewardship which influenced inconsistent levels of private support to public institutions.

One cultural change which developed alongside the extraordinary economic growth of the time was the emergence of a "bourgeois culture," a culture which centered on middle-class values and ideals.[9] These values, including easy access to education, the encouragement of social mobility, and the promotion of personal freedoms, fueled nineteenth-century industrialism but, perhaps more importantly to higher education, created a need for a type of education which would achieve these values. Due to the increase in consumer demand and trends toward urbanization, entrepreneurial activity reacted to the marketplace and million-dollar fortunes were created. As "self-made" men achieved these fortunes a concomitant change occurred with ideas of stewardship.

Stewardship, with its religious overtones, now took on a secular definition.[10] The contrast between these changing conceptions are seen in the philanthropic philosophies of two multimillionaires of the time, John Rockefeller and Andrew Carnegie. The conservative, religious conception of stewardship undergirded Rockefeller's benevolence. A devout Baptist, Rockefeller held to the old-fashioned religious doctrine of stewardship and felt the burden and responsibility of wealth. Rockefeller felt that his wealth was from the "good Lord" and was given for a specific purpose.[11] Further, he felt the responsibility to handle it with care. In contrast, Andrew Carnegie's views epitomized the more secular conception of stewardship referred to as the new "gospel of wealth." Although there were religious overtones to Carnegie's gospel, ". . . he did not believe that under modern conditions much good could be accomplished by imitating the life or methods of Christ."[12] Carnegie referred to philanthropists as "administrators of surplus wealth" who had it in their power to provided lasting benefits for the poor and weak through their benefactions.[13] This new conception of stewardship is articulated in an essay by Carnegie on the "Administration of Wealth":

> This, then, is held to be the duty of the man of wealth: To set an example of modest, unostentatious living, shunning display or extravagance; to provide moderately for the legitimate wants of those dependent upon him; and after doing so, to consider all surplus revenues which came to him simply as trust funds, which he is called upon to administer, and strictly bound as a matter of duty to administer in the manner which, in his judgment, is best calculated to produce the most beneficial results for the community. . . .[14]

Carnegie's redefinition of stewardship fit in neatly with the rise of a bourgeois culture fixed on getting ahead. Carnegie further supported giving to higher education as a need of utmost importance, in particular supporting those institutions already in existence:

> . . . let us endeavor to present some of the best uses to which a millionaire can devote the surplus of which he should regard himself as the only trustee. First. Standing apart by itself there is the founding of a university by men enormously rich, such men as must necessarily be few in any country.
>
> It is reserved for very few to found universities, and, indeed, the use for many, or perhaps, any, new universities does not exist. More good is henceforth to be accomplished by adding to and extending those in existence.[15]

Religious leaders responded adversely to the philanthropy of the millionaires of the period. One illustrative response by Washington Gladden, a Congregational minister, denounced the ways of trade and referred to the self-made men as "robber barons" and "pirates of industry." The money they gave, according to Gladden, was tainted and he asked whether a church or university could accept it without indirectly condoning the standards of the donor.[16] Nevertheless, Americans remained preoccupied with the millionaires and their uses of great wealth. This preoccupation is reflected in a report from the *New York Tribune* in 1892 listing 4,047 men and women reputed to be millionaires.[17] Other articles appearing subsequent to this suggested that some of the millionaires were not givers, thus calling into question the reputation of the wealthy.[18] Of those who were givers, studies indicated that education received near a third of their total giving, that those who had no more than secondary education gave more than those with college degrees, and that self-made men were more philanthropic than those inheriting their wealth.[19] As a strengthening economy and bourgeois culture fueled the creation of wealth, there still appeared to be no effective method for organizing and conducting philanthropy to higher education at the state universities, the institutions which would seem to be in a position to benefit from changing conceptions of stewardship from a religious to a secular motive.

The Changing Federal Interest in Higher Education

Another factor affecting patterns of support to the state universities was the changing Federal interest in higher education during the late nineteenth century. The passage of the Morrill Act in 1862 marked the beginning of a period of increasing Federal support for higher education. Named after Vermont representative Justin Morrill, this act of Congress provided federal lands of 30,000 acres for each senator and representative to each state for establishing

> . . . at least one college where the leading object shall be, without excluding other scientific and classical studies, and including military tactics, to teach such branches of learning as are related to agriculture and the mechanic arts, in such manner as the legislatures of the states may respectively prescribe, in order to promote the liberal and practical education of the industrial classes in the several pursuits and professions of life.[20]

Through this original Morrill Act, 48 state colleges and universities had received aid by 1889, of which 33 had not previously existed.[21] In what has been considered the wisest disposition of the land scrip, in 13 states, including Wisconsin, Minnesota, Missouri, Georgia, North Carolina, and Tennessee, the land scrip went to institutions already in existence.[22] In 20 states the Act prompted a separate college of agriculture and mechanic arts which competed against the state university.[23] The effects on financial support to the state universities were positive. Communities eager to attract the new federally funded state institutions rallied support from individuals often in the form of subscriptions of cash and noncash gifts such as land. Although the movement toward a practical education from a classical liberal arts education may have influenced increasing support, state legislatures might have been forced to consider increasing their levels of support in order to keep the funds created from the federal land grants and to satisfy constituents from communities in support of the nonsectarian institutions.[24] This trend continued as state support stabilized after the passage of the Hatch Act in 1887 and the second Morrill Act in 1890 probably due to guaranteed annual federal appropriations.[25] Despite the stabilization, the land-grant institutions through the latter part of the nineteenth century suffered from slow growth in enrollments, high attrition, low salaries, overworked professors, and primitive facilities.[26] States still appeared unsure of how to raise necessary tax support for a state institution when other organizations needed monies as well. Andrew D. White, colleague to Ezra Cornell while in the New York Legislature, argued persuasively for state support of institutions of higher learning:

> Talk of economy! Go to your state legislatures—what strange ethics in dealing with the public institutions! If asked for money to found an asylum for idiots and lunatics or the blind or the deaf and dumb, you will find legislatures ready to build palaces for them. Millions of dollars are lavished upon your idiots and deaf and dumb and blind and lunatics. Right glad I am it is so; but when you come to ask aid even in measured amounts for the development of the young men of the State, upon whom is to rest its civilization, and from whom is to flow out its prosperity for ages to come, the future makers of your institutions and laws, how are they to be left to the most meager provision during all their preparation?[27]

Of course Ezra Cornell persuaded the state of New York to allocate its land scrip to a private institution named after him to be founded through his donation of half a million dollars in Western Union stock and a site for the institution to be led by Andrew White.[28]

Examples of Trends in Raising Private Support

The origins of the state universities in the latter half of the nineteenth century provide examples of the trends of support during this period and the issues surrounding this support. In the new territories and states of the West the involvement of various citizens in advancing educational opportunities resulted in initial foundations of support. In Washington a primitive territorial university was opened in a building on the outskirts of the village of Seattle in 1861. Reverend Daniel Bagley, a Methodist minister seeking to escape the sectarian rivalries in Oregon, moved to Seattle and began promoting the advantages of having a nonsectarian university in the community.[29] Through Bagley's promotion villagers Arthur and Mary Denny donated eight acres of land which was followed by a gift of two additional acres from Charles and Mary Terry and Edward Lander.[30] As a university in name only, the school had very few students at the collegiate level and would grant its first collegiate degree 25 years later.[31]

While sectarian rivalries possibly delayed the founding of the public university in Oregon, private gifts and publicity initially played important roles. In 1872 the revival of interest in the territorial university endowment from the Northwest Ordinance of 1781 led to the question of the need for a territorial university. There were already seven chartered institutions, all church-related, in the territory, and all lacked adequate funds. A legislative struggle ensued between the existing colleges and a delegation of citizens from Eugene intent on annexing the original university endowment for a newly created institution. The citizens of Eugene shrewdly formed an association with capital stock of $50,000 that was to become available to purchase a site and erect a building if the legislature awarded the endowment to Eugene. This Lane County delegation obtained the necessary support from legislators and a bill approving the location of the state university was signed by the governor in 1872.[32] Following approval, the Lane County delegation formed a committee to solicit subscriptions. Seventeen acres were donated for the original site of the university while the financing was obtained through a $30,000 local bond issue supported by $20,000 in private subscriptions. Letters published in the *Oregon State Journal* promoted a positive impression of the potential impact of the forthcoming university on the community:

> Friends of the university tried to meet the opposition by showing the large sum of money, ($150,000), which would be brought into Lane County by the establishment of the university. The new foundation would also attract wealthy families to the county who would help pay the taxes and put money into circulation. It would also increase the value of farm land at least two and one-half dollars per acre. This for 200,000 acres would make $500,000 of increased valuation of real estate. When once inaugurated, the university would bring into the community 500 new persons a year. It would also exert a wonderful power in elevating the moral standards and improve the condition of the people.[33]

In Colorado, Governor Edward McCook signed a territorial bill in 1870 to establish an agricultural college in order to receive the land grant offered through the Morrill Act of 1862. Larimer County contributed 80 acres after a citizen of Fort Collins, Mr. Robert Dazell, deeded 30 acres to establish a site for the new college. The Territorial Legislature agreed to appropriate $1,000 in 1874 if the Trustees could raise a matching sum. Local citizens, businesses, and the Grange raised the matching funds. The group of farmers from the Grange showed their continued support through holding farm events on the university's land and constructing a small brick building. Colorado Agricultural College, later Colorado State University, welcomed its first students in September of 1879.[34]

A similar start for the University of Colorado led to difficulty with initial subscriptions. Land donations in 1872 from certain citizens of Boulder provided the lead support for the university which would officially open in 1876. These gifts of land from three couples totaled over 130 acres and prompted the Board of Trustees to appoint a committee of seven to solicit donations. This initial drive for private funds raised $1,135 in subscriptions and cash, apparently an amount far short of funding the construction of the first building. A possible reason for this shortfall in private support was a competing drive for funds from citizens to help construct a railroad between Boulder and Denver. Undeterred, J. P. Maxwell, the member of the House of Representatives from Boulder, introduced a bill on January 25, 1872, for appropriating $15,000 of territorial funds to the university. This initial bill failed but was reintroduced after petition by the Board of Trustees in January of 1874, only this time requesting $30,000. The territorial legislature agreed to $15,000 only if the citizens of Boulder could raise a matching amount. Sufficient pledges were raised in dramatic fashion by the speaker of the House, Captain David H. Nichols, who rode on horseback from Denver to Boulder and back in an overnight trip to gather the pledges for the passage of the bill. Although pledges were gathered there still remained some uncertainty regarding their collection. This uncertainty is reflected in the Trustees' enlistment of prominent citizens from Boulder to solicit donations as they traveled in the Eastern states. Included among these citizens were the Presbyterian and Episcopal ministers; their attempts were apparently unfruitful. In November of 1874 the young banker, George Corning, led a vigorous campaign for the Trustees to secure the subscriptions necessary for receipt of the territory's $15,000 appropriation. To avoid the loss of the appropriation, the Trustees arranged for a bank loan to cover the $15,000 needed from Boulder. The state auditor refused to release the legislative funds on the grounds that this loan was not valid as the matching donations. The Trustees then mounted another effort to raise the matching funds and by the spring of 1875 had raised over $16,000.[35]

Among the existing and newer state universities of the Midwest similar themes regarding private support developed during the late nineteenth century. In Michigan a state agricultural college had already been founded in 1855 prior to US Congressman Justin S. Morrill's plea for the land-grant endowment in 1858. Morrill actually used Michigan's agricultural college as a successful example of the type of agricultural college the federal government should support through its land grants. As early as 1849 E. H. Lothrop, the orator for the first State Fair, decried the lack of agricultural training in the young state in an address to an audience at the Fair. One observation of the effects of this speech indicates an awareness of the need for private support but a realization that few people in the state had significant enough wealth at the time to make this a possibility.[36] The state legislature issued an unfruitful plea to the US Congress for 350,000 acres of federal land in 1853 for the purpose of developing agricultural education. In 1855 the state legislature approved a bill to create the agricultural college and authorized payment of 15 dollars per acre for the site. After competition from several communities, Lansing won out with its cheaper land prices. Several farms and tracts of land were offered but A. R. Burr's 677-acre farm was favored by the committee charged with locating a site.

Ohio's bid for a state agricultural and mechanical college began in 1870 and followed a similar pattern of competition from communities. The original Board of Trustees reviewed the initial offers of land and money from various communities. Appointed to their positions by Governor Rutherford B. Hayes, the trustees came from each of the Congressional districts of the state and sought the best interest of their district by soliciting donations from their communities to attract the new college. An example of an appeal by trustee Joseph Sullivant to the citizens of Franklin County illustrates the use of the power of his position coupled with an earnest plea for the cause of higher education and the positive effects on the community:

> The advantages accruing to any county which secures this institution are so obvious that I need not here present any arguments to prove them. Is it not proper that the citizens of Franklin County should move immediately in behalf of their own interests? Shall we, by indifference or supineness, neglect this opportunity, and permit the superior liberality and enterprise of another county to carry away a prize which we can and ought to preserve for ourselves? May I not appeal with confidence to the farmers and mechanics of Franklin County, for a hearty and generous support of an enterprise which is intended to give public recognition and dignity to their professions, and which is to be carried forward in such a manner as to assist in developing all the great industrial interest of the State? I respectfully suggest that a meeting of all parties interested be called at an early day, to consider the important subject here presented.[37]

Sullivant placed further weight on his appeal by closing as follows: "It is evident that without the liberal cooperation of the people of the State, the intentions of Congress and the Legislature cannot be realized."[38] The people from four counties of the state cooperated by actively competing for the college. Each offer combined plans for issuing local bonds with pledges of money and land from prominent citizens. Columbus and Franklin County won the bidding with their offer of $328,000, including private contributions of $28,000 and $300,000 in seven percent bonds; the $28,000 was used as a down payment on a 327-acre farm which would serve as the site for the college.[39]

The promise of federal lands under the Morrill Act prompted the founding of the University of Arkansas in 1871 with a combination of state and private support. A committee appointed to select a site considered the competing bids for the university. Attracted to a "magnificent homestead" of 160 acres in Fayetteville owned by William McIlroy, the committee approved its purchase for $12,000, $1,000 of which was paid by Fayetteville citizens.[40] In neighboring Kansas, competing communities also sought subscriptions to attract a "Free State College" in a politically divided state. Governor Thomas Carney in 1863 expressed his desire to the legislature for creating a university which would make them eligible for the federal land grant. Funds yet to be raised of $15,000 were offered from

Lawrence while Emporia pledged 80 acres of land after the state passed a bill for creating the university.[41] A house committee recommended the Emporia offer which then prompted the Lawrence supporters to furiously raise the $15,000 in 10 days. The citizens then added to their offer 40 acres to secure their plea for the university. The $15,000 included a promise of $10,000 from wealthy Massachusetts manufacturer Amos Lawrence if town leaders raised the additional $5,000.[42] Citizens with connections in the East, such as a Mrs. Emily P. Burke, continued seeking donations from influential Easterners although it is not certain how fruitful these solicitations were.[43]

Illinois's initial call for support of a state university resulted in a unique proposal in 1855. The plan included a form of joint sponsorship of a university by the state and a self-perpetuating board of 12 members who were well-known business leaders. The idea for financing the venture included funding from three sources: a private fund of $20,000 to be raised by the board, a state normal school fund, and a state university fund. This plan further stipulated state funds to be paid out up to $20,000 only if the board were successful in raising their donations; this would continue in $10,000 increments until the state's college and seminary funds created from federal land grants of the Northwest Ordinance were exhausted.[44] Although creative, this proposed plan failed to receive its endorsement from the legislature of 1955. After the passage of the Morrill Act in 1862 the plan for the state university gathered momentum. Several communities desired the university, as demonstrated through promises of land and money. By 1867 the list of competing communities included Bloomington, Champaign-Urbana, Jacksonville, and Lincoln. Champaign-Urbana was able to successfully offer a large building already constructed and used by an educational institute on a 140-acre farm.

In the East, the pattern of raising private support for newly formed universities was repeated. For example, in Pennsylvania the predecessor to Penn State University, the Farmers' High School, received approval in a bill signed by Governor William Bigler in 1854. Trustees searched for a site for this institution and considered proposals from individuals in five counties willing to donate or sell 200 or more acres. James Irvin, a businessman with success in iron furnaces, forges, and rolling mills, offered any one of three 200-acre tracts from his extensive land holdings in Centre County. After two trustees offered to help Irving raise $10,000 from local citizens to combine with the land offer, an isolated site near the Nittany and Penn Valleys was accepted. Following acceptance the trustees mounted another campaign to raise funds. In addition to the $10,000 in subscriptions, the trustees obtained a grant of $10,000 from the state agricultural society and accepted a $5,000 bequest from wealthy Quaker merchant Elliott Cresson of Philadelphia. The trustees implicated themselves further with the institution by donating personal funds for the construction of the first building. Spurred on by the passage of the Morrill Act, the institution changed its name to the Agricultural College of Pennsylvania and successfully obtained the endorsement of the state legislature to become the recipient of the federal land grant.[45]

Several years later, Georgia's bid for an engineering and technology college led to combinations of public and private offers of support from communities. Stimulus for the institution came from the "New South Creed," a social, economic, and intellectual movement of the 1870s and 1880s in the South. Benjamin H. Hill, a proponent of this movement who served as a US Senator, spoke to the Alumni Association of the University of Georgia in 1871 regarding the need for a more practical education which would aid the South in moving away from its dependence on slavery and enable the South to compete equally with the North in industry. Hill's remarks prompted consideration for "schools of agriculture, of commerce, of manufactures, of mining, of technology, and in short, of all polytechnics."[46] In the early 1880s Henry Grady, the influential editor of the *Atlanta Constitution*, joined the plea for a New South in his editorials promoting education and economic development. Macon industrialist John F. Hanson, and Nathaniel E. Harris, a candidate for the state legislature, took up the cause for a state polytechnic college in 1882 through an editorial in Hanson's newspaper, the *Macon Telegraph and Messenger*, lamenting the scarcity of skilled labor for manufacturing in the state. Harris was elected to the legislature later in the year and introduced a successful resolution in the legislature for a school of technology. A committee was formed to travel to the North and inspect several engineering schools. The result was a report "placing technical education in the context of other ways of stimulating industrial and economic development."[47] This committee determined the need for $65,000 to start such a school and provide it with the proper equipment and facilities. After this report and ensuing debates over issues through the editorials of the *Atlanta Constitution*, the bill for the proposed school failed in 1883 but was taken up again in 1885. This time an editorial in the *Atlanta Constitution* urged doubters to support the bill for the school; the bill was passed with the approval of $65,000 in unappropriated funds if available. A commission composed of members whose communities would be likely candidates for the school was created. Macon, Atlanta, Penfield in Greene County, Athens, and Newton County each received representation on the commission. Competing bids from each of the locations included various combinations of public and private support. After a series of private balloting, the school later to be the Georgia Institute of Technology was awarded to Atlanta with its bid of $50,000 from the city, $20,000 from private citizens, a choice of three sites valued at $10,000, and an annual annuity of $2,000 per year for 20 years.[48]

Bequests suggestive of the growing availability of wealth during the latter part of the nineteenth century provided additional funds for some state universities. As the state legislature in Virginia debated over the disposition of the land grant fund in 1869, the University of Virginia received a bequest of $100,000 from the estate of Samuel Miller of Albemarle County to establish a department of scientific and practical agriculture. This bequest combined with an ensuing gift from Thomas Johnson of Augusta County which sparked a request from the University to the state for the land-grant money. The University's request prompted competing responses. For example, Washington College and its president Robert E. Lee formulated a plan for a school of agriculture and obtained financial support from farm equipment inventor and manufacturer Cyrus McCormick; McCormick's $10,000 contribution was less than hoped. Another plan included a joint venture for an agricultural institute between Washington College and the Virginia Military Institute. The smaller colleges in the state also maneuvered for the land-grant fund and in doing so exerted a divisive effect in the state legislature. The bill, which was finally passed on March 19, 1872, gave one-third of the land grant to Hampton Normal and Industrial Institute and two-thirds to the Preston and Olin Institute, which relinquished its charter and donated its property to the state. The newly organized Virginia Agricultural and Mechanical College of Montgomery County relied initially on additional private gifts from local citizens near $20,000.[49]

In South Carolina a bequest to the state produced a different result. At first the availability of land-grant funds initiated a College of Agriculture and Mechanics which would be a part of the existing state college. This emphasis on agricultural education was not received well by the students, as demonstrated by their lackluster participation in the mandatory farm labor.[50] Certain individuals took up the cause for a separate agricultural institution elsewhere, including farmer Benjamin Tillman of Edgefield. Tillman's cause received momentum when in 1888 Thomas G. Clemson died and left his Fort Hill estate of 814 acres and near $80,000 to the state for establishing an agricultural college separate from the existing state college. Incorporated in Clemson's bequest, seven of a 13-member board of trustees were named to protect against political interference. The fact that the existing state college had a school of agriculture presented a problem for the state's acceptance of the bequest; Benjamin Tillman attacked the adequacy of this school in an effort to draw the Morrill and Hatch land-grant funds away from the state college. Debates occurred in the legislature over this issue. During 1888 Tillman rallied support for the Clemson bequest and in 1889 the governor signed a bill accepting the bequest. Another bill followed to establish the Clemson Agricultural College and to award the Morrill and Hatch funds to this institution. In a manner which would seal the fate of both the Clemson Agricultural College and South Carolina College, Tillman ran for and was elected governor in 1890.[51]

Back out West, the University of California received many notable gifts through its initial years indicative of the available wealth in the state at the time. The fourth campus building at Oakland, a gymnasium, was constructed from a private gift by A. K. P. Harmon in 1879.[52] A pioneer citizen of San Francisco, James Lick, invested wisely and became a millionaire near this time. Lick decided to build an observatory with the world's most powerful telescope in 1873. By its completion in 1888, the property was deeded to the university.[53] The university received as a gift the building and facilities of the Toland Medical College in 1873 from Dr. Hugh Toland in San Francisco.[54] The fine arts benefited from the gift of the Mark Hopkins mansion in 1893.

Hopkins, of Central Pacific Railroad fame, spent between two and three million dollars on the mansion on Nob Hill in San Francisco and left it to his wife upon his death. Edward F. Searles later married the widow and inherited the mansion upon her death. Searles gave the mansion to the university on condition that it be used exclusively for the fine arts.[55] In 1894, J. Clute Wilmerding, a wealthy San Francisco liquor merchant, left a bequest of $400,000 to the university to establish a trade school for boys. Although the trade school was not a part of the mission of the institution, the Regents felt such a large gift could not be turned down.[56] Phoebe Hearst, widow of the senator and mother of publisher William Randolph Hearst, contributed $200,000 to fund a competition for an architectural plan for the Berkeley campus in 1896. Hearst's gift and the architect competition drew international attention to the university and made possible the orderly development of the campus.[57]

Conclusion

In Jesse Sears's systematic study of philanthropy and higher education an important question is posed regarding the situation of the state college and university of the late nineteenth century: "Should the State, or private and philanthropic enterprise, determine the character and amount of higher education?"[58] The answer seemed to be a combination of both. Although the pattern of private support to state universities during the latter part of the nineteenth century lacked regularity, the reliance on private gifts appeared to increase at a time that institutions responded to changing social and educational aims. Much like the antebellum period, but perhaps at a greater level, citizens from communities banded together to donate cash and noncash items as an incentive to bring the institution to their community. Economic advances during this time enabled a higher level of private giving to higher education than ever before. Increasing numbers of bequests to the state institutions attest to the economic growth of the nation. Combined with the changing federal interest in supporting higher education through the Morrill Acts, public higher education appeared to gain a more stable means to support its purposes as a more responsive American university emerged.

Notes

1. S. G. Cash (2003), "Private voluntary support to public universities in the United States: An early history," *CASE International Journal of Educational Advancement*, 4, 1, pp. 65–76.
2. W. B. Leslie (1992), *Gentlemen and Scholars: College and Community in the "Age of the University,"* Pennsylvania State University Press, University Park, pp. 1–2.
3. L. R. Veysey (1965), *The Emergence of the American University*, University of Chicago Press, Chicago, p. 439.
4. Ibid., 305–6; quotation p. 306. See also pp. 302–17.
5. Bureau of the Census (1975), *Historical Statistics of the United States, Colonial Times to 1970*, part 1, US Bureau of the Census, Washington, DC, p. 8.
6. Ibid., p. 22.
7. Ibid., p. 11.
8. Ibid., pp. 912–13.
9. J. Hughes and L. P. Cain (1998), *American Economic History*, 5th edn., Addison-Wesley, Reading, MA, pp. 344–5.
10. F. Rudolph (1990), *The American College and University: A History*, reprint with an introductory essay and supplemental bibliography by J. R. Thelin, University of Georgia Press, Athens, p. 425.
11. R. H. Bremner (1988), *American Philanthropy*, 2nd edn., University of Chicago Press, Chicago, p. 106.
12. Ibid., p. 102.
13. Ibid.
14. A. Carnegie (1962), *The Gospel of Wealth and Other Timely Essays*, ed. Edward C. Kirkland, The Belknap Press of Harvard University, Cambridge, UK, p. 25.
15. Ibid., pp. 32, 35.
16. Bremner (1988), *American Philanthropy*, op. cit., p. 107.

17. M. Curti, J. Green, and R. Nash (1963), "Anatomy of giving: Millionaires in the late 19th century," *American Quarterly*, 15, p. 418.

18. Ibid., p. 419.

19. Ibid., pp. 424–5.

20. F. W. Blackmar (1890), *The History of Federal and State Aid to Higher Education*, Bureau of Education, Circular of Information No. 1, Government Printing Office, Washington, DC, p. 48.

21. Ibid., p. 47.

22. R. Hofstadter and C. DeWitt Hardy (1952), *The Development and Scope of Higher Education in the United States*, Columbia University Press, New York, p. 40.

23. J. S. Brubacher and W.s Rudy (1997), *Higher Education in Transition*, 4th edn., Transaction Publishers, New Brunswick, NJ, p. 159.

24. R. L. Geiger (1986), *To Advance Knowledge: The Growth of American Research Universities 1900–1940*, Oxford University Press, Oxford, p. 6.

25. R. L. Williams (1991), *The Origins of Federal Support for Higher Education*, Pennsylvania State University Press, University Park, p. 3.

26. Ibid.

27. Blackmar (1890), *The History of Federal and State Aid to Higher Education*, op. cit., p. 51.

28. M. Curti and R. Nash (1965), *Philanthropy in the Shaping of American Higher Education*, Rutgers University Press, New Brunswick, NJ, p. 121.

29. C. M. Gates (1961), *The First Century at the University of Washington, 1861–1961*, University of Washington Press, Seattle, p. 5.

30. University of Washington Libraries (1998), "The University of Washington's early years," available from http://www.lib.washington.edu/exhibits/site/early.html.

31. Ibid.

32. H. D. Sheldon (1940), *History of University of Oregon*, Binfords & Mort Publishers, Portland, OR, p. 29.

33. Ibid., p. 31.

34. J. Allmendinger (1998), "History of Colorado State University," available from http://welcome.colostate.edu/index.asp?url=history_early1.

35. W. E. Davis (1965), *Glory Colorado! A History of the University of Colorado, 1858–1963*, Pruett Press, Boulder, CO, pp. 10–13; F. S. Allen, P. I. Mitterling, H. L. Scamehorn, E. Andrade, Jr., M. S. Foster (1976), *The University of Colorado, 1876–1976*, Harcourt Brace Jovanovich, New York, pp. 23–6.

36. M. Kuhn (1955), *Michigan State: The First Hundred Years, 1855–1955*, Michigan State University Press, Lansing, p. 5.

37. J. E. Pollard (1952), *History of the Ohio State University*, Ohio State University Press, Columbus, p. 9.

38. Ibid.

39. Ibid., pp. 10–11.

40. H. Hale (1948), *University of Arkansas, 1871–1948*, University of Arkansas Alumni Association, Fayetteville, p. 14.

41. C. S. Griffin (1974), *The University of Kansas: A History*, University of Kansas Press, Lawrence, p. 25.

42. Ibid., p. 28.

43. W. Sterling (ed.) (1891), *Quarter-Centennial History of the University of Kansas, 1866–1891*, George Crane & Company, Topeka, KS, p. 48.

44. W. U. Solberg (1968), *The University of Illinois, 1867–1894: An Intellectual and Cultural History*, University of Illinois Press, Urbana, p. 52.

45. M. Bezilla (1985), *Penn State: An Illustrated History*, Pennsylvania University Press, University Park, pp. 4–6, 12.

46. R. C. McMath, Jr., R. H. Bayor, J. E. Britain, L. Foster et al. (1985), *Engineering the New South: Georgia Tech, 1885–1985*, University of Georgia Press, Athens, p. 12.

47. Ibid., p. 18.

48. Ibid., p. 29.

49. D. L. Kinnear (1972), *The First 100 Years: A History of Virginia Polytechnic Institute and State University*, Virginia Polytechnic Institute Educational Foundation, Blacksburg, pp. 27–37.

50. D. Walker Hollis (1956), *University of South Carolina, Vol. II: College to University*, University of South Carolina Press, Columbia, p. 97.

51. Ibid., p. 157.

52. A. G. Pickerell and M. Dornin (1968), *The University of California: A Pictorial History*, University of California Press, Berkeley, p. 19.

53. Ibid., p. 20.
54. V. A. Stadtman (1970), *The University of California, 1868–1968: A Centennial Publication of the University of California*, McGraw-Hill, New York, p. 108.
55. Ibid., p. 138.
56. Ibid., p. 139.
57. Ibid., p. 119.
58. J. Brundage Sears (1990), *Philanthropy in the History of American Higher Education*, introduction by R. L. Geiger, Transaction Publishers, New Brunswick, NJ, p. 17.

Fund Raising and the College Presidency in an Era of Uncertainty

From 1975 to the Present

W. Bruce Cook

Introduction

When Harvard President Neil Rudenstine took a leave of absence at the end of 1994 in order to recover from exhaustion and to undergo a battery of medical tests, several published reports cited fund-raising stress as one contributing factor [18, 42]. In assessing various analyses offered by the higher education community regarding this event, Robert Hahn, president of Johnson State College, stated, "Most observers have relied on familiar fallacies and myths." Hahn also noted, "The simplistic quality of most of the commentaries on Mr. Rudenstine's leave of absence suggests that much remains to be done to enlarge our understanding of the perils of [academic] leadership" [40, p. A64].

The Rudenstine case—and Hahn's remarks—underscore the need for a comprehensive history of the academic presidency (Joseph N. Crowley's 1994 book, *No Equal in the World*, sets the stage for this). Such a work would provide historians and other scholars as well as journalists and practitioners with a broader context from which to base their understanding and frame their views of current events and trends affecting the academic presidency. Such a work would also help to elevate the level and quality of discourse regarding academic chief executives and fund raising. Unfortunately, space does not allow for such an in-depth treatment of the subject here. Instead, this article will provide a context and overview for the period from 1975 to the present, described by Edward Lilly as the Era of Uncertainty [55].

In so doing, I will attempt to make a number of salient points, including the following:

1. The past 20 years have been correctly called an Era of Uncertainty in higher education because of certain defining characteristics.

2. During this period, both public and private universities have increased their commitment to private fund raising.

3. The increased emphasis given to private fund raising by public universities has changed a tacit, long-standing agreement between public and private institutions.

4. Fund-raising campaigns have become a way of life at many institutions.

5. Academic presidents must devote a significant portion of their time to fund-raising activities.

6. Many presidents have difficulty adjusting to their roles as fund raisers.

7. Fund raising and financial affairs in general are among the most high-profile duties/endeavors of a president and among the skills/attributes most prized by trustees as well as some faculty and alumni, and these issues are widely reported by the media.

8. Due to the increasing complexity of fund raising, presidents and other university personnel must have greater familiarity with tax laws, planned giving, estate planning, and other technical aspects of philanthropy.

9. Fund-raising considerations play a major part in the presidential selection process as well as the length of time incumbents remain in office.

10. There has been a slight trend in recent years toward hiring presidents with a background in development or business, although promotion from within academic ranks is still the norm.

11. Presidents should spend their time and effort in fund raising on the cultivation and solicitation of major gifts and in providing administrative leadership.

12. Presidents must emphasize a team approach to fund raising in which they play the dual roles of quarterback/athletic director.

The Era of Uncertainty

The decades following World War II have been called the Golden Age in American higher education. Federal funds flowed freely, enrollments soared, tremendous sums were expended for construction of new facilities and/or campuses, the community college movement had its flowering, and state university systems were created, to mention but a few notable characteristics [44, 77, 89].

By way of comparison, Whetten and Cameron contrasted this Golden Age with the Era of Uncertainty:

> For at least two decades after World War II, higher education administrators had a relatively easy job. By traditional standards, administrative effectiveness was almost universal. Enrollments were increasing, revenues were growing, innovations in the form of new and experimental programs were common, and almost unprecedented prestige was associated with college professors and administrators in the minds of the public. The environment in which higher education existed was largely protected from outside competition (e.g., almost no corporations offered degree granting programs, and accreditation was restricted, for the most part, to college and university campuses), and costs of college were offset by the availability of large amounts of federal dollars.
>
> All that changed in the 1970s and was magnified in the 1980s: the availability of federal funds was severely curtailed; the legitimacy and usefulness of college degrees was called into question; private corporations began entering the higher education business at a rapid pace and now spend more on education than do colleges and universities; shifting demographics resulted in declining enrollments; and, the public prestige associated with faculty and administrator status plummeted along with their relative earnings [101, p. 35].

For these and other reasons, by the mid-1970s, the postwar boom in higher education had begun to fizzle [44]. According to one source, "Overnight, it seemed, colleges and universities went from a period of plenty to one of poverty" [19, p. 391]. Many factors contributed to this change in the economic climate, and these will be explored in greater detail shortly. However, it is also noteworthy to observe that 1975 spawned several important publications relevant to the topic at hand.

First, a monograph entitled *The President's Role in Development*—apparently the first full-length treatment of this topic—reflected concerns among the nation's higher education leaders over changing expectations for presidential leadership in fund raising and institutional advancement [2].

Second, a study entitled *Giving in America* was published by the Commission on Private Philanthropy and Public Needs, chaired by John Filer of Aetna Life and Casualty Company. The Filer Commission, as it came to be known, had been organized in 1973 in order to document the significance of philanthropy in American life and raise its profile among government and business leaders. The Commission concluded that the nonprofit sector included about six million voluntary organizations with an annual income of some $80 billion and recommended the establishment of a permanent national commission on philanthropy, an expansion of corporate giving, changes in the tax laws to stimulate further giving, and the removal of restrictions on lobbying by charitable organizations other than foundations [12].

And third, 1975 was the year in which a landmark essay, "The Management of Decline," was first published. Its author, economist Kenneth Boulding, predicted a period of slowdown in the American economy for the next fifty to one hundred years and called for a new breed of administrators to oversee this evolution. According to Boulding:

> If this age [of rapid growth] is now coming to an end, large adjustments will have to be made in our ways of thinking, in our habits and standards of decision making, and perhaps even in our institutions. The prospects for the next 50 to 100 years, barring a major catastrophe such as nuclear war, suggest that we are now entering the age of slowdown.
> . . . The implications of all this for education, and especially for higher education, are profound. Education is likely to be the first major segment of the economy to suffer a decline, and management of this decline may very well set the tone for the management of the general slowdown.
> . . . One of education's first priorities, therefore, should be to develop a new generation of academic administrators who are skilled in the process of adjusting to decline. . . . Before we can do this, however, we need to study decline through research programs, beginning perhaps with the educational system, where decline is already upon us. [10, pp. 8–9].

In commenting on this at the time, Clark Kerr stated, "The people who were hired to build in the '50s and early '60s are kind of out of date, and so are the people who were hired in the late '60s and early '70s to handle students and public-relations emergencies. The talents needed now are financial talents, the ability to cut and trim" [88, p. A4]. Kerr later described this presidential type as "a kind of super-accountant" [70, p. 1].

As an example, Dale Corson, former president of Cornell University, wrote a memorandum in 1975 to his board of trustees, faculty, and university senate to explain why the following year's budget included a 10% increase in tuition, a $2.3 million reduction in operating costs, and a $1.3 million deficit. "We are at the end of an era," he commented. "The growth and the affluence of the last three decades, particularly the last two decades, are over" [56, p. A3].

Leon Botstein, president of Bard College, explained this as follows: "By the mid-1970s, the academic job market had collapsed and enrollments at graduate schools declined. The era of growth and expansive, experimental change for the university had come to an end. Retrenchment, early retirement, and faculty development became new enthusiasms." Specifically, he called 1975 a "turning point," citing the beginnings of long-term economic concern about America, doubts regarding the possibilities of a continued American political preeminence in the world, the emergence of a serious environmental movement, and the first warnings about the state of literacy among students [9, p. 39].

Alan Hamlin, in a study of factors associated with the survival of financially endangered private colleges and universities, also stated:

> Several factors combined to erode the financial base of American private colleges and universities during the 1970s: enrollments declined when the "baby boom" generation grew older; national economic trends were generally in decline—evidenced by two devaluations of the dollar, two recessions, and severe bursts of inflation and unemployment; public confidence in the performance of educators began to wane; and the burden of judicial litigation and governmental regulation began to take its toll on higher education [41, p. 2].

In addition, George Keller cited a 1981 study by NACUBO which found that fewer than 50 U.S. colleges and universities had endowments of $100 million or more, and fewer than 200 had an endowment larger than $10 million. According to him, "Nine out of ten institutions in the United States, therefore, are precariously financed, and many live at the brink of jeopardy and instant retrenchment" [44, p. 152]. In citing the source of these difficulties, Keller explained:

> [T]he formation of the OPEC cartel in 1973, and the resulting higher prices for oil, suddenly caused fuel bills to triple or quadruple. Double-digit inflation in the late 1970s brought rapid increases in the costs of library books and periodicals, educational and scientific equipment, and labor. The possible

financial collapse of the social security system mandated higher college contributions to its members in the system. As health care costs ran up, major medical insurance costs escalated. New expenses for the handicapped and for the implementation of affirmative action plans became necessary. As tenure tightened, the number of lawsuits against universities rose, and the size of university legal staffs often had to be tripled, at considerable expense. The computer revolution required costly purchases of new hardware. More detailed federal accounting procedures, the rise of state coordinating agencies and their voracious demands for data, and nervous state budget officials seeking greater accountability forced the expansion of white-collar institutional research, accounting, and reporting staffs. Finances came to dominate campus management [44, pp. 10–11].

As a result of these and other forces, colleges and universities of all varieties increasingly looked to fund raising from private sources to supply a greater percentage of their needs. In particular, many public institutions began private fund-raising programs during the mid-1970s, and by the early 1980s they had learned to look to the private sector for the resources needed to fulfill their aspirations [38, 105].

Growth in Educational Fund Raising

During the 1980s, tuition grew by double digits almost annually at most colleges and universities [38], while the stock market recorded an average annual gain of 17.4% [13]; yet despite this, revenue was still insufficient to balance budgets on most campuses, and as a result, institutions increasingly looked to voluntary support, especially capital campaigns [3, 31, 54, 80, 95, 97]. According to Geiger, "Fund-raising campaigns became virtually ubiquitous: in 1990, 38 of the 55 AAU universities were either conducting or planning such campaigns and at least six envisioned billion-dollar targets" [38, p. 314].

Gains in collegiate fund raising were not distributed equally, however. According to Breneman, "Many small [private] colleges did not have a history of sophisticated fund-raising activities before the 1980s, but most advanced far along the learning curve during that decade, launching campaigns and developing the necessary volunteer support organizations required for success" [13, pp. 33–34]. He then provided a few examples from his 1994 study of 212 liberal arts colleges:

> One tends to think of fund-raising as having a long history in private colleges, and yet, in several of the colleges visited, professionally conducted development efforts are of rather recent origin. At Bowdoin, for example, the development office is located in a former president's home on the edge of the campus, physically removed from the president's office and other parts of the campus. Prior presidents apparently did not look favorably on development, and its location reflects the marginal status accorded to it in the past. The vice president observed that Bowdoin has only had a fully professional development staff for about five years, suggesting that the college has considerable unrealized potential in fund-raising. Dickinson College, founded like Bowdoin in the eighteenth century, is also a fairly recent convert to development, with such efforts conducted by a fully professional staff for less than a decade. Although Dickinson has over 20,000 living alumni of record, the college's annual fund just surpassed the $1 million mark recently. . . .
>
> Every college I visited had just completed a capital campaign, was in the midst of a campaign, or was planning the next one. The dollar amounts of these actual or planned campaigns ranged from a low of $10 million to a high of $150 million. . . . Presidents reported definite expectations in the college community on their role and performance in this aspect of the job, as well as the view that development will require ever-increasing presidential time in the years ahead. Not surprisingly, however, presidents at these colleges (as would be true of any set of institutions) differ in their skill and interest in fund-raising, and development officers were candid with me in expressing such judgments. In earlier years, a president who disliked fund-raising could spend little time doing it, but that is less true today. Tension between the president and the development staff is increasingly common as expectations rise, and I observed several instances of that problem. . . . [13, pp. 108–109].

K. S. Kelly added another reason why the development function has been slow to develop at some private colleges:

[W]hen I assumed the vice presidency of development and public relations at Mount Vernon College in 1982, this small, private, women's college in Washington, DC was approximately $2 million in debt. Contributing to this deficit was the fact that for generations, the college had depended on its relationship with Marjorie Merriweather Post, heiress of the Post Cereal fortune, an alumna, major donor, and trustee of the college. According to fellow administrators, this dependency was so strong that for years before her death Ms. Post would schedule an annual visit to the president to learn the amount of deficit incurred by the college that year, at which time she would write a personal check to cover the deficit.

Convinced that Mrs. Post's role as a trustee would prompt her to provide a major bequest on her death, Mount Vernon continued to operate in the red, failed to build an adequate endowment, and rarely solicited gifts from other alumnae or friends. It is not surprising, then, that when Mrs. Post died and Mount Vernon College received only $100,000 and 10 Cadillac limousines, the college was unprepared to adjust to its new financial circumstances; therefore, in 1982, much of my efforts as vice president were spent trying to convince other wealthy alumnae, who had never been solicited by their alma mater, that the college needed their private support [46, p. 181].

Despite these examples, however, private colleges have historically been much more active in fund raising than their public counterparts [24, 25, 58, 62, 66, 81, 84, 87], although that began to change about 20 years ago, as demonstrated by a 1979 study of capital campaigns at 1,912 U.S. colleges and universities. The study found that during an 11-year period (1974–84) about half of these institutions were either conducting a campaign or planning a campaign for the near future. The study analyzed data on capital campaigns begun or completed during the period 1974–79, and also for the period 1979–84, substituting "contemplated" for "completed." Both periods were 5.5 years in length with 30 June 1979 as a midpoint [22].

Several interesting findings were reported. Roughly 9% of the public and 37% of the private institutions initiated campaigns between 1974 and 1979. The average campaign lasted 3.6 years. The combined total of all campaign goals between 1974 and 1979 was $8.5 billion. Of the institutions completing their campaigns by 1979, 88% of public and 79% of private institutions met or exceeded their goals. The average goal for public institutions was $7 million; for private institutions, $15 million. Private institutions conducted 80% of all campaigns and sought 89% of all funds. Research and doctoral universities—primarily private institutions—received 50% of all funds although they conducted only 10% of all campaigns. Endowment funding was the leading purpose of campaigns, accounting for 50% of all funds sought, followed by construction of new facilities (25%) and renovation (10%). This was true at both public and private institutions. Current operating funds accounted for 9% of public institution goals and 16% of private campaign goals. Only 18 institutions had campaigns of $100 million or more [22].

During the later period (1979–84), a definite trend emerged among public institutions as the percentage of those beginning or planning a campaign doubled (from 9 to 18), whereas among privates, the percentage (37) held constant. The total goal for all public campaigns was about $1 billion, close to a 50% increase over the early period, while the total goal for private campaigns climbed by 30%. It is interesting to note that during 1979–84 only 4% of public community colleges were involved in a campaign [22].

"Twenty years ago, there weren't many public universities, if any, engaged in fund-raising," said Bob Bryan, interim president at the University of South Florida during 1993–94 [108, p. B7]. Gene Budig, former chancellor of the University of Kansas, added, "The country's leading state universities are either in the final stages of large fund drives or about to launch new ones. No one is standing by with indifference. That was not true 25 years ago, when most people in higher education regarded systematic fund raising as the purview of private colleges and universities" [17, p. 39].

In addition, the historical pattern of campaigning has changed, according to Smith:

Traditionally, institutional requirements for capital funds were kept separate from the needs for annual operating support. The financial development programs of most institutions could easily be divided between the need for physical expansion or rehabilitation of facilities and the need for current budgetary support. Building programs were perceived to be inherently discrete, whereas academic programs obviously required continuous funding on an annual basis. In recent years, however, the financial pressures on colleges and universities have led to a change in these perceptions, and the multipurpose fund drive, combining appeals for operating funds and capital funds, has emerged. . . . [94, pp. ix-x].

According to Dove, four distinctive campaign models can be found today: the traditional capital campaign, the comprehensive campaign, the single-purpose campaign, and the continuing major gifts program [30]. This array of titles can be confusing, especially because many institutions fail to differentiate between them. Most large campaigns in the modern era are called capital campaigns but are really comprehensive campaigns. At any rate, the preponderance of these campaigns, both in number and size, has continued to increase in recent years, and this trend shows no sign of slowing.

In the late 1980s, for example, several writers noted that more than 60 of the nation's colleges and universities were then conducting campaigns to raise more than $100 million each [54, 80, 97]. "You're not in the major leagues if your goal is under $100-million," said William P. McGoldrick, former vice president for institute relations at Rensselaer Polytechnic Institute [3, p. A75]. Indeed, several institutions have upped the fund-raising ante by launching campaigns for $1 billion or more.

First out of the blocks was Stanford University with its announcement of a 5-year, $1.1 billion campaign beginning 1 February 1987. Stanford reached its goal ahead of schedule in June 1991 and eventually raised $1.27 billion. This premier feat is even more remarkable when the constant stream of negative publicity generated during this period is considered.

"It isn't every campaign that has a major unfortunate change in the tax laws, a stock market crash, and a $160 million earthquake," said Donald Kennedy, former Stanford president [63, p. A34]. It also isn't every campaign that has a federal investigation over the indirect-cost rate charged for research, a long-time medical educator who resigns after claiming sexual harassment and discrimination by male faculty and administrators at the university's medical school (she later withdrew her resignation), and a presidential resignation and divorce.

Stanford's announcement, and subsequent success, was followed by other campaigns with similarly lofty goals among the elite ranks of American universities. Even Oxford, the stately ancestral monarch of higher education, has since hired its first fund-raising director and recently completed a modest $400 million campaign, its first-ever American-style fund-raising effort [83].

Boston University and New York University launched billion-dollar campaigns in 1988 that will extend to the end of the century. Next to throw its hat into the ring was the University of Pennsylvania, which announced in 1989 a 5-year, $800 million campaign and later raised the goal to an even billion after a series of successes. Late in 1990 two Ivys—Columbia and Cornell—also announced plans for 5-year, record-setting campaigns. Columbia's goal was $1.15 billion and Cornell targeted $1.25 billion. Michigan and Yale also joined the "billion-dollar club," launching in 1992 the public phase of campaigns for $1 billion and $1.5 billion, respectively.

In 1994 Harvard announced a campaign for $2.5 billion, and several other universities are in the planning or early stages of billion-dollar campaigns, including the University of California at Berkeley, the University of Illinois at Urbana, Champaign, the Pennsylvania State University, the University of Southern California, and the University of Texas at Austin.

According to Matthews:

Gone are the days of souvenir mugs and T-shirts; nowadays the focus is on detail, pressure and glitz. Stanford's centennial road show [to 31 cities], for example, paired faculty panels on biomedical ethics with a singing-and-dancing extravaganza requiring a technical crew of 40 to set off lasers, fireworks and an on stage bonfire [57, p. 73].

The 1990s may well become known as the "Billion-Dollar Decade" in higher education fund raising, added former Cornell President Frank Rhodes. According to him:

The move toward billion-dollar campaigns reflects, on the one hand, the fact that there are a substantial number of individuals in our society who are capable of providing multimillion-dollar gifts. Rather than making donors of more modest means feel that their own contributions are insignificant when compared to the need—as some higher education observers had initially feared—billion-dollar campaigns have opened up new levels of giving that campaigns for smaller amounts might never have tapped.

Billion-dollar campaigns reflect, as well, the magnitude of the financial challenges facing many institutions as they seek to attract and retain high-quality faculty and staff; maintain their libraries, computing centers, dormitories, and other facilities; purchase up-to-date equipment for teaching and research; and provide enough financial aid to make their programs accessible to students from a variety of economic circumstances. With a substantial number of institutions charging students more than $20,000 a year for tuition, fees, room, and board, with federal financial aid programs covering only a fraction of the cost, with increased competition for federal research dollars and limited funds for facilities, private support is no longer merely a welcome add-on that can provide a margin of excellence. In many cases, it is essential to institutional survival [79, p. 65].

This success in fund raising has not escaped notice. In an initial ranking of the 400 nonprofit organizations in the U.S. receiving the most private support, the "Philanthropy 400" for 1990 included 141 colleges and universities, "far more than any other kind of organization" [76, p. 20]. Many of those listed indicated that they were involved in a capital campaign.

However, despite their many benefits, campaigns often engender unrealistic expectations, especially among faculty members. Robert S. Shephard offered an insightful and comprehensive analysis of this phenomenon. According to him, campaigns often have a 12-year cash flow spread:

Fund-raising campaigns are typically five-year efforts. That is where the confusion starts, for it is often assumed that solicitation begins in the first year and that by the fifth, all the money has been collected. Actually, however, the cash flow of most campaigns stretches over 12 years or more.

Fund-raising drives are five-year efforts only in their public phases, which begin after the campaigns and financial goals are announced. The public phase typically is preceded by a two-year private effort to collect gifts and pledges from trustees and previous major donors. . . .

Adding to the confusion is that commitments made during both the private and public phases of the campaign are likely to be five-year pledges. Seldom do donors make lump-sum cash gifts. Thus, the cash flow in a typical campaign extends from the first payment in the first year of the private phase to the final payment on a pledge made during the last year of the public phase. Hence the 12-year spread for gift revenues [90, p. A48].

Next, Shephard pointed out that fund-raising totals do not equal available cash:

It is important to understand how campaign gifts are counted, so as not to be led astray by the numbers that appear periodically on the development office's scorecard. The numbers reported reflect a combination of cash received and pledges made. They do not equal cash that is available.

Fund-raising campaigns are not the total answer to the budget woes of colleges and universities. Major gifts, the bread and butter of all successful campaigns, often are designated for specific, restricted purposes. Although we do our best to match donors' interest with university priorities, it is not always easy to find six- and seven-figure gifts that will provide direct budget relief.

. . . Often 50 per cent or more of the gifts made to a campaign are earmarked for the institution's endowment, and most institutions follow a rule of spending only approximately 4 per cent of the endowment's market value each year. Faculty members often forget the tradeoff involved in building endowments: The long-term benefit of a large endowment means the sacrifice of short-term spendable cash [90, p. A48].

Some observers feel that the increasing dependence on private donations is also weakening the distinction between public and private institutions. Brad Choate, former development officer at Ohio State, said, "The difference between a public and a private university is in how you run it—with elected officials or not—rather than in how you fund it" [39, p. A30].

"We had to combat the misconception that Penn State is a university owned and operated by the state and having no need for private gifts," added Roger Williams, assistant vice president and executive director of university relations at Penn State. Only 22% of the University's budget comes from the State of Pennsylvania, he said, making it a "state-related" institution governed by its own board of trustees, only a few of whom are state appointees. "Our goal was to show that private dollars provide the critical academic infrastructure—endowed faculty positions, graduate fellowships, scholarships, research support—that enhances academic quality and allows us to play ball with the nation's best universities," he said [6, p. 20].

"You cannot be a first-rate public university today unless you've got a significant amount of private contributions coming in," said Theodore Saenger, former national chairman of the University of California at Berkeley's "Keeping the Promise" campaign [39, p. A31]. Gene Budig, Baseball Commissioner of the American League, explained this view in more detail:

> [T]he large state university remains only state-assisted, not fully state-supported. Tax-based state assistance, though limited, should be expected to provide the foundation for quality higher education. But it will never offer the full measure of funding required for true and lasting excellence.
>
> Tuition, we must acknowledge, is a limited source of revenue for the state university. It must be held at reasonable levels if the institution is to remain accessible to qualified students, especially minorities.
>
> Research grants and contracts, awarded to a growing number of leading faculty, bring in substantial revenues for the state university. But only private support, realized through an aggressive drive, can bridge the gap between adequate funding and funding for recognized excellence. Through endowment income and annual support, private donors are greatly strengthening progressive state universities. . . .
>
> . . . True quality will emerge only when a public university blends adequate state support with a substantial private endowment. Private dollars can provide a margin of excellence [17, p. 40].

David Riesman, a Harvard sociologist and authority on American higher education, cited the new competition between publics and privates for philanthropic funds as evidence of the demise of a "tacit agreement" that has existed for decades between the two sectors [107, p. B7]. Benezet documented the earlier existence of such agreements as follows:

> A . . . form of indirect yet substantial state university help to the private sector is self-denying ordinances against broadside fund raising among private sources for public colleges. Such restraints are most carefully practiced by public universities located in states with strong private colleges. Midwest state institutions have had full development staffs for many years. . . .
>
> The State University of New York, on the other hand, has not been authorized to employ development officers on its campuses; in fact, no budget lines for campus directors of alumni affairs have yet been approved. In states where the balance of enrollments is less heavy on the public side, the influence of private college fund raising jurisdiction is evident. Even the strong fund-raising state universities espouse politics limiting their solicitation of gifts to their own alumni and immediate business affiliates in response to frequent complaints from nearby private colleges about public college fund raising [4, p. 25].

Boston University's $1 billion campaign includes $500 million for endowment and $150 million for scholarships. Without the extra scholarship money, said former President John Silber, "B.U. simply cannot hope to compete with either subsidized state schools or the much better-endowed Ivy League colleges like Harvard in attracting talented high school graduates" [8, p. 72].

Clark Kerr noted that "all institutions, within their categories and geographic regions, compete for students, for funds, for reputation" and that "private fund-raising by both public and private institutions has, in recent times, increasingly become a mechanism for competitive advantage" [48, p. 15]. At Penn State, where a major campaign was completed several years ago, plans are already well underway for the next one. David Gearhart, former senior vice president for development and university relations, said, "There's no question that Penn State will always be in a fund-raising mode. We have to be, in order to compete with our peer institutions. To stand still is in effect to take a step backward" [6, p. 24].

Barbara Taylor, director of programs and research at the Association of Governing Boards of Universities and Colleges, said, "It used to be that we had annual giving and we had occasional capital campaigns. Now the capital campaign is becoming as constant as the annual campaign has been in the past" [95, p. 10]. "We're always in a campaign," added Kendall Lewis, who recently retired as vice president for alumni relations, development, and public relations at Swarthmore College. "It's just a question of whether we're planning one, in the middle of one, or cleaning one up."

The trend is clear: colleges and universities are raising more money than ever through short-term, high-pressure, high-visibility campaigns, and this is likely to continue for the foreseeable future. Campaigns are held more often and have larger goals than in the past. Also, the use of sophisticated techniques such as prospect research and donor tracking systems has become commonplace, and the size and complexity of fund-raising staffs has greatly increased at many institutions.

In addition to the obvious goal of raising more money for their institutions, however, campaigns may also involve hidden motives. According to Matthews, "One response to the money crunch has been to undertake fund drives for staggering amounts. The size of such campaigns is often a function of prestige as well as an essential part of the annual budget" [57, p. 73]. "More boards of directors are saying, 'It's not what we can raise, but what we have to raise to beat so and so,'" explained Rick Nahm, president of Knox College [37, p. A28].

"Woe be to the fund raiser who wants to set a goal that is less than the competition's," added Gary Evans, former vice chancellor for development and university relations at the University of North Carolina at Chapel Hill. "He can find his job on the line" [3, p. A75]. And according to Wiseman, "A president in whose tenure the university does not raise more money than it did before is a president looking for a new line of work" [102, p. 6].

Terry Holcombe, vice president for development and alumni affairs at Yale, said, "For a place that's raising more than $100 million a year now, anything less than $1 billion would indicate that their plans for the future call for less rather than more money." Yale plans to celebrate its 300th anniversary in 2001, and according to Holcombe, "If we don't raise $2 billion between now and then, people here will worry" [37, p. A26].

"You can't plan a campaign today without thinking about going for a billion dollars," echoed Carol Herring, director of leadership gifts at Princeton [37, p. A25]. And Rose said many presidents feel they can never stop raising money:

> Even at universities worth hundreds of millions, or even billions, of dollars, the presidents I spoke with felt they could never stop raising money. They worried about inflation; that salaries, library, and maintenance costs would rise unchecked. Or, perhaps more troublesome, that they would fall behind in the race for the most up-to-date equipment, i.e., computers. But at least one college president, who declined to be quoted, thinks that colleges have enough for their current needs and beyond. "Many of these college presidents are like squirrels, putting nuts away for the future," he says [80, p. 22].

Fund Raising as a Measure of Presidential Success

According to Rose, another more personal motive driving the culture of college fund raising is that it's "a great way to be remembered" [80, p. 22]. She cited the example of Thomas Reynolds, who retired in 1989 after 20 years of service as president of Bates College. A local news article glossed over his contribution to academics, which had been plentiful, and highlighted his two successful capital campaigns.

Similarly, George M. Harmon, president of Millsaps College, defended his $140,435 salary and $27,174 benefits package (for 1990–91) by explaining that since he arrived in 1978, the endowment had increased more than tenfold, Millsaps had raised almost $50 million in two successful capital campaigns, the faculty had doubled in size, and 50% of the student body now came from outside of Mississippi, up from 20% when he was hired [52, p. A16].

Regarding CEO pay, Pfeffer and Ross, in a study of the compensation of more than 600 college and university presidents, noted that there is a strong relationship between institutional size and executive remuneration, then stated:

> We expect resource-rich schools to pay more than resource-poor schools, other things being equal. This expectation can result from two different reasons. Resource munificence means that there is more to be divided among all the organization's members, and certainly the president will share in these extra rewards. It is also the case that the ability to extract resources from the environment is one important measure of an organization's effectiveness (Yuchtman and Seashore, 1967). Thus, presidents in richer schools may be compensated more highly because the very resource position of the school provides evidence of the president's effectiveness in dealing with at least one important organizational

issue. This is not to say that financial performance is the only or even the most important indicator of a university's success, or that pay always is related to performance. But there is probably enough of both of these connections to argue that we should observe a relationship between financial position and pay [75, p. 81].

In another study, Whetten and Cameron found that successful presidents make an indelible impression on their campuses. According to these scholars:

In our interviews with individuals, especially in small colleges, we have been impressed with the tendency of faculty and administrators to demarcate their institution's history into presidential eras. Frequently, when we would ask a question about campus activities during a specific period of time, before the respondents could formulate an answer, they would have to first identify who the president was at that time. Their memories were clearly indexed by presidential tenure, and their recollections of what transpired on campus during each term was strongly colored by their overall evaluation of the effectiveness of each president. Events that transpired during the term of an uninspiring, ineffective president were described in a bland, colorless manner. In contrast, descriptions of activities during the tenure of spirited, effective presidents were conveyed using very emotional language and with a sense of institutional pride [101, pp. 40–41].

For example, during Leon Botstein's first 17 years as president, Bard College raised more than $82 million. According to one observer, "The last 17 years [1975–1992] have so remade the college that the 'B' on the mat in front of the president's modest yellow house could easily stand for either name" [27, p. 48].

David McLaughlin, former president of Dartmouth, noted that "the success or failure of both a college and an administration is—in the short term—often judged on financial solvency. The fact that campaigns are measurable and many other achievements are not gives fund raising special, tangible significance" [61, p. 7]. Rita Bornstein added, "[A]n ambitious and successful campaign is one of the greatest legacies a president can leave a university or college" [7, p. 202].

Derek Bok, Harvard's long-time helmsman, added that success or failure as a president is defined in part by "how much money you raise, not what you raise the money for" [49, p. 13]. And Gary Evans, vice president for development and alumni relations at Lafayette College, warned that "as long as colleges keep claiming record amounts of money raised, it's hard imagining a college ever cutting back" [36, p. A28].

Former Cornell CEO Edmund Day added the following observations:

The most obvious and best recognized obligation of administration is to add to the institution's resources. The task of obtaining additional funds is, in fact, so characteristic of the role of the college and university president that he is frequently described as more of a cultured mendicant than anything else. It is safe to say that the reputation of many presidents has derived largely from their success or failure as fund-raisers.

The explanation of this is relatively simple. Here is one type of accomplishment which is almost certain to provoke general acclaim. With new funds, the president can implement new undertakings and gain fresh support for his over-all program. A million dollars of new money can quiet a lot of carping criticism of any administration. It is altogether natural that any college or university administration should turn its attention increasingly to the problem of finding additional support for the work of the institution, since the administration's ability to give effect to its own constructive planning may depend largely upon the possibility of finding new financial resources [26, p. 341].

Harold Stoke offered additional insight into the continual, ongoing need for and insatiable, unquenchable nature of fund raising in higher education:

If colleges and universities are by their nature always short of funds, the college president who gets this principle firmly in mind will save himself some psychological problems. It will help him, for example, to accept the fact that he is on a treadmill. He is destined always to approach but never to arrive at the promised land [96, p. 56].

The historic importance of fund raising to higher education has even given academic presidents in the United States a kind of international notoriety. In response to government initiatives to promote greater autonomy and financial independence among French universities, Georges Haddad, president of the Sorbonne, said that he had no intention of becoming a fund raiser "like presidents in the U.S." [14, p. A45].

Fund Raising as a Factor in Presidential Selection

In fact, finance is associated with the academic presidency to such an extent that fund-raising considerations permeate all aspects of the presidential selection process. For example, Tom Ingram, president of the Association of Governing Boards of Universities and Colleges, stated, "I think the majority of boards would perceive that situation [hiring an openly gay or lesbian president] as extremely awkward for the institution, in the fund-raising role in particular" [69, p. A20]. Presidential illness [18, 40, 42, 53] and appearance [51] have also been mentioned as having an impact on fund raising.

Edward Lewis, president of St. Mary's College, noted that while opportunities for women presidents are growing, there "has been a belief that fund raising involves working the old-boy network, which cannot be done as well by women as by the typical 53-year-old male president" [34, p. D25]. William J. Bowen, vice chairman of Heidrick and Struggles, an executive search firm, added that women "are becoming more visible, holding the right chairs, and the perceived pool is much larger than it was 10 years ago" [20, p. B8].

Thompson also cited a pair of recent studies on the presidency by the American Council on Education. The first found that in 1986, 9.3% of college and university presidents in the U.S. were women, while the second found that in 1993, that number was 12%. However, of the 400 female presidents in 1993, only 11 were at major universities.

Thompson noted that "one of the main functions of a college or university president is fund-raising from alumni" [98, p. 26]. One person interviewed by Thompson was Jadwiga Sebrechts, executive director of the Women's College Coalition. According to her, a private, coeducational institution might prefer a male president because most of its graduates are men. On the other hand, a major state university might not think a woman was aggressive enough to fight for legislative appropriations, she said.

Ronald Stead, senior associate for the Academic Search Consultation Service in Washington, D.C., was also interviewed by Thompson. According to him, "In the past few days I heard a board chairman say he thought a man would be in a better position to raise significant funds for the institution than a woman would" [98, p. 26]. Stead, a 15-year veteran of academic searches, said he hears that response less often now than he did 5 years ago.

Milley also addressed this topic in a chapter from a book on women presidents of American Association of State Colleges and Universities member institutions. Her comments were based on 18 responses to a survey she sent to the 25 AASCU women presidents. According to her, 61% of respondents said that when they were appointed, fund raising was mentioned as one of their duties. She also reported:

> This author had hoped to begin to discover, "Is there a difference in fund raising techniques employed by men and women presidents?" But this is not known and probably will not be for some time because presidents, and thus the chief fund raisers, have traditionally been men. Although women presidents have been on the increase, they remain a minority. In 1988, the twenty-five women presidents leading AASCU campuses represented only 7.8 percent of the total presidential population. Thus, despite the growing literature on fund raising and proliferation of material on presidents as chief fund raisers, there is little documentation on women presidents, let alone their role as fund raisers [67, p. 34].

The Reality of Presidential Fund Raising

However, whether candidates are male or female, the prestige and perquisites of the presidency are so enticing for many that they either fail to give serious consideration to or are simply not prepared for what will be expected and required of them in terms of fund raising, as Woodroof so dramatically documented in his study of "first-time" presidents at 36 private nonsectarian colleges and universities. For example, one rookie president stated:

> I knew there would need to be a fund-raising component to the job, but I didn't realize how urgent and intense that really was. The trustees didn't do alot [sic] to prepare me. I had a sense of going in as an educational statesman, a leader, but I realized after I got there that the financial pressures were so acute, that what the college needed from me was to meet the budget. The finances drive everything—I found that out in the first few months on the job. It dawned on me that I had over-romanticized what it was going to be like to be a president [104, pp. 174–175].

Another new president in the study shared the following comments:

> I was told by the board that there was sufficient funds to get the college through the summer. At the end of my first week on the job, the business manager came to me and said, 'We are down to only $2,000 in cash with which to operate.' Given the fact that payroll was due in less than two weeks, reality set in very quickly for me. I've never been that low even in my own bank account [104, p. 175].

A third president stated, "I wasn't informed of the seriousness of the cash flow problem. I didn't know until I was in office for a week that we might not make payroll in 12 days" [104, p. 175]. Finally, a fourth president related, "When I moved here, I thought I had gotten all I needed to know about the status of the institution. However, I found out later that the trustees were deeply concerned about the finances. They decided not to share that with me for fear that I would back out" [104, p. 176].

West penned a thoughtful essay on six areas of concern for presidential candidates: the board of trustees, the faculty and curriculum, the student body, staff, resources, and constituent relations. In regard to trustees, he stated:

> The prospective president should see the contribution record of each individual trustee. Most boards tell a presidential candidate that they expect him or her to raise money—a lot of money—but how much will the trustees themselves pledge toward the needed amount? Unless they are prepared to put up a substantial amount themselves—between one fourth and one third—why should they expect the president to do so, and why should anyone want to seek money on their behalf [100, p. 11]?

He also said, "A presidential candidate should obtain a copy of the last audit and should go over it carefully, preferably with an accountant who is familiar with college fund accounting and who is not connected with the college" [100, p. 12]. West added:

> Some of these questions may seem extremely blunt. Unless they are answered, however, the successful candidate may not be able to be a successful president. Moreover, unless the search committee is willing and able to supply satisfactory answers, its members may not understand their situation well enough to identify the person best qualified to meet its needs. Candidates should not worry about appearing too hard-nosed or demanding. If you are wanted, you are in the strongest position during the interview process that you will ever be in with the college. If you are not wanted, the quality of the answers that you receive to these questions will make that clear [100, p. 13].

Once the decision is made to accept a presidency, candidates commit themselves to care for the institution as if it were their own child, according to McIntosh:

> [I]f one is deeply involved in the college and completely committed to its progress, fund-raising ceases to be a burden. Raising money to increase teaching salaries is especially rewarding since one's efforts in this area are fundamental to the excellence of education now, and in the future. And if a new building is absolutely necessary for the health of the college, one does not resent the necessity of raising money for it any more than a father resents earning money to build a new house for his family, or to send his son through college. Once accepted in its larger framework, the task becomes exciting, and any success truly satisfying [60, p. 22].

Other presidents have used less flattering analogies to describe the presidential fund-raising responsibility. For example, Tolley related how he came to terms with fund raising early in his career during a presidency at Allegheny College:

> Given Allegheny's shaky financial status, I devoted much of my time to fund raising. For many years this was my most difficult task. I disliked it so much that it literally made me sick. One day, however, it dawned on me that "If you can't lick 'em, join 'em."

"This is part of my job," I thought. "It's a disagreeable job, but like washing dishes, making beds, or changing diapers, it needs to be done. Stop complaining about it. Stop getting sick about it. Just do it." After I made that decision, I took fund raising in my stride. It never made me sick again [99, p. 58].

Shuster offered a somewhat more optimistic view, suggesting that presidents must acquire or cultivate a taste for fund raising as in various other activities of life:

Despite the widespread fostering of public higher education, ours is by and large a free enterprise system, which means that the budget is never what it ought to be. Therefore the president is first of all expected to find money somewhere. This is one task he cannot hire anybody else to perform. It is an ornery business which nearly everybody finds extremely unpleasant at the outset. Here nothing helps as does a measure of success. The first check is like a first baby or a first published book. Indeed, I have come to feel that money-raising is like smoking: one's first experiments are sickening, but after a while the thing acquires a fascination quite its own. You have formed the habit. The difficulty is that no matter how much money a president extracts from people, it is never enough either in his own estimation or—what is vastly more oppressive—in that of his colleagues [91, pp. 30–31].

In another description by a former president, Wriston described fund raising as a balancing act that can only be learned through experience—hard experience:

The president who gives too little time to money raising will never have a balanced budget, a salary increase for the faculty, or well-maintained buildings and grounds. The one who pours too much of his time and energy into fund accumulation will lose touch with the faculty, the curriculum, the students—and even worse, with ideas. No man can write a prescription to tell another how much is too much, how little is not enough. The balance is the fruit of experience—hard experience [106, pp. 165–167].

Payton also explained that most academics "detest" fund-raising and often treat the fund-raising staff with "ill-concealed disdain" [73, p. 64]. Because the majority of campus CEOs advance through the academic ranks, this characterization is applicable to many presidents. Several examples of this were provided by Cook in his study of presidential fund raising. For instance, the chief development officer at a major public research university commented:

I think very few people warm naturally to being a fund raiser, particularly among people whose careers have been in the academic world. So I would say that most approach the task rather reluctantly, and what we have been doing in our business is to try to warm the presidents up by giving the presidents some easy fund-raising successes early on and building a sense of confidence that this is not such a hard job after all. But most presidents are not generally extroverted, outgoing, aggressive, sales-marketing type people. They are people who have spent their careers with the life of the mind, and I don't want to say that sales and marketing and the life of the mind are mutually exclusive, but there are some differences there [23, p. 461].

A second chief development officer in Cook's study also shared this viewpoint:

I think one of the strange things we do in academia is we take the best economist or physicist or history professor and make them president, and yet their forte and what got them noticed was their great teaching. So we take them out of their element and turn them into administrators and then fund raisers. It isn't necessarily all that logical. So you get some unevenness but you can't have a president that doesn't have academic credentials. That's the nature of the beast. So you hope the other's there. Sometimes it is and sometimes it isn't [23, p. 461].

College presidents, however, are not the only nonprofit executives who struggle with fund raising. In a national study of excellence in nonprofit organizations, Knauft, Berger, and Gray also found that "by a wide margin, the chief staff officers we surveyed considered fund-raising the most pressing challenge facing their organizations in the coming three to five years. Interestingly, these executives reported that building fund-raising skills was the area where they perceived the greatest need for personal development" [50, pp. 25–26].

The Presidential Fund-Raising Role

Fund raising requires team effort, and an institution's president is typically the central player on the fund-raising team. Using football as an analogy, ideally the chief development officer is the coach or player-coach, the president is the quarterback-athletic director, the offensive line is made up of the "heavy hitters" (trustees and other powerful volunteers) who can open holes (doors), the running backs are the frontline fund-raising staff, and the ends are the deans or department heads of the various academic units [23].

As quarterback, the president is the central player in the fund-raising offense and follows instructions from the head coach (chief development officer) or offensive coordinator (campaign director). At the same time, the president also functions as the athletic director who is responsible for many programs and coaches, of which football is but one. The athletic director may also be more attuned to the external environment than the coach and may have a more intimate relationship with the institution's leadership, top conference officials, or regulatory bodies such as the NCAA or NAIA. Therefore, what usually occurs in fund raising is a blending of the philosophies and strategies of the chief development officer, the president, and a small number of powerful volunteers (trustee and campaign chairmen) [23].

Fund raising is therefore rarely a 50–50 proposition. Many development programs have a dominant personality or a person with superior skills and thus either the president, the chief development officer, or a powerful volunteer (trustee or campaign chairman) may be more or less involved in setting the overall guiding philosophy, strategy, and direction of the program depending on the unique institution, the unique personalities and abilities involved, time constraints, size and expertise of support staff, and other factors [23].

Moreover, presidents should focus their effort and attention in fund raising on two areas: (1) major gifts (although what is "major" varies from institution to institution, this generally refers to gifts of $100,000 and above), and (2) administrative leadership (e.g., policy and strategy decisions, budget and staffing concerns, selection and/or evaluation of the chief development officer, strategic planning, selling a campaign to the trustees, being involved in the selection of a fund-raising consultant, helping to decide on the timing and goal for a campaign, recruiting volunteer campaign leaders, and articulating the institutional vision) [23].

It is not surprising, therefore, that fund-raising ability and experience have become increasingly valued presidential assets in recent years. According to Dorich, "Academic credentials and a clear understanding of how the academy works continue to be vital to aspiring presidents. But in today's uncertain times, many search committees also recognize the value of the fund-raising skills and leadership ability that come with an advancement background" [29, p. 6].

"When governing boards go hunting for presidents, it's often the candidates' fundraising, rather than academic, talents that catch the eye," added Rose [80, p. 19]. Anderson noted, "Nowadays, a president is often hired to ask for money" [1, p. 17]. And Wycliff stated, "For all academic presidents, the job more and more involves what many say is the least enjoyable activity of all: fund raising" [107, p. B7].

"Fundraising is not the only role, but it's a terribly important one in today's time," said Peggy Stock, president of Colby-Sawyer College, who estimated that she spends about 50% of her time on fund raising. "I don't know if any studies have been done but I would bet it would be very difficult, except at the very prestigious institutions, to raise money without having a president who is good at it," she added [92, pp. 28–29].

"As places look around for presidents, the premium on fund-raising ability is getting stronger and stronger," echoed George A. Brakeley III, president of Brakeley, John Price Jones Inc., a fundraising consulting firm. "Fund raisers know the game," explained Steven Ast, a partner in Ast/Bryant, an executive search firm. "If they've been through a capital campaign, they don't have to reinvent the wheel. Every president has to do a capital campaign now, and hiring a development vice president is an advantage" [64, p. A35].

According to Withers, in a capital campaign the president has at least six duties: (1) creating assertive board leadership in fund raising, (2) enunciating the master plan of the institution and obtaining a consensus on mission and goals, (3) using his or her time and appearances wisely, (4) meeting regularly with senior development staff to assess campaign strategy and analyze strengths and weaknesses, (5) spending considerable time in cultivating prospects for major gifts, and 6) insisting on continuity in development strategy rather than zigzagging from one approach to another [103].

Regarding the president's influence on the board, Patton had this to say:

> At most colleges and universities, the president is a member of the board of trustees. The president's involvement in fund raising sets the example for other trustees. If that involvement is positive, enthusiastic, and firmly tied to institutional priorities, trustees are likely to follow suit. If the president is indifferent to development concerns or distant from fund-raising activities, board members are likely to place a lower value on their own participation [72, p. 53].

The president must also be an optimist and encourager during a campaign:

> Every campaign, even the best, will have disappointments. The president is important also in helping the university through the difficult days. Most big campaigns last for five years or so. Inevitably, there will be slow periods when there is nothing much to report. It is then that the president has an additional responsibility: to keep the momentum going. The president may be disappointed, but must not show it. The president must encourage the dean who has just been turned down to try another donor on another day. The trustees' attention may drift away, and the president must invite it back. The professor whose new library wing is still only a dream must be encouraged to keep the faith. Students wondering why tuition is rising, despite all the money being raised, must be patiently educated about the complex realities of university financing [33, p. 76].

Capital campaigns often require huge commitments of time and energy from presidents and contribute to the growing stress level and rapid turnover rate associated with the position. According to G. T. Smith, "It is probably not an overstatement to suggest that no college or university can afford to have less than 60 percent of the chief executive's time dedicated to meaningful development of the institution's major constituencies" [93, p. 703].

McGoldrick added, "During noncampaign periods you should devote at least 20 percent of your time to development activities. During a campaign, that portion of your effort may need to reach 40 or 50 percent" [59, p. 167]. Brown advised presidents to "accept the fact that successful fund raising will require as much as 50 percent of your time and energy at certain times of the year" [16, p. 151]. And Foote stated, "During the height of the campaign, the president will spend as much as a third of his or her time on the campaign itself or directly related responsibilities" [33, p. 76].

At the University of Michigan, former President James Duderstadt spent two thirds of his time generating resources from alumni, corporations, and the state and federal government. Former Cornell President Frank Rhodes spent four days a week wooing donors. Former Stanford President Donald Kennedy took a 3-month sabbatical from his other duties to kick off the Centennial campaign. James Holderman, former head of the University of South Carolina, spent 50% of his time raising money. And the late President James Zumberge at the University of Southern California spent 80% of his time on fund raising [82, 86, 107].

However, not all presidents are willing or able to devote this much time and energy to fund raising. According to Brecher, there are three basic types of "presidents who don't": (1) those who don't know how to raise funds and look to the chief development officer for leadership (the unable), (2) those who don't want to raise funds and assume the chief development officer will handle this unpleasant chore (the unwilling), and (3) those whose performance in fund raising is inadequate but who insist on being involved anyway (the willing but unable) [11, p. 24].

According to Del Martin, vice president of Alexander O'Neill Haas & Martin, Inc., a fund-raising consulting firm, reasons that a president may dislike asking for money include fear of rejection, lack of training, poor solicitation experience, and misplaced pride. "The non-asking president should be given proper training in how to ask and some easy experience to bolster confidence," she said [92, p. 29].

Schoenherr added that many presidents seek to avoid or minimize personal involvement in fund raising because of fear. According to him, "Presidents carry around a catalog of myths about fund-raising, and they are frightened by the thought of asking someone for a donation" [85, p. 46]. Schoenherr listed four fears: (1) the fear that others will see you as a beggar, a person with a tin cup looking for a handout, (2) the fear of being an intruder into the personal life of another, of invading their privacy, (3) the fear of rejection (probably the strongest fear), and (4) the fear of offending people by asking them for a contribution. He then explained:

> As the chief executive officer of your institution, you are responsible for its financial stability. Very few things will bolster the spirit of your institution faster than dollars. You do not have the luxury the

faculty have of dreaming dreams and letting the other guy worry about how the bills are to be paid. The dreams you dream are always tied to the pocketbook [85, pp. 45–46].

Foote added, "Presidents will enjoy fund raising in direct proportion to their enjoyment of people because ultimately a capital campaign is as complex, as fascinating, as exasperating and disappointing, as people themselves" [33, p. 78].

Richard Berendzen, former president of American University, shared both the fascination and the exasperation of fund raising. He began by describing his growing relationship with billionaire Adnan Khashoggi, an international arms dealer and philanthropist. After persuading Khashoggi to join the university's board of trustees, Berendzen introduced the need for a new campus facility—a sports and convocation center. Khashoggi ultimately funded $5 million of the $20 million cost of the 5,000-seat arena, which was named in his honor.

At the other end of the continuum, Berendzen was unusually candid in describing the frustration of working with donors who stall, change their minds, request special favors, and otherwise hinder rather than help progress:

Why are donors so cavalier? Many—maybe even most—mislead and deceive. They ask innumerable favors. Some state directly that they will contribute, citing the amount and the date. Then they do nothing. I remind them but they do not respond. I ask them to put it in writing, but they do not reply. I ask others to approach them, as my surrogates, but they, too, get no response. I ask again where the matter stands, but I am told, "Oh, I'm thinking about it." And so it goes—for weeks, months, years. It is frustrating as hell! [5, p. 171].

Payton summarized the importance of fund raising to the presidency as follows:

For presidents of all sorts of institutions, fund raising is an inescapable part of life. In an increasing number of cases, fund-raising effectiveness is the key to the office—to both getting in and staying in. Intellectual and moral leadership seem to have yielded to the effective marshalling and management of resources. The career path to the presidency is now open to those who enter it from the development function. Like it or not (and I must say that in many respects I don't like it), fund raising is now at the center of the president's responsibilities [74, p. 33].

According to Kerr, another reason why more presidents have advancement/development backgrounds is that applicants from traditional sources (i.e., provosts, deans, and vice presidents for academic affairs) are more reluctant to be considered:

Conversations with individuals who have refused presidencies (sometimes repeatedly), with top academic officers on campuses (who constitute much of the pool from which presidents are drawn), with professional search personnel, and with ex-presidents indicate that the attractiveness of the presidency has deteriorated.

Persons who have refused presidencies frequently note that the management of decline, which many campuses either have experienced or are likely to face, is not as attractive as the management of growth.

At least half of the academic officers note that the presidency has become a heavily external job with more emphasis on fund raising and on public relations, and with less contact with faculty and students and academic issues. Many individuals primarily interested in the academic side of campus life believe they will be better off as a provost or a dean of the faculty or a vice president of academic affairs than as a president [47, pp. 3–4].

In a 1990 interview Kerr explained that "very frequently the provost will make the same amount of money as the president." He also said that academic administrators have jobs which allow them "to be on campus and see their families regularly," in contrast to the frequent travel required of presidents [107, p. B7]. Maimon added, "College administrators, in contrast to their professional colleagues, are much more likely to miss their children's birthday parties. Is it any wonder that many aspire to full professorships as the pinnacle of academic success?" [15, p. 41]. According to Kerr, some academic administrators are also "able to maintain an active scholarly life," something very few presidents manage to do. Finally, Kerr stated that unlike presidents, deans, provosts, and vice presidents are "not directly on the firing line" [107, p. B7].

In addition, there are serious concerns about the impact fund raising has on presidential autonomy and independence. Former Columbia President Michael Sovern claimed that presidents today are speaking out on societal issues as much as ever, but that the "noise level" created by a media-intensive society has drowned out or reduced presidential voices to an inaudible level amid the din of numerous other credible (and incredible) voices in society [43, p. A5]. However, Sovern admitted in another interview the same year that due to the "burdens of the office," it is becoming "increasingly difficult" for presidents to get involved in off-campus issues [28, p. B7].

Sovern rejected the charge that preoccupation with fund raising is responsible for the alleged abdication of social leadership by presidents and said that he had used his office as a "bully pulpit" to speak out on apartheid and divestiture in South Africa, human rights violations, the Solidarity movement in Poland, and free-speech issues [43, p. A5].

However, fund raising is the most frequently cited presidential handicap, and many observers disagree with Sovern. Vartan Gregorian, president of Brown University, stated, "You're frightened to take a stand as an educator because you are afraid that the Federal or state authorities, or your private benefactors, may retaliate against your institution by not giving money" [28, p. B7].

Ernest Boyer, president of the Carnegie Foundation for the Advancement of Teaching, said, "The more dependent you are on the gifts and bequests of others, the more advantageous it is to not get caught up in larger debates that might be viewed as divisive and contentious" [82, p. 54]. He added:

> The job has been powerfully diminished, and I think the nation is the loser. We need people who are able to interpret historically, ethically and socially the issues of the day. But because [presidents] are under such pressure financially, it becomes risky to be prophetic. There is a hazard in offending [32, p. 3D; 43, p. A4].

Similarly, Derek Bok, former Harvard head, commented, "Today, university leaders are largely silent, too heavily burdened with raising funds and administering their huge institutions. There is no one able to communicate a compelling vision of what we are trying to accomplish for our students" [68, p. A18].

However, F. J. Kelly explained that the proliferation of state higher education coordinating boards, national education associations, and university systems in the last 30 years has removed the need (and perhaps the opportunity) for individual presidents to serve as spokesmen on national issues [45]. Further, presidents of all ages have needed an abundant supply of courage and fortitude to resist the special interests of powerful constituencies or the mob mentality of popular opinion.

Finally, increased media attention and its attendant capability of magnifying the impact of any remark through a network of instantaneous global communication are certainly factors inhibiting presidential candor, as is a heightened social consciousness—with its attendant litigious and politically charged climate—regarding comments which focus or touch on race, gender, sexual orientation, religious orientation, age, health, and other differences among individuals and groups of individuals.

Conclusion

During the last 20 years—or the Era of Uncertainty—the level of intensity, the sense of urgency, and the technical sophistication associated with fund raising dramatically increased on the nation's campuses and among nonprofits in general. Fund raising became a definite expectation for every college president, and campaigns became an ongoing way of life on the nation's campuses. Public colleges and universities began development programs *en masse* and launched aggressive, bold campaigns to rival their private counterparts, thus violating a tacit, long-standing agreement.

During the past 20 years, the vast majority of both public and private institutions increased their commitment to private fund raising and enlarged their development staffs and budgets. Nevertheless, academic chief executives must devote a significant portion of their time to fund-raising activities. However, many presidents have difficulty adjusting to their roles as fund raisers. Fund raising and financial affairs in general are among the high profile duties/endeavors of a president and among the skills/attributes most prized by trustees as well as by some faculty and alumni; these issues are also widely reported by the media. Due to the increasing complexity of fund raising, presidents and other university personnel must have greater familiarity with tax laws, planned giving, estate planning, and other technical aspects of philanthropy.

Fund-raising considerations play a major part in the presidential selection process as well as the length of time incumbents remain in office. There has been a slight trend in recent years toward hiring presidents with a background in development or business, although promotion from within academic ranks is still the norm. Ideally, presidents should spend their time and effort in fund raising on the cultivation and solicitation of major gifts and in providing administrative leadership. Presidents should also emphasize a team approach to fund raising in which they play the dual roles of quarterback and athletic director.

As a result of these trends, considerably more critical attention and media coverage has been given to the role of college and university presidents in fund raising. The strident tones and sounds of alarm that characterize this writing certainly have some basis in fact and indicate major shifts in the economy, in higher education, and in the roles of presidents and chief development officers. However, the deeper truth is that leadership has been a scarce commodity in great demand in every era and that presidents have always been called upon to provide this leadership and to preserve intact or move forward their institutions in the midst of difficult circumstances and formidable challenges.

Academic presidents of each era have faced different circumstances and challenges than their predecessors, but two constants that have spanned the years have been the need for leadership and the need for resources. May the presidents of today and tomorrow find the courage, strength, and wisdom to provide both in sufficient amounts.

Reference

1. Anderson, W. Presidents must make fund raising work. *AGB Reports,* 26(6) (1984), 17–19.

2. Association of American Colleges. *The president's role in development.* Washington, DC: AAC, 1975.

3. Bailey, A. L. Fund drives get bigger, broader: 65 college goals top $100-million. *Chronicle of Higher Education* (1987, Sept. 2), A72–73, 74–77.

4. Benezet, L. T. *Private higher education and public funding.* ERIC/Higher Education Research Report No. 5. Washington, DC: George Washington University, 1976.

5. Berendzen, R. *Is my armor straight? A year in the life of a university president.* Bethesda, MD: Adler & Adler, 1986.

6. Bezilla, M. Campaign for Penn State tops $300 million. *Fund Raising Management* (1990, April), 18–24.

7. Bornstein, R. L. The capital campaign: Benefits and hazards. In J. L. Fisher & G. H. Quehl (Eds.), *The president and fund raising* (pp. 202–211). New York: American Council on Education/Macmillan, 1989.

8. Boston U. is trying to raise $1 billion by turn of century. *The New York Times* (1988, December 18), B72.

9. Botstein, L. The college presidency: 1970–1990. *Change,* 22 (1990, March/April), 35–40.

10. Boulding, K. E. The management of decline. *Change,* 7 (1975, June), 8–9, 64.

11. Brecher, B. The fund-raising triangle. *CASE Currents,* 10 (1984, Jan.), 24–26.

12. Bremner, R. H. *American philanthropy* (rev. ed.). Chicago: University of Chicago Press, 1988.

13. Breneman, D. W. *Liberal arts colleges: Thriving, surviving, or endangered?* Washington, DC: The Brookings Institution, 1994.

14. Brett, P. New French minister gets good reviews from university officials. *Chronicle of Higher Education* (1993, May 12), A45–46.

15. Brown, D. G., Chait, R. P., Church, M. E., Clark, K., Clark, M., Levine, A., Maimon, E. P., & Shoenberg, R. E. Preparing the next generation of academic leaders. *Liberal Education,* 76 (1990, January/February), 32–41.

16. Brown, R. W. The presidential role in financial development. In Duane H. Dagley (Ed.), *Courage in mission: Presidential leadership in the church-related college* (pp. 45–55). Washington, DC: Council for Advancement and Support of Education, 1988.

17. Budig, G. A. Campaign Kansas: Driving past the goal. *Fund Raising Management,* 21 (1990, July), 39–41, 63.

18. Bulkeley, W. M., & Stecklow, S. Harvard's president, citing exhaustion, is going on leave during fund drive. *Wall Street Journal* (1994, Nov. 29), B7.

19. Burke, J. C. Coping with the role of college or university president. *Educational Record,* 58 (1977), 388–402.

20. Carmody, D. Turnover speeds search for college presidents. *The New York Times* (1988, February 10), B8.

21. Carnegie Foundation for the Advancement of Teaching. The 1980s: A halcyon decade for voluntary support. *Change,* 21 (1989, March/April), 29–31, 34–35.

22. Coldren, S. L. *The constant quest: Raising billions through capital campaigns*. Washington, DC: American Council on Education, 1982.

23. Cook, W. B. *Courting philanthropy: The role of university presidents in fund raising*. Unpublished doctoral dissertation, The University of Texas at Austin, Austin, TX, 1994.

24. Cook, W. B. *A history of educational philanthropy and the academic presidency*. Unpublished manuscript, The University of Texas at Austin, Austin, TX, 1994.

25. Curti, M., & Nash, R. *Philanthropy in the shaping of American higher education*. New Brunswick, NJ: Rutgers University Press, 1965.

26. Day, E. E. The role of administration in higher education: The obligations of the president. *Journal of Higher Education, 17*(7) (1946, October), 339–343.

27. DePalma, A. The most happy college president: Leon Botstein of Bard. *New York Times Magazine* (1992a, October 4), 22–25, 44–45, 48, 53–54.

28. DePalma, A. University presidents less secure in jobs and stature. *The New York Times* (1992b, June 3), B7.

29. Dorich, D. The making of a president 1991. *CASE Currents, 17* (1991, April), 6–11.

30. Dove, K. E. Changing strategies for meeting campaign goals. In A. W. Rowland (Ed.), *Handbook of institutional advancement*, 2nd ed. (pp. 292–309). San Francisco: Jossey-Bass, 1987.

31. Dove, K. E. *Conducting a successful capital campaign: A comprehensive fundraising guide for nonprofit organizations*. San Francisco: Jossey-Bass, 1988.

32. Dyckman, M. Reaching beyond academia. *St. Petersburg Times* (1993, August 22), 3D.

33. Foote, E. T. II. The president's role in a capital campaign. In H. G. Quigg (Ed.), *The successful capital campaign* (pp. 73–80). Washington, DC: Council for Advancement and Support of Education, 1986.

34. Fowler, E. M. Careers wanted: College presidents. *The New York Times* (1987, November 3), D25.

35. Fowler, E. M. Fund raisers in demand at colleges. *The New York Times* (1989, September 19), C18.

36. Fuchsberg, G. U.S. campus buildings may need $70 billion for renovations. *Chronicle of Higher Education* (1988, October 19), A36.

37. Fuchsberg, G. Fund raisers are asking: Which university will be the next to reach for $1-billion? *Chronicle of Higher Education* (1989, February 1), A25–26.

38. Geiger, R. L. *Research and relevant knowledge: American research universities since World War II*. New York: Oxford University Press, 1993.

39. Grassmuck, K. "History-making" drive expected to raise $500-million in private funds for Ohio State, inspire other colleges. *Chronicle of Higher Education* (1990, January 10), A29–31.

40. Hahn, R. How tough is it to be a college president? *Chronicle of Higher Education* (1995, January 6), A64.

41. Hamlin, A. *Essential factors associated with the survival of financially endangered private colleges and universities*. Unpublished doctoral dissertation, Brigham Young University, Provo, UT, 1987.

42. Heller, S. President Rudenstine's leave stuns Harvard. *Chronicle of Higher Education* (1994, December 7), A18.

43. Jordan, M. Wanted: Presidents for U.S. universities; high-stress, lower prestige and new focus on fundraising contribute to swift turnover. *Washington Post* (1992, June 15), A4.

44. Keller, G. *Academic strategy: The management revolution in American higher education*. Baltimore, MD: Johns Hopkins University Press, 1983.

45. Kelly, F. J. Evolution of leadership in American higher education: A changing paradigm. *Journal for Higher Education Management, 7* (1991), 29–34.

46. Kelly, K. S. *Fund raising and public relations: A critical analysis*. Hillsdale, NJ: Lawrence Erlbaum Associates, 1991.

47. Kerr, C. *Presidents make a difference: Strengthening leadership in colleges and universities*. Washington, DC: Association of Governing Boards of Universities and Colleges, 1984.

48. Kerr, C. The new race to be Harvard or Berkeley or Stanford. *Change, 23* (1991, May/June), 8–15.

49. Kidder, R. M. Raising America's ethical sights. *The Christian Science Monitor* (1990, October 10), 13.

50. Knauft, E. B., Berger, R. A., & Gray, S. T. *Profiles of excellence: Achieving success in the nonprofit sector*. San Francisco: Jossey-Bass, 1991.

51. Leatherman, C. President's hair style, clothing, marriage, and handling of "moral issues" rile older alumnae of Converse College. *Chronicle of Higher Education* (1992, December 16), A17–18.

52. Leatherman, C. What's fair compensation for a university chief? Opinions differ. *Chronicle of Higher Education* (1993, May 5), A13, 16.

53. Leatherman, C. When illness strikes: Colleges face a range of delicate problems when a president dies or falls ill. *Chronicle of Higher Education* (1994, August 10), A15–16.

54. Levine, A. The hard sell behind the ivy. *U.S. News & World Report* (1988, April 11), 54–55.

55. Lilly, E. R. The American college president: The changing roles. *Planning and Giving,* 18(1) (1987), 3–16.

56. Magarell, J. Some top universities retrenching. *Chronicle of Higher Education* (1975, February 3), p. A3.

57. Matthews, A. Alma maters court their daughters. *New York Times Magazine* (1991, April 7), 40, 73, 77–78.

58. McAnear, B. The raising of funds by the colonial colleges. *Mississippi Valley Historical Review,* 48 (1952), 591–612.

59. McGoldrick, W. P. Details you should know. In J. L. Fisher & G. H. Quehl (Eds.), *The president and fund raising* (pp. 160–169). New York: American Council on Education/Macmillan, 1989.

60. McIntosh, M. C. The college presidency. *Pride* (1959, October), 21–22.

61. McLaughlin, D. The president's role in the capital campaign. *CASE Currents,* 10 (1984, January), 7–8.

62. McMahon, C. P. College drives five hundred years old. *School and Society,* 70 (1949, December 24), 423–425.

63. McMillen, L. Stanford's $1.1-billion campaign is on target over all, but ambitions are lowered for vast science complex. *Chronicle of Higher Education* (1990, April 4), A33–35.

64. McMillen, L. More colleges tap fund raisers for presidencies, seeking expertise in strategic thinking about entire institution. *The Chronicle of Higher Education* (1991, September 11), A35–36.

65. McNamee, M. Scaling the salary heights. *CASE Currents,* 12 (1986, Oct.), 7–11.

66. Miller, M. T. *The college president's role in fund raising.* ERIC Document 337 099, 1991.

67. Milley, J. E. Women are used to asking: Women presidents as fund raisers. In J. A. Sturnick, J. E. Milley, & C. A. Tisinger (Eds.), *Women at the helm: Pathfinding presidents at state colleges and universities* (pp. 30–36). San Francisco: Jossey-Bass, 1991.

68. Mooney, C. J. Bok: To avoid bashing, colleges must take a leadership role on national problems. *Chronicle of Higher Education* (1992a, April 8), A17–18.

69. Mooney, C. J. Most colleges seem unready to name openly gay chief. *Chronicle of Higher Education* (1992b, September 13), A19–20.

70. Morganthaler, E. Change on campus: College presidents shift focus from book-keeping to peace-keeping. *Wall Street Journal* (1976, May 18), 1, 41.

71. National Society of Fund Raising Executives. *ESL Employment Opportunities* (1994, September). Alexandria, VA: NSFRE.

72. Patton, S. L. The roles of key individuals. In M. J. Worth (Ed.), *Educational fund raising: Principles and practice* (pp. 51–56). Phoenix, AZ: American Council on Education/Oryx Press, 1993.

73. Payton, R. L. *Philanthropy: Voluntary action for the public good.* New York: American Council on Education/Macmillan, 1988.

74. Payton, R. L. The ethics and values of fund raising. In J. L. Fisher & G. H. Quehl (Eds.), *The president and fund raising* (pp. 33–42). New York: American Council on Education/Macmillan, 1989.

75. Pfeffer, J., & Ross, J. The compensation of college and university presidents. *Research in Higher Education,* 29(1) (1988), 79–91.

76. The Philanthropy 400. *Chronicle of Philanthropy* (1991, November 13), 1, 19–20.

77. Pusey, N. M. *American higher education, 1945–1970: A personal report.* Cambridge, MA: Harvard University Press, 1978.

78. Reagan years: Profound changes for philanthropy. *Chronicle of Philanthropy,* 1 (1988, October 25), 1, 19–20, 22–23.

79. Rhodes, F. H. T. The importance of fund-raising. In G. A. Budig (Ed.), *A higher education map for the 1990s* (pp. 64–70). New York: American Council on Education/Macmillan, 1992.

80. Rose, J. The impossible life of a college president. *Washington Monthly,* 21 (1989, March), 18–24.

81. Rudolph, F. *The American college and university: A history.* Athens, GA: University of Georgia Press, 1990. (Originally published in 1962.)

82. Sanoff, A. P., & Linnon, N. Harvard's helmsman quits the race. *U. S. News & World Report* (1990, June 11), 54.

83. Schmeisser, P., & Anderson, W. Cracks in the ivory tower: Hard times bring the ungentlemanly art of fund raising to Oxford. *U.S. News & World Report* (1988, December 5), 65–66.

84. Schmidt, G. P. *The old time college president.* New York: Columbia University Press, 1930.

85. Schoenherr, C. W. The role of the president in fund raising at church-related colleges. In *Private higher education: The job ahead* (pp. 45–47). Talks from the annual meeting of the American Association of Presidents of Independent Colleges and Universities, Scottsdale, AZ, 1984.

86. Schulze, C. J., Jr. *The role of the community college president in successful fund-raising.* Unpublished doctoral dissertation, Columbia University, New York City, 1991.

87. Sears, J. B. *Philanthropy in the shaping of American higher education.* New Brunswick, NJ: Transaction Publishers, 1990. (Originally published in 1922).

88. Semas, P. W. The perilous presidencies. *Chronicle of Higher Education* (1975, February 3), A1, 4.

89. Sharp, P. F. American college presidents since World War II. *Educational Record*, 65 (1984, Spring), 11–16.

90. Shephard, R. S. How can a university that raises a billion have a tight budget? *Chronicle of Higher Education* (1994, January 12), A48.

91. Shuster, G. N. *The ground I walked on: Reflections of a college president*, rev. ed. Notre Dame: University of Notre Dame Press, 1969.

92. Skelly, M. E. College presidents as fundraisers. *School and College*, 30 (1991, August), 28–29.

93. Smith, G. T. The chief executive and advancement. In A. W. Rowland (Ed.), *Handbook of institutional advancement*, 2nd ed. (pp. 697–705). San Francisco: Jossey-Bass, 1986.

94. Smith, H. W. Foreword. In S. L. Coldren (Ed.), *The constant quest: Raising billions through capital campaigns* (pp. ix–xi). Washington, DC: American Council on Education, 1982.

95. Stehle, V. Capital campaigns: Bigger, broader, bolder. *Chronicle of Philanthropy*, 2 (1990, March 6), 1, 10–12.

96. Stoke, H. W. *The American college president.* New York: Harper & Brothers, 1959.

97. Teltsch, K. The ultimate gift. *The New York Times* (1988, April 10), ED69–70.

98. Thompson, A. Few women chosen as college presidents. *Chicago Sun-Times* (1993, September 19), 26.

99. Tolley, W. P. *At the fountain of youth: Memories of a college president.* Syracuse, NY: Syracuse University, 1989.

100. West, D. C. The presidency of a small college. In A. J. Falander & J. C. Merson (Eds.), *Management techniques for small and specialized institutions* (pp. 11–23). San Francisco: Jossey-Bass, 1983.

101. Whetten, D. A., & Cameron, K. S. Administrative effectiveness in higher education. *Review of Higher Education*, 9(1) (1985), 35–49.

102. Wiseman, L. The university president: Academic leadership in an era of fund raising and legislative affairs. In R. R. Sims & S. J. Sims (Eds.), *Managing institutions of higher education into the 21st Century: Issues and implications* (pp. 3–9). New York: Greenwood Press, 1991.

103. Withers, D. C. Before the campaign begins: An internal audit. In H. G. Quigg (Ed.), *The successful capital campaign* (pp. 13–22). Washington, DC: Council for the Advancement and Support of Education, 1986.

104. Woodroof, R. H. *Internal conflict and the first-time president: An administrative succession model for private colleges seeking "first-time" presidential candidates.* Unpublished doctoral dissertation, University of California-Los Angeles, Los Angeles, CA, 1993.

105. Woods, J. L. *Factors associated with gift income in public research and doctoral-granting institutions.* Unpublished doctoral dissertation, Washington State University, Pullman, WA, 1987.

106. Wriston, H. M. *Academic procession: Reflections of a college president.* New York: Columbia University Press, 1959.

107. Wycliff, D. The short, unhappy life of academic presidents. *The New York Times* (1990, July 25), B7.

108. Yasuda, G. A new class of university president: Academic outsiders can bring important skills to the top job. *Orlando Sentinel* (1993, November 11), B1.

109. Yeomans, H. A. *Abbott Lawrence Lowell, 1856–1943.* Cambridge, MA: Harvard University Press, 1948.

Selected Bibliography

Chapter 8: Origins of Fundraising

Cutlip, Scott M. "From Wholesale to Retail, Philanthropy: 1900–1907." Chapter 2 in *Fund Raising in the United States: Its Role in America's Philanthropy.* New Brunswick, NJ: Rutgers University Press, 1965, pp. 29–63.

———. Cutlip, Scott M. "The 1920s (Continued): Cash for Colleges and Cathedrals." Chapter 7 in *Fund Raising in the United States: Its Role in America's Philanthropy.* New Brunswick, NJ: Rutgers University Press, 1965, pp. 242–295.

"New England's First Fruits." (1643). In *Philanthropy in America: A Comprehensive Historical Encyclopedia*, Dwight F. Burlingame, Editor. Vol. 3. Santa Barbara, CA: ABC-CLIO, pp. 568–569.

CHAPTER 9

ALUMNI/AE GIVING & OTHER RELEVANT INSTITUTIONAL CONSTITUENCIES

DOES INSTITUTIONAL TYPE AFFECT ALUMNAE DONATING PATTERNS IN THE UNITED STATES?

PETER BRIECHLE

Abstract

Women currently comprise over 55 percent of college and university enrollments and control a substantial amount of wealth in the United States. Yet historical research on philanthropy has made little distinction between male and female donors. Are there no differences or have we failed to understand why women give? This study investigated the effect of institutional type (public, private sectarian, or private nonsectarian) on alumnae donating patterns. An anonymous mail survey was used to gather data on the factors that persuaded alumnae to donate to their alma mater and the areas they gave financial support. The results indicate associations between institution type and six of 12 factors that persuaded alumnae to donate and seven of 11 areas they supported financially.

Introduction

Since the early 1990s, scholars have increasingly studied women as a potential source of philanthropic giving. Traditionally they have been perceived as a source of volunteers who gave their time, but not necessarily their money. Older women are especially likely to be viewed this way, since many have never had a career and are often hesitant to contribute what they perceive as their husbands' hard-earned money.[1] This traditional view has changed in the recent past.

As the enrollment of women in institutions of higher education has increased, and surpassed that of men, their influence on American society has evolved.[2] These "career women" have become more financially independent, thereby relying less on men and husbands for economic support. "The average income of working women is increasing at a far greater pace than that of men, according to the U.S. Census Bureau, and two-thirds of all jobs created in the 1990s are expected to be filled by women."[3] And the fact that, on average, women outlive men by approximately seven years should alert fund-raising professionals to the opportunities at hand. This economic evolution creates an opportunity for fund-raising professionals to elicit financial support from women in an effort to advance the mission of their specific institution.

Problem Statement

Fund raising in higher education will become even more important in the future. This is due to a variety of reasons, including the decreased financial support of public institutions of higher education by state governments, reductions in financial aid that are making college unaffordable to a growing segment of the middle class, and increased competition to retain and attract the best faculty. The competition for faculty is not only coming from other universities but also from the private sector, which is able to offer lucrative salaries as well as offering bonuses and stock options.

Since women donors are now an important component of any school's successful fund-raising campaign, more research must be conducted to verify and validate previous findings and make new discoveries. By understanding the factors that persuade women to donate based on institutional type, fund raisers can manage campaigns more effectively and efficiently.

Purpose of the Study

The purpose of this study was to gain information about women's donating patterns and to discover what persuades them to donate based on institution type (public, private sectarian, private non sectarian). It may allow fund-raising marketing efforts to become more focused and institution-specific, thereby reducing costs. Factors that persuade a woman to donate to her public university may be completely different from factors that persuade a woman who graduated from a private college. This would allow fund-raising professionals to gear their marketing plan to a specific niche and possibly increase the yield of women donors.

Research Questions

The following research questions compare alumnae across institutional type (public, private sectarian, and private nonsectarian). The research questions are (1) are there differences, among institutions studied, in the factors that persuade alumnae to donate to their alma mater and (2) are there differences in the programs that women are most likely to support?

Literature Review

Sondra Shaw and Martha Taylor (1995) have conducted extensive research on women as philanthropists. They point out that women and men give for different reasons. Within higher education, men predominantly give because they feel loyalty to their alma mater. Knowing how much a classmate or fraternity brother contributed may heighten a man's competitive nature. Public recognition for donations also seems more important to men than to women. Women view public recognition as unimportant, which can cause frustration for fund raisers, since the positive contributions of women's giving are not influential to other potential women philanthropists.[4]

The University of California at Los Angeles (UCLA) Women and Philanthropy Program attempts to involve women in the UCLA community through involvement, education, support, and leadership. Many important themes have emerged; one was the sense that philanthropy was a responsibility and a family tradition beginning at home.[5] "In some homes philanthropy was consciously taught; in others the children learned by example."[6] Church and youth group affiliations were also a strong influence. These women supported the organizations' causes through the donation of time and money. Although not all were able to donate time, those who did "wanted to serve as role models, to give back to others, to make new friends, to increase their self-esteem, and to give of themselves."[7] In this way philanthropy was passed on from generation to generation. Some women also felt a need to repay, since they at one time were the recipient of a gift.

Rosalie M. Simari's (1995) dissertation entitled "Philanthropy and higher education: Women as donors" examined the factors that may influence women's decisions to support their college or university financially. Her study examined women donors and nondonors who earned an undergraduate degree from a single private nonsectarian institution. She found that a desire "to help the next generation of students and a loyalty to the university were the strongest reasons for providing financial support."[8] The area that received the strongest financial support was student scholarships, awards, and loans. Bressi (1999) found similar results at a large, public, land grant institution in the southeastern United States.[9] Fisher et al. (2000) also found "the most popular reported restricted gifts were scholarships" for alumnae of coeducational institutions included in the study.[10]

Although more research on women donors has recently been conducted, there is a need to continue to validate and refine this area of study.[11] Most studies within the realm of higher education have been institution-specific. This study compares women across institutional type to determine if differences exist. Since fund raising in higher education will gain greater importance, any information that will assist fund-raising professionals to become more efficient and effective in their fund-raising campaigns will be beneficial.

Methodology

The research questions for this study compared women's responses across three different types of institutions. The independent variable was institution type (public, private nonsectarian, and private sectarian) and the dependent variables were (a) factors that persuade women to donate and (b) programs to which they gave financial support.

The three participating institutions were all located in New York State. The public university and the private nonsectarian university are both Research I (Carnegie Classification) universities. The private sectarian institution is a four-year liberal arts college founded by the Free Methodist Church of North America. Women who met the following criteria were potential subjects in the study: (1) alumnae of institution, (2) have donated at least $500 as a single gift in the past five years (1995–99), and (3) currently reside in the United States. The second criterion was important to fund raisers since the donor who made such a gift probably gave it considerable thought, as opposed to someone making a "token" gift. For the purpose of this study the three institutions will be referred to as public (public university), private (private nonsectarian university), and sectarian (private sectarian college).

Both the independent variable and the dependent variables are categorical in nature, therefore Chi-square (χ^2) tests of association were used to analyze the data with a significance level (α) of 0.05. The Statistical Package for the Social Sciences (SPSS) was used to analyze the data.

Since Simari's survey was well developed and permission was granted by the author to use the survey at other universities, it was decided to incorporate a number of themes, with modified questions, into this survey.[12] The Dillman approach to mail surveys was used, resulting in a 73.5 percent response rate.[13]

Results

Factors Persuading Women to Donate

The first research question was: are there differences in the factors that persuade alumnae to donate to their alma mater among institutions studied? Subjects were asked to choose the top three reasons for donating from a list of 12 possible choices. Table 1 lists the choices by institution. The public and private institutions share the same top three choices, although not in the same order. The sectarian institution shares two of the three choices with the public and private; however, the third choice differs. There are associations between the institution type and six of the twelve factors that persuade women to give, which are described below.

Sense of Obligation to Institution

Sense of obligation to the institution was the first choice of the public alumnae, the second choice of the private alumnae, and the fourth choice of sectarian alumnae. There is an association between this factor and institutional type, $\chi^2(2, N = 536) = 28.780, p < 0.05$. Alumnae from the public and private were more than twice as likely to choose "sense of obligation" as a reason to give than were alumnae from the sectarian institution.

Loyalty to Institution

Loyalty to the institution was the first choice of the private alumnae, second most popular choice of the sectarian alumnae, and third most popular choice of public alumnae. There was an association between this factor and institutional type, $\chi^2(2, N - 536) = 14.154, p < 0.05$. Although it was in the top three choices of all alumnae, the sectarian and private alumnae were more likely to choose "loyalty to the institution" as a reason to give than were the public alumnae. Nearly three-quarters

TABLE 1

Factors that Persuade Women to Donate (*N* = 536)

	Institution		
	Public *(N = 203)*	*Private* *(N = 254)*	*Sectarian* *(N = 79)*
Sense of obligation (%)	61.6	59.1	27.8
Positive impact (%)	53.7	54.3	50.6
Loyalty to institution (%)	51.7	65.0	73.4
Knowledge of institutional mission (%)	33.5	33.1	84.8
Tax benefits (%)	21.7	22.8	10.1
Person asking for gift (%)	16.3	8.7	7.6
Involvement in sponsored events (%)	13.3	9.4	10.1
Fund raising literature (%)	4.9	8.7	5.1
Public recognition (%)	4.4	1.2	1.3
Capital campaign under way (%)	3.9	7.1	21.5
Gift level of others (%)	2.5	2.8	0.0
Others (%)	13.3	15.0	5.1

Note: Percentages to not equal 100% because subjects chose their top three choices

of the sectarian alumnae and nearly two-thirds of the private alumnae made this choice. Slightly more than one-half of the public alumnae did the same.

Knowledge of Institutional Mission

Knowledge of institutional mission was the most frequent choice of the sectarian alumnae, with a significant association between this particular factor and institution type, $\chi^2(2, N = 536) = 74.081$, $p < 0.05$. Alumnae of the sectarian institution were more than two-and-a-half times as likely to have chosen "knowledge of institutional mission" as a reason to give than were alumnae from both the public and private institution. Nearly 85 percent of sectarian alumnae made this a top three choice, whereas the public and private alumnae selected this choice only one-third of the time.

Tax Benefits

Although benefiting from federal and/or state tax deductions was not chosen by a majority of alumnae, women from the public and private institution were twice as likely to be persuaded by this choice than the sectarian alumnae. There was an association between this variable and institutional type, $\chi^2(2, N = 536) = 6.232$, $p < 0.05$.

Person Asking for the Gift

The person asking for a gift was nearly twice as important to the public alumnae compared with women at the private or sectarian institutions. Although this choice was not altogether popular, an association between this variable and institutional type did exist, $\chi^2(2, N = 536) = 7.769$, $p < 0.05$.

Knowing that a Capital Campaign Is Under Way

Knowing that a capital campaign was under way was much more important to the sectarian alumnae than to either the public or private alumnae. In fact, the sectarian alumnae chose this factor five times more often than the public alumnae and three times more often than the private alumnae.

Although this choice was not among the top three, an association between this variable and institutional type did exist, $\chi^2(2, N = 536) = 24.387, p < 0.05$.

The factor "making a positive impact with a gift" was chosen at least half the time by alumnae of all institutions. Although there was no association with this variable and institutional type, fund raisers must be aware that this factor is important to alumnae when developing marketing campaigns. All other variables showed no association with institutional type.

Funding Choices

The second research question asked alumnae to select the top three funding choices from a list of 11 areas as displayed in Table 2. Of the 11 areas, seven were found to have an association by institution.

Scholarships, Awards, and Loans

Scholarships, awards, and loans were the first choice of the private and public alumnae and the second choice of the sectarian alumnae. There was an association between this variable and institutional type, $\chi^2(2, N = 528) = 9.904, p < 0.05$. Although "scholarships, awards and loans" was ranked in the top three of all institutions, the private alumnae were most likely to give financial support in this area.

Specific School or Department

A specific school or department was the second most popular choice of the public alumnae, and the third most popular choice of private alumnae. However, only 21.5 percent of the sectarian alumnae made this choice. There was an association between this variable and institutional type, $\chi^2(2, N = 527) = 57.204, p < 0.05$. Alumnae of the public institution were three times more likely to give financial support to a specific school or department than the sectarian alumnae and one and a half times more likely than the private alumnae.

TABLE 2

Areas Alumnae Support Financially (N = 528)

	Institution		
Area	Public (N = 199)	Private (N = 250)	Sectarian (N = 79)
Scholarships, awards, and loans (%)	69.8	81.6	69.6
Specific school or department (%)	67.3	40.8	21.5
General fund (%)	45.7	62.8	86.1
Library (%)	21.1	24.0	7.6
Endowed faculty/chair (%)	18.1	16.8	5.1
Endowment (%)	14.6	20.9	32.9
Technology (%)	12.1	7.2	5.1
Renovations/new buildings (%)	7.0	13.2	49.4
Women's athletics (%)	6.0	6.4	1.3
All athletics (%)	2.5	1.2	3.8
Other support (%)	7.5	8.0	6.3

Note: Percentages do not equal 100% because subjects chose their top three choices

General Fund

The general fund was the most frequent choice of the sectarian alumnae, the second most frequent choice of the private alumnae, and the third most frequent choice of the public alumnae. Although this area was in the top three choices of all institutions, an association between this variable and institutional type did exist, $\chi^2(2, N = 528) = 40.031, p < 0.05$. The sectarian alumnae were nearly twice as likely to give financial support to the general fund, as were the public alumnae.

Library

Financial support of the library system was not in the top three choices of any institution; however, an association between this variable and institutional type did exist, $\chi^2(2, N = 528) = 10.013$, $p < 0.05$. The private and public alumnae were approximately three times as likely to support the library financially than were the sectarian alumnae.

Endowed Faculty Professors and Chairs

Although endowed faculty professors and chairs were not in the top three choices of any institution, an association between this variable and institutional type did exist, $\chi^2(2, N = 528) = 7.899$, $p < 0.05$. The public and private alumnae were more than three times as likely to support endowed faculty professors and chairs financially than were the sectarian alumnae.

Endowment

The endowment was not among the top three choices of any institution; however, there was an association between this variable and institutional type, $\chi^2(2, N = 527) = 11.851, p < 0.05$. The sectarian alumnae were much more likely to support the endowment as compared with the public and private alumnae. In fact, the sectarian alumnae were more than twice as likely as the public alumnae and one and a half times as likely as the private alumnae to support this area.

Renovations and New Buildings

Renovations and new buildings was the third most popular choice of the sectarian alumnae, but ranked much lower at the public and private institutions. An association between this variable and institutional type did exist, $\chi^2(2, N = 528) = 77.643, p < 0.05$. The sectarian alumnae were seven times more likely to support this area than the public and nearly four times more likely than the private alumnae.

All other areas of financial support—women's athletics, all athletics, technology, and other support—showed no association with institutional type.

Significance to Practitioners

The most important implication of this study, for the practitioner, is to realize that differences in alumnae giving may exist at their college or university based on institutional type. Referring to Table 1, the first four factors that persuaded women to donate were chosen most often by all alumnae. However, the degree of importance of each factor differs at each type of institution. The top three factors for the sectarian alumnae are heavily concentrated in (1) knowledge of institutional mission, (2) loyalty to institution, and (3) making a positive impact with the gift. The public and private alumnae share two of the top three choices but not to the same degree. The public and private alumnae's choices are more diversified among all the factors. A number of factors do stand out and are worth special attention.

A sense of obligation was much more popular among the public and private alumnae. Some women indicated, in the "Comments" section of the survey, that they received financial aid in the form of scholarships and awards from their institution, and without that aid they would have been unable to attend. Others noted that they benefited from their education and they felt obligated to pay back. With this in mind, development offices should know which alumnae received financial aid. Specific marketing material could be developed to address this fact when soliciting gifts.

Making a positive impact with a gift was chosen by one half of all the alumnae in the study. This implies that marketing material should state clearly and concisely how alumnae gifts are being used and why it is so important to the institution. Publications should include a letter from the president to alumna and articles that specifically address areas of interest and concern of all alumnae.

Loyalty to the institution was very popular among the sectarian and private alumnae. The question that fund raisers should be asking is: how does an institution instill a sense of loyalty? Loyalty evolves over time; therefore it is a characteristic that must be nurtured when students first begin their college education. For a feeling of loyalty to develop, students must feel connected to the institution and believe in its mission. This can be a daunting task for large institutions such as the two universities in this study; therefore specific schools and departments within the institution must take on this responsibility. Programs should be developed to create a feeling of connectivity (e.g., mentorship, faculty/student research projects, etc.).

The mission of the institution was the first choice of the sectarian alumnae. This may be due to the sectarian nature and the small size of the institution. The sectarian institution serves a very specific niche, where the mission of the institution is used to attract its clientele. All institutions need a clear and concise mission statement. However, the results of this study suggest that alumnae of small private sectarian institutions may place a higher emphasis on this characteristic than public or private nonsectarian institutions.

One last factor worth mentioning is the tax benefits of a gift. Although it was chosen by only just over 20 percent of the public and private alumnae and only 10 percent of the sectarian alumnae, it should be included in the marketing material. If presented properly, the amount of the gift may be increased due to favorable tax treatment.

Table 2 presented the areas that alumnae are most likely to support financially. Factors that persuade women to give may also influence the programs and areas they are most likely to support. Scholarships, awards, and loans were very important to alumnae from all three institutions. As mentioned previously, this may be due to the sense of obligation felt by many alumnae. Therefore, it is not surprising that this area is highly supported. With rising tuition, the demands on this area of support will continue to grow. Again, fund raisers should target alumnae who received institutional aid during their college years. This would offer the alumna an opportunity to repay the institution by supporting a current student who faces the same financial challenges as she did while attending college. Personalizing the scholarship and award program in this manner may strengthen the alumna's sense of obligation. If possible, scholarship recipients should know who the donors are and personally thank them for their gift, which may enhance the donor's satisfaction with regard to the positive impact of the gift.

The general fund is the least restrictive area for the institution in terms of financial allocation. Although institutions are free to spend money where they choose, they take on a greater responsibility of stewardship. It would be to the institutions' benefit to have a clear and concise plan for the general fund. This will make it easier to raise necessary funds, while keeping financial control within the institution. The general fund was the area most supported by the sectarian alumnae. It would be interesting to discover if this is due to the institutional size, type, and/or a well developed and communicated spending plan for the general fund.

A specific school/department was an important area of support at both the public and private institutions. Both these schools are large universities with many areas of study, whereas the sectarian institution is a small liberal arts college. This implies that alumnae at larger institutions are more connected to specific schools or departments compared with the institution as a whole. With this in mind, schools/departments must nurture this support by developing a sense of connectivity, thereby creating a sense of loyalty.

Almost half of the sectarian alumnae supported renovations and new building, which was considerably more than the other institutions. At the time of the study the sectarian institution was conducting a capital campaign, which included raising funds for a new building. This may have influenced the interest in this particular area.

Study Limitations

The study was limited, based on the population and the institutions sampled. Further research should be conducted in other geographical locations, which may yield different outcomes based on local beliefs and/or cultural differences. Other institutions such as single-gender or historically black colleges and universities may also experience different outcomes.

Conclusion

As fund raising continues to grow in the higher education arena, college and university administrators and faculty must explore every opportunity to raise needed funding for the next generation of students. Women are an important and growing part of this complex equation. The job of the institution is to continually refine the message being sent to alumnae with specific marketing campaigns that blend the wishes of the donor with the needs of the institution.

Notes

1. "Women philanthropists support change" (1995), *Women in Higher Education* 4, 10, pp. 8–9.
2. United States Department of Education (2002), *National Center for Education Statistics, Integrated Postsecondary Education Data System, Total Fall Enrollment Survey 1947 to 1999*, Department of Education, Washington, DC, Table 172.
3. S. C. Shaw and M. A. Taylor (1995), *Reinventing Fundraising: Realizing the Potential of Women's Philanthropy*, Jossey-Bass, San Francisco, p. 7.
4. Ibid.
5. UCLA Women and Philanthropy (1992), *Executive Summary*, available at http://women.support.ucla.edu/executive.htm; A. R. Kaminski and M. A. Taylor (1998) "What motivates women to give? A recent survey reveals the answer—and more," *Association of Healthcare Philanthropy Journal*, Spring; A. Radley and M. Kennedy (1995), "Charitable giving by individuals," *Human Relation*, 48, 6, pp. 685–709.
6. UCLA Women and Philanthropy (1992), *Executive Summary*, op. cit.
7. Radley and Kennedy (1995), "Charitable giving by individuals"; Kaminski and Taylor (1998), "What motivates women to give?", p. 8.
8. R. M. Simari (1995), "Philanthropy and higher education: Women as donors," Doctoral dissertation, Hofstra University, p.8.
9. D. E. Bressi, D. E. (1999), "Women and philanthropy: Making a difference in higher education," Doctoral dissertation, The University of Tennessee.
10. C. S. Fisher, C. S. Tidball, & M. E. Tidball (2000), "Women and philanthropy," Council for the Advancement and Support of Education (CASE), Washington, D C/ Tidball Center for the Study of Educational Environments, Hood College, Frederick, MD, p.3.
11. Bressi (1999), "Women and philanthropy" op. cit.; Fisher et al. (2000), "Women and philanthropy" op. cit.; J. M. Shim (2001), "Relationship of selected alumnae characteristics to alumnae financial support at a women's college," Doctoral dissertation, University of Florida; Simari (1995), "Philanthropy and higher education," op. cit.
12. Simari (1995), "Philanthropy and higher education," op. cit. p. 155.
13. D. A. Dillman (1978), *Mail and Telephone Surveys: The Total Design Method*, John Wiley, New York.

Practitioner's Perspective

Dr. Briechle offers an interesting and valuable addition to the growing body of research about the giving patterns of women. He is correct in pointing out that women control an increasing percentage of the potential philanthropic dollar, and that understanding giving patterns from women is a significant lesson for development professionals. Women are an important constituency and growing more important all the time. Both because women tend to live longer and, therefore, often control the final distribution of family wealth, and because women are increasingly entrepreneurs and professionals who control their own resources all along, colleges and universities of all types need to look seriously at women's patterns of giving. Even as we acknowledge this fact, we should, however, also recognize that women give for many reasons and that women's motivations for giving are no more monolithic than they are for men.

Dr. Briechle asks a key question about institutional type and seeks to investigate whether there are any differences in motivation or focus from different kinds of institutions. This work complements the Fisher et al. (2000) study sponsored by CASE several years ago, which studied the motivation and giving patterns of graduates from historically women's colleges versus those from historic coeducational institutions. That study demonstrated that women tend to give more to institutions with which they were personally involved and that volunteer activity was highly correlated with increased giving, as issue which future research might explore even further.

There are a series of valuable and practical suggestions to development professionals to be found in this study. The desire to "give back" is clearly one of the most important of these. Connecting donors who received scholarships as students with scholarship recipients is one specific suggestion that many practitioners could implement with, as this study suggests, potential positive results. As the study also points out, women (and, one might well argue, men also) are increasingly concerned to know the impact of their gifts. Demonstrating the specific way in which a gift has changed the institution is often the best way of generating a comfort level for the donor and, therefore, a basis for the next (and, one would hope, even larger) gift.

This study builds a good foundation for even further research and discussion, as all of us in the profession seek to refine our approach to each of our significant donor groups. Comparative studies, looking at women's motivations side by side with those of men from the same institutions, will give an even better set of guidelines for future initiatives. Likewise, it would be valuable to know more about the influence of institutional size on donor motivations. Although the author points out differences between the small sectarian institution and the large private and public institutions, it is unclear how much of the difference is because of the small size or the sectarian nature of his third institution. The study would have given us more specific and statistically valid information had he used three large institutions and three small institutions, each with a public, private nonsectarian, and private sectarian character. It would also have been valuable had either all of these institutions or none of his institutions been involved in a capital campaign. I suspect that some of his data were skewed by the fact that the small sectarian institution was in a capital campaign and others were not.

Finally, the author makes a passing reference to the potential impact of tax benefits on the size of a gift. Some of the work sponsored by the National Committee on Planned Giving would indicate a strong correlation between tax benefits and gift size. Although this question is beyond the scope of this study, it is also one that is much on the minds of practitioners. We are always interested in what motivates people to give, but we are even more interested in how to turn a relatively small gift into a much larger one. Future research may help to gain an even better handle on this question.

Dr. Briechle adds to our body of knowledge and provides a model for other researchers. Through an expansion and modification of research methodology, we might learn even more about the motivational and giving patterns of our women graduates.

Bruce Bigelow
Senior Vice President for Development and External Relations
Hood College, Frederick, Maryland, USA

Who Are the Alumni Donors? Giving by Two Generations of Alumni from Selective Colleges

Charles T. Clotfelter

Using data on former students of fourteen private colleges and universities, this paper examines patterns of alumni giving. The data are taken from the College and Beyond survey, which covers individuals who entered the institutions in the fall of 1951, 1976, and 1989. Contributions by these former students to these colleges and universities tend to be quite concentrated, with half of all donations being given by the most generous 1 percent of the sample. A higher level of contribution is associated with higher income, with having participated in extracurricular activities in college, with having had a mentor in college, and with the degree of satisfaction in one's undergraduate experience. The projected donations for the most generous of these alumni over the course of a lifetime are quite high, with totals for the 1951 cohort exceeding those from the 1976 cohort.

Donations by alumni are a significant source of revenue for private colleges and universities, and their importance promises to grow in the future. In 1997–98, alumni contributed $3.3 billion to 658 private institutions, representing 7.9 percent of their educational and general expenditures (Morgan, 1999). In the wake of a sustained bull market in stocks, some recent university capital campaigns have easily surpassed their ambitious goals. As market forces cause tuition increases in private institutions to moderate—which they appear to be doing—income from donations seems likely to assume an increasingly important role in total revenue.

Yet some close observers have raised a cautionary flag about the prospects of sustained growth from this source. One fear is that much of the generosity of the current cohort of givers is unique to this generation, that it will be lost when that cohort passes from the scene. In examining the rate of volunteering, for example, Goss (1999) finds that the generation now in its retirement years has volunteered at a pace unlikely to be matched by subsequent generations. Another fear arises from the increasingly meritocratic admissions policy of the most prestigious colleges and universities, whereby the sons and daughters of the social elite increasingly are passed over in favor of applicants with stronger academic credentials. Since the latter tend to come from less wealthy families than the former, this new type of student may give less as an alum than the previous generations of alumni did. This reasoning lies behind speculation by Willemain, Goyal, Van Deven, and Thukral (1994) about what they view as the "democratization" of admissions at Princeton during the 1920s. They argue that changes in admissions practices there reduced the prevalence of students from wealthy families, resulting in a decline in the average gift size. Neither of these fears is inconsistent with previous research on alumni giving, but there is little other work addressing them. More generally, previous studies of alumni giving have not had the luxury of detailed personal information about individual donors at a set of institutions. (For previous statistical analyses of alumni giving, see, for example, Grant and Lindauer, 1986; Leslie and Ramey, 1988; Lindahl and Winship, 1992; and Willemain, Goyal, Van Deven, and Thukral, 1994. For treatment of the normative issues surrounding how many resources to devote to raising funds from alumni, see Rooney, 1999).

Using data on alumni from fourteen selective private colleges and universities, this paper has a threefold purpose. First, it describes some interesting aspects of alumni giving, including constancy, concentration, and pattern over time. Second, it compares the level of giving by alumni from two generations, noting the inherent difficulties in such a comparison. Third, it examines how this giving varies according to other variables. The first section of this article describes the data used and how they trace changes in the type of student who attends these selective institutions. The second section presents information on some of the most striking patterns of alumni contributions made evident in this data set. The third section compares the amount given by alumni in the two oldest cohorts. The last section is a summary and conclusion.

The Sample Institutions and Their Changing Student Bodies

The data used for this study are based on the College and Beyond survey, which assembled information for three cohorts of individuals who enrolled in a sample of thirty-four colleges and universities in 1951, 1976, and 1989. (See Bowen and Bok, 1998, Appendix A, for a description of the survey.) These individuals were surveyed in 1995 and 1996 and were asked questions covering both their college experience and aspects of their current situation. For each former student, the information collected in the survey questionnaire was joined with student records maintained by the institutions, including such items as courses taken, extracurricular activities, and honors received. Although not all of the individuals in the resulting sample graduated from these same colleges and universities, the vast majority did, so they are referred to throughout the paper as alumni. For a subset of fourteen of these institutions (all of them private), additional data were collected from the institution's own administrative files on each person's contributions

TABLE 1

Three Cohorts: A Comparison of Means and Percentages, Weighted by 1976 Enrollment Share

	1951	1976	1989
Social and economic characteristics (%)			
Male	72	52	48
White	98	89	78
Public high school	64	67	63
Father a college graduate	52	74	76
Mother a college graduate	32	52	61
Academic preparation (mean)			
High school percentile rank	77	91	94
SAT combined	1140	1269	1289
State of residence when applied (%)			
Same state as institution	47	34	26
Bordering state	24	31	27

Note: Calculations for each measure are based on institutions with data for all three cohorts. The values for 1976 are unweighted means calculated for all individuals in the institutions applying to each measure. The means for the other two years weight individual observations so as to give each institution the same weight as its actual share in 1976. Where N_{k76} is the number of alumni of institution k in 1976 and N_{76} is the total sample size in that year, its alumni for year t is weighted by $(N_{k76}/N_{76})/(N_{kt}/N_t)$.

for a number of years. These fourteen private colleges and universities constitute the sample for this study.

As has been noted elsewhere, admissions policies at elite private colleges have changed markedly since World War II, resulting in a decline in the prevalence of children of privilege (Lemann, 1999). The data in the current sample are an illuminating reflection of this change. Table 1 presents average values for the sampled alumni from all fourteen institutions for which data were available for all three cohorts. To neutralize the effect of change in relative sample size, the figures are weighted so as to give each institution the same weight in each year.

The table reveals some significant changes over this period. Reflecting the trend toward coeducation in undergraduate schools and colleges, the proportion of males in the sample fell from 72 percent in 1951 to 52 percent in 1976. Equally striking is the effect of opening admissions to racial and ethnic minority groups, which led to a decline in the percentage of whites from 98 to 89 percent, a trend that continued past 1976. In the only trend that was not monotonic over the period, the percentage of students from public high schools rose between 1951 and 1976 and then fell again. A similar increase and decline in the public school percentage was observed among freshmen at all private universities and private nonsectarian colleges between 1966 and 1993 (Clotfelter, 1999).

Students in the sample institutions were more likely over time to have parents who graduated from college, reflecting a societal advance in educational attainment. More striking than this change is improvement in the measured academic quality of students and the broadening geographical appeal of these institutions. Between 1951 and 1976, the average high school rank for these freshmen rose from the 77th to the 91st percentile, and the average SAT score increased by a remarkable 129 points, with the improvement in both measures continuing to 1989. (See Bowen and Bok, 1998, for a similar comparison of average SAT scores at four institutions for the three cohorts.) Both of these trends are consistent with the findings of Cook and Frank (1993) and Hoxby and Terry (1998), who show that top students have become more concentrated in a relatively small number of elite institutions. The proportion who attended college in their home state or a bordering state dropped between 1976 and 1989, reflecting the increasing national character of the elite higher education market, a development analyzed by Hoxby (1997). In short, the enrollment patterns in this group of private colleges and universities did indeed shift over this period. Because most of the 1989 cohort had only just graduated when the survey was conducted and therefore would have had little opportunity to establish giving patterns, this cohort is omitted from the remainder of the analysis. The sample is further limited by the availability of data. Three institutions provided no data on the 1951 cohort. The resulting data set includes a total of 2,910 individuals for the 1951 cohort and 7,995 for the 1976 cohort. In addition, the number of years of giving data covered differs from institution to institution.[1] Most of the institutions offered giving data at a minimum for all of the years from 1991 to 1995.

Giving by Two Cohorts of Alumni: How Much Did They Give?

A natural first question to ask about alumni giving is, simply, How much did they give? Information on giving was collected for four categories: athletics, financial aid, other restricted purposes, and unrestricted. Table 2 shows, by cohort, both the percentage of those who made a contribution in each category and the average amount for those who did so. It is clear that relatively few alumni placed any restriction on their gifts, as shown by the low percentages for the three specified categories. Among those who contributed for those restricted purposes, however, the average gift was in most cases higher than the average for all contributions. Those in the 1951 cohort gave at a higher rate than those in the 1976 cohort; although half of the older cohort made gifts in 1995, only about 32 percent of the younger cohort did. Among those who made donations, the average gift from the 1951 cohort was also much higher ($1,506), more than twice as high on average as that from the younger cohort ($681). Reflecting the degree to which the mean value is influenced by a relatively small number of big gifts, the median giving for those who gave in 1995 was $155 for the 1951 cohort and $98 for the 1976 cohort. Taking into account both the rate of giving and the average donation for those who did make gifts, the average donation for all alumni was $751 in the 1951 cohort, compared to only $216 in the 1976 cohort, almost a 3.5:1 ratio.

Published data on aggregate donations are not broken down by age; however, they can be used as a rough check of the magnitude of the average level of donation, and these figures are in fact similar. Averages based on alumni of all ages in thirteen of the fourteen institutions covered in the College and Beyond sample reveal that 41 percent of alumni in a liberal arts college and 31 percent of those in a private university made a donation in 1995, with average gifts for those who gave of $834 and $1,267, respectively (Morgan, 1996).

Quite clearly, the alumni from the 1951 cohort gave at a much higher level on average than the younger cohort did. This disparity by itself does not indicate, however, that the older alumni were more "generous." When comparing the behavior of the 1951 and 1976 cohorts, it must be remembered that any observed difference in behavior could be the result of one or more of four effects: composition, cohort, life cycle, or income. First, the observed difference in behavior between the cohorts could be due to the kind of change in the composition of the student body—in terms of gender, geography, race, and economic status—that is evident in Table 1. It is possible, as Willemain, Goyal, Van Deven, and Thukral (1994) argue for the case of Princeton, that "democratization" of admissions, that is, reduction in the share of students from wealthy families, leads to reduced donations from younger cohorts.

Second, differences between classes separated by as much as two and a half decades might easily be due to a "cohort effect," one that is generationwide. In the present case, the effect might be present because the members of the 1951 and 1976 cohorts are literally members of different generations—one that experienced World War II, the other the end of the Vietnam War, as teenagers. Such contrasts in historical period envelope differences in life experience of many dimensions, so that the contrast between the generations' worldviews cannot be captured adequately with any set of objectively measured variables.

A third possible reason for observed differences is life-cycle effects, those arising from age alone. At the time this survey was taken, the 1951 and 1976 cohorts were, naturally, at different points in their lives. Those in the cohort entering school in 1951 would have been sixty-two years old and would normally have celebrated their fortieth reunion in 1995. Those in the 1976 cohort would have been only thirty-seven and celebrating their fifteenth reunion year. As documented by many econometric studies of charitable giving, contributions tend to rise with age, independent of income. Auten and Joulfaian (1996), for example, present regression estimates implying that contributions in the fifty-five-to-sixty-four age bracket exceeded those in the under-forty-five bracket by a ratio of 2.4:1.[7]

TABLE 2

Giving by Category, 1995

Cohort	Percentage Who Contributed in 1995		Average Giving by Category for Those Who Gave	
	1951	1976	1951	1976
Athletics	3.8	2.1	462	1,026
Financial aid	2.7	1.5	1,485	1,128
Other restricted	6.0	8.0	5,772	1,303
Unrestricted	46.9	25.8	753	289
Total	49.9	31.7	1,506	681
n	2,910	7,995	2,910	7,995

Source: College and Beyond survey and author's calculations.

The fourth reason we might expect the older cohort of alumni to give more is perhaps the most obvious: their income is likely to be higher. Every empirical study of charitable giving confirms the existence of a strong positive income effect on charitable giving. Before analyzing these four effects in detail, we must acknowledge an additional factor that probably influences the level of alumni giving and that could explain part of the observed difference between cohorts. This is the fundraising effort expended by the school. Although there is little statistical research on this effect, it seems reasonable that these efforts do influence the number of donors and the average gift size.

One yardstick for assessing the 3.5:1 ratio of giving between the 1951 and 1976 cohorts documented in Table 2 is Grant and Lindauer's study (1986) of alumnae contributions to Wellesley, which analyzed average donations for sixty graduating classes. Because their data were essentially a snapshot of giving by a number of classes, one would expect the differences they observed to be a combination of cohort, life-cycle, and income effects. Their estimated regression for average donations suggests that sixty-two-year-old alumnae on average gave roughly three times as much as thirty-seven year olds, slightly less than the gap evident in the College and Beyond data.

Considering that the observed differences between 1951 and 1976 cohorts may contain income and life-cycle effects as well as a cohort effect, it is by no means obvious that one of these cohorts is any more generous than the other. Although there is every reason to think that changing admissions criteria over time have altered the mix of students who attend these selective institutions, these data, as rich as they might appear, cannot isolate a measurable cohort effect.

One logical extension of viewing alumni giving over the life cycle is to ask how much giving adds up to over a lifetime. Since one oft-cited motivation for alumni giving is a desire to "pay back" the institution (see, for example, Leslie and Ramey, 1988), it would be interesting to know the total value of a person's lifetime contributions. Indeed, this is a question of considerable practical importance to university administrators in their long-range financial planning. The current data afford a window (of at least a few years out) of something like five decades of postgraduate life to observe a person's contributions. Using an assumed age-giving profile in which giving rises until about age seventy, I used the observations obtained from the College and Beyond data to infer estimates of lifetime giving. For each person, the present value of this lifetime giving was calculated, as of age twenty-two. For those alumni who made no donations during the period of coverage, lifetime giving was assumed to be zero. More details about this calculation are given in a companion research note in this article.

Table 3 shows the resulting distribution of putative lifetime giving by these alumni. The top portion of the table shows that 30 percent of the 1951 cohort and 42 percent of the 1976 cohort were projected to make no gifts over their lifetime, based on their failure to make any donation during the sample period. At the other end of the distribution, some 4 percent and 1 percent of the alumni, respectively, were projected to give more than $50,000 over the course of their lives. Average lifetime giving was projected to be almost $12,000 for the members of the 1951 cohort, compared to about $7,700 for the 1976 cohort, or about 1.56 times higher for the former. Because of the large number of alumni who are projected to give nothing over their lifetime, the median values for putative lifetime giving are small, $771 for the 1951 cohort and $294 for the 1976 cohort. In judging these figures, one should recall that these calculations assume a person's donations increase over his or her lifetime in a way that is determined by an estimated equation (Grant and Lindauer, 1986). If a higher growth rate were assumed, the 1.56 ratio would decline, and vice versa. In any case, however, the most important implication of the calculation is that only a minority of alumni give a substantial amount over their lifetime.

One yardstick by which these projected quantities can be judged is the tuition level that existed when the alumni entered college. Over a lifetime, how many alumni will donate enough, for example, to pay for one year's worth of tuition, at the level they knew it when they were in college? If ever there were a moving target, this would be it. Still, it seems a particularly apt amount for comparison. Among the fourteen institutions in the current sample, the average tuition in 1951 was a paltry $3,350 in 1997 dollars, but by 1976 it was $10,677 (*Lovejoy's College Guide . . .*, 1952; Cass and Birnbaum, 1977). Comparing those figures to the distribution of projected contributions

TABLE 3

Present Value of Putative Lifetime Giving, by Cohort

	1951 Cohort		1976 Cohort	
	Number	Percentage	Number	Percentage
Present value of putative lifetime contributions (1997 $), age 22				
$0	869	29.9	3,888	41.8
$1–1,000	693	23.8	1,959	21.0
$1,001–5,000	692	23.8	2,146	23.1
$5,001–10,000	224	7.7	614	6.6
$10,001–20,000	154	5.3	359	3.9
$20,001–50,000	156	5.4	217	2.3
Over $50,000	122	4.2	121	1.3
Total	2,910	100.0	9,304	100.0
Mean	$11,969		$7,671	
Median	$771		$294	
Percentage of average tuition in entering year covered by present value of giving				
0	869	29.9	3,888	41.8
1–25	621	21.3	3,286	35.3
26–100	598	20.6	1,476	15.9
101–300	391	13.4	441	4.7
Over 300	431	14.8	213	2.3
Total	2,910	100.0	9,304	100.0

Source: College and Beyond data and author's calculations.

Note: Giving in 1997 dollars estimated for ages twenty-two to eighty, based on fitted values and observed values. Present value of that stream calculated at age twenty-two. See research note in this article for a description of the calculation.

considerably widens the difference between the cohorts. Whereas 28 percent of the 1951 cohort are projected to contribute at least one year's tuition amount, only about 7 percent of the 1976 cohort are.

Patterns of Alumni Giving

Because they contain both yearly data on giving and detailed survey information, the College and Beyond data offer an unusual opportunity to document several interesting features of alumni giving. For example, any director of development or alumni affairs is keenly aware that alumni differ in the regularity of their giving, ranging from the dependable annual giver to the "never-ever." The panel nature of this data set shows a clear picture of how alumni differ in this regard. Table 4 divides the present sample according to the number of years they made contributions during the 1991–1995 period. It shows that most alumni fall into one of the two extreme groups.

An impressive 27.5 percent of those in the 1951 cohort made contributions in each of the five years, while about half that percentage showed the same level of constancy among the younger cohort. At the other end of the spectrum, more than a third of the 1951 cohort and more than half of the 1976 cohort made no contributions at all during this period. Least common among both cohorts were those who made gifts in only a few years. A pattern that one might expect to observe would be giving in only one year, that being the reunion year. Although these data suggest such a pattern, the effect does not appear to be large. The percentage of alumni who gave in only one of the five reunion years was 8 and 11 percent, respectively. As shown in Table 5, although the percentage of giving among both cohorts was indeed highest in 1995 (corresponding to the reunion year for those in both cohorts who finished college in four years), the difference seems

TABLE 4

Constancy of Giving, 1991–1995

Cohort	1951	1976
Percentage who contributed in:		
All five years	27.5	12.6
Four years	12.7	9.3
Three years	8.0	7.6
Two years	6.7	8.5
One year	7.7	11.1
No years	37.5	51.0
Total	100.0	100.0
n	2,910	7,995

Source: College and Beyond survey and author's calculations. One institution for which no 1995 giving data was excluded from these calculations.

TABLE 5

Giving by Year, Combined Sample

Cohort	Percentage Giving		Average Giving, Donors	
	1951	1976	1951	1976
Year				
1991	44.7	30.0	1,577	197
1992	46.6	29.6	1,070	247
1993	45.0	28.8	888	779
1994	46.9	30.8	971	375
1995	49.9	31.7	1,506	681

Source: College and Beyond survey; author's calculations.

Note: Based on 2,910 alumni in the 1951 cohort and 7,995 in the 1976 cohort.

surprisingly small. The more important effect of the reunion year appears to be in the amount given. As Table 5 indicates, the average amount given during 1995 was well above the five-year average for each cohort, although in neither case was 1995 the highest, a finding similar to that of Willemain, Goyal, Van Deven, and Thukral's study of Princeton alumni giving (1994).

One other noteworthy feature of giving that leaps out from the data (and one that is surely not lost on development officers) is its high degree of concentration, a feature noted in previous research, such as Lindahl and Winship (1992). Table 6 shows the percentage of total contributions that donors made during the 1991–1995 period, ranked by size of gift. It is evident that the bottom 40 percent of both cohorts gave virtually nothing over this period. The next 40 percent gave a relatively small fraction of the total, leaving the bulk of the giving for the most generous fifth of alumni. In fact, half of the dollars given by the 1951 cohort were donated by just 1 percent of its members; for the 1976 cohort the top 1 percent gave 65 percent. Considerable concentration exists even among those who donate something. In this group, the top 20 percent contributed 90 percent of all gifts in the 1951 cohort and 88 percent in the 1976 cohort, showing that alumni giving is somewhat more concentrated than the benchmark given by the 80/20 rule in marketing—also known as Pareto's law, or the "law of the heavy half" (Buell, 1986), which states that the most active 20 percent of consumers normally account for 80 percent of total spending on a commodity. It is no wonder that development officers devote a disproportionate share of their attention to a relative handful of alumni donors.

What kind of alumni contribute, and contribute the most? To give a sense of this, Table 7 shows how the giving rate and average size of donation, both defined for the five-year period 1991–1995, differ according to a number of personal characteristics. For the entire sample, 63 percent of the 1951 cohort made at least one contribution in the period, compared to 48 percent for the 1976 cohort, percentages that can also be inferred from Table 4. Average giving over the entire period for those who made any donation—in contrast to 1995 giving only, as in Table 2—was $899 and $270, respectively. By gender, although men and women were about as likely to make any gift, the average size from male donors was over twice as large as that for women.

TABLE 6

Concentration of Giving, 1991–1995

| | Percentage of Cohort's Total Giving | | | |
| | All Alumni | | Alumni Who Gave | |
Cohort	1951	1976	1951	1976
All alumni ranked by giving				
Lowest 20 percent	0.0	0.0	0.5	0.7
Second 20 percent	0.0	0.0	1.0	1.4
Third 20 percent	1.1	0.4	2.4	3.0
Fourth 20 percent	4.4	4.2	6.1	6.6
Next 15 percent	16.8	13.4	19.7	14.6
Next 4 percent	26.1	16.1	27.3	15.2
Highest 1 percent	51.6	65.8	43.0	58.5
All	100.0	100.0	100.0	100.0

Source: College and Beyond survey and author's calculations.

This disparity apparently has been a concern at previously all-male institutions that became co-ed. Giving patterns also differed markedly with income level, with those in the top income class being much more likely to give than those below and having a considerably higher average as well. Political philosophy, on the other hand, shows no systematic relationship to giving. Alumni who once had a leadership position in an extracurricular activity gave more than those who did not. Those who remembered someone who took a special interest in them during college were also more likely to give, and to give more. Having graduated from the institution where they first enrolled was strongly related to giving. Legacies (those with a relative who previously attended the institution) tended to make larger gifts, and they were slightly more likely than other alumni to give at all. Regarding the type of high school attended, there is no clear effect discernible from these averages. SAT score shows little relation to giving among the 1951 cohort, for those who reported such a score. For the 1976 cohort, however, SAT score was positively related to the propensity to give and the average level among donors. Those who had received honors, including Phi Beta Kappa, gave more.

The next three items in Table 7 reflect answers to attitudinal questions. The first among these reveals that an overwhelming majority of respondents were "very satisfied" with their undergraduate institution (though the percentage was lower for the younger cohort). Not surprisingly, those who reported being satisfied were more active contributors than those who were not. Similarly, those who were dissatisfied with various specific aspects were less likely to give, or give a lot.

The last three items refer to characteristics of the institution rather than the respondents. Those who entered a liberal arts college were more likely to give than those who enrolled in a university, but average giving for those making a contribution was higher among college alumni only for the 1951 cohort. When institutions were divided by tuition level, there was no systematic pattern for giving, but there does seem to be a relationship to the institution's degree of selectivity in admissions for 1976. For that cohort, the alumni from the most selective institutions were most likely to give, and those givers had the highest average giving.

It is instructive to examine the interaction between two of the strongest factors noted in Table 7: income and satisfaction with the undergraduate institution. Income, of course, has been shown in previous work on charitable giving to be highly correlated with total contribution. It simply seems intuitive that expressed satisfaction should also be important. Table 8 presents average giving by income class and degree of satisfaction with the undergraduate college where the respondent first enrolled. Almost without exception, in both cohorts, giving rises with income. It is also generally higher within the broad income classes for those who said they were "very satisfied," with the difference being statistically significant overall and in three of the four income classes for each cohort.

In light of the disproportionate share of total giving made by the largest donors, it is especially interesting to focus on the biggest givers. Table 9 compares the top 1 percent of givers to the entire sample, for each cohort. Not surprisingly, those who contributed the most tended to have the highest incomes, with 97 percent making $100,000 or more. Perhaps correspondingly, they tended also to be conservative on economic issues. They also were more likely to be a leader in a volunteer activity, particularly so with alumni activities. Corresponding to the tabulations already shown, the big givers were more likely than average to have had someone who advised them in college, somewhat more likely to have been satisfied with their undergraduate experience, and much more likely to be satisfied with life in general. What may be most surprising, at least to those who feared that increasing emphasis on academic record at the expense of family connections would undermine alumni giving, is that the top givers in both cohorts had higher-than-average SAT scores. All of these differences are statistically significant.

Conclusion

Using a rich data set on two age cohorts of former students from fourteen selective private colleges and universities, this paper examines patterns of alumni donations. The data come from the College and Beyond study, which combines survey data with information from the institutions' own records for two cohorts of former students. The data offer an unusual amount of information describing each former student's past association with his or her undergraduate college.

TABLE 7

1991–1995 Alumni Giving, by Selected Donor Characteristics

Category	Type	n 1951	n 1976	Percentage Who Gave 1951	Percentage Who Gave 1976	Mean Giving for Those Who Gave 1951	Mean Giving for Those Who Gave 1976
All		2,910	9,304	62.5	48.0	899	270*
Gender	Male	2,298	4,943	61.2	47.7	1,036	397*
	Female	612	4,361	67.3	48.3	432	126*
Household income	$150,000+	865	2,418	73.8	61.8	1,866	649*
	$75,000–149,999	987	3,245	61.7	50.5	342	91*
	$30,000–74,999	716	2,667	53.8	37.9	451	57*
	Under $30,000	172	584	47.1	25.9	96	34*
	Unspecified	170	390	62.4	42.8	513	125*
Political philosophy	Conservative	1,622	4,182	62.1	50.0	1,132	242*
	Liberal	548	2,423	65.7	44.6	398	154*
	Moderate	693	2,554	62.1	48.6	804	417
	Unspecified	47	145	46.8	35.9	310	252
Legacy status	Yes	398	1,119	65.3	51.7	1,063	355
	No	2,512	8,185	62.1	47.5	872	257*
Extracurricular activity	Leader or participant	150	140	78.0	67.1	1,290	1,328
	Nonleading participant	223	324	54.7	49.4	803	118*
	Nonparticipant	2,537	8,840	62.3	47.6	877	252*
Someone took an interest?[a]	Yes	1,434	4,530	65.6	51.0	1,110	332*
	No	1,451	4,741	59.6	45.2	680	200*
	Unspecified	25	33	52.0	30.3	164	628
Whether graduated from institution	Yes	2,502	8,064	66.7	53.8	961	275*
	No	408	1,240	37.0	10.5	216	72*
High school type	Public	1,450	6,198	63.4	48.8	1,097	246*
	Private	1,101	2,019	64.0	48.6	784	420
	Other	102	671	62.8	44.1	605	105*
	Unspecified	257	416	51.0	38.2	271	99*
Person's combined SAT Score	More than 1,299	311	3,269	59.2	52.0	675	434
	1,200–1,299	438	2,116	64.6	51.0	1,012	228*
	1,199–1,100	476	1,716	66.8	46.7	1,437	129*

1,000–1,099	320	1,055	60.3	43.2	710	123*
Less than 1,000	219	666	69.0	39.3	864	140*
Unspecified	1,146	482	60.2	34.7	724	143
Was institution person's first choice?						
Yes	2,297	6,185	64.6	52.7	921	268*
No	528	2,968	54.0	38.5	603	274
Unspecified	85	151	58.8	41.1	1,946	262
Received honors/Phi Beta Kappa						
Yes	636	2,878	69.7	60.4	866	401
No	2,156	6,239	62.1	43.2	932	187*
Unspecified	118	187	32.2	14.4	117	42*
Overall satisfaction with institution						
Very	2,128	5,999	66.7	55.5	1,012	323*
Somewhat	555	2,444	55.3	39.1	538	106*
Other	206	828	40.8	20.1	387	129*
Unspecified	21	33	38.1	36.4	64	521
Dissatisfied with research or teaching[b]						
Yes	1,323	4,274	56.7	39.4	686	205*
No	1,543	4,958	67.7	55.5	1,060	309*
Unspecified	44	72	56.8	38.9	563	297
Dissatisfied with other aspects[b]						
Yes	1,975	6,768	59.3	43.4	716	270*
No	895	2,466	69.8	60.9	1,259	269*
Unspecified	40	70	55.0	40.0	401	297
Liberal arts college						
Yes	952	1,673	72.8	61.2	952	162*
No	1,958	7,631	57.5	45.1	866	302*
Institution's tuition[c]						
High	900	3,305	54.1	42.1	494	354
Medium	1,168	2,903	74.1	48.0	1,157	169*
Low	842	3,096	55.3	54.3	842	283
Selectivity of institution						
High		2,961	54.2			355
Medium		5,712	45.0			233
Low		631	46.1			124

Source: College and Beyond survey and author's calculations.

Notes: (a) Based on the survey question "While you were an undergraduate, did anyone associated with your school, other than fellow students, take a special interest in you or your work—that is, was there someone you could turn to for advice or for general support or encouragement?" (Bowen and Bok, 1998, p. 319, question All).

(b) Respondents were asked, "Please indicate how much emphasis you believe your undergraduate school *currently* places on" a number of aspects, ranking each from "a great deal" (5) to "very little/none" (1). Then, for the same list, they were asked how much their institution *should* emphasize each aspect. A respondent was deemed to be dissatisfied with the institution with respect to an aspect if the difference between these two rankings was 2 or more, in either direction. The first measure applies this dissatisfaction criterion to either faculty research or undergraduate teaching. The second applies if the criterion is met for any one of another seven aspects: a broad liberal arts education, intercollegiate athletics, extracurricular activity other than intercollegiate athletics, commitment to intellectual freedom, a racially or ethnically diverse student body, quality of residential life, and alumni or alumnae concerns.

(c) Information on the institution's tuition, contemporaneous to each cohort, was obtained from college guides and summarized in three categorical dichotomous variables for each year. For the 1951 cohort, these were based on tuition figures reported in *Lovejoy's College Guide 1953–54* (1952). The first was assigned the value of 1 for institutions with reported tuition of $700 or more per year, the second for $550–699, and the third for less than $550. The number of institutions in these categories was three, five, and six, respectively. For the 1976 cohort, these dichotomous variables indicating tuition level were based on tuition figures reported in Cass and Birnbaum (1977). The first variable was assigned the value of 1 for institutions with reported tuition and fees of $4,200 for more, the second for $3,600–4,199, and the third for $3,600–4,199, and the third for less than $3,600.

TABLE 8

Average Alumni Donations, 1991–1995, by Cohort, Income, and Satisfaction with Undergraduate Experience

	Household Income					
	Under $30,000	$30,000–$74,999	$75,000–$149,999	$150,000+	Not given	All
1951 cohort						
Very satisfied	123*	543	397*	2,032+	528	1,012*
Not very satisfied	24	200	144	1,233	437	506
No answer	2		114	42		64
All	96	451	342	1,866	513	899
1976 cohort						
Very satisfied	32	61*	103*	743+	151+	323*
Not very satisfied	37	46	57	268	58	109
No answer	11	31	19	1,220	11	521
All	34	57	91	649	125	270

Source: College and Beyond survey and author's calculations.

Notes: The question was, "Overall, how satisfied have you been with the education you received at the school at which you first enrolled?"

An asterisk (*) indicates that the mean for "very satisfied" and "not very satisfied" differs significantly at the 95 percent level; a plus (+) indicates significance at the 90 percent level.

Reflecting a rising emphasis on meritocratic criteria for admission to the nation's most selective colleges and universities, the composition of these fourteen institutions did change perceptibly over the period from 1951 to 1989. The schools became less male, more nonwhite, and less regional, and they enrolled an increasing share of academically high-achieving students. But comparisons of giving between 1951 and 1976 cohorts do not yield any clear reason to worry that these changes reduce the level of alumni giving to such institutions.

Although the act of donating is relatively common among these alumni, the paper reveals that alumni giving is extremely concentrated, with more than half of all donations being given by just 1 percent of all alumni. A surprisingly high proportion of the alumni of these private institutions contribute annually. Based on the amount they contributed over the period of observation, some of these alumni are projected to give a substantial amount over their lifetime.

Of all the variables associated with alumni giving highlighted in this paper, perhaps the two most emphatic effects are those of income and satisfaction. Income, of course, has long been found to be highly correlated to charitable giving. In light of the tendency for more affluent donors to favor higher education as an object of their generosity, this strong correlation should come as no surprise; nor should the effect of expressed satisfaction. Although no similar history of studies documenting the relationship exists, it should be emphasized that this connection has received virtually no statistical support in the literature on charitable giving. (For a detailed analysis of the effect of satisfaction on alumni giving, see Clotfelter, 2000.)

In considering what, if anything, these statistical findings imply for colleges and universities, it is well to begin by noting that increasing the level of alumni donations is not, nor should it be, the primary aim of any institution. A means to achieving ultimate goals, probably; an indirect measure of success, perhaps; but not an ultimate objective. That said, the bulk of donations come from a relatively small number of alumni. Of course, beyond the obvious step of focusing on alumni in high income zip codes, the process of identifying and cultivating them is quite another matter, which is

TABLE 9

Characteristics of Big Givers: Mean Values for Selected Variables, Top 1 Percent and Full Sample, by Cohort

	1951		1976	
	Top 1 Percent of Donors	Full Sample	Top 1 Percent of Donors	Full Sample
SAT-combined	1,188	1,160	1,273	1,230
College cumulative GPA	2.38	2.53	3.20	2.99
Percentages				
Someone took an interest	74	49	59	49
Participated in extracurricular activities[a]	15	13	6	5
Participated in intercollegiate athletics	26	17	29	12
Postgraduate volunteer activity				
Leader 1994–95, any volunteer activity	82	47	65	44
Other past or present participant	18	51	33	52
Leader 1994–95, alumni activities	35	8	31	4
Other past or present alumni participation	61	41	51	28
Personal characteristics				
Married	91	85	88	80
White	100	86	95	82
Male	94	75	70	53
Household income $100,000 or more	97	49	97	46
Attitudes				
Economic conservative	79	56	64	46
Social conservative	29	31	19	20
Very satisfied with life	74	57	74	43
Satisfied with undergraduate education	100	93	97	91
Dissatisfied with research or teaching	13	19	22	24
Dissatisfied with other aspects	24	46	61	53

Source: College and Beyond survey and author's calculations.

Notes: (a) In addition to activities such as publications, government, and cheerleading, also includes resident advisor, ROTC, and volunteering.

Means are unweighted. Hypothesis that the means are equal between top 1 percent and full sample is rejected, at the 95 percent level, for each variable, for both cohorts.

why sophisticated development offices exist in every thriving private college and university and many public ones as well. Within the age groups containing most of today's potential big donors, little can be done to change a central determinant of alumni giving: feelings of satisfaction about the undergraduate experience of decades ago. For such current prospects, the only option besides being courted by development officers that is likely to have an impact in the short run is a policy likely to arouse dissatisfaction, such as a perceived shift in emphasis from teaching to research, or away from sports. Such tradeoffs are necessarily part of every president's ongoing calculus. In contrast to immediate tradeoffs, the paper's most important implications relate to long-run effects. Among them is the likelihood that improvement in teaching and advising has a beneficial effect on eventual alumni giving. Although greatly attenuated by time, the benefit should still offer some comfort to an institution seeking, regardless of the reason, to improve undergraduate education.

Research Note: Calculation of Putative Lifetime Donations

In this article, I present calculations to approximate the present value of individuals' alumni giving over their lifetime, based on limited information on giving. This research note presents a description of the underlying calculations.

To infer the value of an individual's lifetime contributions, I assume that the donations made during the years of observation are representative of the individual's lifetime giving. If the individual makes no gifts during the observation period, I assume he or she never gives. For all other individuals, I make the assumption that everyone's lifetime pattern of giving has the same shape, differing proportionally only in amount. The assumed age-giving profile is based on an estimated relationship for a private women's college on giving per living graduate by year (Grant and Lindauer, 1986, p. 132):

$$\ln g_a = 1.231 + 0.205\ R^* + 0.072\ (a - 21) - 0.00051\ (a - 21)^2$$

where g_a is donations in 1967 dollars, R^* is a dummy variable indicating reunion years (every fifth year from age twenty-six to seventy-six), and a is age. Because it is based on data, collected at one time, on average giving by class, the estimated age-giving profile necessarily conflates life-cycle, cohort, and income effects. According to this function, the real value of alumni giving rises through life, slowing gradually, reaching a peak around age seventy; it features spikes at five-year intervals corresponding with reunion years. Between the ages of thirty-seven and sixty-two, it implies an annual growth rate in giving of 4.4 percent. To correct this equation for expected mortality, each future year's fitted value for donations is multiplied by the probability of survival to the corresponding age, where separate mortality figures are employed for men and women and for members of the 1951 and 1976 cohorts. That is, for members of the 1951 cohort, who are observed in the data at age sixty-two, each year beginning with age sixty-three is multiplied by the probability of surviving to that age, having survived to sixty-two. For members of the 1976 cohort, adjustments for mortality begin with age thirty-eight, the first year after they are observed in the survey.

Calculating an individual's putative lifetime alumni giving follows a five-step procedure. In the first step, the equation and mortality tables already described are used to calculate the expected present value of donations, stated in 1997 constant dollars, evaluated at age twenty-two. Call this the present value V_k where k indexes two cohorts, each with two genders.

Steps two through four are applied separately to each individual in the sample. For each individual i, we have observations on giving for years $a1$ to $a2$, denoted $g_{ia1} \cdot g_{ia2}$. In step two, the present value of this giving, calculated at age twenty-two in 1997 dollars, is calculated. In step three, a second present value is calculated for the same ages, but now using the estimated giving from the estimated equation above, $g_{ia1} \cdot g_{ia2}$.

In step four, the ratio between these two present values is computed:

$$X_i = PV(g_{ia1} \cdot g_{ia2}) / PV(g_{ia1} \cdot g_{ia2})$$

If the individual makes no contributions during the years covered by the data, $X_i = 0$.

In the final step, the present value of the individual's lifetime giving is estimated to be

$$V_i = X_i V_k$$

If, for example, the present value of a man's giving over the span of ages from fifty-six to sixty-two is 85 percent of the present value of predicted giving for ages fifty-six to sixty-two, then the present value of his expected lifetime giving is taken to be 85 percent of the age-and gender-appropriate V_k calculated from the estimated equation.

Charles T. Clotfelter is Z. Smith Reynolds Professor of Public Policy Studies and professor of economics and law at Duke University. He is also director of the Center for the Study of Philanthropy and Voluntarism at Duke and a research associate of the National Bureau of Economic Research.

References

Auten, G., and Joulfaian, D. "Charitable Contributions and Intergenerational Transfers." *Journal of Public Economics*, 1996, 59, 55–68.

Bowen, W. G., and Bok, D. *The Shape of the River: Long-Term Consequences of Considering Race in College and University Admissions*. Princeton, N.J.: Princeton University Press, 1998.

Buell, V. P. (ed.). *Handbook of Modern Marketing*. New York: McGraw-Hill, 1986.

Cass, J., and Birnbaum, M. *Comparative Guide to American Colleges*. (8th ed.) New York: Harper and Row, 1977.

Clotfelter, C. T. *Federal Tax Policy and Charitable Giving*. Chicago: University of Chicago Press, 1985.

Clotfelter, C. T. "The Familiar but Curious Economics of Higher Education: Introduction to a Symposium." *Journal of Economic Perspectives*, Winter 1999, 13, 3–12.

Clotfelter, C. T. "Alumni Giving to Elite Private Colleges and Universities." Unpublished paper, Apr. 2000.

Cook, P. J., and Frank, R. H. "The Growing Concentration of Top Students at Elite Schools." In C. T. Clotfelter and M. Rothschild (eds.), *Studies of Supply and Demand in Higher Education*. Chicago: University of Chicago Press, 1993.

Goss, K. A. "Volunteering and the Long Civic Generation." *Nonprofit and Voluntary Sector Quarterly*, 1999, 28, 378–415.

Grant, J. H., and Lindauer, D. L. "The Economics of Charity: Life-Cycle Patterns of Alumnae Contributions." *Eastern Economic Journal*, Apr.–June 1986, 2, 129–141.

Hoxby, C. M. "The Changing Market Structure of U.S. Higher Education." Unpublished working paper, Harvard University, 1997.

Hoxby, C. M., and Terry, B. "Explaining Rising Incomes and Wage Inequality Among the College Educated." Unpublished working paper, Harvard University, 1998.

Lemann, N. *The Big Test: The Secret History of American Meritocracy*. New York: Farrar, Strauss and Giroux, 1999.

Leslie, L. L., and Ramey, G. "Donor Behavior and Voluntary Support for Higher Education Institutions." *Journal of Higher Education*, Mar.–Apr. 1988, 59, 115–132.

Lindahl, W. E., and Winship, C. "Predictive Models for Annual Fundraising and Major Gift Fundraising." *Nonprofit Management and Leadership*, Fall 1992, 3, 43–64.

Lovejoy's College Guide 1953–54. New York: Simon & Schuster, 1952.

Morgan, D. R. *Voluntary Support of Education 1995, 1998*. New York: Council for Aid to Education, 1996, 1999.

Rooney, P. M. "A Better Method for Analyzing the Costs and Benefits of Fundraising at Universities." *Nonprofit Management and Leadership*, Fall 1999, 10, 39–56.

Willemain, T. R., Goyal, A., Van Deven, M., and Thukral, I. S. "Alumni Giving: The Influences of Reunion, Class, and Year." *Research in Higher Education*, Oct. 1994, 35, 609–629.

Notes

1. An important practical question that arose in using the data on alumni giving presented by institutions was how to determine whether the absence of recorded giving by an individual reflected no contributions by the individual or merely lack of data on giving. Institutions were asked to indicate for each individual whether giving data were available; conversations with those who provided and collected the data suggested that this indicator was not reliable. Instead, the assumption was made that missing data would indicate true zero giving except in cases in which the institution offered no giving data for any donors, as was the case with three institutions for all of the 1951 cohort and several other institutions for some years and cohorts.

2. The ratio 2:4:1 is based on logarithmic coefficients of –.399 and .474 in equation (1) (Auten and Joulfaian, 1996, Table 2), where sixty-five and over is the omitted age category. For a review of estimated age effects in studies of charitable giving, see Clotfelter (1985). Since they rely on cross-section differences, however, these estimated effects could include both generational effects as well as pure life-cycle effects.

Note: I am grateful to Thomas Anderson, Chi Leng, Margaret Lieberman, Cathleen McHugh, and Robert Malme for research assistance; to Philip Cook, Gordon Winston, and several anonymous referees for helpful comments on an earlier draft; and to the Andrew W. Mellon Foundation for providing data and financial support. The views expressed here are mine and do not necessarily represent those of any organization.

College Relations and Fund-Raising Expenditures: Influencing the Probability of Alumni Giving to Higher Education

William B. Harrison

Abstract

Costs of fund raising and college relations data for each of three years from 17 colleges and universities have been combined with the schools' institutional characteristics to predict ratios of alumni donors to total alumni for each school. With factor analysis, expenditure and institutional variables were classified into three descriptor influences on giving: fund-raising effort, donor wealth, and school resources. The expected ratio of donors to number of available alumni for each school was then projected with the use of logit coefficients derived from the limited factor model. [JEL I21]

Introduction

My research addresses empirically a question about which there is little information. Are larger expenditures upon college and university development justified, and in particular do alumni activities pay off?

This study concerns a subset source of giving to higher education, the alumni, and specifically, the proportion of alumni on record who may be expected to give in any school year. The resources available for the promotion of alumni giving are professional and clerical personnel, office equipment and supplies, university space, and outside consultants or other services. These are employed in fundraising, alumni relations and similar activities conducted with the business and general community, faculty and students, and not-for-profit organizations. Such resources are constrained by each school's type, size, endowment, ability to use resources effectively, donor wealth, and educational and general (E & G) budget.

For more than 30 years. The New York-based Council for Aid to Education (CAE) has published its annual report *Voluntary Support of Education*.[1] This has greatly facilitated motivational studies of college philanthropy. While most research has focused on donor characteristics and behavior, *Voluntary Support* data has supplemented studies of colleges influence on philanthropy with extensive institutional information. Sources of support, restrictions on gifts, and vital statistics about the receiving institutions are provided for most American colleges and universities, which are grouped into ten "Carnegie" peer classifications.[2]

Statistics reported by CAE. however, do not yet include information about collegiate expenditures for the purpose of promoting gifts. Generally, these fall into three cost categories. Fundraising costs include those designed to obtain private gifts from all sources, for all purposes, and for immediate or deferred purposes (such as bequests). Alumni relations costs cover informational activities for the benefit of alumni(ae) and especially encourage participation in and support for college activities and plans. Other relations costs arise from informational activities concerned with attracting support for the institution from non-alumni, including parents, faculty, staff, students, government officials, and the business community.

Costs associated with the three activities just mentioned are not usually available to researchers. For one reason, schools may not be willing to share details about successes or shortcomings in their efforts to secure funds and other support.[3] They may be uncertain as to how public release of their data on fund-raising costs or methods would affect their own support or share of support relative to others.

In 1990, The Council for Advancement and Support of Education (CASE) published *Expenditures in Fund Raising, Alumni Relations, and other Constituent (Public) Relations*. This study which was funded by a grant from Lilly Endowment, Inc., included central tendency data for 51 participating colleges and universities for each of three years. Instructions to participating schools provided definitions for each of the three classes of costs to be reported and thoroughly described specific types of expenditure. The result was a uniform and consistent report on cost allocations.

By obtaining the CASE "Expenditures" data directly from 18 of the 51 reporting schools, most of them reporting for each of the academic years 1985–86, 1986–87 and 1987–88, I was able to perform statistical analysis of relationships between various kinds of giving associated with combinations of fund-raising costs and institutional variables. My specific concern in this research was with the decision of alumni to give or not to give.

The goal of this study is to estimate, insofar as possible, the proportion of alumni of record who actually donate to any given school (a dependent variable). Explanatory (independent) variables include fundraising and constituent relations costs, along with a number of institutional variables.

State of the Literature on Giving to Higher Education

Because giving for educational purposes is a philanthropic activity, it is useful to review studies that deal with altruism. Many investigators, especially economists, search for motives—whether altruistic or not—that explain giving as an act of consumer behavior. They assume that the act of giving creates positive utility for the giver.

Much literature in recent years has focused on an *interdependence thesis* (Andreoni and Scholz, 1990; Becker, 1974; Boulding, 1962; Hochman and Rodgers, 1973; Reece, 1979; Schwartz, 1970; Scott, 1972). The economic person gives as a response to others whose income or wealth is less than his or hers. Such acts are Pareto-optimal as long as the income or wealth of the recipient remains below that of the donor. Some have even classified giving as a luxury good to the donor, citing recipient income elasticity greater than one with respect to giving (Becker, 1974; Reece; 1979).

Many who have included a price variable in their studies have used a taxation rate for this purpose, because giving is believed to be directly related to the marginal tax rate on donor income (Boskin and Feldstein, 1977; Clotfelder and Feldstein, 1986; Feldstein, 1975; Hood et al., 1977; Reece, 1979; Schwartz, 1970).

While most studies of philanthropy are concerned with donor behavior as exemplified by those just cited, giving to educational institutions has been examined also for influences on giving that are generated by recipients. This orientation is not surprising given the schools abilities to shape the perceptions people have about them and the reactions of donors to different fund-raising approaches by school development offices.

Studies of educational philanthropy that deal with donor characteristics have stimulated efforts by college development officers to know more about their pools of alumni(ae) and other potential donors. Colleges then have sought to appeal to their principal characteristics. Some have found, for example, that *emotional attachment* to the school is important (Beeler, 1982). Also, donor *attitudes toward their own educational experiences* are significant (Beeler, 1982). The latter is the basis for findings of connections between giving and *involvement in student activities* (Haddad, 1986; Hall, 1967; Keller, 1982), *residence on campus* (Widick, 1985), *scholarship or grant awards* (Beeler, 1982), *major subject* (Deel, 1971; Haddad, 1986), and *year of graduation* (Beeler, 1982; Haddad, 1986; Keller, 1982; Yankelovich, 1987).

Studies on the receiving end are less numerous. These incorporate institutional features of colleges, such as endowment, E & G expenditures, enrollment, and "prestige", a more nebulous factor that may be proxied by the institution's age or research funds available.

Additionally, a number of variable costs are associated with fundraising, alumni relations, and community relations, which are assumed to be justified by their direct relationship to giving. Some of the most revealing work in this area has been produced in recent years by doctoral dissertations dealing with the economics of education. For example, recent theses have emphasized that maintaining close contact with alumni and producing high-quality alumni publications with information about college plans, philosophy, and objectives encourage giving (Aug, 1987; Carlson, 1978).

One dissertation—winner of a CASE Grenzebach award—examines a comprehensive range of college-determined variables that are associated with gifts received by public, research/doctoral universities (Woods, 1987). This work, covering 77 schools, combines dozens of variables into six categories *a priori*:

Financial resources—number of alumni, federally-sponsored research grants, legislative appropriations, and student aid funds.

Inherent institutional characteristics—age, endowment, in-state and total enrollment, cost of attendance. E & G expenditures, number of advancement professional staff.

Organizational components—fund-raising and constituent relations goals, planning, staffing, budget, experience, and structure.

Method components—solicitation techniques such as direct mail, telephone, written proposal, capital campaign, and use of trustees, faculty, president, students, volunteers.

Gift emphasis components—Annual, deferred, corporate, foundation, and major giving emphasis.

U.S. regional locations.

Wood's research finds that, in general, two factors are especially crucial to success in fundraising: financial resources and inherent institutional characteristics. Some aspects of the organizational structure of the college development office also were significant.

Proposing a model in which donations to colleges are the outcome of the simultaneous solution of supply and demand functions, Yoo and Harrison (1989) tested the model with cross-section data from 13 private colleges. Donors were said to demand the attention and prestige supplied by colleges. The donors try to maximize recipient services while colleges maximize donations. Equations were estimated with two and three-stage least squares techniques. Yoo and Harrison found that their price variable, donations per donor, explained significantly the value of recipient services rendered by colleges to donors, in both supply and demand equations.

Despite the increase in research into giving to higher education, more is required. Notably lacking are findings on developmental activity influences on (1) proportions of alumni who give to their *alma mater*, as well as (2) amounts given per alumnus or alumna. The identification by Woods of "components", which are groups of variables to account for giving, suggests a more formal procedure, factor analysis, as a basis for formulating the groups. Her findings that financial resource variables and inherent institutional research variables, along with the Yoo-Harrison conclusions also suggest some of the influences to be examined in this study.

Empirical Approach

Colleges wish to maximize an objective function consisting of some measure of success in attracting money and property gifts from corporations (matching or otherwise), from alumni and other individuals (current and bequests), and from other organizations. These schools must allocate scarce resources to fundraising, alumni relations, and other relations activities. These costs, along with selected institutional variables, are arguments for determining colleges' alumni participation rates.

A preliminary correlation matrix exhibited a strong linear relationship among a number of our variables. When a large number of explanatory variables present such a multicollinearity problem, the relative contributions of some variables are clouded. In these circumstances, a solution is to omit some variables that are collinear. However, dropping variables may result in information loss, and the model may in consequence be misspecified. Factor analysis goes a long way toward solving the problem.

Factor analysis is employed here as a means to identify a few broad influences (factors) underlying the large number of institutional variables contained in my constraints. By clustering a larger number of variables into a few homogeneous sets, each set is identified as a *factor*. This accomplishes two objectives. First, I reduced the number of variables used in the study, because any one variable may he substituted for a number of other homogeneous ones. Also, I established a few broad, interpretable characteristics to identify my objective function.[4]

Once the set of "super variables" representing factors are produced, they are used to extend my analysis of the *proportion of alumni on record that gives to its alma mater*. The next task is to predict this proportion for any school (i), given its fund-raising and relations expenses and institutional factors.

The logit procedure provides a response probability to be modeled (Rubinfeld and Pindyck, 1981). In this case, it is the proportion (P_i) of alumni that will donate to a school, given information (X_i) about the costs of fundraising, costs of constituent relations, and certain institutional characteristics of the school. The logistic probability function is defined as:

$$P_i = 1(1 + e^{-z}),$$

where z is a linear function of X_i, namely.

$$z = a + B \, X_i.$$

Solving for e^z.

$$e^z = P_i/(1 - P_i).$$

By taking the natural log of e^z.

$$z_i = \log (P_i/(1 - P_i)) = a + B \, X_i.$$

The regression parameters provide an estimate of the logarithm of the odds that a particular choice to give will be made. From that I have a predicted proportion of alumni making a donation to a specific school, given the school's characteristics.

The final and most important task is performed with logit regressions which produce the ratio predictions just described, based on my sample of colleges and universities. These predictions may be compared with the actual ratios of alumni giving to alumni of record for each school.

Data Sources

Eighteen schools gave me copies of data that they had submitted to CASE for its 1990 report. One school could supply only the 1987–88 data, and one supplied only the 1985–86 and 1986–87 data. The other 16 colleges and universities furnished data on costs of fundraising and college relations for each of the three years as summarized in the CASE report. For statistical analysis, I treated data from each school for one year as a separate observation. In consequence, there are 51 observations in the analysis: 48 for 16 schools, 2 for one school and one for another.

The data set consists of figures for the three years from both CAE and CASE reports. Collectively, these sources supplied information about various sources and amounts given to higher education, institutional characteristics of the schools including endowment, enrollment, and educational and general expenditures (E & G). Each school is identified by a dummy variable with its Carnegie class. Table 1 provides the data used, variable designations, and sources, and major characteristics of the data.

The college development costs for fundraising, alumni relations and other constituent relations were obtained for 1986, 1987 and 1988 from the 1990 CASE report. The remaining data (gift amounts from different sources and institutional characteristics) came from CAE reports for 1985–86, 1986–87 and 1987–88 as indicated above.

Empirical Results

The enrollment of full-time equivalent (F.T.E.) students is the conventional way of denoting size of schools and, indeed, is the primary basis for funds allocation to public schools. In order to abstract from the dominant influence of size, each of the independent variables, except Carnegie classification dummies, are expressed in total dollars, and all were denominated in terms of the schools' full-time enrollment.

Classical factor analysis was employed to classify these variables into several broad categories that influence the proportion of alumni who gave.[5] The dominant influence of size in association with number of donors relative to total number of alumni, led to a search for a way to abstract from size altogether. Three factors were finally specified—after experimenting with the size-denominated variables—as most representative of broad, non-size characteristics that would describe schools influence on giving.

Table 2 includes most of the variables found in Table 1 taken from CASE and CAE reports for our 51 observations from 1985–86 through 1987–88. Setting the number of factors equal to three, thirteen variables—plus the Carnegie classifications—are shown as they loaded into the three factors. Observe the loadings: these are the correlations between the factors and the variables. Note also the proportion of the variability explained by the factors.

TABLE 1

Data Used, Variable Names and Data Sources

CASE 1990 Report for 1985–86, 1986–87 and 1987–88
TOTGIV—Total giving in $(000)
FRCOST—Fund raising costs $(000)
ALCOST—Alumni (as) relations costs $(000)
OTHCOST—Other constituent costs $(000)
CAE Annual Reports for 1985–86, 1986–87, 1987–88
ENDOW—Endowment market value $(000)
EG—Educational and general expenses $(000)
ENROLL—College enrollment in full—time equivalent students
ALUMREC—Number of alumni(ae) of record
ALUMDON—Number of alumni(ae) donors
ALUMGIV—Aulmni(ae) gifts $(000)
OTHIND—Other individual gifts $(000)
ORGGIV—Gifts from organizations $(000)
CURROPNS—Current operations support $(000)
CAPSUPP—Capital purposes support $(000)
CORPMAT—Corporate matching gifts $(000)
PLANGIV—Planned gifts $(000)
PROPGIV—Property gifts $(000)
ALRELTOT—Revenues from alumi(ae) activities
Carnegie Classifications
RSDOCPUB—Public research/doctoral institutions
COMPPUB—Public comprehensive institutions
LBARTPUB—Public liberal arts institutions
PROFPUB—Public professional and specialized institutions
RSDOCPRV—Private research/doctoral institutions
COMPPRV—Private comprehensive institutions
LBARTPRV—Private liberal arts Institutions
PROFPRV—Private professional and specialized institutions

TABLE 2

Rotated Factor Matrix

Variables (*)	F1: Fund Raising Effort	F2: Donor Wealth	F3: Resource Availability
FRCOST/ENROLL	0.86*	0.28	0.14
ALCOST/ENROLL	0.82*	0.31	0.13
ENDOW/ENROLL	0.70*	0.29	0.01
ALUMGIV/ENROLL	0.79*	0.35	−0.01
CAPSUPP/ENROLL	0.66*	0.46	0.37
CORPMAT/ENROLL	0.94*	0.04	0.09
OTHIND/ENROLL	0.37	0.88*	0.20
CURROPNS/ENROLL	0.41	0.77*	0.35
PLANGIV/ENROLL	0.43	0.85*	0.09
PROPGIV/ENROLL	0.31	−0.57*	0.40
EG/ENROLL	−0.08	0.02	0.94*
OTHCOST/ENROLL	−0.07	0.26	0.90*
ORGGIV/ENROLL	0.31	0.02	0.86*

*Primary factor loadings.

Table 2 is the rotated factor matrix obtained from intercorrelation among the variables. Factor one contains six variables, most of which are clearly connected with school fund-raising efforts: fund-raising costs; endowment; alumni giving and cost of alumni relations; and corporate matching gifts.

Factor two includes four variables, three of which are linked to donor wealth characteristics: bequests, property gifts and gifts of other individuals besides the alumni pool. The latter group is not targeted as extensively as alumni, and, because of diversity of interests, is thought to be motivated to contribute more as a result of being wealthy than because of anything the school does.

The third factor includes educational and general expenditures and other relations expenditures over and above alumni relations and fund-raising activities. Including organizational giving in this category is consistent with the appropriations character of these gifts. This category provides information about the availability and use of funds on a more or less regular basis and the efficiency with which the school uses its resources.

As a comparison with the factor-analytic method, I prepared a stepwise regression with the maximum R^2 improvement procedure. Because this model looks for the "best" one-variable model, the "best" two-variable model, etc., I wished to see if representative variables from each of the three factor classes would enter the "best" explanatory equations at an early stage. The stepwise regression results confirmed the use of these variables.

By using only one selected variable per factor, my experiments with several regression equations indicate the results are almost as good with three variables—one for each factor—as with all thirteen variables shown in Table 1. These are: ALCOST/ENROLL, representing factor one and fund-raising effort; PLANGIV/ENROLL, representing factor two and donor wealth; and OTHCOST/ENROLL, representing resource availability. In addition, the dummy variables representing Carnegie classifications are included.

Using the parameter estimates, *Logistic Procedure* calculates the estimated logit of the proportion of alumni of record—for any given school—that will donate to that school. Recall that each of our 51 school observations exhibits its own number of response observations in terms of donors per 100 alumni.

Using a base of 100% of the alumni per school for 51 schools, the dependent variable predicted by the model parameters is the ratio of donors per 100 alumni of record, 26.67%. By summing the number of donors per 100 alumni for each of our 51 schools there are 1360 donors (26.67% of 5100) and 3740 nondonor observations.

The logit procedure computes an index of rank correlation for assessing the predictive ability of the model as follows:

$$c = (nc + 0.5 (6 - nc - nd)/t.$$

where t is the total number of pairs with different responses. With 5100 alumni responses as our basis, we have 1360 donor events times 3760 no-donor events, or

$$t = 5,086,400.$$

nc is the number of "concordant" pairs and nd is the number of "discordant" pairs (explained below).

In our use of an "events/trials" model—the ratio of donors to total alumni—P_i is the *observed* response ratio of donors to alumni for school i, and $P^{\wedge}_i$ is the ratio *predicted* by the model for that school. In any pair of trials—e.g., comparing ratios for School A with School B's ratios—if the *predicted* ratio for School A ($P^{\wedge}_A$) is larger than the *Predicted* ratio for School B ($P^{\wedge}_B$), then the pair comparison is said to be *concordant* if the *observed* ratio for School A (P_A) is also larger than the *observed* ratio for School B (P_B).

Symbolically, the following three terms are indicated by these conditions:

Concordant if

$$P^{\wedge}_A > P^{\wedge}_B \text{ and } P_A > P_B.$$

or if

$$P^{\wedge}_A < P^{\wedge}_B \text{ and } P_A < P_B;$$

Discordant if

$$P^{\wedge}_A > P^{\wedge}_B \text{ and } P_A > P_B,$$

or if

$$P^{\wedge}_A < P^{\wedge}_B \text{ and } P_A < P_B;$$

Tied if

$$P^{\wedge}_A = P^{\wedge}_B \text{ and } P_A = P_B.$$

In this case, the index value (c = 0.69) and percentage of concordant pairs (68%) show a high degree of predictive probability for the model.

Table 3 provides the logit regression results, including the parameter estimates and test of the estimates for all thirteen variables along with data for the three preferred variables. Observe first that all of the coefficients on the variables except two of the Carnegie classification dummies are significant at the 1% level.[6]

Findings of Interest to College Development Officers

Table 3 shows that each of the three variables chosen to represent principal factors are significantly different from zero at the 1% level. These variables are: (1) (ALCOST/ENROLL) representing fund-raising effort. (2) (OTHCOST/ENROLL) for resource availability, and (3) (PLANGIV/ENROLL) for donor wealth. Moreover, the same three variables, along with the Carnegie classifications, are the only ones with significant coefficients when all 13 variables are included.

Recall that the dependent variable is a response probability to be modeled. In this study, it is the expected ratio of alumni donors to alumni of record for each school. The results show that the reduced factor analytic model is as successful in predicting which schools are likely to have above average alumni participation as the full variable model.

Our earlier discriminant analysis revealed that the factor, fund-raising effort discriminates between low- and high-donation schools with the greatest magnitude. This is consistent with the large, significant, and positive relationship between alumni costs per full-time student enrolled and the ratio of donors to alumni of record shown in Table 3. This is the most striking result of our study: that expenditures on alumni activities have greatest significance in explaining success for this sample of schools.

What are the activities for which these *alumni costs* are incurred? They are informational activities for alumni such as plans and activities of the school, promotion of contacts among alumni, and encouragement of alumni to participate in school affairs. We learn from CASE's guidelines that such activities include alumni records maintenance; alumni newsletters; promoting membership in clubs; participation in events such as reunions and committee meetings; organizing alumni travel, job placement, non-credit instructional programs; and recognition of alumni.

Our second major finding is that expenditures on "other" development activities is negatively related to success in securing a higher participation rate among alumni. *Other relations costs* relate to non-alumni. According to CASE, these include, ". . . the general public, parents, faculty, staff, students, elected and appointed officials, church groups (in the case of church-affiliated institutions), and the business community." The objective of these activities is to cultivate support among all of these groups.

This finding that other activities have a significant negative impact on alumni participation suggests that alumni expenditures are more likely to be substitutes for rather than complements to costs of other constituent relations. Our personal contacts with some of the schools in our sample found very low staffing levels with tendencies to specialize and concentrate limited resources on particular constituencies.

Fund-raising costs are associated with activities to secure private gifts of all types and for all purposes occurring in the development office, athletic associations, academic units, fund-raising consortia, and other affiliates of the school. These include contracts for external services; fund-raising events such as dinners, auctions, phonathons, and concerts; and research and cultivation of donor prospects. Also included are production and distribution of fund-raising literature, expenses for volunteer groups, and tangible recognition of donors.

Surprisingly, our schools exhibit no significant relationship between fund-raising activities and percentage of alumni of record contributing. Although our study shows a significant net dollar return to fund-raising activities, alumni contacts providing information and recognition on a continuing basis are seen as far more important to participation than intermittent festivals and special fund raisers.

Planned giving (bequests) is negatively and significantly related to the alumni participation rate, both in the full equation model and the factor analytic model. This is not surprising, given the formal nature of many contracts between donor and school. Though bequests reveal wealth and are often an indicator of sizable annual gifts from some alumni, bequests act to reduce the number of annual gifts. Planned giving can provide the donor with income for life, a charitable income tax deduction and a way to avoid capital gains taxes. In the circumstances, many alumni making bequests are likely to forego annual giving.

In general, *private schools* in our sample revealed a significantly better participation rate than did *public* schools. However, being identified as a *research/doctoral public* school raised the probability that alumni of record would donate. Our sample is small, however; only three schools with eight data observations were identified as *research/doctoral public*.

TABLE 3

Logit Regression Results for Full-variable and Factor Analytic Models A Response Probability Model: Ratio of Donors to Alumni of Record

Variable	Full-Variable Model*	Factor-Analyte Model*
Intercept	−4.617	−3.834
	1.689	1.258
EG/ENROLL	−0.004	
	0.006	
FRCOST/ENROLL	−0.254	
	0.615	
ALCOST/ENROLL	5.410	7.158
	1.161	0.616
OTHCOST/ENROLL	−0.732	−1.685
	0.736	0.435
ENDOW/ENROLL	−0.003	
	0.002	
ALUGIV/ENROLL	−1.210	
	6.503	
OTHIND/ENROLL	−1.172	
	6.494	
ORGGIV/ENROLL	−1.529	
	6.488	
CURROPNS/ENROLL	1.382	
	6.481	
CAPSUPP/ENROLL	1.484	
	6.488	
CORPMAT/ENROLL	3.659	
	2.040	
PLANGIV/ENROLL	−0.265	−0.039
	0.079	0.012
PROPGIV/ENROLL	0.187	
	0.280	
RSDOCPUB	0.785	0.580
	0.285	0.207
COMPPUB	0.061	−0.153
	0.336	0.268
RSDOCPRV	0.430	0.229
	0.296	0.206
COMPPRV	0.583	0.440
	0.302	0.222
LBARTPRV	0.630	0.850
	0.247	0.190
Model chi-square ratio test**	460.838	412.382
Association of predicted probabilities and observed responses	0.675	0.667
(percentage concordant pairs among 1360 × 3740)		
Number of donors relative to a base of 5100 alumni of record	1360.000	1360.000
(51 schools and a base of 100 per school)		
Number of non-donors per 100 × 51	3740.000	3740.000

*Standard errors are listed below each coefficient.

**Chi-square statistic significant at 0.01 level.

Calculating a Change in Participation Rate for a Particular School

Logistic Procedure, as explained above, provides predicted proportions of alumni at each school in our sample who would donate to their school. Table 3 provides a logit regression model developed from the "preferred" variables of the factor analytic model for each school and a dependent variable which is the ratio of that school's donors to alumni of record. With the regression coefficients derived from all of the schools, logistic procedure calculates a predicted alumni participation ratio for each school which can then be compared with its actual rate.

How might a development office influence participation? Consider a change in one of the variables. *Alumni Costs*, for example. Let's use from Table 3 the coefficient on *Alumni Costs per F.T.E.* to calculate the effect on the alumni participation rate at one of our research/doctoral public universities from an increase of say $10.00 in alumni expenditures per student.[7]

Recall that the natural log (Y) of a schools (i) alumni participation rate (P) is a linear function of the change in the log of the participation rate (X) when alumni cost per student changes:

In symbolic terms:

$$Log_e(P_{i1}/(1 - P_{i1})) = Y_1 \pm X_i = Y_2,$$

and

$$\text{Anti Log } Y_2/(1 + \text{Anti Log } Y_2) = P_{i2}$$

and

$$\Delta P_i = P_{i2} - P_{i1}$$

In numerical terms:

$$Log_e(0.25067/0.74933) = -1.09504 + 0.071575 = -1.02347.$$

and

$$\text{Anti Log}_e(-1.02347) = 0.35935/1.35935 = 0.26436.$$

and

$$0.26436 - 0.25067 = 0.014.$$

Consequently, a ten dollar change in this university's alumni relations expenditures per full time equivalent student could increase the alumni participation ratio from about 25% to about 26.4%.

Implications for Development Officers

Use of these parameters, such as the logit change of 0.071575 used above, is based on our particular sample and historical time period of observations. It would not be so useful therefore to use these coefficients to predict a particular school's outcome from future alumni relations expenditures. A better procedure for the school development officer assisted by a statistician would involve building their own model along lines of ours but with their own historical time series data or with current cross-section data from a consortium of peer schools.

Development officers though they may recognize special factors in their own schools that lead to donation results quite different from our schools experience can nonetheless apply our methodology to their own data.

Table 4 lists the predicted proportions of alumni at each school for a given year who would contribute to that school. These predictions are based on the logit regression model of Table 3.

An index of "efficiency" is constructed as the actual ratio of the donor alumni percentage for each school to the predicted response rate of donors for that school. Any index above 100% implies that the school is performing well or at least better than the limited factor-logit model would predict.

Summary and Conclusion

The inclusion of fund-raising and college relations costs in studies of how schools influence alumni gift decisions is of paramount importance. A pre-pondereance of education philanthropy research has focused on the characteristics of donors. Investigating the recipients roles in giving to higher education has been limited generally to institutional characteristics.

In collecting and merging both institutional characteristics and college expenditure data this study makes possible a more comprehensive explanation of how colleges influence giving. In terms of the statistical analysis performed here the most influential variables on the school side were identified, and cross-section models were developed from 18 schools' data for three years. These models go a long way toward explaining why smaller or larger proportions of alumni donate to their schools.

Facilitated by factor analysis, thirteen variables—each one uniquely related to each school—were reduced to a set of three groups of variables. Within groups, homogeneity is indicated by the high degree of intercorrelation among cross-section variables. This procedure allowed selection of one variable from each group and, in consequence, the reduction of variables from thirteen to three. The analysis suggested that a generalized identity could be ascribed to each of the three groups and that each group could be proxied by a selected variable. Based on the variables contained, the three groups were identified as: Fund-Raising Effort, Resource Use, and Donor Wealth.

A logistic model was then used to predict the proportion of any school's alumni of record that would make a donation to the school. The observed response—a school's actual percentage of alumni who were donors in any one of the three years under study—was compared to the predicted percentage of donors giving to that school for that particular year as computed by the model. Consistent with the factor analysis procedure, logit analysis performed equally as well with a single-variable-per-factor model as with use of all thirteen variables.

The three-factor analytic variables used to predict the number of donors per 100 alumni of record were alumni costs per full-time equivalent student, other college relations costs per student, and planned giving per student. Each of these variables' coefficients were significant at the 0.01 level of statistical significance.

The effectiveness of the model's predicting ability was only slightly enhanced by adding the school Carnegie classifications. These were added to the logit model as dummy variables on which the coefficients were significant at the 1% level for research, doctoral-granting public schools and liberal arts private schools and significant at the 5% level for comprehensive private schools.

This study has provided useful knowledge about particular results of college and university spending on alumni relations and fund-raising activities. The findings fail to support any null hypothesis that such expenditures have little influence on the number of giving alumni relative to total number of alumni.

Besides analysis of participation, similar analysis is needed to discover the distinguishing characteristics of high-dollar gift schools and low-dollar gift schools. As more information is developed relative to college and university characteristics and behavior, development units on campuses may discover more effective ways to generate philanthropic responses.

Acknowledgements—The author acknowledges with appreciation the contributions and assistance of the following: David R. Morgan, Director of Research: Council for Aid to Education. Mary Joan McCarthy, Vice President, Educational Fund Raising; Council for Advancement and Support of Education. Alfred University. Asbury Theological Seminary. Ball State University. Baylor College of Medicine. Berea College. Briar Cliff College. Georgia Tech Foundation, Inc. Hampden-Sydney

TABLE 4

Logit Probabilities That Alumni Will Give and Efficiency Indexes of Schools

School and Carnegie Class	1986%				1987%				1988%			
	Full Model	Limited Model	Actual Ratio	Index	Full Model	Limited Model	Actual Ratio	Index	Full Model	Limited Model	Actual Ratio	Index
106	30	31	51	1.65	33	35	31	0.89	29	30	25	0.83
201	22	23	26	1.13	23	24	26	1.08	23	24	26	1.08
308	7	8	9	1.13	5	7	5	0.71	6	7	7	1.00
407	53	45	60	1.33	72	58	67	1.16	56	55	63	1.15
506	19	21	15	0.71	20	21	17	0.81	19	21	14	0.67
602	12	12	2	0.17	12	12	5	0.42	12	12	10	0.83
705	16	15	18	1.20	16	16	18	1.13	16	16	22	1.38
805	33	36	30	0.83	34	35	30	0.86	31	36	32	0.89
906	28	28	27	0.96	24	23	27	1.17	37	32	31	0.97
1006	27	27	29	1.07	27	27	27	1.00	30	27	29	1.07
1102	12	12	16	1.33	12	12	22	1.83	12	12	16	1.33
1207	18	20	10	0.50	18	19	16	0.84	21	18	18	1.00
1307	41	44	43	0.98	23	31	23	0.74	23	30	23	0.77
1401	37	36	31	0.86	39	36	37	1.03	40	35	39	1.11
1507	44	41	45	1.10	50	55	50	0.91	42	46	43	0.93
1605	25	18	25	1.39	24	18	25	1.39	24	18	24	1.33
1705									35	46	31	0.67
1801	23	25	24	0.96	24	25	20	0.80				

College. University of Detroit Mercy. Pomona College. Rensselaer Polytechnic Institute. Saginaw Valley State College. Texas Christian University. The University of Chicago. The University of Georgia. University of North Carolina at Asheville. University of Pennsylvania. University of Richmond.

Notes

1. The Council for Aid to Education, Inc. is a non-profit organization which promotes financial and advisory aid from business enterprise in support of education at all levels.
2. The Carnegie Foundation for the Advancement of Teaching classifies four-year colleges into eight classifications, public and private: Research/Doctoral, Comprehensive, Liberal Arts, and Specialized.
3. In our earlier study (Yoo and Harrison, 1989), we found that schools for which we had data were reluctant to have these statistics identified with them. In consequence, I have assured schools participating in this study that individual school data would not be revealed.
4. I assume that (1) there is a causal relationship linking the limited number of factors to each of the numerous observed institutional variables, and that (2) these variables are expressed as linear functions of at least one factor that is common to all variables and one factor that is uniquely associated with each variable. The SAS computational package produces factors based on correlations between variables. The highly correlated variables tend to be associated with the same factor.
5. The Statistical Analysis System (SAS), version 66, PROC FACTOR procedure was used to classify these variables. The model used is principal axis factor analysis with an equamax rotation technique and the number of factors equal to four.
6. In this version of the SAS *Logistic Procedure*, I use a model in which the dependent variable is a ratio of the number of events (Donors) to a number of trials (Alumni of Record). The score statistic gives a test for the joint significance of all of the explanatory variables in the model. The combined effect here of the independent variables is significant with a p value of 0.01. The -2LOG L statistic provides a Chi-Square test for the effects of the variables based on -2LOG Likelihood. Again, the combined effects of the variables are significant with $p = 0.01$.
7. Our coefficient of 7.158 on Alumni Costs per F.T.E., for example, represents the change in the log of the participation rate per $1,000 change in Alumni Cost per F.T.E. A $10.00 change converts the coefficient to 0.071575. This school's actual participation rate for the year was 0.25067.

References

Andreoni, J. and Scholz, J.K. (1990) An econometric analysis of charitable giving with interdependent preferences. Madison, Wisconsin: Social Systems Research Institute, Workshop Series, Paper No. 9023, University of Wisconsin.

Aug, M.A.C. (1987) Applying marketing principles to institutional advancement in higher education. Ph.D. dissertation, University of Pittsburg.

Becker, G.S. (1974) A theory of social interactions. *Journal of Political Economy* 82, 1063–1073.

Beeler, K.J. (1982) A study of predictors of alumni philanthropy in private universities. Ph.D. dissertation, University of Connecticut.

Boulding, K.E. (1962) Notes on a theory of philanthropy. In *Philanthropy and Public Policy* (Edited by Dickenson, F.G.). New York, 57–59.

Carlson, J. (1978) The role of alumni in the financial survival of independent education. Ed.D. dissertation, University of California, Los Angeles.

Clotfelder, C. and Feldstein, M. (1986) Tax incentives and charitable contributions in the U.S. *Journal of Public Economics* 29, 1–26.

Council for Advancement and Support of Education (1990) *Expenditures in Fund Raising. Alumni Relations, and Other Constituent (Public) Relations*. Washington, D.C.

Council for Financial Aid to Education (1986, 1987, 1988) *Voluntary Support of Education (1985–1986, 1986–1987, 1987–1988)*, New York.

Feldstein, M. (1975) The income tax and charitable contributions: Part 1—Aggregate and Distributional, *National Tax Journal* 28, 81–100.

Haddad, F.D. (1986) An analysis of the characteristics of alumni donors and non-donors at Butler University. Ed.D. dissertation. Butler University.

Heeman, W. (1979) (Ed.) New directions for institutional advancement. *Analyzing the Cost Effectiveness of Fund Raising*. San Francisco: Jossey-Bass.

Hochman, H.M. and Rodgers, J.D. (1973) Utility interdependence and income transfers through charity. In *Transfers in an Urbanized Economy* (Edited by BOULDING, K.E. *et al.*). Belmont, pp. 63–77.

Hood, R.D., Martin, S.A. and Osberg, L.S. (1977) Economic determinants of charitable donations in Canada. *Canadian Journal of Economics* 10, 653–677.

Kachigan, S.K. (1986) *Statistical Analysis*. New York: Radius Press.

Kelifr, M.J.C. (1982) An analysis of alumni donor and non-donor characteristics at the University of Montevallo. Ph.D. dissertation, University of Alabama.

Pickett, W.L. (1977) An assessment of the effectiveness of fund raising policies of private undergraduate colleges. Ph.D. dissertation, University of Denver.

Pindyck, R.S. and Rubinfeld, D.L. (1981) *Econometric Models and Economic Forecasts*, 2nd Edn. New York: McGraw-Hill Book Company.

Reece, W.S. (1979) Charitable contributions: new evidence on household behavior. *American Economic Review* 69, 142–151.

Schwartz, R.A. (1970) Personal philanthropic contributions. *Journal of Political Economy* 78, 1264–1291.

Scort, R.H. (1972) Avarice, altruism and second party preferences, *Quarterly Journal of Economics* 86, 1–18.

Shadoian, H.L. (1989) A study of predictors of alumni philanthropy in public colleges. Ph.D. dissertation, The University of Connecticut.

Woods, J.L. (1987) Factors associated with gift income in public research and doctoral granting universities. Ph.D. dissertation, Washington State University.

Yankelovich, D. (1987) Bridging the gap. *CASE Currents*. Washington: Council for Advancement and Support of Education, October.

Yoo, J.H. and Harrison, W.B. (1989) Altruism in the market for giving and receiving: a case of higher education. *Economics of Education Review*, Vol. 8, No. 4.

WINNING AND GIVING: FOOTBALL RESULTS AND ALUMNI GIVING AT SELECTIVE PRIVATE COLLEGES AND UNIVERSITIES

SARAH E. TURNER, LAUREN A. MESERVE, & WILLIAM G. BOWEN

Objective. Our central question is how changes in an institution's football success affect giving behavior. Also, we consider whether former varsity athletes are more or less sensitive in their giving behavior than other alumni to the competitive success of their school and whether such effects differ by type of institution. *Methods.* Using micro data from 15 academically selective private colleges and universities, the analysis presents fixed-effects estimates of how football winning percentages affect giving behavior. *Results.* General giving rates are unaffected by won-lost records at the high-profile Division IA schools and at the Ivy League schools. Increases in winning percentages yield modest positive increases in giving rates, particularly among former athletes, at the lower-profile Division III liberal arts colleges. *Conclusions.* While there is a modest positive effect at Division III colleges, our results do not support the notion that winning and giving go hand-in-hand at the selective private universities that play big-time football.

Intercollegiate athletics is expensive, especially at universities that support big-time programs. Notre Dame and Stanford reported total expenditures ranging from $30 to $36 million for fiscal year 1997–1998. Even in the Ivy League, where no athletic scholarships are given, annual expenditures on intercollegiate athletics generally exceed $10 million; Division III liberal arts colleges such as Kenyon and Williams spend between $2 and $3 million fielding intercollegiate teams.[1] There are other kinds of "costs" as well, including both the effects of scandals and alleged abuses on institutional reputations and the opportunity cost involved in admitting recruited athletes in lieu of other applicants who might take fuller advantage of the academic opportunities offered by the schools. The offsetting benefits that are thought to justify these costs include large presumed financial returns to the most successful football and basketball programs; the pleasure of competing; positive effects on school spirit; stronger ties to alumni as well as local communities; and increased visibility for the school. Increasingly, however, scholars and critics have raised questions about whether these programs are worth what they cost.[2]

An important element of this debate focuses on the effects of intercollegiate athletics on support by alumni, who are a critically important constituency at these schools, even though they are not the only source of donations. In particular, it is important to know if what Noll (1999) refers to as "the high cost of winning" can be justified simply in terms of increased donations from alumni. Although there have been perhaps a dozen studies of this question, the behavioral evidence has been limited by the availability of data and the difficulty in identifying exogenous changes in giving behavior. With access to a rich new database (described below) that provides a wealth of information about individual schools and the actual or potential donors who attended these schools, we are in a position to answer some very basic queries more definitively than has been possible before. Our claim, then, is not that we are posing an entirely new set of questions, but that we are able to provide some new answers as a result of new evidence.

The principal questions that we explore are (1) Do variations in the won-lost records of the most visible athletic teams affect the percentage of graduates who make general gifts (the "general giving rate")? (2) Does variation in won-lost records affect the amount that donors contribute for general purposes? (3) How are "athletic giving rates" (percentages of graduates who make gifts specifically for athletics) and the amounts given to athletics affected by won-lost records? In addition to these standard questions, we also explore two new questions: (4) In their giving behavior, are former varsity athletes more or less sensitive than other former students to the competitive success of their school? (5) Are graduates of schools that sponsor big-time, Division IA programs more or less sensitive to won-lost records than graduates of schools with the lower-profile programs found in the Ivy League and Division III liberal arts colleges?

Access to the College and Beyond[3] database provides considerable new information to address these questions. In particular, these data allow us to "tag" former athletes, that is, to look at their giving patterns separately from the giving patterns of other graduates. Data for 15 private institutions that compete at three very different levels of athletic intensity permit direct comparisons of "winning and giving" relationships at these different levels of athletic intensity. Five of the 15 are universities that compete actively in big-time collegiate sports at the NCAA Division IA level (Duke, Notre Dame, Northwestern, Rice, and Vanderbilt); four are members of the NCAA Division IAA Ivy League (Columbia, University of Pennsylvania, Princeton, and Yale); the remaining six are liberal arts colleges that compete in NCAA Division III (Denison, Hamilton, Oberlin, Swarthmore, Wesleyan, and Williams).

To be sure, these 15 institutions are far from representative of higher education, in that all of them are both private and academically selective. Different patterns might well be found at other types of institutions. Also, some might argue that intercollegiate athletics matter much less at the Ivies and the Division III colleges than they do at the "big-time" schools. But recent experiences and a new study rebut this proposition. The high-decibel controversy at Swarthmore sparked by that school's decision to drop football illustrates vividly the powerful emotions associated with athletics at even this highly "academic" liberal arts college. More generally, the widely quoted empirical findings in Shulman and Bowen (2001) demonstrate that athletics has a more important overall impact on many of the smaller colleges than it does on an institution such as the University of Michigan.[4] An additional reason for studying these schools is that alumni giving is a particularly compelling subject in schools where alumni-driven private philanthropy subsidizes a substantial share of total costs. Such schools have reason to be highly sensitive to factors affecting their overall level of private support and to be aware that a dollar given to support the football team could be a dollar that otherwise might have gone to the library.

In focusing solely on donations by individual alumni, we miss effects of winning athletic programs on contributions by "boosters" and other non-alumni. This omission is in large measure unavoidable, in that there are no systematic data on these other sources of donations. In any case, anecdotal evidence suggests that "boosters" are rarely major sources of donations for general purposes and are often less important to athletic programs than one might suspect.[5]

Why Might Winning Affect Giving?

Economists and other social scientists tend to begin with the basic question of why success (or failure) on the playing field should be expected to affect alumni giving. One explanation, following earlier work on enrollment and application behavior, is that success on the playing field creates exceptionally good publicity for the college or university (McCormick and Tinsley, 1987). This "advertising effect" might be thought to raise the profile of a college or university relative to other potential candidates for charitable giving, thus increasing the likelihood that alumni read and respond to solicitations from the college or university. Individuals may also see success on the playing field as a direct reflection of the extent to which administrators and trustees are preserving the "quality" of their alma mater. Whereas alumni may lose track of changes in the faculty, the state of the core curriculum, or the amenities in college dorm rooms, scores and standings permeate the media. For some graduates, these results may be the subject of idle conversation; for others, a losing season may stimulate intense reactions, including even threats to "never make another gift." The sign of such effects is not, however, unambiguously clear. Some individuals might see success on the athletic field (especially if it is associated with scandals of one kind or another) as a degradation of a school's academic reputation, whereas others may see athletic success as a straightforward indication of institutional "competence" and ability to achieve results in every kind of arena.

Another explanation considers the role played by the ancillary "benefits" of giving—such as preferred seats in the football stadium, opportunities to hobnob with coaches, or parking privileges at basketball games—all of which become more valuable as a consequence of winning. In this context, "giving" is really a form of "consuming," and the effects of a change in athletic fortunes might be particularly evident in giving that is restricted to athletics (e.g., donations to varsity clubs and the like).

Winning seasons could also affect giving behavior indirectly through what might be called the "bundling" programs of schools. That is, schools often schedule a variety of events on the same weekends that home football games are played. The prospect of a strong showing on the football field may encourage alumni to come back to campus and participate in a variety of programs, some initiated or sponsored by the fund-raising office.

Results from Other Research

Far more has been written about the purported link between athletic success and alumni giving than is justified by the available empirical evidence. A wide array of researchers, including both economists and others, have examined the question, and they have reported empirical results that, on the whole, are far from conclusive. An earlier summary of the available research by Frey (1985) notes six studies of alumni giving showing no effects of athletic performance and three identifying a positive relationship.

Among the studies widely cited in this literature are the studies of giving behavior at Division IA schools by Sigelman and Carter (1979), Brooker and Klastorin (1981), and Sigelman and Bookheimer (1983). Sigelman and Carter (1979) examined a series of repeated cross-sectional regressions and found little relation between athletic success and giving. Brooker and Klastorin (1981) estimated regressions pooled over time and found a positive and significant relationship between football success and alumni giving, particularly in private schools. Sigelman and Bookheimer (1983) revisited the question with a particular focus on athletic giving at 57 big-time programs and concluded that football success is a strong determinant of voluntary contributions to athletic programs. However, Sigelman and Bookheimer (1983), as well as Coughlin and Erekson (1985), are unable to distinguish between contributions made by alumni to athletics and those made by others without connections to the institutions.

This body of research is limited in several respects. First, as noted by Baade and Sundberg (1996a), the focus on Division IA schools presents an incomplete picture of the relationship between winning and giving, as other types of colleges and universities make substantial investments in athletic programs, particularly football. Moreover, many of the previous empirical analyses are methodologically suspect because of their overreliance on cross-sectional variation—differences in football performance across institutions at a point in time—to identify the parameter of interest. Although it is possible to include a set of explanatory variables to control for observed differences in the academic standing and athletic emphasis of institutions, there are substantial differences in the general willingness of alumni to give that remain unmeasured. To the extent that these unmeasured or omitted factors may be correlated with athletic performance, estimates relying on cross-sectional variation may be biased and inconsistent.

Data Used in This Study

The individual-level data used in this analysis include alumni giving records compiled for 15,351 full-time students who entered the 15 colleges and universities in this study (listed earlier) in the fall of 1976. Data were provided by each school, and gifts were divided into two categories: those restricted to athletics ("athletic giving") and all other gifts (which we group together as "general giving"). The giving data span the 10-year period beginning in the 1988–89 academic year and ending with 1997–1998.[6] Won-lost records provided by sports information offices were matched to individual giving records for each of these years. That is, the 1997 fall football winning percentage was matched to giving during the 1997–1998 fiscal year, for example.

Although we were able to collect detailed won-lost records for both football and men's basketball, we use only the won-lost records for the football teams in the final regressions presented below. At the majority of schools in the study, alumni are most likely to be aware of the success (or failure) of the football team. Duke, with its highly successful basketball program, is clearly an exception. Recognizing that success in basketball as well as football is important at a number of institutions, we included won-lost records for both football and men's basketball in earlier work. The results were unaffected, however, by adding basketball, and so we elected to simplify the exposition by presenting the results for football only.

The actual and potential donors included in the study consist of all members of the 1976 entering cohorts at the 15 schools in the College and Beyond database participating in this study. We have focused our analysis on the 1976 entering cohort primarily because roughly 20 years have passed since this cohort graduated from college. Thus, a sufficiently long time has passed for them to have settled into jobs and established giving patterns, which we are able to observe over the 10 years for which we have giving records.

This unusual data set, comprised of extensive micro data, offers several notable advantages over the more commonly used institutional aggregates. First, we are able to examine the behavior of a well-defined cohort of same-age contributors rather than a changing mix of "old" and "young" classes. Second, identifying gifts with individual donors allows us to avoid the commingling of individual gifts with gifts from corporate or foundation sources that often confounds the interpretation of institutional aggregates. Third, as already noted, these data allow us to distinguish general giving from athletic giving, thus permitting us to determine if athletic giving is more (or less) sensitive to competitive success than giving in general. Finally, the detailed demographic information that is in the database allows us to see if the giving of particular types of individuals (such as former athletes) is especially responsive to changes in athletic performance.

Framing the Analysis

To examine the relationship between athletic success and the giving behavior of alumni, it is desirable to observe variation in athletic fortunes over time, not just across institutions at a point in time. Fortunately, from the standpoint of the objectives of this study, the degree of athletic success at nearly all of the schools that we observe has in fact varied substantially over the 10 years for which we have giving data. For example, one season in which the football program at the University of Pennsylvania won only 2 of 10 games is balanced by several perfect seasons. Even teams with widely known histories of athletic success, such as the Notre Dame football program, experienced relative ups and downs over this interval, with Notre Dame football experiencing both a perfect season and a season in which it won only slightly more than half its games.

Giving behavior is less one-dimensional than won-lost records. Development officers are concerned with both participation rates—the share of any group of former students who make contributions—and the total amount of dollars contributed. Participation rates are often thought to be important indicators of "connection" to the university or college and also as important precursors of giving patterns later in life. In this regard, young alumni are sometimes encouraged to make token gifts (e.g., $19.99 for those graduating in 1999) so that they may begin a habit of giving back. Thus, we look at both giving rates and the overall level of giving.[7]

General giving rates are not so different across the three athletic divisions included in our study. The Division III liberal arts colleges did modestly better as a group (with 32 percent of men and 33 percent of women making contributions) than either the Ivies (26 percent for men and 30 percent for women) or the Division IA private universities (28 percent for men and 25 percent for women). Average athletic giving rates are low everywhere but slightly higher in the Ivies than in the other

TABLE 1

Means of Winning and Giving Variables

	Division IA (Universities)			Division IAA (Ivy)			Division III (Colleges)		
	N	Mean	SD	N	Mean	SD	N	Mean	SD
Men									
Football W%	50	0.44	0.27	40	0.54	0.26	52	0.43	0.31
General participation (%)	38,948	0.28	0.45	31,024	0.26	0.44	13,455	0.32	0.47
Athletic giving participation (%)		0.02	0.12		0.03	0.17		0.01	0.11
Average general giving ($)		96	5764		131	3690		100	1051
Average athletic giving ($)		10	193		17	837		1	18
Women									
Football W%	50	0.44	0.27	29	0.64	0.22	52	0.43	0.31
General participation (%)	24,805	0.25	0.43	13,654	0.30	0.46	11,535	0.33	0.47
Athletic giving participation (%)		0.01	0.09		0.02	0.12		0.00	0.07
Average general giving ($)		166	17828		67	434		54	289
Average athletic giving ($)		6	361		2	67		0	4

The tabulations reflect data from 15 colleges and universities over 10 years (or as indicated), playing in three football divisions. In Division IA, we observe Duke University (89–98), University of Notre Dame (89–97), Northwestern University (89–97), Rice University (89–96), and Vanderbilt University (91–97). In Division IAA, we observe Columbia University (89–98), University of Pennsylvania (89–94, 96–98), Princeton University (89–98), and Yale University (89–96). In Division III, we observe Denison University (89–96), Hamilton College (95–98), Oberlin College (89–98), Swarthmore College (90–98), Wesleyan University (92–98), and Williams College (89–96).

divisions; overall, women graduates are as likely to be general givers as their male classmates (though usually making somewhat smaller gifts), but they are less likely to give to athletics. Table 1 summarizes average giving rates (general and athletic) and average dollar levels of giving (again, both general and athletic), by division, and separately for men and women graduates. Average won-lost percentages for football are also shown in this table.

The empirical analysis presents fixed-effects estimates of how football winning percentages affect the aggregate giving behavior for each group of institutions, as well as for subsets of students within each group. Explicitly, with y_{it} as the measure of giving behavior at institution i in year t, we estimate the relationship:

$$y_{it} = \mu_i + \lambda_t + \sum_k \beta_k D_k F_{it} + \epsilon_{it}$$

where the μ_i are the institution fixed effects, λ_t are year-specific effects, and the parameters β_k indicate the relationship between football performance (F) and giving behavior for a school in athletic division k, where D_k are dummy variables indicating the division in which a school's football program competes. The institution-specific fixed effects capture dimensions of institutional culture and resources that are unlikely to vary appreciably over time. Football performance (F_{it}) is measured by the percentage of games a team won in a given season. We distinguish the effects of athletic success according to the level of NCAA competition by including interactions between winning percentage and dummy variables (D_k) indicating division of competition (Division IA, Division IAA, or Division III). This approach yields what are, in effect, separate measures of the sensitivity of giving to winning by division.

Regression analysis with a straightforward fixed-effects model (which is computationally equivalent to including a dummy variable for each of the 15 institutions) provides a formal test of the underlying relationship between winning and giving. Year-to-year changes in the winning percentage of an institution's football team are used to predict changes in aggregate measures of giving behavior. In addition, we include a full set of year-specific dummy variables that are intended to pick up the effects of any broad events that might have affected all institutions in a particular year (such as the timing of major reunions, which were the same for members of the 1976 entering cohorts at all of our schools). We also include a "Campaign" dummy variable that indicates whether an institution was conducting a major fund-raising campaign during the year in question, and we have experimented with other measures varying over time within institutions that might plausibly affect contributions.[8]

We focus this analysis on variations over time within specified institutions, because the effects of unobserved variables are particularly likely to plague cross-sectional regressions. In seeking to analyze differences in contributions across colleges and universities at a single point in time, it may be very difficult to separate the effects of differences in athletic performance from the effects of other institution-specific factors that are correlated with athletic success and difficult for researchers to observe. The direction of causation can also be hard to discern: Do schools with winning athletic programs attract students who go on to be highly successful in their professions and therefore generous to the school, or do schools with generous alumni have more successful athletic programs in part because of the wealth and influence of their graduates? Even in studying giving behavior over time within the confines of a single institution, it may be difficult to disentangle the effects of changes in won-lost records from changes in other external factors, but at least more things are reasonably constant (Notre Dame is still Notre Dame). Our central question is how changes in an institution's athletic fortunes affect giving behavior, not the more general subject of the relationship between individual characteristics and giving behavior, which is studied more appropriately using cross-sectional analysis.

Findings

Contrary to much of the mythology about winning and giving, we find no relationship of any kind between won-lost records in football and general giving rates at either the Division IA universities that operate high-profile programs or among the Ivies (Table 2, column 1). The general giving coefficient for the Division III schools, on the other hand, is positive and statistically significant. The apparent impact of even a substantial change in competitive results would be described by some as relatively modest. The coefficient of .050 implies that an increase in the winning percentage of .5 (moving from a 50–50 record to an unbeaten season) is associated with an increase in the general giving rate of 2.5 percentage points—which is, however, equivalent to roughly an 8 percent increase in the share of graduates making a donation. We believe we understand why—contrary to what one might have expected to find—football victories are more consequential for giving rates in Division III than elsewhere, but we defer a discussion of the forces at work until later in the article.

Changes in won-lost records at the Division IA schools and in the Ivies also have no discernible effect on athletic giving rates (Table 2, column 2). In the case of the Division III colleges, there appears to be a negative association between changes in won-lost records and (athletic) giving rates, but the overall frequency of athletic giving at these colleges is so low (with only 1 percent of all members of the 1976 cohort making an athletic gift in a typical year) that we do not attach any real meaning to this relationship.

When we do a parallel analysis and focus not on giving rates but on the amounts given, there is only one significant result that deserves consideration (Table 2, column 3). Improvements in Division IA football performance are associated with an average *decline* of more than $200 per person in general giving.[9] There is not, however, an offsetting increase in athletic contributions; we observe no significant association at any level of competition between won-lost records and athletic contributions (Table 2, column 4).

The patterns just described can be understood much better when we interact changes in football won-lost records with a key variable available to us from the College and Beyond database: whether the potential donor did or did not play on an intercollegiate team in college (which we refer to simply as prior athletic participation).

Although it is common to think of football as a "men's" sport, gender plays virtually no role in determining giving participation or amount.[10] On the other hand, giving behavior is definitely influenced by status as a former athlete. The athletic-participation component of the systematic variation of giving behavior and football performance is shown in Table 3. Improvements in the performance of the football team clearly increase the propensity to give for those who participated in varsity athletics as undergraduates. Among former athletes from the Ivy League schools and Division III colleges, participation in general giving increases. Among Division IA athletes, on the other hand, it is participation in athletic giving that increases, with former athletes from Division IAA also responding positively to athletic success.

A key finding: There is no statistically significant association between football won-lost records and the general giving rates for *any* group of nonathletes—those members of the cohort who did not play on intercollegiate teams, regardless of gender or the division in which they competed (Table 3, column 1). The positive relationship between winning and giving rates found in the data for Division III does not appear among the nonathletes who attended these schools.

TABLE 2

Fixed Effects Estimates of the Effect of Football Performance on Giving, College and Beyond Data, 1976 Cohort and Giving Years 1989–1998

	Giving Rate		Giving Level	
	General (1)	Athletic (2)	General (3)	Athletic (4)
Football (% W)*Div IA	–0.01	0.00	–270.00**	–2.90
	(0.02)	(0.00)	(79.91)	(5.09)
Football (% W)*Div IAA	0.01	0.01	–26.05	–1.48
	(0.02)	(0.00)	(81.95)	(5.22)
Football (% W)*Div III	0.05*	–0.01**	56.26	1.88
	(0.03)	(0.00)	(98.62)	(6.28)
Campaign dummy	0.02**	0.00	19.36	2.65*
	(0.01)	(0.00)	(22.20)	(1.41)
R^2	.15	.13	.22	.16

Each regression includes 125 institution-year observations, representing 15 institutions; see Table 1 for data availability. Each regression includes a constant and fixed effects for individual institutions and years. The reported R^2 measures reflect the share of the within-institution variation over the time explained in the model.

* indicates significance at the 10% level; ** indicates significance at the 5% level.

TABLE 3

Fixed Effects Estimates of the Effect of Football Performance on Giving by Athletes and Other Students, College and Beyond Data, 1976 Cohort and Giving Years 1989–1998

	General Level		Giving Level	
	General (1)	Athletic (2)	General (3)	Athletic (4)
Football (% W)*Athlete*Div IA	−0.02	0.06**	−117.63**	33.60**
	(0.03)	(0.03)	(54.51)	(17.05)
Football (% W)* Athlete*Div IAA	0.06**	0.10**	10.96	39.26
	(0.03)	(0.03)	(55.39)	(17.32)
Football (% W)* Athlete*Div III	0.15**	0.00	41.87	6.88
	(0.03)	(0.03)	(65.73)	(20.55)
Football (% W)*Not Ath*Div IA	−0.02	−0.05	−144.09**	−2.11
	(0.03)	(0.03)	(54.51)	(17.05)
Football (% W)*Not Ath*Div IAA	−0.01	−0.07**	−50.77	−17.21
	(0.03)	(0.03)	(55.39)	(17.32)
Football (% W)*Not Ath*Div III	0.01	−0.03	18.27	6.20
	(0.03)	(0.03)	(65.73)	(20.55)
Campaign dummy	0.02**	0.01	17.29	8.70**
	(0.01)	(0.01)	(14.24)	(4.45)
R^2	.34	.41	.12	.21

Each regression includes 250 institution-year athletic status observations, representing 15 institutions; see Table 1 for data availability. Each regression includes a constant and fixed effects for individual institutions and year. The reported R^2 measures reflect the share of the within-institution variation over the time explained in the model.

* indicates significance at the 10% level; ** indicates significance at the 5% level.

Our interpretation of this clear pattern is that the athletes at the Division III liberal arts colleges identify most strongly with their schools, following success and failure on the playing field more closely than students from other types of institutions. As such, these alumni are more inclined to adjust their general gifts to success and failure than are the former athletes who participated in the big-time programs at the Division IA schools and the men who played sports in the Ivy League.[11] It is also true that former athletes, men and women, comprise *much* higher proportions of the student bodies of the Division III liberal arts colleges than they do of the student bodies at the Division IA schools. Harkening back to the overall relationship between winning and giving at the Division III colleges that we described earlier, we now see that it is the former athletes who drive these results. Their giving behavior has a strong impact because of the combination of their greater sensitivity to won-lost records and their much larger presence in the student bodies of these colleges.

Improving won-lost records *depressed* general giving levels among nonathletes at Division IA schools; the coefficients are significant and far from trivial in size. Some graduates may assume (erroneously, in almost all instances) that winning football teams generate so much revenue that they don't need to make as large a gift as they would have made otherwise. We know from other data that nonathletes at these schools believe that intercollegiate athletics is, if anything, overemphasized (Shulman and Bowen, 2001:204), and it is possible that better results by the football team feed this impression and then lead to resentment and to reduced giving. A related possibility is that some nonathletes may have taken genuine pride in the fact that their school was *not* an athletic power and may then have interpreted greater success on the field as an indication that values have changed and that their school is not the same place that they attended. Whatever the underlying explanation, it is the behavior of these nonathletes that is driving the negative coefficient for the amount of giving at the Division IA schools that we reported in Table 2.

The second aspect of these results is the negative impact of winning on general giving levels among the male athletes who attended Division IA schools. A different explanation for this relationship is required, and it may be found in Table 3 (column 4), which focuses on levels of *athletic* giving. Whereas winning has no impact on the average amount given to athletics by nonathletes, it has a clearly positive effect on the size of athletic gifts made by former athletes from Division IA schools (men and women alike). The combination of these positive effects of winning on the size of athletic gifts and the negative effects on the size of general gifts is consistent with the view that some shifting of gifts is occurring. That is, the reduced level of general giving by former Division IA athletes may be explained, at least in part, by their increased support of athletics (Table 3, columns 3 and 4).[12]

Conclusions

In assessing the arguments for and against the large investments in intercollegiate athletics generally thought to be necessary in order to produce winning teams, there is no evidence to suggest that "paybacks" will come in the form of enhanced generosity by alumni. It is, of course, entirely possible that the relationship between alumni giving and success on the football field follows a more complex dynamic path than the simple model we are able to explore with our data. Although we have experimented with the introduction of simple lag structures (and obtained no different results), we are not able to explore questions such as whether a decade of poor performance on the gridiron would have a larger effect on alumni support than intermittent years of poor performance. Nonetheless, the evidence presented in this article seems sufficiently robust to put to rest the notion that winning and giving go hand in hand at the selective private universities that play big-time football. Our results suggest that, in fact, there is a stronger positive relationship between football performance and giving among Division III colleges.

At the most competitive level (NCAA Division IA), our data suggest an even stronger conclusion: winning appears to have, if anything, a *negative* effect on the overall level of alumni support. The giving behavior of the great majority of the former students at these schools who were not themselves varsity athletes suggests that, overall, these graduates are likely to give less, not more, when the football team does better. And the graduates who were intercollegiate athletes as undergraduates show some tendency to substitute larger athletic gifts for general gifts when the won-lost record improves. Of course, as we have said, this analysis does not take account of gifts from local boosters and corporate sponsors. We would expect winning in big-time programs to lead to greater revenue from these sources.

An even more interesting story, at least from our perspective, is the very different picture that emerges from the winning and giving patterns at the Division III liberal arts colleges. Anyone tempted to downplay the role of intercollegiate athletics at the Division III level should ponder the evidence presented here. From the perspective of the frequency of alumni donations, winning actually turns out to be more important at these schools than at their much higher-profile counterparts. This result is really not so surprising when one thinks of both the institutional "bonding" effect of athletics, which is likely to be especially strong in these schools (leading many students who play sports to feel a closer identity to their schools than they would feel otherwise) and the relatively large number of undergraduates who play intercollegiate sports at the leading liberal arts colleges.

The positive relationship between winning and giving in the liberal arts colleges suggests that successful athletic programs may well encourage more of the former athletes who attended these schools to contribute. But there could also be a downside to this set of findings. The recruited athlete of today is the alumnus of tomorrow, and if this large group of potential donors regard winning as important, the pressures to continue to win may be very great. This might be fine if the school could respond to such pressures without incurring costs of various kinds, of which dollar costs may be the least important. But that is not the case.

References

Baade, Robert, and Jeffrey Sundberg. 1996a. "Fourth Down and Gold to Go? Assessing the Link between Athletics and Alumni Giving." *Social Science Quarterly* 77(4):75–81.

———. 1996b. "What Determines Alumni Generosity?" *Economics of Education Review* 15(1).75–81.

Bowen, William G., and Derek Bok. 1998. *The Shape of the River: Long-Term Consequences of Considering Race in College and University Admissions*. Princeton, NJ: Princeton University Press.

Brooker, George and T. Klostorin. 1981. "To the Victors Belong the Spoils? College Athletics and Alumni Giving." *Social Science Quarterly* 62(4):744–50.

Cough, Cletus, and O. Homer Erekson. 1985. "Contributions to Intercollegiate Athletic Programs: Further Evidence." *Social Science Quarterly* 66(March):194–202.

Cronin, Don. 2001. "Donations up since Louisville Hired Pitano." *USA Today* April 3, p. 1c.

Frey, James. 1985. "The Winning Team Myth." *Currents* (January):132.

Groen, Jeff, and Michelle White. 2001. "In-State versus Out-of-State Students: The Divergence of Interest between Public Universities and State Governments." Mimeo. University of Michigan.

McCormick, Robert, and Maurice Tinsley. 1987. "Athletics versus Academics? Evidence from SAT Scores." *Journal of Political Economy* 95(5):1103–16.

Menand, Louis. 2001. "Sporting Chances." *The New Yorker*, January 22, pp. 84–88.

Noll, Roger. 1999. "The Business of College Sports and the High Cost of Winning." *Milken Institute Review* (Fall):24–37.

Shulman, James, and William Bowen. 2001. *The Game of Life: College Sports and Educational Values*. Princeton, NJ: Princeton University Press.

Sigelman, Lee, and Samuel Bookheimer. 1983. "Is It Whether You Win or Lose? Monetary Contributions to Big-Time College Athletic Programs." *Social Science Quarterly* 64(June):347–59.

Sigelman, Lee, and Robert Carter. 1979. "Win One for the Giver? Alumni Giving and Big-Time College Sports." *Social Science Quarterly* 60:284–94.

Sperber, Murray. 2000. *Beer and Circus: How Big-Time College Sports Is Crippling Undergraduate Education*. Henry Holt & Company, Inc.

Zimbalist, Andrew. 1999. *Unpaid Professionals*. Princeton, NJ: Princeton University Press.

Notes

1. The figures for Notre Dame and Stanford are taken directly from reports filed by the schools under the Equity in Athletics Disclosure Act (EADA). Figures for the smaller programs are our estimates based on the EADA reports and other information. These figures underestimate true costs in that they ignore most if not all of the capital costs invested in athletic facilities.

2. One recent full-length study is Zimbalist (1999); see also Noll (1999). Sperber (2001) focuses on the problems of Division I athletics.

3. The College and Beyond database is a restricted access database that was built by the Andrew W. Mellon Foundation to facilitate study of various outcomes of the undergraduate education provided by academically selective colleges and universities. The database contains records of approximately 90,000 students who matriculated at 34 colleges and universities in the fall of 1951, 1976, and 1989. The College and Beyond database was first used extensively in Bowen and Bok (1998), and it is described at length in Appendix A of that book. In this study we have also used supplementary data on giving histories supplied by the participating schools.

4. Menand's (2001) review of Shulman and Bowen (2001) makes this point emphatically.

5. The EADA forms lump all sources of voluntary support together, and an extended search reveals no other sources. Nonalumni "booster" revenues are exceedingly modest at the Ivies and the Division III liberal arts colleges. Donations from booster groups are more important at Division IA schools such as Notre Dame and Duke, but even there they pale in relation to alumni contributions. Booster donations tend (not surprisingly) to be directed primarily to support of athletic budgets. A story in *USA Today* (2001) reports that the University of Louisville's athletic department has received $850,000 in donations since Rick Pitino was hired as basketball coach; according to the story: "The money has come from basketball season ticket holders, who must increase their donations to get the best seats in Freedom Hall next season."

6. Giving data correspond to July–June fiscal years at 12 of the 15 institutions. Data from three schools (Notre Dame, Oberlin, Williams) correspond to calendar years.

7. Giving rates are defined here as the average annual percentage of individuals in a category who made a gift. Thus, if 50 percent never gave and the other 50 percent averaged one gift every two years, the average giving rate would be 25 percent. Giving levels are defined analogously to giving rates: as the average annual gift made by individuals in a defined category.

8. We are grateful to Susan Anderson for her efforts in collecting the campaign data by contacting individual institutions. We have also considered the impact of changes in the *U.S. News and World Report* college rankings (compiled by Ron Ehrenberg and James Monks) on giving behavior and do not find any significant relationship between these rankings and giving behavior.

9. The magnitude of this coefficient is affected by the presence of an unusually large (multimillion-dollar) contribution to an institution during an "off" football year. We do not eliminate such outliers, precisely because they do not appear to be related to athletic performance.

10. The effects of football performance on general giving behavior are not significantly different for men and women. An interesting question raised by one reviewer concerns the extent to which giving behavior of women has changed as their participation in athletics increased in the aftermath of the enforcement of Title IX requirements. To address this question, a researcher would need panel data on the giving of multiple cohorts of students.

11. This finding and this interpretation are consistent with extensive cross-sectional evidence about the giving behavior of the various groups and their attitudes toward intercollegiate athletics (Shulman and Bowen, 2001:chap. 10). The Shulman and Bowen data also show that men who played the high-profile sports of football, basketball, and hockey in the Ivy League are less inclined to make general gifts than are those who played other sports.

12. There are, of course, other variables that may explain some part of the relationship between winning and giving. For example, we found that the giving of those graduates who continued to live in the state where their school is located was more likely than that of graduates living out of state to be affected positively by winning football records. Adding this "residence" variable does not, however, change any of the other results and, because of space constraints, we do not present the regressions including the location variable. They are available from the authors on request. Groen and White (2001) probe the question of academic performance and location choice in more detail.

The authors wish to thank James Shulman, Steven Haider, and Charlie Brown for helpful comments. We are also grateful to Susan Anderson for her help in putting the manuscript in final form.

Bibliography

Chapter 9: Alumni/ae Giving & Other Relevant Institutional Constituencies

Buggink, Thomas H., and Kamran Siddiqui. "An Econometric Model of Alumni Giving: A Case Study for a Liberal Arts College." *American Economist*, Vol. 39, No. 2 (1995), pp. 53–60.

Conley, Aaron and Tempel, Gene. "The Student Foundation as a Community of Participation: A Study of Its Impact on Alumni Giving Rates." *The CASE International Journal of Educational Advancement*, Vol. 1, No. 2 (2000), pp. 120–134.

Grimes, Paul W., and George A. Chressanthis. "Alumni Contributions to Academics: The Role of Intercollegiate Sports and NCAA Sanctions." *American Journal of Economics and Sociology*, Vol. 53, No. 1 (1994), pp. 27–40.

Knight, William E. "Influences on Participation in University Faculty and Staff Annual Giving Campaign." *The CASE International Journal of Educational Advancement*. Vol. 4, No. 3 (2004), pp. 221–232.

Okunade, A.A., and R.L. Berl. "Determinants of Charitable Giving of Business School Alumni." *Research in Higher Education*, Vol. 38, No. 2, pp. 201–214.

Patouillet, Leland D. "Alumni Association Members: Attitudes Toward University Life and Giving at a Public AAU Institutions." *The CASE International Journal of Educational Advancement*. Vol. 2, No. 1 (2001), pp. 53–66.

Schervish, P. "The Dependent Variable of the Independent Sector: The Definition and Measurement of Giving and Volunteering." *Voluntas: International Journal of Voluntary and Nonprofit Organizations*, Vol. 4, No. 2 (1993), pp. 223–232.

Schervish, P. and J. Havens. "Social Participation and Charitable Giving: A Multivariate Analysis." *Voluntas: International Journal of Voluntary and Nonprofit Organizations*, Vol. 8, No. 3 (1997), pp. 235–260.

Taylor, A.L. and J.C. Martin. "Characteristics of Alumni Donors and Non-Donors at a Research I, Public University." *Research in Higher Education*, Vol. 36, No. 3, (1995), pp. 283–302.

Terrell, Melvin C., James A. Gold, and James C. Renick. "Student Affairs Professionals and Fund-Raisers: An Untapped Resource." *NASPA Journal*, Vol. 30, No. 3 (1993), pp. 190–195.

Tucker, Irvin B. "A Reexamination of the Effect of Big-Time Football and Basketball Success on Graduation Rates and Alumni Giving Rates." *Economics of Education Review*, Vol. 23 (2004), pp. 655–661.

Webb, Charles H. "The Role of Alumni Relations in Fund Raising." In *New Strategies for Educational Fund Raising*, Michael J. Worth, ed. Westport, CT: Praeger Press, 2002, pp. 332–338.

Willemain, Thomas R., Anil Goyal, Mark Van Deven, and Inderpreet S. Thukral. "Alumni Giving: The Influences of Reunion, Class, and Year". *Research in Higher Education*, Vol. 35, No. 5 (1994), pp. 609–629.

CHAPTER 10
THE MECHANICS OF FUNDRAISING

INSTITUTIONAL ADVANCEMENT AND COMMUNITY COLLEGES: A REVIEW OF THE LITERATURE

S. RENEA AKIN

Abstract

Community colleges are increasingly turning to fund raising to replace declining federal and state appropriations. This paper provides a review of the higher education literature related to community college fund raising. The review examines the history of public and private financial support of community colleges, describes the differences between fund-raising practices of two- and four-year colleges and universities, and examines development strategies currently recommended for use by community colleges. Such strategies include integrating resource development with institutional planning, staffing foundation boards with individuals who are interested in the college and who are able to solicit donations, and providing strong presidential leadership and support to fund-raising efforts. Recommendations for future research are discussed.

Introduction

American society is characterized by private individuals voluntarily giving to promote the public good.[1] As a result, nearly every aspect of American life, including higher education, has benefited from philanthropy.[2] Private donations, however, have not been evenly distributed across all segments of higher education. Even though community colleges comprise the largest sector of higher education in the United States, they receive only about 2 percent of all private financial support.[3] This disparity is unfortunate as community colleges typically serve large numbers of individuals with low incomes,[4] and over the past decade have experienced a decline in federal and state appropriations.[5]

As federal and state appropriations to higher education are tied to the economy, during periods of economic downturn, public appropriations tend to decline.[6] Periods of economic decline, however, are nearly always associated with an increase in enrollment at community colleges.[7] In light of increasing enrollment in the face of declining federal and state appropriations,[8] publicly supported community colleges are increasingly challenged to find alternative means of obtaining adequate financial support.[9] Finally recognizing that doing more with less is not a viable long-term strategy,[10] community colleges are increasingly seeking to augment their budgets with private donations.[11]

As fund raising is well established in four-year colleges and universities,[12] community colleges face stiff competition for philanthropic leadership, sponsorships, and gifts.[13] Unfortunately, fund raising in the community college setting has not been consistently implemented or thoroughly investigated.[14] The body of knowledge related to two-year institutions varies in nature, purpose, content, and accessibility,[15] and little is written about these institutions in the traditional higher education literature. The purpose of this paper is to explore the literature in order to identify strategic development practices employed by two-year institutions to increase private sector support.

Literature Review

The framework for this paper will be bounded by the areas of community college finance and development practices. The review of the literature presented here examines higher education scholarship

698

in an attempt to identify successful strategic development practices of two-year institutions. The literature review will begin with a discussion of the history of both public and private financial support of community colleges. It will also describe the differences between fund-raising practices of two- and four-year colleges and universities, and will examine strategies currently recommended to tailor development strategies to the community college setting. The literature review will conclude by identifying recommendations for further research.

Community College Finances

Publicly supported two-year colleges are a relatively recent and uniquely American phenomenon.[16] Although the majority of publicly supported four-year colleges and universities were founded in the mid- to late 1800s following passage of the Morrill Acts of 1862 and 1890,[17] the nation's first two-year college only came into existence in 1907.[18] Until the early 1950s, two-year colleges were commonly referred to as "junior" colleges,[19] and were considered to be an extension of the 1–12 public school system.[20] As a result, funding for two-year colleges was based on the public school system model rather than on traditional college and university funding formulas.[21]

In 1918, 94 percent of public support for junior colleges originated from local taxes and 6 percent of support came from tuition.[22] Although states did not become a revenue source for two-year colleges until 1942,[23] by 1965 states provided the largest source of revenue for these institutions.[24] The trend for the state to assume responsibility for funding an ever-increasing percentage of community college operating costs[25] may be explained in part to passage of legislation such as California's Proposition 13 which limited local property taxes.[26] Although state revenue remains the largest source of income for two-year colleges, this source of funding peaked in 1980 and has since been steadily declining,[27] further reinforcing the premise that community colleges need to seek additional sources of revenue to fulfill their mission.

Community College Fund Raising

Publicly supported community colleges are increasingly challenged to find alternative means of obtaining adequate financial support[28] to sustain increased enrollment in light of declining federal and state appropriations.[29] Although public and private four-year institutions have successfully augmented their budgets with charitable donations, community colleges lag behind other institutions of higher education in this area.[30] While the majority of community colleges now have foundations,[31] most are small and generate significantly less income than their four-year counterparts.[32] Glass and Jackson found only 45 percent of community colleges that use foundations to expand sources of revenue consider fund raising on their campus to be successful.[33] According to MacArthur, in 1996 the American Association of Community Colleges reported that the average community college endowment was valued at $2.1m compared with the average four-year college and university endowment of $350m.[34] Not surprisingly, unlike foundations at four-year institutions, community college foundations fail to make a significant impact on the financial stability of these institutions.[35] The historical development of community college foundations will be examined below.

History of Fund Raising

Public funding appeared plentiful when the majority of community colleges were founded in the early 1960s and 1970s.[36] The percentage of revenue from states increased from 34 percent of the total budget in 1965 to 60 percent in 1980.[37] Because state funding appeared to be plentiful and ongoing, many community college presidents and trustees failed to appreciate the need to seek private funds.[38] Other community college leaders deliberately chose not to solicit private funding because they feared a proportional decrease in state funding, and competition from four-year institutions.[39] As a result, community colleges were not only late in joining the higher education establishment; they were also the last segment in higher education to engage seriously in fund-raising endeavors.[40]

Even though community colleges began developing foundations in the 1970s and 1980s,[41] by 1987, only 53 percent of colleges had established foundations.[42] The next decade saw a significant increase in foundation growth so that by 1997, 88 percent of community colleges had established a foundation.[43] Unfortunately, most community college foundations were not actively involved in seeking financial support for the colleges, but instead functioned as passive conduits for donors who sought out the colleges.[44] As a result, income from private gifts and grants from 1965 to 1997 remained steady at 1 percent of total income.[45]

Differences in Fund-raising Practices

As fund-raising challenges in the community college setting differ from those experienced by traditional universities,[46] the structural and organizational support systems employed by community colleges to pursue donations also differ from traditional university fund-raising models.[47] For instance, community colleges do not staff development offices in the same manner as four-year institutions,[48] and alumni relations in the community college setting differ significantly from four-year institutions.[49] The dissimilarities in staffing and alumni relations will be discussed more fully below.

One of the more obvious differences in two- and four-year institutions is the number of individuals employed by the development office. Four-year institutions typically employ dozens of development staff who specialize in areas such as alumni affairs, planned giving, corporate and foundation relations, or communications.[50] In stark contrast, community college development offices typically employ one or two full-time professional staff members who are responsible for all fund-raising functions.[51] Keener et al. examined the staffing patterns of community college foundations and found the number of development staff is proportional to the size of the college.[52] Eighty percent of colleges in their study employed only one full-time staff member, while the largest development office in their study employed seven full-time professional staff, far fewer than the typical four-year institution. The size of the college, the number of development staff, and the amount of funds collected appear to have a symbiotic relationship. For instance, the number of development staff is reported to be related to the size of foundation[53] and the college,[54] and the size of the college appears to be related to the amount of funds collected annually.[55]

The second area in which two-year and four-year institutions differ significantly is alumni relations. This is not surprising considering two- and four-year institutions serve different populations. Compared with four-year institutions, community colleges serve a larger number of minorities, people with low incomes, and first-generation college students.[56] Community college students approach academics with a different, more consumer-oriented, point of view than do typical four-year college or university students,[57] and also approach higher education with different expectations. For instance, 63 percent of community college students are enrolled part-time, and only 39 percent plan to pursue postbaccalaureate education.[58] In public four-year institutions, 22 percent of students attend part-time, and 79 percent plan to purse postbaccalaureate education.[59]

In addition to coming from different backgrounds and approaching higher education with differing expectations, postgraduate alliances, earnings and contacts of these two groups also differ. Alumni who continue their education and graduate from four-year institutions usually transfer their allegiance to those institutions.[60] Pokrass theorized that as the community colleges themselves are relatively new, alumni are not sufficiently well established in their careers to be able to offer significant support to these institutions.[61] As community colleges typically do not keep good records of alumni,[62] possibly because of the small size of development offices, contacting alumni for support is difficult at best. Alumni giving is not considered to be successful at community colleges,[63] and is usually not emphasized.[64] Data from the Council for Aid to Education[65] (as reported by Glass and Jackson)[66] show that in 1995, alumni contributions accounted for only 3.3 percent of community college donations compared to 39.8 percent at four-year institutions.

Fund-raising Strategies

Four strategies for tailoring fund raising to the two-year college setting consistently appear in the community college literature. The strategies identified include integrating resource development with institutional planning,[67] staffing foundation boards with individuals who are interested in the college and are able to solicit donations,[68] building relationships with the community,[69] and providing strong presidential leadership and support to fund-raising efforts.[70] Each of these suggestions will be described in detail below.

Institutional Planning

The first strategy recommended for fund raising is to form a link between the mission of the college, the mission of the foundation, and the strategic plan.[71] The strategic plan should be flexible enough to allow the institution to take advantage of unforeseen opportunities,[72] and allow the creation of an institutional atmosphere that both fosters and celebrates giving.[73]

Boards

Unlike Regents at private institutions who are often selected for their ability to contribute to the institution,[74] governing board members of publicly supported community colleges are usually politically appointed.[75] Their primary duties include establishing the mission and goals of the institution,[76] setting policy, determining fund-raising priorities, and representing and promoting the college favorably to the local community.[77] Members of the governing board may,[78] or may not fully appreciate the importance of fund raising to the institution.[79] Most community college governing board members are not wealthy,[80] personally contribute an average of $999 per year to the college, and have no plans to leave money to the college after their death.[81] In short, governing board members of community colleges are not active fund raisers,[82] do not view fund raising as their responsibility,[83] and generally agree that a separate foundation board should deal with private sector fund raising.[84]

The members of the foundation board are the driving force behind a successful foundation.[85] Successful foundations strive to support the mission of the college and maintain a good relationship with the governing board.[86] Unlike politically appointed governing board members, foundation board members may be selected based on their ability to contribute to the institution.[87] Ideally, foundation boards should be staffed with individuals who have resources such as personal wealth, personal connections, business acumen, or technical knowledge in areas such as banking, finance, or the law.[88]

The primary duties of the foundation board members include setting foundation policy, representing and promoting the college favorably to the community,[89] providing financial support, and actively participating in the fund-raising process by identifying and cultivating donors.[90]

Relationships

Successful fund raising at two-year institutions often begins with "friend-raising."[91] The purpose of "friend-raising" is not necessarily to immediately raise funds, but is instead designed to make potential donors aware of the college, its mission, and the benefits the college provides to the local community.[92] With the exception of research universities,[93] businesses support community colleges more than any other segment of higher education,[94] and are often the recipient of "friend-raising" endeavors.[95] Businesses contribute to community colleges because the colleges provide trained workers for the business[96] and provide training for existing workers.[97]

Even though community college alumni do not provide a significant amount of monetary support,[98] MacArthur[99] and Smith[100] recommend exploring ways to increase alumni support. Pokrass recommends using "friend-raising" strategies with alumni by providing job placement assistance, discounts to cultural events, and recognition of alumni achievements as a means of strengthening alumni relations.[101] Alumni who are not able to provide financial support may contribute to the college by providing volunteer services,[102] contacting employers for donations, lobbying on behalf of the college, or by serving as curriculum advisory committee members.[103]

Strong Presidents

Presidential involvement is crucial for successful fund raising.[104] Presidential responsibilities include providing leadership,[105] supervising the development staff and process,[106] facilitating communication between the governing and foundation boards,[107] and building relationships with individuals and businesses in the community.[108] The college president must be committed to fund raising, serve as the point person in public relations,[109] and personally contribute both time and money to ensure success.[110] Unlike leaders of major research universities, community college presidents must be able to articulate the institutional mission and make the case that their institutions are worthy of support.[111] For this reason, fund raising is a threat to many community college presidents because it puts them at risk of publicly failing.[112]

Recommendations for Further Research

Glass and Jackson noted that successful community college development offices do not model four-year colleges, but instead emulate advancement models used by successful community colleges.[113] Identifying two-year institutions that have a successful history of fund raising, however, is challenging. Although the Council for Aid to Education (CAE) annually publishes a report based on the results of the Voluntary Support of Education Survey, in 2003, fewer than 8 percent of the 1,101 publicly supported two-year colleges identified in 2002 by the National Center for Education Statistics participated in the CAE survey. Participation rates for other voluntary surveys are similar. Of the 717 colleges and universities that participated in the annual endowment survey conducted by the National Association of College and University Business Officers, community colleges accounted for only 11 of the responses. As low participation rates result in inconsistent and possibly inaccurate data for research, several authors have strongly recommended that community colleges participate in national surveys to provide consistent data for future research.[114]

Conclusion

As state support for higher education is expected to continue to decline,[115] community colleges should actively pursue other avenues of revenue, including philanthropic giving. This paper identified four strategies for tailoring fund raising to the community college setting: integrating resource development with institutional planning,[116] staffing foundation boards with individuals who are interested in the college and are able to solicit donations,[117] building relationships with the community,[118] and providing strong presidential leadership and support to fund-raising efforts.[119]

Notes

1. J. C. Glass, Jr. and K. L. Jackson (1998a), "A new role for community college presidents: Private fund raiser and development team leader," *Community College Journal of Research and Practice*, 22, pp. 575–90; L. S. Miller (1994), "Community college resource development: Foundations and fund-raising" in G. A. Baker (Ed.), *A Handbook on the Community College in America: Its History, Mission, and Management*, Greenwood Press, Westport, CT, pp. 360–74.

2. B. Babitz (2003), "Strategies for leveraging a community college foundation," in M. D. Milliron, G. E. de los Santos, and B. Browning (Eds.), *New Directions for Community Colleges: Successful Approaches to Fundraising and Development*, Jossey-Bass, San Francisco, pp. 5–14.

3. B. J. Keener, S. M. Carrier, and S. J. Meaders (2002), "Resource development in community colleges: A national overview," *Community College Journal of Research and Practice*, 26, pp. 7–23.

4. C. Q. Sheldon (2003), ERIC review: "The impact of financial crisis on access and support services in community colleges," *Community College Review*, 31, pp. 73–0; S. R. Wise and M. W. Camper (1985), "Fund raising for two-year colleges," in M. J. Worth (ed.), *Public College and University Development: Fund Raising at State Universities, State Colleges, and Community Colleges*, Onyx Press, Phoenix, AZ, pp. 131–40.

5. D. Bass (2003), "From the foundations up: Contexts for change in community college advancement" in M. D. Milliron, G. E. de los Santos, and B. Browning (Eds.), *New Directions for Community Colleges: Successful Approaches to Fundraising and Development*, Jossey-Bass, San Francisco, pp. 15–26; Keener et al. (2002), "Resource development in community colleges," op. cit.; L. W. Jenkin and J. C. Glass, Jr. (1999), "Inception, growth, and development of a community college foundation: Lessons to be learned," *Community College Journal of Research and Practice*, 23, pp. 593–612; K. Phillippe and I. R. Eblinger (1998), "Community

college foundations: Funding the community college future." American Association of Community Colleges, Research Brief, AACC-RB-98–3; Sheldon (2003), ERIC review, op. cit.; T. G. Watkins (2000), "Public community college revenues, 1989–1994," *Community College Journal of Research and Practice*, 24, pp. 95–106.

6. D. Hossler, J. P. Lund, and J. Ramin (1997), "State funding for higher education: The Sisyphean task," *The Journal of Higher Education*, 68, pp. 160–90; Sheldon (2003), ERIC review, op. cit.

7. K. L. Pennington, D. McGinty, and M. R. Williams (2002), "Community college enrollment as a function of economic indicators," *Community College Journal of Research and Practice*, 22, pp. 431–7; Sheldon (2003), ERIC review, op. cit.

8. Bass (2003), "From the foundations up," op. cit.; Jenkin and Glass (1999), "Inception, growth, and development of a community college foundation," op. cit.; Keener et al. (2002), "Resource development in community colleges," op cit.; Phillippe and Eblinger (1998), "Community college foundations," op. cit.; W. E. Piland and B. G. Rees (1995), "Community college foundations and fundraising: A national view," *Trustees Quarterly*, Spring, pp. 9–12; Sheldon (2003), ERIC review, op. cit.; Watkins (2000), "Public community college revenues," op. cit.

9. Jenkin and Glass (1999), "Inception, growth, and development of a community college foundation," op. cit.; J. C. Glass, Jr. and K. L. Jackson (1998b), "Integrating resource development and institutional planning," *Community College Journal of Research and Practice*, 22, pp. 715–39; K. L. Jackson and J. C. Glass, Jr. (2000), "Emerging trends and critical issues affecting private fund-raising among community colleges," *Community College Journal of Research and Practice*, 24, pp. 729–44; Watkins (2000), "Public community college revenues," op. cit.

10. Glass and Jackson (1998b), "Integrating resource development and institutional planning," op. cit.

11. Ibid.; Miller (1994), "Community college resource development," op. cit.; Piland and Rees (1995), "Community college foundations and fundraising," op. cit.; R. K. Smith (1994), "Building budgets for effective resource allocation," in G. A. Baker (Ed.), *A Handbook on the Community College in America: Its History, Mission, and Management*, Greenwood Press, Westport, CT, pp. 350–9; M. J. Worth (1993), "The historical overview," in M. J. Worth (Ed.), *Public College and University Development: Fund Raising at State Universities, State Colleges, and Community Colleges*, Onyx Press, Phoenix, AZ, pp. 131–40.

12. Keener et al. (2002), "Resource development in community colleges," op. cit.; Worth (1993), "The historical overview," op. cit.; Piland and Rees (1995), "Community college foundations and fundraising," op. cit.

13. Babitz, (2003), "Strategies for leveraging a community college foundation," op. cit.; CASE (1988), "Initiating a fund-raising program: A model for the community college," Council for Advancement and Support of Education, Washington, DC (ERIC Document Reproduction Service No. ED 314134); K. M. MacArthur (2000), "Advancement in community colleges," in P. M. Buchanan, (Ed.), *Handbook of Institutional Advancement*, 4th edn., Council for Advancement and Support of Education, Washington, DC, pp. 487–90; Miller (1994), "Community college resource development," op. cit.; Piland and Rees (1995), "Community college foundations and fundraising," op. cit.

14. Jackson and Glass (2000), "Emerging trends and critical issues affecting private fund-raising among community colleges," op. cit.; K. L. Jackson and B. J. Keener (2002), "Introduction to community college resource development: Creating preferred futures," *Community College Journal of Research and Practice*, 26, pp. 1–6; Jenkin and Glass (1999), "Inception, growth, and development of a community college foundation," op. cit.; Miller (1994), "Community college resource development," op. cit.

15. T. H. Bers and H. D. Calhoun (2002), "Literature on community colleges: An overview," in T. H. Bers and H. D. Calhoun (Eds.), *New Directions for Community Colleges: Next Steps for the Community Colleges*, Jossey-Bass, San Francisco, pp. 5–12.

16. A. M. Cohen and F. B. Brawer (2003), *The American Community College*, Jossey-Bass, San Francisco.

17. M. J. Bowman (1962), "The land grant colleges and universities in human resource development," *The Journal of Economic History*, 22, pp. 523–46; Cohen and Brawer (2003), *The American Community College*, op. cit.; R. V. Herren and M. C. Edwards (2002), "Whence we came: The land-grant tradition—origins, evolution, and implications for the 21st century," *Journal of Agricultural Education*, 43, 4, pp. 88–100.

18. Cohen and Brawer (2003), *The American Community College*, op. cit.

19. Ibid.; J. H. Frye (1995), "Women in the two-year college, 1900 to 1970," in A. M. Cohen (Series Ed.), and B. K. Townsend (Vol. Ed.), *New Directions for Community Colleges: No. 89. Gender and Power in the Community College*, Jossey-Bass, San Francisco, pp. 5–14.

20. J. L. Wattenbarger (1994), "Resource development in the community college: The evolution of resource policy development for community colleges as related to support from local, state, and federal government," in G. A. Baker (Ed.), *A Handbook on the Community College in America: Its History, Mission, and Management*, Greenwood Press, Westport, CT, pp. 333–9.

21. Ibid.
22. Cohen and Brawer (2003), *The American Community College*, op. cit.; Smith (1994), "Building budgets for effective resource allocation," op. cit.
23. Cohen and Brawer (2003), *The American Community College*, op. cit.
24. Ibid.; Smith (1994), "Building budgets for effective resource allocation," op. cit.
25. C. D. Lovell and C. Trouth (2002), "State governance patterns for community colleges," in T. H. Bers and H. D. Calhoun (Eds.), *New Directions for Community Colleges: Next Steps for the Community Colleges*, Jossey-Bass, San Francisco, pp. 91–100.
26. Cohen and Brawer (2003), *The American Community College*, op. cit.
27. Ibid.
28. Glass and Jackson (1998a), "A new role for community college presidents" op. cit.; Glass and Jackson (1998b), "Integrating resource development and institutional planning," op. cit.; Jackson and Glass (2000), "Emerging trends and critical issues affecting private fund-raising among community colleges," op. cit.; Piland and Rees (1995), "Community college foundations and fundraising," op. cit.; Watkins (2000), "Public community college revenues," op. cit.
29. Bass (2003), "From the foundations up," op. cit.; Jenkin and Glass (1999), "Inception, growth, and development of a community college foundation," op. cit.; Keener et al. (2002), "Resource development in community colleges," op. cit.; Sheldon (2003), ERIC review, op. cit.; Watkins (2000), "Public community college revenues," op. cit.
30. J. L. Catanzaro and L. G. Miller (1994), "Strategic alliance: A key tool for institutional advancement" (ERIC Document Reproduction Service No. ED 374872.); K. A. Phillippe and M. Patton (2000), *National Profile of Community Colleges: Trends & Statistics*, 3rd edn., Community College Press, American Association of Community Colleges, Washington, DC; Piland and Rees (1995), "Community college foundations and fundraising," op. cit.; Worth (1993), "The historical overview," op. cit.
31. Babitz (2003), "Strategies for leveraging a community college foundation," op. cit.
32. Catanzaro and Miller (1994), "Strategic alliance," op. cit.; MacArthur (2000), "Advancement in community colleges," op. cit.; Phillippe and Patton (2000), *National Profile of Community Colleges*, op. cit.; Jackson and Glass (2000), "Emerging trends and critical issues affecting private fund-raising among community colleges," op. cit.
33. Glass and Jackson (1998b), "Integrating resource development and institutional planning," op. cit.
34. MacArthur (2000), "Advancement in community colleges," op. cit.
35. Babitz (2003), "Strategies for leveraging a community college foundation," op. cit.
36. Jenkin and Glass (1999), "Inception, growth, and development of a community college foundation," op. cit.
37. Cohen and Brawer (2003), *The American Community College*, op. cit.
38. Jenkin and Glass (1999), "Inception, growth, and development of a community college foundation," op. cit.
39. Glass and Jackson (1998b), "Integrating resource development and institutional planning," op. cit.
40. Ibid.
41. Jenkin and Glass (1999), "Inception, growth, and development of a community college foundation," op. cit.; Keener et al. (2002), "Resource development in community colleges," op. cit.
42. Glass and Jackson (1998b), "Integrating resource development and institutional planning," op. cit.
43. Phillippe and Eblinger (1998), "Community college foundations," op. cit.
44. D. Angel and D. Gares (1989), "History, characteristics, and assets," in J. L. Catanzaro and A. D. Arnold (Eds.), *New Directions for Community Colleges: Alternative Funding Sources*, Jossey-Bass, San Francisco, pp. 7–14; Glass and Jackson (1998b), "Integrating resource development and institutional planning," op. cit.; Miller (1994), "Community college resource development," op. cit.
45. Cohen and Brawer (2003), *The American Community College*, op. cit.
46. Glass and Jackson (1998b), "Integrating resource development and institutional planning," op. cit.; Smith (1994), "Building budgets for effective resource allocation," op. cit.
47. Bass (2003), "From the foundations up," op. cit.; Jackson and Glass (2000), "Emerging trends and critical issues affecting private fund-raising among community colleges," op. cit.; Keener et al. (2002), "Resource development in community colleges," op. cit.; Miller (1994), "Community college resource development," op. cit.; Smith (1994), "Building budgets for effective resource allocation," op. cit.
48. Bass (2003), "From the foundations up," op. cit.; Keener et al. (2002), "Resource development in community colleges," op. cit.; Miller (1994), "Community college resource development," op. cit.
49. CASE (1988), "Initiating a fund-raising program," op. cit.; Catanzaro and Miller (1994), "Strategic alliance," op. cit.; Glass and Jackson (1998b), "Integrating resource development and institutional planning,"

op. cit.; R. J. Pokrass (1989), "Alumni: Friends and funds for your institution," in J. L. Catanzaro and A. D. Arnold (Eds.), *New Directions for Community Colleges: Alternative Funding Sources*, Jossey-Bass, San Francisco, pp. 29–34; Smith (1994), "Building budgets for effective resource allocation," op. cit.

50. Bass (2003), "From the foundations up," op. cit.; Keener et al. (2002), "Resource development in community colleges," op. cit.; Miller (1994), "Community college resource development," op. cit.

51. Bass (2003), "From the foundations up," op. cit.; Keener et al. (2002), "Resource development in community colleges," op. cit.; Piland and Rees (1995), "Community college foundations and fundraising," op. cit.

52. Keener et al. (2002), "Resource development in community colleges," op. cit.

53. Phillippe and Eblinger (1998), "Community college foundations," op. cit.

54. Keener et al. (2002), "Resource development in community colleges," op. cit.

55. Piland and Rees (1995), "Community college foundations and fundraising," op. cit.

56. Sheldon (2003), ERIC review, op. cit.; Wise and Camper (1985), "Fund raising for two-year colleges," op. cit.

57. Glass and Jackson (1998b), "Integrating resource development and institutional planning," op. cit.

58. Phillippe and Patton (2000), *National Profile of Community Colleges*, op. cit.

59. Ibid.

60. Catanzaro and Miller (1994), "Strategic alliance," op. cit.

61. Pokrass (1989), "Alumni," op. cit.

62. CASE (1988), "Initiating a fund-raising program," op. cit.

63. Glass and Jackson (1998b), "Integrating resource development and institutional planning," op. cit.; Smith (1994), "Building budgets for effective resource allocation," op. cit.

64. Keener et al. (2002), "Resource development in community colleges," op. cit.; Smith (1994), "Building budgets for effective resource allocation," op. cit.

65. CASE (1988), "Initiating a fund-raising program," op. cit.

66. Glass and Jackson (1998b), "Integrating resource development and institutional planning," op. cit.

67. S. Anderson (2003), "Fundraising programs in community colleges: Factors that contribute to effectiveness," *Digital Dissertation, AAT 3110089*; Bass (2003), "From the foundations up," op. cit.; M. A. Brumbach and A. W. Villadsen (2002), "At the edge of chaos: The essentials of resource development for the community's college," *Community College Journal of Research and Practice*, 26, pp. 77–86; CASE (1988), "Initiating a fundraising program," op. cit.; Glass and Jackson (1998b), "Integrating resource development and institutional planning," op. cit.; Miller (1994), "Community college resource development," op. cit.; Piland and Rees (1995), "Community college foundations and fundraising," op. cit.

68. Anderson (2003), "Fundraising programs in community colleges," op. cit.; Angel and Gares (1989), "History, characteristics, and assets," op. cit.; Babitz (2003), "Strategies for leveraging a community college foundation," op. cit.; D. E. Bock and W. R. Sullins (1987), "The search for alternative sources of funding: Community colleges and private fund-raising," *Community College Review*, 15, pp. 13–20; CASE (1988), "Initiating a fund-raising program," op. cit.; Miller (1994), "Community college resource development," op. cit.; N. Nielson, W. Newton, and C. W. Mitvalsky (2003), "The role of community college trustees in supporting the foundation," in M. D. Milliron, G. E. de los Santos, and B. Browning (Eds.), *New Directions for Community Colleges: Successful Approaches to Fundraising and Development*, Jossey-Bass, San Francisco, pp. 33–9; Piland and Rees (1995), "Community college foundations and fundraising," op. cit.; Smith (1994), "Building budgets for effective resource allocation," op. cit.; Wise and Camper (1985), "Fund raising for two-year colleges," op. cit.

69. Anderson (2003), "Fundraising programs in community colleges," op. cit.; Bock and Sullins (1987), "The search for alternative sources of funding," op. cit.; CASE (1988), "Initiating a fundraising program," op. cit.; M. R. Hall (2002), "Building on relationships: A fundraising approach for community colleges," *Community College Journal of Research and Practice*, 26, pp. 47–60; M. J. Pastorella (2003), "Keeping in touch: Alumni development in community colleges," in M. D. Milliron, G. E. de los Santos, and B. Browning (Eds.), *New Directions for Community Colleges: Successful Approaches to Fundraising and Development*, Jossey-Bass, San Francisco, pp. 75–9; Pokrass (1989), "Alumni," op. cit.; Wise and Camper (1985), "Fund raising for two-year colleges," op. cit.

70. Anderson (2003), "Fundraising programs in community colleges," op. cit.; Babitz (2003), "Strategies for leveraging a community college foundation," op. cit.; Bock and Sullins (1987), "The search for alternative sources of funding," op. cit.; CASE (1988), "Initiating a fund-raising program," op. cit.; Glass and Jackson (1998a), "A new role for community college presidents," op. cit.; E. A. McGee (2003), "The role of the president in supporting the college's foundation," in M. D. Milliron, G. E. de los Santos, and B. Browning (Eds.), *New Directions for Community Colleges: Successful Approaches to Fundraising and*

Development, Jossey-Bass, San Francisco, pp. 41–6; Miller (1994), "Community college resource development," op. cit.; Phillippe and Eblinger (1998), "Community college foundations," op. cit.; Piland and Rees (1995), "Community college foundations and fundraising," op. cit.; G. J. Ryan (1989), "Reasons for success," in J. L. Catanzaro and A. D. Arnold (Eds.), *New Directions for Community Colleges: Alternative Funding Sources*, Jossey-Bass, San Francisco, pp. 15–20; Smith (1994), "Building budgets for effective resource allocation," op. cit.; J. W. Wenrich and B. L. Reid (2003), "It's not the race I signed up for, but it's the race I'm in: The role of community college presidents," in M. D. Milliron, G. E. de los Santos, and B. Browning (Eds.), *New Directions for Community Colleges: Successful Approaches to Fundraising and Development*, Jossey-Bass, San Francisco, pp. 27–32; Wise and Camper (1985), "Fund raising for two-year colleges," op. cit.

71. Anderson (2003), "Fundraising programs in community colleges," op. cit.; C. J. Carlsen (2003), "Weaving the foundation into the culture of a community college," in M. D. Milliron, G. E. de los Santos, and B. Browning (Eds.), *New Directions for Community Colleges: Successful Approaches to Fundraising and Development*, Jossey-Bass, San Francisco, pp. 47–51; Glass and Jackson (1998b), "Integrating resource development and institutional planning," op. cit.; Miller (1994), "Community college resource development," op. cit.

72. Wenrich and Reid (2003), "It's not the race I signed up for, but it's the race I'm in," op. cit.

73. Babitz (2003), "Strategies for leveraging a community college foundation," op. cit.; Miller (1994), "Community college resource development," op. cit.

74. Glass and Jackson (1998a), "A new role for community college presidents," op. cit.

75. Bass (2003), "From the foundations up," op. cit.; Jenkin and Glass (1999), "Inception, growth, and development of a community college foundation," op. cit.

76. Glass and Jackson (1998a), "A new role for community college presidents," op. cit.

77. CASE (1988), "Initiating a fund-raising program," op. cit.

78. A. R. Southerland and M. S. Graham (1994), "Fundraising from the private sector: Trustee perceptions," *Trustee Quarterly*, Fall, pp. 5–8.

79. Jackson and Glass (2000), "Emerging trends and critical issues affecting private fund-raising among community colleges," op. cit.

80. Bass (2003), "From the foundations up," op. cit.; Jenkin and Glass (1999), "Inception, growth, and development of a community college foundation," op. cit.

81. Southerland and Graham (1994), "Fundraising from the private sector," op. cit.

82. Glass and Jackson (1998a), "A new role for community college presidents," op. cit.; Ryan (1989), "Reasons for success," op. cit.

83. R. J. Kopecek and S. K. Kubik (1997), "Successful fundraising at a two-year community college with a foundation: Northampton County Area Community College," in F. H. T. Rhodes (Ed.), *Successful Fund Raising for Higher Education: The Advancement of Learning*, The American Council on Education and The Oryx Press, Phoenix, AZ, pp. 75–88.

84. Southerland and Graham (1994), "Fundraising from the private sector," op. cit.

85. R. Taylor (1994), "The community college board and the foundation board: The role relationship in the context of 'Policy Governance.'" *Trustees Quarterly*, Fall, pp. 9–14.

86. Ibid.

87. Anderson (2003), "Fundraising programs in community colleges," op. cit.; McGee (2003), "The role of the president in supporting the college's foundation," op. cit.; Miller (1994), "Community college resource development," op. cit.; Smith (1994), "Building budgets for effective resource allocation," op. cit.

88. CASE (1988), "Initiating a fund-raising program," op. cit.

89. Ibid; Nielson et al. (2003), "The role of community college trustees in supporting the foundation," op. cit.

90. "Initiating a fund-raising program: A model for the community college" (1988), op. cit.

91. Babitz (2003), "Strategies for leveraging a community college foundation," op. cit.; MacArthur (2000), "Advancement in community colleges," op. cit.; Pokrass (1989), "Alumni," op. cit.; Wise and Camper (1985), "Fund raising for two-year colleges," op. cit.

92. Phillippe and Eblinger (1998), "Community college foundations," op. cit.

93. Glass and Jackson (1998a), "A new role for community college presidents," op. cit.; MacArthur (2000), "Advancement in community colleges," op. cit.

94. CASE (1988), "Initiating a fund-raising program," op. cit.; Glass and Jackson (1998b), "Integrating resource development and institutional planning," op. cit.

95. Dock and Sullins (1987), "The search for alternative sources of funding," op. cit.; CASE (1988), "Initiating a fund-raising program," op. cit.; Piland and Rees (1995), "Community college foundations and fundraising," op. cit.

96. CASE (1988), "Initiating a fund-raising program," op. cit.; MacArthur (2000), "Advancement in community colleges," op. cit.

97. CASE (1988), "Initiating a fund-raising program," op. cit.

98. Glass and Jackson (1998b), "Integrating resource development and institutional planning," op. cit.

99. MacArthur (2000), "Advancement in community colleges," op. cit.

100. Smith (1994), "Building budgets for effective resource allocation," op. cit.

101. Pokrass (1989), "Alumni," op. cit.

102. Bock and Sullins (1987), "The search for alternative sources of funding," op. cit.; Pastorella (2003), "Keeping in touch," op. cit.; Pokrass (1989), "Alumni," op. cit.; Smith (1994), "Building budgets for effective resource allocation," op. cit.

103. MacArthur (2000), "Advancement in community colleges," op. cit.

104. Ryan (1989), "Reasons for success," op. cit.; Smith (1994), "Building budgets for effective resource allocation," op. cit.; Wenrich and Reid (2003), "It's not the race I signed up for, but it's the race I'm in," op. cit.

105. CASE (1988), "Initiating a fund-raising program," op. cit.; Glass and Jackson (1998a), "A new role for community college presidents," op. cit.

106. Ibid.

107. CASE (1988), "Initiating a fund-raising program," op. cit.

108. Carlsen (2003), "Weaving the foundation into the culture of a community college," op. cit.; CASE (1988), "Initiating a fund-raising program," op. cit.; Glass and Jackson (1998a), "A new role for community college presidents," op. cit.

109. Smith (1994), "Building budgets for effective resource allocation," op. cit.; Wenrich and Reid (2003), "It's not the race I signed up for, but it's the race I'm in," op. cit.

110. Glass and Jackson (1998a), "A new role for community college presidents," op. cit.

111. Ibid.

112. Ibid.

113. Glass and Jackson (1998b), "Integrating resource development and institutional planning," op. cit.

114. Jackson and Glass (2000), "Emerging trends and critical issues affecting private fund-raising among community colleges," op. cit.; Jackson and Keener (2002), "Introduction to community college resource development," op. cit.; Keener et al. (2002), "Resource development in community colleges," op. cit.

115. Keener et al. (2002), "Resource development in community colleges," op. cit.

116. Anderson (2003), "Fundraising programs in community colleges," op. cit.; Bass (2003), "From the foundations up," op. cit.; Brumbach and Villadsen (2002), "At the edge of chaos," op. cit.; CASE (1988), "Initiating a fund-raising program," op. cit.; Glass and Jackson (1998b), "Integrating resource development and institutional planning," op. cit.; Miller (1994), "Community college resource development," op. cit.; Piland and Rees (1995), "Community college foundations and fundraising," op. cit.

117. Anderson (2003), "Fundraising programs in community colleges," op. cit.; Angel and Gares (1989), "History, characteristics, and assets," op. cit.; Babitz (2003), "Strategies for leveraging a community college foundation," op. cit.; Bock and Sullins (1987), "The search for alternative sources of funding," op. cit.; CASE (1988), "Initiating a fund-raising program," op. cit.; Miller (1994), "Community college resource development," op. cit.; Nielson et al. (2003), "The role of community college trustees in supporting the foundation," op. cit.; Piland and Rees (1995), "Community college foundations and fundraising," op. cit.; Smith (1994), "Building budgets for effective resource allocation," op. cit.; Wise and Camper (1985), "Fund raising for two-year colleges," op. cit.

118. Anderson (2003), "Fundraising programs in community colleges," op. cit.; Bock and Sullins (1987), "The search for alternative sources of funding," op. cit.; CASE (1988), "Initiating a fund-raising program," op. cit.; Hall (2002), "Building on relationships," op. cit.; Pastorella (2003), "Keeping in touch," op. cit.; Pokrass (1989), "Alumni," op. cit.; Wise and Camper (1985), "Fund raising for two-year colleges," op. cit.

119. Anderson (2003), "Fundraising programs in community colleges," op. cit.; Babitz (2003), "Strategies for leveraging a community college foundation," op. cit.; Bock and Sullins (1987), "The search for alternative sources of funding," op. cit.; CASE (1988), "Initiating a fund-raising program," op. cit.; Glass and Jackson (1998a), "A new role for community college presidents," op. cit.; McGee (2003), "The role of the president in supporting the college's foundation," op. cit.; Miller (1994), "Community college resource development," op. cit.; Phillippe and Eblinger (1998), "Community college foundations," op. cit.; Piland and Rees (1995), "Community college foundations and fundraising," op. cit.; Ryan (1989), "Reasons for success," op. cit.; Smith (1994), "Building budgets for effective resource allocation," op. cit.; Wenrich and Reid (2003), "It's not the race I signed up for, but it's the race I'm in," op. cit.; Wise and Camper (1985), "Fund raising for two-year colleges," op. cit.

TOWARD A THEORY OF CHARITABLE FUND-RAISING

JAMES ANDREONI

Private providers of public goods, such as charities, invariably enlist fund-raisers to organize and collect contributions. Common in charitable fund-raising is seed money, either from a government grant or from a group of "leadership givers," that launches the fund drive and generates additional gifts. This paper provides a theoretical basis for fund-raisers and seeds to charity. The primary assumption is that there is a range of increasing returns at low levels of provision of the public good. It is shown that fund-raisers have a natural and important role, and that sometimes only a small amount of seed money can grow into a substantial charity.

I. Introduction

Economic research on altruism, public goods, and charitable giving has flourished over the past decade. The analysis to date has focused almost exclusively on donors—the supply side of charity—and has left unexplored the role played by fund-raisers—the demand side. Yet fund-raising is a vibrant, innovative, and highly professional industry. According to one estimate, about 115,000 organizations hire fund-raising staff and consultants, spending $2 billion per year on fund-raising. In 1995 the 25 largest charities spent an average of over $25 million each on fund-raising, or about 14 percent of charitable gifts.[1]

Understanding fund-raising may be important for improving policy predictions. In the 1980s several policy changes resulted in reduced government grants to charities and a reduced tax preference for donations. While economists predicted dire consequences for charities, contributions continued to rise in the 1980s. Several authors have conjectured that, had the models accounted for the vigorous response by fund-raisers, the predictions might have been better.[2]

This paper begins the task of including fund-raisers by modeling them alongside donors as active participants in the market for privately provided public goods. In doing so, I distinguish between two different types of fund drives, each with different incentives, constraints, and strategies. The first type is capital campaigns. They characterize new charities, or major new initiatives of existing charities, and, as the name implies, involve projects with large fixed costs of capitalization. Examples include buying expensive equipment or constructing new buildings. The second type is continuing campaigns. They raise the operating funds for items such as salaries, supplies, and maintenance for charities that are already capitalized.

This paper, the first in a research program, will focus exclusively on capital campaigns. I begin here because capital campaigns are generally the origins of charitable organizations. In addition, they are characterized by several features that appear to conflict with the intuition of free riding. Foremost among them is that capital campaigns rely heavily on "seed grants" and large "leadership gifts" that are publicly announced before the general fund drive begins. In fact, a well-known rule of thumb for capital campaigns is that one-third of the goal must be raised in a "quiet phase" before the public fund drive is launched. One might guess that such leadership gifts would only encourage free riding among later givers, whereas fund-raisers surely believe that they encourage gifts. By contrast, continuing campaigns turn directly to general fund-raising, without relying on the leadership phase.

While the discussion will be carried out in terms of capital campaigns, the application of the model is much broader. The key to the model is the assumption that there are initially some economies of scale in producing the public good. This is obviously true of capital investments, such as buildings, which must meet some critical threshold before they become productive. However, any public good that has increasing returns at low levels of provision will fit into the model presented here and can form the basis for fund-raising and leadership giving.

Note that one obvious way to explain leadership gifts is to consider social pressures and warm glows to giving. While they are clearly important, this paper will begin with the focus on purely economic variables. This is done for simplicity and to motivate more general results. Adding social effects, as is shown later in the paper, only strengthens the findings.

In Section II, I discuss some central features of capital campaigns that the model must explain. Section III provides important theoretical background, and Section IV presents the basic model. Sections V and VI look at the role of seed grants and leadership gifts. Section VII expands the model to include social effects, and Section VIII considers the possibility of seed subsidies.

II. Capital Campaigns

In the spring of 1995, Wisconsin Governor Tommy Thompson offered $27 million in state bonds to finance a new $72 million basketball arena for the University of Wisconsin, on the condition that the rest of the money be raised by private donations. A few days later, on April 1, 1995, Wisconsin's U.S. Senator Herb Kohl, who is also a wealthy entrepreneur, pledged $25 million to the project, which would now be called the Kohl Center. On June 27, 1995, Ab Nichols, a former University of Wisconsin basketball star, pledged $10 million. In November of 1995 the Kellner family pledged $2.5 million. By the time the university formally announced its public fund-raising campaign in February of 1996, it needed only $7 million to reach its goal. Building for the arena began in May of 1996, a little more than a year after the governor's offer.[3]

The Lawrenceville School, a private high school in New Jersey, just completed a 5-year, $125 million capital campaign. The drive was described in the October 1992 issue of *Fund Raising Management* magazine as "a technical and diplomatic juggling act requiring a timetable divided into three phases: Preparation, Nucleus Fund and the Public Campaign" (p. 21). During the preparation phase, the fund-raisers gathered information about potential donors, especially those who would be capable of contributing $25,000 or more. In the nucleus fund stage, the school set out to raise one-third of the goal from these large donors. After quietly securing $42 million in the nucleus fund stage, the fund-raisers were ready for the public campaign phase. With a lavish kickoff banquet and public relations blitz, the school announced its campaign. It then relied on small contributions raised from mailings, phone solicitations, and class reunions to complete the drive (see *Fund Raising Management*, October 1992, pp. 19–25; August 1996, pp. 21–24).

These two examples are typical of many capital campaigns. Skimming recent issues of *Fund Raising Management* yields many similar cases in which large donations from governments or from a small group of "leadership givers" act as a seed to grow a successful major capital fund drive. The phenomenon is so prevalent that experts in fund-raising have developed rules of thumb to describe it. For instance, Robert F. Hartsook in *Fund Raising Management* (August 1994, p. 32) advised that "the leadership commitment . . . should represent no less than 20 percent of the capital campaign goal." Jerold Panas, a professional fund-raiser and author of "how-to" books for fund-raisers, suggests that "if . . . there is not the potential for receiving 40 percent of your objective from your top twenty gifts, your campaign is likely to be moribund" (*Fund Raising Management*, August 1994, p. 27). The Lawrenceville School was following a similar and often-quoted rule: raise one-third of the goal in a "quiet phase" before announcing the general public fund drive.

In the economic models, charities are generally treated as inert organizations without goals, strategies, or influence.[4] However, the fund-raising apparatus appears to play a very important role in providing public goods.[5] Complicating the role of fund-raisers in capital campaigns is the fact that the charitable goods require significant fixed costs. For instance, a basketball arena or a school building needs to be of a certain minimum size and quality before it can be useful. Similarly, a public television or radio station needs expensive equipment before a minute of broadcasting can be produced. Unless there is a single large benefactor who is willing to guarantee this minimum quality, an equilibrium will spring up at zero contributions, even though another equilibrium exists at an interior point. Until the charity is sure to reach the threshold, no one has an incentive to give, meaning, of course, that without certain efforts the threshold may never be exceeded.

This paper will discuss the origins of privately provided public goods and, in particular, the role of seed money. In one version of the model, a government grant provides seed money. In a second version, fund-raisers solicit the seed money from donors. To make the model interesting, I consider two additional assumptions. First, the public good must meet a minimum quality threshold before it yields any services. Second, fund-raising is costly. The result is that the seed money is often necessary, but need be only a small fraction of the ultimate equilibrium level of contributions, and in fact need be only a small fraction of the minimum threshold, in order to push the economy off the zero provision level of the public good. Just as in the Kohl Center or the Lawrenceville School, help from the government or from large private donors—each well below the amount required to build the good—can seed the millions of dollars of small private contributions needed to complete the project.

It is important to note that this is not a paper about mechanism design. Rather, this is a positive look at the role of seeds and fund-raisers in starting charitable organizations. Why don't charities simply adopt one of the many mechanisms suggested in the economics literature? Aside from the fact that these mechanisms can be complicated and abstract, charities rely on many donors, perhaps thousands, and the organizational activity of the charity is costly. Organizing such a mechanism with so many people involved could be prohibitively expensive. The objective here is to understand why charities invest in organizing only a relatively small band of major contributors and then count on them to jump-start a general fund drive.

III. Theoretical Foundation

This section reviews the model of privately provided public goods that forms the basis for the later analysis. This model was introduced by Warr (1982, 1983) and developed further by others.[6] Individuals are each endowed with money m_i, which they can allocate between consumption of a private good, x_i, and gifts to the public good, g_i. Assume that units are normalized so that x and g can be expressed in dollars; hence each person faces a budget $x_i + g_i = m_i$. Let $G = \sum_{i=1}^{n} g_i$ be the total contributions to the public good. Individuals are taken to have preferences $u_i = u_i(x_i, G)$, which are continuous and strictly quasi-concave. Note that so far I have not assumed that there is a minimum threshold for the production of the public good; hence there is no range of increasing returns. As we shall see, the assumption of a threshold will create an important nonconvexity. For that reason, I shall refer to this standard model as the *convex case* throughout the paper. It will serve as an important reference point.

The provision of the public good is modeled as a simultaneous play Nash equilibrium game. Define $G_{-i} = \sum_{j \neq i} g_j$ as the contributions of everyone except person i. Alternatively, we can write $G = G_{-i} + g_i$. Under Nash equilibrium, each person's strategy is a contribution g_i, $0 \leq g_i \leq m_i$, with G_{-i} taken as given. With this framework, an individual's maximization problem can be written as

$$\max_{x_i, g_i} u_i (x_i, g_i + G_{-i})$$
$$\text{subject to } x_i + g_i = m_i,$$
$$g_i \geq 0.$$

Since gifts of others are treated as exogenous in the individual's maximization problem, it is equivalent to add the constant G_{-i} to both sides of the constraints and then to think of individuals as choosing G rather than g_i. Hence, the maximization above is equivalent to

$$\max_{x_i, G} u_i(x_i, G)$$

$$\text{subject to } x_i + G = m_i + G_{-i},$$

$$G \geq G_{-i}.$$

Ignoring the inequality constraint, one can easily see that each individual will have a solution to this problem of the form $G = f_i(m_i + G_{-i})$ or, equivalently, $g_i = f_i(m_i + G_{-i}) - G_{-i}$. However, keeping the inequality constraint in mind, we can write the individual supply function as

$$g_i = \max\{f_i(m_i + G_{-i}) - G_{-i}, 0\}. \tag{1}$$

We can add the further assumption that both the public good and the private good are normal; hence $0 < f_i' < 1$.

Given these supply functions, we can define a Nash equilibrium as a vector of gifts $(g_1^*, g_2^*, \dots, g_n^*)$ such that the supply functions in (1) map this vector into itself. Under the assumptions made, it can be shown that a Nash equilibrium will exist and that it will be unique. Both of these propositions have been shown by Bergstrom et al. (1986) and follow directly from the assumption of normal goods. For brevity, interested readers are referred to the original source.

Before continuing with the new model, I need to add two more assumptions. First, assume that if we were to remove any threshold, the equilibrium $G^* = \sum_{i=1}^{n} g_i^*$ would always be positive. Furthermore, let G^* be the equilibrium set of contributors to the public good in the convex case. Then assume that the number of people in this set is at least two.

IV. A Model

In this section and in the remainder of the paper, I shall often refer to the model above as an important reference point. Hence, any mention of G^* or g_i^* will be referring to the Nash equilibrium in the convex case.

For the new model, keep all the same assumptions used above, but now define the technology for producing the public good G as including an important nonconvexity:

$$G = \begin{cases} \sum_{i=1}^{n} g_i & \text{if } \sum_{i=1}^{n} g_i \geq \overline{G} \\ 0 & \text{if } \sum_{i=1}^{n} g_i < \overline{G}. \end{cases}$$

There is now a minimum threshold $\overline{G}$ that contributions must meet or surpass before any benefits of the public good can be consumed.[7] Note that this implies that there are some fixed costs involved in producing the good or, alternatively, there are increasing returns around the point at which contributions approach $\overline{G}$.[8]

The interesting feature of having fixed costs is that the economy could get "stuck" at an equilibrium of zero contributions. First notice that when $\overline{G} = 0$, we are back in the convex case; hence $g_i = g_i^*$ for all i is the unique equilibrium. As $\overline{G}$ increases from zero, the threshold may have absolutely no impact on g_i. In fact, it is easy to see that if $\overline{G}$ is below the g_i^* of any individual, then $\overline{G}$ will have no effect on the existence or uniqueness of any equilibrium.

How big does $\overline{G}$ need to be? Define g_i^o as the solution to the following for all i: $u_i(m_i - g_i^o, g_i^o) \equiv u_i(m_i, 0)$. Then g_i^o is the threshold such that if $\overline{G} = g_i^o$, person i would be just willing to provide all the public good alone, if need be; whereas if the threshold is above g_i^o, this person would not. The solution for g_i^o can be shown graphically in figure 1. Clearly, an equilibrium will spring up at $G = 0$ if no one is willing to make a solo gift. Hence, define $g_{max}^o = \max\{g_1^o, g_2^o, \dots, g_n^o\}$ as the highest of these values across all individuals. Then we can make the following proposition.

PROPOSITION 1. The allocation $G = 0$ is a Nash equilibrium iff $g_{max}^o \leq \overline{G}$.

Proof. If $g_i^o \leq \overline{G}$, then the best response to $G_{-i} = 0$ will be $g_i = 0$ for all i. Hence, $g_i = 0$ for all i is a Nash equilibrium. Likewise, suppose that $G = 0$ is a Nash equilibrium but $g_{max}^o > \overline{G}$. Then for at

CHARITABLE FUND-RAISING

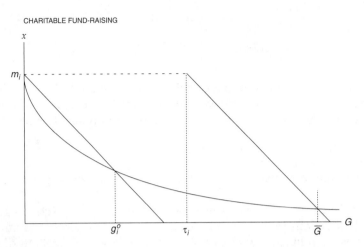

Figure 1 Defining g_i^* and τ_i

least one person k there exists a $g_k > \bar{G}$ that yields higher utility than $g_k = 0$, which contradicts the assumption that $G = 0$ is a Nash equilibrium. Q.E.D.

If $\bar{G}$ is too large, then there may be only one equilibrium at $G = 0$. The interesting case is one in which $\bar{G}$ is large enough to possibly prevent a charity from springing up, but not so large as to keep it from ever being provided. It turns out that if $\bar{G} < G^*$, then we are guaranteed to have two and only two Nash equilibria. This is stated formally in the following proposition.

PROPOSITION 2. If $g_{max}^o \le \bar{G} \le G^*$, then there will be exactly two Nash equilibria: one at $G = 0$ and another at $G = G^*$.

Proof. If follows obviously from proposition 1 that both $G = 0$ and $G = G^*$ are Nash equilibria. What we need to establish is that there are no other Nash equilibria. Since any $G > \bar{G}$ would have been available in the convex case (where $\bar{G} = 0$), we have to rule out possibilities for $\bar{G}$ as an equilibrium only when $\bar{G} < G^*$.

Consider a $\bar{G} < G^*$ and a vector $(\bar{g}_1, \bar{g}_2, \ldots, \bar{g}_n)$ such that $\bar{g}_i \ge 0$ for all i and $\sum_{i=1}^{n} \bar{g}_i = \bar{G}$. Suppose that this allocation is an equilibrium. Let $\hat{g}_i = f_i(m_i + \bar{G}_{-i}) - G_{-i}$. If $\bar{g}_i$ is an equilibrium, then it must be that the best response to $\bar{G}_{-i}$ is not a number greater than $\bar{g}_i$; that is, $\hat{g}_i \le \bar{g}_i$ for all i. Since $f_i(m_i + \bar{G}_{-i}) \le \bar{G} < G^* = f_i(m_i + G_{-i}^*)$ for all $i \in C^*$ and since f is monotonically increasing, we know that $\bar{G}_{-i} < G_{-i}^*$ for all $i \in C^*$. Finally, by the assumption that all goods are normal, $-1 < f'$ $-1 < 0$. It follows that $\hat{g}_i > g_i^*$ for all $i \in C^*$. Since $\bar{g}_i \ge \hat{g}_i$, it follows that $\bar{g}_i > g_i^*$ *for* $i \in C^*$. But this would imply that $\bar{G} > G^*$, a contradiction. Q.E.D.

The next two results follow easily from the discussion above.

COROLLARY 1. If $\bar{G} = G^*$, then $(g_1^*, g_2^*, \ldots, g_n^*)$ is the unique interior equilibrium.

Proof. Consider any allocation $(\bar{g}_1, \bar{g}_2, \ldots, \bar{g}_n)$ not equal to $(g_1^*, g_2^*, \ldots, g_n^*)$ such that $\sum_{i=1}^{n} \bar{g}_i = \sum_{i=1}^{n} g_i^*$. Suppose that $(\bar{g}_1, \bar{g}_2, \ldots, \bar{g}_n)$ is a Nash equilibrium. Then there must be at least one $j \in C^*$ such that $\bar{g}_j < g_j^*$, and hence $\bar{G}_{-j} > G_{-j}^*$. By monotonicity, $f_j(m_j + \bar{G}_{-j}) > f_j(m_j + G_{-j}^*) = G^*$ for j, which contradicts the assumption that $(\bar{g}_1, \bar{g}_2, \ldots, \bar{g}_n)$ is a Nash equilibrium. Q.E.D.

COROLLARY 2. If $g_{max}^o > \bar{G}$, then $(g_1^*, g_2^*, \ldots, g_n^*)$ is the unique Nash equilibrium.

Proof. When g_{max}^o is above the threshold $\bar{G}$, then for some k there is a $g_k > 0$ that is a best response to $G_{-k} = 0$. Hence, $G = 0$ is no longer a Nash equilibrium. The proof that $(g_1^*, g_2^*, \ldots, g_n^*)$ is the unique Nash equilibrium is exactly the same as that in corollary 1, which showed it to be the unique interior equilibrium.

Proposition 2 shows that if the threshold $\bar{G}$ is big enough, it will create another Nash equilibrium at $G = 0$; but as long as the threshold is not above G^*, it will not create any more Nash equilibria. This is true even if by chance the threshold actually equals G^*. Of course, it is still possible for two Nash equilibria to exist if $\bar{G} > G^*$. It is obvious that a threshold $\bar{G} > G^*$ means that G^* is unavailable as an equilibrium. It is also clear that no equilibrium G will develop above $\bar{G}$. However, it is possible that $\bar{G}$ itself may become an equilibrium. In particular, as long as there exists a Pareto-improving way to allocate gifts such that $\sum g_i = \bar{G}$, there will exist a Nash equilibrium at $\bar{G}$. This is shown next.

Proposition 3. Assume $\bar{G} > G^*$. If there exists a $(\bar{g}_1, \bar{g}_2, \ldots, \bar{g}_n)$ such that $g_i^* < \bar{g}_i \leq g_i^o$ for each i and $\sum_{i=1}^{n} \bar{g}_i = \bar{G}$, then $(\bar{g}_1, \bar{g}_2, \ldots, \bar{g}_n)$ is a Nash equilibrium.

Proof. First note that since $\sum_{i=1}^{n} \bar{g}_i = \bar{G}$, everyone is pivotal; that is, if anyone provides less than $\bar{g}_i$, then no public good will be provided. But since $\bar{g}_i \leq g_i^o$ for all i, no one has an incentive to provide less than $\bar{g}_i$; then is, $\bar{G}$ is Pareto improving. Furthermore, since $g_i^* < \bar{g}_i$ for all i, $G_{-i}^* < \bar{G}_{-i}$ for all i. By normal goods, no one can increase utility by providing more than $\bar{g}_i$. Hence, $\bar{g}_i$ is a best response for all i. Q.E.D.

An interesting contrast between propositions 2 and 3 is that when $\bar{G} \leq G^*$, there is only one nonzero equilibrium at G^*. However, when $\bar{G} > G^*$, any set of contributions that are between g_i^o and g_i^* for all i and sum to $\bar{G}$ may be a Nash equilibrium. In general, there will be a continuum of such equilibria. This case is very similar to the "provision point" models considered by Bagnoli and Lipman (1989). Typically in these models the public good is provided only at the threshold, not above or below, and any contributions above the threshold are either wasted or refunded in some manner. If an interior equilibrium exists, however, it is always at contributions that sum to exactly $\bar{G}$. In our model, the case in which $\bar{G} > G^*$ is much like the Bagnoli and Lipman framework since no one has an incentive to give more than the assigned $\bar{g}_i$; hence models of provision points can be applied to the fund-raising problem.

This naturally raises the point of what to assume in the event that contributions fail to meet the threshold, $\Sigma g_i < \bar{G}$. There are several possibilities. Funds could be wasted, refunded, or applied to some other (inferior) project. The provision point models often also allow that contributions below the threshold are refunded to the donor. Applying the funds to an alternative project would require a more general model than that presented here but would have consequences similar to those of a refund as long as utility is continuous in the contributions to the inferior project. As far as equilibria are concerned, they are the same regardless of whether a refund is given, the funds are wasted, or an alternative project is built. Because it is simpler, and perhaps more realistic, assume that if gifts do not meet the threshold, the funds are used for some other project that the contributors do not care about and in this sense are wasted.[9]

The next two sections examine how a small grant by government or individuals can result in big growth for charity, that is, can remove $G = 0$ as an equilibrium. It is assumed throughout that $\bar{G}$ is large enough that a Nash equilibrium exists at $G \equiv 0$.

V. Government Grants

Imagine that the government levies lump-sum taxes t_i on each individual and contributes a grant $T = \sum_{i-1}^{n} t_i$ to the public good. It is well known that if $t_i \leq g_i^*$ for all i, then the lump-sum tax will be completely crowded out. That is, total giving $G + T$ will remain unchanged (Warr 1982). Since the individual's voluntary gift, g_i^* is greater than the involuntary gift, t_i, the individual can simply reduce the voluntary component of the gift so that the total gift, voluntary plus involuntary, equals the value of the pretax gift g_i^*. By the definition of the equilibrium, this is optimal for everyone, and hence, private contributions are completely crowded out by the public grant. This crowding-out hypothesis will greatly simplify the analysis below.

Note that the crowding-out proposition has been the subject of many papers, which show that it is unrealistic and easily rejected when confronted with data. It is used here for its analytical ease. Later I show that qualitatively similar, although technically more complicated, results follow from more general and realistic models of giving, such as warm glow and prestige giving. Likewise, using income or commodity taxes would be more descriptive than simple lump-sum taxes. Similar results follow from more complex taxes but are much more easily shown using lump-sum taxation.[10]

For each i let τ_i be the amount of exogenous giving at which person i is just willing to bring the public good up to the threshold value by acting alone. That is, τ_i is determined implicitly as the solution to

$$u_i(m_i + \tau_i - \bar{G}, \bar{G}) \equiv u_i(m_i, 0), \tag{2}$$

where $g_i = \bar{G} - \tau_i$ is the individual's gift. An illustration of τ_i is shown in figure 1.

The quantity τ_i will be an important variable in determining the necessary size of seeds to charitable giving. This is illustrated in the next proposition.

PROPOSITION 4. Suppose $\overline{G} < G^*$ and $g^0_{max} < \overline{G}$. For any lump-sum tax scheme $(t_1, t_2, \ldots, t_n)$ such that $t_i \le g^*_i$ for all $i \in C^*$, $t_i = 0$ for all $i \notin C^*$, and $\sum_{j \ne k} t_j > \tau_k$ for at least one $k \in C^*$, there will exist a unique interior Nash equilibrium G', where $g'_i = g^*_i - t_i$ for all i and $G^* = G' + T$.

PROOF. As in proposition 1, for some k there exists a $g_k > 0$ that is a best reply to $G_{-k} = 0$; hence $G = 0$ is no longer a Nash equilibrium. It is also clear, by the crowding-out hypothesis, that $g'_i = g^*_i - t_i$ for all i is also a Nash equilibrium. We need to show that this equilibrium is unique.

As before, we need to verify that the threshold is not an equilibrium. Consider person k for whom $\sum_{j \ne k} t_j > \tau_k$. For this person, $G_{-k} + \sum_{j \ne k} t_j > \tau_k$. By the assumption of normal goods and by the definition of τ, person k will have a best response $g_k > \overline{G} - \tau_k$ Hence, there is not an equilibrium at the threshold.

To complete the proof, we need to show that it is indeed possible to find a tax vector that satisfies the conditions of the proposition, that is, $t_i \le g^*_i$ for all i and $\sum_{j \ne k} t_j > \tau_k$ for some k. Suppose $\tau_k = \min\{\tau_1, \tau_2, \ldots, \tau_n\}$. It is easy to show (see Andreoni and McGuire 1993) that the assumption of normal goods implies that $G^*_{-k} > \tau_k$. Hence, set $t_i = g^*_i \cdot [(\tau_k + \epsilon)/G^*_{-k}]$ for all $i \ne k$ and for some positive ϵ arbitrarily close to zero, and let t_k be any nonnegative number less than g^*_k. Then $t_i < g^*_i$ for all i, and $\sum_{j \ne k} t_j > \tau_k$. Q.E.D.

This proposition states that if the government raises taxes *on people other than i* by an amount at least as high as τ_i, then there will be a unique Nash equilibrium in which the total provision, private gifts plus taxes, will be identical to the Nash equilibrium in the original convex version of this economy. Notice that, by definition, τ_i will be less than g^0_i for each i; hence, τ_i will be less than $\overline{G}$. The implication of this is that the seed provided by the government can be below the threshold $\overline{G}$. In fact, the seed can be chosen with the most generous person, that is, with the lowest τ, in mind.

Several other interesting things can be noted. First, if $\overline{G} > G^*$ but there still exists an interior Nash equilibrium at $\overline{G}$ and if the government contributes a grant T that is large enough to induce one person to give to the public good, then in equilibrium that person need not be the sole contributor to the public good. As in proposition 3, as long as there is a Pareto-improving way to allocate contributions such that the threshold is met, such an allocation can be an equilibrium. In general there may be a continuum of such equilibria. All that the government seed does is to guarantee that $G = 0$ is no longer an equilibrium.[11]

A second interesting point is that giving can also be seeded in situations less restrictive than those spelled out in this proposition. In fact, as shown by Bergstrom et al. (1986), taxing nongivers will increase the equilibrium level of public goods. The implication for this model is that if nongivers are taxed, then the seed will generate even greater gifts. All that is needed is that the tax on individuals other than i be greater than τ_i for at least one i in order to rule out a Nash equilibrium at the origin. If this is accomplished, the resulting Nash equilibrium will be whatever the unique interior Nash equilibrium would have been for that tax scheme in the ordinary convex case. As we know from Bergstrom et al., if nongivers are taxed or if individuals are taxed in excess of their original gift, then the Nash equilibrium will be higher than if only givers had been taxed and at an amount lower than the original gift. This is shown next.

COROLLARY 3. Assume $\overline{G} < G^*$. Let G^{**} be the interior Nash equilibrium in the convex case that would result from a lump-sum tax scheme $(t_1, t_2, \ldots, t_n)$. If $t_i \ge 0$ for all i and if $\sum_{j \ne k} t_j > \tau_k$ for at least one k, then G^{**} will be the unique Nash equilibrium and $G^{**} + T \ge G^*$.

Proof. First find a vector of taxes that satisfies the conditions in proposition 4. Hence, only givers are taxed. Now adjust that vector of taxes to the desired new vector. Since all changes either will be neutral (by completely crowding out givers) or will be increases in taxes on nongivers and hence cause a nonneutral increase in total giving, $G^{**} + T \ge G^*$. Q.E.D.

This corollary has the natural interpretation that if free riders are taxed, we can get an even bigger bang for each tax dollar collected. What is important, and perhaps surprising, is that τ need not be large compared with $\overline{G}$. If $\overline{G}$ is close to g^0_i, then the τ may be quite small. As $\overline{G}$ moves farther above g^0_i, the τ will grow as well, but the return from government tax dollars in terms of seeding and promoting private gifts may still be substantial. Only when $\overline{G}$ is many times g^0_i will the seed need to be a significant fraction of the total public good.

TABLE 1

Example

	Case 1: $\bar{G} = 50$	Case 2: $\bar{G} = 75$	Case 3: $\bar{G} = 100$	Case 4: $\bar{G} = 150$	Case 5: $\bar{G} = 250$
τ	1.20	13.47	29.62	68.65	112.50
$t_i = \tau/(n-1)$	.012	.136	.299	.693	1.136
Equilibrium $G + T$	97.08	97.08	100	150	200
Bang for the buck: G/T	79.10	6.14	2.34	1.16	.76

Note:— $u_i = x^{25}(G + 200)^{75}$ for all i, $m = 100$, $n = 100$, $G^* = 97.08$, and $g_i^0 = 46.75$. Identical individuals and identical taxation $t_i = \tau/(n-1)$ are assumed.

These propositions can be illustrated with a simple example. Consider an economy of 100 individuals with identical utility functions $u_i = (1 - \alpha)\ln x + \alpha \ln(G + \gamma)$. In this example, set $\alpha = 0.75$, $\gamma = 200$, and income $m = 100$ for all 100 individuals. These parameters imply an interior Nash equilibrium, in the case with no threshold, at $G^* = 97.09$; hence $g_i^* = 0.9709$ for all i, which is about 1 percent of income. The critical value for the threshold is $g_i^0 = 46.75$. Suppose for simplicity that the government levies an identical tax on each individual such that $(n - 1)\,t = \tau$, and hence $T = n\tau/(n - 1)$. Table 1 shows a number of different outcomes based on different assumptions about the threshold $\bar{G}$.

Look first at case 1, where $\bar{G}$ is 50, only 3.25 above g_i^0. Here a total tax of only $T = 1.21$ will guarantee that $G^* = 97.08$ is the unique Nash equilibrium. Every dollar of taxes collected generates $79.10 of private charity, a substantial bang for the buck. In case 2, a $\bar{G}$ of 75 is 28.5 above g_i^0, and here taxes $T = 13.61$ are enough to guarantee the unique equilibrium at G^*, with each dollar of taxes generating over $6.00 of charity. As the threshold $\bar{G}$ rises above G^*, as in the last three cases, the threshold itself becomes the equilibrium. But as we can see in case 5, even when the threshold is more than twice G^*, each dollar of tax revenue still raises an additional 76 cents of private charity.

I can also illustrate corollary 3. Suppose in the example above that an amount of income equal to g_i^* is transferred from half the population to the other half; hence the richer half will have income of $100.97 and the poorer half $99.03. Now, because of the crowding-out hypothesis, only the rich half will give, but the equilibrium G^* will stay the same. If we retain the assumption of taxing everyone equally, then in case 1 the τ_i for the givers falls to 0.73; hence the tax t_i falls as well and the bang for the buck rises to $131.35. Providing any level of G now requires less total taxation. For instance, the bang for the buck in the case $\bar{G} = 75$ is 6.46, for $\bar{G} = 100$ is 2.42, and for $\bar{G} =$ is 0.77.

VI. Fund-Raising

Imagine again the convex case. Here there is no role for fund-raising. To understand it in this context we might turn to models of advertising and information, or perhaps appeal to ad hoc models of social pressure. With the existence of a nonconvexity, however, fund-raising plays a natural role in coordinating givers to overcome the equilibrium at zero contributions.

Fund-raising is modeled in three stages. The first stage is the *selection* stage. Here the charity selects a subset of the population to act as leaders. This stage is done "quietly" by the charity. One can think of this as the time at which the fund-raiser assesses the feasibility of the project and does "market research" into the potential donors. In the second stage, called the *leadership* phase, the charity organizes the leaders and allows them to make pledges of contributions. Just as with real fund-raising, these pledges are binding.[12] The leadership phase is thus a game among the leaders. An interesting aspect of the leadership phase is that being a leader is voluntary; hence the charity cannot make people worse off by being leaders. Models of the sequential provision of public goods can be exploited to analyze this stage of the game. It should also be added that organizing leaders is costly, and the greater the number of leaders the greater the cost of the fund-raising. This gives charities (and leaders) an incentive to keep the group small. The final stage is called the *contribution* stage. In this stage the charity turns to the general public for massive fund-raising. This stage is modeled as a simultaneous contribution public goods game. The charity announces the leadership pledges and then collects contributions to the public good. The crux of the model is that the charity will choose leaders, and select a game to run among the leaders, so that when they turn to the general contributions stage they have omitted zero as a Nash equilibrium.

A. Fund-Raising in a Pure-Altruism Model

Define the set of leaders, $\mathscr{L}$, as those who are approached by the charity. Let 1 be the number of people in the set $\mathscr{L}$. Then define $\mathscr{F}$ to be the set of followers, where $\mathscr{F}$ is the complement of $\mathscr{L}$. Since the people who are chosen to be leaders must agree to do it, they must all be at least as well off being a leader as not. Of course, there are many ways a charity can make a leader better off than nonleaders. It can, for instance, offer a quid pro quo such as choice seats in return for a major gift to the opera. Or it can provide a warm glow or prestige in the form of an award or mention in the symphony program. At this point I shall not consider any of these effects, although I shall return to this possibility later. Instead, assume that the charity can affect utility only through consumption of x and G.

Selecting the leaders amounts to letting this group collude to be first movers. What is the advantage in this? Varian (1994) analyzed a very simple model of sequential provision of public goods and found that the first mover is always better off. The reason is that a first mover can commit to more free riding than a second mover. Through a similar means, the charity can give its first movers just such an advantage.

Before I provide a more general model, let us look at some examples to illustrate the issues. For ease of exposition, assume that everyone has identical preferences and identical wealth and, hence, everyone has identical τ. In each of the three examples to follow, the fund drives will be allowed to have a leadership stage in which a game among the leaders results in binding commitments. These pledges are then announced to the community, at which time a Nash equilibrium contribution game is played among the rest of society. For these examples the cost of fund-raising will be ignored.

Example 1: $\sum_{i \in \mathscr{L}} g_i^* = \tau$. In this case the charity would ask all the members of the group of leaders to pledge g_i^*. Looking ahead, the leaders know that if they all do this, then the result will be an equilibrium with total contributions of G^*. Since this is better than the Nash equilibrium of $G = 0$ and since none of the leaders would rather be followers, all members of the leaders will pledge to give g_i^*. Note that there is also an equilibrium at $g_i = 0$ for all the leaders in the leadership stage. However, if the fund-raiser collects pledges of the form "I will pledge y_l only if all other leaders pledge $(y_2, \ldots, y_l)$," then, as discussed later, a subgame perfect equilibrium in the leadership stage will have every leader pledging g_i^*, conditional on the pledge of g_j^* from other leaders (Admati and Perry 1991).

Example 2: $\sum_{i \in \mathscr{L}} g_i^* < \tau$. In this case there is no way for the charity to specify any contributions by the leaders that would both meet the threshold of τ and make each of the leaders better off than if they had been followers. Hence, the group of leaders is too small.

Example 3: $\sum_{i \in \mathscr{L}} g_i^* > \tau$. Here the leaders will each be better off committing to some g_i such that $g_i^* \geq g_i$ and $\sum_{i \in \mathscr{L}} g_i^* \geq \tau$. Since those members of $\mathscr{F}$, the followers, each have donation functions $g_i = f_i(m_i + G_{-i}) - G_{-i}$ and $-1 < f_i' - 1 < 0$, if the members of $\mathscr{L}$ give a little less than g_i^*, then the members of $\mathscr{F}$ will each give a little more. Hence, G will not fall in equilibrium by the amount by which the leaders reduce their contributions. Since we know from the definition of g_i^* that each individual's marginal rate of substitution equals one when everyone gives g_i^*, the members of $\mathscr{L}$ can be made better off by committing to giving an amount below g_i^*. As long as their gifts are large enough to surpass τ, they will all be better off for agreeing to be leaders, and the public good will be provided at an interior point.

Notice that the outcome of example 3 is that, while the public good is provided, it is somewhat below G^*. This result matches the predictions in Varian (1994). Hence, while the provision of public goods will be greater than zero in equilibrium with fund-raisers, it may also be less than G^*. Next this model will be solved in more detail.

B. The Game among the Leaders

Generalize the examples above in two ways. First, imagine that individuals are heterogeneous; hence each g_i^* and τ_i is unique. Second, assume that the charity faces costs of fund-raising that increase with the size of the leadership group,[13] so $c = c(l)$ and $c' > 0$. Furthermore, assume that the cost of organizing everyone, $c(n)$, is prohibitively high.

Assume that the costs of fund-raising must be paid with the funds collected. So if l is the number of leaders and total contributions are G, then consumption of charity by everyone will be $G - c(l)$. Also assume that the objective of the charity is to provide the greatest level of these net contributions, $G - c(l)$, as possible. This now changes the calculus of the problem slightly. For a given cost, the equilibrium in the convex case will now be below G^*. This adds one more reason for the charity to want to minimize on costs. For complete generality we should now think of G^* as a function of the costs, that is, $G^* = G^*(c)$ and $G^{*\prime} < 0$. Likewise, we should also think of τ as depending on costs: $\tau_i = \tau_i(c)$ and $\tau_i' > 0$.

In constructing the game among the leaders, we need to keep in mind the subgame played by the followers. They will take the pledges of the leaders as given and play a simultaneous contributions game. For instance, for a given $c(l)$, if the leaders by coincidence were each to give $g_i^*(c(l))$ and if $\sum_{i \in \mathcal{L}} g_i^* - c(l) \geq \tau_k$ for some k in $\mathcal{F}$, then the followers would each give $g_i^*(c(l))$ as well. This follows from the definition of Nash equilibrium. However, if the leaders were each to give an amount below $g_i^*(c(l))$, but with a total still above the τ necessary to get an interior equilibrium, then, as shown earlier, the followers would respond with gifts greater than $g_i^*(c(l))$ and hence make up some of the difference. As long as $\sum_{i \in \mathcal{L}} g_i^* - c > \tau_k$, there will be room for the leaders to make smaller gifts and increase their own utility.

The objective of the fund-raiser will be to find the set of leaders, set a goal for leadership contributions, and choose a game among the leaders that will guarantee that the goal is met. The ultimate objective is to reach the highest net contributions. Once again, let us build up the logic of the model by starting with a special case. Suppose that the charity has identified the optimal set $\mathcal{L}$ and that $\sum_{i \in \mathcal{L}} g_i^*(c(l)) - c(l) = \tau_{\min}(c(l))$, where $\tau_{\min}$ is the lowest τ among the set of followers. Now the charity needs to implement a game among the leaders that will have each member giving g_i^*.

There are at least two games that the charity could choose from. First, notice that this problem is identical to a game in which a group of individuals $\mathcal{L}$ must provide a discrete public good at the level $\tau_k + c(l)$. A mechanism suggested by Bagnoli and Lipman (1989) shows that in a simultaneous play game, $g_i = g_i^*$ is an equilibrium. However, $g_i = 0$ is also an equilibrium. An alternative is presented by Admati and Perry (1991). They derive a model with two agents who alternate making gifts. On an agent's turn he can increase, but not decrease, his contribution. Admati and Perry show that under reasonable assumptions this game will have an equilibrium at the desired level, although it also cannot be guaranteed. However, if agents are allowed to make contributions with conditional statements of the form "I will give X if the other person gives Y," then the desired equilibrium will always be met. Moreover, the equilibrium is identical to that of an alternating offers bargaining problem.[14]

There are many other mechanisms that the charity could use in this case to get the members of $\mathcal{L}$ to give $g_i^*(c(l))$. Which mechanism the charities use is beside the point of this analysis. Hence, the mechanism used among the leaders will be treated as a black box.

How do things change when the optimal $\mathcal{L}$ is such that $\sum_{i \in \mathcal{L}} g_i^*(c(l)) - c(l) > \tau_{\min}(c(l))$? The leaders can look ahead to the contribution stage and know that their contributions will determine the ultimate equilibrium. They could collude to set their contributions at the level that will maximize their own utility, taking the followers as Nash responders to their leadership gift. Now define $\tau^* + c(l)$ as the collusive level of giving by the leadership givers that maximizes their collective welfare as first movers. That is, if the leadership givers *commit* to giving an aggregate level τ^*, with an implied allocation of gifts so that $\sum_{i \in \mathcal{L}} g_i - c(l) = \tau^*$, then when the followers move to the contribution stage, the result will maximize the utility of the leaders. Hence, in the leadership phase, the charity should set the goal of the leaders at $\tau^L = \max\{\tau^*, \tau_{\min}\}$. With the goal for the leaders at τ^L, the charity then runs a game among these leaders to meet this goal.

Finally, how does the charity choose the members of $\mathcal{L}$? The charity now faces a difficult non-linear problem. One complication is the tension between τ and g^*. To keep the contributions of the leaders as high as possible, the charity should choose those with the highest g^*'s. But they should leave out people with low τ's since they need to surpass the τ of only one individual in $\mathfrak{F}$. But people with high g^*'s are also likely to have low τ's, and they are likely to be the wealthy. Hence, depending on the distribution of preferences and incomes, the charity can adopt any number of strategies. Unless we make stricter assumptions about preferences and income distributions, it is impossible to present a solution to the charity's problem.[15]

The model now generally characterizes the behavior of charities and fund-raisers in the economy. Fund-raisers organize their most generous givers and coordinate their contributions before announcing a general fund drive. The fund-raiser's rule of thumb—variously stated as raising one-third of the goal or as getting commitments from the 20 top contributors before announcing the general fund drive—is also captured by this model. The only assumptions made here to distinguish the model from prior models of privately provided public goods are, first, that there is a range of increasing returns in the production of the public good and, second, that fund-raising is costly.

C. A Note about Commitment

A key assumption in the model just described is that the first movers are able to commit to their actions. There has been an active discussion in the game theory literature on commitment in sequential games. Bagwell (1995), for instance, shows that in a two-person game, if the second mover has any degree of uncertainty (over an infinite support) about the first mover's choice, then the simultaneous play Nash equilibrium will result, even though the game is played sequentially. Intuitively, this holds because the second mover must be willing to choose the sequential-game equilibrium move regardless of the information he gets about the choice of the first mover. This in turn gives the first mover an incentive to cheat on the sequential-game equilibrium outcome. As a result, the second mover will assume, regardless of information, that the first mover has indeed cheated. Hence, subgame perfection leads to the simultaneous play equilibrium. Bagwell's results are naturally extended to games with many first and second movers. The only way for first movers to maintain an advantage is to make their moves perfectly observable.

In the models presented above, the first mover is either the government or the leadership givers. The government can make its contribution observable by issuing the cash ex ante. Indeed, this is often how the government works. Even in so-called challenge grants the government will typically give money contingent only on a *plan* to raise privately three or four times the challenge grant funds.[16]

For leaders to commit is a bit more complicated. The fact that general fund drives are often initiated with large press conferences and major donors make legally enforceable pledges can be seen as an effort to make the leadership gifts credible and known. However, it is difficult to credibly prevent first movers from giving again. While leadership givers may not be able to commit to not giving more than the leadership gift, they can clearly commit to giving no less.[17] If we allow that leaders, in the contribution stage, can increase their gifts as part of the simultaneous provision game, then the results in this paper remain the same. The only difference would be that leaders will have no particular first-mover advantage, except the possible social effects discussed below. If, on the other hand, leaders and followers are allowed to alternate moves ad infinitum, then the game becomes far more complex.[18] There may be a benefit to future research that explores these alternatives.

VII. Warm Glow, Prestige, and Social Effects

Several authors have argued that a model of warm-glow giving, in which individuals behave as though there is some private goods benefit from the act of giving, captures the data much better than the "pure altruism" model just described.[19] The warm glow may enter the model through any number of mechanisms, but the important component is that utility depends, at a minimum, on one's own contribution, so $u_i = u_i(x_i, G, g_i)$.

How would warm glow giving affect the results just stated? The answer is that the basic result would remain unchanged: if the government or fund-raisers can reach some critical mass of provision, they can eliminate the zero equilibrium. The difference is that such efforts can have an even bigger bang for the buck with a warm glow. The reason is that, as shown in Andreoni (1989), lump-sum taxes on warm-glow givers will generally be incompletely crowded out. Hence, if the government raises an amount of tax T to get the economy off the zero equilibrium, the resultant equilibrium will be above the G^* defined as the unique interior equilibrium in the convex case.[20]

Related work by Harbaugh (1998) introduces the concept of prestige as the benefit individuals might get from having the size of their gifts known to others. A distinguishing feature of leadership gifts is that the givers are often named publicly and, as Harbaugh notes, the sizes of their gifts are often revealed. Prestige may matter because, for instance, there are benefits to business owners in advertising their companies or to lawyers or accountants in signaling their honesty and integrity; or, as Glazer and Konrad (1996) hypothesize, people may simply get consumption value from sending signals of their wealth. All of these are various ways of saying that if there is a warm glow, then there may be an additional glow to the members of $\mathscr{L}$; hence they may be willing to pay more to the public good as leaders than as followers. As a result, an even smaller group of leaders may be needed in order to reach the threshold.[21] Moreover, the amount collected from these people may easily exceed the convex case; hence, total contributions could be larger as well. Thus warm glow and prestige can generate an even bigger impact for fund-raising than in the case of perfect altruism and pure public goods.

A third possible effect is "social comparison." Sociologists and other social scientists stress how one person's gift may act as a model for another's. People who want to do their "fair share" may look to others around them to get an idea of what gift is appropriate. One might imagine that leadership gifts serve to set some standard for fair share. Let $G^{\mathscr{L}}$ be the contributions of the leadership group, and let $d_i = d(g_i, G^{\mathscr{L}})$ be some distance function between one's own gift and a standard set by the leadership gifts. Then utility could look something like $u_i = u_i(x_i, G, 1/d_i)$. Analysis of this model would proceed just as in the warm-glow case, except now G^* and τ_i, will also depend on the $G^{\mathscr{L}}$ determined in the leadership stage, with G^* increasing and τ_i decreasing in the leadership gifts.

One final word about social effects is that they may be creating a nonconvexity in themselves. If certain charities become fads or if people want to get involved only if enough others show interest, then there may be a cascading effect of participation in charity. If this is so, then it shows one more role for seed money, that is, to create social momentum behind a cause.

VIII. Subsidizing Gifts

In addition to direct grants, another instrument available to both government and leaders is subsidies or, as they are sometimes called, matching grants. Subsidies are, of course, already a part of government policy. By giving to tax-exempt organizations, givers who itemize their taxes gain a subsidy. Much less common, however, are matching grants by the government to specific charities.

In private fund-raising campaigns, matching gifts are occasionally observed. Some corporations offer to match their employees' contributions. A common tool in fund-raising for public broadcasting is the "challenge grant," where an individual promises to give, for instance, $1,000 if a certain number or amount of pledges is received by a specified deadline. Still, general offers of matching grants, where the more an individual gives the more another will give in return, remain relatively rare.

In this section I discuss generalizations of the model above to include the possibility for subsidies in addition to direct grants. I shall look at both government subsidies and leadership subsidies. The result is that indeed subsidies should be rare.

A. Government Subsidies

There are several ways in which the government could offer a subsidy. It could, for instance, earmark a certain group of philanthropists and offer a subsidy to just those people. In a way this is like making the government part of the group of leaders described in the last section. Rather, what I have in mind here is a general offer by the government to give s dollars to the charity for every dollar the charity raises privately, with the subsidy paid from general tax revenues. This subsidy could be combined with direct grants or used alone. It is important to note that the question being asked here is not whether there is an optimal subsidy. This has been addressed elsewhere. Instead, the question is whether the government could get a bigger bang for the buck by using some of its money on subsidies rather than on direct grants.[22]

First, could government remove the zero equilibrium with a subsidy alone? The answer here is clearly no. From the logic of Section V, to guarantee that $\bar{G}$ will be met, the government must offer a subsidy of at least $\bar{s}$, where $\bar{s}$ solves

$$u_i(m_i - (1 - \bar{s})\, \bar{G}, \bar{G}) \equiv u_i(m_i, 0)$$

for at least one i. Since $\bar{G}$ may be many times m_i for most i, the subsidy may need to be quite high. But to get one person to prefer to give, the government will have to subsidize all individuals by $\bar{s}$. This is an unlikely scenario.

Next turn the question to one of incremental changes. Imagine that the government has chosen lump-sum taxes t_i as described in Section V so that they just reach the minimum t necessary to get an interior equilibrium. Now let us ask whether they can shave some revenue from the t_i's to devote the money to subsidies and increase welfare.

An individual's budget constraint is now $x_i + (1 - s)g_i = m_i - t_i$. Next, determine the taxes on others, τ_i, necessary to make an individual willing to provide $\bar{G}$ for this given s. To provide $\bar{G}$ he must make a gift of $g_i = \bar{G} - \tau_i - t_i$. Substituting this into the budget constraint, we see that $\tau_i = \tau_i(s)$ is defined implicitly as the solution to

$$u_i(m_i - st_i - (1 - s)(\bar{G} - \tau_i), \bar{G}) \equiv u_i(m_i, 0).$$

This subsidy will imply a new Nash equilibrium, $G^N(s)$. Hence, the new subsidy will cost the government revenue in the amount $R(s) = sG^N(s)$.

Does $\tau(s)$ fall fast enough to free up tax revenues to pay for the subsidy $R(s)$? It is easy to verify that $d\tau(s)/ds = (T - G)/(1 - s)$ and $dR(s)/ds = G^N(s) + [sdG^N(s)/ds]$. Evaluating both of these at $s = 0$, we see that

$$\frac{d\tau(s)}{ds}\Big|_{s=0} = -(\bar{G} - T),$$

$$\frac{dR(s)}{ds}\Big|_{s=0} = G^N. \tag{3}$$

However, by definition, $G^N \geq \bar{G}$, so clearly $G^N > \bar{G} - T$. This means that there is no room for the government to convert tax dollars from seed grants to subsidies.[23] If the total budget that the government can devote to the charity is T, it is best to spend it all as a direct grant. Only when the government's budget is large should it consider adding subsidies.

The result is that indeed government matching grants to specific charities are likely to be rare and will not replace seed grants. One should emphasize again that this is not a normative exercise, but a positive one. If a government is constrained and cannot afford Pigouvian subsidies to all deserving public goods, it may be best to provide seed grants to several charities to nudge them into existence. This indeed appears to capture the behavior of the government.

B. Leadership Subsidies

Now consider whether leadership givers would ever choose to subsidize the followers by offering a matching grant. Note first that we must look only at subsidies that operate at the margin. For instance, an offer to match dollar for dollar the first million dollars of gifts to a $10 million fund drive is inframarginal and hence should operate as an ordinary direct grant. To be true subsidies, they must match the *last* dollars given.

As in the case with government subsidies, it is unlikely that subsidies alone will be sufficient for the leaders to eliminate the zero equilibrium. So again, we can start at a solution found in Section V to see whether it can be adjusted to include a subsidy from the leaders to the followers.

Begin by redefining $\tau_i(s)$ among the followers as the solution to

$$u_i(m_i - (1 - s) (\bar{G} - \tau_i), \bar{G}) \equiv u_i(m_i, 0).$$

Assume for simplicity that the leaders provide the optimal τ given an announced s. Then the cost of the subsidy to the leaders will be $R(s) = s[G^N (s) - \tau (s)]$. Analogously to (3), differentiating $\tau (s)$ and $R(s)$ and evaluating at $s = 0$, we find

$$\frac{d\tau(s)}{ds}\bigg|_{s=0} = -(\bar{G} - \tau),$$

$$\frac{dR(s)}{ds}\bigg|_{s=0} = G^N - \tau.$$

Hence, the net cost to the leaders of introducing a subsidy is simply $G^N - \bar{G}$. Again by definition, $G^N \geq \bar{G}$, so adding a subsidy will cost the leaders more money.[24] This clearly stacks the deck against a leadership-sponsored subsidy. However, the shape of the $G^N(s)$ function may restore some chance. As s increases, presumably G^N will rise as well. There may be some $s > 0$ such that the leaders are willing to pay the extra cost in order to get the extra public goods. I cannot tell for sure whether this will happen, however, without more assumptions on preferences and distributions of income. Hence, except for extremely small s, one cannot rule out subsidies by leaders, although one can say that subsidies, if they are used at all, will complement and not replace ordinary seed gifts. Again, this is in line with the observed facts.

IX. Conclusion

This paper shows that models of privately provided public goods can include a role for fund—raising. Moreover, the results of the model accord quite nicely with the actual role that fund—raising and seed money seem to play. Also, many of the troubling features of prior models of charitable giving, such as complete crowding out and neutrality of income redistribution, no longer hold under some circumstances in this model, and the addition of warm—glow givers has a natural application. Hence, further work that looks more carefully at the role of fund—raising may ultimately help us to gain better understanding of charitable institutions, private initiatives, and government policies to encourage them.

The model presented here relied entirely on the fact of a nonconvexity in the production of the public good for the result. While it was assumed that the nonconvexity came from the technology of producing the public good, it might also be possible for the nonconvexity to be the result of preferences as well. For instance, suppose that individuals want to give to a fund-raising campaign but would value their gift more if the campaign were "successful," that is, met its goals. Hence, the marginal rate of substitution could be increasing with donations over a range until it becomes clear that indeed the campaign goals will be met. In the extreme case, the marginal utility could be zero until the goal, $\bar{G}$, is reached and positive thereafter. Thus this nonconvexity in preferences could be represented in a model formally identical to the model in which the nonconvexity comes from technology. In this sense, continuing campaigns that are able to create "bandwagon effects" of this kind could also exhibit qualities of leadership givers even in the absence of any increasing returns in the production of the public good.

In addition to exploring nonconvexities in preferences, there are many other fruitful ways for research on fund-raising to continue. One important avenue is to study continuing campaigns. Harbaugh (1998) has noticed that law schools and operas, for instance, often announce contributions of donors and that the donations are reported in "bracket" amounts rather than the actual amounts. He finds that, under certain assumptions on preferences, such a strategy is optimal for fund-raisers. Other attempts to capture the stylized facts of fund-raising in a theoretical model of continuing campaigns would be useful. Ultimately, the models can address important policy questions, such as how fund-raisers' strategies change as levels of government grants and tax subsidies change.

Another possible area of research is to model more carefully the sequential nature of donations. Perhaps early donations or large donations convey some information about the quality of the charity.[25] How a charity chooses the sequence of donor solicitations, or the order in which individuals volunteer to contribute, may be a critical factor in the fund-raising strategy.

Finally, it will also be important to devote more research, both theoretical and empirical, to understanding the motives and objectives of charitable entrepreneurs, and whether they are compatible with the views of donors.[26] There are also more subtle issues, such as whether a charitable organization is incentive compatible, whether charities are able to act as private implementation mechanisms, why some charity markets are "contested" by competing charities versus "collusive" with a single charity, and whether united fund drives are better than competing fund drives. Addressing these issues fully will require a fundamental understanding of charities and their interactions with donors. Understanding this interaction will help form better policy regarding the charitable sector of the economy.

Notes

I am grateful to the National Science Foundation and the University of Wisconsin Vilas Associates Fund for financial support; to Marc Bilodeau, Peter Cramton, Preston McAfee, Larry Samuelson, Al Slivinski, Rich Steinberg, Lise Vesterlund, the editor, and an anonymous referee for helpful comments; and to Deena Ackerman for valuable research assistance.

1. The figures on the overall industry are taken from Kelly (1997). The 25 largest charities are those identified by Money Magazine Online: http://money/features/charity_1196/top25.html.

2. See Clotfelter (1990) and Auten, Cilke, and Randolph (1992) for discussions of the effects of the tax reforms of the 1980s on charitable giving. Economists did accurately predict the effect of tax changes on the *timing* of gifts, however, as seen in Randolph (1995).

3. This information was drawn from various issues of Wisconsin newspapers: the *Wisconsin State Journal* (June 27, 1995, p. 1A; September 12, 1995, p. 1B; October 28, 1995, p. 2D), the *Capital Times* (January 17, 1996, p. 1B), and the *Milwaukee Sentinel* (November 13, 1995, sports page 4).

4. Several authors have looked at nonprofit entrepreneurship. Recent contributions include Bilodeau and Slivinski (1996a). Earlier theoretical models of fund-raising have focused on maintaining the proper incentives of the fund-raisers and managers from the point of view of donors (see Rose-Ackerman 1982, 1987).

5. Studies of charitable organizations have found fund-raising to be positively related to donations. The most recent study, by Khanna, Posnett, and Sandler (1995), shows that government grants and large "legacies" also appear to increase the donations of others. The type of effect will be illustrated in Sec. V.

6. Examples include Roberts (1984, 1987), Bergstrom, Blume, and Varian (1986), and Andreoni (1988). See Sandler (1992) for a detailed discussion of this literature.

7. Note that a more general model would assume that $G = \alpha \Sigma_{i=1}^{n} g_i$ if $\Sigma_{i=1}^{n} g_i < \overline{G}$, where $0 < \alpha < 1$. For instance, if the project fails to reach the threshold, then an inferior alternative public good will be built. Similar results would follow as long as α is small enough to create an additional equilibrium at $G = 0$.

8. Clearly, there are many other less dramatic ways in which increasing returns could have been introduced. However, it is easy to show that equilibria would never occur on an area of increasing returns; hence the assumption of this technology is a simplifying, if extreme, form of increasing returns.

9. It is interesting to note, however, that experiments run by Bagnoli and McKee (1991) reveal that a refund greatly increases the chance of providing the good. In practice, therefore, charities may find it in their interest to get pledges that will be refunded if the goal is not met. I return to this point in Sec. VI.

10. Andreoni (1988, 1993) examines the validity of the crowding-out hypothesis, and Andreoni and Bergstrom (1996) discuss distortionary taxes in models of privately provided public goods.

11. At this point one could consider other assumptions on fund-raising, such as sequential giving among givers. As Admati and Perry (1991) show, this will also lead to an equilibrium that meets the threshold. This will be discussed more later.

12. It is not uncommon for fund-raisers who gather large pledges to have a legal contract drawn up between the donor and the organization. The reason for this is that fund-raisers make many plans contingent on the anticipation of the promised cash; hence they cannot risk a change of heart. As we shall see, the leaders would actually prefer to have their pledge binding as well.

13. For instance, the more people there are to organize as leaders, the higher the cost in terms of meetings, negotiations, and legal advice; whereas certain economies of scale, such as billboards, advertisements, and mailings, will prevent much cost savings among the followers as l grows.

14. A related mechanism designed by Cornelli (1996) deals with providing a private good with large fixed costs in which individuals have unitary demands, such as a concert series. Cornelli finds individuals paying different amounts in equilibrium. She considers a generalization of her model to privately provided public goods. Unfortunately, she shows that her mechanism is impractical for large populations. If we think of τ_{min} as a public good among leaders, however, Cornelli's mechanism could also be considered as another means to raise the critical threshold.

15. It is, however, possible to characterize that solution. Consider some arbitrary partition of individuals into leaders and followers. Define $\tau_{min} = \min \{\tau_f j \in \mathfrak{F}\}$ as the lowest τ among the followers. Then if $\Sigma_{i \in \mathscr{L}} g_i^*(c(l)) - c(l) \geq \tau_{min}(c(l))$, where l is the number of members of $\mathscr{L}$, this partition is "viable"; i.e., it is capable of overcoming the zero equilibrium. The charity must then search among all the viable partitions such that it chooses the partition that will result in the highest $G - c(l)$.

16. See Challenge (1996) regarding challenge grants. The only penalty for failure to meet goals for private fund-raising is a lower likelihood of future federal grants.

17. Large gifts are often secured with contracts and legally binding letters of intent. Failure to meet these obligations has resulted in lawsuits.

18. Work by Bilodeau and Slivinski (1996a) indicates that such a situation may give leaders an incentive to actually increase their gift in the first stage. Also, games with alternating moves in two-person provision point models, such as Admati and Perry (1991), show a first-mover advantage, although the mechanism is not generally Pareto efficient.

19. See Cornes and Sandler (1984), Steinberg (1987), and Andreoni (1989, 1990). This view has been supported by various experimental and econometric studies (see, e.g., Kingma 1989; Andreoni 1995).

20. Technically, all that we need to get results similar to those discussed above is to assume that all goods are normal. Preferences with a warm glow, $u_i(x_i, G, g_i)$, generate a demand function $g_i = f_i(m_i + G_{-i}, G_{-i}) - G_{-i}$. As long as $-1 < dg_i/dG_{-i} = [\partial f/\partial(m_i + G_{-i})] + (\partial f/\partial G_{-i}) - < 0$, the principal results hold, with those that rely on complete crowding out excluded. The propositions using complete crowding out are even stronger than those using incomplete crowding. Hence, the general result regarding government taxation (under the assumption that there is no warm glow from paying taxes) has the flavor of corollary 3. It is interesting to note that this holds whether one assumes that the warm glow is felt only when $G \geq \bar{G}$ or for all levels of G.

21. In fact, if the value of being a leader is large enough, then adding leaders may have other benefits above simply meeting a threshold. Such strategies are, unfortunately, beyond the scope of this paper.

22. There has been discussion in the literature about whether subsidies can crowd out other giving. Andreoni and Bergstrom (1996) show that, while complete crowding out is possible, it is also possible to choose subsidy schemes that are effective. The details of any subsidy scheme are not essential for this discussion, although it is clearly assumed that an effective subsidy would be chosen.

23. This does not rule out more complicated subsidy schemes, such as subsidizing only gifts above a certain minimum. Such a step subsidy is implicit in the test for itemized deductions. However, designing such a step subsidy for specific charities would be unwieldy and, again, is virtually never done.

24. Notice that this mathematics implicitly assumes that leaders subsidize their own direct gifts as well as those of the followers. There is no loss of generality in doing so if the gifts of the leaders are redefined to account for this "double giving" of subsidizing themselves.

25. For instance, Vesterlund (1998) examines a model in which asymmetric information about the quality of a charity leads to gifts as signals of that quality.

26. Some authors have begun to ask these questions. Bilodeau and Slivinski (1996a), for instance, ask whether it is "rational" to impose a nondistribution constraint voluntarily, i.e., to choose to charter the firm as nonprofit rather than for profit. Bilodeau and Slivinski (1996b) look at selection of heterogeneous agents into becoming charity managers. Finally, Bilodeau and Slivinski (1997) study charities that provide a varied mix of charitable services, and entrepreneurs enter the charity market in order to influence that mix.

References

Admati, Anat R., and Perry, Motty. "Joint Projects without Commitment." *Rev. Econ. Studies* 58 (April 1991): 259–76.

Andreoni, James. "Privately Provided Public Goods in a Large Economy: The Limits of Altruism." *J. Public Econ.* 35 (February 1988): 57–73.

———. "Giving with Impure Altruism: Applications to Charity and Ricardian Equivalence." *J.P.E.* 97 (December 1989): 1447–58.

————. "Impure Altruism and Donations to Public Goods: A Theory of Warm-Glow Giving." *Econ. J.* 100 (June 1990): 464–77.

————. "An Experimental Test of the Public-Goods Crowding-Out Hypothesis." *A.E.R.* 83 (December 1993): 1317–27.

————. "Cooperation in Public Goods Experiments: Kindness or Confusion?" *A.E.R.* 85 (September 1995): 891–904.

Andreoni, James, and Bergstrom, Theodore C. "Do Government Subsidies Increase the Private Supply of Public Goods?" *Public Choice* 88 (September 1996): 295–308.

Andreoni, James, and McGuire, Martin C. "Identifying the Free Riders: A Simple Algorithm for Determining Who Will Contribute to a Public Good." *J. Public Econ.* 51 (July 1993): 447–54.

Auten, Gerald E.; Cilke, James M.; and Randolph, William C. "The Effects of Tax Reform on Charitable Contributions." *Nal. Tax J.* 45 (September 1992): 267–90.

Bagnoli, Mark, and Lipman, Barton L. "Provision of Public Goods: Fully Implementing the Core through Private Contributions." *Rev. Econ. Studies* 56 (October 1989): 583–601.

Bagnoli, Mark, and McKee, Michael. "Voluntary Contribution Games: Efficient Private Provision of Public Goods." *Econ. Inquiry* 29 (April 1991): 351–66.

Bagwell, Kyle. "Commitment and Observability in Games." *Games and Econ. Behavior* 8 (February 1995): 271–80.

Bergstrom, Theodore C.; Blume, Lawrence E.; and Varian, Hal R. "On the Private Provision of Public Goods." *J. Public Econ.* 29 (February 1986): 25–49.

Bilodeau, Marc, and Slivinski, Al. "Rational Nonprofit Entrepreneurship." Manuscript. Indianapolis: Indiana University–Purdue University; London: Univ. Western Ontario, 1996. (*a*)

————. "Volunteering Nonprofit Entrepreneurial Services." *J. Econ. Behavior and Organization* 31 (October 1996): 117–27. (*b*)

————. "Rival Charities." *J. Public Econ.* 66 (December 1997): 449–67.

Challenge: Application Guidelines for Fiscal Year 1996. Washington: Nat. Endowment Arts, 1996.

Clotfelter, Charles T. "The Impact of Tax Reform on Charitable Giving: A 1989 Perspective." In *Do Taxes Matter? The Impact of the Tax Reform Act of 1986*, edited by Joel E. Slemrod. Cambridge, Mass.: MIT Press, 1990.

Cornelli, Francesca. "Optimal Selling Procedures with Fixed Costs." *J. Econ. Theory* 71 (October 1996): 1–30.

Cornes, Richard, and Sandler, Todd. "Easy Riders, Joint Production, and Public Goods." *Econ. J.* 94 (September 1984): 580–98.

Glazer, Amihai, and Konrad, Kai A. "A Signaling Explanation for Charity." *A.E.R.* 86 (September 1996): 1019–28.

Harbaugh, William T. "What Do Donations Buy? A Model of Philanthropy Based on Prestige and Warm Glow." *J. Public Econ.* 67 (February 1998): 269–84

Kelly, Kathleen S. "From Motivation to Mutual Understanding: Shifting the Domain of Donor Research." In *Critical Issues in Fundraising*, edited by Dwight Burlingame. New York: Wiley, 1997.

Khanna, Jyoti; Posnett, John; and Sandler, Todd. "Charity Donations in the UK: New Evidence Based on Panel Data." *J. Public Econ.* 56 (February 1995): 257–72.

Kingma, Bruce Robert. "An Accurate Measurement of the Crowd-Out Effect, Income Effect, and Price Effect for Charitable Contributions." *J.P.E.* 97 (October 1989): 1197–1207.

Randolph, William C. "Dynamic Income, Progressive Taxes, and the Timing of Charitable Contributions." *J.P.E.* 103 (August 1995): 709–38.

Roberts, Russell D. "A Positive Model of Private Charity and Public Transfers." *J.P.E.* 92 (February 1984): 136–48.

————. "Financing Public Goods." *J.P.E.* 95 (April 1987): 420–37.

Rose-Ackerman, Susan. "Charitable Giving and 'Excessive' Fundraising." *Q.J.E.* 97 (May 1982): 193–212.

————. "Ideals versus Dollars: Donors, Charity Managers, and Government Grants." *J.P.E.* 95 (August 1987): 810–23.

Sandler, Todd. *Collective Action: Theory and Applications*. Ann Arbor: Univ. Michigan Press, 1992.

Steinberg, Richard S. "Voluntary Donations and Public Expenditures in a Federalist System." *A.E.R.* 77 (March 1987): 24–36.

Varian, Hal R. "Sequential Contributions to Public Goods." *J. Public Econ.* 53 (February 1994): 165–86.

Vesterlund, Lise. "The Information Value of Sequential Fundraising." Manuscript. Ames: Iowa State Univ., Dept. Econ., 1998.

Warr, Peter G. "Pareto Optimal Redistribution and Private Charity." *J. Public Econ.* 19 (October 1982): 131–38.

————. "The Private Provision of a Public Good Is Independent of the Distribution of Income." *Econ. Letters* 13, nos. 2–3 (1983): 207–11.

Toward Professionalization: Fund Raising Norms and Their Implications for Practice

Timothy C. Caboni

Abstract

This article outlines the core traits of professions and discusses the extent to which fund raising possesses these traits. Three inviolable and six admonitory normative patterns of fund-raising behavior are described and their implications for the practice of fund raising are discussed. This article reexamines the fund-raising profession in comparison with the markers of true professions as suggested in the sociological literature. First, the core traits of professions and their relationship to fund raising is examined. Second, professional self-regulation is discussed. Third, the informal norms that fund raisers use to self-regulate are described. Finally, the importance of these norms to the profession and their use for practitioners is outlined.

Sociological Inquiry and Professions

Carr-Saunders and Wilson outlined the historical progression of professions in Great Britain over two centuries.[1] Within their work emerges the notion that a profession is defined by its members having a set of specialized skills, charging set fees, having a professional association and a code of ethics. Since the 1933 study by Carr-Saunders and Wilson, the study of professions has remained an important part of sociological inquiry.

There are certain attributes by which one can determine if an occupation is a profession. Greenwood describes five attributes that are possessed by an ideal profession.[2] First, it will have a body of systematic theory on which it draws. This body of knowledge requires an extensive period of training. Second, its professional authority is recognized by the profession's clients. In the client/professional relationship, the client believes that what the professional judges to be appropriate should not be questioned. Professionals, because of their extensive training (and because the client does not possess that training), are perceived as knowing what is best for the client. Third, the community at large agrees that the profession has this authority. Fourth, a profession will have a code of ethics that is used by members of a profession to self-regulate their behavior. Finally, a profession will have a formal association to which its members belong.

Greenwood also suggests that professions should be seen as being distributed along a continuum of professionalism. Additionally, Greenwood asserts that, "the crucial distinction between professions and nonprofessions is this: the skills that characterize a profession flow from and are supported by a fund of knowledge that has been organized into an internally consistent system called a body of theory."[3]

Theories of professions frequently focus on one of two main characteristics; first, is it knowledge-based? And second, does it establish a monopoly in the market for its services? Parsons claimed that professions serve an altruistic, social function: "a full-fledged profession must have some institutional means of making sure that such [professional] competence will be put to socially responsible uses."[4] This view was attacked by Johnson and others who emphasized the power of professions.[5]

Instead of altruism, some suggest that professions aim to create "market shelters"[6] and market monopolies.[7] From this point of view, it is important for a profession to seek to license its particular professional practices.[8]

In contrast to approaches focusing on professional knowledge or market monopolies, Abbott claims that the professions have to be seen as a system.[9] The system is based around work and consists of professions and their links to particular tasks. Abbott calls the link between a profession and its tasks "jurisdiction." The professions compete with one another for control of particular tasks. "In claiming jurisdiction, a profession asks society to recognize its cognitive structure through exclusive rights."[10] Knowledge is one means in professional competition; it is the "currency of competition."[11]

Brint suggests that professions now more frequently define themselves in terms of the skills and knowledge possessed by members of the profession.[12] Rarely do members of a profession turn to the social importance of their work as a justification of social status. However, because of the lack of a well-developed body of knowledge, for fund raising to claim professional status it must look to the other characteristics of professions that it might possess.

Professionalization of Fund Raising and Professional Traits

Professions possess a number of characteristics and traits. These include: an extensive period of training and socialization, the possession of a systematic body of theory, the formation of professional associations, and the existence of a code of conduct. Additionally, members of a profession adhere to an ideal of service, and conduct their work with autonomy from external review.[13] The degree to which fund raising meets each of these criteria is discussed below.

Extensive Period of Training

While there is no certification required for practicing as a fund raiser, there has been a recent proliferation of programs designed to prepare individuals who choose fund raising as a career. This is in addition to the certificate offered by the Association of Fundraising Professionals (AFP) to individuals who have been practicing in the field for over five years and who have met the necessary criteria. Carbone reports that many practicing fund raisers view this certificate with disdain. Others, however, view the certificate as helpful when entering the profession.[14]

Fund raisers, according to practitioners in the field, possess no specialized knowledge for doing their jobs. Carbone also found that while fund raisers believe that there is a codified body of knowledge, most were of the opinion that these principles were best learned on the job, rather than through formal educational instruction, as done in most true professions.[15] However, there are informal paths through which individuals progress through the fund-raising ranks. Entry level fund raisers rarely have contact with an institution's top donors. Frequently they spend much of their time designing direct-mail appeals in annual fund offices, or doing research on individuals who have the capacity to make large gifts.

After some time, an individual may rise to the level of manager of an annual fund or may shift to major gifts as a development officer. Even in these positions, at some institutions fund raisers rarely interact with prospects who have been targeted for the largest gifts. At others, all major gift officers have access to the largest prospects. This is evidence of on-the-job training that may last for many years.

Additionally, because there is a nascent group of programs in fund raising beginning to appear at colleges and universities across the country, this is not an area in which additional research is needed to argue for the professionalization of the field.

Formation of Professional Associations

Fund raisers have two primary professional organizations that serve their professional needs. For fund raisers engaged in fund raising primarily for colleges and universities (although private secondary schools are members) the Council for Advancement and Support of Education (CASE) serves as these individuals' primary professional organization. An umbrella group, CASE counts among its members individuals who are also responsible for alumni relations, public relations, publications, government relations, and enrollment management. CASE was formed in 1974 through a merger of the American Alumni Council (AAC, founded in 1913) and the American College Public Relations Association (ACPRA, founded in 1917).

The Association of Fundraising Professionals (AFP, founded as the National Society of Fund-Raising Executives in 1960) is a national organization whose membership contains fund raisers for educational institutions as well as those fund raisers who work for social service organizations and other not-for-profit organizations.

A number of secondary professional organizations exist to support fund raisers. These include the Association of Lutheran Development Executives (ALDE), Association for Healthcare Philanthropy (AHP), Association of Professional Researchers for Advancement (APRA), and others.

The existence of these professional associations is another marker of professionalization for fund raising. For the purposes of this article, attention will be concentrated on AFP and CASE.

Existence of a Code of Conduct

Both AFP and CASE have adopted codes of conduct that apply to their members. CASE adopted the Donor Bill of Rights in 1982. AFP's *Code of Ethical Principals* was adopted in 1991 and the *Principles for Practice* were added in 1992. The existence of these codes is an additional marker of professionalism possessed by the field. It should be noted that these are of relatively recent origin.

Systematic Body of Theory and Mastery of Knowledge

One of the challenges for fund raising as it progresses toward professional status is the lack of inquiry into the fund-raising function within the college and university environment. One of the markers of professionalism is the existence of a knowledge base in which practitioners are well versed. Typically, this knowledge is mastered through an extended period of training.

Carbone writes that fund raisers themselves report that the knowledge they use in doing their duties as development officers is primarily general knowledge that is possessed by anyone.[16] They also believe that such knowledge is best learned on the job rather than in formal education.

Rowland states that "the systematic study of institutional advancement, employing social science and management-based research methodologies, is of comparatively recent origin."[17] Kelly notes that of the studies that appear in Rowland's work, "there are few, if any studies on basic research or theory building."[18] The research that does exist is limited, fragmented, and of marginal quality.[19] Additionally, the majority of articles focus on the motivators that exist for donors of a particular institution.[20] With vast differences among higher education institutions, a broader inquiry is needed across the spectrum of colleges and universities. Payton suggests that "a lot of people don't want to be bothered with fund-raising, don't like it, find it distasteful and don't want to be involved with it at all."[21]

This lack of a well-developed body of knowledge poses an important challenge to those interested in fund raising moving toward professionalization. As discussed previously, Brint suggests that technical knowledge is becoming the most important marker that differentiates professions from occupations.[22] If this is the case, fund raising as a profession must begin to encourage scholarly inquiry into fund raising for colleges and universities. CASE has addressed this need through the annual award program for outstanding dissertations focused on fund raising in higher education. The journal in which this article appears is another vehicle through which the professional organization may encourage scholarly inquiry. Other steps that might be of value to increasing the knowledge base include: encouraging current scholars to pursue research on issues of fund raising within higher education through research grants; increasing the number of faculty members presenting research on fund raising at annual professional conferences; and supporting emerging programs designed to prepare scholars whose primary research focus will be fund raising within the context of postsecondary education.

Because the fund-raising profession lacks a substantial knowledge base, focus must be placed upon the professional characteristic of the ideal of service if fund raising is to lay claim to status as a profession.

Ideal of Service and Fund Raising

Goode suggests that members of a profession must base their individual decisions on what will serve the needs and protect the welfare of their clients.[23] If viewed through this lens, the fund-raising profession has two separate clients for whom it is responsible: the institution and the donor.

Professional fund raisers are responsible for the welfare of their institutional clients. Development officers are charged with providing necessary capital for the operations of their institutions and for raising money to create endowed funds to provide support for specific projects, programs, scholarships, and professorships in perpetuity. Rosso suggests that development officers should be hired for their ability to clearly articulate the mission and values of the organization, and because of a personal commitment to the institutional mission.[24] This commitment to the college or university mission separates professional fund raisers from salespeople. The fund raiser should believe strongly in the institution and its goals, and view fund raising as a way of advancing the institution. Along with this responsibility comes the potential for causing great harm to the institution. This harm may be caused in a number of ways.

First, because there is great latitude afforded to development officers in soliciting gifts, a development officer might be tempted to enter into an agreement with a donor to create a specific program for which the university has no need or want. While accepting such a donation might help the institution reach its capital campaign or yearly fund-raising goals, it may move the college or university in an academic direction that its leaders had not intended. The task of crafting academic policy is best left to provosts, deans, and department chairs, not donors and development officers.

A second possible way in which the institutional client might be harmed is through inappropriate behavior on the part of the fund raiser. Because the role of fund raiser is one of boundary spanner, the development officer represents the organization to individuals who are outside of the organization and in the community. Because the development officer is the embodiment of the university, his or her actions will reflect directly on the institution's reputation. This is another instance where a fund raiser may cause harm to an institutional client.

Fund raisers must also protect the individuals who provide funds to their institutions. In order to know as much as possible about potential donors, college and university development offices conduct research into the financial and personal backgrounds of these individual donors. Much of this information could be potentially damaging if revealed to the general public. Some donors also desire some degree of confidentiality about their gifts. Development officers are responsible for ensuring that this information is protected.

One area of fund raising that poses a potential threat to the welfare of the donor client is planned giving. Planned gifts are structured toward the later years of a prospect's life and in many cases provide income for that person until the time of his or her death. This type of gift can be potentially damaging to the donor if the amount of income guaranteed by the institution is not enough for the donor to meet expenses. Additionally, with uncertain health, a problem in elderly donors, those individuals who tie up a large percentage of their capital in a structured gift may run into problems taking care of themselves when unforeseen health problems arise.

Because of the potential financial and reputational damage that may be inflicted on a potential donor through a development officer's behavior, fund raisers do bear a responsibility for the welfare of their donor clients.

Autonomy

One of the privileges granted to members of a profession is autonomy. This autonomy from external review is granted by society with the expectation that members of a profession will police their own behavior. A failure to regulate misconduct results in a loss of trust of the profession and its members by the public.[25] Consequently, the profession's autonomy is threatened. By sanctioning those who engage in misconduct, a profession reassures the public that its faith in the profession is justified.

Professional fund raisers who are employed in higher education do enjoy some degree of autonomy in the performance of their duties. While most development officers are accountable to someone in the university hierarchy, there is a great deal of latitude in the methods by which individuals are solicited for gifts. Most development officers devise their own strategies for cultivating and soliciting individual prospects. Additionally, they are responsible for determining the best time to ask for a gift based upon a relationship developed with the prospect.

Interrelationship among Core Traits

The professional traits of mastery of knowledge, ideal of service, and autonomy are interrelated. If individuals in a profession are granted the privilege of operating autonomously, the public expects that the profession will regulate its members' behaviors. Specifically, to ensure that the profession's members adhere to the ideal of service to its clients, the profession must sanction those behaviors that are not in the best interest of clients. Additionally, those members of the profession are expected to have mastered the knowledge base that will allow them to make decisions that will not cause harm to their clients.

For the fund-raising profession, this interrelationship is reflected in the formulation of how individuals progress from entry-level fund-raising positions to more senior positions. Individuals who are involved in major gifts work have typically been involved in the profession for a number of years. They may have progressed from asking for smaller gifts, which have little potential for doing harm to the donor, to soliciting donors for large structured gifts that have important tax implications. While the profession's formal knowledge base may be lacking, there is an extended period of on-the-job training as individuals move into different areas of fund raising with additional responsibility.

In the course of this progression, individuals are granted more autonomy as the solicitations become more intricate and the potential for harm to the individual and the institution increases. With this increased exposure to making decisions that could have serious negative consequences, the fund raiser must be even more strongly committed to the ideal of service to both the donor and institutional client. The profession must also ensure that as more autonomy is granted, individual fund-raiser behavior is regulated.

Professional Self-regulation

The notion of ideal of service to both donor and institutional clients by fund raisers is evidenced in their codes of conduct and the *Donor Bill of Rights*. The code of ethics protects the interests of both donor and institutional clients. In a discussion of the regulation of the fund-raising profession in 1985 at the Greenbrier II conference, the decision was made not to develop a body responsible for imposing sanctions on those individuals who have violated the code of ethics. However, at this gathering, it was decided that the statement of ethics should be promoted and guidelines, along with illustrative cases, should be developed for each area outlined in the *Code of Ethics* and *Donor Bill of Rights*.

Without a sanctioning body, or a formal way of regulating the actions of fund raisers, the profession would necessarily rely upon informal self-regulation of its membership.[26] Professions ensure that members adhere to the ideal of service through the use of formal and informal social control mechanisms.[27] Goode suggests that these rules are taught to new members of a profession through the socialization process. These social control mechanisms define what behaviors by members of a profession are appropriate and inappropriate.[28]

Formal Social Control Mechanisms

One marker of the degree of professionalism an occupation has attained is the existence of a code of conduct.[29] Published codes of ethics by which professionals are expected to abide are an example of a formal social control mechanism. These codes assist a profession in attaining professional autonomy and self-regulation.[30] They also serve as a measuring stick against which members of a profession may judge the relative impropriety of certain demands.[31] "Through its ethical code, a profession's commitment to the social welfare becomes a matter of public record, thereby insuring for itself the continued confidence of the community."[32]

As discussed previously, both of the major professional organizations to which college and university fund raisers belong have explicitly stated codes of ethics for their members. However, Kelly found that less than half (44%) of the organizations represented in AFP had policies regarding the acquisition of gifts, and 50 percent count on professional fund raisers to abide by a code of professional ethics when receiving gifts or to judge gifts on an individual basis.[33] Lombardo found that only four of the 12 charitable institutions she studied had formal guidelines to deal with cases of conflict of interest between fund raisers and donors.[34] In his study of fund raisers who are members of CASE, Carbone found that 30 percent of them were unsure if their national organization played a role in setting standards and protecting the right to practice. Additionally, he found that "28% are unsure if this function is important and 10% thought it was unimportant for the organization to do this."[35]

Informal Social Control Mechanisms

In the absence of formal social control mechanisms, fund raisers must rely upon informal mechanisms to ensure that members of the profession are conforming to what are considered appropriate behaviors. Carlin and Freidson both found that informal rules are more important social control mechanisms than formal controls.[36]

Norms are one mechanism through which professions self-regulate using informal social controls. Norms are shared beliefs about how an individual should act in a particular situation.[37] Merton suggests that norms function as mechanisms of social control because they consist of prescribed and proscribed patterns of behavior.[38] This concept is derived from Durkheim's statement that the natural human condition is unregulated passion, whereas conforming requires social regulation.[39] Without a normative structure, individuals in the profession would be free to act as they saw fit, with individuals deciding for themselves what behaviors constituted appropriate and inappropriate behavior. Additionally, "norms assure that professional choices adhere to the ideal of service."[40] By self-regulating, a profession communicates to its members the necessity of stewarding the welfare of its clients.

The degree of moral outrage that accompanies the violation of a norm indicates the social significance of the norm.[41] Norm-violating behaviors that individuals view as highly inappropriate carry a higher penalty and increased social significance as compared to those behaviors which are not as inappropriate.

Morris writes that "norms are generally accepted, sanctioned prescriptions for or prohibitions against, others' behavior, belief or feeling, i.e. what others *ought* to do, believe, feel—*or else*."[42] He goes on to state that violation of accepted norms always involve sanctions. Norms serve as a guide to how fund raisers perform the roles associated with the fund-raising profession. They represent the "collective conscience" of the profession and dictate what is appropriate and inappropriate behavior for its members.[43] Violation of these norms by development officers may result in sanctioning by peers, institutions, and the government.

Fund-raising Norms

In a study of CASE fund raisers, Caboni found three inviolable and six admonitory norms.[44]

Inviolable Norms

The violation of inviolable norms is perceived as being the most egregious and warranting the most severe sanctions.[45] The three violations of these norms, in alphabetical order, are: exploitation of institutional resources, institutional disregard, and misappropriation of gifts. Each of these is described below.

Exploitation of Institutional Resources

This normative pattern proscribes behaviors by fund raisers that take advantage of an institution's funds, or other things of value that the institution possesses (including offers of admission), for personal gain. Three examples of prohibitive behavior are: a fund raiser makes personal charges on an institutional credit card and submits them as business expenses; a fund raiser agrees to get a student admitted to the institution if a gift is made; and a fund raiser pads a call report with visits he or she did not make.

Institutional Disregard

The normative pattern of institutional disregard proscribes behaviors by fund raisers that would damage the reputation of the fund raiser's employing institution. As discussed earlier, the institution for which a fund raiser works is a client of the fund raiser. Violating this norm puts at risk the welfare of the fund raiser's institutional client. Four examples of prohibited behaviors are: a fund raiser speaks poorly about the institution to a prospect; a fund raiser provides a copy of a prospect list to another institution; a fund raiser tells someone outside of the institution private information about a donor; and a fund raiser gets drunk at an official institution function.

Misappropriation of Gifts

The inviolable norm regarding misappropriation of gifts includes transgressions by fund raisers in which donations are used for purposes that were not intended by the donor. Violation of this normative pattern could cause damage both to the donor–client relationship (by misusing the funds given by the individual) and the institutional client (if the donor relationship is compromised because the donation was not used for its intended purpose, the donor might never make another gift to the college). Three examples of prohibited behaviors are: a fund raiser allows the income from a restricted scholarship fund to be used for a purpose other than scholarships; a fund raiser uses restricted funds to support an institution's operating budget; and a fund raiser allows a donor's gift to be used for something other than for what it was intended.

Admonitory Fund-Raising Norms

Caboni also found six admonitory norms in his study of CASE fund raisers.[46] The violation of admonitory norms is perceived as being inappropriate, but not requiring the severity of sanctioning reserved for the violation of inviolable norms.[47] The six violations of admonitory norms, in alphabetical order, are: commission-based compensation, dishonest solicitation, donor manipulation, exaggeration of professional experience, institutional mission abandonment, and unreasonable enforcement of pledges. Each of these is explained below.

Commission-based Compensation

The admonitory norm regarding commission-based compensation includes transgressions by fund raisers in which an individual's salary is paid in part or in full as a percentage of the dollar total raised by that fund raiser. Violation of this normative pattern is in direct conflict with the code of ethical standards for fund raisers. The purpose of discouraging these types of compensation packages is to ensure that an individual raising funds for an institution does not take advantage of a donor for financial gain (e.g., pushing a donor to make a gift that will do harm to the individual's financial standing because a large gift will result in a large commission). An additional argument against commission-based compensation is that placing pressure on a donor to make a gift solely for the purposes of meeting a dollar goal may jeopardize the receipt of a larger gift from the donor in the future. Two prohibited behaviors are: a fund raiser works on a commission basis; and a fund raiser agrees to base a part of his or her annual salary as a percentage of total dollars raised.

Dishonest Solicitation

The normative pattern of dishonest solicitation proscribes behaviors by fund raisers that involve untruthfulness while a fund raiser asks a prospect for a gift. By violating this norm, a fund raiser takes advantage of the autonomy granted to development officers in the conduct of their professional duties. By lying or bending the truth, the fund raiser puts at risk the relationship with the potential donor. Four examples of prohibited behaviors are: a fund raiser knows that a donor received double credit for a gift, but does not tell anyone; a fund raiser tells a donor their gift will solve a particular institutional problem when, in reality, the gift will not solve the problem; a fund raiser makes a mistake and blames an administrative assistant; and a fund raiser intentionally uses confusing language when describing the details of a planned gift to a donor.

Donor Manipulation

The normative factor dealing with donor manipulation involves a fund raiser's handling of delicate relationships with a donor. Individuals who have lost or are losing the capacity to make sound decisions for themselves should not be solicited for gifts. By exploiting these individuals, a fund raiser is potentially causing harm to the donor client. Donor manipulation consists of two prohibited behaviors: a fund raiser attempts to solicit a planned gift from a prospect, even though it is not in the prospect's best interest and a fund raiser asks a prospect whose mental faculties are in question to make a gift because it would be of benefit to the institution.

Exaggeration of Professional Experience

The normative array with respect to exaggeration of professional experience centers on fund raisers who embellish the fund-raising work they have done either at a previous institution or for their current employer. Four disapproved behaviors are: a fund raiser inflates his or her dollar raised totals in a previous position; a fund raiser exaggerates his or her professional experience; a fund raiser takes credit for a gift brought in by another development officer; and a fund raiser takes credit for another staff member's idea.

Institutional Mission Abandonment

The behaviors associated with institutional mission abandonment are focussed on fund raisers attracting gifts for activities and programs for which the institution has no need. Because fund raisers are not involved directly in the academic enterprise of the institution, they should not create or change academic programs according to the whim of donors. Doing so infringes upon the institution's autonomy to make programmatic decisions based upon the best interest of enrolled students. Three examples of disapproved behaviors are: a fund raiser allows a donor to make a gift that creates a program the institution does not need or want; a fund raiser agrees to accept a gift from a donor, the use of which is too narrowly defined to be of use to the institution; and a fund raiser accepts a gift because it adds to fund-raising totals, even though the institution has no need for the program the gift will fund.

Unreasonable Enforcement of Pledges

The admonitory norm that proscribes the unreasonable enforcement of pledges is the final admonitory norm that emerged from the data. This norm prohibits fund raisers from taking legal action against a donor or their families in the pursuit of gifts promised to an institution, or from refusing to return a gift made by a donor who is unhappy with how the gift is being used. While a pledge may be considered a legally binding document, this norm advises fund raisers (and in turn their institutions) from pursuing legal action against donors and their families. Two behaviors that violate this norm are: a fund raiser takes a deceased donor's family to court to force them to fulfill the donor's pledge because the gift would benefit the institution, and a fund raiser refuses to return a gift to a donor who is upset with how the funds are being used and has asked for the gift to be returned.

Discussion

From the nine norms listed above, the following four conclusions may be drawn. First, moral boundaries for the practice of fund raising in colleges and universities do exist. Braxton and Bayer suggest that normative patterns establish moral boundaries for members of a profession.[48] These normative patterns espoused by members of the fund-raising profession establish boundaries that should not be crossed in the conduct of their duties. These boundaries restrict the autonomy they have in how they solicit donors (unreasonable enforcement of pledges and dishonest solicitation), how they represent their institutions (institutional disregard), how they steward university funds (exploitation of institutional resources and misappropriation of gifts), how they persuade prospects to make donations (commission-based compensation and donor manipulation), how they decide for what individuals should be solicited (institutional mission abandonment), and how they represent themselves professionally (exaggeration of professional experience).

Second, because fund raisers within higher education presumably use norms to self-regulate, it is a marker of additional professionalism for the fund-raising profession. College and university development officers enjoy latitude in the approaches that they use to solicit individuals for gifts to their institutions. This professional autonomy is granted to a profession with the expectation that that profession's members will regulate their own behavior and the behavior of their colleagues.[49] One way a profession ensures that its members behave appropriately is through the use of informal social control mechanisms. Norms are one device used by members of a profession to self-regulate. Because a normative structure does exist for college and university fund raisers, it suggests that fund raising is maturing as a profession.

Third, the identified normative patterns protect the welfare of both institutional clients and donor clients. Goode suggests that members of a profession must base their individual decisions on what will serve the needs and protect the welfare of their clients.[50] The inviolable and admonitory norms that emerged from this study serve to protect the interests of both sets of clients for fund-raising professionals. However, the institutional client receives more protection, because the inviolable norms tend not to prohibit behaviors that might cause harm to the fund raiser's donor client. The donor client is protected through five of the six admonitory norms.

The welfare of donor clients is protected by one inviolable norm (misappropriation of gifts) and five admonitory norms (commission-based compensation, dishonest solicitation, donor manipulation, exaggeration of professional experience, and unreasonable enforcement of pledges). Institutional clients are protected by three inviolable norms (exploitation of institutional resources, institutional disregard, and misappropriation of gifts) and one admonitory norm (exaggeration of professional experience).

While both individual donor clients and institutional clients are protected by these norms, the most severe sanctions are reserved for those transgressions that pose the threat of harm to an institutional client. All three of the inviolable norms serve to protect institutional clients. Only one protects the welfare of donor clients. Of the six admonitory norms, which require less severe sanctions than inviolable norms, five protect the welfare of donors. Only one admonitory norm proscribes behaviors that could cause harm to the fund raiser's institution.

The norms show that the protection of institutional clients occurs primarily through inviolable normative patterns and the protection of donor clients occurs primarily through admonitory normative patterns. A possible explanation for this involves the pressure on development officers to meet annual dollar goals. The easiest and most common way to evaluate the performance of fund raisers is an examination of total dollars raised compared with previous year totals. As a result, a fund raiser's primary concern is frequently the total amount of money he or she has raised. If a fund raiser were to violate any of the three inviolable norms, his or her chances of getting a gift would not increase. However, if a fund raiser violates admonitory norms, he or she may have an increased opportunity to receive a gift from a donor, even though the gift may have come through what some would perceive as inappropriate fund-raising behaviors.

Finally, the normative patterns that emerged in this study parallel the formal codes of ethics for CASE and AFP. The norms that protect the donor are codified in the donor bill of rights adopted by CASE. However, the norms that prohibit transgressions against the fund raiser's institution are represented in the CASE Statement of Ethics only in generalities. AFP's code of ethical principles is much more thorough in its treatment of inappropriate behaviors. Each of the three inviolable and five of the admonitory norms appear in the code. The admonitory norm against institutional mission abandonment does not appear in any of the discussed codes. This is an example of neglect on the part of the profession to incorporate what are informal norms into the written ethical codes.

This reflects the focus (especially by CASE) on the welfare of the donor. However, CASE's statement of ethics is more broadly constructed than that of AFP because many different functional areas are represented within the organization. Members of CASE may be responsible for other institutional advancement areas including public relations, publications, and alumni relations. AFP's membership, in contrast to CASE's, comprises primarily individuals whose sole responsibility is fund raising. This narrow focus allows for a more detailed description of fund-raising behaviors that are proscribed by the profession in its ethical code.

Practical Implications

The normative patterns discussed above suggest a number of implications for those individuals engaged in professional fund-raising activities, for those involved in the preparation of future development officers, and for institutional policy makers who are responsible for institutional advancement or development operations. Six implications for practice are described below.

First, fund raising is progressing to professionalization. Carbone suggests that fund raising is an emerging profession, possessing some of the markers of a full profession; it is "an *emerging* profession—an occupation that has moved steadily along the professional continuum; a profession with the potential to attain greater professional stature."[51] This study demonstrates that the fund-raising profession possesses another marker of a profession not previously identified. Because fund raisers espouse the normative patterns that protect both donor and institutional clients, the existence of a concern for client welfare does exist within the profession.

Second, the ethical code for CASE should have more specific language added to describe fund raiser responsibility to the institutional client. The focus of the *Donor Bill of Rights* is obviously on the welfare of the donor client. Specific responsibilities are not delineated for the institutional client. However, it is interesting to note that although an entire document exists outlining the rights of a donor, the normative patterns prohibiting behaviors that might cause harm to a donor are almost exclusively in the admonitory category. Those norms that proscribe behaviors that place the institution in jeopardy are primarily inviolable. This is not surprising; after all, the institution pays the fund raiser's salary.

Third, those college and university administrators might use the College Fund Raising Behaviors Instrument as a tool to evaluate the development staff within their institutions. CASE and AFP could also develop a kit for fund-raising managers that would include the instrument and the national average for each fund-raising norm. By administering the instrument to those individuals involved in the solicitation of gifts and comparing the results for the institution with the results reported in this study, individuals who are responsible for fund raising may begin a dialogue with staff fund raisers about similarities and differences between the organization's results and the perception of other fund raisers. By stating explicitly those behaviors that colleagues consider inappropriate, those individuals who are not aware of informal norms will be made aware of them.

Fourth, with the recent increase in the number of courses and degree programs in nonprofit management and institutional advancement, these identified normative patterns should be taught to individuals who plan on entering the profession. Additionally, they should be included in sessions presented at various professional conferences. Goode suggested that norms are inculcated through the process of socialization.[52] One period of intense socialization is graduate school. If students in these programs are made aware of the formal codes of ethics and well as the informal codes, perhaps variation in espousal of these norms will be reduced.

Fifth, CASE could add the presentation of these norms to those newcomers who attend the national assembly and district conferences each year. As part of the socialization process, formally introducing newcomers to the norms presented above would give concrete boundaries for what fund raisers consider inappropriate behaviors. Additionally, discussions could be structured around each norm so that newcomers might more fully understand the responsibilities placed upon fund raisers for the welfare of both donors and institutions.

A final implication for the practice of fund raising involves the need to establish mentorships for those individuals who are entering the profession. By developing relationships between neophyte fund raisers and those who have been practicing members of the profession for many years, the profession will decrease the chance that those behaviors that are perceived as inappropriate by those in the profession will be adopted by those who are new. Mentors could be assigned as individuals are hired into an organization. Professional organizations may also engage in this practice.

Notes

1. A. M. Carr-Saunders and P. A. Wilson (1933), *The Professions*, Clarendon Press, Oxford.
2. E. Greenwood (1957), "Attributes of a profession," *Social Work*, 2, pp. 44–55.
3. Ibid., p.46.
4. T. Parsons (1939), "The professions and social structure," *Social Forces*, 17, pp. 457–67, quote p.463.
5. T. J. Johnson (1972), *Professions and Power*, Macmillan, London.
6. E. Freidson (1970), *Professional Dominance*, Aldine, Chicago.
7. J. L. Berlant (1975), *Profession and Monopoly*, University of California Press, Berkeley; M. S. Larson (1977), *The Rise of Professionalism*, University of California Press, Berkeley.
8. E. Freidson (1975), *Doctoring Together: A Study of Professional Social Control*, Elsevier, New York.
9. A. Abbott (1988), *The System of Professions*, University of Chicago Press, Chicago.
10. Ibid., p. 59.
11. Ibid., p. 102.
12. S. Brint (1994), *The Changing Roles of Professionals in Politics and Public Life*, Princeton University Press, Princeton, NJ.
13. W. J. Goode (1969), "The theoretical limits of professionalization," in Amati Etzoni (Ed.), *The Semiprofessions and their Organization*, New York: Free Press, pp. 266–313.
14. R. F. Carbone (1989), *Fund Raising as a Profession*, Monograph No. 3, University of Maryland, Clearinghouse for Research on Fund Raising, College Park.
15. Ibid.
16. R. F. Carbone (1989), *An Agenda for Research on Fund Raising*, University of Maryland, Clearinghouse for Research on Fund Raising, College Park.
17. A. W. Rowland (1983), *Research in Institutional Advancement: A Selected, Annotated Compendium of Doctoral Dissertations*, Council for the Advancement and Support of Education, Washington, DC, p. iii.
18. K. S. Kelly (1991), *Fund Raising and Public Relations: A Critical Analysis*, Lawrence Erlbaum Associates, Hillsdale, NJ, p.114; Rowland (1983), *Research in Institutional Advancement* op. cit.; A. W. Rowland (1986), *Research in Institutional Advancement: Addendum*, Council for the Advancement and Support of Education, Washington, DC.
19. B. E. Brittingham and T. R. Pezzullo (1990), *The Campus Green: Fund Raising in Higher Education*, ERIC Clearinghouse on Higher Education, Washington, DC.
20. K. E. Burke (1988), "Institutional image and alumni giving," unpublished doctoral dissertation, University of Maryland, College Park.
21. R. L. Payton (1987), "American values and private philanthropy; Philanthropic values," in K. W. Thompson (Ed.), *Philanthropy: Private Means, Public Ends*, University Press of America, Lanham, MD, pp. 3–46, 123–36, quote p.133.
22. Brint (1994), *The Changing Roles of Professionals in Politics and Public Life*, op. cit.
23. Goode (1969), "The theoretical limits of professionalization," op. cit.
24. H. A. Rosso (1996), *Rosso on Fund Raising: Lessons from a Master's Lifetime Experience*, Jossey-Bass, San Francisco.
25. Goode (1969), "The theoretical limits of professionalization," op. cit.
26. Ibid.
27. J. M. Braxton (1986), "The normative structure of science: Social control in the academic profession," in J. C. Smart (Ed.), *Higher Education: Handbook of Theory and Research*, vol. 2., Agathon Press, New York, pp. 309–57; J. M. Braxton, A. E. Bayer, and M. J. Finkelstein (1992), "Teaching performance norms in academia," *Research in Higher Education*, 33, October, pp. 553–69; R. Bucher and A. Strauss (1961), "Professions in process," *American Journal of Sociology*, 66, November, pp. 325–34; W. J. Goode (1957), "Community within a community: The professions," *American Sociological Review*, 22, pp. 194–200.
28. Goode (1957), "Community within a community," op. cit.

29. Carr-Saunders and Wilson (1933), *The Professions*, op. cit.; B. Barber (1962), *Science and the Social Order*, Collier, New York; G. Harries-Jenkins (1970), "Professionals in organizations," in J. A. Jackson (Ed.), *Professions and Professionalization*, Cambridge University Press, New York, pp. 53–107; A. Abbott (1983), "Professional ethics," *American Journal of Sociology*, 88, 5, pp. 855–85.

30. J. R. Cohen and L. W. Pant (1991), "Beyond bean counting: Establishing high ethical standards in the accounting profession," *Journal of Business Ethics*, 10, pp. 45–6.

31. M. S. Frankel (1989), "Professional codes: Why, how and with what impact?" *Journal of Business Ethics*, 8, pp. 109–115.

32. E. Greenwood (1966), "The elements of professionalism," in H. M. Vollmer and D. L. Mills (Eds.), *Professionalization*, Prentice-Hall, Englewood Cliffs, NJ, pp. 9–19, quote p.14.

33. K. S. Kelly (1995), "The fund-raising behavior of U.S. charitable organizations," *Journal of Public Relations Research*, 7, 2, pp. 111–37.

34. B. J. Lombardo (1991), "Conflicts of interest between nonprofits and corporate donors," in D. F. Burlingame and L. J. Hulse (Eds.), *Taking Fund-raising Seriously: Advancing the Profession and Practice of Raising Money*, Jossey-Bass, San Francisco, pp. 83–99.

35. Carbone (1989), *Fund Raising as a Profession*, op. cit. p. 32.

36. J. Carlin (1966), *Lawyer's Ethics*, Sage, New York; Freidson (1975), *Doctoring Together*.

37. R. K. Merton (1968), *Social Theory and Social Structure*, Free Press, New York; R. K. Merton (1973), *The Sociology of Science: Theoretical and Empirical Investigations*, University of Chicago Press, Chicago.

38. R. K. Merton (1957), "Priorities in scientific discovery," *American Sociological Review*, 2, pp. 635–59; Merton (1968), *Social Theory and Social Structure*.

39. E. Durkheim (1951), *Suicide*, trans. John H. Saulding and George Simpson, Free Press, New York.

40. J. M. Braxton and A. E. Bayer (1999), *Faculty Misconduct in Collegiate Teaching*, Johns Hopkins University Press, Baltimore, MD, p. 4.

41. E. Durkheim (1995), *The Elementary Forms of Religious Life*, trans. K. E. Fields, Free Press, New York.

42. R. T. Morris (1956), "A typology of norms," *American Sociological Review*, 21, 5, pp. 610–13, quote p.610.

43. Durkheim (1951), *Suicide*, op. cit.

44. T. C. Caboni (2001), "The normative structure of college and university fund raising," Unpublished doctoral dissertation, Vanderbilt University, Nashville, TN.

45. Braxton and Bayer (1999), *Faculty Misconduct in Collegiate Teaching*, op. cit.

46. Caboni (2001), "The normative structure of college and university fund raising," op. cit.

47. Braxton and Bayer (1999), *Faculty Misconduct in Collegiate Teaching*, op. cit.

48. Ibid.

49. W. J. Goode (1969), "The theoretical limits of professionalization," op. cit.

50. Ibid.

51. Carbone (1989), *Fund Raising as a Profession*, op. cit. p.46.

52. Goode (1957), "Community within a community," op. cit.

Practitioner's Perspective

Is fund raising a "true profession"? In this article the author compares fund raising as a profession against standard characteristics that sociologists have identified to determine whether a particular occupation is a "profession" and concludes that yes, fund raising is "an emerging profession." Moreover it is "an occupation that has moved steadily along the professional continuum; a profession with the potential to attain greater professional stature."

In taking a comprehensive look at the characteristics that true professions possess and comparing the fund-raising profession against those characteristics, the article is both informative and timely. Our institutional fund-raising programs are under growing pressure to increase the private gift support as our state budgets continue to shrink and our endowments continue to slide in the current economy. The author identifies four key characteristics of a profession: (1) an intensive period of training and socialization, (2) the possession of a systematic body of theory, (3) the formation of professional associations, and (4) the existence of a code of conduct.

The profession of fund raising meets each of these criteria, albeit in varying degrees. The strength of this article is the road map the author has prepared for us to study as we continue in our drive for increased professionalism. Two areas of particular interest are his discussion of formal and informal training programs and a growing systematic body of theory. I believe there is a strong connection between these two areas. As fund raisers we serve our institutions in positions of privilege. The author refers to this role as one of "boundary spanner"—representing both the institution and the donor. To best serve both the institution and the donor our growing skills as fund raisers should be based on solid research that in turn leads to best practices. We need to clearly understand effective and appropriate fund-raising techniques for our work with donors. We also need to be fully integrated into our institutions in order to represent true academic priorities and goals. As our fund-raising programs continue to grow in size and scope, we owe it to our institutions to become more sophisticated, professional, and effective.

As fund-raising managers, we are responsible for guiding the progress of our fund-raising staff from entry level to more senior positions. This has been largely an informal process, but there are increased signs of more formal career paths being established, especially at large institutions. There are increasing sources of educational opportunities available for training and development of our fund-raising staff, through CASE, AFP, and other organizations. The better we can articulate appropriate skills, experience, and career steps necessary for fund raisers, the closer we will be in our drive toward professionalism.

As a profession, fund raising has made significant progress over the past 20 years; however, there is much we can continue to do to ensure we are meeting our responsibilities to both our institutions and our donors. With his solid review and analysis of our "emerging" profession of fund raising, in comparison with other, "true" professions, the author has given us several key guideposts as we continue our journey.

Myrna Hall
Vice President of Development, University of Colorado Foundation, Boulder, USA

Surveying the Major Gifts Literature: Observations and Reflections

W. Bruce Cook

This article gives only cursory attention to generally accepted and widely known principles that provide the foundation and the context for the major gifts effort; instead, the author focuses more broadly and strategically on the critical importance of mission, quality, leadership, and prestige; the dichotomy between annual and major gift fundraising; and the need for an empirically derived and theoretically driven model of fundraising and philanthropic behavior to inform the major gifts effort.

In recent years, journalists, practitioners, and scholars have increasingly focused and written extensively on philanthropy, fundraising, and nonprofit leadership, and, in the process, the topic of major gifts has been addressed in considerable detail. However, this growing literature focuses almost exclusively on gifts from individuals (including bequests) and virtually ignores two additional sources of gifts: corporations and foundations. Furthermore, despite this abundance of research studies, much remains to be discovered—and applied—since what is already known about major gifts has yet to be put into practice by many nonprofit organizations.

A 1991 study by the Association for Healthcare Philanthropy, for example, found, among other things, that the top two concerns of association members were "poor understanding of fund raising by administrators" and "insufficient involvement in fund raising by administrators" (Childress, 1992). Herman and Heimovics (1991, pp. 2–3) have observed, "The most fundamental problem facing many of the leaders of nonprofit organizations is the continuing effort needed to find and sustain financial resources sufficient to carry out the mission of the organization during a time of declining government support and intensifying competition for available funds." And, in a national study of excellence in nonprofit organizations, Knauft, Berger, and Gray (1991, pp. 25–26) found that "by a wide margin, the chief staff officers we surveyed considered fund raising the most pressing challenge facing their organizations in the coming three to five years. Interestingly, these executives reported that building fundraising skills was the area where they perceived the greatest need for personal development."

Kathleen S. Kelly conceptualized and tested four models of fund-raising—press agentry, public information, two-way asymmetrical, and two-way symmetrical—that are practiced by nonprofit organizations and estimated that only 5 percent of all U.S. nonprofits practice the most enlightened model, the two-way symmetrical:

> The purpose of the two-way symmetrical model of fund raising is to reach mutual understanding. The nature of its communication is two-way between groups with balanced, or symmetrical, effects. Rather than source to receiver, the group-to-group distinction emphasizes this model's orientation to systems theory and the environmental interdependencies of donors and charitable organizations. Unlike the press agentry model of fund raising, which is dependent on the emotions of its publics, or the public information model, which is dependent on their enlightenment, the two-way symmetrical model is dependent on congruency with its donor publics.
>
> This latest model uses formative research to balance the needs of the charitable organization and its donor publics (i.e., research is used to identify opportunities for private funding and issues that the charitable organization is not addressing). Its practice is based on principles of negotiation, compromise, and conflict resolution. The effectiveness of this model is evaluated by its contribution to enhancing and protecting organizational autonomy through the fund-raising process [1995, p. 109].

Kelly (1995) concluded from her quantitative research that fundraisers practice the two-way symmetrical model more when raising major gifts than when raising annual gifts, and that most managerial tasks in fundraising are more highly correlated with the two-way symmetrical model than other models. She also concluded that most fundraisers practice a mixed-motive model, which includes both symmetrical and asymmetrical elements. This latter conclusion is not surprising, since most fundraising programs include both annual and major gift components, and since mutual understanding, balanced effects, and congruence are goals held by a small minority of organizations, while organizational autonomy is a goal held by the vast majority of organizations.

But despite the widespread failure among nonprofits to maximize their fundraising and major gifts potential, what is even more striking from a review of the literature are the absence of and the critical need for an empirically derived and theoretically driven model of fundraising and philanthropic behavior. Despite claims to the contrary by many practitioners, fundraising is a science and can be observed, measured, and analyzed. As Kelly (1997, p. 33) so aptly has stated, "Without theory, fund raising is relegated to an occupation without scientific explanation, predictable outcomes, or any claim to professionalism."

Since 1975, the fundraising model developed by Smith (1975, 1977, 1993) has gained widespread acceptance among practitioners and has served unofficially as the standard model for the industry. Smith named his major gifts continuum the cultivation cycle (popularly known as the "Five I's" of fundraising), which includes the steps of identification, information, interest, involvement, and investment, in that order. Others have used modified versions of Smith's continuum. Dunlop (1993), for example, included the steps of identification, information, awareness, understanding, caring, involvement, and commitment in his schematic of the major gift process.

Prather (1981) included the five steps of identification, cultivation, planning the approach, solicitation, and follow-up. Dailey (1986) identified seven steps in the major gifts process: prospect research, research and qualification, strategizing the approach, involving the prospect, making the ask, closing the solicitation, and after-solicitation follow-up. Dailey explained that every major gift solicitation is a separate minicampaign and noted, "People make small annual gifts to projects in which they are 'interested' or 'involved.' But they make large major gifts only to projects to which they are 'committed'" (p. 82).

Wood (1989) offered the four-step fundraising process of research, cultivation, solicitation, and recognition and described the major gifts process as 25 percent research, 60 percent cultivation, 5 percent solicitation, and 10 percent recognition. Tempel (1991) envisioned six steps: analysis, planning, cultivation, execution, control, and evaluation, whereas Steele and Elder (1992) presented a five-step development cycle: identification, cultivation, solicitation, stewardship, and resolicitation.

A central tenet of Smith's continuum is that major gift success is accomplished over a period of years and involves a series of well-planned and well-coordinated moves orchestrated by individuals designated as "primes" and "secondaries" who are close to the donor prospect and have some linkage with the institution. In this scheme, short-term gifts are less important than progress in moving the prospect closer to the institution.

Smith also enunciated the concepts of foreground and background activities. According to Dunlop (1986, p. 326), "Background activities are those initiatives that, although they do have an impact on individual prospects, are conceived and carried out for groups." Foreground activities, on the other hand, are initiatives that are conceived, planned, and carried out for specific individual major gift prospects. Dunlop added, "Major gift fund-raising derives benefits from initiatives directed toward individual prospects as well as initiatives directed toward groups; in other words, in major gift fund-raising, background activities are as important as foreground activities" (p. 335).

In contrast, Kelly (1991, 1997) pioneered the development of a theoretical framework for fundraising and, drawing on systems theory, reconceptualized fundraising as donor relations. This view is significant because it refutes the common misperception that fundraising is a marketing or sales function and instead places fundraising within the domain of public relations, adding donors as a seventh public in need of strategic two-way communication and donor relations as a seventh specialization, along with media, employee, community, government, consumer, and investor relations. Within this conceptual framework, relationships between charitable organizations and donors are viewed as environmental interdependencies, fundraising is defined as the management of relationships between a charitable organization and its donor publics, and the major principles and tenets on which fundraising rests are linked to particular communication theories.

Kelly (1997) also conceptualized the ROPES (research, objectives, programming, evaluation, stewardship) typology to describe the fundraising process. ROPES describes the process by which both annual and major gifts are raised. Specifically, the annual giving program involves a large number of prospects and thus requires group analysis and the use of controlled and mass media techniques. The major gifts program, on the other hand, deals with a small number of prospects, which allows for individual attention and interpersonal techniques.

This dichotomy or dual emphasis can be observed in the fund-raising programs of many nonprofit organizations and is one indication of organizational and programmatic maturity and viability, since annual and major gift programs are potentially complementary and synergistic. However, major gifts account for a high (that is, majority) percentage of private gift totals each year for most nonprofits, and this pattern reflects the fundamental reality underlying major gifts, which is economic inequality.

For example, Brossman (1981) cited a study by Levy and Steinbach for the American Council on Education that found that more than 70 percent of the gift dollars received by colleges and universities in 1973–74 came from fewer than 0.5 percent of the donors. Brossman concluded, "The key to successful fund raising for higher education lies in attracting big gifts" (p. 69). Moreover, Kelly (1991, p. 266) found that most large gifts go to a small percentage of institutions: "Whereas 77 percent of corporate dollars and 68 percent of foundation dollars went to the 183 research universities in CFAE's [Council for Aid to Education's] 1987–1988 survey of gifts, 62 percent of the individual dollars also went to those same institutions. It can, therefore, be stated . . . that the majority of gift dollars to higher education from all three sources of private support is funnelled to a very small percentage of institutions."

Just how small a percentage is illustrated in the data from a 1990 survey by the Council for Aid to Education. The study revealed that 60 institutions—less than 6 percent of the 1,066 included in the survey—raised half of all donations to higher education, accounting for $4.1 billion. In terms of specific categories of private support, 37 institutions—or 3.5 percent of those surveyed—received half of all foundation dollars contributed to higher education; 40 institutions—or 3.8 percent of those surveyed—received half of all corporate dollars; 50 institutions—or 4.7 percent of those surveyed—received half of all alumni gifts; and 64 institutions—or 6 percent of those surveyed—raised half of all gifts from other individuals (Goss, 1991). Of the 60 institutions that raised half of all contributions, 29 were private and 31 were public universities. And nearly all of the universities with the largest fundraising totals were doctorate-granting research institutions. Furthermore, the study claimed that these results reflect "virtually no change over the last two decades in the fraction of higher-education institutions that receive the bulk of all private contributions" (Goss, 1991, p. 8).

The same forces that govern institutional wealth apply to individuals as well, with the net result that in terms of the society as a whole, the rich tend to get richer and the poor poorer (Allen, 1987; Blau, 1993; Braun, 1991; Goss, 1991; Kelly, 1991; Packard, 1989; Phillips, 1990). Dove (1988, p. 75) explained this phenomenon as follows: "Wealth is not distributed democratically in this society. If everyone is asked to make a gift that is 'generous within their own means,' each donor will not be expected to give the same amount; much will be expected of a few, and many more will be expected to do as much as they can. Not only will everyone not give the same amount to any given campaign, many will choose to give nothing at all. In addition, this approach limits the amount asked from those who could give more, and seldom do donors give more than they are asked to give."

A nationally prominent fundraising consultant has observed that as a result of the shrinking middle class, nonprofit organizations that desire anything more than incremental growth must focus their time, attention, and effort on the top 2 to 5 percent of donor prospects:

> There's the concept of a donor pyramid where people start out at the bottom—large numbers of people make these smaller gifts—and there's essentially a trickle-up kind of theory that people will move through the ranks as they become more wealthy and eventually they'll become major donors to the institution. The studies that I have done, basically looking at the results of capital campaigns, suggest that that old

way of thinking is not going to work in the future primarily because the middle class—the American white-collar middle class—is not varied in the way it used to be. . . . If you will look at statistics—I think it's the last 12 to 15 years—8 percent of the American middle class has left the middle class; 6 percent's gone down, 2 percent's gone up. And the bottom line is, if you start with the Arab oil embargo, you find that the group of people who were in that middle class, not only are they disappearing, but they have less disposable discretionary income. . . . My bottom line is this: the demographics and the economics and the sociology have shifted but I don't think fund-raising methodology has. And I think that many people are simply using the methods of the past without understanding the trends of the future. The whole premise I'm moving to is if you want to be cost effective, cost efficient, if you want to be success-ful with a fund-raising program, if you want to get quantum growth, or anything more than incremen-tal growth which basically keeps pace with inflation, you're going to turn more and more time, attention, and focus to the top 2 to 5 percent of your donor population, where you will probably get as much as 80 to 90 percent of the total dollars you're going to get in your program on an annual basis. . . . Again, the old annual giving-based, donor pyramid-driven philosophy of fund raising is going to give way to a major gifts-focused, tiered concept of fund raising [Cook, 1994, p. 129].

An example of this viewpoint was provided by Martin Grenzebach, a fundraising consultant and chair of Grenzebach Glier & Associates, who assisted the University of Illinois with a campaign during the late 1980s. According to him, securing each gift of $100,000 or more for the campaign required an average of seven to nine visits with the donor over a two-year period. Since 300 major donors were involved, approximately 2,400 visits were required. "That took time," said Grenzebach. Ultimately, 129 donors gave 99.6 percent of the $132.4 million raised in the campaign (Bailey, 1987, p. A76). A second example was provided by the chief development officer of a private university: "In our campaign that just finished, 91 percent of the money came from 507 out of 32,000 donors. So we're trying to get the president focused on those 507, not on the 32,000. He deals with the larger groups through mass communications, but his personal commitment is to the 1,200 to 1,500 prospects whose derivative becomes the 507 who were worth 90 percent of the money. So it's the focus on the critical few that has been heightened in the last several years" (Cook, 1994, p. 351).

Basically, these examples illustrate the difference between the lower-level and major gift approaches to fundraising. Jencks (1987) has referred to this dichotomy as "paying your dues" versus "giving away your surplus." Annual giving refers to the less personalized strategy and methodology employed by fundraisers to obtain gifts ranging from $1 to $100, or in some cases $1,000 or $10,000, depending on individual donor capacity. Major gifts, on the other hand, typically refer to the more personalized strategy and methodology employed by fundraisers seeking six- or seven-figure gifts.

Moreover, major gifts are more likely to favor museums, hospitals and medical centers, arts orga-nizations, research institutes, and colleges and universities rather than other types of nonprofits (Brittingham and Pezzullo, 1990; Caton, 1991; Cook, 1994; Kelly, 1991, 1997; Panas, 1984; Silberg, 1990; Ostrower, 1991). This is because prestige is a critical factor in major gift considerations. As Kelly (1991, p. 189) commented, "Private gifts are not distributed equally (e.g., major gifts are rarely given to small, unknown organizations even if their need is great—such as feeding starving children, but are instead generally made to the most prestigious organizations, such as doctoral universities, museums, and hospitals)."

In 1995, the most recent year for which figures are available, Americans gave an estimated $143.9 billion to charity, with the largest totals by categories as follows: religion, $63.45 billion, or 44.1 percent; education, $17.94 billion, or 12.5 percent; health, $12.59 billion, or 8.8 percent; human services, $11.70 billion, or 8.1 percent; and the arts, $9.96 billion, or 6.9 percent (Murawski, 1996, pp. 28–29). However, despite its relatively modest share of the philanthropic pie, higher education attracts the majority of gifts of $1 million or more each year (Sterne, 1990; Ostrower, 1991). Accord-ing to Kelly (1991, p. 180), one explanation for this is that "colleges and universities are of particu-lar interest to groups and organizations in their environment because of the resources they hold (e.g., knowledge, trained manpower, scientific innovation, prestige, and even athletics)."

Caton (1991, p. 228) also noted that, in common with alumni, the prestige of a given nonprofit organization is a public good for its major donors: "Major donors are drawn to institutions with a reputation for quality and seek to associate themselves with the achievement of higher quality in ways that can be appreciated by their peers." Caton explained that in addition to pride of association and making a difference, major donors also feel that projects with which they are associated are a personal reflection on them and their concept of quality. In other words, major donors must have a high level of respect for and trust in an organization and its leadership because such donors invest a portion of their identities and values in the organization along with actual gifts of money and property. "Donors look for ways to enhance institutional quality even as they also consider the ways a project might reflect their own appreciation of quality to others. Obviously, nonprofit organizations seeking big gifts must devote some attention to identifying projects associated with higher institutional quality and to considering what a project might convey about the donor to others who appreciate quality. In other words, institutional and personal prestige are often intimately intertwined in the case of major gifts" (1991, p. 197).

Caton's findings are consistent in many respects with those of other studies of major donors (for example, Panas, 1984; Odendahl, 1990; Silberg, 1990; Ostrower, 1991; Gibbons, 1992; Reilly, 1992). Ostrower (1991, pp. 337, 340–341), for example, addressed the importance of institutional prestige in fundraising in her study of elite philanthropy in New York City: "The prestige of nonprofits in the eyes of a particular group affects who gets donations. . . . Donors are very much aware of the power of prestige to attract donations, and indeed regularly use this to elicit contributions from one another. . . . Among donors as a whole, the bulk of largest gifts are directed towards prestigious educational and cultural organizations that are a part of elite life. Regardless of their public significance, these institutions have a special place among elites. Identification with them is a symbol of social standing. Involvement with them brings the individual into contact with his or her social peers."

As mentioned previously, studies of major donors by Panas (1984) and Gibbons (1992) indicate that belief in mission is at or near the top of donor motives. In the Panas study, for example, belief in the mission of the organization rated first among both major donors and development professionals on a list of twenty-two possible motives. In the Gibbons study, which used the Panas list to compare the motives of major donors at the University of Utah and Brigham Young University, belief in the mission of the institution was rated third by the University of Utah donors and second by the Brigham Young University donors. It is noteworthy that the University of Utah donors chose two separate measures of prestige—institutional respect/wide circle and institutional respect/local—as their first and second choices, respectively, with interest in a specific program ranked fourth. The Brigham Young donors predictably ranked religious affiliation first on their list of motives, but institutional respect/local was ranked third and institutional respect/wide circle, fourth. In other words, belief in mission and two separate measures of institutional prestige were ranked as three of the top four motives for giving by the major donors at the two largest universities (a Doctorate I private and a Research I public) in Utah.

Similarly, Hunter (1968) found that "conviction as to the merits of the project" was ranked first among possible motives by a national sample of thirty donors who gave gifts of $1 million or more. Hunter summarized his findings by stating that donors tend to give generously "to causes which they believe to be worthwhile" (pp. 41, 45). And in a study of thirteen donors who gave $1 million or more to institutions of higher education, Silberg (1990) found that one of nine primary themes (mentioned by all thirteen donors) was that major donors give according to the issues and causes in which they are interested. Such donors "seek organizations whose missions support the same causes and issues that interest them" (p. 137).

These findings support the fundraising maxim that belief in mission is the strongest reason for giving. As Kelly (1997, p. 32) noted, "If real estate is dependent on the three factors of location, location, and location, then fund raising is dependent on mission, mission, and mission."

Other studies of major donors—Boris and Odendahl (1987), Odendahl (1990), Ostrower (1991), Prince and File (1994), and Schervish and Herman (1988)—have used more of a sociological approach and found that philanthropy is an important part of elite life, that wealthy donors tend to give to high-prestige organizations that play a major role in maintaining elite culture, that major donors tend to have a dominant giving style, and that wealthy donors are creators or producers rather than mere supporters of philanthropic outcomes. In summary, they found that elite philanthropy is a form of identity and group membership and that social setting and culture profoundly influence donor motive.

Taken together, these studies reveal that belief in mission, organizational prestige, and interest in a particular program or project are factors given considerable weight by major donors in their gift decisions. On the other hand, low-prestige institutions occasionally receive major gifts—even unrestricted ones—from someone giving out of community pride or loyalty to alma mater or gratitude or desire to make a difference or because of the influence a doctor or nurse or social worker or professor had on his or her life (for example, the $100 million Mr. and Mrs. Henry Rowan gave to Glassboro State College [now Rowan College] in New Jersey).

Obviously, there are many commodities other than prestige that donors may purchase with their gifts, such as pride of association, social status, recognition, gratitude, immortality, and a sense of satisfaction or joy from giving something back or doing good. Equally obvious is the fact that other factors are often involved in major gift decisions, including donor capacity, timing, momentum, executive leadership, a relationship between the donor and someone associated with the institution, effort, planning, an adequate fundraising infrastructure, competent staff, donor recognition program, tax considerations, state of the economy and nation, and so on. Apparently, however, what is not as obvious is that *it is the interaction or intersection of donor motives and organizational prerequisites that produces major gifts*.

Greenfield (1991, p. 12) summarized the rationale for research on donor motivation as follows: "The lists of motives for giving only confirm that there is no single reason why people or institutions make gifts, but motives are important to study because they trigger the gift response." However, Schervish and Herman (1988) and Kelly (1991) downplayed the importance or usefulness of research on motivation. The former stated, "such research is of questionable insight and utility" (p. 56), while the latter added, "Previous fund-raising studies, which focus on characteristics, attitudes, and motivations of donors, are limited to their explanation of the fund-raising process" (p. 197). In addition, Brittingham and Pezzullo (1990, p. iii) noted, "Studies of institutional effectiveness . . . and analyses of donors' behavior have dominated research in fund raising for the last 20 years." They concluded, "The cumulative results of these studies have been somewhat disappointing, given their relatively high numbers" (p. 90). In summary, while disagreeing on the relative importance of research on donor motives, most practitioners and scholars agree that multiple motives are involved and somehow converge or coalesce in the case of a major gift (Bakal, 1979; Brakeley, 1980; Greenfield, 1991; Panas, 1984; Prince and File, 1994).

In regard to organizational prerequisites for fundraising, Cook and Lasher (1996) developed a list of the top dozen prerequisites for a program of sustained fundraising in higher education as well as a social exchange model of academic fundraising based on the ROPES typology described earlier. This model incorporates both donor motives and organizational prerequisites as well as donor responses to ROPES initiatives, and both the model and prerequisites appear to have relevance and application to other types of nonprofit organizations. Further, social exchange theory (see Cook, 1994; Kelly, 1991) provides the legal rationale and justification for the tax-exempt status of nonprofit organizations as well as the charitable deduction donors are allowed for gifts to 501(c)(3) organizations.

Cook and Lasher's (1996) twelve prerequisites include leadership; financial capacity and capability of constituency; clarity and strength of organizational mission; personal relationship between donors and someone associated with the organization; involvement of donors in the life of the organization; prestige, reputation, and image of the organization or individual programs or operating units; history, age, maturity, consistency, and tradition of both the organization and its development program; informed and committed constituency; donor predisposition to give (philanthropic impulse in society as a whole as well as established patterns of generosity in particular regions and cities); continued public confidence in the nonprofit sector; state of the economy and nation; and tax policy. These prerequisites were derived from an extensive review of the literature and from numerous interviews with knowledgeable individuals; therefore, individual elements are not weighted or ranked. Moreover, the prerequisites create a synergistic effect since each element is important for sustained fundraising effectiveness, and the absence or dilution of an element or elements reduces the overall impact of the others.

However, few if any programs enjoy the luxury of being strong in all twelve prerequisites at any one time (especially since the last four items are beyond the control of individual organizations). Fortunately, as Duronio and Loessin (1991) indicated, institutions can experience a measure or degree of fundraising success under less than ideal or perfect conditions. (In fact, of the sixteen variables they measured that contribute to fundraising effectiveness, the successful institutions in their study were on average strong in only eight.)

This is encouraging news for nonprofit fundraisers and executives because fundraising is one area where leadership can have a significant, and at times transforming, effect on an organization. And although change is more often evolutionary, or incremental, rather than revolutionary, leaders can still make a difference—and exert considerable influence—on their organizations. Donor confidence in leadership is, of course, a prerequisite for major gifts and is based on personality, style, ethics, vision, personal and fiscal integrity, communication skills, and managerial ability, among other things. This applies to the governing board as well as the chief executive, and, quite naturally, board members of effective organizations contribute a significant percentage of total giving each year. In terms of fundraising, nonprofit chief executives should focus their efforts on two areas: major gifts (say, gifts of $10,000 or more, though this varies depending on organizational type and other factors) and administrative leadership (for example, policy and strategy decisions, budget and staffing concerns, selection and evaluation of the chief development officer, strategic planning, selling a campaign to the board, involvement in the selection of a consultant, helping to decide on the timing and goal for a campaign, recruiting volunteer leaders, and articulating the institutional vision) (Cook, 1994).

Leaders can also help to set the tone, style, and focus of their fundraising programs through their attitudes, values, and decisions, as well as their personal involvement and time. For example, major gifts veteran David Dunlop of Cornell University described the need for long-term thinking in fundraising as follows: "Many contend that fund raising, like selling, is primarily a matter of getting the order to commitment. This focuses a great deal of reliance on asking for the gift and it suggests that a campaign prospect's decision is largely conditioned by the 'ask.' This view may serve in the short run and for the objectives of a single campaign, but our institutions function in the long run and that perspective must also be taken into account. In the long run the campaign fund raiser who focuses only on the 'task,' caring nothing for the institution's on-going relationship with the donor, does a disservice to the school [or other type of nonprofit organization] and its benefactors [as well as the fundraising profession]" (1980, p. 31). An example of the short-term thinking criticized by Dunlop was offered by Tripp Carter, former director of development research at Rice University: "The secret to making the pieces fit is finding who holds the power. I can make anybody a donor if I can find someone with social, economic, or political influence over them" (Leslie and others, 1988, p. 66).

While Carter may or may not be correct in his assumption that anyone can be led to give when exposed to the right influences, his statement ignores social exchange theory and implies that donors are puppets to be manipulated by hidden fundraisers who pull invisible strings. Such an approach may produce donors, but it will not produce philanthropists. Likewise, fundraising programs that emphasize short-term goals and asymmetrical communication with donors rather than long-term relationships and balanced, two-way communication will fall short of their potential, no matter what particular giving totals or campaign results might indicate, and over time may cost organizations more than they earn in lost goodwill and other, more tangible benefits.

In conclusion, social exchange theory, and social exchange models of fundraising, appear to offer a promising alternative to nonprofits in need of philanthropic resources. As Ostrander and Schervish (1990, p. 93) observed, "Donors have needs to be fulfilled as well as resources to grant, and recipients have resources to give as well as needs to be met. In other words, donors and recipients both give and get in the social relation that is philanthropy." Similarly, Lord (1983, p. 5) has commented, "The fact is that people give in order to *get*. They don't want to feel that they are 'giving away' their money. They want to feel they are investing it, and getting something in return." Dove (1988, p. 91) also noted that major donors "view giving as an investment, and through their investments they desire to solve a problem or issue, seek ways to express themselves (self-actualization), and expect to see and understand the 'return on the investment.'"

Nonprofits must rise to the challenge of making major donors partners in the true sense of the word. A university president said of major donors to his institution, "They're supposed to be family members, having some stock in its success, and so when they contribute, we point out that they're really part of a community, and as part of a community, we know they're interested in what happens, so we keep them well-informed as to how their dollars are being used" (Cook, 1994, p. 419). Another academic chief executive provided the following summary statement: "How do you motivate donors? You bring them into the dream. You make them a part of the vision. You make them a part of something bigger than themselves, which is what these wonderful places {nonprofits are. And you not only help them understand it, but you allow them a way to identify with it. If you don't bring them into the center and they don't feel a part of it, then you will not have a very large donor" (Cook, 1994, p. 420). Ultimately, major donors invest not only their time and money but also, and of even greater worth to them, their identity, prestige, and reputation in the nonprofits that they so ably serve.

References

Allen, M. P. *The Founding Fortunes*. New York: Talley Books, 1987.

Bailey, A. L. "Fund Drives Get Bigger, Broader: 65 College Goals to $100 Million." *Chronicle of Higher Education*, Sept. 2, 1987, pp. A72–73, 74–77.

Bakal, C. *Charity U.S.A.: An Investigation into the Hidden World of the Multi-Billion-Dollar Charity Industry.* New York: Times Books, 1979.

Blau, J. R. *Social Contracts and Economic Markets*. New York: Plenum Press, 1993.

Boris, E. T., and Odendahl, T. J. (eds.). *America's Wealthy and the Future of Foundations*. New York: Foundation Center, 1987.

Brakeley, G. A., Jr. *Tested Ways to Successful Fund Raising*. New York: AMACOM, 1980.

Braun, D. *The Rich Get Richer: The Rise of Income Inequality in the United States and the World*. Chicago: Nelson-Hall, 1991.

Brittingham, B. E., and Pezzullo, T. R. *The Campus Green: Fund Raising in Higher Education*. ASHE-ERIC Higher Education Report No. 1. Washington, D.C.: George Washington University, 1990.

Brossman, W. R. "The Central Importance of Large Gifts." In F. C. Pray (ed.), *Handbook for Educational Fund Raising: A Guide to Successful Principles and Practices for Colleges, Universities, and Schools*. San Francisco: Jossey-Bass, 1981.

Caton, C. S. "A Preference for Prestige? Commentary on the Behavior of Universities and Their Benefactors." Unpublished doctoral dissertation, Department of Education, University of Toronto, 1991.

Childress, R. *USA Report on Giving, FY 1991*. Falls Church, Va.: Association for Healthcare Philanthropy, 1992.

Cook, W. B. "Courting Philanthropy: The Role of University Presidents and Chancellors in Fund Raising." Unpublished doctoral dissertation, Department of Educational Administration, University of Texas, Austin, 1994.

Cook, W. B., and Lasher, W. F. "Toward a Theory of Fund Raising in Higher Education." *Review of Higher Education*, 1996, *20* (1), 33–51.

Dailey, W. F. "Organizing Yourself for Major Gift Success," In H. G. Quigg (ed.), *The Successful Capital Campaign*. Washington, D. C.: Council for Advancement and Support of Education, 1986.

Dove, K. E. *Conducting a Successful Capital Campaign: A Comprehensive Fundraising Guide for Nonprofit Organizations*. San Francisco: Jossey-Bass, 1988.

Dunlop, D. R. "The Changing Role of Volunteers in Capital Campaigns." In L. A. Maddalena (ed.), *Encouraging Voluntarism and Volunteers*. San Francisco: Jossey-Bass, 1980.

Dunlop, D. R. "Special Concerns of Major Gift Fund-Raising." In A. W. Rowland (ed.), *Handbook of Institutional Advancement: A Modern Guide to Executive Management, Institutional Relations, Fund Raising, Alumni Administration, Government Relations, Publications, Periodicals, and Enrollment Management*. (2nd ed.) San Francisco: Jossey-Bass, 1986.

Dunlop, D. R. "Strategic Management of a Major Gift Program." In R. Muir and J. May (eds.), *Developing an Effective Major Gift Program*. Washington, D.C.: Council for Advancement and Support of Education, 1993.

Duronio, M. A., and Loessin, B. A. *Effective Fund Raising in Higher Education: Ten Success Stories*. San Francisco: Jossey-Bass, 1991.

Gibbons, L. "Philanthropy in Higher Education: Motivations of Major Donors to Two Utah Universities." Unpublished doctoral dissertation, Department of Education Leadership, Brigham Young University, 1992.

Goss, K. A. "Sixty Institutions Get Half of Gifts to Colleges, Survey Finds." *Chronicle of Philanthropy*, June 4, 1991, p. 8.

Greenfield, J. M. *Fund-Raising: Evaluating and Managing the Fund Development Process*. New York: Wiley, 1991.

Herman, R. D., and Heimovics, R. D. *Executive Leadership in Nonprofit Organizations: New Strategies for Shaping Executive-Board Dynamics.* San Francisco: Jossey-Bass, 1991.

Hunter, T. W. "The Million-Dollar Gift." *College and University Journal,* 1968, 7 (4), 35–45.

Jencks, C. "Who Gives to What?" In W. W. Powell (ed.), *The Nonprofit Sector: A Research Handbook.* New Haven, Conn.: Yale University Press, 1987.

Kelly, K. S. *Fund Raising and Public Relations: A Critical Analysis.* Hillsdale, N.J.: Erlbaum, 1991.

Kelly, K. S. "Utilizing Public Relations Theory to Conceptualize and Test Models of Fund Raising." *Journalism and Mass Communication Quarterly,* 1995, 72 (1), 106–127.

Kelly, K. S. *Effective Fund-Raising Management.* Hillsdale, N.J.: Erlbaum, 1997.

Knauft, E. B., Berger, R. A., and Gray, S. T. *Profiles of Excellence: Achieving Success in the Nonprofit Sector.* San Francisco: Jossey-Bass, 1991.

Leslie, C., Harrison, J., Hutchison, S., Joseph, N., King, P., and Rosenberg, D. "Prospecting for Alumni Gold." Sept. 5, 1988, pp. 66–67.

Lord, J. G. *The Raising of Money: Thirty-Five Essentials Every Trustee Should Know.* Cleveland: Third Sector Press, 1983.

Murawski, J. "A Banner Year for Giving." *Chronicle of Philanthropy,* May 30, 1996, pp. 1, 27–30.

Odendahl, T. J. *Charity Begins at Home: Generosity and Self-Interest Among the Philanthropic Elite.* New York: Basic Books, 1990.

Ostrander, S. A., and Schervish, P. G. "Giving and Getting: Philanthropy as a Social Relation." In J. Van Til (ed.), *Critical Issues in American Philanthropy: Strengthening Theory and Practice.* San Francisco: Jossey-Bass, 1990.

Ostrower, F. L. "Why the Wealthy Give: A Study of Elite Philanthropy in New York City." Unpublished doctoral dissertation, Department of Sociology, Yale University, 1991.

Packard, V. *The Ultra Rich.* Boston: Little, Brown, 1989.

Panas, J. *Mega Gifts: Who Gives Them, Who Gets Them.* Chicago: Pluribus Press, 1984.

Phillips, K. *The Politics of Rich and Poor.* New York: Random House, 1990.

Prather, R. F. "The Private Liberal Arts College and the Major Gift." Unpublished doctoral dissertation, Teachers College, Columbia University, 1981.

Prince, R. A., and File, K. M. *The Seven Faces of Philanthropy: A New Approach to Cultivating Major Donors.* San Francisco: Jossey-Bass, 1994.

Reilly, T. J. "Motivations, Bilateral Relationships, and One Million Dollar Contributors: A Case Study of a Southwestern University." Unpublished doctoral dissertation, Department of Educational Administration and Higher Education, University of Arizona, 1992.

Schervish, P. G., and Herman, A. *The Study on Wealth and Philanthropy Final Report.* Chestnut Hill, Mass.: Social Welfare Research Institute, Boston College, 1988.

Silberg, C. S. "Factors Associated with the Philanthropic Behaviors of Major Donors." Unpublished doctoral dissertation, Department of Education Policy, Planning, and Administration, University of Maryland, 1990.

Smith, G. T. "Developing Private Support: Three Issues." In F. W. Ness (ed.), *The President's Role in Development.* Washington, D.C.: Association of American Colleges, 1975.

Smith, G. T. "The Development Program." In A. W. Rowland (ed.), *Handbook of Institutional Advancement.* San Francisco: Jossey-Bass, 1977.

Smith, G. T. "The Cultivation Cycle and Moves Management Concept." Paper presented at a seminar sponsored by the Institute for Charitable Giving, Chicago, 1993.

Steele, V., and Elder, S. *Becoming a Fundraiser: The Principles and Practice of Library Development.* Chicago: American Library Association, 1992.

Sterne, L. "Giving USA Report: Religion, Arts, and Environment Help Push Giving Up 10 Percent." *NonProfit Times,* June 1990, pp. 1, 13–16, 44.

Tempel, E. R. "Assessing Organizational Strengths and Vulnerabilities." In H. A. Rosso and Associates, *Achieving Excellence in Fund Raising: A Comprehensive Guide to Principles, Strategies, and Methods.* San Francisco: Jossey-Bass, 1991.

Wood, E. W. "The Four R's of Major Gift Solicitation." *Reid Report,* 1989, *141,* 1, 6.

Major Donors, Major Motives: The People and Purposes Behind Major Gifts

Paul G. Schervish

The motives of donors of large gifts are both simple and complex. What motivates the wealthy is very much what motivates someone at any point along the economic spectrum, but complexities of ability spirituality, and association come into play in the making of major gifts.

In this chapter, I explain what motivates the charitable giving of the wealthy, or more succinctly, the major motives of major donors. My research over the past twelve years has enabled me to distill an answer that is both simple and complex. The simple part is that what motivates the wealthy is very much what motivates someone at any point along the economic spectrum. Identify any motive that might inspire concern—from heartfelt empathy to self-promotion, from religious obligation to business networking, from passion to prestige, from political philosophy to tax incentives—and some millionaires (as well as some nonmillionaires) will make it the cornerstone of their giving. The complex part about the charitable motivation of the wealthy is that those who hold great wealth and consciously direct it to social purposes invariably want to shape rather than merely support a charitable cause. Although everyone who makes a gift wants it to make a difference, those who make a big gift want it to make a big difference. This raises the question, then, about what distinctive additional or complementary mobilizing factors come into play when major donors make major gifts.

Our research on giving and volunteering over the past decade has enabled my colleagues and me to develop several interconnected sets of findings and to specify their practical implications for generating charitable giving. In this chapter, I elaborate on three sets of research findings that are directly related to charting the motivational matrix of the wealthy.

The first set helps us specify an additional motivational vector that is peculiar to those who are able to allocate substantial resources to charity. The distinguishing characteristic of wealth holders is that they are "hyperagents." By this I mean that in addition to being agents alongside the rest of us, living within a given institutional framework in many realms—from business to politics to philanthropy—they are capable of establishing the institutional framework within which they and others live.

The second set of findings concern what we call the *identification model of caritas*. We have found that the spiritual foundations for charitable giving revolve around identification with the needs of others. Drawing on the writings of Thomas Aquinas and other thinkers, and on an analysis of intensive interviews with millionaires, we perceive that the key to the practice of care is how people link their destiny to the destiny of others. The practice of care derives from the disposition that meeting the needs of others fulfills one's own needs *and* connects one to the deeper dimensions of life, often experienced and expressed in religious terms as the unity of love of self, love of neighbor, and love of God.

Our third set of findings concerns the *associational dynamics of charity*. Our empirical research demonstrates that the forces of identification are generated, nurtured, and manifested through the associational relations of individuals. Generosity of time and money derives not from one's level of income or wealth but from the physical and moral density of one's associational life and horizons of identification.

In this chapter, I draw on the research findings that my colleagues and I have uncovered regarding motivations for charitable giving. My intention is to chart the unique juncture where general charitable motivations intersect with the motivations that are particular to the distinctive financial capacities and social-psychological dispositions of the wealthy. In the first section, I discuss the empowering class trait of the wealthy, which I call hyperagency. In the second section, I illustrate the mobilizing factors that we have found to be at the heart of the identification and association models of charitable giving. Although these factors apply in a general way to donors at all levels of income and wealth, I draw on my intensive interviews with the wealthy to portray how the factors apply specifically to holders of wealth. In the third section I address two topics. First, I describe how the class trait of hyperagency leads wealth holders to an *inclination* to be producers rather than simply supporters of philanthropic projects. Second, I explore how the growing levels of wealth and the estate tax code, as modified by the 1986 Federal Tax Code revisions, combine to become an unprecedented ally of philanthropy. With charitable contributions having become the principal alternative to paying an effective estate tax rate of 60 percent, no discussion of the determinants of major gifts can omit the operation of estate taxes in generating charitable giving. In the conclusion, I indicate some practical implications for encouraging wealth holders to become major donors.

I base the analysis largely on the findings from the Study on Wealth and Philanthropy. This multiyear research project, funded by the T. B. Murphy Foundation, focused on the meaning and practice of money management among individuals with a net worth of $1 million or more who have earned or inherited their wealth. During the course of the research, we conducted 130 intensive interviews with individuals spread over eleven metropolitan areas of the United States. (See Schervish and Herman, 1988, for details on the sample and methodology of the Study on Wealth and Philanthropy.)

Major Donors: Determination and Dominion

"Just who, exactly, did the Dutch think they were?" asks Simon Schama (1988, p. 51) as he begins his exploration of the cultural setting and moral identity of the sixteenth-century and seventeenth-century Dutch who, for the first time in history, composed a whole class of people who were wealthy without being aristocratic. There is in that question, of course, a bit of the acerbic overtone we find in the parental admonition, "Just who do you think you are?" But Schama's question is also an opening for a serious answer. In that spirit, I explore the question "Just who, exactly, do the wealthy think they are?" My answer requires a look at the attributes of determination and dominion that characterize the empowerment of wealth holders.

Hyperagency

In a famous statement, Karl Marx argued that although people do indeed make their own history, they are not able to choose the conditions under which they do so. Although Marx was referring to collective action, the same dictum holds for individual actors as well. However, the capacity to "make history" is not equally distributed. Some, including wealth holders, make more history than others. I call this history-making capacity of individuals *hyperagency*. For sure, not every hyperagent is wealthy. Some financially common folk make history by virtue of being profound, creative, or spiritual. But in the material realm, every wealth holder is at least potentially a hyperagent.

Hyperagency refers to the enhanced capacity of wealthy individuals to establish or control substantially the conditions under which they and others live. For most individuals, agency is limited to choosing among and acting within the constraints of those situations in which they find themselves. As monarchs of agency, the wealthy can circumscribe such constraints and, for good or ill, create for themselves a world of their own design. As everyday agents, most of us strive to *find* the best possible place to live or the best job to hold, within a given field of possibilities. As hyperagents, the wealthy—when they choose to do so—can *found* a broad array of the field of possibilities within which they will live and work.

Whenever a respondent is asked to identify the most important attribute of wealth, the answer is invariably the same: *freedom*. Such freedom is both a negative release *from* constraint and a positive capacity *to* secure desire. Negative freedom refers to the loosening or negation of constraints, especially from the immediate pressures surrounding stable provision of material well-being.

At the extreme, it is liberty from having to work in order to survive. In contrast, positive freedom refers to the capacity to accomplish desires in the face of constraints. In the material realm, such freedom is the ability to experience virtually every situation, from housing and vacations to education and work, as opportunities for choice rather than conditions of compromise or deprivation. For instance, the fact that the wealthy do not *have* to work ironically results often enough in their *wanting* to work. Freed *from* the obligation to work, they are free *to* select and shape their work so that it becomes a source of satisfaction, self-actualization, and effective accomplishment. Attorney Rebecca Austin (a pseudonym, as are all the vignette names and identifying details in this chapter) expresses this duality of freedom in her assessment of how wealth "smoothes out" the everyday toils of life and enables her to set her "own agenda":

> Everything is easier when you have money. It's a shame because it's such a hard thing to get. It is the one item that smoothes out what everyone is struggling for: security, good health, fitness, good relationships, taking care of your children. Work choices are easier. Life is easier. You can do anything you want. You can take a vacation whenever and wherever you want. And even though I have a job, it's the kind of job that I can get there when I want to get there, because I want to be there rather than having to be there. The reason I work at [a public interest firm with the pseudonym] Citizen Law is that I can integrate my life. It allows me to focus on issues and do things that can become all-encompassing in terms of things that I care about. I don't work on anything I don't care about. I don't take assignments from anybody else. I set my own agenda.

To set one's own agenda, especially in those areas where it is usually set by others, is the fundamental endowment of wealth. Wealth enables individuals to freely conceive of and choose from among a wheel of alternatives. It would, of course, be foolish to assert that the possession of wealth dissolves all the fetters of time, health, and social constraint. The wealthy do indeed face constraints and rightly feel bounded in certain ways by obligation and responsibility (see Schervish, 1994). They have concerns with continued and expanded accumulation of wealth, organizational pressures of business, strategies of investment, generational reproduction of family wealth, preservation of a congenial political and economic climate, and moral and social responsibilities of philanthropy. Such concerns do indeed demand their time, money, and consciousness. As Norman Stryker, the Houston-born heir to an oil fortune, says, being granted an inheritance is a surprisingly alien burden. Without quotidian necessity to shape his life, he is forced to "carve out every goddamn day." Still, we find that even those who first flounder about with an inheritance overcome the obstacles and eventually learn the advantages of carving out rather than receiving their daily round.

Determination: The Individuality of Psychological Empowerment

Although the success of wealthy individuals in making the world requires material riches, it is also contingent upon a constellation of emotional, intellectual, and moral dispositions that enable the rich to act with determination. To be world builders in the spheres of business, consumption, and philanthropy, wealth holders need to learn repertoires of knowledge and sentiment. Del Garrison, a prominent Hollywood actor, describes the impact of wealth upon his consciousness and behavior as having "opened up a world to me that I never knew existed, a world that is not just one of consumption but of understanding! Of seeing the world in a different way. It's an education." The transformation provoked by wealth, he clarifies, "is not so much a value thing as it is a very basic thing" in that he became introduced to a way of life he "either didn't know existed or knew existed but [I thought was only] for somebody else." In the area of food, for instance, his wealth opened up not just new tastes, "some of which I liked and some I didn't," but a whole new cultural horizon. It was "a real mind expander":

> As a result of exploring [various foods] I found out about them, where they come from, a little about the cultures they're derived from, and so forth. So that what I meant in a sense is that everything like that, whether it be food or an understanding of the further distance between where I was now and where I had been, I was beginning to be more aware of what I had been and of others who lived that way and would never be out of living that way. It was a real mind expander and I can understand, I think, why often times poverty is such a narrowing thing. Now, I'm not saying I was in poverty, as I

never considered myself in poverty, but how poverty can be such a crushing and narrowing thing because it limits all kinds of opportunities so much. I did have a wonderful thing.

Garrison goes on to exemplify this "wonderful thing" by describing an especially satisfying episode in which he kept his underlying empowerment of wealth hidden in reserve until the proper dramatic moment.

> I had on an old pair of ratty jeans and a work shirt and some beat up boots. And I was driving down the street and I saw this 4-wheel drive Toyota Land Cruiser in the window of a place and I said "that's what I want, that's what I need." And I walked up in my semi-hippiness and asked the salesman how much it was and he kind of looked at me like, "It's out of your reach, fella." And I kept walking around looking at it, and I said, "Well, how much is it and if I bought it how soon could I get it?" He said, "If you pay cash for it, I'll have it ready for you in an hour." And I said, "OK, I want it." He said, "What?" And I pulled the cash out of my pocket and paid for it. At that time it was a real bubble to be able to do something like that. I haven't done anything like that since. I had to sort of do it once.

Individuality is psychological empowerment. It revolves around the premise of great expectations, the right to pursue them, and conviction about one's ability to achieve them. Individuality is not only a matter of conception; it is a matter of perception: of oneself as a minor demigod who has, at least in some local sphere, burst the bonds of normal agency in constructing the environment. Shaping the world is always in reference to how it shapes or expresses one's self. As Benjamin Ellman, the owner of a hotel supply company in Chicago, says, "I've never thought of doing things because it's the particularly right thing to do—except if it was the right thing for me to do. I've always been a doer. I've always been a leader."

In a world where most individuals are limited to carving out the best possible niche in an organizational scheme designed by others, the wealthy are able to conceive and create a world tailored to their specification. Detroit importer Rebecca Jacobs captures this close affiliation between uninhibited imagination and determined purpose: "I'm a winner, and I believe in winning in life. And I set my own goals. And I'm a dreamer—I think that's one of the big assets that I have, my imagination. It's the most wonderful thing in the world that I have—and I just try to make those dreams come true. I just know I'm going to win. I've been a winner and a dreamer since I was a little girl, and I knew that. You are what you think about. You are what you believe."

A key element of this individuality is a posture of emotional distance from the trials and tribulations of certain daily affairs. The distance from the mundane, explains Detroit heir Hillary Blake, may be so alluring as to be like "magic":

> I feel like a little girl and I feel like this is just pie in the sky. You know, this is like Fantasy Land or something like that. It's magic. And I think I should be responsible about it, but I don't want to be. You know what analogy comes to mind? This is going to sound crazy, but it's always fascinated me how radios work because if you're driving in your car and you just turn the knob, a different song comes from nowhere. I'm sure that somebody could explain to me how that happens. But I don't want them to because I like the image that it's—that it's just magic. And that's exactly how I feel when it comes to this part of the money: I know intellectually where all the dividends come from and approximately what they are. And I know what my annual income is, and I know what my expenses are, and I know how much money I give away, and I know how much I pay in taxes, and I know it all. And then all of this stuff gets split off and I live in this fantasy world. I had a girlfriend say to me one time, "You know, there's nothing that you'll be able to do in your life that will earn you more money than staying at home in bed and eating bon-bons." Now I thought, "Well, you know, that's true."

But despite the magical lures of opulence, such emotional liberty seldom if ever leads to the confection-filled complacency she fantasizes. Far from sitting home eating bon-bons, Blake established and helps run the Forest Grove women's foundation in the Detroit area. Emotional liberty, it turns out, actually expedites involvement. For activist attorney Allison Randall, what is "wonderful" about freedom from "financial restrictions" is that it enables her to think expansively about her "next career": "My next career could be anything. I have that freedom and I'm not afraid to sort of think, well, maybe you could do *that*."

"That's the nature of privilege," notes Bradley Stark, thirty-two-year-old heir of a distinguished American family. As though he were answering Randall, Stark advocates a *responsibility* to do things that are as defining as having the potential to do them: "If it's privilege, it's not something [you can abandon]. I mean, obviously you can get rid of money. You can give all your money away and then you're not privileged anymore. But you were privileged to be in that position. So that your giving it away is in itself an exercise of that privilege. So there's really no way of getting around it."

As we have seen with Garrison's purchase of the Land Cruiser, cognitive empowerment provides the orientation that the world is subject to amendment. This is eloquently underscored by attorney Austin, who recognizes that not "dealing with day-to-day" life makes her "a different kind of person"—one more able to deal deliberately with "substantive issues":

> The difference for the wealthy is that they are so far removed from the [mundane kind of] struggle to do what they are doing that it becomes a qualitatively different way of life. And the reason that I know that is that I can see the changes even at my home. We have a housekeeper. One of the things that she does is clean. Every day. I used to clean myself, a lot of years ago. But now I am so used to having it done for me that I take it for granted. [I have reached] that level of beginning to have such a different lifestyle that you have no idea of what people are dealing with day to day. It sure makes a big difference when you get to the top. And when you have generation after generation that has no contact with those kinds of things, it has to make you a different kind of person. I don't know what all of that is like except by watching myself and the kind of freedom that I have to deal with substantive issues.

Dominion: The Principality of Temporal and Spatial Empowerment

The worldly domain in and through which the wealthy "deal with substantive issues" is their *principality*. If individuality revolves around psychological empowerment, principality revolves around temporal and spatial empowerment. If individuality is self-construction, principality is world building.

Temporal empowerment is the longitudinal dimension of principality. It is the ability to influence significant stretches of the past and future, and to make concrete arrangements to extend one's control over the present. This is clear to Detroit wholesaler Brendan Dwyer, who explains that one key to his success is that "I allocate my time. I allocate my time," he repeats, "where I think it will make a difference." Following the adage that "20 percent of the events account for 80 percent of the results," he purposefully tries to "shy away from allocating time to the 80 percent that are only going to account for 20 percent of the results." In this way he can "influence results" *and* retain "a certain amount of time for leisure."

Another expression of temporal empowerment is the familiar penchant of the wealthy to perpetuate their family legacy by arranging for intergenerational transfer of wealth through trusts and other intrafamily mechanisms of inheritance. As Eileen Case Wilson notes, her family wealth, derived from the past, is legally arranged in the present to sustain her lineage into the future:

> No non-Case may own stock [in my grandfather's company]. So I cannot pass my stock to my husband, for instance; only to a blood Case, not to their spouses. My mother, for instance, has no stock. She's not a relative. That was grandfather's intent: to safeguard and preserve the family's corporation. He couldn't control their lives, but he could control who owns Case Chapter, so he only gave stock to his own issue. It still is a condition today. My grandparents left their shares of the business to the five grandchildren in trust, the income of which was to go to my father for the duration of his life. Upon my father's death, those trusts are dissolved and they will come directly to my sister and me— not including what will pass from my father to my children. That income will come to me for the duration of my life, even though the children will own his stock.

Austin and her husband introduce their son to the prospects of temporal empowerment as they counsel him about how his forthcoming inheritance will allow him to freely choose his career. They tell him about "the kind of money he can expect to have" so that he can begin "thinking about career choices and what he wants to do." Because her husband "has worked very hard," says Austin, he "likes the idea of my son being able to choose what he wants to do and not what he feels he has to do. So we have let him know that as he's making his decision, he should be thinking about what it is that he wants to do."

But in addition to extending family and opportunity over time, temporal empowerment provides the capacity to shape the future. According to New York interior decorator Carol Layton, this means perpetuating herself through her business. "I have a need for ongoing things," she explains. "I want the business to go on. I want to build something that doesn't die when I die. So we're building something that we hope will have continuity." Scanning the temporal horizon, the wealthy articulate a range of possible trajectories for practices in different spheres of activity. They project possible futures not only for themselves and their families, but for the businesses and organizations to which they are tied.

Spatial empowerment is the geographical counterpart of temporal empowerment. It marks the territorial boundaries of principality. Spatial empowerment refers to both the vertical power exercised within a sphere and horizontal power exercised across spheres of institutional life. In the exercise of spatial power, the wealthy direct and coordinate the monetary and human resources of organizations, strategically mobilizing the use of these resources as material extensions of their will and physical incarnations of their presence. "The [hotel supply] company was built around me," reports Chicagoan Benjamin Ellman. "Everybody in the United States thinks about this company as me personally. I once felt that was wrong, and that there's no way you can be successful in business if things revolve around one individual and you want to grow larger. That's not necessarily true. Look what's happening today. What's happening today with Lee Iacocca and other people. Individuals who are heading up businesses are becoming more connected with their businesses."

"The most important thing money gives me is power to get through time and red-tape barriers," explains real estate magnate Graham Reynolds. Connecting spatial to temporal empowerment, he explains how his wealth reduces the time and distance for getting things done: "I can pick up the phone and call a congressman who's heard my name, and I can have the impact of one million votes on the issue with a phone call. You always have the upper hand in negotiating, and it allows you to do in one-tenth the time what it would take somebody else ten times the time because of the credibility he'd have to develop."

The same is true for another real estate developer, David Stephanov, who also "picks up the phone" to set his will in motion. Exemplifying his Golden Rule—"them with the gold makes the rules"—Stephanov describes how, in addition to injecting himself into the world, spatial empowerment enables him to bring the world to himself. "When I want something, [politicians] come here and meet me for breakfast, and I tell them what I want. When I have to convey a message to the governor, he comes here, or he'll have one of his top two or three aides come down, and I'll tell them what I think should be done. And then we go from there." Whether running a business, exercising executive power in a corporation, or disbursing the funds through a family foundation, the wealthy command actors and resources as they carve out a custom-made dominion.

Major Motives: Identification and Association

I have summarized in several publications what my colleagues and I have found to be the major mobilizing factors that generate charitable giving (Schervish 1995, 1997). Taken together, these mobilizing factors compose what I call the identification model of charitable giving. We have published our first empirical test of the theory (Schervish and Havens, 1997) based on an analysis of the 1991 Survey of Giving and Volunteering (Hodgkinson and Weitzman, 1992). Our findings are that the level of contributions depends on the frequency and intensity of participation, volunteering, and being asked to contribute. Our findings also indicate that larger gifts are generated from those already making substantial gifts. Taken together, our general conclusion is that charitable giving derives from forging an associational and psychological connection between donors and recipients (Ostrander and Schervish, 1990).

I illustrate the identification theory by returning to the data from which I originally generated the theory. This first effort to ascertain the determinants of charitable giving that constitute the identification model was an analysis of intensive interviews with 130 millionaires in the Study on Wealth and Philanthropy. During the course of these interviews, we obtained information both about the modes of empowerment discussed in the previous section and about the factors that motivate giving among millionaires. What we learned provided the basis for inductively mapping a constellation of seven variable-sets that were positively related to charitable giving. These eight sets of variables are listed and briefly described in Exhibit 1. Here I illustrate in detail only four of these variable sets, and even then I tend to concentrate on one specific aspect of each set. In this section, I discuss frameworks of consciousness, especially under the cardinal rubric *identification*, and

EXHIBIT 1

Determinants of Charitable Giving

1. *Communities of participation*: groups and organizations in which one participates
2. *Frameworks of consciousness*: beliefs, goals, and orientations that shape the values and priorities that determine people's activities
3. *Invitations to participate*: requests by persons or organizations to directly participate in philanthropy
4. *Discretionary resources*: the quantitative and psychological wherewithal of time and money that can be mobilized for philanthropic purposes
5. *Models and experiences from one's youth*: the people or experiences from one's youth that serve as positive exemplars for one's adult engagements
6. *Urgency and effectiveness*: a desire to make a difference; a sense of how necessary or useful charitable assistance will be in the face of people's needs
7. *Demographic characteristics*: the geographic, organizational, and individual circumstances of one's self, family, and community that affect one's philanthropic commitment
8. *Intrinsic and extrinsic rewards*: the array of positive experiences and outcomes (including taxation) of one's current engagement that draws one deeper into a philanthropic identity

Note: See Schervish and Havens (1998) for a fuller description of these sets of variables.

communities of participation, especially under the principal rubric *association*. In the next section, I examine the factors of wanting to make a difference as well as tax incentives.

Identification: Love of Neighbor and Love of Self

The social-psychological dispositions referred to in Exhibit 1 as "frameworks of consciousness" range from religious and political aspirations on the one hand to guilt and desire for control on the other. But the most formative, durable, and effective framework of consciousness—and the eventual outcome of guilt, duty, and other motives—is captured by the notion of identification. For wholesaler Dwyer, identifying with a cause is the criterion he uses to determine the causes to which his major contributions go. For instance, the fact that he "can fully identify" with the one-on-one drug rehabilitation program started by a local judge leads him to support the program with a series of major gifts. "I feel like I'm involved and a participant and I feel I can identify with the project, and I've learned enough about it to have some feeling that it's worth doing."

The key to care and philanthropy, as I have written elsewhere (for example, Schervish, 1993), is not the absence of self that motivates charitable giving but the presence of self-identification with others. This is what Thomas Aquinas teaches as the convergence of love of neighbor, love of self, and love of God. In its civic expression, it is what Tocqueville meant by "self-interest properly understood," and what Washington, D.C., respondent Dean Ehrlich expresses in personalistic terms as his and his wife's attraction to those causes "we can be identified with in order to give part of ourselves to." Recognizing the unity of self-development and community development has become the touchstone for Malcolm Hirsch's modest assessment of his giving, which he characterizes as "no big deal" and "not particularly generous." Rather, says the Tacoma environmental activist, "giving was just a front for figuring out who I was."

In this way, the inspiration for charitable giving and care in general is a function of the social-psychological processes of personal identification. It is for this reason that I have found that donors contribute the bulk of their charitable dollars to causes from whose services the donors directly benefit. It is not by coincidence that schools, health and arts organizations, and (especially) churches attract so much giving. For it is here that donors, because they are also recipients, most identify with the individuals—namely themselves, their families, and people much like them—whose needs are being met by the contributions. Although describing this form of giving as *consumption philanthropy* (Schervish, in press) may seem to discount its value, my intention is just the opposite. Within the identification model, consumption philanthropy is an honorable prototype of motivation to be emulated rather than a regrettable stereotype to be eschewed. Consumption philanthropy mobilizes charitable giving so formidably because it is here that identification between donor and recipient is strongest.

For generating generosity, the question is how to expand those same sentiments of identification to human beings in wider fields of space and time, that is, to extend the sentiments of family-feeling to the realms of fellow-feeling. This is the key to *adoption philanthropy* (see Schervish, 1992), where donors support individuals on the basis of a feeling of surrogate kinship. Again, it is not by coincidence that the golden rule entreats us to love our neighbor as ourselves.

"I listen and I go where I'm needed," says New York philanthropist Laura Madison. "The only thing I'm interested in in the world is the health of humanity. To be human is to be a spiritual person as well as a physical, mental, emotional person. This means to really relate to other human beings all over the world—whoever they are, wherever they are," she explains, highlighting how she extends her identification beyond her immediate sphere. Her goal is "making a oneness in every way that's there but isn't seen by most people—healing the earth, healing the rifts between people, all that sort of thing: that's what I'm really interested in. And wherever I see any chance or see that I'm supposed to be doing something about it, that's what I'm interested in." For Madison, the sentiments of identification derive from her perception of being needed; for Chicagoan Nancy Shaw they derive from her humanistic rendition of the golden rule, which she "professes" as her only religion. "I feel that you have a certain debt to society, and if you are comfortable, you pay it. And this is my way of doing it. I treat people as I would like to be treated. And that's as close to a religion as I can get." The religious undertones and concrete expressions of identification are what New York industrialist Stryker recalls his father teaching him as the way human beings live on after their deaths. "My father used to say—and this is not original with him—that he believed that each human being has a hereafter, and that it is not amorphous, not in heaven. It is tangible, palpable, measurable. And it consists of all the people who you've touched in your life for better or worse and who live on after."

Association: The School of Identification

The disposition of identification does not grow in isolation. The school of identification is the constellation of communities and organizations in which donors learn about the needs of the people with whom they (the donors) come to identify. Among our most consistent findings from over a decade of research is that the greatest portion of giving and volunteering takes place in one's own community and church and helps support activities from which the donor is directly associated. This means that the basis for higher giving and volunteering is in large part a function of the mix and intensity of the network of formal and informal associations both within and beyond one's local community. Over the course of our research, it has become increasingly clear that differences in levels of giving of time and money are due to more than differences in income, wealth, religion, gender, and race. When it comes to philanthropy, it is less a matter of financial capital, or even moral capital in the form of some kind of intrinsic faculty of generosity. What matters more is one's abundance of *associational capital* in the form of social networks, invitation, and identification.

For instance, 53-year-old hotel supplier Benjamin Ellman became ever more serious about volunteering his time and money to the Association of Jewish Community Centers as he came to associate with the clients of the centers. "It was unbelievable what I learned about the numbers of people in this community literally whose life depended on that agency," says Ellman. "I mean [they would have suffered gravely] if they didn't get the subvention so their kids could go to camps, or their kids could be in day care centers, or some of their older people could be taken care of in the elderly homes and got meals. I mean, their whole life depended on this institution." Indeed, it meant so much to him that he was able to see "where children have gone on from very humble beginnings to becoming major contributors not only to themselves but back to the community," that he eventually served two terms as president of the association.

New York philanthropist Janet Arnold traces her empathy for the least advantaged to her childhood when she and her siblings "were exposed to a wide variety of people and taught by both our parents the dignity of the human being. I think that was the foundation of my attitudes," she explains. The people who worked for her parents were always treated well. When she was young, her father took her along on his Latin American travels, where he would "go into the villages and talk to the people": "He loved going into the villages. He was wonderful with these people. He used to take us on trips, he worked in Latin America, and because of that, we were exposed to people who were not wealthy. We didn't move in a very narrow circle the way most people of wealth do, but a much wider circle through travel and because of my father's constantly reaching out to the people. And all of us, my brothers and sisters and I, worked in Latin America in summer jobs."

Arnold also spent years living among the poor and disguising her wealth on the east side of Detroit: "I loved being there and I loved working with those people. I guess I discovered that I had a very abiding belief in the potential of human beings, and that was something I wanted to affirm in my philanthropic work," she recalls. To this day, Arnold grounds her substantial philanthropic efforts on these formative experiences and has come to direct all her endeavors to "enabling people to grow and to achieve their potential." Again, it is her associational relations that put her face-to-face with those in need and that are the occasion for developing the necessary knowledge and desire for her major efforts to initiate small beginnings. "There are people who do small entrepreneurial things in their neighborhoods and they could use help," she explains. "To make their lives somehow successful [on their] own terms seems to me to be very important. You know, having better schools for children so that the children who grow up in Detroit or in Harlem, so their lives won't be circumscribed because they can't read."

Association also turns out to be the training ground of identification for Boston condominium builder Walter Adams, who purposefully guides his charitable giving by the maxim that "charity begins at home." He is grateful to his alma mater for making him conscientious, and to his employees for making him prosperous. So he directs his wealth to improving their fortunes. His major conventional charity is Boston College. But even closer to home and more worthy of Adams's attention are his workers, especially those at the lower end of the pay scale. He tells how instead of giving $100,000 to the United Way, he prefers to allocate that sum in order "to help some of [my] people who are in the lower end. Give them a bonus, I mean, or take $100,000 and hire a couple of truly nonemployables."

Ultimately there is nothing mysterious or extraordinary about the centrality of association in determining the amount and kinds of charitable engagements. "All giving is local" is an accurate portrayal of how charitable activity gets mobilized in and around the formal and informal social relations with which one is incorporated. Such incorporation may be direct, as occurs in and around one's church and university, or one's children's school or sports team. Incorporation may also be more indirect, for instance when the medical or mental illness suffered by a family member induces support for medical research to cure that illness. Association is even more indirect, but equally powerful, when the inspiration for contributions of time and money arrives through the media, as often occurs when news of famines and natural disasters attracts our care. Indeed, our own research (Schervish and Havens, 1997) and that of others (for example, Jackson, Bachmeier, Wood, and Craft, 1995) indicate that among all the variables listed in Exhibit 7.1, the strongest immediate determinant of charitable giving is the level of formal and informal engagement.

Major Purposes, Major Wealth, Major Taxes

I have described the individuality and principality that constitute the hyperagency of determination and dominion by which wealth holders shape the world. I have also explored the forces of identification and association that motivate their philanthropic engagement. In this section, I spell out how hyperagency and philanthropic motivation interact as wealth holders become major donors. First, I address the great expectations by which major donors seek to make a major difference. Second, I look at how growth in wealth and the estate tax code unite to mold a relatively powerful incentive for wealth holders to allocate large sums to philanthropy.

Major purposes: Great expectations to make a major difference

The definition of wealth holders as hyperagents with personal determination and institutional dominion directly applies to their activity in the realm of philanthropy. Self-construction and world building do not stop at the doors to their homes or their businesses. It extends to all their involvements, including (for those who so choose) politics, community, religion, and philanthropy. By dint of personality, the wealthy are no more egoistically myopic or socially responsible than anyone else. Great expectations and grand aspirations occupy people across the financial spectrum. What is different for wealth holders is that they can legitimately be more confident about actualizing their expectations and aspirations because they are able to directly effect the fulfillment of their desires. It's a matter of realizing "how much a little money can make a difference," as Californian Francis Toppler puts it.

Hyperagency in philanthropy does not mean that the wealthy always and everywhere conceive or achieve major innovative interventions. It means they tend to think more about doing so, and to partake more in bringing them about. Entrepreneurs, said Brendan Dwyer, are investors who have two characteristics. First, they have a creative idea. They discern an area of output for which demand outstrips supply. Second, entrepreneurs are investors who actively affect the rate of return on their investment by directly commanding production. Correspondingly, venture capitalists are investors who bolster the capacity for others to be entrepreneurs. In business, wealth is an output. In philanthropy, wealth is an input. As such, wealth holders are the entrepreneurs and venture capitalists of philanthropic endeavors.

The distinctive class trait of the wealthy in philanthropy is the ability to bring into being, and not just support, particular charitable projects. Hyperagency in the field of philanthropy assigns financial resources to fabricating major outcomes. When exercising this capacity, wealth holders are *producers* rather than supporters of philanthropy, underwriters rather than just contributors. Finding neglected social niches where needs are great and resources are scarce is precisely Janet Arnold's craft: "I am involved in human rights and I tend to be more involved with the American Indian, at this particular time, than I am with other minorities," says the third-generation guardian of a Detroit fortune. She contributes to many other causes, but her "main focus is on the American Indian" and other "unpopular" issues. "I gravitate to areas that have need and have no access to support," she says, because it is especially there "I feel like I can make a difference."

In common parlance, we regularly speak of large and small contributors. Distinguishing between producers and supporters of philanthropy is a more functional distinction. Each philanthropic enterprise pursues resources in order to produce outcomes in response to social needs and interests. Most individuals respond to appeals for contributions in a manner parallel to how a consumer responds to the products or services of a business. That is, they are consumers or supporters rather than creators or architects of the enterprise whose goods and services they wish to receive. Only as a group acting formally or informally in concert can consumers and contributors determine the fate of a charitable endeavor. Because it is the accumulated support of many individuals, rather than of any particular single individual, that determines the existence and direction of a venture, each separate individual is at most a joint or collateral producer.

It is a different story altogether, however, when a wealthy contributor provides a sizable enough gift to actually shape the agenda of a charity or nonprofit institution. In this instance, the contributor may be termed a direct producer or architect. Such direct production, of course, cuts two ways, and so it is always important to discern the conditions under which philanthropic hyperagency produces care rather than control (see Schervish, in press).

Laura Madison clearly appreciates the productive potential of her charitable giving. "Because I have a large amount of money to put in," she explains, "I have an opportunity to really make a difference if I see something that a large amount of money could do more for than a small amount of money could." The extreme case of direct production is the personal founding of an original philanthropic organization or project. Such hyperagency gets exercised formally through creation of a private or working foundation, or through contribution of enough resources to establish within an existing organization a novel direction, such as a clinic, endowed chair, or hospital wing. Less formally, individuals of means can directly produce philanthropic outcomes by "adopting" specific individuals (including family members), organizations, or causes that they assist in a sufficiently large manner so as to "make a difference."

It is precisely the possibility and practice of "making a difference" that undergirds the determination and dominion of hyperagency that marks Brendan Dwyer's charitable giving. "Whatever success I've got, and whatever I've learned, and whatever I get my satisfaction from come from being able to make a difference," says Dwyer. "That's what makes me happy: when I've felt I've made a difference in a beneficial way." Establishing a personal foundation as one vehicle for his charitable giving is only a small part of his institution-shaping philanthropy. He also contributes substantially enough to be considered a producer of the work of two university-based research institutes, a metro Detroit prison rehabilitation program, an inner-city charter school, and an inner-city church-based community organization. In the end, Dwyer counsels, there are two fairly straightforward questions that, if answered in the affirmative, mark the path of inclination that leads to philanthropy: "Is there something valuable you want to do that needs to be done in society? And can you do it better than Uncle Sam?"

Major Wealth: The Expanding Horizon of Riches

Coupled to this inclination to make a difference in a major way is the opportunity to do so. Major donors have the inclination to fashion society; they also have the material wherewithal and tax incentive to do so.

The notion that philanthropy is indispensable for innovation in providing material goods and services for people in need, and for promoting cultural, social, and human capital for all members of society, is neither new nor controversial. What is new is the remarkable burgeoning in the material and (as I discuss in the conclusion) spiritual resources that may be devoted to philanthropy.

At the material level, there is clear evidence of growth in wealth. Despite a bifurcation between the lower and upper ends of the income and wealth distributions, growth in national wealth is outpacing growth in population by a factor of two, with per capita wealth growing around 5 percent per year. There are now close to four million millionaires and dramatically new conditions of affluence among the top 30 percent of the income and wealth distributions. There is much important rethinking and policy work to be done regarding issues of equity. For instance, contrary to conventional opinion, there is some indication that, when social security and private pensions are included, wealth has not become dramatically more concentrated in the seven decades since the depression (Wolff, 1996). But even among those who remain concerned about the level of concentration of wealth, no one seriously expects that major changes in the distribution of wealth are in the offing, even if we were to institute the most progressive *realistic* tax and transfer reforms.

On the contrary, there is every indication that the percentage of affluent and wealthy households will continue to grow, as every 1,000-point jump in the Dow Jones Industrial Average represents an increment of $1 trillion of wealth. The upshot is that there are larger and larger numbers of American households with the resources for modest-to-substantial philanthropic giving. It is the first time in history that large proportions of a population can materially afford to consider charitable giving as a principal component of their financial strategy and moral agency. A parallel trend is revealed in the 1993 study of Federal Reserve wealth data by researchers at Cornell University (Avery and Rendall, 1993). Avery and Rendall estimate that baby boomers ranging in age from thirty to forty-nine will share a $10 trillion transfer from their aging parents. Not surprisingly, much attention in philanthropic circles has been devoted to this transfer, which is projected to occur over the next three decades. (The dollar figure for this intergenerational transfer varies depending in part on how far into the future one is forecasting and on the rate of growth in wealth one assumes.)

Hoping to secure their share of this windfall, fundraisers and nonprofit professionals understandably have riveted their attention on three ideas. First, a disproportionate share (25–35 percent) of the intergenerational transfer will occur among the wealthiest 1.5–2 percent of the population (those with assets over $600,000). Second, this intergenerational transfer has the potential to unleash vast sums of money for philanthropic purposes. Third, because those who possess an inordinately high percentage of wealth have a considerably broader range of choices, it is therefore imperative to remind the patrons of this windfall about their choices and acquaint them with their charitable responsibilities. A fourth point, one made by financial planner Stephen Nill, is that "the bell curve of wealth release is already rapidly expanding, climbing from $39.4 billion in 1990 to $84.3 billion in 1995. The release will peak in 2015" (personal communication with author). Finally, a significant finding from our most recent research is that between 32 and 42 percent (depending upon the method of calculation) of all charitable contributions are currently given by the wealthiest 3.5 percent of the population (Schervish and Havens,

1998). But even among the super-wealthy and upper affluent who make up this 3.5 percent of the population, there is surprising variation in the amounts given—suggesting a potential for increased giving among many at the upper reaches of income and wealth (see also Auten and Rudney, 1990).

Major Taxes: Incentives for Major Gifts

Perhaps the strongest material incentive for channeling this burgeoning major wealth to major gifts revolves around making positive use of the current estate tax laws. Much research has explored the effect of marginal income tax rates and other factors on the level of charitable giving from *income*, most recently a report prepared by Price Waterhouse for the Council on Foundations and INDEPENDENT SECTOR (1997) that confirms the positive effect of the charitable deduction on the amount of income given by individuals. However, we are only now beginning to recognize the implications of the growth in wealth for charitable giving from *wealth*. As I said, one of the emerging determinants of substantial giving from *wealth* among upper-income earners and wealth holders is the estate tax environment instituted by the 1986 changes in the federal tax code. Something that is now patently obvious to financial planners, tax accountants, and increasing numbers of wealthy individuals (especially small-business holders) is that the 1986 tax code dramatically increased the incentives of wealthy individuals to make substantial contributions to charity in lieu of paying an effective minimum wealth tax of at least 60 percent (see Murphy and Schervish, 1995). It is crucial to learn how current estate tax laws influence wealth holders to choose to dedicate their wealth (both while alive and at their death) to charity rather than government. As experienced financial planners such as Richard Haas, Scott Fithian, and Stuart Miller all insist, the only significant tax shelter for the very wealthy is philanthropy. Therefore, informing the affluent and wealthy about the practical tax advantages of the estate tax codes and about corresponding financial planning strategies that highlight charitable giving is one increasingly crucial and productive task.

Conclusion: Spirituality in the Age of Affluence

Many wealthy and affluent individuals (especially among professionals and first-generation entrepreneurs) have not been adequately called upon to chart their resources for philanthropy. For the most part, the philanthropic community has not initiated effective strategies to persuade the financially well-off to make philanthropy the positive cornerstone for innovative and efficient production of valuable social outcomes. There are many reasons for this. In addition to not realizing their level of discretionary wealth (see for example Rosenberg, 1994, and Havens, 1996a, 1996b) and the positive implications of the current estate tax code, another serious obstacle is that potential major donors simply do not appreciate fully enough how effective charitable organizations are in generating valuable outcomes. As I said, one direction is to encourage fundraisers to become educated and then to educate their donors about the new social conditions of wealth and estate planning. But equally important is making donors cognizant of the effectiveness of their contributions. We believe this can best be achieved by incorporating donors into the associational relations that occur in and around charitable organizations. This is clearly congruent with our findings on participation and identification, which show the strategic importance of (1) involving donors in increasingly more engaging and rewarding participatory activities, (2) closely listening to what donors say about their areas of interest and welcoming them to contribute to such areas, and (3) bringing donors into relations of identification with the ultimate beneficiaries of their gifts.

This chapter has reviewed the material dominion and psychological determination of wealth holders. It has also discussed how growth in wealth in conjunction with the estate tax codes and the inclination of the wealthy to make a difference are positive vectors in the "physics of philanthropy." But as powerful as the forces are, it is the expansion of the spiritual potential for philanthropy that may prove to be the most significant factor. In a provocative 1930 essay entitled "Economic Possibilities for Our Grandchildren," John Maynard Keynes predicted that material wealth has the potential for releasing spiritual wealth. "The *economic problem* [of scarcity] may be solved, or at least within sight of solution, within a hundred years," Keynes wrote. "When the accumulation of wealth is no longer of high social importance, there will be great changes in the code of morals . . . such that the love of money as a possession—as distinguished from the love of money as a means to the enjoyments and realities of life—will be recognized for what it is, a somewhat disgusting morbidity, one of those semi-criminal, semi-pathological propensities which one hands over with a shudder to the specialists in mental disease" (1933, pp. 369–370).

For those concerned with understanding the spiritual potential in the new "code of morals" and mobilizing it in the service of philanthropy, much needs to be learned about harnessing what I call *spirituality in the age of affluence*. One strategy is to help fashion a philanthropic vocation for Keynes's grandchildren, who are now coming of financial age. To the extent that the affluent and wealth holders desire to search out their philanthropic vocation, there is a verdant opportunity to assist them in determining the socially beneficial charitable projects through which they may forge their moral identity. Given the tax environment, it is not unreasonable to expect that when they stop to reflect, the affluent and wealth holders will increasingly entertain the two questions formulated by Brendan Dwyer: Do you have something you want to accomplish for society? And do you think that philanthropic institutions can do a better job than government in accomplishing it?

The practical matter before us, then, is how to increase the probability that the answers to these questions are in the affirmative and in the service of society. This means working to produce and distribute a denser *social* capital of associational ties and a deeper *spiritual* capital of care. It also means doing so not just in the conventionally designated realms of giving and volunteering but in all the nooks—great and small—of our homes, communities, and world.

Note

I am grateful to the T. B. Murphy Foundation Charitable Trust and the Lilly Endowment for supporting the research reported here, and to Platon E. Coutsoukis, John J. Havens, and Andrew Herman, who graciously worked with me on various aspects of the research reported here. All the names and identifying information about the persons interviewed in this chapter have been changed. Where real institutions are mentioned, they represent the type of rather than the particular institution.

References

Auten, G., and Rudney, G. "The Variability of Individual Charitable Giving in the U.S." *Voluntas: International Journal of Voluntary and Nonprofit Organizations*, 1990, 1(2), 80–97.

Avery, R. B., and Rendall, M. S. "Estimating the Size and Distribution of Baby Boomers' Prospective Inheritances." Ithaca, N.Y.: Department of Economics, Cornell University, 1993.

Council on Foundations and INDEPENDENT SECTOR. *Impact of Tax Restructuring on Tax-Exempt Organizations.* Report prepared by the Washington National Tax Service of Price Waterhouse and by Caplin and Drysdale Chartered. Washington, D.C.: INDEPENDENT SECTOR, 1997.

Havens, J. J. "The Composition of Wealth and Charitable Giving." Working chapter. Boston College Social Welfare Research Institute, 1996a.

Havens, J. J. "Consumer Finances as Basis for Estimating Discretionary Income." Report submitted for the Indiana University Center on Philanthropy Discretionary Income Study, 1996b.

Hodgkinson, V. A., and Weitzman, M. A. Giving and Volunteering in the United States: Findings from a National Survey. Washington, D.C.: INDEPENDENT SECTOR, 1992.

Jackson, E. F., Bachmeier, M. D., Wood, J. R., and Craft, E. A. "Volunteering and Charitable Giving: Do Religious and Associational Ties Promote Helping Behavior?" *Nonprofit and Voluntary Sector Quarterly*, 1995, 24 (1), 59–78.

Keynes, J. M. "Economic Possibilities for our Grandchildren." *Essays in Persuasion*. London: Macmillan, 1933.

Murphy, T. B., and Schervish, P. G. "The Dynamics of Wealth Transfer: Behavioral Implications of Tax Policy for the $10 Trillion Transfer." Presented at the INDEPENDENT SECTOR 1995 Spring Research Forum, "Nonprofit Organizations as Public Actors: Rising to New Public Policy Challenges," Alexandria, Va., Mar. 23–24, 1995.

Ostrander, S. A., and Schervish, P. G. "Giving and Getting: Philanthropy as a Social Relation." In J. Van Til (ed.), *Critical Issues in American Philanthropy: Strengthening Theory and Practice*. San Francisco: Jossey-Bass, 1990.

Rosenberg, C., Jr. *Wealthy and Wise: How You and America Can Get the Most out of Your Giving.* New York: Little, Brown, 1994.

Schama, S. *The Embarrassment of Riches: An Interpretation of Dutch Culture in the Golden Age.* Berkeley: University of California Press, 1988.

Schervish, P. G. "Adoption and Altruism: Those with Whom I Want to Share a Dream." *Nonprofit and Voluntary Sector Quarterly,* 1992, *21* (4), 327–350.

Schervish, P. G. "Philanthropy as a Moral Identity of *Caritas.*" In P. G. Schervish with O. Benz, P. Dulany, T. B. Murphy, and S. Salett, *Taking Giving Seriously.* Indianapolis: Indiana University, Center on Philanthropy, 1993.

Schervish, P. G. "The Moral Biographies of the Wealthy and the Cultural Scripture of Wealth." In P. G. Schervish (ed.), *Wealth in Western Thought: The Case for and Against Riches.* New York: Praeger, 1994.

Schervish, P. G. "Gentle as Doves and Wise as Serpents: The Philosophy of Care and the Sociology of Transmission." In P. G. Schervish, V. A. Hodgkinson, and M. Gates (eds.), *Care and Community in Modern Society: Passing on the Tradition of Care to the Next Generation.* San Francisco: Jossey-Bass, 1995.

Schervish, P. G. "Inclination, Obligation, and Association: What We Know and What We Need to Learn about Donor Motivation." In D. F. Burlingame (ed.), *Critical Issues in Fund Raising.* New York: Wiley, 1997.

Schervish, P. G. *The Modern Medicis: Strategies of Philanthropy Among the Wealthy.* San Francisco: Jossey-Bass, in press.

Schervish, P. G., and Havens, J. J. "Social Participation and Charitable Giving: A Multivariate Analysis." *Voluntas: International Journal of Voluntary and Nonprofit Organizations,* 1997, *8* (3).

Schervish, P. G., and Havens, J. J. "Money and Magnanimity: New Findings on the Distribution of Income, Wealth, and Philanthropy." *Nonprofit Management & Leadership,* 1998, *8* (4), 421–434.

Schervish, P. G., and Herman, A. *Empowerment and Beneficence: Strategies of Living and Giving Among the Wealthy.* Final report, the Study on Wealth and Philanthropy. Presentation of findings from the Study on Wealth and Philanthropy, submitted to the T. B. Murphy Foundation Charitable Trust, 1988.

Wolff, E. N. "International Comparisons of Wealth Inequality." *Review of Income and Wealth,* 1996, *42* (4), 433–451.

Paul G. Schervish *is Professor of Sociology and Director of the Center on Wealth and Philanthropy at Boston College, and National Research Fellow at the Indiana University Center on Philanthropy. He is also Senior Advisor to the Wealth & Giving Forum, a peer-directed endeavor to deepen the philanthropic engagement of the nation's 7000 wealthiest families.*

Originally published in *New Directions for Philanthropic Fundraising,* No. 16, Summer 1997.

Charles S. Johnson and Johnnetta Cole: Successful Role Models for Fund-raising at Historically Black Colleges and Universities

Marybeth Gasman

Abstract

Johnnetta Cole at Spelman College and Charles S. Johnson at Fisk University offer two powerful examples of the leadership that is needed in fund-raising at HBCUs. This paper will examine their innovative strategies and program ideas. It will suggest ways in which current presidents can emulate their practices. Most importantly, it will approach this task from the perspective of black leaders by highlighting their ability to generate innovative ideas and solicit funding to support them.

Introduction

In the past few years, several historically black colleges and universities (HBCUs) have staged successful multimillion-dollar fund-raising campaigns. In their wake, others have announced similar efforts. HBCUs are making attempts to capitalize on the USA's strong economy and the growing number of generous donors. Because even the wealthiest of black colleges do not have the large endowments or access to wealthy benefactors that predominantly white institutions do, they must find innovative approaches to the task of fund-raising. Perhaps the best publicized of these fund-raising efforts has been that of Johnnetta Cole at Spelman College in Atlanta. Her efforts received widespread attention in the mainstream media including The *New York Times*. Cole, who until recently was president of Spelman, led a campaign which raised $114 million toward the endowment of the college from 1993–96.[1] Although this amount would not be unusual at many predominantly white institutions, it was a first for a historically black college. What makes President Cole's feat particularly interesting is the way in which she went about raising the money. Whereas predominantly white colleges in the same category as Spelman (Wellesley or Bryn Mawr are two similarly sized women's colleges) receive 80 percent of their endowment monies from alumnae, Spelman acquired only $3.2 million of its total endowment money from this source.[2] Because of the current economic barriers to the earning potential of black women, Johnnetta Cole was forced to look in many directions for funds.[3]

Cole was not the first HBCU president to meet such a challenge successfully. During his tenure as president of Fisk University in the 1950s, Charles S. Johnson, who was president of the university from 1946–56, was considered the leader to emulate in the area of fund-raising for HBCUs. Johnson raised Fisk University to a level unsurpassed by any private HBCU at the time, when measured by prestige and endowment.[4] Under Johnson's leadership, Fisk became an incubator for African-American intellectuals and leaders; its graduates include historian David Levering Lewis and former Secretary of Energy, Hazel O' Leary. Johnnetta Cole herself was a student during Johnson's tenure at Fisk. Johnson's unique approach to fund-raising, which included carrying program proposals to nearly every meeting he attended, was a key element in his success. He was well connected and, like Johnnetta Cole, tenacious. Cole's and Johnson's accomplishments are particularly important given the troubled financial history of HBCUs.

Historically black colleges and universities are uniquely rooted in American history. Prior to the Civil War and because of the oppression of slavery, very few blacks were allowed to be educated. (Exceptions are those black colleges established in the North prior to the Civil War such as Wilberforce College in Ohio and Lincoln University in Pennsylvania.) However, at the close of the war, through the assistance of the Freedmen's Bureau and missionary organizations (both white and black), small private black colleges appeared rapidly. The white missionaries feared that blacks would become a menace to society unless they were freed from the ignorance which slavery had imposed on them.[5] As church funding dried up, white northern industrialists took control of the funding and curriculum at most black colleges. With the enormous power they held, they imposed a program of industrial education on the institutions. This included classes in cooking, cleaning, horseshoeing, and so forth. Booker T. Washington, the chief African-American supporter of industrial education, urged blacks to "cast down your bucket where you are" and accept the current situation of discrimination. He believed that if blacks committed themselves to economic improvement, eventually civil rights would follow. Economic improvement would come through a steadfast commitment to manual labor and the dignity of hard work. Washington received unprecedented support from white philanthropists. Although not opposed to Washington's "industrial education," sociologist W.E.B. Du Bois wanted more for at least a "talented tenth" of the black population. Du Bois spoke out vehemently against the white philanthropists and their "pawn" Booker T. Washington.[6] Eventually, the industrial philanthropists began to support a liberal arts curriculum for black colleges. However, they maintained a close watch on the recipients of their money.[7]

The existence and monetary support of HBCUs has been a subject of debate since their inception. From the start, these institutions have been providing educational opportunities to African-Americans who, for most of their history, have been denied access to historically white institutions (HWIs). Although the nation's HWIs are making strides toward diversification on their campuses, HBCUs still provide a valuable and much needed choice for African-American college students. Not only do HBCUs provide a nurturing, supportive environment for their students, but they are also dedicated to serving low-income families.[8] According to Kenneth Redd of the USAGroup Foundation:

> In 1995–96, about 40 percent of the African-American undergraduates at HBCUs were first-generation college students . . . 62 percent came from families with annual incomes of less than $30,000 . . . and 80 percent of the students received financial assistance to help pay their costs of attending college . . .[9]

Given the particular problems of funding at HBCUs, the task faced by Johnson and Cole was unique.[10] Not only did they have to raise money, but they had continually to deal with questions of the need and mission of their colleges. Knowing that much of their funding would come from white philanthropic foundations and corporations, they also had to contend with problems of outside control and racial hegemony—real or imagined.

Both Cole and Johnson created a niche, knew their institutions and alumni, and were influential contributors in both the black and white worlds. Neither, however, has been studied in depth as a fund-raiser. This exploration of Charles S. Johnson and Johnnetta Cole's approach to fund-raising will provide a better understanding of the ways in which philanthropies, corporations, and black education can work together. Further, it will suggest concrete solutions for those HBCUs that continue to struggle for financial security.

Theoretical Framework and Methodology

Because many black colleges were, in their early years, dependent on white philanthropy, scholars of higher education have looked at the actions and motives of the white philanthropists rather than exploring the agency of black college presidents.[11] This paper, however, approaches the study of black higher education from the perspective of black leaders, demonstrating their ability to generate original ideas and solicit the funding to support them. Much of the previous scholarship on the topic of black college presidents has tended to evaluate their success or failure based on the question of whether or not they were a pawn of white philanthropy. Black college presidents who garner funds from whites are often lumped together with Booker T. Washington—they are labeled as victims of white control. In taking this perspective, scholars lose sight of the specific accomplishments and innovations of these presidents.

This study uses a historical methodology, including but not limited to a review of personal and professional correspondence, official university reports, speeches, newspaper articles, and miscellaneous written materials found in the Fisk University archives in Nashville, Tennessee. Information pertaining to Johnnetta Cole was gleaned from newspaper articles, speeches, special reports, Spelman College fund-raising materials, and autobiographical pieces. Interviews were conducted with past colleagues and students of the two individuals discussed. Although there is merit in reviewing the strategies and experiences of Charles S. Johnson and Johnnetta Cole individually, this paper will look at their cases together in order to provide a better-rounded example for today's HBCU practitioner. Studying Johnson in conjunction with Cole points out the relevance of history to today's fund-raisers and demonstrates how contemporary fund-raising situations, tactics, and strategies are rooted in the past. Because fund-raising often requires long-term relationships between the donor and recipient, it is important to study the record of individual fund-raisers over time. For this reason, the paper will provide a biographical overview of both Cole and Johnson. This is essential to understanding their style and skills.

Preparing for the Role of Fund-raiser

According to historian and former Fisk board member John Hope Franklin (in an interview by the author, June 5, 1999), Charles Johnson came to the presidency of Fisk with well-developed relationships with most of the prominent philanthropists of his generation. Remembered primarily as a University of Chicago-trained sociologist and an "architect" of the Harlem Renaissance,[12] Charles S. Johnson made great contributions to black higher education. Adept at working with philanthropists, Johnson was not only able to collaborate with individual organizations but could also initiate cooperative efforts among various philanthropic institutions. Because the Laura Spelman Rockefeller Memorial had funded his position as chair of the social science department at Fisk and was instrumental in his selection for the post, Johnson had a strong relationship with the Rockefeller philanthropies. He knew Edwin Embree, president of the Julius Rosenwald Fund, from his days with the Chicago Race Relations Commission, and had nurtured the relationship over many years. Embree and the Rosenwald Fund were the chief supporters of Johnson's sociological research. Johnson's ability to work with white philanthropy was the main reason he was selected for the presidency. Fisk desperately needed to increase its endowment and although Johnson was not the first choice of many black leaders, they knew that he could bring in the much needed funding. Although Embree, too, would have preferred that Johnson remain in his role of researcher, he supported him in his presidency. Johnson was highly regarded for his sociological research and the white philanthropists with whom he associated wanted him to remain in this role.

Not only did Embree serve as a university trustee, but within one week after the inauguration, he made a $15,000 contribution to the Fisk president's office—to be used at the discretion of Johnson.[13] Despite Johnson's close ties to philanthropic organizations, he was able to maintain control of the Fisk campus and its curriculum. After many years of struggle, Fisk had established itself as a liberal arts institution and Johnson, as will be demonstrated, was able to maintain this focus and build upon it.[14]

While Johnnetta Cole received grants to support faculty research in anthropology, she did not have the long-standing personal relationships that Johnson had developed with individual philanthropists.[15] Unlike Johnson, Cole did not have the experience of building an entire academic department with the assistance of philanthropy. Her lack of expertise in this area made her doubt whether she would be selected for the Spelman presidency. According to Cole,

> . . . at one point I almost guaranteed that I would not become Spelman's seventh president. During the course of a meeting with the faculty, one professor asked, "Dr. Cole, what has been your experience as a fund-raiser? What can we expect from you?" Drawing on nothing but sheer honesty I replied, "Well, I have certainly raised funds as a faculty member, but I have to say that in the sense in which you mean fund-raising, I have never raised a dime. But," I added, "I think I am capable of raising millions."[16]

Despite her lack of philanthropic connections, Cole was persistent in her pursuit of funds and had the type of personality appropriate for educational fund-raising. Perhaps she gained these interpersonal skills in her past positions within academe. A graduate of Northwestern's doctoral program in anthropology, Cole began her academic career at Washington State University in 1964 as an assistant professor and director of black studies. From 1970 to 1983, she served as the associate provost for undergraduate education at the University of Massachusetts. In 1983, she moved on to Hunter College in New York City to serve as the director of Latin American and Caribbean Studies. In each of these positions, Cole was known as someone who was assertive in her desires to make change and able to build coalitions across gender and race.[17]

The Challenge of Alumni Giving

One of the greatest challenges for both Cole and Johnson in their quest for funds was the support of alumni. Johnson, for example, found that most foundations were unwilling to give money toward an endowment when alumni support was lacking. Similarly, while most foundations and corporations were impressed with Spelman's ability to secure a $20 million gift from Camille and Bill Cosby, they still asked, "How much are the alumni giving?" According to Charles Stephens, a staff member in external relations at Clark Atlanta University (an HBCU), "Alumni are the proof in the pudding. If we're going to get support from the larger community, we've got to demonstrate that the people who have benefited from us directly do care."[18] This is particularly important to HBCUs because of the continual questioning of their existence.[19] The support and accomplishments of alumni help to solidify the foundation of these institutions.

In their efforts to raise funds from alumni, both Johnson and Cole were helped by the fact that their presidencies broke new ground. Cole, for example, was the first black female president of the all-female college. Spelman College was founded in 1881 as the Atlanta Baptist Seminary. Its first classes took place in the basement of the Friendship Baptist Church. Spelman's mission for its first students, all freed slaves, was to "teach them to read the Bible and write well enough to send letters to their families in the North."[20] Today, however, Spelman is considered a highly selective college and is ranked by *U.S. News & World Report* as one of the best liberal arts colleges in the country—black or white.[21] Johnnetta Cole's selection as president pleased alumnae who were asking, "When will a black woman lead Spelman?" Upon her selection, 77 Spelman alumnae contributed a total of $1.7 million with gifts of over $10,000 each. This feat set a new standard in the world of African-American philanthropy.[22]

Cole's accomplishments are particularly impressive given that Spelman lagged behind most liberal arts institutions in the area of fund-raising staff and supportive technology.[23] They had "no consistent annual giving program, no ongoing stewardship program, no planned giving or major gifts program, and an out-of-date computer system."[24] Cole had to establish avenues for regular communication with alumnae. Instead of organizing their alumnae campaign in a traditional manner such as identifying donors based on past giving habits, categorizing them, and approaching them all using the same strategy, Spelman developed individual strategies for its various constituencies: "Each constituent group had a financial goal and a distinct strategy."[25] For example, in order to cultivate alumnae donors for the future, Cole encouraged students to become involved in the campaign. One student who led a campaign was 1996 graduate Johnita Mizelle, who noted, "It was the feeling of empowering other sisters to give of themselves for future Spelman sisters that was most important to me." Not only did the women at Spelman learn about fund-raising, they gave $78,000 to the institution.[26] A key to Cole's success with alumnae was her positive approach. While some fund-raising campaigns ask donors to give money to make up for the institution's deficiencies—decaying buildings, inadequate staffing, poor library facilities—Cole's approach was to focus on Spelman's strengths, particularly its science programs. For example, Cole was quick to point out that 40 percent of Spelman's students are science majors. Given the fact that African-Americans are poorly represented in the sciences, this was a very strong selling point.[27]

As with Johnnetta Cole, when Johnson was selected for the presidency, it was used as an occasion to renew a long-standing endowment campaign. Johnson was the first black president of Fisk.

Founded in 1866 under the auspices of the American Missionary Association, Fisk was originally located in an old Nashville army barracks. Its mission was to provide free education to the former slaves.[28] Fisk went from teaching basic reading and writing classes to being one of the premier black institutions in the country, producing graduates such as W.E.B. Du Bois and John Hope Franklin. At the time that Johnson became president, alumni had been calling for black leadership of their institution. To capitalize on the new energy at Fisk and to gain the support of blacks, Marts and Lundy, a prominent national fund-raising firm that had been hired to assist Johnson, encouraged several of the black Fisk trustees to match dollar for dollar each contribution made by alumni. According to Marts and Lundy,

> . . . this would put the negroes out in the front of the procession carrying the flag—instead of drag-ging along in the rear in a place of inferiority. It would put the flag in the hands of the new negro president and strengthen him in his leadership. And it would encourage the proper philosophy of cooperation between the whites and negroes, that of white encouragement to the negroes to work out their own destiny—in the best Fisk tradition.[30]

Ernest Alexander, one of the alumni trustees, used Johnson's prestige to aid in this effort. For example, in a letter to alumni, Alexander wrote:

> Those of us, and particularly you as parents, who know Fisk and its President-Elect, Dr. Charles S. Johnson (Fisk's first Negro president) have the promise that any such investment which may be made in the education of our boys and girls will bring rich returns to our American democracy and culture.[30]

Recruiting alumni support at HBCUs proves to be a very difficult task. The problem lies in the financial situation of blacks. According to the U.S. Census Bureau, even today the median black fam-ily income is 62 percent of the median white family income; and the median net worth of black families is one-tenth that of white families. Until these financial gaps are narrowed, HBCUs will have a difficult time soliciting funds from their alumni.[29]

Because the alumni did not have enough resources to give large amounts of money to Fisk, President Johnson looked to the faculty, staff, and students as well. Together, this group pledged to raise $15,000. The Nashville black community was also asked to support the campaign. Under the auspices of architect Calvin McKissack, the black community pledged to raise $25,000 as "evidence of its support of Dr. Johnson and Fisk University." Although many doubted its ability to raise this amount, the black community successfully fulfilled its pledge.[30]

Attracting White Donors

According to an article in the *Chronicle on Higher Education*, what matters most to trustees and com-mittees when searching for a new president is "the ability to think strategically about the entire col-lege, its financial needs and its future."[31] However, at HBCUs, presidents must also be able to bridge the cultural gap that exists between them and the majority culture—the majority culture that could potentially support the institution financially. Most college fund-raisers want the donor to feel like part of the "college family," but this becomes a difficult task when the traditions and culture of the family are unlike that of the potential donor. Charles S. Johnson and Johnnetta Cole were able to bridge this gap successfully.

Because of Johnson's national stature, it was hoped that his inauguration would bring support from the white community. White members of the board of trustees were asked to use their ties in their own community to raise support for the university—support that had not been seen since the mid-1920s. In this effort, the fund-raisers appealed to the white citizen's concerns regarding blacks—economics, loyalty to the South, and morality. Some of the reasons given to persuade whites to give to Fisk were progressive and pragmatic in their tone. For example, reason number one of Marts and Lundy's document, "Twelve Reasons Why Nashville Should Support Fisk," asks white citizens to consider the economic contributions of blacks to the local community:

  1. The University itself and the student body spend approximately $500,000 in Nashville each year. This means that amount is brought in from the outside every year . . .[32]

However, many of the other reasons fed into the attitudes of racist Southern whites. Reason six, for example, conveys the idea that blacks should be indoctrinated in the segregated way of life by educating them in the South:

6. The Negro people must have ministers, doctors, teachers, and social workers. These professional leaders must be trained either in the South in a place like Fisk, or they must go to a northern University. Would we not prefer to train our own, here in our midst, where they can continue sympathetic to southern life?[32]

And reason twelve taps into the racial stereotype that blacks that are uneducated or educated in the North are immoral, lawless, and rebellious:

12. The sound religious program at Fisk makes for a sober, sane, constructive, and moral citizenship. Fisk students do not get into trouble. They are law-abiding and they make citizens who cooperate with the best element—white or black—in the communities where they live.[33]

It may be difficult today to understand Johnson's willingness to include language that appeased Southern whites. However, in light of Fisk's past history of strained town-gown relations, it was perhaps the only way he could garner funds from the local white citizens. In an effort to be pragmatic, this fund-raising campaign may have belittled the people whom it was trying to benefit. Perhaps this is one reason why the appeal to local whites bore Marts and Lundy's signature rather than Johnson's.

Despite the perils involved, the fact that Charles Johnson and Johnnetta Cole were both interested in reaching out to white donors is one of the most important elements of their success. President Johnson positioned himself strategically by accepting invitations to be on several philanthropic boards. He was director of race relations for both the American Missionary Association and the Julius Rosenwald Fund. On behalf of the John Hay Whitney Foundation, Johnson directed the Opportunity Scholars Program—a program that aimed to develop black scholars and leaders. Johnson made every effort to establish relationships with the leaders of both white and black organizations. Since several leaders in the black community, including W.E.B. Du Bois and E. Franklin Frazier, did not condone his high-profile interactions with white philanthropists, he was more successful in his relationships with whites. Frazier and Du Bois, both sociologists, received very little philanthropic funding throughout their careers, primarily because they spoke out so vehemently about philanthropic support and the strings attached to it. They saw Johnson as someone who capitalized on white philanthropy—using it to create a sociological "empire" at Fisk. Johnson was able to shape Fisk into a center for scholarship because of his interactions with many of the major foundations. Likewise, President Cole, who is an advocate of "the power of people engaging across communities to solve problems," serves, or has served on the boards of five major corporations including Home Depot, Merck, and Coca-Cola.[34] Her connections to these companies were instrumental in her successful fund-raising.

Understanding the Donor

The mere willingness to work "across communities," however, did not propel Johnson and Cole to the forefront of educational fund-raising. These two presidents made concerted efforts to understand the point of view and needs of the donors. A representative of Burger King who gave Spelman $100,000 said of Johnnetta Cole:

She knew exactly how to pitch me. She invited me to breakfast at her home and she had a tax attorney there who specializes in handling gift taxes. She knew I'd be interested in any tax advantage which could help me make the gift.[35]

According to Cole, what appeals to most corporate donors is

reciprocity—the idea that we each have something the other needs. They know they will need a diverse work force in the future. They know they need to help us educate these black women.[36]

Just as industrial philanthropists of the late nineteenth and early twentieth century wanted a skilled black labor force for their companies, today's corporations want to employ skilled, educated people.

Aware of the changing racial and ethnic demographics in future years which are projected by the U.S. Census Bureau, corporate leaders are eager to make sure that the pool of workers is prepared to meet the demands placed upon them. Both Johnnetta Cole and Charles Johnson used the quality of the workforce as a leveraging tool when soliciting corporations and foundations.

Charles Johnson, like Cole, was skilled at learning the likes and dislikes of philanthropists. He knew what motivated them and what would make the difference between getting and not getting a donation.[37] For example, knowing the Rockefeller Foundation leaders were absolutely meticulous about their record keeping and administration of grants—undoubtedly a holdover from the reign of John D. Rockefeller, Sr.—Johnson would compile the most detailed reports possible. He would write letters almost every other day to the foundation and call often. He knew that the Rockefeller Foundation would look more favorably upon an institution when it was providing copious documentation of its efforts. Perhaps Johnson's most successful use of his skills of persuasion was his relationship with John Hay Whitney. While serving on the United States Commission for UNESCO (United Nations Educational, Scientific, and Cultural Organization) in the early 1950s, Johnson met philanthropist and socialite John Hay Whitney. Born into one of America's wealthiest families, Whitney was a colorful figure in the worlds of business, media, and politics. He was the chief editor and publisher of the *New York Herald Tribune* that, despite the $40 million he poured into to it, failed. Whitney's name and persona carried great political clout. He used his influence in the Republican Party to help elect Dwight Eisenhower, who returned the favor by appointing him ambassador to Great Britain. Recognizing Johnson as a person with innovative ideas and strong ambition, Whitney soon took a liking to him and solicited his opinion on a variety of issues. Johnson saw in Whitney a person who had vast material wealth but lacked personal fulfillment. When Whitney complained, "He had wasted too many years, put too much money into things that had no deeper purpose," Johnson quickly volunteered to assist the philanthropist in his quest to do something meaningful. Johnson saw a need to nurture black talent, not only at Fisk but also throughout the country—at both black and white institutions. Through the financial help of Whitney, he was able to realize his vision. With the creation of both the John Hay Whitney Foundation, and more specifically, the Opportunity Fellows Program, Johnson helped Whitney to align himself with interracial education and human relations.[38]

In addition to their persuasion skills, both Johnson and Cole used very personal approaches and sometimes even odd peculiarities to influence donors. Johnnetta Cole, who frequently wears a scarf of kente cloth, a multicolored West African weaving, gives these scarves to corporate and foundation donors as a sign of racial harmony. For example, after a meeting with executives of the Chase Manhattan Bank in 1994, Cole gave each of the white, middle-aged men a stole made of kente cloth. She considered it a positive way to solidify their relationship and make them feel included in the Spelman community. Cole has also been known to present the stoles to the college's alumnae, noting that the stoles are the "stripe of royalty" and that the alumnae are the "royalty" of Spelman. Cole's very personal, down-to-earth approach has served her well.[39]

Although persuasive, Johnson did not have Cole's warmth. He has been described as being aloof and possessing a very dry sense of humor. However, he was adept at controlling the dynamics of a meeting. He used personal peculiarities to his advantage when meeting with donors. One such peculiarity was a stuttering problem:

> He was [often] overheard talking to someone about money and he could deliver a solicitation without stuttering one time for several minutes. It was a mannerism that he developed. Sometimes he would use the stuttering to cause silent moments in the conversation when asking for donations. When the potential donor looked like she was most vulnerable, he would pop the question and stop stuttering. (Joe Taylor in interview by author, April 29, 1999.)

Maintaining Independence in Philanthropic Relationships

According to Billie Sue Schultz, fund-raising consultant for the Kresge Foundation and head of the advancement division at Spelman during Cole's presidency, "Black colleges have been practicing reactive fund-raising: Filling out applications for whatever programs foundations and the federal government announced. But sometimes these programs [don't] have a thing to do with the priorities of the colleges."[40] Perhaps the most important lesson to be learned from the experiences of Charles S. Johnson and Johnnetta Cole is their ability to maintain independence in their decision making. Because they approached foundations and corporations with ideas, they were able to set the priorities for their institutions. Universities must consider the potential encroachments on their means of governance, principles of academic freedom, and institutional integrity before accepting contributions from philanthropic organizations and corporations.[41] As noted earlier, this is especially important at HBCUs that have a past marred by incidents of philanthropists imposing their ideas on desperate colleges. With a few exceptions, HBCUs are, even today, at the mercy of the foundations and corporations because of their financial status. Whereas most HWIs have enough funds to cover operating costs and substantial endowments, HBCUs must be frugal about their spending. Even Howard University in Washington, DC, which has the largest endowment of any HBCU—$291,468,000—lags far behind 131 predominantly white institutions in terms of endowment. It even falls behind Phillips Academy, a private preparatory high school, which has a $535 million endowment.[42] HBCU leaders must be diligent about taking the lead in the area of fund-raising so as not to be exploited.

The Basic College is perhaps the best example of Charles S. Johnson's ability to set his own priorities in the use of philanthropic dollars. Unsure of the possibility of integrated black education in the South, Johnson created the Basic College, to give promising black students the opportunity to learn in a nurturing, stimulating environment. An early entry program, the Basic College recruited high school juniors and seniors and placed them in cohesive learning groups that benefited from the presence of artistic, literary, and political figures that Johnson invited to the Fisk campus. They studied together, ate together, and lived together in small cohorts that provided support within the academic setting. By going to the Ford and Whitney Foundations with the Basic College idea, Johnson was able to create the learning environment that he had envisioned. These foundations collaborated with Johnson and he implemented his program with few modifications.

Cole tried to find donors who were sympathetic to the mission of Spelman. She accepted funds from those who supported her ideas and her methods of change and advancement. In Cole's mind, Spelman was producing tomorrow's female leaders and it was just as reputable as Wellesley, Williams, Amherst, and Oberlin[43] in terms of faculty and students. One of Cole's initiatives was to raise support for a $22 million science complex. Although 40 percent of Spelman's students were science majors, the large amounts of money necessary to support the latest science facilities were missing.[43] She approached funders with this in mind—emphasizing the prestige of the institution and its proven ability to educate young women.

Although imperative to the success of their respective institutions, both Johnnetta Cole's and Charles Johnson's fund-raising efforts took a toll on their relationships on campus. President Cole was away from the campus for large periods of time—making an average of two solicitation visits per week. Because of her personality, Cole seemed better able to handle the time away and was good at regrouping with faculty and staff upon her return. However, Charles Johnson had a more difficult time and felt the need to apologize to the faculty:

> It is necessary for someone to go out into the country and pick it up [the money]. It is a long and tedious business, because you can't walk into an office and asked for $10,000 cold . . . That is my interpretation and my apology to you for what must have been my great loss.[44]

According to Mary Thompson, the former director of the Fisk International Center, the faculty opinion of Johnson was one of great respect coupled with frustration. Leslie Collins, a professor of English, described Johnson as someone who "enjoyed building fences around himself and [who] was not easily accessible." There is no doubt that Johnson's frequent absence from the campus exacted a cost from his relationships with faculty members.[45]

Conclusions and Recommendations

As today's black colleges and universities continue to struggle to garner funding for operating costs and endowments, it is important to look at the successes of their predecessors. Both Johnnetta Cole and Charles S. Johnson offer powerful examples of the type of leadership that is needed on HBCU campuses. Johnson, for instance, would study prospective donors—learning their inner motivations, obsessions, and personal quirks. He would then use this information to craft an approach that made donors feel as if they were accomplishing their goals. While this kind of management of donor interactions is important for any fund-raiser, it is imperative at an HBCU where there is a history of outside manipulation. By controlling his interactions with the philanthropists, he ensured that he would not be controlled by them. Cole, on the other hand, dealt with the problem of cultural gaps and lack of familiarity with the HBCU environment. She used gestures of inclusion to attract interest from those who might not otherwise understand the importance of historically black colleges.

Both Johnson and Cole were cognizant of the important role that alumni play at HBCUs. Alumni giving is essential as a financial resource, but most importantly as a testimony to the effectiveness and uniqueness of an HBCU education. For many HBCUs, soliciting alumni "formally" is a new undertaking. For years, HBCUs have only solicited alumni when specific needs arose. Cole provides an example of how to cultivate ongoing support and educate alumnae donors not only after they graduate but also while they are students.[46] Once they understand the structure of the giving process, black college alumni begin to give and support their alma maters. Emmett D. Carson, president of the Minnesota Foundation and former fellow at the Joint Center for Political and Economic Studies, has suggested that HBCUs introduce "general information about the role of philanthropy in our society into undergraduate liberal arts programs." This seems almost a given considering that since "we encourage people to participate in the democratic process another important aspect of being a good citizen [in addition to voting] is active participation in some form of philanthropy."[47]

Johnnetta Cole demonstrates that it is necessary for leaders of HBCUs to use nontraditional approaches to fund-raising. What might work for predominantly white institutions may not be appropriate at an HBCU. She recognized that focusing on the college's deficiencies—a frequent strategy at HBCUs—would not work when the institution's mere existence was being questioned. Corporations and foundations want to be associated with successful, proven endeavors. Cole rightfully positioned Spelman in a positive light when conveying its story to potential donors. Further, both leaders used the occasion of their selection as a way to bolster support for the institution. Both were firsts at their respective colleges and both emphasized this in their solicitations.

Most importantly, Johnson and Cole show that it is necessary to bring ideas to funders and that it is crucial to search actively for innovative funding sources. An organized, deliberate approach to fund-raising enables an institution to maintain integrity in its efforts to garner funds. This approach must be delivered by leaders who are dynamic, outreaching, and comfortable in their social interactions—leaders who are willing to bring their institution's goals to a wider audience. Again, this point is particularly important at HBCUs given their troubled history of outside control. The fund-raising strategies and perseverance of Cole and Johnson can and should be mirrored by current HBCU presidents.

Legal scholar Derrick Bell has pointed out that the only significant advancement for African-Americans has taken place when there has also been an opportunity for whites to benefit. Understanding historical realities, Johnson and Cole have taken a pragmatic approach, gaining the support of both the white and black communities. For Johnson, this was a difficult balance to strike—he had to spend a great amount of time socializing with white philanthropists instead of his family and the Fisk faculty. Occasionally his relationships with white philanthropists led to distrust by faculty members and black intellectuals. However, in the end, he was able to establish a premier educational institution through the use of philanthropy. This strategy is key to the future of black colleges. Particularly in a time when affirmative action is in decline, the continued existence of, and monetary support for, historically black colleges are important for both African-Americans and the country as a whole. Not only do HBCUs respond to the unique needs of today's black students, but they also cultivate new leaders in American society and abroad. The support for historically black colleges is a positive statement by the public and private sectors that reinforces their commitment to the education of all citizens, including African-Americans.[48] HBCU presidents and their staffs must convey this message to potential donors.

Notes

1. William H. Honan (1996), "$114 million campaign lifts a black college to the elite of fund-raisers," The *New York Times*, July 31, Education section.

2. Johnnetta Cole joined Emory University's department of anthropology in 1998 as Presidential Distinguished Professor of Anthropology, Women's Studies, and African-American Studies. Johnnetta B. Cole to author, August 9, 1999; "Endowments over $100-million," the Nation section. The *Chronicle of Higher Education*, Almanac Issue, September 1, 2000, XLVII (1).

3. Honan (1996), "$114 million campaign"; U.S. Census Bureau (1988), Population Income Documents; Frank Rhodes (1997), *Successful Fund Raising for Higher Education*, The Advancement of Learning Series on Higher Education, American Council on Education, Washington, DC.

4. Patrick Gilpin (1973), "Charles S. Johnson: An intellectual biography," Ph.D. dissertation, Vanderbilt University, Nashville, TN.

5. James Anderson (1988), *Black Education in the South, 1860–1935*. University of North Carolina Press, Chapel Hill.

6. Booker T. Washington, *Up From Slavery*. New York: A. L. Burt, 1901; Booker T. Washington, "Atlanta Compromise," Cotton States and International Exposition, September 1895, Atlanta, GA; Louis R. Harlan, *Booker T. Washington, I, The Making of a Black Leader, 1856–1901*, New York: Oxford University Press, 1972; Louis R. Harlan, *Booker T. Washington, II, The Wizard of Tuskegee, 1901–1915*. New York: Oxford University Press, 1983; W. E. B. Du Bois, *The Souls of Black Folk*. New York: Signet Classics, 1995, originally published 1903.

7. Anderson (1988), *Black Education in the South*. Issues of philanthropic control, as they pertain to black colleges, were rarely discussed in history of fund-raising literature. Instead, most discussions were left to black intellectuals and later historians of black education and philanthropy. For example, Scott M. Cutlip's *Fund Raising in the United States* glorifies the contributions of white philanthropists to black colleges. Cutlip fails to take a critical look at the philanthropists' motives for giving. See Scott M. Cutlip (1965), *Fund Raising in the United States. Its Role in America's Philanthropy*, Rutgers University Press, New Brunswisk, NJ.

8. Jacqueline Fleming (1984), *Blacks in College*, Jossey-Bass, San Francisco, CA.

9. Kenneth E. Redd (2000), "HBCU graduates: Employment, earnings and success after college," *USA Group Foundation New Agenda Series*, 2(4), p. 7. The 1994–95 statistics are the latest available from the U.S. Department of Education at time of publication. If the focus is moved to only UNCF schools, approximately 90% of the students require financial assistance, 50% are from families with a gross income level of less that $35,000, 55% are from single parent homes, and 60% are first generation college students. For more information see, www.uncf.org/about/facts.html, United Negro College Fund, Inc. website, September 27, 2000.

10. Alan H. Kirschner (1991), *Perspectives on the Current Status of and Emerging Policy Issues for Private, Historically Black Colleges*, AGB White Paper, No. 1, Association of Governing Boards of Universities and Colleges, Washington, DC.

11. Frederick Rudolph (1962), *The American College and University: A History*, University of Georgia, Athens, GA; Christopher Jencks and David Riesman (1968), *The Academic Revolution*, University of Chicago Press, Chicago; John Stanfield (1985), *Philanthropy and Jim Crow in American Social Science*, Greenwood Press, Westport, CT; Stephen Peeps (1981), "Northern philanthropy and the emergence of black higher education—do-gooders, compromisers, or co-conspirators?" *Journal of Negro Education*, 50, 3, pp. 251–69; Edward Berman (1983), *The Influence of the Carnegie, Ford, and Rockefeller Foundations on American Foreign Policy: The Ideology of Philanthropy*, State University of New York Press, Albany, NY; Robert Bremmer (1988), *American Philanthropy*, University of Chicago Press, Chicago; John Brubacher and Willis Rudy (1976), *Higher Education in Transition: A History of American Colleges and Universities, 1636–1976*, Harper & Row, New York; Merle Curti and Roderick Nash (1965), *Philanthropy in the Shaping of American Higher Education*, Rutgers University Press, New Brunswick, NJ.

12. The Harlem Renaissance took place between 1920 and 1930 in New York. It was a celebration of African-American art, literature, and music. See David L. Lewis (1981), *When Harlem Was in Vogue*, Oxford University Press, New York; Steven Watson (1995), *The Harlem Renaissance. Hub of African-American Culture*, Pantheon Books, New York.

13. Gilpin (1973), "Charles S. Johnson: An intellectual biography"; Richard Robbins (1996), *Sidelines Activist: Charles S. Johnson and the Struggle for Civil Rights*, University of Mississippi Press, Jackson, MS.

14. Ibid.; see also Marybeth Gasman (2000), "A renaissance in Nashville: Charles S. Johnson's use of philanthropy to build Fisk University in the postwar era," Ph.D. dissertation, Indiana University.

15. Hollingsworth Wood to Edwin Embree, November 18, 1947, Edwin Embree Papers, Julius Rosenwald Fund Papers, Fisk University archives, Nashville, Tennessee.

16. Johnnetta B. Cole (1993), *Conversations. Straight Talk With America's Sister President*, Doubleday, New York, pp. 37–38.

17. Allison O. Adams (1998), "Johnnetta Cole: Challenging the status quo," *Emory Magazine*. Spring 1998.

18. Courtney Leatherman (1989), "Black colleges step up efforts to win alumni gifts," *The Chronicle of Higher Education*, October 25, p. A31.

19. See John A. Moore (2000), "Are state-supported historically black colleges and universities justifiable after Fordice? A higher education dilemma," *Florida State University Law Review*, 27, p. 547; Anthony Ngula Luti (1999), "When a door closes, a window opens: Do today's private historically black colleges and universities run afoul of conventional equal protection analysis?" *Howard Law Journal*, 42, p. 479; Theodore Cross and Robert Bruce Slater (1996), "Once again, Mississippi take aim at black higher education," *Journal of Blacks in Higher Education* Vol. 12, pp. 92–6; Jacquelin A. Stefkovich and Terrence Leas (1994) "A legal history of desegregation in higher education," *Journal of Negro Education*, 63, 3, pp. 406–20; Grace L. Butler (1944), "Legal and policy issues in higher education," *Journal of Negro Education*, 63, 3, pp. 451–59.

20. *Herald Sun* (1999), "Fighting to survive. On the brink. A school without peer: Spelman rides wave of success. *Herald Sun*, http://herald-sun.com/hbcu/docs/brink_2.html, March 1.

21. See www.usnews.com/usnews/educ/college/rankings. *U.S. News Online*. September 29, 2000.

22. Cole (1993), *Conversations*.

23. Even today, Spelman has not been able to catch up with institutions similar to it in the area of alumni giving. According to *U.S. News and World Report*, only 15% of Spelman alumni support the institution. This percentage is the lowest of any national liberal arts college. It will take Spelman even more hard work to reach the typical levels of 25–55% held by most institutions of the same caliber. See www.usnews.com/usnews/educ/college/rankings. *U.S. News Online*. September 29, 2000.

24. Donald E. Winbush (1996), "Spelman mission was not impossible," *Black Issues in Higher Education*, 13, September 19, p. 19.

25. Ibid., p. 20.

26. Ibid., p. 21.

27. Ibid.

28. *American Missionary* (1866), March 10, pp. 59–60; Editor (1866), *Nashville Daily Union and American*, January 10; Jane Browning and John Williams (1978), "History and goals of black institutions of higher learning," in C. Willie and R. Edmonds (Eds.), *Black Colleges in America: Challenge, Development, Survival*, Teacher's College Press, New York; Joe M. Richardson (1980), *A History of Fisk University, 1865–1946*, The University of Alabama Press, 1980, AL; Julian Roebuck and Komanduri Murty (1993), *Historically Black Colleges and Universities: Their Place in American Higher Education*, Praeger, Westport, CT.

29. Marybeth Gasman (1988), "Supporting HBCUs. An alternative proposal for funding historically black colleges and universities," *Business Today*, Fall, pp. 25–26; U.S. Census Bureau (1999), Population Income Documents, www.census.gov/hhes/income/income99.

30. A.C. Marts to Theodore Yoder, Director of Public Relations, October 30, 1946, box 53, folder 10; Ernest R. Alexander to alumni, March 1947, box 56, folder 10.

31. Liz McMillin (1991), "More colleges tap fund raisers for presidencies," *The Chronicle of Higher Education*, September 11, Online Chronicle Archive. www.chronicle.com.

32. J. L. Mandell to Dean W. J. Faulkner, February 25, 1947, box 53, folder 16, Charles S. Johnson Papers, Fisk University Archives, Nashville, Tennessee.

33. J. L. Mandell to Dean W. J. Faulkner, February 25, 1947, box 53, folder 16, Charles S. Johnson Papers, Fisk University Archives, Nashville, Tennessee.

34. Johnnetta B. Cole (1996), Commencement Speech at Emory University, May 13.

35. Honan (1996), "$114 million campaign," p. B6.

36. Cole (1993), *Conversations*, p. 41.

37. Russ Alan Prince and Karen Maru File (1994), *The Seven Faces of Philanthropy: A New Approach to Cultivating Major Donors*, Jossey-Bass, San Francisco, CA.

38. Ely Kahn (1981), *The Life and Times of John Hay Whitney*, Doubleday, New York, p. 178; Charles S. Johnson to John Hay Whitney, October 1, 1952, box 51, folder 3, Charles S. Johnson Papers, Fisk University Archives, Nashville, Tennessee.

39. Honan (1996), "$114 million campaign," p. B6.

40. Michele N. K. Collison (2000), "Jump-starting black college fund-raising. It takes money to raise money," *Black Issues in Higher Education*, 17, 7, p. 22.

41. Barbara E. Brittingham and Thomas R. Pezzullo (1990), *The Campus Green. Fund Raising in Higher Education 1990*, ASHE-ERIC Higher Education Report No. 1, School of Education and Human Development, The George Washington University, Washington, DC.

42. Theodore Cross and Robert Bruce Slater (1995), "The financial footings of the black colleges," *Journal of Blacks in Higher Education*, Vol. 6, 7–9. Phillips Academy, www.andover.edu.

43. Winbush (1996), "Spelman mission was not impossible," p. 18.

44. Fisk Faculty Meeting Minutes, February 10, 1948, box 38, folder 10, Charles S. Johnson Papers, Fisk University Archives, Nashville, Tennessee.

45. Leslie M. Collins, interview by Patrick Gilpin, November 17, 1970; Professor Collins's opinions were reiterated in a short conversation with the author, May 15, 1999, Mary Thompson to author, March 28, 1999.

46. Leatherman (1989), "Black colleges step up efforts to win alumni gifts."

47. Emmett D. Carson (1988), "Black philanthropy," *Liberal Education*, 74, p. 8.

48. Derrick Bell (1997), *Confronting Authority. Reflections of an Ardent Protester*, Beacon Press, Boston; Derrick Bell, conversation with author, Lincoln, Nebraska, April 18, 1997.

Practitioners' Perspectives

In her paper, Marybeth Gasman masterfully parallels the core success characteristics of two prominent African-American CEOs: Presidents Johnnetta Cole at Spelman College and Charles S. Johnson at Fisk University. Gasman's seminal work illustrates the effectiveness of Cole and Johnson in their philanthropic efforts, clearly outlining the intricacies of effective fund-raising and leadership.

Nearly fifty years separated Cole's and Johnson's endeavors at garnering support for their institutions—institutions that historically struggled to match the successes of their white counterparts—yet their styles are surprisingly similar and equally effective. During their tenures, each set a precedence of excellence and offered needed templates and prescriptions for CEOs of historically black colleges and universities (HBCUs) interested in effectively advancing their institutions.

Gasman's work articulates the success factors shaping the superior contributions made by Cole and Johnson. The work is intriguing, for it effectively illustrates the inherited challenges each of these leaders faced during their presidencies.

Undoubtedly, Gasman's insights parallel many of the needed characteristics for one to be successful in any organization serious about fund-raising. However, she artfully tailors those characteristics to the realities present within HBCUs—both during Johnson's tenure in the 1950s and most recently while Johnnetta Cole was at Spelman's helm. Ultimately, Gasman's work reinforces the most important elements needed to advance an institution or cause effectively.

Certainly, Cole and Johnson were masters in their craft of educational fund-raising, possessing well-honed skills and talents in support of their leadership goals. Gasman's work reinforces the benefits associated with HBCU CEOs understanding and practicing educational fund-raising basics. Obviously, the successes of Johnnetta Cole and Charles S. Johnson would not have come to fruition if their personalities did not include initiative, integrity, and positive mental attitude—the main staples of effective fund-raising. As illustrated, Cole and Johnson knew the art of effective stewardship, and whenever possible aligned their efforts to meet the needs of the donors with whom they were working. Without Cole's and Johnson's thoughtful and deliberate professional fund-raising strategies, it is doubtful their efforts would have been as successful as they were.

A macro approach to Gasman's work quickly gives relevance to the contributions made by these African-American CEOs. Through Cole's and Johnson's successes, it is clear that self-confidence, vision, intuition, and persistence, coupled with an unyielding pursuit of excellence, brought their institutions' dreams to fruition. Undoubtedly the leadership of Presidents Johnnetta Cole and Charles S. Johnson earned them their historical place in educational fund-raising.

Ralph Amos
Assistant Vice President
Ohio University Alumni Association

CHAPTER 11

FUNDRAISING FROM DIVERSE COMMUNITIES

Black Philanthropy's Past, Present, and Future

Emmett D. Carson

> A brief look at the past and present helps inform speculation about the future of black philanthropy and how it may affect America's nonprofit sector.

In the past ten years, black philanthropy has moved from relative obscurity to become the focus of national and regional conferences as well as a growing area of study by scholars. This is a welcome change brought about by the growing recognition that African Americans have a rich philanthropic tradition and that the changing demographics of American society coupled with greater socioeconomic equality will result in African American philanthropy's playing an ever greater role in shaping the direction and contours of the American nonprofit sector.

This chapter explores black philanthropy's proud past and the socioeconomic forces that helped to shape it, examines black philanthropy today and how it differs from the past, and speculates about the future of black philanthropy and its impact on nonprofit organizations interested in soliciting gifts from African Americans.

It is important to provide some context at the start for the issues expressed in this chapter, as well as two critical definitions. It is increasingly difficult to have segregated conversations within a racial or ethnic group that are not overheard and possibly taken out of context by other racial and ethnic groups. For example, comments by entertainer Bill Cosby that some African American parents are too young and are not adequately fulfilling their parental responsibilities caused a national stir. Cosby's comments, in a May 2004 speech, were directed to an African American audience and were widely taken out of context by both right-wing conservatives and advocates of the African American community. The ideas put forward in this chapter are meant to provoke a candid discussion about the current state and future of black philanthropy by those who want to promote knowledge and open discussion and not whether they are the right or wrong choices for the African American community.

While black philanthropy is often discussed, few provide a working definition. Black philanthropy is defined here to mean the giving of time, talent, goods, and services or money by African Americans for charitable purposes. Black philanthropy should not be viewed as limited to charitable donations by African Americans to African American causes or organizations, as some believe. After all, white philanthropy has never been defined by the recipient of the charity or the charitable gift. Is a gift no less black philanthropy when it comes from African American hands but supports such institutions as Harvard University?

The second concept to convey is that black philanthropy is not a static concept but rather an evolving, fluid concept that adapts based on its environment. Carson's axiom, modestly named, is that black philanthropy is shaped by the social, economic, and legal climates faced by African Americans at different points in history. As the social context changes, so does black philanthropy.

Black Philanthropy's Past

The roots of black philanthropy can be traced to Africa. It arrived in America with the first slaves, embedded in their cultural and communal traditions of self-help. The pernicious institution of slavery forced Africans from different lands to band together for mutual survival and reinforced their self-help practices.

For African Americans, black philanthropy has been the economic engine that helped them create and sustain the first black mutual aid associations and churches. These institutions, especially the black church, were of special importance during slavery and Jim Crow because their leaders were supported and financed by the African American community. As a result, these leaders were able to voice the concerns of their constituents without fear of economic reprisal, although they were constantly under physical threat and intimidation. Denied access to goods and services from all manner of white institutions, African Americans saw to their own needs through the establishment of their own religious and nonprofit organizations. In many ways, the black church was the first community foundation, aggregating the community's resources across class lines and directing the resources to provide the services and institutions that were needed.

During its earliest years, black philanthropy was directed at social empowerment and transformation. In addition to schools and financial institutions, it gave life to the Underground Railroad and, later, Marcus Garvey's Back to Africa movement and the civil rights movement. Make no mistake; although the various freedom movements received contributions from white donors and their philanthropic institutions, these efforts were predominantly sustained by the lives, volunteer efforts, donations, and money of African Americans.

By 1835, white America had become so afraid of black philanthropy that Virginia, Maryland, and North Carolina had laws banning mutual aid societies and fraternal organizations (Carson, 1993). This is a principal reason that African Americans developed secret societies and nonprofit organizations with dual purposes. One example of a dual-purpose organization is the women's bridge clubs of the South, which had the public purpose of providing social interaction for its members but a secret purpose of engaging in charitable efforts to support the community.

In the face of demeaning, humiliating segregation in which separate was never equal, African American churches and other nonprofit organizations used black philanthropy to turn the impossible into possible and make Martin Luther King Jr.'s dream of an integrated society a reality. In the 1970s, the National Black United Fund won access to the federal workplace campaign as well as to other groups, such as women and the environment.

For three centuries, from the late 1600s to the 1970s, black philanthropy had three defining characteristics. First, African Americans used their collective philanthropy, often through the church, to promote common interests rather than individual interests. Second, black philanthropy was characterized by pooling together relatively modest amounts from multiple individuals rather than relying on a few donors who could give large amounts. Third, black philanthropy was transformative: it was directed at improving the socioeconomic status of African Americans through both self-help and social protest.

Black Philanthropy Today

Today, black philanthropy is at a crossroads because the African American community is at a crossroads. Fifty years after the momentous *Brown* v. *Board of Education* (1954) decision, things are better for African Americans. Based on the 2000 Census, there are forty-one thousand African American doctors, forty-three thousand African American lawyers, and ninety-one thousand African American engineers. This does not include the large number of African American athletes, entertainers, the new U.S. secretary of state (Condoleezza Rice), the former secretary of state (Colin Powell), or Justice Clarence Thomas. Whether it is broadly acknowledged in the African American community or not, it was King's dream that African Americans would be judged by the content of their character and not the color of their skin.

African Americans today represent the full spectrum of class, wealth, and political ideology. The realization of King's dream has meant that African Americans no longer have identical experiences, and therefore they hold views that are increasingly heterogeneous rather than homogeneous. Although there are those who lament these developments, I would remind them that this is what King, Medgar Evers, and countless others gave their lives to achieve and what millions of African Americans over generations hoped for.

It is equally true that fifty years since *Brown* v. *Board of Education*, African Americans have not yet achieved socioeconomic justice. Consider the following statistics:

- Health outcomes in Harlem, New York, are equal to those of Bangladesh.

- There are more African American men in prison than in college.

- There continues to be ongoing discrimination in corporate America, as evidenced by discrimination suits settled by such corporations as Microsoft, Coca Cola, Eddie Bauer, and Denny's, among others.

Today African Americans no longer share a commonality of experiences even though we share history and skin color. As the axiom would suggest, the focus and direction of black philanthropy are changing. Black philanthropy is more likely to be driven by individual interests rather than communal needs.

This shift is primarily due to three reasons. First, the African American community now has individuals of significant wealth who can make significant gifts consistent with their personal charitable interests. Second, the diminished racial discrimination in America has released African Americans from the burden of having their philanthropy be race focused. Third, black philanthropy is no longer centered through the black church or even other African American nonprofit organizations. Weekly church attendance by African Americans declined from 38 percent in 1970 to 25 percent in 2002 (University of Michigan, n.d.).

More than ever before, black philanthropy reflects what W.E.B. DuBois referred to in *Souls of Black Folks* (1969) as two-ness: the idea that African Americans lived in two worlds—one white, the other black. For many African Americans, these worlds are no longer separate. Music, fashion, and other areas of life that have what is termed crossover appeal, economically and socially, increasingly dominate our society. African Americans increasingly see themselves as part of a global community, and their philanthropy—their time and money—is beginning to reflect these realities. For example, actor Danny Glover and others were arrested in Washington, D.C., in 2004 while protesting the genocide that has occurred in the Sudan.

The Future of Black Philanthropy

The question facing people of African descent in the United States is to what extent we see ourselves as African Americans as opposed to Americanized Africans. African Americans see themselves as having a common history and, more important, an intertwined common destiny. Yet Americanized Africans recognize their common past but see a future in which they are individuals with no obligations or responsibilities to the race. This is not to say that they cannot or will not support African American causes; rather, they do not feel an obligation to have to do so. As the axiom would suggest, the current crossroads has significant implications for the future of black philanthropy. Due to diminished discrimination, more so than at any other point in history, African Americans are free to support their individual interests and pursuits.

Tremendous socioeconomic challenges remain in the African American community. There is an important fundraising case to be made by African American nonprofit organizations focused on traditional civil rights issues inclusive of social justice, education, employment, housing, and health care, among others. These organizations must demonstrate excellence in their programs and their donor relations. Unfortunately, this has not always been the case, as some of these organizations have relied on African Americans to support their organization, even when the service provided has been lacking. Such behavior will no longer be tolerated.

For nonprofit organizations that do not have an African American focus, there exist new opportunities to recruit African American donors in support of their work. To achieve this, these organizations must walk the talk in terms of what they claim to do and deliver excellence in their programming and donor relations. Unlike in decades past, there is more receptivity among African Americans to consider supporting nonprofit organizations that are not focused on African American causes. Nonprofit organizations that want to solicit gifts from African Americans without their input and without boards and staff who fully represent the diversity of the community will ultimately not be successful.

Conclusion

The future of black philanthropy looks brighter than it has ever before. At one end of the spectrum, there is the wonderful example of Oseola McCarty. In 1995, at eighty-seven years of age, McCarty, a washerwoman, donated $150,000 to the University of Southern Mississippi to establish college scholarships; at the time, it was the largest single gift it had ever received ("Oseola McCarty Donates $150,000 to USM," 1995). Later, McCarty stated, "I can't do everything, but I can do something to help somebody. And what I can do, I will do. I wish I could do more." In 2004, Alphonse Fletcher, a thirty-eight-year-old investment professional, announced that he will distribute $50 million in honor of *Brown* v. *Board of Education* (Rimer, 2004). It is worth noting that at age twenty-eight, he gave $4.8 million to Harvard University, his alma mater. These two examples indicate that black philanthropy remains an important community value and is poised to make an even greater impact on America's nonprofit sector in the years ahead.

References

Brown v. *Board of Education of Topeka*. 347 U.S. 483. 1954.

Carson, E. D. *A Hand Up: Black Philanthropy and Self-Help in America*, Washington, D.C.: Joint Center for Political and Economic Studies, 1993.

DuBois, W.E.B. *Souls of Black Folks*. New York: New American Library, 1969. (Originally published 1903.)

NAACP Legal Defense Fund v. *Campbell*. 504 F. Supp. 1365, 1981.

National Black United Fund v. *Campbell*. 494 F. Supp. 748, 1980.

"Oseola McCarty Donates $150,000 to USM." University of Southern Mississippi, press release, July 1995.

Rimer, S. "$50 Million Gift Aims to Build on Legacy of *Brown* v. *Board*." *New York Times*, May 18, 2004, p. A23.

University of Michigan. *The National Election Studies*. N.d. [www.umich.edu/~nes/].

An Untapped Resource: Bringing African Americans into the College and University Giving Process

Marybeth Gasman

Abstract

Often overlooked by scholars of philanthropy and practitioners in the area of advancement, black giving has a rich history. This paper will discuss the specific nature of black giving patterns and make recommendations to advancement and alumni staff on how to better include African Americans in the college and university giving process.

Introduction

Fund raising is . . . an acquired talent. You must train yourself to look for possible donors in areas others would see as simply the passing parade of life.[1] African-American giving is an untapped resource in college and university fund-raising campaigns, at both predominantly white institutions (PWIs) and historically black institutions (HBIs). One reason for the scant attention is that black giving potential is underestimated. However, given that more African Americans have moved and are moving into the middle class, it is apparent that many are, or will be, in a position to donate money to philanthropic causes. According to the latest Census data (1999), the black median family income for those with a head of household between ages 35 and 64 years is $40,392 (married couples).[2] More importantly, the long history of giving within the black community (often in ways that fall outside of traditional definitions of philanthropy) suggests that blacks are deeply concerned with giving back to the community and have great potential to support education.

Because black giving does not receive the exposure offered to "white" giving, the public, including college and university advancement officers, is generally unaware of it.[3] Those who study philanthropic giving are often unacquainted with the patterns and traditions of minority communities.[4] Even some of the most comprehensive studies on giving in communities of color have neglected aspects of black philanthropy.[5] In fact, blacks have a rich legacy of giving both monetarily and through volunteerism. The purpose of this paper is to explore the tradition of giving in the African-American community in an effort to understand how more blacks might be successfully brought into the educational giving process. This paper examines black giving in multiple settings (i.e., the church, fraternal organizations, neighborhood associations, mutual aid societies, women's organizations, etc.). Most importantly, it points to the prevailing motivations for giving among African Americans in order to assist college and university advancement staffs in their efforts to raise funds from their black alumni.

Methodology

According to Marilyn Fisher, "To understand an individual [one must] understand the social and historical contexts through which he or she shapes a life."[6] Understanding an individual and individuals who make up the collective alumni of a college or university is crucial to fund-raising success.[7] Specifically, it is necessary to be cognizant of alumni behavior and motivations in order to bring new donors into the university "family."[8] Although scholars in the fields of history, African-American studies, education, and sociology have explored black giving, those professionals doing the actual fund raising have rarely applied this research. With this in mind, the author has used a historical lens to examine the traditions and history of giving in the black community as a way to inform the field of advancement. By synthesizing research from different academic disciplines, this paper will foster an understanding of the long history, traditions, and motivations associated with African-American philanthropy, the author will use this research to make recommendations pertaining to the inclusion of African Americans in the alumni giving process.

Theoretical Framework

African Americans are often looked upon as recipients of philanthropic efforts but scholars rarely examine the philanthropic contributions made by members of this group. For example, scholarship on the history of historically black colleges and universities has tended to focus on the problematic role of white industrial philanthropists in building institutional curriculum. While this is an important topic, it neglects to consider the role of blacks in shaping their own institutions. Historian James D. Anderson, however, has successfully demonstrated the agency of black leaders in the establishment of education for African Americans.[9] This paper will follow Anderson's lead and view African Americans as active participants in the giving process. They will be shown to be fund raisers and philanthropic givers who support both their own needs and the needs of the country as a whole.

A Brief Overview of Alumni Giving

> New generations of alumni provide the continuity that perpetuates a university. Its officers come and go, its faculties change, its programs and buildings are replaced, but its alumni maintain a lifelong relationship with the university. They are keepers of the tradition, preferred stockholders of the enterprise, the mark of accomplishment.[10]

The concept of alumni giving, as it is now known, is for the most part a twentieth century phenomenon. Alumni associations, however, date back to the colonial period, with colleges such as Harvard, Yale, and Williams forming organizations to help alumni maintain contact with their friends. By the last decade of the nineteenth century, 117 alumni associations had been created and class reunions were being held regularly. Nonetheless, it was not until the twentieth century, around the mid-1930s, that alumni giving came to resemble what people are familiar with today. Just prior to World War II, alumni began to play roles on college and university governing boards; annual funds were initiated nationally. After the war, with the influx of veterans, the baby boom, and increased access to education, alumni solicitation became more systematic. Universities began to create polished alumni publications and found ever more creative ways to involve their alumni in campus events.[11] According to Robert A. Reichley,

> A new kind of professional appeared in alumni, institutional relations, and development offices. This professional was faced with new responsibilities and accountabilities, a difficult fight against impersonality in what was supposed to be a highly personal endeavor, and ever greater demands for efficiency and evaluation.[12]

Today's alumni professionals work hand in hand with the advancement office. The relationships that they establish are crucial to the philanthropic success of institutions of higher learning. Currently, alumni giving ranges from 6 percent at Morris Brown College in Atlanta, Georgia to 37 percent at Washington University in St. Louis, Missouri to 68 percent at Amherst College in Williamstown, Massachusetts. Most institutions fall somewhere in the middle of this continuum.[13]

Colleges and universities have typically used "high profile" spokespeople, glossy publications, special events, recognition, and telemarketing to attract their alumni into the giving process.

Traditions of Black Giving in the Community

The origins of black giving and the organizations around which it is focused are rooted in efforts to overcome oppression. The history of black philanthropy shows that blacks are motivated by those who are close to them and efforts that make a difference in the daily lives of other African Americans. In many cases, their philanthropy has been a response to discrimination—in the past, slavery and segregation—today, inequality in education and the workplace.

The tradition of giving "tithes and offerings" began as early as the colonial period when free blacks in the North established black churches to aid needy African Americans. According to C. Eric Lincoln and Lawrence H. Mamiya in their book, *The Black Church in the African American Experience,*

> The tradition of mutual aid lay deep in the African heritage, which stressed a greater communalism and social solidarity than either European or American customs allowed. These incipient traditions of mutual aid and self-help in the slave quarters were formalized and legitimated with the Christian-izing of the slaves in the eighteenth and nineteenth centuries.[14]

The growth of separate black churches gave African Americans the opportunity to establish the "first black-owned and operated institutions."[15] Since its inception, the black church has been the single most important institution involved in black philanthropy.[16] It has also been the chief beneficiary of the black community's giving efforts.[17] According to Ann Abbe, "Clergy are often the most influential members of their communities, and church members are expected to support the church with frequent and/or large gifts."[18]

The majority of African Americans are taught from a young age that they have an obligation to give to the church. Through personal engagement and the establishment of a trusting bond, black preachers convey the needs of the church and consistently encourage their parishioners to support the work of the church—the will of God.[19] This obligation to give has provided the backbone for many black social movements in the United States, including the Civil Rights Movement.[20] Black church ministers were cognizant of the effect of racism on economic mobility in the United States, and hence sought to create a sound financial base from which political and social change could take place.[21] Since their beginnings, black churches have acted as collection points for money, services, and goods that are pooled and redistributed.[22] According to Smith et al.,

> The creation and evolution of the black church has been the most significant factor in the political, social, cultural, spiritual, educational and philanthropic development of African Americans in this country.[23]

Thus, the black church is a key example of African-American agency. Although forced upon blacks by white slave owners, in the hands of black leaders, Christianity became an instrument for black emancipation.[24]

Often created as an arm of the church, mutual aid societies were also among the earliest organizations created by African Americans.[25] These societies began in the North and were typically founded by freedmen. In addition to meeting the spiritual needs of blacks, they also addressed their physical and social needs.[26] The first recorded mutual aid society was the Free African Society, which was established in 1787 in Philadelphia by the African Methodist Episcopal and the African Protestant Episcopal churches. Other organizations included the New York Society, the Union Society of Brooklyn, the African Union Society, the Wilberforce Benevolent Society, the Woolman Society, and the Clarkson Society.[27] Eventually, the mutual aid societies developed into cultural, economic, and political forces that helped to advance blacks. Under the aegis of these organizations, African Americans joined together—trusting and relying on one another in dire circumstances. According to Lincoln and Mamiya, these loosely organized societies were the forerunners of national organizations such as the Urban League and the National Association for the Advancement of Colored People (NAACP)[28] Further, Smith et al. note that influential black businesses such as the "National Benefit Life Insurance and the Central Life Insurance companies also owe their origins to mutual aid organizations."[29]

Beginning in 1775 with the establishment of the Prince Hall Masons, fraternal organizations began to work closely with the black church. These organizations were, first and foremost, communal and social, but were also committed to healing social ills and contributing to the community. On many occasions they secured funds and gifts in kind from their members for indigent women and children. Black fraternal organizations consisted of two types: those that were black versions of already existing white organizations and those that were established specifically for African Americans. Blacks created their own versions of the Masons (as mentioned), the Odd Fellows, Knights of Pythias, Eastern Star, Household of Ruth, Foresters, Shriners, and the Elks. Those organizations created by blacks for blacks included the Grand United. Order of Galilean Fishermen, the Colored Brotherhood and Sisterhood of Honor, the Friends of Negro Freedom, the International Order of Twelve, the African Blood Brotherhood, the Colored Consolidated Brotherhood, the African Legion, and the Knights of the Invisible Colored Kingdom. Many of the fraternal organizations established an auxiliary group of women such as the Daughters of the Eastern Star for Masons.[30] Fraternal organizations were most prevalent in northeastern cities including Boston, Philadelphia, and New York. These organizations contributed to a culture of "giving back" and "uplifting the race."

During the antebellum period, black women devised a variety of means of supporting causes important to the community. For example, they participated in "fairs" with white abolitionist women to support antislavery legislation. These black women also sponsored their own fairs to support the African Methodist Episcopal Church, the abolitionist Frederick Douglass, and the Union Anti-Slavery Society. Still other African-American women's organizations held fairs to support the black press as well as orphaned black children.[31] These efforts by black women are yet another example of the importance of "uplifting the race" as a motivation for giving.

African-American "elites" (business and professional circles) have also created many social and service organizations for themselves. Because of the secretive nature of these organizations and the fact that their membership is exclusively black, their philanthropic efforts go unnoticed by nonblacks, and are thus overlooked in discussions of African-American philanthropy. Among them are the Links, the Girl Friends, National Smart Set, the Drifters, and the Northeasterners for women. For men, the organizations include the Boulé (Sigma Pi Phi), the Comus Club, the Reveille Club, the Ramblers, the Bachelor-Benedicts, and the Guardsmen. African-American children also belong to elite organizations—the most prominent being Jack and Jill.

According to a member of the Links, "Once you are a part of one of these groups, you end up knowing many more people in all the other groups too."[32] Because most of the elite organizations were founded on a premise of volunteerism and charitable giving, the potential for black philanthropy in these groups is obvious. For example, the Links proudly claim,

> [Our] tradition is based on volunteerism. For over fifty years, the organization has gathered momentum, continuously redefined its purposes, sharpened its focus, and expanded its program dimensions in order to make the name "Links" synonymous with not only a chain of friendship, but also a chain of purposeful service.[33]

Within these elite organizations, giving is an expectation—a requirement of membership. For example, each local Links chapter is called to participate in philanthropic activities in four areas: youth, arts, national issues, and international issues. A Links chapter in New Orleans created and sponsors a citywide boys choir, hosts art exhibitions to promote new artists, contributes on a national level to bone marrow research, and provides school supplies and uniforms to school children in Belize.[34] The Links and other black elite organizations collect money from their members, not only to support their own operating budgets and projects, but for the NAACP, the National Urban League, and the United Negro College Fund. The success of these black elite organizations in supporting a wide variety of philanthropic endeavors is made possible by the strong bonds of trust within the organization.[35]

Traditions of Black Giving Within Educational Settings

Although northern white missionaries and industrial philanthropists are most often credited with the establishment of black education in the United States, the freedmen played a significant role. According to historian James Anderson, they "spurred the establishment of widespread elementary and literacy education."[36] Likewise, several churches, including the African Methodist Episcopal Church, founded colleges for the purpose of educating the former slaves. These educational efforts for blacks were made possible by money saved—sometimes one penny at a time—by African-American communities and churches. As a result of the "obligation to give" instilled in them by their churches, blacks supported their own advancement in society. As they had been excluded from education during the period of slavery, and segregation was keeping them out of the white educational system, the need for blacks to develop separate educational institutions was particularly acute.

One of the most successful efforts to bring blacks together in support of their own institutions was the United Negro College Fund (UNCF). An umbrella organization, originally consisting of 27 member colleges and a combined enrollment of 14,000 students, the UNCF encouraged giving among blacks and supported disadvantaged African Americans through advocacy and scholarships. The Fund was established on April 25, 1944 and appealed to both black and nonblack donors in a systematic way. According to Frederick D. Patterson, the Fund's founder,

> The coming together of the private black colleges out of concern for our needs; the fact that we were not going to get the amount of money we had been receiving from our former sources; and the innovative fund-raising practices of other organizations—all of these factors contributed to the formation of the UNCF.[37]

The UNCF is an excellent example of autonomous action by blacks. African-American educational leaders saw one type of funding (industrial philanthropy) drying up, so they sought to create their own funding mechanism. Today, many African Americans who give to black colleges also give to the UNCF.[38]

In the early 1900s, African Americans began organizing exclusively black fraternities and sororities on college campuses. In most cases, these organizations began with a social focus but eventually placed an emphasis on scholarly discussion and activism on behalf of the race. Alpha Phi Alpha, which was established in 1906 at Cornell University, was the first black fraternity. From that time until 1924, eight other fraternities and sororities were created on college campuses. Although varied in their characteristics and goals, these organizations banded together during the 1950s and 1960s to support the Civil Rights Movement.[39]

Black sororities and fraternities are quite different from their white counterparts. Although in both cases, membership is lifelong, in the black Greek system it has much greater importance after graduation. That fraternity and sorority membership is important for older participants is shown by the induction of members into graduate chapters. These members need not join as undergraduates. Graduate and undergraduate members share a common commitment to philanthropic giving and volunteerism.[40] For example, the sisters of Delta Sigma Theta focus their public service on five specific areas: educational development, economic development, physical and mental health, political awareness and involvement, and international awareness and involvement. Individual chapters are charged with sponsoring programs that support these initiatives. However, local chapters have the "flexibility to create programs that will meet the needs of their individual communities as long as they have these foci as their central charge."[41] Some of Delta Sigma Theta's programs include the support of research on hypertension among blacks, the sponsorship of voter education and registration drives, the promotion of black-owned businesses, the support of computer literacy training, and assistance to Haitian refugees.[42] In addition to their philanthropic efforts, African-American fraternities and sororities provide "a forum, postcollege, through which some of the best-educated blacks in America can discuss an agenda to fight racism and improve conditions for other less-advantaged blacks."[43]

Black fraternity and sorority membership includes many influential African Americans: President Clinton's Secretary of Labor Alexis Herman (Delta Sigma Theta), Congresswoman Sheila Jackson Lee (Alpha Kappa Alpha), Atlanta Mayor Bill Campbell (Omega Psi Phi), Rensselaer Polytechnic Institute President Shirley Jackson (Delta Sigma Theta) and Executive Director of the UNCF William Gray (Alpha Phi Alpha). These organizations have a significant impact on politics, education, business, and philanthropy.

Traditions of Black Giving Within the Family Setting

The African-American family reunion has become an important occasion for charitable giving—the Black Family Reunion Institute at Temple University is currently studying this phenomenon. Black family reunion organizations are sprouting up throughout the United States. One of these, in New York, was established on the premise that,

> It will echo the themes of family, unity, and community, as well as self-empowerment. . . . Through collectivity, we can make a stronger impact on the surrounding urban neighborhoods. . . . We will hold clothing, food, and book drives, perform different types of service, expose our members to cultural arts activities, develop creative workshops and increase social and political awareness and involvement. We hope all this will serve to nourish the minds, bodies, and souls of us all.[44]

Many black family reunions connect philanthropy with local, state, and national issues. With each gathering, members select a "favorite" cause (typically African American in nature) to which to donate money. All in attendance are expected to support the chosen charity.

In the black community, family means more than just the immediate family. It also includes "fictive kin" such as neighbors, friends of parents, close friends at school, and others. According to Smith et al., "African American families are often characterized by large kinship networks related both by blood and association."[45] Because much giving in the African-American community is between these "family" members, it goes unreported and is not included in national giving surveys. Close relationships of this sort lead to keen expectations that those who "make it" will help those who have not. Thus, the family, as understood by blacks, helps to instill in many African-American children a sense that one must "give back" to the community.

Discovering African American Motivations for Giving

According to Ernest E. Rydell,

> When people are better informed about the institution, they will be more interested in what it has to offer; they will take pride in it and support its purpose. But different people have different interests. [Advancement] programs and activities should be directed at specific audiences with interests in a particular aspect of the institution.[46]

A review of the history of black giving reveals several key themes: personal engagement, giving back, and uplifting the race. These themes help in understanding motivations for black giving as well as to overcome obstacles to successful fund raising among alumni.

For African Americans, trust is particularly important when making monetary contributions.[47] Although a personal relationship with potential donors is helpful when working with the white community, it is essential in the black community. The experience of blacks in the United States—that of discrimination—makes them less inclined to trust unfamiliar institutions and their representatives.[48] Instead, the record shows that blacks give in settings that inspire their trust. When a revered figure in the community, such as a pastor, makes an appeal on behalf of a charitable cause, blacks are more likely to contribute. African Americans are motivated and mobilized by their clergy, beginning at an early age. The message conveyed is personal and consistent. The obligation to give, and the call to uplift the race, originally came from the pulpit in the black church.[49]

The same kind of personal appeal that explains the success of the black church is present in black "elite" organizations, fraternities, and sororities. If their friends belong to, or are willing to give to, a particular organization, African Americans are more likely to get involved.[50] Although often unnoticed by the nonblack community, these organizations have clearly been successful in raising funds and organizing the donation of time and resources.[51]

When African Americans give they favor causes that uplift their race. This pattern was established during the antebellum period when blacks banded together in support of mutual aid societies, abolitionist movements, and fraternal organizations. The tradition continues today with the support of institutions such as the United Negro College Fund, the National Urban League, historically black colleges, and the NAACP. However, racial uplift could also include support for a PWI that is producing a cadre of influential black leaders or is paying special attention to pertinent black issues. Historical data also shows that African-American donors respond to urgent needs in their community (e.g., the Civil Rights Movement).[52] They are motivated by tangible, concrete causes and are frustrated when they are not kept informed as to how their contributions are being used. This has made raising endowment monies difficult in the black community. African Americans want to see the results of their giving, and endowments are not visible on the campus during alumni gatherings.[53]

Recommendations

> When [colleges and universities] have involved all those who share the purposes of their institution and can contribute to them, they will indeed have realized [Henry T.] Heald's description of the alumni as the salvation of higher education.[54]

If advancement personnel tap into the motivations for black giving, they will enhance their ability to garner funds from their alumni.[55] An awareness of these motivations and the creation of fund-raising campaigns that speak to these motivations will bolster the response of black college alumni. In order to cultivate more alumni giving within the African-American community, the author offers the following recommendations:

1. Give black alumni a sense of ownership in the university. Draw them into the institution—perhaps by including them on important committees and at intimate gatherings. Far too often, black alumni are asked to "stay on the porch." Invite them into the alumni family. It is evident from the research that African Americans contribute to organizations and causes to which they have a strong connection.

2. Colleges and universities can benefit from the lessons of African-American churches, which nurture philanthropic giving from a young age. With this in mind, it is important to educate black students on alumni giving. Include discussions pertaining to university philanthropic support at convocations, student activities, and athletic events. Create student alumni councils, with black representatives, to nurture the spirit of giving in students prior to their departure from an institution. Potential black donors are more likely to give to their alma mater if they are familiar with the giving process and trusting of the institution's goals.

3. *Ask* African-American alumni for support. Too often, black alumni are not asked to give to their alma mater on a regular basis. Organizations that benefit from the most successful African-American giving are those that continually ask for support (e.g., the black church).

4. Once African-American donors make a contribution, maintain communication with them and inform them of the effect of their gift. Knowing that their gift was used for the intended purpose may motivate them to give again. Publicize the nature of their gift in alumni magazines, perhaps side by side with their stated motivations for giving.

5. As demonstrated by the research, African-American organizations have considerable influence on their members and may be able to assist an institution in its fund-raising efforts. Consider group-giving activities that show potential donors who else is donating to one's institution. Typically advancement staffs have organized opportunities for specific classes or traditionally white fraternities/sororities to give in unison. It would be advantageous to do the same for black groups. Tapping into black organizations can link a university, for example, to a network of black giving that is strong, organized, and stretches from state to state (i.e., elite organizations, fraternities, and sororities).

6. The most successful fund-raising efforts among African Americans have been those geared toward the uplifting of the race. Advancement publications need to focus on campus policies and practices that support progress within the black campus community and highlight African-American alumni successes. Black alumni profiles should be used in African-American-specific publications as well as general publications. Knowing that friends or classmates gave to the institution may motivate other African Americans to give.

7. Design specific publicity materials to appeal to black alumni.[56] This is not to say that general publicity materials should not speak to black alumni; however, targeted publicity is effective. Use language that speaks to their concerns—future leaders in the African-American community, a better racial climate on the campus, and diversity among the faculty and students.

These issues, on a larger scale, are those that have been emphasized historically by black social, educational, and political organizations.

8. Help your advancement staff to acquire an understanding of issues of importance to the African-American donor. This can be accomplished by reading *Black Issues in Higher Education*, the *Journal of Blacks in Higher Education*, and popular magazines such as *Savoy*, and *Ebony*. The black newspapers found in many large metropolitan areas are also an important resource. Caring about the interests of black alumni and conveying this message aids in the establishment of trust with the potential donor.

9. Draw attention to campus improvements that are important to African Americans, such as a new black culture center, library collections, art collections, new black faculty, and academic programs. Communicate these changes to black alumni.

10. Learn from the success stories of African-American giving: the United Negro College Fund, Spelman College, and Hampton University have all completed very successful fund-raising campaigns. Just as much can be learned from a historical examination of black giving, these current examples offer valuable information on black giving.

11. Most importantly, gauge the public attitudes regarding the climate for African Americans on campus. Talk to young alumni and current students about their experiences on campus. If their experiences were or are negative, they will not support the institution. Make it a priority to change the racial climate on campus—it affects alumni just as much as it affects current students. Again, if black alumni feel that their alma mater is contributing to the uplift of the race they will be more likely to give.

Acknowledgement

An earlier version of this paper was presented at the Southern History of Education Society in Atlanta, Georgia. The author would like to thank Vida Avery, Sibby Anderson-Thompkins, Serena Wilson, Nia Woods Haydel, and Edward Epstein for their comments on several earlier versions of this paper.

Notes

1. R. L. Lowenstein (1997), *Pragmatic Fund-Raising for College Administrators and Development Officers*, University Press of Florida, Gainsville, p. 31.
2. U.S. Census Bureau, (2001) Census Tables, http://www.census.gov/prod/2000pubs/p60–209.pdf, May 1, 2001.
3. M. Fischer (1997), "Respecting the individual, valuing diversity. Equity in philanthropy and fund raising," in D. Burlingame (Ed.), *Critical Issues in Fund Raising*, John Wiley & Sons, New York, pp. 65–74.
4. B. E. Brittingham and T. R. Pezzullo (1990), *The Campus Green. Fund Raising in Higher Education*, ASHE-ERIC Higher Education Report No. 1, The George Washington University, Washington, DC; F. E. Andrews (1953), *Attitudes Toward Giving*, Russell Sage Foundation, New York.
5. B. Smith, S. Shue, J. L. Vest, and J. Villarreal (1999), *Philanthropy in Communities of Color*, Indiana University Press, Bloomington, IN; Council on Foundations (1999), *Cultures of Caring: Philanthropy in Diverse American Communities*, Council on Foundations, Washington, DC.
6. Fischer (1997), "Respecting the individual, valuing diversity," p. 65.
7. R. Thomas (1994), "Managing diversity and the philanthropic community," *Advancing Philanthropy*, 2, pp. 31–3.
8. Brittingham and Pezzullo (1990), *The Campus Green*.
9. J. D. Anderson (1988), *The Education of Blacks in the South, 1860–1935*, University of North Carolina Press, Chapel Hill, NC.
10. H. T. Heald, Ford Foundation, 1960, cited in R. A. Reichley (1986), "The alumni movement: An overview," in A. Westley Rowland. (Ed), *Handbook of Institutional Advancement*, Jossey-Bass, San Francisco, pp. 275–6.
11. Reichley (1986), "The alumni movement."
12. Ibid., p. 278.
13. *Chronicle of Higher Education* (2000–2001), Almanac.
14. C. E. Lincoln and L. H. Mamiya (1990), *The Black Church in the African American Experience*, Duke University Press, Durham, North Carolina, p. 242. See also J. A. Joseph (1995), *Remaking America. How the Benevolent Traditions of Many Cultures are Transforming Our National Life*, Jossey-Bass, San Francisco.

15. Smith et al. (1999), *Philanthropy in Communities*, p. 10.
16. Ibid; A. Byrd (Ed) (1990), *Philanthropy and the Black Church*, Council on Foundations, Washington, DC; E. F. Frazier (1963), *The Negro Church in America*, Schocken Books, New York; C. E. Lincoln (1974), *The Black Church Since Frazier*, Schocken Books, New York; E. F. Frazier (1997), *Black Bourgeoisie*, Free Press Paperbacks, Simon & Schuster, New York.
17. M. A. Abbe (2000), "The roots of minority giving. Understand the philanthropic traditions of different cultures to solicit them more effectively," *CASE Currents*, July, at http://www.case.org/currents.
18. Ibid., p. 4.
19. Lincoln and Mamiya (1990), *The Black Church*.
20. D. Garrow (1987), *Philanthropy and the Civil Rights Movement*, Center for the Study of Philanthropy, New York.
21. E. Anderson and A. A. Moss, Jr, (1999), *Dangerous Donations. Northern Philanthropy and Southern Black Education, 1902–1930*, University of Missouri Press, Columbia.
22. Lincoln and Mamiya (1990), *The Black Church*; E. Brooks Higginbotham (1993), *Righteous Discontent. The Women's Movement in the Black Baptist Church 1880–1920*, Harvard University Press, Cambridge, MA.
23. Smith et al. (1999), *Philanthropy in Communities*, p. 9.
24. Anderson and Moss (1999), *Dangerous Donations*.
25. Lincoln and Mamiya (1990), *The Black Church*.
26. E. D. Carson (1989), *A Charitable Appeals Fact Book: How Black and White Americans Respond to Different Types of Fund-Raising Efforts*, Joint Center for Political Studies, Washington, DC; E. D. Carson (1993), *A Hand Up: Black Philanthropy and Self-Help in America*, Joint Center for Political and Economic Studies Press, Washington, DC; E. D. Carson (1989), "Black philanthropy: Shaping tomorrow's nonprofit sector," *The NSFRE Journal*, Summer, pp. 23–31; E. D. Carson (1987), "Despite long history, black philanthropy gets little credit as 'self-help' tool," *Focus*, 15, 6, pp. 3, 4, 76.
27. Smith et al. (1999), *Philanthropy in Communities*.
28. Lincoln and Mamiya (1990), *The Black Church*. See also V. P. Franklin (1992), *Black Self-Determination: A History of African American Resistance*, Lawrence Hill Books, New York.
29. Smith et al. (1999), *Philanthropy in Communities*, p. 11.
30. L. O. Graham (2000), *Our Kind of People. Inside America's Black Upper Class*, HarperPerennial, New York.
31. B. Gordon (1998), *Bazaars and Fair Ladies. The History of the American Fundraising Fair*, The University of Tennessee Press, Knoxville, TN.
32. Graham (2000), *Our Kind of People*, p. 113.
33. Links, Inc. (2001), publicity materials.
34. N. Haydel, personal communication, July 12, 2001.
35. Graham (2000), *Our Kind of People*.
36. Anderson (1988), *The Education of Blacks in the South*, p. 15.
37. M. G. Goodson (Ed.) (1991), *Chronicles of Faith: The Autobiography of Frederick D. Patterson*, The University of Alabama Press, Tuscaloosa, AL, p. 135.
38. Abbe (2000), "The roots of minority giving."
39. L. C. Ross, Jr. (2000), *The Divine Nine. The History of the African American Fraternities and Sororities*, Kensington Publishing, New York; Smith et al. (1999), *Philanthropy in Communities*.
40. Ibid.
41. N. Haydel, personal communication, July 12, 2001.
42. Ibid.
43. Graham (1999), *Our Kind of People*, p. 85; see also M.-F. Winters (1999), "Reflections on endowment building in the African American community," in Council on Foundations, *Cultures of Caring. Philanthropy in Diverse American Communities*, Council on Foundations, Washington, DC; W. B. Gatewood (1990), *Aristocrats of Color: the Black Elite, 1925–1960*, Indiana University Press, Bloomington, IN.
44. New York University Black Family Reunion (2001), *www.clubs.nyu.edu/detail.cfm* (March 2, 2001).
45. Smith et al. (1999), *Philanthropy in Communities*, p. 12.
46. E. E. Rydell (1986), "External relations," in A. W. Rowland (Ed), *Handbook of Institutional Advancement*, Jossey-Bass, San Francisco, pp. 47–59.
47. Smith et al. (1999), *Philanthropy in Communities*.
48. Abbe (2000), "The roots of minority giving."
49. Lincoln and Mamiya (1990), *The Black Church*.
50. P. G. Schervish (1997), "Inclination, obligation, and association. What we know and what we need to learn about donor motivation," in D. F. Burlingame (Ed.) *Critical Issues in Fundraising*, John Wiley & Sons, New York, pp. 110–38.

51. S. A. Ostrander and P. G. Schervish (1990), "Giving and getting: Philanthropy as a social relation," in J. Van Til (Ed.), *Critical Issues in American Philanthropy: Strengthening Theory and Practice*, Jossey-Bass, San Francisco.
52. Smith et al. (1999), *Philanthropy in Communities*.
53. E. L. Yates (2001), "Capital campaigns," *Black Issues in Higher Education*, 18, 10, pp. 18–27.
54. Reichley (1986), "The alumni movement," p. 285.
55. L. L. Leslie (1985), "What appeals to whom? Donors respond to different approaches," *CASE Currents*, 11, 7, pp. 34–7.
56. A. R. Crawford (1986), "Publications for key audiences," in A. W. Rowland (Ed) *Handbook of Institutional Advancement*, Jossey-Bass, San Francisco, pp. 389–98.

Practitioners' Perspectives

As a white fund-raising practitioner at a predominantly white institution (PWI) (in a predominantly white state), this practitioner found the author's study of African-American philanthropy both revealing and obvious.

This practitioner had little knowledge or understanding of the traditions of black giving, rooted in the church, based on a firmly held belief in giving back to the community and always influenced by the desire to lift up the black race by supporting black causes. Likewise, she was unaware of differences in black and white sororities and fraternities (with black Greeks considering their organizations to have an even greater importance after graduation as a forum to fight racism), as well as the particular role that black social service agencies and opinion leaders play in framing black giving.

Being sensitive to these nuances and aware of these distinct motivations will no doubt assist anyone charged with raising money is to build relationship, or a bridge with the donor or prospect. The first rule of relationship building is to establish a common ground, an understanding of the person(s) being reached out to.

With that being said, some of the author's recommendations for cultivating increased giving among black alumni are not different than what one would suggest for alumni of all races. Educating African-American alumni on the fund-raising and financial needs of the university as well as its goals, maintaining communication with them, particularly about the effect of their gift considering group giving activities that show potential donors who else is donating to a particular university capitalizing on connections black alumni have giving black alumni a sense of ownership in the university and highlighting African-American success stories, are sound strategies foundational— strategies—for practitioners working with any lace of alumni. If these basis aren't being covered one would suggest it is a result of an immature fund-raising program more than an insensitivity to distinct motivations within a particular population.

Still the author makes a final recommendation—a key to black fund-raising success—that one would suspect is easily overlooked on many white campuses. Most importantly gauge the public attitudes regarding the climate for African Americans on campus. Tall to young alumni and current students about their experiences on campus. If their experiences were or are negative they will not support the institution. Make it a priority to change the racial climate on campus.

That is s tall order and one that cannot be accomplished solely by the advancement staff. To overlook it though, is to for felt the lifelong affiliation financial support and goodwill of the preferred stockholders of the enterprise.

Joan Nesbitt
Direclor of Major Gifts,
University of Tulsa

Indians Giving: The New Philanthropy in Indian Country

Marjane Ambler

Abstract (Document Summary)

Such confusion represents one of many barriers to giving in Indian Country. Philanthropists provide disproportionately few grants for Indian causes, and sometimes those are ineffective. This is true despite good intentions: Ever since contact, at least some Europeans have been concerned enough about the welfare of their indigenous neighbors to make substantial monetary gifts. The importance of these contributions cannot be overstated; they helped save Indian people from possible extinction. Yet initially their objective was akin to Richard Henry Pratt's goal at the Carlisle Indian School—to make "real Americans" out of Indians. Essentially, that goal for philanthropic efforts continued: To help the Indian people become more like their benefactors—educated and prosperous.

Referring to the number of Indian people on boards of foundations, Lucille Echohawk (Pawnee) says, "Although it's not happening fast enough, we've come a long way." A couple dozen Indian people serve on foundation staffs—enough that they and the Indian board members formed an organization in 1990. Native Americans in Philanthropy (NAP), an affinity group of the Council on Foundations, is based in Lumberton, North Carolina. Echohawk, a director at the Council of Energy Resource Tribes, and Elouise Cobell (Blackfeet) both serve on the board of Women and Foundations/ Corporate Philanthropy, which co-sponsored a meeting with NAP between Native women and foundations on the Flathead Reservation in October 1993. To help them with Indian projects, more foundations have begun visiting reservations and establishing Indian advisory councils.

The collaborative will regrant about two-thirds of the money to projects, and most of the rest will go toward technical assistance. Technical assistance represents a key objective of the collaborative. "Many of the letters of intent we have received would have been denied outright by foundations even though the ideas are good," says [Sherry Salway Black]. Instead, the collaborative staff calls applicants to discuss program development issues and questions that funding officers might ask. "They are so thankful for even a phone call," Salway Black says. "Foundations' officers don't have the time and don't have the mandate."

Indians Giving: The New Philanthropy in Indian Country

In the nation's mind, two images compete. One, a tiny, ragged American Indian child with enormous eyes, accompanied by a plea for food and shoes. The other, a well dressed Mashantucket Pequot handing over a check for $10 million to the National Museum of the American Indian. No wonder people find the subject of American Indians and philanthropy bewildering.

Such confusion represents one of many barriers to giving in Indian Country. Philanthropists provide disproportionately few grants for Indian causes, and sometimes those are ineffective. This is true despite good intentions: Ever since contact, at least some Europeans have been concerned enough about the welfare of their indigenous neighbors to make substantial monetary gifts. The importance of these contributions cannot be overstated; they helped save Indian people from possible extinction. Yet initially their objective was akin to Richard Henry Pratt's goal at the Carlisle Indian School—to make "real Americans" out of Indians. Essentially, that goal for philanthropic efforts continued: To help the Indian people become more like their benefactors—educated and prosperous.

Nevertheless, the first Americans today rank dead last in monetary, health, and education statistics. Although many foundations have enjoyed fruitful projects, others have been frustrated by projects that died after the seed money was gone and by an apparent lack of commitment by participants, who neglected to file reports or to attend project meetings.

Why? What barriers stand in the way of effective philanthropy in Indian Country? A small but growing number of foundations are working with Indian organizations and communities to answer those questions. They are helping to finance models conceived by Indian people, five of which are discussed in this issue (the Seventh Generation Fund, the American Indian College Fund, the Eagle Staff Fund Collaborative, the Michigan Native American Foundation, and a Montana Community Foundation project on the Blackfeet Reservation).

At the same time, some foundations are initiating changes in their own organizations to better hear the Native voice. They are finding Native people with ideas about how to rebuild individual self-esteem and reservation social and economic health.

Referring to the number of Indian people on boards of foundations, Lucille Echohawk (Pawnee) says, "Although it's not happening fast enough, we've come a long way." A couple dozen Indian people serve on foundation staffs—enough that they and the Indian board members formed an organization in 1990. Native Americans in Philanthropy (NAP), an affinity group of the Council on Foundations, is based in Lumberton, North Carolina. Echohawk, a director at the Council of Energy Resource Tribes, and Elouise Cobell (Blackfeet) both serve on the board of Women and Foundations/Corporate Philanthropy, which co-sponsored a meeting with NAP between Native women and foundations on the Flathead Reservation in October 1993. To help them with Indian projects, more foundations have begun visiting reservations and establishing Indian advisory councils.

By listening, the foundations are discovering that the capabilities, the needs, and the cultures of the 500 tribes differ. Some tribes have casinos and can afford to assist not only their own people but also their neighbors. Others have to choose between sending a child to Head Start or an adult for dialysis treatment. By listening, foundations are being reminded they can't just go to the reservation communities and say, "I've got the solution, what's your problem?" Such generic ideas do not suit the individual circumstances. Nor does a community feel committed to a project if the foundations name is the only one over the door.

On the Fort Peck Reservation in northeastern Montana, for example, the unemployment rate jumped to 70 percent when the tribal industry shut down. "If someone offered us a $50,000 grant to count cans on the highway, we would take it, even if we questioned the value of counting cans. It puts people to work," says James Shanley (Assiniboine), president of Fort Peck Community College and a veteran fundraiser.

"But when the money dies, the solution dies, too, because people who receive it don't necessarily believe in the program," he says.

Another veteran fundraiser, Norbert S. Hill, Jr., (Oneida) says, "I question whether we need foundations to provide ambulances to pick up bodies at the bottom of the cliff or fences at the top to keep us from jumping." Hill is the executive director and principal fundraiser for the American Indian Science and Engineering Society and the head of a family foundation. He says, "We've been picking up bodies for 500 years. We need to empower people so they don't jump."

Ask a typical foundation program officer what the biggest problem is in Indian Country, the answer will likely be poverty. Many Indian experts agree with Buffy Sainte-Marie, who says the biggest problem is low self-esteem. People without self-esteem tend to jump.

What makes a good fence? What is just an ambulance approach? How can degrading charity be transformed into empowering philanthropy? How can anyone bridge the cultural gap separating the foundation culture from those of the tribes? Aware of the wealth of a few casino tribes, some philanthropists say they are considering opting out, leaving Indian problems in the laps of Indian philanthropists and such questions unanswered. Outside benefactors will always be needed, however, to provide both ambulances and fences. Thus tactics for effective assistance must be discovered.

The models created by Indian people themselves provide some answers. In addition to the five featured here, other nonprofit organizations with Indian boards and/or staffs also help direct gifts toward effective: programs. Native people active in philanthropy offer suggestions for future models, as will be discussed later.

Each of the models provides distinct mechanisms for addressing various barriers to effective philanthropy. They target disparate groups and differ in their political viewpoints. Participants in the models even vary in what they call themselves—Indians or Natives. Two specifically address the need to increase philanthropic efforts by Indians for Indians.

The models hold several essential qualities in common: They affirm rather than undercut tribal cultures; they build self-esteem instead of dependence and shame; and Indian people control decision making. Such models make it easier for foundations and corporate givers to learn about Indian Country and thus to fund the right proposals.

Seventh Generation Fund

Since its creation seventeen years ago, the Seventh Generation Fund for Indian Development, Inc., has filled a unique niche. It funnels grant funds into Native communities for work that once would have been called anti-establishment. The late Daniel Bomberry (Salish-Cayuga) established the public foundation under the name of Tribal Sovereignty in 1976. Now based in Arcata, California, the fund has an all-Native board and an all-Native staff, making it perhaps the only national Native foundation, according to Donna Chavis of Native Americans in Philanthropy. Its name derives from the Great Law of the Iroquois Confederacy—to consider the impact of every decision on the seventh generation.

Despite its small staff and relatively low budget, the fund has had a far reaching impact. "Our purpose is to keep Native people Native," according to Executive Director Chris Peters (Yurok-Karuk). "Much of the nonprofit world is oriented toward improving Natives' socio-economic status by Euro-American standards," according to Peters, who has been on the staff since 1989. In contrast, he says, "We do what we can to not empower mainstreaming."

Although the Seventh Generation Fund has a community development component, it focuses most of its efforts upon sustaining traditional customs and traditional communities. Most of its grants are small, starting with the price of an airline ticket and averaging $3,000–$5,000. The grants support efforts such as opposing nuclear waste dumping on reservations, supporting religious freedom, and renewing language and culture. At least two grants have gone to projects sponsored by tribal colleges. Seventh Generation has provided support for the Hopi Foundation, a small foundation established by Hopi community members in 1985, whose main emphasis now is providing solar panels to Hopi villages that refuse to depend upon outside sources of electricity. In recent years, the fund has supported what Peters calls an especially neglected arena—Natives in Central and South America. In 1993, it helped sponsor Earth Day when the theme included honoring indigenous peoples.

It is harder to raise money for such causes than for business development, Peters says. (A study commissioned by Native Americans in Philanthropy confirmed that the largest area of foundations' giving from 1984–1989 was under the broad category of "development." The next largest was education.) Contributions and grants to the Seventh Generation Fund each year total about half a million dollars, Peters says. The staff leverages more dollars into Indian Country by helping local people with fundraising strategies and by advocating on their behalf to foundations. Often the fund has provided the first outside help for projects that became national models, Peters says.

Because the communities it serves face immediate crises, fattening the endowment fund is not a priority. "I try to get as much as possible into the communities instead. Ultimately, in the long run it would be better to have a several million dollar endowment. But endowment funds are difficult to raise, and our staff is very small (four and a half people)," Peters says. Consequently, the Seventh Generation endowment totals $306,000.

The Seventh Generation board is made up of Native activists. Mindful of their credibility among traditional Native communities, the board would not accept money from just anyone, Peters says. The board is adamant against the casino industry, for example. "We would have problems with taking money from casinos—or from Union Carbide or Standard Oil," he says. Despite its iconoclasm, the Seventh Generation Fund has attracted support from major foundations such as MacArthur, Mott, Veatch, as well as Lannan.

Each year through the Combined Federal Campaign, the fund receives $15,000–$20,000 in payroll deductions, some of which no doubt derives from Indian employees of federal agencies. Peters does not believe in trying to raise money from the grassroots communities in which the organization works. "The resource base is not there. There is a lot of giving within extended families and communities; they would be digging into pockets that are nearly empty. To seek foundation support from them would be asking too much," he says.

American Indian College Fund

In the late 1980s, the nation's tribal college presidents realized they needed a new way to raise funds. Although the first college had been created by the Navajo Tribe in 1968 and there were 26 tribal colleges by 1988, few people knew they existed. Nor was it easy to explain to potential funders the rationale behind their dual mission: teaching both academic and cultural classes.

Each tribal college's funding from Congress and short-term grants vacillated from year to year; but the students, faculty, and accreditation boards required continuity. The colleges' individual endowment funds (created by Congress in 1983) were too small to provide any assurance of continuity. Fighting daily for enough money to keep their doors open, the colleges individually could not afford expensive fundraising campaigns.

In 1988, the college presidents created the American Indian College Fund (AICF), a tax-exempt, non-profit organization based in New York City. The fund helps both the colleges and the contributors. Foundations and other contributors can deal with a single voice rather than the voices of the 29 colleges that now benefit from the fund. In 1993 alone, the fund spent $1.6 million on public education, in addition to donated time and space. Its sophisticated campaign included direct mail; advertisements on billboards, television, Time magazine, and the New York Times; and cross country speaking tours by the fund's president, who is now Ronald S. McNeil (Lakota). In 1993, AICF raised close to $4 million, half of it from individuals, generally the hardest money to raise. It received grants from 84 corporations and foundations.

As a result of a change made in 1989, the by-laws clearly state that college presidents will always hold a majority on the board, according to AICF Executive Director Barbara Bratone, a non-Indian. Foundations rarely try to impose their own programs upon the fund. "Our by-laws clearly state what our mission is," Bratone says. That mission is providing scholarships and emergency aid to students and creating an endowment. In 1993, AICF awarded $810,000 in such grants, divided equally amongst the 27 colleges. Because of the AICF endowment, the colleges will be able to count on continuing help in the future. The fund has raised $7 million for its general endowment, almost half of its goal of $15 million. When the goal is reached, all the revenue from the endowment will be available to the colleges for scholarships and developmental needs.

By supporting the students, the college fund supports the colleges indirectly, but it does not alleviate their serious cash problems. The colleges and their organization, the American Indian Higher Education Consortium, must raise their own capital expansion and operation funds. With many foundations reluctant to provide endowment funds, some of the colleges cannot even raise enough for their individual endowments to earn federal matching dollars. James Shanley (Assiniboine), chairman of the AICF board, believes foundations should rethink this. "Five hundred thousand dollars in an endowment in the long run is much more effective than the same amount in a program grant," he says.

Both the fundraising campaign and the allocation of grants reflect the thinking of the American Indian College Fund's board of directors. Publicity material focuses upon students' achievements, their bright, smiling faces appealing for partners, not pity. Instead of trying to make potential donors feel guilty, as charity drives often do, the advertisements elicit respect and pride: "Help Save a Culture that Could Save Ours."

Shanley says Native studies have been largely ignored by the private sector in the past, with pressure from some foundations to focus upon math and science instead. However, AICF applied for and was awarded a $775,000 challenge grant from the National Endowment for the Humanities to establish a $3 million Native studies endowment. The colleges recognize the importance of the sciences, and they see no conflict. "They (outsiders) cannot imagine electrical engineers who can speak their own language and practice their own culture and traditions," he says. The colleges have a more holistic perspective. Shanley points out, for example, that emerging technologies benefit cultural studies. Several Native language programs across the country utilize CD-ROM and other computer technology.

Some have questioned the board's insistence upon allocating AICF funds equally among the colleges, which vary greatly in their size and their neediness. Shanley says, "Equity is absolutely essential to the future of the college fund. . . . Everyone had special needs that could be used to divide the funds. If we have equity, there is never any argument." Shanley says the policy derives from Indian tribes' cultural values of sharing and caring. "It is very democratic. Everyone is equal. By maintaining equity, we enable ourselves to share and care into the future," he says.

Eagle Staff Fund Collaborative

In October of 1993, the First Nations Development Institute announced the most ambitious effort yet to reform philanthropy in Indian Country. The Eagle Staff Fund: a Collaborative for Native American Development. During more than fifteen years as a Native ambassador to the world of foundations, Rebecca Adamson (Cherokee) frequently heard foundations express concern that they had not received Indian proposals directed at the structural causes of native American poverty. Adamson is the founder and president of First Nations Development Institute, a national native American economic development organization based in Fredericksburg, Virginia.

First Nations designed the Eagle Staff collaborative to address that concern and to help bridge the gaps in understanding between the foundation world and the Indian people. In the past, she said, foundations have required applicants to adopt assimilationist goals. The collaborative asks grant applicants to attack poverty with culturally appropriate strategies. Instead of forcing Indian people to disregard their cultural values, the collaborative requires applicants to use such values as the foundation of grant proposals.

Both funders and applicants have responded favorably to the three-year pilot program, according to Sherry Salway Black, director of the Eagle Staff collaborative and vice president of First Nations. The collaborative had received over 500 requests for guidelines by September 1994. Although the collaborative had to reduce its goal from $12 million down to $10 million, it had already raised half of that amount—$5 million—by then.

First Nations spent years laying the groundwork for the initiative. Both Adamson and Salway Black have extensive involvement in philanthropy, with Salway Black on the Hitachi Foundation board and Adamson on the Ms. Foundation board. Contributing foundations include mostly faces familiar in Indian Country with a few new ones: Charles Stewart Mort, Ford, W.K. Kellogg, William and Flora Hewlett, U.S. WEST, Fannie Mae, Coca-Cola, Hitachi, Bay, Tides, Joyce, and Levi Strauss as of May 1994.

The collaborative will regrant about two-thirds of the money to projects, and most of the rest will go toward technical assistance. Technical assistance represents a key objective of the collaborative. "Many of the letters of intent we have received would have been denied outright by foundations even though the ideas are good," says Salway Black. Instead, the collaborative staff calls applicants to discuss program development issues and questions that funding officers might ask. "They are so thankful for even a phone call," Salway Black says. "Foundations' officers don't have the time and don't have the mandate."

If the proposal does not fit the collaborative's criteria, the staff tries to direct applicants to other funders. To receive funding, proposals must have an economic focus. Educational institutions or health clinics can apply, but only if the project would help them become self-supporting, according to Salway Black. Applicants need not be tax exempt, but they must be controlled by native Americans. The collaborative does not fund endowments. To meet the needs of both sophisticated tribal institutions and individuals with the nucleus of an idea, the collaborative offers four different levels of grants, ranging from a minimum of $5,000 to a maximum of $150,000 per year.

The three-year pilot will educate both participating foundations and applicants about one another's worlds. Foundation representatives serve on the grants review committee along side Eagle Staff board members, who are all native Americans except one. Periodically, program officers from the participating foundations meet with the collaborative to discuss the letters of intent and their ramifications, such as how to recognize good proposals and why the letters might not be as polished as expected. Foundation participants will also visit the reservation sites of potential and selected grantees.

Foundation representatives have told First Nations they like the opportunity to support such an innovative approach while spreading the risk over several projects and among several foundations. How much they like the idea will be demonstrated after three years when they will decide whether to fund the Eagle Staff Fund for its full ten-year term.

Eventually, Salway Black says, the collaborative would like to raise money from casino tribes also. "It would be ideal to have tribes sitting around the table as funders, too, being philanthropic with our own people," she says.

Community Foundations: Browning Beacon Project

Giving is nothing new to Blackfeet tribal members. "You'll find people here who save enough to pay their bills and give the rest away," says Elouise Cobell (Blackfeet). Cobell treasures that quality in her people, and she hopes her work with the Montana Community Foundation will enhance its impact.

The Montana Community Foundation has selected Browning, Montana, as a "beacon community" under a rural initiative of the Ford Foundation. Twenty proposals were submitted to the Montana Community Foundation board, which selected three. The Blackfeet Tribe submitted the proposal for a regional landfill and recycling hub in Browning. The project will involve both Indians and non-Indians. "When you're doing philanthropy, you're not seeing color. You're seeing community and seeing needs," Cobell says.

As a trustee of the tribally owned bank, Cobell is intimately familiar with her community and its needs. In recent years, she has also become familiar with the needs of the foundation world as a board member of the Montana Community Foundation and of Women and Foundations/Corporate Philanthropy.

She sees the Browning project as an opportunity to address the needs of both. Browning, the capital of the Blackfeet Nation, ranks along side other reservation towns in poverty. Yet despite the economic poverty, the Montana Community Foundation board intends—just as other community foundations—to involve local people in philanthropy.

The project leaders will raise money locally toward an endowment, which will be managed by the Montana Community Foundation. In addition, they will depend upon contributions of time by local people like herself, whom Cobell refers to as "philanthropists with no money." Before becoming a board member two years ago, Cobell served for several years as a community representative to the Montana Community Foundation.

The recycling project will also need assistance from other funders outside the community, in addition to Ford's match. The local, personal contributions will build pride and stability in the community, Cobell believes, which has depended too long upon the tribal government to meet all its needs. "The Ford Foundation should be commended for this. They haven't made all those little hoops to jump through. They allow the Montana Community Foundation to do the structuring," Cobell says. The Aspen Institute will give technical assistance to the community foundation for three years.

The project could be a model for community foundations in other states, where their involvement with Native projects varies greatly. In Montana there are seven Indian reservations and in South Dakota there are nine. The South Dakota Community Foundation has included Indian board members since it was established in 1989 because tribal members represent one-fourth of the state's population, according to Art Zimiga (Lakota). A board member there, Zimiga also serves on the national Council of Foundations' committee on community foundations.

The South Dakota Community Foundation has funded several Indian projects on reservations and in cities. Although the work takes time, Zimiga believes it is important for Indian people to get actively involved on community foundation boards. He is executive director of public relations and marketing at Oglala Lakota College.

In New Mexico, with 134,000 American Indians and 22 reservations, no native Americans serve on the board of the New Mexico Community Foundation. The foundation has supported dozens of reservation projects, however, since it was founded in 1980, according to Sue Rundstrom.

Community Foundations: Michigan Native American Foundation

When Carolee Dodge Francis looked at health statistics for Indian people in Michigan, she saw some disturbing trends. Although native American life expectancy was growing gradually, it was still far below that of the general population. "Part of it has to do with funding cycles and the lack of dollars," says Dodge Francis, an Oneida Indian and a county health department employee.

Meanwhile, the gaming revenues of Michigan's tribes were increasing, and some of the tribes were also enjoying the fruits of other good investments. Gaming receipts alone for the seven federally recognized tribes totaled $70.7 million in 1993, according to an economic impact study conducted by the tribes.

"I wanted to see some type of vehicle to allow native American people to insure their health and social services for years to come," says Dodge Francis. To her, the answer was dear: a native American foundation. In 1992, she contacted the tribes and Pat Babcock, program director at the W.K. Kellogg Foundation.

The tribes had already demonstrated their concern for neighboring communities by generous giving. In addition to supporting their own government programs, they paid nearly $6 million in state and federal taxes in 1993 and made donations to charitable causes in other communities such as educational programs, service clubs, athletic events, shelter residences, museums and cultural events.

Six of the seven tribes agreed to form the Michigan Native American Foundation. Kellogg provided technical assistance and a small $10,000 grant for development. Later, Kellogg awarded $150,000 to be used as endowment and for start-up administrative costs. Dodge Francis serves part-time as the administrative liaison for the foundation, which is temporarily being administered through the Michigan Intertribal Council. Funds will be raised from other foundations, the tribes, and tribal payroll deductions. Two more tribes have since won federal recognition, and Dodge Francis hopes they will participate, too. The Grand Traverse Band of Ottawa and Chippewa Indians has chosen not to participate. Within ten years, the foundation hopes to have an $8 million endowment.

Babcock is proud of Kellogg's participation in what he says is the first endowed foundation involving several tribes, and he hopes other foundations will support the Michigan tribes' foundation, too. Babcock says, "We see it as a way to stimulate new philanthropic activity by foundations and develop the concept of philanthropy in native American communities."

The seven tribes have discussed several possible priorities for the foundation, including the elderly, substance abuse, cardio-vascular disease, diabetes, smoking, and hypertension. "We want to preserve the traditional and cultural family values and at the same time improve minimum social and health conditions," Dodge Francis says.

The tribes' new creation is a "community foundation" serving the community of native American families within the state. The Internal Revenue Service classifies it as a "public charity" with 501(c)(3) status. The tribal chairs of each of the participating tribes will sit on the board along with four at-large board members with expertise in areas such as Native traditions, banking, or philanthropy. The four do not have to be Native.

A foundation provides a strategic vehicle for giving as well as tax advantages, Dodge Francis says. The board can set short and long-term objectives and evaluate progress toward those objectives, somewhat separate from the political arena. It can also leverage additional contributions into the reservations.

"The foundation is now an infant and needs to take small steps. But five to ten years from now I expect it to be making major contributions to the Native communities in Michigan," says Dodge Francis.

Future of Philanthropy in Indian Country

Indian philanthropy experts expect more collaboration and more giving by Indians in the future. "Tribal foundations are a fast growing trend, and not all related to gaming," according to Donna Chavis of Native Americans in Philanthropy. Chavis receives a telephone call each week from someone considering establishing a foundation, both from tribes, including the Mashantucket Pequot Tribe in Connecticut, and from other Indian groups. In most cases the foundations plan to seek support from other foundations as well as from tribes.

In interviews with Tribal College, several Indian philanthropy experts mentioned the need for a national Indian-controlled foundation, making grants to Indians and receiving some of its funds from Indians. Sherry Salway Black also would like to see a national alternative giving program similar to Earthshare where donations would be sought from the nation at large and would be divided amongst many different Indian organizations.

Gaming will never solve all of the needs in Indian Country, despite flamboyant gifts such as the Mashantucket Pequot Tribe's $10 million to the National Museum of the American Indian last October. Less than 20 percent of the tribes in the nation have casinos, and none net as much as the Pequot's Foxwoods Casino. Because of political pressures and the growing number of non-Indian gaming enterprises, most experts predict only a few years of significant revenues for many tribes.

Individuals and tribes involved in philanthropy must be oriented toward the future, which makes endowments especially important. A growing number of Indian organizations have established endowment funds, including the American Indian Science and Engineering Society, the Native American Rights Fund, the tribal colleges, and those models previously mentioned.

Philanthropy work requires people who can build hope and self-esteem, according to Art Zimiga of Oglala Lakota College. "We need to have people who can close their eyes and see us as prosperous people living healthier lifestyles. We need that type of vision to help start local community foundations to work on economic development, quality of life, health, and environmental stewardship. We have to have vision," he says.

EDUCATION AND HISPANIC PHILANTHROPY: FAMILY, SACRIFICE, AND COMMUNITY

CHARLES G. RODRIGUEZ

The Hispanic community is stalemated in its progress toward school retention and graduation. For too many years academic dropout rates have hovered close to 50 percent, even as the total Hispanic population continues to grow rapidly. From the perspective of dollars contributed, philanthropy among Hispanics is modest and not increasing relative to the community's demographic growth. This chapter offers a more comprehensive definition of philanthropy and, with it, the hope that Hispanics might reassess their strengths and forfeit debilitating attitudes. Hispanic philanthropy in dollar terms may well depend on working out sacrifice philanthropy in their hearts and minds.

MAMA ROSA: This meeting won't take too long. The principal will be ready to talk with me as soon as he gets done with that telephone call. Now, don't be nervous sitting here, *mi hijo*. We'll get this right, you'll see. You're not embarrassed that I'm doing this, are you?

HIJO CARLITOS: No, mom. It's just that the high school counselor said I had to take wood and auto shop and there is nothing else to talk about. Do you think the principal will let me take college prep courses with my friends?

MAMA ROSA: You just watch. *Mi hijo* has a B+ average and is not going to be kept out of college prep courses. *De ninguna manera*. You watch. I'll talk with the principal, you'll see. . . .

Ask hispanic graduates from college who it was that nurtured their enthusiasm for academic achievement. Most will say mom, or an older sister, or perhaps papá. The truth of this became evident for me as I sat with my Mama Rosa at Eisenhower High School in Rialto, California, in 1967. The turning point was her standing up to the "professional" counselors who had consigned me to a general studies class schedule in tenth grade in spite of my good grades. Although she maintained her usual patient and courteous demeanor, Mama Rosa turned into an unyielding advocate for her son; we didn't leave the principal's office that day until I had been scheduled for college prep classes.

Says Roberto Villarreal, M.D., "Lots of people ask what motivated me to become a medical doctor. My mom was always on my case to study, do my homework, and get great grades—not just the minimum. And if I didn't do well, I'd have a big price to pay. She was demanding! It was easier on me to study hard than face her correction when mom saw me bring home a bad grade from school. Truly, I never even thought about missing school. Are you kidding? The studying hard just became a habit. After a while, she didn't need to be supervising my academic progress anymore. Then I was on autopilot. Yet, I still wanted to please her by bringing home good grades. It was mom's influence that made the difference for me" (Roberto Villarreal, associate director, South Texas Health Research Center, San Antonio, interview with author, January 1999).

There are now thousands of such stories. Hispanic professionals and college presidents serving with distinction today all have stories similar to the two noted. However, tens of thousands of other stories tell of how the road to college is actually obstructed by Hispanic parents.

Says Kenia Magallanes, "Mine was a traditional Mexican American household in Brawley, California. Mom and stepfather wanted me to stay at home and commute to a local community college. My stepdad thought I was just going to get pregnant and drop out of school. They didn't know why I had to go so far away. We had so many arguments over this" (Reisberg, 1999).

The attitude toward college that Kenia's parents communicated was overtly negative. Maybe that negative attitude was based on different cultural expectations for boys and girls. Perhaps it reflects other cultural-social dynamics, thus precluding a close comparison with the first two stories. What it does show is the tremendous impact that the attitudes held by Hispanic parents have on the academic success and economic future of their children. Dr. Villarreal and I were blessed with parents who not only expected us to go to college but became personally involved and relentless, removing barriers, and then demanding the best performances we could give. Kenia Magallanes's ongoing challenge is to stay in college, despite previously persistent objections from her parents. Other Hispanic students face obstacles less vocal, but equally real and very discouraging.

Hispanic School Dropout Rate Parallels Perceived Shallowness of Hispanic Philanthropy

The high dropout rate from school among Hispanics has resisted improvement for several decades. Hispanics drop out at nearly double the rate of other major population groups and find themselves not as well prepared and less frequently hired for jobs that pay well. For society, this means an ever-growing economic underclass in an increasingly competitive job market. Hispanics face challenging obstacles to attaining middle-class status, not the least of which is academic underachievement.

For philanthropy in America, the Hispanic dropout problem coupled with the Hispanic community's rapid population increase is creating a group of outsiders that is growing exponentially. This group requires, in aggregate, an increasing amount of tax-supported child assistance and emergency health services. The overall number of "safety net" program dependencies increases as Hispanic school dropout numbers continue to grow. At the same time, there is a corresponding reduction in the overall percentage of Americans with disposable incomes sufficient to help others and fortify the economy as net contributors to the tax-paying and gift-making bases. This state of affairs is especially grim in the context of the not-too-distant retirement of millions of baby boomers, who will inflate the ranks of Social Security recipients.

In other words, the trends are going in the wrong direction, and this has been a pattern for more than thirty years. From a macroeconomic perspective, what America needs is more young people who are adequately educated, prepared, and positioned to earn middle- and upper-middle-class incomes. Such a prosperous younger population base could then adequately support the aging and demographically large baby boom generation as it enters retirement. In reality, what we have is a fast-growing Hispanic population with an alarmingly large number and high percentage of high school dropouts who are placing additional requirements on tax-based entitlement systems and on philanthropy. This adverse macroeconomic trend points to a time of extreme strain and threat to the economic well-being of the nation within the next twenty years.

Research seems to indicate that fewer philanthropic dollars are contributed overall by people who have not earned a college degree. A report from the Russ Reid Company entitled *The Heart of the Donor* (1995, p. 5) shows "Who gives the most?" Selected entries are reproduced here:

Personal characteristic	Median cumulative annual giving
Leaves nonprofit organization in will	$558
Has annual income of $50,000 to $75,000	289
Is a college graduate	270
Volunteers in a nonprofit organization	248
Is in fifties	229
Is in thirties	197
Gives to church	196
National average	173

(*continued*)

Doesn't give to church	118
Is not a college graduate	95
Has annual income under $30,000	55

These donor statistics, taken together with the demographic reality of a fast-growing Hispanic community making up an ever-larger percentage of the total U.S. population and the persistently high Hispanic academic dropout rate, lead the casual observer to conclude that in the next decade or two fewer people (as a percentage of the overall population) will be earning an amount of money to permit them to contribute generously. The donor statistics from Russ Reid also show a remarkably close association between high dollar amounts of philanthropic giving, higher income, and college education. Similarly, lower dollar amounts of charitable giving, lower income, and lack of college education are closely associated.

Although much more research should be conducted to validate these as closely linked characteristics, this research supports the commonly held presumption that college graduates give more in dollar terms than people without college degrees. Assuming this to be true, then the logical extension would be that high school dropouts are even less philanthropically beneficent in dollar terms than those who have earned at least a high school diploma. Subject to additional research, it seems reasonable to advance the conjecture that unless the Hispanic community significantly, and soon, reduces its academic dropout rate and succeeds in graduating more students from college, its philanthropic characteristics in dollar terms will become even shallower. Also, given the growing U.S. population of Hispanics, it would follow that even the overall number of individuals who give generous dollar amounts might decline beginning in the next ten to twenty years.

The search for solutions to the Hispanic school dropout problem deserves much more commitment and money from individuals of means, corporations, and mainstream private foundations (especially to help replicate, not just start and then abandon, activities with measurable retention-graduation improvement). Proposed solutions (for example, offering early childhood reading interventions; providing after-school alternatives for young people who might be tempted by gang membership; engaging adult, senior, and college-age mentors to assist students in public elementary, junior high, and high schools; encouraging parental involvement with their children to complete their homework every day; and so on) can be successful to varying degrees for different barrios and Hispanic subgroups. However, such "successful" solutions are usually very expensive on a per person basis and many, even the most effective, seldom survive beyond the life of the program grant or appropriation. Too few tax-supported school districts can long afford to incorporate programs that work into their own heavily committed and politically driven operating budgets. This is not to say that innovative stay-in-school programs are undeserving of support—quite the contrary. But relying on programs of one to five years—even great programs—has not yielded sustainable results when it comes to the ultimate solution to the Hispanic school dropout crisis.

The Hispanic retention-in-school and graduation-from-school rates remain significantly lower than those for other population groups (and most others have shown measurable improvement during the past thirty years). In his keynote address at the Third Annual Symposium of the National Community College Hispanic Council in July 1998, Augustine Gallego said that the completion rates for the bachelor's degree for individuals twenty-five years and older shows non-Hispanic whites at 25.6 percent, blacks at 13.0 percent, and Hispanics at 10.0 percent. One is compelled to ask whether something in the Hispanic community has stifled numerous well-intentioned programs to promote higher school retention and graduation rates. In the Hispanic community today, do we see an ethic that genuinely and broadly values academic excellence? Is such an ethic appreciably more operative than it was thirty years ago? Why not?

Philanthropy as Values Transfer

Western civilization's valuation of charity and philanthropy is historically significant. The Hebrew traditions of gleaning (that is, leaving a remnant of the harvest for the destitute to gather and eat) and accepting foreigners and strangers into the community (because the children of Israel were themselves once foreigners during their sojourn in Egypt) provide biblical precedent. Early Christian church groups that flourished under the Roman Empire actively practiced the corporate care of widows and orphans and distinguished themselves from secular society through communal sharing of resources with one another, especially to help their weaker members. Even pagan Roman society placed great value on caring for the helpless. One of the Romans' esteemed gods stood for the love of humanity.

In its U.S. incarnation, Western-style charity is characterized by a focus on alleviating suffering and meeting crucial survival needs. At both the individual level (for example, the outpouring of private financial contributions to establish turn-of-the-twentieth-century orphanages, the establishment of contemporary battered wives' and children's shelters, the feeding and clothing of those left destitute after natural flood disasters in Honduras and south Texas in 1998) and the community level (for example, the response of an entire Alaskan citizenry to contain oil spill damage to a pristine aquatic environment after the Exxon Valdez accident), there is a willingness and an eagerness to improve the human condition and the lot of the less fortunate. But providing bandage solutions (charity) to today's suffering differs from promoting preventive behavior (philanthropy) that mitigates the effects of future calamity.

Philanthropy aims to do more than simply relieve difficult conditions; its purpose is to improve the quality of life and lifestyles so that future environments and conditions are more benign and give rise to less devastating or painful situations. An example of philanthropy is improving understanding between people and communities through art and music. Another example is providing free instruction to develop skills and knowledge about how best to treat or prevent illness. Such good works improve the human condition and the lot of disadvantaged people.

Benefits to the acknowledged recipients of philanthropy are evident: more civilized behavior, productive livelihood, improved health, and greater opportunity to improve themselves. The benefits are no less real to the less acknowledged recipients of philanthropy (that is, the donors): a sense of fulfilled gratitude for the good others have done for you (that is, payback), the feeling of being right with self or right with God, and the comfort derived from knowing that one's philanthropic good works offset perceived loss or guilt one may harbor. In the end, a significant transaction occurs between donor and donee, and vice versa. Philanthropists gain emotional, psychic, and social satisfaction (and perhaps even financial satisfaction in the form of a tax benefit from the IRS), whereas donees have their personal situations and aptitudes enhanced, perhaps for the rest of their lives.

The exchange of values that defines philanthropy is usually understood in terms of money given and money received. The traditional way to measure the extent of philanthropy going on is to look at dollars contributed, such as in the Russ Reid report previously mentioned. However, philanthropy is also understood as volunteer time and effort. Sociologist Bradford Smith (1999) of the University of San Francisco observes that researchers should take more seriously informal minority group giving traditions, such as donating to family members. He argues that ignoring such good works results in an inaccurate picture and an underestimate of the amount of minority giving. Even less discussed is philanthropy in which other values—neither money nor time—are the operative elements of exchange. Specifically, *philanthropy can also involve the surrender of deeply held convictions and self-perceptions in exchange for the creation and perpetuation of new identities and ways of being that have inherent worth.* This is no less a real exchange of values, and far more than a vague concept. This less discussed philanthropy, referred to hereafter as *surrender philanthropy*, is not so intangible as it might at first appear. For example, on an individual level, people engage in this kind of philanthropy, at least theoretically, when they marry in the American style.

Each of the two people in a marriage surrenders elements of his or her self-identity, some long-cultivated preferences, and even some favored individual behaviors in exchange for a "more perfect union," a new way of being that promises a better environment for child rearing or for simple mutual encouragement and support between the married couple. By surrendering some things they individually value, a bride and groom make room in their lives for birth and the growth of a new reality, the "us" that has a peculiar life of its own. In this example of surrender philanthropy, the donors are the single members of the premarried couple who give up cherished independence and habits and the beneficiaries are the married members of the husband-wife team, the couple, who come to enjoy a new and different existence with its attendant identity of perceived but not necessarily monetary great worth.

Marriages that falter and fail often do so because promises of surrender that were made during courtship, the wedding ceremony, and subsequently, are not kept—surrendering or sublimating old preferences, habits, and behaviors, for example. In crumbling marriages, the critical commodities of surrender promises made and fulfilled, the stuff of surrender philanthropy, are withdrawn and broken. The "us" so carefully crafted between husband and wife ceases to be or becomes a ghost of its best self when the surrendered values once held dear by either the bride or the groom resurface and undermine the wedded union. It is then that the philanthropic values exchange underpinning a healthy marriage evaporates or becomes fraught with distrust and retribution. Unfortunately, this is not an unfamiliar occurrence in America.

The marriage example of surrender philanthropy has a parallel among population groups in the collective. Sociologists and anthropologists have their own terminologies for behaviors when population groups adapt to survive better, perpetuate themselves, and dominate others. Those who study populations observe that groups exhibit sacrificial behavior to satisfy their own requirements and desires (the rational economic person) and to benefit others (the philanthropic person), especially their offspring. Parents act philanthropically when they give up their right to enjoy the fruits of their own labor in exchange for a deferred benefit, the promise of a better tomorrow for their children.

The sacrifice of parents—their investment in the future of children—often makes possible more prosperous conditions for family line and name. This is the sacrificial philanthropy of scores of immigrant groups who have come to America from Europe, Africa, and Asia over the past five hundred years. This is a nearly universal and shared value. To a certain extent, the story of sacrificial philanthropy is repeated today by many migrants and seasonal workers *pasando al norte* to the United States from Central and South America and, most prominently, from Mexico.

Values Transfer with Negative Results: When Philanthropic Surrender is not Evenly Applied

Population groups are relatively successful in their cross-generation sacrificial behavior to the degree they succeed in transferring constructive elements and minimize transferring self-destructive elements of their collective personality. When behaviors and attitudes that people hold dear and refuse to surrender actually impede the process of adaptation by their children, then difficulties can result. If the fruits of parental hard work are to be transferred to children successfully, there should be a successful transfer of constructive values and sublimation of self-destructive values.

One example of a Hispanic community value producing unintended damage is the strong Catholic value placed on large families and a tradition of having babies beginning at a young age. When children imitate the life patterns of their ancestors, for instance, by becoming pregnant and impregnating at young ages, yet fail to subscribe to other parental values like aversion to divorce (because the church's practical influence is degraded or lost from one generation to the next), then genuine trouble can result. High out-of-wedlock birthrates and increasing numbers of single-parent, predominately single-mother households result. Witness in consequence the far too high percentage of Hispanic children who live in poverty. The unintended destructive results of unmarried children having many babies in the Hispanic community stems partially from an uneven or incomplete transfer of Catholic parental values.

Another example of a values transfer that is both constructive and self-destructive is the great worth placed on working with one's hands—"honest work." Many Mexican American children have come to accept from their parents or grandparents a high regard for hard physical labor. Many young Hispanics replay in their minds stories about first jobs taken by their immigrant ancestors who came to the United States to earn money in a job, any job, usually domestic work or a job in the lowest-paying field. Nearly all Mexican American immigrants, whether legal or illegal, started with physically demanding work. However, when children identify with the relatively high value their elders place on manual labor and providing food and shelter for the family, there is often another value inherited: a subtle aversion to work as a manager or supervisor.

There remain vestiges, recollections, and daily reminders of mean-spirited taskmasters who made life miserable for humble workers like grandfather, *mis abuelos*, those who worked on the rancho or in small pueblos earning subsistence wages. Young Hispanics who inherit a strong motivation to work hard often hold an accompanying conviction that they do not want to become one of the oppressive first-line supervisors, and even less the distant and all-powerful boss, *caudillo*, or *politico*. The result is a generation of young people who would rather work at low wages than prepare themselves to become one of the less-esteemed middle managers and leaders—no longer a constructive values transfer from an economic perspective.

Young Latinos in Washington Heights (New York City) give several reasons why they drop out: trouble with gangs, difficulties with English, inattentive or prejudiced teachers. The girls often leave to care for their brothers and sisters, or to have babies of their own. The boys take jobs—or deal drugs—to help pay bills or to buy expensive clothes or gold chains.

Ramon, age nineteen, left George Washington High School in the ninth grade. Now, he says, he sells drugs to support his diabetic mother and three siblings.

The tall, serious young man in the puffy Tommy Hilfiger parka thinks school is important and says he makes his siblings go. But he doesn't question his decision to leave (school), and neither do his parents. "They understand because they need to live," he says. "Once I get enough money to keep up the family, I'll go back."

Reasons vary for the high dropout rate. For one, many immigrants speak no English and are reluctant to endure the embarrassments inherent in the struggle to catch up. (Perlstein, 1998, p. B1)

Reasons why Hispanics drop out of school as teenagers include satisfying their financial obligations to their young and extended families, which typically include several babies; the natural inclination to find an honest job in manual labor (and resignation to the fact that they are unqualified for jobs other than unskilled or low-paying ones); reluctance to consider the institution of marriage as inviolable, resulting in far too many young single mothers; and reluctance or lack of desire, *falta de ganas*, to study and graduate from high school and college in preparation for jobs as managers, owners, and organizational leaders. *Furthermore, Hispanic parents often don't demand that their children graduate from high school and then college.* Although there are other psychological and sociological factors that contribute to the phenomenon of Hispanic school dropouts, much can be attributed to an incomplete transfer of values that results in self-destructive behaviors and attitudes.

An unfortunate outcome of unevenly transferred surrender philanthropy from parent to child is a sense of pride, *el orgullo*, a puffed-up sense of self-sufficiency and an unwillingness to admit a need for or accept assistance from others outside the family. Passed from one generation to the next, this kind of pride compels many Mexican American school dropouts to resist: "I don't need nobody's help. I got a job. Anyway, I could get one easy. Somebody's got to earn money to feed the babies. There's no sense in studying to catch up in school. Heck, I'm just as good as the next guy. Forget school. Anyway, even if I graduated, there is no future for me in the Anglo world—I'll always be second-class there, no matter what I do. Why try? I'll be all right with my people, my family. That's all that matters." This "composite" opinion is typical of many Hispanic school dropouts.

Is There a Remedy? Perhaps One Is at Hand and Within

The parable about teaching people how to fish rather than simply giving them fish to eat is perhaps one of the most poetic and instructive descriptions of philanthropy that changes a situation for the better rather than simply satisfying a present need that will only be felt again tomorrow. This parable has application for Hispanics and the school dropout problem as follows: Overcome self-defeating behaviors and reverse notions that prevent them from "learning how to fish"—from graduating from high school and college. Recognize that an important precondition to improving the situation for all Hispanics is for individual Hispanics, one at a time, to set aside self-destructive aspects of deeply held values and focus on applying their constructive aspects.

There is nothing wrong with wanting large families; wanting to work with one's hands; wishing to satisfy one's family's needs for food, clothing, and shelter; and respecting oneself and one's autonomy. These values characterize Hispanics as a people and add to the health, diversity, and dignity of society at large. However, the negative consequences of these and other unevenly applied values transfers deserve examination. Such a review need not be considered "blaming the victim." Rather, it might include identifying and better celebrating the ways in which Hispanics are breaking out of the dropout predicament. There are Hispanic success stories in college retention and graduation, even in the midst of persistently high dropout rates.

The most notable Hispanic success—imperfect still but undeniably a way out of the community's destructive dropout cycle—is through community colleges and technical schools. The challenge is to build on this success and move toward more four-year college and professional school graduates, leading ultimately to a thoroughgoing respect in the Hispanic community for academic achievement.

"Because they are geographically and academically accessible, community and technical colleges are the institutions of choice for many underrepresented students. With their open admissions policies and wide range of course offerings, community and technical colleges are an excellent academic beginning for those who want baccalaureate degrees, and excellent vocational training for those moving directly into the workforce. But many of the students who begin community and technical college do not receive a degree of any kind. Improvements should be made to remove barriers in the pathway to a degree" (Texas Commission on a Representative Student Body, 1998, p. 22).

The following information from the *Chronicle of Higher Education Almanac* (1998, p. 10) shows minority enrollments in higher education during the 1996–97 academic year:

Public two-year colleges	424,000 (42 percent of enrollments)
Public four-year universities	414,000 (34 percent of enrollments)
Private two-year vocational	10,000 (48 percent of enrollments)

Many Hispanics whose parents did not graduate from high school are making significant and life-changing progress by attending and graduating from community college. Their children are then more likely to pursue four-year degrees. Perhaps by the third generation, significant numbers of Hispanics will earn bachelor's, legal, medical, and doctoral degrees. However, the process must start where it is possible to start: locally, at a reasonable price, and flexibly. My father received his associate's degree in architecture at San Bernardino Valley College, and he was the first in his family to earn a degree in higher education. His children took the next steps up the educational ladder, with his encouragement.

My own story, inspired by my father's counsel, includes graduating from West Point, continuing service as an officer in the National Guard twenty-four years later, earning an M.B.A. at night school, and then attaining a Ph.D. in philanthropic leadership. When I left active military service in 1983, I backed into fundraising as a career. One of my professors, Dr. Wesley Willmer, encouraged me to take a college development job. Hispanics were then, and still are, very underrepresented in the profession.

The destructive vestiges of insecurity and ambivalence I might have had about being able to succeed in an Anglo world were eclipsed by an entire youth subject to persistent admonishments from Mama Rosa to "stand up tall because you can do anything and be anybody you want to be if you put your mind to it" and gentle advice and reflections from my father that "I wish I had applied myself better in school," and "Learning is so wonderful; don't grow up to regret that you missed any chance to learn." In their own ways, my parents helped shape my priorities and my faith in the possible. College, career opportunities, and philanthropic sacrifice on the part of my parents made it possible for me to be where I am today. Gratitude is too small a word to describe my feelings for the sacrifices they made.

There is still much to do before the Hispanic community even approaches a critical mass of college graduates, which would indicate that the community's school dropout problem is nearly over. But a reasonable solution may be at hand. Applying surrender philanthropy to Hispanic education is quite appropriate. A new Hispanic philanthropy focused on contributing, or surrendering, negative self-perceptions in the pursuit of educational achievement makes common sense, especially from the point of view of disposable resources. One can give only what one has available to give. Although it might be argued that a good philanthropic goal would be for Hispanics to make big cash contributions to needy Hispanics and others, the money we can give as a group is limited and will remain quite limited until many more of us earn higher incomes and begin to accumulate significantly larger amounts of wealth. Until then, what Hispanics can most readily give—or give up—are self-destructive, closely held perceptions about who they are and what they are capable of doing.

Next Step

A suggestion that results from this consideration of Hispanics, education, and philanthropy is that Hispanic leaders should be forthright in helping the Hispanic community focus its combined and united resources, including the notion of surrender philanthropy, to the achievable task of significantly multiplying the number of Hispanic college graduates. We need to find ways to place more Hispanic academic role models in front of Hispanic children, on television, and in their schools as teachers and speakers. Hispanic organizations and private foundations need to collaborate more extensively to match Hispanic academic "success story" role models to schoolchildren. High school students can serve as role models to children of elementary school age. College students can often best inspire junior high or high school students. Most importantly, there should be more extensive efforts made to help Hispanic parents become academic role models for their own children. My father, with a two-year college degree, and my mother, with a high school diploma, inspired this Ph.D. to set goals high and then pursue them without reluctance. Such mentor skills can be taught and caught by others.

Unity of effort, concentration of will, and serious commitment of resources that comes from within the Hispanic community itself are critical shortcomings today. Available time, energy, money, and attention should be invested from all quarters and from all organized Hispanics in a serious new millennial campaign to create a pervasive climate—one that values and celebrates staying in school and graduating from high school *and* college as *the minimum* acceptable standard. *La gente,* the people, will surrender self-destructive values resulting from uneven values transfer in a genuine act of philanthropy if academic role models are active and the "Graduate! Graduate! Graduate!" message is communicated without apology. Hispanics will sacrifice for the good of their children. They will likely need honest and consistent reminders that anything less will prevent their children from fully participating in American society.

Speaking the truth often comes at great cost. For those who do, it can carry the risk of being labeled antiethnic. However, in this instance hard truth may be part of the school dropout solution. The message is unequivocal: Graduate from high school or perish financially. Graduate from college or be treated as a second-class person for the rest of your life. It is quite simple and easy enough to comprehend, just hard to say. Do our Hispanic leaders and our Hispanic parents have the fortitude to communicate this honestly and constructively within the Hispanic community? My faith in the possible remains unshaken.

References

Chronicle of Higher Education Almanac, 1998–1999. Chicago: University of Chicago Press, Aug. 28, 1998.

Perlstein, L. "Steep Dropout Rate of Latinos Is Tough Challenge for U.S." *Washington Post,* Dec. 2, 1998, p. B1.

Reisberg, L. "To Help Latino Students, a College Looks to Parents." *Chronicle of Higher Education,* Jan. 15, 1999, p. A45.

Russ Reid Company. *The Heart of the Donor.* Pasadena, Calif.: Russ Reid Company, 1995.

Smith, B. *Ethnic Philanthropy.* Bloomington: Indiana University Press, 1999. Texas Commission on a Representative Student Body. Report. State of Texas, Oct. 1998.

Charles G. Rodriguez *is executive director for development and public affairs at the University of Texas Health Science Center in San Antonio.*

A BRIEF EXAMINATION OF INSTITUTIONAL ADVANCEMENT ACTIVITIES AT HISPANIC SERVING INSTITUTIONS

MICHAEL WILLIAM MULNIX, RANDALL G. BOWDEN, & ESTHER ELENA LÓPEZ

Abstract

Clearly, increased funding at the local, state, and federal levels would go a long way to ensure the future success of Hispanic Serving Institutions (HSIs) of higher education in the United States. Private funding and strong support from alumni groups are also a critical part of this funding mix. In addition, sophisticated and adequately funded marketing, public relations, and enrollment management efforts are needed. The funding of most HSIs is closely tied to the political process. Successful lobbying efforts and the structuring of a strong advancement effort is instrumental in building healthy institutions and ensuring high graduation rates. With this in mind, the goal of this study was to determine what level of importance is placed on institutional advancement activities by college and university presidents at select HSIs throughout the United States.

Resumen

Claro que el incremento de fondos monetario a niveles estatal y federal harían mucho por asegurar el futuro éxito de instituciones de educación superior que sirven a Hispanos (HSIs) en los Estados Unidos de América. Fondos monetarios privados y apoyo fuerte de grupos de ex-alumnos son también partes criticas de este fondo mixto. Aún más, fondos adecuados y sofisticados en la bolsa de valores, relaciones públicas y esfuerzos de reclutamiento son necesarios. Los fondos económicos de la mayoría de las HSIs están atados de manera cercana al proceso politico. Esfuerzos exitosos de "lobbying" y la estructuración de un fuerte esfuerzo de desarrollo son instrumentales para construir instituciones saludables y asegurar altos porcentajes de graduación. Pensando en todo la anterior, la meta de este estudio ha sido el determinar el nivel de importancia al que los presidentes de colegios o universidades selectas HSIs en Estados Unidos de América ponen las actividades de desarrollo institucional.

Overview

Disparities in institutional advancement activities (for purposes of this study: fund raising, public relations, alumni affairs, marketing, enrollment management, and government relations) between Hispanic Serving Institutions (HSIs) and their majority counterparts are extreme. For example, a majority of HSIs are almost entirely dependent on state and federal funds and many have virtually no endowment. Information provided by the U.S. Department of Education (1998) shows that:

- the total revenues of HSIs are 42% less per full-time equivalent (FTE) student than at other institutions,
- endowment revenues at HSIs per FTE student are 91% less than at other institutions,
- HSIs spend 43% less on instruction per FTE student than other colleges and universities,

- HSIs spend 51% less on academic support functions per FTE than other schools, and
- HSIs spend 27% less on student services per FTE student than other institutions.

According to Benítez (1998),

> It is no exaggeration to describe the financial condition of a large number of HSIs as precarious. Many HSIs are underequipped and understaffed, and they are unable to do competitive hiring, develop baccalaureate or graduate programs, maintain modern research facilities, or offer high-tech learning and working environments.
>
> In light of these problems, some questions may be raised about the quality of instruction and the possibilities for student and faculty advancement at HSIs. Do HSIs have adequate resources to face up to the difficult task of educating a student population that lags behind in practically every academic indicator? Are Hispanic students better off at HSIs than at other institutions that are stronger financially and academically? (p. 61)

According to the President's Advisory Commission on Educational Excellence for Hispanic Americans (1996), if present rates of population growth continue, by 2030 one in five persons in the United States will be Hispanic. Hispanics, then, will make up 25% of the total school population and Hispanics aged 5 to 18 will number almost 16 million. A study commissioned by the Association of American Colleges and Universities (1995) reported that

> into the 1960s, the nation's system of higher education was *de facto* almost completely racially segregated, basically either all-white or all-black with at best a 1 to 2 percent variation at some major institutions. As late as the fall of 1970, nearly 87 percent of college students in the United States were white. Nine percent were black and the combined total of Asian Americans, American Indians, and others was a mere 2.2 percent. The curriculum at majority institutions was as "white" as the student body. (p. 10)

It is interesting to note that the study of the Association of American Colleges and Universities failed to mention Hispanic students and their particular educational needs. And yet Hispanics are the fastest growing population in the United States. Whereas Hispanics totaled a mere 3% of the population in 1960 (U.S. Census Bureau statistics), the number more than quadrupled in less than three decades. Benítez (1998) wrote,

> Although Hispanics are the fastest-growing minority in the United States, their numbers at all levels of the educational system in this country have not kept pace with their population growth. Dropout rates for Hispanics are higher and dropping out occurs earlier than for most other groups. (p. 58)

According to the 1996 report of the President's Advisory Commission on Educational Excellence for Hispanic Americans, "40 percent of 16- to 24-year-old Hispanic dropouts left school with less than a 9th grade education, compared with 13 percent of white dropouts and 11 percent of black dropouts" (p. 36). And the National Education Goals Panel (1996) stated that in 1995 the disparity between White and Hispanic students with regard to high school completion was 27%, whereas it was 5% between White and Black students. The panel also found that disparities in college completion rates between White and Hispanic students are growing. In 1992, the gap between the proportions of Hispanic and White high school graduates who completed a college degree was 15 percentage points. In 1996, the gap had increased to 21%.

According to the President's Advisory Commission on Educational Excellence for Hispanic Americans (1996), in 1993 Hispanic students earned only 6% of all associate degrees, 4% of bachelor's degrees, 3% of master's degrees, and 2% of all doctorates. Enrollment of Hispanic students, however, continues to climb, doubling from 520,000 in 1992 to 1,045,600 in 1997 (U.S. Department of Education, 1998).

Without question, added resources would assist HSIs to recruit and retain more students. Educated Hispanic students are key to America's future vitality. According to the Commission on Minority Participation in Education and American Life (Education Commission of the States, 1988),

> America is moving backward—not forward—in its efforts to achieve the full participation of minority citizens in the life and prosperity of the nation. In education, employment, income, health, longevity, and other basic measures of individual and social well-being, gaps persist—and in some cases are widening—between members of minority groups and the majority population. If we allow these

disparities to continue, the United States inevitably will suffer a compromised quality of life and a lower standard of living. Social conflict will intensify. Our ability to compete in world markets will decline, our domestic economy will falter, our national security will be endangered. In brief, we will find ourselves unable to fulfill the promise of the American dream. (p. 1)

And according to Benítez (1998),

It is fair to say that HSIs as a group are presently at the front line of American postsecondary education. They are dealing with the population mix that will dominate the twenty-first century, and they
appear to be doing better than any other group of institutions at meeting the educational needs of
Hispanics. Whether their efforts and resources suffice to meet the challenge of educating Hispanics in
the United States is another question. HSIs at present are seriously under-funded, and most do not go
beyond the undergraduate level. That is not sufficient to serve the needs of the population, or of the
nation in the future. (p. 64)

The gravity of the state of Hispanic higher education was spelled out in a recent *Report on the White House Strategy Session on Improving Hispanic Student Achievement* (2001) stating

the urgency of these troubling gaps between Hispanic youth and their peers in educational achievement demands concerted awareness and effort because the disparities signal not just diminished possibilities for individual Hispanics, but squandered potential for the economic strength of the nation
as a whole. (Achievement Academic Gaps section, para. 1)

This report asserted as one of its goals to "double the percentage of Hispanic Americans who earn Associate's and Bachelor's degrees by 2010" (Challenging the Nation section, para. 6).

Although gaps in federal funding for HSIs and Historically Black Colleges and Universities (HBCUs) has narrowed in recent years, there is still a disparity in the amount of money awarded to these two types of institutions. According to Benítez (1998),

In the case of HBCUs, the congressional intent was to remedy past injustices and acknowledge and
support the efforts of these institutions to educate blacks in the United States under very difficult
conditions. Congress therefore established an entitlement program for HBCUs, with eligibility criteria including that the school be accredited and established prior to 1964 with a mission to educate black
Americans. (p. 64)

By law, the minimum award for an individual HBCU is $500,000 each year. Prior to 1995, Con-
gressional funding levels for HBCUs remained stable at $108.9 million, whereas appropriations for HSIs decreased from $12 million in 1995 to $10.8 million in 1996 and 1997.

Lobbying efforts to increase federal entitlement money for HSIs has been intensified and better coordinated in recent years, resulting in many instances in a keen sense of competition between HSIs and HBCUs. A 1998 article in *The Washington Post* quoted Henry Ponder, president of the National Association for Equal Opportunity in Higher Education (representing Black colleges and universities), who said,

They [HSIs] can get everything they want under the current structure. They don't need a separate
part in the law. I know Hispanics have had an unfavorable history in terms of discrimination, but it
in no way compares to what has happened to African Americans. (Fletcher, 1998, p. A10)

Lobbyists for Hispanic higher education gained their biggest victory to date when, in 1999, they convinced Congress to establish a separate entitlement program aimed specifically at helping HSIs. Prior to that, HSIs were grouped with HBCUs under the Title III program and competition for Congressional attention was intense. Since then, HSIs have fared much better in the Congressional arena. For example, President Bush's FY 2003 budget request has asked for more than $89 mil-
lion to support HSIs to help close the funding gap. This is a $3.1 million or 3.6% increase over 2002 funding levels. He has further pledged to increase funding for both HBCUs and HSIs by 30% between 2001 and 2005 in an effort to expand access to postsecondary education for students from minority and disadvantaged backgrounds.

A separate entitlement program (Title III) and additional increases in other governmental fund-
ing areas at both the state and federal level has significant implications for HSIs. Without question, the huge increase in the number of Hispanic students seeking higher education warrants such large

funding increases. Prior to 2000, there were approximately 14.5 million Hispanic college students in the United States. There were 62 million such students in 2001. As mentioned, total investment in HSIs has gone from $12 million in 1995 to $42.25 million in 2000 to Bush's request for $89 million in 2003. Thus, the outlook appears promising from a federal perspective, and it appears that campus lobbying efforts in the nation's capital are succeeding beyond what many had forecasted. Each year, the Hispanic Association of Colleges and Universities (HACU) holds a well-attended government relations seminar in Washington, D.C., and coordinates efforts by college and university presidents to lobby members of Congress. The results appear to be paying off.

This brief overview brings up several interesting questions: Precisely how much funding will be needed to accomplish the goal of recruiting and retaining Hispanic college and university students? And just as important, where will the money be found? The federal government can only be expected to fund up to certain levels and that, in large part, will always be influenced by party politics. Money from the private sector—corporations, foundations, alumni, and others—will be increasingly important to offset years of funding neglect at HSIs. With this in mind, this study set out to determine the level of support that college and university presidents give to the overall institutional advancement effort in their attempt to build a solid funding base and ensure the future growth and development of their institutions.

Method and Limitations

Little has been written on the overall subject of Hispanic higher education, and almost nothing in the area of institutional advancement at HSIs. An ERIC database search conducted in January 2002—going back to 1966—resulted in less than a dozen articles or chapters in books dealing with this subject. We therefore designed a survey to increase the field of knowledge about advancement activities at HSIs in the United States.

For purposes of this study, surveys were sent to approximately 250 college and university presidents at HSIs who are members of the HACU headquartered in San Antonio, Texas. HACU-member institutions collectively enroll two thirds of all Hispanics in higher education and are located in 10 states including Arizona, California, Colorado, Florida, Illinois, New Jersey, New Mexico, New York, Texas, and Washington. Members are also located in Puerto Rico, Argentina, Brazil, Costa Rica, El Salvador, Spain, Mexico, Nicaragua, and Venezuela.

Collecting data for this study was accomplished using a measure of self-assessment. A survey was designed that contained 18 statements and questions with answers often given in a Likert scale. Topics related to a variety of institutional advancement issues centering around fund raising, public relations, alumni affairs, marketing, enrollment management, and government relations. An up-to-date mailing list was obtained from HACU and a cover letter endorsing the project was written by the president of HACU. A prominent HSI university president also wrote a letter endorsing the project.

Eighty completed surveys were returned for a 32% return rate. Although a substantial number of international surveys were also returned, they are not the focus of this particular article.

The mailing took place in the spring of 2001. Follow-up e-mails were sent to encourage campus CEOs to return the surveys. Data were entered in the Statistical Package for Social Sciences (SPSS) for analysis. Results from the survey were calculated according to frequencies and descriptive statistics.

The primary limitation of the study is the relatively low response rate. Open-ended questions would have yielded rich data. This brief study, however, provides future researchers with interesting core data on which to build.

The Importance of Institutional Advancement Activities

The first question on the survey asked chancellors and presidents to gauge the relative importance of key institutional advancement activities on their campuses. As indicated in Table 1, the 80 college and university CEOs who responded to the survey agree overwhelmingly in the importance of institutional advancement activities.

Although the numbers are perhaps too close to draw any hard and fast conclusions, it is interesting nonetheless to note that the most important advancement activity—ranked together as being either "extremely" or "very" important—is enrollment management followed by public relations, fund raising, marketing, sponsored programs, government relations, and, lastly, alumni relations. Conclusions likely can be drawn by the disparity of responses between, say, fund raising and alumni relations, as those two advancement activities are very much interrelated. For example, the question can be asked. Is it possible to have a strong development (fund raising) program without a strong alumni base? In this instance, more than 5% of campus CEOs went so far as to say that alumni relations is *not important*—the only category in the group to receive such dubious distinction—and another 21% to describe the activity as only *somewhat important*.

It is also illuminating to find such a clear majority of chancellors and presidents indicating the importance of effective enrollment management, allowing one to hypothesize that many HSIs are almost exclusively tuition-driven and that funding from private sources has yet to supplant the importance of tuition revenue. With this in mind, it is interesting to note that government relations was listed by 14% of campus CEOs as being only *somewhat important* even though effective lobbying is generally seen as a way to increase state and federal revenue and to slow the mandate for hikes in tuition.

Outside Consulting

In an attempt to clarify further the importance that chancellors and presidents place on various elements of institutional advancement, they were asked if they ever employed outside consultants to assist in various advancement activities (see Table 2).

It is, perhaps, not surprising that a majority of CEOs hired consultants to assist first in fund-raising efforts, closely following by marketing. There is a fairly significant drop, then, in the number who hired consultants for the next highest ranked activity: public relations. Yet again, alumni

TABLE 1

Institutional Advancement Activities of Importance to CEOs (in percentages)

	Not Important	Somewhat Important	Unsure	Very Important	Extremely Important
Fund raising	0	8.5	0	31.9	59.6
Alumni relations	5.5	20.9	3.3	35.2	35.2
Public relations	0	1.1	0	41.8	57.1
Government relations	0	14.0	1.1	37.6	47.3
Marketing	0	5.5	4.3	32.3	58.1
Enrollment management	0	2.2	2.2	26.9	68.8
Sponsored programs (grants and contracts)	0	6.5	2.2	41.9	49.5

TABLE 2

Employed Outside Consultant for Various Advancement Activities (in percentages)

	Yes	No	Not Applicable
Fund raising	61.7	37.2	1.1
Alumni relations	14.3	83.5	2.2
Public relations	39.8	60.2	0
Government relations	24.7	73.0	2.2
Marketing	57.1	42.9	0
Enrollment management	34.8	64.0	1.1
Sponsored programs	32.6	65.2	2.2

relations remains at the bottom of the list. It also appears significant that although enrollment management was ranked as the most important of all advancement activities (see Table 1), a relatively small number of campus CEOs had hired a consultant to assist in this activity.

Sponsored Programs

It was originally hypothesized that a clear majority of chancellors and presidents would believe strongly in the importance of government relations and, in turn, in the importance of having an effective sponsored programs office dealing with federal and state grants as well as interacting with private foundations (see Table 3). A question was therefore asked: "Does your institution presently have a sponsored programs office solely responsible for (a) writing federal grants and (b) interfacing with private foundations?"

As can be seen, approximately 70% of campus CEOs who responded see the importance of having sponsored programs officers who write federal grants. And 65% have program officers who interface with private foundations.

In an attempt to find out just how sophisticated these program officers were in monitoring federal grants and contracts, CEOs were asked if someone from their institutions regularly monitored the *Federal Register* and/or several well-known federal Web sites (see Table 4).

Although the data would indicate that a fair proportion of program officers read the *Federal Register* and monitor various federal Web sites, it is intriguing to find that a number do not. It is difficult to imagine a successful sponsored programs office not monitoring these sites. It is also highly interesting that a good number of chancellors and presidents simply "don't know" if their program officers are monitoring the sites and/or reading the *Federal Register*.

In an attempt to further measure the overall sophistication and effectiveness of sponsored programs offices at HSIs, we asked CEOs to name the type(s) of federal grants their institutions have both applied for and received during the past 5 years (see Tables 5 and 6).

As can be seen, the federal programs receiving the most attention from HSIs are TRIO (designed to retain and graduate low-income, disadvantaged students), Title V (established in 2000 and targeted specifically to help HSIs), and the Fund for the Improvement of Postsecondary Education (FIPSE). Following these three, there is a significant drop-off in the amount of attention paid to other federal aid programs, particularly those outside of the Department of Education. It would appear that a majority of sponsored programs officers are concentrating primarily on education grants.

TABLE 3

Sponsored Programs for Federal Grants and Private Foundations (in percentages)

	Yes	No	Not Applicable
Federal grants	69.1	29.8	1.1
Interfacing with private foundations	64.9	33.0	2.1

TABLE 4

Regularly Monitoring Federal Web Sites (in percentages)

	Yes	No	Do Not Know
Federal Register	71.7	19.6	8.7
www.ed.gov	60.4	19.8	19.8
www.nsf.gov	68.9	17.8	13.3
Other federal Web sites	69.0	17.2	13.8

TABLE 5

Type of Federal Grant Applied for in the Past 5 Years

	Applied for—Yes	Applied for—No	NA	Do Not Know
FIPSE	68.8	18.2	0	
Title VI (BIE)	23.5	51.5	.5	
Title V (ED)	76.7	19.2	.4	2.7
Teacher Quality Enhancement (ED)	43.1	44.4	.4	
TOP (Commerce)		67.1	0	25.7
TRIO or McNair (ED)	77.3	17.3	0	5.3
Eisenhower (ED)	31.6	40.8	0	14.3

Note: FIPSE = Fund for the Improvement of Postsecondary Education, BIE = Business and International Education, ED = Department of Education, TOP = Technology Opportunity Program.

TABLE 6

Type of Federal Grant Received in the Past 5 Years

	Received-Yes	Received—No	NA	Do Not Know
FIPSE	33.8	50.0	2.9	
Title VI (BIE)	9.7	59.7	9.7	
Title V (ED)	60.3	31.5	5.5	2.7
Teacher Quality Enhancement (ED)	35.3	45.6	8.8	10.3
TOP (Commerce)	6.2	58.5	12.3	23.1
TRIO or McNair (ED)	61.2	25.4	3.0	10.4
Eisenhower (ED)	30.3	50.0	7.6	12.1

Note: FIPSE = Fund for the Improvement of Postsecondary Education, BIE = Business and International Education, ED = Department of Education, TOP = Technology Opportunity Program.

The attention being paid, in particular, to Title V and TRIO appear to be paying off. Fully 55% of those institutions that have applied for a Title V award have received one, whereas more than 50% of those applying for TRIO have been successful. Following those two programs there is, however, a significant drop-off in success rates.

It was hypothesized that many campus CEOs—believing in the importance of lobbying as a way to increase federal funding and to more effectively interact with program officers for key entitlement programs—would have a lobbying presence in the nation's capital. As Table 7 indicates, this is not necessarily true (see also Table 8).

Fully 50% of those who responded said that they do not have a lobbying presence in Washington, D.C. Of those who responded that they do have a lobbying presence, it is interesting to note that only 6 (9.3%) of those who responded rely primarily on HACU, generally considered the primary "voice" of HSIs in the United States. What this may indicate is that HSIs remain at a disadvantage when lobbying members of Congress due to a lack of a centrally organized lobbying group.

TABLE 7

Lobbying Presence in Washington, D.C. (in percentages)

	Yes	No	NA	Do Not Know
Percentage	45.1	50.5	2.2	

TABLE 8

Type of Presence in Washington, D.C. (in percentages)

	Private Firm	AASCU	HACU	Other	AAU	NAICU	NASULGC
Percentage	12.4		9.3	19.6		0	

Note: AASCU = HACU = Hispanic Association of Colleges and Universities, AAU = Association of American Universities, NAICU = National Association of Independent Colleges, and NASULGC = National Assocation of State Universities and Land Grant Colleges.

TABLE 9

Conducted Formal Research to Determine Public Perception of Institution Within the Past 5 Years

	Yes	No	Do Not Know
Percentage	64.9	34.0	1.1

TABLE 10

Satisfied with Current Image (in percentages)

	Not Very	Somewhat Satisfied	Satisfied	Very Unsure	Extremely Satisfied	Satisfied
Percentage		15.8	44.2	2.1	32.6	5.3

Marketing and Public Relations

Development of a positive image and effective interaction with a wide variety of constituent groups is key to successful efforts in institutional advancement. Thus, it was hypothesized that a majority of college and university presidents at the nation's HSIs would have worked to establish what they considered to be strong and effective public relations and marketing offices. As outlined in Table 9, approximately 65% of those who responded to the survey indicated that they have conducted formal research to determine public perception of their institutions within the past 5 years. Half of the respondents went so far as to hire an outside consulting firm to conduct the research. Clearly, a majority of those college and university presidents who responded feel that "image" is important and needs to be monitored closely.

Although a majority of CEOs see the importance of using research to track public perception of their institutions, it is highly interesting to note that 60% are *not very satisfied* or only *somewhat satisfied* with their current image. A mere 5% are *extremely satisfied* with their image (see Table 10).

It appears that there would be a strong relationship between satisfaction with institutional image and expertise of institutional marketing and public relations activities. It is interesting to note, therefore, that more than half of those who responded believe their marketing efforts as either *very professional* or *extremely professional* and that more than 70% believe the same regarding expertise of their

TABLE 11

Level of Expertise (in percentages)

	Marketing Activities
Not very professional	4.2
Somewhat professional	34.7
Unsure	6.3
Very professional	41.1
Extremely professional	13.7

TABLE 12

Institution Conducted a Major Advertising/Publicity Campaign Within the Past 5 Years (in percentages)

	Yes	No	Do Not Know
Percentage	62.8	36.2	1.1

TABLE 13

Institution's Current Fundraising Efforts (in percentages)

Not Very	Somewhat Effective	Effective	Very Unsure	Extremely Effective	Effective
Fund-raising efforts	7.4	52.1	3.2		5.3

public relations efforts. Thus, although a clear majority are not all that satisfied with their current image, a majority also believe in the expertise of their public relations and marketing efforts. Thus, there appears to be a disparity between the two responses (see Table 11).

A majority of college and university CEOs appear to be trying to do something about the image of their institutions. As indicated in Table 12, more than 62% have conducted major advertising and publicity campaigns within the past 5 years.

It is interesting to note that although a majority of campus CEOs are not very satisfied with the image of their campuses, they believe in the expertise of their marketing and public relations departments and have conducted major advertising/public relations campaigns within the past several years. Again, there seems to be somewhat of a disparity among these answers.

Fund Raising

As previously mentioned, increases in private funding would go a long way in reducing the reliance of HSIs on tax dollars. Private money allows for a certain "margin of excellence" for state institutions and is, of course, mandatory for the survival of private schools. Our working hypothesis was therefore that college and university presidents at HSIs would put a great deal of emphasis on development/fund raising efforts at their institutions. Although this appears to be true (see Table 1), we found it highly interesting to discover that nearly 58% of those CEOs who responded to the survey rated their fund-raising efforts as *not very effective* or only *somewhat effective*. As Table 13 shows, only 5% rated their efforts at raising money as *extremely effective*.

In an attempt to discover the sophistication of fund-raising efforts at HSIs, CEOs were asked if they have a formal, written investment policy at their institutions. As indicated in Table 14, a sizeable majority have such a policy. What is surprising, however, is that fully 11% of those who responded

TABLE 14

Institutions With a Formal, Written Investment Policy (in percentages)

	Yes	No	Do Not Know	Not Applicable
Percentage	70.8	11.5	11.5	6.3

TABLE 15

Employment and Number of Full-Time Development/Fund-Raising Officers (in percentages)

			Yes	No
Percentage			87.5	12.5
	1 to	4 to 6	7 to 9	10 or More
Percentage	61.4	18.	12.0	8.4

TABLE 16

Approximate Endowment Size in Millions of Dollars (in percentages)

Less than $1 million	22.6
$1 to $3 million	11.8
$3 + 1111 to $5 million	10.8
$5 + 1111 to $10 million	8.6
$10 + 1111 to $15 million	11.8
$15 + 1111 to $25 million	2.2
$25 + 1111 to $40 million	5.4
$40 + 1111 to $60 million	6.5
$60 + 1111 to $100 million	4.3
More than $100 million	7.5
Not applicable	5.4
Do not know	3.2

said they "didn't know" if such a policy existed. And more than 11% said that they did not have a formal investment policy, leading one to question just how their endowments are being managed and what, precisely, is being said to donors and potential donors.

As Table 15 indicates, more than 12% of the CEOs said that they do not employ full-time development officers at their institutions. It is logical to conclude that the same 12% who do not have a formal investment policy also do not employ full-time development officers; in other words, fund raising is likely nonexistent at these institutions. Of those who responded, a clear majority had rather small development staffs, with more than 61% saying that they employed only 1 to 3 fund-raising officers. Four of those who responded had quite large staffs, employing more than 10 full-time development officers.

As Table 16 indicates, a majority of those who responded said the endowment at their institution was rather small; nearly 70% have endowments less than $15 million. It is rather illuminating to discover that two of those who responded "didn't know" the size of their endowments, again indicating that perhaps an endowment is nonexistent.

TABLE 17

Institutions Endowment Annual Growth Rate (in percentages)

	Less than 5%	5% + to 10%	10% + to 15%	15% + to 20%	20% + to 25%	More than 25%
Percentage	18.7	46.7	25.3	5.3	4.0	0

TABLE 18

Satisfied With Institution's Current Growth Rate of the Endowment (in percentages)

	Not Very Satisfied	Somewhat Satisfied	Unsure	Very Satisfied	Extremely Satisfied	Do Not Know	Not Applicable
Percentage	16.7	28.9	11.1	25.6	6.7	4.4	6.7

TABLE 19

Institutions Need to Make Overall Advancement Activities More Successful (in percentages)

Clearer goals and objectives	34.7
Integrated advancement plan	49.5
Revision of organizational structure	20.0
Significant increase of resources	54.7
Presidential involvement	20
More research	24.2

The growth of the endowments at many of the HSIs appears to be quite healthy, as indicated in Table 17. More than 45% have percentage growth rates between 5% and 10%, and more than 25% have growth rates between 10% and 15%.

Despite what appears to be effective management of a majority of endowment funds at these HSIs, nearly 50% of those college and university presidents who responded to the survey were *not very satisfied* or only *somewhat satisfied* with the current growth rate. Only 6% responded that they were *extremely satisfied* with the growth rate of their endowment (see Table 18).

Finally, CEOs were asked what was needed to make their overall advancement efforts more successful. A majority of those who responded listed "significant increase of resources" as their number one answer, followed by development of an "integrated advancement plan" (see Table 19).

Conclusions and Directions for Future Research

Results from this brief survey reveal that, clearly, college and university CEOs at HSIs across the United States believe in the importance of institutional advancement activities (for purposes of this study listed as fund raising, public relations, marketing, enrollment management, alumni affairs, government relations, and sponsored programs). However, a majority believe that their efforts in such key areas as fund raising, marketing, and public relations are not very satisfactory. One of the most illuminating discoveries is that a large number of campus chief executives at these HSIs do not believe in the importance of alumni relations in the overall advancement effort. And the fact that enrollment management is listed by most as the most important of all advancement activities indicates that the raising of private money lags behind tuition as the primary concern of most CEOs.

Limitations of the study include a return rate of less than 50% and also the effect of volunteerism (the sample collected may or may not represent the target population).

Future researchers may find it worthwhile to take this primary data and expand on it. Particularly interesting will be comparative studies across cultures; for example, comparing advancement activities at HSIs in the United States with similar institutions in Mexico and beyond. Finally, qualitative data would enrich the information obtained about institutional trends in institutional advancement at HSIs.

References

Association of American Colleges and Universities. (1995). *The drama of diversity and democracy: Higher education and American commitments*. Washington, DC: Author.

Benitez, M. (1998). Hispanic Serving Institutions: Challenges and opportunities. In J. P. Merisotis & C. T. O'Brien (Eds.), *Minority Serving Institutions: Distinct purposes, common goals, 102*, (pp. 57–68). San Francisco: Jossey-Bass.

Education Commission of the States. (1988). *One-third of a nation* (Report of the Commission on Minority Participation in Education and American Life). Washington, DC: American Council on Education, Government Printing Office.

Fletcher, M. A. (1998, February 1). White House backs plan to aid Hispanic-serving colleges. *Washington Post*, p. A10.

National Education Goals Panel. (1996). *The national education goals report: Building a nation of learners*. Washington, DC: Government Printing Office.

President's Advisory Commission on Educational Excellence for Hispanic Americans. (1996). *Our nation on the fault line: Hispanic American education*. Washington, DC: Government Printing Office.

Report on the White House Strategy Session on Improving Hispanic Student Achievement. (2001, December). Retrieved January 23, 2002, from http://www.ed.gov/offices/OIIA/Hispanic/report2001jan/report2001Jan.doc

U.S. Department of Education. (1998). *Fact sheet: Title III institutions*. Washington, DC: Government Printing Office.

WHAT IS CHINESE AMERICAN PHILANTHROPY?

JESSICA CHAO

Philanthropy in America is the public expression of one's social and civic values. It barters in financial, human and social capital, and empowers common citizens of all financial means to take private action on behalf of community good. Philanthropy is essential to a vibrant democracy because it brings attention to important causes and innovative remedies for which government and business are often less effective. It ensures community ownership of these remedies and guards against total dominance of "top down" national policies and majority rule.

According to Giving USA, Americans gave about $212 billion in charitable donations in 2001. Of this extraordinary generosity, the vast majority comes from individuals across the entire economic spectrum through direct donations (75.8 percent of the total) and bequests (another 7.7 percent). Contrary to popular thought, foundation grants only accounted for 12.2 percent and corporate giving a mere 4.3 percent.

In America, various cultural groups have created honored traditions of philanthropy, which have contributed to their identity as well as given them a civic voice. These include the building of libraries and universities by the early industrialists, the socially conscious philanthropy of Jewish donors, the politically empowered African American church and even the budding venture philanthropy experiments of young high tech entrepreneurs.

Chinese American philanthropy does not appear to have developed a unifying theme at this point. It is old and new, personal and institutional, extremely ethnic and paradoxically assimilated. This is not a surprise, because the way one gives and shares assets is influenced not only by level of disposable income and assets, but also by the perception of stability, cultural values and the social and business networks one joins.

We Chinese, however, did not all arrive during the same period under the same circumstances. In fact, since the 1965 Immigration Act, our population is not only growing at an incredible rate, but our diversity is also increasing. While we can be proud of our growing income base, there are still many among us who are disadvantaged. According to U.S. Census 2000, the average income of the Asian American household was $51,205 compared to $44,366 for white non-Hispanic households. We have come a long way, but our poverty rates are also high—as much as 12 percent in New York City and even higher some inner cities compared to 7.7 percent for the majority population. While a growing number are American born who cannot even speak Chinese, the foreign born among us is as high as 70% in many areas.

Because of our diversity we practice a robust tradition of mutual aid through myriad social, civic and fraternal associations, even while there is a growing trend in establishing family or corporate foundations, and giving major gifts to mainstream institutions. Many immigrants and a few American-born Chinese continue to support extended family, friends and public works in home countries and villages, which are estimated in the billions of dollars annually.

Noted scholars such as Him Mark Lai, Sucheng Chang, Peter Kwong and Anna Saxenian researched various Chinese mutual aid associations. While the oldest village, family and Consolidated Benevolent associations were founded in the 1880's and were almost exclusively Cantonese, the contemporary versions reflect the diverse ethnic backgrounds of newer immigrants as well as a variety of professions and businesses including medical, engineering, and high technology. People with similar interests and needs share their collective knowledge, contacts and financial resources. The most organized run credit unions and social services such as day care centers, programs for the elderly and business development mentoring. They all serve the purpose of social and business networking, especially to help newcomers begin their ascent up the American ladder of economic opportunity.

The civil rights, anti-war and cultural identity movements of the 1960s and 1970s were an unusual confluence of events for Chinese Americans. In addition to the Immigration Act of 1965, the end of the Vietnam War, and the opening of China, for the first time in U.S. history there was a critical mass of Asian college students. Influenced by the political activism and call to civic participation on campuses across the country, several community and student activists created nonprofits led by Chinese and other Asian Americans to address the economic, social and educational needs of the immigrant enclaves. These nonprofits challenged the social order of the older associations, increased professionalism and bridged community needs with the outside world.

These community organizations include San Francisco's Self-Help for the Elderly, New York's Charles B. Wang Community Health Center (formerly Chinatown Health Clinic), and the Chinese-American Planning Council among many others, as well as civic associations such as the Organization of Chinese Americans. Scholars William Wei and Yen Le Espiratu observed and documented the development of community institutions stemming from this era. They also observed the development of an Asian American identity created both by external forces (Census, media, welfare programs, etc.) and internal motivations (political empowerment and decreasing ethnic-specific identity with growing acculturation).

As American-born and immigrant Chinese Americans attained educational milestones, entered elite professions and built successful national and international corporations, they also slowly gained acceptance by mainstream philanthropic institutions. Today, although not common enough, there are Chinese Americans on the boards of several elite universities, research hospitals, private foundations and cultural institutions. Generally, they represent major donors of these institutions. Some also volunteer and support community nonprofits. A few continue to socialize in alumni or professional associations. Affluent Chinese American donors rarely limit their giving to Asian-related causes and nonprofits. In fact, numerous donors including An Wang, Oscar Tang, Charles B. Wang, Kenneth Fong and many others with more modest gifts are known for their generosity to universities and museums.

From my numerous interviews with affluent philanthropically-minded Chinese Americans over the last several years, I have learned that there is a growing, but as yet "unorganized" interest in cultivating philanthropic leadership in our community. These philanthropists are asking critical, self-reflective questions. After all, with fairly modest means, our parents and families have achieved so much both for themselves as well as their expanding definition of community. Much of our success has been due to their generosity and informal philanthropy as well as to the benefits of the civil rights movement and the opening of elite institutions of higher education.

Many of us have gained prominence through this success. According to the U.S. Census Bureau, between 1992 and 1997 $591.3 billion in revenues was generated from minority-owned businesses, of which 52 percent were reaped by Asian Americans, and the revenues rose by 60% compared to 40% for all U.S. firms. With greater assets, education and acculturation, can we and should we have a greater impact on public policy, social issues and civil society, especially on those issues that impact our families, communities and businesses?

What philanthropic legacy will Chinese Americans collectively make as we transition from mutual aid to major charitable investments? Will we exert philanthropic leadership on international relations and sensitivity to the domestic conditions of immigrants and the disadvantaged? Will we leave behind the 12 percent among us who still live below the poverty line? While there may be a perception that we are insular and should not give to "ourselves" only, there is a competing perception that if we do not help ourselves given our wealth, how can we ask mainstream America to "bail us out"? In fact, studies conducted by the Foundation Center and the National Committee for Responsive Philanthropy suggest that we cannot rely on the mainstream to speak for us. Only 0.3 percent of foundation grants and corporate contributions supported programs targeting Asian Americans, and this trend held steady throughout the 1990s.

While we are at the mercy of our own consciences and obligations to our loved ones in creating our personal legacies, clearly nonprofits such as the Chinese American Forum, Committee of 100, and Organization of Chinese Americans could lead the way in directing our collective legacy and social identity. With institutional support and community focus, our spirit of voluntarism and cultural pride can be channeled to reflect our unique combination of experiences. Given our energy and talent, our bi-cultural and entrepreneurial perspectives can have an impact on the greater U.S. Social consciousness and should continue to shape our civic vision.

Advancing Gallaudet: Alumni Support for the Nation's University for the Deaf and Hard-of-hearing and its Similarities to Black Colleges and Universities

Noah D. Drezner

Abstract

Gallaudet University, originally chartered by the US Congress as the Columbia Institute for the Deaf and Dumb and Blind in 1864, recently began to solicit donations from their alumni through formal fund-raising campaigns. Using a combination of historical and qualitative analysis coupled with descriptive statistics from institutional data and the Voluntary Support of Education Survey, Gallaudet's advancement story becomes apparent. Working within the Deaf culture and its nontraditional view of philanthropy, Gallaudet's fund-raising experiences and results are similar to those of historically black colleges and universities.

Introduction

John Havens and Paul Schervish note that over the next 55 years America will experience a "great wealth transfer" where $41 trillion will likely be passed on from one generation to the next—through bequest, philanthropy, and taxes. A conservative estimate by Havens and Schervish approximates that of the "great wealth transfer" 15 percent, or $6 trillion, will be given to nonprofit organizations.[1] Havens and Schervish conducted their study in 1999 before the Bush tax cuts that propose an elimination of estate taxes and the tax advantage for charitable giving at death. It is unclear how the $6 trillion estimate will be affected if the tax cuts are adopted permanently. David Joulfaian, from the US Treasury Department, found that the estate tax deduction given for charitable bequests is "budget efficient," in that it encourages giving at a rate higher than the revenue lost by the government. Joulfaian estimates in the absence of the estate tax, charitable bequests might decline by 12 percent. However, Stuart Butler, vice-president of domestic and economic policy studies at the Heritage Foundation, citing Milton Friedman's permanent income/overlapping generations theory, where a person's residual wealth, after heirs are taken care of, goes to philanthropic causes, believes that by eliminating the estate tax charitable bequests will increase since the "after-tax cost of planned contributions to heirs would be reduced."[2]

As philanthropic organizations and foundations prepare for this phenomenon, many have focused their interests on learning more about traditions of giving outside of the majority communities. Scholars and foundations have concentrated their research efforts on ethnic minorities, women, and religions, but have not studied those populations with differing abilities.[3] For instance, these reports and studies have neglected to look at the uniqueness of the American Deaf community, its role in giving, and its own culture of philanthropy.[4] In an era of decreased Federal support of higher education and higher cost of education, Gallaudet University has turned to its graduate deaf alumni to cover the institution's budget differential in a concerted effort recently for the first time. Gallaudet's first formal capital campaign began in 1997.

This paper will examine formal fund raising at Gallaudet University, explore the culture of giving within the Deaf community, and finally draw out the similarities between Gallaudet's development story with other minority communities, specifically, historically black colleges and universities.

Methods

Both oral histories and primary document analyses were used in this study. Oral histories were gathered by informational interviews and electronic correspondences through "conversation[s] with a purpose."[5] The intention of these communications was to obtain information that was not otherwise available through written documents, policies, or records of Gallaudet University's institutional advancement office.[6] A "mix of more- and less-structured questions" were used in semistructured interviews and emails.[7] The queries in the protocol were intended to be open-ended, conversational, and "guided by a list of questions," yet flexible.[8] They were hypothetical, ideal position, interpretive as well as exploratory in nature.[9] Interviews, where permission was granted, were audiotaped, transcribed, and additional notes were taken throughout the interview. Detailed notes of interviews that were not taped were taken as well. American Sign Language (ASL) interpreters were used to facilitate discussion with deaf interviewees where the author's ASL knowledge was not adequate. The transcriptions, notes, institutional records, and archival documents, from Gallaudet University and the Library of Congress, are the dataset for this historical study.[10] Finally, the dataset was analyzed for content.[11]

History and Context

In order to educate the deaf, residential schools were opened throughout the United States. In the early portion of 1857 Amos Kendall and others convinced the US Congress to incorporate the Columbia Institution for the Instruction for the Deaf, Dumb, and Blind.[12] Congress began its financial connection to the education of the deaf from day one. The legislature appropriated $150 per year for local children attending the school in order to cover their maintenance and tuition costs.[13] Additional support for the newly established school came from its founder. Kendall donated a house and two acres of land, and finances to cover the start-up costs and salary of the superintendent.[14] Kendall's wealth and influence undoubtedly helped the then Columbia Institute gain favor in the Congress and within the Jackson administration's eyes. Kendall was a political powerhouse of sorts. He had for six years served as the fourth auditor of the United States Treasury and was Postmaster General for five years. This influence was captured in an 1860 report in *The Washington Evening Star*: "At that time, next to [President Andrew] Jackson, [Kendall's] mind was the controlling one in the Government, stamping the impress of its patriotism and will more indelibly upon the future of the United States than those of all the rest of Jackson's advisors."[15]

It was this influence that led to the inception of the Columbia Institution for the Deaf and Dumb as a college, in 1864. The college was later renamed after its first president Edward Miner Gallaudet and has received the vast majority of its operating budget from the Federal government.[16] The government funding was put in place because the institution was given collegial powers, including the ability to confer degrees, by an Act of Congress—that after some debate passed unanimously by the Senate—and was signed by President Lincoln on April 8, 1864.[17] Upon passing the authorization Congress allocated $26,000 to cover the cost of purchasing an additional 13 acres of land. $26,000 was nearly 400 percent of the Institution's total receipts for its first year of operation ($6,513.25; $5,263.25 from Congress and $1,250 from private subscriptions).[18]

Edward Gallaudet, reflecting on the government's involvement, later pointed out in a speech given to the Columbia Historical Society in 1911 that it was a unique show of support and investment to deaf education that Congress acted "in providing for a national college for the Deaf at a time when the burdens of [the Civil War] were pressing heavily upon the Government." Gallaudet continues by pointing out that the very day that the $26,000 of support was "drawn from the Treasury, all communication, either by rail or telegraph, between the Capitol and the country was cut off by the operations of the Civil War."[19] While this action was indeed significant, that monies were allocated during the war effort to support the creation of a college for the deaf, it is important to note that because of the succession of 11 states from the Union, the true voice of the nation was not part of this decision.

Upon Kendall's death in 1869, only a few months after the College held its first graduation, his estate sold the adjoining 81 acres of land to the institution for $85,000; the campus was now a full 100 acres.[20] The larger campus allowed for expansion and construction. At a January 29, 1871 dedication of Chapel Hall, US President Ulysses S. Grant and then General James A. Garfield spoke about the "courage of the government" to fund the institution while the Country was at war with itself.[21] Gallaudet quoted Garfield as saying: "Congress took half a million dollars from the public Treasury and devoted it to this work—I hailed it as a nobler expression of the faith and virtue of the American people, and of the statesmanship of their representatives, than I ever before witnessed."[22]

Garfield continued this "noble expression" himself. The future US President had a continued interest in the College and its progress for the last 15 years of his life. One of Garfield's greatest accomplishments on behalf of the institution was securing the funds for the purchase of the portion of the Kendall estate. Garfield helped raise $10,000 from private subscriptions and successfully lobbied Congress for the remaining $70,000.[23]

As a result of this Congressional relationship, Gallaudet's situation, throughout its history and still today, closely resembled that of a service academy. In addition to Federal funding of the operating budget, students received Congressional appointments for study, diplomas hold the signature of the President of the United States in the position of Patron of the University, and the Federal General Services Administration is given the task of building the campus.[24]

However, Congressional support of the College was not always as strong as it was under Kendall and Gallaudet. During the College's second president's tenure (Percival Hall 1910–45) Federal support fell amid two world wars and the Depression. Congress, which supported the College generously during the war between the states, was hesitant to fund building and at times even debated whether to continue the school or not.[25] This decreased funding made it difficult to expand the enrollment, faculty, curriculum, and physical plant. As a result, President Hall considered approaching others for private funding. Nina Van Oss reported this contemplation in the *Gallaudet Alumni Bulletin*: "He [President Hall] felt that *if the alumni could in some way interest* the Ford, Rockefeller, Carnegie or such foundations in the College and obtain grants to the College funds for expanding the curriculum, research, and the like, as is done for other noteworthy and deserving institutions, then much progress could be made. . . ."[26] That alumni were thought of first as those who could help connect the institution to the foundations rather than as a form of support is evidence of the administration's acknowledgement that their deaf alumni were not in a real position to support the institution. This fund-raising reliance on corporations and foundations is evident today. Alumni only made up 7.27 percent of the total income from private support while corporation and foundation gifts accounted for 5.7 percent and 30.7 percent respectively in fiscal year 2004.[27]

While President Hall never saw this connection to foundations happen, his successor, Leonard Elstad, did help reconnect the institution with Congress. Soon after entering the presidency in 1945, Elstad was told that Gallaudet needed to become accredited by the Middle States Association. The resulting report commended the College on its faculty, students, and strategic plans, but found that the College had inadequate facilities.[28] Additionally, in 1949, the United States Office of Education and the Federal Security Agency (FSA), the division of the government that the College reported to at the time, decided to review the College as well. The resulting report, *The Federal Government and the Higher Education of the Deaf*, was very positive. The study found that the Federal government had an obligation to continue the financing of postsecondary education of the deaf simply because it was not economically possible for states to fund this obligation. The report continued that in order for Gallaudet to become a first-rate institution a stronger relationship between the government and the institution would be necessary.[29] In response to the two reports, FSA acting administrator John L. Thurston recommended that Congress and the Bureau of the Budget increase their funding and involvement in the College.[30] At a May 5, 1954 Congressional hearing, President Elstad used the results of each report to ask for increased support. The result was a new relationship between the Federal government and the College in the passage of *Public Law 420* (83rd Congress of the United States). Through *Public Law 420*, Congress funded increased faculty, curricular development, and improvements to the physical plant. Additionally, the law officially changed the name of the institution to Gallaudet College. One example of the Federal government's increased involvement in

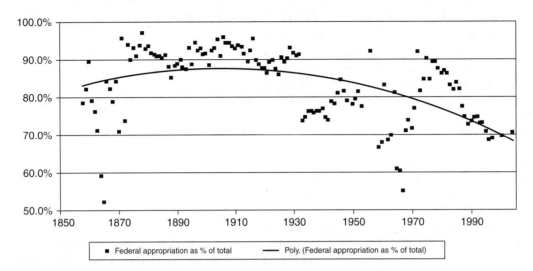

Figure 1 Federal Appropriation to Gallaudet as Percentage of Total Budget

Source: Gallaudet University. Office of Budget, Administration and Finance. Annual Reports of Columbia Institute, Gallaudet College, and Gallaudet University and Congressional Budget Data.

Note: Cost associated with the Model Secondary School for the Deaf and the Kendall Demonstration Elementary School are included in the Federal appropriations. These institutions receive full funding from Congress.

Gallaudet was the size of the annual budgets appropriated to the college. In Elstad's first year, 1945, Congress appropriated $270,000. By 1969, as Elstad left office the Federal appropriation was $6,900,000.[31] This was a 1,192 percent increase after accounting for inflation.[32]

The Federal government has only fully or majority supported a small number of institutions, including the military academies, Howard University, and Gallaudet University. States have long supported colleges and universities.[33] While Congressional support still remains a large source of funding at Gallaudet, Federal support, like with many other government-sponsored programs, has dropped significantly (see Figure 1). In the fiscal year 2000 budget appropriations from Congress only covered 70 percent of the institution's costs.[34] The Department of Education has asked Gallaudet to be more self-sufficient. Additionally, Congress has given a caveat to its subvention; the institution must keep its tuition at an equivalent level to the land-grant institutions.[35] This hinders Gallaudet's ability to increase revenues through tuition.

Gallaudet's Fund Raising

As Federal and state subvention has declined, more and more public and private two- and four-year colleges and universities have started asking for gifts from individual donors. Administrators are searching for all possible nontax revenue sources to help meet budget requirements. Supplemental private dollars "often [provide] the bulk of discretionary income for publicly supported institutions, and hence has been referred to as their margin of excellence."[36] Gallaudet is no different. In order to mend the gap in funding, the University has moved to development. Fund raising, in the past, was not central to the institution as it is at other universities around the United States. Where donations were once used as a margin of excellence Gallaudet now uses them to stay afloat. The current president and first deaf leader of the institution, I. King Jordan, was appointed in 1988, when the University's endowment was only $5m. Jordan knew it was time to plan Gallaudet's first formal *capital* campaign.

However, it was not the institution's first formal campaign; alumni support for Gallaudet did not begin with the institution's first campaign of nearly a decade ago. In 1907, to mark President Gallaudet's 50th anniversary as the institution's executive and his 70th birthday, alumni, without solicitation, announced that they would establish the Edward Miner Gallaudet Fund. The former students left the purpose of the fund open to their honoree's choice. Gallaudet later decided that the fund should be used to finance the library that would bear his name.[37] Later, in 1919, alumni raised a total of $10,000 in memory of their first president. The money was pledged toward the building of College Hall, a comprehensive administration building that included the president's office, faculty offices, storerooms, the library, an auditorium, alumni office, and a men's residence.[38]

Additionally, in the early 1960s a self-motivated alumnus, Dave Piekoff, began a centennial campaign with his wife that ended in the purchase, renovation, and endowment of an alumni house— now bearing his name—and the establishment of two additional permanent endowments: the Laurent Clerc Cultural Fund and Graduate Fellowship Fund. Piekoff raised $1m from fellow alumni by traveling the nation and asking for their support for Gallaudet in honor of its significant anniversary.[39]

The golden age in American higher education, when Federal money was abundant, enrollments were on the rise, and large sums of money were spent on institutions' physical plants, lasted for the decades following the Second World War.[40] However, this golden age ended in the 1970s and 1980s when Federal funds were not as readily available as they once were due to the increases in Federal deficits. As a result many small private liberal arts institutions, such as Gallaudet, began to engage in professionally conducted advancement efforts in the decade of the 1980s.[41]

Historically, there was a development discussion on campus, prior to the 1988 "Deaf President Now" protests, which brought the institution's current president, I. King Jordan on campus. These deliberations focused on what the fund-raising message of the college should be. There was a segment of the administration that thought that the message should be one of charity—that giving to Gallaudet was an action of social justice. Another view, and the one that is currently in place, is that giving to Gallaudet is a philanthropic act of supporting higher education, just as it is at any other institution.[42] This debate over the approach of fund raising, within the rest of higher education, ended in the last 100 years. Early colleges with religious backgrounds appealed to prospects through a charitable lens—donors should give to the disadvantaged. However, around the turn of the century, institutions began to appeal to donors with a philanthropic approach.[43] Even though discussions took place in the 1980s, Gallaudet did not formalize its development activities until 1990, shortly after President Jordan came to Gallaudet.[44]

The institution hired Grenzebach Glier & Associates, Inc., a philanthropic management-consulting firm known for its work within higher education, to conduct a campaign feasibility study in 1990. Grenzebach's report informed Gallaudet that, in their infancy with respect to development, they were not ready to proceed with a campaign. The consultants found that, at the time, the Board of Trustees was not committed to the pursuit of private support; Gallaudet's was not yet raising enough funds annually compared with its peers; the institution's cost for dollar raised was too high (27%); and that their case for support was not clearly articulated.[45] Over the next seven years Gallaudet's development staff grew and became more experienced and worked to resolve the list concerns presented in the 1990 Grenzebach report.

Gallaudet's first formal campaign was launched in January 1997 without the commission of another feasibility study. The development office and president believed that they had accomplished all of the tasks identified by the Grenzebach report and therefore were ready to proceed with a campaign.[46] They were. The campaign opened publicly with a goal of $30m and closed five years later nearly $10m above the goal. From initial data most of the success was due to corporate and foundation support and only a small percentage was from alumni. At its height alumni participation in the campaign reached only 15 percent, a low figure for traditional annual funds at private liberal arts colleges that historically reach 33 percent alumni participation, let alone during a capital campaign.[47] As a result in part of the campaign Gallaudet's endowment, at the end of fiscal year 2003, was $115m.[48]

Cathy Sweet-Windham, Gallaudet's executive director of institutional advancement, recognizes that "Gallaudet does not have a long history of philanthropy." As a result of the current state of Federal budgeting "the Federal government is looking more closely at how [the institution is] fund raising and making sure that we are receiving a substantial amount [from fund raising]."[49] Therefore, Gallaudet has identified the need to engage its alumni and identify and develop fund-raising strategies that will increase alumni participation within their annual fund, designated, and comprehensive campaigns.[50] As with many development offices, Gallaudet has recognized difficulties in achieving these goals. Senior advancement officers identify two major roadblocks in their work with Gallaudet alumni. The first—a common misconception of many institutions' alumni—is the myth that the institution does not need support. Gallaudet alumni, like many alumni from historically black colleges and universities (HBCUs), simply believe that their alma mater is strongly funded by the Federal government and supplemented by corporations and foundations, and therefore is not in need of alumni support.[51] The second barrier to increased alumni support and participation, as identified by the Office of Institutional Advancement, is the culture of giving within the Deaf community.[52]

Philanthropy in the United States has historically been viewed through the lens of the wealthy-white-hearing-man.[53] Marybeth Gasman and Sibby Anderson Thompkins, who studied fund raising at HBCUs, suggest that when looking at the culture of giving in the African American community the traditional definition of philanthropy is too narrow.[54] This is the case when looking at giving in the Deaf community as well.

Director of Development Lynne Murray believes that the Deaf community's culture of giving is not one of monetary philanthropy because of historic aspects of the community. Based on her work with Gallaudet alumni, she contends that participation and dollars received are both low for three reasons. The first is that historically deaf adults do not have access to well-paying jobs and therefore do not have the disposable income to donate. The second is that members of the Deaf community are "used to receiving instead of giving."[55] The final reason is that the idea of giving is not passed down within families. Ninety percent of members of the Deaf community have hearing parents.[56] Additionally, the vast majority of deaf elementary and secondary students attend residential schools.[57] Sweet-Windham believes that communication barriers between hearing parents and deaf children, as well as the fact that most deaf children do not regularly see their parents give donations due to them living away from home, affects the ability for a culture of philanthropy to flourish in the Deaf community.[58]

Gallaudet's Office of Institutional Advancement has realized that in order to teach a culture of giving—one that goes beyond monetary giving—it is important to begin at the youngest age possible.[59] Through Gallaudet University's residential schools, the Kendall Demonstration Elementary School and the Model Secondary School for the Deaf, the Office of Institutional Advancement has begun to teach the importance of volunteerism and community service as forms of philanthropy. Elementary school students participate in activities centered on the University's Campus Community Campaign, which successfully raises funds from nearly half of the institution's faculty and staff. Interestingly the development office finds equal support and participation from hearing and deaf faculty and staff in the Campus Community Campaign. Lynne Murray believes that this might be partially due to Gallaudet's faculty and staff being well compensated.[60]

Realizing that "developing a lifelong relationship with alumni can't be magically turned on as your graduating seniors cross the bridge between their lives as students and their lives as alumni,"[61] Gallaudet has begun to work with its college students. In addition to celebrating the importance of philanthropy with precollege students, the importance of cultivating the next generation of donors and philanthropists has led the development office to team with alumni affairs to begin traditional student and young alumni advancement programs in the past year, including senior class gift drives and young alumni targeted events.[62]

The advancement office realizes the importance of having deaf development officers and volunteers. Currently, there is only one deaf fund raiser on staff at Gallaudet. In order to increase this number the institution realizes that it needs to "grow its own."[63] In order to continue to teach about philanthropy, and more specifically about development, the advancement office recently has begun two internships with students, one from the Model Secondary School and another from the graduate school. The hope is that these students consider a job within Gallaudet's development office in the future.[64]

Deaf Higher Education and Its Similarities to HBCUs

Much like HBCUs, Gallaudet University was established to serve a section of the population that was excluded from traditional American higher education. Deaf students were almost fully relegated to deaf-serving institutions, such as Gallaudet and the National Technical Institute for the Deaf (NTID) at the Rochester Institute of Technology, until the passage of the Education of the Deaf Act of 1986 (EDA), its amendments, and the Americans with Disabilities Act of 1990 (ADA). The EDA (which officially changed the name of Gallaudet College to Gallaudet University), and even more so the ADA, opened the door for deaf students to attend any institution of higher education in the country, requiring the institutions to provide interpreters and other needed facilities for deaf students should they attend.

The similarities between Gallaudet and HBCUs go well beyond those of their origin and necessity; they are peers with respect to development and fund raising as well. For example, alumni participation in FY 2004 at HBCUs averaged 7.8 percent, while at Gallaudet in the same year participation reached 7.6 percent, both well below the national average for FY 2004 of 21.2 percent.[65] Gallaudet has closely resembled HBCUs' alumni participation for at least the past 10 years—consistently being between five and ten percentage points below the national average (see Figure 2).

Additionally, the average alumni gift (see Figure 3) and alumni support per student (see Figure 4) were comparable over the last 10 years as well, with each also below the national average.

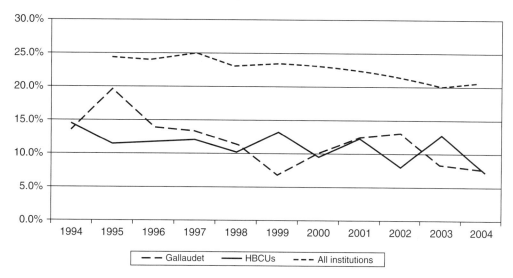

Figure 2 Alumni Donors as Percentage of Total Budget
Source: Voluntary Support of Education Survey, Council for Aid to Education, New York
Note: Reliable data for 1994 not available.

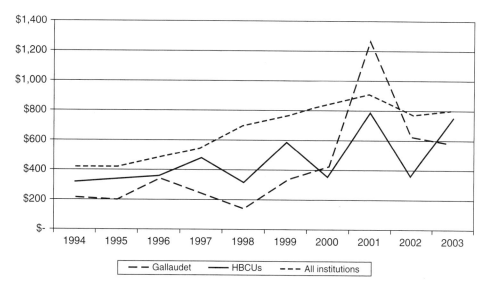

Figure 3 Average Alumni Gift
Source: Voluntary Support of Education Survey, Council for Aid to Education, New York

Gallaudet's average alumni gift surpassed the national average in FY 2001 at the height of its last campaign. Interestingly both HBCUs and Gallaudet experience inconsistent average gifts (indicated by the peak and valley nature of the graph) while the national average shows a much more consistent and increasing average alumni gift. The decrease between FY 2001 and FY 2002 can be explained by the shift of donor dollars after the September 11, 2001 terrorist attacks. The AAFRC found that nonprofit organizations, such as Gallaudet, in the cities that were attacked on September 11, 2001, were affected most by the shift of donor funding. *Giving USA* reports that nonprofits in Washington, DC had difficulty raising funds for the six months after the attacks. The obstacles to fund raising are attributed in part to the canceling of special events and mailings, as well as the increased expense for direct mailings associated with the treatment of mail by radiation in response to the threat of anthrax.[66]

Foundation support as a percentage of the total giving (see Figure 5) between Gallaudet and HBCUs—the proposed comparison group—was equivalent in the same 10-year period, save fiscal

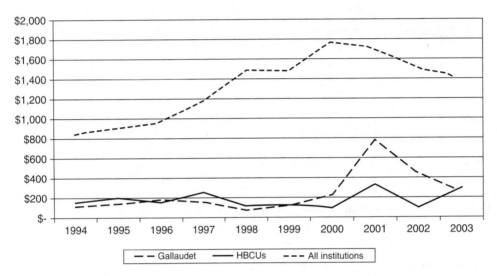

Figure 4 Alumni Support Per Student
Source: Voluntary Support of Education Survey, Council for Aid to Education, New York

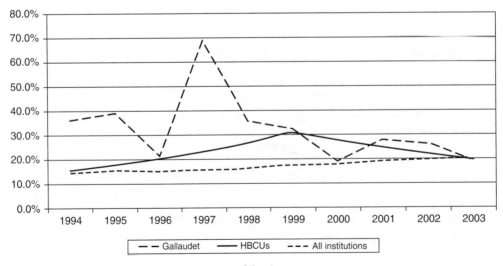

Figure 5 Foundation Giving as Percentage of Total
Source: Voluntary Support of Education Survey, Council for Aid to Education, New York

year 1997, where Gallaudet's foundation support reached 68.8 percent while the HBCUs were 19.7 percent.[67] The 1997 outlier could be explained by the fact that this was the first year of Gallaudet's capital campaign and foundation support increased for that reason. It is interesting to note that, for both Gallaudet and HBCUs, foundation support as a percentage of total dollars raised is higher than that of the national average. Therefore, it is reasonable to infer that Gallaudet and HBCUs rely on foundation support more than the average higher education institution. This is of concern since the data indicates that FY 2002 and 2003 (the latest data available) marked a point where foundation giving toward Gallaudet and HBCUs was on a decline and was about to level out or even dip beneath the national average.

Recommendations

Kim Kein found that historically, within the private sector, individuals donate most of the money given to the third sector.[68] Within higher education those individuals that give the most are alumni of the institutions.[69] This is not the case at Gallaudet University. Parents and friends of the University combine to account for 83 percent of individual donations, while alumni and faculty/staff lag behind at 12 percent and 5 percent of individual giving respectively.[70]

M. Starita Boyce, in her dissertation, found that HBCUs would need to increase their market effectiveness among individual donors in order to shield themselves from their financial hardships based on decreasing public subsidies and relatively small investments.[71] Gallaudet, like historically black colleges and universities, is threatened by reductions and changes in funding policies from their traditional sources of funding (e.g., corporations and foundation).[72] Therefore, it is important that both HBCUs and Gallaudet move to increase their individual donor base.

In order to increase the individual donor base it is essential that Gallaudet consider moving their advancement program forward by implementing the following recommendations. Trust is extremely important to African Americans when considering monetary donations.[73] This is the case for the Deaf community as well.[74] A personal relationship between the donor and development officer is essential. Deaf identity is highly important within the Deaf culture. Hearing people, even those allies considered part of the "third culture," have trouble being accepted or trusted by the Deaf community. The "third culture" is a term developed by Bienvenu and Colonomos that describes the four growing populations of hearing allies that have arrived at the fringe of the Deaf community in the past 20 years (a period referred to as the Deaf resurgence): (1) professionals (linguists, teachers, and interpreters); (2) hearing parents of deaf children who are engaged with the Deaf community; (3) hearing people who have learned sign language; (4) children of deaf adults (CODAs).[75] Deaf donors are more likely to donate to an accepted member of their community, or a revered figure, such as Gallaudet President I. King Jordan, than to an outsider.[76] It is the personal appeal that leads to the successful attainment of a gift. Therefore, it is important that Gallaudet increase the number of deaf development officers and work closely with engaged deaf alumni in solicitations.

Gallaudet should continue, and perhaps increase, its internship program with students from the graduate school and Model Secondary School for the Deaf. A simple way to increase this program would be to include an undergraduate internship in addition to the high school and graduate school positions.

Since the institution's president is so revered within the Deaf community it is important that Gallaudet be cautious in its approach of highlighting his achievements and successes with deaf higher education. While Dr. Jordan is a powerful fund raiser and a compelling reason to support the University, in preparation for the eventual leadership change, Gallaudet should emphasize the leadership of the institution and its president rather than focusing on the specific individual. It is important to show prospective donors that not only the current president is a leader in deaf education but also the president's office in general is one of prestige within the Deaf community.

While educating current alumni about the importance and need for support of deaf education, Gallaudet must continue to teach the importance of philanthropy to its current students—their future alumni. By educating current students, Gallaudet will likely have an easier time gaining alumni participation in the future.

Conclusion

Gallaudet has a strong and unique history within American higher education, one with great Federal support. As Congressional funding begins to decrease, calls for self-sufficiency are on the horizon. As corporations and foundations change their funding priorities, it is important that Gallaudet begin to look more closely at its alumni as perspective donors to the nation's university for the deaf.

Since Gallaudet is relatively new in the advancement arena and has many similarities to HBCUs, it is important that the University embraces its past and look to its colleagues at the HBCUs who are successful at fund raising to share ideas. The Deaf community, like the African American community and other cultural groups, has its own culture of giving. Gallaudet has the opportunity to educate its alumni and students and become a more successful part of this culture.

Notes

1. J. J. Havens and P. G. Schervish (1999), *Millionaires and the Millennium: New Estimates of the Forthcoming Wealth Transfer and the Prospects for a Golden Age of Philanthropy*, Boston College Social Welfare Research Institute, Boston; J. J. Havens and P. G. Schervish (2003), "Why the $41 trillion wealth transfer estimate is still valid: A review of challenges and questions," *The Journal of Gift Planning*, 7, 1, pp. 11–15.

2. D. Joulfaian (2000), "Estate taxes and charitable bequests by the wealthy," Working Paper 7663, National Bureau of Economic Research, Cambridge, MA; S. M. Butler, "Why the Bush tax cuts are no threat to philanthropy," *The Heritage Foundation Backgrounder*, 1417, 8 March. Online at Website

3. B. Smith, S. Shue, J. L. Vest, and J. Villarreal (1999), *Philanthropy in Communities of Color*, Indiana University Press, Bloomington; Council on Foundations (1999), *Cultures of Caring: Philanthropy in Diverse American Communities*, Council on Foundations, Washington, DC; W. K. Kellogg Foundation (1999), *Emerging Philanthropy in Communities of Color: A Report on Current Trends*. W. K. Kellogg Foundation, Battle Creek, MI. Available online at <http://www.wkkf.org/Programming/RenderRes.aspx?CID=12&ID=687>.

4. P. Ladd (2003), *Understanding Deaf Culture: In Search of Deafhood*, Multilingual Matters LTD, Tonawanda, NY.

5. L. A. Dexter (1970), *Elite and Specialized Interviewing*, Northwestern University Press, Evanston, IL, p. 136.

6. S. B. Merriam (1998), *Qualitative Research and Case Study Applications in Education: Revised and Expanded from "Case Study Research in Education,"* Jossey-Bass Publishers, San Francisco.

7. Ibid., p. 73.

8. Ibid., p. 74.

9. A. Strauss, L. Schatzman, R. Bucher, D. Erlich and M. Sobshin (1981), *Psychiatric Ideologies and Institutions*, 2nd edn., Transaction, New Brunswick, NJ; Merriam (1998), *Qualitative Research and Case Study Applications in Education*, op. cit.

10. M. Q. Patton (1990), *Qualitative Evaluation Methods*, 2nd edn. Sage, Thousand Oaks, CA.

11. Merriam (1998), *Qualitative Research and Case Study Applications in Education*, op. cit.

12. A. W. Attwood (1964), *Gallaudet College: Its First One Hundred Years*, Gallaudet College, Washington, DC; *US Statues at Large* 11 (1857): 161.

13. H. O. Bishop (1922), "Where the deaf and mute overcome their handicaps," *The National Republican*, June 17.

14. Attwood (1964), *Gallaudet College*, op. cit.

15. Attwood (1964), *Gallaudet College*, op. cit., p. 4, quoting *The Washington Evening Star*, 1860; N. B. Tadie (1979), "A history of drama at Gallaudet College: 1864 to 1969," Ph.D. Dissertation, New York University, 1979.

16. Attwood (1964), *Gallaudet College*, op. cit.; John L. Pulley (2003), "The sign language of fund raising: Gallaudet University, an institution founded for the deaf, aims for donors' hearts," *The Chronicle of Higher Education*, July 11, p. A23.

17. "An Act to Authorize the Columbia Institute for the Deaf and Dumb and the Blind to Confer Degrees," *U.S. Statutes at Large* (1864): 45; Attwood (1964), *Gallaudet College*, op. cit.; Tadie (1979), "A History of Drama at Gallaudet College," op. cit.

18. E. M. Gallaudet (1911), "A history of the Columbia Institution for the Deaf and Dumb," Speech to the Columbia Historical Society, January 17, 1911, *Records of the Columbia Historical Society*, Washington, DC, XV; Attwood, *Gallaudet College*, op. cit.

19. Gallaudet (1911), "A history," op. cit, p. 6.

20. F. Peet (1949), "The building of Gallaudet," *Gallaudet Alumni Bulletin*, July, p. 3.

21. Tadie (1979), "A history of drama at Gallaudet College," op. cit.; "Interesting dedicatory exercises at the Columbia Institution" (1871), *Daily Patriot*, Washington, DC, July 30, p. 1.

22. Gallaudet (1911), "A history," op. cit, p. 12.

23. E. M. Gallaudet (1882), "President Garfield's connection with the deaf-mute college" (pamphlet), Gibson Brothers, Washington, DC, pp. 7–11.

24. J. Gannon (Ed.) (1994), *Gallaudet Almanac*, Gallaudet Press, Washington, DC.; Gallaudet University Archives. *Gallaudet College Catalogues, 1975–1976*; Pulley (2003), "The sign language of fund raising," op. cit.

25. Tadie (1979), "A history of drama at Gallaudet College," op. cit.; Nina B. Van Oss (1953), "On Dr. Hall's long range plans," *Gallaudet Alumni Bulletin*, November.

26. Van Oss (1953), "On Dr. Hall's long range plans," p. 12, emphasis added.

27. Gallaudet University (2004), Office of Institutional Advancement. "Board of Associates Briefing Book," November 4.

28. Attwood (1964), *Gallaudet College*, op. cit.

29. United States Office of Education (1949), *The Federal Government and the Higher Education of the Deaf: a progress report on the Columbia Institution for the Deaf, with proposals for action*, United States Office of Education, Washington, DC.

30. Attwood (1964), *Gallaudet College*, op. cit.

31. R. N. Pacto (1969), "Reminiscences of Dr. Leonard M. Elstad," *Buff and Blue*, May 8, p. 2.

32. *Historical Statistics of the United States* (1975), The United States Government Printing Office, Washington DC, retrieved electronically from <http://www.westegg.com/inflation>

33. J. R. Thelin (2004), *A History of American Higher Education*, The Johns Hopkins University Press, Baltimore, MD.

34. Gallaudet University (2004), Office of Budget, Administration and Finance, May 1.

35. Pulley (2003), "The sign language of fund raising," op. cit.; Cathy Sweet-Windham, interview with author, Washington, DC, November 3, 2004.

36. C. C. Garvin, Jr. (1978), *Corporate Philanthropy: The Third Aspect of Social Responsibility*, Council for Financial Aid to Education, New York.

37. Attwood, Attwood (1964), *Gallaudet College*, op. cit., pp. 38, 44.

38. Ibid., p. 45.

39. Cathy Sweet-Windham, interview.

40. N. M. Pusey (1978), *American Higher Education, 1945–1970: A Personal Report*, Harvard University Press, Cambridge, MA; Thelin (2004), *A History of American Higher Education*, op. cit.; W. B. Cook (1997), "Fund raising and the college presidency in an era of uncertainty: From 1975 to the present," *Journal of Higher Education*, 68, 1, pp. 53–86.

41. D. W. Breneman (1994), *Liberal Arts Colleges: Thriving, Surviving, or Endangered?* The Brookings Institution, Washington, DC.

42. David Armstrong, interview with author, Washington, DC, November 3, 2004.

43. B. E. Brittingham and T. R. Pezzullo (1990), *The Campus Green: Fund Raising in Higher Education. ASHE-ERIC higher Education Report No. 1*, The George Washington University, School of Education and Human Development, Washington, DC.

44. Cathy Sweet-Windham, interview.

45. Gallaudet University (1997). Office of Institutional Advancement, "Grenzebach Feasibility Study review and update."

46. Ibid.

47. Gallaudet University (2004). Office of Institutional Advancement. "Board of Associates Briefing Book," op. cit; C. S. Hunter, E. B. Jones, and C. Boger (1999), "A study of the relationship between alumni giving and selected characteristics of alumni donors of Livingstone College, NC," *Journal of Black Studies*, 29, 4, pp. 523–39.

48. Pulley (2003), "The sign language of fund raising," op. cit.

49. Cathy Sweet-Windham, interview.

50. Lynne Murray, interview with author, Washington, DC, November 3, 2004.

51. Ibid.; M. Gasman and S. Anderson-Thompkins (2003), *Fund Raising from Black-College Alumni: Successful Strategies for Supporting Alma Mater*, Council for the Advancement and Support of Education, Washington, DC.

52. Lynne Murray, interview.

53. Council on Foundations (1999), *Cultures of Caring*, op. cit.

54. Gasman and Anderson-Thompkins (2003), *Fund Raising from Black-College Alumni*, op. cit.

55. Lynne Murray, interview, op. cit.

56. Ladd (2003), *Understanding Deaf Culture*, op. cit.

57. Ibid.; Lynne Murray, interview.

58. Cathy Sweet-Windham, interview.

59. P. B. Chewning (1993), "The ultimate goal: Installing the volunteer and philanthropic ethic," in B. T. Todd (Ed.), *Student Advancement Programs: Shaping Tomorrow's Alumni Leaders Today*, Council for the Advancement and Support of Education, Washington, DC, pp. 147–8.
60. Lynne Murray, interview.
61. B. T. Todd (Ed.) (1993), *Student Advancement Programs: Shaping Tomorrow's Alumni Leaders Today*, Council for the Advancement and Support of Education, Washington, DC, p. iii.
62. Todd (1993), *Student Advancement Programs*, op. cit; Innes van Nostrand (1999), "Young alumni programming," in J. Feudo (Ed.), *Alumni Relations: A Newcomer's Guide to Success*, Council for the Advancement and Support of Education, Washington, DC, pp. 127–36.
63. Lynne Murray, interview.
64. Ibid.; L. H. Nakada (1993), "Student interns: Cultivating the next generation of advancement professionals," in B. T. Todd (Ed.), *Student Advancement Programs: Shaping Tomorrow's Alumni Leaders Today*, Council for the Advancement and Support of Education, Washington, DC, pp. 141–5.
65. Council for Aid to Education, "Voluntary Support of Education Survey-Data Miner," <http://vse.cae.org>
66. American Association of Fundraising Counsel (2003), *Giving USA 2003: The Annual Report on Philanthropy for the Year 2002*, American Association of Fundraising Counsel, New York.
67. Council for Aid to Education, op. cit.
68. K. Kein (1994), *Fundraising for Social Change*, 3rd edn. Chardon Press, Inverness, CA.
69. American Association of Fundraising Counsel (2003), *Giving USA* 2003, op. cit., p. 116.
70. Gallaudet University (2004). Office of Institutional Advancement. "Board of Associates Briefing Book," op. cit.
71. M. S. Boyce (1992), "Fund-raising and market effectiveness at historically black colleges and universities," Ed.D. dissertation, State University of New York at Albany.
72. Cathy Sweet-Windham, interview.
73. Smith, Shue, Vest, and Villarreal (1999), *Philanthropy in Communities of Color*, op. cit.
74. Cathy Sweet-Windham, interview.
75. Ladd (2000), *Understanding Deaf Culture*, op. cit.
76. Cathy Sweet-Windham, interview.

WOMEN'S PHILANTHROPY PROGRAMS AT COEDUCATIONAL COLLEGES AND UNIVERSITIES

JEANIE LOVELL

Many programs that work at universities and colleges to successfully engage more women as donors can be applied to any other nonprofit organization.

A growing number of coeducational colleges and universities are seeing the untapped philanthropic potential of alumnae donors. In response, some institutions have established women's philanthropy programs in order to educate and engage more women as leaders and donors. This study compares existing alumnae initiatives at a variety of coeducational institutions, ranging from large public research universities to small private liberal arts colleges, in order to identify effective models and components. The conclusions from this study will be useful to institutions of all sizes that want to engage their alumnae more actively and help these women reach their full potential as philanthropists.

Alumnae Giving in Higher Education

The success of fundraising programs at colleges and universities relies in large part on the generosity of graduates of their institutions. According to Judith E. Nichols in her book *Pinpointing Affluence in the Twenty-First Century* (2001), male and female "alumni provide nearly 40 percent of contributions at both colleges and secondary schools" (p. 10). Therefore it is important for institutions of higher education to pay particular attention to the changing demographics of this primary donor constituency.

The National Center for Education Statistics reports that U.S. college and university enrollment of both sexes has increased in the past three decades. But women's enrollment has increased at such a pace that the proportion of undergraduate men and women is nearly the reverse of what it was thirty years ago. In 1970, 56 percent of the students who earned bachelor's degrees were men and 44 percent were women. By 2001, women were 56 percent of undergraduates nationwide (Bickel, 2002, p. 34).

More than a decade before, in the early 1990s, higher education began taking notice of alumnae donors. In "Alma Maters Court Their Daughters," a 1991 article in the *New York Times*, author Anne Matthews wrote:

Many campus administrations have long assumed that "donor" primarily means "male donor." No more. As alumnae move into prominence and power in business and the professions (often becoming, in the process, major giving prospects), their views on college philanthropy are creating bewilderment, even alarm, on many campuses. The reasons why women give, or refuse to give, or give sporadically, or donate to one institution attended but not another are proving far more complex than previously believed—and far different from the giving decisions of their male counterparts [p. 73].

One year later, the *Chronicle of Higher Education* noted:

Many colleges and universities, eager for new sources of support and aware that women represent an untapped donor market, are beginning to court their daughters in the same way they have pursued their sons: aggressively. They are setting up special fund-raising programs to woo female donors and are paying much closer attention to the views of alumnae about their institutions [McMillen, 1992, p. A31].

Without a doubt, this was a formative period in which fundraisers began to take serious note of women's potential as donors in their own names. The media attention directed at the successful fundraising efforts of women's colleges in the early 1990s prompted comparisons of alumnae support at coeducational institutions. Data showing less support by women graduates of coeducational colleges and universities were viewed by some as a warning sign. Select institutions recognized this as an opportunity and began looking for new ways to engage and involve their alumnae as donors and leaders.

The women's philanthropy movement as a whole gained momentum throughout the 1990s, which sparked a growing number of coeducational institutions to implement philanthropy initiatives designed to involve more alumnae. Today more and more institutions are seeing the potential of women's philanthropy to higher education. According to M. Ann Abbe, "As the forces of education and career choices, business acumen, accumulation of wealth and charitable attitude converge, women possess a greater capacity to make major contributions to universities than any time in our history" (2001, para. 19). Yet the creation of a women's philanthropy program is still a relatively unexplored idea among the vast majority of U.S. colleges and universities.

With the exception of the handful of coeducational institutions whose women's philanthropy programs received significant media attention in the 1990s (for example, UCLA, the University of Wisconsin-Madison, Colgate) or have been highlighted more recently by the Council for Advancement and Support of Education (CASE) or the Women's Philanthropy Institute, little published documentation is available regarding the impact of women's philanthropy programs at coeducational colleges and universities. Yet a growing number of colleges and universities are implementing alumnae initiatives and exploring ways to involve more women as donors and leaders at their institutions. Interviews conducted as part of a thesis study of women's philanthropy programs (Lovell, 2004) sought to learn from some of their collective experiences.

Interview Findings

To gather firsthand information regarding the benefits and challenges of establishing a women's philanthropy program, telephone interviews were conducted with development representatives from eight coeducational colleges and universities from throughout the United States: Denison University (Ohio), Iowa State University, Mount Mercy College (Iowa), Purdue University (Indiana), South Dakota State University, University of Mississippi, University of Tennessee, and University of Wisconsin-Madison. Of these eight, five were founded as coeducational universities (several of which were land grant institutions), two were founded as men's universities, and one was founded as a women's college. All eight institutions currently enroll men and women.

Each of the institutions interviewed currently has an established women's philanthropy program. Information reflects a full range of program histories, spanning from two to seventeen years. The oldest program, founded in 1988, is at the University of Wisconsin-Madison, which was the first coeducational institution to create a major gift organization for women. Three of the institutions interviewed established their programs in the mid-1990s, and four have programs that have been begun since 2000.

All college and university representatives who participated in the telephone interviews were asked a series of open-ended questions focused on the women's philanthropy programs at their respective institutions. The interviews provided a snapshot of eight unique programs at different stages of implementation. The participants shared detailed feedback specific to their respective programs, which offer a full range of models that could be applied at other institutions.

In order to present the findings, each question is listed with a narrative summary of the participants' responses.

- *What is the mission/purpose of the women's philanthropy program at your institution? What are the primary goals of your women's philanthropy program?* In defining the mission or purpose of their respective women's philanthropy programs, all institutional representatives stated that educating women about finances, raising their awareness about philanthropy, and identifying and encouraging women as leaders are primary program goals. Several also said their programs seek to inspire and motivate women to think more broadly about major gifts and to increase giving by women donors. Some representatives cited additional goals of providing networking opportunities for women of all ages and seeking women who can be role models in philanthropy. One institution also includes a leadership mentoring program as a key part of its women's philanthropy initiative.

The women's philanthropy programs at all eight of the institutions are open to all women associated with the college or university: alumnae, faculty, trustees, spouses, and friends of the institution. Two universities stated that their women's philanthropy programs serve primarily alumnae, but all women are welcome to participate.

- *Briefly describe the women's philanthropy program at your institution including an overview of the key components (e.g., meetings, mailings, seminars, minimum donation, annual celebration).* All institutions stated that they hold educational seminars or forums for women on topics such as finance, estate planning, or leadership. Often these seminars are part of an annual event hosted on their respective campuses. The scope of participation ranges from 40 to 350 participants. Many programs feature primarily women speakers at their seminars and events. One institution indicated that its founding group mandated "women teaching women" to increase women's comfort levels.

  All of the institutions interviewed have a steering committee, board, or council that meets at least once annually to advise their women's philanthropy programs. The memberships range from ten to thirty-three members. Some advisory groups meet as many as four times each year; most meet only once or twice annually.

  The financial expectations associated with the women's giving programs vary significantly. Mount Mercy College and South Dakota State University have giving circles that require gifts at a level of five hundred dollars annually. At the University of Wisconsin-Madison, the women's philanthropy program encourages all alumnae giving but focuses on major gifts of twenty-five thousand dollars or more to the area of the donor's interest. The council has an annual collaborative giving project to support women on campus and a Women's Leadership Fund. The University of Mississippi is the only institution to request dues for membership; it also receives corporate and foundation grant support for the program's annual operating budget and its endowed scholarship. Several institutions, including Denison University, indicated that they do not have specific solicitations as part of their women's philanthropy programs, but use the programs as a cultivation tool to encourage women to consider more major gifts.

  Marketing and communication efforts vary among the institutions. While two universities noted sending regular newsletters to highlight women's impact, other institutions use their existing alumni publications to publicize the women's philanthropy program and spotlight women as donors and leaders.

  Iowa State University and the University of Wisconsin-Madison noted that they conduct in-house staff training regarding gender sensitivity as part of their women's philanthropy programs.

- *What was the biggest challenge in establishing a women's philanthropy program at your institution?* According to the interviews, one of the biggest challenges in establishing a women's philanthropy program was getting the administration and top leadership to buy in to the concept of a program focused on women. One representative indicated that some people within her institution were initially concerned about discrimination and feared that women would be "belittled" by the segmenting. Another representative stated that her institution's biggest challenge was overcoming the internal and external skepticism of the need for such a program aimed at women. One person said some individuals within her university doubted a women's philanthropy program could raise significant blocks of money, which has since been disproved.

Several institutions noted the challenges of staffing and managing a women's philanthropy program. According to Debra Engle, vice president for development at Iowa State University Foundation, its biggest challenge has been "determining how to share responsibility and make sure it is a coordinated, collaborative effort," so it is not just one staff member doing everything. Determining the financial success of the program can also be a challenge, according to Martha Taylor, vice president of the University of Wisconsin Foundation, Madison, who said it is difficult to trace "credit" for the money raised to the women's philanthropy program in particular.

Another big challenge, according to the interviews, was getting women to think differently about their own giving. One institution stated that older women had the capacity to give but were afraid of having financial advisers "jump on them" when they have limited financial background. Acknowledging generational differences, one university indicated the ongoing challenge of "trying to appeal to young and old" within one program aimed at women.

- *What has been the most positive outcome?* Several institutions commented that the most positive outcome of their women's philanthropy programs is the women's response in terms of their giving and involvement. The University of Wisconsin-Madison said one positive outcome is "the new donors we have brought into the fold." South Dakota State University said its program has "unearthed women who were wanting to get involved." Denison University noted that several women are now members of the university's highly selective board of trustees.

  According to Engle, one of the positive outcomes of the women's philanthropy program at Iowa State University is "seeing women step up in leadership positions and taking their role in philanthropy much more seriously," which has resulted in "larger, more-focused gifts." Purdue University and Denison University also noted that many women have made major gifts as a result of their involvement, citing gifts of $1 million or more from participants in their women's philanthropy programs. At Mount Mercy College, women have experienced "joy in allocating money and seeing what it could do" as part of its giving circle, which the college said is the most positive outcome of its women's philanthropy program.

  Many institutions also noted the positive outcomes involving campus awareness and gender sensitivity. Iowa State University noted a cultural change with the "sensitivity of men looking at family philanthropy, not just who is sitting in the corporate office." The University of Tennessee said its most positive outcome was the "realization that we need more women involved." Taylor also acknowledged the "level of awareness by the dean and colleagues who really supported the concept of involving women on advisory boards" as a positive outcome at the University of Wisconsin-Madison. At South Dakota State University, "collaborating with women across campus for a common goal" has been a plus as well.

  For the University of Mississippi, the leadership mentoring program that is part of its women's philanthropy initiative is the most positive outcome.

- *Have there been outcomes that you would consider "problematic" or "negative"? If yes, what are they, and why do you consider them problematic or negative?* Responses to this question varied considerably. Three institutions said getting people to recognize the need for a program was somewhat problematic initially. "Dealing with the perception of women's giving and why it's necessary to have a separate group" was a challenge, according to one university. Another representative noted that her institution had gotten "a few complaints that it was 'all women,'" although men are welcome to attend program events. Cheryl Altinkemer, senior director of development at Purdue University, said the development community is "interested intellectually, but action may take some time. Education and success [of the women's philanthropy program] get their attention."

  One university expressed concern that the development staff "go at alums with so many asks, we may be shifting allegiance rather than expanding on top of current commitments." Another institution shared frustration with how to get the word out and encourage women to participate in a women's philanthropy program. The difficulty of having a common agenda for women of diverse backgrounds and generations was also noted.

Staffing was identified as problematic by one representative, who said the women's philanthropy program is labor intensive and acknowledged that women donors "need lots of attention."

One of the eight institutions interviewed said there were no "problematic" or negative outcomes resulting from the establishment of its women's philanthropy program.

- *Did you receive any criticism for targeting women? Please explain.* None of the institutions interviewed reported any direct criticism for targeting women with a women's philanthropy program. Some representatives indicated that they did experience skepticism about the need for a women's philanthropy program, but felt *criticism* was too strong of a word.

  One person said that while none of the women were negative about the concept, some questioned if it was good to separate men and women donors. Another representative said she had fielded similar concerns from some of her development colleagues who were concerned about targeting by gender.

  One university pointed out that generation makes a significant difference, noting that "many fifty-year-olds don't want to segment." The representative added that a women's philanthropy program "is not for everyone" but is another way of involving potential donors.

- *Have you experienced a growth in alumnae giving (dollars and/or participation) as a result of the women's philanthropy program?* While most institutions interviewed acknowledged that it is hard to quantify and pinpoint giving to a particular program, all thought their women's philanthropy programs have resulted in some level of growth in giving among their alumnae. One university noted growth particularly at the "largest-end capital gifts," where, after removing couples, now almost half of their top one hundred donors are women. Most of these gifts were bequests, yet the university anticipates it is "likely to see more women making outright gifts" in the future. Another institution said its program had experienced growth in giving and participation, saying it had found "new donor pockets" and "opened a new market segment" for the university.

  Two institutions commented that because they split gifts between couples (attributing a portion of the gift to both wife and husband), it is more difficult to track giving directly resulting from involvement with their women's philanthropy programs. One university said that it is a struggle to answer the question of growth and that perhaps institutions need to find a new way to get at the issue of program success. According to Martha Taylor, the challenge is how to establish a direct line of credit to know what gifts resulted from the women's philanthropy program. Given the multiple contacts and multiple involvements most donors have with an institution, there is typically not one particular incident that is solely responsible for a gift.

  Some of the newer programs said it is too early to tell if there has been growth in giving, especially since women generally take longer to become major donors; however, one representative predicts there will be a growth in giving because the women's philanthropy program has "struck a chord with some women who weren't donors before." Another university representative emphasized that it is best to view a women's philanthropy program as a "long-term thing, not an annual review."

- *What words of wisdom would you offer to institutions considering a women's philanthropy program?* All representatives were very encouraging and highly recommended establishing a women's philanthropy program. They offered a full range of advice in response to the closing question on words of wisdom. Their comments appear under the general categories that emerged as themes:

Goals and Expectations

"Have realistic expectations—this requires a longer process."
"Start small—the program will require huge time and effort."
"Tailor the program to your institution."
"Know your institution's culture."

"Evaluate as you go."
"Be clear about purpose and goals."
"Look at women's giving and benchmarking to determine goals."
"Determine how to show the program has made a difference; gather baseline data on women's giving to show a change has happened."

Staffing and Budget

"You don't have to spend a lot of money to start a program; don't go extravagant."
"Have a budget on which to operate."
"Be sure to have staff to handle the program; will need a full-time staff person ('staff champion') devoted to the initiative; very rewarding and very labor intensive."
"Must be able to manage the volunteers; an all-female group can be harder to manage because they want more accountability."

To begin planning for a women's philanthropy program, those interviewed recommended establishing a committee or starting with a small planning group. One representative suggested identifying a core group of ten to twenty women to gather ideas. Getting the right people involved (staff, leadership, and volunteers) was also noted. Several institutions emphasized the importance of having a diverse group, including younger members and minorities. It was also recommended that each group be approached differently.

Regarding institutional buy-in, several institutions interviewed noted the importance of having the endorsement of leadership, with support from the highest levels. Others emphasized the need for buy-in from colleagues and raised awareness across the institution. One representative acknowledged, "There is a huge learning curve."

Finally, regarding presentations and events offered as part of a women's philanthropy program, several of the institutions interviewed noted the importance of including breakout sessions and networking time to get women talking. Women want sessions to be interactive and want to be able to ask questions. According to one representative, the best presenters are those who want to interact with the women, not lecture them.

Summary of Recommendations

Based on the findings of this study, it is evident that women's philanthropy programs can and do have a positive impact on fundraising at coeducational institutions.

While most women's philanthropy programs share some basic components, many different models are being implemented nationwide. Budgets, staffing, and participation all vary considerably, depending on the size of the institution and the scope of the program. It is clear that in order to be effective, a women's philanthropy program or initiative must be tailored to fit the institution's culture.

Plan First

The key to success seems to be to begin with comprehensive planning. It is evident that an institution must clearly define goals and thoroughly plan before launching a women's philanthropy program. The importance of proceeding slowly in order to educate people and build necessary support for the concept was emphasized by those interviewed.

Build Institutional Buy-in

As noted in the interviews, overcoming internal and external skepticism can be a major challenge that must be addressed up front. According to the institutions interviewed, it is important to have both the endorsement of leadership and buy-in from colleagues. Gaining support from the highest levels of administration helps to convey the importance of having a program or initiative aimed specifically at women donors.

Start Small

Unlike the major universities, which have larger staffs and greater financial resources to support a comprehensive program aimed at women's philanthropy, smaller institutions may be better served by beginning their efforts on a smaller scale as part of existing fundraising programs. This idea of starting small was supported by comments from some of the newer women's philanthropy programs, including South Dakota State University and Mount Mercy College.

Gather Data

As recommended in the interviews, institutions need to do a formal assessment of giving trends before moving forward. It is likely that both the administration and alumnae will want to see data that demonstrate a need for a women's philanthropy program and evidence it will work. Many of the institutions interviewed suggested using baseline data to help define the goals and purpose from the beginning. Future data comparisons will help determine if the program is a success.

Educate, Educate, Educate

Education will be imperative to the successful implementation of women's philanthropy initiatives. Insights shared in the interviews affirmed the importance of educating the development staff, alumnae and other women participants, and the institution as a whole about women's philanthropy.

According to the interviews, women who choose to participate in women's philanthropy programs do become more engaged, involved, and invested. The challenge is to find compelling ways to encourage alumnae and other potential women donors to participate so they will be educated about finances and philanthropy.

Discuss Gender Bias

The institutions interviewed cited varying viewpoints at their respective colleges and universities regarding questions of gender difference. Most ranged from enthusiasm to skepticism. Some people see a real need for programs aimed at women; others view these same programs as unnecessary. Although the interviews did not address the history of gender bias in traditional fundraising programs and in society as a whole, these issues are worthy of future discussion in order to educate people about their potential implications for fundraising initiatives.

Acknowledge Generational Differences

As noted in the interviews, developing programs that appeal to women across generations can be challenging. This study concludes that programming associated with a women's philanthropy initiative must be tailored to appeal to multiple age groups in order to relate to women at different life stages.

Conclusion

Women's philanthropy will play an increasingly significant role in the future of colleges and universities. Coeducational institutions in particular must recognize the growing potential of alumnae giving and nurture relationships that engage more women as leaders and donors in their own names.

Through specific programs and initiatives aimed at educating and empowering women, institutions of higher education can broaden their donor bases and increase philanthropic support. According to the interviews, women's philanthropy programs have been well received by the women who participate. The impact in terms of both involvement and investment is positive and worth emulating. Learning from the successes and challenges experienced by existing women's philanthropy programs, this study affirms the role of women's philanthropy and encourages more coeducational colleges and universities to explore ways to realize the untapped potential of women philanthropists.

The interviews cited in this chapter were conducted as part of a 2004 thesis study that examined women's philanthropy programs currently under way at coeducational institutions in order to identify effective components for a model that can be applied and implemented at Luther College, a four-year, private, coeducational liberal arts institution located in Decorah, Iowa. The study also included an extensive literature review and two focus groups: one with Luther College alumnae and one with the Luther College Alumni and Development staff.

References

Abbe, M. A. "Converging Forces Enhance Women's Philanthropy." Abbe & Associates, Mar. 1, 2001. http://www.philanthropy-solutions.com/Articles/thearticles.asp?ID=13.

Bickel, K. "Alumnae: In Numbers Too Big to Ignore." *CASE Currents*, Mar. 2002, pp. 34–38.

Lovell, J. M. "Women's Philanthropy Programs at Coeducational Colleges and Universities: Exploring the Concept at Luther College." Unpublished master's thesis, Saint Mary's University of Minnesota, 2004.

Matthews, A. "Alma Maters Court Their Daughters." *New York Times*, Apr. 7, 1991, pp. 40, 73,77.

McMillen, L. "Many College Fund Raisers See Alumnae as Untapped Donors." *Chronicle of Higher Education*, Apr. 1, 1992, pp. A31–A32.

Nichols, J. E. *Pinpointing Affluence in the Twenty-First Century.* Chicago: Precept Press, 2001.

Bibliography
Chapter 11: Fundraising from Non-Traditional Communities

Barrett, Gregory T. "Institutional Culture, Life-cycle Issues and Other Factors: Issues Selected Alumnae Who Are Actively Involved in Spelman College Self-Report as Being Influential in Their Giving Decisions." *The CASE International Journal of Educational Advancement*, Vol. 3, No. 3 (2002), pp. 259–279.

Cortés, Mike. "Questions about Hispanics and Fundraising." *New Directions for Philanthropic Fundraising*, No. 37 (2002), pp. 45–54.

Fischer, Marilyn. "Respecting the Individual, Valuing Diversity: Equity in Philanthropy and Fund Raising." In *Critical Issues in Fund Raising*, Dwight F. Burlingame, ed. New York: John Wiley & Sons, 1997, pp. 65–72.

Gasman, Marybeth. "The Role of Black Faculty in Fund Raising at Black Colleges: What Is It and What Can It Become?" *The CASE International Journal of Educational Advancement*, Vol. 5, No. 2 (2005), pp. 171–179.

Gough, Jr., Samuel N. "Diverse Fundraising and Philanthropy Today." In *Cultivating Diversity in Fundraising*, Janice Gow Pettey, ed. New York: John Wiley & Sons, 2002, pp. 95–127.

Havens, John F., and Paul G. Schervish. "Wealth Transfer Estimates for African American Households." New Directions for Philanthropic Fundraising, No. 48 (2005), pp. 47–55.

Kaminski, Andrea. "Women as Philanthropists." In *New Strategies for Educational Fund Raising*, Michael J. Worth, ed. Westport, CT: Praeger Press, 2002, pp. 187–196.

Minter, Michele. "Women's Volunteerism and Philanthropy at Princeton University." *New Directions for Philanthropic Fundraising*, No. 50 (2005), pp. 125–139.

Patterson, Frederick D. "Would It Not Be Wise for Some Negro Schools to Make Joint Appeal to Public for Funds?" *The Pittsburg Courier*, "Southern Viewpoint" (January 30, 1943).

Scanlan, Joanne B., and John Abrahams. "Giving Traditions of Minority Communities." In *New Strategies for Educational Fund Raising*, Michael J. Worth, ed. Westport, CT: Praeger Press, 2002, pp. 197–205.

Shaw, Sondra C., and Martha A. Taylor. "How and Why Women Give." Chapter 4 in *Reinventing Fundraising: Realizing the Potential of Women's Philanthropy.* San Francisco, CA: Jossey-Bass, 1995, pp. 83–100.

Wagner, Lilya, and J. Patrick Ryan. "Achieving Diversity among Fundraising Professionals." *New Directions for Philanthropic Fundraising*, No. 43 (2004), pp. 63–84.

CHAPTER 12

DONOR MOTIVATION

INCLINATION, OBLIGATION, AND ASSOCIATION

WHAT WE KNOW AND WHAT WE NEED TO LEARN ABOUT DONOR MOTIVATION

Paul G. Schervish, PhD

This chapter reviews the *status quaestionis* surrounding the issue of motivation for charitable gifts of money and assets—what I will call *financial philanthropy*. By *motivation*, I refer not to the moralistic distinction between so-called noble and base intentions, or between altruistic and self-serving aspirations. Rather, by motivation I refer to the array of associations, experiences, goals, and orientations that generate people's charitable giving—what I like to refer to as *mobilizing factors*. Because the same factors (such as volunteering or organizational membership) may lead to giving *and* increased giving, it is always necessary to bear in mind what place in the "pipeline" of giving we are speaking about at each point in the discussion. Therefore, in exploring the mobilizing factors that induce financial philanthropy, it is important to distinguish between those influences that lead people to become givers in the first place and those that lead some donors to make larger than average gifts or to increase their giving.

In all instances, the guiding principle of my approach to charitable giving is represented by an *identification* model rather than an *altruism* model of motivation. The altruism model is best known through the various studies on extraordinary heroism and on blood and organ donations. I have elaborated my view of the identification model in various places (Ostrander & Schervish, 1990; Schervish, 1993, 1995) and find it well articulated in a parallel fashion by Martin (1994) and Langdon (forthcoming). My fullest case for the theoretical and empirical superiority of the identification model over the altruism model is in the first chapter of my book *The Modern Medicis* (Schervish, forthcoming). Both my intensive interviews with wealthy donors and survey analyses of giving and volunteering persuade me that it makes little theoretical or practical sense to chase down forces of *selflessness* precisely in the areas of life in which dedication and commitment of *self-identification* are so crucial. Thus instead of investigating the quantitative *absence* of the self, I prefer to investigate the qualitative presence of the self.

I address the issue of motivation and charitable giving in four sections. First, I summarize the literature on motivations for giving. I do not intend this review to be exhaustive. Rather in reviewing a range of conceptual and empirical writings, my goal is to present a useful topical survey of the kinds of variables designated by researchers as important. Second, I will present the empirical findings my colleague John Havens and I have thus far discovered from our ongoing multivariate research on the factors that induce charitable giving. In the third section, I elaborate a research agenda aimed at substantiating what we and others have already found and at uncovering what we still need to learn. I conclude by suggesting the implications for encouraging a less judgmental and more fruitful fund raising attitude, especially in regard to wealthy donors.

Mobilizing Factors for Charitable Giving

The current literature on the motivating factors for charitable giving is extensive; however, it is uneven in its level of theoretical sophistication and empirical complexity. For a number of reasons, including that volunteering is tied to charitable giving, the literature on motivations for volunteering is always indirectly, if not directly, relevant to the discussion of charitable giving. Also, the fund raising and prospect research literature is invariably related to the mobilizing factors for giving insofar as this literature addresses the organizational techniques and personal strategies fund raisers employ to induce donors to contribute. Also, this literature is both repetitive and partial. Although much of the literature offers useful information, the key findings seem to be periodically "rediscovered." As a result, we have a litany of well-documented factors that appear to motivate charitable giving. In the absence of more complex research, we know little about the *relative importance* of these factors; that is, how the factors are linked together in a causal chain, and which factors turn out to be more important and which turn out to be less important in the light of multivariate statistical analyses. This is true for qualitative as well as quantitative research efforts. To date, neither approach for studying charitable giving has endeavored to produce anything even approaching normal science. We have not yet reached the point at which the theories, conceptual frameworks, measurement techniques, statistical analyses, and findings of one research effort build explicitly on previous research and become the basis for subsequent research designed to confirm, disprove, or amend previous findings.

So what can we learn from the current literature? Platon Coutsoukis, a research associate at the Social Welfare Research Institute, and I have undertaken a systematic review of the literature on the factors inducing charitable giving. As yet, our efforts have not progressed sufficiently to provide an appropriately complete and coherent account of this literature. However, I am able to outline the major categories of factors found to be influential in inducing charitable giving and to indicate the most important specific variables studied within each of the categories. We have generally limited our review to the literature that deals with charitable giving. In some instances, however, we report findings from studies on the factors that lead to "charitable acts" in general, without distinguishing between volunteering and giving.[1]

As I stated, I have not found a comprehensive literature review summarizing the empirical findings concerning charitable giving parallel to what David Horton Smith (1994) and Fischer and Schaffer (1993) have provided regarding the theory and research on volunteering. The two broadest conceptual outlines of factors contributing to giving are presented in Mixer (1993) and Schervish and Havens (1997). Although developed independently, the latter two frameworks are similar. Because I am understandably more familiar with the schema I developed, and because we have now carried out a substantial amount of empirical research based on it, I have chosen to summarize current research findings according to the rubrics of my framework. My debt to Mixer's good review, however, is great. Finally, I want to mention that Virginia A. Hodgkinson is currently completing a prodigious tome in which she provides a comprehensive review not just of the research findings on motivation for charitable giving but on the full range of religious, philosophical, sociological, psychological, legal, and institutional factors that lead to care and community participation. At this point, I have not drawn upon her work.

The major categories of variables comprising my conceptual framework grew out of my analysis of intensive interviews with millionaires in the Study on Wealth and Philanthropy (Schervish & Herman, 1988) and further elaborated in the course of subsequent research. Although the specific motivations of wealthy donors differ in significant ways from those of nonwealthy donors, the broad categories of variables I found to be relevant for millionaires seem to provide an effective conceptual framework for understanding giving in general. My research indicated the following eight variables:

1. *Communities of participation.* Groups and organizations in which one participates.
2. *Frameworks of consciousness.* Beliefs, goals, and orientations that shape the values and priorities that determine people's activities.
3. *Direct requests.* Invitations by persons or organizations to directly participate in philanthropy.

4. *Discretionary resources.* The quantitative and psychological wherewithal of time and money that can be mobilized for philanthropic purposes.

5. *Models and experiences from one's youth.* The people or experiences from one's youth that serve as positive exemplars for one's adult engagements.

6. *Urgency and effectiveness.* A sense of how necessary and/or useful charitable assistance will be in the face of the onset of an unanticipated or previously unrecognized family, community, national, or international crisis.

7. *Demographic characteristics.* The geographic, organizational, and individual circumstance of one's self, family, and community that affect one's philanthropic commitment.

8. *Intrinsic and extrinsic rewards.* The array of positive experiences and outcomes of one's current engagement that draws one deeper into a philanthropic identity.

The first seven variables work both to induce charitable involvement in the first place and, once in place, to increase one's level of commitment. The eighth variable—reinforcing rewards—is by definition relevant in regard to increasing the level of participation of those who have already become involved and, as such, may be in the form of one or more of the first seven variables. For a particular individual, any one of the first seven factors may be sufficient to induce at least a minimal level of philanthropic care, but in most cases the path to philanthropic care is via the influence of several if not all the factors.

Elaboration of Variables[2]

Communities of participation are the networks of formal and informal relationships with which people are associated. Communities of participation may be formal organizations such as schools, soup kitchens, or weekend soccer leagues. Communities of participation may also be quite informal, such as an extended family visiting and caring for an elderly grandparent or neighbors rallying to help a family burned out of its home. Some communities of participation (such as a political party) require little voluntary activity while others (such as a cooperative nursery school) require participation as a condition of membership. Some communities of participation are entered only out of choice, such as a volunteer fire department or volunteer counseling at a shelter for battered women. Others are entered as a result of circumstances; for example, parents with school-age children are automatically put into contact with numerous school, extracurricular, and sports programs that offer opportunities to volunteer time and to contribute money. As I indicated, many communities of participation directly request and sometimes require time and money from their participants. But the important point is that being connected to an array of such life-settings is the basis for people becoming aware of needs and choosing to respond.

Frameworks of consciousness are ways of thinking and feeling that are rooted deeply enough in one's awareness to induce a commitment to a cause based on political ideology, religious beliefs, social concerns, or other values. An awareness of the redemptive value of Alcoholics Anonymous' twelve-step program in one's own or a family member's life is one example. Equally common are the deeply felt convictions about political prisoners that lead concerned citizens to join Amnesty International, about homeless people or battered women that lead volunteers to work at shelters, about community violence that lead parents to patrol the streets as part of a neighborhood watch, about the value of religious faith that lead church members to work in a food bank or a program for racial justice. The list of motivating concerns is as long as the list of deeply cherished beliefs. Just as there are different types of organizations in which one may participate, there are different types of beliefs. Some mobilizing beliefs are in fact better described as general values, other beliefs are really fundamental orientations, while still other beliefs concern causes to which one is dedicated. Again, there are no impermeable boundaries separating these kinds of beliefs any more than there is a sharp demarcation between what one does because of heartfelt feelings, on the one hand, and communities of participation, on the other. Communities of participation and frameworks of consciousness almost always occur together.

The third mobilizing factor comprises *direct requests* made to individuals for contributions of time and money. Many of these invitations arise directly as a result of one's participation in an organization. Certainly, some people volunteer their time and money without being asked. For the majority of givers, being asked is cited as a major reason for their charitable efforts. We are finding evidence that while telephone and mail solicitations do get results (otherwise they would not be so incessant), those who contribute higher percentages of their income state they are not influenced by such impersonal methods. Still, there is every reason to believe that people in all income groups follow what I found among wealthy contributors, namely that being asked directly by someone the contributor knows personally or by a representative of an organization the contributor participates in is a major mobilizing factor. Once again, the linkages among the mobilizing factors are apparent. Being asked to contribute largely occurs from within existing communities of participation and appeals to existing frameworks of consciousness.

The presence of *discretionary resources* is a fourth factor leading to charitable commitment. The level of one's discretionary resources of time and money is a mixture of objective and subjective considerations. The amount of time retired people, with children out of the house, consider discretionary is likely to be greater than the amount felt to be available by members of the labor force who are still raising children. Similarly, a family of four with a household income of $75,000 presumably enjoys more discretionary spending than a family of four with an income of $25,000. Nevertheless, there are a good number of complicating factors including the amount of time needed to care for a sick spouse and the amount of money devoted to necessary expenditures such as college tuition and taxes. One family's necessity is another family's luxury, which highlights that the amount of discretionary resources is also a matter of subjective disposition. What may appear to some as a desperately urgent need for which they should sacrifice time and money may appear less compelling to others with the same objective resources. The organizations in which we participate, the cultural frameworks we embrace, the pleas to which we are attuned, and the resources we deem able to give are inextricably linked.

The same is true for the fifth determinant, namely the positive *models and experiences from one's youth* that animate adult philanthropy. By speaking of models from one's youth, I do not mean to neglect those exemplars from adulthood. But for the sake of clarity, I include such adult models (be they friends, business associates, or colleagues on a board of directors) as part of one's community of participation. To be emphasized here are those activities and lives that people are more or less drawn into in the course of growing up. To some extent, such contacts are voluntary choices. But the majority of them are more likely to have been unavoidable, put in the person's path by parents, grandparents, churches, youth groups, and schools. As such, they are occasions for initiation into the child's earliest communities of participation and frameworks of consciousness. They are part of a moral education that molds children's lives at a period when they are less guarded about priorities and more apt to accrue a feel for the charitable impulse.

The sixth mobilizing factor is the *urgency* with which needs are presented to potential donors and the effectiveness these donors perceive their charitable response to have. Such urgency usually revolves around the actual onset or introduction into an individual's purview of an unanticipated highly salient family, community, national, or international need. Such emergency needs are thrust on individuals by such events as illness, deaths, fires, and other tragedies that befall relatives and friends. But equally important are the local, national, and international natural disasters, famines, and epidemics that strike people as particularly compelling because of the dire nature of a situation and the lack of normal channels of provision. Here, perhaps more than in any other circumstance, people sense and respond to the realization, "There but for fortune go I." A response to urgency is connected to the perceived effectiveness of a response. An urgent need about which potential donors feel they can make no difference is unlikely to mobilize their time and money. In many ways, the now familiar "compassion fatigue" is a result of an emotional stalemate resulting from the intersection of repeated urgent appeals coupled with the perception that intervention is ineffective in curtailing suffering.

Demographic variables comprise the seventh category of influences. Such demographic variables include individuals' personal characteristics of age, education, gender, and race as well as various background or contextual characteristics associated with one's employment, community, home ownership, tenure living in a locale, and so forth. Most demographic characteristics are introduced into analyses as control variables and so are not accorded much explanatory substance. Many so-called demographic controls, however, represent important underlying causal dynamics. For example, education and age are not simply control variables. Rather they are indicators of a person's array of relationships, experiences, networks, organizational involvements, and time commitments that set in motion a range of consequences for charitable participation.

An eighth variable comes into play when we are seeking to explain the intensity of people's philanthropic commitment. This is the set of *intrinsic and extrinsic rewards* that accrue to individuals who are already active in philanthropy. The source and intensity of such satisfactions are connected to the additional communities of participation and frameworks of consciousness that philanthropists encounter in carrying out their commitments. Such reinforcing factors include getting to know other givers, formal and informal expressions of gratitude, public recognition of various sorts, and direct material benefits such as preferred seating at the symphony and decision-making clout at a welfare agency. But most important among such reinforcing rewards is the personal satisfaction from helping others and from seeing one's money and time used as an effective investment to accomplish cherished goals. In this regard, less involved philanthropists might do well to take a page from Jane Addams and from those who work directly with the beneficiaries of their philanthropy. One of the richest sources of reinforcing satisfaction is to ascertain firsthand the positive effect of one's care on the lives of others and to be able to more fully identify with one's beneficiaries as radical ends.

Exhibit 8.1 is a compendium of the various categories of mobilizing factors and specific variables examined in empirical research on the determinants of charitable giving.

Multivariate Analysis of Charitable Giving

To my knowledge, our research at the Social Welfare Research Institute is the only effort to carry out a multivariate analysis of variables representing nearly all the general factors catalogued in the preceding section. The major exception is that we have not yet modeled how intrinsic and extrinsic rewards advance additional giving. In regard to demographic variables, we have not yet attempted to incorporate the contextual variables of community and geography that Wolpert (1994, 1995a, 1995b) has skillfully analyzed.

We explored the causal relationship between the foregoing variable sets and charitable giving through a multivariate analysis of a subset of the "National Survey of Giving and Volunteering in the U.S." collected in 1992 by the Gallup Organization for the INDEPENDENT SECTOR (Schervish & Havens, 1994). The survey is of a representative cross-sectional sample of 2,671 American households whose respondent was 18 years of age or older. The survey obtains information on giving and volunteering, numerous indicators of relevant motivations and attitudes, household social characteristics, economic factors, and selected demographic descriptors. To increase the likelihood of accurate responses, we restricted our analysis to the subsample of 2,065 households in which the respondent, often jointly with their spouse, was both "most involved in deciding which charities your household will give to" and "primarily responsible for giving donations to charity."[3]

Operationalization of Variable Clusters

We briefly considered defining our dependent variable, charitable giving, (1) as two variables (participation and total amount contributed); (2) as the amount given to religious organizations and amount given to nonreligious organizations; or (3) as total amount contributed. In the end, we decided on the percentage of income contributed by the household as the dependent variable in our investigation.[4] Among the major considerations for this choice was that it is a continuous variable which is not, itself, overwhelmingly influenced by household income—as is the case with the total amount contributed. In addition, it has the historical advantage that we and others have worked extensively with this measure in previous research efforts.[5]

EXHIBIT 8.1

Determinants of Charitable Giving

I. Communities of Participation
   1. Church
      a. Denominational Affiliation
      b. Church Attendance
      c. General Church Involvement
      d. Volunteering for Church Organizations
   2. School (school's religious orientation and emphasis of community service, student's organizational memberships and academic performance)
   3. Work (size of business and organizational culture)
   4. Civic Institutions (membership and general involvement)
   5. Government and Political Organizations (sense of power and influence)

II. Framework of Consciousness
   1. General Values
   2. Religious Beliefs and Values
   3. Political Beliefs and Values
   4. Attitudes about Social Responsibility
   5. Attitudes about Volunteering
   6. Attitudes toward the Recipient Organization

III. Direct Requests
   1. Medium of Request (face-to-face meeting, telephone call, mail)
   2. Strategies of Approach (determine needs and wants of donor, describe need, use mix of rational arguments and emotional appeals, convey organizational vision, provide opportunities for donor involvement, show the example of leading supporters)
   3. Mode of Petition (ask or encourage to give, document organizational efficiency and effectiveness of gift,* offer additional information and convenient financial arrangements)
   4. Closure: Foundations of an ongoing Relationship (feedback on accomplishments and appropriate recognition and personal rewards—see VIII.2. Extrinsic Rewards)

IV. Discretionary Resources
   1. Income
   2. Wealth and Composition of Wealth (real estate, equities, and other properties)
   3. Time (hours per week, weeks per year, employment—part time, stage of entrepreneurship, retirement, age of children)
   4. Expectations about Future Financial Capacity

V. Models and Experiences from One's Youth
   1. Parental Example
   2. Example of Other Role Models
   3. Membership in a Youth Group
   4. Was a Volunteer
   5. Door-to-Door Fund raising
   6. Helped by Others
   7. Active in Student Government

VI. Urgency and Effectiveness
   1. Demonstration of Pressing Need
   2. Belief in the Effectiveness of Gift
   3. Perceived Organizational Efficiency

(continued)

EXHIBIT 8.1

Determinants of Charitable Giving (continued)

VII. Demographic

1. Location (geographic location, urban/rural type, size and economic status of community)
2. Age
3. Gender
4. Education
5. Race
6. Marital Status
7. Children (presence and number of)
8. Employment (part or full-time)
9. Occupational Prestige
10. Length of Residence
11. Home Ownership
12. Health

VIII. Intrinsic and Extrinsic Rewards

1. Intrinsic Rewards
   a. Personal Elements (self-esteem, achievement, cognitive interest, growth, meaning, or purpose in life)
   b. Configurations of Personal Elements
   c. Social Elements (status, affiliation, group endeavor, interdependence, power)
   d. Negative Elements (guilt reduction or guilt avoidance, frustration, insecurity)
2. Extrinsic Rewards
   a. Recognition Rewards (introductions in meetings, invitations to elite gatherings, publicity)
   b. Personal Rewards (Immediate thank-you letters, telephone calls from leaders and officials, awards, membership in elite groups, and peer acknowledgments)
   c. Social Rewards (development of new personal relationships, an increased sense of community and status, and new awareness of group cohesion)
   d. Tax Incentives (e.g., income, estate, and capital gains taxes)

*Determinant(s) cited in more than one category.

We reviewed the questions asked in the survey several times to map particular questions into one of the conceptual clusters. At the conclusion of this process we had mapped 107 variables into the seven clusters. For a number of methodological reasons, 107 variables is too large a number even for multivariate analysis.[6] We used a highly empirical procedure to reduce the number of variables to a more manageable size. We ran a series of multiple regressions to estimate (1) the relationship between charitable giving (i.e., percentage of household income given to charity) and the variables associated with each theoretical cluster, estimated independently of variables in any other cluster; (2) the relationship between charitable giving and all 107 variables, entered in hierarchical order by cluster; (3) the relationship between giving and all 107 variables entered simultaneously; and (4) the relationship between giving and all 107 variables with the least significant variables successively eliminated until the remaining variables were all significant at the .10 level. At the end of this procedure, we included all variables that were theoretically significant at .10 level and several nonstatistically significant variables that we judged to be the most theoretically important. The resulting number of variables was reduced from 107 to 48; these are listed by theoretical cluster in Exhibit 8.2.

EXHIBIT 8.2

Independent Variables within Theoretical Clusters

Communities of Participation

Q27	Length of time living in community
Q33e	Directly helped a needy person other than relative, friend, neighbor, homeless, or street person
Q37	Average number of hours per week respondent spent helping friends or relatives who don't live with respondent
Q87	Frequency of attending church or synagogue
Q901	Number of people living in household
Nvol	The number of different types of organization in which the respondent volunteers time
Hvol	The number of hours per month that the respondent volunteers
Ngiv	The number of different types of organization to which the respondent's household makes a contribution in money and/or in kind
Rfix	Gives a fixed proportion of income to church, synagogue, or mosque
Ofix	Gives a fixed proportion of income to nonreligious organization(s)

Frameworks of Consciousness

Q67b	Giving back to society some of benefits it gave you is a personal motivation that may involve both charitable giving of money and volunteering time in general, not just last year
Q67f	Fulfilling a business or community obligation is a personal motivation that may involve . . .
Q67i	Meeting religious beliefs or commitments is a personal motivation that may involve . . .
Q68b	Teaching people to be more self-sufficient is a major, a minor, or not a goal of charitable giving of money and volunteering time
Q68e	Enhancing the moral basis of society is a major, a minor, . . .
Q68f	Changing the way society works is a major, a minor, . . .

Direct Requests

Q26	Has been asked to give money or other property to charitable organizations, including religious organizations, in the past year
Q66b	Receiving a phone call asking you to give is (very important, somewhat important, not too important, or not at all important) to you for contributing to a charitable organization
Q66c	Someone coming to the door asking you to give is (very important, . . .)
Q66j	Being asked by clergy to give is (very important, . . .)
Q67a	Being asked to contribute or volunteer by a personal friend or business associate was a (major motivation, minor motivation, or not a motivation) for your charitable giving and volunteering
Q67j	Being encouraged by an employer was a (major motivation, . . .)

Discretionary Resources

Q3	Degree respondent worries about not having enough money—a lot, moderate amount, or only a little
Q4	Respondent has (more, less, or the same amount of) money left over after paying bills this year compared with last year
Q77	Will be claiming a deduction for charitable contribution on federal income tax return for 1991
Q83	Is financially (better off, about the same, worse off) now compared with a year ago
Q84	Expect at this time next year to be financially (better off, the same, worse off) then than now
Inc	Household gross income
Nemp	The number of people currently employed in the household

(continued)

EXHIBIT 8.2

Independent Variables within Theoretical Clusters (continued)

Models and Experiences from One's Youth

Q82A	One or both parents did volunteer work in community when young
Q82j	Helped by others in the past when young
Q82k	Saw somebody in family help others when young

Urgency and Effectiveness

Q47a	The need for charitable organizations is greater now than five years ago—strongly agree, agree, disagree, strongly disagree
Q47b	Charitable organizations are more effective now in providing services than five years ago—strongly agree, . . .
Q47c	I place a low degree of trust in charitable organizations—strongly agree, . . .
Q47g	Generally, the U.S. is in more trouble now than 5 years ago—strongly agree, . . .
Q47h	Generally, charitable organizations play a major role in making our communities better places to live—strongly agree, . . .
Q47i	On the whole, charitable organizations do not do a very good job in helping those who need help—strongly agree, . . .
Q69h	Most people with serious problems brought their problems on themselves—strongly agree, . . .
Q69i	It is in my power to do things that improve the welfare of others—strongly agree, . . .

Demographic Characteristics

Age	Respondent's age
Heduc	Education of Chief Wage Earner
Hret	Retirement Status of Chief Wage Earner
Race	Race Dichotomy (nonwhite or white)
Prot	Religious Affiliation Dichotomy (non-Protestant or Protestant)
Cath	Religious Affiliation Dichotomy (non-Catholic or Catholic)
Jwsh	Religious Affiliation Dichotomy (non-Jewish or Jewish)
Orel	Religious Affiliation Dichotomy (not other religion or other religion)

Findings about Individual Clusters

Details of our multivariate analysis are presented in Schervish and Havens (1994). Our central finding is that there is broad quantitative support for major tenets of the identification theory of philanthropy. We came to this conclusion as a result of investigating two questions: (1) whether each of the clusters of variables was separately related to charitable giving and (2) which specific variables determine charitable giving when variables from all the clusters are examined simultaneously. The first step was to run multiple regressions[7] of the specific subset of variables associated with each theoretical cluster to determine whether a subset explained giving behavior as represented by the percentage of household income contributed. Each separate regression analysis estimates the combined direct and indirect impacts of the cluster of variables on percentage of income contributed. It also estimates the relative combined direct and indirect impact of each of the variables associated with the cluster.

Communities of Participation

Our analysis also demonstrates that participation in associational communities induces charitable contribution. The set of 10 variables corresponding to participation in a variety of communities is significant at the .0001 level of statistical significance. The strength of the relationship, measured by

R-Squared, is a rather substantial .288. Given the empirical methods used to reduce the number of variables in the analysis, it is interesting that most variables measuring general levels of social participation (e.g., membership in a variety of clubs and organizations) were not sufficiently strongly related to giving behavior to be included in this analysis. Most of the variables that are relatively strongly related to giving behavior are measures of either (a) participation and/or commitment to organizations and institutions that serve as channels for giving and volunteering or (b) informal activities that involve helping others. Eight of the 10 variables are associated with giving behavior in the expected direction (greater participation and/or greater opportunities for participation lead to larger percentages of income contributed). However, two are not: (1) households that allocate a fixed proportion of their income to donate to nonreligious organizations tend to allocate smaller proportions than those that do not structure their donations so formally; and (2) larger households (which presumably have more opportunities for participation because of the activities of their members) tend to give smaller proportions of their incomes than do smaller households. In this case, larger households may not have sufficient financial resources to support larger proportions of income contributed after meeting the needs of members, especially since larger households tend also to have lower incomes.

Framework of Consciousness

Based on multiple regression analysis of the available information in the survey data, we found that strongly held frameworks of consciousness advance charitable giving. The set of six variables corresponding to relatively stable beliefs and motives for giving is significantly related to giving behavior at the .0001 level of statistical significance. The strength of the relationship as measured by *R*-Squared is .073, nearly double that of youthful experiences—indicating that even partial measures of one's current framework of consciousness are more strongly related to current giving behavior than are youthful experiences, which are more distant in time. The substance of the relationship is also rather interesting. Those who are motivated mainly either (1) to fulfill a business or community obligation or (2) to change the way society works, tend to give smaller percentages of their income than those who are motivated by (1) meeting religious beliefs or commitments, (2) enhancing the moral basis of society, (3) teaching people to be more self-sufficient, or (4) giving back to society some of the benefits it gave the respondent. This pattern is phenomenologically consistent with the definition of framework of consciousness.

Direct Requests

Regression analysis of the relevant survey data indicates that the mode of petition affects the level of charitable response. The set of six variables corresponding to the direct invitation cluster is significant at the .0001 level; and its strength, measured as usual by *R*-Squared, is .052. However, only three of the variables indicate that direct invitation leads to higher percentages of income contributed while three others indicate that direct invitation is actually associated with lower, if any, percentage of income contributed (Q66b, Q66c, Q67j).

Closer inspection of each subset of three variables implies that the method of direct contact may be more important than just the contact itself. The three direct invitations that seem to lead to higher levels of contribution imply a personal contact by a previously known individual—a personal friend, business associate, or clergyperson. The three direct invitations that seem to lead to small if any contributions are associated with less intimate contact—phone call, someone coming to the door, or workplace-based encouragement by an employer.

Discretionary Resources

Regression analysis shows that the set of seven variables corresponding to the discretionary resources cluster is significant at the .0001 level of statistical significance. The strength of the relationship, as measured by *R*-Squared, is .062. Variables that indicate increases in income or optimism concerning one's financial future are associated with higher percentages of income contributed.

Two variables that we associated with greater household resources, however, had signs that implied lower rather than higher percentages of income contributed. The first of these variables was the number of people employed in the household—the more people employed, according to this analysis, the lower the percentage of income contributed. One might speculate that households have a larger than average number of people employed because the household's income is not sufficient to meet the basic needs of the household and additional people have to work just to make ends meet—leaving very little left over for philanthropy. A more mean-spirited speculation would be that the members of some households are so materialistic and selfish that more of their members go to work and keep all of their increased earnings for themselves.

The second variable was gross household income, whose sign indicated lower percentages of income are contributed by households with higher gross incomes. This sign, however, makes some sense when one considers that another resource variable was the respondent's intentions to list charitable contributions as an itemized deduction. This variable would tend to pick up moderate and higher income households who made significant charitable contributions, leaving moderate and higher income households who made small or no charitable contributions to be reflected in the sign of the gross household income variable.

Models and Experiences from One's Youth

Multiple regression analysis of the information available in the survey data indicates that youthful experiences are related to current giving behavior. The set of three variables corresponding to this cluster is significantly related to giving behavior at the .0001 level of statistical significance. Although significant, the strength of the relationship is relatively modest with an R-Squared of .038, but the coefficients of each of the three variables are associated with higher levels of household giving at the current time.

Urgency and Effectiveness

Do the urgency of the cause and perception of the donation's effectiveness lead to *giving behavior?* Here, the answer is more ambiguous, and perhaps closer to "maybe." The set of eight variables corresponding to the urgency/effectiveness cluster is significant at the .045 level rather than the .0001 level as in the previous theoretical clusters. The strength of relationship is quite small at .0144, as measured by R-Squared. Of the eight variables, five have signs consistent with greater urgency and/or effectiveness being associated with larger proportions of income contributed; one is ambiguous (Q47b); and two are negative (Q47g, Q69h). Thus this cluster is less internally consistent than the other theoretical clusters, but once again there is evidence that confidence in charitable organizations is related to increased giving (Q47h).

Demographic Characteristics

Multiple regression analysis shows that the set of eight demographic factors is significant at the .0001 level of statistical significance and the strength of relationship, as measured by R-Squared, is .064. These variables were the age of the respondent, the education of the chief wage earner, the retirement status of the chief wage earner, the race of the respondent, and religious affiliation (represented as four dummy variables). It should be noted that the first three of these demographic variables survived the variable reduction process while the last two were included because of the special interest of the researchers. Demographic characteristics that were related to giving behavior but were only weakly related when considered jointly with other demographic factors include marital status, presence of teens in the household, and Hispanic origin.

Findings from Joint Analysis of Variable Clusters

The multiple regression analysis provides strong statistical evidence that five of the theoretical factors identified in the conceptual framework are, in some sequence and/or causal structure, related to giving behavior. The one theoretical factor, urgency/effectiveness, that emerged during the course of the analysis, in fact, seems also to be related to giving behavior. In this case, however, the empirical evidence is borderline at best. In view of the findings about the individual clusters, our second major question is *When the many factors relevant to the theory are taken into account simultaneously, which factors are most strongly related to giving behavior?* Multiple regression was again used to investigate this research question. As described earlier, variables from all clusters were entered into an initial analysis, which were then reduced to a smaller set of the 25 variables most relevant for the remaining research questions. As one would expect from the foregoing results, the reduced set of variables were significantly related to giving behavior at .0001 level of statistical significance (see Exhibit 8.3). The strength of the relationship, as measured by R-Squared, was .276,[8] which is in the moderate range for social science research based on survey data.

In this joint analysis, three of the five variables with the strongest relation to giving behavior, as measured by their standardized beta coefficients, are community of participation variables. All three are closely related to participation in institutions and organizations that already contain formal channels through which they may receive charitable contributions (Exhibit 8.3). One of the five is a resource variable and one is a demographic characteristic. Of the four remaining variables significant at the .05 level, two are general community of participation variables and the other two are invitation to participate variables. Thus of the nine variables significant at the .05 level, five are communities of participation variables, two are invitation to participate variables, one is a resource variable, and one is a demographic characteristic.

The lack of variables from the youthful experiences, framework of consciousness, and effectiveness/urgency clusters means only that these clusters, as reflected in the variables contained in the Survey of Giving and Volunteering, are not strongly or consistently related to the percentage of income contributed once participation, resource, and demographic variables are taken into account. It does not necessarily mean that these clusters are only minor factors in giving behavior, indeed they may critical factors in causal sequences involved in giving behavior but they may be either (1) less proximate factors than participation, discretionary resources, and demographic factors or (2) more proximately related to giving behavior but only for selected segments of the population. Hypothetically, youthful experiences might influence framework of consciousness, and jointly they may influence the pattern and magnitude of community of participation so that the community of participation variable may already capture the effects of youthful experiences and framework of consciousness. This hypothetical sequence is one of many that are consistent with both the five-variable theory and the multivariate regression results.

Discussion

Reviewing these findings from the broad theoretical standpoint of identification theory, it appears that for the population as a whole, participation, especially participation that already embodies a commitment to philanthropy or to a philanthropic organization, is directly related to giving behavior. Within community of participation, religious commitment and participation in religious organizations have a strong influence on general giving behavior. Variables from other theoretical clusters do not have as central and consistent impact on giving behavior: Retirement status appears to influence the percentage of income contributed mainly through reductions in income that are proportionately much less than reductions in contributions; the impact of income appears to filter out those middle and higher income households that make relatively small contributions which they do not intend to deduct on their income taxes; the impact of direct invitations to participate appears to be to filter out those households contributing small percentages of their income who are prodded into making a small donation by door-to-door contact or a general contribution campaign (e.g., United Way) at their place of work.

The impact of household income (together with charitable deductions) seems less an indicator of discretionary resources than the delineator of higher income households making smaller donations; direct invitation variables seem less indicators of the impact of direct invitation to participate in the general population as delineators of households that are prodded into making a small

EXHIBIT 8.3

Joint Regression Analysis of All Clusters for Total Population

N = 1375	R-Squared* = 0.276		Significance Level = 0.0001
Variable Name	Non-Standardized Coefficient	Statistical Coefficient	Standardized Significance Level
Independent Variables with the Five Largest Standardized Coefficients			
Rfix	Gives a fixed proportion of income to church, synagogue, or mosque	2.865	0.289	0.0001
Ngiv	The number of different types of organization to which the respondent's household makes a contribution in money and/or in kind	0.361	0.193	0.0001
Inc	Household gross income ($1000's)	–0.019	–0.130	0.0001
Q87	Frequency of attending church or synagogue	0.368	0.110	0.0001
Hret	Retirement Status of Chief Wage Earner	0.011	0.101	0.0002
Other Independent Variables Significant at the .05 Level			
Q27	Length of time living in community	0.238	0.066	0.0081
Q67j	Being encouraged by an employer was motivation for charitable giving and volunteering time	–0.361	–0.062	0.0150
Q66c	Importance for charitable giving of someone coming to the door asking you to give	–0.264	–0.059	0.0356
Hvol	The number of hours per month that the respondent volunteers	0.020	0.055	0.0282

* This value of R-Squared is based on all 25 independent variables in the analysis—in the interest of space only the values statistically significant at the .05 level or lower are presented in this exhibit; none of the variables excluded had standardized coefficients as large as .100.

contribution and are not in general internally motivated to give to charitable institutions; and the only demographic variable seems an indicator of reduced household income without commensurate reductions in the pattern of contribution.

The only variable in the empirical analysis that has theoretical significance is community of participation. To understand giving behavior in the total population, it turns out one should focus on understanding the community of participation, with special emphasis on the role of religious participation. A major task for future research on causal sequences affecting giving behavior should be the investigation of the relationship between communities of participation and the other theoretical clusters of variables in the five-variable theory—youthful experiences, frameworks of consciousness, discretionary resources, invitation to participate, and possibly urgency/effectiveness.

Summary of Findings

The findings can be summarized as follows:

- Each of the five theoretical variable clusters that could be operationalized within the limits of the data from the Survey of Giving and Volunteering (youthful experiences, framework of consciousness, communities of participation, invitation to participate, and discretionary resources) are significantly related to giving behavior.

- While there are variations in the strength of the relationships between each cluster and giving behavior, communities of participation is the cluster with the strongest and most consistent relationship to giving behavior.

- When considered jointly with other variable clusters, communities of participation is the only cluster that evinces a distinctive relationship to giving behavior.

- Two dimensions of communities of participation seem especially important for giving behavior: (1) a general level of participation and (2) religious participation and commitment.

- Two subgroups of higher income households (the retired and those intending to claim a charitable deduction at higher income levels) give a larger than average percentage of their incomes to charity.

- Participation and commitment, especially religious participation and commitment, are centrally and strongly related to giving behavior. Moreover, there is reason to believe that this cluster may operate, at least in part, as an intervening variable through which other clusters affect giving behavior.

Research Agenda

The foregoing literature and multivariate analysis provide several significant empirical findings on the factors that induce charitable giving. Taken together, the findings about the impact of participation and frequency of participation, being asked, volunteering, generosity across income groups, and the fact that larger gifts are generated from those who have given large gifts—all indicate that charitable giving is largely a consequence of forging a connection between the existing inclinations and involvement of individuals and the needs of recipients. It is not the absence of self that must be generated but the presence of self-identification with others. This is what Thomas Aquinas teaches as the convergence of love of neighbor, love of self, and love of God. It is also, in its civic expression, what Tocqueville meant by self-interest properly understood. In this way, the inspiration for charitable giving is a function of the social-psychological processes of associational density, group incorporation, personal identification, and the satisfying experience of making an important difference.

Despite these solid initial findings, a weighty research agenda needs to be addressed—not simply because of the never-to-be-minimized vocation of intellectual discovery "for its own sake," but because there are important practical implications. In the study of charitable giving, there is a fortunate convergence between the discovery of the most technical detail and the invigoration of the equally honorable vocation of generosity and care.

The research agenda on the factors mobilizing charitable giving includes the following items.

Confirmatory Population Studies

There must be continuing *confirmation and amendment* of existing findings, such as those generated in the foregoing analysis. This includes continued *application of multivariate statistical techniques* that enable researchers to distinguish between the more and less important determinants of charitable giving by measuring the relative effects of numerous variables simultaneously.

Segmentation Analyses

Researchers need to develop *separate analyses for differing segments* of the population. John Havens and I have undertaken (1994) such an analysis and have some preliminary findings to report. We hypothesized that the population of givers must reflect the national population in being segmented roughly along the lines of liberal and conservative policy orientations. Our major finding is that the seven-variable model explored in the previous section appears to be even more fully supported for each segment than it is for the population as a whole. That is, the impact of several mobilizing factors that tend to cancel out for the population as a whole are revealed when either of the segments is analyzed separately.

To discover an effective segmenting variable, we identified more than a dozen variables as potential components of sociopolitical ideological orientation. Originally, we anticipated developing a measure that would distinguish between "liberal" and "conservative" lifestyles and ideologies. A variety of indices were constructed using several methods. Cross-validation with other variables and descriptions of other behavior indicated that none of the indices adequately captured the essence of the "conservative" versus "liberal" dimension we had originally conceived.

One of the measures derived after item and item-index analysis appears to come as close to the desired categorization as any of the others and, empirically, leads to relatively more homogeneous giving behavior "within group" compared with "between groups" than did the other measures. We then used this measure to segment the sample in assessing whether the explanatory power of the seven-variable model increased when the two groups were analyzed separately.

The measure identifies one group as those households whose respondent indicated that "keeping taxes or other costs down" was a more major goal of their giving money and volunteering time than was the goal of "helping individuals meet their material needs." It identifies a second group as those households whose respondent indicated that "helping individuals meet their material needs" was a more major goal of their giving money and volunteering time than was the goal of "keeping taxes or other costs down." For convenience of presentation, we refer to the first group as "tax-motivated" and to the second group as "needs-motivated." We believe, however, that each group embodies a constellation of societal and political goals, motives, attitudes, and behavior that may not be appropriately captured by these convenient labels.[9]

For both tax-motivated and need-motivated households, the regression analyses reveal many elements that operate identically for each segment of households and for the population of all households. Communities of participation variables, with special emphasis on participation in and commitment to religious organizations, are the most prominent feature of the regression analysis among both tax-motivated households and the population of all households. A second common feature is that several of the variables seem not to operate on a broad theoretical basis but to delineate two of the same special groups: (1) households with moderate-to-high incomes that give relatively small proportions of their income to charity compared with households with similar incomes that give larger-than-average proportions of their income and expect to claim a charitable deduction, and (2) households whose chief wage earner is retired compared with other low-to-moderate-income households whose chief wage earner is not retired.

The regression analyses, however, do reveal important new features idiosyncratic to the way the theory manifests among each segment of households. Among the tax-motivated segment, three new groupings of variables are prominent on a broad theoretical basis: framework of consciousness, a psychological continuum ranging from less to more generous, and (less prominently) youthful experiences. Among the needs-motivated segment, three groupings of variables are also prominent: framework of consciousness, youthful experiences, and (less prominently) invitation to participate.

There are differences between the way that common clusters of variables manifest themselves in the two segments:

- Among tax-motivated households, the important dimensions of framework of consciousness, in regard to different levels of giving behavior, are (1) a sense of social indebtedness expressed as variations in a desire to give back to society some of the beneficence received from society and (2) a consistency of the framework at either a psychological or behavioral level. Among need-motivated households, the important dimension of framework of consciousness is the degree to which religious commitment has been internalized.

- Among both tax-motivated and need-motivated households, the same youthful experience dimension is revealed as important—being helped when young, rather than youthful experiences helping others or the importance of philanthropically oriented role models when young. However, among tax-motivated households this dimension has a minor impact compared with its prominence among need-motivated households.

- Religious participation and commitment are important factors among both tax-motivated and need-motivated segments. Among tax-motivated households, religious behavior is the important facet of the dimension, but among need-motivated households both religious behavior and internalized commitment to religious principles are strongly related to giving behavior.

For each segment, there is also one cluster that is important for that segment but not the other:

- Among tax-motivated households, an important dimension related to giving behavior is the psychological continuum that we have labeled as the nongenerous/generous continuum. This dimension does not appear to affect the giving behavior of need-motivated households.[10]

- Among need-motivated households, invitation to participate is an important dimension that identifies a subgroup that appears to be prodded to give a token contribution, much as this cluster operates in the population of all households. This variable is not at all prominent among tax-motivated households—it neither directly affects giving behavior nor delineates special groups.

These findings are preliminary in every sense with the exception that it is now clear that it is worth pursuing such segmented analyses. To do so we need to continue to explore what sociopolitical orientation scales should be included among the questions in the IS/Gallup surveys, and to pursue theoretical thinking and empirical analyses regarding relevant demarcations in the population.

Analyses of Sectoral Giving

An additional area for exploration is analyses of sectoral giving patterns. The major sectoral distinction is between religious (approximately 45%–50% of individual giving) and nonreligious giving. The explanatory determinants of religious giving need to be distinguished from the determinants of nonreligious giving in general, and specific areas of nonreligious giving, in particular. For example, it would be intellectually and practically important to carry out a multivariate analysis of the variables that predict level of giving to educational institutions.

Causal Path Analyses

Virtually absent from the research literature, but implied in almost every conceptual depiction of the giving process is the notion that charitable giving is the outcome of a series of influences and forces. Two additional directions of causal analysis are warranted in addition to the determination of the factors that lead to levels of giving. The first is the development of a first-stage model that explains how people become givers in the first place. Although several variables that are significant determinants of giving in the analysis of individual clusters are not significant in the joint analysis, this does not mean that the specific variables in the cluster analyses are not important. Rather, we believe, the correct interpretation is that their impact is mediated by the participation cluster. That is, these apparently "insignificant" variables affect participation, which, in turn, affects giving behavior. For example, if volunteering and other variables associated with communities of participation induce giving, the next question becomes what factors induced volunteering and participation. Therefore, just because, as Havens and I found, most of the variables in the seven-variable model "dropped out" in favor of the communities of participation variable, these "dropped" variables probably remain extremely important for inducting people into communities of participation in the first place. The second venue for further causal analysis is to develop and test measures of the factors, such as intrinsic and extrinsic rewards and various forms of deeper personal engagement that lead to *increased* giving. The elaboration of such expanded causal pathways applies to each of the three foregoing research domains.

Analyses of Giving Patterns by Income and Wealth

It is of no surprise to anyone who has followed the research and popular literature on giving patterns by income and wealth that there remains much work to be done by way of settling the debate about the relative generosity of the rich and poor. My colleague, John Havens, and I have written several papers on this topic (Schervish & Havens 1995a, 1995b). In our recent paper, entitled "Wherewithal and

Beneficence: Charitable Giving by Income and Wealth" (1995c), we extend the analysis of the upper income groups contained in the IS/Gallup studies to the very wealthy by analyzing the Survey of Consumer Finances that contains information on charitable giving of approximately 400 individuals at the upper extremes of income and wealth. In the income range up to $100,000, there is a relative equality of generosity measured by percentage of income contributed. Above $100,000, there is a dramatic increase in percentage of income contributed. Thus the popular notion of the generous poor and the stingy rich is simply incorrect. Our analysis of the Survey of Consumer Finances also enables us to conclude that virtually all the rich are contributors, that they donate very large amounts to charity, and that they give higher proportions of their income to charity than do the poor or affluent. That this pattern represents "generosity," however, is not for us to say. But it certainly contradicts the statistical portrait harbored by those who refer to the wealthy as "ungenerous" and "stingy" (Nielsen, 1992).

In view of these findings, I identify four specific research tasks:

1. Investment in acquiring larger and more detailed *datasets* on the charitable giving patterns of the individuals at the uppermost ends of wealth and income, the primary source of charitable contributions, especially nonreligious contributions.

2. Analysis of the *variation* of giving by income and wealth. Our preliminary research from the Survey of Consumer Finances and the IS/Gallup data confirm the earlier finding by Auten and Rudney (1990). While Auten and Rudney emphasized that only a small portion of the superwealthy are truly generous givers, we have found that in *every category* of income and wealth, there is a small proportion of extraordinary givers and that there is some evidence that among the highest income and wealth groups there may in fact be a greater proportion of such extraordinary givers.

3. Given our finding that income and wealth are not in themselves the source of generosity or stinginess, an important research question is to determine *what other factors distinguish the extraordinary from ordinary givers* within each income and wealth group.

4. We have thus far found that it is possible to chart the relationship between percentage of income given and level of income, and percentage of income given and level of wealth. We have not yet discovered a pattern, however, when the dependent variable is *percentage of wealth given to charity*. We suspect this is because wealth is not a unidimensional resource. This implies a research effort to discern how the relative distribution of one's wealth into liquid and nonliquid assets as well as the period in one's business and investment life cycle are connected to one's timing and level of giving.

Capacity to Give

An important research effort that has been begun under the auspices of the Center on Philanthropy and in a different way by John Havens, Thomas Murphy, and me at Boston College (Murphy & Schervish 1996) is to derive micro- and macromeasures of the capacity to give. To date, the Center on Philanthropy has directed efforts to establish an aggregate figure of the capacity to give by compiling an aggregate measure of a modified notion of the discretionary income for the wealthy. The Boston College effort has focused instead on developing micromeasures of the capacity to give that focus on a combination of discretionary wealth and discretionary income as well as on the subjective orientations and tax policies that advance the psychological capacity to give.

New Horizons of Tax Incentives

Perhaps the most neglected yet most consequential determinant of substantial giving among the upper income earners and wealth holders is the estate tax environment instituted by the Tax Reform Act of 1986. Much research has been conducted on the effect of marginal income tax rates and of the role of charitable deductions for the level of charitable giving. But in both of these cases, the question remains about the effect of such tax regulations on charitable contributions from income. Far more important, and therefore worthy of extensive research, is the consequence of existing and prospective federal and state estate taxes for charitable giving. The most neglected fact among researchers and commentators on charitable giving is something that is now patently obvious to financial planners, tax accountants, and increasing numbers of wealthy individuals (especially small business holders). This is that the 1986 tax code has dramatically increased the incentives of wealthy individuals to make substantial contributions to charity in lieu of paying an effective minimum wealth tax of at least 60%. Research would be very fruitfully directed toward studying the requirement embedded in the current estate tax laws for wealth holders to choose between dedicating their wealth (both while alive and at their death) to government uses or to charitable uses. As Richard Haas, an experienced financial planner, has put it, the only substantial tax shelter for the very wealthy is philanthropy. How to communicate to wealth holders this unanticipated and heretofore unappreciated convergence between a Republican tax reform and philanthropy is just one of several important research topics. Perhaps even more important will be research that helps us understand how to develop an entrepreneurial philanthropic agenda whereby the wealthy come to discern which socially beneficial projects they wish to undertake and how they wish to dedicate their wealth to such endeavors.

Conclusion: Associational Density, Inclination, Obligation, and Invitation

The major implication of the foregoing is that much research has been initiated on the determinants of charitable giving, and that much more needs to be done. I would be pleased if the foregoing research agenda be viewed as more than just another of those self-serving global calls for more research that we have grown to expect at the end of research chapters. Rather, I believe the foregoing tenders a sensible, practical, and targeted research agenda that picks up where current research leaves off and has direct implications for advancing charitable giving. Current research offers many leads about what makes a difference in generating generosity. These leads, I am happy to note, are usually in concert with what fund raisers and donors know from their personal experience. However, the following four tasks require attention: (1) to draw together in a systematic manner those findings on which research and experience concur, (2) to examine in more detail the simultaneous interplay of factors so as to attribute fund raising successes and failures to their fundamental rather than apparent sources; (3) to explore the workings of new factors such as estate-tax changes introduced in the 1986 tax legislation; and (4) to correct down-right mistakes and misconceptions about the determinants of charitable giving. As our current research has indicated, generosity is not a function of income but of the personal and social aspects of associational density, inclination, obligation, and invitation. Therefore, it is of great practical significance and, hence, a worthy investment of resources to improve our understanding of those determinants.

Notes

1. I recognize that I am skimming the surface of the vast literature on charitable giving and so apologize to those whose work we have thus far neglected, and request that they let us know about their work and how it relates to our conceptual framework.
2. My discussion of the first five and the eighth variables in the following paragraphs is taken with only slight revision from my article "Gentle as Doves and Wise as Serpents: The Philosophy of Care and the Sociology of Transmission" (Schervish, 1995b).
3. Due to missing data in the 25 independent variables used in the final regression analysis, the sample size for this regression was reduced further to 1,375 households.
4. Based on the subsample of households in which the respondent either solely or jointly with others (usually their spouse) in the household make decisions regarding philanthropic contributions, we estimate that 77 percent of the population of households contribute to one or more philanthropic organizations. The average of total annual contributions is $733 per household—$440 to religious organizations and $293 to nonreligious organizations. The annual total of all contributions amounts to 2.0 percent of household gross income—1.3 percent being given to religious organizations and .7 percent being given to nonreligious organizations.
5. The contribution variables for the survey contained missing data for approximately 10 percent of the households that made a contribution. Among these households, one component of giving was usually missing,

but there were often nonmissing values for several other components. Consequently, the missing values were imputed for the missing components and then added together with the nonmissing components to arrive at an estimate of total contribution. These imputations were based on multiple regressions of age of respondent, sex of respondent, education of respondent, residential location, and household income. This method assumes that missing values within each category follow the trend relationship for that category.

6. First, such a large number of variables is difficult for the researcher and the reader to keep straight, even within cluster groupings. Second, the 107 variables are interrelated among themselves which has the effect that the impact of any one variable is in part obfuscated by each of the others—the more variables beyond 15 to 20 in this particular analysis, the greater the degree of obfuscation. Third, each of the 107 variables were not answered by a small percentage of the sample; when any of the answers were missing, the case was eliminated from the analysis; less than 900 cases had substantive answers to all 107 variables; consequently the sample was reduced to less than 48 percent of the original subsample size. Fourth, because of the high degree of intercorrelation, the statistical methods could not, in most instances, identify which of the variables were statistically significant (although this does not necessarily cause major problems in early stages of research).

7. Unless otherwise noted, all multiple regressions reported in this chapter used the population weights developed by the Gallup organization; casewise deletion when any variable was missing data; and ordinary least squares estimation of the regression coefficients on the independent variables. The values of R-Squared reported are not adjusted for the number of independent variables in the analysis.

8. This value is less than the value of .288 for the communities of participation analysis reported under question A3. However, the two analyses are not comparable in the strict mathematical sense: The first analysis included all participation variables that had survived the first stage of the variable reduction process resulting in a sample size of 1,099 cases, while the second analysis included a smaller subset of variables surviving the second stage of the data reduction process and is based on an expanded sample size of 1,375 cases.

9. We know that this grouping is empirically important, but we are not yet entirely confident that we understand the composition of the groups. Indeed, we believe that each group may actually be a combination of several other groups with similar giving behavior.

10. In a sense, the definition of the segments facilitates this finding for the tax-motivated households but does not facilitate the finding for need-motivated households. In this sense, the analysis is biased toward this finding among tax-motivated households—or, more correctly, biased against this finding among need-motivated households. It may still be the case that this dimension or its analog is important among need-motivated households but limited data does not adequately permit its measurement; consequently analysis cannot reveal its importance.

I am grateful to the T. B. Murphy Foundation Charitable Trust for supporting the research reported here, and to Platon Coutsoukis who graciously and competently assisted in the preparation of this paper.

Reference

Auten, Gerald, and Rudney, Gabriel. "The Variability of Individual Charitable Giving in the U.S." *Voluntas: International Journal of Voluntary and Nonprofit Organizations*, 1990, 1(2), 80–97.

Fischer, Rose Lucy, and Schaffer, Kay Banister. *Older Volunteers: A Guide to Research and Practice*. Newbury Park, CA: Sage, 1993.

Langdon, John P. *Capitalism and the Moral Life*. Forthcoming.

Martin, Mike W. *Virtuous Giving: Philanthropy, Voluntary Service, and Caring*. Bloomington: Indiana University Press, 1994.

Mixer, Joseph R. *Principles of Professional Fundraising: Useful Foundations for Successful Practice*. San Francisco: Jossey-Bass, 1993.

Murphy, Thomas B., and Schervish, Paul G. "The Dynamics of Wealth Transfer: Behavioral Implications of Tax Policy for the $10 Trillion Transfer." In *Nonprofit Organizations as Public Actors*. Eds. Astrid Merget, Ed Weaver, and Virginia H. Hodgkinson. San Francisco: Jossey-Bass, 1996.

Nielsen, W. A. "A Reason to Have Fund-Raisers: Our Stingy Rich People." *Chronicle of Philanthropy*, Oct. 6, 1992, 41.

Ostrander, Susan A., and Schervish, Paul G. "Giving and Getting: Philanthropy as a Social Relation." In *Critical Issues in American Philanthropy: Strengthening Theory and Practice*. Ed. Jon Van Til. San Francisco: Jossey-Bass, 1990.

Schervish, Paul G. "Gentle as Doves and Wise as Serpents: The Philosophy of Care and the Sociology of Transmission." In *Care and Community in Modern Society: Passing on the Tradition of Care to the Next Generation*. Eds. Paul G. Schervish, Virginia A. Hodgkinson, and Margaret Gates. San Francisco: Jossey-Bass, 1995.

Schervish, Paul G. *The Modern Medicis: Strategies of Philanthropy among the Wealthy*. San Francisco: Jossey-Bass: Forthcoming.

Schervish, Paul G., with Benz, Obie, Dulany, Peggy, Murphy Thomas B., and Salett, Stanley. *Taking Giving Seriously*. Indianapolis: Indiana University, Center on Philanthropy, 1993.

Schervish, Paul G., and Havens, John J. "Do the Poor Pay More? Is the U-shaped Curve Correct?" *Nonprofit and Voluntary Sector Quarterly*, 1995a, 24(1), 79–90.

Schervish, Paul G., and Havens, John J. "Explaining the U in the U-Shaped Curve." *Voluntas: International Journal of Voluntary and Nonprofit Organizations*, 1995b, 6(2), 202–225.

Schervish, Paul G., and Havens, John J. "Social Participation and Charitable Giving: A Multivariate Analysis." *Voluntas: International Journal of Voluntary and Nonprofit Organizations*, 8(1), Winter, 1997.

Schervish, Paul G., and Havens, John J. "Wherewithal and Beneficence: Charitable Giving by Income and Wealth." In *Cultures of Giving II: How Heritage, Gender, Wealth, and Values Influence Philanthropy*, Summer issue of *New Directions for Philanthropic Fundraising*. Eds. Charles H. Hamilton and Warren F. Ilchman, 1995c, 8, 81–109.

Schervish, Paul G., and Herman, Andrew. *Empowerment and Beneficence: Strategies of Living and Giving among the Wealthy*. Final Report: The Study on Wealth and Philanthropy. Presentation of findings from the Study on Wealth and Philanthropy submitted to the T. B. Murphy Foundation Charitable Trust. July 1988.

Smith, David Horton. "Determinants of Voluntary Association Participation and Volunteering: A Literature Review." *Nonprofit and Voluntary Sector Quarterly*, 1994, 23(3), 243–263.

Wolpert, Julian. "The Demographics of Giving Patterns." Draft chapter for the 1995 Think Tank on Fund-Raising Research, Indianapolis: Indiana University, Center on Philanthropy. 1995a.

Wolpert, Julian. "Fragmentation in America's Nonprofit Sector." In *Care and Community in Modern Society: Passing on the Tradition of Care to the Next Generation*. Eds. Paul G. Schervish, Virginia A. Hodgkinson, and Margaret Gates. San Francisco: Jossey-Bass, 1995b.

Wolpert, Julian. *Patterns of Generosity in America: Who's Holding the Safety Net?* New York: Twentieth Century Fund, 1994.

"TO BIND THE UNIVERSITY TO NOTHING": THE GIVING OF CLEMENTINE MILLER TANGEMAN AS A CASE STUDY IN DONOR MOTIVATION

ANDREA WALTON

Abstract

This paper uses oral history and biography to study the philanthropic motivations and contributions of Clementine Miller Tangeman (1905–96). Born in Columbus, Indiana, Mrs. Tangeman gave generously to church, to youth initiatives, and to higher education—Smith College, Butler University, Christian Theological Seminary, and the Yale School of Sacred Music. Her story reveals the importance of family and church as educative institutions or what Paul Schervish has called "mobilizing factors" that shape the "philanthropic identity." This paper argues that biography is an important pedagogical tool for "educating" and inspiring a new generation of givers and for illustrating to practitioners the types of factors that nurture philanthropic sensibilities and commitments. In addition, this study contributes to documenting women's philanthropy, and, hence, will address a gap in the historical record and enrich contemporary discussion of women's giving.

Introduction

> This letter is intended to bind the University to nothing . . . Our aim is rather to suggest a broad, and, one might even hope, timeless purpose to the enterprise, all the while recognizing that succeeding generations . . . will themselves have varieties of understandings of the valid meaning of the purpose.[1]

Since John Harvard's gift to a struggling colonial college in 1638, private giving has been crucial in shaping the nature, scope, and character of higher education in the United States. In the 1990s, the multidisciplinary field of philanthropic studies made strides in analyzing patterns of giving to education—namely, who gives, what dollar amount, and to what causes. Additional research is needed to further an understanding of another aspect of the phenomenon of giving: why do people give?[2]

Such research on the ideas, experiences, and circumstances that educate and inspire donors will be of particular interest to academicians who study the role of philanthropy as a cultural phenomenon that has consequences on social policy but will also be of direct interest to development officers and scholar-practitioners as they meet the challenge of a new context for giving in the USA. Despite the ongoing turbulence of the financial markets in the first year and a half of the twenty-first century, the wealth amassed through investments during the last 20 years still suggests the possibility of a new, dramatic wave of philanthropy. New segments of the population are gaining access to greater financial resources and baby boomers stand poised to inherit substantial financial assets (estimated, conservatively, at over 10 trillion dollars by 2040) as a graying population transfers its wealth to a younger generation.[3] (The conservative estimate of 10.4 trillion was arrived at by Robert B. Avery and Michael S. Rendall in 1990. In 1999 researchers John J. Havens and Paul G. Schervish estimated the imminent transfer of wealth to be in the range of $41 to $136 trillion dollars.)

Of course, the question of whether this vast economic potential will translate into increased giving in the decades ahead remains to be answered. Fund raisers and scholars of philanthropy are aware that economic wherewithal alone does not necessarily a "golden age" of philanthropy make.[4] The promising financial news comes at a moment in the nation's history when a number of scholars and social commentators, most notably Robert Putnam, author of *Bowling Alone,* have raised probing questions about the continued vitality and inclusiveness of traditions of community and philanthropic giving.[5] Will the values of giving for the common good and of institutional loyalty that have guided earlier generations of benefactors be transmitted to the next? Will individuals who are able to lend financial support to education be inclined to do so, and will these new donors give wisely? What values will they bring?

This paper examines the philanthropy of Mrs. Clementine Tangeman (1905–96) as a case study in donor motivation and the life experiences that shape giving.[6] Although Mrs. Tangeman gave widely, the focus here will be on her giving to higher education that culminated in her understanding of the ideal that philanthropy in its most empowering mode, as the paper's title suggests, should "bind the university to nothing." The author chose biography as the preferred method to arrive at the impulses embedded in an individual's giving, although there are other ways to study donor motivation—such as surveys.[7]

Whereas surveys can suggest trends over time, the full investigation of a philanthropic life, drawn from research on the donor and the recipient, adds a crucial dimension of personal and institutional history to the study of philanthropy.[8] A particularly useful lens for biography, and one that will inform this study of Clementine Tangeman, is the theory of education developed by the historian, Lawrence Cremin, that locates the education of individuals as occurring within multiple educative institutions, both formal and nonformal, such as the school, family, church, workplace, and community.[9] Informed by this theory of education, the study of philanthropic lives will, the author believes, provide insights into the motivation of the giver and, moreover, can illuminate the values and assumptions guiding donor-recipient interactions. The purpose of developing biographical case studies of philanthropists is not to write hagiography, but rather, to balance history's preoccupation with great foundation builders, the likes of Andrew Carnegie and John D. Rockefeller, with an understanding of the significant contribution of scores of men and women who have supported higher education and the variety of paths these individuals traveled in identifying and committing themselves as philanthropists.

Biography can be used to study all donors—regardless of gender, class, ethnicity, and religious or regional traditions. In relation to women's giving, biography holds the possibility of recovering a legacy of women's giving to higher education that is relatively unrecognized and understudied.[10] The author has argued elsewhere that not only will closer study "discover" the contributions of women philanthropists in higher education, but that such analysis will help people rethink the history of the research university.[11] Simply put, studies of philanthropic women, such as the biography of Mrs. Tangeman presented here, can challenge a misconception that women are "new donors" and will help people rethink the current narrative of philanthropy, which is documented by the "great" foundation builders. Furthermore, biography can underscore the complexity-of giving and help refine generalizations that compare the giving of women and men and attribute any differences to gender alone. Biography as a method lends itself to grappling with the differences among women and to exploring how other factors might affect giving, for men and women alike—faith, family, education, personal financial resources, and an appreciation of regional traditions, among them.

Efforts to preserve the history of women's philanthropy and to produce biographical studies of philanthropic lives are particularly timely given the growing numbers of organizations, professional networks, websites, and conferences devoted to women's philanthropy.[12] The growing interest in women's philanthropy and the power of biography as a method notwithstanding, writing the biographies of women donors presents significant challenges. Published and archival sources on women donors tend to be fewer than those about their male counterparts and restrictions on confidential donor-recipient files prove another obstacle to research. In such instances, oral history narratives can supplement the public record by providing more developed insights into the personal motivations and satisfactions of giving.[13]

Additionally, oral history provides a means for the experienced donor to educate others about giving, and records impressions of the donor-recipient relations and decision making, which are an integral part of an institution's memory. Further, at a time when there is concern about the inter-generational transmission of the values of giving, oral histories and biographical portraits can not only provide a powerful pedagogical tool to educate the current generation about giving but can also help achieve a richer understanding of the formative experiences that shape and give coherence to an individual's philanthropic sensibilities and commitments—what Boston College researcher Paul Schervish has called a "philanthropic identity." According to Schervish, "To say that one has a phi-lanthropic identity means that one's moral biography is shaped in large measure by devotion to the quantity and quality of one's charity."[14]

Based on interviews he and Andrew Herman conducted with 130 wealthy individuals,[15] Paul Schervish identified a "working model" of six "mobilizing" factors that commonly motivate an indi-vidual to engage in philanthropy as follows: (1) *community of participation*—involvement in an orga-nizational setting where philanthropy is expected (e.g., alumnae association, board of trustees); (2) *framework of consciousness*—exposure to a world view or set of values that promote the idea of giving (e.g., religion); (3) the effects of *early childhood experiences*; (4) the influence of a *socializing agent*—an individual who introduces the adult to the value of giving and to avenues for philanthropic action; (5) *reinforcing intrinsic rewards*—the satisfactions of making a difference in the lives of people and institutions; and (6) *realization that one has resources* to devote—time, money, creativity, and access to relevant networks.[16] (Schervish has continued to elaborate upon this working model and has under-taken a multivariate analysis of charitable giving.[17]) Drawing upon an oral history, archival research, and site visits, this brief portrait of the philanthropist Clementine Miller Tangeman substantiates Schervish's findings about the factors that influence people to give, but beyond that depicts a life where philanthropy was guided by purposefulness and critical reflection. The portrait draws from printed sources and interviews with Mrs. Tangeman's associates. The author also conducted an oral history interview with Mrs. Tangeman, at the Irwin mansion in Columbus, Indiana, on September 19 and 20, 1995, hereafter cited as Tangeman Interview.

The Shaping of Philanthropic Sensibilities: Family, Church, and Hometown

Elizabeth Clementine Miller (1905–96), known more commonly by her middle name, Clementine, was born in the southern Indiana town of Columbus, on February 17, 1905. Together with her younger brother, J. Irwin Miller (b. 1909), Clementine Miller (later Mrs. Clementine Tangeman, after her 1951 marriage to musicologist Robert Stone Tangeman) represented the fourth generation of a Hoosier family of ministers (Disciples of Christ), lay church leaders, civic-minded industrialists, and phi-lanthropists. The Disciples of Christ grew out of a purification movement in Christianity that was inspired by Alexander Campbell, founder of Bethany College in West Virginia. Disciples character-istically value "deeds not creeds."[18] In her own time, she would become a generous and well-respected practitioner of the art of giving.

Clementine Tangeman's approach to philanthropy and service cannot be understood apart from her small-town Midwestern upbringing, her formation in faith as a Disciple of Christ, and the influ-ential adults who figured prominently in her youth and young adulthood as models of giving and service. Mrs. Tangeman's philanthropic career took her to New York City (where she worked with the Girl Scouts of the USA) and to wartime Italy (where she served as a volunteer in the Gray Ladies), yet she always remained anchored in Indiana, in her hometown of Columbus, and in her family tradition.

Mrs. Tangeman's extended family—the Irwins, Sweeneys, and the Millers—were active early in the religious, business, and civic life of Columbus. (In fact, both of Mrs. Tangeman's grandfa-thers were pioneer preachers.) Although this Columbus, Indiana, family today is most often associ-ated in the media with Cummins Engine, a diesel manufacturing company founded in 1919, by the 1880s the Irwin men had already built their fortune as bankers and industrialists. As civic leaders in local, state, and national Republican politics, they had helped to extend southern Indiana's role in the state economy and politics, effectively connecting the small town of Columbus to the state capital of Indianapolis (approximately 60 miles to the north), to the national economy, and to wider circles of commerce and intellectual and religious debate. Within their family tradition, belief in civic involvement was anchored in a religious outlook that, as Mrs. Tangeman's uncle Will Irwin, a noted lay religious leader and founder of Cummins Engine, might have put it, went hand in hand with "good business sense." The women of the family, for their part, received formal education in the local public schools and like the men were encouraged to continue to college. Female members routinely joined in the household decision making and, as trustees, participated in the family's philanthropic and (to a lesser extent) business decisions. They actively engaged in church committees and Sunday school teaching and achieved reputations as patrons of civic life and the arts.

The youngest members of this multigeneration household, Clementine and Irwin Miller, acquired an ethic of service early in life. The youngsters were ceaselessly prepared for the contributions they would make as responsible citizens, as churchgoers, and as adult members of the Irwin-Sweeney-Miller family. In Irwin Miller's words:

> There was considerable uneasiness in my family at having possessions, and most of the uneasiness probably came from our religion. There was a feeling that maybe you didn't have any right to wealth unless you personally took charge and worked it, and unless you handled it as a trust, rather than as a possession. If you didn't work it yourself, if you didn't work it in the general interest, then maybe you shouldn't have it.[19]

This familial sense of obligation was reinforced for the Miller children at school and at church. The consonant values of church, school, and family gave the siblings a shared understanding of their heritage and an interconnected sense of self and service for public well-being. While their individual paths to leadership would ultimately, in some respects, diverge—he becoming a lay church leader and board member of corporations as well as educational institutions, she achieving recognition as an active trustee and volunteer in education and as head of the family foundations—their childhood homelife imbued them both with an abiding appreciation of excellence and offered them models and possibilities for its attainment.

A Philanthropic Education, On Giving Wisely

The most important informal education in giving that young Clementine Miller and Irwin Miller received was at the family dining room table. Two times daily, sometimes three, the children would join their parents, grandparents, and great-grandparents for a meal and conversation. The conversation was adult conversation, not children's conversation, recalled Clementine Tangeman. Still, "Early on we became interested. We didn't resent that" (Tangeman interview). Topics included church matters, the arts (particularly music or painting), Republican politics, and the larger realm of current events and ideas.

During these discussions, brother and sister also received firsthand instruction in the ways grantees and donors might confer and reach a mutual goal. In the early years (before the incorporation of the Irwin-Sweeney-Miller Foundation and The Christian Foundation), the family's charitable gifts were distributed on an individual or ad-hoc basis. The adults generally did not consider written appeals for money from acquaintances or "begging letters" from strangers as seriously as solicitations that were made in person. On many occasions, visitors who had journeyed to Columbus for a day's business were invited to join the family for the evening meal. These men of affairs—college presidents, politicians, church leaders, inventors, and investors alike—came seeking advice and, more often than not, the Irwin family's financial support for a particular project or cause. Afterward, family discussion focused on the merits and weaknesses of these proposed ventures: "Did this person have a well-reasoned plan? Did they have the wherewithal to ensure its success? We would hear all these pitches for contributions and growth and expansion," recalled Mrs. Tangeman. "One thing and another. The people who came down and wanted their money would do their best. In those days I don't think they had any printed material; they relied on persuasion." Such exchanges educated the family about wise giving. "From a lot of exposure, my family became astute, and they could tell when a person didn't have good enough plans, a good enough grip on their responsibilities to be able to carry the plans forward." But most of all, she remarked, "It was sizing up a person's personality—people's intentions, their responsible attitudes. It's what they *didn't* say as much as what they *did* say" (Tangeman interview).

The family's thoughtful discussions about these in-person requests and the nature of the relationship between donor and recipient conveyed to the Miller youngsters the seriousness of giving wisely and impressed upon them two related lessons which Mrs. Tangeman, by her own account, tried to draw upon in her philanthropic decision making: first, that a carefully formulated plan is essential to a successful enterprise, and that it is therefore the donor's obligation to ask the most telling questions; and secondly, that after studying the issue and asking good questions, philanthropists need to trust their own judgment and exercise leadership by their resolute willingness to take what others might consider "a risk." She deemed both principles integral to a grant maker's or benefactor's effectiveness, and to his or her ability to make a substantive difference (Tangeman interview).

The Thoughtful Question, a Call to Philanthropic Leadership

By her own recollection, Clementine Tangeman's homecoming after her graduation from Smith College marked the beginning of her adult understanding of philanthropy. As a youngster she had learned about giving from the dining table and from observing her relatives play a central role in building the local church and in supporting Disciples' education. Now, as a young college graduate, she was expected to reflect upon her own obligations and opportunities to serve. As Mrs. Tangeman later recalled, her father urged her to remember how she and her classmates had benefited from the generosity of earlier Smith alumnae. "Somebody gave to Smith College so that you could go there. Now what are you doing for it?" he asked, conveying his personal sense of the communal obligation of adulthood and prompting his daughter to consider the direction and goals of her personal giving (Tangeman interview). In the years that followed, Clementine Tangeman lived up to this expectation of "giving back" to a valued institution. She served as class secretary, an alumnae club member, an organizer of her thirty-fifth reunion, and, from the late 1960s onward, a generous contributor to a number of Smith College capital campaigns.

Clementine Tangeman's commitment to the education of girls and young women was also evident in her extensive involvement in Girl Scouts of the USA and the Emma Willard School. Her scouting activities, including membership on a number of international committees and national boards of directors, helped forge global connections in scouting. In fact, she was most proud of her fundraising efforts for the construction of the Our Cabana world center in Cuernavaca, Mexico, which brought scouting within the reach of girls living in Latin American countries.

From Mrs. Tangeman's perspective, the distinctive worldwide appeal of Girl Scouts lay in its broad range of programs, as well as in the organization's commitment to providing learning experiences for both the young participants and their adult volunteer leaders. Scouting offered girls from different family circumstances and backgrounds a similar opportunity to pursue their individual interests freely. Adult leaders could, in turn, benefit from the experience of helping others and gain greater understanding of the situations girls encounter in their lives. From Mrs. Tangeman's perspective, scouting's organizational structure seemed to make no hierarchical distinction between "professional" salaried workers and volunteers. Moreover, the leadership training designed and sponsored by the Girl Scouts organization offered its women volunteers a gratifying, balanced experience. As she put it, "So many programs for today's young people are just honing their skills so they'll get a good job or be better liked by their peers. The Girl Scout program says to learn, yes, and enjoy what you are doing, but to also use what you have learned for other people's benefit. Not just to get ahead. To help others."[20]

The skills and experience that were gained from scouting carried over to Mrs. Tangeman's service to the Emma Willard School. She was elected to the board of directors of the Emma Willard School Alumnae Association in 1958, and to the school's board of trustees two years later. In 1963, she cochaired the school's National Development Council and led its first capital campaign, endowing a foreign language chair in memory of her parents. Most notably, in 1965, Clementine Tangeman became the first female chairperson of the board in Emma Willard's 150-year history.

In accepting board leadership at Emma Willard, Mrs. Tangeman drew upon principles of business she learned from the family dining table and as a shareholder in Cummins Engine. As chair, she focused attention on capital needs and launched a capital campaign with a generous personal contribution, thereby effectively galvanizing the commitment and financial support of her colleagues. On the interpersonal side, she demonstrated a style of engaging others in the decision-making process through questions that welcomed an open, imaginative exchange. By combining business savvy with an understanding of collaboration, she was able to initiate a board discussion about ways to preserve the best of Emma Willard's history while reaching toward the future. She drew upon her family's experience with public architecture in Columbus to begin a discussion with her colleagues about modern aesthetics. Her gift of the Tangeman Apartments, designed by the noted modern architect Edward Larrabee Barnes to be in harmony with Emma Willard's neo-Gothic structures, were among the earliest examples of nondormitory accommodations for single boarding school faculty. Mrs. Tangeman's benefactions also made possible the William Moore Dietel Library, the Snell Music Wing, the Maquire Art Wing, and lighting and a pipe organ for the Chapel.

Faith, Family, and the Higher Learning: Butler University and Christian Theological Seminary

From the 1950s onward, Clementine Tangeman, while still deeply involved in scouting and in board activities at Emma Willard, assumed an increasingly prominent role in the family's foundations (The Christian Foundation and the Irwin Sweeney Miller Foundation, known by the abbreviations TCF and ISMF, respectively) and in the family's personal support of Indiana's leading Disciples institutions of higher education: Butler University and Christian Theological Seminary. This particular commitment appealed to her sense of family, church, and history. In fact, with brief exception, a member of the Irwin-Sweeney-Miller family was actively involved in Butler University's governance, from its opening as Northwest Christian University in 1855 until Clementine Tangeman stepped down from Butler's board in 1970. The family's varied service as benefactors, trustees, faculty, and loyal graduates provided a vital thread of continuity, helping to assure Butler's academic caliber, financial viability, and its association with the Disciples of Christ. (Disciples' belief precludes "owning" an institution. Butler did not sever its affiliation with the Disciples until 1971.) Furthermore, the family's ties to Butler, and particularly its School of Religion, which separated from Butler in 1958 to become Christian Theological Seminary, provides a prism for understanding the intersecting religious ideals and social concerns that motivated the giving of the Irwin, Sweeney, and Miller families and the instrumental role of their philanthropy in evangelizing through education.

In the 1930s, Butler's relationship with the Disciples became strained, as a group within the institution directed its attention toward building a more secular city university. Once assured of Butler's continued service to the church, The Christian Foundation in 1938 gave more than $400,000 (a sizable portion donated by the Irwins) toward the building of Butler's College of Religion.[21] In the 20 years that followed, however, circumstances at Butler, generational differences within the Disciples, and changing needs and opportunities in religious higher education pointed to the advantages of an independent seminary.

Clementine Tangeman did not attend Butler; neither did her brother, J. Irwin Miller. Yet both served on Butler's board, following the example of their uncle Will Irwin and their grandmother Linnie Sweeney, as well as of their parents, Hugh Th. and Nettie Miller. The brother and sister were mindful of the importance of maintaining their family's ties to this Disciples' institution and of guiding its response to changes within society and the Church. Mrs. Tangeman became a trustee in 1947 (briefly overlapping with both her brother and her mother in 1951) and was emerita from 1970 onward.

In 1958, Irwin Miller was Chair of the Butler University Board of Trustees and Mrs. Tangeman (then living in Manhattan) was President of The Christian Foundation. Together, they were instrumental in funding and negotiating the separation of the School of Religion from Butler and overseeing its incorporation as a graduate institution, Christian Theological Seminary (CTS), on

September 17, 1958. The Irwin-Sweeney-Miller Foundation and The Christian Foundation collaborated in the effort by providing funds to purchase the 36-acre site to which the seminary would move in 1966.

Mrs. Tangeman's association with CTS as a donor and member of the board opens up a lens on her ideas of trusteeship, her views on the intimate ties between religion and the arts, and her ability to elaborate upon the heritage of her family's philanthropy. While maintaining its long-standing ties to Butler, the Irwin-Sweeney-Miller family's ever-strengthening commitment to CTS helped make possible the seminary's financial stability and leadership in the ecumenical movement. Working in partnership with successive CTS administrations, providing leadership in periods of uncertainty, and constructively addressing a measure of ambivalence toward philanthropy on campuses in the late 1960s, their involvement is a striking chapter in the history of seminary education in the USA. While the Luce family's generosity was important to Princeton Theological Seminary and the McCormick family's was important to Chicago, the partnership between CTS and successive generations of the Irwin-Sweeney-Miller family was rare in its duration and intensity.

True to its founding mission, The Christian Foundation provided much of the fiscal stability that CTS required to help meet the national need for Disciples' ministers and to establish its standing within seminary circles. In the ten-month period that ended in June 1960, CTS received $195,267 from The Christian Foundation and an additional $89,100 from the Indianapolis-based Lilly Endowment to support special research projects. Continuing to provide crucial ground-level support to the young seminary, The Christian Foundation pledged $269,000 the following year, representing over half of the CTS operating budget. This cooperation between the foundation and the fledgling seminary in building a first-class institution devoted to ministerial education offered, as one CTS official described it, "an imperative Christian opportunity for meaningful sacrifice through purposeful stewardship."[22]

In October 1963, The Christian Foundation demonstrated its staunch confidence in the CTS administration and faculty by turning over control of the capital funds to the seminary. In a partnership reminiscent of their grandmother and great-uncle's, Clementine Tangeman and her brother, Irwin Miller, worked together to support CTS—he as chair of the CTS board, she as a member of the CTS board and as President of The Christian Foundation.[23]

In May 1968, Mrs. Tangeman's term of service on the CTS board ended. Stepping down, she made a challenge gift of $125,000 to launch a drive toward $281,000 to complete the building project and air conditioning installation.[24] Her aunt, Elsie Sweeney, as head of the Irwin-Sweeney-Miller Foundation, also announced a $1,197,284 grant to retire the seminary's building debt on the two-year-old campus. Matthew E. Welsh, Chair of the CTS board and a former governor of Indiana, welcomed the grant as making it "possible for the Seminary trustees to take decisive action on the completion of the campus."[25]

Completing the Campus

By the twenty-fifth anniversary of its founding, CTS was relatively well positioned. The seminary had overcome numerous obstacles to exert leadership within the ecumenical movement and to counter declining Disciples' membership.[26] Yet financial constraints had stalled completion of the campus, as originally designed by the noted architect Edward Larrabee Barnes. To the regret of the CTS community, worship services were being held in an auditorium and the library had not yet been built. Under the leadership of its third president, T. J. Liggett, who joined the seminary in 1974–75, CTS was able to weather these financial difficulties and challenges. The building of the much-needed library, completed in September 1977, was made possible by a $1.8 million grant from the Krannert Charitable Trust of Indianapolis and a matching grant for endowment from the Irwin-Sweeney-Miller Foundation.[27] In 1982, in a concerted effort to reach new donors, Liggett and school officials launched what was described as the largest capital campaign ever undertaken by a nonuniversity-related seminary. The capital campaign was significantly aided by challenge grants from The Christian Foundation and the Krannert Charitable Trust. Over six million dollars were raised for endowment, faculty chairs and salaries, and student scholarships.[28]

A Donor's Sense of History and the Aesthetic: The Sweeney Chapel

Deeply pleased with the seminary's educational advances and its broadened base of support, Clementine Tangeman, by now retired from the board, though still an interested donor and friend of the seminary, turned her attention to bringing the first phase of campus development to completion.[29] She was particularly enthusiastic about this project because it would invite the input of two men she admired, both nearing retirement, with whom she had already worked closely and whose visions and skills would complement each other's: T. J. Liggett and Edward Barnes. In a November 1983 letter to President Liggett, Mrs. Tangeman broached the subject of building a chapel. She wrote:

> The time is ripe for such an undertaking. We understand that enrollment is at an all time high, that the new programs are under way and flourishing, that new faculty have been added and that the interest of the public as well as that of Disciples is at a peak. We are also impressed by the excellent financial management of assets on the part of the trustees and their money-managers, putting the institution in a sound financial position.[30]

Mrs. Tangeman proposed to fund completion of the east wing of the CTS quadrangle, including the Chapel, which she regarded as a "major element in the design."[31]

Given the nature of the gift, Mrs. Tangeman and President Liggett believed that it would be important to solicit perspectives on chapel design from various members of the CTS community. In these early discussions, Mrs. Tangeman's own sense of the role and requisite qualities of a chapel was crystalline, reflecting her awareness of the evolving nature of religion and her characteristic appreciation of the aesthetic. The chapel was to be a dignified place, "suitable for the range of existing worship—from low church to high church," and its structure was to accommodate new types of worship. The chapel would be designed to transcend time and space. Mrs. Tangeman encouraged the CTS faculty and trustees to engage in an exercise in creative thinking: "What might users of this space in the year 2000 wish had been built?"[32]

In late spring 1984, a joint task force from CTS and The Christian Foundation met with architect Edward Larrabee Barnes to consider plans for the chapel. Original plans had been drawn in the 1960s and needed to be discussed and revised.[33] When completed, the chapel would contain a specially designed pipe organ, a bell tower, and prism-like light-catching windows. It was meant to be, in Barnes's view, "a place of mystery where we encounter the Infinite."[34]

On the inaugural Founder's Day, September 13, 1987, Clementine Tangeman dedicated the East Wing, Irwin Tower, and Sweeney Chapel, named for her preacher grandfather, Z. T. Sweeney. Over the years, the family had funded the annual Hugh Th. Miller Lectureship, the William G. Irwin Chair of Church History, and the Nettie Sweeney and Hugh Th. Miller Chair of New Testament. The Chapel's dedication marked the completion of the new campus. Its chosen name, suggested by the CTS community, symbolized the enduring ties between the Irwin-Sweeney-Miller family and the seminary, going back to the early Sweeney Chapel at Butler and to the study of religion at that university. In accepting the Founder's Day medal, Mrs. Tangeman asked CTS officials to recognize her in her capacity as the president of The Christian Foundation, whose members, all Disciples and residents of Columbus, had been instrumental in supporting the seminary.

Mrs. Tangeman's final pledge to CTS, part of the 1994–98 capital campaign, was used to fund the Frederick Doyle Kershner Chair in Religion and the Arts, to support a permanent endowment for ongoing professional development of staff and professors, and to provide scholarships for students preparing for Church Music, Christian Education, and the Master's of Divinity. These categories reflected two of Mrs. Tangeman's own lifelong priorities: the importance of the arts, particularly music, in exalting the spirituality of the worshiper, and the importance of investing in people. A Clementine Miller Tangeman Scholarship was announced by CTS in the fall of 1996, after Mrs. Tangeman's death.

Irwin-Sweeney-Miller Foundation

The family tradition of charitable contributions that had once centered on conversations around the dining table in the Irwin mansion became more formally organized in 1952, with the founding of the Irwin-Sweeney-Miller Foundation. Intended as a vehicle for administering the various gifts and charitable contributions of family members, the Irwin-Sweeney-Miller Foundation (ISMF) has no endowment. In its early years, ISMF gifts were numerous and small in size, generally given to organizations, activities, projects, and groups that were already well-known to the family. (In 1958, grants equaled $120,000. In 1961, giving reached $334,119. The following year, ISMF surpassed the million dollar mark ($1,105,375).) Over time, however, the ISMF enlarged its conception of grant making to support the public good, defined more broadly. As the Foundation's first published annual report, which appeared in 1971, explained, "It was the conviction of the incorporators that if family philanthropy was to be more effective it must involve broad social concern rather than primarily personal interest." A vehicle for one family's charitable gifts thus became "a structure through which goals and objectives could be articulated, analyzed and evaluated."[35]

Historically, two generations of family members have served together on the ISMF board. The foundation's grant-making deliberations have thus transmitted a particular ethos and art of philanthropic giving across generations and helped to maintain the family's ties to Columbus and the surrounding areas of Bartholomew County. Notably, too, the women in the family have assumed responsibility for chairing and administering both foundations (TCF and the ISMF), though the ISMF had a brief period of additional professional management in the 1960s and early 1970s. Nettie Sweeney Miller, the founding Director, was succeeded by her sister, Elsie Sweeney, who served until her death in 1972 and who was, in turn, followed by Clementine Miller Tangeman. J. Irwin Miller currently heads the ISMF.

Having learned much about philanthropy from her mother and aunt, Mrs. Tangeman respected the importance of historical perspectives in guiding philanthropic judgment. In 1988 she prepared a memorandum to provide board members (among them a number of members of the family's younger generation) with a brief history of the Irwin-Sweeney-Miller Foundation. As she recalled, the 1960s had been a pivotal time for the Foundation: its size, focus, grant making, and administration were deeply influenced by the social and cultural challenges of that period. During its first decade and a half, too, the ISMF had been a family enterprise. Now, in response to the changing tax laws for individual gifts and foundations, as well as to the influential rise of professional philanthropy, the small private foundation had begun hiring professional staff members.

The annual reports of the ISMF in the early 1970s asserted that institutions had failed to serve individuals and called for a "regeneration of the spirit."[36] During this time, the foundation began making grants in three broad categories: justice, religion, and the arts. The first emphasized cultural diversity and "equity in the distribution of power"; the second supported innovations in theological training, particularly in black and Latino communities, and efforts to combat racism within religious institutions; and the third promoted arts as "a cohesive social force."[37] The driving belief behind the grant making was the conviction that foundations could address the distribution of power within society and promote social change. This imperative was supported by the ISMF's willingness to fund the "new" and "untried."[38]

The ISMF's prescient grant making during this period included considerable support for several Civil Rights initiatives, among them Marian Wright Edelman's work in the Washington Research Project prior to the start of the Children's Defense Fund, Frederico Pena's Chicano education project, and the Black Women's Community Development Fund. These grants typified the risk taking that Mrs. Tangeman, in agreement with her brother, Irwin Miller, believed essential to fulfilling the social mission of philanthropy.

By the early 1970s, the ISMF had a national staff of 17 and an annual pay-out of $4.5 million dollars. In 1972, Clementine Tangeman succeeded her aunt, Elsie Sweeney, as chair. She assumed this position just as the ISMF entered a period of transition. The late 1960s saw severe public criticisms of foundations, and the 1970s brought a decline in the stock market and the economy. A substantial gift to fund the Institute of Sacred Music at Yale University in 1973 and the coinciding economic downturn significantly reduced the ISMF's finances.

The circumstances of the 1970s brought a re-evaluation of the ISMF's national role vis-à-vis the interests and grant-making capacities of the nation's larger foundations. Aware that few other foundations had funded programs addressing the interrelated issues of race, religion, and the arts, and that tough social issues were yet to be resolved, ISMF administered terminal grants to its national grantees and, where possible, helped grantees pursue new funding.

The Donor's Letter of Intent: A Pedagogical Tool

Perhaps the best example of Mrs. Tangeman's ideas about the relationship between the giver and receiver in the philanthropic relationship and her purposefulness as a grant maker—all sensibilities shaped by family, faith, and extensive experience in both the nonprofit and business worlds—is to be found in her efforts to help found the Institute of Sacred Music at Yale University. The Institute was established in 1973–74 with a ten million dollar gift from the ISMF and the transfer of several faculty and administrators from its antecedent, the School of Sacred Music at Union Theological Seminary, in Manhattan. Mrs. Tangeman's role in facilitating this shift from one institution to the other—both of them with long-standing associations to the Columbus, Indiana, family—opens a window onto her diplomacy as a trustee and donor, as well as her commitment to the integrity and mission of a project. Mrs. Tangeman served on the board of trustees at Union Theological Seminary from 1969 to 1974.

The School of Sacred Music (SSM) had been founded at Union Theological Seminary in 1928. It drew on the cultural resources of New York City's music community, the library collections of nearby Columbia University, and in later years the resources of Lincoln Center. The School built a fine reputation in preparing musicians for liturgical work and as teachers of sacred music.

In the late 1960s, Union Theological Seminary, like its neighbor Columbia University, struggled to address volatile social concerns and student voices and to define its future at the same time. Amidst the fiscal constraints of the early 1970s, plans were made for restructuring Union, and the niche held by the School of Sacred Music became uncertain. Dean Robert S. Baker, an SSM faculty member and former colleague of Robert Tangeman (Clementine Miller Tangeman's late husband), was concerned about the school's precarious financial and institutional standing. Hoping to secure an endowment for the School, Baker broached the matter with Mrs. Tangeman, a Union trustee and Chairman of the Irwin-Sweeney-Miller Foundation. The ISMF regarded the school's impending closure at Union as exceedingly unfortunate, especially given the "promising renaissance of interest in the interweaving of religious expression and the arts." This was a time in which, the foundation believed, "established institutions might play an important role in both preserving the best of the past and developing new forms of expression."[39]

Sensing "a major opportunity" to promote their long-standing interest in the field of religion and music, Clementine Tangeman and Irwin Miller, a Yale alumnus and a member of the university's Governing Board, proposed that the ISMF help to establish a new entity at Yale, an Institute of Sacred Music. The Institute would be directed by a "few key" faculty from Union and would draw creatively from Yale's Music and Divinity faculties. The shift from Manhattan to New Haven would be accompanied by a shift in curriculum as well, toward intellectual study and theory.

Clementine Tangeman's letter to Yale President Kingman Brewster, Jr., describing the intention of the ISMF gift, was reprinted in the February 1993 *Prism*, in celebration of the Institute's twentieth anniversary. It is a superb example of the educative value of a donor's letter of intent. Mrs. Tangeman's discussion reflected a philosophical understanding of the debates, going back to Hobshouse, arguing that philanthropy should enable rather than prescribe or circumscribe future actions on the recipient's part.[40] She wrote,

> This letter is intended to bind the University to nothing. Even our predominately Christian vocabulary is not intended to limit the proposed Institute. . . . We make this statement then, not to limit or hamper the officers of the University in administering the funds, nor is it our intent to lay a dead hand upon future generations. Our aim is rather to suggest a broad, and, one might even hope, timeless purpose to the enterprise, all the while recognizing that succeeding generations will choose to carry out that purpose in a variety of ways, and will themselves have varieties of understandings of the valid meaning of the purpose.[41]

Mrs. Tangeman's letter was also one of the few public documents that articulated her belief in art as a compelling expression of religious conviction and her conceptualization of philanthropy as part of social education:

> Man communicates also by his physical expression, by gesture, by work, by poems, by pictures, by the structures and monuments he erects, by dancing before the ark (as David did), by music, and by

any effective means he can discover. . . . Insofar as the artist in each of us is liberated and encouraged to full development, so each of us is fulfilled in no other ways. . . . A peculiar danger of our society is that so many of us are now so well off. The "do-it-yourself" society is in danger of developing a contempt for the minority of the poor and disadvantaged, and helpless. In recalling us to such concern and to unpalatable truth that we save our lives only by losing them, the compassionate artist has often been the best preacher among us.[42]

Concluding Thoughts on a Philanthropic Life

Mrs. Tangeman's biography illustrates three significant points: first, the role of educative institutions in teaching philanthropic values; secondly, as a donor, her upbringing imbued her with an unusual degree of awareness about philanthropy's potential and led her to make philanthropy an object of reflection; and thirdly, the importance of the transmission of philanthropic values.

Mrs. Tangeman's giving during her lengthy career reflected the influences of two institutions whose lessons about giving were reinforcing—family and church. From her family of lay church leaders and businessmen and women, she learned about the importance of giving back and of carrying forth family obligations to community, church, and to institutions of higher education. From her church activities, she grew in faith and learned about the concept of stewardship and Christian humility. In addition, she gained an understanding of the qualities of mind and heart to be cultivated in seminary training and Disciples' education, as well as the importance of music and art to religious expression and the elevation of spiritual life. In all, her biography provides a poignant example of a religiously inspired education in giving that began in childhood, as philanthropic values were transmitted by example and explicit teaching from one generation to the next. These values provided the coherence in Mrs. Tangeman's giving and were reflected in her pattern of support to higher education—particularly to Butler, Christian Theological Seminary, and to Yale.

In addition to capturing the formative experiences that motivated Mrs. Tangeman's giving, her biography captures an approach to philanthropy that was as deliberate as it was generous. Having grown up in an extended family of givers—men and women—she made philanthropy an object of reflection. From her vantage point, how one gave was as important as why one gave: both impulses were in fact intimately connected. The example of family members and scripture had inculcated Mrs. Tangeman with the belief that philanthropy should not be intrusive; it should instead inspire, challenge, and enable. These ideas guided her own giving, and had found consistent expression in her leadership of her family's foundations—as her discussion of the design for the Sweeney Chapel and the Institute of Sacred Music at Yale best illustrate.

The same inclination toward reflection that was evident in her practice led Mrs. Tangeman to consider broader issues related to the role of philanthropy in society and the transmission of philanthropic values to younger generations. In her youth, the town, the church, and the family dining table had all provided an education in the connections between individual and society. It was a moment in the nation's past when, to borrow the philosopher Jean Bethke Elshtain's apt historical description of society, daily life was "honeycombed by a vast network that offered a densely textured social ecology for the growing citizen."[43] From Mrs. Tangeman's perspective the institutions she supported financially and through service—notably, scouting, church, and higher education—aimed to fulfill a similar philanthropic and educative function: they sought to educate, to connect people to their past and to their common future, and to one another. Within this social framework, giving ascended to a personal obligation to work for the common good. Wealth that was directed solely to individual pursuits and comfort, Mrs. Tangeman asserted, brought isolation and detracted from community life. Speaking informally among colleagues at a conference on the past and future of philanthropy held in 1993, she underscored the social relevance of philanthropy:

> [People] are getting farther and farther away from each other. They are getting less and less sympathetic to each other than they were in the days when people lived closer together and you knew the grocer and the carpenter as well as your next-door neighbor. I think it is a serious trend in society. A part of it is because of the real affluence we have had in the last couple of decades. So people have been able to develop life styles and interests that separate them by great distances from the people who

live differently—people who don't have education. That is a very serious thing—that the American society is kind of splitting apart.[44]

Her concerns were not unlike those raised today by Putnam and other scholars who are concerned with the vitality of civil society and the possibilities of capitalizing on wealth to achieve social good. The external social changes she witnessed provided a new motivation for philanthropy—leading her to conceptualize more clearly philanthropy as an important avenue for addressing social divisions and reinvigorating her long-standing philanthropic commitments to religious higher education. Equally important, she became concerned about continuing to educate the younger generation of her family about giving. (One recalls that it was her decision as president of ISMF to prepare a history of the foundation for family members.) In fact, it was this concern that made her decision to participate in the oral history interviews that have contributed vitally to this biography.

Implications for Practice

As stated in the introduction to this study, biography can be both a research and a pedagogical tool for understanding the factors that shape donor motivation. Individuals in the world of practice—whether prospective donors or development officers—can draw inspiration and lessons from the study of exemplary philanthropic lives and of documents that reflect the values underlying giving, such as Mrs. Tangeman's eloquent letter of intent in establishing the Yale Institute of Sacred Music. Both biography and historical documents can be used as case studies to generate discussion about the personal element of giving and the importance of reflection in practice: what motivates an individual to give, and how do donors conceptualize their relationship to the institutions and causes that they support? Further, in learning more about donor motivation through the collection and study of such materials—"stories" about giving or portraits of philanthropic style—institutions come to learn more about their own history and the personalities who have shaped decisions and contributed to their advancement. As Smith College president Jill Ker Conway underscored in urging Mrs. Tangeman to attach her name to what had been intended as an anonymous gift, "First, it is good for the faculty morale to know who the friends of the College are who recognize the need to improve salaries. Secondly, a college is the history of its benefactors, and these should be named at some point in its history."[45]

Understanding donor motivation is an important step in nurturing existing philanthropic relationships, in engaging the interest and cultivating the commitment of prospective donors, and in developing the types of circumstances that introduce new generations to giving. The effort to collect and to provide research access to oral histories related to philanthropy and fund raising is just beginning and will provide crucial tools to inform practice and further understanding of the role of philanthropy in shaping institutions of higher education. Some of these efforts focus on institution-specific initiatives. See, for example, the collection of interviews related to fund raising and the founding of the Indiana Center on Philanthropy, available at Special Collections at Indiana University-Purdue University at Indianapolis (IUPUI) campus. A more established effort to document the history and underpinnings of philanthropy is the Carnegie Corporation of New York Oral History Project at the Oral History Research Office, Columbia University. This collection is currently being augmented with 250 hours of new interviews.

One can discern in Mrs. Tangeman's life, even in this brief biography, the factors and types of experiences that Paul Schervish described as "mobilizing forces." As has been described, Mrs. Tangeman and her brother as children were introduced by family members and church leaders (*a community of participation; childhood experience*) to examples of philanthropy and to explicit discussions about wise giving. The family's deep faith and leadership in the Disciples of Christ provided a framework for understanding giving (*framework of consciousness*) that fostered a sense of purposefulness and moral consistency. Several family members, including women, provided models of giving (*socializing agent*) that encouraged the young Clementine Tangeman to translate the values that had been inculcated by her family into her own decision making and action. "What are you going to do . . .?," the simple question from father to his daughter upon her graduation from Smith College (Tangeman interview), underscored for the young woman her responsibility as an adult to live by the principle of giving back that she had been taught as a young child.

One cannot study the life of a woman like Mrs. Tangeman, whose philanthropic contributions were so significant, without relating the historical perspectives derived from her biography to contemporary discussions of women's philanthropy. First, the story of Mrs. Tangeman's philanthropic career and family history provides useful examples of women who have used wealth and service effectively to provide leadership in higher education. Secondly, her life suggests that the influence of gender on giving must be viewed within the context of other variables. Indeed, the historical record demonstrates the complexity of women's giving. There is no one particular way that women give nor is there an inherently female approach to philanthropy. Thirdly, as this biography has shown, models from family and faith deeply influenced Mrs. Tangeman in her thinking about giving and guided her in helping to perpetuate long-standing family ties to church, community, and to Indiana's Butler University and Christian Theological Seminary. These sentiments in fact provided coherence to the range of her philanthropic commitments. Her lengthy involvement with the Emma Willard School and the Girl Scouts of the USA enabled her to hone the leadership skills she had learned from the family's giving; and, in turn, the substantial lessons she learned from her work in women's education were applied to her leadership in her family's foundations and her contributions to higher education considered here.

"To bind the university to nothing" is indeed a great ideal for a philanthropist to carry. It seeks to enable rather than infringe upon the autonomy of the recipient institution. It is an ideal that speaks to the core of donor motivation and, hence, is exceedingly relevant both to a discussion of philanthropy and higher education and to current concerns about educating the next generation of philanthropists. The author has tried in this biography to outline the life circumstances that led Clementine Tangeman to arrive at this understanding of the crux of philanthropy's ideal power. What other lessons will the lives of other men and women hold?

Notes

1. A copy of this letter appeared in the February 1993 *Prism*, published by the Yale Institute of Sacred Music on the occasion of the 20th anniversary of the Institute. The author would like to thank Gale L. Pollen, Alumni editor, for providing her with a copy.

2. See, e.g., Paul Schervish (1997), "Inclination, obligation and association: What we need to learn about donor motivation," in Burlingame, D (Ed) *Critical Issues in Fund Raising*, Jossey-Bass, San Francisco, pp. 110–38. See also the website of the Social Welfare Research Institute at Boston College, see <http://www.bc.edu/swri>. See also Hamilton, C. H. and Illchman, W. F. (Eds) (1995), *Cultures of Giving: How Heritage, Gender, Wealth, and Values Influence Giving*, Jossey-Bass, San Francisco; Hamilton, C. H. and Illchman, W. F. (Eds.) (1995), *Cultures of Giving: How Region and Religion Influence Philanthropy*, Jossey-Bass, San Francisco.

3. See Havens, J. J. and Schervish, P. G. (2001), "Millionaires and the millennium: New estimates of the forthcoming wealth transfer and the prospects for a golden age of philanthropy," retrieved from *http://www.bc.edu/srwi*, March 27, 2001.

4. Ibid.

5. Putnam, R. D. (2000), *Bowling Alone: The Collapse and Revival of American Community*, Simon and Schuster, New York.

6. See Walton, A. (1998), "'With the strength to reason and the warmth to feel': A portrait of Clementine Miller Tangeman, philanthropist and educator," Working Paper No. 1, Center for the Study of American Culture and Education, New York University.

7. See, e.g., information on Indiana Gives and the Philanthropic Giving Index available at *www.phil.iupui.edu*, as well as *Taking the Pulse of American's Attitudes Toward Charities*, available at www.independentsector.org.

8. See, e.g., Parks Daloz, L. A., Keen, C. H., Keen, J. P., and Daloz Parks, S. (1996), *Common Fire: Lives of Commitment in a Complex World*, Beacon Press, Boston; Williams, L. E. (1996), *Servants of the People: The 1960s Legacy of African-American Leadership*, St. Martin's Press, New York.

9. Cremin, L. A. (1990), *Popular Education and its Discontents*, Harper and Row, New York, pp. 59–65; Cremin, L. A. (1988), *American Education: The Metropolitan Experience, 1876–1980*, Harper and Row, New York, 1988, p. x. Cremin, L. A. (1976), *Public Education*, Basic Books, New York.

10. McCarthy, K. D. (Ed) (1990), *Lady Bountiful Revisited: Women, Philanthropy and Power*, Rutgers University Press, New Brunswick, NJ; Scott, A. F. (1991), *Natural Allies: Women's Associations in American History*, University of Illinois, Urbana. To date, scholars have generally assumed women's influence, particularly their financial influence, was limited in the sphere of higher education.

11. Walton, A. (2000), "Rethinking boundaries: The history of women, philanthropy, and higher education," *History of Higher Education Annual*, 20, pp. 29–57.

12. See, e.g., www.women.phil.org, *www.women-philanthropy.umich.edu*, and www.philanthropy.org.; Ettinger, H. R. (2000), "Shattering the glass floor: Women donors as leaders of fundamental change," *Vital Speeches of the Day*, 65, pp. 727–31; Gutner, T. (2000), "Philanthropy with a woman's touch," *Business Week*, 3705, p. 200; Wilkerson, B., "Women's philanthropy: The changing face of giving," *Journal of Business*, 15, 23, p. 8.

13. See Kridel, C. (2000), *Writing Educational Biography: Explorations in Qualitative Research*, Farland, New York; Dougherty, J. (1999) "From anecdote to analysis: Oral interviews and new scholarship in educational history," *Journal of American History*, 86, pp. 712–23.

14. Schervish, P. G. (1993) "Taking giving seriously," in Dean, P. (Ed), *Taking Giving Seriously*, Indianapolis: Indiana Center on Philanthropy, pp. 11–41; quotation from p. 12.

15. Schervish, P. G. and Herman, A. (1988), *Final Report: The Study on Wealth and Philanthropy*. Boston College, Chestnut Hill, MA.

16. Schervish, P. G. (1993), "Taking giving seriously," especially pp. 36–8; and Schervish, P. G., "Gentle as doves and wise as serpents: The philosophy of care and the sociology of transmission," in Schervish, P. G., Hodgkinson, V. A., Gates, M., and Associates (1995), *Care and Community in Modern Society: Passing on the Tradition of Service to Future Generations*, San Francisco, Jossey Bass, pp. 1–20; "Passing it on: The transmission of wealth and financial care," in Schervish et al. (1995), *Care and Community in Modern Society*, pp. 109–33.

17. Schervish (1997), "Inclination, obligation, and association," pp. 112–13.

18. Imbler, J. (1996), "The disciples of Christ," in Hunt, T. C. and Carper, J. C. (Eds.), *Religious Higher Education in the United States: A Sourcebook*, Garland, New York, p. 225.

19. Quoted in Roberts, S. V. (1967), "Is it too late for a man of honesty, high purpose and intelligence to be elected president?," *Esquire*, 68, October, p. 183.

20. Quoted in "Volunteer for a Lifetime" (1996), *Tulip Topics*, 10, March, p. 1.

21. Morrison, C. (1941), *Christian Century*, September 17, pp. 1136–7; "Creed Row at Butler," (1941), *Newsweek* 18, October 6, p. 57.

22. "For the work of the ministry" (1962), *CTS Bulletin*, 3, May, p. 1.

23. "CTS receives securities transfer" (1963), *CTS Bulletin* 7, December, pp. 1, 3.

24. "Trustees drive tops $82,000 in response to Tangeman challenge" (1968), *CTS Bulletin*, 9, September, p. 1.

25. See e.g., "Columbus grant helps" (1968), *The Republic*, May 11; "Grant clears building debt of seminary" (1968) *Indianapolis Star*, April 19.

26. Noll, M. A. (1992), *A History of Christianity in the United States and Canada*, William B. Eerdmann, Grand Rapids, MI, p. 468.

27. "Seminary gets library gift, new president" (1974), *Indianapolis News*, October 17; "CTS tells plans for $4.8-million library" (1974) *Indianapolis Star*, October, 18; "Begin new library by May, financing assured" (1976), *CTS Bulletin* 17, February, pp. 1, 3; "$1 million grant provides salary support" (1978) *"CTS Bulletin*, 19, May, p.1.

28. "Capital campaign at five million and climbing" (1982), *CTS Bulletin*, 23, January, p. 1; "Campaign now over six million" (1982), *CTS Bulletin*, 23, May, p. 4.

29. "25 year old CTS expansive thanks to success in capital drive" (1983), *CTS Bulletin*, 24, September, p. 1.

30. Clementine Miller Tangeman to President T. J. Liggett, November 7, 1983, Office of the President, Christian Theological Seminary, Indianapolis.

31. Ibid.

32. Ibid.

33. "The chapel at last! Thanks to The Christian Fdn" (1984), *CTS Bulletin* 25, March, p. 1; "Plans move ahead on chapel and East Wing" (1984). *CTS Bulletin*, 25, June, p. 1.

34. "Sweeney Chapel dedicated" (1987), *CTS Bulletin*, 28, December, p. 4; "Sweeney Chapel to be dedicated" (1987), *Indianapolis Star*, September 12, p. 23.

35. ISMF *Annual Report*, 1971–72, p. 3.

36. Ibid., p. 5.

37. ISMF *Annual Report*, 1973–74, pp. 5–6.

38. Ibid., p. 6.

39. Ibid., p. 12.

40. Hobshouse, Sir A. (1880), *Deadhand: Address on the Subject of Endowments and Settlement of Property*, London, Chatto & Windus.

41. Tangeman (1973), letter to Kingman Brewster.

42. Ibid.

43. Elshstain, J. B. (1995), *Democracy on Trial*, Basic Books, New York, p. 6.

44. Quoted in "An overview of the CEP Conference, June 28–29, 1993," p. 6, unpublished manuscript in author's possession.

45. Excerpted in "A Letter from Smith College," December, 1981, in author's possession.

Practitioner's Perspectives

"Telling her story" has become a nearly universal agenda for any aspect of the women's movement. There is good reason for this when it comes to women's philanthropy. The historical record of American philanthropy is woefully limited when it comes to acknowledging women donors. For too long women were discouraged from speaking openly about their accomplishments or their money, leaving very few first-hand accounts. Thus the motivations of women donors may only be revealed by biographies or oral histories. With this case study, the author makes a useful contribution to filling in a gap in the knowledge about women philanthropists.

Clementine Miller Tangeman is a worthy subject for a biographical account aimed at revealing donor motivation. She was a dream donor in many ways. She came from a family with strong values and a philanthropic tradition which she carried forward. She believed in active involvement and in "doing her homework." Because she held leadership positions, there are some records of her concerns and intentions. Because she gave through a family foundation one can find records with which to document her stewardship of the family's association with religious and educational institutions. Although she also developed her own interests, they did not push beyond acceptable boundaries for a woman of her time and status.

As a philanthropist, Mrs. Tangeman certainly can be viewed as a role model for women (and men) with inherited wealth. But does her story have a wider application? The "mobilizing" factors described by the author from the work of Paul Schervish and his associates at Boston College are useful here. They allow readers to assess how the culture and values of the Irwin. Sweeney, and Miller families influenced Mrs. Tangeman's eleemosynary activities. Of even more interest are the personal statements quoted by the author in which Mrs. Tangeman reveals her thoughts about the world. Placing the projects she supported in the context of these philosophical statements gives readers a glimpse into the translation of thought into action—the process every donor and fund raiser strives to understand.

Sally Randel
Vice President Institutional Advancement
Mills College, CA.

Acknowledgement

The biographical section of this paper is a condensed version of an earlier study, focusing on philanthropy and education, and is used here with permission from the Center for the Study of American Culture and Education at New York University. The views presented in this discussion of donor motivation belong solely to the author. The author would like to thank Gale L. Pollen, Alumni editor, for providing her with a copy of *Prism*, and Mr. J. Irwin Miller for giving her permission to cite from the Tangeman interview.

WHEN VENTURE PHILANTHROPY ROCKS THE IVORY TOWER

LUISA BOVERINI

Abstract

This essay explores the implication of venture philanthropy for higher education fund raising. The author provides a detailed description of venture philanthropy, including the social context driving its development. Then, the benefits brought to higher education by this style of philanthropy are explored. Finally, a single example of venture philanthropy is described in detail. The paper then outlines the issues for institutions seeking support from this new generation of funders.
International Journal of Educational Advancement (2006) **6**, 84–106. doi:10.1057/palgrave.ijea.2150011

Setting the Stage for Venture Philanthropy

In 2001, Vance T. Peterson, President of the Council for the Advancement and Support of Education, predicted "the last half of the final decade of the twentieth century will go down in history as one of the greatest periods of giving to American higher education" (Pulley, 2001). Peterson was right. Between 1999 and 2000, American universities amassed a record $23.2 billion, marking the fifth consecutive year of double-digit percentage increase in private giving to higher education (Pulley, 2001).

Amazingly, despite a tanking stock market and an economy that slipped into recession, giving to higher education continued to grow 4.3 percent during 2000–01, as total private contributions to American colleges and universities reached a record $24.2 billion. The year 2001–02 witnessed the first decline in giving to higher education in more than 15 years to $23.9 billion, representing a 1.2 percent drop in total giving (Blumenstyk, 2003). The Council for Aid to Education found that higher education contributions again totaled $23.9 billion for 2002–03 (Strout, 2004). Although this figure is the same as that for 2001–02, it represents a 2.2 percent decline from the prior year after adjusting for an inflation of 1.9 percent (Wolverton, 2004). Giving to higher education spiked again in 2004 to $24.2 billion, surpassing the high that was reached in 2001 (Strout, 2001).

Even with the slight slowdown in percentage growth in 2001–02 and fiscal year 2002–03, annual voluntary support for higher education has more than doubled since 1994 when total giving was about $12 billion (Pulley, 2002). Furthermore, education's K-16 market share of total philanthropy has increased about 3 percent during the last two decades, as compared with other sectors that have dropped in market share or barely held their own. This suggests that donors continue to place a great value on education as a critically important investment in the future (Peterson, 2003).

These billions of dollars raised today for higher education from private coffers are no longer luxuries to provide "margins of excellence," but vital sources of annual operating funds as colleges and universities are seeing an overall retrenchment from other income sources. Recently, the weak economy and stock market of the United States have depressed other revenue streams that institutions rely upon, namely endowments.

Furthermore, state and federal budgets have come under intense pressure to cut support to higher education. These same economic factors also make it difficult to make up budget shortfalls through higher tuition. In addition, geopolitical changes in the world such as September 11, 2001; the tsunami disaster that hit SouthEast Asia in December 2004; and most recently Hurricane Katrina have affected the psychology of donors, threatening to alter their priorities and impact their decision to move away from giving to higher education in favor of human needs they consider more urgent (Brower, 2001). At the same time, costs are rising in areas such as student services and business operations. These trends have resulted in a reliance on alternative revenue sources, mainly fund raising from private sources (Miller, 1994).

Just as private funding has recently become a vital source of revenue for the future of higher education, so has a new type of giving known as "venture or high-impact philanthropy." Using multiple sources, a preliminary definition of the term follows:

> *Venture/High Impact Philanthropy* (ven'cher fi lan'thro pe), n. Grant making based on principles used by venture capitalists for investing in new businesses; Activity is called the "new philanthropy" and is characterized by a challenging, rigorous, better-measured and entrepreneurial approach to giving; Grantors do not give only money, but give their time to organizations in the areas of accounting, marketing, operations management and whatever else they have expertise in. (Brower, 2001)

What makes venture philanthropy unique? Four key characteristics of venture philanthropy can help to answer this question. First of all, a close relationship between investor and investee is essential. Second, venture philanthropy requires a long-term commitment between donor and institution. These relationships often last between three and seven years. Venture philanthropists believe that large blocks of capital delivered over an extended period of time are needed to build the capacity of nonprofit organizations (Frumkin, 2003). Third, venture philanthropists seek to strengthen the organization to meet its mission. Therefore, they focus on organizational capacity and infrastructure building, working on improving an organization's potential for lasting success. Finally, venture philanthropists seek to measure both the means and the ends of their contribution (Savage, 2002). This means that the social return on investment has become something that is measured and evaluated as an outcome of philanthropy.

The individuals practicing this type of philanthropy are known as venture philanthropists or new donors. These new donors practice what Sprinkel and Wendroff (2001) call "high-impact philanthropy," a new style of giving that rivals the revolution in private giving generated by John D. Rockefeller and Andrew Carnegie a century ago. New donors bring not just money but their time and experience. They desire clear benchmarks of performance to be developed jointly with the institution, with future support contingent on meeting those goals (Kramer, 2002). Venture philanthropy has brought the discipline of the investment world to a field that for over a century relied on good faith and trust (Frumkin, 2003).

Although venture philanthropy remains relatively small today, as recent surveys have estimated (there are about 40 institutional funders committed to the approach investing around $60 million a year, compared with the total $200 billion dollars given away each year by all donors), its influence is considerable. It has been the subject of growing media attention and the profile of its early practitioners has risen within the field. Most significantly, several of the largest private foundations have recently begun to experiment with the language and practices of venture philanthropy (Frumkin, 2003). Regardless of size, this group is likely to remake or at least modify philanthropy. For colleges and universities in particular, this new type of giving will influence the way in which higher education will attract and use major gifts. Understanding what Sprinkel and Wendroff call "transformational giving," which focuses on the impact of the gift and the renewing relationship with the donor, will be the key to success in higher education fund raising, especially as the new donors are knocking at the door.

Some predict that there will be many more new donors knocking on the doors of the academy in the near future. Consider the observation made by two researchers, John Havens and Paul Schervish at the Boston College Social Welfare Research Institute. They project that from 1998 to 2052, close to $41 trillion (in 1998 dollars) will move from one generation to another. Table 1 shows three different

TABLE 1

Projections for Intergenerational Wealth Transfer: 1998–2052[a]

Total	Low Estimate (2% Real Growth in Wealth)	Middle Estimate (3% Real Growth in Wealth)	High Estimate (4% Real Growth in Wealth)
Number of estates	87,839,311	87,839,311	87,839,311
Value of estates ($)	40.6	72.9	136.2
Estate fees ($)	1.6	2.9	5.5
Estate taxes ($)	8.5	18.0	40.6
Bequest to charity ($)	6.0	11.6	24.8
Bequest to heirs ($)	24.6	40.4	65.3

[a]Derived from tables in Schervish and Havens (1999)
All dollar values are in trillions of 1998 dollars

estimates of wealth transfer based on varying real growth in wealth. The middle, moderate estimate shows a total of $40.4 in the last row, which illustrates the transfer of wealth to younger generations. They estimate that during this 55-year period, our economy will produce 10.1 million new millionaires.

Importantly, Havens and Schervish conclude that there is a "golden age of philanthropy" dawning as a result of both this growth in wealth and the economic and emotional incentives to devote financial resources to charitable purposes that increasingly shape the moral sentiments of wealth holders (Havens and Schervish, 1999). It is likely that these individuals will share the philosophy of the recent venture philanthropists (Gaudiani, 2003). In fact, these future millionaires will quite possibly become the prospects of colleges and universities for funds vital to their operation and overall existence.

At the same time as this trend is taking hold, many of the large foundations have announced that they plan to substantially reduce their grants to colleges and universities. Some may stop giving altogether. They indicate a lack of common goals for innovation, few measurable results, and changes having little effect on the overall fabric of higher education as reasons for their decision to withdraw support (Marcy, 2003). This trend suggests that the tenets of venture philanthropy may be pervading all private revenue sources for the support of higher education, as more traditional donors and philanthropic organizations begin to focus more on results like the new donors (Gose, 2003a, b). This suggests that developing a clear understanding of this phenomenon and its implications for the academy may be critical.

"The business of fundraising is not about money, but about people." Although this quote can be found in Howard J. Seymour's 1966 classic *Designs for Fund-Raising*, the message could not be more important today. As people change, it is necessary for the business of fund raising to adapt as well. Surprisingly, the increased importance of private fund raising in higher education has not been matched by increasing research into the practices of fund raising and the techniques to bring about success in the field. An understanding of what venture philanthropy is, who these new donors are, and how they are motivated to give and managed once they do is not currently available.

Regarding the motivations of venture philanthropists in particular, although there has been limited recent literature attempting to define what high-impact or activist philanthropy is and generally discuss the topic, this literature rarely looks at this type of giving in the context of higher education. Bornstein (2001) writes, "Although venture philanthropy is generating considerable buzz in the fields of business and philanthropy, it garners little notice in higher education." At the moment, the best information can be obtained by looking at profiles where venture philanthropy has broken down the walls of the ivory tower and high-impact donors have been successfully motivated to give to higher education. The growing importance of private funding for the future of higher education combined with the emergence of this new type of donor creates a need to understand more about this donor group: their characteristics, motivations, goals for how the academy uses their dollars, and finally their current and potential impact on higher education.

What Motivates Venture Philanthropists and Why Are They Different?

We want to use our brainpower, not just our checkbooks. (Paul Brainerd, Founder, Social Venture Partners, 1997)

The new philanthropists do not fit a common mold. They are the cyber and venture capital rich, women, ethnic and racial groups previously underrepresented or unrecognized in philanthropy, and those who have become wealthy through the intergenerational transfer of trillions of dollars over the recent years. New donors may be young, middle-aged, or older, and they may come from a tradition of giving or from a culture and tradition where giving is new (Sprinkel and Wendroff, 2001). This group may be diverse, but they seem to share one defining characteristic: they represent a group of peers who became interested in philanthropy and how to give more than just money, but were frustrated by some of the existing structures (Gose, 2003a, b).

"Nontraditional donors," or venture philanthropists, have joined but not replaced more traditional givers (Sprinkel and Wendroff, 2001). Their gifts, in many cases, represent significant shifts from previous donor profiles. The way in which they want to be cultivated, solicited, and acknowledged is different, and they view their gifts more as investments than donations. Brower (2001) emphasizes these differences especially in the early stages of donor cultivation, defining the new donors as "highly individualistic, often eccentric, and sometimes even chaotic." Their desire for involvement in the organizations in which they are investing is greater than that of traditional donors and is often a point of concern or even anxiety for the recipient organization. Regardless, the varying coordinates provide a rich set of opportunities for organizations that wish to cultivate and access these potential investors (Sprinkel and Wendroff, 2001).

New donors give to issues. They like values-driven organizations with values woven into their mission. They want acceptance of their ideas and opinions, not just their money (Sprinkel and Wendroff, 2001). This focus on broad issues represents a major difference in the new philanthropy when compared with the old-style pattern of philanthropy that was more localized or institutionalized. For example, a gift to a school, a museum, or a community does not do much to attack a major issue in higher education. A good example of this issues-driven giving style is Bill Gates, with the largest single donation since the start of the millennium ($1 billion) to the United Negro College Fund to establish the Gates Millennium Scholars Program. The goal of the funding is to address issues of racial and ethnic minorities in America through providing higher education for these individuals. Another example was the Gates' launching of the US Library Program in 1997, with an issue-based goal to "give back with technology" (Brower, 2001). The projects that attract venture philanthropists, therefore, are more often designed to ameliorate educational, social, or behavioral conditions (Bornstein, 2001).

Although venture philanthropists will not replace the more traditional donor, they may represent a new challenge for higher education. On a positive note, the opportunities for the academy to harness the resources and know-how of these new donors are abundant, provided that higher education is willing to open the doors necessary to collaboration with this type of philanthropist. To summarize and further clarify what makes the venture philanthropist unique, the chart below highlights the differences in motivational factors among various donor types.

Another unique characteristic of the venture philanthropist is that there seems to be little connection between the new donor's career and goals for philanthropic endeavors. For example, entertainment industry mogul David Geffen gave $200 million in 2002 to UCLA's School of Medicine. Their desire for involvement in the institution over the long term is definitely a departure from the donor who gives to the institution "at a distance" and desires no benchmarking or measurement reporting after giving. The type of institution that attracts venture philanthropists may also be unique. The new donor is interested in the transparency and flexibility of the institution and its mission. How

The Higher Education Donor Motivation Matrix

Donor Type	Why Give?	For What Goal?	To What Type of Institution?
Individuals	When societal needs rise, giving normally rises in turn	"Indirect" benefits such as enhancing the institution	
Alumni	Type of school/prestige; emotional attachment to institution	Prior participation in school events	Alma mater
Nonalumni	Combination of altruism and egoism; if giving has an impact on their own interests	Tangible outcomes (endowed professorship)	Financially struggling institutions
Corporations	To address social problems, to "do what is right" (but usually when economic conditions are stable); if it is related to what they do	Peer pressure (Seattle, where one corporate gift fuels another)	Wealthy, financially stable institutions
Foundations	To affect change in society; aligns with donor's mission	An overall effect on higher education	Well-defined, advantaged institutions
Venture philanthropist	Desire involvement in the organization; attracted by an investment with greater risk	Intangible outcomes/big picture issues (race in America)	Institutions that are willing to change

willing is the institution to change from within? How easy is it to communicate to the leadership and obtain information from an institution? These are the questions that the venture philanthropist will ask when giving. These qualities need to be understood within the higher education development community to achieve success in soliciting and managing gifts from venture philanthropists.

Is Venture Philanthropy Really New?

Our field has had strategic, broadly focused partnership models of giving long before the term "venture philanthropy" arose during the dot-com revolution. (Susan V. Berresford, President of the Ford Foundation)

Many authors, while illuminating the differences in the new donor, also point out the similarities to a more traditional style of giving. Brower argues that over the twentieth century, effective philanthropy has come to depend on professional management as defined by a clear mission, experienced staff, and effective control of funds. Although the venture philanthropists may tweak this "giving philosophy" already established, there may not be major changes in the management of gifts once given (Brower, 2001). Kramer (2002) argues that the three main elements of venture philanthropy—building operating capacity, close engagement between donors and recipients, and clear performance expectations—are not new at all. He emphasizes that venture philanthropy's greatest lasting effect may be to reinforce a few basic principles of effective philanthropy that were already emerging.

Some of these basic principles may have been formed a century ago. In fact, it is clear that Andrew Carnegie and John D. Rockefeller also shared many of the same characteristics of today's venture philanthropists. For example, they were noted for using their contributions to dictate various administrative functions of the agencies they chose to give to, resulting in a more business like approach to the raising of money (Goldin, 1988). Just as Carnegie and Rockefeller, who accumulated fortunes in the late nineteenth century, were compelled to think about their philanthropy, so are similar conditions compelling people to think in the late twentieth and early twenty-first centuries about how they are going to organize their philanthropy as well (Think Tank, 2001). The similarities of the Rockefeller's and other late nineteenth century donors to today's late twentieth and early twenty-first century "venture philanthropists" can be explained through some brief examples.

When John D. Rockefeller helped to support what would later be Spelman College in the mid-1880s, he is reported to have sent his own landscape architects to redesign the campus and he selected the trees and shrubbery himself (Allen, 2002). This is akin to the due diligence that is performed by today's venture philanthropist. For example, when considering a grantee organization's capacity, is it common for venture philanthropists to send their own analysts out to examine in detail the business plan and financial records of the organization (Firstenberg, 2003).

Another example is provided by railroad baron Leland Stanford. When creating their university for Ivy League-quality education on the West Coast, he and his wife were intimately involved in the details, which ranged from construction of the physical plant to hiring faculty (Allen, 2002). This is a main characteristic of today's venture philanthropy, where the making of the grant is really the beginning of the process. Today's venture philanthropist, like Leland Stanford the century before, will remain engaged with the organization long after the money has changed hands (Firstenberg, 2003).

A second similarity of today's venture philanthropist to yesterday's industrial capitalist is the desire to give to issues. Just as Bill Gates is trying to solve problems of "race" in American higher education, from their beginnings the activities of giant philanthropic foundations like Rockefeller, Carnegie, and Ford were concerned with promoting the issues of "stability and orderly change in an emergent national society" (Arnove, 1980). In fact, the Ford Foundation was often described as "the world's largest investor in new ideas."

Finally, a third similarity is the explosion in millionaires that is predicted to take place today, which parallels what happened at the same time a century ago. By one estimate, the number of millionaires in the United States increased from 100 in 1880 to 40,000 in 1916 (Howe in Arnove, 1980). This dramatic increase in the number of wealthy individuals is similar to that predicted by Havens and Schervish today (Havens and Schervish, 1999). The new millionaires at the turn of the twentieth century, like today's new donors, had unprecedented latitude in deciding how to distribute their personal fortunes. Like Rockefeller, the new donors are looking for the best means to use their resources to promote human progress, in Rockefeller's words, "to enrich and sustain the lives and livelihoods of people throughout the world" (www.rockfound.org, 2005). Carnegie, like Rockefeller, gave to broad issues, such as the Carnegie Hero Fund Commission (see notes) he established in 1904 "to recognize those heroes of peace who had tried, successfully or unsuccessfully, to save human life." These ideals are not unlike those addressed by the Gates Foundation, George Soros' Open Society Institute, or the United Nations Foundation of today.

The impact that the new donor can have on higher education is significant, as was the impact that the industrial capitalists had on higher education at the time. The Rockefellers came to view education, especially higher education, as an important building block for the new social and economic order (Watkins, 2001). This may suggest that as more venture philanthropists emerge from this predicted transfer of wealth, they will look toward higher education in the same way.

Whereas some of the literature points to the notion of venture philanthropy as not new but rooted in industrial capitalism, other authors are more blatantly critical of those calling themselves venture philanthropists. For example, author Brendan Koerner believes that many business leaders assume that applying business skills to nonprofit work is all that is needed, but Koerner believes that dot-commers err in assuming that instant NASDAQ success qualifies them as nonprofit geniuses (Koerner, 2001). Some even discount the entire foundation that venture philanthropy is built upon and that "pure philanthropy is giving without strings in areas that offer minimal chance of personal recognition" (Allis, 2000). Allis prefers the more "classic giving" of Paul Mellon or John D. Rockefeller Jr., both of whom "performed lengthy due diligence but then gave away their money with the belief that it would be spent well" (Allis, 2000).

Nonetheless, leaders of venture philanthropy organizations contend that their approaches are indeed unique because of certain principles, such as helping to pay for an organization's operating costs rather than programs and rigorously assessing results. Paul Shoemaker, executive director of Social Venture Partners in Seattle, calls the hands-on relationship a comprehensive "venture plan."

Today's venture philanthropy, however, is less radical than it was when it first came on the scene a few years ago. "There's now a much better level of dialogue between what people think of as the new school and what people think of as the old school," says Phil Buchanan, executive director of the Center for Effective Philanthropy" (Gose, 2003a, b). Venture philanthropists, acknowledging that they practice a different type of philanthropy, also recognize that their approach is not a template for all of philanthropy. Vartan Gregorian, president of the Carnegie Corporation of New York, emphasized, "American philanthropy's strength does not lie in its uniformity, but in its diversity" (Gregorian, 2001). Although some of the more traditional donor types, such as foundations, are incorporating some entrepreneurial approaches to grant making in their own work, "proponents of both the traditional and the 'new' philanthropies can learn from each other" (Bornstein 2001).

What Do Venture Philanthropists Bring To the Ivory Tower?

It is believed that these new philanthropists offer what some more traditional philanthropists have not provided. Their giving is both pragmatic *and* idealistic; and the combination, when used to cement partnerships, can have high-impact results (Sprinkel and Wendroff, 2001). It is widely reported that the first time the term "venture philanthropy" was used was in the 1997 seminal *Harvard Business Review* article "Virtuous Capital: What Foundations Can Learn From Venture Capitalists." In this piece, the authors lay out six "lessons" or defining characteristics of this type of philanthropy. These six characteristics are discussed below, followed by the potential opportunity or challenge for higher education.

Risk: Venture philanthropists like to "manage" risk in return for high reward. Therefore, they are more likely to donate for riskier goals but a potential larger impact. This characteristic suggests that venture philanthropists are often interested in less definite funding opportunities. These may be more challenging to implement than such gifts as a building naming opportunity or an endowed chair.

Performance measures: Performance is measured and rewarded to achieve long-term goals rather than short-term outcomes. Measuring performance over the long term may require recording and reporting practices that are new to the higher education enterprise. Also, the measure of performance of venture philanthropy is often tied to a private-sector model, which may ignore the "unique needs and culture of nonprofits" (Allen, 2002). Finally, institutions of higher education focus on teaching, conducting research, and sharing knowledge on a wide scale, and tend to address problems comprehensively. Therefore, a measurable result may be difficult to achieve.

Close relationships: Venture philanthropists work closely with organizations, sit on boards, and get involved in strategic planning. Many nonprofit groups that have worked with venture funds say the advice and aid in strategic planning they have received goes well beyond the support they have received from traditional foundations. Donors' experiences may be valuable in strategic planning, but where strategic planning in higher education is often an insulated exercise, this may be a departure from the norm. Also, unlike other organizations, colleges and universities are often well staffed and may have less need for this type of relationship.

Size of funding: The funding is more of a continuum rather than a one-time gift. Financing for subsequent needs is critical. This type of funding may alter the way the college or university manages money and develops financial projections.

Length of Relationship: The relationship between a new donor and an institution often spans several years, rather than the more traditional one-time grants. Donor relations departments may have to alter their current, shorter-term strategies to better build lasting, long-term relationships with their prospects.

Exit strategy: Venture philanthropists have exit strategies in place at the outset. The college or university, therefore, would be required to become more self-sufficient and sustainable through this type of philanthropy.

To assess whether these defining characteristics are actually present in venture philanthropists today, we look to the story of one donor who embodies these traits today.

The Jane Brown Story: Venture Philanthropy in Action

Jane Brown is an alumna of the University of Maryland (UMD) College Park. Like many other alumnae, Jane had not returned to her college campus in 25 years. She had been busy with her own career in journalism, serving as managing editor of the newly independent *Baltimore Magazine* and overseeing special features at *The Baltimore Sun*. But the grueling schedule of the 24/7 news cycle coupled with the birth of her son prompted Brown to leave the news business in search of more fulfilling work. She gravitated toward the world of philanthropy, and now runs the Robert W. Deutsch Foundation, a private philanthropy funded by her technologist father. In fact, when we sat down to talk, she spoke extensively of her father's higher education experience, which was typical for those young people, mostly male, who attended college immediately after World War II to about 1970. "At that time, higher education was seen as a benefit to society," Jane emphasized. The federal government took a strong hand in building higher education, and subjects like physics, her Dad's major at the Massachusetts Institute of Technology (MIT), were strongly supported. Higher education in post-World War II America was an exciting realm, presenting new opportunities for many young people who would have never had the chance for a college education. Jane's father was one of these young people, enabled by the GI Bill to graduate from MIT and then on to the University of California at Berkeley to earn his Ph.D. in physics. "The goal of higher education back then was to build the defense infrastructure and capitalize on the growing scientific know-how within the universities for the betterment of the country as a whole," Jane explained. For example, the research that was funded in areas like physics provided the foundation for the advancement of society as a whole, not the individual, and although men like Robert Deutsch went on to become wealthy individuals running successful companies, the goal of the government-subsidized, advanced technical education he received was to build the United States' competitive advantage in a global economy.

"This is not the case today," Jane claims.

First the federal dollars began to decline, then the state's contribution to public education began to recede and in Maryland, higher education is the largest discretionary item in the State budget. That means that funding for higher education is at risk every year and has no protection from the budget knife. As tuitions have risen by more than 30% to make up for some portion of the declining federal and state support, the need for private philanthropy is greater than ever.

Today, close to one-third of the funds from private sources go to cover the operating budgets of colleges and universities, so it is critical that universities reconnect with alumni and other types of donors. This shift in funding sources has gone hand in hand with a shift in the perceived goal of higher education from providing a benefit to society to a benefit to the individual. "This trend began around the mid 1970's and holds today." Jane laments this trend, as the pressure from mounting student loans prevents students from choosing such vital career paths as teaching or social work and opting for degrees they perceive will allow them to earn more money when they graduate. More specifically, Jane viewed her own alma mater as symbolic of the more general trend in higher education.

Reconnecting with UMD College Park: the Importance of Leadership

These are the views Jane held when, in 1999, she was invited back to her alma mater after 25 years to attend the inauguration of its new president, Dr. C.D. (Dan) Mote Jr.

> Dr. Mote insisted on creating a new foundation dedicated to the flagship campus with its own board holding fiduciary oversight and responsibility for the foundation. While many large university systems have system-wide foundations, President Mote felt the need for a board passionately dedicated to College Park and thus created the University of Maryland College Park Foundation.

There was a UMD College Park Foundation Board established to oversee the activities of the foundation. Jane was approached by Brodie Remington, director of university relations, to sit on this newly established board. Although Jane had negative experiences with other institutions within the University System of Maryland, she decided to accept the invitation, seeing the ability to now make a difference.

Jane credits President Mote with bringing her back to her alma mater and the dynamic development staff for her growing involvement in a variety of initiatives. Ultimately, she stresses,

> Dan Mote is a remarkable individual who recognizes the large and small contributions of external stakeholders and is truly a joy to work with. It is difficult for me to give my time or money to an institution with which I have no rapport with the institution's president. If I didn't have this feeling for Dan I wouldn't do what I do.

Jane's initial motivation therefore was not spurred by the institution's prestige or the economic success it has brought her (Leslie and Ramey, 1988), but rather by establishing a personal connection with President Mote and Brodie Remington (Adams-Chau, 1988). "It's critical to have the top leadership on the same page when dealing with venture philanthropists," Jane emphasized. She feels that President Mote's responsiveness, emulated by Brodie Remington with whom she deals with on a more regular basis, has had everything to do with her relationship with UMD College Park. "There's no price tag for deep satisfaction and personal service," Jane said in explaining how President Mote often sends a handwritten note to thank her for something she has done. Jane credits Mote for having a broad vision and a deep understanding of the trends in higher education. "Dan has the ability to see how small investments over the long term can yield big results," which embodies Jane's style of philanthropy.

Jane's relationship with President Mote illustrates the importance of strong leadership that understands venture philanthropy and knows how to attract and nurture this type of donor. However, it is just as important to have a team that embodies this vision. In Jane's view, "a fish rots from the head down, so if the leader is not a visionary, it's likely their staff won't be either." The UMD College Park's development team "gets it" in Jane's words. "If an institution doesn't ask for feedback, then there's something wrong." Jane said that she feels the greatest strength of a development officer is to listen. Brodie sincerely wants to know what excites her. "As time has gone on, every new initiative that Brodie introduces me to is more incredible than the last."

When I asked Brodie and Barbara to comment on this issue, they both stressed that when working with a donor like Jane, it is imperative to understand what is motivating that person. Brodie emphasized that when soliciting funds from a venture philanthropist, "You go in and ask at the right time, for the right reason, and with the right people." In fact, Brodie has made it a priority to recruit a team of good listeners, collaborative team players, and unique individuals who have the ability to understand donors like Jane. Brodie also echoed the importance of relationship building, emphasizing that after establishing a strong relationship with a donor like Jane, the need to ask for funds is often eliminated, as donors will identify what they want to fund and, if motivated enough, will also identify other funding sources. This relationship symbolizes the positive outcome that has arisen when high-impact donors feel that their ideas and opinions are being accepted (Sprinkel and Wendroff, 2001).

Establishing a Long-term, Multifaceted Relationship

The long-term conversation that Jane feels is so crucial to a donor—development officer relationship has paid off in a number of ways on a number of levels. For example, Brodie created the initial spark that ignited Jane's interest and involvement in the creation of the Baltimore Incentive Awards, a scholarship program that supports students from nine Baltimore city high schools to attend UMD. "President Mote wanted to reconnect the Baltimore public school students to UMD College Park, which recently has become more and more selective," Jane said. The mission of the Awards was to recruit talented students from the Baltimore public schools to attend UMD College Park, but the university had limited influence in Baltimore city. Jane saw this as a way to help by using not only her wallet but also her address book to make contacts on behalf of the university to help make this program a success.

Since Jane, like many other activist donors, works with so many community organizations, she has been able to get them connected to each other. Taking the networks of a donor and making them work for the good of the institution is something that development officers are doing more and more with activist donors like Jane. "If a development officer can harness the door-opening potential of a donor it can be very powerful for an institution as well as motivational for the donor," Jane stressed. In Jane's case, it was connecting research and ideas to the community by way of the people she knows to create partnerships that did not exist before.

Jane has been encouraged to expand her influence at UMD College Park by initiating and becoming involved in a wider array of initiatives. She is involved in *J-Lab*, an initiative at the School of Journalism to make journalism more interactive, something that she feels strongly about. Also, Jane is working with the Democracy Collaborative, an interdisciplinary center at the university that explores options for economic development in poor communities and issues of university engagement in their home communities. Finally, Jane has taken a leadership role on the College Park Foundation's Board of Directors. She has become involved in educating and motivating other board members on how to streamline their activities as a board and have a greater impact on the institution. In this way, Jane is fostering a spirit of venture philanthropy from within. "I see great power in university partnerships and the ability of a university to connect donor interests with exciting initiatives." Like Bornstein (2001) observes, Jane's projects, like other venture philanthropists of today and industrial capitalists of the last century, have largely centered on ameliorating educational, social, or behavioral conditions in the community around them. Over the course of the last five years, Jane's involvement has translated into approximately $500,000 in gifts to four different projects at the university. Currently she is working on a $1,000,000 gift for a department at the university, but in structuring the deal the department has to agree to hit certain benchmarks.

Jane heralded President Mote's move toward establishing a dedicated board at UMD. "The College Park Board has given me a way to be involved without dealing with the big brother of a large university system." She said that College Park's development team, under Brodie, is making great strides to get connected to other activist donors like her. She believes that board structure is critical to facilitating these connections. She stressed the importance of a "leaner and hungrier university" to activist donors like her. Jane has spurred an even more decentralized structure, breaking down the College Park Foundation to strengthen individual school boards so donors' efforts can be more focused and results realized more quickly and efficiently, creating a more streamlined structure that appeals to high-impact donors (Sprinkel and Wendroff, 2001).

Challenges for the Venture Philanthropist and the Institution

When I asked Jane what her biggest challenges were in working with an institution like UMD College Park, she said the most formidable challenge is tenured faculty. "Tenured faculty are so antithetical to a productive and dynamic system." Protecting donors from faculty is sometimes very important. On the development side, Brodie stressed that sometimes the biggest challenge is educating donors so they get to the point where "their idea is your idea," focusing their interests so that the college is benefited as well without exhausting unnecessary resources. Therefore, although the activist donor can often present a challenge to the institution, the results can often be quite significant both financially and in other areas.

When I asked Jane what characterizes her style of giving as a venture philanthropist, she spoke extensively about the level of engagement of the new donor. "The way the new donors will operate as philanthropists is the way they operate in their day to day business, with a high level of involvement." Like a venture capitalist, the venture philanthropist will not put all of the funds in up front, but will "invest" and establish a longer term relationship that is more intense, but also more rewarding. "I believe that a highly engaged approach is a personal choice, and can vary from person to person." When I asked Jane if she believed that venture philanthropists required a similarly unique approach to development, she enthusiastically agreed. "This type of giving is very different from, say, donating an endowed chair to a school, which is a very passive form of giving." Most importantly, she believes the trend toward venture philanthropy is not something that is going to go away. "As younger, more engaged philanthropists emerge on the higher education scene, they will serve as an example to other potential donors to 'cross the chasm' and become involved."

Jane continues to become more and more involved with UMD College Park. "The relationship has become more complex, but also more rewarding," she said. Although she has given a relatively small amount in total funds to the institution, her ability to create "networks from networks" and open doors to additional funding and support for a host of initiatives has proved extremely valuable for the university. Of course, Jane is poised to give much larger gifts when the time is right. When asked about the future of her alma mater, UMD College Park, Jane emphasized that "although it has become a dynamic and great institution, they are only now beginning to tap their vast philanthropic potential."

> The practices of these new philanthropists are challenging more experienced leaders in philanthropy to think about *changing roles and relationships* with grantee partners, using *new tools and approaches* that stretch philanthropy *beyond traditional grant making* and into more opportunistic and market-based models.
>
> (W.K. Kellogg Foundation, January 1999 Report)

Changing Roles and Relationships

Thinking about the way in which a venture philanthropist like Jane Brown and a college or university collaborate leads to a set of new and unique roles that present both opportunities and challenges for the academy.

The Idea Generator vs. the Idea Processor

The venture philanthropist, similar to an entrepreneur, approaches philanthropy with a full docket of ideas. These ideas are often in the form of broad, issue-based goals that have, as the desired outcome, a social return on investment. An important characteristic of higher education that has plagued these high-impact philanthropists, according to Gose (2003a, b), is an existing rigidity within the academy that traditionally does not allow for this type of input of ideas from donors. Options for philanthropy in higher education have often been generated by the institutions themselves as opposed to the donors. However, for venture philanthropists, one of the most important qualifications for organizations with which they will work is the ability, in Jane Brown's words, to listen and respond to a philanthropist's ideas in creative and thoughtful ways.

This suggests that development officers, who are often used to being the *idea generators*, will have to become the *idea processors*, possessing the ability to craft a solution to fulfill what the venture philanthropist determines as a perceived need for the institution. This means that development officers will have to, in New Schools Venture Fund's CEO Kim Smith's words, "acknowledge the power of venture philanthropists as entrepreneurs, who are a special kind of change agent" (The Philanthropy Roundtable, 2003). Smith explains that the challenge is to harness the new energy and insight brought by these individuals—that unique way of approaching problems and tackling change—and focus it on higher education's problems.

The Jane Brown story presents a good example of how a successful development officer–venture philanthropist relationship can work. Brown emphasizes that the key characteristics embodied by the university's president, Dan Mote, and development head Brodie Remington are strong listening skills and responsiveness to her ideas. She further explains that it is essential for the institution to have a broad vision and a deep understanding of the trends in higher education and an ability to react quickly to these trends.

Although there has been a necessary role reversal in the donor–development officer relationship when working with the high-impact donor, this does not imply that the development officer has no influence over their donor subject. Nor does it mean that the venture philanthropist's ideas are always the right fit for an institution, or for higher education in general. In the case of UMD's relationship with Jane Brown, Brodie Remington emphasized that even though it is imperative to understand what motivates Jane Brown, it does not mean that a fit cannot be made between the institution's goals and Brown's ideas. As Brodie emphasized, "a good development officer has the ability to make a venture philanthropist believe that the institution's goals are her own."

Investor–investee

Sprinkel and Wendroff (2001) explain that venture philanthropists view their gifts as investments in the future. Like choosing a long-term partner, venture philanthropists enter the playing field with trepidation, afraid of getting hurt. As confidence builds, so does the investment, but this investment is a two-way street and requires significant work on the institution's part, similar to the way an investor works with a financial manager. In the groundbreaking *Harvard Business Review* article on venture philanthropy, the authors relate venture philanthropists to venture capitalists to explain this relationship. "As an industry, venture capitalist firms fund a very small percentage of the businesses that are started each year, but the impact that venture capitalists have on their chosen companies is quite significant" (Letts *et al.*, 1997). The impact is significant because there has been extreme due diligence and care taken during the screening process (Frumkin 2003).

This investment must be explained in more than just financial terms. For example, as Jane Brown explained how she defined her role with UMD, she discussed her ability to "build networks". Brown's relationship with UMD started many years ago when she was a student in the 1970s. Although her role as a venture philanthropist began only six years ago, this role has grown and developed since that time. Through a successful *idea generator–idea processor* relationship with the university's president and his development staff, Jane has become more invested both financially and otherwise, contributing not only her ideas, but her time and her Rolodex of contacts to benefit the institution, building the networks that have helped to launch a series of initiatives on campus. Financially, Jane has already invested $500,000 into four different projects at the university and is close to making a $1 million gift in the coming year, but it is also the nonmonetary benefits that make Jane such a valuable part of the UMD.

Consultant–client

Looking at the way in which many donors carry out their giving, venture philanthropists observed that a tremendous amount of effort was being sunk into the process of selecting grant recipients and very little effort was being devoted to helping organizations succeed once the check was sent (Frumkin, 2003). Through this lens, another adaptation of roles and relationships has emerged with the advent of today's venture philanthropist. The institution has had to assume the role of client and the venture philanthropist has become more of a consultant, providing not only ideas but also ways to implement these ideas and the desire to measure the results of initiatives funded. This is akin to venture philanthropy pioneer Paul Shoemaker's "venture plan" at his organization, Social Venture Partners, which includes helping to pay for an organization's operating costs rather than programs. Kim Smith calls them "wrap-around services" to help organizations succeed (*Philanthropy Magazine*, 2003).

The venture philanthropist comes with not only ideas but also expertise and a "for-profit attitude" to maximize resources for the best possible result. Venture philanthropists, like consultants, are motivated by the quality of an institution more than the prestige of an institution, similar to the findings of Marcy (2001) in her review of nonalumni donors to higher education. For example, in Jane Brown's case, a further motivation may be that the institution was also her alma mater. Additionally, she spoke extensively of her connections to Baltimore and the proximity of UMD to her "area of interest." This indicates that characteristics such as location could be a factor.

New Tools and Approaches

The venture philanthropist is not bound by financial coffers, but possesses many other resources that the academy must tap into. Therefore, the practice of "profiling" potential prospects for solicitation by colleges and universities based upon their financial wealth is no longer as valuable as it once was. From the research provided by Schervish and Havens at Boston College (1999 and 2001), it is clear that the number of millionaires that will be created over the next four to five decades will dramatically alter the playing field for potential donors. As the transfer of millions from one generation to another takes place, the profile of donors will change at a rapid pace, requiring the academy to adapt in different ways.

For example, we see Jane Brown becoming one of UMD's most influential donors before she has even given over $1 million to her alma mater. Her influence is felt not only through the financial assistance she has provided the institution, but by the depth of her contact list and her ability to use it to help the institution in a number of ways—from recruiting and motivating other trustees to think creatively and boldly to helping young people in Baltimore, where UMD has been criticized for not doing enough.

Although most venture philanthropists will agree that their approach is not new in history, since the Carnegies and Rockefellers that came before them probably also viewed their philanthropy as a good investment, there is something that is clearly distinctive about venture philanthropy. This distinctiveness has been called "agent-animated philanthropy," where high-impact donors strive to be productive of outcomes in the same way they have been, or continue to be, formative of outcomes in their business ventures in the new economy (Schervish, O'Herlihy and Havens 2001). In this way, venture philanthropy is both market conscious and knowledge based.

Stretching Philanthropy Beyond Traditional Grant Making

The venture donor is often ready to be an active spokesperson for the initiative. This can be valuable for an institution, because it helps them reach into places and communities to which they may have not had prior access. The venture philanthropist will become actively engaged in the institution, whether through participating on the board of directors, volunteering on-site at the organization, or encouraging others to support the cause or the organization (www.kirschfoundation.org). Beyond the grant, benchmarks are another way that venture philanthropists go beyond the traditional giving style. Susan Berresford, president of the Ford Foundation, explains that "We (the donors) are not so good at describing the short-term changes we expect from a series of grants that will ultimately contribute to the larger change". She explains that it is healthy to spell out a series of assumptions that underlie grants. Rather than "giving a person a fish rather than teaching that person to fish," venture philanthropists will not see their gift as purely monetary, but rather a gift of their network, their experience, and their desire to support organizations that are working to change to a model of self-sufficiency rather than dependency.

Recommendations to the Academy

Taking chances, thinking outside the box, investing time, money, and expertise . . . these are, in Sprinkel Grace's words, the "new models for action" of the venture philanthropist that the literature puts forth. The new era of philanthropists are looking for a very specific return on their investment and a benefit from their philanthropy. Now higher education needs to respond. How can the academy better prepare for the new donor, the venture philanthropist? Three recommendations, or lessons, can be learned from this research.

Develop a Clear Understanding of the Motivations of Venture Philanthropists

Drawing from the "motivation matrix" that I created to distinguish the motivations of other types of donors from venture philanthropists, it is interesting to note how many "I" words emerge. This phenomenon is very similar to what Sprinkel and Wendroff (2000) call the "5 I's" to understanding Twenty-first Century Motivators for Major Giving. These are *issues, ideas, involvement, impact,* and *investment.*

Venture philanthropists want to tackle big issues, like Jane Brown's desire to connect UMD to the inner city youth in Baltimore. These issues often take the shape of broad and lofty ideas, but represent the starting point for most venture philanthropists as they connect with higher education. Venture philanthropists' involvement in their cause can be significant. "I feel very strongly that you want to be involved with an organization in a way that goes beyond simply writing a check," says Charles Simoyi, a venture philanthropist who Forbes estimates is worth around $1 billion. Simonyi goes on to explain, "Certainly, before you make the commitment, you want to really understand the organization. Typically, I become close friends with the principals" (Corporation for Public

Broadcasting Leadership Development Meeting, 2004). This level of involvement will go far beyond the doors of the development director. The venture philanthropist will sometimes even take a seat on the college's board to help shape strategy (Letts *et al.*, 1997). Jane Brown exemplified this level of involvement by sitting on UMD College Park's board. The new donor will be motivated by an impact that is concrete and measurable. There must be clear objectives that provide a focus for the relationship between the donor and the institution. Finally, the size, length, and type of investment may be different from the traditional donor and new to the higher education institution.

Alter the Engagement and Asking Process

The unique motivations of venture philanthropists require the higher education development community to alter the way donors are managed. New donors see their investment as much more than a financial "transaction." Rather, donors view a gift as an opportunity to fuel a "transformation" at the institution with their style of giving. These donors seek transformation of themselves to become not only donors but also social investors. Similarly, they seek transformation of the institutions they fund and of the issues they support.

The way in which higher education development has historically functioned is through a step-by-step transactional process beginning with the identification of the donor, also called "prospecting." The process moves through the qualification and cultivation of the donor, then on to soliciting the donor for a gift, and then to acknowledgment, recognition, and donor maintenance. This method for acquiring new donors does not meet the motivations of the new donor. Therefore, the method is structured to have limited success with this group of individuals.

However, the propensity for venture philanthropists to use a transformational approach to giving has given way to a new strategy for attracting and nurturing them, called the *Transformational Infinity Loop*, which Kay Sprinkel Grace and Alan Wendroff first developed and presented in their recent work on high-impact philanthropy (Sprinkel and Wendroff, 2001).

Using this strategy responds to the motivations of the venture philanthropist, including the desire to have the investment tied to an issue, a clear impact, and ongoing measurement and evaluation. Rather than adhering to a linear, step-by-step traditional formula, the development officer's strategy will be defined by the cornerstone of ongoing communication and an inevitably longer and richer relationship with the donor.

Create the Organizational Conditions that Attract Venture Philanthropists

Colleges and universities that seek to attract venture philanthropists to knock on their doors must take stock of their institutional environment. Do they have the right qualifications to attract this group of donors? Do they send the right message to this donor community?

First, an institution must clearly communicate a results-oriented message to donors, including values-obvious outreach. This can be done through a number of mediums, including written materials like catalogues and brochures, the school's mission statement, its development officers, and, importantly, its alumni base. Clear statements of, and action on, mission—why you exist, not just what you do; vision—what you desire to accomplish both within and beyond the institution's walls; and values are key.

Second, an institution must have a visibly strong staff, as evidenced in the case of Jane Brown and UMD and her reliance on key staff members at the institution to make their partnership work. Third, the institution must offer the donor the opportunity to become involved beyond making a financial gift. These opportunities often appear, as in the case of Jane Brown, after intense collaboration between the donor and the development officer. As more opportunities emerge, the donor will become more deeply rooted into the institution. Finally, the institution must make a commitment to stewardship, the ongoing relationship with donors after the gift is made. If this step in the development process is left behind, effectiveness is lost.

Venture philanthropy may not be a "necessary evil" for all higher education institutions. Larger, more prestigious colleges and universities may not have the immediate need to alter their fund-raising strategies to attract the new donor community, as endowments and financial solvency vary greatly in the higher education playing field. This study shows that one of the most unique and often the most challenging traits of the new donor is their need to keep a tight lid on donations not only as a way of asserting one's will but also as a way of imposing accountability. Venture philanthropists believe that if they are giving of their time and money, they are entitled to a certain amount of control that makes them comfortable. This intrusive and controlling style of interaction and a demand for compelling near term results may be more than some institutions can handle or actually need to handle.

In fact, large, wealthy colleges and universities can, and do, turn down all kinds of offers and, in rare cases, return gifts accompanied by conditions that they cannot accept or that do not fit a particular fund-raising plan (Strom, 2004). Larger institutions are more accustomed to the capital campaign structure, which are by nature restrictive to external influences in the form of ideas from venture philanthropists. Many established institutions of higher education prefer the capital campaign structure because they usually raise big sums of money that are dedicated to an agenda they control.

Nevertheless, it is important to remember the forecasting done by Schervish and Havens on the transfer of wealth that will be happening in the next 50 years. As the pool of new donors becomes larger, it is inevitable that they will become a bigger contender in the philanthropic community at large and a force for even the most prestigious higher education institutions to contend with. At present, inviting venture philanthropists into the donor mix is clearly a choice for some institutions, but for other types of institutions, venture philanthropy may present a great opportunity for raising funds.

It is hoped that this study will form the basis for future research on the topic of venture philanthropy in higher education. The Jane Brown story provides a limited look at how venture philanthropy has taken root in higher education, but additional profiles of venture philanthropists will serve to inform and prepare the academy to become more effective in their fundraising efforts. Secondly, a closer look at the different types of venture philanthropy initiatives is warranted. An examination and critique of the value that different models of venture philanthropy bring to colleges and universities will not only broaden the definition of venture philanthropy but also provide potential avenues for higher education development. This study suggests that venture philanthropy has evolved since the early part of the millennium, and will continue to evolve. A few years ago, the concepts of venture philanthropy and high engagement grant making—as it is more commonly referred to today—were overinflated with airy promises to transform philanthropy as we know it. Today, we can see that although there is clear progress toward that promise, venture philanthropy has not been revolutionary, as it comprises a small percentage of total grant making to higher education. However, having the tools to define the characteristics and motivations of venture philanthropists will be a skill that may be required for the future growth of the academy. As Mario Morino, one of the foremost experts on venture philanthropy, explains,

> Venture philanthropy is important because if successful, a few, small, high-impact grantmakers can influence the other philanthropic activities of an institution's investors. They can model a way of partnering with grant recipients that may be worthy of emulation by large donors and foundations alike. In this way tens of millions of dollars can be leveraged to influence tens of billions, and philanthropy's vulnerability can be transformed into strength.

It is still unclear as to whether venture philanthropy will have the level of impact that Morino suggests within the higher education realm, but it is clear that further research needs to be done to provide the academy with a better understanding of this trend.

Note

1. The twofold mission of the Carnegie Hero Fund Commission is to recognize persons who perform acts of heroism in civilian life in the United States and Canada, and to provide financial assistance for those disabled and the dependants of those killed helping others.

References

Adams-Chau, L.L. (1988), *The Professionals' Guide to Fundraising, Corporate Giving, and Philanthropy*, Connecticut: Greenwood Press.

Allen, K. (2002, November/December), "The mechanics of venture philanthropy," *PROFILE Currents*, pp. 16–21.

Allis, S. (2000, November 19), "Tiptoeing the line between giving and meddling: A new generation of philanthropists has yet to grasp that giving is about letting go," *The Boston Globe*, p. J11.

Arnove, R.F. (Ed.) (1980), *Philanthropy and Cultural Imperialism*, Bloomington: Indiana University Press.

Blumenstyk, G. (2003, March 21), "Donations to colleges decline for the first time since 1988," *The Chronicle of Higher Education*, p. A29.

Bornstein, R. (2001, September/October), "Venture philanthropy: A boon to academe? *Trusteeship* 5, 9, pp. 1–4.

Brower, B. (2001), *The New Philanthropists and the Emergence of Venture Philanthropy*, Washington, DC: CSIS Press.

Frumkin, P. (2003, May/June), "Inside venture philanthropy," *Society*, 40, 4, pp. 7–15.

Gaudiani, C. (2003, October 2), "Sustaining America's tradition of generosity," *The Chronicle of Philanthropy*. Retrieved August 10, 2004, from http://philanthropy.com/premium/articles/v15/i24/24004801.htm.

Goldin, M. (1988, June), "The founding fathers of modern philanthropy," *Fundraising Management* 28, 7, pp. 48–51.

Gose, B. (2003, August 21), "Cornering a franchise on giving," *The Chronicle of Philanthropy*. Retrieved January 5, 2004, from http://philanthropy.com/premium/articles/v15/i21/21000701.htm.

Gose, B. (2003, August 21), "A revolution was ventured, but what did it gain? *The Chronicle of Philanthropy*. Retrieved January 5, 2004, from http://philanthropy.com/premium/articles/v15/i21/21000601.htm.

Gregorian, V. (2001, April 19), "Putting venture philanthropy into perspective," *The Chronicle of Philanthropy*. Retrieved March 13, 2004, from http://philanthropy.com/premium/articles/v13/i13/13004302.htm.

Havens, J.J. and Schervish, P.G. (1999), *Millionaires and the Millennium: New Estimates of the Forthcoming Wealth Transfer and the Prospects for a Golden Age of Philanthropy*, Boston, MA: Boston College Social Welfare Research Institute.

Koerner, B. (2001, January/February), "Press clippings: 'Washington Monthly': The new rich.," *The Chronicle of Philanthropy*. Retrieved October 10, 2003, from http://philanthropy.com/premium/articles/v13/i07/07004703.htm.

Kramer, M. (2002, May 2), "Will 'venture philanthropy' leave a lasting mark on charitable giving? *The Chronicle of Philanthropy*. Retrieved November 16, 2003, from http://philanthropy.com/premium/articles/v14/i14/14003801.

Leslie, L. and Ramey, G. (1988), "Donor behavior and voluntary support for higher education," *Journal of Higher Education*, 59, 2, pp. 115–132.

Letts, C., Ryan, W. and Grossman, A. (1997, March/April), "Virtuous capital: What foundations can learn from venture capitalists," *Harvard Business Review* 75, 2, pp. 1–7.

Marcy, M. (2001, July 6), "How to reach the new donors," *The Chronicle of Higher Education*, p. B13.

Marcy, M. (2003, July 25), "Why foundations have cut back in higher education," *The Chronicle of Higher Education*, p. B16.

Miller, M.T. (1994), *Overview of literature related to the study and practice of academic fundraising*. ERIC Document Reproduction Service No. ED378866.

Peterson, V.T. (2003, October 17), "Giving to colleges: There's reason for hope," *The Chronicle of Higher Education*, p. B16.

Pulley, J. (2001, May 4), "College fundraising reached record $23.2 billion in 1999–2000," *The Chronicle of Higher Education*, p. A28.

Pulley, J. (2002, April 5), "Private giving to colleges surpassed expectations in 2000–2001," *The Chronicle of Higher Education*, p. A24.

Savage, C. (2002, June 4), "Venture philanthropy: Applying venture capital model to grant-making can better serve nonprofits," *Pittsburgh Post Gazette*, p. E3.

Schervish, P.G., O'Herlihy, M.A. and Havens, J. (2001), *Agent Animated Wealth and Philanthropy: The Dynamics of Accumulation and Allocation among High-Tech Donors*, Final Report of the 2001 High Tech Donors Study Boston, MA: Boston College Social Welfare Research Institute.

Schervish, P.G. and Havens, J.J. (1999, October), "Millionaires and the Millennium:," *New Estimates of the Forthcoming Wealth Transfer and the Prospects for a Golden Age of Philanthropy*, Boston College, MA: Social Welfare Research Institute.

Sprinkel Grace, K. and Wendroff, A. (2001), *High Impact Philanthropy: How Donors, Boards, and Nonprofit Organizations Can Transform Communities*, New York, NY: John Wiley and Sons Inc.

Strom, S. (2004, November 15), "Accountability: Big but not easy: As donors set terms, some charities resist," *New York Times*. Retrieved November 15, 2004, from http://nytimes. com/2004/11/15/giving.

Strout, E. (2004, June 25), "Charitable giving rose in 2003, but gifts to education foundered," *The Chronicle of Higher Education*, p. A34.

Strout, E. (2001), "The Giving Boom: How the New Philanthropy Will Change America. *Think Tank* with Ben Wattenberg, PBS Weekly Special, July 12.

Watkins, W.H. (2001), *The White Architects of Black Education: Ideology and Power in America, 1865–1954*, New York, NY: Teachers College Press, Columbia University.

Wolverton, B. (2004, March 18), "Giving to colleges, private school drops for second year in a row," *The Chronicle of Philanthropy*. Retrieved October 14, 2004, from http://philanthropy.com/premium/articles/v16/i11/11002901.htm.

Bibliography

Chapter 12: Donor Motivation

Drezner, N. "Recessions and Tax-Cuts: The Impact of Economic Cycles on Individual Giving, Philanthropy, and Higher Education." *International Journal of Educational Advancement*, Vol. 6, No. 4 (2007).

APPENDIX

New England's First Fruits (1643)

The first systematic fund-raising appeal to raise money for an American institution was probably that for Harvard College. In 1641, the Massachusetts Bay Colony sent three clergy to England to solicit money so they could educate the "heathen Indian" among other things. Fund-raisers Well and Peter requested the best selling points and the New England's First Fruits was the result.

The History of the Founding of Harvard College

After God had carried us safe to New England, and we had built our houses, provided necessaries for our livelihood, reared convenient places for God's worship, and led the civil government, one of the next things we longed for and looked after was to advance learning and perpetuate it to posterity; dreading to leave an illiterate ministry to the churches, when our present ministers shall lie in the dust. And as we were thinking and consulting how to effect this great work, it pleased God to stir up the heart of one Mr. Harvard (a godly gentleman and a lover of learning, there living among us) to give the one-half of his estate (it being in all about £700) toward the founding of a college, and all his library. After him, another gave £300; others after them cast in more; and the public hand of the state added the rest. The college was, by common consent, appointed to be at Cambridge (a place very pleasant and accommodate) and is called (according to the name of the first founder) Harvard College.

The edifice is very fair and comely within and without, having in it a spacious hall where they daily meet at commons, lectures, and exercises; and a large library with some books to it, the gifts of diverse of our friends, their chambers and studies also fitted for and possessed by the students, and all other rooms of office necessary and convenient with all needful offices thereto belonging. And by the side of the college, a fair grammar school, for the training up of young scholars and fitting of them for academical learning, that still as they are judged ripe they may be received into the college of this school. Master Corlet is the master who has very well approved himself for his abilities, dexterity, and painfulness in teaching and education of the youths under him.

Over the college is Master Dunster placed as president, a learned, a conscionable, and industrious man, who has so trained up his pupils in the tongues and arts, and so seasoned them with the principles of divinity and Christianity, that we have to our great comfort (and in truth) beyond our hopes, beheld their progress in learning and godliness also. The former of these has appeared in their public declamations in Latin and Greek, and disputations logic and philosophy which they have been wonted (besides their ordinary exercises in the college hall) in the audience of the magistrates, ministers, and other scholars for the probation of their growth in learning, upon set days, constantly once every month to make and uphold. The latter has been manifested in sundry of them by the savory things of their spirits in their godly versation; insomuch that we are confident, if these early blossoms may be cherished and warmed with the influence of the friends of learning and lovers of this pious work, they will, by the help of God, come to happy maturity in a short time.

Over the college are twelve overseers chosen by the General Court, six of them are of the magistrates, the other six of the ministers, who are to promote the best good of it and (having a power of influence into all persons in it) are to see that everyone be diligent and proficient in his proper place.

Reference

Collections of the Massachusetts Historical Society. 1792. 1:242–248.

Would It Not Be Wise for Some Negro Schools to Make Joint Appeal to Public for Funds?

Frederick D. Patterson

One of the most severe catastrophies of the present war, so far as the American people are concerned, is what is happening to our private colleges throughout the length and breadth of our nation today. They are receiving a double assault—that which comes from the loss of the majority of the male student population and that which comes through inability to receive adequate support through the taxing program now necessary to fight this war and to insure the broad social programs upon which this nation has engaged for the past seven or eight years.

If this is true of private colleges in general where it may be said that these colleges have a definite constituency upon which upon which they place a financial claim, the situation is trebly more grave with the Negro colleges of a private nature which heretofore have relied largely on gifts from substantial members of the white race for their support and maintenance. There is occasion therefore for serious alarm as to what may happen to such institutions as Atlanta, Fisk, Dillard, Morehouse, Hampton and Tuskegee to say nothing of a large number of smaller church schools.

Is Public Interested?

The handwriting is on the wall so far as substantial northern support is concerned. The question remains as to whether or not these institutions have sufficiently impressed their worth on the general public and there has been sufficient growth in the public conscience to permit the quality of widespread, if small, individual generosity that is necessary to offset the substantial gifts of the past.

The general public probably does not realize that most of the substantial progress for human betterment has come through the aegis of private and charitable institutions. In the case of education the freedom to experiment and blaze new trails was a pioneering service responsible for much of the progress we know in this field today. Even now, this service is needed because of the more or less fixed pattern which governs the educational programs of most publicly supported educational institutions. In not a few instances the political pot boils incessantly that anything beyond the merest traditional routine is out of the question.

Unified Appeals

Private colleges for Negroes have carried the brunt of our educational effort for the better part of this experience. They yet educate to the extent of their means nearly 50% of those who receive college training. They have provided the bulk of the educational leadership administering to colleges both public and private. They, too, have pioneered in areas, until recently, hardly possible in few if any state supported institutions.

These Negro institutions may well take a cure from the general program of organization which seems to involve most charitable efforts today. Various and sundry drives are being unified with a reduction in overhead for publicity and in behalf of a more purposeful and pointed approach to the giving public. The idea may not be new but it seems most propitious at this time that the several institutions which they are spending for campaign and publicity and that they make a unified appeal to national conscience.

How to Split Gifts

The first question which naturally arises is who will get how much of the funds collected. The only reasonable way to handle this would be to work out certain range limits of individual budgets and then see that the given percentage of a dollar that went to any institution was in terms of this range in its ratio to the whole. If there is included approximately ten institutions this should not be a too difficult mathematical problem. A given institutional range could be determined for a base period similar to that used in the cotton allotment program so as to be sure that a fair estimate of the operating budget is taken.

Negroes Should Start

Such a campaign might well begin with Negro people of America. There are few of us who have any sort of employment who haven't enough intelligence and interest, I am sure, to appreciate the importance of a such a program to these institutions of higher learning. The fact that all types of education would be involved would overcome the objections which might result if a single institution were to make an appeal. In addition to this there would be the savory feeling that this contribution would be made so that a large number of individuals would benefit regardless of their educational choice.

It is also possible that by starting with the Negro people in a campaign of this kind each individual institution could continue to appeal to the donors and special friends it had developed over a period of years. The nominal contribution of one dollar per person could be sought over this wider range without any important conflict. At least during these critical times, a unified financial campaign for several Negro colleges seems to be an idea worth toying with.